THE

ANTE-NICENE FATHERS

TRANSLATIONS OF

The Writings of the Fathers down to A.D. 325

THE REV. ALEXANDER ROBERTS, D.D.,

AND

JAMES DONALDSON, LL.D.,

EDITORS

AMERICAN REPRINT OF THE EDINBURGH EDITION

REVISED AND CHRONOLOGICALLY ARRANGED, WITH BRIEF PREFACES AND
OCCASIONAL NOTES,

BY

A. CLEVELAND COXE, D.D.

VOLUME V

HIPPOLYTUS, CYPRIAN, CAIUS, NOVATIAN, APPENDIX.

AUTHORIZED EDITION

T&T CLARK
EDINBURGH

WM. B. EERDMANS PUBLISHING COMPANY
GRAND RAPIDS, MICHIGAN

British Library Cataloguing in Publication Data
Ante-Nicene Fathers.
1. Fathers of the church
I. Robertson, Alexander   II. Donaldson, James
230'.13   BR60.A62

Reprinted 1995

T&T Clark ISBN 0 567 09378 6

Eerdmans ISBN 0-8028-8091-6

FATHERS OF THE THIRD CENTURY:

HIPPOLYTUS, CYPRIAN, CAIUS, NOVATIAN, APPENDIX.

AMERICAN EDITION.

CHRONOLOGICALLY ARRANGED, WITH BRIEF NOTES AND PREFACES,

BY

A. CLEVELAND COXE, D.D.

Τὰ ἀρχαῖα ἔθη κρατείτω.
THE NICENE COUNCIL.

PREFACE

THIS fifth volume will be found a work complete in itself, *simplex et unum*. At first, indeed, it might look otherwise. The formation of Latin Christianity in the school of North Africa seems interrupted by the interpolation, between Tertullian and his great pupil Cyprian, of a Western bishop and doctor, who writes in Greek. A little reflection, however, will suggest to the thoughtful student, that, even if our chronological plan admitted of it, we should divest the works of Cyprian of a very great advantage should we deprive them of the new and all-important light shed upon Cyprian and his conflicts with Stephen by the discovery of the *Philosophumena* of Hippolytus. That discovery, as Dr. Bunsen reminds us, more than once, has *duplicated* our information concerning the Western Church of the ante-Nicene period. It gives us overwhelming evidence on many points heretofore imperfectly understood, and confirms the surmises of the learned and candid authors who have endeavoured to disentangle certain complications of history. It meets some questions of our own day with most conclusive testimony, and probably had not a little to do with the ultimate conclusions of Döllinger, and the rise of the Old Catholic school, among the Latins. We cannot fail to observe in all this the hand of a wise and paternal Providence, which is never wanting to the faithful in the day of trial. "I believe, with Niebuhr," says Dr. Bunsen, "that Providence always furnishes every generation with the necessary means of arriving at the truth and at the solution of its doubts." This consideration has inspired me with great hopes from the publication of this series in America, where the aggressions of an alien element are forcing us to renewed study of that virgin antiquity which is so fatal to its pretensions. I can adopt with a grateful heart the language of Bunsen, when he adds :[1] "I cannot help thinking it of importance that we have *just now* so unexpectedly got our knowledge of facts respecting early Christianity *doubled*."

To show some tokens of this new light on old difficulties, I shall be obliged to throw one or two of my *Elucidations* almost into the form of dissertations. It will appear, as we proceed, that we have reached a most critical point in the ante-Nicene history, and one on which that period itself depends for its complete exposition. Let me adduce conclusive evidence of this by reference to two fundamental facts, which need only to be mentioned to be admitted : —

1. The Council of Nice did not pretend to be setting forth a new creed, or making anything doctrine which was not doctrine before. Hence the period we are now studying is to be interpreted by the testimony of the Nicene Fathers, who were able to state historically, and with great felicity, in idioms gradually framed by the Alexandrian theologians, *the precise intent and purport of their teaching*. The learned Bull has demonstrated this ; demolishing alike the sophistry of Petavius the Jesuit, and the efforts of latitudinarians to make capital out of some of those *obiter dicta* of orthodox Fathers, which, like certain passages of Holy Scripture itself, may be wrested into contradictory and self-stultifying declarations. Note, therefore, that the Nicene Creed must be studied not so much in the controvertists of the fourth century as in the doctors of preceding ages, whom we are reviewing in these pages.

---

[1] *Hippol.*, vol. i. p. 7. Ed. London, 1851.

2. A like statement is true of the Nicene constitutions and discipline. The synodical rule, alike in faith and discipline, was Τὰ ἀρχαῖα ἔθη κρατείτο: "Let the (ancient) primitive examples prevail." Observe, therefore, what they ruled as to Rome and other churches was already *ancient*. Now, the "duplicated" light thrown upon the position of the North-African churches, and others in the West, at this period, by the discovery of long-lost portions of Hippolytus, will be found to settle many groundless assertions of Roman controvertists as to what these ἀρχαῖα ἔθη were.

Bearing this in mind, let us return to the point with which this Preface starts. We are pausing for a moment, in the North-African history, to take a contemporary survey of Rome, and to mark just where it stands, and what it is, at this moment. The earliest of the great Roman Fathers now comes forward, but not as a Latin Father. He writes in Greek; he continues the Greek line of thought brought into the West by Irenæus; he maintains the Johannean rather than the Petrine traditions and idioms, which are distinct but not clashing; he stands only in the third generation from St. John himself, through Polycarp, and his master Irenæus; and, like his master, he confronts the Roman bishops of his time with a superior orthodoxy and with an authority more apostolic.[1] He illustrates in his own conduct the maxim of Irenæus, that "the Catholic faith is preserved in Rome by the testimony *imported into it* by those who visit it from every side;" that is, who thus keep alive in it the common faith, as witnessed in all the churches of Christendom.

Thus, Hippolytus, once "torn to pieces as by horses," in his works, if not in his person, comes to life again in our times, to shed new light upon the history of Latin Christianity, and to show that Rome had no place nor hand in its creation. He appears as a Greek Father in a church which was yet a "Greek colony;"[2] and he shows to what an estate of feebleness and humiliation the Roman Church had been brought, probably by the neglect of preaching, which is an anomaly in its history, and hardly less probably by its adherence to a Greek liturgy long after the Christians of Rome had ceased to understand Greek familiarly. At such a moment Hippolytus proves himself a reformer. His historical elucidations of the period, therefore, form an admirable introduction to Cyprian, and will explain the entire independence of Roman dictation, with which he maintained his own opinions against that Church and its bishops.

And lastly we have Novatian as a sequel to the works of Cyprian; and truly, the light upon his sad history is "duplicated" by what Hippolytus shows us of the times and circumstances which made his schism possible, and which somewhat relieve his character from its darker shades.

Such, then, is the volume now given to the reader, — Hippolytus, Cyprian, Novatian, — affording the fullest information ever yet brought together in one volume, upon the rise of Latin Christianity, the decline of the Greek period of the Roman See, and the restricted limits of the Roman province not yet elevated to the technical position of a Nicene patriarchate.

---

[1] See this series, vol. iii. Elucid. II. p. 630.
[2] See this series, vol. i. pp. 309, 360; also vol. ii. p. 166, and Milman (vol. i. pp. 28, 29), *Latin Christianity*.

Contents of Volume V

HIPPOLYTUS

INTRODUCTORY NOTICE TO HIPPOLYTUS

[A.D. 170–236.]

THE first great Christian Father whose history is Roman is, nevertheless, not a Roman, but a Greek. He is the disciple of Irenæus, and the spirit of his life-work reflects that of his master. In his personal character he so much resembles Irenæus risen again,[1] that the great Bishop of Lyons must be well studied and understood if we would do full justice to the conduct of Hippolytus. Especially did he follow his master's example in withstanding contemporary bishops of Rome, who, like Victor, "deserved to be blamed," but who, much more than any of their predecessors, merited rebuke alike for error in doctrine and viciousness of life.

In the year 1551, while some excavations were in progress near the ancient Church of St. Lawrence at Rome, on the Tiburtine Road, there was found an ancient statue, in marble, of a figure seated in a chair, and wearing over the Roman tunic the *pallium* of Tertullian's eulogy. It was in 1851, just three hundred years after its discovery, and in the year of the publication of the newly discovered *Philosophumena* at Oxford, that I saw it in the Vatican. As a specimen of early Christian art it is a most interesting work, and possesses a higher merit than almost any similar production of a period subsequent to that of the Antonines.[2] It represents a grave personage, of noble features and a high, commanding forehead, slightly bearded, his right hand resting over his heart, while under it his left arm crosses the body to reach a book placed at his side. There is no reason to doubt that this is, indeed, the statue of Hippolytus, as is stated in the inscription of Pius IV., who calls him "Saint Hippolytus, Bishop of Portus," and states that he lived in the reign of the Emperor Alexander; i.e., Severus.

Of this there is evidence on the chair itself, which represents his episcopal *cathedra*, and has a modest symbol of lions at "the stays," as if borrowed from the throne of Solomon. It is a work of later date than the age of Severus, no doubt; but Wordsworth, who admirably illustrates the means by which such a statue may have been provided, gives us good reasons for supposing that it may have been the grateful tribute of contemporaries, and all the more trustworthy as a portrait of the man himself. The chair has carved upon it, no doubt for use in the Church, a calendar indicating the Paschal full moons for seven cycles of sixteen years each; answering, according to the science of the period, to similar tables in the Anglican Book of Common Prayer. It indicates the days on which Easter must fall, from A.D. 222 to A.D. 333. On the back of the chair is a list of the author's works.[3]

Not less interesting, and vastly more important, was the discovery, at Mount Athos, in 1842, of the long-lost *Philosophumena* of this author, concerning which the important facts will appear below. Its learned editor, Emmanuel Miller, published it at Oxford under the name of Origen, which was inscribed on the MS. Like the Epistle of Clement, its composition in the Greek language had given it currency among the Easterns long after it was forgotten in the West; and very naturally they had ascribed to Origen an anonymous treatise containing much in coincidence

---

[1] In *pseudo-Chrysost.* called γλυκύτατος καὶ εὐνούστατος. See Wordsworth, *St. Hippolytus*, etc., p. 92.

[2] A very good representation of it may be seen in Bunsen's *Hippolytus and his Age*, as a frontispiece to vol. i. London, 1852.

[3] The learned Dr. Wordsworth deals with all the difficulties of the case with judicial impartiality, but enforces his conclusions with irrefragable cogency. See also Dr. Jarvis, learned *Introduction*, p. 339.

with his teachings, and supplying the place of one of his works of a similar kind. It is now sufficiently established as the work of Hippolytus, and has been providentially brought to light just when it was most needed.[1]   In fact, the statue rose from its grave as if to rebuke the reigning pontiff (Pius IV.), who just then imposed upon the Latin churches the novel " Creed " which bears his name ; and now the *Philosophumena* comes forth as if to breathe a last warning to that namesake of the former Pius who, in the very teeth of its testimony, so recently forged and uttered the dogma of " papal infallibility " conferring this attribute upon himself, and retro-spectively upon the very bishops of Rome whom St. Hippolytus resisted as heretics, and has transmitted to posterity, in his writings, branded with the shame alike of false doctrine and of heinous crimes.   Dr. Döllinger, who for a time lent his learning and genius to an apologetic effort in behalf of the Papacy, was no doubt prepared, by this very struggle of his heart *versus* head, for that rejection of the new dogma which overloaded alike his intellect and his conscience, and made it impossible for him any longer to bear the lashes of Rehoboam [2] in communion with modern Rome.

In the biographical *data* which will be found below, enough is supplied for the needs of the reader of the present series, who, if he wishes further to investigate the subject, will find the fullest information in the works to which reference has been made, or which will be hereafter indicated.[3] But this is the place to recur to the much-abused passage of Irenæus which I have discussed in a former volume.[4]   Strange to say, I was forced to correct, from a Roman-Catholic writer, the very unsatisfactory rendering of our Edinburgh editors, and to elucidate at some length the pal-pable absurdity of attributing to Irenæus any other than a geographical and imperial reference to the importance of Rome, and its usefulness to the West, more especially, as its only see of apos-tolic origin.   Quoting the Ninth Antiochian Canon, I gave good reasons for my conjecture that the Latin *convenire* represents συντρέχειν in the original ; and now it remains to be noted how strongly the real meaning of Irenæus is illustrated in the life and services of his pupil Hippolytus.

1. That neither Hippolytus nor his master had any conception that the See of Rome possesses any pre-eminent authority, to which others are obliged to defer, is conspicuously evident from the history of both.   Alike they convicted Roman bishops of error, and alike they rebuked them for their misconduct.

2. Hippolytus is the author of a work called the *Little Labyrinth*, which, like the recently discovered *Philosophumena*, attributes to the Roman See anything but the " infallibility " which the quotation from Irenæus is so ingeniously wrested to sustain.[5]   How he did *not* understand the passage is, therefore, sufficiently apparent.   Let us next inquire what appears, from his con-duct, to be the true understanding of Irenæus.

3. I have shown, in the elucidation already referred to, how Irenæus affirms that Rome is the city which everybody visits from all parts, and that Christians, resorting thither, because it is the Imperial City, *carry into it* the testimony of all other churches.   Thus it becomes a competent witness to the *quod ab omnibus*, because it cannot be ignorant of what all the churches teach with one accord.   This argument, therefore, reverses the modern Roman dogma ; primitive Rome *received* orthodoxy instead of prescribing it.   She embosomed the Catholic testimony *brought into* it from all the churches, and gave it forth as reflected light ; not primarily her own, but what she faithfully preserved in coincidence with older and more learned churches than her-self.   Doubtless she had been planted and watered by St. Paul and St. Peter ; but doubtless, also, she had been expressly warned by the former of her liability to error and to final severance [6]

---

[1] The valuable treatise of Dr. Bunsen must be compared with the luminous reviewal of Wordsworth, *St. Hippolytus and the Church of Rome*, London, 1853 ; enlarged 1880.

[2] 1 Kings xii. 14.

[3] *A Bibliographical* account of all the ante-Nicene literature, from the learned pen of Dr. M. B. Riddle, will be given in the concluding volume of this series.

[4] Vol. i. pp. 415, 460, this series.

[5] See Eusebius, *Hist.*, v. 28 ; also Routh, *Script. Eccles. Opusc.*, vol. ii. pp. 153-160.   [6] Rom. xi. 17-21.

from apostolic communion. Hippolytus lived at a critical moment, when this awful admonition seemed about to be realized.

4. Now, then, from Portus and from Lyons, Hippolytus brought into Rome the Catholic doctrine, and convicted two of its bishops of pernicious heresies and evil living. And thus, as Irenæus teaches, the faith was preserved in Rome by the testimony of those *from every side resorting thither*, not by any prerogative of the See itself. All this will appear clearly enough as the student proceeds in the examination of this volume.

But it is now time to avail ourselves of the information given us by the translator in his INTRODUCTORY NOTICE, as follows : —

THE entire of *The Refutation of all Heresies*, with the exception of book i., was found in a MS. brought from a convent on Mount Athos so recently as the year 1842. The discoverer of this treasure — for treasure it certainly is — was Minöides Mynas, an erudite Greek, who had visited his native country in search of ancient MSS., by direction of M. Abel Villemain, Minister of Public Instruction under Louis Philippe. The French Government have thus the credit of being instrumental in bringing to light this valuable work, while the University of Oxford shares the distinction by being its earliest publishers. *The Refutation* was printed at the Clarendon Press in 1851, under the editorship of M. Emmanuel Miller,[1] whose labours have proved serviceable to all subsequent commentators. One generally acknowledged mistake was committed by Miller in ascribing the work to Origen. He was right in affirming that the discovered MS. was the continuation of the fragment, *The Philosophumena*, inserted in the Benedictine copy of Origen's works. In the volume, however, containing the *Philosophumena*, we have dissertations by Huet, in which he questions Origen's authorship in favour of Epiphanius. Heuman attributed the *Philosophumena* to Didymus of Alexandria, Gale to Aetius ;[2] and it, with the rest of *The Refutation*, Fessler and Baur ascribed to Caius, but the Abbe Jellabert to Tertullian. The last hypothesis is untenable, if for no other reason, because the work is in Greek. In many respects, Caius, who was a presbyter of Rome in the time of Victor and Zephyrinus, would seem the probable author ; but a fatal argument — one applicable to those named above, except Epiphanius — against Caius is his not being, as the author of *The Refutation* in the *Proœmium* declares himself to be, a bishop. Epiphanius no doubt filled the episcopal office ; but when we have a large work of his on the heresies, with a summary,[3] it would seem scarcely probable that he composed likewise, on the same topic, an extended treatise like the present, with two abridgments. Whatever diversity of opinion, however, existed as to these claimants, most critics, though not all, now agree in denying the authorship of Origen. Neither the style nor tone of *The Refutation* is Origenian. Its compilatory process is foreign to Origen's plan of composition ; while the subject-matter itself, for many reasons, would not be likely to have occupied the pen of the Alexandrine Father. It is almost impossible but that Origen would have made some allusions in *The Refutation* to his other writings, or in them to it. Not only, however, is there no such allusion, but the derivation of the word " Ebionites," in *The Refutation*, and an expressed belief in the (orthodox) doctrine of eternal punishment, are at variance with Origen's authorship. Again, no work answering the description is awarded to Origen in catalogues of his extant or lost writings. These arguments are strengthened by the facts, that Origen was never a bishop, and that he did not reside for any length of time at Rome. He once paid a hurried visit to the capital of the West, whereas the author of *The Refutation* asserts his presence at Rome during the occurrence of events which occupied a period of some twenty years. And not only was he a spectator, but took part in these transactions in such an official and authoritative manner as Origen could never have assumed, either at Rome or elsewhere.

---

[1] In addition to Miller, the translator has made use of the Göttingen edition, by Duncker and Schneidewin, 1859; and the Abbe Cruice's edition, Paris, 1860.

[2] An Arian bishop of the first half of the fourth century.

[3] See pp. 126–157, tom. ii., of Epiphanius' collected works, edited by Dionysius Petavius.

In this state of the controversy, commentators turned their attention towards Hippolytus, in favour of whose authorship the majority of modern scholars have decided. The arguments that have led to this conclusion, and those alleged by others against it, could not be adequately discussed in a notice like the present. Suffice it to say, that such names as Jacobi, Gieseler, Duncker, Schneidewin, Bernays, Bunsen, Wordsworth, and Döllinger, support the claims of Hippolytus. The testimony of Dr. Döllinger, considering the extent of his theological learning, and in particular his intimate acquaintance with the apostolic period in church history, virtually, we submit, decides the question.[1]

For a biography of Hippolytus we have not much authentic materials. There can be no reasonable doubt but that he was a bishop, and passed the greater portion of his life in Rome and its vicinity. This assertion corresponds with the conclusion adopted by Dr. Döllinger, who, however, refuses to allow that Hippolytus was, as is generally maintained, Bishop of Portus, a harbour of Rome at the northern mouth of the Tiber, opposite Ostia. However, it is satisfactory to establish, and especially upon such eminent authority as that of Dr. Döllinger, the fact of Hippolytus' connection with the Western Church, not only because it bears on the investigation of the authorship of *The Refutation*, the writer of which affirms his personal observation of what he records as occurring in his own time at Rome, but also because it overthrows the hypothesis of those who contend that there were more Hippolytuses than one — Dr. Döllinger shows that there is only one historical Hippolytus — or that the East, and not Italy, was the sphere of his episcopal labours. Thus Le Moyne, in the seventeenth century, a French writer resident in Leyden, ingeniously argues that Hippolytus was bishop of *Portus Romanorum* (Aden), in Arabia. Le Moyne's theory was adopted by some celebrities, viz., Dupin, Tillemont, Spanheim, Basnage, and our own Dr. Cave. To this position are opposed, among others, the names of Nicephorus, Syncellus, Baronius, Bellarmine, Dodwell, Beveridge, Bull, and Archbishop Ussher. The judgment and critical accuracy of Ussher is, on a point of this kind, of the highest value. Wherefore the question of Hippolytus being bishop of Portus near Rome would also appear established, for the reasons laid down in Bunsen's *Letters to Archdeacon Hare*, and Canon Wordsworth's *St. Hippolytus*. The mind of inquirers appears to have been primarily unsettled in consequence of Eusebius' mentioning Hippolytus (*Ecclesiast. Hist.*, vi. 10) in company with Beryllus (of Bostra), an Arabian, expressing at the same time his uncertainty as to where Hippolytus was bishop. This indecision is easily explained, and cannot invalidate the tradition and historical testimony which assign the bishopric of Portus near Rome to Hippolytus, a saint and martyr of the Church. Of his martyrdom, though the fact itself is certain, the details, furnished in Prudentius' hymn, are not historic. Thus the mode of Hippolytus' death is stated by Prudentius to have been identical with that of Hippolytus the son of Theseus, who was torn limb from limb by being tied to wild horses. St. Hippolytus, however, is known on historical testimony to have been thrown into a canal and drowned; but whether the scene of his martyrdom was Sardinia, to which he was undoubtedly banished along with the Roman bishop Pontianus, or Rome, or Portus, has not as yet been definitively proved. The time of his martyrdom, however, is probably a year or two, perhaps less or more, after the commencement of the reign of Maximin the Thracian, that is, somewhere about A.D. 235–39. This enables us to determine the age of Hippolytus; and as some statements in *The Refutation* evince the work to be the composition of an old man, and as the work itself was written after the death of Callistus in A.D. 222, this would transfer the period of his birth to not very long after the last half of the second century.

The contents of *The Refutation*, as they originally stood, seem to have been arranged thus:

---

[1] Those who are desirous of examining it for themselves may consult Gieseler's paper on Hippolytus, etc., in the *Theologische Studien und Kritiken*, 1853; Hergenröther, *Theologische Quartalschrift*, Tübingen, 1852; Bunsen's *Hippolytus and his Age;* Wordsworth's *St. Hippolytus;* Dr. Döllinger's *Hippolytus und Kallistus: oder die Römische Kirche in der ersten Hälfte des dritten Jahrhunderts*, 1853; and Cruice's *Études sur de Nouveaux Documents Historiques empruntés au livre des Φιλοσοφούμενα*, 1853. See also articles in the *Quarterly Review*, 1851; *Ecclesiastic and Theologian*, 1852, 1853; the *Westminster Review*, 1853; the *Dublin Review*, 1853, 1854; *Le Correspondent*, t. xxxi.; and the *Revue des Deux Mondes*, 1865.

The first book (which we have) contained an account of the different schools of ancient philosophers; the second (which is missing), the doctrines and mysteries of the Egyptians; the third (likewise missing), the Chaldean science and astrology; and the fourth (the beginning of which is missing), the system of the Chaldean horoscope, and the magical rites and incantations of the Babylonian Theurgists. Next came the portion of the work relating more immediately to the heresies of the Church, which is contained in books v.-ix. The tenth book is the *résumé* of the entire, together with the exposition of the author's own religious opinions. The heresies enumerated by Hippolytus comprehend a period starting from an age prior to the composition of St. John's Gospel, and terminating with the death of Callistus. The heresies are explained according to chronological development, and may be ranged under five leading schools: (1) The Ophites; (1) Simonists; (3) Basilidians; (4) Docetæ; (5) Noetians. Hippolytus ascends to the origin of heresy, not only in assigning heterodoxy a derivative nature from heathenism, but in pointing out in the *Gnosis* elements of abnormal opinions antecedent to the promulgation of Christianity. We have thus a most interesting account of the early heresies, which in some respects supplies many *desiderata* in the ecclesiastical history of this epoch.

We can scarcely over-estimate the value of *The Refutation*, on account of the propinquity of its author to the apostolic age. Hippolytus was a disciple of St. Irenæus, St. Irenæus of St. Polycarp, St. Polycarp of St. John. Indeed, one fact of grave importance connected with the writings of St. John, is elicited from Hippolytus' *Refutation*. The passage given out of Basilides' work, containing a quotation by the heretic from St. John i. 9, settles the period of the composition of the fourth Gospel, as of greater antiquity by at least thirty years than is allowed to it by the Tübingen school. It is therefore obvious that Basilides formed his system out of the prologue of St. John's Gospel; thus for ever setting at rest the allegation of these critics, that St. John's Gospel was written at a later date, and assigned an apostolic author, in order to silence the Basilidian Gnostics.[1] In the case of Irenæus, too, *The Refutation* has restored the Greek text of much of his book *Against Heresies*, hitherto only known to us in a Latin version. Nor is the value of Hippolytus' work seriously impaired, even on the supposition of the authorship not being proved, — a concession, however, in no wise justified by the evidence. Whoever the writer of *The Refutation* be, he belonged to the early portion of the third century, formed his compilations from primitive sources, made conscientious preparation for his undertaking, delivered statements confirmed by early writers of note,[2] and lastly, in the execution of his task, furnished indubitable marks of information and research, and of having thoroughly mastered the relations and affinities, each to other, of the various heresies of the first two and a quarter centuries. These heresies, whether deducible from attempts to Christianize the philosophy of Paganism, or to interpret the Doctrines and Life of our Lord by the tenets of Gnosticism and Oriental speculation generally, or to create a compromise with the pretensions of Judaism, — these heresies, amid all their complexity and diversity, St. Hippolytus[3] reduces to one common ground of censure — antagonism to Holy Scripture. Heresy, thus branded, he leaves to wither under the condemnatory sentence of the Church.

---

[1] It settles the period of the composition of St. John's Gospel only, of course, on the supposition that Hippolytus is giving a correct account as regards Basilides' work. The mode, however, in which Hippolytus introduces the quotation, appears to place its authenticity beyond reasonable doubt. He represents Basilides (see book vii. chap. 10) as notifying his reference to St. John's Gospel thus, " And this," he says, " is what has been stated in the Gospels: ' He was the true light, which lighteneth every man that cometh into the world.' " Now this is precisely the mode of reference we should expect that Basilides would employ; whereas, if Hippolytus had either fabricated the passage or adduced it from hearsay, it is almost certain he would have said " in the Gospel of St. John," and not indefinitely " the Gospels." And more than this, the formulary " in the Gospels," adopted by Basilides, reads very like a recognition of an agreed collection of authorized accounts of our Lord's life and sayings. It is also remarkable that the word " stated " (λεγόμενον) Basilides has just used in quoting (Gen. i. 3) as interchangeable with " written " (γέγραπται), the word exclusively applied to what is included within the canon of Scripture.

[2] For instance, St. Irenæus, whom Hippolytus professes to follow, Epiphanius, Theodoret, St. Augustine, etc.

[3] The translator desires to acknowledge obligations to Dr. Lottner, Professor of Sanskrit and sub-librarian in Trinity College, Dublin, — a gentleman of extensive historical erudition as well as of accurate and comprehensive scholarship.

THE REFUTATION OF ALL HERESIES

[TRANSLATED BY THE REV. J. H. MACMAHON, M.A.]

BOOK I.

CONTENTS.

THE following are the contents of the first book of *The Refutation of all Heresies*.[1]

We propose to furnish an account of the tenets of natural philosophers, and who these are, as well as the tenets of moral philosophers, and who these are; and thirdly, the tenets of logicians, and who these logicians are.

Among natural philosophers[2] may be enumerated Thales, Pythagoras, Empedocles, Heraclitus, Anaximander, Anaximenes, Anaxagoras, Archelaus, Parmenides, Leucippus, Democritus, Xenophanes, Ecphantus, Hippo.

Among moral philosophers are Socrates, pupil of Archelaus the physicist, (and) Plato the pupil of Socrates. This (speculator) combined three systems of philosophy.

Among logicians is Aristotle, pupil of Plato. He systematized the art of dialectics. Among the Stoic (logicians) were Chrysippus (and) Zeno. Epicurus, however, advanced an opinion almost contrary to all philosophers. Pyrrho was an Academic;[3] this (speculator) taught the incomprehensibility of everything. The Brahmins among the Indians, and the Druids among the Celts, and Hesiod (devoted themselves to philosophic pursuits).

THE PROŒMIUM. — MOTIVES FOR UNDERTAKING THE REFUTATION; EXPOSURE OF THE ANCIENT MYSTERIES; PLAN OF THE WORK; COMPLETENESS OF THE REFUTATION; VALUE OF THE TREATISE TO FUTURE AGES.

We must not overlook[4] any figment devised by those denominated philosophers among the Greeks. For even their incoherent tenets must be received as worthy of credit, on account of the excessive madness of the heretics; who, from the observance of silence, and from concealing their own ineffable mysteries, have by many been supposed worshippers of God.[5] We have likewise, on a former occasion,[6] expounded the doctrines of these briefly, not illustrating them with any degree of minuteness, but refuting them in coarse digest; not having considered it requisite to bring to light their secret[7] doctrines, in order that, when we have explained their tenets by enigmas, they, becoming ashamed, lest also, by our divulging their mysteries, we should convict them of atheism, might be induced to desist in some degree from their un-

---

[1] The four of the MSS. of the first book extant prior to the recent discovery of seven out of the remaining nine books of *The Refutation*, concur in ascribing it to Origen. These inscriptions run thus: 1. "Refutation by Origen of all Heresies;" 2. "Of Origen's Philosophumena . . . these are the contents;" 3. "Being estimable (Dissertations) by Origen, a man of the greatest wisdom." The recently discovered MS. itself in the margin has the words, "Origen, and Origen's opinion." The title, as agreed upon by modern commentators, is: 1. "Book I. of Origen's Refutation of all Heresies" (Wolf and Gronovius); 2. "A Refutation of all Heresies;" 3. "Origen's Philosophumena, or the Refutation of all Heresies." The last is Miller's in his Oxford edition, 1851. The title might have been, "Philosophumena, and the Refutation (therefrom) of all Heresies." There were obviously two divisions of the work: (1) A *résumé* of the tenets of the philosophers (books i., ii., iii., iv.), preparatory to (2) the refutation of heresies, on the ground of their derivative character from Greek and Egyptian speculation. Bunsen would denominate the work "St. Hippolytus' (Bishop and Martyr) Refutation of all Heresies; what remains of the ten books."

[2] Most of what follows in book i. is a compilation from ancient sources. The ablest *résumé* followed by Cicero in the *De Nat. Deor.*, of the tenets of the ancient philosophers, is to be found in Aristotle's *Metaphysics*. The English reader is referred to the *Metaphysics*, book i. pp. 13–46 (Bohn's Classical Library), also to the translator's analysis prefixed to this work, pp. 17–25. See also Diogenes' *Lives of the Philosophers*, and Tenneman's *Manual of Philosophy* (translated in Bohn's Library); Plutarch, *De Placitis Philosophorum*; Lewes' *Biographical History of (Ancient) Philosophy;* and Rev. Dr. F. D. Maurice's *History of (Ancient) Metaphysical and Moral Philosophy*. The same subject is discussed in Ritter's *History of Philosophy* (translated by Morrison).

[3] This word is variously given thus: Academian, Academeian, Academaic, Academe, Cademian, and Cadimian. The two last would seem to indicate the character rather than the philosophy of Pyrrho. To favour this view, the text should be altered into καὶ ἄδημος, i.e., ἀπόδημος = from home, not domestic.

[4] Some hiatus at the beginning of this sentence is apparent.

[5] An elaborate defence of this position forms the subject of Cudworth's great work, *The True Intellectual System of the Universe*.

[6] This statement has been urged against Origen's authorship, in favour of Epiphanius, who wrote an extended treatise on the *Heresies*, with an abridgment.

[7] That is, their esoteric mysteries, intended only for a favoured few, as contrasted with the exoteric, designed for more general diffusion.

9

reasonable opinion and their profane attempt.[1] But since I perceive that they have not been abashed by our forbearance, and have made no account of how God is long-suffering, though blasphemed by them, in order that either from shame they may repent, or should they persevere, be justly condemned, I am forced to proceed in my intention of exposing those secret mysteries of theirs, which, to the initiated, with a vast amount of plausibility they deliver who are not accustomed first to disclose (to any one), till, by keeping such in suspense during a period (of necessary preparation), and by rendering him blasphemous towards the true God, they have acquired complete ascendancy over him, and perceive him eagerly panting after the promised disclosure. And then, when they have tested him to be enslaved by sin, they initiate him, putting him in possession of the perfection of wicked things. Previously, however, they bind him with an oath neither to divulge (the mysteries), nor to hold communication with any person whatsoever, unless he first undergo similar subjection, though, when the doctrine has been simply delivered (to any one), there was no longer any need of an oath. For he who was content to submit to the necessary purgation,[2] and so receive the perfect mysteries of these men, by the very act itself, as well as in reference to his own conscience, will feel himself sufficiently under an obligation not to divulge to others ; for if he once disclose wickedness of this description to any man, he would neither be reckoned among men, nor be deemed worthy to behold the light, since not even irrational animals[3] would attempt such an enormity, as we shall explain when we come to treat of such topics.

Since, however, reason compels us to plunge[4] into the very depth of narrative, we conceive we should not be silent, but, expounding the tenets of the several schools with minuteness, we shall evince reserve in nothing. Now it seems expedient, even at the expense of a more protracted investigation, not to shrink from labour ; for we shall leave behind us no trifling auxiliary to human life against the recurrence of error, when all are made to behold, in an obvious light, the clandestine rites of these men, and the secret orgies which, retaining under their management, they deliver to the initiated only. But none will refute these, save the Holy Spirit bequeathed unto the Church, which the Apostles, having in the first instance received, have transmitted to those who have rightly believed. But we, as being their successors, and as participators in this grace, high-priesthood, and office of teaching,[5] as well as being reputed guardians of the Church, must not be found deficient in vigilance,[6] or disposed to suppress correct doctrine.[7] Not even, however, labouring with every energy of body and soul, do we tire in our attempt adequately to render our Divine Benefactor a fitting return ; and yet withal we do not so requite Him in a becoming manner, except we are not remiss in discharging the trust committed to us, but careful to complete the measure of our particular opportunity, and to impart to all without grudging whatever the Holy Ghost supplies, not only bringing to light,[8] by means of our refutation, matters foreign (to our subject), but also whatsoever things the truth has received by the grace of the Father,[9] and ministered to men. These also, illustrating by argument and creating testimony[10] by letters, we shall unabashed proclaim.

In order, then, as we have already stated, that we may prove them atheists, both in opinion and their mode (of treating a question) and in fact, and (in order to show) whence it is that their attempted theories have accrued unto them, and that they have endeavoured to establish their tenets, taking nothing from the holy Scriptures —nor is it from preserving the succession of any saint that they have hurried headlong into these opinions ; — but that their doctrines have derived their origin[11] from the wisdom of the Greeks, from the conclusions of those who have formed systems of philosophy, and from would-be mysteries, and the vagaries of astrologers, — it seems, then, advisable, in the first instance, by explaining the opinions advanced by the philosophers of the Greeks, to satisfy our readers that such are of greater antiquity than these (heresies), and more deserving of reverence in reference to their views respecting the divinity ; in the next place, to compare each heresy with the system of each speculator, so as to show that the earliest champion of the heresy availing himself[12] of these attempted theories, has turned them to advantage by appropriating their principles, and, impelled from these into worse, has constructed his own doctrine. The undertaking

---

[1] One MS. has — " the profane opinion and unreasonable attempt."
[2] " To learn " (Roeper).
[3] " And those that are irrational animals do not attempt," (or) " because irrational," etc. The last is Sancroft's reading; that in the text, Roeper's.
[4] " Ascend up to " (Roeper).

[5] This passage is quoted by those who impugn the authorship of Origen on the ground of his never having been a bishop of the Church. It is not, however, quite certain that the words refer to the episcopal office exclusively.
[6] The common reading is in the future, but the present tense is adopted by Richter in his *Critical Observations*, p. 77.
[7] It might be, " any opinion that may be subservient to the subject taken in hand." This is Cruice's rendering in his Latin version. A different reading is, " we must not be silent as regards reasons that hold good," or, " as regards rational distinctions," or, " refrain from utterances through the instrument of reasoning." The last is Roeper's.
[8] Another reading is, " bringing into a collection."
[9] Or, " the Spirit."
[10] Or, " indicating a witness; " or, " having adduced testimony."
[11] Or, " a starting-point."
[12] Or, " devoting his attention to; " or, " having lighted upon."

admittedly is full of labour, and (is one) requiring extended research. We shall not, however, be wanting in exertion; for afterwards it will be a source of joy, just like an athlete obtaining with much toil the crown, or a merchant after a huge swell of sea compassing gain, or a husbandman after sweat of brow enjoying the fruits, or a prophet after reproaches and insults seeing his predictions turning out true. In the commencement, therefore, we shall declare who first, among the Greeks, pointed out (the principles of) natural philosophy. For from these especially have they furtively taken their views who have first propounded these heresies,[1] as we shall subsequently prove when we come to compare them one with another. Assigning to each of those who take the lead among philosophers their own peculiar tenets, we shall publicly exhibit these heresiarchs as naked and unseemly.

CHAP. I. — THALES; HIS PHYSICS AND THEOLOGY; FOUNDER OF GREEK ASTRONOMY.

It is said that Thales of Miletus, one of the seven[2] wise men, first attempted to frame a system of natural philosophy. This person said that some such thing as water is the generative principle of the universe, and its end; — for that out of this, solidified and again dissolved, all things consist, and that all things are supported on it; from which also arise both earthquakes and changes of the winds and atmospheric movements,[3] and that all things are both produced[4] and are in a state of flux corresponding with the nature of the primary author of generation; — and that the Deity[5] is that which has neither beginning nor end. This person, having been occupied with an hypothesis and investigation concerning the stars, became the earliest author to the Greeks of this kind of learning. And he, looking towards heaven, alleging that he was carefully examining supernal objects, fell into a well; and a certain maid, by name Thratta, remarked of him derisively, that while intent on beholding things in heaven, he did not know[6] what was at his feet. And he lived about the time of Crœsus.

CHAP. II. — PYTHAGORAS; HIS COSMOGONY; RULES OF HIS SECT; DISCOVERER OF PHYSIOGNOMY; HIS PHILOSOPHY OF NUMBERS; HIS SYSTEM OF THE TRANSMIGRATION OF SOULS; ZARATAS ON DEMONS; WHY PYTHAGORAS FORBADE THE EATING OF BEANS; THE MODE OF LIVING ADOPTED BY HIS DISCIPLES.

But there was also, not far from these times, another philosophy which Pythagoras originated (who some say was a native of Samos), which they have denominated Italian, because that Pythagoras, flying from Polycrates the king of Samos, took up his residence in a city of Italy, and there passed the entire of his remaining years. And they who received in succession his doctrine, did not much differ from the same opinion. And this person, instituting an investigation concerning natural phenomena,[7] combined together astronomy, and geometry, and music.[8] And so he proclaimed that the Deity is a monad; and carefully acquainting himself with the nature of number, he affirmed that the world sings, and that its system corresponds with harmony, and he first resolved the motion of the seven stars into rhythm and melody. And being astonished at the management of the entire fabric, he required that at first his disciples should keep silence, as if persons coming into the world initiated in (the secrets of) the universe; next, when it seemed that they were sufficiently conversant with his mode of teaching his doctrine, and could forcibly philosophize concerning the stars and nature, then, considering them pure, he enjoins them to speak. This man distributed his pupils in two orders, and called the one esoteric, but the other exoteric. And to the former he confided more advanced doctrines, and to the latter a more moderate amount of instruction.

And he also touched on magic — as they say — and himself[9] discovered an art of physiogony,[10] laying down as a basis certain numbers and measures, saying that they comprised the principle of arithmetical philosophy by composition after this manner. The first number became an originating principle, which is one, indefinable, incomprehensible, having in itself all numbers that, according to plurality, can go on *ad infinitum*. But the primary monad became a principle of numbers, according to substance,[11] — which is a male monad, begetting after the manner of a parent all the rest of the numbers. Secondly, the duad is a female number, and the same also is by arithmeticians termed even. Thirdly, the triad is a male number. This also has been classified by arithmeti-

---

[1] The chief writers on the early heresies are: Irenæus, of the second century; Hippolytus, his pupil, of the third; Philastrius, Epiphanius, and St. Augustine, of the fourth century. The learned need scarcely be reminded of the comprehensive digest furnished by Ittigius in the preface to his dissertation on the heresies of the apostolic and post-apostolic ages. A book more within the reach of the general reader is Dr. Burton's *Inquiry into the Heresies of the Apostolic Age*.

[2] [These were: Periander of Corinth, B.C. 585; Pittacus of Mitylene, B.C. 570; Thales of Miletus, B.C. 548; Solon of Athens, B.C. 540; Chilo of Sparta, B.C. 597; Bias of Priene; Cleobulus of Lindus, B.C. 564.]

[3] Or, "motions of the stars" (Roeper).

[4] Or, "carried along" (Roeper).

[5] Or, "that which is divine." See Clemens Alexandrinus, *Strom.*, v. pp. 461, 463 (Heinsius and Sylburgius' ed.). Thales, on being asked, "What is God?" "That," replied he, "which has neither beginning nor end."

[6] Or, "see."

[7] Or, "nature."

[8] "And arithmetic" (added by Roeper).

[9] Or, "and he first."

[10] Or, "physiognomy."

[11] Or, "in conformity with his hypothesis."

cians under the denomination uneven. And in addition to all these is the tetrad, a female number; and the same also is called even, because it is female. Therefore all the numbers that have been derived from the genus are four; but number is the indefinite genus, from which was constituted, according to them, the perfect [1] number, viz., the decade. For one, two, three, four, become ten, if its proper denomination be preserved essentially for each of the numbers. Pythagoras affirmed this to be a sacred quaternion, source of everlasting nature,[2] having, as it were, roots in itself; and that from this number all the numbers receive their originating principle. For eleven, and twelve, and the rest, partake of the origin of existence[3] from ten. Of this decade, the perfect number, there are termed four divisions, — namely, number, monad,[4] square, (and) cube. And the connections and blendings of these are performed, according to nature, for the generation of growth completing the productive number. For when the square itself is multiplied[5] into itself, a biquadratic is the result. But when the square is multiplied into the cube, the result is the product of a square and cube; and when the cube is multiplied into the cube, the product of two cubes is the result. So that all the numbers from which the production of existing (numbers) arises, are seven, — namely, number, monad, square, cube, biquadratic, quadratic-cube, cubo-cube.

This philosopher likewise said that the soul is immortal, and that it subsists in successive bodies. Wherefore he asserted that before the Trojan era he was Æthalides,[6] and during the Trojan epoch Euphorbus, and subsequent to this Hermotimus of Samos, and after him Pyrrhus of Delos; fifth, Pythagoras. And Diodorus the Eretrian,[7] and Aristoxenus[8] the musician, assert

that Pythagoras came to Zaratas[9] the Chaldean, and that he explained to him that there are two original causes of things, father and mother, and that father is light, but mother darkness; and that of the light the parts are hot, dry, not heavy, light, swift; but of darkness, cold, moist, weighty, slow; and that out of all these, from female and male, the world consists. But the world, he says, is a musical harmony;[10] wherefore, also, that the sun performs a circuit in accordance with harmony. And as regards the things that are produced from earth and the cosmical system, they maintain that Zaratas[11] makes the following statements: that there are two demons, the one celestial and the other terrestrial; and that the terrestrial sends up a production from earth, and that this is water; and that the celestial is a fire, partaking of the nature of air, hot and cold.[12] And he therefore affirms that none of these destroys or sullies the soul, for these constitute the substance of all things. And he is reported to have ordered his followers not to eat beans, because that Zaratas said that, at the origin and concretion of all things, when the earth was still undergoing its process of solidification,[13] and that of putrefaction had set in, the bean was produced.[14] And of this he mentions the following indication, that if any one, after having chewed a bean without the husk, places it opposite the sun for a certain period, — for this immediately will aid in the result, — it yields the smell of human seed. And he mentions also another clearer instance to be this: if, when the bean is blossoming, we take the bean and its flower, and deposit them in a jar, smear this over, and bury it in the ground, and after a few days uncover it, we shall see it wearing the appearance, first of a woman's *pudendum*, and after this, when closely examined, of the head of a child growing in along with it. This person, being burned along with his disciples in Croton, a town of Italy, perished. And this was a habit with him, whenever one repaired to him with a view of becoming his follower, (the candidate disciple was compelled) to sell his possessions, and lodge the money sealed with Pythagoras, and he continued in silence to un-

---

[1] Or, "the third."

[2] Or, "an everlasting nature;" or, "having the roots of an everlasting nature in itself," the words "as it were" being omitted in some MSS.

[3] Or, "production."

[4] It should be probably, "monad, number." The monad was with Pythagoras, and in imitation of him with Leibnitz, the highest generalization of number, and a conception in abstraction, commensurate with what we call essence, whether of matter or spirit.

[5] Κοβιϲθῇ in text must be rendered "multiplied." The formulary is self-evident: $(a^2)^2 = a^4$, $(a^2)^3 = a^6$, $(a^3)^3 = a^9$.

[6] Or Thallis. Æthalides, a son of Hermes, was herald of the Argonauts, and said never to have forgotten anything. In this way his soul remembered its successive migrations into the bodies of Euphorbus, Hermotimus, Pyrrhus, and Pythagoras. (See Diogenes' *Lives*, book viii. chap. i. sec. 4.)

[7] No name occurs more frequently in the annals of Greek literature than that of Diodorus. One, however, with the title "of Eretria," as far as the translator knows, is mentioned only by Hippolytus; so that this is likely another Diodorus to be added to the long list already existing. It may be that Diodorus Eretriensis is the same as Diodorus Crotoniates, a Pythagorean philosopher. See Fabricius' *Biblioth. Græc.*, lib ii. cap. iii., lib. iii. cap. xxxi.; also Meursius' *Annotations*, p. 20, *on Chalcidius' Commentary on Plato's Timæus*. The article in *Smith's Dictionary* is a transcript of these.

[8] Aristoxenus is mentioned by Cicero in his *Tusculan Questions*, book i. chap. xviii., as having broached a theory in psychology, which may have suggested, in modern times, to David Hartley his hypothesis of sensation being the result of nerval vibrations. Cicero says of Aristoxenus, "that he was so charmed with his own harmonies, that he sought to transfer them into investigations concerning our corporeal and spiritual nature."

[9] Zaratas is another form of the name Zoroaster.

[10] Or, "is a nature according to musical harmony" (preceding note); or, "The cosmical system is nature and a musical harmony."

[11] Zaratas, or Zoroaster, is employed as a sort of generic denomination for philosopher by the Orientals, who, whatever portions of Asia they inhabit, mostly ascribe their speculative systems to a Zoroaster. No less than six individuals bearing this name are spoken of. Arnobius (*Contr. Gentes.*, i. 52) mentions four — (1) a Chaldean, (2) Bactrian, (3) Pamphylian, (4) Armenian. Pliny mentions a fifth as a native of Proconnesus (*Nat. Hist.*, xxx. 1), while Apuleius (*Florida*, ii. 15) a sixth Zoroaster, a native of Babylon, and contemporary with Pythagoras, the one evidently alluded to by Hippolytus. (See translator's *Treatise on Metaphysics*, chap. ii.)

[12] Or, "that it was hot and cold," or "hot of moist."

[13] Or it might be rendered, "a process of arrangement." The Abbe Cruice (in his edition of *Hippolytus*, Paris, 1860) suggests a different reading, which would make the words translate thus, "when the earth was an undigested and solid mass."

[14] [See book vi. cap. xxii., *infra*, and note. But Clement gives another explanation. See vol. ii. p. 385, this series.]

dergo instruction, sometimes for three, but sometimes for five years. And again, on being released, he was permitted to associate with the rest, and remained as a disciple, and took his meals along with them ; if otherwise, however, he received back his property, and was rejected. These persons, then, were styled Esoteric Pythagoreans, whereas the rest, Pythagoristæ.

Among his followers, however, who escaped the conflagration were Lysis and Archippus, and the servant of Pythagoras, Zamolxis,[1] who also is said to have taught the Celtic Druids to cultivate the philosophy of Pythagoras. And they assert that Pythagoras learned from the Egyptians his system of numbers and measures ; and being struck by the plausible, fanciful, and not easily revealed wisdom of the priests, he himself likewise, in imitation of them, enjoined silence, and made his disciples lead a solitary life in underground chapels.[2]

CHAP. III. — EMPEDOCLES ; HIS TWOFOLD CAUSE ;
TENET OF TRANSMIGRATION.

But Empedocles, born after these, advanced likewise many statements respecting the nature of demons, to the effect that, being very numerous, they pass their time in managing earthly concerns. This person affirmed the originating principle of the universe to be discord and friendship, and that the intelligible fire of the monad is the Deity, and that all things consist of fire, and will be resolved into fire ; with which opinion the Stoics likewise almost agree, expecting a conflagration. But most of all does he concur with the tenet of transition of souls from body to body, expressing himself thus : —

" For surely both youth and maid I was,
And shrub, and bird,[3] and fish, from ocean stray'd."[4]

This (philosopher) maintained the transmutation of all souls into any description of animal. For Pythagoras, the instructor of these (sages),[5] asserted that himself had been Euphorbus, who served in the expedition against Ilium, alleging that he recognised his shield. The foregoing are the tenets of Empedocles.

CHAP. IV. — HERACLITUS ; HIS UNIVERSAL DOGMATISM ; HIS THEORY OF FLUX ; OTHER SYSTEMS.

But Heraclitus, a natural philosopher of Ephesus, surrendered himself to universal grief, condemning the ignorance of the entire of life, and of all men ; nay, commiserating the (very) exist-ence of mortals, for he asserted that he himself knew everything, whereas the rest of mankind nothing.[6] But he also advanced statements almost in concert with Empedocles, saying that the originating principle of all things is discord and friendship, and that the Deity is a fire endued with intelligence, and that all things are borne one upon another, and never are at a standstill ; and just as Empedocles, he affirmed that the entire locality about us is full of evil things, and that these evil things reach as far as the moon, being extended from the quarter situated around the earth, and that they do not advance further, inasmuch as the entire space above the moon is more pure. So also it seemed to Heraclitus.

After these arose also other natural philosophers, whose opinions we have not deemed it necessary to declare, (inasmuch as) they present no diversity to those already specified. Since, however, upon the whole, a not inconsiderable school has sprung (from thence), and many natural philosophers subsequently have arisen from them, each advancing different accounts of the nature of the universe, it seems also to us advisable, that, explaining the philosophy that has come down by succession from Pythagoras, we should recur to the opinions entertained by those living after the time of Thales, and that, furnishing a narrative of these, we should approach the consideration of the ethical and logical philosophy which Socrates and Aristotle originated, the former ethical, and the latter logical.[7]

CHAP. V. — ANAXIMANDER ; HIS THEORY OF THE
INFINITE ; HIS ASTRONOMIC OPINIONS ; HIS
PHYSICS.

Anaximander, then, was the hearer of Thales. Anaximander was son of Praxiadas, and a native of Miletus. This man said that the originating principle of existing things is a certain constitution of the Infinite, out of which the heavens are generated, and the worlds therein ; and that this principle is eternal and undecaying, and comprising all the worlds. And he speaks of time as something of limited generation, and subsistence, and destruction. This person declared the Infinite to be an originating principle and element of existing things, being the first to employ such a denomination of the originating principle. But, moreover, he asserted that there is an eternal motion, by the agency of which it happens that the heavens[8] are generated ; but that the earth is poised aloft, upheld by nothing,

---

[1] Or, "Zametus."
[2] Or, "leading them down into cells, made them," etc.; or, "made his disciples observe silence," etc.
[3] Or, "and beast," more in keeping with the sense of the name; or "a lamb" has been suggested in the Gottingen edition of Hippolytus.
[4] Or, "traveller into the sea ;" or, "mute ones from the sea ;" or, "from the sea a glittering fish."
[5] Or, "being the instructor of this (philosopher)."

[6] Proclus, in his commentary on Plato's *Timæus*, uses almost the same words: "but Heraclitus, in asserting his own universal knowledge, makes out all the rest of mankind ignorant."
[7] Or, "and among these, Socrates a moral philosopher, and Aristotle a logician, originated systems."
[8] Or, "men."

continuing (so) on account of its equal distance from all (the heavenly bodies) ; and that the figure of it is curved, circular,[1] similar to a column of stone.[2]   And one of the surfaces we tread upon, but the other is opposite.[3]   And that the stars are a circle of fire, separated from the fire which is in the vicinity of the world, and encompassed by air.   And that certain atmospheric exhalations arise in places where the stars shine ; wherefore, also, when these exhalations are obstructed, that eclipses take place.   And that the moon sometimes appears full and sometimes waning, according to the obstruction or opening of its (orbital) paths.   But that the circle of the sun is twenty-seven times[4] larger than the moon, and that the sun is situated in the highest (quarter of the firmament) ; whereas the orbs of the fixed stars in the lowest.   And that animals are produced (in moisture[5]) by evaporation from the sun.   And that man was, óriginally, similar to a different animal, that is, a fish.   And that winds are caused by the separation of very rarified exhalations of the atmosphere, and by their motion after they have been condensed.   And that rain arises from earth's giving back (the vapours which it receives) from the (clouds[6]) under the sun.   And that there are flashes of lightning when the wind coming down severs the clouds.   This person was born in the third year of the XLII. Olympiad.[7]

CHAP. VI. — ANAXIMENES ; HIS SYSTEM OF " AN INFINITE AIR ; " HIS VIEWS OF ASTRONOMY AND NATURAL PHENOMENA.

But Anaximenes, who himself was also a native of Miletus, and son of Eurystratus, affirmed that the originating principle is infinite air, out of which are generated things existing, those which have existed, and those that will be, as well as gods and divine (entities), and that the rest arise from the offspring of this.   But that there is such a species of air, when it is most even, which is imperceptible to vision, but capable of being manifested by cold and heat, and moisture and motion, and that it is continually in motion ; for that whatsoever things undergo alteration, do not change if there is not motion. For that it presents a different appearance according as it is condensed and attenuated, for when it is dissolved into what is more attenuated that fire is produced, and that when it is moderately condensed again into air that a cloud

is formed from the air by virtue of the contraction ;[8] but when condensed still more, water, (and) that when the condensation is carried still further, earth is formed ; and when condensed to the very highest degree, stones.   Wherefore, that the dominant principles of generation are contraries, — namely, heat and cold.   And that the expanded earth is wafted along upon the air, and in like manner both sun and moon and the rest of the stars ; for all things being of the nature of fire, are wafted about through the expanse of space, upon the air.   And that the stars are produced from earth by reason of the mist which arises from this *earth ;* and when this is attenuated, that fire is produced, and that the stars consist of the fire which is being borne aloft. But also that there are terrestrial natures in the region of the stars carried on along with them. And he says that the stars do not move under the earth, as some have supposed, but around the earth,[9] just as a cap is turned round our head ; and that the sun is hid, not by being under the earth, but because covered by the higher portions of the earth, and on account of the greater distance that he is from us.   But that the stars do not emit heat on account of the length of distance ; and that the winds are produced when the condensed air, becoming rarified, is borne on ; and that when collected and thickened still further, clouds are generated, and thus a change made into water.   And that hail is produced when the water borne down from the clouds becomes congealed ; and that snow is generated when these very clouds, being more moist, acquire congelation ; and that lightning is caused when the clouds are parted by force of the winds ; for when these are sundered there is produced a brilliant and fiery flash.   And that a rainbow is produced by reason of the rays of the sun falling on the collected air.   And that an earthquake takes place when the earth is altered into a larger (bulk) by heat and cold.   These indeed, then, were the opinions of Anaximenes.   This (philosopher) flourished about the first year of the LVIII. Olympiad.[10]

CHAP. VII. — ANAXAGORAS ; HIS THEORY OF MIND ; RECOGNISES AN EFFICIENT CAUSE ; HIS COSMOGONY AND ASTRONOMY.

After this (thinker) comes Anaxagoras,[11] son of Hegesibulus,[12] a native of Clazomenæ.   This person affirmed the originating principle of the universe to be mind and matter ; mind being

[1] Or, " moist."
[2] Or, " congealed snow."
[3] That is, Antipodes.   Diogenes Laertius was of opinion that Plato first indicated by name the Antipodes.
[4] Or, " 727 times," an improbable reading.
[5] " In moisture" is properly added, as Plutarch, in his *De Placitis,* v. xix., remarks that " Anaximander affirms that primary animals were produced in moisture."
[6] This word seems requisite to the sense of the passage.
[7] [B.C. 610.   On *Olympiads,* see Jarvis, *Introd.,* p. 21.]

[8] Or, " revolutionary motion."
[9] Plutarch, in his *De Placitis Philosophorum,* attributes both opinions to Anaximenes, viz., that the sun was moved both under and around the earth.
[10] [B.C. 556.]
[11] Aristotle considers that Anaxagoras was the first to broach the existence of efficient causes in nature.   He states, however, that Hermotimus received the credit of so doing at an earlier date.
[12] Or, Hegesephontus.

the efficient cause, whereas matter that which was being formed. For all things coming into existence simultaneously, mind supervening introduced order. And material principles, he says, are infinite ; even the smaller of these are infinite.[1] And that all things partake of motion by being moved by mind, and that similar bodies coalesce. And that celestial bodies were arranged by orbicular motion. That, therefore, what was thick and moist, and dark and cold, and all things heavy, came together into the centre, from the solidification of which earth derived support ; but that the things opposite to these — namely, heat and brilliancy, and dryness and lightness — hurried impetuously into the farther portion of the atmosphere. And that the earth is in figure plane ; and that it continues suspended aloft, by reason of its magnitude, and by reason of there being no vacuum, and by reason of the air, which was most powerful, bearing along the wafted earth. But that among moist substances on earth, was the sea, and the waters in it ; and when these evaporated (from the sun), or had settled under, that the ocean was formed in this manner, as well as from the rivers that from time to time flow into it. And that the rivers also derive support from the rains and from the actual waters in the earth ; for that this is hollow, and contains water in its caverns. And that the Nile is inundated in summer, by reason of the waters carried down into it from the snows in northern (latitudes).[2] And that the sun and moon and all the stars are fiery stones, that were rolled round by the rotation of the atmosphere. And that beneath the stars are sun and moon, and certain invisible bodies that are carried along with us ; and that we have no perception of the heat of the stars, both on account of their being so far away, and on account of their distance from the earth ; and further, they are not to the same degree hot as the sun, on account of their occupying a colder situation. And that the moon, being lower than the sun, is nearer us. And that the sun surpasses the Peloponnesus in size. And that the moon has not light of its own, but from the sun. But that the revolution of the stars takes place under the earth. And that the moon is eclipsed when the earth is interposed, and occasionally also those (stars) that are underneath the moon. And that the sun (is eclipsed) when, at the beginning of the month, the moon is interposed. And that the solstices are caused by both sun and moon being repulsed by the air. And that the moon is often turned, by its not

being able to make head against the cold. This person was the first to frame definitions regarding eclipses and illuminations. And he affirmed that the moon is earthy, and has in it plains and ravines. And that the milky way is a reflection of the light of the stars which do not derive their radiance from the sun ;[3] and that the stars, coursing (the firmament) as shooting sparks, arise out of the motion of the pole. And that winds are caused when the atmosphere is rarified by the sun, and by those burning orbs that advance under the pole, and are borne from (it). And that thunder and lightning are caused by heat falling on the clouds. And that earthquakes are produced by the air above falling on that under the earth ; for when this is moved, that the earth also, being wafted by it, is shaken. And that animals originally came into existence[4] in moisture, and after this one from another ; and that males are procreated when the seed secreted from the right parts adhered to the right parts of the womb, and that females are born when the contrary took place. This philosopher flourished in the first year of the LXXXVIII. Olympiad,[5] at which time they say that Plato also was born. They maintain that Anaxagoras was likewise prescient.

CHAP. VIII. — ARCHELAUS ; SYSTEM AKIN TO THAT OF ANAXAGORAS ; HIS ORIGIN OF THE EARTH AND OF ANIMALS ; OTHER SYSTEMS.

Archelaus was by birth an Athenian, and son of Apollodorus.[6] This person, similarly with Anaxagoras, asserted the mixture of matter, and enunciated his first principles in the same manner. This philosopher, however, held that there is inherent immediately in mind a certain mixture ; and that the originating principle of motion is the mutual separation of heat and cold, and that the heat is moved, and that the cold remains at rest. And that the water, being dissolved, flows towards the centre, where the scorched air and earth are produced, of which the one is borne upwards and the other remains beneath. And that the earth is at rest, and that on this account it came into existence ; and that it lies in the centre, being no part, so to speak, of the universe, delivered from the conflagration ; and that from this, first in a state of ignition, is the nature of the stars, of which indeed the largest is the sun, and next to this the moon ; and of the rest some less, but some greater. And he says that the heaven was inclined at an angle, and so that the sun diffused light over the earth, and made the atmosphere transparent, and the ground dry ; for that at first it was a sea,

---

[1] Simplicius, in his *Commentary on Aristotle's Physics*, where (book i. c. 2) Anaxagoras is spoken of, says that the latter maintained that " all things existed simultaneously — infinite things, and plurality, and diminutiveness, for even what was diminutive was infinite." (See Aristotle's *Metaphysics*, iii. 4, Macmahon's translation, p. 93.) This explains Hippolytus' remark, while it suggests an emendation of the text.
[2] Or, " in the Antipodes; " or, " from the snow in Æthiopia."

[3] Or, " overpowered by the sun," that is, whose light was lost in the superior brilliancy of the sun.
[4] Or, " were generated."
[5] [Died B.C. 428 or 429.]
[6] [B.C. 440.]

inasmuch as it is lofty at the horizon and hollow in the middle. And he adduces, as an indication of the hollowness, that the sun does not rise and set to all at the same time, which ought to happen if the earth was even. And with regard to animals, he affirms that the earth, being originally fire in its lower part, where the heat and cold were intermingled, both the rest of animals made their appearance, numerous and dissimilar,[1] all having the same food, being nourished from mud ; and their existence was of short duration, but afterwards also generation from one another arose unto them ; and men were separated from the rest (of the animal creation), and they appointed rulers, and laws, and arts, and cities, and the rest. And he asserts that mind is innate in all animals alike ; for that each, according to the difference of their physical constitution, employed (mind), at one time slower, at another faster.[2]

Natural philosophy, then, continued from Thales until Archelaus. Socrates was the hearer of this (latter philosopher). There are, however, also very many others, introducing various opinions respecting both the divinity and the nature of the universe ; and if we were disposed to adduce all the opinions of these, it would be necessary to compose a vast quantity of books. But, reminding the reader of those whom we especially ought — who are deserving of mention from their fame, and from being, so to speak, the leaders to those who have subsequently framed systems of philosophy, and from their supplying them with a starting-point towards such undertakings — let us hasten on our investigations towards what remains for consideration.

CHAP. IX. — PARMENIDES ; HIS THEORY OF "UNITY ;" HIS ESCHATOLOGY.

For Parmenides[3] likewise supposes the universe to be one, both eternal and unbegotten, and of a spherical form. And neither did he escape the opinion of the great body (of speculators), affirming fire and earth to be the originating principles of the universe — the earth as matter, but the fire as cause, even an efficient one. He asserted that the world would be destroyed, but in what way he does not mention.[4] The same (philosopher), however, affirmed the universe to be eternal, and not generated, and of spherical form and homogeneous, but not having a figure in itself, and immoveable and limited.

CHAP. X. — LEUCIPPUS ; HIS ATOMIC THEORY.

But Leucippus,[5] an associate of Zeno, did not maintain the same opinion, but affirms things to be infinite, and always in motion, and that generation and change exist continuously. And he affirms plenitude and vacuum to be elements. And he asserts that worlds are produced when many bodies are congregated and flow together from the surrounding space to a common point, so that by mutual contact they made substances of the same figure and similar in form come into connection ; and when thus intertwined,[6] there are transmutations into other bodies, and that created things wax and wane through necessity. But what the nature of necessity is, (Parmenides) did not define.

CHAP. XI. — DEMOCRITUS ; HIS DUALITY OF PRINCIPLES ; HIS COSMOGONY.

And Democritus[7] was an acquaintance of Leucippus. Democritus, son of Damasippus, a native of Abdera,[8] conferring with many gymnosophists among the Indians, and with priests in Egypt, and with astrologers and magi in Babylon, (propounded his system). Now he makes statements similarly with Leucippus concerning elements, viz., plenitude and vacuum, denominating plenitude entity, and vacuum nonentity ; and this he asserted, since existing things are continually moved in the vacuum. And he maintained worlds to be infinite, and varying in bulk ; and that in some there is neither sun nor moon, while in others that they are larger than with us, and with others more numerous. And that intervals between worlds are unequal ; and that in one quarter of space (worlds) are more numerous, and in another less so ; and that some of them increase in bulk, but that others attain their full size, while others dwindle away ; and that in one quarter they are coming into existence, whilst in another they are failing ; and that they are destroyed by clashing one with another. And that some worlds are destitute of animals and plants, and every species of moisture. And that the earth of our world was created before that of the stars, and that the moon is underneath ; next (to it) the sun ; then the fixed stars. And that (neither) the planets nor these (fixed stars) possess an equal elevation. And that the world flourishes, until no longer it can receive anything from without. This (philosopher) turned all things into ridicule, as if all the concerns of humanity were deserving of laughter.

---

[1] Or, "both many of the rest of the animal kingdom, and man himself." (See Diogenes Laertius' *Lives*, ii. 17.)
[2] There is some confusion in the text here, but the rendering given above, though conjectural, is highly probable. One proposed emendation would make the passage run thus: "for that each body employed mind, sometimes slower, sometimes faster."
[3] [B.C. 500.]
[4] The next sentence is regarded by some as not genuine.

[5] [B.C. 370.]
[6] Or, "when again mutually connected, that different entities were generated." (See Diogenes Laertius' *Lives*, ix. 30-32.)
[7] [Died in his hundred and ninth year, B.C. 361.]
[8] Or, "Audera."

CHAP. XII. — XENOPHANES; HIS SCEPTICISM; HIS NOTIONS OF GOD AND NATURE; BELIEVES IN A FLOOD.

But Xenophanes, a native of Colophon,[1] was son of Orthomenes. This man survived to the time of Cyrus.[2] This (philosopher) first asserted that there is no possibility of comprehending anything, expressing himself thus : —

"For if for the most part of perfection man may speak,
Yet he knows it not himself, and in all attains surmise."

And he affirms that nothing is generated or perishes, or is moved; and that the universe, being one, is beyond change. But he says that the deity is eternal, and one and altogether homogeneous and limited, and of a spherical form, and endued with perception in all parts. And that the sun exists during each day from a conglomeration of small sparks, and that the earth is infinite, and is surrounded neither by an atmosphere nor by the heaven. And that there are infinite suns and moons, and that all things spring from earth. This man affirmed that the sea is salt, on account of the many mixtures that flow into it. Metrodorus, however, from the fact of its being filtered through earth, asserts that it is on account of this that it is made salt. And Xenophanes is of opinion that there had been a mixture of the earth with the sea, and that in process of time it was disengaged from the moisture, alleging that he could produce such proofs as the following: that in the midst of earth, and in mountains, shells are discovered; and also in Syracuse he affirms was found in the quarries the print of a fish and of seals, and in Paros an image of a laurel[3] in the bottom of a stone, and in Melita[4] parts of all sorts of marine animals. And he says that these were generated when all things originally were embedded in mud, and that an impression of them was dried in the mud, but that all men had perished[5] when the earth, being precipitated into the sea, was converted into mud; then, again, that it originated generation, and that this overthrow occurred to all worlds.

CHAP. XIII. — ECPHANTUS; HIS SCEPTICISM; TENET OF INFINITY.

One Ecphantus, a native of Syracuse, affirmed that it is not possible to attain a true knowledge of things. He defines, however, as he thinks, primary bodies to be indivisible,[6] and that there are three variations of these, viz., bulk, figure, capacity, from which are generated the objects of sense. But that there is a determinable multitude of these, and that this is infinite.[7] And that bodies are moved neither by weight nor by impact, but by divine power, which he calls mind and soul; and that of this the world is a representation; wherefore also it has been made in the form of a sphere by divine power.[8] And that the earth in the middle of the cosmical system is moved round its own centre towards the east.[9]

CHAP. XIV. — HIPPO; HIS DUALITY OF PRINCIPLES; HIS PSYCHOLOGY.

Hippo, a native of Rhegium, asserted as originating principles, coldness, for instance water, and heat, for instance fire. And that fire, when produced by water, subdued the power of its generator, and formed the world. And the soul, he said, is[10] sometimes brain, but sometimes water; for that also the seed is that which appears to us to arise out of moisture, from which, he says, the soul is produced.

So far, then, we think we have sufficiently adduced (the opinions of) these; wherefore, inasmuch as we have adequately gone in review through the tenets of physical speculators, it seems to remain that we now turn to Socrates and Plato, who gave especial preference to moral philosophy.

CHAP. XV. — SOCRATES; HIS PHILOSOPHY REPRODUCED BY PLATO.

Socrates, then, was a hearer of Archelaus, the natural philosopher; and he, reverencing the rule, "Know thyself," and having assembled a large school, had Plato (there), who was far superior to all his pupils. (Socrates) himself left no writings[11] after him. Plato, however, taking notes[12] of all his (lectures on) wisdom, established a school, combining together natural, ethical, (and) logical (philosophy). But the points Plato determined are these following.

---

[1] [Born 556 B.C.]
[2] [Incredible. Cyrus the younger, fell at Cunaxa B.C. 401. Cyrus the elder was a contemporary of Xenophanes.]
[3] Or, "anchovy."
[4] Or, "Melitus."
[5] The textual reading is in the present, but obviously requires a past tense.

[6] Some confusion has crept into the text. The first clause of the second sentence belongs probably to the first. The sense would then run thus: "Ecphantus affirmed the impossibility of dogmatic truth, for that every one was permitted to frame definitions as he thought proper."
[7] Or, "that there is, according to this, a multitude of defined existences, and that such is infinite."
[8] Or, "a single power."
[9] [So far anticipating modern science.]
[10] Or, "holds."
[11] Or, "writing." Still Socrates may be called the father of the Greek philosophy. "From the age of Aristotle and Plato, the rise of the several Greek sects may be estimated as so many successful or abortive efforts to carry out the principles enunciated by Socrates." — Translator's Treatise on Metaphysics, chap. iii. p. 45.
[12] This word signifies to take impressions from anything, which justifies the translation, historically correct, given above. Its literal import is "wipe clean," and in this sense Hippolytus may intend to assert that Plato wholly appropriated the philosophy of Socrates. (See Diogenes Laertius, xi. 61, where the same word occurs.)

CHAP. XVI. — PLATO ; THREEFOLD CLASSIFICATION OF PRINCIPLES ; HIS IDEA OF GOD ; DIFFERENT OPINIONS REGARDING HIS THEOLOGY AND PSYCHOLOGY ; HIS ESCHATOLOGY AND SYSTEM OF METEMPSYCHOSIS ; HIS ETHICAL DOCTRINES ; NOTIONS ON THE FREE-WILL QUESTION.

Plato (lays down) that there are three originating principles of the universe, (namely) God, and matter, and exemplar ; God as the Maker and Regulator of this universe, and the Being who exercises providence over it ; but matter, as that which underlies all (phenomena), which (matter) he styles both receptive and a nurse, out of the arrangement of which proceeded the four elements of which the world consists ; (I mean) fire, air, earth, water, from which all the rest of what are denominated concrete substances, as well as animals and plants, have been formed. And that the exemplar, which he likewise calls ideas, is the intelligence of the Deity, to which, as to an image in the soul, the Deity attending, fabricated all things. God, he says, is both incorporeal and shapeless, and comprehensible by wise men solely ; whereas matter is body potentially, but with potentiality not as yet passing into action, for being itself without form and without quality, by assuming forms and qualities, it became body. That matter, therefore, is an originating principle, and coeval with the Deity, and that in this respect the world is uncreated. For (Plato) affirms that (the world) was made out of it. And that (the attribute of) imperishableness necessarily belongs to (literally " follows ") that which is uncreated. So far forth, however, as body is supposed to be compounded out of both many qualities and ideas, so far forth it is both created and perishable. But some of the followers of Plato mingled both of these, employing some such example as the following : That as a waggon can always continue undestroyed, though undergoing partial repairs from time to time, so that even the parts each in turn perish, yet itself remains always complete ; so after this manner the world also, although in parts it perishes, yet the things that are removed, being repaired, and equivalents for them being introduced, it remains eternal.

Some maintain that Plato asserts the Deity to be one, ingenerable and incorruptible, as he says in *The Laws :* [1] " God, therefore, as the ancient account has it, possesses both the beginning, and end, and middle of all things." Thus he shows God to be one, on account of His having pervaded all things. Others, however, maintain that Plato affirms the existence of many gods indefinitely, when he uses these words : " God of gods, of whom I am both the Creator

and Father." [2] But others say that he speaks of a definite number of deities in the following passage : " Therefore the mighty Jupiter, wheeling his swift chariot in heaven ; " and when he enumerates the offspring of the children of heaven and earth. But others assert that (Plato) constituted the gods as generable ; and on account of their having been produced, that altogether they were subject to the necessity of corruption, but that on account of the will of God they are immortal, (maintaining this) in the passage already quoted, where, to the words, " God of gods, of whom I am Creator and Father," he adds, " indissoluble through the fiat of My will ; " so that if (God) were disposed that these should be dissolved, they would easily be dissolved.

And he admits natures (such as those) of demons, and says that some of them are good, but others worthless. And some affirm that he states the soul to be uncreated and immortal, when he uses the following words, " Every soul is immortal, for that which is always moved is immortal ; " and when he demonstrates that the soul is self-moved, and capable of originating motion. Others, however, (say that Plato asserted that the soul was) created, but rendered imperishable through the will of God. But some (will have it that he considered the soul) a composite (essence), and generable and corruptible ; for even he supposes that there is a receptacle for it,[3] and that it possesses a luminous body, but that everything generated involves a necessity of corruption.[4] Those, however, who assert the immortality of the soul are especially strengthened in their opinion by those passages [5] (in Plato's writings), where he says, that both there are judgments after death, and tribunals of justice in Hades, and that the virtuous (souls) receive a good reward, while the wicked (ones) suitable punishment. Some notwithstanding assert, that he also acknowledges a transition of souls from one body to another, and that different souls, those that were marked out for such a purpose, pass into different bodies,[6] according to the desert of each, and that after [7] certain definite periods they are sent up into this world to furnish once more a proof of their choice. Others, however, (do not admit this to

---

[1] *De Legibus,* iv. 7 (p. 109, vol. viii. ed. Bekker).

[2] *Timæus,* c. xvi. (p. 277, vol. vii. ed. Bekker). The passage runs thus in the original : "Gods of gods, of whom I am Creator and Father of works, which having been formed by Me, are indissoluble, through, at all events, My will."
[3] The word is literally a cup or bowl, and, being employed by Plato in an allegorical sense, is evidently intended to signify the *anima mundi* (soul of the world), which constituted a sort of depository for all spiritual existences in the world.
[4] Or, " that there exists a necessity for the corruption of everything created."
[5] Or, " are confirmed by that (philosopher Plato), because he asserts," etc.: or, " those who assert the soul's immortality are especially confirmed in their opinion, as many as affirm the existence of a future state of retribution."
[6] Or, " that he changes different souls," etc.
[7] Or, " during."

be his doctrine, but will have it that Plato affirms that the souls) obtain a place according to the desert of each ; and they employ as a testimony the saying of his, that some good men are with Jove, and that others are ranging abroad (through heaven) with other gods ; whereas that others are involved in eternal punishments, as many as during this life have committed wicked and unjust deeds.

And people affirm that Plato says, that some things are without a mean, that others have a mean, that others are a mean. (For example, that) waking and sleep, and such like, are conditions without an intermediate state ; but that there are things that had means, for instance virtue and vice ; and there are means (between extremes), for instance grey between white and black, or some other colour. And they say, that he affirms that the things pertaining to the soul are absolutely alone good, but that the things pertaining to the body, and those external (to it), are not any longer absolutely good, but reputed blessings. And that frequently he names these means also, for that it is possible to use them both well and ill. Some virtues, therefore, he says, are extremes in regard of intrinsic worth, but in regard of their essential nature means, for nothing is more estimable than virtue. But whatever excels or falls short of these terminates in vice. For instance, he says that there are four virtues — prudence, temperance, justice, fortitude — and that on each of these is attendant two vices, according to excess and defect : for example, on prudence, recklessness according to defect, and knavery according to excess ; and on temperance, licentiousness according to defect, stupidity according to excess ; and on justice, foregoing a claim according to defect, unduly pressing it according to excess ; and on fortitude, cowardice according to defect, foolhardiness according to excess. And that these virtues, when inherent in a man, render him perfect, and afford him happiness. And happiness, he says, is assimilation to the Deity, as far as this is possible ; and that assimilation to God takes place when any one combines holiness and justice with prudence. For this he supposes the end of supreme wisdom and virtue. And he affirms that the virtues follow one another in turn,[1] and are uniform, and are never antagonistic to each other ; whereas that vices are multiform, and sometimes follow one the other, and sometimes are antagonistic to each other. He asserts that fate exists ; not, to be sure, that all things are produced according to fate, but that there is even something in our power, as in the passages where he says, "The fault is his who chooses, God is blame-

less ;" and "the following law[2] of Adrasteia."[3] And thus some (contend for his upholding) a system of fate, whereas others one of free-will. He asserts, however, that sins are involuntary. For into what is most glorious of the things in our power, which is the soul, no one would (deliberately) admit what is vicious, that is, transgression, but that from ignorance and an erroneous conception of virtue, supposing that they were achieving something honourable, they pass into vice. And his doctrine on this point is most clear in *The Republic*,[4] where he says, " But, again, you presume to assert that vice is disgraceful and abhorred of God ; how then, I may ask, would one choose such an evil thing? He, you reply, (would do so) who is worsted by pleasures.[5] Therefore this also is involuntary, if to gain a victory be voluntary ; so that, in every point of view, the committing an act of turpitude, reason proves[6] to be involuntary." Some one, however, in opposition to this (Plato), advances the contrary statement, "Why then are men punished if they sin involuntary?" But he replies, that he himself also, as soon as possible, may be emancipated from vice, and undergo punishment. For that the undergoing punishment is not an evil, but a good thing, if it is likely to prove a purification of evils ; and that the rest of mankind, hearing of it, may not transgress, but guard against such an error. (Plato, however, maintains) that the nature of evil is neither created by the Deity, nor possesses subsistence of itself, but that it derives existence from contrariety to what is good, and from attendance upon it, either by excess and defect, as we have previously affirmed concerning the virtues. Plato unquestionably then, as we have already stated, collecting together the three departments of universal philosophy, in this manner formed his speculative system.

CHAP. XVII. — ARISTOTLE ; DUALITY OF PRINCIPLES ; HIS CATEGORIES ; HIS PSYCHOLOGY ; HIS ETHICAL DOCTRINES ; ORIGIN OF THE EPITHET " PERIPATETIC."

Aristotle, who was a pupil of this (Plato), reduced philosophy into an art, and was distinguished rather for his proficiency in logical science, supposing as the elements of all things substance and accident ; that there is one substance underlying all things, but nine accidents, — namely, quantity, quality, relation, where,

---

[1] Diogenes Laertius, in describing the system of the Stoics, employs the same word in the case of their view of virtue.

[2] This is supplied from the original ; the passage occurs in the *Phædrus*, c. lx. (p. 86, vol. i. ed. Bekker).
[3] The word Adrasteia was a name for Nemesis, and means here unalterable destiny.
[4] The passage occurs in *Clitophon* (p. 244, vol. vi ed. Bekker).
[5] The text, as given by Miller, is scarcely capable of any meaning. The translation is therefore conjectural, in accordance with alterations proposed by Schneidewin.
[6] Or, "declares."

when, possession, posture, action, passion; and that substance is of some such description as God, man, and each of the beings that can fall under a similar denomination. But in regard of accidents, quality is seen in, for instance, white, black; and quantity, for instance two cubits, three cubits; and relation, for instance father, son; and where, for instance at Athens, Megara; and when, for instance during the tenth Olympiad; and possession, for instance to have acquired; and action, for instance to write, and in general to evince any practical powers; and posture, for instance to lie down; and passion, for instance to be struck. He also supposes that some things have means, but that others are without means, as we have declared concerning Plato likewise. And in most points he is in agreement with Plato, except the opinion concerning soul. For Plato affirms it to be immortal, but Aristotle that it involves permanence; and after these things, that this also vanishes in the fifth body,[1] which he supposes, along with the other four (elements), — viz., fire, and earth, and water, and air, — to be a something more subtle (than these), of the nature of spirit. Plato therefore says, that the only really good things are those pertaining to the soul, and that they are sufficient for happiness; whereas Aristotle introduces a threefold classification of good things, and asserts that the wise man is not perfect, unless there are present to him both the good things of the body and those extrinsic to it.[2] The former are beauty, strength, vigour of the senses, soundness; while the things extrinsic (to the body) are wealth, nobility, glory, power, peace, friendship.[3] And the inner qualities of the soul he classifies, as it was the opinion of Plato, under prudence, temperance, justice, fortitude. This (philosopher) also affirms that evils arise according to an opposition of the things that are good, and that they exist beneath the quarter around the moon, but reach no farther beyond the moon; and that the soul of the entire world is immortal, and that the world itself is eternal, but that (the soul) in an individual, as we have before stated, vanishes (in the fifth body). This (speculator), then holding discussions in the Lyceum, drew up from time to time his system of philosophy; but Zeno (held his school) in the porch called *Poecilé*. And the followers of Zeno obtained their name from the place — that is, from *Stoa* — (i.e., a porch), being styled Stoics; whereas Aristotle's followers (were denominated) from their mode of employ-

ing themselves while teaching. For since they were accustomed walking about in the Lyceum to pursue their investigations, on this account they were called Peripatetics. These indeed, then, were the doctrines of Aristotle.

CHAP. XVIII. — THE STOICS; THEIR SUPERIORITY IN LOGIC; FATALISTS; THEIR DOCTRINE OF CONFLAGRATIONS.

The Stoics themselves also imparted growth to philosophy, in respect of a greater development of the art of syllogism, and included almost everything under definitions, both Chrysippus and Zeno being coincident in opinion on this point. And they likewise supposed God to be the one originating principle of all things, being a body of the utmost refinement, and that His providential care pervaded everything; and these speculators were positive about the existence of fate everywhere, employing some such example as the following: that just as a dog, supposing him attached to a car, if indeed he is disposed to follow, both is drawn,[4] or follows voluntarily, making an exercise also of free power, in combination with necessity, that is, fate; but if he may not be disposed to follow, he will altogether be coerced to do so. And the same, of course, holds good in the case of men. For though not willing to follow, they will altogether be compelled to enter upon what has been decreed for them. (The Stoics), however, assert that the soul abides after death,[5] but that it is a body, and that such is formed from the refrigeration of the surrounding atmosphere; wherefore, also, that it was called *psyche* (i.e., soul). And they acknowledge likewise, that there is a transition of souls from one body to another, that is, for those souls for whom this migration has been destined. And they accept the doctrine, that there will be a conflagration, a purification of this world, some say the entire of it, but others a portion, and that (the world) itself is undergoing partial destruction; and this all but corruption, and the generation from it of another world, they term purgation. And they assume the existence of all bodies, and that body does not pass through body,[6] but that a refraction[7] takes place, and that all things involve plenitude, and that there is no vacuum. The foregoing are the opinions of the Stoics also.

---

[1] Or, "the fifth body, in which it is supposed to be, along with the other four (elements);" or, "the fifth body, which is supposed to be (composed) of the other four."
[2] Hippolytus expresses himself in the words of Stobæus, who says (*Eclog.*, ii. 274): "And among reputed external blessings are nobility, wealth, glory, peace, freedom, friendship."
[3] Or, "glory, the confirmed power of friends."

[4] One of the MSS. elucidates the simile in the text thus: "But if he is not disposed, there is absolutely a necessity for his being drawn along. And in like manner men, if they do not follow fate, seem to be free agents, though the reason of (their being) fate holds assuredly valid. If, however, they do not wish to follow, they will absolutely be coerced to enter upon what has been fore-ordained."
[5] Or, "is immortal." Diogenes Laertius (book vii.) notices, in his section on Zeno, as part of the Stoic doctrine, "that the soul abides after death, but that it is perishable."
[6] Or, "through what is incorporeal;" that is, through what is void or empty space.
[7] Or, "resurrection;" or, "resistance;" that is, a resisting medium.

CHAP. XIX. — EPICURUS ; ADOPTS THE DEMOCRITIC ATOMISM ; DENIAL OF DIVINE PROVIDENCE ; THE PRINCIPLE OF HIS ETHICAL SYSTEM.

Epicurus, however, advanced an opinion almost contrary to all. He supposed, as originating principles of all things, atoms and vacuity.[1] He considered vacuity as the place that would contain the things that will exist, and atoms the matter out of which all things could be formed ; and that from the concourse of atoms both the Deity derived existence, and all the elements, and all things inherent in them, as well as animals and other (creatures) ; so that nothing was generated or existed, unless it be from atoms. And he affirmed that these atoms were composed of extremely small particles, in which there could not exist either a point or a sign, or any division ; wherefore also he called them atoms. Acknowledging the Deity to be eternal and incorruptible, he says that God has providential care for nothing, and that there is no such thing at all as providence or fate, but that all things are made by chance. For that the Deity reposed in the intermundane spaces, (as they) are thus styled by him ; for outside the world he determined that there is a certain habitation of God, denominated " the intermundane spaces," and that the Deity surrendered Himself to pleasure, and took His ease in the midst of supreme happiness ; and that neither has He any concerns of business, nor does He devote His attention to them.[2] As a consequence on these opinions, he also propounded his theory concerning wise men, asserting that the end of wisdom is pleasure. Different persons, however, received the term "pleasure" in different acceptations ; for some (among the Gentiles [3] understood) the passions, but others the satisfaction resulting from virtue. And he concluded that the souls of men are dissolved along with their bodies, just as also they were produced along with them, for that they are blood, and that when this has gone forth or been altered, the entire man perishes ; and in keeping with this tenet, (Epicurus maintained) that there are neither trials in Hades, nor tribunals of justice ; so that whatsoever any one may commit in this life, that, provided he may escape detection, he is altogether beyond any liability of trial (for it in a future state). In this way, then, Epicurus also formed his opinions.

CHAP. XX. — THE ACADEMICS ; DIFFERENCE OF OPINION AMONG THEM.

And another opinion of the philosophers was called that of the Academics,[4] on account of those holding their discussions in the Academy, of whom the founder Pyrrho, from whom they were called Pyrrhonean philosophers, first introduced the notion of the incomprehensibility of all things, so as to (be ready to) attempt an argument on either side of a question, but not to assert anything for certain ; for that there is nothing of things intelligible or sensible true, but that they appear to men to be so ; and that all substance is in a state of flux and change, and never continues in the same (condition). Some followers, then, of the Academics say that one ought not to declare an opinion on the principle of anything, but simply making the attempt to give it up ; whereas others subjoined the formulary " not rather " [5] (this than that), saying that the fire is not rather fire than anything else. But they did not declare what this is, but what sort it is.[6]

CHAP. XXI. — THE BRACHMANS ; THEIR MODE OF LIFE ; IDEAS OF DEITY ; DIFFERENT SORTS OF ; THEIR ETHICAL NOTIONS.

But there is also with the Indians a sect composed of those philosophizing among the Brachmans. They spend a contented existence, abstain both from living creatures and all cooked food, being satisfied with fruits ; and not gathering these from the trees, but carrying off those that have fallen to the earth. They subsist upon them, drinking the water of the river Tazabena.[7] But they pass their life naked, affirming that the body has been constituted a covering to the soul by the Deity. These affirm that God is light, not such as one sees, nor such as the sun and fire ; but to them the Deity is discourse, not that which finds expression in articulate sounds, but that of the knowledge through which the secret mysteries of nature [8] are perceived by the wise. And this light which they say is discourse, their god, they assert that the Brachmans only know on account of their alone rejecting all vanity of opinion which is the soul's ultimate covering.[9] These despise death, and always in their own peculiar language [10] call God

---

[1] The atomic theory is, as already mentioned by Hippolytus, of more ancient date than Epicurus' age, being first broached by Leucippus and Democritus. This fact, however, has, as Cudworth argues, been frequently overlooked by those who trace the doctrine to no older a source than the founder of the Epicurean philosophy.

[2] Or, "that neither has He business to do, nor does He attend to any. As a consequence of which fact," etc.

[3] "Among the Gentiles" seems a mistake. One reading proposed is, " some (intended) our sensuous passions;" or, " some understood the passions." The words "among the Gentiles," the French commentator, the Abbe Cruice, is of opinion, were added by Christian hands, in order to draw a contrast between the virtuous Christian and the vicious pagan.

[4] See Diogenes Laertius' *Lives,* x. 63 (Bohn's Library) ; Plutarch, *De Placitis Philosophorum,* iv. 3.

[5] Diogenes Laertius, *Lives,* ix. 75 ; Sextus Empiricus, *Hypotyp.,* i. 188-192.

[6] This is what the Academics called " the phenomenon " (Sextus Empiricus, *Pyrrh. Hyp.,* i. 19-22).

[7] This is a mistake in the manuscript for Ganges, according to Roeper.

[8] Or, "knowledge." (See Clemens Alexandrinus, *Strom.,* i., xv., lxxii.; Eusebius, *Præparat. Evang.,* ix. 6.)

[9] Athenæus (*Deipn.,* book ix) ascribes this opinion to Plato, who, he tells us, " asserted that the soul was so constituted, that it should reject its last covering, that of vanity."

[10] Or, " they name light their god;" or, " they celebrate in their own peculiar language God, whom they name," etc.

by the name which we have mentioned previously, and they send up hymns (to him). But neither are there women among them, nor do they beget children. But they who aim at a life similar to these, after they have crossed over to the country on the opposite side of the river, continue to reside there, returning no more; and these also are called Brachmans. But they do not pass their life similarly, for there are also in the place women, of whom those that dwell there are born, and in turn beget children. And this discourse which [1] they name God they assert to be corporeal, and enveloped in a body outside himself, just as if one were wearing a sheep's skin, but that on divesting himself of body that he would appear clear to the eye. But the Brachmans say that there is a conflict in the body that surrounds them, (and they consider that the body is for them full of conflicts); [2] in opposition to which, as if marshalled for battle against enemies, they contend, as we have already explained. And they say that all men are captive to their own congenital struggles, viz., sensuality and inchastity, gluttony, anger, joy, sorrow, concupiscence, and such like. And he who has reared a trophy over these, alone goes to God; wherefore the Brachmans deify Dandamis, to whom Alexander the Macedonian paid a visit, as one who had proved victorious in the bodily conflict. But they bear down on Calanus as having profanely withdrawn from their philosophy. But the Brachmans, putting off the body, like fishes jumping out of water into the pure air, behold the sun.

CHAP. XXII. — THE DRUIDS; PROGENITORS OF THEIR SYSTEM.

And the Celtic Druids investigated to the very highest point the Pythagorean philosophy, after Zamolxis, [3] by birth a Thracian, [4] a servant of Pythagoras, became to them the originator of this discipline. Now after the death of Pythagoras, Zamolxis, repairing thither, became to them the originator of this philosophy. The Celts esteem these as prophets and seers, on account of their foretelling to them certain (events), from calculations and numbers by the

Pythagorean art; on the methods of which very art also we shall not keep silence, since also from these some have presumed to introduce heresies; but the Druids resort to magical rites likewise.

CHAP. XXIII. — HESIOD; THE NINE MUSES; THE HESIODIC COSMOGONY; THE ANCIENT SPECULATORS, MATERIALISTS; DERIVATIVE CHARACTER OF THE HERESIES FROM HEATHEN PHILOSOPHY.

But Hesiod the poet asserts himself also that he thus heard from the Muses concerning nature, and that the Muses are the daughters of Jupiter. For when for nine nights and days together, Jupiter, through excess of passion, had uninterruptedly lain with Mnemosyne, that Mnemosyne conceived in one womb those nine Muses, becoming pregnant with one during each night. Having then summoned the nine Muses from Pieria, that is, Olympus, he exhorted them to undergo instruction: —

"How first both gods and earth were made, [5]
And rivers, and boundless deep, and ocean's surge,
And glittering stars, and spacious heaven above;
How they grasped the crown and shared the glory,
And how at first they held the many-valed Olympus.
These (truths), ye Muses, tell me of, saith he,
From first, and next which of them first arose.
Chaos, no doubt, the very first, arose; but next
Wide-stretching Earth, ever the throne secure of all
Immortals, who hold the peaks of white Olympus;
And breezy Tartarus in wide earth's recess;
And Love, who is most beauteous of the gods immortal,
Chasing care away from all the gods and men,
Quells in breasts the mind and counsel sage.
But Erebus from Chaos and gloomy Night arose;
And, in turn, from Night both Air and Day were born;
But primal Earth, equal to self in sooth begot
The stormy sky to veil it round on every side,
Ever to be for happy gods a throne secure.
And forth she brought the towering hills, the pleasant haunts
Of nymphs who dwell throughout the woody heights.
And also barren Sea begat the surge-tossed
Flood, apart from luscious Love; but next
Embracing Heaven, she Ocean bred with eddies deep,
And Cæus, and Crius, and Hyperian, and Iapetus,
And Thia, and Rhea, and Themis, and Mnemosyne,
And gold-crowned Phœbe, and comely Tethys.
But after these was born last [6] the wiley Cronus,
Fiercest of sons; but he abhorred his blooming sire,
And in turn the Cyclops bred, who owned a savage breast."

And all the rest of the giants from Cronus, Hesiod enumerates, and somewhere afterwards that Jupiter was born of Rhea. All these, then, made

---

[1] The text here would seem rather confused. The above translation agrees with Cruice's and Schneidewin's Latin version. I have doubts about its correctness, however, and would render it thus: " . . . enveloped in a body extrinsic to the divine essence, just as if one wore a sheepskin covering; but that his body, on being divested of this (covering), would appear visible to the naked eye." Or, " This discourse whom they name God they affirm to be incorporeal, but enveloped in a body outside himself (or his own body) (just as if one carried a covering of sheepskin to have it seen); but having stripped off the body in which he is enveloped, that he no longer appears visible to the naked eye." (Roeper.) I am not very confident that this exactly conveys the meaning of Roeper's somewhat obscure Greek paraphrase.

[2] The parenthetical words Roeper considers introduced into the text from a marginal note.

[3] Or " Zamalxis," or " Zametris" (see Menagius on Diogenes Laertius, viii. 2).

[4] Or, " of Thracian origin." The words are omitted in two MSS.

[5] There are several verbal differences from the original in Hippolytus' version. These may be seen on comparing it with Hesiod's own text. The particular place which Hesiod occupies in the history of philosophy is pointed out by Aristotle in his *Metaphysics*. The Stagyrite detects in the Hesiodic cosmogony, in the principle of " love," the dawn of a recognition of the necessity of an efficient cause to account for the phenomena of nature. It was Aristotle himself, however, who built up the science of causation; and in this respect humanity owes that extraordinary man a deep debt of gratitude.

[6] Or " youngest," or " most vigorous." This is Hesiod's word, which signifies literally, " fittest for bearing arms " (for service, as we say).

the foregoing statements in their doctrine regarding both the nature and generation of the universe.   But all, sinking below what is divine, busied themselves concerning the substance of existing things,[1] being astonished at the magnitude of creation, and supposing that it constituted the Deity, each speculator selecting in preference a different portion of the world ; failing, however, to discern the God and maker of these.

---

[1] "The majority of those who first formed systems of philosophy, consider those that subsist in a form of matter, to be alone the principle of all things." — ARISTOTLE'S *Metaphysics*, book i. c. iii. p. 13 (Bohn's ed.).

The opinions, therefore, of those who have attempted to frame systems of philosophy among the Greeks, I consider that we have sufficiently explained ; and from these the heretics, taking occasion, have endeavoured to establish the tenets that will be after a short time declared.   It seems, however, expedient, that first explaining the mystical rites and whatever imaginary doctrines some have laboriously framed concerning the stars, or magnitudes, to declare these ; for heretics likewise, taking occasion from them, are considered by the multitude to utter prodigies. Next in order we shall elucidate the feeble opinions advanced by these.

BOOKS II. AND III. ARE AWANTING.

THE REFUTATION OF ALL HERESIES

BOOK IV.

CHAP. I. — SYSTEM OF THE ASTROLOGERS; SIDERE-
AL INFLUENCE; CONFIGURATION OF THE STARS.

BUT in each zodiacal sign they call limits of
the stars those in which each of the stars, from
any one quarter to another, can exert the greatest amount of influence; in regard of which
there is among them, according to their writings,
no mere casual divergency of opinion. But
they say that the stars are attended as if by satellites when they are in the midst of other stars,
in continuity with the signs of the Zodiac; as
if, when any particular star may have occupied
the first portions of the same sign of the Zodiac,
and another the last, and another those portions
in the middle, that which is in the middle is said
to be guarded by those holding the portions at
the extremities. And they are said to look upon
one another, and to be in conjunction with one
another, as if appearing in a triangular or quad-
rangular figure. They assume, therefore, the
figure of a triangle, and look upon one another,
which have an intervening distance [1] extending
for three zodiacal signs; and they assume the
figure of a square those which have an interval
extending for two signs. But as the underlying
parts smpathize with the head, and the head
with the underlying parts,[2] so also things terrestrial with superlunar objects.[3] But there is of
these a certain difference and want of sympathy,
so that they do not involve one and the same
point of juncture.

CHAP. II. — DOCTRINES CONCERNING ÆONS; THE
CHALDEAN ASTROLOGY; HERESY DERIVABLE FROM
IT.

Employing these (as analogies), Euphrates
the Peratic, and Acembes [4] the Carystian, and

the rest of the crowd of these (speculators),
imposing names different from the doctrine of
the truth, speak of a sedition of Æons, and of
a revolt of good powers over to evil (ones), and
of the concord of good with wicked (Æons),
calling them *Toparchai* and *Proastioi*, and very
many other names. But the entire of this heresy, as attempted by them, I shall explain and
refute when we come to treat of the subject of
these (Æons). But now, lest any one suppose
the opinions propounded by the Chaldeans respecting astrological doctrine to be trustworthy
and secure, we shall not hesitate to furnish a
brief refutation respecting these, establishing
that the futile art is calculated both to deceive
and blind the soul indulging in vain expectations,
rather than to profit it. And we urge our case
with these, not according to any experience of
the art, but from knowledge based on practical
principles. Those who have cultivated the art,
becoming disciples of the Chaldeans, and communicating mysteries as if strange and astonishing to men, having changed the names (merely),
have from this source concocted their heresy.
But since, estimating the astrological art as a
powerful one, and availing themselves of the
testimonies adduced by its patrons, they wish to
gain reliance for their own attempted conclusions,
we shall at present, as it has seemed expedient,
prove the astrological art to be untenable, as our
intention next is to invalidate also the Peratic
system, as a branch growing out of an unstable
root.

CHAP. III. — THE HOROSCOPE THE FOUNDATION OF
ASTROLOGY; INDISCOVERABILITY OF THE HORO-
SCOPE; THEREFORE THE FUTILITY OF THE CHAL-
DEAN ART.

The originating principle,[5] and, as it were,
foundation, of the entire art, is fixing [6] the horo-

---

[1] Or, "interval."
[2] Hippolytus gives the substance of Sextus Empiricus' remarks,
omitting, however, a portion of the passage followed. (See Sextus
Empiricus' *Mathem.*, v. 44.)
[3] Or, "celestial."
[4] Or, "Celbes," or "Ademes." The first is the form of the name
employed in book v. c. viii.; the second in book x. c. vi.

[5] This passage occurs in Sextus Empiricus.
[6] Or, "the knowledge of."

scope.[1] For from this are derived the rest of the cardinal points, as well as the declinations and ascensions, the triangles and squares, and the configurations of the stars in accordance with these ; and from all these the predictions are taken. Whence, if the horoscope be removed, it necessarily follows that neither any celestial object is recognisable in the meridian, or at the horizon, or in the point of the heavens opposite the meridian ; but if these be not comprehended, the entire system of the Chaldeans vanishes along with (them). But that the sign of the horoscope is indiscoverable by them, we may show by a variety of arguments. For in order that this (horoscope) may be found, it is first requisite that the (time of) birth of the person falling under inspection should be firmly fixed ; and secondly, that the horoscope which is to signify this should be infallible ; and thirdly, that the ascension[2] of the zodiacal sign should be observed with accuracy. For from[3] (the moment) of birth[4] the ascension of the zodiacal sign rising in the heaven should be closely watched,[5] since the Chaldeans, determining (from this) the horoscope, frame the configuration of the stars in accordance with the ascension (of the sign) ; and they term this — disposition, in accordance with which they devise their predictions. But neither is it possible to take the birth of persons falling under consideration, as I shall explain, nor is the horoscope infallible, nor is the rising zodiacal sign apprehended with accuracy.

How it is, then, that the system of the Chaldeans[6] is unstable, let us now declare. Having, then, previously marked it out for investigation, they draw the birth of persons falling under consideration from, unquestionably, the depositing of the seed, and (from) conception or from parturition. And if one will attempt to take (the horoscope) from conception, the accurate account of this is incomprehensible, the time (occupied) passing quickly, and naturally (so). For we are not able to say whether conception takes place upon the transference[7] of the seed or not. For this can happen even as quick as thought, just also as leaven, when put into heated jars, immediately is reduced to a glutinous state. But conception can also (take place) after a lapse of duration. For there being an interval

from the mouth of the womb to the fundament, where physicians[8] say conceptions take place, it is altogether the nature of the seed deposited to occupy some time in traversing[9] this interval. The Chaldeans, therefore, being ignorant of the quantity of duration to a nicety, never will comprehend the (moment of) conception ; the seed at one time being injected straight forward, and falling at one spot upon actual parts of the womb well disposed for conception, and at another time dropping into it dispersedly, and being collected into one place by uterine energies. Now, while these matters are unknown, (namely), as to when the first takes place, and when the second, and how much time is spent in that particular conception, and how much in this; while, I say, ignorance on these points prevails on the part of these (astrologers), an accurate comprehension of conception is put out of the question.[10] And if, as some natural philosophers have asserted, the seed, remaining stationary first, and undergoing alteration in the womb, then enters the (womb's) opened blood-vessels, as the seeds of the earth[11] sink into the ground ; from this it will follow, that those who are not acquainted with the quantity of time occupied by the change, will not be aware of the precise moment of conception either. And, moreover, as women[12] differ from one another in the other parts of the body, both as regards energy and in other respects, so also (it is reasonable to suppose that they differ from one another) in respect of energy of womb, some conceiving quicker, and others slower. And this is not strange, since also women, when themselves compared with themselves, at times are observed having a strong disposition towards conception, but at times with no such tendency. And when this is so, it is impossible to say with accuracy when the deposited seed coalesces, in order that from this time the Chaldeans may fix the horoscope of the birth.

CHAP. IV. — IMPOSSIBILITY OF FIXING THE HOROSCOPE ; FAILURE OF AN ATTEMPT TO DO THIS AT THE PERIOD OF BIRTH.

For this reason it is impossible to fix the horoscope from the (period of) conception. But neither can this be done from (that of) birth. For, in the first place, there exists the difficulty as to when it can be declared that there is a birth ; whether it is when the foetus begins to incline towards the orifice,[13] or when it may project a little, or when it may be borne to the

---

[1] Horoscope (from ὥρα σκοπός) is the act of observing the aspect of the heavens at the moment of any particular birth. Hereby the astrologer alleged his ability of foretelling the future career of the person so born. The most important part of the sky for the astrologer's consideration was that sign of the Zodiac which rose above the horizon at the moment of parturition. This was the " horoscope ascendant," or " first house." The circuit of the heavens was divided into twelve " houses," or zodiacal signs.
[2] Or, " difference."
[3] Or, " during."
[4] ἀποτέξεως; some would read ἀποτάξεως.
[5] The passage is given more explicitly in Sextus Empiricus. (See *Adversus Astrol.*, v. 53.)
[6] Sextus uses almost these words.
[7] Or " lodgment " (Sextus), or " deposition."

[8] Or, " attendants of physicians."
[9] Or, " make."
[10] Or, " vanishes."
[11] Not in Sextus Empiricus.
[12] The passage is more clearly given in Sextus.
[13] Or, " the cold atmosphere."

ground. Neither is it in each of these cases possible to comprehend the precise moment of parturition,[1] or to define the time. For also on account of disposition of soul, and on account of suitableness of body, and on account of choice of the parts, and on account of experience in the midwife, and other endless causes, the time is not the same at which the fœtus inclines towards the orifice, when the membranes are ruptured, or when it projects a little, or is deposited on the ground ; but the period is different in the case of different individuals. And when the Chaldeans are not able definitely and accurately to calculate this, they will fail, as they ought, to determine the period of emergence.

That, then, the Chaldeans profess to be acquainted with the horoscope at the periods of birth,[1] but in reality do not know it, is evident from these considerations. But that neither is their horoscope infallible, it is easy to conclude. For when they allege that the person sitting beside the woman in travail at the time of parturition gives, by striking a metallic rim, a sign to the Chaldean, who from an elevated place is contemplating the stars, and he, looking towards heaven, marks down the rising zodiacal sign ; in the first place, we shall prove to them, that when parturition happens indefinitely, as we have shown a little before, neither is it easy[2] to signify this (birth) by striking the metallic rim. However, grant that the birth is comprehensible, yet neither is it possible to signify this at the exact time ; for as the noise of the metallic plate is capable of being divided by a longer time and one protracted, in reference to perception, it happens that the sound is carried to the height (with proportionate delay). And the following proof may be observed in the case of those felling timber at a distance. For a sufficiently long time after the descent of the axe, the sound of the stroke is heard, so that it takes a longer time to reach the listener. And for this reason, therefore, it is not possible for the Chaldeans accurately to take the time of the rising zodiacal sign, and consequently the time when one can make the horoscope with truth. And not only does more time seem to elapse after parturition, when he who is sitting beside the woman in labour strikes the metallic plate, and next after the sound reaches the listener, that is, the person who has gone up to the elevated position ; but also, while he is glancing around and looking to ascertain in which of the zodiacal signs is the moon, and in which appears each of the rest of the stars, it necessarily follows that there is a different position in regard of the stars, the

motion[3] of the pole whirling them on with incalculable velocity, before what is seen in the heavens[4] is carefully adjusted to the moment when the person is born.

CHAP. V. — ANOTHER METHOD OF FIXING THE HOROSCOPE AT BIRTH ; EQUALLY FUTILE ; USE OF THE CLEPSYDRA IN ASTROLOGY ; THE PREDICTIONS OF THE CHALDEANS NOT VERIFIED.

In this way, the art practised by the Chaldeans will be shown to be unstable. Should any one, however, allege that, by questions put to him who inquires from the Chaldeans,[5] the birth can be ascertained, not even by this plan is it possible to arrive at the precise period. For if, supposing any such attention on their part in reference to their art to be on record, even these do not attain — as we have proved — unto accuracy either, how, we ask, can an unsophisticated individual comprehend precisely the time of parturition, in order that the Chaldean acquiring the requisite information from this person may set[6] the horoscope correctly? But neither from the appearance of the horizon will the rising star seem the same everywhere ; but in one place its declination will be supposed to be the horoscope, and in another the ascension (will be thought) the horoscope, according as the places come into view, being either lower or higher. Wherefore, also, from this quarter an accurate prediction will not appear, since many may be born throughout the entire world at the same hour, each from a different direction observing the stars.

But the supposed comprehension (of the period of parturition) by means of clepsydras[7] is likewise futile. For the contents of the jar will not flow out in the same time when it is full as when it is half empty ; yet, according to their own account, the pole itself by a single impulse is whirled along at an equable velocity. If, however, evading the argument,[8] they should affirm that they do not take the time precisely, but as it happens in any particular latitude,[9] they will be refuted almost by the sidereal influences themselves. For those who have been born at the same time do not spend the same life, but some, for example, have been made kings, and others have grown old in fetters.

---

[1] Or, " manifestation."
[2] Or, " reasonable."

[3] Or, " but the motion . . . is whirled on with velocity."
[4] This rendering of the passage may be deduced from Sextus Empiricus.
[5] The text is corrupt, but the above seems probably the meaning, and agrees with the rendering of Schneidewin and Cruice.
[6] Or, " view."
[7] The clepsydra, an instrument for measuring duration, was with the sun-dial, invented by the Egyptians under the Ptolemies. It was employed not only for the measurement of time, but for making astronomical calculations. Water, as the name imports, was the fluid employed, though mercury has been likewise used. The inherent defect of an instrument of this description is mentioned by Hippolytus.
[8] Literally, " twisting, tergiversating."
[9] This seems the meaning, as deducible from a comparison of Hippolytus with the corresponding passage in Sextus Empiricus.

There has been born none equal, at all events, to Alexander the Macedonian, though many were brought forth along with him throughout the earth ; (and) none equal to the philosopher Plato. Wherefore the Chaldean, examining the time of the birth in any particular latitude, will not be able to say accurately, whether a person born at this time will be prosperous. Many, I take it, born at this time, have been unfortunate, so that the similarity according to dispositions is futile.

Having, then, by different reasons and various methods, refuted the ineffectual mode of examination adopted by the Chaldeans, neither shall we omit this, namely, to show that their predictions will eventuate in inexplicable difficulties. For if, as the mathematicians assert, it is necessary that one born under the barb of Sagittarius' arrow should meet with a violent death, how was it that so many myriads of the Barbarians that fought with the Greeks at Marathon or Salamis [1] were simultaneously slaughtered? For unquestionably there was not the same horoscope in the case, at all events, of them all. And again, it is said that one born under the urn of Aquarius will suffer shipwreck : (yet) how is it that so many [2] of the Greeks that returned from Troy were overwhelmed in the deep around the indented shores of Euboea? For it is incredible that all, distant from one another by a long interval of duration, should have been born under the urn of Aquarius. For it is not reasonable to say, that frequently, for one whose fate it was to be destroyed in the sea, all who were with him in the same vessel should perish. For why should the doom of this man subdue the (destinies) of all? Nay, but why, on account of one for whom it was allotted to die on land, should not all be preserved?

CHAP. VI. — ZODIACAL INFLUENCE ; ORIGIN OF SIDEREAL NAMES.

But since also they frame an account concerning the action of the zodiacal signs, to which they say the creatures that are procreated are assimilated,[3] neither shall we omit this : as, for instance, that one born in Leo will be brave ; and that one born in Virgo will have long straight hair,[4] be of a fair complexion, childless, modest. These statements, however, and others similar to them, are rather deserving of laughter than serious consideration. For, according to them, it is possible for no Æthiopian to be born in Virgo ; otherwise he would allow that such a one is white, with long straight hair and the rest. But I am rather of opinion,[5] that the ancients imposed the names of received animals upon certain specified stars, for the purpose of knowing them better, not from any similarity of nature ; for what have the seven stars, distant one from another, in common with a bear, or the five stars with the head of a dragon? — in regard of which Aratus [6] says : —

"But two his temples, and two his eyes, and one beneath
Reaches the end of the huge monster's jaw."

CHAP. VII. — PRACTICAL ABSURDITY OF THE CHALDAIC ART ; DEVELOPMENT OF THE ART.

In this manner also, that these points are not deserving so much labour, is evident to those who prefer to think correctly, and do not attend to the bombast of the Chaldeans, who consign monarchs to utter obscurity, by perfecting cowardice [7] in them, and rouse private individuals to dare great exploits. But if any one, surrendering himself to evil, is guilty of delinquency, he who has been thus deceived does not become a teacher to all whom the Chaldeans are disposed to mislead by their mistakes. (Far from it) ; (these astrologers) impel the minds (of their dupes, as they would have them), into endless perturbation, (when) they affirm that a configuration of the same stars could not return to a similar position, otherwise than by the renewal of the Great Year, through a space of seven thousand seven hundred and seventy and seven years.[8] How then, I ask, will human observation for one birth be able to harmonize with so many ages ; and this not once, (but oftentimes,

---

[1] Omitted by Sextus.

[2] The Abbe Cruice observes, in regard of some verbal difference here in the text from that of Sextus, that the MS. of *The Refutation* was probably executed by one who heard the extracts from other writers read to him, and frequently mistook the sound. The transcriber of the MS. was one Michael, as we learn from a marginal note at the end.

[3] This was the great doctrine of astrology, the forerunner of the science of astronomy. Astrology seems to have arisen first among the Chaldeans, out of the fundamental principle of their religion — the assimilation of the divine nature to light. This tenet introduced another, the worship of the stars, which was developed into astrology. Others suppose astrology to have been of Arabian or Egyptian origin. From some of these sources it reached the Greeks, and through them the Romans, who held the astrologic art in high repute. The art, after having become almost extinct, was revived by the Arabians at the verge of the middle ages. For the history of astrology one must consult the writings of Manilius, Julius Firmicus, and Ptolemy. Its greatest mediæval apologist is Cardan, the famous physician of Pavia (see his work, *De Astron. Judic.*, lib. vi.-ix. tom. v. of his collected works).

[4] Sextus adds, " bright-eyed."

[5] Hippolytus here follows Sextus.

[6] Aratus, from whom Hippolytus quotes so frequently in this chapter, was a poet and astronomer of antiquity, born at Soli in Cilicia. He afterwards became physician to Gonatus, son of Demetrius Poliorcetes, king of Macedon, at whose court he rose high into favour. The work alluded to by Hippolytus is Aratus' *Phænomena*, — a versified account of the motions of the stars, and of sidereal influence over men. This work seems to have been a great favourite with scholars, if we are to judge from the many excellent annotated editions of it that have appeared. Two of these deserve notice, viz., Grotius' Leyden edition, 1600, in Greek and Latin ; and Buhle's edition, Leipsic, 1803. See also Dionysius Petavius' *Uranologion.* Aratus must always be famous, from the fact that St. Paul (Acts xvii. 28) quotes the fifth line of the *Phænomena.* Cicero considered Aratus a noble poet, and translated the *Phænomena* into Latin, a fragment of which has been preserved, and is in Grotius' edition. Aratus has been translated into English verse, with notes by Dr. Lamb, Dean of Bristol (London: J. W. Parker, 1858).

[7] The Abbe Cruice suggests "freedom from danger," instead of " cowardice," and translates thus: " whereby kings are slain, by having impunity promised in the predictions of these seers."

[8] Sextus makes the number " nine thousand nine hundred and seventy and seven years."

when a destruction of the world, as some have stated, would intercept the progress of this Great Year ; or a terrestrial convulsion, though partial, would utterly break the continuity of the historical tradition) ? [1] The Chaldaic art must necessarily be refuted by a greater number of arguments, although we have been reminding (our readers) of it on account of other circumstances, not peculiarly on account of the art itself.

Since, however, we have determined to omit none of the opinions advanced by Gentile philosophers, on account of the notorious knavery of the heretics, let us see what they also say who have attempted to propound doctrines concerning magnitudes, — who, observing the fruitless labour of the majority (of speculators), where each after a different fashion coined his own falsehoods and attained celebrity, have ventured to make some greater assertion, in order that they might be highly magnified by those who mightily extol their contemptible lies. These suppose the existence of circles, and measures, and triangles, and squares, both in twofold and threefold array. Their argumentation, however, in regard of this matter, is extensive, yet it is not necessary in reference to the subject which we have taken in hand.

CHAP. VIII. — PRODIGIES OF THE ASTROLOGERS ; SYSTEM OF THE ASTRONOMERS ; CHALDEAN DOCTRINE OF CIRCLES ; DISTANCES OF THE HEAVENLY BODIES.

I reckon it then sufficient to declare the prodigies [2] detailed by these men. Wherefore, employing condensed accounts of what they affirm, I shall turn my attention to the other points (that remain to be considered). Now they make the following statements.[3] The Creator communicated pre-eminent power to the orbital motion of the identical and similar (circle), for He permitted the revolution of it to be one and indivisible ; but after dividing this internally into six parts, (and thus having formed) seven unequal circles, according to each interval of a twofold and threefold dimension, He commanded, since there were three of each, that the circles should travel in orbits contrary to one another, three indeed (out of the aggregate of seven) being whirled along with equal velocity, and four of them with a speed dissimilar to each

other and to the remaining three, yet (all) according to a definite principle. For he affirms that the mastery was communicated to the orbital motion of the same (circle), not only since it embraces the motion of the other, that is, the erratic stars, but because also it possesses so great mastery, that is, so great power, that even it leads round, along with itself, by a peculiar strength of its own, those heavenly bodies — that is, the erratic stars — that are whirled along in contrary directions from west to east, and, in like manner, from east to west.

And he asserts that this motion was allowed to be one and indivisible, in the first place, inasmuch as the revolutions of all the fixed stars were accomplished in equal periods of time, and were not distinguished according to greater or less portions of duration. In the next place, they all present the same phase as that which belongs to the outermost motion ; whereas the erratic stars have been distributed into greater and varying periods for the accomplishment of their movements, and into unequal distances from earth. And he asserts that the motion in six parts of the other has been distributed probably into seven circles. For as many as' are sections of each (circle) — I allude to monads of the sections [4] — become segments ; for example, if the division be by one section, there will be two segments ; if by two, three segments ; and so, if anything be cut into six parts, there will be seven segments. And he says that the distances of these are alternately arranged both in double and triple order, there being three of each, — a principle which, he has attempted to prove, holds good of the composition of the soul likewise, as depending upon the seven numbers. For among them there are from the monad three double (numbers), viz., 2, 4, 8, and three triple ones, viz., 3, 9, 27. But the diameter of Earth is 80,108 stadii ; and the perimeter of Earth, 250,543 stadii ; and the distance also from the surface of the Earth to the lunar circle, Aristarchus the Samian computes at 8,000,178 stadii, but Apollonius 5,000,000, whereas Archimedes computes [5] it at 5,544,130. And from the lunar to solar circle, (according to the last authority,) are 50,262,065 stadii ; and from this to the circle of Venus, 20,272,065 stadii ; and from this to the circle of Mercury, 50,817,165 stadii ; and from this to the circle of Mars, 40,541,108 stadii ; and from this to the circle of Jupiter, 20,275,065

---

[1] The parenthetical words are taken from Sextus Empiricus, as introduced into his text by the Abbe Cruice. Schneidewin alludes to the passage in Sextus as proof of some confusion in Hippolytus' text, which he thinks is signified by the transcriber in the words, " I think there is some deficiency or omissions," which occur in the MS. of *The Refutation.*

[2] As regards astrological predictions, see Origen's *Comment. on Gen.;* Diodorus of Tarsus, *De Fato ;* Photii *Biblioth.,* cod. ccxxiii.; and Bardesanis, *De Legibus Nationum,* in Cureton's *Spicilegium Syriacum.*

[3] See Plato's *Timæus.*

[4] Schneidewin, on Roeper's suggestion, amends the passage thus, though I am not sure that I exactly render his almost unintelligible Latin version: " For as many sections as there are of each, there are educible from the monad more segments than sections; for example, if," etc. The Abbe Cruice would seemingly adopt the following version: " For whatsoever are sections of each, now there are more segments than sections of a monad, will become; for example, if," etc.

[5] Schneidewin, on mathematical authority, discredits the numerical calculations ascribed to Archimedes.

stadii ; and from this to the circle of Saturn, 40,-372,065 stadii ; and from this to the Zodiac and the furthest periphery, 20,082,005 stadii.[1]

CHAP. IX. — FURTHER ASTRONOMIC CALCULATIONS.

The mutual distances of the circles and spheres, and the depths, are rendered by Archimedes. He takes the perimeter of the Zodiac at 447,310,000 stadii ; so that it follows that a straight line from the centre of the Earth to the most outward superficies would be the sixth of the aforesaid number, but that the line from the surface of the Earth on which we tread to the Zodiac would be a sixth of the aforesaid number, less by four myriads of stadii, which is the distance from the centre of the Earth to its surface. And from the circle of Saturn to the Earth he says the distance is 2,226,912,711 stadii ; and from the circle of Jupiter to Earth, 202,770,646 stadii ; and from the circle of Mars to Earth, 132,418,-581. From the Sun to Earth, 121,604,454 ; and from Mercury to the Earth, 526,882,259 ; and from Venus to Earth, 50,815,160.

CHAP. X. — THEORY OF STELLAR MOTION AND DISTANCE IN ACCORDANCE WITH HARMONY.

Concerning the Moon, however, a statement has been previously made. The distances and profundities of the spheres Archimedes thus renders ; but a different declaration regarding them has been made by Hipparchus ; and a different one still by Apollonius the mathematician. It is sufficient, however, for us, following the Platonic opinion, to suppose twofold and threefold distances from one another of the erratic stars ; for the doctrine is thus preserved of the composition of the universe out of harmony, on concordant principles[2] in keeping with these distances. The numbers, however, advanced by Archimedes,[3] and the accounts rendered by the rest concerning the distances, if they be not on principles of symphony, — that is, the double and triple (distances) spoken of by Plato, — but are discovered independent of harmonies, would not preserve the doctrine of the formation of the universe according to harmony. For it is neither credible nor possible that the distances of these should be both contrary to some reasonable plan, and independent of harmonious and proportional principles, except perhaps only the Moon, on account of wanings and the shadow of the Earth,

in regard also of the distance of which alone — that is, the lunar (planet) from earth — one may trust Archimedes. It will, however, be easy for those who, according to the Platonic dogma itself, adopt this distance to comprehend by numerical calculation (intervals) according to what is double and triple, as Plato requires, and the rest of the distances. If, then, according to Archimedes, the Moon is distant from the surface of the Earth 5,544,130 stadii, by increasing these numbers double and triple, (it will be) easy to find also the distances of the rest, as if subtracting one part of the number of stadii which the Moon is distant from the Earth.

But because the rest of the numbers — those alleged by Archimedes concerning the distance of the erratic stars — are not based on principles of concord, it is easy to understand — that is, for those who attend to the matter — how the numbers are mutually related, and on what principles they depend. That, however, they should not be in harmony and symphony — I mean those that are parts of the world which consists according to harmony — this is impossible. Since, therefore, the first number which the Moon is distant from the earth is 5,544,130, the second number which the Sun is distant from the Moon being 50,272,065, subsists by a greater computation than ninefold. But the higher number in reference to this, being 20,272,065, is (comprised) in a greater computation than half. The number, however, superior to this, which is 50,817,165, is contained in a greater computation than half. But the number superior to this, which is 40,541,108, is contained in a less computation than two-fifths. But the number superior to this, which is 20,275,065, is contained in a greater computation than half. The final number, however, which is 40,372,065, is comprised in a less computation than double.

CHAP. XI. — THEORY OF THE SIZE OF THE HEAVENLY BODIES IN ACCORDANCE WITH NUMERICAL HARMONIES.

These (numerical) relations, therefore, the greater than ninefold, and less than half, and greater than double, and less than two-fifths, and greater than half, and less than double, are beyond all symphonies, from which not any proportionate or harmonic system could be produced. But the whole world, and the parts of it, are in all respects similarly framed in conformity with proportion and harmony. The proportionate and harmonic relations, however, are preserved — as we have previously stated — by double and triple intervals. If, therefore, we consider Archimedes reliable in the case of only the first distance, that from the Moon to the Earth, it is easy also to find the rest (of the intervals), by multiplying (them) by double and

---

[1] This is manifestly erroneous; the total could only be "four myriads!"

[2] The Abbe Cruice thinks that the word should be " tones," supporting his emendation on the authority of Pliny, who states that Pythagoras called the distance of the Moon from the Earth a tone, deriving the term from musical science (see Pliny's *Hist. Nat.*, ii. 20).

[3] These numerical speculations are treated of by Archimedes in his work *On the Number of the Sand*, in which he maintains the possibility of counting the sands, even on the supposition of the world's being much larger than it is (see Archimedes, τὰ μεχρὶ νῦν σωζόμενα ἄπαντα, Treatise Ψαμμίτης, p. 120, ed. Eustoc. Ascalon., Basil, 1544).

treble. Let then the distance, according to Archimedes, from Earth to Moon be 5,544,130 stadii ; there will therefore be the double number of this of stadii which the Sun is distant from the Moon, viz., 11,088,260. But the Sun is distant from the Earth 16,632,390 stadii ; and Venus is likewise distant from the Sun 16,632,-390 stadii, but from the Earth 33,264,780 stadii ; and Mercury is distant from Venus 22,176,520 stadii, but from Earth 55,441,300 stadii ; and Mars is distant from Mercury 49,897,170 stadii, and from Earth 105,338,470 stadii ; and Jupiter is distant from Mars 44,353,040 stadii, but from Earth 149,691,510 stadii ; Saturn is distant from Jupiter 149,691,510 stadii, but from Earth 299,383,020 stadii.

CHAP. XII. — WASTE OF MENTAL ENERGY IN THE SYSTEMS OF THE ASTROLOGERS.

Who will not feel astonishment at the exertion of so much deep thought with so much toil? This Ptolemy, however — a careful investigator of these matters — does not seem to me to be useless ; but only this grieves (one), that being recently born, he could not be of service to the sons of the giants, who, being ignorant of these measures, and supposing that the heights of heaven were near, endeavoured in vain to construct a tower. And so, if at that time he were present to explain to them these measures, they would not have made the daring attempt ineffectually. But if any one profess not to have confidence in this (astronomer's calculations), let him by measuring be persuaded (of their accuracy) ; for in reference to those incredulous on the point, one cannot have a more manifest proof than this. O, pride of vain-toiling soul, and incredible belief, that Ptolemy should be considered pre-eminently wise among those who have cultivated similar wisdom !

CHAP. XIII. — MENTION OF THE HERETIC COLARBASUS ; ALLIANCE BETWEEN HERESY AND THE PYTHAGOREAN PHILOSOPHY.

Certain, adhering partly to these, as if having propounded great conclusions, and supposed things worthy of reason, have framed enormous and endless heresies ; and one of these is Colarbasus,[1] who attempts to explain religion by measures and numbers. And others there are (who act) in like manner, whose tenets we shall explain when we commence to speak of what concerns those who give heed to Pythagorean calculation as possible ; and uttering vain prophecies, hastily assume[2] as secure the philosophy by numbers

and elements. Now certain (speculators), appropriating[3] similar reasonings from these, deceive unsophisticated individuals, alleging themselves endued with foresight ;[4] sometimes, after uttering many predictions, happening on a single fulfilment, and not abashed by many failures, but making their boast in this one. Neither shall I pass over the witless philosophy of these men ; but, after explaining it, I shall prove that those who attempt to form a system of religion out of these (aforesaid elements), are disciples of a school[5] weak and full of knavery.

CHAP. XIV. — SYSTEM OF THE ARITHMETICIANS ; PREDICTIONS THROUGH CALCULATIONS ; NUMERICAL ROOTS ; TRANSFERENCE OF THESE DOCTRINES TO LETTERS ; EXAMPLES IN PARTICULAR NAMES ; DIFFERENT METHODS OF CALCULATION ; PRESCIENCE POSSIBLE BY THESE.

Those, then, who suppose that they prophesy by means of calculations and numbers,[6] and elements and names, constitute the origin of their attempted system to be as follows. They affirm that there is a root of each of the numbers ; in the case of thousands, so many monads as there are thousands : for example, the root of six thousand, six monads ; of seven thousand, seven monads ; of eight thousand, eight monads ; and in the case of the rest, in like manner, according to the same (proportion). And in the case of hundreds, as many hundreds as there are, so many monads are the root of them : for instance, of seven hundred there are seven hundreds ; the root of these is seven monads : of six hundred, six hundreds ; the root of these, six monads. And it is similar respecting decades : for of eighty (the root is) eight monads ; and of sixty, six monads ; of forty, four monads ; of ten, one monad. And in the case of monads, the monads themselves are a root : for instance, of nine, nine ; of eight, eight ; of seven, seven. In this way, also, ought we therefore to act in the case of the elements (of words), for each letter has been arranged according to a certain number : for instance, the letter *n* according to fifty monads ; but of fifty monads five is the root, and the root of the letter *n* is (therefore) five. Grant that from some name we take certain roots of it. For instance, (from) the name

---

[1] Colarbasus is afterwards mentioned in company with Marcus the heretic, at the beginning and end of book vi. of *The Refutation*.
[2] This word (σχεδιάζουσι), more than once used by Hippolytus, is applied to anything done offhand, e.g , an *extempore* speech. It therefore might be made to designate immaturity of opinion. Σχεδια means something hastily put together, viz., a raft ; σχέδιος, sudden.

[3] Schneidewin suggests ὅμως instead of οἱμοίως. The word (ἐρανισάμενοι) translated "appropriating" is derived from ἔρανος, which signifies a meal to which those who partake of it have each contributed some dish (pic-nic). The term, therefore, is an expressive one for Hippolytus' purpose.
[4] προγνωστικούς. Some would read πρὸς γνωστικούς.
[5] Some propose δόξης, "opinion." Hippolytus, however, used the word ῥίζης (translated "school") in a similar way at the end of chap. i. of book iv. "Novelty" is read instead of "knavery ;" and for ἀναπλέου, "full," is proposed (1) ἀναπλέοντας, (2) ἀναπτεροῦντας.
[6] The subject of the numerical system employed by the Gnostics, and their occult mysteries, is treated of by the learned Kircher, (*Œdipi Ægypt.*, tom. ii. part i , *de Cabalâ Hebræorum ;* also in his *Arithmolog..* in the book *De Arithmomantia Gnosticor.*, cap. viii., *de Cabalâ Pythagoreâ.* See also Mersennes, *Comment. on Genes.*

Agamemnon, there is of the *a*, one monad; and of the *g*, three monads; and of the other *a*, one monad; of the *m*, four monads; of the *e*, five monads; of the *m*, four monads; of the *n*, five monads; of the (long) *o*, eight monads; of the *n*, five monads; which, brought together into one series, will be 1, 3, 1, 4, 5, 4, 5, 8, 5; and these added together make up 36 monads. Again, they take the roots of these, and they become three in the case of the number thirty, but actually six in the case of the number six. The three and the six, then, added together, constitute nine; but the root of nine is nine: therefore the name Agamemnon terminates in the root nine.

Let us do the same with another name — Hector. The name (H)ector has five letters — *e*, and *k*, and *t*, and *o*, and *r*. The roots of these are 5, 2, 3, 8, 1; and these added together make up 19 monads. Again, of the ten the root is one; and of the nine, nine; which added together make up ten: the root of ten is a monad. The name Hector, therefore, when made the subject of computation, has formed a root, namely a monad. It would, however, be easier[1] to conduct the calculation thus: Divide the ascertained roots from the letters — as now in the case of the name Hector we have found nineteen monads — into nine, and treat what remains over as roots. For example, if I divide 19 into 9, the remainder is 1, for 9 times 2 are 18, and there is a remaining monad: for if I subtract 18 from 19, there is a remaining monad; so that the root of the name Hector will be a monad. Again, of the name Patroclus these numbers are roots: 8, 1, 3, 1, 7, 2, 3, 7, 2; added together, they make up 34 monads. And of these the remainder is 7 monads: of the 30, 3; and of the 4, 4. Seven monads, therefore, are the root of the name Patroclus.

Those, then, that conduct their calculations according to the rule of the number nine,[2] take the ninth part of the aggregate number of roots, and define what is left over as the sum of the roots. They, on the other hand, (who conduct their calculations) according to the rule of the number seven, take the seventh (part of the aggregate number of roots); for example, in the case of the name Patroclus, the aggregate in the matter of roots is 34 monads. This divided into seven parts makes four, which (multiplied into each other) are 28. There are six remaining monads; (so that a person using this method) says, according to the rule of the number seven, that six monads are the root of the

name Patroclus. If, however, it be 43, (six) taken seven times,[3] he says, are 42, for seven times six are 42, and one is the remainder. A monad, therefore, is the root of the number 43, according to the rule of the number seven. But one ought to observe if the assumed number, when divided, has no remainder; for example, if from any name, after having added together the roots, I find, to give an instance, 36 monads. But the number 36 divided into nine makes exactly 4 enneads; for nine times 4 are 36, and nothing is over. It is evident, then, that the actual root is 9. And again, dividing the number forty-five, we find nine[4] and nothing over — for nine times five are forty-five, and nothing remains; (wherefore) in the case of such they assert the root itself to be nine. And as regards the number seven, the case is similar: if, for example we divide 28 into 7, we have nothing over; for seven times four are 28, and nothing remains; (wherefore) they say that seven is the root. But when one computes names, and finds the same letter occurring twice, he calculates it once; for instance, the name Patroclus has the *pa* twice,[5] and the *o* twice: they therefore calculate the *a* once and the *o* once. According to this, then, the roots will be 8, 1, 3, 1, 7, 2, 3, 2, and added together they make 27 monads; and the root of the name will be, according to the rule of the number nine, nine itself, but according to the rule of the number seven, six.

In like manner, (the name) Sarpedon, when made the subject of calculation, produces as a root, according to the rule of the number nine, two monads. Patroclus, however, produces nine monads; Patroclus gains the victory. For when one number is uneven, but the other even, the uneven number, if it is larger, prevails. But again, when there is an even number, eight, and five an uneven number, the eight prevails, for it is larger. If, however, there were two numbers, for example, both of them even, or both of them odd, the smaller prevails. But how does (the name) Sarpedon, according to the rule of the number nine, make two monads, since the letter (long) *o* is omitted? For when there may be in a name the letter (long) *o* and (long) *e*, they leave out the (long) *o*, using one letter, because they say both are equipollent; and the same must not be computed twice over, as has been above declared. Again, (the name) Ajax makes four monads; (but the name) Hector, according to the rule of the ninth number, makes one

[1] This subject is examined by Cornelius Agrippa in his celebrated work, *De vanitate et incertitudine Scientiarum*, chap. xi., *De Sorte Pythagoricâ.* Terentius Maurus has also a versified work on *Letters and Syllables and Metres*, in which he alludes to similar interpretations educible from the names Hector and Patroclus.

[2] That is, the division by nine.

[3] That is, calculated according to the rule of a division by seven.

[4] We should expect rather five instead of 9, if the division be by nine.

[5] There is some confusion in the text. Miller conjectures that the reading should be: "As, for instance, the name Patroclus has the letter *o* occurring twice in it, they therefore take it into calculation once." Schneidewin suggests that the form of the name may be Papatroclus.

monad. And the tetrad is even, whereas the monad odd. And in the case of such, we say, the greater prevails — Ajax gains the victory. Again, Alexander and Menelaus (may be adduced as examples). Alexander has a proper name (Paris). But Paris, according to the rule of the number nine, makes four monads; and Menelaus, according to the rule of the number nine, makes nine monads. The nine, however, conquer the four (monads): for it has been declared, when the one number is odd and the other even, the greater prevails; but when both are even or both odd, the less (prevails). Again, Amycus and Polydeuces (may be adduced as examples). Amycus, according to the rule of the number nine, makes two monads, and Polydeuces, however, seven: Polydeuces gains the victory. Ajax and Ulysses contended at the funeral games. Ajax, according to the rule of the number nine, makes four monads; Ulysses, according to the rule of the number nine, (makes) eight.[1] Is there, then, not any annexed, and (is there) not a proper name for Ulysses?[2] for he has gained the victory. According to the numbers, no doubt, Ajax is victorious, but history hands down the name of Ulysses as the conqueror. Achilles and Hector (may be adduced as examples). Achilles, according to the rule of the number nine, makes four monads; Hector one: Achilles gains the victory. Again, Achilles and Asteropæus (are instances). Achilles makes four monads, Asteropæus three: Achilles conquers. Again, Menelaus and Euphorbus (may be adduced as examples). Menelaus has nine monads, Euphorbus eight: Menelaus gains the victory.

Some, however, according to the rule of the number seven, employ the vowels only, but others distinguish by themselves the vowels, and by themselves the semi-vowels, and by themselves the mutes; and, having formed three orders, they take the roots by themselves of the vowels, and by themselves of the semi-vowels, and by themselves of the mutes, and they compare each apart. Others, however, do not employ even these customary numbers, but different ones: for instance, as an example, they no not wish to allow that the letter p has as a root 8 monads, but 5, and that the (letter) x (si) has as a root four monads; and turning in every direction, they discover nothing sound. When, however, they contend about the second (letter), from each name they take away the first letter; but when they contend about the third (letter), they take away two letters of each name, and calculating the rest, compare them.

CHAP. XV. — QUIBBLES OF THE NUMERICAL THEORISTS; THE ART OF THE FRONTISPICISTS (PHYSIOGNOMY); CONNECTION OF THIS ART WITH ASTROLOGY; TYPE OF THOSE BORN UNDER ARIES.

I think that there has been clearly expounded the mind of arithmeticians, who, by means of numbers and of names, suppose that they interpret life. Now I perceive that these, enjoying leisure, and being trained in calculation, have been desirous that, through the art[3] delivered to them from childhood, they, acquiring celebrity, should be styled prophets. And they, measuring the letters up (and) down, have wandered into trifling. For if they fail, they say, in putting forward the difficulty, Perhaps this name was not a family one, but imposed, as also lighting in the instance they argue in the case of (the names) Ulysses and Ajax. Who, taking occasion from this astonishing philosophy, and desirous of being styled "Heresiarch," will not be extolled?

But since, also, there is another more profound art among the all-wise speculators of the Greeks — to whom heretical individuals boast that they attach themselves as disciples, on account of their employing the opinions of these (ancient philosophers) in reference to the doctrines attempted (to be established) by themselves, as shall a little afterwards be proved; but this is an art of divination, by examination of the forehead,[4] or rather, I should say, it is madness: yet we shall not be silent as regards this (system) There are some who ascribe to the stars figures that mould the ideas[5] and dispositions of men, assigning the reason of this to births (that have taken place) under particular stars; they thus express themselves: Those who[6] are born under Aries will be of the following kind: long head, red hair, contracted eyebrows, pointed forehead, eyes grey and lively,[7] drawn cheeks, long-nosed, expanded nostrils, thin lips, tapering chin, wide mouth. These, he says, will partake of the following nature: cautious, subtle, perspicuous,[8] prudent, indulgent, gentle, over-anxious, persons of secret resolves, fitted for every undertaking, prevailing more by prudence than strength, deriders for the time being, scholars,

---

[1] Miller says there is an error in the calculation here.
[2] This is as near the sense of the passage as a translation in some respects conjectural can make it.

[3] The word θέλειν occurs in this sentence, but is obviously superfluous.
[4] In the margin of the MS. is the note, "Opinion of the Metopiscopists."
[5] These words are out of place. See next note.
[6] There is evidently some displacement of words here. Miller and Schneidewin suggest: "There are some who ascribe to the influence of the stars the natures of men; since, in computing the births of individuals, they thus express themselves as if they were moulding the species of men." The Abbe Cruice would leave the text as it is, altering only τυποῦντες ἰδέας into τύπων τε ἰδέας.
[7] Literally, "jumping;" others read "blackish," or "expressive" (literally, "talking"). The vulgar reading, ὑπὸ ἄλλοις, is evidently untenable.
[8] Or "cowardly," or "cowards at heart;" or some read, χαροποιοί, i.e., "causative of gl

trustworthy, contentious, quarrellers in a fray, concupiscent, inflamed with unnatural lust, reflective, estranged [1] from their own homes, giving dissatisfaction in everything, accusers, like madmen in their cups, scorners, year by year losing something [2] serviceable in friendship through goodness; they, in the majority of cases, end their days in a foreign land.

CHAP. XVI. — TYPE OF THOSE BORN UNDER TAURUS.

Those, however, who are born in Taurus will be of the following description: round head, thick hair, broad forehead, square eyes, and large black eyebrows; in a white man, thin veins, sanguine, long eyelids, coarse huge ears, round mouths, thick nose, round nostrils, thick lips, strong in the upper parts, formed straight from the legs.[3] The same are by nature pleasing, reflective, of a goodly disposition, devout, just, uncouth, complaisant, labourers from twelve years, quarrelsome, dull. The stomach of these is small, they are quickly filled, forming many designs, prudent, niggardly towards themselves, liberal towards others, beneficent, of a slow [4] body: they are partly sorrowful, heedless as regards friendship, useful on account of mind, unfortunate.

CHAP. XVII. — TYPE OF THOSE BORN UNDER GEMINI.

Those who are born in Gemini will be of the following description: red countenance, size not very large, evenly proportioned limbs,[5] black eyes as if anointed with oil, cheeks turned down,[6] and large mouth, contracted eyebrows; they conquer all things, they retain whatever possessions they acquire,[7] they are extremely rich, penurious, niggardly of what is peculiarly their own, profuse in the pleasures of women,[8] equitable, musical, liars. And the same by nature are learned, reflective, inquisitive, arriving at their own decisions, concupiscent, sparing of what belongs to themselves, liberal, quiet, prudent, crafty, they form many designs, calculators, accusers, importunate, not prosperous, they are beloved by the fair sex, merchants; as regards friendship, not to any considerable extent useful.

CHAP. XVIII. — TYPE OF THOSE BORN UNDER CANCER.

Those born in Cancer are of the following description: size not large, hair like a dog, of a reddish colour, small mouth, round head, pointed forehead, grey eyes, sufficiently beautiful, limbs somewhat varying. The same by nature are wicked, crafty, proficients in plans, insatiable, stingy, ungracious, illiberal, useless, forgetful; they neither restore what is another's, nor do they ask back what is their own; [9] as regards friendship, useful.

CHAP. XIX. — TYPE OF THOSE BORN UNDER LEO.

Those born in Leo are of the following description: round head, reddish hair, huge wrinkled forehead, coarse ears, large development of neck, partly bald, red complexion, grey eyes, large jaws, coarse mouth, gross in the upper parts,[10] huge breast, the under limbs tapering. The same are by nature persons who allow nothing to interfere with their own decision, pleasing themselves, irascible, passionate, scorners, obstinate, forming no design, not loquacious,[11] indolent, making an improper use of leisure, familiar,[12] wholly abandoned to pleasures of women, adulterers, immodest, in faith untrue, importunate, daring, penurious, spoliators, remarkable; as regards fellowship, useful; as regards friendship,[13] useless.

CHAP. XX. — TYPE OF THOSE BORN UNDER VIRGO.

Those born in Virgo are of the following description: fair appearance, eyes not large, fascinating, dark, compact [14] eyebrows, cheerful, swimmers; they are, however, slight in frame,[15] beautiful in aspect, with hair prettily adjusted, large forehead, prominent nose. The same by nature are docile, moderate, intelligent, sportive, rational, slow to speak, forming many plans; in regard of a favour, importunate; [16] gladly observing everything; and well-disposed pupils, they master whatever they learn; moderate, scorners, victims of unnatural lusts, companionable, of a noble soul, despisers, careless in practical matters, attending to instruction, more honourable in what concerns others than what relates to themselves; as regards friendship, useful.

CHAP. XXI. — TYPE OF THOSE BORN UNDER LIBRA.

Those born in Libra will be of the following description: hair thin, drooping, reddish and

---

[1] Or, " diseased with unnatural lust," i.e., νοσοῦντες for νοοῦντες.
[2] Or, κατ᾽ ἔπος, " verbally rejecting anything."
[3] Or better, " weak in the limbs."
[4] Or, " short."
[5] Or, " parts."
[6] Some read καλῶ γεγεννημένων, or καλῶ τετενννημένων.
[7] Or, " they are given to hoarding, they have possessions."
[8] This is an amended reading of the text, which is obviously confused. The correction necessary is introduced lower down in the MS., which makes the same characteristic be twice mentioned. The Abbé Cruice, however, accounts for such a twofold mention, on the ground that the whole subject is treated by Hippolytus in such a way as to expose the absurdities of the astrologic predictions. He therefore quotes the opinions of various astrologers, in order to expose the diversities of opinion existing among them.

[9] Manilius maintains that persons born under Cancer are of an avaricious and usurious disposition. (See *Astronom.*, iv. 5.)
[10] Or, " having the upper parts larger than the lower."
[11] Some read ἀναλοι.
[12] Schneidewin conjectures ἀσυνήθεις, i.e., inexperienced.
[13] Or, " succour."
[14] Or, " straight, compact."
[15] Miller gives an additional sentence: " They are of equal measurement at the (same) age, and possess a body perfect and erect."
[16] Or, " careful observers."

longish, forehead pointed (and) wrinkled, fair compact eyebrows, beautiful eyes, dark pupils, long thin ears, head inclined, wide mouth. The same by nature are intelligent, God-fearing, communicative to one another,[1] traders, toilers, not retaining gain, liars, not of an amiable disposition, in business or principle true, free-spoken, beneficent, illiterate, deceivers, friendly, careless, (to whom it is not profitable to do any act of injustice) ;[2] they are scorners, scoffers, satirical,[3] illustrious, listeners, and nothing succeeds with these ; as regards friendship, useful.

CHAP. XXII. — TYPE OF THOSE BORN UNDER SCORPIO.

Those born in Scorpio are of the following description : a maidenish countenance, comely, pungent, blackish hair, well-shaped eyes, forehead not broad, and sharp nostril, small contracted ears, wrinkled foreheads, narrow eyebrows, drawn cheeks. The same by nature are crafty, sedulous, liars, communicating their particular designs to no one, of a deceitful spirit, wicked, scorners, victims to adultery, well-grown, docile ; as regards friendship, useless.

CHAP. XXIII. — TYPE OF THOSE BORN UNDER SAGITTARIUS.

Those born in Sagittarius will be of the following description : great length, square forehead, profuse eyebrows, indicative of strength, well-arranged projection of hair, reddish (in complexion). The same by nature are gracious, as educated persons, simple, beneficent ; given to unnatural lusts, companionable, toil-worn, lovers, beloved, jovial in their cups, clean, passionate, careless, wicked ; as regards friendship, useless ; scorners, with noble souls, insolent, crafty ; for fellowship, useful.

CHAP. XXIV. — TYPE OF THOSE BORN UNDER CAPRICORN.

Those born in Capricorn will be of the following description : reddish body, projection of greyish hair, round mouth,[4] eyes as of an eagle, contracted brows, open forehead, somewhat bald, in the upper parts of the body endued with more strength. The same by nature are philosophic, scorners, and scoffers at the existing state of things, passionate, persons that can make concessions, honourable, beneficent, lovers of the practice of music, passionate in their cups, mirthful, familiar, talkative, given to unnatural lusts, genial, amiable, quarrelsome lovers, for fellowship well disposed.

CHAP. XXV. — TYPE OF THOSE BORN UNDER AQUARIUS.

Those born in Aquarius will be of the following description : square in size, of a diminutive body ; sharp, small, fierce eyes ; imperious, ungenial, severe, readily making acquisitions, for friendship and fellowship well disposed ; moreover, for maritime[5] enterprises they make voyages, and perish. The same by nature are taciturn, modest, sociable, adulterers, penurious, practised in business,[6] tumultuous, pure, well-disposed, honourable, large eyebrows ; frequently they are born in the midst of trifling events, but (in after life) follow a different pursuit ; though they may have shown kindness to any one, still no one returns them thanks.

CHAP. XXVI. — TYPE OF THOSE BORN UNDER PISCES.

Those born in Pisces will be of the following description : of moderate dimensions, pointed forehead like fishes, shaggy hair, frequently they become soon grey. The same by nature are of exalted soul, simple, passionate, penurious, talkative ; in the first period of life they will be drowsy ; they are desirous of managing business by themselves, of high repute, venturesome, emulous, accusers, changing their locality, lovers, dancers ; for friendship, useful.

CHAP. XXVII. — FUTILITY OF THIS THEORY OF STELLAR INFLUENCE.

Since, therefore, we have explained the astonishing wisdom of these men, and have not concealed their overwrought art of divination by means of contemplation, neither shall I be silent as regards (undertakings) in the case of which those that are deceived act foolishly. For, comparing the forms and dispositions of men with names of stars, how impotent their system is ! For we know that those originally conversant with such investigations have called the stars by names given in reference to propriety of signification and facility for future recognition. For what similarity is there of these (heavenly bodies) with the likeness of animals, or what community of nature as regards conduct and energy (is there in the two cases), that one should allege that a person born in Leo should be irascible, and one born in Virgo moderate, or one born in Cancer wicked, but that those born in . . .

---

[1] Or, " speaking falsehoods, they will be believed."
[2] The parenthetical words are obviously an interpolation.
[3] Or, " spies."
[4] Or, " body."

[5] Literally " moist," or " difficult ; " or, the Abbe Cruice suggests, fortuitous."
[6] Or, " pragmatic, mild, not violent."

CHAP. XXVIII.[1] — SYSTEM OF THE MAGICIANS; INCANTATIONS OF DEMONS; SECRET MAGICAL RITES.

. . . And (the sorcerer), taking (a paper), directs the inquirer[2] to write down with water whatever questions he may desire to have asked from the demons. Then, folding up the paper, and delivering it to the attendant, he sends him away to commit it to the flames, that the ascending smoke may waft the letters to demons. While, however, the attendant is executing this order, (the sorcerer) first removes equal portions of the paper, and on some more parts of it he pretends that demons write in Hebrew characters. Then burning an incense of the Egyptian magicians, termed Cyphi, he takes these (portions of paper) away, and places them near the incense. But (that paper) which the inquirer happens to have written (upon), having placed on the coals, he has burned. Then (the sorcerer), appearing to be borne away under divine influence, (and) hurrying into a corner (of the house), utters a loud and harsh cry, and unintelligible to all, . . . and orders all those present to enter, crying out (at the same time), and invoking Phryn, or some other demon. But after passing into the house, and when those that were present stood side by side, the sorcerer, flinging the attendant upon a bed,[3] utters to him several words, partly in the Greek, and partly, as it were, the Hebrew language, (embodying) the customary incantations employed by the magicians. (The attendant), however, goes away[4] to make the inquiry. And within (the house), into a vessel full of water (the sorcerer) infusing copperas mixture, and melting the drug, having with it sprinkled the paper that forsooth had (the characters upon it) obliterated, he forces the latent and concealed letters to come once more into light; and by these he ascertains what the inquirer has written down. And if one write with copperas mixture likewise, and having ground a gall nut, use its vapour as a fumigator, the concealed letters would become plain. And if one write with milk, (and) then scorch the paper, and scraping it, sprinkle and rub (what is thus scraped off) upon the letters traced with the milk, these will become plain. And urine likewise, and sauce of brine, and juice of euphorbia, and of a fig, produce a similar result. But when

(the sorcerer) has ascertained the question in this mode, he makes provision for the manner in which he ought to give the reply. And next he orders those that are present to enter, holding laurel branches and shaking them, and uttering cries, and invoking the demon Phryn. For also it becomes these to invoke him;[5] and it is worthy that they make this request from demons, which they do not wish of themselves to put forward, having lost their minds. The confused noise, however, and the tumult, prevent them directing attention to those things which it is supposed (the sorcerer) does in secret. But what these are, the present is a fair opportunity for us to declare.

Considerable darkness, then, prevails. For the (sorcerer) affirms that it is impossible for mortal nature to behold divine things, for that to hold converse (with these mysteries) is sufficient. Making, however, the attendant lie down (upon the couch), head foremost, and placing by each side two of those little tablets, upon which had been inscribed in, forsooth, Hebrew characters, as it were names of demons, he says that (a demon) will deposit the rest in their ears. But this (statement) is requisite, in order that some instrument may be placed beside the ears of the attendant, by which it is possible that he signify everything which he chooses. First, however, he produces a sound that the (attendant) youth may be terrified; and secondly, he makes a humming noise; then, thirdly, he speaks[6] through the instrument what he wishes the youth to say, and remains in expectation of the issue of the affair; next, he makes those present remain still, and directs the (attendant) to signify what he has heard from the demons. But the instrument that is placed beside his ears is a natural instrument, viz., the windpipe of long-necked cranes, or storks, or swans. And if none of these is at hand, there are also some different artificial instruments (employed); for certain pipes of brass, ten in number, (and) fitting into one another, terminating in a narrow point, are adapted (for the purpose), and through these is spoken into the ear whatsoever the (magician) wishes. And the youth hearing these (words) with terror as uttered by demons, when ordered, speaks them out. If any one, however, putting around a stick a moist hide, and having dried it and drawn it together, close it up, and by removing the rod fashion the hide into the form of a pipe, he attains a similar end. Should any of these, however, be not at hand, he takes a book, and, opening it inside, stretches it out as far as

---

[1] Hippolytus, having exposed the system of sidereal influence over men, proceeds to detail the magical rites and operations of the sorcerers. This arrangement is in conformity with the technical divisions of astrology into (1) judiciary, (2) natural. The former related to the prediction of future events, and the latter of the phenomena of nature, being thus akin to the art of magic.

[2] The text here and at the end of the last chapter is somewhat imperfect.

[3] Or "cushion" (Cruice), or "couch," or "a recess."

[4] Or "goes up," or "commences," or "enters in before the others, bearing the oblation" (Cruice).

[5] Or, "deride."

[6] The Abbe Cruice considers that this passage, as attributing all this jugglery to the artifice of sorcerers, militates against the authorship of Origen, who ascribes (Περὶ Ἀρχῶν, lib. iii. p. 144, ed. Benedict.) the same results not to the frauds of magicians, but to demons.

he think requisite, (and thus) achieves the same result.

But if he knows beforehand that one is present who is about to ask a question, he is the more ready for all (contingencies). If, however, he may also previously ascertain the question, he writes (it) with the drug, and, as being prepared, he is considered [1] more skilful, on account of having clearly written out what is (about) being asked. If, however, he is ignorant of the question, he forms conjectures, and puts forth something capable of a doubtful and varied interpretation, in order that the oracular response, being originally unintelligible, may serve for numerous purposes, and in the issue of events the prediction may be considered correspondent with what actually occurs. Next, having filled a vessel with water, he puts down (into it) the paper, as if uninscribed, at the same time infusing along with it copperas mixture. For in this way the paper written upon floats [2] upwards (to the surface), bearing the response. Accordingly there ensue frequently to the attendant formidable fancies, for also he strikes blows plentifully on the terrified (bystanders). For, casting incense into the fire, he again operates after the following method. Covering a lump of what are called "fossil salts" with Etruscan wax, and dividing the piece itself of incense into two parts, he throws in a grain of salt; and again joining (the piece) together, and placing it on the burning coals, he leaves it there. And when this is consumed, the salts, bounding upwards, create the impression of, as it were, a strange vision taking place. And the dark-blue dye which has been deposited in the incense produces a blood-red flame, as we have already declared. But (the sorcerer) makes a scarlet liquid, by mixing wax with alkanet, and, as I said, depositing the wax in the incense. And he makes the coals [3] be moved, placing underneath powdered alum; and when this is dissolved and swells up like bubbles, the coals are moved.

CHAP. XXIX. — DISPLAY OF DIFFERENT EGGS.

But different eggs they display after this manner. Perforating the top at both ends, and extracting the white, (and) having again dipped it, throw in some minium and some writing ink. Close, however, the openings with refined scrapings of the eggs, smearing them with fig-juice.

CHAP. XXX. — SELF-SLAUGHTER OF SHEEP.

By those who cause sheep to cut off their own heads, the following plan is adopted. Secretly smearing the throat (of the animal) with a cau-

terizing drug, he places a sword near, and leaves it there.[4] The sheep, desirous of scratching himself, rushes against the blade, and in the act of rubbing is slaughtered, while the head is almost severed from the trunk. There is, however, a compound of the drug, bryony and salt and squills, made up in equal parts. In order that the person bringing the drug may escape notice, he carries a box with two compartments constructed of horn, the visible one of which contains frankincense, but the secret one (the aforesaid) drug. He, however, likewise insinuates into the ears of the sheep about to meet death quicksilver; but this is a poisonous drug.

CHAP. XXXI. — METHOD OF POISONING GOATS.

And if one smear [5] the ears of goats over with cerate, they say that they expire a little afterwards, by having their breathing obstructed. For this to them is the way — as these affirm — of their drawing their breath in an act of respiration. And a ram, they assert, dies,[6] if one bends back (its neck)[7] opposite the sun. And they accomplish the burning of a house, by daubing it over with the juice of a certain fish called *dactylus*. And this effect, which it has by reason of the sea-water, is very useful. Likewise foam of the ocean is boiled in an earthen jar along with some sweet ingredients; and if you apply a lighted candle to this while in a seething state, it catches the fire and is consumed; and (yet though the mixture) be poured upon the head, it does not burn it at all. If, however, you also smear it over with heated resin,[8] it is consumed far more effectually. But he accomplishes his object better still, if also he takes some sulphur.

CHAP. XXXII. — IMITATIONS OF THUNDER, AND OTHER ILLUSIONS.

Thunder is produced in many ways; for stones very numerous and unusually large, being rolled downwards along wooden planks, fall upon plates of brass, and cause a sound similar to thunder. And also around the thin plank with which carders thicken cloth, they coil a thin rope; and then drawing away the cord with a whirr, they spin the plank round, and in its revolution it emits a sound like thunder. These farces, verily, are played off thus.

There are, however, other practices which I shall explain, which those who execute these

---

[1] Or, "denominated."
[2] Or, "rises up."
[3] On the margin of the MS. we find the words, "concerning coals," "concerning magical signs," "concerning sheep."

[4] Or, παραδοθείς, "he delivers it a sword, and departs."
[5] Or, "close up."
[6] The words "death of a goat" occur on the margin of the MS.
[7] A similar statement is made, on the authority of Alcmæon, by Aristotle in his *Histor. Animal.*, i. 2.
[8] Μαννή is the word in the text. But manna in the ordinary acceptation of the term can scarcely be intended. Pliny, however, mentions it as a proper name of grains of incense and resin. The Abbe Cruice suggests the very probable emendation of μαλθη, which signifies a mixture of wax and resin for caulking ships.

ludicrous performances estimate as great exploits. Placing a cauldron full of pitch upon burning coals, when it boils up, (though) laying their hands down upon it, they are not burned; nay, even while walking on coals of fire with naked feet, they are not scorched. But also setting a pyramid of stone on a hearth, (the sorcerer) makes it get on fire, and from the mouth it disgorges a volume of smoke, and that of a fiery description. Then also putting a linen cloth upon a pot of water, throwing on (at the same time) a quantity of blazing coals, (the magician) keeps the linen cloth unconsumed. Creating also darkness in the house, (the sorcerer) alleges that he can introduce gods or demons; and if any requires him to show Æsculapius, he uses an invocation couched in the following words:—

"The child once slain, again of Phœbus deathless made,
   I call to come, and aid my sacrificial rites;
Who, also, once the countless tribes of fleeting dead,
   In ever-mournful homes of Tartarus wide,
The fatal billow breasting, and the inky [1] flood
Surmounting, where all of mortal mould must float,
Torn, beside the lake, with endless [2] grief and woe,
Thyself didst snatch from gloomy Proserpine.
Or whether the seat of Holy Thrace thou haunt, or lovely
Pergamos, or besides Ionian Epidaurus,
The chief of seers, O happy God, invites thee here."

CHAP. XXXIII.—THE BURNING ÆSCULAPIUS; TRICKS WITH FIRE.

But after he discontinues uttering these jests, a fiery Æsculapius [3] appears upon the floor. Then, placing in the midst a pot full of water, he invokes all the deities, and they are present. For any one who is by, glancing into the pot, will behold them all, and Diana leading on her baying hounds. We shall not, however, shrink from narrating the account (of the devices) of these men, how they attempt (to accomplish their jugglery). For (the magician) lays his hand upon the cauldron of pitch,[4] which is in, as it were, a boiling state; and throwing in (at the same time) vinegar and nitre and moist pitch, he kindles a fire beneath the cauldron. The vinegar, however, being mixed along with the nitre, on receiving a small accession of heat, moves the pitch, so as to cause bubbles to rise to the surface, and afford the mere semblance of a seething (pot). The (sorcerer), however, previously washes his hands frequently in brine; the consequence being, that the contents of the cauldron do not in any wise, though in reality

boiling, burn him very much. But if, having smeared his hands with a tincture of myrtle [5] and nitre and myrrh, along with vinegar, he wash them in brine frequently, he is not scorched; and he does not burn his feet, provided he smear them with isinglass and a salamander.

As regards, however, the burning like a taper of the pyramid, though composed of stone, the cause of this is the following. Chalky earth is fashioned into the shape of a pyramid, but its colour is that of a milk-white stone, and it is prepared after this fashion. Having anointed the piece of clay with plenty of oil, and put it upon coals, and baked it, by smearing it afresh, and scorching it a second and third time, and frequently, (the sorcerer) contrives that it can be burned, even though he should plunge it in water; for it contains in itself abundance of oil. The hearth, however, is spontaneously kindled, while the magician pours out [6] a libation, by having lime instead of ashes burning underneath, and refined frankincense and a large quantity *of tow*,[7] and a bundle [8] of anointed tapers and of gall nuts, hollow within, and supplied with (concealed) fire. And after some delay, (the sorcerer) makes (the pyramid) emit smoke from the mouth, by both putting fire in the gall nut, and encircling it with tow, and blowing into the mouth. The linen cloth, however, that has been placed round the cauldron, (and) on which he deposits the coals, on account of the underlying brine, would not be burned; besides, that it has itself been washed in brine, and then smeared with the white of an egg, along with moist alum. And if, likewise, one mix in these the juice of house-leek along with vinegar, and for a long time previously smear it (with this preparation), after being washed in this drug, it continues altogether fire-proof.

CHAP. XXXIV.—THE ILLUSION OF THE SEALED LETTERS; OBJECT IN DETAILING THESE JUGGLERIES.

After, then,[9] we have succinctly explained the powers of the secret arts practised among these (magicians), and have shown their easy plan for the acquisition of knowledge,[10] neither are we disposed to be silent on the following point,

---

[1] δίαυλον in the text has been altered into κελαινὸν. The translator has followed the latter.
[2] Or "indissoluble," or "inseparable."
[3] Marsilius Ficinus (in his *Commentary on Plotinus*, p. 504 et seq., vol. ii. Creuzer's edition), who here discusses the subject of demons and magical art, mentions, on the authority of Porphyry, that sorcerers had the power of evoking demons, and that a magician, in the presence of many, had shown to Plotinus his guardian demon (angel). This constitutes the Goetic department of magic.
[4] Or, "full of pitch."

[5] Μυρσίνη. This word is evidently not the right one, for we have (σμύρνη) myrrh mentioned. Perhaps the word μάλθη, suggested in a previous passage, is the one employed here likewise.
[6] Or, "makes speedy preparation;" or, "resorts to the contrivance of."
[7] The words in italics are added by the Abbe Cruice. There is obviously some hiatus in the original.
[8] Or, "the refuse of."
[9] In the margin of the MS. occur the words, "concerning the breaking of the seals."
[10] Or, "exposed their method of proceeding in accordance with the system of Gnosticism." Schneidewin, following C. Fr. Hermann, is of opinion that what follows is taken from Celsus' work on magic, to which Origen alludes in the *Contra Celsum*, lib. i. p. 53 (Spencer's edition). Lucian (the well-known satirist), in his *Alexander*, or *Pseudomantis*, gives an account of the jugglery of these magicians. See note, chap. xlii. of this book.

which is a necessary one, — how that, loosing the seals, they restore the sealed letters, with the actual seals themselves. Melting pitch, resin, and sulphur, and moreover asphalt, in equal parts, (and) forming the ointment into a figure, they keep it by them. When, however, it is time to loose a small tablet, smearing with oil their tongue, next with the latter anointing the seal, (and) heating the drug with a moderate fire, (the sorcerers) place it upon the seal; and they leave it there until it has acquired complete consistence, and they use it in this condition as a seal. But they say, likewise, that wax itself with fir-wood gum possesses a similar potency, as well as two parts of mastich with one part of dry asphalt. But sulphur also by itself effects the purpose tolerably well, and flower of gypsum strained with water, and of gum. Now this (last mixture) certainly answers most admirably also for sealing molten lead. And that which is accomplished by the Tuscan wax, and refuse[1] of resin, and pitch, and asphalt, and mastich, and powdered spar, all being boiled together in equal parts, is superior to the rest of the drugs which I have mentioned, while that which is effected by the gum is not inferior. In this manner, then, also, they attempt to loose the seals, endeavouring to learn the letters written within.

These contrivances, however, I hesitated to narrate[2] in this book, perceiving the danger lest, perchance, any knavish person, taking occasion (from my account), should attempt (to practise these juggleries). Solicitude, however, for many young persons, who could be preserved from such practices, has persuaded me to teach and publish, for security's sake, (the foregoing statements). For although one person may make use of these for gaining instruction in evil, in this way somebody else will, by being instructed (in these practices), be preserved from them. And the magicians themselves, corrupters of life, will be ashamed in plying their art. And learning these points that have been previously elucidated[3] by us, they will possibly be restrained from their folly. But that this seal may not be broken, let me seal it with hog's lard and hair mixed with wax.[4]

CHAP. XXXV. — THE DIVINATION BY A CAULDRON; ILLUSION OF FIERY DEMONS; SPECIMEN OF A MAGICAL INVOCATION.

But neither shall I be silent respecting that piece of knavery of these (sorcerers), which

consists in the divination by means of the cauldron. For, making a closed chamber, and anointing the ceiling with cyanus for present use,[5] they introduce certain vessels of cyanus,[6] and stretch them upwards. The cauldron, however, full of water, is placed in the middle on the ground; and the reflection of the cyanus falling upon it, presents the appearance of heaven. But the floor also has a certain concealed aperture, on which the cauldron is laid, having been (previously, supplied with a bottom of crystal, while itself is composed of stone.[7] Underneath, however, unnoticed (by the spectators), is a compartment, into which the accomplices, assembling, appear invested with the figures of such gods and demons as the magician wishes to exhibit. Now the dupe, beholding these, becomes astonished at the knavery of the magician, and subsequently believes all things that are likely to be stated by him. But (the sorcerer) produces a burning demon, by tracing on the wall whatever figure he wishes, and then covertly smearing it with a drug mixed according to this manner, viz., of Laconian[8] and Zacynthian asphalt, — — while next, as if under the influence of prophetic frenzy, he moves the lamp towards the wall. The drug, however, is burned with considerable splendour. And that a fiery Hecate seems to career through air, he contrives in the mode following. Concealing a certain accomplice in a place which he wishes, (and) taking aside his dupes, he persuades them (to believe himself), alleging that he will exhibit a flaming demon riding through the air. Now he exhorts them immediately to keep their eyes fixed until they see the flame in the air, and that (then), veiling themselves, they should fall on their face until he himself should call them; and after having given them these instructions, he, on a moonless night, in verses speaks thus: —

"Infernal, and earthy, and supernal Bombo, come!
Saint of streets, and brilliant one, that strays by night;
Foe of radiance, but friend and mate of gloom;
In howl of dogs rejoicing, and in crimson gore,
Wading 'mid corpses through tombs of lifeless dust,
Panting for blood; with fear convulsing men.
Gorgo, and Mormo, and Luna,[9] and of many shapes,
Come, propitious, to our sacrificial rites!"

CHAP. XXXVI. — MODE OF MANAGING AN APPARITION.

And while speaking these words, fire is seen borne through the air; but the (spectators) being horrified at the strange apparition, (and) cover-

---

[1] Or, "ground" — φορυκτῆς, (al.) φορυτῆς, (al.) φρυκτῆς, (al.) φρικτῆς.
[2] Or, "insert."
[3] Or "taught," or "adduced," or "delivered."
[4] This sentence is obviously out of place, and should properly come in probably before the words, "These contrivances, however, I hesitated to narrate," etc., a few lines above in this chapter. The Abbe Cruice conjectures that it may have been written on the margin by some reader acquainted with chemistry, and that afterwards it found its way into the text.

[5] Some read φανερὸν for παρὸν.
[6] What cyanus was is not exactly known. It was employed in the Homeric age for the adornment of implements of war. Whatever the nature of the substance be, it was of a dark-blue colour. Some suppose it to have been blue steel, others blue copper. Theophrastus' account of it makes it a stone like a dark sapphire.
[7] Or, "with the head downwards."
[8] There is some hiatus here.
[9] Or, "memory."

ing their eyes, fling themselves speechless to earth. But the success of the artifice is enhanced by the following contrivance. The accomplice whom I have spoken of as being concealed, when he hears the incantation ceasing, holding a kite or hawk enveloped with tow, sets fire to it and releases it. The bird, however, frightened by the flame, is borne aloft, and makes a (proportionably) quicker flight, which these deluded persons beholding, conceal themselves, as if they had seen something divine. The winged creature, however, being whirled round by the fire, is borne whithersoever chance may have it, and burns now the houses, and now the courtyards. Such is the divination of the sorcerers.

CHAP. XXXVII. — ILLUSIVE APPEARANCE OF THE MOON.

And they make moon and stars appear on the ceiling after this manner. In the central part of the ceiling, having fastened a mirror, placing a dish full of water equally (with the mirror) in the central portion of the floor, and setting in a central place likewise a candle, emitting a faint light from a higher position than the dish, — in this way, by reflection, (the magician) causes the moon to appear by the mirror. But frequently, also, they suspend on high from the ceiling, at a distance, a drum,[1] but which, being covered with some garment, is concealed by the accomplice, in order that (the heavenly body) may not appear before the (proper) time. And afterwards placing a candle (within the drum), when the magician gives the signal to the accomplice, he removes so much of the covering as may be sufficient for effecting an imitation representing the figure of the moon as it is at that particular time. He smears, however, the luminous parts of the drum with cinnabar and gum ;[2] and having pared around the neck and bottom of a flagon[3] of glass ready behind, he puts a candle in it, and places around it some of the requisite contrivances for making the figures shine, which some one of the accomplices has concealed on high ; and on receiving the signal, he throws down from above the contrivances, so to make the moon appear descending from the sky.

And the same result is achieved by means of a jar in sylvan localities.[4] For it is by means of a jar that the tricks in a house are performed. For having set up an altar, subsequently is (placed upon it) the jar, having a lighted lamp ; when, however, there are a greater number of lamps, no such sight is displayed. After then the enchanter invokes the moon, he orders all the lights to be extinguished, yet that one be left faintly burning ; and then the light, that which streams from the jar, is reflected on the ceiling, and furnishes to those present a representation of the moon ; the mouth of the jar being kept covered for the time which it would seem to require, in order that the representation of full moon should be exhibited on the ceiling.

CHAP. XXXVIII. — ILLUSIVE APPEARANCE OF THE STARS.

But the scales of fishes — for instance, the seahorse — cause the stars to appear to be ; the scales being steeped in a mixture of water and gum, and fastened on the ceiling at intervals.

CHAP. XXXIX. — IMITATION OF AN EARTHQUAKE.

The sensation of an earthquake they cause in such a way, as that all things seem set in motion ; ordure of a weasel burned with a magnet upon coals (has this effect).[5]

CHAP. XL. — TRICK WITH THE LIVER.

And they exhibit a liver seemingly bearing an inscription in this manner. With the left hand he writes what he wishes, appending it to the question, and the letters are traced with gall juice and strong vinegar. Then taking up the liver, retaining it in the left hand, he makes some delay, and then it draws away the impression, and it is supposed to have, as it were, writing upon it.

CHAP. XLI. — MAKING A SKULL SPEAK.

But putting a skull on the ground, they make it speak in this manner. The skull itself is made out of the caul of an ox ;[6] and when fashioned into the requisite figure, by means of Etruscan wax and prepared gum,[7] (and) when this membrane is placed around, it presents the appearance of a skull, which seems to all[8] to speak when the contrivance operates ; in the same manner as we have explained in the case of the (attendant) youths, when, having procured the windpipe of a crane,[9] or some such long-necked animal, and attaching it covertly to the skull, the accomplice utters what he wishes. And when he desires (the skull) to become invisible, he

---

1 Or, "suspending a drum, etc., covered with," etc.; or "frequently placing on an elevated position a drum." For πόρρωθεν, which is not here easy of explanation, some read τορνωθὲν, others πορπωθὲν, i.e , fastened with buckles; others, πόρρω τεθὲν.

2 Schneidewin, but not the Abbe Cruice, thinks there is a hiatus here.

3 There are different readings: (1) ἐτυμολογικῆς ; (2) ἔτι ὁλοκλήρου ; (3) ὑαλουργικῆς, i e., composed of glass. (See next note.)

4 The Abbe Cruice properly remarks that this has no meaning here. He would read ὑαλώδεσι τοποις, or by means of glass images.

5 There is a hiatus here.

6 The Abbe Cruice suggests ἐπίπλεον βώλου, which he thinks corresponds with the material of which the pyramid mentioned in a previous chapter was composed. He, however, makes no attempt at translating ἐπίπλεον. Does he mean that the skull was filled with clay ? His emendation is forced.

7 Or, "rubbings of" (Cruice).

8 Or, "they say."

9 Some similar juggleries are mentioned by Lucian in his Alexander, or Pseudomantis, xxxii. 26, — a work of a kindred nature to Celsus' Treatise on Magic (the latter alluded to by Origen, Contr. Cels., lib. i p 53, ed. Spenc.), and dedicated by Lucian to Celsus.

appears as if burning incense, placing around, (for this purpose,) a quantity of coals; and when the wax catches the heat of these, it melts, and in this way the skull is supposed to become invisible.

CHAP. XLII. — THE FRAUD OF THE FOREGOING PRACTICES; THEIR CONNECTION WITH HERESY.

These are the deeds of the magicians,[1] and innumerable other such (tricks) there are which work on the credulity of the dupes, by fair balanced words, and the appearance of plausible acts. And the heresiarchs, astonished at the art of these (sorcerers), have imitated them, partly by delivering their doctrines in secrecy and darkness, and partly by advancing (these tenets) as their own. For this reason, being desirous of warning the multitude, we have been the more painstaking, in order not to omit any expedient[2] practised by the magicians, for those who may be disposed to be deceived. We have been however drawn, not unreasonably, into a detail of some of the secret (mysteries) of the sorcerers, which are not very requisite, to be sure, in reference to the subject taken in hand; yet, for the purpose of guarding against the villanous and incoherent art of magicians, may be supposed useful. Since, therefore, as far as delineation is feasible, we have explained the opinions of all (speculators), exerting especial attention towards the elucidation of the opinions introduced as novelties by the heresiarchs; (opinions) which, as far as piety is concerned, are futile and spurious, and which are not, even among themselves, perhaps[3] deemed worthy of serious consideration. (Having pursued this course of inquiry), it seems expedient that, by means of a compendious discourse, we should recall to the (reader's) memory statements that have been previously made.

CHAP. XLIII. — RECAPITULATION OF THEOLOGIES AND COSMOGONIES; SYSTEM OF THE PERSIANS; OF THE BABYLONIANS; THE EGYPTIAN NOTION OF DEITY; THEIR THEOLOGY BASED ON A THEORY OF NUMBERS; THEIR SYSTEM OF COSMOGONY.

Among all those who throughout the earth, as philosophers and theologians, have carried on investigations, has prevailed diversity of opinion[4] concerning the Deity, as to His essence or nature. For some affirm Him to be fire, and some spirit, and some water, while others say that He is earth. And each of the elements labours under some deficiency, and one is worsted by the other. To the wise men of the world, this, however, has occurred, which is obvious to persons possessing intelligence; (I mean) that, beholding the stupendous works of creation, they were confused respecting the substance of existing things, supposing that these were too vast to admit of deriving generation from another, and at the same time (asserting) that neither the universe itself is God. As far as theology was concerned, they declared, however, a single cause for things that fall under the cognizance of vision, each supposing the cause which he adjudged the most reasonable; and so, when gazing on the objects made by God, and on those which are the most insignificant in comparison with His overpowering majesty, not, however, being able to extend the mind to the magnitude of God as He really is, they deified these (works of the external world).

But the Persians,[5] supposing that they had penetrated more within the confines of the truth, asserted that the Deity is luminous, a light contained in air. The Babylonians, however, affirmed that the Deity is dark, which very opinion also appears the consequence of the other; for day follows night, and night day. Do not the Egyptians, however,[6] who suppose themselves more ancient than all, speak of the power of the Deity? (This power they estimate by) calculating these intervals of the parts (of the zodiac; and, as if) by a most divine inspiration,[7] they asserted that the Deity is an indivisible monad, both itself generating itself, and that out of this were formed all things. For this, say they,[8] being unbegotten, produces the succeeding numbers; for instance, the monad, superadded into itself, generates the duad; and in like manner, when superadded (into duad, triad, and so forth), produces the triad and tetrad, up to the decade, which is the beginning and end of numbers. Wherefore it is that the first and tenth monad is generated, on account of the decade being equipollent, and being reckoned for a monad, and (because) this multiplied ten times will become a hundred, and

---

[1] The word magic, or magician, at its origin, had no sinister meaning, as being the science professed by the Magi, who were an exclusive religious sect of great antiquity in Persia, universally venerated for their mathematical skill and erudition generally. It was persons who practised wicked arts, and assumed the name of Magi, that brought the term into disrepute. The origin of magic has been ascribed to Zoroaster, and once devised, it made rapid progress; because, as Pliny reminds us, it includes three systems of the greatest influence among men — (1) the art of medicine, (2) religion, (3) divination. This corresponds with Agrippa's division of magic into (1) natural, (2) celestial, (3) ceremonial, or superstitious. This last has been also called "goetic" (full of imposture), and relates to the invocation of devils. This originated probably in Egypt, and quickly spread all over the world.

[2] Or, "topic discussed;" or, "not leave any place (subterfuge) for these," etc.

[3] Or, "you will suppose."

[4] See Aristotle's *Metaphysics*, book i.; Cicero, *De Natura Deorum*, book i. (both translated in Bohn's Classical Library); and Plutarch, *De Placitis Philosophorum*, lib. i.

[5] The mention of the Persians, Babylonians, and Egyptians shows the subject-matter of the lost books to have been concerning the speculative systems of these nations.

[6] This rendering follows Miller's text. Schneidewin thinks there is a hiatus, which the Abbe Cruice fills up, the latter translating the passage without an interrogation: "The Egyptians, who think themselves more ancient than all, have formed their ideas of the power of the Deity by calculations and computing," etc.

[7] Or, "meditation on the divine nature," or "godlike reflection."

[8] The MS. has "says he."

again becomes a monad, and the hundred multiplied ten times will produce a thousand, and this will be a monad. In this manner also the thousand multiplied ten times make up the full sum of a myriad; in like manner will it be a monad. But by a comparison of indivisible quantities, the kindred numbers of the monad comprehend 3, 5, 7, 9.[1]

There is also, however, a more natural relation of a different number to the monad, according to the arrangement of the orbit of six days' duration,[2] (that is), of the duad, according to the position and division of even numbers. But the kindred number is 4 and 8. These, however, taking from the monad of the numbers[3] an idea of virtue, progressed up to the four elements; (I allude), of course, to spirit, and fire, and water, and earth. And out of these having made the world, (God) framed it an ermaphrodite, and allocated two elements for the upper hemisphere, namely spirit and fire; and this is styled the hemisphere of the monad, (a hemisphere) beneficent, and ascending, and masculine. For, being composed of small particles, the monad soars into the most rarified and purest part of the atmosphere; and the other two elements, earth and water, being more gross, he assigned to the duad; and this is termed the descending hemisphere, both feminine and mischievous. And likewise, again, the upper elements themselves, when compared one with another, comprise in one another both male and female for fruitfulness and increase of the whole creation. And the fire is masculine, and the spirit feminine. And again the water is masculine, and the earth feminine. And so from the beginning fire consorted with spirit, and water with earth. For as the power of spirit is fire, so also that of earth is water;[4] . . . and the elements themselves, when computed and resolved by subtraction of enneads, terminate properly, some of them in the masculine number, and others of them in the feminine. And, again, the ennead is subtracted for this cause, because the three hundred and sixty parts of the entire (circle) consist of enneads, and for this reason the four regions of the world are circumscribed by ninety perfect parts. And light has been appropriated to the monad, and darkness to the duad, and life to light, according to nature, and death to the duad. And to life (has been appropriated) justice; and to death, injustice. Wherefore everything generated among masculine numbers is beneficent, while that (produced) among feminine (numbers) is mischievous. For instance, they pursue their calculations thus: monad — that we may commence from this — becomes 361, which (numbers) terminate in a monad by the subtraction of the ennead. In like manner, reckon thus: Duad becomes 605; take away the enneads, it ends in a duad, and each reverts into its own peculiar (function).

CHAP. XLIV. — EGYPTIAN THEORY OF NATURE; THEIR AMULETS.

For the monad, therefore, as being beneficent, they assert that there are consequently[5] names ascending, and beneficent, and masculine, and carefully observed, terminating in an uneven number;[6] whereas that those terminating in the even number have been supposed to be both descending, and feminine and malicious. For they affirm that nature is made up of contraries, namely bad and good, as right and left, light and darkness, night and day, life and death. And moreover they make this assertion, that they have calculated the word "Deity," (and found that it reverts into a pentad with an ennead subtracted). Now this name is an even number, and when it is written down (on some material) they attach it to the body, and accomplish cures[7] by it. In this manner, likewise, a certain herb, terminating in this number, being similarly fastened around (the frame), operates by reason of a similar calculation of the number. Nay, even a doctor cures sickly people by a similar calculation. If, however, the calculation is contrary, it does not heal with facility.[8] Persons attending to these numbers reckon as many as are homogeneous according to this principle; some, however, according to vowels alone; whereas others according to the entire number. Such also is the wisdom of the Egyptians, by which, as they boast, they suppose that they cognise the divine nature.

CHAP. XLV. — USE OF THE FOREGOING DISCUSSIONS.

It appears, then, that these speculations also have been sufficiently explained by us. But since I think that I have omitted no opinion found in this earthly and grovelling Wisdom, I

---

[1] The Abbe Cruice suggests the elimination of 9, on account of its being a divisible number.

[2] Miller considers some reference here to the six days' creation (Hexaëmeron), on account of the word φυσικωτέρα, i.e., more natural. The Abbe Cruice considers that there is an allusion to an astronomic instrument used for exhibiting harmonic combinations; see Ptolem., *Harmon*, i. 2. Bunsen reads τοῦ ἐξακύκλου ὑλικοῦ.

[3] The text is obviously corrupt. As given by Schneidewin, it might be rendered thus: "These deriving from the monad a numerical symbol, a virtue, have progressed up to the elements." He makes no attempt at a Latin version. The Abbe Cruice would suggest the introduction of the word προστεθεῖσαν, on account of the statement already made, that "the monad, superadded into itself, produces a duad."

[4] There is a hiatus here. Hippolytus has said nothing concerning enneads.

[5] Or, "names have been allocated," or "distributed."

[6] Miller thinks it should be "even number" (περιττόν). The Abbe Cruice would retain "uneven" (ἀπερίζυγον), on the ground that the duad being a περίζυξ ἀριθμὸς, the monad will be ἀπερίζυγος.

[7] Servius on the *Eclogues of Virgil* (viii. 75) and Pliny (*Hist. Nat*, xxxviii. 2) make similar statements.

[8] This is Miller and Schneidewin's emendation for "uneven" in the MS.

perceive that the solicitude expended by us on these subjects has not been useless. For we observe that our discourse has been serviceable not only for a refutation of heresies, but also in reference to those who entertain these opinions. Now these, when they encounter the extreme care evinced by us, will even be struck with admiration of our earnestness, and will not despise our industry and condemn Christians as fools when they discern the opinions to which they themselves have stupidly accorded their belief. And furthermore, those who, desirous of learning, addict themselves to the truth, will be assisted by our discourse to become, when they have learned the fundamental principles of the heresies, more intelligent not only for the easy refutation of those who have attempted to deceive them, but that also, when they have ascertained the avowed opinions of the wise men, and have been made acquainted with them, that they shall neither be confused by them as ignorant persons would, nor become the dupes of certain individuals acting as if from some authority ; nay, more than this, they shall be on their guard against those that are allowing themselves to become victims to these delusions.

CHAP. XLVI. — THE ASTROTHEOSOPHISTS ; ARATUS IMITATED BY THE HERESIARCHS ; HIS SYSTEM OF THE DISPOSITION OF THE STARS.

Having sufficiently explained these opinions, let us next pass on to a consideration of the subject taken in hand, in order that, by proving what we have determined concerning heresies, and by compelling their (champions) to return to these several (speculators) their peculiar tenets, we may show the heresiarchs destitute (of a system) ; and by proclaiming the folly of those who are persuaded (by these heterodox tenets), we shall prevail on them to retrace their course to the serene haven of the truth. In order, however, that the statements about to follow may seem more clear to the readers, it is expedient also to declare the opinions advanced by Aratus concerning the disposition of the stars of the heavens. (And this is necessary), inasmuch as some persons, assimilating these (doctrines) to those declared by the Scriptures, convert (the holy writings) into allegories, and endeavour to seduce the mind of those who give heed to their (tenets), drawing them on by plausible words into the admission of whatever opinions they wish, (and) exhibiting a strange marvel, as if the assertions made by them were fixed among the stars. They, however, gazing intently on the very extraordinary wonder, admirers as they are of trifles, are fascinated like a bird called the owl, which example it is proper to mention, on account of the statements that are about to follow. The animal (I speak of) is, however, not very different from an eagle, either in size or figure, and it is captured in the following way : — The hunter of these birds, when he sees a flock of them lighting anywhere, shaking his hands, at a distance pretends to dance, and so by little and little draws near the birds. But they, struck with amazement at the strange sight, are rendered unobservant of everything passing around them. But others of the party, who have come into the country equipped for such a purpose, coming from behind upon the birds, easily lay hold on them as they are gazing on the dancer.

Wherefore I desire that no one, astonished by similar wonders of those who interpret the (aspect of) heaven, should, like the owl, be taken captive. For the knavery practised by such speculators may be considered dancing and silliness, but not truth. Aratus,[1] therefore, expresses himself thus : —

" Just as many are they ; hither and thither they roll
Day by day o'er heav'n, endless, ever, (that is, every star),
Yet this declines not even little ; but thus exactly
E'er remains with axis fixed and poised in every part
Holds earth midway, and heaven itself around conducts."

CHAP. XLVII. — OPINIONS OF THE HERETICS BORROWED FROM ARATUS.

Aratus says that there are in the sky revolving, that is, gyrating stars, because from east to west, and west to east, they journey perpetually, (and) in an orbicular figure. And he says that there revolves towards [2] " The Bears " themselves, like some stream of a river, an enormous and prodigious monster, (the) Serpent ; and that this is what the devil says in the book of Job to the Deity, when (Satan) uses these words : " I have traversed earth under heaven, and have gone around (it)," [3] that is, that I have been turned around, and thereby have been able to survey the worlds. For they suppose that towards the North Pole is situated the Dragon, the Serpent, from the highest pole looking upon all (the objects), and gazing on all the works of creation, in order that nothing of the things that are being made may escape his notice. For though all the stars in the firmament set, the pole of this (luminary) alone never sets, but, careering high above the horizon, surveys and beholds all things, and none of the works of creation, he says, can escape his notice.

" Where chiefly
Settings mingle and risings one with other." [4]

(Here Aratus) says that the head of this (constellation) is placed. For towards the west and

---

[1] Arat., *Phænom.*, v. 19 et seq.
[2] *Ibid*, v. 45, 46.
[3] This refers to Job i. 7, but is at once recognised as not a correct quotation.
[4] Arat., *Phænom.*, v. 61.

east of the two hemispheres is situated the head of the Dragon, in order, he says, that nothing may escape his notice throughout the same quarter, either of objects in the west or those in the east, but that the Beast may know all things at the same time. And near the head itself of the Dragon is the appearance of a man, conspicuous by means of the stars, which Aratus styles a wearied image, and like one oppressed with labour, and he is denominated "Engonasis." Aratus [1] then affirms that he does not know what this toil is, and what this prodigy is that revolves in heaven. The heretics, however, wishing by means of this account of the stars to establish their own doctrines, (and) with more than ordinary earnestness devoting their attention to these (astronomic systems), assert that Engonasis is Adam, according to the commandment of God as Moses declared, guarding the head of the Dragon, and the Dragon (guarding) his heel. For so Aratus expresses himself : —

" The right-foot's track of the Dragon fierce possessing." [2]

CHAP. XLVIII. — INVENTION OF THE LYRE ; ALLEGORIZING THE APPEARANCE AND POSITION OF THE STARS ; ORIGIN OF THE PHŒNICIANS ; THE LOGOS IDENTIFIED BY ARATUS WITH THE CONSTELLATION CANIS ; INFLUENCE OF CANIS ON FERTILITY AND LIFE GENERALLY.

And (Aratus) says that (the constellations) Lyra and Corona have been placed on both sides near him, — now I mean Engonasis, — but that he bends the knee, and stretches forth both hands, as if making a confession of sin. And that the lyre is a musical instrument fashioned by Logos while still altogether an infant, and that Logos is the same as he who is denominated Mercury among the Greeks. And Aratus, with regard to the construction of the lyre, observes : —

" Then, further, also near the cradle,[3]
Hermes pierced it through, and said, Call it Lyre." [4]

It consists of seven strings, signifying by these seven strings the entire harmony and construction of the world as it is melodiously constituted. For in six days the world was made, and (the Creator) rested on the seventh. If, then, says (Aratus), Adam, acknowledging (his guilt) and guarding the head of the Beast, according to the

commandment of the Deity, will imitate Lyra, that is, obey the Logos of God, that is, submit to the law, he will receive Corona that is situated near him. If, however, he neglect his duty, he shall be hurled downwards in company with the Beast that lies underneath, and shall have, he says, his portion with the Beast. And Engonasis seems on both sides to extend his hands, and on one to touch Lyra, and on the other Corona — and this is his confession ; — so that it is possible to distinguish him by means of this (sidereal) configuration itself. But Corona nevertheless is plotted against, and forcibly drawn away by another beast, a smaller Dragon, which is the offspring of him who is guarded by the foot [5] of Engonasis. A man also stands firmly grasping with both hands, and dragging towards the space behind the Serpent from Corona ; and he does not permit the Beast to touch Corona. though making a violent effort to do so. And Aratus styles him Anguitenens, because he restrains the impetuosity of the Serpent in his attempt to reach Corona. But Logos, he says, is he who, in the figure of a man, hinders the Beast from reaching Corona, commiserating him who is being plotted against by the Dragon and his offspring simultaneously.

These (constellations), "The Bears," however, he says, are two hebdomads, composed of seven stars, images of two creations. For the first creation, he affirms, is that according to Adam in labours, this is he who is seen " on his knees " (Engonasis). The second creation, however, is that according to Christ, by which we are regenerated ; and this is Anguitenens, who struggles against the Beast, and hinders him from reaching Corona, which is reserved for the man. But "The Great Bear " is, he says, Helice,[6] symbol of a mighty world towards which the Greeks steer their course, that is, for which they are being disciplined. And, wafted by the waves of life, they follow onwards, (having in prospect) some such revolving world or discipline or wisdom which conducts those back that follow in pursuit of such a world. For the term Helice seems to signify a certain circling and revolution towards the same points. There is likewise a certain other "Small Bear " (Cynosuris), as it were some image of the second creation — that formed according to God. For few, he says, there are that journey by the narrow path.[7] But they assert that Cynosuris is narrow, towards·which Aratus[8] says that the Si-

---

[1] Arat., *Phænom.*, v. 63 et seq.
[2] Arat., *Phænom.*, v. 70.
[3] " Pierced it through," i.e., bored the holes for the strings, or, in other words, constructed the instrument. The Latin version in Buhle's edition of Aratus is *ad cunam (cunabulam) compegit*, i.e., he fastened the strings into the shell of the tortoise near his bed. The tortoise is mentioned by Aratus in the first part of the line, which fact removes the obscurity of the passage as quoted by Hippolytus. The general tradition corresponds with this, in representing Mercury on the shores of the Nile forming a lyre out of a dried tortoise. The word translated bed might be also rendered fan, which was used as a cradle, its size and construction being suitable. [See note, p. 46, *infra*.]
[4] Arat., *Phænom.*, v. 268.

[5] Or, "son of" (see Arat., *Phænom.*, v. 70).
[6] The Abbe Cruice considers that these interpretations, as well as what follows, are taken not from a Greek writer, but a Jewish heretic. No Greek, he supposes, would write, as is stated lower down, that the Greeks were a Phœnician colony. The Jewish heresies were impregnated by these silly doctrines about the stars (see Epiphan., *Adv. Hæres.*, lib. i. *De Pharisæis*).
[7] Reference is here made to Matt. vii. 14.
[8] Arat., *Phænom.*, v. 44.

donians navigate. But Aratus has spoken partly of the Sidonians, (but means) the Phœnicians, on account of the existence of the admirable wisdom of the Phœnicians. The Greeks, however, assert that they are Phœnicians, who have migrated from (the shores of) the Red Sea into this country where they even at present dwell, for this is the opinion of Herodotus.[1]   Now Cynosura, he says, is this (lesser) Bear, the second creation; the one of limited dimensions, the narrow way, and not Helice. For he does not lead them back, but guides forward by a straight path, those that follow him being (the tail) of Canis. For Canis is the Logos,[2] partly guarding and preserving the flock, that is plotted against by the wolves; and partly like a dog, hunting the beasts from the creation, and destroying them; and partly producing all things, and being what they express by the name "Cyon" (Canis), that is, generator. Hence it is said, Aratus has spoken of the rising of Canis, expressing himself thus: "When, however, Canis has risen, no longer do the crops miss." This is what he says: Plants that have been put into the earth up to the period of Canis' rising, frequently, though not having struck root, are yet covered with a profusion of leaves, and afford indications to spectators that they will be productive, and that they appear full of life, (though in reality) not having vitality in themselves from the root. But when the rising of Canis takes place, the living are separated from the dead by Canis; for whatsoever plants have not taken root, really undergo putrefaction. This Canis, therefore, he says, as being a certain divine Logos, has been appointed judge of quick and dead. And as (the influence of) Canis is observable in the vegetable productions of this world, so in plants of celestial growth — in men — is beheld the (power of the) Logos. From some such cause, then, Cynosura, the second creation, is set in the firmament as an image of a creation by the Logos. The Dragon, however, in the centre reclines between the two creations, preventing a transition of whatever things are from the great creation to the small creation; and in guarding those that are fixed in the (great) creation, as for instance Engonasis, observing (at the same time) how and in what manner each is constituted in the small creation. And (the Dragon) himself is watched at the head, he says, by Anguitenens. This image, he affirms, is fixed in heaven, being a certain wisdom to those capable of discerning it. If, however, this is obscure, by means of some other image, he says the creation teaches (men) to

philosophize, in regard to which Aratus has expressed himself thus : —

"Neither of Cepheus Iasidas are we the wretched brood." [3]

CHAP. XLIX. — SYMBOL OF THE CREATURE ; AND OF SPIRIT ; AND OF THE DIFFERENT ORDERS OF ANIMALS.

But Aratus says, near this (constellation) is Cepheus, and Cassiepea, and Andromeda, and Perseus, great lineaments of the creation to those who are able to discern them. For he asserts that Cepheus is Adam, Cassiepea Eve, Andromeda the soul of both of these, Perseus the Logos, winged offspring of Jove, and Cetos[4] the plotting monster. Not to any of these, but to Andromeda only does he repair, who slays the Beast; from whom, likewise taking unto himself Andromeda, who had been delivered (and) chained to the Beast, the Logos — that is, Perseus — achieves, he says, her liberation. Perseus, however, is the winged axle that pierces both poles through the centre of the earth, and turns the world round. The spirit also, that which is in the world, is (symbolized by) Cycnus, a bird — a musical animal near "The Bears" — type of the Divine Spirit, because that when it approaches the end itself of life,[5] it alone is fitted by nature to sing, on departing with good hope from the wicked creation, (and) offering up hymns unto God. But crabs, and bulls, and lions, and rams, and goats, and kids, and as many other beasts as have their names used for denominating the stars in the firmament, are, he says, images, and exemplars from which the creation, subject to change, obtaining (the different) species, becomes replete with animals of this description.

CHAP. L. — FOLLY OF ASTROLOGY.

Employing these accounts, (the heretics) think to deceive as many of these as devote themselves over-sedulously to the astrologers, from thence striving to construct a system of religion that is widely divergent from the thoughts of these (speculators). Wherefore, beloved, let us avoid the habit of admiring trifles, secured by which the bird (styled) the owl (is captured). For these and other such speculations are, (as it were), dancing, and not Truth. For neither do the stars yield these points of information ; but men of their own accord, for the designation of certain stars, thus called them by names, in order that they might become to them easily

---

[1] Herod., *Hist.*, i. 1.
[2] Or, "for creation is the Logos" (see Arat., *Phænom.*, v. 332 et seq.).

[3] Arat., *Phænom.*, v. 179.
[4] i.e., literally a sea-monster (Cicero's *Pistrix*) : Arat., *Phænom.*, v. 353 et seq.
[5] πρὸς αὐτοῖς ἤδη τοῖς τέρμασι γενόμενον τοῦ βίου. Some read τοῖς σπέρμασι, which yields no intelligible meaning.

distinguishable. For what similarity with a bear, or lion, or kid, or waterman, or Cepheus, or Andromeda, or the spectres that have names given them in Hades, have the stars that are scattered over the firmament — for we must remember that these men, and the titles themselves, came into existence long after the origin of man, — (what, I say, is in common between the two), that the heretics, astonished at the marvel, should thus strive by means of such discourses to strengthen their own opinions?

CHAP. LI. — THE HEBDOMADARII; SYSTEM OF THE ARITHMETICIANS; PRESSED INTO THE SERVICE OF HERESY; INSTANCES OF, IN SIMON AND VALENTINUS; THE NATURE OF THE UNIVERSE DEDUCIBLE FROM THE PHYSIOLOGY OF THE BRAIN.

But since almost every heresy (that has sprung up) through the arithmetical art has discovered measures of hebdomads and certain projections of Æons, each rending the art differently, while whatever variation prevailed was in the names merely; and (since) Pythagoras became the instructor of these, first introducing numbers of this sort among the Greeks from Egypt, it seems expedient not to omit even this, but, after we have given a compendious elucidation, to approach the demonstration of those things that we propose to investigate.

Arithmeticians and geometers arose, to whom especially Pythagoras first seems to have furnished principles. And from numbers that can continually progress *ad infinitum* by multiplication, and from figures, these derived their first principles,[1] as capable of being discerned by reason alone; for a principle of geometry, as one may perceive, is an indivisible point. From that point, however, by means of the art, the generation of endless figures from the point is discovered. For the point being drawn into length becomes a line, after being thus continued, having a point for its extremity. And a line flowing out into breadth begets a surface, and the limits of the surface are lines; but a surface flowing out into breadth becomes body. And when what is solid has in this manner derived existence from, altogether, the smallest point, the nature of a huge body is constituted; and this is what Simon expresses thus: "The little will be great, being as a point, and the great illimitable." Now this coincides with the geometrical doctrine of a point.

But of the arithmetical[2] art, which by composition contains philosophy, number became a first principle, which is an indefinable and incomprehensible (entity), comprising in itself all the numbers that can go on *ad infinitum* by aggregation. But the first monad became a principle, according to substance, of the numbers, which (principle) is a male[3] monad, procreating paternally all the rest of the numbers. Secondly, the duad is a female number, which by the arithmeticians is also itself denominated even. Thirdly, the triad is a male number; this also it has been the usual custom of arithmeticians to style odd. In addition to all these, the tetrad is a female number; and this same, because it is feminine, is likewise denominated even. All the numbers therefore, taken generically, are four — number, however, as regards genus, is indefinite — from which, according to their system, is formed the perfect number — I mean the decade. For one, two, three, four, become ten — as has been previously proved — if the proper denomination be preserved, according to substance, for each of the numbers. This is the sacred quaternion, according to Pythagoras, having in itself roots of an endless nature, that is, all other numbers; for eleven, and twelve, and the rest, derive the principle of generation from the ten. Of this decade — the perfect number — there are called four parts — number, monad, power, cube — whose connections and mixtures take place for the generation of increase, according to nature completing the productive number. For when the square is multiplied into itself, it becomes a biquadratic; but when the square is multiplied into a cube, it becomes the product of a quadratic and cube; but when a cube is multiplied into a cube, it becomes the product of cube multiplied by cube. Wherefore all the numbers are seven; so that the generation of things produced may be from the hebdomad — which is number, monad, power, cube, biquadratic, product of quadratic multiplied by cube, product of cube multiplied by cube.

Of this hebdomad Simon and Valentinus, having altered the names, detailed marvellous stories, from thence hastily adopting a system for themselves. For Simon employs his denominations thus: Mind, Intelligence, Name, Voice, Ratiocination, Reflection; and He who stood, stands, will stand. And Valentinus (enumerates them thus): Mind, Truth, Word, Life, Man, Church, and the Father, reckoned along with these, according to the same principles as those advanced by the cultivators of arithmetical philosophy. And (heresiarchs) admiring, as if unknown to the multitude, (this philosophy, and) following it, have framed heterodox doctrines devised by themselves.

Some indeed, then, attempt likewise to form

---

[1] Sextus Empiricus, *adv. Geom.*, 29 et seq. (See book vi. chap. xviii. of *The Refutation*.)

[2] The observations following have already been made in book i. of *The Refutation*.

[3] Some read ἄρσις.

the hebdomads from the medical[1] (art), being astonished at the dissection of the brain, asserting that the substance of the universe and the power of procreation and the Godhead could be ascertained from the arrangement of the brain. For the brain, being the dominant portion of the entire body, reposes calm and unmoved, containing within itself the spirit. Such an account, then, is not incredible, but widely differs from the conclusions which these (heretics) attempt to deduce from it. For the brain, on being dissected, has within it what may be called a vaulted chamber. And on either side of this are thin membranes, which they term little wings. Now these are gently moved by the spirit, and in turn propel towards the cerebellum the spirit, which, careering through a certain blood-vessel like a reed, advances towards the pineal gland. And near this is situated the entrance of the cerebellum, which admits the current of spirit, and distributes it into what is styled the spinal marrow. But from them the whole frame participates in the spiritual energy, inasmuch as all the arteries, like a branch, are fastened on from this blood-vessel, the ex-

tremity of which terminates in the genital blood-vessels, whence all the (animal) seeds proceeding from the brain through the loin are secreted (in the seminal glands). The form, however, of the brain is like the head of a serpent, respecting which a lengthened discussion is maintained by the professors of knowledge, falsely so named, as we shall prove. Six other coupling ligaments grow out of the brain, which, traversing round the head, and having their termination in (the head) itself, hold bodies together; but the seventh (ligament) proceeds from the cerebellum to the lower parts of the rest of the frame, as we have declared.

And respecting this there is an enlarged discussion, whence both Simon and Valentinus will be found both to have derived from this source starting-points for their opinions, and, though they may not acknowledge it, to be in the first instance liars, then heretics. Since, then, it appears that we have sufficiently explained these tenets likewise, and that all the reputed opinions of this earthly philosophy have been comprised in four books; it seems expedient to proceed to a consideration of the disciples of these men, nay rather, those who have furtively appropriated their doctrines.[2]

---

[1] The Abbe Cruice refers to Censorinus (*De Die Natali*, cap. vii. et xiv.), who mentions that two numbers were held in veneration, the seventh (hebdomad) and ninth (ennead). The former was of use in curing corporeal disease, and ascribed to Apollo; the latter healed the diseases of the mind, and was attributed to the Muses.

[2] At foot of MS. occur the words, "Fourth Book of Philosophumena."

NOTE.

[On p. 43 *supra* I omitted to direct attention to the desirable enlargement of note 3 by a reference to Homer's Hymn of Mercury and its minute description of the invention of the Lyre. The passage is given in Henry Nelson Coleridge's *Introduction*, etc., p. 202. The versified translation of Shelley is inimitable; in *ottava rima*, but instinct with the *ethos* of the original.]

THE REFUTATION OF ALL HERESIES

BOOK V.

CHAP. I. — RECAPITULATION ; CHARACTERISTICS OF HERESY ; ORIGIN OF THE NAME NAASSENI ; THE SYSTEM OF THE NAASSENI.

I think that in the four preceding books I have very elaborately explained the opinions propounded by all the speculators among both Greeks and Barbarians, respecting the Divine Nature and the creation of the world ; and not even have I omitted[4] the consideration of their systems of magic. So that I have for my readers undergone no ordinary amount of toil, in my anxiety to urge many forward into a desire of learning, and into stedfastness of knowledge in regard of the truth. It remains, therefore, to hasten on to the refutation of the heresies ; but it is for the purpose of furnishing this (refutation) that we have put forward the statements already made by us. For from philosophers the heresiarchs deriving[5] starting-points, (and) like cobblers patching together, according to their own particular interpretation, the blunders of the ancients, have advanced them as novelties to those that are capable of being deceived, as we shall prove in the following books. In the remainder (of our work), the opportunity invites us to approach the treatment of our proposed subjects, and to begin from those who have presumed to celebrate a serpent,[6] the originator of the error (in question), through certain expressions devised by the energy of his own (ingenuity). The priests, then, and champions of the system, have been first those who have been called Naasseni,[7] being so denominated from the Hebrew language, for the serpent is called *naas*[8] (in Hebrew). Subsequently, however, they have styled themselves Gnostics, alleging that they alone have sounded the depths of knowledge. Now, from the system of these (speculators), many, detaching parts, have constructed a heresy which, though with several subdivisions, is essentially one, and they explain precisely the same (tenets) ; though conveyed under the guise of different opinions, as the following discussion, according as it progresses, will prove.

---

1 [Consult Bunsen, vol. i. p. 35, always interesting and ingeniously critical; nobody should neglect his work. But for a judicial mind, compare Dr. Wordsworth, p. 182.]
2 The MS. employs the form Sithians, which is obviously not the correct one.
3 This term κλεψίλογος is frequently applied by Hippolytus to the heretics.
4 Miller has ἀποκαλύψας for παραλείψας. This, however, can bear no intelligible meaning, except we add some other word, as thus: "not even have I failed to disclose." Schneidewin's correction of ἀποκαλυψας into παραλειψας is obviously an improvement.

5 Μεταλαβόντες; some read μετασχόντες, which it is presumed might be rendered, "sharing in the opinions which gave occasion to these heterodox doctrines."
6 i.e., ὄφις. This term has created the title "Ophites," which may be regarded as the generic denomination for all the advocates of this phase of Gnosticism.
7 The heresy of the Naasseni is adverted to by the other leading writers on heresy in the early age of the Church. See St. Irenæus, i. 34; Origen, *Contr. Cels.*, vi 28 (p. 291 et seq. ed. Spenc.) ; Tertullian, *Præscr.*, c. 47; Theodoret, *Hæretic. Fabul* , i. 14; Epiphanius, *Advers. Hæreses.*, xxv. and xxxvii.; St. Augustine, *De Hæres.*, xvii.: Jerome, *Comment. Epist. ad Galat.*, lib. ii. The Abbe Cruice reminds his readers that the Naasseni carried their doctrines into India, and refers to the *Asiatic Researches* (vol. x. p. 39).
8 The Hebrew word is נָחָשׁ (*nachash*).

These (Naasseni), then, according to the system[1] advanced by them, magnify, (as the originating cause) of all things else, a man and a son of man. And this man is a hermaphrodite, and is denominated among them Adam ; and hymns many and various are made to him. The hymns,[2] however — to be brief — are couched among them in some such form as this : " From thee (comes) father, and through thee (comes) mother, two names immortal, progenitors of Æons, O denizen of heaven, thou illustrious man." But they divide him as Geryon[3] into three parts. For, say they, of this man one part is rational, another psychical, another earthly. And they suppose that the knowledge of him is the originating principle of the capacity for a knowledge of God, expressing themselves thus : " The originating principle of perfection is the knowledge[4] of man, while the knowledge of God is absolute perfection." All these qualities, however — rational, and psychical, and earthly — have, (the Naassene) says, retired and descended into one man simultaneously — Jesus,[5] who was born of Mary. And these three men (the Naassene) says, are in the habit of speaking (through Jesus) at the same time together, each from their own proper substances to those peculiarly their own. For, according to these, there are three kinds of all existent things — angelic, psychical, earthly ; and there are three churches — angelic, psychical, earthly ; and the names of these are elect, called, captive.

CHAP. II. — NAASSENI ASCRIBE THEIR SYSTEM, THROUGH MARIAMNE, TO JAMES THE LORD'S BROTHER ; REALLY TRACEABLE TO THE ANCIENT MYSTERIES ; THEIR PSYCHOLOGY AS GIVEN IN THE " GOSPEL ACCORDING TO THOMAS ; " ASSYRIAN THEORY OF THE SOUL ; THE SYSTEMS OF THE NAASSENI AND THE ASSYRIANS COMPARED ; SUPPORT DRAWN BY THE NAASSENI FROM THE PHRYGIAN AND EGYPTIAN MYSTERIES ; THE MYSTERIES OF ISIS ; THESE MYSTERIES ALLEGORIZED BY THE NAASSENI.

These are the heads of very numerous discourses which (the Naassene) asserts James the brother of the Lord handed down to Mariamne.[6] In order, then, that these impious (heretics) may no longer belie Mariamne or James, or the Saviour Himself, let us come to the mystic rites (whence these have derived their figment), — to a consideration, if it seems right, of both the Barbarian and Grecian (mysteries), — and let us see how these (heretics), collecting together the secret and ineffable mysteries of all the Gentiles, are uttering falsehoods against Christ, and are making dupes of those who are not acquainted with these orgies of the Gentiles. For since the foundation of the doctrine with them is the man Adam, and they say that concerning him it has been written, " Who shall declare his generation? "[7] learn how, partly deriving from the Gentiles the undiscoverable and diversified[8] generation of the man, they fictitiously apply it to Christ.

" Now earth,"[9] say the Greeks, " gave forth a man, (earth) first bearing a goodly gift, wishing to become mother not of plants devoid of sense, nor beasts without reason, but of a gentle and highly favoured creature." " It, however, is difficult," (the Naassene) says, " to ascertain whether Alalcomeneus,[10] first of men, rose upon the Bœotians over Lake Cephisus ; or whether it were the Idæan Curetes, a divine race ; or the Phrygian Corybantes, whom first the sun beheld springing up after the manner of the growth of trees ; or whether Arcadia brought forth Pelasgus, of greater antiquity than the moon ; or Eleusis (produced) Diaulus, an inhabitant of Raria ; or Lemnus begot Cabirus, fair child of secret orgies ; or Pallene (brought forth) the Phlegræan Alcyoneus, oldest of the giants. But the Libyans affirm that Iarbas, first born, on emerging from arid plains, commenced eating the sweet acorn of Jupiter. But the Nile of the Egyptians," he says, " up to this day fertilizing mud, (and therefore) generating animals, renders up living bodies, which acquire flesh from moist vapour." The Assyrians, however, say that fish-eating Oannes[11] was (the first man, and) produced among themselves. The Chaldeans, however, say that this Adam is the man whom

---

[1] παρὰ τὸν αὐτῶν λόγον. Bernaysius suggests for these words, πατέρα τῷ αὐτῷ λόγῳ. Schneidewin regards the emendation as an error, and Bunsen partly so. The latter would read, πατέρα τὸν αὐτῶν λόγον, i.e., " The Naasseni honour the Father of all existent things, the Logos, as man and the Son of Man."

[2] See Irenæus, *Hær.*, i. 1.

[3] Geryon (see note, chap. iii.) is afterwards mentioned as a synonyme with Jordan, i.e., " flowing from earth " (γῆ ῥύων).

[4] γνῶσις, — a term often alluded to by St. John, and which gives its name " Gnosticism " to the various forms of the Ophitic heresy. The aphorism in the text is one that embodies a grand principle which lies at the root of all correct philosophy. In this and other instances it will be found that the system, however wild and incoherent in its theology, of the Naasseni and of some of the other Gnostic sects, was one which was constructed by a subtle analysis of thought, and by observation of nature.

[5] The Abbe Cruice remarks on this passage, that, as the statement here as regards Jesus Christ does not correspond with Origen's remarks on the opinions of the Naasseni in reference to our Lord, the *Philosophumena* cannot be the work of Origen.

[6] The Abbe Cruice observes that we have here another proof that the *Philosophumena* is not the work of Origen, who in his *Contra Celsum* mentions Mariamne, but professes not to have met with any of his followers (see *Contr. Cels.*, lib. v. p. 272, ed. Spenc.). This confirms the opinion mostly entertained of Origen, that neither the bent of his mind nor the direction of his studies justify the supposition that he would write a detailed history of heresy.

[7] Isa. liii. 8.

[8] Or ἀδιάφ ρον, equivocal.

[9] This has been by the best critics regarded as a fragment of a hymn of Pindar's on Jupiter Ammon. Schneidewin furnishes a restored poetic version of it by Bergk. This hymn, we believe, first suggested to M. Miller an idea of the possible value and importance of the MS. of *The Refutation* brought by Minöides Mynas from Greece.

[10] The usual form is Alalcomenes. He was a Bœotian Autocthon.

[11] Or, " Iannes." The Abbe Cruice refers to Berosus, *Chald. Hist.*, pp. 48, 49, and to his own dissertation (Paris, 1844) on the authority to be attached to Josephus, as regards the writers adduced by him in his treatise *Contr. Apion*.

alone earth brought forth. And that he lay in-animate, unmoved, (and) still as a statue ; being an image of him who is above, who is celebrated as the man Adam,[1] having been begotten by many powers, concerning whom individually is an enlarged discussion.

In order, therefore, that finally the Great Man from above may be overpowered, "from whom," as they say, "the whole family named on earth and in the heavens" has been formed, to him was given also a soul, that through the soul he might suffer ; and that the enslaved image may be punished of the Great and most Glorious and Perfect Man, for even so they call him. Again, then, they ask what is the soul, and whence, and what kind in its nature, that, coming to the man and moving him,[2] it should enslave and punish the image of the Perfect Man. They do not, however, (on this point) institute an inquiry from the Scriptures, but ask this (question) also from the mystic (rites). And they affirm that the soul is very difficult to discover, and hard to understand ; for it does not remain in the same figure or the same form invariably, or in one passive condition, that either one could express it by a sign, or comprehend it substantially.

But they have these varied changes (of the soul) set down in the gospel inscribed "accord-ing to the Egyptians."[3] They are, then, in doubt, as all the rest of men among the Gen-tiles, whether (the soul) is at all from something pre-existent, or whether from the self-produced (one),[4] or from a widespread Chaos. And first they fly for refuge to the mysteries of the Assy-rians, perceiving the threefold division of the man ; for the Assyrians first advanced the opin-ion that the soul has three parts, and yet (is essentially) one. For of soul, say they, is every nature desirous, and each in a different manner. For soul is cause of all things made ; all things that are nourished, (the Naassene) says, and that grow, require soul. For it is not possible, he says, to obtain any nourishment or growth where soul is not present. For even stones, he affirms, are animated, for they possess what is capable of increase ; but increase would not at any time take place without nourishment, for it is by accession that things which are being in-creased grow, but accession is the nourishment of things that are nurtured. Every nature, then, (the Naassene) says, of things celestial, and earthly, and infernal, desires a soul. And an entity of this description the Assyrians call Adonis or Endymion ;[5] and when it is styled Adonis, Venus, he says, loves and desires the soul when styled by such a name. But Venus is production, according to them. But when-ever Proserpine or Cora becomes enamoured with Adonis, there results, he says, a certain mortal soul separated from Venus (that is, from generation). But should the Moon pass into concupiscence for Endymion, and into love of her form, the nature,[6] he says, of the higher beings requires a soul likewise. But if, he says, the mother of the gods emasculate Attis,[7] and herself has this (person) as an object of affec-tion, the blessed nature, he says, of the supernal and everlasting (beings) alone recalls the male power of the soul to itself.

For (the Naassene) says, there is the her-maphrodite man. According to this account of theirs, the intercourse of woman with man is demonstrated, in conformity with such teach-ing, to be an exceedingly wicked and filthy (practice).[8] For, says (the Naassene), Attis has been emasculated, that is, he has passed over from the earthly parts of the nether world to the everlasting substance above, where, he says, there is neither female or male,[9] but a new creature,[10] a new man, which is hermaphrodite. As to where, however, they use the expression "above," I shall show when I come to the prop-er place (for treating this subject). But they assert that, by their account, they testify that Rhea is not absolutely isolated, but — for so I may say — the universal creature ; and this they declare to be what is affirmed by the Word. "For the invisible things of Him are seen from the creation of the world, being understood by the things that are made by Him, even His eternal power and Godhead, for the purpose of leaving them without excuse. Wherefore, know-ing God, they glorified Him not as God, nor gave Him thanks ; but their foolish heart was rendered vain. For, professing themselves to be wise, they became fools, and changed the glory of the uncorruptible God into images of the likeness of corruptible man, and of birds, and four-footed beasts, and creeping things. Wherefore also God gave them up unto vile af-

---

[1] The Rabbins, probably deriving their notions from the Chal-deans, entertained the most exaggerated ideas respecting the per-fection of Adam. Thus Gerson, in his *Commentary on Abarbanel*, says that "Adam was endued with the very perfection of wisdom, and was chief of philosophers, that he was an immediate disciple of the Deity, also a physician and astrologer, and the originator of all the arts and sciences." This spirit of exaggeration passed from the Jews to the Christians (see *Clementine Homilies*, ii.). Aquinas (*Sum. Theol.*, pars i 94) says of Adam, " Since the first man was appointed perfect, he ought to have possessed a knowledge of everything capa-ble of being ascertained by natural means."

[2] Or, "vanquishing him" (Roeper).

[3] This is known to us only by some ancient quotations. The Naasseni had another work of repute among them, the "Gospel ac-cording to Thomas." Bunsen conjectures that the two "Gospels" may be the same.

[4] αὐτογενοῦς. Miller has αὐτοῦ γένους, which Bunsen rejects in favour of the reading "self-begotten."

[5] Schneidewin considers that there have been left out in the MS. the words "or Attis" after Endymion. Attis is subsequently men-tioned with some degree of particularity.

[6] Or, "creation."

[7] Or, "Apis." See Diodorus Siculus, iii. 58, 59. Pausanias, vii. 20, writes the word Attes. See also Minucius Felix, *Octav.*, cap. xxi.

[8] Or, "forbidden."

[9] Gal. iii. 28, and Clement's *Epist. ad Rom.*, ii. 12. [This is the apocryphal Clement reserved for vol. viii. of this series. See also same text, Ignatius, vol. i. p. 81.]

[10] See 2 Cor. v. 17, Gal. vi. 15.

fections ; for even their women did change the natural use into that which is against nature." What, however, the natural use is, according to them, we shall afterwards declare. "And likewise also the men, leaving the natural use of the woman, burned in their lust one toward another ; men with men working that which is unseemly" — now the expression "that which is unseemly" signifies, according to these (Naasseni), the first and blessed substance, figureless, the cause of all figures to those things that are moulded into shapes, — "and receiving in themselves that recompense of their error which was meet." [1] For in these words which Paul has spoken they say the entire secret of theirs, and a hidden mystery of blessed pleasure, are comprised. For the promise of washing is not any other, according to them, than the introduction of him that is washed in, according to them, life-giving water, and anointed with ineffable [2] ointment (than his introduction) into unfading bliss

But they assert that not only is there in favour of their doctrine, testimony to be drawn from the mysteries of the Assyrians, but also from those of the Phrygians concerning the happy nature — concealed, and yet at the same time disclosed — of things that have been, and are coming into existence, and moreover will be, — (a happy nature) which, (the Naassene) says, is the kingdom of heaven to be sought for within a man.[3] And concerning this (nature) they hand down an explicit passage, occurring[4] in the Gospel inscribed according to Thomas,[5] expressing themselves thus : "He who seeks me, will find me in children from seven years old ; for there concealed, I shall in the fourteenth age be made manifest." This, however, is not (the teaching) of Christ, but of Hippocrates, who uses these words : "A child of seven years is half of a father." And so it is that these (heretics), placing the originative nature of the universe in causative seed, (and) having ascertained the (aphorism) of Hippocrates,[6] that a child of seven years old is half of a father, say that in fourteen years, according to Thomas, he is manifested. This, with them, is the ineffable and mystical Logos. They assert, then, that the Egyptians, who after the Phrygians,[7] it is established, are of greater antiquity than all mankind, and who confessedly were the first to proclaim to all the rest of men the rites and orgies of, at the same time, all the gods, as well as the species and energies (of things), have the sacred and august, and for those who are not initiated, unspeakable mysteries of Isis. These, however, are not anything else than what by her of the seven dresses and sable robe was sought and snatched away, namely, the *pudendum* of Osiris. And they say that Osiris is water.[8] But the seven-robed nature, encircled and arrayed with seven mantles of ethereal texture — for so they call the planetary stars, allegorizing and denominating them ethereal[9] robes, — is as it were the changeable generation, and is exhibited as the creature transformed by the ineffable and unportrayable,[10] and inconceivable and figureless one. And this, (the Naassene) says, is what is declared in Scripture, "The just will fall seven times, and rise again."[11] For these falls, he says, are the changes of the stars, moved by Him who puts all things in motion.

They affirm, then, concerning the substance[12] of the seed which is a cause of all existent things, that it is none of these, but that it produces and forms all things that are made, expressing themselves thus : "I become what I wish, and I am what I am : on account of this I say, that what puts all things in motion is itself unmoved. For what exists remains forming all things, and nought of existing things is made."[13] He says that this (one) alone is good, and that what is spoken by the Saviour[14] is declared concerning this (one) : "Why do you say that I am good? One is good, my Father which is in the heavens, who causeth His sun to rise upon the just and unjust, and sendeth rain upon saints and sinners."[15] But who the saintly ones are on whom He sends the rain, and the sinners on whom the same sends the rain, this likewise we shall afterwards declare with the rest. And this is the great and secret and unknown mystery of the universe, concealed and revealed among the Egyptians. For Osiris,[16] (the Naassene) says, is in temples in front of Isis ;[17] and his *pudendum* stands exposed, looking downwards, and crowned with all its own fruits of things that are made. And (he affirms) that such stands not only in the most hallowed temples chief of idols, but that also, for the information of all, it is as it were a light not set under a bushel, but upon a candlestick, proclaiming its message upon the housetops,[18] in all by-

---

[1] Rom. i. 20–27.
[2] ἀλάλῳ; some read ἄλλῳ.
[3] Luke xvii. 21.
[4] These words do not occur in the "Gospel of Thomas concerning the Saviour's infancy," as given by Fabricius and Thilo.
[5] The Abbe Cruice mentions the following works as of authority among the Naasseni, and from whence they derived their system: *The Gospel of Perfection, Gospel of Eve, The Questions of Mary, Concerning the Offspring of Mary, The Gospel of Philip, The Gospel according to* (1) *Thomas,* (2) *the Egyptians.* (See Epiphanius, *Hæres.,* c. xxvi., and Origen, *Contr. Cels.,* vi. 30, p. 296, ed. Spenc.) These heretics likewise make use of the Old Testament, St. John's Gospel, and some of the Pauline epistles.
[6] Miller refers to Littré, *Traduct. des Œuvres d'Hippocrate,* t. i. p. 396.   [7] See Herodotus, ii. 2, 5.

[8] See Origen, *Contr. Cels.,* v. 38 (p. 257, ed. Spenc.).
[9] Or, "brilliant."
[10] Or, "untraceable."
[11] Prov. xxiv. 16; Luke xvii. 4.
[12] Or, "spirit."
[13] See Epiphanius, *Hæres.,* xxvi. 8.
[14] Matt. xix. 17; Mark x. 18; Luke xviii. 19.
[15] Matt. v. 45.
[16] Miller has οὐδείς. See Plutarch, *De Isid. et Osirid.,* c. li. p. 371.
[17] Or, εἰσόδου, i.e., entrance.
[18] Matt. v. 15, x. 27.

ways, and all streets, and near the actual dwellings, placed in front as a certain appointed limit and termination of the dwelling, and that this is denominated the good (entity) by all. For they style this good-producing, not knowing what they say. And the Greeks, deriving this mystical (expression) from the Egyptians, preserve it until this day. For we behold, says (the Naassene), statues of Mercury, of such a figure honoured among them.

Worshipping, however, Cyllenius with especial distinction, they style him Logios. For Mercury is Logos, who being interpreter and fabricator of the things that have been made simultaneously, and that are being produced, and that will exist, stands honoured among them, fashioned into some such figure as is the *pudendum* of a man, having an impulsive power from the parts below towards those above. And that this (deity) — that is, a Mercury of this description — is, (the Naassene) says, a conjurer of the dead, and a guide of departed spirits, and an originator of souls; nor does this escape the notice of the poets, who express themselves thus : —

> "Cyllenian Hermes also called
> The souls of mortal suitors."[1]

Not Penelope's suitors, says he, O wretches ! but (souls) awakened and brought to recollection of themselves,

> "From honour so great, and from bliss so long."[2]

That is, from the blessed man from above, or the primal man or Adam, as it seems to them, *souls* have been conveyed down here into a creation of clay, that they may serve the Demiurge of this creation, Ialdabaoth,[3] a fiery God, a fourth number; for so they call the Demiurge and father of the formal world : —

> "And in hand he held a lovely
> Wand of gold that human eyes enchants,
> Of whom he will, and those again who slumber rouses."[4]

This, he says, is he who alone has power of life and death. Concerning this, he says, it has been written, "Thou shalt rule them with a rod of iron."[5] The poet, however, he says, being desirous of adorning the incomprehensible (potency) of the blessed nature of the Logos, invested him with not an iron, but golden wand. And he enchants the eyes of the dead, as he says, and raises up again those that are slumbering, after having been roused from sleep, and after having been suitors. And concerning these, he says, the Scripture speaks : "Awake thou that sleepest, and arise, and Christ will give thee light."[6]

This is the Christ who, he says, in all that have been generated, is the portrayed Son of Man from the unportrayable Logos. This, he says, is the great and unspeakable mystery of the Eleusinian rites, Hye, Cye.[7] And he affirms that all things have been subjected unto him, and this is that which has been spoken, "Their sound is gone forth unto all the earth,"[8] just as it agrees with the expressions, "Mercury[9] waving his wand, *guides the souls*, but they twittering follow." I mean the disembodied spirits follow continuously in such a way as the poet by his imagery delineates, using these words : —

> "And as when in the magic cave's recess
> Bats humming fly, and when one drops
> From ridge of rock, and each to other closely clings."[10]

The expression "rock," he says, he uses of Adam. This, he affirms, is Adam : "The chief corner-stone become the head of the corner."[11] For that in the head the substance is the formative brain from which the entire family is fashioned.[12] "Whom," he says, "I place as a rock at the foundations of Zion." Allegorizing, he says, he speaks of the creation of the man. The rock is interposed (within) the teeth, as Homer[13] says, "enclosure of teeth," that is, a wall and fortress, in which exists the inner man, who thither has fallen from Adam, the primal man above. And he has been "severed without hands to effect the division,"[14] and has been borne down into the image of oblivion, *being earthly and clayish*. And he asserts that the twittering spirits follow him, that is, the Logos : —

> "Thus these, twittering, came together : and then the souls

That is, he guides them ;

> Gentle Hermes led through wide-extended paths."[15]

That is, he says, into the eternal places separated from all wickedness. For whither, he says, did they come : —

> "O'er ocean's streams they came, and Leuca's cliff,
> And by the portals of the sun and land of dreams."

This, he says, is ocean, "generation of gods and generation of men"[16] ever whirled round by the eddies of water, at one time upwards, at another time downwards. But he says there ensues a generation of men when the ocean flows downwards; but when upwards to the wall and fortress and the cliff of Luecas, a generation

---

[1] *Odyssey*, xxiv. 1.
[2] Empedocles, v. 390, Stein.
[3] Esaldaius, Miller (see Origen, *Contr. Cels.*, v. 76, p. 297, ed. Spenc.).
[4] *Odyssey*, xxiv. 2.
[5] Ps. ii. 9.
[6] Eph. v. 14.

[7] See Plutarch, *De Iside et Osiride*, c. xxxiv.
[8] Rom. x. 18.
[9] *Odyssey*, xxiv. 5.
[10] *Ibid.*, xxiv. 6 et seq.
[11] Ps. cxviii. 22; Isa. xxviii. 16.
[12] Eph. iii. 15.
[13] *Iliad*, iv. 350, ἕρκος ὀδόντων : —
> "What word hath 'scaped the ivory guard that should
> Have fenced it in."
[14] Dan. ii. 45.
[15] *Odyssey*, xxiv. 9.
[16] *Iliad*, v. 246, xxiv. 201.

of gods takes place. This, he asserts, is that which has been written : " I said, Ye are gods, and all children of the highest ; " [1] " If ye hasten to fly out of Egypt, and repair beyond the Red Sea into the wilderness," that is, from earthly intercourse to the Jerusalem above, which is the mother of the living ; [2] " If, moreover, again you return into Egypt," that is, into earthly intercourse,[3] " ye shall die as men." For mortal, he says, is every generation below, but immortal that which is begotten above, for it is born of water only, and of spirit, being spiritual, not carnal. But what (is born) below is carnal, that is, he says, what is written. " That which is born of the flesh is flesh, and that which is born of the spirit is spirit." [4] This, according to them, is the spiritual genera- tion. This, he says, is the great Jordan [5] which, flowing on (here) below, and preventing the children of Israel from departing out of Egypt — I mean from terrestrial intercourse, for Egypt is with them the body, — Jesus drove back, and made it flow upwards.

CHAP. III. — FURTHER EXPOSITION OF THE HERESY OF THE NAASSENI ; PROFESS TO FOLLOW HOMER ; ACKNOWLEDGE A TRIAD OF PRINCIPLES ; THEIR TECHNICAL NAMES OF THE TRIAD ; SUPPORT THESE ON THE AUTHORITY OF GREEK POETS ; ALLEGORIZE OUR SAVIOUR'S MIRACLES ; THE MYSTERY OF THE SAMOTHRACIANS ; WHY THE LORD CHOSE TWELVE DISCIPLES ; THE NAME CORYBAS, USED BY THRACIANS AND PHRYGIANS, EXPLAINED ; NAASSENI PROFESS TO FIND THEIR SYSTEM IN SCRIPTURE ; THEIR INTERPRETATION OF JACOB'S VISION ; THEIR IDEA OF THE " PER- FECT MAN ; " THE " PERFECT MAN " CALLED " PAPA " BY THE PHRYGIANS ; THE NAASSENI AND PHRYGIANS ON THE RESURRECTION ; THE ECSTASIS OF ST. PAUL ; THE MYSTERIES OF RELI- GION AS ALLUDED TO BY CHRIST ; INTERPRE- TATION OF THE PARABLE OF THE SOWER ; ALLEGORY OF THE PROMISED LAND ; COMPARI- SON OF THE SYSTEM OF THE PHRYGIANS WITH THE STATEMENTS OF SCRIPTURE ; EXPOSITION OF THE MEANING OF THE HIGHER AND LOWER ELEUSINIAN MYSTERIES ; THE INCARNATION DIS- COVERABLE HERE ACCORDING TO THE NAASSENI.

Adopting these and such like (opinions), these most marvellous Gnostics, inventors of a novel [6] grammatical art, magnify Homer as their prophet — as one, (according to them,) who, after the mode adopted in the mysteries, an- nounces these truths ; and they mock those who

are not indoctrinated into the holy Scriptures, by betraying them into such notions. They make, however, the following assertion : he who says that all things derive consistence from one, is in error ; but he who says that they are of three, is in possession of the truth, and will fur- nish a solution of the (phonomena of the) uni- verse. For there is, says (the Naassene), one blessed nature of the Blessed Man, of him who is above, (namely) Adam ; and there is one mortal nature, that which is below ; and there is one kingless generation, which is begotten above, where, he says, is Mariam [7] the sought- for one, and Iothor the mighty sage, and Seph- ora the gazing one, and Moses whose generation is not in Egypt, for children were born unto him in Madian ; and not even this, he says, has es- caped the notice of the poets.

" Threefold was our partition ; each obtained
His meed of honour due." [8]

For, says he, it is necessary that the magnitudes be declared, and that they thus be declared by all everywhere, " in order that hearing they may not hear, and seeing they may not see." [9] For if, he says, the magnitudes were not declared, the world could not have obtained consistence. These are the three tumid expressions (of these heretics), CAULACAU,[10] SAULASAU, ZEESAR. CAU- LACAU, i.e., Adam, who is farthest above ; SAULA- SAU, that is, the mortal one below ; ZEESAR, that is, Jordan that flows upwards. This, he says, is the hermaphrodite man (present) in all. But those who are ignorant of him, call him Geryon with the threefold body — Geryon, i.e., as if (in the sense of) flowing from earth — but (whom) the Greeks by common consent (style) " celestial horn of the moon," because he mixed and blended all things in all. " For all things," he says, " were made by him, and not even one thing was made without him, and what was made in him is life." [11] This, says he, is the life, the ineffable generation of perfect men, which was not known by preceding generations. But the passage, " nothing was made without him," refers to the formal world, for it was created without his instrumentality by the third and fourth (of the quaternion named above). For says he, this is the cup " CONDY, out of which the king, while he quaffs, draws his omens." [12] This, he says, has been discovered hid in the beauteous seeds of Benjamin. And the Greeks

---

[1] Ps. lxxxii. 6; Luke vi. 35; John x. 34.
[2] Gal. iv. 26.
[3] Philo Judæus adopts the same imagery (see his *De Agricult.*, lib. i.).
[4] John iii. 6.
[5] Josh. iii. 7–17.
[6] Or, " empty."

[7] The Abbe Cruice considers that this is taken from verses of Ezekiel, founding his opinion on fragments of these verses to be found in Eusebius' *Præparat. Evang.*, ix. 38.
[8] *Iliad*, xv. 189.
[9] Matt. xiii. 13.
[10] The commentators refer to Isa. xxviii. 10. Epiphanius, *Hæres.*, xxv., mentions these expressions, but assigns them a different mean- ing. *Saulasau* is tribulation, *Caulacau* hope, and *Zeesar* " hope, as yet, little." [See my note on *Irenæus*, p. 350, this series, and see Elucidation II.]
[11] John i. 3, 4.
[12] Gen. xliv. 2–5.

likewise, he says, speak of this in the following terms : —

"Water to the raging mouth bring; thou slave, bring
    wine;
Intoxicate and plunge me into stupor.
My tankard tells me
The sort I must become."[1]

This, says he, was alone sufficient for its being understood by men ; (I mean) the cup of Anacreon declaring, (albeit) mutely, an ineffable mystery. For dumb, says he, is Anacreon's cup ; and (yet) Anacreon affirms that it speaks to himself, in language mute, as to what sort he must become — that is spiritual, not carnal — if he shall listen in silence to the concealed mystery. And this is the water in those fair nuptials which Jesus changing made into wine. This, he says, is the mighty and true beginning of miracles[2] which Jesus performed in Cana of Galilee, and (thus) manifested the kingdom of heaven. This, says he, is the kingdom of heaven that reposes within us as a treasure, as leaven hid in the three measures of meal.[3]

This is, he says, the great and ineffable mystery of the Samothracians, which it is allowable, he says, for us only who are initiated to know. For the Samothracians expressly hand down, in the mysteries that are celebrated among them, that (same) Adam as the primal man. And habitually there stand in the temple of the Samothracians two images of naked men, having both hands stretched aloft towards heaven, and their *pudenda erecta, as with* the statue of Mercury on Mount Cyllene. And the aforesaid images are figures of the primal man, and of that spiritual one that is born again, in every respect of the same substance with that man. This, he says, is what is spoken by the Saviour : "If ye do not drink my blood, and eat my flesh, ye will not enter into the kingdom of heaven ; but even though," He says, "ye drink of the cup which I drink of, whither I go, ye cannot enter there."[4] For He says He was aware of what sort of nature each of His disciples was, and that there was a necessity that each of them should attain unto His own peculiar nature. For He says He chose twelve disciples from the twelve tribes, and spoke by them to each tribe. On this account, He says, the preachings of the twelve disciples neither did all hear, nor, if they heard, could they receive. For the things that are not according to nature, are with them contrary to nature.

This, he says, the Thracians who dwell around Hæmus, and the Phrygians similarly with the Thracians, denominate Corybas, because, (though) deriving the beginning of his descent

from the head above and from the unportrayed brain, and (though) permeating all the principles of the existing state of things, (yet) we do not perceive how and in what manner he comes down. This, says he, is what is spoken : "We have heard his voice, no doubt, but we have not seen his shape."[5] For the voice of him that is set apart[6] and portrayed is heard ; but (his) shape, which descends from above from the unportrayed one, — what sort it is, nobody knows. It resides, however, in an earthly mould, yet no one recognises it. This, he says, is "the god that inhabiteth the flood," according to the Psalter, "and who speaketh and crieth from many waters."[7] The "many waters," he says, are the diversified generation of mortal men, from which (generation) he cries and vociferates to the unportrayed man, saying, "Preserve my only-begotten from the lions."[8] In reply to him, it has, says he, been declared, "Israel, thou art my child : fear not ; even though thou passest through rivers, they shall not drown thee ; even though thou passest through fire, it shall not scorch thee."[9] By rivers he means, says he, the moist substance of generation, and by fire the impulsive principle and desire for generation. "Thou art mine ; fear not." And again, he says, "If a mother forget her children, so as not to have pity on them and give them food, I also will forget you."[10] Adam, he says, speaks to his own men : "But even though a woman forget these things, yet I will not forget you. I have painted you on my hands." In regard, however, of his ascension, that is his regeneration, that he may become spiritual, not carnal, the Scripture, he says, speaks (thus) : "Open the gates, ye who are your rulers ; and be ye lift up, ye everlasting doors, and the King of glory shall come in," that is a wonder of wonders.[11] "For who," he says, "is this King of glory? A worm, and not a man ; a reproach of man, and an outcast of the people ; himself is the King of glory, and powerful in war."[12]

And by war he means the war that is in the body, because its frame has been made out of hostile elements ; as it has been written, he says, "Remember the conflict that exists in the body."[13] Jacob, he says, saw this entrance and this gate in his journey into Mesopotamia, that is, when from a child he was now becoming a youth and a man ; that is, (the entrance and gate) were made known unto him as he journeyed into Mesopotamia. But Mesopotamia, he

---

[1] Taken from Anacreon.
[2] John ii. 1-11.
[3] Matt. xiii. 33, 34: Luke xvii. 21.
[4] John vi. 53; Mark x. 38.

[5] John v. 37.
[6] ἀποτεταγμένου: some read ἀποτεταμένου.
[7] Ps. xxix. 3, 10.
[8] Ps. xxii. 20, 21, xxxv. 17.
[9] Isa. xli. 8, xliii. 1, 2.
[10] Isa. xlix. 15.
[11] Ps. xxiv. 7-9.
[12] Ps. xxii. 6, xxiv. 8.
[13] This is a quotation from the Septuagint, Job xl. 27. The reference to the authorized (English) version would be xli. 8.

says, is the current of the great ocean flowing from the midst of the Perfect Man ; and he was astonished at the celestial gate, exclaiming, "How terrible is this place ! it is nought else than the house of God, and this (is) the gate of heaven." [1] On account of this, he says, Jesus uses the words, "I am the true gate." [2] Now he who makes these statements is, he says, the Perfect Man that is imaged from the unportrayable one from above. The Perfect Man therefore cannot, he says, be saved, unless, entering in through this gate, he be born again. But this very one the Phrygians, he says, call also PAPA, because he tranquillized all things which, prior to his manifestation, were confusedly and dissonantly moved. For the name, he says, of PAPA belongs simultaneously to all creatures [3] — celestial, and terrestrial, and infernal — who exclaim, *Cause to cease, cause to cease the discord of the world, and make* "peace for those that are afar off," that is, for material and earthly beings ; and "peace for those that are near," [4] that is, for perfect men that are spiritual and endued with reason. But the Phrygians denominate this same also "corpse" — buried in the body, as it were, in a mausoleum and tomb. This, he says, is what has been declared, "Ye are whited sepulchres, full," he says, "of dead men's bones within," [5] because there is not in you the living man. And again he exclaims, "The dead shall start forth from the graves," [6] that is, from the earthly bodies, being born again spiritual, not carnal. For this, he says, is the Resurrection that takes place through the gate of heaven, through which, he says, all those that do not enter remain dead. These same Phrygians, however, he says, affirm again that this very (man), as a consequence of the change, (becomes) a god. For, he says, he becomes a god when, having risen from the dead, he will enter into heaven through a gate of this kind. Paul the apostle, he says, knew of this gate, partially opening it in a mystery, and stating "that he was caught up by an angel, and ascended as far as the second and third heaven into paradise itself ; and that he beheld sights and heard unspeakable words which it would not be possible for man to declare." [7]

These are, he says, what are by all called the secret mysteries, "which (also we speak), not in words taught of human wisdom, but in those taught of the Spirit, comparing spiritual things with spiritual. But the natural man receiveth not the things of the Spirit of God, for they are

foolishness unto him." [8] And these are, he says, the ineffable mysteries of the Spirit, which we alone are acquainted with. Concerning these, he says, the Saviour has declared, "No one can come unto me, except my heavenly Father draw some one unto me." [9] For it is very difficult, he says, to accept and receive this great and ineffable mystery. And again, it is said, the Saviour has declared, "Not every one that saith unto me, Lord, Lord, shall enter into the kingdom of heaven, but he that doeth the will of my Father which is in heaven." [10] And it is necessary that they who perform this (will), not hear it merely, should enter into the kingdom of heaven. And again, he says, the Saviour has declared, "The publicans and the harlots go into the kingdom of heaven before you." [11] For "the publicans," he says, are those who receive the revenues [12] of all things ; [13] but we, he says, are the publicans, "unto whom the ends of the ages have come." [14] For "the ends," he says, are the seeds scattered from the unportrayable one upon the world, through which the whole cosmical system is completed ; for through these also it began to exist. And this, he says, is what has been declared : "The sower went forth to sow. And some fell by the wayside, and was trodden down ; and some on the rocky places, and sprang up," he says, "and on account of its having no depth (of soil), it withered and died ; and some," he says, "fell on fair and good ground, and brought forth fruit, some a hundred, some sixty, and some thirty fold. Who hath ears," he says, "to hear, let him hear." [15] The meaning of this, he says, is as follows, that none becomes a hearer of these mysteries, unless only the perfect Gnostics. This, he says, is the fair and good land which Moses speaks of : "I will bring you into a fair and good land, into a land flowing with milk and honey." [16] This, he says, is the honey and the milk, by tasting which those that are perfect become kingless, and share in the Pleroma. This, he says, is the Pleroma, through which all existent things that are produced [17] have from the ingenerable one been both produced and completed.

And this same (one) is styled also by [18] the Phrygians "unfruitful." For he is unfruitful when he is carnal, and causes the desire of the flesh. This, he says, is what is spoken : "Every tree not producing good fruit, is cut down and

---

[1] Gen. xxviii. 7, 17.
[2] John x. 9; Matt. vii. 13.
[3] [A strange amplifying of the word, which is now claimed exclusively for one. Elucidation III.]
[4] Eph. ii. 17.
[5] Matt. xxiii. 27.
[6] Matt. xxvii. 52, 53.
[7] 2 Cor. xii. 2.

[8] 1 Cor. ii. 13, 14.
[9] John vi. 44.
[10] Matt. vii. 21.
[11] Matt. xxi. 31.
[12] The word translated "revenues" and "ends" is the same—τέλη.
[13] Τῶν ὅλων: some read τῶν ὠνίων.
[14] 1 Cor. x. 11.
[15] Matt. xiii. 3-9; Mark iv. 3-9; Luke viii. 5-8.
[16] Deut. xxxi. 20.
[17] Or, "genera."
[18] ὑπὸ: Miller reads ἀπὸ.

cast into the fire." [1] For these fruits, he says, are only rational living men, who enter in through the third gate. They say, forsooth, "Ye devour the dead, and make the living; (but) if ye eat the living, what will ye do?" They assert, however, that the living "are rational faculties and minds, and men — pearls of that unportrayable one cast before the creature below." [2] This, he says, is what (Jesus) asserts: "Throw not that which is holy unto the dogs, nor pearls unto the swine." [3] Now they allege that the work of swine and dogs is the intercourse of the woman with a man. And the Phrygians, he says, call this very one "goat-herd" (Aipolis), not because, he says, he is accustomed to feed the goats female and male, as the natural (men) use the name, but because, he says, he is "Aipolis" — that is, always ranging over, — who both revolves and carries around the entire cosmical system by his revolutionary motion. For the word "Polein" signifies to turn and change things; whence, he says, they all call the twos centre of the heaven poles (Poloi). And the poet says: —

"What sea-born sinless sage comes hither,
Undying Egyptian Proteus?" [4]

He is not undone, [5] he says, [6] but revolves as it were, and goes round himself. Moreover, also, cities in which we dwell, because we turn and go round in them, are denominated "Poleis." In this manner, he says, the Phrygians call this one "Aipolis," inasmuch as he everywhere ceaselessly turns all things, and changes them into their own peculiar (functions). And the Phrygians style him, he says, "very fruitful" likewise, "because," says he, "more numerous are the children of the desolate one, than those of her which hath an husband;" [7] that is, things by being born again become immortal, and abide for ever in great numbers, even though the things that are produced may be few; whereas things carnal, he says, are all corruptible, even though very many things (of this type) are produced. For this reason, he says, "Rachel wept [8] for her children, and would not," says (the prophet), "be comforted; sorrowing for them, for she knew," says he, "that they are not." [9] But Jeremiah likewise utters lamentation for Jerusalem below, not the city in Phœnicia, but the corruptible generation below. For Jeremiah likewise, he says, was aware of the Perfect Man, of him that is born again — of water and the

Spirit not carnal. At least Jeremiah himself remarked: "He is a man, and who shall know him?" [10] In this manner, (the Naassene) says, the knowledge of the Perfect Man is exceedingly profound, and difficult of comprehension. For, he says, the beginning of perfection is a knowledge of man, whereas knowledge of God is absolute perfection.

The Phrygians, however, assert, he says, that he is likewise "a green ear of corn reaped." And after the Phrygians, the Athenians, while initiating people into the Eleusinian rites, likewise display to those who are being admitted to the highest grade at these mysteries, the mighty, and marvellous, and most perfect secret suitable for one initiated into the highest mystic truths: (I allude to) an ear of corn in silence reaped. But this ear of corn is also (considered) among the Athenians to constitute the perfect enormous illumination (that has descended) from the unportrayable one, just as the Hierophant himself (declares); not, indeed, emasculated like Attis, [11] but made a eunuch by means of hemlock, and despising [12] all carnal generation. (Now) by night in Eleusis, beneath a huge fire, (the Celebrant,) enacting the great and secret mysteries, vociferates and cries aloud, saying, "August Brimo has brought forth a consecrated son, Brimus;" that is, a potent (mother has been delivered of) a potent child. But revered, he says, is the generation that is spiritual, heavenly, from above, and potent is he that is so born. For the mystery is called "Eleusin" and "Anactorium." "Eleusin," because, he says, we who are spiritual come flowing down from Adam above; for the word "eleusesthai" is, he says, of the same import with the expression "to come." But "Anactorium" is of the same import with the expression "to ascend upwards." This, he says, is what they affirm who have been initiated in the mysteries of the Eleusinians. It is, however, a regulation of law, that those who have been admitted into the lesser should again be initiated into the Great Mysteries. For greater destinies obtain greater portions. But the inferior mysteries, he says, are those of Proserpine below; in regard of which mysteries, and the path which leads thither, which is wide and spacious, and conducts those that are perishing to Proserpine, the poet likewise says: —

"But under her a fearful path extends,
Hollow, miry, yet best guide to
Highly-honoured Aphrodite's lovely grove." [13]

These, he says, are the inferior mysteries, those appertaining to carnal generation. Now, those

---

[1] Matt. iii. 10; Luke iii. 9.
[2] κάτω: some read κάρπου.
[3] Matt. vii. 6.
[4] Odyssey, iv. 384.
[5] πιπράσκεται: literally, bought and sold, i.e., ruined.
[6] λέγει: some read ἀμέλει, i.e., doubtless, of course.
[7] Isa. liv. 1; Gal. iv. 27.
[8] ἔκλαιε: this is in the margin; ἔλαβε is in the MS. The marginal reading is the proper correction of that of the MS.
[9] Jer. xxxi. 15; Matt. ii. 18.

[10] Jer. xvii. 9.
[11] [The Phrygian Atys (see cap. iv. infra), whose history should have saved Origen from an imitation of heathenism.]
[12] παρητημένος: some read ἀπηρτισμένος, i.e., perfecting.
[13] These verses have been ascribed to Parmenides.

men who are initiated into these inferior (mysteries) ought to pause, and (then) be admitted into the great (and) heavenly (ones). For they, he says, who obtain their shares (in this mystery), receive greater portions. For this, he says, is the gate of heaven; and this a house of God, where the Good Deity dwells alone. And into this (gate), he says, no unclean person shall enter, nor one that is natural or carnal; but it is reserved for the spiritual only. And those who come hither ought to cast off[1] their garments, and become all of them bridegrooms, emasculated through the virginal spirit. For this is the virgin[2] who carries in her womb and conceives and brings forth a son, not animal, not corporeal, but blessed for evermore. Concerning these, it is said, the Saviour has expressly declared that "straight and narrow is the way that leadeth unto life, and few there are that enter upon it; whereas broad and spacious is the way that leadeth unto destruction, and many there are that pass through it."[3]

CHAP. IV. — FURTHER USE MADE OF THE SYSTEM OF THE PHRYGIANS; MODE OF CELEBRATING THE MYSTERIES; THE MYSTERY OF THE "GREAT MOTHER;" THESE MYSTERIES HAVE A JOINT OBJECT OF WORSHIP WITH THE NAASSENI; THE NAASSENI ALLEGORIZE THE SCRIPTURAL ACCOUNT OF THE GARDEN OF EDEN; THE ALLEGORY APPLIED TO THE LIFE OF JESUS.

The Phrygians, however, further assert that the father of the universe is "Amygdalus," not a tree, he says, but that he is "Amygdalus" who previously existed; and he having in himself the perfect fruit, as it were, throbbing and moving in the depth, rent his breasts, and produced his now invisible, and nameless, and ineffable child, respecting whom we shall speak. For the word "Amyxai" signifies, as it were, to burst and sever through, as he says (happens) in the case of inflamed bodies, and which have in themselves any tumour; and when doctors have cut this, they call it "Amychai." In this way, he says, the Phrygians call him "Amygdalus," from which proceeded and was born the Invisible (One), "by whom all things were made, and nothing was made without Him."[4] And the Phrygians say that what has been thence produced is "Syrictas" (piper), because the Spirit that is born is harmonious. "For God," he says, "is Spirit; wherefore," he affirms, "neither in this mountain do the true worshippers worship, nor in Jerusalem, but in spirit. For the adoration of the perfect ones," he says, "is spiritual, not carnal."[5] The Spirit, however, he

says, is there where likewise the Father is named, and the Son is there born from this Father. This, he says, is the many-named, thousand-eyed Incomprehensible One, of whom every nature — each, however, differently — is desirous. This, he says, is the word of God, which, he says, is a word of revelation of the Great Power. Wherefore it will be sealed, and hid, and concealed, lying in the habitation where lies the basis of the root of the universe, viz., Æons, Powers, Intelligences, Gods, Angels, delegated Spirits, Entities, Nonentities, Generables, Ingenerables, Incomprehensibles, Comprehensibles, Years, Months, Days, Hours, (and) Invisible Point from which[6] what is least begins to increase gradually. That which is, he says, nothing, and which consists of nothing, inasmuch as it is indivisible — (I mean) a point — will become through its own reflective power a certain incomprehensible magnitude. This, he says, is the kingdom of heaven, the grain of mustard seed,[7] the point which is indivisible in the body; and, he says, no one knows this (point) save the spiritual only. This, he says, is what has been spoken: "There is no speech nor language where their voice is not heard."[8]

They rashly assume in this manner, that whatsoever things have been said and done by all men, (may be made to harmonize) with their own particular mental view, alleging that all things become spiritual. Whence likewise they assert, that those exhibiting themselves in theatres, — not even these say or do anything without premeditation. Therefore, he says, when, on the people assembling in the theatres, any one enters clad in a remarkable robe, carrying a harp and playing a tune (upon it, accompanying it) with a song of the great mysteries, he speaks as follows, not knowing what he says: "Whether (thou art) the race of Saturn or happy Jupiter,[9] or mighty Rhea, Hail, Attis, gloomy mutilation of Rhea. Assyrians style thee thrice-longed-for Adonis, and the whole of Egypt (calls thee) Osiris, celestial horn of the moon; Greeks denominate (thee) Wisdom; Samothracians, venerable Adam; Hæmonians, Corybas; and the Phrygians (name thee) at one time Papa, at another time Corpse, or God, or Fruitless, or Aipolos, or green Ear of Corn that has been reaped, or whom the very fertile Amygdalus produced — a man, a musician." This, he says, is multiform Attis, whom while they celebrate in a hymn, they utter these words: "I will hymn Attis, son of Rhea, not with the buzzing sounds of trumpets, or of Idæan pipers, which accord with (the voices of) the Curetes;

but I will mingle (my song) with Apollo's music of harps, 'evoe, evan,' inasmuch as thou art Pan, as thou art Bacchus, as thou art shepherd of brilliant stars."

On account of these and such like reasons, these constantly attend the mysteries called those of the "Great Mother," supposing especially that they behold by means of the ceremonies performed there the entire mystery. For these have nothing more than the ceremonies that are performed there, except that they are not emasculated : they merely complete the work of the emasculated. For with the utmost severity and vigilance they enjoin (on their votaries) to abstain, as if they were emasculated, from intercourse with a woman. The rest, however, of the proceeding (observed in these mysteries), as we have declared at some length, (they follow) just as (if they were) emasculated persons. And they do not worship any other object but Naas, (from thence) being styled Naasseni. But Naas is the serpent from whom, i.e., from the word Naas, (the Naassene) says, are all that under heaven are denominated temples (Naous). And (he states) that to him alone — that is, Naas — is dedicated every shrine and every initiatory rite, and every mystery ; and, in general, that a religious ceremony could not be discovered under heaven, in which a temple (Naos) has no existence ; and in the temple itself is Naas, from whom it has received its denomination of temple (Naos). And these affirm that the serpent is a moist substance, just as Thales also, the Milesian, (spoke of water as an originating principle,) and that nothing of existing things, immortal or mortal, animate or inanimate, could consist at all without him. And that all things are subject unto him, and that he is good, and that he has all things in himself, as in the horn of the one-horned bull ;[1] so as that he imparts beauty and bloom to all things that exist according to their own nature and peculiarity, as if passing through all, just as ("the river) proceeding forth from Edem, and dividing itself into four heads."[2]

They assert, however, that Edem is the brain, as it were, bound and tightly fastened in encircling robes, as if (in) heaven. But they suppose that man, as far as the head only, is Paradise, therefore that "this river, which proceeds out of Edem," that is, from the brain, "is divided into four heads,[3] and that the name of the first river is called Phison ; this is that which encompasseth all the land of Havilath : there is gold, and the gold of that land is excellent, and there is bdellium and the onyx stone." This, he says, is the eye, which, by its honour (among the rest

of the bodily organs), and its colours, furnishes testimony to what is spoken. "But the name of the second river is Gihon : this is that which compasseth the land of Ethiopia." This, he says, is hearing, since Gihon is (a tortuous stream), resembling a sort of labyrinth. "And the name of the third is Tigris. This is that which floweth over against (the country of) the Assyrians." This, he says,[4] is smelling, employing the exceedingly rapid current of the stream (as an analogy of this sense). But it flows over against (the country of) the Assyrians, because in every act of respiration following upon expiration, the breath drawn in from the external atmosphere enters with swifter motion and greater force. For this, he says, is the nature of respiration. "But the fourth river is Euphrates." This, they assert, is the mouth, through which are the passage outwards of prayer, and the passage inwards of nourishment. (The mouth) makes glad, and nurtures and fashions the Spiritual Perfect Man. This, he says, is "the water that is above the firmament,"[5] concerning which, he says, the Saviour has declared, "If thou knewest who it is that asks, thou wouldst have asked from Him, and He would have given you to drink living, bubbling water."[6] Into this water, he says, every nature enters, choosing its own substances ; and its peculiar quality comes to each nature from this water, he says, more than iron does to the magnet, and the gold to the backbone[7] of the sea falcon, and the chaff to the amber.

But if any one, he says, is blind from birth, and has never beheld the true light, "which lighteneth every man that cometh into the world,"[8] by us let him recover his sight, and behold, as it were, through some paradise planted with every description of tree, and supplied with abundance of fruits, water coursing its way through all the trees and fruits ; and he will see that from one and the same water the olive chooses for itself and draws the oil, and the vine the wine ; and (so is it with) the rest of plants, according to each *genus*. That Man, however, he says, is of no reputation in the world, but of illustrious fame in heaven, being betrayed by those who are ignorant (of his perfections) to those who know him not, being accounted as a drop from a cask.[9] We, however, he says, are spiritual, who, from the life-giving water of Eu-

---

[1] Deut. xxxiii. 17.
[2] Gen. ii. 10.
[3] Gen. ii. 11-14.

[4] Or, "they say."
[5] Gen. i. 7.
[6] John iv. 10.
[7] κερκίς. This word literally means the rod; or, in later times, the comb fixed into the ἱστός (i.e., the upright loom), for the purpose of driving the threads of the woof home, thus making the web even and close. It is, among other significations, applied to bones in the leg or arm. Cruice and Schneidewin translate κερκίς by *spina*, a rendering adopted above. The allusion is made again in chap. xii. and chap. xvi. In the last passage, κέντρον (spur) is used instead of κερκίς.
[8] John i. 9, ix. 1.
[9] Isa. xl. 15.

phrates, which flows through the midst of Babylon, choose our own peculiar quality as we pass
through the true gate, which is the blessed Jesus.
And of all men, we Christians alone are those
who in the third gate celebrate the mystery, and
are anointed there with the unspeakable chrism
from a horn, as David (was anointed), not from
an earthen vessel,[1] he says, as (was) Saul, who
held converse with the evil demon[2] of carnal
concupiscence.

CHAP. V. — EXPLANATION OF THE SYSTEM OF THE NAASSENI TAKEN FROM ONE OF THEIR HYMNS.

The foregoing remarks, then, though few out
of many, we have thought proper to bring forward. For innumerable are the silly and crazy
attempts of folly. But since, to the best of our
ability, we have explained the unknown Gnosis,
it seemed expedient likewise to adduce the following point. This psalm of theirs has been
composed, by which they seem to celebrate all
the mysteries of the error (advanced by) them
in a hymn, couched in the following terms : —

> The world's producing law was Primal Mind,[3]
> And next was First-born's outpoured Chaos;
> And third, the soul received its law of toil :
> Encircl'd, therefore, with an aqueous[4] form,
> With care o'erpowered it succumbs to death.
> Now holding sway, it eyes the light,
> And now it weeps on misery flung;
> Now it mourns, now it thrills with joy;
> Now it wails, now it hears its doom;
> Now it hears its doom, now it dies,
> And now it leaves us, never to return.
> It, hapless straying, treads the maze of ills.
> But Jesus said, Father, behold,
> A strife of ills across the earth
> Wanders from thy breath (of wrath);
> But bitter Chaos (man) seeks to shun,
> And knows not how to pass it through.
> On this account, O Father, send me;
> Bearing seals, I shall descend;
> Through ages whole I'll sweep,
> All mysteries I'll unravel,
> And forms of Gods I'll show;
> And secrets of the saintly path,
> Styled " Gnosis," I'll impart.

CHAP. VI. — THE OPHITES THE GRAND SOURCE OF HERESY.

These doctrines, then, the Naasseni attempt
to establish, calling themselves Gnostics. But
since the error is many-headed and diversified,
resembling, in truth, the hydra that we read of
in history ; when, at one blow, we have struck
off the heads of this (delusion) by means of
refutation, employing the wand of truth, we shall
entirely exterminate the monster. For neither

do the remaining heresies present much difference of aspect from this, having a mutual connection through (the same) spirit of error. But
since, altering the words and the names of the
serpent, they wish that there should be many
heads of the serpent, neither thus shall we fail
thoroughly to refute them as they desire.

CHAP. VII. — THE SYSTEM OF THE PERATÆ ; THEIR TRITHEISM ; EXPLANATION OF THE INCARNATION.

There is also unquestionably a certain other
(head of the hydra,[5] namely, the heresy) of the
Peratæ,[6] whose blasphemy against Christ has for
many years escaped notice. And the present is
a fitting opportunity for bringing to light the
secret mysteries of such (heretics). These allege
that the world is one, triply divided. And of
the triple division with them, one portion is a
certain single originating principle, just as it were
a huge fountain, which can be divided mentally
into infinite segments. Now the first segment,
and that which, according to them, is (a segment) in preference (to others),[7] is a triad, and
it is called a Perfect Good, (and) a Paternal
Magnitude. And the second portion of the
triad of these is, as it were, a certain infinite
crowd of potentialities that are generated[8] from
themselves, (while) the third is formal.[9] And
the first, which is good, is unbegotten, and the
second is a self-producing good, and the third
is created ; and hence it is that they expressly
declare that there are three Gods, three Logoi,
three Minds, three Men. For to each portion
of the world, after the division has been made,
they assign both Gods, and Logoi, and Minds,
and Men, and the rest ; but that from unorigination and the first segment[10] of the world, when
afterwards the world had attained unto its completion, there came down from above, for causes
that we shall afterwards declare, in the time of

---

[1] 1 Sam. x. 1, xvi. 13.
[2] 1 Sam. xvi. 14.
[3] The text of this hymn is very corrupt. The Abbe Cruice explains the connection of the hymn with the foregoing exposition, and
considers it to have a reference to the Metempsychosis, which forms
part of the system of the Naasseni. [Bunsen, i. 36.]
[4] Or, " nimble."

[5] Something is wanting after Περατική in the text. Miller supplies the deficiency, and his conjecture is adopted above. Literally,
it should be rendered — " the Peratic heresy, the blasphemy of which
(heretics)," etc.
[6] Most of what is mentioned by Hippolytus concerning this sect
is new, as the chief writers on the early heresies are comparatively
silent concerning the Peratæ; indeed, Irenæus, Tertullian, and Epiphanius completely so. Clemens Alexandrinus, Strom., vii.; (vol.
ii. p. 555), mentions the Peratics, and Theodoret more fully than
the rest speaks of them (Hæret. fabul., i. 17). Theodoret, however,
as the Abbe Cruice thinks, has appropriated his remarks from Hippolytus.
[7] προεχεστέρα or προσεχεστέρα, contiguous. This is Miller's
reading, but is devoid of sense. Προεχεστέρα, adopted by Schneidewin and Cruice, might bear the meaning of the expression par excellence.
[8] γεγεννημένων: Miller reads γεγεννημένον, agreeing with
πλῆθος. Bernays, in his Epistola Critica addressed to Bunsen,
proposes the former reading.
[9] εἰδικοῦ: some read ἰδικοῦ. This term, adopted from the Platonic philosophy, is translated specialis by logicians, and transcen-
dentalis by metaphysicians. It expresses the pre-existent form in the
divine mind, according to which material objects were fashioned. The
term seems out of place as used by the Peratics to denominate a corruptible and perishing world. We should rather expect ὑλικοῦ, i.e ,
material. (See Aristotle's masterly exposition of the subject of the
εἶδος and ὕλη in his Metaphysics, book vi., and p. 64 of the analysis
prefixed to the translation in Bohn's Library.)
[10] πρώτης or πρὸ τῆς, " antecedent to the segment."

Herod a certain man called Christ, with a three-fold nature, and a threefold body, and a three-fold power, (and) having in himself all (species of) concretions and potentialities (derivable) from the three divisions of the world ; and that this, says (the Peratic), is what is spoken : " It pleased him that in him should dwell all fulness bodily," [1] and in Him the entire Divinity resides of the triad as thus divided. For, he says, that from the two superjacent worlds — namely, from that (portion of the triad) which is unbegotten, and from that which is self-producing — there have been conveyed down into this world in which we are, seeds of all sorts of potentialities. What, however, the mode of the descent is, we shall afterwards declare.

(The Peratic) then says that Christ descended from above from unorigination, that by His descent all things triply divided might be saved. For some things, he says, being borne down from above, will ascend through Him, whereas whatever (beings) form plots against those which are carried down from above are cast off,[2] and being placed in a state of punishment, are renounced. This, he says, is what is spoken : " For the Son of man came not into the world to destory the world, but that the world through Him might be saved." The world, he says, he denominates those two parts that are situated above, viz., both the unbegotten (portion of the triad), and the self-produced one. And when Scripture, he says, uses the words, " that we may not be condemned with the world," it alludes to the third portion of (the triad, that is) the formal world. For the third portion, which he styles the world (in which we are), must perish ; but the two (remaining portions), which are situated above, must be rescued from corruption.

CHAP. VIII. — THE PERATÆ DERIVE THEIR SYSTEM FROM THE ASTROLOGERS ; THIS PROVED BY A STATEMENT OF THE ASTROLOGICAL THEORIES OF THE ZODIAC ; HENCE THE TERMINOLOGY OF THE PERATIC HERETICS.

Let us, then, in the first place, learn how (the Peratists), deriving this doctrine from astrologers, act despitefully towards Christ, working destruction for those who follow them in an error of this description. For the astrologers, alleging that there is one world, divide it into the twelve fixed portions of the zodiacal signs, and call the world of the fixed zodiacal signs one immoveable world ; and the other they

affirm to be a world of erratic (signs), both in power, and position, and number, and that it extends as far as the moon.[3] And (they lay down), that (one) world derives from (the other) world a certain power, and mutual participation (in that power), and that the subjacent obtain this participation from the superjacent (portions). In order, however, that what is (here) asserted may be perspicuous, I shall one by one employ those very expressions of the astrologers ; (and in doing so) I shall only be reminding my readers of statements previously made in the department of the work where we have explained the entire art of the astrologers. What, then, the opinions are which those (speculators) entertain, are as follow : —

(Their doctrine is), that from an emanation of the stars the generations of the subjacent (parts) is consummated. For, as they wistfully gazed upward upon heaven, the Chaldeans asserted that (the seven stars)[4] contain a reason for the efficient causes of the occurrence of all the events that happen unto us, and that the parts of the fixed zodiacal signs co-operate (in this influence). Into twelve (parts they divide the zodiacal circle), and each zodiacal sign into thirty portions, and each portion into sixty diminutive parts ; for so they denominate the very smallest parts, and those that are indivisible. And of the zodiacal signs, they term some male, but others feminine ; and some with two bodies, but others not so ; and some tropical, whereas others firm. The male signs, then, are either feminine, which possess a co-operative nature for the procreation of males, (or are themselves productive of females.) For Aries is a male zodiacal sign, but Taurus female ; and the rest (are denominated) according to the same analogy, some male, but others female. And I suppose that the Pythagoreans, being swayed from such (considerations), style the Monad male, and the Duad female ; and, again, the Triad male, and analogically the remainder of the even and odd numbers. Some, however, dividing each zodiacal sign into twelve parts, employ almost the same method. For example, in Aries, they style the first of the twelve parts both Aries and a male, but the second both Taurus and a female, and the third both Gemini and a male ; and the same plan is pursued in the case of the rest of the parts. And they assert that there are signs with two bodies, viz., Gemini and the signs diametrically opposite, namely Sagittarius, and Virgo, and Pisces, and that the rest have not two bodies. And (they state) that some are likewise tropical, and when the sun stands in these, he causes great turnings[5] of the surrounding (sign). Aries is a sign of this

---

[1] σωματικῶς, i.e, substantially. See Col. i. 19, ii. 9.
[2] ἀφίεται: some read ἀφίει, i.e., dismisses ; some ἀφιεῖ εἰκῆ, i.e., heedlessly casts off. Hippolytus, in his *Summary of the Peratic Heresy* in book x., has ἀφίεται εἰκῆ, which Cruice translates *temere absolvuntur*. Schneidewin has in the same passage ἀφίεται merely, and translates it *abjiciuntur*. In both places Bernays suggests ὀφιοειδῆ, i.e., those of the nature of the Serpent.

[3] Or, " is part of the moon."
[4] Some omissions here are supplied from Sextus Empiricus.
[5] Or, " produces alterations and causes turnings."

description, and that which is diametrically opposite to it, just as Libra, and Capricorn, and Cancer. For in Aries is the vernal turning, and in Capricorn that of winter, and in Cancer that of summer, and in Libra that of autumn.

The details, however, concerning this system we have minutely explained in the book preceding this; and from it any one who wishes instruction (on the point), may learn how it is that the originators of this Peratic heresy, viz., Euphrates the Peratic, and Celbes the Carystian,[1] have, in the transference (into their own system of opinions from these sources), made alterations in name only, while in reality they have put forward similar tenets. (Nay more), they have, with immoderate zeal, themselves devoted (their attention) to the art (of the astrologers). For also the astrologers speak of the limits of the stars, in which they assert that the dominant stars have greater influence; as, for instance, on some they act injuriously, while on others they act well. And of these they denominate some malicious, and some beneficent. And (stars) are said to look upon one another, and to harmonize with each other, so that they appear according to (the shape of) a triangle or square. The stars, looking on one another, are figured according to (the shape of[2]) a triangle, having an intervening distance of the extent of three zodiacal signs; whereas (those that have an interval of) two zodiacal signs are figured according to (the shape of) a square. And (their doctrine is), that as in the same way as in a man, the subjacent parts sympathize with the head, and the head likewise sympathizes with the subjacent parts, so all terrestrial (sympathize) with superlunar[3] objects. But (the astrologers go further than this[4]); for there exists (according to them) a certain difference and incompatibility[5] between these, so as that they do not involve one and the same union. This combination and divergence of the stars, which is a Chaldean (tenet), has been arrogated to themselves by those of whom we have previously spoken.

Now these, falsifying the name of truth, proclaim as a doctrine of Christ an insurrection of Æons and revolts of good into (the ranks of) evil powers; and they speak of the confederations of good powers with wicked ones. Denominating them, therefore, Toparchai and Proastioi,[6] and (though thus) framing for themselves very many other names not suggested (to them from other sources), they have yet unskilfully systematized the entire imaginary doctrine of the astrologers concerning the stars. And since they have introduced a supposition pregnant with immense error, they shall be refuted through the instrumentality of our admirable arrangement. For I shall set down, in contrast with the previously mentioned Chaldaic art of the astrologers, some of the Peratic[7] treatises, from which, by means of comparison, there will be an opportunity of perceiving how the Peratic doctrines are those confessedly of the astrologers, not of Christ.

CHAP. IX. — SYSTEM OF THE PERATÆ EXPLAINED OUT OF ONE OF THEIR OWN BOOKS.

It seems, then, expedient to set forth a certain one of the books held[8] in repute amongst them, in which the following passage[9] occurs: " I am a voice of arousal from slumber in the age of night. Henceforward I commence to strip the power which is from chaos. The power is that of the lowest depth of mud, which uprears the slime of the incorruptible (and) humid expanse of space. And it is the entire power of the convulsion, which, ever in motion, and presenting the colour of water, whirls things on that are stationary, restrains things tremulous, sets things free as they proceed, lightens[10] things as they abide, removes things on the increase, a faithful steward of the track of the breezes, enjoying the things disgorged from the twelve eyes of the law,[11] (and) manifesting a seal[12] to the power which along with itself distributes the downborne invisible waters, and has been called Thalassa. This power ignorance has been accustomed to denominate Cronus, guarded with chains because he tightly bound the fold of the

---

[1] Celbes, as observed in a former note, has two other forms in *The Refutation*, viz., Acembes and Ademes. He is called Carystius, and the other founder of the heresy Peraticus. As the latter term is frequently used to designate Eubœa, i.e., the country beyond (πέραν) the continent, it is inferred that Carystius has a similar import. This would seem placed beyond conjecture by a passage (*Strom.*, vii. vol. ii. p. 555) in Clemens Alexandrinus, already alluded to, who says that some heresies, e.g., those of the Marcionites and Basilidians, derived their denomination from the names, whereas others from the country, of their founders. As an instance of the latter, he mentions the Peratics (see note 4, p. 62, [and note 6, p. 58]).

[2] Some deficiencies in the text are filled up from Sextus Empiricus.

[3] Or, "celestial."

[4] This expression ἀλλὰ γάρ requires to have the ellipsis supplied as above. It may be freely rendered " nay more." Miller reads Ἀλλη γάρ, i.e. " There is some other difference," etc.; but this does not agree with Sextus Empiricus.

[5] Or, "sympathy:" συμπάθεια is, however, properly altered into ἀσυμπάθεια on the authority of Sextus.

[6] i.e., " Rulers of localities and suburbans."

[7] The Peratic heresy both Hippolytus and Theodoret state to have originated from Euphrates. Origen, on the other hand, states (*Contr. Cels.*, vi. 28, [vol. iv. p. 586]) that Euphrates was founder of the Ophites. The inference from this is, that Origen was not author of *The Refutation*.

[8] Hippolytus at the end of this chapter mentions the title of one of their books, Οἱ προάστειοι ἕως αἰθέρος, " The Suburbans up to the Air." Bunsen suggests Περάται ἕως αἰθέρος, " The Transcendental Etherians." (See note 1 *supra*.)

[9] The Abbe Cruice considers that the following system of cosmogony is translated into Greek from some Chaldaic or Syriac work. He recognises in it likewise a Jewish element, to be accounted for from the fact that the Jews during the Babylonish captivity imbibed the principles of the Oriental philosophy. What, therefore, is given by Hippolytus may have a Judaistic origin.

[10] Schneidewin considers the text here corrupt.

[11] The Abbe Cruice observes that the reference here is to the second book of the law (Ex. xv. 27), where mention is made of the twelve fountains of Elim. The Hebrew word (עין) stands for both an eye and a fountain. Hence the error by the Greek translator.

[12] i.e., a poetic expression, as Cruice remarks, for closing the seal. (See Job ix. 7.)

dense and misty and obscure and murky Tartarus. According to the image of this were produced Cepheus, Prometheus, (and) Japetus. The Power to which has been entrusted Thalassa[1] is hermaphrodite. And it fastens the hissing sound arising from the twelve mouths into twelve pipes, and pours it forth. And the power itself is subtle, and removes the controlling, boisterous, upward motion (of the sea), and seals the tracks of its paths, lest (any antagonistic power) should wage war or introduce any alteration. The tempestuous daughter of this one is a faithful protectress of all sorts of waters. Her name is Chorzar. Ignorance is in the habit of styling this (power) Neptune, according to whose image was produced Glaucus, Melicertes, Ino, Nebroë.[2] He that is encircled with the pyramid of twelve angels,[3] and darkens the gate into the pyramid with various colours, and completes the entire in the sable hues of Night: this one ignorance denominated Cronus.[4] And his ministers were five, — first U, second Aoai, third Uo, fourth Uoab, fifth . . . Other trustworthy managers (there are) of his province of night and day, who repose in their own power. Ignorance denominated these the erratic stars, from whom depends a corruptible generation. Manager of the rising of the star[5] is Carphacasemeocheir, (and) Eccabbacara (is the same). Ignorance is in the habit of denominating these Curetes chief of the winds; third in order is Ariel, according to whose image was generated Æolus, Briares. And chief of the twelve-houred nocturnal (power) is Soclan, whom ignorance is accustomed to style Osiris; (and) according to the image of this one was born Admetus, Medea, Helen, Æthusa. Chief of the twelve-houred diurnal power is Euno. This is manager of the rising of the star Protocamarus and of the ethereal (region), but ignorance has denominated him Isis. A sign of this one is the Dog-star, according to whose image were born Ptolemæus son of Arsinoe, Didyma, Cleopatra, and Olympias. God's right-hand power is that which ignorance has denominated Rhea, according to whose image were produced Attis, Mygdon,[6] (and) Œnone. The left-hand power has lordship over sustenance, and ignorance is in the habit of styling this Ceres, (while) her name is Bena; and according to the image of this one were born Celeus, Trip-

tolemus, Misyr, and Praxidica.[7] The right-hand power has lordship over fruits. This one ignorance has denominated Mena, according to whose image were born Bumegas,[8] Ostanes, Mercury Trismegistus, Curites, Petosiris, Zodarium, Berosus, Astrampsuchus, (and) Zoroaster. The left-hand power is (lord) of fire, (and) ignorance has denominated this one Vulcan, according to whose image were born Erichthonius, Achilles, Capaneus, Phaëthon,[9] Meleager, Tydeus, Enceladus, Raphael, Suriel, (and) Omphale. There are three intermediate powers suspended from air, authors of generation. These ignorance has been in the habit of denominating Fates; and according to the image of these were produced the house of Priam, the house of Laius, Ino, Autonoe, Agave, Athamas, Procne, Danaides, and Peliades. A power (there is) hermaphrodite, always continuing in infancy, never waxing old, cause of beauty, pleasure, maturity, desire, and concupiscence; and ignorance has been accustomed to style this Eros, according to whose image were born Paris, Narcissus, Ganymede, Endymion, Tithonus, Icarius, Leda, Amymone, Thetis, Hesperides, Jason, Leander, (and) Hero." These are PRO-ASTIOI up to Æther, for with this title also he inscribes the book.

CHAP. X. — THE PERATIC HERESY NOMINALLY DIFFERENT FROM ASTROLOGY, BUT REALLY THE SAME SYSTEM ALLEGORIZED.

It has been easily made evident to all, that the heresy of the Peratæ is altered in name only from the (art) of the astrologers. And the rest of the books of these (heretics) contain the same method, if it were agreeable to any one to wade through them all. For, as I said, they suppose that the causes of the generation of all begotten things are things unbegotten and superjacent, and that the world with us has been produced after the mode of emanation, which (world) they denominate formal. And (they maintain) that all those stars together which are beheld in the firmament have been causes of the generation of this world. They have, however, altered the name of these, as one may perceive from the PROASTIOI by means of a comparison (of the two systems). And secondly, according to the same method as that whereby the world was made from a supernal emanation, they affirm that in this manner objects here derive from the emanation of the stars their generation, and corruption, and arrangement. Since, then, astrologers are acquainted with the horoscope, and meridian, and setting, and the point opposite the meridian; and since these stars occupy at different

---

[1] Schneidewin refers us to a passage from Berosus, who affirms that this person was styled Thalatta by the Greeks, Thalath by the Chaldeans; another denomination being Omorka, or Omoroka, or Marcaia. The Abbe Cruice, however, sets little value on these names, which, following the judgment of Scaliger, he pronounces spurious. It is unnecessary to remind scholars that the authenticity of Berosus has collapsed under the attacks of modern criticism.
[2] Miller suggests Νεφέλη, Cruice Nebo.
[3] Cruice thinks this may be a figure of the year and of twelve months.
[4] Miller has Κόρην.
[5] Or, "air."
[6] Miller reads Μυγδώνη, others Μυγδόνη.

[7] Miller has Ἀπραξία.
[8] Miller suggests Βουζύγης.
[9] Miller reads Φλέγων.

times different positions[1] in space, on account of the perpetual revolution of the universe, there are (necessarily) at different periods different declinations towards a centre, and (different) ascensions to centres.[2] (Now the Peratic heretics), affixing an allegorical import to this arrangement of the astrologers, delineate the centre, as it were, a god and monad and lord over universal generation, whereas the declination (is regarded by them as a power) on the left, and ascension on the right. When any one, therefore, falling in with the treatises of these (heretics), finds mention among them of right or left power, let him recur to the centre, and the declination, and the ascension (of the Chaldean sages, and) he will clearly observe that the entire system of these (Peratæ) consists of the astrological doctrine.

CHAP. XI. — WHY THEY CALL THEMSELVES PERATÆ ; THEIR THEORY OF GENERATION SUPPORTED BY AN APPEAL TO ANTIQUITY ; THEIR INTERPRETATION OF THE EXODUS OF ISRAEL ; THEIR SYSTEM OF "THE SERPENT ;" DEDUCED BY THEM FROM SCRIPTURE ; THIS THE REAL IMPORT OF THE DOCTRINES OF THE ASTROLOGERS.

They denominate themselves, however, Peratæ, imagining that none of those things existing by generation can escape the determined lot for those things that derive their existence from generation. For if, says (the Peratic), anything be altogether begotten, it also perishes, as also is the opinion of the Sibyl.[3] But we alone, he says, who are conversant with the necessity of generation, and the paths through which man has entered into the world, and who have been accurately instructed (in these matters), we alone are competent to proceed through and pass beyond destruction.[4] But water, he says, is destruction ; nor did the world, he says, perish by any other thing quicker than by water. Water, however, is that which rolls around among the PRO-ASTIOI, (and) they assert (it to be) Cronus. For such a power, he says, is of the colour of water ; and this power, he says — that is, Cronus — none of those things existent by generation can escape. For Cronus is a cause to every generation, in regard of succumbing under destruction, and there could not exist (an instance of) generation in which Cronus does not interfere. This, he says, is what the poets also affirm, and what even appals the gods : —

"For know, he says, this earth and spacious heaven above,
And Styx' flooded water, which is the oath
That greatest is, and dreaded most by gods of happy life."

And not only, he says, do the poets make this statement, but already also the very wisest men among the Greeks. And Heraclitus is even one of these, employing the following words : " For to souls water becomes death." This death, (the Peratic) says, seizes the Egyptians in the Red Sea, along with their chariots. All, however, who are ignorant (of this fact), he says, are Egyptians. And this, they assert, is the departure from Egypt, (that is,) from the body. For they suppose little Egypt to be body, and that it crosses the Red Sea — that is, the water of corruption, which is Cronus — and that it reaches a place beyond the Red Sea, that is, generation ; and that it comes into the wilderness, that is, that it attains a condition independent of generation, where there exist promiscuously all the gods of destruction and the God of salvation.

Now, he says, the stars are the gods of destruction, which impose upon existent things the necessity of alterable generation. These, he says, Moses denominated serpents of the wilderness, which gnaw and utterly ruin those who imagined that they had crossed the Red Sea. To those, then, he says, who of the children of Israel were bitten in the wilderness, Moses exhibited the real and perfect serpent ; and they who believed on this serpent were not bitten in the wilderness, that is, (were not assailed) by (evil) powers. No one therefore, he says, is there who is able to save and deliver those that come forth from Egypt, that is, from the body and from this world, unless alone the serpent that is perfect and replete with fulness. Upon this (serpent), he says, he who fixes his hope is not destroyed by the snakes of the wilderness, that is, by the gods of generation. (This statement) is written, he says, in a book of Moses. This serpent, he says, is the power that attended Moses,[5] the rod that was turned into a serpent. The serpents, however, of the magicians — (that is,) the gods of destruction — withstood the power of Moses in Egypt, but the rod of Moses reduced them all to subjection and slew them. This universal serpent is, he says, the wise discourse of Eve. This, he says, is the mystery of Edem, this the river of Edem ; this the mark that was set upon Cain, that any one who findeth him might not kill him. This, he says,[6] is Cain,[7] whose sacrifice[8] the god of this world did not accept. The gory sacrifice, however, of Abel he

---

[1] γινομένων; some read κινουμένων, i.e , have different motions.
[2] κέντροις: Schneidewin suggests κέντρων.
[3] See *Oracula Sibyllina Fragm.*, ii. ver. 1.
[4] περᾶσαι; hence their name Peratics, i.e., Transcendentalists. Bunsen considers, however, that such a derivation as this was not the true one (see note 1, p. 60), but merely an after-thought. The title of one of the Peratic treatises, as altered by Bunsen from Οἱ προάστειοι ἕως αἰθέρος into Οἱ Περάται ἕως αἰθέρος, i.e., "the Transcendental Etherians," would agree with their subsequent assumption of this title. [Bunsen, i. p. 37.]

[5] Ex. iv. 2-4, 17, vii. 9-13.
[6] Or, " they say."
[7] Gen. iv. 15.
[8] Gen. iv. 5.

approved of; for the ruler of this world rejoices in (offerings of) blood. This, he says, is he who appeared in the last days, in form of a man, in the times of Herod, being born after the likeness of Joseph, who was sold by the hand of his brethren, to whom alone belonged the coat of many colours. This, he says, is he who is according to the likeness of Esau, whose garment — he not being himself present — was blessed; who did not receive, he says, the benediction uttered by him of enfeebled vision.[1] He acquired, however, wealth from a source independent of this, receiving nothing from him whose eyes were dim; and Jacob saw his countenance,[2] as a man beholds the face of God. In regard of this, he says, it has been written that "Nebrod was a mighty hunter before the Lord."[3] And there are, he says, many who closely imitate this (Nimrod): as numerous are they as the gnawing (serpents) which were seen in the wilderness by the children of Israel, from which that perfect serpent which Moses set up delivered those that were bitten. This, he says, is that which has been declared: "In the same manner as Moses lifted up the serpent in the wilderness, so also must the Son of man be lifted up."[4] According to the likeness of this was made in the desert the brazen serpent which Moses set up. Of this alone, he says, the image is in heaven, always conspicuous in light.

This, he says, is the great beginning respecting which Scripture has spoken. Concerning this, he says it has been declared: "In the beginning was the Word, and the Word was with God, and the Word was God. This was in the beginning with God, all things were made by Him, and without Him was not one thing that was made. And what was formed in Him is life."[5] And in Him, he says, has been formed Eve; (now) Eve is life. This, however, he says, is Eve, mother of all living,[6] — a common nature, that is, of gods, angels, immortals, mortals, irrational creatures, (and) rational ones. For, he says, the expression "all" he uttered of all (existences). And if the eyes of any, he says, are blessed, this one, looking upward on the firmament, will behold at the mighty summit[7] of heaven the beauteous image of the serpent, turning itself, and becoming an originating principle of every (species of) motion to all things that are being produced. He will (thereby) know that without him nothing consists, either of things in heaven, or things on earth, or things under the earth. Not night, not

moon, not fruits, not generation, not wealth, not sustenance, not anything at all of existent things, is without his guidance. In regard of this, he says, is the great wonder which is beheld in the firmament by those who are able to observe it. For, he says, at this top of his head, a fact which is more incredible than all things to those who are ignorant, "are setting and rising mingled one with other." This it is in regard of which ignorance is in the habit of affirming: in heaven

"Draco revolves, marvel mighty of monster dread."[8]

And on both sides of him have been placed Corona and Lyra; and above, near the top itself of the head, is visible the piteous man "Engonasis,"

"Holding the right foot's end of Draco fierce."[9]

And at the back of Engonasis is an imperfect serpent, with both hands tightly secured by Anguitenens, and being hindered from touching Corona that lies beside the perfect serpent.

CHAP. XII. — COMPENDIOUS STATEMENT OF THE DOCTRINES OF THE PERATÆ.

This is the diversified wisdom of the Peratic heresy, which it is difficult to declare in its entirety, so intricate is it on account of its seeming to consist of the astrological art. As far forth, then, as this is possible, we shall briefly explain the whole force of this (heresy). In order, however, that we may by a compendious statement elucidate the entire doctrine of these persons, it appears expedient to subjoin the following observations. According to them, the universe is Father, Son, (and) Matter; (but) each of these three has endless capacities in itself. Intermediate, then, between the Matter and the Father sits the Son, the Word, the Serpent, always being in motion towards the unmoved Father, and (towards) Matter itself in motion. And at one time he is turned towards the Father, and receives the powers into his own person; but at another time takes up these powers, and is turned towards Matter. And Matter, (though) devoid of attribute, and being unfashioned, moulds (into itself) forms from the Son which the Son moulded from the Father.

But the Son derives shape from the Father after a mode ineffable, and unspeakable, and unchangeable; (that is,) in such a manner as Moses says that the colours of the conceived (kine) flowed from the rods[10] which were fixed in the drinking-troughs. And in like manner, again, that capacities flowed also from the Son into Matter, similarly to the power in reference to conception which came from the rods upon the conceived (kine). And the difference of

---

[1] Gen. xxvii. 1.
[2] Gen. xxxiii. 10.
[3] Gen. x. 9.
[4] John iii. 14, 15.
[5] John i. 1-4.
[6] The Abbe Cruice thinks that Hippolytus is here quoting from the *Gospel of Eve* (see Epiph., *Hær.*, xxvi. 2).
[7] ἄκρῳ: this is a conjectural reading instead of ἀρχῇ.

[8] Aratus, *Phænom.*, v. 62.
[9] *Ibid.*, v. 46.
[10] Gen. xxx. 37-39.

colours, and the dissimilarity which flowed from the rods through the waters upon the sheep, is, he says, the difference of corruptible and incorruptible generation. As, however, one who paints from nature, though he takes nothing away from animals, transfers by his pencil all forms to the canvas; so the Son, by a power which belongs to himself, transfers paternal marks from the Father into Matter. All the paternal marks are here, and there are not any more. For if any one, he says, of those (beings) which are here will have strength to perceive that he is a paternal mark transferred hither from above, (and that he is) incarnate — just as by the conception resulting from the rod a something white is produced, — he is of the same substance altogether with the Father in heaven, and returns thither. If, however, he may not happen upon this doctrine, neither will he understand the necessity of generation, just as an abortion born at night will perish at night. When, therefore, he says, the Saviour observes, "your Father which is in heaven,"[1] he alludes to that one from whom the Son deriving his characteristics has transferred them hither. When, however, (Jesus) remarks, "Your father is a murderer from the beginning,"[2] he alludes to the Ruler and Demiurge of matter, who, appropriating the marks delivered from the Son, generated him here who from the beginning was a murderer, for his work causes corruption and death.

No one, then, he says, can be saved or return (into heaven) without the Son, and the Son is the Serpent. For as he brought down from above the paternal marks, so again he carries up from thence those marks roused from a dormant condition and rendered paternal characteristics, substantial ones from the unsubstantial Being, transferring them hither from thence. This, he says, is what is spoken: "I am the door."[3] And he transfers (those marks), he says,[4] to those who close the eyelid, as the naphtha drawing the fire in every direction towards itself; nay rather, as the magnet (attracting) the iron and not anything else, or just as the backbone of the sea falcon, the gold and nothing else, or as the chaff is led by the amber. In this manner, he says, is the portrayed, perfect, and consubstantial genus drawn again from the world by the Serpent; nor does he (attract) anything else, as it has been sent down by him. For a proof of this, they adduce the anatomy[5] of the brain, assimilating, from the fact of its immobility, the

brain itself to the Father, and the cerebellum to the Son, because of its being moved and being of the form of (the head of) a serpent. And they allege that this (cerebellum), by an ineffable and inscrutable process, attracts through the pineal gland the spiritual and life-giving substance emanating from the vaulted chamber[6] (in which the brain is embedded). And on receiving this, the cerebellum in an ineffable manner imparts the ideas, just as the Son does, to matter; or, in other words, the seeds and the genera of the things produced according to the flesh flow along into the spinal marrow. Employing this exemplar, (the heretics) seem to adroitly introduce their secret mysteries, which are delivered in silence. Now it would be impious for us to declare these; yet it is easy to form an idea of them, by reason of the many statements that have been made.

CHAP. XIII. — THE PERATIC HERESY NOT GENERALLY KNOWN.

But since I consider that I have plainly explained the Peratic heresy, and by many (arguments) have rendered evident (a system that hitherto) has always escaped notice, and is altogether[7] a tissue of fable, and one that disguises its own peculiar venom, it seems expedient to advance no further statement beyond those already put forward; for the opinions propounded by (the heretics) themselves are sufficient for their own condemnation.

CHAP. XIV. — THE SYSTEM OF THE SETHIANS; THEIR TRIAD OF INFINITE PRINCIPLES; THEIR HERESY EXPLAINED; THEIR INTERPRETATION OF THE INCARNATION.

Let us then see what the Sithians[8] affirm. To these it appears that there are three definite principles of the universe, and that each of these principles possesses infinite powers. And when they speak of powers[9] let him that heareth take into account that they make this statement. Everything whatsoever you discern by an act of intelligence, or also omit (to discern) as not being understood, this by nature is fitted to become each of the principles, as in the human soul every art whatsoever which is made the subject of instruction. Just for instance, he says, this child will be a musician, having waited

---

[1] Matt. vii. 11.
[2] John viii. 44.
[3] John x. 7.
[4] There is a hiatus here. Miller, who also suggests διαφέρει instead of μεταφέρει, supplies the deficiency as translated above. The Abbe Cruice fills up the hiatus by words taken from a somewhat similar passage in the third chapter of book viii., but the obscurity still remains. Miller thinks there is a reference to Isa vi. 10.
[5] This theory has been previously alluded to by Hippolytus in the last chapter of book iv.

[6] καμαρίου: some would read μακαρίου ["the dome of thought, the palace of the soul"].
[7] παντάπασι: some read πάντα πᾶσι. Cruice suggests πᾶσιν ἐπιτιθειμένην, i.e., one that plots against all.
[8] This is the form in which the name occurs in Hippolytus, but the correct one is Sethians. As regards this sect, see Irenæus, Contr. Hæres., i. 30; Tertullian, Præscript., c. lxvii.; Theodoret, Hæret. Fabul., i. 14; Epiphanius, Advers. Hæres., c. xxviii., xxxvii; and xxxix.; Augustine, De Hæret., c. xix.; Josephus, Antiq. Judaic., i. 2; Suidas on the word "Seth."
[9] For δυνάμεις . . . λογιζέσθω, Bernays reads δυνάται . . . λογίζεσθαι: "While these make (such) assertions, he is able to calculate," etc.

the requisite time for (acquiring a knowledge of) the harp; or a geometrician, (having previously undergone the necessary study for acquiring a knowledge) of geometry; (or) a grammarian, (after having sufficiently studied) grammar; (or) a workman, (having acquired a practical acquaintance) with a handicraftsman's business; and to one brought into contact with the rest of the arts a similar occurrence will take place. Now of principles, he says, the substances are light and darkness; and of these, spirit is intermediate without admixture. The spirit, however, is that which has its appointed place in the midst of darkness which is below, and light which is above. It is not spirit as a current of wind, or some gentle breeze that can be felt; but, as it were, some odour of ointment or of incense formed out of a compound. (It is) a subtle power, that insinuates itself by means of some impulsive quality in a fragrance, which is inconceivable and better than could be expressed by words. Since, however, light is above and darkness below, and spirit is intermediate in such a way as stated between these; and since light is so constituted, that, like a ray of the sun, it shines from above upon the underlying darkness; and again, since the fragrance of the spirit, holding an intermediate place, is extended and carried in every direction, as in the case of incense-offerings placed upon fire, we detect the fragrance that is being wafted in every direction: when, I say, there is a power of this description belonging unto the principles which are classified under three divisions, the power of spirit and light simultaneously exists in the darkness that is situated underneath them. But the darkness is a terrible water, into which light is absorbed and translated into a nature of the same description with spirit. The darkness, however, is not devoid of intelligence, but altogether reflective, and is conscious that, where the light has been abstracted from the darkness, the darkness remains isolated, invisible, obscure, impotent, inoperative, (and) feeble. Wherefore it is constrained, by all its reflection and understanding, to collect into itself the lustre and scintillation of light with the fragrance of the spirit. And it is possible to behold an image of the nature of these in the human countenance; for instance, the pupil of the eye, dark from the subjacent humours, (but) illuminated with spirit. As, then, the darkness seeks after the splendour, that it may keep in bondage the spark, and may have perceptive power, so the light and spirit seek after the power that belongs to themselves, and strive to uprear, and towards each other to carry up their intermingled powers into the dark and formidable water lying underneath.

But all the powers of the three originating principles, which are as regards number indefi-nitely infinite, are each according to its own substance reflective and intelligent, unnumbered in multitude. And since what are reflective and intelligent are numberless in multitude, while they continue by themselves, they are all at rest. If, however, power approaches power, the dissimilarity of (what is set in) juxtaposition produces a certain motion and energy, which are formed from the motion resulting from the concourse effected by the juxtaposition of the coalescing powers. For the concourse of the powers ensues, just like any mark of a seal that is impressed by means of the concourse correspondingly with (the seal) which prints the figure on the substances that are brought up (into contact with it). Since, therefore, the powers of the three principles are infinite in number, and from infinite powers (arise) infinite concourses, images of infinite seals are necessarily produced. These images, therefore, are the forms of the different sorts of animals. From the first great concourse, then, of the three principles, ensues a certain great form, a seal of heaven and earth. The heaven and the earth have a figure similar to the womb, having a navel in the midst; and if, he says, any one is desirous of bringing this figure under the organ of vision, let him artfully scrutinize the pregnant womb of whatsoever animal he wishes, and he will discover an image of the heaven and the earth, and of the things which in the midst of all are unalterably situated underneath.

(And so it is, that the first great concourse of the three principles) has produced such a figure of heaven and earth as is similar to a womb after the first coition. But, again, in the midst of the heaven and the earth have been generated infinite concourses of powers. And each concourse did not effect and fashion anything else than a seal of heaven and earth similar to a womb. But, again, in the earth, from the infinite seals are produced infinite crowds of various animals. But into all this infinity of the different animals under heaven is diffused and distributed, along with the light, the fragrance of the Spirit from above. From the water, therefore, has been produced a first-begotten originating principle, viz., wind, (which is) violent and boisterous, and a cause of all generation. For producing a sort of ferment in the waters, (the wind) uplifts waves out of the waters; and the motion[2] of the waves, just as when some impulsive power of pregnancy is the origin of the production of a man or mind,[3] is caused when (the ocean), excited by the impulsive power of spirit, is propelled forward. When, however, this wave that

---

[1] Or, "form of a seal."
[2] Or, "production."
[3] This is Cruice's mode of supplying the hiatus. Miller has "man or ox."

has been raised out of the water by the wind, and rendered pregnant in its nature, has within itself obtained the power, possessed by the female, of generation, it holds together the light scattered from above along with the fragrance of the spirit — that is, mind moulded in the different species. And this (light) is a perfect God, who from the unbegotten radiance above, and from the spirit, is borne down into human nature as into a temple, by the impulsive power of Nature, and by the motion of wind. And it is produced from water being commingled[1] and blended with bodies as if it were a salt[2] of existent things, and a light of darkness. And it struggles to be released from bodies, and is not able to find liberation and an egress for itself. For a very diminutive spark, a severed splinter from above like the ray of a star, has been mingled in the much compounded waters of many (existences),[3] as, says he, (David) remarks in a psalm.[4] Every thought, then, and solicitude actuating the supernal light is as to how and in what manner mind may be liberated, by the death of the depraved and dark body, from the Father that is below, which is the wind that with noise[5] and tumult uplifted the waves, and who generated a perfect mind his own Son; not, however, being his peculiar (offspring) substantially. For he was a ray (sent down) from above, from that perfect light, (and) was overpowered in the dark,[6] and formidable, and bitter, and defiled water; and he is a luminous spirit borne down over the water.[7] When, therefore, the waves that have been upreared from the waters have received within themselves the power of generation possessed by females, they contain, as a certain womb, in different species, the infused radiance, so as that it is visible in the case of all animals.[8] But the wind, at the same time fierce and formidable,[9] whirling along, is, in respect of its hissing sound, like a serpent.[10]

First, then, from the wind — that is, from the serpent — has resulted the originating principle of generation in the manner declared, all things having simultaneously received the principle of generation. After, then, the light and the spirit

had been received, he says, into the polluted and baneful (and) disordered womb, the serpent — the wind of the darkness, the first-begotten of the waters — enters within and produces man, and the impure womb neither loves nor recognises any other form. The perfect Word of supernal light being therefore assimilated (in form) to the beast, (that is,) the serpent, entered into the defiled womb, having deceived (the womb) through the similitude of the beast itself, in order that (the Word) may loose the chains that encircle the perfect mind which has been begotten amidst impurity of womb by the primal offspring of water, (namely,) serpent, wind, (and) beast.[11] This, he says, is the form of the servant,[12] and this the necessity of the Word of God coming down into the womb of a virgin. But he says it is not sufficient that the Perfect Man, the Word, has entered into the womb of a virgin, and loosed the pangs[13] which were in that darkness. Nay, more than this was requisite; for after his entrance[14] into the foul mysteries of the womb, he was washed, and drank of the cup of life-giving bubbling water.[15] And it was altogether needful that he should drink who was about to strip off the servile form, and assume celestial raiment.

CHAP. XV. — THE SETHIANS SUPPORT THEIR DOCTRINES BY AN ALLEGORICAL INTERPRETATION OF SCRIPTURE; THEIR SYSTEM REALLY DERIVED FROM NATURAL PHILOSOPHERS AND FROM THE ORPHIC RITES; ADOPT THE HOMERIC COSMOGONY.

These are the statements which the patrons[16] of the Sethian doctrines make, as far as it is possible to declare in a few words. Their system, however, is made up (of tenets) from natural (philosophers), and of expressions uttered in reference to different other subjects; and transferring (the sense of) these to the Eternal[17] Logos, they explain them as we have declared. But they assert likewise that Moses confirms their doctrine when he says, "Darkness, and mist, and tempest." These, (the Sethian) says, are the three principles (of our system); or when he states that three were born in paradise — Adam, Eve, the serpent; or when he speaks of three (persons, namely) Cain, Abel, Seth;

---

[1] Or, "concealed."

[2] ἅλας τῶν γενομένων: Miller reads ἀλάλων.

[3] The hiatus, as filled up by Miller, is adopted above. The Abbe Cruice suggests the following emendation: "For there has been intermingled a certain very diminutive spark from the light (subsisting) along with the supernal fragrance, from the spirit producing, like a ray, composition in things dissolved, and dissolution in things compounded."

[4] Ps. xxix. 3.

[5] βρόμῳ: some read βρασμῷ, i.e., agitation, literally a boiling up.

[6] σκοτεινῷ: some read σκολιῷ (which is of similar import), crooked, i.e., involved, obscure.

[7] Or, "the light."

[8] A hiatus occurs here. The deficiency is supplied by Cruice from previous statements of Hippolytus, and is adopted above.

[9] Or, "strong."

[10] This passage is obscure. The translation above follows Schneidewin and Cruice. Miller's text would seem capable of this meaning: "The wind, simultaneously fierce and formidable, is whirled along like a trailing serpent supplied with wings." His text is, τῷ σύρματι ὄφει παραπλήσιος πτερωτός, but suggests πτερωτῷ ὡς ἀπὸ.

[11] Schneidewin has a full stop after "wind," and begins the next sentence with θηρίου (beast).

[12] Phil. ii. 7.

[13] Acts ii. 24.

[14] Miller would read μετὰ τὰ . . . ἐξελθὼν, "after the foul mysteries of the womb he went forth," etc.

[15] John iv. 7-14. For πιεῖν some read ποιεῖν, "a course which he must pursue who," etc.

[16] προστάται. This is a military expression applied to those placed in the foremost ranks of a battalion of soldiers; but it was also employed in civil affairs, to designate, for instance at Athens, those who protected the μέτοικοι (aliens), and others without the rights of citizenship. Προστάτης was the Roman Patronus.

[17] Or, "their own peculiar."

and again of three (others) — Shem, Ham,[1] Japheth ; or when he mentions three patriarchs — Abraham, Isaac, Jacob ; or when he speaks of the existence of three days before sun and moon ; or when he mentions three laws — prohibitory, permissive, and adjudicatory of punishment. Now, a prohibitory law is as follows : "Of every tree that is in paradise thou mayest freely eat ; but of the tree of the knowledge of good and evil thou mayest not eat."[2] But in the passage, "Come forth from thy land and from thy kindred, and hither into a land which I shall show thee,"[3] this law, he says, is permissive ; for one who is so disposed may depart, and one who is not so disposed may remain. But a law adjudicatory of punishment is that which makes the following declaration : "Thou shalt not commit adultery, thou shalt not kill, thou shalt not steal ; "[4] for a penalty is awarded to each of these acts of wickedness.

The entire system of their doctrine, however, is (derived) from[5] the ancient theologians Musæus, and Linus, and Orpheus,[6] who elucidates especially the ceremonies of initiation, as well as the mysteries themselves. For their doctrine concerning the womb is also the tenet of Orpheus ; and the (idea of the) navel,[7] which is harmony,[8] is (to be found) with the same symbolism attached to it in the Bacchanalian orgies of Orpheus. But prior to the observance of the mystic rite of Celeus, and Triptolemus, and Ceres, and Proserpine, and Bacchus in Eleusis, these orgies have been celebrated and handed down to men in Phlium of Attica.[9] For antecedent to the Eleusinian mysteries, there are (enacted) in Phlium the orgies[10] of her denominated the "Great (Mother)." There is, however, a portico in this (city), and on the portico is inscribed a representation, (visible) up to the present day, of all the words which are spoken (on such occasions). Many, then, of the words inscribed upon that portico are those respecting

which Plutarch institutes discussions in his ten books against[11] Empedocles. And in the greater[12] number of these books is also drawn the representation of a certain aged man, grey-haired, winged,[13] having his *pudendum erectum*, pursuing a retreating woman of azure colour.[14] And over the aged man is the inscription "phaos ruentes," and over the woman "pereëphicola."[15] But "phaos ruentes"[16] appears to be the light (which exists), according to the doctrine of the Sethians, and "phicola" the darkish water ; while the space in the midst of these seems to be a harmony constituted from the spirit that is placed between. The name, however, of "phaos ruentes" manifests, as they allege, the flow from above of the light downwards. Wherefore one may reasonably assert that the Sethians celebrate rites among themselves, very closely bordering upon those orgies of the "Great (Mother)" which are observed among) the Phliasians. And the poet likewise seems to bear his testimony to this triple division, when he remarks, "And all things have been triply divided, and everything obtains its (proper) distinction ; "[17] that is, each member of the threefold division has obtained (a particular) capacity. But now, as regards the tenet that the subjacent water below, which is dark, ought, because the light has set (over it), to convey upwards and receive the spark borne down from (the light) itself ; in the assertion of this tenet, I say, the all-wise Sethians appear to derive (their opinion) from Homer : —

"By earth I sware, and yon broad Heaven above,
And Stygian stream beneath, the weightiest oath
Of solemn power, to bind the blessed gods."[18]

That is, according to Homer, the gods suppose water to be loathsome and horrible. Now, similar to this is the doctrine of the Sethians, which affirms (water) to be formidable to the mind.[19]

CHAP. XVI. — THE SETHIAN THEORY CONCERNING "MIXTURE" AND "COMPOSITION ; " APPLICATION OF IT TO CHRIST ; ILLUSTRATION FROM THE WELL OF AMPA.

These, and other assertions similar to these, are made (by the Sethians) in their interminable

---

[1] It is written Cham in the text.
[2] Gen. ii. 16, 17.
[3] Gen. xii. 1.
[4] Ex. xx. 13-15 ; Deut. v. 17-19.
[5] ὑπὸ, Miller.
[6] These belong to the legendary period of Greek philosophy. Musæus flourished among the Athenians, Linus among the Thebans, and Orpheus among the Thracians. They weaved their physical theories into crude theological systems, which subsequently suggested the cosmogony and theogony of Hesiod. See the translator's *Treatise on Metaphysics*, chap. ii. pp. 33, 34.
[7] ὀμφαλός : some read with greater probability φαλλὸς, which means the figure, generally wooden, of a *membrum virile*. This harmonizes with what Hippolytus has already mentioned respecting Osiris. A figure of this description was carried in solemn procession in the orgies of Bacchus as a symbol of the generative power of nature. The worship of the Lingam among the Hindoos is of the same description.
[8] ἁρμονία (Schneidewin). Cruice reads ἀνδρεία (manliness), which agrees with φαλλὸς (see preceding note). For φαλλὸς Schneidewin reads ὀμφαλὸς (navel).
[9] "Of Achaia" (Meinekius, *Vindic. Strab.*, p. 242).
[10] The reading in Miller is obviously incorrect, viz., λεγομένη μεγαληγορια, for which he suggests μεγάλη ἑορτή. Several other emendations have been proposed, but they scarcely differ from the rendering given above, which is coincident with what may be learned of these mysteries from other sources.

[11] πρὸς, or it might be rendered "respecting." A reference, however, to the catalogue of Empedocles' works, given by Fabricius (t. v. p. 160), shows that for πρὸς we should read εἰς.
[12] πλείοστι : Miller would read πυλεωσι, i.e., gateways.
[13] Or πετρωτὸς, intended for πετρώδης, "made of stone." [A winged *phallus* was worn by the women of Pompeii as an ornament, for which Christian women substituted a cross. See vol. iii., this series, p. 104.]
[14] κυανοειδῆ : some read κυνοειδῆ, i.e., like a dog.
[15] Some read Persephone (Proserpine) Phlya.
[16] For "phaos ruentes" some read "Phanes rueis," which is the expression found in the Orphic hymn (see Cruice's note).
[17] *Iliad*, xv. 189. (See the passage from Hesiod given at the end of book i. of *The Refutation*.)
[18] *Iliad*, xv. 36-38 (Lord Derby's translation) ; *Odyssey*, v. 185-187.
[19] Miller reasonably proposes for τῷ νοῒ the reading στοιχεῖον, "which affirms water to be a formidable element."

commentaries. They, however, persuade their disciples to become conversant with the theory respecting composition and mixture. But this theory has formed a subject of meditation to many, but (among others) also to Andronicus the Peripatetic. The Sethians, then, affirm that the theory concerning composition and mixture is constituted according to the following method : The luminous ray from above is intermingled, and the very diminutive spark is delicately blended in the dark waters beneath ; and (both of these) become united, and are formed into one compound mass, just as a single savour (results) from the mixture of many incense-offerings in the fire, and (just as) an adept, by having a test in an acute sense of smell, ought to be able from the single odour of the incense to distinguish accurately each (ingredient) of the incense-offerings that have been mingled in the fire, — whether, for example, storax, and myrrh, and frankincense, or whatever other (ingredient) n.ay be mixed (in the incense). They, however, employ also other examples, saying both that brass is mixed with gold, and that some art has been discovered which separates the brass from the gold. And, in like manner, if tin or brass, or any substance homogeneous with it, be discovered mixed with silver, these likewise, by some art superior to that of mixing, are distinguished. But already some one also distinguishes water mingled with wine.[1] So, say they, though all things are commingled, they are capable of being separated. Nay, but, he says, derive the same lesson from the case of animals. For when the animal is dead, each of its parts is separated ; and when dissolution takes place, the animal in this way vanishes. This is, he says, what has been spoken : " I came not to send peace on the earth, but a sword,"[2] — that is, the division and separation of the things that have been commingled. For each of the things that have been commingled is separated and divided when it reaches its proper place. For as there is one place of mixture for all animals, so also has there been established one (locality) of separation. And, he says, no one is aware of this (place), save we alone that have been born again, spiritual, not carnal, whose citizenship is in heaven above.

In this manner insinuating themselves, they corrupt their pupils, partly by misusing the words spoken (by themselves), while they wickedly pervert, to serve any purpose they wish, what has been admirably said (in Scripture) ; and

partly by concealing their nefarious conduct, by means of whatever comparisons they please. All these things, then, he says, that have been commingled, possess, as has been declared, their own particular place, and hurry towards their own peculiar (substances), as iron towards the magnet, and the chaff to the vicinity of amber, and the gold to the spur[3] of the sea falcon. In like manner, the *ray*[4] of light which has been commingled with the water, having obtained from discipline and instruction its own proper locality, hastens towards the Logos that comes from above in servile form ; and along with the Logos exists as a logos in that place where the Logos is still : (the light, I say, hastens to the Logos with greater speed) than the iron towards the magnet.

And that these things, he says, are so, and that all things that have been commingled are separated in their proper places, learn. There is among the Persians in a city Ampa,[5] near the river Tigris, a well ; and near the well, at the top, has been constructed a certain reservoir, supplied with three outlets ; and when one pumps from this well, and draws off some of its contents in a vessel, what is thus pumped out of the well, whatever it is at all, he pours into the reservoir hard by. And when what is thus infused reaches the outlets, and when what is taken up (out of each outlet) in a single vessel is examined, a separation is observed to have taken place. And in the first of the outlets is exhibited a concretion of salt, and in the second of asphalt, and in the third of oil ; and the oil is black, just as, he says, Herodotus[6] also narrates, and it yields a heavy smell, and the Persians call this " rhadinace." The similitude of the well is, say the Sethians, more sufficient for the demonstration of their proposition than all the statements that have been previously made.

CHAP. XVII. — THE SETHIAN DOCTRINES TO BE LEARNED FROM THE " PARAPHRASE OF SETH."

The opinion of the Sethians appears to us to have been sufficiently elucidated. If, however, any one is desirous of learning the entire doctrine according to them, let him read a book inscribed *Paraphrase of Seth ;* for all their secret tenets he will find deposited there. But since we have explained the opinions entertained by the Sethians, let us see also what are the doctrines advanced by Justinus.

---

[1] ὕδωρ μεμιγμένον οἴνῳ διακρίνει: Miller's text is ὕδωρ μεμιγμένον αἰνωδία κρήνη, which is obviously corrupt. His emendation of the passage may be translated thus: "And now some one observes water from a wayside fountain, mixed, so they say ; and even though all things be intermingled, a separation is effected."
[2] Matt. x. 34.

[3] κέντρῳ. In other passages the word κερκίς is used, i.e., the backbone.
[4] Or, " power "
[5] Or, " Ama."
[6] Herodotus, vi. 119.

CHAP. XVIII. — THE SYSTEM OF JUSTINUS ANTI-SCRIPTURAL AND ESSENTIALLY PAGAN.

Justinus [1] was entirely opposed to the teaching of the holy Scriptures, and moreover to the written or oral teaching of the blessed evangelists, according as the Logos was accustomed to instruct His disciples, saying, " Go not into the way of the Gentiles ; " [2] and this signifies that they should not attend to the futile doctrine of the Gentiles. This (heretic) endeavours to lead on his hearers into an acknowledgment of prodigies detailed by the Gentiles, and of doctrines inculcated by them. And he narrates, word for word, legendary accounts prevalent among the Greeks, and does not previously teach or deliver his perfect mystery, unless he has bound his dupe by an oath. Then he brings forward (these) fables for the purpose of persuasion, in order that they who are conversant with the incalculable trifling of these books may have some consolation in the details of these legends. Thus it happens as when in like manner one making a long journey deems it expedient, on having fallen in with an inn, to take repose. And so it is that, when once more they are induced to turn towards studying the diffuse doctrine of these lectures, they may not abhor them while they, undergoing instruction unnecessarily prolix, rush stupified into the transgression devised by (Justinus) ; and previously he binds his followers with horrible oaths, neither to publish nor abjure these doctrines, and forces upon them an acknowledgment (of their truth). And in this manner he delivers the mysteries impiously discovered by himself, partly, according to the statements previously made, availing himself of the Hellenic legends, and partly of those pretended books which, to some extent, bear a resemblance to the foresaid heresies. For all, forced together by one spirit, are drawn into one profound abyss of pollution, inculcating the same tenets, and detailing the same legends, each after a different method. All those, however, style themselves Gnostics in this peculiar sense, that they alone themselves have imbibed the marvellous knowledge of the Perfect and Good (Being).

---

[1] What Hippolytus here states respecting Justinus is quite new. No mention occurs of this heretic in ecclesiastical history. It is evident, however, that, like Simon Magus, he was contemporary with St. Peter and St. Paul. Justinus, however, and the Ophitic sect to which he belonged, are assigned by Hippolytus and Irenæus a prior position as regards the order of their appearance to the system of Simon, or its offshoot Valentinianism. The Ophites engrafted Phrygian Judaism, and the Valentinians Gentilism, upon Christianity : the former not rejecting the speculations and mysteries of Asiatic paganism, and the latter availing themselves of the cabalistic corruptions of Judaism. The Judaistic element soon became prominent in successive phases of Valentinianism, which produced a fusion of the sects of the old Gnostics and of Simon. Hippolytus, however, now places the Ophitic sect before us prior to its amalgamation with Valentinianism. Here, for the first time, we have an authentic delineation of the primitive Ophites. This is of great value. [See Irenæus, vol. i., this series, p. 354 ; also Bunsen (on Baur), vol. i. p. 42.]

[2] Matt. x. 5.

CHAP. XIX. — THE JUSTINIAN HERESY UNFOLDED IN THE " BOOK OF BARUCH."

But swear, says Justinus, if you wish to know " what eye hath not seen, and ear hath not heard, and the things which have not entered into the heart ; " [3] that is, if you wish to know Him who is good above all, Him who is more exalted, (swear) that you will preserve the secrets (of the Justinian) discipline, as intended to be kept silent. For also our Father, on beholding the Good One, and on being initiated with Him, preserved the mysteries respecting which silence is enjoined, and sware, as it has been written, " The Lord sware, and will not repent." [4] Having, then, in this way set the seal to these tenets, he seeks to inveigle (his followers) with more legends, (which are detailed) through a greater number of books ; and so he conducts (his readers) to the Good One, consummating the initiated (by admitting them into) the unspeakable Mysteries.[5] In order, however, that we may not wade through more of their volumes, we shall illustrate the ineffable Mysteries (of Justinus) from one book of his, inasmuch as, according to his supposition, it is (a work) of high repute. Now this volume is inscribed *Baruch ;* and one fabulous account out of many which is explained by (Justinus) in this (volume), we shall point out, inasmuch as it is to be found in Herodotus. But after imparting a different shape to this (account), he explains it to his pupils as if it were something novel, being under the impression that the entire arrangement of his doctrine (springs) out of it.

CHAP. XX. — THE COSMOGONY OF JUSTINUS AN ALLEGORICAL EXPLANATION OF HERODOTUS' LEGEND OF HERCULES.

Herodotus,[6] then, asserts that Hercules, when driving the oxen of Geryon from Erytheia,[7] came into Scythia, and that, being wearied with travelling, he retired into some desert spot and slept for a short time. But while he slumbered his horse disappeared, seated on which he had performed his lengthened journey. On being aroused from repose, he, however, instituted a diligent search through the desert, endeavouring to discover his horse. And though he is unsuccessful in his search after the horse, he yet finds in the desert a certain damsel, half of whose form was that of woman, and proceeded to question her if she had seen the horse anywhere. The girl, however, replies that she had seen (the animal), but that she would not show him unless

---

[3] Isa. lxiv. 4 ; 1 Cor. ii. 9.

[4] Ps. cx. 4 ; Heb. vii. 21.

[5] Or, " the rest of the Mysteries."

[6] Herodotus, iv. 8-10.

[7] Erytheia (Eretheia) was the island which Geryon inhabited. Miller's text has Ἐρυθᾶς (i.e., sc. Θαλάσσης), " the Red Sea." This, however, is a mistake.

Hercules previously would come along with her for the purpose of sexual intercourse. Now Herodotus informs us that her upper parts as far as the groin were those of a virgin, but that everything below the body after the groin presented some horrible appearance of a snake. In anxiety, however, for the discovery of his horse, Hercules complies with the monster's request; for he knew her (carnally), and made her pregnant. And he foretold, after coition, that she had by him in her womb three children at the same time, who were destined to become illustrious. And he ordered that she, on bringing forth, should impose on the children as soon as born the following names: Agathyrsus, Gelonus, and Scytha. And as the reward of this (favour) receiving his horse from the beast-like damsel, he went on his way, taking with him the cattle also. But after these (details), Herodotus has a protracted account; adieu, however, to it for the present.[1] But what the opinions are of Justinus, who transfers this legend into (his account of) the generation of the universe, we shall explain.

CHAP. XXI. — JUSTINUS' TRIAD OF PRINCIPLES; HIS ANGELOGRAPHY FOUNDED ON THIS TRIAD; HIS EXPLANATION OF THE BIRTH, LIFE, AND DEATH OF OUR LORD.

This (heresiarch) makes the following statement. There are three unbegotten principles of the universe, two male (and) one female. Of the male (principles), however, a certain one is denominated good, and it alone is called after this manner, and possesses a power of prescience concerning the universe. But the other is father[2] of all begotten things, devoid of prescience,[3] and invisible. And the female (principle) is devoid of prescience, passionate, two-minded,[4] two-bodied, in every respect answering (the description of) the girl in the legend of Herodotus, as far as the groin a virgin, and (in) the parts below (resembling) a snake, as Justinus says. But this girl is styled Edem and Israel. And these principles of the universe are, he says, roots and fountains from which existing things have been produced, but that there was not anything else. The Father, then, who is devoid of prescience, beholding that half-woman Edem, passed into a concupiscent desire for her. But this Father, he says, is called Elohim. Not less did Edem also long for Elohim, and the mutual passion brought them together into the one nuptial couch of love.[5]

And from such an intercourse the Father generates out of Edem unto himself twelve angels. And the names of the angels begotten by the Father are these: Michaël, Amen,[6] Baruch, Gabriel, Esaddæus. . . . And of the maternal angels which Edem brought forth, the names in like manner have been subjoined, and they are as follows: Babel,[7] Achamoth, Naas, Bel, Belias, Satan, Saël, Adonæus, Leviathan,[8] Pharao, Carcamenos, (and) Lathen.

Of these twenty-four angels the paternal ones are associated with the Father, and do all things according to His will; and the maternal (angels are associated with) Edem the Mother. And the multitude of all these angels together is Paradise, he says, concerning which Moses speaks: "God planted a garden in Eden towards the east,"[9] that is, towards the face of Edem, that Edem might behold the garden — that is, the angels — continually. Allegorically the angels are styled trees of this garden, and the tree of life is the third of the paternal angels — Baruch. And the tree of the knowledge of good and evil is the third of the maternal angels — Naas. For so,[10] says (Justinus), one ought to interpret the words of Moses, observing, "Moses said these things disguisedly, from the fact that all do not attain the truth." And, he says, Paradise being formed from the conjugal joy of Elohim and Edem, the angels of Elohim receiving from the most beauteous earth, that is, not from the portion of Edem resembling a monster, but from the parts above the groin of human shape, and gentle — in aspect, — make man out of the earth. But out of the parts resembling a monster are produced wild beasts, and the rest of the animal creation. They made man, therefore, as a symbol of the unity and love (subsisting) between them; and they depute their own powers unto him, Edem the soul, but Elohim the spirit. And the man Adam is produced as some actual seal and memento of love, and as an everlasting emblem of the marriage of Edem and Elohim. And in like manner also Eve was produced, he says, as Moses has described, an image and emblem (as well as) a seal, to be preserved for ever, of Edem. And in like manner also a soul was deposited in Eve, — an image — from Edem, but a spirit from Elohim. And there were given to them commandments, "Be fruitful, and multiply, and replenish the earth,"[11] that is, Edem; for so he wishes that it had been written. For the entire of the power belonging unto herself, Edem conferred upon Elohim as a sort of nuptial dowry. Whence, he says, from imitation of that

---

[1] Some read τὸν νοῦν, which has been properly altered into τὸ νῦν, as translated above.
[2] Or, "mother."
[3] καὶ ἄγνωστος, "and unknown," is added in Cruice's and Schneidewin's text, as this word occurs in Hippolytus' epitome of Justinus' heresy in book x. of *The Refutation*.
[4] διγνώμος: some read ἀγνώμων, i.e., devoid of judgment.
[5] εὐνήν: some read εὔνοιαν, i.e., goodwill, but this seems pleonastic where φιλίας precedes.

[6] See Rev. iii. 14. [Bunsen, i. 39.]
[7] Or, "Babelachamos," or "Babel, Achamos."
[8] Or, "Kaviathan."
[9] Gen. ii. 8.
[10] Or, "this one."
[11] Gen. i. 28.

primary marriage up to this day, women bring a dowry to their husbands, complying with a certain divine and paternal law that came into existence on the part of Edem towards Elohim.

And when all things were created as has been described by Moses — both heaven and earth, and the things therein [1] — the twelve angels of the Mother were divided into four principles, and each fourth part of them is called a river — Phison, and Gehon, and Tigris, and Euphrates, as, he says, Moses states. These twelve angels, being mutually connected, go about into four parts, and manage the world, holding from Edem a sort of viceregal [2] authority over the world. But they do not always continue in the same places, but move around as if in a circular dance, changing place after place, and at set times and intervals retiring to the localities subject to themselves. And when Phison holds sway over places, famine, distress, and affliction prevail in that part of the earth, for the battalion of these angels is niggardly. In like manner also there belong to each part of the four, according to the power and nature of each, evil times and hosts of diseases. And continually, according to the dominion [3] of each fourth part, this stream of evil, just (like a current) of rivers, careers, according to the will of Edem, uninterruptedly around the world. And from some cause of this description has arisen the necessity of evil.

When Elohim had prepared and created the world as a result from joint pleasure, He wished to ascend up to the elevated parts of heaven, and to see that not anything of what pertained to the creation laboured under deficiency. And He took His Own angels with Him, for His nature was to mount aloft, leaving Edem below: [4] for inasmuch as she was earth, she was not disposed to follow upward her spouse. Elohim, then, coming to the highest part of heaven above, and beholding a light superior to that which He Himself had created, exclaimed, "Open me the gates, that entering in I may acknowledge the Lord; for I considered Myself to be Lord." [5] A voice was returned to Him from the light, saying, "This is the gate of the Lord: through this the righteous enter in." [6] And immediately the gate was opened, and the Father, without the angels, entered, (advancing) towards the Good One, and beheld "what eye hath not seen, and ear hath not heard, and what hath not entered into the heart of man to (conceive)." [7]

Then the Good One says to him, "Sit thou on my right hand." [8] And the Father says to the Good One, "Permit me, Lord, to overturn the world which I have made, for my spirit is bound to men.[9] And I wish to receive it back (from them)." Then the Good One replies to him, "No evil canst thou do while thou art with me, for both thou and Edem made the world as a result of conjugal joy. Permit Edem, then, to hold possession of the world as long as she wishes; but do you remain with me." Then Edem, knowing that she had been deserted by Elohim, was seized with grief, and placed beside herself her own angels. And she adorned herself after a comely fashion, if by any means Elohim, passing into concupiscent desire, might descend (from heaven) to her.

When, however, Elohim, overpowered by the Good One, no longer descended to Edem, Edem commanded Babel, which is Venus, to cause adulteries and dissolutions of marriages among men. (And she adopted this expedient) in order that, as she had been divorced from Elohim, so also the spirit of Elohim, which is in men, being wrung with sorrow, might be punished by such separations, and might undergo precisely the sufferings which (were being endured by) the deserted Edem. And Edem gives great power to her third angel, Naas, that by every species of punishment she might chasten the spirit of Elohim which is in men, in order that Elohim, through the spirit, might be punished for having deserted his spouse, in violation of the agreements entered into between them. Elohim the father, seeing these things, sends forth Baruch, the third angel among his own, to succour the spirit that is in all men.[10] Baruch then coming, stood in the midst of the angels of Edem, that is, in the midst of paradise — for paradise is the angels, in the midst of whom he stood, — and issued to the man the following injunction : "Of every tree that is in paradise thou mayest freely eat, but thou mayest not eat of the tree of the knowledge of good and evil," [11] which is Naas. Now the meaning is, that he should obey the rest of the eleven angels of Edem, for the eleven possess passions, but are not guilty of transgression. Naas, however, has committed sin, for he went in unto Eve, deceiving her, and debauched her ; and (such an act as) this is a violation of law. He, however, likewise went in unto Adam, and had unnatural intercourse with him ; and this is itself also a piece of turpitude, whence have arisen adultery and sodomy.

Henceforward vice and virtue were prevalent among men, arising from a single source — that

---

[1] ἐν αὐτῇ: some read ἐν ἀρχῇ, i.e., in the beginning.
[2] σατραπικήν. The common reading ἀστραπικήν is obviously corrupt.
[3] Or, "mixture."
[4] κάτω: some read κατώγη, i.e., κατώγαιος, earthly; some κατωφερής, with a downward tendency.
[5] Ps. cxvii. 19.
[6] Ps. cxviii. 20.
[7] Isa. lxiv. 4; 1 Cor. ii. 9.

[8] Ps. cx. 1.
[9] Or, "the heavens."
[10] ἀνθρώποις πᾶσιν. Ἐλθών. Some read: ἀνθρώποις. Πάλιν ἐλθών.
[11] Gen. ii. 16, 17.

of the Father. For the Father having ascended to the Good One, points out from time to time the way to those desirous of ascending (to him likewise). After having, however, departed from Edem, he caused an originating principle of evil for the spirit of the Father that is in men.[1] Baruch therefore was despatched to Moses, and through him spoke to the children of Israel, that they might be converted unto the Good One. But the third angel (Naas), by the soul which came from Edem upon Moses, as also upon all men, obscured the precepts of Baruch, and caused his own peculiar injunctions to be hearkened unto. For this reason the soul is arrayed against the spirit, and the spirit against the soul.[2] For the soul is Edem, but the spirit Elohim, and each of these exists in all men, both females and males. Again, after these (occurrences), Baruch was sent to the Prophets, that through the Prophets the spirit that dwelleth in men[3] might hear (words of warning), and might avoid Edem and the wicked fiction, just as the Father had fled from Elohim. In like manner also — by the prophets[4] — Naas, by a similar device, through the soul[5] that dwells in man, along with the spirit of the Father, enticed away the prophets, and all (of them) were allured after him, and did not follow the words of Baruch, which Elohim enjoined.

Ultimately Elohim selected Hercules, an uncircumcised prophet, and sent him to quell the twelve angels of Edem, and release the Father from the twelve angels, those wicked ones of the creation. These are the twelve conflicts of Hercules which Hercules underwent, in order, from first to last, viz., Lion, and Hydra, and Boar, and the others successively. For they say that these are the names (of them) among the Gentiles, and they have been derived with altered denominations from the energy of the maternal angels. When he seemed to have vanquished his antagonists, Omphale — now she is Babel or Venus — clings to him and entices away Hercules, and divests him of his power, viz., the commands of Baruch which Elohim issued. And in place (of this power, Babel) envelopes him in her own peculiar robe, that is, in the power of Edem, who is the power below; and in this way the prophecy of Hercules remained unfulfilled, and his works.

Finally, however, in the days of Herod the king, Baruch is despatched, being sent down once more by Elohim; and coming to Nazareth, he found Jesus, son of Joseph and Mary, a child of twelve years, feeding sheep. And he announces to him all things from the beginning, whatsoever had been done by Edem and Elohim, and whatsoever would be likely to take place hereafter, and spoke the following words : " All the prophets anterior to you have been enticed. Put forth an effort, therefore, Jesus, Son of man, not to be allured, but preach this word unto men, and carry back tidings to them of things pertaining to the Father, and things pertaining to the Good One, and ascend to the Good One, and sit there with Elohim, Father of us all." And Jesus was obedient unto the angel, saying that, " I shall do all things, Lord," and proceeded to preach. Naas therefore wished to entice this one also. (Jesus, however, was not disposed to listen to his overtures[6]), for he remained faithful to Baruch. Therefore Naas, being inflamed with anger because he was not able to seduce him, caused him to be crucified. He, however, leaving the body of Edem on the (accursed) tree, ascended to the Good One ; saying, however, to Edem, " Woman, thou retainest thy son,"[7] that is, the natural and the earthly man. But (Jesus) himself commending his spirit into the hands of the Father, ascended to the Good One. Now the Good One is Priapus, (and) he it is who antecedently caused the production of everything that exists. On this account he is styled Priapus, because he previously fashioned all things (according to his own design). For this reason, he says, in every temple is placed his statue, which is revered by every creature ; and (there are images of him) in the highways, carrying over his head ripened fruits, that is, the produce of the creation, of which he is the cause, having in the first instance formed, (according to His own design), the creation, when as yet it had no existence. When, therefore, he says, you hear men asserting that the swan went in unto Leda, and begat a child from her, (learn that) the swan is Elohim, and Leda Edem. And when people allege that an eagle went in unto Ganymede, (know that) the eagle is Naas, and Ganymede Adam. And when they assert that gold (in a shower) went in unto Danaë and begat a child from her, (recollect that) the gold is Elohim, and Danaë is Edem. And similarly, in the same manner adducing all accounts of this description, which correspond with (the nature of) legends, they pursue the work of instruction. When, therefore, the prophet says, " Hearken, O heaven, and give ear, O earth ; the Lord hath spoken," he means by heaven, (Justinus) says, the spirit which is in man from Elohim ; and by earth, the soul which is in man along with the spirit ; and by Lord, Baruch ; and by Israel, Edem, for Israel as well as Edem

---

[1] Or, " in heaven."
[2] Gal. v. 17.
[3] Or, " in heaven."
[4] These words are superfluous here, and are repeated from the preceding sentence by mistake.
[5] ψυχῆς: some read εὐχῆς, i.e., prayer.

[6] Miller conjectures that the parenthetical words should be added to the text.
[7] John xix. 26.

is called the spouse of Elohim. "Israel," he says, "did not know me (Elohim) ; for had he known me, that I am with the Good One, he would not have punished through paternal ignorance the spirit which is in men."

CHAP. XXII. — OATH USED BY THE JUSTINIAN HERETICS ; THE BOOK OF BARUCH ; THE REPERTORY OF THEIR SYSTEM.

Hence [1] also, in the first book inscribed "Baruch," has been written the oath which they compel those to swear who are about to hear these mysteries, and be initiated with the Good One.[2] And this oath, (Justinus) says, our Father Elohim sware when He was beside the Good One, and having sworn He did not repent (of the oath), respecting which, he says, it has been written, "The Lord sware, and will not repent." [3] Now the oath is couched in these [4] terms : "I swear by that Good One who is above all, to guard these mysteries, and to divulge them to no one, and not to relapse from the Good One to the creature." And when he has sworn this oath, he goes on to the Good One, and beholds "whatever things eye hath not seen, and ear hath not heard, and which have not entered into the heart of man ; " [5] and he drinks from life-giving water, which is to them, as they suppose, a bath,[6] a fountain of life-giving, bubbling water.[7] For there has been a separation made between water and water ; and there is water, that below the firmament of the wicked creation, in which earthly and animal men are washed ; and there is life-giving water, (that) above the firmament,[8] of the Good One, in which spiritual (and) living men are washed ; and in this Elohim washed Himself, and having washed did not repent. And when, he says, the prophet affirms, "Take unto yourself a wife of whoredom, since the earth has abandoned itself to fornication, (departing) from (following) after the Lord ; " [9] that is, Edem (departs) from Elohim. (Now) in these words, he says, the prophet clearly declares the entire mystery, and is not hearkened unto by reason of the wicked machinations of Naas. According to that same manner, they deliver other prophetical passages in a similar spirit of interpretation throughout numerous books. The volume, however, inscribed "Baruch," is pre-eminently to them the one in which the reader [10] will ascertain the entire explanation of their legendary system (to be contained). Beloved, though I have encountered many heresies, yet with no wicked (heresiarch) worse than this (Justinus) has it been my lot to meet. But, in truth, (the followers of Justinus) ought to imitate [11] the example of his Hercules, and to cleanse, as the saying is, the cattle-shed of Augias, or rather I should say, a ditch,[12] into which, as soon as the adherents of this (heresiarch) have fallen, they can never be cleansed ; nay, they will not be able even to raise their heads.

CHAP. XXIII. — SUBSEQUENT HERESIES DEDUCIBLE FROM THE SYSTEM OF JUSTINUS.

Since, then, we have explained the attempts (at a system) of the pseudo-gnostic Justinus, it appears likewise expedient in the following books to elucidate the opinions put forward in heresies following (in the way of consequence upon the doctrines of Justinus), and to leave not a single one of these (speculators) unrefuted. Our refutation will be accomplished by adducing the assertions made by them ; such (at least of their statements) as are sufficient for making a public example (of these heretics). (And we shall attain our purpose), even though there should only be condemned [13] the secret and ineffable (mysteries) practised amongst them, into which, silly mortals that they are, scarcely (even) with considerable labour are they initiated. Let us then see what also Simon affirms.

---

1 ἐντεῦθεν: this word stands at the end of the last chapter in the text of Miller, who suspects that there is here some hiatus. In this opinion the Abbe Cruice concurs. Schneidewin, however, transfers ἐντεῦθεν to the beginning of this chapter as above.
2 παρὰ τῷ ἀγαθῷ; or rather, we should expect, into a knowledge of the Good One.
3 Ps. cx. 4; Heb. vii. 21.
4 οὕτως: some read οὗτος.
5 1 Cor. ii. 9.
6 λουτρὸν: the ecclesiastical use of this word makes it stand for baptism.
7 John iv. 14.
8 Gen. i. 6, 7.

9 Hos. i. 2.
10 ἐντυχών: some read εὐτυχῶν, i.e., one who is fortunate enough to meet with the book.
11 Literally "ought, according to his Hercules, by imitating," etc.
12 ἀμάραν. This word means a trench or channel in a field, for the purpose either of irrigation or drainage. Schneidewin and Cruice render it by the Latin *Sentinam,* an expression applied, for example, to bilge water.
13 ἐκρηθείη, i.e., ἐκριθείη: some read ἐκκριθείη, which might be rendered, "even though, (for the purpose of holding these heretics up to public shame,) there should be made a selection only," etc.

THE REFUTATION OF ALL HERESIES

BOOK VI.

CONTENTS.

THE following are the contents of the sixth book of the *Refutation of all Heresies:* —

What the opinions are that are attempted (to be established) by Simon, and that his doctrine derives its force from the (lucubrations) of magicians and poets.

What are the opinions propounded by Valentinus, and that his system is not constructed out of the Scriptures, but out of the Platonic and Pythagorean tenets.

And what are the opinions of Secundus, and Ptolemæus, and Heracleon, as persons also who themselves advanced the same doctrines as the philosophers among the Greeks, but enunciated them in different phraseology.

And what are the suppositions put forward by Marcus and Colarbasus, and that some of them devoted their attention to magical arts and the Pythagorean numbers.

CHAP. I.[1] — THE OPHITES THE PROGENITORS OF SUBSEQUENT HERESIES.

Whatever opinions, then, were entertained by those who derived the first principles (of their doctrine) from the serpent, and in process of time[2] deliberately[3] brought forward into public notice their tenets, we have explained in the book preceding this, (and) which is the fifth of the *Refutation of Heresies.* But now also I shall not be silent as regards the opinions of (heresiarchs) who follow these (Ophites in succession); nay, not one (speculation) will I leave unrefuted, if it is possible to remember all (their tenets), and the secret orgies of these (heretics) which one may fairly style orgies, — for they who propagate such audacious opinions are not far distant from the anger (of God), — that I may avail myself of the assistance of etymology.

CHAP. II. — SIMON MAGUS.

It seems, then, expedient likewise to explain now the opinions of Simon,[4] a native of Gitta, a village of Samaria; and we shall also prove that his successors, taking a starting-point from him, have endeavoured (to establish) similar opinions under a change of name. This Simon being an adept in sorceries, both making a mockery of many, partly according to the art of Thrasymedes, in the manner in which we have explained above,[5] and partly also by the assistance of demons perpetrating his villany, attempted to deify himself. (But) the man was a (mere) cheat, and full of folly, and the Apostles reproved him in the Acts.[6] With much greater wisdom and moderation than Simon, did Apsethus the Libyan, inflamed with a similar wish, endeavour to have himself considered a god in Libya. And inasmuch as his legendary system does not present any wide divergence from the inordinate desire of that silly Simon, it seems expedient to furnish an explanation of it, as one worthy of the attempt made by this man.

CHAP. III. — STORY OF APSETHUS THE LIBYAN.

Apsethus[7] the Libyan inordinately longed to become a god; but when, after repeated intrigues, he altogether failed to accomplish his desire, he nevertheless wished to appear to have become *a god;* and he did at all events appear, as time wore on, to have in reality become a god. For the foolish Libyans were accustomed

---

[1] [Presuming that all who are disposed to study this work will turn to Dr. Bunsen's first volume (*Hippol.*), I have not thought it wise to load these pages with references to his interesting review.]

[2] κατὰ τελείωσιν τῶν χρόνων. This is Bunsen's emendation. The textual reading is μείωσιν.

[3] ἐκουσίως: Bunsen suggests ἀνοσίως, i.e., profanely.

[4] See Irenæus, *Hæres.*, i. 19, 20; Tertullian, *Præscript.*, c. xlvi.; Epiphanius, *Hæres.*, xxi.; Theodoret, *Hæret. Fab.*, i. 1; St. Augustine, *De Hæres.*, 1. See the apology of Justin Martyr (vol. i., this series, p. 171), who says, "There was a Samaritan, Simon, a native of the village called Gitto, who, in the reign of Claudius Cæsar, and in your royal city of Rome, did mighty acts of magic, by virtue of the art of the devils operating in him." Simon's history and opinions are treated of largely in the *Recogvitions of Clement.* See vol. iii. of the Edinburgh series, pp. 156–271; [vol. viii. of this series].

[5] In book iv. of *The Refutation.*

[6] Acts viii. 9–24.

[7] Miller refers us to Apostolius' *Proverb.*, s.v. ψαφῶν. Schneidewin remarks that Maximus Tyrius relates almost a similar story concerning one Psapho, a Libyan, in his *Dissert.* (xxxv.), and that Apostolius extracted this account and inserted it in his *Cent.*, xviii. p. 730, ed. Leutsch, mentioning at the same time a similar narrative from Ælian's *Hist.*, xiv. 30. See Justin., xxi. 4, and Pliny, *Nat. Hist.*, viii. 16.

to sacrifice unto him as to some divine power, supposing that they were yielding credence to a voice that came down from above, from heaven. For, collecting into one and the same cage a great number of birds, — parrots, — he shut them up. Now there are very many parrots throughout Libya, and very distinctly these imitate the human voice. This man, having for a time nourished the birds, was in the habit of teaching them to say, "Apsethus is a god." After, however, the birds had practised this for a long period, and were accustomed to the utterance of that which he thought, when said, would make it supposed that Apsethus was a god, then, opening the habitation (of the birds), he let forth the parrots, each in a different direction. While the birds, however, were on the wing, their sound went out into all Libya, and the expressions of these reached as far as the Hellenic country. And thus the Libyans, being astonished at the voice of the birds, and not perceiving the knavery perpetrated by Apsethus, held Apsethus to be a god. Some one, however, of the Greeks, by accurate examination, perceiving the trick of the supposed god, by means of those same parrots not only refutes, but also utterly destroys, that boastful and tiresome fellow. Now the Greek, by confining many of the parrots, taught them anew to say, "Apsethus, having caged us, compelled us to say, Apsethus is a god." But having heard of the recantation of the parrots, the Libyans, coming together, all unanimously decided on burning Apsethus.

CHAP. IV. — SIMON'S FORCED INTERPRETATION OF SCRIPTURE; PLAGIARIZES FROM HERACLITUS AND ARISTOTLE; SIMON'S SYSTEM OF SENSIBLE AND INTELLIGIBLE EXISTENCES.

In this way we must think concerning Simon the magician, so that we may compare him unto the Libyan, far sooner than unto Him who, though made man,[1] was in reality God. If, however, the assertion of this likeness is in itself accurate, and the sorcerer was the subject of a passion similar to Apsethus, let us endeavour to teach anew the parrots of Simon, that Christ, who stood, stands, and will stand, (that is, was, is, and is to come,) was not Simon. But (Jesus) was man, offspring of the seed of a woman, born of blood and the will of the flesh, as also the rest (of humanity). And that these things are so, we shall easily prove as the discussion proceeds.

Now Simon, both foolishly and knavishly paraphrasing the law of Moses, makes his statements (in the manner following) : For when Moses asserts that " God is a burning and consuming fire," [2] taking what is said by Moses not in its correct sense, he affirms that fire is the originating principle of the universe. (But Simon) does not consider what the statement is which is made, namely, that it is not that God is a fire, but a burning and consuming fire, (thereby) not only putting a violent sense upon the actual law of Moses, but even plagiarizing from Heraclitus the Obscure. And Simon denominates the originating principle of the universe an indefinite power, expressing himself thus : " This is the treatise of a revelation of (the) voice and name (recognisable) by means of intellectual apprehension of the Great Indefinite Power. Wherefore it will be sealed, (and) kept secret, (and) hid, (and) will repose in the habitation, at the foundation of which lies the root of all things." And he asserts that this man who is born of blood is (the aforesaid) habitation, and that in him resides an indefinite power, which he affirms to be the root of the universe.

Now the indefinite power which is fire, constitutes, according to Simon, not any uncompounded (essence, in conformity with the opinion of those who) assert that the four elements are simple, and who have (therefore) likewise imagined that fire, (which is one of the four,) is simple. But (this is far from being the case) : for there is, (he maintains,) a certain twofold nature of fire ;[3] and of this twofold (nature) he denominates one part a something secret, and another a something manifest, and that the secret are hidden in the manifest portions of the fire, and that the manifest portions of the fire derive their being from its secret (portions). This, however, is what Aristotle denominates by (the expressions) "potentiality" and "energy," or (what) Plato (styles) "intelligible" and "sensible." And the manifest portion of the fire comprises all things in itself, whatsoever any one might discern, or even whatever objects of the visible creation[4] he may happen to overlook. But the entire secret (portion of the fire) which one may discern is cognised by intellect, and evades the power of the senses ; or one fails to observe it, from want of a capacity for that particular sort of perception. In general, however, inasmuch as all existing things fall under the categories, namely, of what are objects of Sense, and what are objects of Intellect, and as for the denomination of these (Simon) employs the terms secret and manifest ; it may, (I say, in general,) be affirmed that the fire, (I mean) the super-celestial (fire), is a treasure, as it were a large tree, just such a one as in a dream

---

[1] The text here is corrupt. The above is Miller's emendation. Cruice's reading may thus be rendered: " So that far sooner we may compare him unto the Libyan, who was a mere man, and not the true God."

[2] Deut. iv. 24.
[3] The Abbe Cruice considers that Theodoret has made use of this passage. (See *Hæret. Fab.*, i. 1.)
[4] Or, τὸν ἀόρατον, the invisible one.

was seen by Nabuchodonosor,[1] out of which all flesh is nourished. And the manifest portion of the fire he regards as the stem, the branches, the leaves, (and) the external rind which overlaps them. All these (appendages), he says, of the Great Tree being kindled, are made to disappear by reason of the blaze of the all-devouring fire. The fruit, however, of the tree, when it is fully grown, and has received its own form, is deposited in a granary, not (flung) into the fire. For, he says, the fruit has been produced for the purpose of being laid in the storehouse, whereas the chaff that it may be delivered over to the fire.[2] (Now the chaff) is stem, (and is) generated not for its own sake, but for that of the fruit.

CHAP. V. — SIMON APPEALS TO SCRIPTURE IN SUPPORT OF HIS SYSTEM.

And this, he says, is what has been written in Scripture : "For the vineyard of the Lord of Sabaoth is the house of Israel, and the man of Judah is His beloved plant." If, however, the man of Judah (is) the beloved plant, it has been proved, he says, that there is not any other tree but that man. But concerning the secretion and dissolution of this (tree), Scripture, he says, has spoken sufficiently. And as regards instruction for those who have been fashioned after the image (of him), that statement is enough which is made (in Scripture), that "all flesh is grass, and all the glory of flesh, as it were, a flower of grass. The grass withereth, and its flower falleth ; but the word of the Lord abideth for ever."[3] The word of the Lord, he says, is that word which is produced in the mouth, and (is) a Logos, but nowhere else exists there a place of generation.

CHAP. VI. — SIMON'S SYSTEM EXPOUNDED IN THE WORK, GREAT ANNOUNCEMENT ; FOLLOWS EMPEDOCLES.

Now, to express myself briefly, inasmuch as the fire is of this description, according to Simon, and since all things are visible and invisible, (and) in like manner resonant and not resonant, numerable and not subjects of numeration ; he denominates in the *Great Announcement* a perfect intelligible (entity), after such a mode, that each of those things which, existing indefinitely, may be infinitely comprehended, both speaks, and understands, and acts in such a manner as Empedocles[4] speaks of : —

"For earth, indeed, bv earth we see, and water by water,
And air divine by air, and fire fierce by fire,
And love by love, and also strife by gloomy strife."

CHAP. VII. — SIMON'S SYSTEM OF A THREEFOLD EMANATION BY PAIRS.

For, he says, he is in the habit of considering that all these portions of the fire, both visible and invisible, are possessed of perception and a share of intelligence.[5] The world, therefore, that which is generated, was produced from the unbegotten fire. It began, however, to exist, he says, according to the following manner. He who was begotten from the principle of that fire took six roots, and those primary ones, of the originating principle of generation. And, he says, that the roots were made from the fire in pairs, which roots he terms "Mind" and "Intelligence," "Voice" and "Name," "Ratiocination" and "Reflection." And that in these six roots resides simultaneously the entire indefinite power potentially, (however) not actually. And this indefinite power, he says, is he who stood, stands, and will stand. Wherefore, whensoever he may be made into an image, inasmuch as he exists in the six powers, he will exist (there) substantially, potentially, quantitively, (and) completely. (And he will be a power) one and the same with the unbegotten and indefinite power, and not labouring under any greater deficiency than that unbegotten and unalterable (and) indefinite power. If, however, he may continue only potentially in the six powers, and has not been formed into an image, he vanishes, he says, and is destroyed in such a way as the grammatical or geometrical capacity in man's soul. For when the capacity takes unto itself an art, a light of existent things is produced ; but when (the capacity) does not take unto itself (an art), unskilfulness and ignorance are the results ; and just as when (the power) was non-existent, it perishes along with the expiring man.

CHAP. VIII. — FURTHER PROGRESSION OF THIS THREEFOLD EMANATION ; CO-EXISTENCE WITH THE DOUBLE TRIAD OF A SEVENTH EXISTENCE.

And of those six powers,[6] and of the seventh which co-exists with them, the first pair, Mind and Intelligence, he calls Heaven and Earth. And that one of these, being of male sex, beholds from above and takes care of his partner, but that the earth receives below the rational fruits, akin to the earth, which are borne down from the heaven. On this account, he says, the Logos, frequently looking towards the things that are being generated from Mind and Intelligence, that is, from Heaven and Earth, exclaims, "Hear, O heaven, and give ear, O earth, because

---

[1] Dan iv. 10-12.
[2] Matt iii. 12; Luke iii. 17.
[3] 1 Pet. i. 24.
[4] Emped., ed. Karst. v. 324.

[5] νώματος αἶσαν: Miller has γνώμην ἴσην, which yields but little sense.
[6] These powers are thus arranged : —
1. Mind and Intelligence : termed also, — 1. Heaven and Earth.
2. Voice and Name,   "   "   2. Sun and Moon.
3. Ratiocination and Reflection, "   3. Air and Water.

the Lord has spoken. I have brought forth children, and exalted them; and these have rejected me." Now, he who utters these words, he says, is the seventh power—he who stood, stands, and will stand; for he himself is cause of those beauteous objects of creation which Moses commended, and said that they were very good. But Voice and Name (the second of the three pairs) are Sun and Moon; and Ratiocination and Reflection (the third of the three pairs) are Air and Water. And in all these is intermingled and blended, as I have declared, the great, the indefinite, the (self-) existing power.

CHAP. IX.—SIMON'S INTERPRETATION OF THE MOSAIC HEXAËMERON; HIS ALLEGORICAL REPRESENTATION OF PARADISE.

When, therefore, Moses has spoken of "the six days in which God made heaven and earth, and rested on the seventh from all His works,"[1] Simon, in a manner already specified, giving (these and other passages of Scripture) a different application (from the one intended by the holy writers), deifies himself. When, therefore, (the followers of Simon) affirm that there are three days begotten before sun and moon, they speak enigmatically of Mind and Intelligence, that is, Heaven and Earth, and of the seventh power, (I mean) the indefinite one. For these three powers are produced antecedent to all the rest. But when they say, "He begot me prior to all the Ages,"[2] such statements, he says, are alleged to hold good concerning the seventh power. Now this seventh power, which was a power existing in the indefinite power, which was produced prior to all the Ages, this is, he says, the seventh power, respecting which Moses utters the following words: "And the Spirit of God was wafted over[3] the water;" that is, says (the Simonian), the Spirit which contains all things in itself, and is an image of the indefinite power about which Simon speaks, —"an image from an incorruptible form, that alone reduces all things into order." For this power that is wafted over the water, being begotten, he says, from an incorruptible form alone, reduces all things into order. When, therefore, according to these (heretics), there ensued some such arrangement, and (one) similar (to it) of the world, the Deity, he says, proceeded to form man, taking clay from the earth. And He formed him not uncompounded, but twofold, according to (His own) image and likeness.[4] Now the image is the Spirit that is wafted over the water; and whosoever is not fashioned into

a figure of this, will perish with the world, inasmuch as he continues only potentially, and does exist actually. This, he says, is what has been spoken, "that we should not be condemned with the world."[5] If one, however, be made into the figure of (the Spirit), and be generated from an indivisible point, as it has been written in the *Announcement*, (such a one, albeit) small, will become great. But what is great will continue unto infinite and unalterable duration, as being that which no longer is subject to the conditions of a generated entity.

How then, he says, and in what manner, does God form man? In Paradise; for so it seems to him. Grant Paradise, he says, to be the womb; and that this is a true (assumption) the Scripture will teach, when it utters the words, "I am He who forms thee in thy mother's womb."[6] For this also he wishes to have been written so. Moses, he says, resorting to allegory, has declared Paradise to be the womb, if we ought to rely on his statement. If, however, God forms man in his mother's womb—that is, in Paradise—as I have affirmed, let Paradise be the womb, and Edem the after-birth,[7] "a river flowing forth from Edem, for the purpose of irrigating Paradise,"[8] (meaning by this) the navel. This navel, he says, is separated into four principles; for on either side of the navel are situated two arteries, channels of spirit, and two veins, channels of blood. But when, he says, the umbilical vessels[9] proceed forth from Edem, that is, the caul in which the fœtus is enveloped grows into the (fœtus) that is being formed in the vicinity of the epigastrium,—(now) all in common denominate this a navel,—these two veins through which the blood flows, and is conveyed from Edem. the after-birth, to what are styled the gates of the liver; (these veins, I say,) nourish the fœtus. But the arteries which we have spoken of as being channels of spirit, embrace the bladder on both sides, around the pelvis, and connect it with the great artery, called the aorta, in the vicinity of the dorsal ridge. And in this way the spirit, making its way through the ventricles to the heart, produces a movement of the fœtus. For the infant that was formed in Paradise neither receives nourishment through the mouth, nor breathes through the nostrils: for as it lay in the midst of moisture, at its feet was death, if it attempted to breathe; for it would (thus) have been drawn away from moisture, and perished (accordingly). But (one may go further than this); for the entire (fœtus) is

---

[1] Gen. ii. 2.
[2] Prov. viii. 22–24.
[3] "Brooded over" (see Gen. i. 2).
[4] Gen. ii. 7.

[5] 1 Cor. xi. 32.
[6] Jer. i. 5.
[7] χωρίον (i.e., locality) is the reading in Miller, which Cruice ingeniously alters into χόριον, the caul in which the fœtus is enclosed, which is called the "after-birth."
[8] Gen. ii. 10.
[9] This rendering follows Cruice, who has succeeded in clearing away the obscurity of the passage as given in Miller.

bound tightly round by a covering styled the caul, and is nourished by a navel, and it receives through the (aorta), in the vicinity of the dorsal ridge, as I have stated, the substance of the spirit.

CHAP. X. — SIMON'S EXPLANATION OF THE FIRST TWO BOOKS OF MOSES.

The river, therefore, he says, which proceeds out of Edem is divided into four principles, four channels — that is, into four senses, belonging to the creature that is being born, viz., seeing, smelling, taste, and touch ; for the child formed in Paradise has these senses only. This, he says, is the law which Moses appointed ; and in reference to this very law, each of his books has been written, as the inscriptions evince. The first book is Genesis. The inscription of the book is, he says, sufficient for a knowledge of the universe. For this is (equivalent in meaning with) generation, (that is,) vision, into which one section of the river is divided. For the world was seen by the power of vision. Again, the inscription of the second book is Exodus. For what has been produced, passing through the Red Sea, must come into the wilderness, — now they say he calls the Red (Sea) blood, — and taste bitter water. For bitter, he says, is the water which is (drunk) after (crossing) the Red Sea ; which (water) is a path to be trodden, that leads (us) to a knowledge in (this) life of (our) toilsome and bitter lot. Altered, however, by Moses — that is, by the Logos — that bitter (water) becomes sweet. And that this is so we may hear in common from all who express themselves according to the (sentiments of the) poets : —

> " Dark at the root, like milk, the flower,
> Gods call it ' Moly,' and hard for mortal men
> To dig, but power divine is boundless." [1]

CHAP. XI. — SIMON'S EXPLANATION OF THE THREE LAST BOOKS OF THE PENTATEUCH.

What is spoken by the Gentiles is sufficient for a knowledge of the universe to those who have ears (capable) of hearing. For whosoever, he says, has tasted this fruit, is not the only one that is changed by Circe into a beast ; but also, employing the power of such a fruit, he forms anew and moulds afresh, and re-entices into that primary peculiar character of theirs, those that already have been altered into beasts. But a faithful man, and beloved by that sorceress, is, he says, discovered through that milk-like and divine fruit. In like manner, the third book is Leviticus, which is smelling, or respiration. For the entire of that book is (an account) of sacrifices and offerings. Where, however, there is a sacrifice, a certain savour of the fragrance

arises from the sacrifice through the incense-offerings ; and in regard of this fragrance (the sense of) smelling is a test. Numbers, the fourth of the books, signifies taste, where the discourse is operative. For, from the fact of its speaking all things, it is denominated by numerical arrangement. But Deuteronomy, he says, is written in reference to the (sense of) touch possessed by the child that is being formed. For as touch, by seizing the things that are seen by the other senses, sums them up and ratifies them, testing what is rough, or warm, or clammy, (or cold) ; so the fifth book of the law constitutes a summary of the four books preceding this.

All things, therefore, he says, when unbegotten, are in us potentially, not actually, as the grammatical or geometrical (art). If, then, one receives proper instruction and teaching, and (where consequently) what is bitter will be altered into what is sweet, — that is, the spears into pruning-hooks, and the swords into ploughshares,[2] — there will not be chaff and wood begotten for fire, but mature fruit, fully formed, as I said, equal and similar to the unbegotten and indefinite power. If, however, a tree continues alone, not producing fruit fully formed, it is utterly destroyed. For somewhere near, he says, is the axe (which is laid) at the roots of the tree. Every tree, he says, which does not produce good fruit, is hewn down and cast into fire.[3]

CHAP. XII. — FIRE A PRIMAL PRINCIPLE, ACCORDING TO SIMON.

According to Simon, therefore, there exists that which is blessed and incorruptible in a latent condition in every one — (that is,) potentially, not actually ; and that this is He who stood, stands,[4] and is to stand.[5] He has stood above in unbegotten power. He stands below, when in the stream of waters He was begotten in a likeness. He is to stand above, beside the blessed indefinite power, if He be fashioned into an image. For, he says, there are three who have stood ; and except there were three Æons who have stood, the unbegotten one is not adorned. (Now the unbegotten one) is, according to them, wafted over the water, and is re-made, according to the similitude (of an

---

[1] *Odyssey*, x. 304 et seq. [See Butcher and Lang, p. 163.]

[2] Isa. ii. 4.
[3] Matt. iii. 10; Luke iii. 9.
[4] In the *Recognitions of Clement* we have this passage: " He (Simon) wishes himself to be believed to be an exalted power, which is above God the Creator, and to be thought to be the Christ, and to be called the standing one" (Ante-Nicene Library, ed. Edinburgh, vol. iii. p. 196).
[5] The expression *stans* (standing) was used by the scholastics as applicable to the divine nature. Interpreted in this manner, the words in the text would be equivalent with " which was, and is, and is to come " (Rev. i. 8). The *Recognitions of Clement* explain the term thus: " He (Simon) uses this name as implying that he can never be dissolved, asserting that his flesh is so compacted by the power of his divinity, that it can endure to eternity. Hence, therefore, he is called the *standing one*, as though he cannot fall by any corruption " (Ante-Nicene Library, vol. iii. p. 196). [To be found in vol. viii. of this series, with the other apocryphal Clementines.]

eternal nature), a perfect celestial (being), in no (quality of) intelligence formed inferior to the unbegotten power: that is what they say— I and you, one; you, before me; I, that which is after you. This, he says, is one power divided above (and) below, generating itself, making itself grow, seeking itself, finding itself, being mother of itself, father of itself, sister of itself, spouse of itself, daughter of itself, son of itself, mother, father, a unit, being a root of the entire circle of existence.

And that, he says, the originating principle of the generation of things begotten is from fire, he discerns after some such method as the following. Of all things, (i.e.) of whatsoever there is a generation, the beginning of the desire of the generation is from fire. Wherefore the desire after mutable generation is denominated "to be inflamed." For when the fire is one, it admits of two conversions. For, he says, blood in the man being both warm and yellow, is converted as a figured flame into seed; but in the woman this same blood is converted into milk. And the conversion of the male becomes generation, but the conversion of the female nourishment for the fœtus. This, he says, is "the flaming sword, which turned to guard the way of the tree of life."[1] For the blood is converted into seed and milk, and this power becomes mother and father — father of those things that are in process of generation, and the augmentation of those things that are being nourished; (and this power is) without further want, (and) self-sufficient. And, he says, the tree of life is guarded, as we have stated, by the brandished flaming sword. And it is the seventh power, that which (is produced) from itself, (and) which contains all (powers, and) which reposes in the six powers. For if the flaming sword be not brandished, that good tree will be destroyed, and perish. If, however, these be converted into seed and milk, the principle that resides in these potentially, and is in possession of a proper position, in which is evolved a principle of souls, (such a principle,) beginning, as it were, from a very small spark, will be altogether magnified, and will increase and become a power indefinite (and) unalterable, (equal and similar) to an unalterable age, which no longer passes into the indefinite age.

CHAP. XIII. — HIS DOCTRINE OF EMANATION FURTHER EXPANDED.

Therefore, according to this reasoning, Simon became confessedly a god to his silly followers, as that Libyan, namely, Apsethus — begotten, no doubt, and subject to passion, when he may

exist potentially, but devoid of propensions. (And this too, though born from one having propensions, and uncreated though born) from one that is begotten, when He may be fashioned into a figure, and, becoming perfect, may come forth from two of the primary powers, that is, Heaven and Earth. For Simon expressly speaks of this in the "Revelation" after this manner: "To you, then, I address the things which I speak, and (to you) I write what I write. The writing is this: there are two offshoots from all the Æons, having neither beginning nor end, from one root. And this is a power, viz., Sige, (who is) invisible (and) incomprehensible. And one of these (offshoots) appears from above, which constitutes a great power, (the creative) Mind of the universe, which manages all things, (and is) a male. The other (offshoot), however, is from below, (and constitutes) a great Intelligence, and is a female which produces all things. From whence, ranged in pairs opposite each other, they undergo conjugal union, and manifest an intermediate interval, namely, an incomprehensible air, which has neither beginning nor end. But in this is a father who sustains all things, and nourishes things that have beginning and end. This is he who stood, stands, and will stand, being an hermaphrodite power according to the pre-existent indefinite power, which has neither beginning nor end. Now this (power) exists in isolation. For Intelligence, (that subsists) in unity, proceeded forth from this (power), (and) became two. And that (father) was one, for having in himself this (power) he was isolated, and, however, He was not primal though pre-existent; but being rendered manifest to himself from himself, he passed into a state of duality. But neither was he denominated father before this (power) would style him father. As, therefore, he himself, bringing forward himself by means of himself, manifested unto himself his own peculiar intelligence, so also the intelligence, when it was manifested, did not exercise the function of creation. But beholding him, she concealed the Father within herself, that is, the power; and it is an hermaphrodite power, and an intelligence. And hence it is that they are ranged in pairs, one opposite the other; for power is in no wise different from intelligence, inasmuch as they are one. For from those things that are above is discovered power; and from those below, intelligence. So it is, therefore, that likewise what is manifested from these, being unity, is discovered (to be) duality, an hermaphrodite having the female in itself. This, (therefore,) is Mind (subsisting) in Intelligence; and these are separable one from the other, (though both taken together) are one, (and) are discovered in a state of duality."

---

[1] Gen. iii. 24.

CHAP. XIV. — SIMON INTERPRETS HIS SYSTEM BY THE MYTHOLOGICAL REPRESENTATION OF HELEN OF TROY ; GIVES AN ACCOUNT OF HIMSELF IN CONNECTION WITH THE TROJAN HEROINE ; IMMORALITY OF HIS FOLLOWERS ; SIMON'S VIEW OF CHRIST ; THE SIMONISTS' APOLOGY FOR THEIR VICE.

Simon then, after inventing these (tenets), not only by evil devices interpreted the writings of Moses in whatever way he wished, but even the (works) of the poets.[1] For also he fastens an allegorical meaning on (the story of) the wooden horse and Helen with the torch, and on very many other (accounts), which he transfers to what relates to himself and to Intelligence, and (thus) furnishes a fictitious explanation of them. He said, however, that this (Helen) was the lost sheep. And she, always abiding among women, confounded the powers in the world by reason of her surpassing beauty. Whence, likewise, the Trojan war arose on her account. For in the Helen born at that time resided this Intelligence ; and thus, when all the powers were for claiming her (for themselves), sedition and war arose, during which (this chief power) was manifested to nations. And from this circumstance, without doubt, we may believe that Stesichorus, who had through (some) verses reviled her, was deprived of the use of his eyes ; and that, again, when he repented and composed recantations, in which he sung (Helen's) praises, he recovered the power of vision. But the angels and the powers below — who, he says, created the world — caused the transference from one body to another of (Helen's soul) ; and subsequently she stood on the roof of a house in Tyre, a city of Phœnicia, and on going down thither (Simon professed to have) found her. For he stated that, principally for the purpose of searching after this (woman), he had arrived (in Tyre), in order that he might rescue her from bondage. And after having thus redeemed her, he was in the habit of conducting her about with himself, alleging that this (girl) was the lost sheep, and affirming himself to be the Power above all things. But the filthy[2] fellow, becoming enamoured of this miserable woman called Helen, purchased her (as his slave), and enjoyed her person.[3] He, (however,) was likewise moved with shame towards his disciples, and concocted this figment.

But, again, those who become followers of this impostor — I mean Simon the sorcerer — indulge in similar practices, and irrationally allege the necessity of promiscuous intercourse. They express themselves in the manner following : " All earth is earth, and there is no difference where any one sows, provided he does sow." But even they congratulate themselves on account of this indiscriminate intercourse, asserting that this is perfect love, and employing the expressions, " holy of holies," and " sanctify one another." [4] For (they would have us believe) that they are not overcome by the supposed vice, for that they have been redeemed. " And (Jesus), by having redeemed Helen in this way," (Simon says,) " has afforded salvation to men through his own peculiar intelligence. For inasmuch as the angels, by reason of their lust for pre-eminence, improperly managed the world, (Jesus Christ) being transformed, and being assimilated to the rulers and powers and angels, came for the restoration (of things). And so (it was that Jesus) appeared as man, when in reality he was not a man. And (so it was) that likewise he suffered — though not actually undergoing suffering, but appearing to the Jews to do so[5] — in Judea as ' Son,' and in Samaria as ' Father,'[6] and among the rest of the Gentiles as ' Holy Spirit.' " And (Simon alleges) that Jesus tolerated being styled by whichever name (of the three just mentioned) men might wish to call him. " And that the prophets, deriving their inspiration from the world-making angels, uttered predictions (concerning him)." Wherefore, (Simon said,) that towards these (prophets) those felt no concern up to the present, who believe on Simon and Helen, and that they do whatsoever they please, as persons free ; for they allege that they are saved by grace. For that there is no reason for punishment, even though one shall act wickedly ; for such a one is not wicked by nature, but by enactment. " For the angels who created the world made," he says, " whatever enactments they pleased," thinking by such (legislative) words to enslave those who listened to them. But, again, they speak of a dissolution[7] of the world, for the redemption of his own particular adherents.

CHAP. XV. — SIMON'S DISCIPLES ADOPT THE MYSTERIES ; SIMON MEETS ST. PETER AT ROME ; ACCOUNT OF SIMON'S CLOSING YEARS.

The disciples, then, of this (Magus), celebrate magical rites, and resort to incantations. And

---

[1] Homer, for instance (See Epiphanius, *Hæres.*, xxi. 3).
[2] μιαρὸς, Bunsen's emendation for ψυχρὸς, the reading in Miller and Schneidewin. Some read ψυδρὸς, i.e., lying; others ψευδόχριστος, i.e., counterfeit Christ. Cruice considers Bunsen's emendation unnecessary, as ψυχρὸς may be translated "absurd fellow." The word, literally meaning cold, is applied in a derived sense to persons who were heartless, — an import suitable to Hippolytus' meaning.
[3] [See Irenæus, vol. i. p. 348, and Bunsen's ideas, p. 50 of his first volume.]

[4] This rendering is according to Bunsen's emendation of the text.
[5] Cruice omits the word δεδοκηκέναι, which seems an interpolation. The above rendering adopts the proposed emendation.
[6] Bunsen thinks that there is an allusion here to the conversation of our Lord with the woman of Samaria, and if so, that Menander, a disciple of Simon, and not Simon himself, was the author of *The Great Announcement*, as the heretic did not outlive St. Peter and St. Paul, and therefore died before the period at which St John's Gospel was written.
[7] Miller reads φύσιν, which makes no sense. The rendering above follows Bunsen's emendation of the text. [Here it is equally interesting to the student of our author or of Irenæus to turn to Bunsen (p. 51), and to observe his parallels.]

(they profess to) transmit both love-spells and charms, and the demons said to be senders of dreams, for the purpose of distracting whomsoever they please. But they also employ those denominated Paredroi. "And they have an image of Simon (fashioned) into the figure of Jupiter, and (an image) of Helen in the form of Minerva; and they pay adoration to these." But they call the one Lord and the other Lady. And if any one amongst them, on seeing the images of either Simon or Helen, would call them by name, he is cast off, as being ignorant of the mysteries. This Simon, deceiving many[1] in Samaria by his sorceries, was reproved by the Apostles, and was laid under a curse, as it has been written in the Acts. But he afterwards abjured the faith, and attempted these (aforesaid practices). And journeying as far as Rome,[2] he fell in with the Apostles; and to him, deceiving many by his sorceries, Peter offered repeated opposition. This man, ultimately repairing to . . . (and) sitting under a plane tree, continued to give instruction (in his doctrines). And in truth at last, when conviction was imminent, in case he delayed longer, he stated that, if he were buried alive, he would rise the third day. And accordingly, having ordered a trench to be dug by his disciples,[3] he directed himself to be interred there. They, then, executed the injunction given; whereas he remained (in that grave) until this day, for he was not the Christ. This constitutes the legendary system advanced by Simon, and from this Valentinus derived a starting-point (for his own doctrine. This doctrine, in point of fact, was the same with the Simonian, though Valentinus denominated it under different titles: for "Nous," and "Aletheia," and "Logos," and "Zoe," and "Anthropos," and "Ecclesia," and Æons of Valenti-

nus, are confessedly the six roots of Simon, viz., "Mind" and "Intelligence," "Voice" and "Name," "Ratiocination" and "Reflection." But since it seems to us that we have sufficiently explained Simon's tissue of legends, let us see what also Valentinus asserts.

CHAP. XVI. — HERESY OF VALENTINUS; DERIVED FROM PLATO AND PYTHAGORAS.

The heresy of Valentinus[4] is certainly, then, connected with the Pythagorean and Platonic theory. For Plato, in the *Timæus*, altogether derives his impressions from Pythagoras, and therefore Timæus himself is his Pythagorean stranger. Wherefore, it appears expedient that we should commence by reminding (the reader) of a few points of the Pythagorean and Platonic theory, and that (then we should proceed) to declare the opinions of Valentinus.[5] For even although in the books previously finished by us with so much pains, are contained the opinions advanced by both Pythagoras and Plato, yet at all events I shall not be acting unreasonably, in now also calling to the recollection of the reader, by means of an epitome, the principal heads of the favourite tenets of these (speculators). And this (recapitulation) will facilitate our knowledge of the doctrines of Valentinus, by means of a nearer comparison, and by similarity of composition (of the two systems). For (Pythagoras and Plato) derived these tenets originally from the Egyptians, and introduced their novel opinions among the Greeks. But (Valentinus took his opinions) from these, because, although he has suppressed the truth regarding his obligations to (the Greek philosophers), and in this way has endeavoured to construct a doctrine, (as it were,) peculiarly his own, yet, in point of fact, he has altered the doctrines of those (thinkers) in names only, and numbers, and has adopted a peculiar terminology (of his own). Valentinus has formed his definitions by meas-

---

[1] The Abbe Cruice considers that the statements made by Origen (*Contr. Celsum*, lib. i. p. 44, ed Spenc.), respecting the followers of Simon in respect of number, militates against Origen's authorship of *The Refutation*.

[2] This rendering follows the text of Schneidewin and Cruice. The *Clementine Recognitions* (Ante-Nicene Library, ed. Edinb., vol. iii. p. 273) represent Simon Magus as leaving for Rome, and St. Peter resolving to follow him thither. Miller's text is different; and as emended by him, Hippolytus' account would harmonize with that given in the Acts. Miller's text may be thus translated: "And having been laid under a curse, as has been written in the Acts, he subsequently disapproved of his practices, and made an attempt to journey as far as Rome, but he fell in with the apostles," etc. The text of Cruice and Schneidewin seems less forced; while the statement itself — a new witness to this controverted point in ecclesiastical history concerning St. Peter — corroborates Hippolytus' authorship of *The Refutation*.

[3] Justin Martyr mentions, as an instance of the estimation in which Simon Magus was held among his followers, that a statue was erected to him at Rome. Bunsen considers that the rejection of this fable of Justin Martyr's, points to the author of *The Refutation* being a Roman, who would therefore, as he shows himself in the case of the statue, be better informed than the Eastern writer of any event occurring in the capital of the West. [Bunsen's magisterial decision (p. 53) is very amusingly characteristic.] Hippolytus' silence is a presumption against the existence of such a statue, though it is very possible he might omit to mention it, supposing it to be at Rome. At all events, the very precise statement of Justin Martyr ought not to be rejected on slight or conjectural grounds. [See vol. i., this series, pp. 171, 172, 182, 187, and 193. But our author relies on Irenæus, same vol., p. 348. Why reject positive testimony?]

[4] Valentinus came from Alexandria to Rome during the pontificate of Hyginus, and established a school there. His desire seems to have been to remain in communion with Rome, which he did for many years, as Tertullian informs us. Epiphanius, however, tells that Valentinus, towards the end of his life, when living in Cyprus, separated entirely from the Church. Irenæus, book i.; Tertullian on Valentinus, and chap. xxx. of his *Præscript.*; Clemens Alexandrinus, *Strom.*, iv. 13, vi. 6; Theodoret, *Hæret. Fab.*, i 7; Epiphanius, *Hær.*, xxxi.; St. Augustine, *Hær.*, xl.; Philastrius, *Hist. Hæres.*, c. viii.; Photius, *Biblioth.*, cap. ccxxx.; Clemens Alexandrinus' *Epitome of Theodotus* (pp. 789-809, ed. Sylburg). The title is, Ἐκ τῶν Θεοδότου καὶ τῆς ἀνατολικῆς καλουμένης διδασκαλίας, κατὰ τοὺς Οὐαλεντίνου χρόνους ἐπιτομαί. See likewise Neander's *Church History*, vol. ii. Bohn's edition.

[5] These opinions are mostly given in extracts from Valentinus' work *Sophia*, a book of great repute among Gnostics, and not named by Hippolytus, probably as being so well known at the time. The *Gospel of Truth*, mentioned by Irenæus as used among the Valentinians, is not, however, considered to be from the pen of· Valentinus. In the extracts given by Hippolytus from Valentinus, it is important (as in the case of Basilides: see translator's introduction) to find that he quotes St. John's Gospel, and St. Paul's Epistle to the Ephesians. The latter had been pronounced by the Tübingen school as belonging to the period of the Montanistic disputes in the middle of the second century, that is, somewhere about 25-30 years after Valentinus.

ures, in order that he may establish an Hellenic heresy, diversified no doubt, but unstable, and not connected with Christ.

CHAP. XVII. — ORIGIN OF THE GREEK PHILOSOPHY.

The origin, then, from which Plato derived his theory in the *Timæus*, is (the) wisdom of the Egyptians.[1] For from this source, by some ancient and prophetical tradition, Solon[2] taught his entire system concerning the generation and destruction of the world, as Plato says, to the Greeks, who were (in knowledge) young children, and were acquainted with no theological doctrine of greater antiquity. In order, therefore, that we may trace accurately the arguments by which Valentinus established his tenets, I shall now explain what are the principles of the philosophy of Pythagoras of Samos, — a philosophy (coupled) with that Silence so celebrated by the Greeks. And next in this manner (I shall elucidate) those (opinions) which Valentinus derives from Pythagoras and Plato, but refers with all solemnity of speech to Christ, and before Christ to the Father of the universe, and to Silence conjoined with the Father.

CHAP. XVIII. — PYTHAGORAS' SYSTEM OF NUMBERS.

Pythagoras, then, declared the originating principle of the universe to be the unbegotten monad, and the generated duad, and the rest of the numbers. And he says that the monad is the father of the duad, and the duad the mother of all things that are being begotten — the begotten one (being mother) of the things that are begotten. And Zaratas, the pupil of Pythagoras, was in the habit of denominating unity a father, and duality a mother. For the duad has been generated from the monad, according to Pythagoras; and the monad is male and primary, but the duad female (and secondary). And from the duad, again, as Pythagoras states, (are generated) the triad and the succeeding numbers up to ten. For Pythagoras is aware that this is the only perfect number — I mean the decade — for that eleven and twelve are an addition and repetition of the decade; not, however, that what is added[3] constitutes the generation of another number. And all solid bodies he generates from incorporeal (essences). For he asserts that an element and principle of both corporeal and incorporeal entities is the point which is indivisible. And from a point, he says, is generated a line, and from a line a surface; and a surface flowing out into a height becomes, he says, a solid body. Whence also the Pythagoreans have a certain object of adjuration, viz.,

the concord of the four elements. And they swear in these words : —

" By him who to our head quaternion gives,
A font that has the roots of everlasting nature."[4]

Now the quaternion is the originating principle of natural and solid bodies, as the monad of intelligible ones. And that likewise the quaternion generates,[5] he says, the perfect number, as in the case of intelligibles (the monad) does the decade, they teach thus. If any, beginning to number, says one, and adds two, then in like manner three, these (together) will be six, and to these (add) moreover four, the entire (sum), in like manner, will be ten. For one, two, three, four, become ten, the perfect number. Thus, he says, the quaternion in every respect imitated the intelligible monad, which was able to generate a perfect number.

CHAP. XIX. — PYTHAGORAS' DUALITY OF SUBSTANCES ; HIS " CATEGORIES."

There are, then, according to Pythagoras, two worlds : one intelligible, which has the monad for an originating principle ; and the other sensible. But of this (latter) is the quaternion having the iota, the one tittle,[6] a perfect number. And there likewise is, according to the Pythagoreans, the *i*, the one tittle, which is chief and most dominant, and enables us to apprehend the substance of those intelligible entities which are capable of being understood through the medium of intellect and of sense. (And in this substance inhere) the nine incorporeal accidents which cannot exist without substance, viz., " quality," and " quantity," and " relation," and " where," and " when," and " position," and " possession," and " action," and " passion." These, then, are the nine accidents (inhering in) substance, and when reckoned with these (substances), contains the perfect number, the *i*. Wherefore, the universe being divided, as we said, into the intelligible and sensible world, we have also reason from the intelligible (world), in order that by reason we may behold the substance of things that are cognised by intellect, and are incorporeal and divine. But we have, he says, five senses — smelling, seeing, hearing, taste, and touch. Now, by these we arrive at a knowledge of things that are discerned by sense ; and so, he says, the sensible is divided from the intelligible world. And that we have for each of these an instrument for attaining knowledge, we perceive from the following consideration. Nothing, he says, of intelligibles can

---

[1] See *Timæus*, c. vii. ed. Bekker.
[2] Or, " Solomon," evidently a mistake.
[3] Miller would read for προστιθέμενον, νομιστέον or νομίζει.

[4] Respecting these lines, Miller refers us to Fabricius, *in Sextum Empiricum*, p. 332.
[5] The Abbe Cruice adduces a passage from Suidas (on the word ἀριθμός) which contains a similar statement to that furnished by Hippolytus.
[6] Matt. v. 18.

be known to us from sense. For he says neither eye has seen, nor ear heard, nor any whatsoever of the other senses known that (which is cognised by mind). Neither, again, by reason is it possible to arrive at a knowledge of any of the things discernible by sense. But one must see that a thing is white, and taste that it is sweet, and know by hearing that it is musical or out of tune. And whether any odour is fragrant or disagreeable, is the function of smell, not of reason. It is the same with objects of touch; for anything rough, or soft, or warm, or cold, it is not possible to know by hearing, but (far from it), for touch is the judge of such (sensations). Things being thus constituted, the arrangement of things that have been made and are being made is observed to happen in conformity with numerical (combinations). For in the same manner as, commencing from monad, by an addition of monads or triads, and a collection of the succeeding numbers, we make some one very large complex whole of number; (and) then, again, from an amassed number thus formed by addition, we accomplish, by means of a certain subtraction and re-calculation, a solution of the totality of the aggregate numbers; so likewise he asserts that the world, bound by a certain arithmetical and musical chain, was, by its tension and relaxation, and by addition and subtraction, always and for ever preserved incorrupt.

CHAP. XX. — PYTHAGORAS' COSMOGONY; SIMILAR TO THAT OF EMPEDOCLES.

The Pythagoreans therefore declare their opinion concerning the continuance of the world in some such manner as this : —

"For heretofore it was and will be; never, I ween,
Of both of these will void the age eternal be."

"Of these;" but what are they? Discord and Love. Now, in their system, Love forms the world incorruptible (and) eternal, as they suppose. For substance and the world are one. Discord, however, separates and puts asunder, and evinces numerous attempts by subdividing to form the world. It is just as if one severs into small parts, and divides arithmetically, the myriad into thousands, and hundreds, and tens; and drachmæ into oboli and small farthings. In this manner, he says, Discord severs the substance of the world into animals, plants, metals, and things similar to these. And the fabricator of the generation of all things produced is, according to them, Discord; whereas Love, on the other hand, manages and provides for the universe in such a manner that it enjoys permanence. And conducting together[1] into unity the divided and scattered parts of the universe, and leading them forth from their (separate) mode of existence, (Love) unites and adds to the universe, in order that it may enjoy permanence; and it thus constitutes one system. They will not therefore cease, — neither Discord dividing the world, nor Love attaching to the world the divided parts. Of some such description as this, so it appears, is the distribution of the world according to Pythagoras. But Pythagoras says that the stars are fragments from the sun, and that the souls[2] of animals are conveyed from the stars; and that these are mortal when they are in the body, just as if buried, as it were, in a tomb: whereas that they rise (out of this world) and become immortal, when we are separated from our bodies. Whence Plato, being asked by some one, "What is philosophy?" replied, "It is a separation of soul from body."

CHAP. XXI. — OTHER OPINIONS OF PYTHAGORAS.

Pythagoras, then, became a student of these doctrines likewise, in which he speaks both by enigmas and some such expressions as these: "When you depart from your own (tabernacle), return not;[3] if, however, (you act) not (thus), the Furies, auxiliaries to justice, will overtake you," — denominating the body one's own (tabernacle), and its passions the Furies. When, therefore, he says, you depart, that is, when you go forth from the body, do not earnestly crave for this; but if you are eagerly desirous (for departure), the passions will once more confine you within the body. For these suppose that there is a transition of souls from one body to another, as also Empedocles, adopting the principles of Pythagoras, affirms. For, says he, souls that are lovers of pleasure, as Plato states,[4] if, when they are in the condition of suffering incidental to man, they do not evolve theories of philosophy, must pass through all animals and plants (back) again into a human body. And when (the soul) may form a system of speculation thrice in the same body, (he maintains) that it ascends up to the nature of some kindred star. If, however, (the soul) does not philosophize, (it must pass) through the same (succession of changes once more). He affirms, then, that the soul sometimes may become even mortal, if it is overcome by the Furies, that is, the passions (of the body); and immortal, if it succeeds in escaping the Furies, which are the passions.

---

[1] Or, συνάγει, leads together.

[2] The Abbe Cruice considers that the writer of *The Refutation* did not agree with Pythagoras' opinion regarding the soul, — a fact that negatives the authorship of Origen, who assented to the Pythagorean psychology. The question concerning the pre-existence of the soul is stated in a passage often quoted, viz., St. Jerome's *Letter to Marcellina* (Ep. 82).

[3] Cruice thinks that the following words are taken from Heraclitus, and refers to Plutarch, *De Exilio*, c. xi.

[4] *Phædo*, vol. i. p. 89, ed. Bekker.

CHAP. XXII. — THE "SAYINGS" OF PYTHAGORAS.

But since also we have chosen to mention the sayings darkly expressed by Pythagoras to his disciples by means of symbols, it seems likewise expedient to remind (the reader) of the rest (of his doctrines. And we touch on this subject) on account also of the heresiarchs, who attempt by some method of this description to converse by means of symbols ; and these are not their own, but they have, (in propounding them,) taken advantage of expressions employed by the Pythagoreans.[1] Pythagoras then instructs his disciples, addressing them as follows : "Bind up the sack that carries the bedding." (Now,) inasmuch as they who intend going upon a journey tie their clothes into a wallet, to be ready for the road ; so, (in like manner,) he wishes his disciples to be prepared, since every moment death is likely to come upon them by surprise.[2] (In this way Pythagoras sought to effect) that (his followers) should labour under no deficiency in the qualifications required in his pupils.[3] Wherefore of necessity he was in the habit, with the dawn of day, of instructing the Pythagoreans to encourage one another to bind up the sack that carries the bedding, that is, to be ready for death. "Do not stir fire with a sword ; "[4] (meaning,) do not, by addressing him, quarrel with an enraged man ; for a person in a passion is like fire, whereas the sword is the uttered expression. "Do not trample on a besom ; "[5] (meaning,) despise not a small matter. "Plant not a palm tree in a house ; " (meaning,) foment not discord in a family, for the palm tree is a symbol of battle and slaughter.[6] "Eat not from a stool ; " (meaning,) do not undertake an ignoble art, in order that you may not be a slave to the body, which is corruptible, but make a livelihood from literature.

For it lies within your reach both to nourish the body, and make the soul better.[7] "Don't take a bite out of an uncut loaf ; " (meaning,) diminish not thy possessions, but live on the profit (of them), and guard thy substance as an entire loaf.[8] "Feed not on beans ; " (meaning,) accept not the government of a city, for with beans they at that time were accustomed to ballot for their magistrates.[9]

CHAP. XXIII. — PYTHAGORAS' ASTRONOMIC SYSTEM.

These, then, and such like assertions, the Pythagoreans put forward ; and the heretics, imitating these, are supposed by some to utter important truths. The Pythagorean system, however, lays down that the Creator of all alleged existences is the Great Geometrician and Calculator — a sun ; and that this one has been fixed in the whole world, just as in the bodies a soul, according to the statement of Plato. For the sun (being of the nature of) fire,[10] resembles the soul, but the earth (resembles the) body. And, separated from fire, there would be nothing visible, nor would there be any object of touch without something solid ; but not any solid body exists without earth. Whence the Deity, locating air in the midst, fashioned the body of the universe out of fire and earth. And the Sun, he says, calculates and geometrically measures the world in some such manner as the following : The world is a unity cognizable by sense ; and concerning this (world) we now make these assertions. But one who is an adept in the science of numbers, and a geometrician, has divided it into twelve parts. And the names of these parts are as follow : Aries, Taurus, Gemini, Cancer, Leo, Virgo, Libra, Scorpio, Sagittarius, Capricorn, Aquarius, Pisces. Again, he divides each of the twelve parts into thirty parts, and these are days of the month. Again, he divides each part of the thirty parts into sixty small divisions,

---

[1] These sayings (*Symbola Pythagorica*) have been collected by, amongst others, Thomas Stanley, and more recently by Gaspar Orellius. The meaning and the form of the proverbs given by Hippolytus do not always correspond with, e.g., Jamblichus (the biographer of Pythagoras), Porphyry, and Plutarch. The curious reader can see the *Proverbs*, in all their variety of readings and explanations, in the edition of L. Gyraldus.

[2] This has been explained by Erasmus as a precept enjoining habits of tidiness and modesty.

[3] Miller's text here yields a different but not very intelligible meaning.

[4] Horace quotes this proverb (2 *Serm.*, iii. 274) with a somewhat different meaning. Porphyry considers it a precept against irreverent language towards the Deity, the fire being a symbol — for instance, the vestal fire — of the everlasting nature of God. Σκάλευε in Hippolytus is also read, e.g., by Basil, ζαίνοντες, that is, cleaving. This alludes to some ancient game in which fire was struck at and severed.

[5] Σάρον. This word also signifies "sweepings" or "refuse." Some say it means a Chaldean or Babylonian measure. The meaning would then be: Neglect not giving good measure, i e., practise fair dealing. This agrees with another form of the proverb, reading ζυγόν for σάρον — that is, overlook not the balance or scales.

[6] Another meaning assigned to this proverb is, "Labour to no purpose." The palm, it is alleged, when it grows of itself, produces fruit, but sterility ensues upon transplantation. The proverb is also said to mean: Avoid what may seem agreeable, but really is injurious. This alludes to the quality of the wine (see Xenophon's *Anab.*, ii.), which, pleasant in appearance, produced severe headache in those partaking of it.

[7] "Eat not from a stool." This proverb is also differently read and interpreted. Another form is, "Eat not from a chariot," of which the import is variously given, as, Do not tamper with your health, because food swallowed in haste, as it must be when one is driving a team of horses, cannot be salutary or nutritive: or, Do not be careless, because one should attend to the business in hand; if that be guiding a chariot, one should not at the same time try to eat his meals.

[8] The word "entire" Plutarch adds to this proverb. Its ancient form would seem to inculcate patience and courtesy, as if one should not, when at meals, snap at food before others. As read in Plutarch, it has been also interpreted as a precept to avoid creating dissension, the unbroken bread being a symbol of unity. It has likewise been explained as an injunction against greediness. The loaf was marked by two intersecting lines into four parts, and one was not to devour all of these. (See Horace, 1 *Epist.*, xvii. 49.)

[9] This is the generally received import of the proverb. Ancient writers, however, put forward other meanings, connected chiefly with certain effects of beans, e.g., disturbing the mind, and producing melancholy, which Pythagoras is said to have noticed. Horace had no such idea concerning beans (see 2 *Serm.*, vi. 63), but evidently alludes to a belief of the magi that disembodied spirits resided in beans. (See Lucian, *Micyll.*: Plutarch, Περὶ Παίδ. Ἀγωγ. 17; Aulus Gellius, iv. 11; and Guigniaut's Cruiser's *Symbolik*, i. 160.) [See p. 12 *supra*, and compare vol. ii., this series, p. 383, and Elucidation III. p. 403.]

[10] The text seems doubtful. Some would read, "The sun is (to be compared with) soul, and the moon with body."

and (each) of these small (divisions) he sub-divides into minute portions, and (these again) into portions still more minute. And always doing this, and not intermitting, but collecting from these divided portions (an aggregate), and constituting it a year; and again resolving and dividing the compound, (the sun) completely finishes the great and everlasting world.[1]

CHAP. XXIV. — VALENTINUS CONVICTED OF PLAGI-ARISMS FROM THE PLATONIC AND PYTHAGORIC PHILOSOPHY; THE VALENTINIAN THEORY OF EMANATION BY DUADS.

Of some such nature, as I who have accurately examined their systems (have attempted) to state compendiously, is the opinion of Pythagoras and Plato. And from this (system), not from the Gospels, Valentinus, as we have proved, has collected the (materials of) heresy — I mean his own (heresy) — and may (therefore) justly be reckoned a Pythagorean and Platonist, not a Christian. Valentinus, therefore, and Heracleon, and Ptolemæus, and the entire school of these (heretics), as disciples of Pythagoras and Plato, (and) following these guides, have laid down as the fundamental principle of their doctrine the arithmetical system. For, likewise, according to these (Valentinians), the originating cause of the universe is a Monad, unbegotten, imperishable, incomprehensible, inconceivable, productive, and a cause of the generation of all existent things. And the aforesaid Monad is styled by them Father. There is, however, discoverable among them some considerable diversity of opinion. For some of them, in order that the Pythagorean doctrine of Valentinus may be altogether free from admixture (with other tenets), suppose that the Father is unfeminine, and unwedded, and solitary. But others, imagining it to be impossible that from a male only there could proceed a generation at all of any of those things that have been made to exist, necessarily reckon along with the Father of the universe, in order that he may be a father, Sige as a spouse. But as to Sige, whether at any time she is united in marriage (to the Father) or not, this is a point which we leave them to wrangle about among themselves. We at present, keeping to the Pythagorean principle, which is one, and unwedded, unfeminine, (and) deficient in nothing, shall proceed to give an account of their doctrines, as they themselves inculcate them. There is, says (Valentinus), not anything at all begotten, but the Father is alone unbegotten, not subject to the condition of place, not (subject to the condition of) time, having no counsellor, (and) not being any other substance that could be realized

according to the ordinary methods of perception. (The Father,) however, was solitary, subsisting, as they say, in a state of quietude, and Himself reposing in isolation within Himself. When, however, He became productive,[2] it seemed to Him expedient at one time to generate and lead forth the most beautiful and perfect (of those germs of existence) which He possessed within Him-self, for (the Father) was not fond of solitari-ness. For, says he, He was all love, but love is not love except there may be some object of affection. The Father Himself, then, as He was solitary, projected and produced Nous and Ale-theia, that is, a duad which became mistress,[3] and origin, and mother of all the Æons com-puted by them (as existing) within the Pleroma. Nous and Aletheia being projected from the Father,[4] one capable of continuing generation, deriving existence from a productive being, (Nous) himself likewise, in imitation of the Father, projected Logos and Zoe; and Logos and Zoe project Anthropos and Ecclesia. But Nous and Aletheia, when they beheld that their own offspring had been born productive, returned thanks to the Father of the universe, and offer unto Him a perfect number, viz., ten Æons. For, he says, Nous and Aletheia could not offer unto the Father a more perfect (one) than this number. For the Father, who is perfect, ought to be celebrated by a perfect number, and ten is a perfect number, because this is first of those (numbers) that are formed by plurality, (and therefore) perfect.[5] The Father, however, being more perfect, because being alone unbegotten, by means of the one primary conjugal union of Nous and Aletheia, found means of projecting all the roots of existent things.

CHAP. XXV. — THE TENET OF THE DUAD MADE THE FOUNDATION OF VALENTINUS' SYSTEM OF THE EMANATION OF ÆONS.

Logos himself also, and Zoe, then saw that Nous and Aletheia had celebrated the Father of the universe by a perfect number; and Logos him-

---

[1] Or, "completes the great year of the world" (see book iv. chap. vii. of The Refutation).

[2] Valentinus' system, if purged of the glosses put upon it by his disciples, appears to have been constructed out of a grand conception of Deity, and evidences much power of abstraction. Between the essence of God, dwelling in the midst of isolation prior to an exercise of the creative energy, and the material worlds, Valentinus interposes an ideal world. Through the latter, the soul — of a kindred nature — is enabled to mount up to God. This is the import of the terms Bythus (depth) and Sige (silence, i.e., solitariness) afterwards used.

[3] κυρία: instead of this has been suggested the reading καὶ ρίζα, i.e., "which is both the root," etc.

[4] In all this Valentinus intends to delineate the progress from absolute to phenomenal being. There are three developments in this transition. Absolute being (Bythus and Sige) is the same as the eternal thought and consciousness of God's own essence. Here we have the primary emanation, viz., Nous, i.e., Mind (called also Mono-genes, only-begotten), and Aletheia, i.e., Truth. Next comes the ideal manifestation through the Logos, i e., Word (obviously bor-rowed from the prologue to St. John's Gospel), and Zoe, i.e., Life (taken from the same source). We have then the passage from the ideal to the actual in Anthropos, i.e., Man, and Ecclesia, i.e., Church. These last are the phenomenal manifestations of the divine mind.

[5] τέλειος: Bunsen would read τέλος, which Cruice objects to on account of the word τελειότερος occurring in the next sentence.

self likewise with Zoe wished to magnify their own father and mother, Nous and Aletheia. Since, however, Nous and Aletheia were begotten, and did not possess paternal (and) perfect uncreatedness, Logos and Zoe do not glorify Nous their father with a perfect number, but far from it, with an imperfect one.[1] For Logos and Zoe offer twelve Æons unto Nous and Aletheia. For, according to Valentinus, these — namely, Nous and Aletheia, Logos and Zoe, Anthropos and Ecclesia — have been the primary roots of the Æons. But there are ten Æons proceeding from Nous and Aletheia, and twelve from Logos and Zoe — twenty and eight in all.[2] And to these (ten) they give these following denominations : [3] Bythus and Mixis, Ageratus and Henosis, Autophyes and Hedone, Acinetus and Syncrasis, Monogenes and Macaria.[4] These are ten Æons whom some say (have been projected) by Nous and Aletheia, but some by Logos and Zoe. Others, however, affirm that the twelve (Æons have been projected) by Anthropos and Ecclesia, while others by Logos and Zoe. And upon these they bestow these following names : [5] Paracletus and Pistis, Patricus and Elpis, Metricus and Agape, Æinous and Synesis, Ecclesiasticus and Macariotes, Theletus and Sophia. But of the twelve, the twelfth and youngest of all the twenty-eight Æons, being a female, and called Sophia, observed the multitude and power of the begetting Æons, and hurried back into the depth of the Father. And she perceived that all the rest of the Æons, as being begotten, generate by conjugal intercourse. The Father, on the other hand, alone, without copulation, has produced (an offspring). She wished to emulate the Father,[6] and to produce (offspring) of herself without a marital partner, that she might achieve a work in no wise inferior [7] to (that of)

the Father. (Sophia, however,) was ignorant that the Unbegotten One, being an originating principle of the universe, as well as root and depth and abyss, alone possesses the power of self-generation. But Sophia, being begotten, and born after many more (Æons), is not able to acquire possession of the power inherent in the Unbegotten One. For in the Unbegotten One, he says, all things exist simultaneously, but in the begotten (Æons) the female is projective of substance, and the male is formative of the substance which is projected by the female. Sophia, therefore, prepared to project that only which she was capable (of projecting), viz., a formless and undigested substance.[8] And this, he says, is what Moses asserts : "The earth was invisible, and unfashioned." This (substance) is, he says, the good (and) the heavenly Jerusalem, into which God has promised to conduct the children of Israel, saying, "I will bring you into a land flowing with milk and honey."

CHAP. XXVI. — VALENTINUS' EXPLANATION OF THE EXISTENCE OF CHRIST AND THE SPIRIT.

Ignorance, therefore, having arisen within the Pleroma in consequence of Sophia, and shapelessness in consequence of the offspring of Sophia, confusion arose in the Pleroma. (For all) the Æons that were begotten (became overwhelmed with apprehension, imagining) that in like manner formless and incomplete progenies of the Æons should be generated; and that some destruction, at no distant period, should at length seize upon the Æons. All the Æons, then, betook themselves to supplication of the Father, that he would tranquillize the sorrowing Sophia; for she continued weeping and bewailing on account of the abortion produced by her, — for so they term it. The Father, then, compassioning the tears of Sophia, and accepting the supplication of the Æons, orders a further projection. For he did not, (Valentinus) says, himself project, but Nous and Aletheia (projected) Christ and the Holy Spirit for the restoration of Form, and the destruction of the abortion, and (for) the consolation and cessation of the groans of Sophia. And thirty Æons came into existence along with Christ and the Holy Spirit. Some of these (Valentinians) wish that this should be a triacontad of Æons, whereas others desire that Sige should exist along with the Father, and that the Æons should be reckoned along with them.

---

[1] This follows the text as emended by Bernays.

[2] The number properly should be thirty, as there were two tetrads: (1) Bythus, Sige, Nous, and Aletheia; (2) Logos, Zoe, Ecclesia, and Anthropos. Some, as we learn from Hippolytus, made up the number to thirty, by the addition of Christ and the Holy Ghost, — a fact which Bunsen thinks conclusively proves that the alleged generation of Æons was a subsequent addition to Valentinus' system.

[3] There is some confusion in Hippolytus' text, which is, however, removeable by a reference to Irenæus (i. 1).

[4] We subjoin the meanings of these names: —

Ten Æons from Nous and Aletheia, (or) Logos and Zoe, viz.: —

1. Bythus　= Profundity.
2. Mixis　= Mixture.
3. Ageratos　= Ever-young.
4. Henosis　= Unification.
5. Autophyes = Self-grown.
6. Hedone　= Voluptuousness.
7. Acinetus　= Motionless.
8. Syncrasis　= Composition.
9. Monogenes = Only-begotten.
10. Macaria　= Blessedness.

[5] The following are the meanings of these names: —

Twelve Æons from Anthropos and Ecclesia, (or) Logos and Zoe: —

1. Paracletus　= Comforter.
2. Pistis　= Faith.
3. Patricus　= Paternal.
4. Elpis　= Hope.
5. Metricus　= Temperate.
6. Agape　= Love.
7. Æinous　= Ever-thinking.
8. Synesis　= Intelligence.
19. Ecclesiasticus = Ecclesiastical.
10. Makariotes　= Felicity.
11. Theletus　= Volition.
12. Sophia　= Wisdom.

[6] [Rev ii 24. It belongs to the "depths of Satan" to create mythologies that caricature the Divine mysteries. Cf. 2 Cor. ii. 11.]

[7] This Sophia was, so to speak, the bridge which spanned the abyss between God and Reality. Under an aspect of this kind Solomon (Prov. viii.) views Wisdom; and Valentinus introduces it into his system, according to the old Judaistic interpretation of Sophia, as the

instrument for God's creative energy. But Sophia thought to pass beyond her function as the connecting link between limited and illimitable existence, by an attempt to evolve the infinite from herself. She fails, and an abortive image of the true Wisdom is procreated, while Sophia herself sinks into this nether world.

[8] Miller's text has, "a well-formed and properly-digested substance." This reading is, however, obviously wrong, as is proved by a reference to what Epiphanius states (Hær., xxxi.) concerning Valentinus.

Christ, therefore, being additionally projected, and the Holy Spirit, by Nous and Aletheia, immediately this abortion of Sophia, (which was) shapeless, (and) born of herself only, and generated without conjugal intercourse, separates from the entire of the Æons, lest the perfect Æons, beholding this (abortion), should be disturbed by reason of its shapelessness. In order, then, that the shapelessness of the abortion might not at all manifest itself to the perfect Æons, the Father also again projects additionally one Æon, viz., Staurus. And he being begotten great, as from a mighty and perfect father, and being projected for the guardianship and defence of the Æons, becomes a limit of the Pleroma, having within itself all the thirty Æons together, for these are they that had been projected. Now this (Æon) is styled Horos, because he separates from the Pleroma the Hysterema that is outside. And (he is called) Metocheus, because he shares also in the Hysterema. And (he is denominated) Staurus, because he is fixed inflexibly and inexorably, so that nothing of the Hysterema can come near the Æons who are within the Pleroma. Outside, then, Horos, (or) Metocheus,[1] (or) Staurus, is the Ogdoad, as it is called, according to them, and is that Sophia which is outside the Pleroma, which (Sophia) Christ, who was additionally projected by Nous and Aletheia, formed and made a perfect Æon, so that in no respect she should be inferior in power to any of the Æons within the Pleroma.[2] Since, however, Sophia was formed outside, and it was not possible and equitable that Christ and the Holy Spirit, who were projected from Nous and Aletheia, should remain outside the Pleroma, Christ hurried away, and the Holy Spirit, from her who had had shape imparted to her, unto Nous and Aletheia within the Limit, in order that with the rest of the Æons they might glorify the Father.

CHAP. XXVII. — VALENTINUS' EXPLANATION OF THE EXISTENCE OF JESUS; POWER OF JESUS OVER HUMANITY.

After, then, there ensued some one (treaty of) peace and harmony between all the Æons within the Pleroma, it appeared expedient to them not only by a conjugal union to have magnified the Son, but also that by an offering of ripe fruits they should glorify the Father. Then all the thirty Æons consented to project one Æon, joint fruit of the Pleroma, that he might be (an earnest) of their union,[3] and unanimity, and peace. And he alone was projected by all the Æons in honour of the Father. This (one) is styled among them "Joint Fruit of the Pleroma." These (matters), then, took place within the Pleroma in this way. And the "Joint Fruit of the Pleroma" was projected, (that is,) Jesus, — for this is his name, — the great High Priest. Sophia, however, who was outside the Pleroma in search of Christ, who had given her form, and of the Holy Spirit, became involved in great terror that she would perish, if he should separate from her, who had given her form and consistency. And she was seized with grief, and fell into a state of considerable perplexity, (while) reflecting who was he who had given her form, what the Holy Spirit was, whither he had departed, who it was that had hindered them from being present, who it was that had been envious of that glorious and blessed spectacle. While involved in sufferings such as these, she turns herself to prayer and supplication of him who had deserted her. During the utterance of her entreaties, Christ, who is within the Pleroma, had mercy upon (her), and all the rest of the Æons (were similarly affected); and they send forth beyond the Pleroma "the Joint Fruit of the Pleroma" as a spouse for Sophia, who was outside, and as a rectifier of those sufferings which she underwent in searching after Christ.

"The Fruit," then, arriving outside the Pleroma, and discovering (Sophia) in the midst of those four primary passions, both fear and sorrow, and perplexity and entreaty, he rectified her affections. While, however, correcting them, he observed that it would not be proper to destroy these, inasmuch as they are (in their nature) eternal, and peculiar to Sophia; and yet that neither was it seemly that Sophia should exist in the midst of such passions, in fear and sorrow, supplication (and) perplexity. He therefore, as an Æon so great, and (as) offspring of the entire Pleroma, caused the passions to depart from her, and he made these substantially-existent essences.[4] He altered fear into animal desire,[5] and (made) grief material, and (rendered) perplexity (the passion) of demons. But conversion,[6] and entreaty, and supplication, he constituted as a path to repentance and power over the animal essence, which is denominated right.[7] The Creator[8] (acted) from fear; (and) that is what, he says, Scripture affirms: "The fear of the Lord is the beginning of wisdom."[9] For this is the beginning of the

---

[1] Or, "Metagogeus" (see Irenæus, i. 1, 2, iii. 1).
[2] Bunsen corrects the passage, "So that she should not be inferior to any of the Æons, or unequal (in power) to any (of them)."
[3] ἑνότητος: Miller has νεότητος, i.e., youth. The former is the emendation of Bernays.

[4] This is Bunsen's text, ὑποστάτους. Duncker reads ὑποστατικὰς, hypostatic.
[5] Some read οὐσίαν (see Theodoret, Hær., c. vii.).
[6] ἐπιστροφὴν; or it may be rendered "solicitude." Literally, it means a turning towards, as in this instance, for the purpose of prayer (see Irenæus, i. 5).
[7] Valentinus denominates what is psychical (natural) right, and what is material or pathematic left (see Irenæus, i. 5).
[8] Cruice renders the passage thus: "which is denominated right, or Demiurge, while fear it is that accomplishes this transformation." The Demiurge is of course called "right," as being the power of the psychical essence (see Clemens Alexandrinus, Hypot. excerpta e Theod., c. 43).
[9] Ps. cxi. 10; Prov. i. 7, ix. 10.

affections of Sophia, for she was seized with fear, next with grief, then with perplexity, and so she sought refuge in entreaty and supplication. And the animal essence is, he says, of a fiery nature, and is also termed by them the super-celestial Topos, and Hebdomad,[1] and "Ancient of Days."[2] And whatever other such statements they advance respecting this (Æon), these they allege to hold good of the animalish (one), whom they assert to be creator of the world. Now he is of the appearance of fire. Moses also, he says, expresses himself thus : " The Lord thy God is a burning and consuming fire."[3] For he, likewise, wishes (to think) that it has been so written. There is, however, he says, a twofold power of the fire ; for fire is all-consuming, (and) cannot be quenched. According, therefore, to this division, there exists, subject to death, a certain soul which is a sort of mediator, for it is a Hebdomad and Cessation.[4] For underneath the Ogdoad, where Sophia is, but above Matter, which is the Creator, a day has been formed,[5] and the " Joint Fruit of the Pleroma." If the soul has been fashioned in the image of those above, that is, the Ogdoad, it became immortal and repaired to the Ogdoad, which is, he says, heavenly Jerusalem. If, however, it has been fashioned in the image of Matter, that is, the corporeal passions, the soul is of a perishable nature, and is (accordingly) destroyed.

CHAP. XXVIII. — THE VALENTINIAN ORIGIN OF THE CREATION.

As, therefore, the primary and greatest power[6] of the animal essence came into existence, an image (of the only begotten Son) ; so also the devil, who is the ruler of this world, constitutes the power of the material essence, as Beelzebub is of the essence of demons which emanates from anxiety. (In consequence of this,) Sophia from above exerted her energy from the Ogdoad to the Hebdomad. For the Demiurge, they say, knows nothing at all, but is, according to them, devoid of understanding, and silly, and is not conscious of what he is doing or working at. But in him, while thus in a state of ignorance that even he is producing, Sophia wrought all sorts of energy, and infused vigour (into him). And (although Sophia) was really the operating cause, he himself imagines that he evolves the creation of the world out of himself : whence

he commenced, saying, " I am God, and beside me there is no other."[7]

CHAP. XXIX. — THE OTHER VALENTINIAN EMANATIONS IN CONFORMITY WITH THE PYTHAGOREAN SYSTEM OF NUMBERS.

The quaternion, then, advocated by Valentinus, is " a source of the everlasting nature having roots ; "[8] and Sophia (is the power) from whom the animal and material creation has derived its present condition. But Sophia is called "Spirit," and the Demiurge "Soul," and the Devil "the ruler of this world," and Beelzebub "the (ruler) of demons." These are the statements which they put forward. But further, in addition to these, rendering, as I have previously mentioned, their entire system of doctrine (akin to the) arithmetical (art), (they determine) that the thirty Æons within the Pleroma have again, in addition to these, projected other Æons, according to the (numerical) proportion (adopted by the Pythagoreans), in order that the Pleroma might be formed into an aggregate, according to a perfect number. For how the Pythagoreans divided (the celestial sphere) into twelve and thirty and sixty parts, and how they have minute parts of diminutive portions, has been made evident.

In this manner these (followers of Valentinus) subdivide the parts within the Pleroma. Now likewise the parts in the Ogdoad have been subdivided, and there has been projected Sophia, which is, according to them, mother of all living creatures, and the " Joint Fruit of the Pleroma," (who is) the Logos,[9] (and other Æons,) who are celestial angels that have their citizenship in Jerusalem which is above, which is in heaven. For this Jerusalem is Sophia, she (that is) outside (the Pleroma), and her spouse is the " Joint Fruit of the Pleroma." And the Demiurge projected souls ; for this (Sophia) is the essence of souls. This (Demiurge), according to them, is Abraham, and these (souls) the children of Abraham. From the material and devilish essence the Demiurge fashioned bodies for the souls. This is what has been declared : " And God formed man, taking clay from the earth, and breathed upon his face the breath of life, and man was made into a living soul."[10] This, according to them, is the inner man, the natural (man), residing in the material body. Now a material (man) is perishable, incomplete, (and) formed out of the devilish essence. And this is

---

[1] Schneidewin fills up the hiatus thus: " Place of Mediation." The above translation adopts the emendation of Cruice (see Irenæus, i. 5).
[2] Dan. vii. 9, 13, 22.
[3] Deut. ix. 3; Ps. l. 3; Heb. xii. 29.
[4] Gen. ii. 2.
[5] See *Epistle of Barnabas*, chap. xv. vol. i. p. 146, and *Ignatius' Letter to the Magnesians*, chap. ix. p. 63, this series.
[6] The opening sentence in this chapter is confused in Miller's text. The sense, however, as given above, is deducible from a reference to a corresponding passage in Irenæus (i. 5).

[7] Deut. iv. 35; Isa. xlv. 5, 14, 18, 21, 22.
[8] These words are a line out of Pythagoras' *Golden Verses:* —
Πηγή τις ἀενάου φύσεως ῥιζώματ' ἔχουσα — (48).
[9] The Abbe Cruice thinks that a comparison of this passage with the corresponding one in Irenæus suggests the addition of οἱ δορυφόροι after Λόγος, i.e., the Logos and his satellites. [Vol. i. p. 381, this series.]
[10] Gen. ii. 7.

the material man, as it were, according to them an inn [1] or domicile, at one time of soul only, at another time of soul and demons, at another time of soul and Logoi.[2]   And these are the Logoi that have been dispersed from above, from the "Joint Fruit of the Pleroma" and (from) Sophia, into this world.   And they dwell in an earthly body, with a soul, and when demons do not take up their abode with that soul.   This, he says, is what has been written in Scripture : "On this account I bend my knees to the God and Father and Lord of our Lord Jesus Christ, that God would grant you to have Christ dwelling in the inner man," [3] — that is, the natural (man), not the corporeal (one), — "that you may be able to understand what is the depth," which is the Father of the universe, "and what is the breadth," which is Staurus, the limit of the Pleroma, "or what is the length," that is, the Pleroma of the Æons.   Wherefore, he says, "the natural man receiveth not the things of the Spirit of God, for they are foolishness unto him;" [4] but folly, he says, is the power of the Demiurge, for he was foolish and devoid of understanding, and imagined himself to be fabricating the world.   He was, however, ignorant that Sophia, the Mother, the Ogdoad, was really the cause of all the operations performed by him who had no consciousness in reference to the creation of the world.

CHAP. XXX. — VALENTINUS' EXPLANATION OF THE BIRTH OF JESUS ; TWOFOLD DOCTRINE ON THE NATURE OF JESUS' BODY ; OPINION OF THE ITALIANS, THAT IS, HERACLEON AND PTOLEMÆUS ; OPINION OF THE ORIENTALS, THAT IS, AXIONICUS AND BARDESANES.

All the prophets, therefore, and the law, spoke by means of the Demiurge, — a silly god,[5] he says, (and themselves) fools, who knew nothing. On account of this, he says, the Saviour observes : "All that came before me are thieves and robbers." [6]   And the apostle (uses these words) : "The mystery which was not made known to former generations." [7]   For none of the prophets, he says, said anything concerning the things of which we speak ; for (a prophet) could not but be ignorant of all (these) things, inasmuch as they certainly had been uttered by the Demiurge only.   When, therefore, the creation received completion, and when after (this) there ought to have been the revelation of the sons of God — that is, of the Demiurge, which up to this had been concealed, and in which obscurity the

natural man was hid, and had a veil upon the heart ; — when (it was time), then, that the veil should be taken away, and that these mysteries should be seen, Jesus was born of Mary the virgin, according to the declaration (in Scripture), "The Holy Ghost will come upon thee" — Sophia is the Spirit — "and the power of the Highest will overshadow thee," — the Highest is the Demiurge, — "wherefore that which shall be born of thee shall be called holy." [8]   For he has been generated not from the highest alone, as those created in (the likeness of) Adam have been created from the highest alone — that is, (from) Sophia and the Demiurge.   Jesus, however, the new man, (has been generated) from the Holy Spirit — that is, Sophia and the Demiurge — in order that the Demiurge may complete the conformation and constitution of his body, and that the Holy Spirit may supply his essence, and that a celestial Logos may proceed from the Ogdoad being born of Mary.

Concerning this (Logos) they have a great question amongst them — an occasion both of divisions and dissension.   And hence the doctrine of these has become divided : and one doctrine, according to them, is termed Oriental, and the other Italian.   They from Italy, of whom is Heracleon and Ptolemæus, say that the body of Jesus was (an) animal (one).   And on account of this, (they maintain) that at his baptism the Holy Spirit as a dove came down — that is, the Logos of the mother above, (I mean Sophia) — and became (a voice) to the animal (man), and raised him from the dead.   This, he says, is what has been declared : "He who raised Christ from the dead will also quicken your mortal and natural bodies." [9]   For loam has come under a curse ; "for," says he, "dust thou art, and unto dust shalt thou return." [10]   The Orientals, on the other hand, of whom is Axionicus [11] and Bardesianes,[12] assert that the body of the Saviour was spiritual ; for there came upon Mary the Holy Spirit — that is, Sophia and the power of the highest.   This is the creative art, (and was vouchsafed) in order that what was given to Mary by the Spirit might be fashioned.

CHAP. XXXI. — FURTHER DOCTRINES OF VALENTINUS RESPECTING THE ÆONS ; REASONS FOR THE INCARNATION.

Let, then, those (heretics) pursue these inquiries among themselves, (and let others do so likewise,) if it should prove agreeable to anybody else to investigate (such points.   Valen-

---

[1] Or, "subterranean" (Cruice).
[2] Epiphanius, Hær., xxxi. sec. 7.
[3] Eph. iii. 14–18.
[4] 1 Cor. ii. 14.
[5] Epiphanius, Hær., xxxi. 22,
[6] John x. 8.
[7] Col. i. 26.

[8] Luke i. 35.
[9] Rom. viii. 11, 12.
[10] Gen. iii. 19.
[11] Axionicus is mentioned by Tertullian only (see Tertullian, Contr. Valent., c. iv; [vol. iii. p. 505, this series]).
[12] Bardesianes (or Ardesianes, as Miller's text has it) is evidently the same with Bardesanes, mentioned by Eusebius and St. Jerome.

tinus) subjoins, however, the following statement : That the trespasses appertaining to the Æons within (the Pleroma) had been corrected ; and likewise had been rectified the trespasses appertaining to the Ogdoad, (that is,) Sophia, outside (the Pleroma) ; and also (the trespasses) appertaining to the Hebdomad (had been rectified). For the Demiurge had been taught by Sophia that He is not Himself God alone, as He imagined, and that except Himself there is not another (Deity). But when taught by Sophia, He was made to recognise the superior (Deity). For He was instructed [1] by her, and initiated and indoctrinated into the great mystery of the Father and of the Æons, and divulged this to none. This is, as he says, what (God) declares to Moses : " I am the God of Abraham, and the God of Isaac, and the God of Jacob ; and my name I have not announced to them ; " [2] that is, I have not declared the mystery, nor explained who is God, but I have preserved the mystery which I have heard from Sophia in secrecy with myself. When, then, the trespasses of those above had been rectified, it was necessary, according to the same consequence, that the (transgressions) here likewise should obtain rectification. On this account Jesus the Saviour was born of Mary, that he might rectify (the trespasses committed) here ; as the Christ who, having been projected additionally from above by Nous and Aletheia, had corrected the passions of Sophia — that is, the abortion (who was) outside (the Pleroma). And, again, the Saviour who was born of Mary came to rectify the passions [3] of the soul. There are therefore, according to these (heretics), three Christs : (the first the) one additionally projected by Nous and Aletheia, along with the Holy Spirit ; and (the second) the " Joint Fruit of the Pleroma," spouse of Sophia, who was outside (the Pleroma). And she herself is likewise styled Holy Spirit, but one inferior to the first (projection). And the third (Christ is) He who was born of Mary for the restoration of this world of ours.

CHAP. XXXII. — VALENTINUS CONVICTED OF PLAGIARISMS FROM PLATO.

I think that the heresy of Valentinus, which is of Pythagorean (origin), has been sufficiently, indeed more than sufficiently, delineated. It therefore seems also expedient, that having explained his opinions, we should desist from (further) refutation (of his system). Plato, then, in expounding mysteries concerning the universe, writes to Dionysius expressing himself after some

such manner [4] as this : " I must speak to you by riddles,[5] in order that if the letter may meet with any accident in its leaves by either sea or land, he who reads (what falls into his hands) may not understand it. For so it is. All things are about the King of all, and on his account are all things, and he is cause of all the glorious (objects of creation). The second is about the second, and the third about the third. But pertaining to the King there is none of those things of which I have spoken. But after this the soul earnestly desires to learn what sort these are, looking upon those things that are akin to itself, and not one of these is (in itself) sufficient. This is, O son of Dionysius and Doris, the question (of yours) which is a cause of all evil things. Nay, but rather the solicitude concerning this is innate in the soul ; and if one does not remove this, he will never really attain truth.[6] But what is astonishing in this matter, listen. For there are men who have heard these things — (men) furnished with capacities for learning, and furnished with capacities of memory, and persons who altogether in every way are endued with an aptitude for investigation with a view to inference. (These are) at present aged speculators.[7] And they assert that opinions which at one time were credible are now incredible, and that things once incredible are now the contrary. While, therefore, turning the eye of examination towards these (inquiries), exercise caution, lest at any time you should have reason to repent in regard of those things should they happen in a manner unbecoming to your dignity. On this account I have written nothing concerning these (points) ; nor is there any treatise of Plato's (upon them), nor ever shall there be. The observations, however, now made are those of Socrates, conspicuous for virtue even while he was a young man."

Valentinus, falling in with these (remarks), has made a fundamental principle in his system " the King of all," whom Plato mentioned, and whom this heretic styles Pater, and Bythos, and Proarche [8] over the rest of the Æons. And when Plato uses the words, " what is second about things that are second," Valentinus supposes to be second all the Æons that are within the limit (of the Pleroma, as well as) the limit (itself). And when Plato uses the words, " what is third about what is third," he has (constituted as third)

---

[1] κατηχήθη. Miller's text has κατήχθη, which is properly corrected by Bunsen into the word as translated above.
[2] Ex. vi. 2, 3.
[3] Or, " the multitudes."

[4] Cruice thinks that the following extract from Plato's epistles has been added by a second hand. [Cf vol. iii. p. 181, this series.]
[5] There are some verbal diversities between the texts of Plato and Hippolytus, which a reference will show (see Plat., *Epist.*, t. ix. p. 76, ed. Bekker).
[6] Some forty lines that follow in Plato's letter are omitted here.
[7] Here likewise there is another deficiency as compared with the original letter.
[8] Miller's text is, καὶ πᾶσι γῆν, etc. In the German and French edition of Hippolytus we have, instead of this, καὶ Προαρχην. The latter word is introduced on the authority of Epiphanius and Theodoret. Bernays proposes Σιγὴν, and Scott Πλάστην. The Abbe Cruice considers Πλάστην an incongruous word as applied to the creation of spiritual beings.

the entire of the arrangement (existing) outside the limit [1] and the Pleroma. And Valentinus has elucidated this (arrangement) very succinctly, in a psalm commencing from below, not as Plato does, from above, expressing himself thus : " I behold [2] all things suspended in air by spirit, and I perceive all things wafted by spirit ; the flesh (I see) suspended from soul, but the soul shining out from air, and air depending from æther, and fruits produced from Bythus, and the fœtus borne from the womb." Thus (Valentinus) formed his opinion on such (points). Flesh, according to these (heretics), is matter which is suspended from the soul of the Demiurge. And soul shines out from air ; that is, the Demiurge emerges from the spirit, (which is) outside the Pleroma. But air springs forth from æther ; that is, Sophia, which is outside (the Pleroma, is projected from the Pleroma) which is within the limit, and (from) the entire Pleroma (generally). And from Bythus fruits are produced ; (that is,) the entire projection of the Æons is made from the Father. The opinions, then, advanced by Valentinus have been sufficiently declared. It remains for us to explain the tenets of those who have emanated from his school, though each adherent (of Valentinus) entertains different opinions. [3]

CHAP. XXXIII. — SECUNDUS' SYSTEM OF ÆONS ; EPIPHANES ; PTOLEMÆUS.

A certain (heretic) Secundus, [4] born about the same time with Ptolemæus, expresses himself thus : (he says) that there is a right tetrad and a left tetrad, — namely, light and darkness. And he affirms that the power which withdrew and laboured under deficiency, was not produced from the thirty Æons, but from the fruits of these. Some other (heretic), however — Epiphanes, a teacher among them — expresses himself thus : " The earliest originating principle was inconceivable, ineffable, and unnameable ; " and he calls this Monotes. And (he maintains) that there co-exists with this (principle) a power which he denominates Henotes. This Henotes and this Monotes, not by projection (from themselves), sent forth a principle (that should preside) over all intelligibles ; (and this was) both

unbegotten and invisible, and he styles it a Monad. "With this power co-exists a power of the same essence, which very (power) I call Unity. These four powers sent forth the remainder of the projections of the Æons." But others, again, denominate the chief and originating Ogdoad, (which is) fourth (and) invisible, by the following names : first, Proarche ; next, Anennoetus ; third, Arrhetus ; and fourth, Aoratus. And that from the first, Proarche, was projected by a first and fifth place, Arche ; and from Anennoetus, by a second and sixth place, Acataleptus ; and from Arrhetus, by a third and seventh place, Anonomastus ; and from Aoratus, Agennetus, a complement of the first Ogdoad. They wish that these powers should exist before Bythus and Sige. Concerning, however, Bythus himself, there are many different opinions. Some affirm him to be unwedded, neither male nor female ; but others (maintain) that Sige, who is a female, is present with him, and that this constitutes the first conjugal union.

But the followers of Ptolemæus [5] assert that (Bythus) has two spouses, which they call likewise dispositions, viz., Ennoia and Thelesis (conception and volition). For first the notion was conceived of projecting anything ; next followed, as they say, the will to do so. Wherefore also these two dispositions and powers — namely, Ennoia and Thelesis — being, as it were, mingled one with the other, there ensued a projection of Monogenes and Aletheia by means of a conjugal union. And the consequence was, that visible types and images of those two dispositions of the Father came forth from the invisible (Æons), viz., from Thelema, Nous, and from Ennoia, Aletheia. And on this account the image of the subsequently generated Thelema is (that of a) male ; but (the image) of the unbegotten Ennoia is (that of a) female, since volition is, as it were, a power of conception. For conception always cherished the idea of a projection, yet was not of itself at least able to project itself, but cherished the idea (of doing so). When, however, the power of volition (would be present), then it projects the idea which had been conceived.

CHAP. XXXIV. — SYSTEM OF MARCUS ; A MERE IMPOSTOR ; HIS WICKED DEVICES UPON THE EUCHARISTIC CUP.

A certain other teacher among them, Marcus, [6] an adept in sorcery, carrying on operations [7]

---

[1] The word "limit" occurs twice in this sentence, and Bunsen alters the second into " Pleroma," so that the words may be rendered thus: "Valentinus supposes to be second all the Æons that are within the Pleroma."

[2] This is a Gnostic hymn, and is arranged metrically by Cruice, of which the following is a translation : —
> All things whirled on by spirit I see,
> Flesh from soul depending,
> And soul from air forth flashing,
> And air from æther hanging,
> And fruits from Bythus streaming,
> And from womb the infant growing.

[3] The text here is corrupt, but the above rendering follows the Abbe Cruice's version. Bunsen's emendation would, however, seem untenable.

[4] Concerning Secundus and Epiphanes, see Irenæus, i. 11 ; Theodoret, Hær. Fab., i. 5-9 ; Epiphanius, xxxii. 1, 3, 4 ; Tertullian, Adv. Valent., c. xxxviii. ; and St. Augustine, Hær., xi. Hippolytus, in his remarks on Secundus and Epiphanes, borrows from St. Irenæus.

[5] Concerning Ptolemæus, see Irenæus, i. 12 ; Tertullian, De Præscript., c. xlix. ; and Advers. Valent., c. viii. ; Epiphanius, Hær., xxxiii. 3-7 ; and Theodoret, Hæret. Fab., i. 8.

[6] Concerning Marcus, see Irenæus, i. 12-18 ; Tertullian, Præscript., c. l. ; Epiphanius, Hær., xxxiv. ; Theodoret, Hæret. Fab., i. 9 ; St. Augustine, Hær., c. xiv. ; and St. Jerome's 29th Epistle.

[7] ἐνεργῶν: Bunsen reads δρῶν, which has the same meaning. Cruice reads αἰωρῶν, but makes no attempt at translation. Miller's reading is δώρων, which is obviously corrupt, but for which δόλων has been suggested, and with good show of reason.

partly by sleight of hand and partly by demons, deceived many from time to time. This (heretic) alleged that there resided in him the mightiest power from invisible and unnameable places. And very often, taking the Cup, as if offering up the Eucharistic prayer, and prolonging to a greater length than usual the word of invocation, he would cause the appearance of a purple, and sometimes of a red mixture, so that his dupes imagined that a certain Grace descended and communicated to the potion a blood-red potency. The knave, however, at that time succeeded in escaping detection from many; but now, being convicted (of the imposture), he will be forced to desist from it. For, infusing secretly into the mixture some drug that possessed the power of imparting such a colour (as that alluded to above), uttering for a considerable time nonsensical expressions, he was in the habit of waiting, (in expectation) that the (drug), obtaining a supply of moisture, might be dissolved, and, being intermingled with the potion, might impart its colour to it. The drugs, however, that possess the quality of furnishing this effect, we have previously mentioned in the book on magicians.[1] And here we have taken occasion to explain how they make dupes of many, and thoroughly ruin them. And if it should prove agreeable to them to apply their attention with greater accuracy to the statement made by us, they will become aware of the deceit of Marcus.

CHAP. XXXV. — FURTHER ACTS OF JUGGLERY ON THE PART OF MARCUS.

And this (Marcus), infusing (the aforesaid) mixture into a smaller cup, was in the habit of delivering it to a woman to offer up the Eucharistic prayer, while he himself stood by, and held (in his hand) another empty (chalice) larger than that. And after his female dupe had pronounced the sentence of Consecration,[2] having received (the cup from her), he proceeded to infuse (its contents) into the larger (chalice), and, pouring them frequently from one cup to the other, was accustomed at the same time to utter the following invocation: " Grant that the inconceivable and ineffable Grace which existed prior to the universe, may fill thine inner man, and make to abound in thee the knowledge of this (grace), as She disseminates the seed of the mustard-tree upon the good soil." And simultaneously pronouncing some such words as these, and astonishing both his female dupe and those that are present, he was regarded as one performing a miracle; while the larger was being filled from the smaller chalice, in such a way as

that (the contents), being superabundant, flowed over. And the contrivance of this (juggler) we have likewise explained in the aforesaid (fourth) book, where we have proved that very many drugs, when mingled in this way with liquid substances, are endued with the quality of yielding augmentation, more particularly when diluted in wine. Now, when (one of these impostors) previously smears, in a clandestine manner, an empty cup with any one of these drugs, and shows it (to the spectators) as if it contained nothing, by infusing into it (the contents) from the other cup, and pouring them back again, the drug, as it is of a flatulent nature, is dissolved[3] by being blended with the moist substance. And the effect of this was, that a superabundance of the mixture ensued, and was so far augmented, that what was infused was put in motion, such being the nature of the drug. And if one stow away (the chalice) when it has been filled, (what has been poured into it) will after no long time return to its natural dimensions, inasmuch as the potency of the drug becomes extinct by reason of the continuance of moisture. Wherefore he was in the habit of hurriedly presenting the cup to those present, to drink; but they, horrified at the same time, and eager (to taste the contents of the cup), proceeded to drink (the mixture), as if it were something divine, and devised by the Deity.[4]

CHAP. XXXVI. — THE HERETICAL PRACTICES OF THE MARCITES IN REGARD OF BAPTISM.

Such and other (tricks) this impostor attempted to perform. And so it was that he was magnified by his dupes, and sometimes he was supposed to utter predictions. But sometimes he tried to make others (prophesy), partly by demons carrying on these operations, and partly by practising sleight of hand, as we have previously stated. Hoodwinking therefore multitudes, he led on (into enormities) many (dupes) of this description who had become his disciples, by teaching them that they were prone, no doubt, to sin, but beyond the reach of danger, from the fact of their belonging to the perfect power, and of their being participators in the inconceivable potency. And subsequent to the (first) baptism, to these they promise another, which they call Redemption. And by this (other baptism) they wickedly subvert those that remain with them in expectation of redemption, as if persons, after they had once been baptized, could again obtain remission. Now, it is by means of such knavery as this that they seem to retain their

---

[1] [The lost book upon the Witch of Endor, possibly. " Against the Magi" is the title of the text, and is taken to refer to book iv. cap. xxviii. p. 35, *supra:* the more probable opinion.]
[5] Or, " had given thanks."

[3] ἀναλυομένου : some read ἀναδυομένου, which is obviously untenable.
[4] [Here was an awful travesty of the heresy of a later day which introduced " the miracle of Bolsena" and the *Corpus-Christi* celebration. See Robertson, *Hist.*, vol. iii. p. 604.]

hearers. And when they consider that these have been tested, and are able to keep (secret the mysteries) committed unto them, they then admit them to this (baptism). They, however, do not rest satisfied with this alone, but promise (their votaries) some other (boon) for the purpose of confirming them in hope, in order that they may be inseparable (adherents of their sect). For they utter something in an inexpressible (tone of) voice, after having laid hands on him who is receiving the redemption. And they allege that they could not easily declare (to another) what is thus spoken unless one were highly tested, or one were at the hour of death, (when) the bishop comes and whispers (it) into the (expiring one's) ear. And this knavish device (is undertaken) for the purpose of securing the constant attendance upon the bishop of (Marcus') disciples, as individuals eagerly panting to learn what that may be which is spoken at the last, by (the knowledge of) which the learner will be advanced to the rank of those admitted into the higher mysteries. And in regard of these I have maintained a silence for this reason, lest at any time one should suppose that I was guilty of disparaging these (heretics). For this does not come within the scope of our present work, only so far as it may contribute to prove from what source (the heretics) have derived the standing-point from which they have taken occasion to introduce the opinions advanced by them.[1]

CHAP. XXXVII. — MARCUS' SYSTEM EXPLAINED BY IRENÆUS; MARCUS' VISION; THE VISION OF VALENTINUS REVEALING TO HIM HIS SYSTEM.

For also the blessed presbyter Irenæus, having approached the subject of a refutation in a more unconstrained spirit, has explained such washings and redemptions, stating more in the way of a rough digest[2] what are their practices. (And it appears that some of the Marcosians,) on meeting with (Irenæus' work,) deny that they have so received (the secret word just alluded to), but they have learned that always they should deny. Wherefore our anxiety has been more accurately to investigate, and to discover minutely what are the (instructions) which they deliver in the case of the first bath, styling it by some such name; and in the case of the second, which they denominate Redemption. But not even has this secret of theirs escaped

(our scrutiny). For these opinions, however, we consent to pardon Valentinus and his school.

But Marcus, imitating his teacher, himself also feigns a vision, imagining that in this way he would be magnified. For Valentinus likewise alleges that he had seen an infant child lately born; and questioning (this child), he proceeded to inquire who it might be. And (the child) replied, saying that he himself is the Logos, and then subjoined a sort of tragic legend; and out of this (Valentinus) wishes the heresy attempted by him to consist. Marcus, making a similar attempt[3] with this (heretic), asserts that the Tetrad came to him in the form of a woman, — since the world could not bear, he says, the male (form) of this Tetrad, — and that she revealed herself who she was, and explained to this (Marcus) alone the generation of the universe, which she never had revealed to any, either of gods or of men, expressing herself after this mode: When first the self-existent Father, He who is inconceivable and without substance, He who is neither male nor female, willed that His own ineffability should become realized in something spoken, and that His invisibility should become realized in form, He opened His mouth, and sent forth similar to Himself a Logos. And this (Logos) stood by Him, and showed unto Him who he was, viz., that he himself had been manifested as a (realization in) form of the Invisible One. And the pronunciation of the name was of the following description. He was accustomed to utter the first word of the name itself, which was Arche, and the syllable of this was (composed) of four[4] letters. Then he subjoined the second (syllable), and this was also (composed) of four letters. Next he uttered the third (syllable), which was (composed) of ten letters; and he uttered the fourth (syllable), and this was (composed) of twelve letters. Then ensued the pronunciation of the entire name, (composed) of thirty letters, but of four syllables. And each of the elements had its own peculiar letters, and its own peculiar form, and its own peculiar pronunciation, as well as figures and images. And not one of these was there that beholds the form of that (letter) of which this was an element. And of course none of them could know the pronunciation of the (letter) next to this, but (only) as he himself pronounces it, (and that in such a way) as that, in pro-

---

[1] [Buusen (vol. i. p 72–75) makes useful comments.]

[2] Hippolytus has already employed this word, ἀδρομέστερον, in the *Proœmium*. It literally means, of strong or compact parts. Hippolytus, however, uses it in contrast to the expression λεπτομέρης, in reference to his *Summary of Heresies*. Bunsen thinks that Hippolytus means to say that Irenæus expressed himself rather too strongly, and that the Marcosians, on meeting with Irenæus' assertions, indignantly repudiated them. Dr. Wordsworth translates ἀδρομερῶς (in the *Proœmium*), "with rude generality," — a rendering scarcely in keeping with the passage above.

[3] The largest extract from Irenæus is that which follows— the explanation of the heresy of Marcus. From this to the end of book vi. occurs in Irenæus likewise. Hippolytus' text does not always accurately correspond with that of his master. The divergence, however, is inconsiderable, and may sometimes be traceable to the error of the transcriber.

[4] Hippolytus uses two words to signify letters, στοιχεῖον and γράμμα. The former strictly means an articulate sound as the basis of language or of written words, and the latter the sound itself when represented by a particular symbol or sign.

nouncing the whole (word), he supposed that he was uttering the entire (name). For each of these (elements), being part of the entire (name), he denominates (according to) its own peculiar sound, as if the whole (of the word). And he does not intermit sounding until he arrived at the last letter of the last element, and uttered it in a single articulation. Then he said, that the restoration of the entire ensued when all the (elements), coming down into the one letter, sounded one and the same pronunciation, and an image of the pronunciation he supposed to exist when we simultaneously utter the word *Amen.*[1] And that these sounds are those which gave form to the insubstantial and unbegotten Æon, and that those forms are what the Lord declared to be angels — the (forms) that uninterruptedly behold the face of the Father.

CHAP. XXXVIII. — MARCUS' SYSTEM OF LETTERS.

But the generic and expressed names of the elements he called Æons, and Logoi, and Roots, and Seeds, and Pleromas, and Fruits. (And he maintains) that every one of these, and what was peculiar to each, is perceived as being contained in the name of "Ecclesia." And the final letter of the last element sent forth its own peculiar articulation. And the sound of this (letter) came forth and produced, in accordance with images of the elements, its own peculiar elements. And from these he says that things existing here were garnished, and the things antecedent to these were produced. The letter itself certainly, of which the sound was concomitant with the sound below, he says, was received up by its own syllable into the complement of the entire (name) ; but that the sound, as if cast outside, remained below. And that the element itself, from which the letter along with its own pronunciation descended below, he says, is (composed) of thirty letters, and that each one of the thirty letters contains in itself other letters, by means of which the title of the letter is named. And again, that the other (letters) are named by different letters, and the rest by different (ones still). So that by writing down the letters individually, the number would eventuate in infinity. In this way one may more clearly understand what is spoken. The element Delta, (he says,) has five letters in itself, (viz.), Delta, and Epsilon, and Lambda, and Tau, and Alpha ; and these very letters are (written) by means of other letters. If, therefore, the entire substance of the Delta eventuates in infinity, (and if) different letters invariably produce different letters, and succeed one another, by how much greater

than that element is the more enormous sea[2] of the letters? And if one letter is thus infinite, behold the entire name's depth of the letters out of which the patient industry, nay, rather (I should say,) the vain toil of Marcus wishes that the Progenitor (of things) should consist ! Wherefore also (he maintains) that the Father, who knew that He was inseparable from Himself, gave (this depth) to the elements, which he likewise denominates Æons. And he uttered aloud to each one of them its own peculiar pronunciation, from the fact that one could not pronounce the entire.

CHAP. XXXIX. — THE QUATERNION EXHIBITS "TRUTH."

And (Marcus alleged) that the Quaternion, after having explained these things, spoke as follows : "Now, I wish also to exhibit to you Truth herself, for I have brought her down from the mansions above, in order that you may behold her naked, and become acquainted with her beauty ; nay, also that you may hear her speak, and may marvel at her wisdom. Observe," says the Quaternion, "then, first, the head above, Alpha (and long) O ; the neck, B and P[si] ; shoulders, along with hands, G and C[hi] ; breasts, Delta and P[hi] ; diaphragm,[3] Eu ; belly, Z and T ; *pudenda,* Eta and S ; thighs, T[h] and R ; knees, Ip ; calves, Ko ; ankles, Lx[si] ; feet, M and N." This is in the body of Truth, according to Marcus. This is the figure of the element ; this the character of the letter. And he styles this element Man, and affirms it to be the source of every word, and the originating principle of every sound, and the realization in speech of everything that is ineffable, and a mouth of taciturn silence. And this is the body of (Truth) herself. But do you, raising aloft the conceiving power of the understanding, hear from the mouths of Truth (of) the Logos, who is Self-generator[4] and Progenitor.[5]

CHAP. XL. — THE NAME OF CHRIST JESUS.

But, after uttering these words, (Marcus details) that Truth, gazing upon him, and opening her mouth, spoke the discourse (just alluded to). And (he tells us) that the discourse became a name, and that the name was that which we know and utter, viz., Christ Jesus, and that as soon as she had named this (name) she remained silent. While Marcus, however, was expecting that she was about to say more, the

---

[1] [Rev. iii. 14. A name of Christ. This word is travestied as the name *Logos* also, most profanely.]

[2] This is Duncker's emendation, suggested by Irenæus' text. Miller reads τὸν τόπον, which yields scarcely any meaning.
[3] Hippolytus' text has been here corrected from that of Irenæus.
[4] This is a correction from Progenitor, on the authority of Irenæus and Epiphanius.
[5] Προπάτορα: Irenæus reads Πατρόδορα, which is adopted by Schneidewin, and translated *patrium.*

Quaternion, again advancing into the midst, speaks as follows : "Thou didst regard as contemptible [1] this discourse which you have heard from the mouth of Truth. And yet this which you know and seem long since to possess is not the name ; for you have merely the sound of it, but are ignorant of the power. For Jesus is a remarkable name, having six letters,[2] invoked[3] by all belonging to the called (of Christ) ; whereas the other (name, that is, Christ,) consists of many parts, and is among the (five) Æons of the Pleroma. (This name) is of another form and a different type, and is recognised by those existences who are connate with him, and whose magnitudes subsist with him continually.

CHAP. XLI. — MARCUS' MYSTIC INTERPRETATION OF THE ALPHABET.

Know, (therefore,) that these letters which with you are (reckoned at) twenty-four, are emanations from the three powers, and are representative[4] of those (powers) which embrace even the entire number of the elements. For suppose that there are some letters that are mute — nine of them — of Pater and Aletheia, from the fact that these are mute — that is, ineffable and unutterable. And (again, assume) that there are other (letters that are) semi-vowels — eight of them — of the Logos and of Zoe, from the fact that these are intermediate between consonants and vowels, and receive the emanation[5] of the (letters) above them, but the reflux of those below them.[6] And (likewise take for granted) that there are vowels — and these are seven — of Anthropos and Ecclesia, inasmuch as the voice of Anthropos proceeded forth, and imparted form to the (objects of the) universe. For the sound of the voice produced figure, and invested them with it. From this it follows that there are Logos and Zoe, which have eight (semi-vowels) ; and Anthropos and Ecclesia, which have seven (vowels) ; and Pater and Aletheia, which have nine (mutes). But from the fact that Logos wanted[7] (one of being an ogdoad), he who is in the Father was removed (from his seat on God's right hand), and came down (to earth). And he was sent forth (by the Father) to him from whom he was separated,

for the rectification of actions that had been committed. (And his descent took place) in order that the unifying process, which is inherent in Agathos, of the Pleromas might produce in all the single power that emanates from all. And thus he who is of the seven (vowels) acquired the power of the eight[8] (semi-vowels) ; and there were produced three *topoi*, corresponding with the (three) numbers (nine, seven, and eight), — (these *topoi*) being ogdoads. And these three being added one to the other, exhibited the number of the twenty-four (letters). And (he maintains), of course, that the three elements, — (which he himself affirms to be (allied) with the three powers by conjugal union, and which (by this state of duality) become six, and from which have emanated the twenty-four elements, — being rendered fourfold by the Quaternion's ineffable word, produce the same number (twenty-four) with these. And these, he says, belong to Anonomastus. And (he asserts) that these are conveyed by the six powers into a similarity with Aoratus. And (he says) that there are six double letters of these elements, images of images, which, being reckoned along with the twenty-four letters, produce, by an analogical power, the number thirty.

CHAP. XLII. — HIS SYSTEM APPLIED TO EXPLAIN OUR LORD'S LIFE AND DEATH.

And he says, as the result of this computation and that proportion,[9] that in the similitude of an image He appeared who after the six days Himself ascended the mountain a fourth person, and became the sixth.[10] And (he asserts) that He (likewise) descended and was detained by the Hebdomad, and thus became an illustrious Ogdoad. And He contains in Himself of the elements the entire number which He manifested, as He came to His baptism. (And the symbol of manifestation was) the descent of the dove, which is O[mega] and Alpha, and which by the number manifested (by these is) 801.[11] And for this reason (he maintains) that Moses says that man was created on the sixth day. And (he asserts)

---

[1] The reading is doubtful. The translator adopts Scott's emendation.

[2] [See note 1, p. 94 *supra*, on "Amen." Comp. Irenæus, vol. i. p. 393, this series. This name of Jesus does, indeed, run through all Scripture, in verbal and other forms; Gen. xlix. 18 and in *Joshua*, as a foreshadowing.]

[3] Irenæus has "known."

[4] εἰκονικάς. This is Irenæus' reading. Miller has εἰκόνας (representations).

[5] ἀπόρροιαν: some read ἀπορίαν, which is obviously erroneous.

⁖ ὑπ' αὐτά: Irenæus reads ὑπὲρ αὐτήν, and Massuet ὑπένερθεν.

[7] The deficiency consisted in there not being three ogdoads. The sum total was twenty-four, but there was only one ogdoad — Logos and Zoe. The other two — Pater and Aletheia, and Anthropos and Ecclesia — had one above and one below an ogdoad.

[8] τῶν ὀκτὼ has been substituted for τῷ νοητῷ, an obviously corrupt reading. The correction is supplied by Irenæus.

[9] Or, "economy."

[10] Christ went up with the three apostles, and was therefore the fourth Himself; by the presence of Moses and Elias, He became the sixth: Matt. xvii. 1; Mark ix. 2.

[11] The Greek word for dove is περίστερα, the letters of which represent 801, as may be seen thus : —

$$\pi = 80$$
$$\epsilon = 5$$
$$\rho = 100$$
$$\iota = 10$$
$$\sigma = 200$$
$$\tau = 300$$
$$\epsilon = 5$$
$$\rho = 100$$
$$a = 1$$

$$801$$

This, therefore, is equipollent with Alpha and Omega, as a is equal to 1, and ω to 800. [Stuff! Bunsen, very naturally, exclaims.]

that the dispensation of suffering (took place) on the sixth day, which is the preparation ; (and so it was) that on this (day) appeared the last man for the regeneration of the first man. And that the beginning and end of this dispensation is the sixth hour, at which He was nailed to the (accursed) tree. For (he says) that perfect Nous, knowing the sixfold number to be possessed of the power of production and regeneration, manifested to the sons of light the regeneration that had been introduced into this number by that illustrious one who had appeared. Whence also he says that the double letters[1] involve the remarkable number. For the illustrious number, being intermingled with the twenty-four elements, produced the name (consisting) of the thirty letters.

CHAP. XLIII. — LETTERS, SYMBOLS OF THE HEAVENS.

He has, however, employed the instrumentality of the aggregate of the seven numbers, in order that the result of the self-devised (counsel)[2] might be manifested. Understand, he says, for the present, that remarkable number to be Him who was formed by the illustrious one, and who was, as it were, divided, and remained outside. And He, through both His Own power and wisdom, by means of the projection of Himself, imparted, in imitation of the seven powers,[3] animation to this world, so as to make it consist of seven powers, and constituted (this world) the soul of the visible universe. And therefore this one has resorted to such an operation as what was spontaneously undertaken by Himself; and these minister,[4] inasmuch as they are imitations of things inimitable, unto the intelligence of the Mother. And the first heaven sounds Alpha,[5] and the one after that E[psilon], and the third Eta, and the fourth, even that in the midst of the seven (vowels, enunciates) the power of Iota, and the fifth of O[micron], and the sixth of U[psilon], and the seventh and fourth from the central[6] one, O[mega]. And all the powers, when they are connected together in one, emit a sound, and glorify that (Being) from whom they have been projected. And the glory of that sound is transmitted upwards to the Progenitor. And furthermore, he says that the sound of this ascription of glory being conveyed to the earth, became a creator and producer of terrestrial objects. And (he maintains) that the proof of this (may be drawn) from the case of infants recently born, whose soul, simultaneously with exit from the womb, utters similarly this

sound of each one of the elements. As, then, he says, the seven powers glorify the Logos, so also does the sorrowing soul in babes (magnify Him).[7] And on account of this, he says, David likewise has declared, "Out of the mouths of babes and sucklings Thou hast perfected praise."[8] And again, "The heavens declare the glory of God."[9] When,[10] however, the soul is involved in hardships, it utters no other exclamation than the O[mega], inasmuch as it is afflicted in order that the soul above, becoming aware of what is akin to herself (below), may send down one to help this (earthly soul).

CHAP. XLIV — RESPECTING THE GENERATION OF THE TWENTY-FOUR LETTERS.

And so far for these points. Respecting, however, the generation of the twenty-four elements, he expresses himself thus: that Henotes co-exists with Monotes, and that from these issue two projections, viz., Monas and Hen, and that these being added together[11] become four, for twice two are four. And again, the two and four (projections) being added together, manifested the number six ; and these six made fourfold, produce the twenty-four forms.[12] And these are the names of the first tetrad, and they are understood as Holy of Holies, and cannot be expressed, and they are recognised by the Son alone. These the Father knows which they are. Those names which with Him are pronounced in silence and with faith, are Arrhetus and Sige, Pater and Aletheia. And of this tetrad the entire number is (that) of twenty-four letters. For Arrhetus has seven elements, Sige five, and Pater five, and Aletheia seven.[13] And in like manner also (is it with) the second tetrad ; (for) Logos and Zoe, Anthropos and Ecclesia, exhibited the same number of elements. And (he says) that the expressed name — (that is, Jesus)[14] — of the Saviour consists of six letters, but that His ineffable[15] name, according to the number of the letters, one by one,[16] consists of twenty-four elements, but Christ a Son of twelve. And (he says) that the ineffable (name) in Christ consists of thirty

---

[7] Irenæus has the sentence thus: "so also the soul in babes, lamenting and bewailing Marcus, glorifies him."
[8] Ps. viii. 2.
[9] Ps. xix. 1.
[10] Hippolytus here omits some passages which are to be found in Irenæus.
[11] Literally, "being twice two:" some for οὖσαι read οὐσίαι. Irenæus has ἐπὶ δύο οὖσαι, i.e., "which being (added) into two."
[12] Hippolytus has only the word "twenty-four," to which Schneidewin supplies "letters," and Irenæus "forms," as given above. Hippolytus likewise omits the word "produced," which Irenæus supplies. The text of the latter is τὰς εἰκοσιτέσσαρας ἀπεκύησαν μορφάς.
[13] Irenæus adds, "which being added together, I mean the twice five and twice seven, complete the number of the twenty-four (forms)."
[14] The parenthetical words had fallen into a wrong part of the sentence, and are placed here by Schneidewin.
[15] This is a correction for "expressed" from Irenæus. Marcus observes the distinction afterwards.
[16] κατὰ ἕν γραμμάτων. The MS. has ἐγγραμάτων. Irenæus omits these words.

---

[1] γράμματα: some read πράγματα.
[2] Supplied from Irenæus.
[3] This should be altered into Hebdomad if we follow Irenæus.
[4] τάδε διακονεῖ. This is the text of Irenæus, and corrects the common reading, τὰ δὲ εἰκόνων.
[5] φθέγγεται (Irenæus). The common reading is φαίνεται.
[6] μέσου: in Irenæus we have μέρους.

letters, and this exists, according to the letters which are in Him, the elements being counted one by one. For the (name) Christ[1] consists of eight elements; for Chi[2] consists of three, and R[ho] of two, and EI of two, and I[ota] of four, S[igma] of five, and T[au] of three, and OU of two, and San of three. Thus the ineffable name in Christ consists, they allege, of thirty letters. And they assert that for this reason He utters the words, "I am Alpha and Omega," displaying the dove, which (symbolically) has this number, which is eight hundred and one.[3]

CHAP. XLV. — WHY JESUS IS CALLED ALPHA.

Now Jesus possesses this ineffable generation. For from the mother of the universe, I mean the first tetrad, proceeded forth, in the manner of a daughter, the second tetrad. And it became an ogdoad, from which proceeded forth the decade; and thus was produced ten, and next eighteen. The decade, therefore, coming in along with the ogdoad, and rendering it tenfold, produced the number eighty; and again making eighty tenfold, generated the number eight hundred.[4] And so it is that the entire number of letters that proceeded forth from ogdoad into decade is eight hundred and eighty-eight, which is Jesus; for the name Jesus, according to the number in letters, is eight hundred and eighty-eight. Now likewise the Greek alphabet has eight monads and eight decades, and eight hecatontads; and these exhibit the calculated sum of eight hundred and eighty-eight, that is, Jesus, who consists of all numbers. And that on this account He is called Alpha (and Omega), indicating His generation (to be) from all.[5]

CHAP. XLVI. — MARCUS' ACCOUNT OF THE BIRTH AND LIFE OF OUR LORD.

But concerning the creation of this (Jesus), he expresses himself thus: That powers emanating from the second tetrad fashioned Jesus, who appeared on earth, and that the angel Gabriel[6] filled the place of the Logos, and the Holy Spirit that of Zoe, and the "Power of the Highest"[7] that of Anthropos, and the Virgin that of Ecclesia.[8] And so it was, in Marcus' system, that the man (who appeared) in accordance with the dis-

pensation was born through Mary.[9] And when He came to the water, (he says) that He descended like a dove upon him who had ascended above and filled the twelfth number. And in Him resides the seed of these, that is, such as are sown along with Him, and that descend with (Him), and ascend with (Him). And that this power which descended upon Him, he says, is the seed of the Pleroma, which contains in itself both the Father and the Son, and the unnameable power of Sige, which is recognised through these and all the Æons. And that this (seed) is the spirit which is in Him and spoke in Him through the mouth of the Son, the confession of Himself as Son of man, and of His being one who would manifest the Father; (and that) when this spirit came down upon Jesus, He was united with Him. The Saviour, who was of the dispensation, he says, destroyed death, whereas He made known (as) the Father Christ (Jesus). He says that Jesus, therefore, is the name of the man of the dispensation, and that it has been set forth for the assimilation and formation of Anthropos, who was about to descend upon Him; and that when He had received Him unto Himself, He retained possession of Him. And (he says) that He was Anthropos, (that) He (was) Logos, (that) He (was) Pater, and Arrhetus, and Sige, and Aletheia, and Ecclesia, and Zoe.

CHAP. XLVII. — THE SYSTEM OF MARCUS SHOWN TO BE THAT OF PYTHAGORAS, BY QUOTATIONS FROM THE WRITINGS' OF MARCUS' FOLLOWERS.

I trust, therefore, that as regards these doctrines it is obvious to all possessed of a sound mind, that (these tenets) are unauthoritative, and far removed from the knowledge that is in accordance with Religion, and are mere portions of astrological discovery, and the arithmetical art of the Pythagoreans. And this assertion, ye who are desirous of learning shall ascertain (to be true, by a reference to the previous books, where,) amongst other opinions elucidated by us, we have explained these doctrines likewise. In order, however, that we may prove it a more clear statement, viz., that these (Marcosians) are disciples not of Christ but of Pythagoras, I shall proceed to explain those opinions that have been derived (by these heretics) from Pythagoras concerning the meteoric (phenomena) of the stars[10] as far as it is possible (to do so) by an epitome.

Now the Pythagoreans make the following statements: that the universe consists of a Mon-

---

[1] This entire sentence is wanting in Irenæus.
[2] Corrected from Chri, which is in the MS.
[3] Irenæus has the passage thus: "And for this reason He says that He is Alpha and Omega, that He may manifest the dove, inasmuch as this bird (symbolically) involves this number (801)." See a previous note in chap. xlii. p. 95, *supra*.
[4] Part of this sentence is supplied from Irenæus.
[5] Hippolytus here omits the following sentence found in Irenæus: "And again thus — of the first quarternion, when added into itself, in accordance with a progression of number, appeared the number ten, and so forth."
[6] Luke i. 26–38.
[7] Or, "of the Son," an obvious mistake.
[8] Irenæus has, "And the Virgin exhibited the place of Ecclesia."

[9] Irenæus adds, "whom the Father of the universe selected, for passage through the womb, by means of the Logos, for recognition of Himself."
[10] Cruice thinks that for stars we should read "numbers," but gives no explanation of the meaning of μετέωρα. This word, as applied to numbers, might refer to "the astrological phenomena" deducible by means of numerical calculations.

ad and Duad, and that by reckoning from a monad as far as four they thus generate a decade. And again,[1] a duad coming forth as far as the remarkable (letter), — for instance, two and four and six, — exhibited the (number) twelve. And again, if we reckon from the duad to the decade, thirty is produced; and in this are comprised the ogdoad, and decade, and dodecade. And therefore, on account of its having the remarkable (letter), the dodecade has concomitant[2] with it a remarkable passion.[3] And for this reason (they maintain) that when an error had arisen respecting the twelfth number, the sheep skipped from the flock and wandered away;[4] for that the apostasy took place, they say, in like manner from the decade. And with a similar reference to the dodecade, they speak of the piece of money which, on losing, a woman, having lit a candle, searched for diligently. (And they make a similar application) of the loss (sustained) in the case of the one sheep out of the ninety and nine; and adding these one into the other, they give a fabulous account of numbers. And in this way, they affirm, when the eleven is multiplied into nine, that it produces the number ninety and nine; and on this account that it is said that the word Amen embraces the number ninety-nine. And in regard of another number they express themselves in this manner: that the letter Eta along with the remarkable one constitutes an ogdoad, as it is situated in the eighth place from Alpha. Then, again, computing the number of these elements without the remarkable (letter), and adding them together up to Eta, they exhibit the number thirty. For any one beginning from the Alpha[5] to the Eta will, after subtracting the remarkable (letter), discover the number of the elements to be the number thirty. Since, therefore, the number thirty is unified from the three powers; when multiplied thrice into itself it produced ninety, for thrice thirty is ninety, (and this triad when multiplied into itself produced nine). In this way the Ogdoad brought forth the number ninety-nine from the first Ogdoad, and Decade, and Dodecade. And at one time they collect the number of this (trio) into an entire sum, and produce a triacontad; whereas at another time they subtract twelve, and reckon it at eleven. And in like manner, (they subtract) ten and make it nine. And connecting these one into the other, and multiplying them tenfold, they complete the number ninety-nine. Since, however, the twelfth Æon, having left the eleven (Æons above), and departing downwards, withdrew, they allege that even this is correlative (with the letters). For the figure of the letters teaches (us as much). For L is placed eleventh of the letters, and this L is the number thirty. And (they say) that this is placed according to an image of the dispensation above; since from Alpha, irrespective of the remarkable (letter), the number of the letters themselves, added together up to L, according to the augmentation of the letters with the L itself, produces the number ninety-nine. But that the L, situated in the eleventh (of the alphabet), came down to search after the number similar to itself, in order that it might fill up the twelfth number, and that when it was discovered it was filled up, is manifest from the shape itself of the letter. For Lambda, when it attained unto, as it were, the investigation of what is similar to itself, and when it found such and snatched it away, filled up the place of the twelfth, the letter M, which is composed of two Lambdas. And for this reason (it was) that these (adherents of Marcus), through their knowledge, avoid the place of the ninety-nine, that is, the Hysterema, a type of the left hand,[6] and follow after the one which, added to ninety-nine, they say was transferred to his own right hand

CHAP. XLVIII. — THEIR COSMOGONY FRAMED ACCORDING TO THESE MYSTIC DOCTRINES OF LETTERS.

And by the Mother, they allege, were created first the four elements, which, they say, are fire, water, earth, air; and these have been projected as an image of the tetrad above; and reckoning the energies of these — for instance, as hot, cold, moist, dry — they assert that they accurately portray the Ogdoad. And next they compute ten powers thus. (There are, they say,) seven orbicular bodies, which they likewise call heavens. There is next a circle containing these within its compass, and this also they name an eighth heaven; and in addition to these, they affirm the existence of both a sun and moon. And these being ten in number, they say, are images of the invisible decade that (emanated) from

---

[1] A comparison of Hippolytus with Irenæus, as regards what follows, manifests many omissions in the former.

[2] Following Irenæus, the passage would be rendered thus: "And therefore, on account of its having the remarkable (letter) concomitant with it, they style the dodecade a remarkable passion." Massuet, in his *Annotations on Irenæus*, gives the following explanation of the above statement, which is made by Hippolytus likewise. From the twelfth number, by once abstracting the remarkable (number), which does not come into the order and number of the letters, eleven letters remain. Hence in the dodecade, the πάθος, or what elsewhere the heretics call the "Hysterema," is a defect of one letter. And this is a symbol of the defect or suffering which, upon the withdrawal of one Æon, happened unto the last dodecade of Æons.

[3] Hippolytus' statement is less copious and less clear than that of Irenæus, who explains the defect of the letter to be symbolical of an apostasy of one of the Æons, and that this one was a female.

[4] Luke xv. 4-10.

[5] Marcus' explanation of this, as furnished by Irenæus, is more copious than Hippolytus'.

[6] The allusion here seems to be to the habit among the ancients of employing the fingers for counting, those of the left hand being used for all numbers under 100, and those of the right for the numbers above it. To this custom the poet Juvenal alludes, when he says of Nestor: —

"Atque suos jam dextera computat annos."

That is, that he was one hundred years old.

Logos and Zoe. (They affirm,) however, that the dodecade is indicated by what is termed the zodiacal circle. For these twelve zodiacal signs, they say, most evidently shadowed forth [1] the daughter of Anthropos and Ecclesia, namely the Dodecade. And since, he says, the upper heaven has been united from an opposite direction to the revolutionary motion, which is most rapid, of the entire (of the signs) ; and since (this heaven) within its cavity retards, and by its slowness counterpoises, the velocity of those (signs), so that in thirty years it accomplishes its circuit from sign to sign, — they therefore assert that this (heaven) is an image of Horos, who encircles the mother of these, who has thirty names. And, again, (they affirm) that the moon, which traverses the heaven in thirty days, by reason of (these) days portrays the number of the Æons. And (they say) that the sun, performing its circuit, and terminating its exact return to its first position in its orbit in twelve months, manifests the dodecade. And also (they say) that the days themselves, involving the measure of twelve hours, constitute a type of the empty [2] dodecade ; and that the circumference of the actual zodiacal circle consists of three hundred and sixty degrees, and that each zodiacal sign possesses thirty divisions. In this way, therefore, even by means of the circle, they maintain that the image is preserved [3] of the connection of the twelve with the thirty.[4] But, moreover, alleging that the earth was divided into twelve regions, and that according to each particular region it receives one power by the latter's being sent down from the heavens, and that it produces children corresponding in likeness [5] unto the power which transmitted (the likeness) by emanation ; (for this reason) they assert that earth is a type of the Dodecade above.

CHAP. XLIX. — THE WORK OF THE DEMIURGE PERISHABLE.

And in addition to these (points, they lay down) that the Demiurge of the supernal Ogdoad, desirous of imitating the indefinite, and everlasting, and illimitable (one), and (the one) not subject to the condition of time ; and (the Demiurge) not being able to represent the stability [6] and eternity of this (Ogdoad), on account of his being the fruit of the Hysterema, to this end appointed times, and seasons, and numbers, measuring many years in reference to the eternity of this (Ogdoad), thinking by the multitude of times to imitate its indefiniteness. And here they say, when Truth eluded his pursuit, that Falsehood followed close upon him ; and that on account of this, when the times were fulfilled, his work underwent dissolution.

CHAP. L. — MARCUS AND COLARBASUS REFUTED BY IRENÆUS.

These assertions, then, those who are of the school of Valentinus advance concerning both the creation and the universe, in each case propagating opinions still more empty.[7] And they suppose this to constitute productiveness (in their system), if any one in like manner, making some greater discovery, will appear to work wonders. And finding, (as they insinuate,) each of the particulars of Scripture to accord with the aforesaid numbers, they (attempt to) criminate Moses and the prophets, alleging that these speak allegorically of the measures of the Æons. And inasmuch as these statements are trifling and unstable, it does not appear to me expedient to bring them before (the reader. This, however, is the less requisite,) as now the blessed presbyter [8] Irenæus has powerfully and elaborately refuted the opinions of these (heretics). And to him we are indebted for a knowledge of their inventions, (and have thereby succeeded in) proving that these heretics, appropriating these opinions from the Pythagorean philosophy, and from over-spun theories of the astrologers, cast an imputation upon Christ, as though He had delivered these (doctrines). But since I suppose that the worthless opinions of these men have been sufficiently explained, and that it has been clearly proved whose disciples are Marcus and Colarbasus, who were successors of the school of Valentinus, let us see what statement likewise Basilides advances.

---

[1] Or, " sketched out " (Irenæus).
[2] Or, " radiant."
[3] Or, " measured."
[4] Massuet gives the following explanation: The sun each day describes a circle which is divided into twelve parts of 30 degrees each, and consists of 360 degrees. And as for each of the hours, where days and nights are equal, 15 degrees are allowed, it follows that in two hours, that is, in the twelfth part of a day, the sun completes a progress of 30 degrees.
[5] Or, " of the same substance."

[6] Or, " blamelessness."
[7] Or, " strange."
[8] [The Apostle John delights to call himself a presbyter, and St. Peter claims to be co-presbyter with the elders whom he exhorts. The Johannean school of primitive theologians seem to love this expression pre-eminently. It was almost as little specific in the primitive age as that of *pastor* or *minister* in our own.]

THE REFUTATION OF ALL HERESIES

BOOK VII.

CONTENTS.

THE following are the contents of the seventh book of the *Refutation of all Heresies :* —

What the opinion of Basilides is, and that, being struck with the doctrines of Aristotle, he out of these framed his heresy.[1]

And what are the statements of Saturnilus,[2] who flourished much about the time of Basilides.

And how Menander advanced the assertion that the world was made by angels.

What is the folly of Marcion, and that his tenet is not new, nor (taken) out of the Holy Scriptures, but that he obtains it from Empedocles.

How Carpocrates acts sillily, in himself also alleging that existing things were made by angels.

That Cerinthus, in no wise indebted to the Scriptures, formed his opinion (not out of them), but from the tenets of the Egyptians.[3]

What are the opinions propounded by the Ebionæans, and that they in preference adhere to Jewish customs.

How Theodotus has been a victim of error, deriving contributions to his system partly from the Ebionæans, (partly from Cerinthus.)[4]

And what were the opinions of Cerdon,[5] who both enunciated the doctrines of Empedocles, and who wickedly induced Marcion to step forward.

And how Lucian, when he had become a disciple of Marcion,[6] having divested himself of all shame, blasphemed God from time to time.

And Apelles also, having become a disciple of this (heretic), was not in the habit of advancing the same opinions with his preceptor; but being actuated (in the formation of his system) from the tenets of natural philosophers, assumed the substance of the universe as the fundamental principle of things.[7]

CHAP. I. — HERESY COMPARED TO (1) THE STORMY OCEAN, (2) THE ROCKS OF THE SIRENS ; MORAL FROM ULYSSES AND THE SIRENS.

The pupils of these men, when they perceive the doctrines of the heretics to be like unto the ocean when tossed into waves by violence of the winds, ought to sail past in quest of the tranquil haven. For a sea of this description is both infested with wild beasts and difficult of navigation, like, as we may say, the Sicilian (Sea), in which the legend reports were Cyclops, and Charybdis, and Scylla, and the rock[8] of the Sirens. Now, the poets of the Greeks allege that Ulysses sailed through (this channel), adroitly using (to his own purpose) the terribleness of these strange monsters.[9] For the savage cruelty (in the aspect) of these towards those who were sailing through was remarkable. The Sirens, however, singing sweetly and harmoniously, beguiled the voyagers, luring, by reason of their melodious voice, those who heard it, to steer their vessels towards (the promontory). The (poets) report that Ulysses, on ascertaining this, smeared with wax the ears of his companions, and, lashing himself to the mast, sailed, free of danger, past the Sirens, hearing their chant distinctly. And my advice to my readers is to adopt a similar expedient, viz., either on account of their infirmity to smear their ears with wax, and sail (straight on) through the

---

[1] [Here our author's theory concerning the origin of heresy in heathen philosophy begins to be elaborated.]

[2] Satronilus (Miller).

[3] Or, " in no respect formed his system from the Scriptures, but from the tenets propounded by the Egyptians."

[4] Cruice would prefer, " from the Gnostics," on account of Cerinthus being coupled with the Gnostics and Ebionæans by Hippolytus, when he afterwards indicates the source from which Theodotus derived his heretical notions of Christ.

[5] Miller has " Sacerdon."

[6] The word μόνος occurs in Miller's text, but ought obviously to be expunged. It has probably, as Cruice conjectures, crept into the MS. from the termination of γενόμενος. Duncker suggests ὁμοίως.

[7] This rendering would ascribe Pantheism to Apelles. The passage might also be construed, " supposed there to exist an essence (that formed the basis) of the universe."

[8] A hiatus here has given rise to conjecture. Cruice suggests χορός (band) instead of ὅρος.

[9] Or, " practices of the monsters," or " inhospitable beasts." Abbe Cruice suggests παροξέων, and Roeper ἐμπλάστων.

tenets of the heretics, not even listening to (doctrines) that are easily capable of enticing them into pleasure, like the luscious lay of the Sirens, or, by binding one's self to the Cross [1] of Christ, (and) hearkening with fidelity (to His words), not to be distracted, inasmuch as he has reposed his trust in Him to whom ere this he has been firmly knit, and (I admonish that man) to continue stedfastly (in this faith).

CHAP. II. — THE SYSTEM OF BASILIDES DERIVED FROM ARISTOTLE.

Since, therefore, in the six books preceding this, we have explained previous (heretical opinions), it now seems proper not to be silent respecting the (doctrines) of Basilides,[2] which are the tenets of Aristotle the Stagyrite, not (those) of Christ. But even though on a former occasion the opinions propounded by Aristotle have been elucidated, we shall not even now scruple to set them down beforehand in a sort of synopsis, for the purpose of enabling my readers, by means of a nearer comparison of the two systems, to perceive with facility that the doctrines advanced by Basilides are (in reality) the clever quibbles of Aristotle.

CHAP. III. — SKETCH OF ARISTOTLE'S PHILOSOPHY.

Aristotle, then, makes a threefold division of substance. For one portion of it is a certain genus, and another a certain species, as that (philosopher) expresses it, and a third a certain individual. What is individual, however, (is so) not through any minuteness of body, but because by nature it cannot admit of any division whatsoever. The genus, on the other hand, is a sort of aggregate, made up of many and different germs. And from this genus, just as (from) a certain heap, all the species of existent things derive their distinctions.[3] And the genus constitutes a competent cause for (the production of) all generated entities. In order, however, that the foregoing statement may be clear, I shall prove (my position) through an example. And by means of this it will be possible for us to retrace our steps over the entire speculation of the Peripatetic (sage).

CHAP. IV. — ARISTOTLE'S GENERAL IDEA.

We affirm the existence of animal absolutely, not some animal. And this animal is neither ox, nor horse, nor man, nor god; nor is it sig-

nificant of any of these at all, but is animal absolutely. From this animal the species of all particular animals derive their subsistence. And this animality, itself the *summum genus*,[4] constitutes (the originating principle) for all animals produced in those (particular) species, and (yet is) not (itself any one) of the things generated. For man is an animal deriving the principle (of existence) from that animality, and horse is an animal deriving the principle of existence from that animality. The horse, and ox, and dog, and each of the rest of the animals, derive the principle (of existence) from the absolute animal, while animality itself is not any of these.

CHAP. V. — NONENTITY AS A CAUSE.

If, however, this animality is not any of these (species), the subsistence, according to Aristotle, of the things that are generated, derived its reality from non-existent entities. For animality, from whence these singly have been derived, is not any one (of them); and though it is not any one of them, it has yet become some one originating principle of existing things. But who it is that has established this substance as an originating cause of what is subsequently produced, we shall declare when we arrive at the proper place for entertaining a discussion of this sort.

CHAP. VI. — SUBSTANCE, ACCORDING TO ARISTOTLE; THE PREDICATES.

Since, however, as I have stated, substance is threefold, viz., genus, species, (and) individual; and (since) we have set down animality as being the genus, and man the species, as being already distinct from the majority of animals, but notwithstanding still to be identified (with animals of his own kind), inasmuch as not being yet moulded into a species of realized substance, — (therefore it is, that) when I impart form under a name to a man derived from the genus, I style him Socrates or Diogenes, or some one of the many denominations (in use). And since (in this way, I repeat,) I comprehend under a name the man who constitutes a species that is generated from the genus, I denominate a substance of this description individual. For genus has been divided into species, and species into individual. But (as regards) the individual, since it has been comprehended under a name, it is not possible that, according to its own nature, it could be divided into anything else, as we have divided each of the fore-mentioned (genus and species).[5]

Aristotle primarily, and especially, and preeminently entitles this — substance, inasmuch as

---

[1] Literally, the (accursed) tree.
[2] What Hippolytus now states in regard of the opinions of Basilides, is quite new (compare Irenæus, i. 24; Clemens Alexandrinus, *Strom.*, iii. and vii.; Tertullian, *Præscript.*, xlvi.; Epiphanius, *Hær.*, xxiv.; Theodoret, i. 4; Eusebius, *Ecclesiast. Hist.*, iv. 7; and Philastrius, c. xxxii.). Abbe Cruice refers us to *Basilidis philosophi Gnostici Sententiæ*, by Jacobi (Berlin, 1852), and to *Das Basilidianische System*, etc., by Ulhorn (Gottingen, 1855).
[3] Or, "dispositions."

[4] Compare Porphyry's *Isagoge*, c. ii., and Aristotle's *Categ.*, c.
[5] Aristotle's *Categ.*, c. v.

it cannot either be predicated of any Subject, or exist in a Subject. He, however, predicates of the Subject, just as with the genus, what I said constituted animality, (and which is) predicated by means of a common name of all particular animals, such as ox, horse, and the rest that are placed under (this genus). For it is true to say that man is an animal, and horse an animal, and that ox is an animal, and each of the rest. Now the meaning of the expression " predicated of a Subject " is this, that inasmuch as it is one, it can be predicated in like manner of many (particulars), even though these happen to be diversified in species. For neither does horse nor ox differ from man so far forth as he is an animal, for the definition of animal is said to suit all animals alike. For what is an animal? If we define it, a general definition will comprehend all animals. For animal is an animated Substance, endued with Sensation. Such are ox, man, horse, and each of the rest (of the animal kingdom). But the meaning of the expression " in a Subject " is this, that what is inherent in anything, not as a part, it is impossible should exist separately from that in which it is. But this constitutes each of the accidents (resident) in Substance, and is what is termed Quality. Now, according to this, we say that certain persons are of such a quality ; for instance, white, grey, black, just, unjust, temperate, and other (characteristics) similar to these. But it is impossible for any one of these to subsist itself by itself ; but it must inhere in something else. If, however, neither animal which I predicate of all individual animals, nor accidents which are discoverable in all things of which they are non-essential qualities, can subsist themselves by themselves, and (yet if) individuals are formed out of these, (it follows, therefore, that) the triply divided Substance, which is not made up out of other things, consists of nonentities. If, then, what is primarily, and pre-eminently, and particularly denominated Substance consists of these, it derives existence from nonentities, according to Aristotle.

CHAP. VII. — ARISTOTLE'S COSMOGONY ; HIS " PSYCHOLOGY ; " HIS " ENTELECHEIA ; " HIS THEOLOGY ; HIS ETHICS ; BASILIDES FOLLOWS ARISTOTLE.

But concerning Substance, the statements now made will suffice. But not only is Substance denominated genus, species, (and) individual, but also matter, and form, and privation. There is, however, (as regards the substance,) in these no difference, even though the division be allowed to stand. Now, inasmuch as Substance is of this description, the arrangement of the world has taken place according to some such plan as the following. The world is divided,

according to Aristotle, into very numerous and diversified parts. Now the portion of the world which extends from the earth to the moon is devoid of foresight, guideless, and is under the sway[1] of that nature alone which belongs to itself. But another (part of the world which lies) beyond the moon, and extends to the surface of heaven, is arranged in the midst of all order and foresight and governance. Now, the (celestial) superficies constitutes a certain fifth substance, and is remote from all those natural elements out of which the cosmical system derives consistence. And this is a certain fifth Substance, according to Aristotle, — as it were, a certain super-mundane essence. And (this essence) has become (a logical necessity) in his system, in order to accord with the (Peripatetic) division of the world. And (the topic of this fifth nature) constitutes a distinct investigation in philosophy. For there is extant a certain disquisition, styled A Lecture on Physical (Phenomena), in which he has elaborately treated[2] concerning the operations which are conducted by nature and not providence, (in the quarter of space extending) from the earth as far as the moon. And there is also extant by him a certain other peculiar treatise on the principles of things (in the region) beyond the moon, and it bears the following inscription : Metaphysics.[3] And another peculiar dissertation has been (written) by him, entitled Concerning a Fifth Substance, and in this work Aristotle unfolds his theological opinions.

There exists some such division of the universe as we have now attempted to delineate in outline, and (corresponding with it is the division) of the Aristotelian philosophy. His work, however, (styled) Concerning the Soul, is obscure. For in the entire three books (where he treats of this subject) it is not possible to say clearly what is Aristotle's opinion concerning the soul. For, as regards the definition which he furnishes of soul, it is easy (enough) to declare this ; but what it is that is signified by the definition[4] is difficult to discover. For soul, he says, is an entelecheia of a natural organic body ; (but to explain) what this is at all, would require a very great number of arguments and a lengthened investigation. As regards, however, the Deity, the Originator of all those glorious objects in creation, (the nature of) this (First Cause) — even to one conducting his speculations by a more prolonged inquiry than that concerning (the soul) — is more difficult to know than the soul itself. The definition, however, which Aris-

---

[1] Or, " is sufficient."
[2] Or, " the question is discussed."
[3] [This word, not yet technical, as with us, is thus noted as curious. Of its force see Professor Caird, Encyc. Britannic., sub voce " Metaphysic."]
[4] See Aristotle, De Anim., ii. 1.

totle furnishes of the Deity is, I admit, not difficult to ascertain, but it is impossible to comprehend the meaning of it. For, he says, (the Deity) is a "conception of conception;" but this is altogether a non-existent (entity). The world, however, is incorruptible (and) eternal, according to Aristotle. For it has in itself nothing faulty,[1] inasmuch as it is directed by Providence and Nature. And Aristotle has laid down doctrines not only concerning Nature and a cosmical system, and Providence, and God,[2] but he has written (more than this) ; for there is extant by him likewise a certain treatise on ethical subjects, and these he inscribes *Books of Ethics*.[3] But throughout these he aims at rendering the habits of his hearers excellent from being worthless. When, therefore, Basilides has been discovered, not in spirit alone, but also in the actual expressions and names, transferring the tenets of Aristotle into our evangelical and saving doctrine, what remains, but that, by restoring what he has appropriated from others, we should prove to the disciples of this (heretic) that Christ will in no wise profit them, inasmuch as they are heathenish?

CHAP. VIII. — BASILIDES AND ISIDORUS ALLEGE APOSTOLIC SANCTION FOR THEIR SYSTEMS ; THEY REALLY FOLLOW ARISTOTLE.

Basilides, therefore, and Isidorus, the true son and disciple of Basilides, say that Matthias[4] communicated to them secret discourses, which, being specially instructed, he heard from the Saviour. Let us, then, see how clearly Basilides, simultaneously with Isidorus, and the entire band of these (heretics), not only absolutely belies Matthias, but even the Saviour Himself. (Time) was, says (Basilides), when there was nothing. Not even, however, did that nothing constitute anything of existent things ; but, to express myself undisguisedly and candidly, and without any quibbling, it is altogether nothing. But when, he says, I employ the expression "was," I do not say that it was ; but (I speak in this way) in order to signify the meaning of what I wish to elucidate. I affirm then, he says, that it was "altogether nothing." For, he says, that is not absolutely ineffable which is named (so),—although undoubtedly we call this ineffable,—but that which is "non-ineffable." For that which is "non-ineffable" is not denominated ineffable, but is, he says, above every name that is named.

For, he says, by no means for the world are these names sufficient, but so manifold are its divisions that there is a deficiency (of names). And I do not take it upon myself to discover, he says, proper denominations for all things. Undoubtedly, however, one ought mentally, not by means of names, to conceive, after an ineffable manner, the peculiarities (of things) denominated. For an equivocal terminology, (when employed by teachers,) has created for their pupils confusion and a source of error concerning objects. (The Basilidians), in the first instance, laying hold on this borrowed and furtively derived tenet from the Peripatetic (sage), play upon the folly of those who herd together with them. For Aristotle, born many generations before Basilides, first lays down a system in *The Categories* concerning homonymous words. And these heretics bring this (system) to light as if it were peculiarly their own, and as if it were some novel (doctrine), and some secret disclosure from the discourses of Matthias.[5]

CHAP. IX. — BASILIDES ADOPTS THE ARISTOTELIAN DOCTRINE OF "NONENTITY."

Since, therefore, "nothing" existed, — (I mean) not matter, nor substance, nor what is insubstantial, nor is absolute, nor composite,[6] (nor conceivable, nor inconceivable, (nor what is sensible,) nor devoid of senses, nor man, nor angel, nor a god, nor, in short, any of those objects that have names, or are apprehended by sense, or that are cognised by intellect, but (are) thus (cognised), even with greater minuteness, still, when all things are absolutely removed, — (since, I say, "nothing" existed,) God, "non-existent," —whom Aristotle styles "conception of conception," but these (Basilidians) "non-existent," — inconceivably, insensibly, indeterminately, involuntarily, impassively, (and) unactuated by desire, willed to create a world. Now I employ, he says, the expression "willed" for the purpose of signifying (that he did so) involuntarily, and inconceivably, and insensibly. And by the expression "world" I do not mean that which was subsequently formed according to breadth and division, and which stood apart ; nay, (far from this,) for (I mean) the germ of a world. The germ, however, of the world had all things in itself. Just as the grain of mustard comprises all things simultaneously, holding them (collected) together within the very smallest (compass), viz., roots, stem, branches, leaves, and innumerable grains which are produced from the plant, (as) seeds again of other plants, and

---

[1] Literally, "out of tune."

[2] These works must be among Aristotle's lost writings (see Fabricius' *Bibl. Græc.*, t. iii. pp. 232, 404). We have no work of Aristotle's expressly treating "of God." However, the Stagyrite's theology, such as it is, is unfolded in his *Metaphysics*. See Macmahon's analysis prefixed to his translation of Aristotle's *Metaphysics*, Bohn's Classical Library.

[3] Aristotle composed three treatises on ethical subjects: (1) *Ethics to Nicomachus;* (2) *Great Morals;* (3) *Morals to Eudemus.*

[4] Miller erroneously reads "Matthew."

[5] [See Bunsen, i. v. 86. A fabulous reference may convey a truth. This implies that Matthias was supposed to have preached and left results of his teachings.]

[6] This emendation is made by Abbe Cruice. The MS. has "incomposite," an obviously untenable reading.

frequently of others (still), that are produced (from them). In this way, " non-existent " God made the world out of nonentities, casting and depositing some one Seed that contained in itself a conglomeration of the germs of the world. But in order that I may render more clear what it is those (heretics) affirm, (I shall mention the following illustration of theirs.) As an egg of some variegated and particoloured bird, — for instance the peacock, or some other (bird) still more manifold and particoloured, — being one in reality, contains in itself numerous forms of manifold, and particoloured, and much compounded substances ; so, he says, the non-existent seed of the world, which has been deposited by the non-existent God, constitutes at the same time the germ of a multitude of forms and a multitude of substances.

CHAP. X. — ORIGIN OF THE WORLD ; BASILIDES' ACCOUNT OF THE " SONSHIP."

All things, therefore, whatsoever it is possible to declare, and whatever, being not as yet discovered, one must omit, were likely to receive adaptation to the world which was about to be generated from the Seed. And this (Seed), at the requisite seasons, increases in bulk in a peculiar manner, according to accession, as through the instrumentality of a Deity so great, and of this description. (But this Deity) the creature can neither express nor grasp by perception. (Now, all these things) were inherent, treasured in the Seed, as we afterwards observe in a new-born child the growth of teeth, and paternal substance, and intellect, and everything which, though previously having no existence, accrues unto a man, growing little by little, from a youthful period of life. But since it would be absurd to say that any projection of a non-existent God became anything non-existent (for Basilides altogether shuns and dreads the Substances of things generated in the way of projection : for, (he asks,) of what sort of projection is there a necessity, or of what sort of matter [1] must we assume the previous existence, in order that God should construct a world, as the spider his web ; or (as) a mortal man, for the purpose of working it, takes a (piece of) brass or of wood, or some other of the parts of matter?), — (projection, I say, being out of the question,) certainly, says (Basilides), God spoke the word, and it was carried into effect. And this, as these men assert, is that which has been stated by Moses : " Let there be light, and there was light." [2] Whence, he says, came the light? From nothing. For it has not been written, he says, whence, but this only, (that it came) from

the voice of him who speaks the word. And he who speaks the word, he says, was non-existent ; nor was that existent which was being produced.[3] The seed of the cosmical system was generated, he says, from nonentities ; (and I mean by the seed,) the word which was spoken, " Let there be light." And this, he says, is that which has been stated in the Gospels : " He was the true light, which lighteth every man that cometh into the world." [4] He derives his originating principles from that Seed, and obtains from the same source his illuminating power. This is that seed which has in itself the entire conglomeration of germs. And Aristotle affirms this to be genius, and it is distributed by him into infinite species ; just as from animal, which is non-existent, we sever ox, horse, (and) man. When, therefore, the cosmical Seed becomes the basis (for a subsequent development), those (heretics) assert, (to quote Basilides' own words :) " Whatsoever I affirm," he says, " to have been made after these, ask no question as to whence. For (the Seed) had all seeds treasured and reposing in itself, just as non-existent entities, and which were designed to be produced by a non-existent Deity."

Let us see, therefore, what they say is first, or what second, or what third, (in the development of) what is generated from the cosmical Seed. There existed, he says, in the Seed itself, a Sonship, threefold, in every respect of the same Substance with the non-existent God, (and) begotten from nonentities. Of this Sonship (thus) involving a threefold division, one part was refined, (another gross,) and another requiring purification. The refined portion, therefore, in the first place, simultaneously with the earliest deposition of the Seed by the non-existent one, immediately burst forth [5] and went upwards and hurried above from below, employing a sort of velocity described in poetry, —

" . . . As wing or thought," [6] —

and attained, he says, unto him that is non-existent. For every nature desires that (non-existent one), on account of a superabundance of beauty and bloom. Each (nature desires this), however, after a different mode. The more gross portion, however, (of the Sonship) continuing still in the Seed, (and) being a certain imitative (principle), was not able to hurry upwards. For (this portion) was much more deficient in the refinement that the Sonship possessed, which through itself hurried upwards, (and so the more gross portion) was left behind. Therefore the more gross Sonship equipped it-

---

[1] Or, " of what sort of material substance," etc.
[2] Gen. i. 3.

[3] Or, " being declared."
[4] John i. 9. [See translator's important note (1), p. 7, *supra*.]
[5] Literally, " throbbed."
[6] *Odyssey*, vii. 36.

self with some such wing as Plato, the Preceptor of Aristotle, fastens on the soul in (his) *Phædrus*.[1] And Basilides styles such, not a wing, but Holy Spirit; and Sonship invested in this (Spirit) confers benefits, and receives them in turn. He confers benefits, because, as a wing of a bird, when removed from the bird, would not of itself soar high up and aloft; nor, again, would a bird, when disengaged from its pinion, at any time soar high up and aloft; (so, in like manner,) the Sonship involved some such relation in reference to the Holy Spirit, and the Spirit in reference to the Sonship. For the Sonship, carried upwards by the Spirit as by a wing, bears aloft (in turn) its pinion, that is, the Spirit. And it approaches the refined Sonship, and the non-existent God,[2] even Him who fabricated the world out of nonentities. He was not, (however,) able to have this (spirit) with (the Sonship) itself; for it was not of the same substance (with God), nor has it (any) nature (in common) with the Sonship. But as pure and dry air is contrary to (their) nature, and destructive to fishes; so, in contrariety to the nature of the Holy Spirit, was that place simultaneously of non-existent Deity and Sonship, — (a place) more ineffable than ineffable (entities), and higher up than all names.

Sonship, therefore, left this (spirit) near that Blessed Place, which cannot be conceived or represented by any expression. (He left the spirit) not altogether deserted or separated from the Sonship; nay, (far from it,) for it is just as when a most fragrant ointment is put into a vessel, that, even though (the vessel) be emptied (of it) with ever so much care, nevertheless some odour of the ointment still remains, and is left behind, even after (the ointment) is separated from the vessel; and the vessel retains an odour of ointment, though (it contain) not the ointment (itself). So the Holy Spirit has continued without any share in the Sonship, and separated (from it), and has in itself, similarly with ointment, its own power, a savour of Sonship. And this is what has been declared: "As the ointment upon the head which descended to the beard of Aaron."[3] This is the savour from the Holy Spirit borne down from above, as far as formlessness, and the interval (of space) in the vicinity of our world. And from this the Son began to ascend, sustained as it were, says (Basilides), upon eagles' wings, and upon the back. For, he says, all (entities) hasten upwards from below, from things inferior to those that are superior. For not one of those things that are among things superior, is so silly as to descend beneath. The third Sonship, however, that which requires purification, has continued, he says, in the vast conglomeration of all germs conferring benefits and receiving them. But in what manner it is that (the third Sonship) receives benefits and confers them, we shall afterwards declare when we come to the proper place for discussing this question.

CHAP. XI.—THE "GREAT ARCHON" OF BASILIDES.

When, therefore, a first and second ascension of the Sonship took place, and the Holy Spirit itself also remained after the mode mentioned, the firmament was placed between the supermundane (spaces) and the world. For existing things were distributed by Basilides into two continuous and primary divisions, and are, according to him, denominated partly in a certain (respect) world, and partly in a certain (respect) super-mundane (spaces). But the spirit, a line of demarcation between the world and supermundane (spaces), is that which is both holy, and has abiding in itself the savour of Sonship. While, therefore, the firmament which is above the heaven is coming into existence, there burst forth, and was begotten from the cosmical Seed, and the conglomeration of all germs, the Great Archon (and) Head of the world, (who constitutes) a certain (species of) beauty, and magnitude, and indissoluble power.[4] For, says he, he is more ineffable than ineffable entities, and more potent than potent ones, and more wise than wise ones, and superior to all the beautiful ones whatever you could mention. This (Archon), when begotten, raised Himself up and soared aloft, and was carried up entire as far as the firmament. And there He paused, supposing the firmament to be the termination of His ascension and elevation, and considering that there existed nothing at all beyond these. And than all the subjacent (entities) whatsoever there were among them which remained mundane, He became more wise, more powerful, more comely, more lustrous, (in fact,) pre-eminent for beauty above any entities you could mention with the exception of the Sonship alone, which is still left in the (conglomeration of) all germs. For he was not aware that there is (a Sonship) wiser and more powerful, and better than Himself. Therefore imagining Himself to be Lord, and Governor, and a wise Master Builder, He turns Himself to (the work of) the creation of every object in the cosmical system. And first, he deemed it proper not to be alone, but made unto Himself, and generated from adjacent (entities), a Son far superior to Himself, and wiser. For all these things had the non-existent Deity previously determined upon,

---

[1] See Plato, vol. i. p. 75 et seq., ed. Bekker. Miller has " Phædo;" an obvious mistake.
[2] [Foretaste of Cent. IV.] Miller's text has, instead of τοῦ οὐκ ὄντος (non-existent), οἰκοῦντος (who dwells *above*).
[3] Ps. cxxxiii. 2.

[3] Or, "unspeakable power."

when He cast down the (conglomeration of) all germs. Beholding, therefore, the Son, He was seized with astonishment, and loved (Him), and was struck with amazement. For some beauty of this description appeared [1] to the Great Archon to belong to the Son, and the Archon caused Him to sit on his right (hand). This is, according to these (heretics), what is denominated the Ogdoad, where the Great Archon has his throne. The entire celestial creation, then, that is, the Æther, He Himself, the Great Wise Demiurge formed. The Son, however, begotten of this (Archon), operates in Him, and offered Him suggestions, being endued with far greater wisdom than the Demiurge Himself.

CHAP. XII. — BASILIDES ADOPTS THE "ENTELECHEIA" OF ARISTOTLE.

This, then, constitutes the *entelecheia* of the natural organic body, according to Aristotle, (viz.,) a soul operating in the body, without which the body is able to accomplish nothing ; (I mean nothing) that is greater, and more illustrious, and more powerful, and more wise than the body.[2] The account, therefore, which Aristotle has previously rendered concerning the soul and the body, Basilides elucidates as applied to the Great Archon and his Son. For the Archon has generated, according to Basilides, a son ; and the soul as an operation and completion, Aristotle asserts to be an *entelecheia* of a natural organic body. As, therefore, the *entelecheia* controls the body, so the Son, according to Basilides, controls the God that is more ineffable than ineffable (entities). All things, therefore, have been provided for, and managed by the majesty [3] of the Great Archon ; (I mean) whatever objects exist in the æthereal region of space as far as the moon, for from that quarter onwards air is separated from æther. When all objects in the æthereal regions, then, were arranged, again from (the conglomeration of) all germs another Archon ascended, greater, of course, than all subjacent (entities), with the exception, however, of the Sonship that had been left behind, but far inferior to the First Archon. And this (second Archon) is called by them Rhetus.[4] And this Topos is styled Hebdomad, and this (Archon) is the manager and fabricator of all subjacent (entities). And He has likewise made unto Himself out (of the conglomeration of) all germs, a son who is more prudent and wise than Himself, similarly to what has been stated to have taken place in the case of the First Archon. That which exists in this quarter (of the universe) constitutes, he says, the actual conglomeration and collection of all seeds ; and the things which are generated are produced according to nature, as has been declared already by Him who calculates on things future, when they ought [5] (to be), and what sort they ought (to be), and how they ought (to be). And of these no one is Chief, or Guardian, or Creator. For (a) sufficient (cause of existence) for them is that calculation which the Non-Existent One formed when He exercised the function of creation.

CHAP. XIII. — FURTHER EXPLANATION OF THE "SONSHIP."

When, therefore, according to these (heretics), the entire world and super-mundane entities were finished, and (when) nothing exists labouring under deficiency, there still remains in the (conglomeration of) all germs the third Sonship, which had been left behind in the Seed to confer benefits and receive them. And it must needs be that the Sonship which had been left behind ought likewise to be revealed and reinstated above. And His place should be above the Conterminous Spirit, near the refined and imitative Sonship and the Non-Existent One. But this would be in accordance with what has been written, he says : " And the creation itself groaneth together, and travaileth in pain together, waiting for the manifestation of the sons of God." [6] Now, we who are spiritual are sons, he says, who have been left here to arrange, and mould, and rectify, and complete the souls which, according to nature, are so constituted as to continue in this quarter of the universe. " Sin, then, reigned from Adam unto Moses," [7] as it has been written. For the Great Archon exercised dominion and possesses an empire with limits extending as far as the firmament. And He imagines Himself alone to be God, and that there exists nothing above Him, for (the reason that) all things have been guarded by unrevealed Siope. This, he says, is the mystery which has not been made known to former generations ; but in those days the Great Archon, the Ogdoad, was King and Lord, as it seemed, of the universe. But (in reality) the Hebdomad was king and lord of this quarter of the universe, and the Ogdoad is Arrhetus, whereas the Hebdomad is Rhetus. This, he says, is the Archon of the Hebdomad, who has spoken to Moses, and says : " I am the God of Abraham, and Isaac, and Jacob, and I have not manifested unto them the name of God " [8] (for so they wish that it had been written) — that is, the God, Arrhetus,

---

[1] Or, " was produced unto."
[2] Miller's text has " the soul," which Duncker and Cruice properly correct into " body."
[3] Μεγαλειότητος, a correction from μεγάλης.
[4] A correction from " Arrhetus."

[5] This passage is very obscure, and is variously rendered by the commentators. The above translation follows Schneidewin's version, which yields a tolerably clear meaning.
[6] Rom. viii. 19, 22.
[7] Rom. v. 14.
[8] Ex. vi. 2, 3.

Archon of the Ogdoad. All the prophets, therefore, who were before the Saviour uttered their predictions, he says, from this source (of inspiration). Since, therefore, it was requisite, he says, that we should be revealed as the children of God, in expectation of whose manifestation, he says, the creation habitually groans and travails in pain, the Gospel came into the world, and passed through every Principality, and Power, and Dominion, and every Name that is named.[1] And (the Gospel) came in reality, though nothing descended from above ; nor did the blessed Sonship retire from that Inconceivable, and Blessed, (and) Non-Existent God. Nay, (far from it ;) for as Indian naphtha, when lighted merely[2] from a considerably long distance, nevertheless attracts fire (towards it), so from below, from the formlessness of the conglomeration (of all germs), the powers pass upwards as far as the Sonship. For, according to the illustration of the Indian naphtha, the Son of the Great Archon of the Ogdoad, as if he were some (sort of) naphtha, apprehends and seizes conceptions from the Blessed Sonship, whose place of habitation is situated after that of the Conterminous (Spirit). For the power of the Sonship which is in the midst of the Holy Spirit, (that is,) in the midst of the (Conterminous) Spirit, shares the flowing and rushing thoughts of the Sonship with the Son of the Great Archon.

CHAP. XIV. — WHENCE CAME THE GOSPEL ; THE NUMBER OF HEAVENS ACCORDING TO BASILIDES ; EXPLANATION OF CHRIST'S MIRACULOUS CONCEPTION.

The Gospel then came, says (Basilides), first from the Sonship through the Son, that was seated beside the Archon, to the Archon, and the Archon learned that He was not God of the universe, but was begotten. But (ascertaining that) He has above Himself the deposited treasure of that Ineffable and Unnameable (and) Non-existent One, and of the Sonship, He was both converted and filled with terror, when He was brought to understand in what ignorance He was (involved). This, he says, is what has been declared : " The fear of the Lord is the beginning of wisdom."[3] For, being orally instructed by Christ, who was seated near, he began to acquire wisdom, (inasmuch as he thereby) learns who is the Non-Existent One, what the Sonship (is), what the Holy Spirit (is), what the apparatus of the universe (is), and what is likely to be the consummation of things. This is the wisdom spoken in a mystery, concerning which, says (Basilides), Scripture uses the following expressions : " Not in words taught of human wisdom, but in (those) taught of the Spirit."[4] The Archon, then, being orally instructed, and taught, and being (thereby) filled with fear, proceeded to make confession concerning the sin which He had committed in magnifying Himself. This, he says, is what is declared : " I have recognised my sin, and I know my transgression, (and) about this I shall confess for ever."[5] When, then, the Great Archon had been orally instructed, and every creature of the Ogdoad had been orally instructed and taught, and (after) the mystery became known to the celestial (powers), it was also necessary that afterwards the Gospel should come to the Hebdomad, in order likewise that the Archon of the Hebdomad might be similarly instructed and indoctrinated into the Gospel. The Son of the Great Archon (therefore) kindled in the Son of the Archon of Hebdomad the light which Himself possessed and had kindled from above from the Sonship. And the Son of the Archon of the Hebdomad had radiance imparted to Him, and He proclaimed the Gospel to the Archon of the Hebdomad. And in like manner, according to the previous account, He Himself was both terrified and induced to make confession. When, therefore, all (beings) in the Hebdomad had been likewise enlightened, and had the Gospel announced to them (for in these regions of the universe there exist, according to these heretics, creatures infinite (in number), viz., Principalities and Powers and Rulers, in regard of which there is extant among the (Basilidians)[6] a very prolix and verbose treatise, where they allege that there are three hundred and sixty-five heavens, and that the great Archon of these is Abrasax,[7] from the fact that his name comprises the computed number 365, so that, of course, the calculation of the title includes all (existing) things, and that for these reasons the year consists of so many days) ; — but when, he says, these (two events, viz., the illumination of the Hebdomad and the manifestation of the Gospel) had thus taken place, it was necessary, likewise, that afterwards the Formlessness existent in our quarter of creation should have radiance imparted to it, and that the mystery should be revealed to the Sonship, which had been left behind in Formlessness, just like an abortion.

Now this (mystery) was not made known to previous generations, as he says, it has been written, " By revelation was made known unto me the mystery ; "[8] and, " I have heard inex-

---

[1] Eph. i. 21.
[2] Or, " seen merely."
[3] Prov. i. 7.
[4] 1 Cor. ii. 13.
[5] Ps. xxxii. 5, li. 3.
[6] κατ' αὐτούς. Ulhorn fills up the ellipsis thus: " And in reference to these localities of the Archons," etc.
[7] This is a more correct form than that occasionally given, viz., Abraxas. See Beausobre, Hist. Manich., lib. ii. p. 51.
[8] Eph. iii. 3-5.

pressible words which it is not possible for man to declare." [1] The light, (therefore,) which came down from the Ogdoad above to the Son of the Hebdomad, descended from the Hebdomad upon Jesus the son of Mary, and he had radiance imparted to him by being illuminated with the light that shone upon him. This, he says, is that which has been declared: "The Holy Spirit will come upon thee," [2] (meaning) that which proceeded from the Sonship through the conterminous spirit upon the Ogdoad and Hebdomad, as far as Mary; "and the power of the Highest will overshadow thee," (meaning) the power of the anointing,[3] (which streamed) from the (celestial) height above (through) the Demiurge, as far as the creation, which is (as far as) the Son. And as far as that (Son) he says the world consisted thus. And as far as this, the entire Sonship, which is left behind for benefiting the souls in Formlessness, and for being the recipient in turn of benefits, — (this Sonship, I say,) when it is transformed, followed Jesus, and hastened upwards, and came forth purified. And it becomes most refined, so that it could, as the first (Sonship), hasten upwards through its own instrumentality. For it possesses all the power that, according to nature, is firmly connected with the light which from above shone down (upon earth).

CHAP. XV. — GOD'S DEALINGS WITH THE CREATURE; BASILIDES' NOTION OF (1) THE INNER MAN, (2) THE GOSPEL; HIS INTERPRETATION OF THE LIFE AND SUFFERINGS OF OUR LORD.

When, therefore, he says, the entire Sonship shall have come, and shall be above the conterminous spirit, then the creature will become the object of mercy. For (the creature) groans until now,[4] and is tormented, and waits for the manifestation of the sons of God, in order that all who are men of the Sonship may ascend from thence. When this takes place, God, he says, will bring upon the whole world enormous ignorance, that all things may continue according to nature, and that nothing may inordinately desire anything of the things that are contrary to nature. But (far from it); for all the souls of this quarter of creation, as many as possess the nature of remaining immortal in this (region) only, continue (in it), aware of nothing superior or better (than their present state). And there will not prevail any rumour or knowledge in regions below, concerning beings whose dwelling is placed above, lest subjacent souls should be wrung with torture from longing after impossi-

bilities. (It would be) just as if a fish were to crave to feed on the mountains along with sheep. (For) a wish of this description would, he says, be their destruction. All things, therefore, that abide in (this) quarter [5] are incorruptible, but corruptible if they are disposed to wander and cross over from the things that are according to nature. In this way the Archon of the Hebdomad will know nothing of superjacent entities. For enormous ignorance will lay hold on this one likewise, in order that sorrow, and grief, and groaning may depart from him; for he will not desire aught of impossible things, nor will he be visited with anguish. In like manner, however, the same ignorance will lay hold also on the Great Archon of the Ogdoad, and similarly on all the creatures that are subject unto him, in order that in no respect anything may desire aught of those things that are contrary to nature, and may not (thus) be overwhelmed with sorrow. And so there will be the restitution of all things which, in conformity with nature, have from the beginning a foundation in the seed of the universe, but will be restored at (their own) proper periods. And that each thing, says (Basilides), has its own particular times, the Saviour is a sufficient (witness [6]) when He observes, "Mine hour is not yet come." [7] And the Magi (afford similar testimony) when they gaze wistfully upon the (Saviour's) star.[8] For (Jesus) Himself was, he says, mentally preconceived at the time of the generation of the stars, and of the complete return to their starting-point of the seasons in the vast conglomeration (of all germs). This is, according to these (Basilidians), he who has been conceived as the inner spiritual man in what is natural (now this is the Sonship which left there the soul, not (that it might be) mortal, but that it might abide here according to nature, just as the first Sonship left above in its proper locality the Holy Spirit, (that is, the spirit) which is conterminous), — (this, I say, is he who has been conceived as the inner spiritual man, and) has then been arrayed in his own peculiar soul.

In order, however, that we may not omit any of the doctrines of this (Basilides), I shall likewise explain whatever statements they put forward respecting a gospel. For gospel with them, as has been elucidated, is of super-mundane entities the knowledge which the Great Archon did not understand. As, then, it was manifested unto him that there are likewise the Holy Spirit — that is, the conterminous (spirit) — and the Sonship, and the Non-Existent God, the cause of all these, he rejoiced at the communications made to him, and was filled with exultation.

---

[1] 2 Cor. xii. 4.
[2] Luke i. 35.
[3] Miller's text has "judgment," which yields no meaning. Roeper suggests "Ogdoad."
[4] Rom. viii. 19–22.

[5] Or, "their own peculiar locality" (Bunsen).
[6] This word is added by Bunsen.
[7] John ii. 4.
[8] Matt. ii. 1, 2.

According to them, this constitutes the gospel. Jesus, however, was born, according to these (heretics), as we have already declared. And when the generation which has been previously explained took place, all the events in our Lord's life occurred, according to them, in the same manner as they have been described in the Gospels. And these things happened, he says, in order that Jesus might become the first-fruits of a distinction of the different orders (of created objects) that had been confused together.[1] For when the world had been divided into an Ogdoad, which is the head of the entire world, — now the great Archon is head of the entire world, — and into a Hebdomad, — which is the head of the Hebdomad, the Demiurge of subjacent entities, — and into this order of creatures (that prevails) amongst us, where exists Formlessness, it was requisite that the various orders of created objects that had been confounded together should be distinguished by a separating process performed by Jesus. (Now this separation) that which was his corporeal part suffered, and this was (the part) of Formlessness, and reverted into Formlessness. And that was resuscitated which was his psychical part, and this was (part) of the Hebdomad, and reverted into the Hebdomad. And he revived that (element in his nature) which was the peculiar property of the elevated region where dwells the Great Archon, and (that element) remained beside the Great Archon. And he carried upwards as far as (that which is) above that which was (the peculiar property) of the conterminous spirit, and he remained in the conterminous spirit. And through him there was purified the third Sonship, which had been left for conferring benefits, and receiving them. And (through Jesus) it ascended towards the blessed Sonship, and passed through all these. For the entire purpose of these was the blending together of, as it were, the conglomeration of all germs, and the distinction of the various orders of created objects, and the restoration into their proper component parts of things that had been blended together. Jesus, therefore, became the first-fruits of the distinction of the various orders of created objects, and his Passion took place for not any other reason than the distinction which was thereby brought about in the various orders of created objects that had been confounded together. For in this manner (Basilides) says that the entire Sonship, which had been left in Formlessness for the purpose of conferring benefits and receiving them, was divided into its component elements, according to the manner in which also the distinction of natures had taken place in Jesus. These, then, are the

legends which likewise Basilides details after his sojourn in Egypt;[2] and being instructed by the (sages of this country) in so great a system of wisdom, (the heretic) produced fruits of this description.

CHAP. XVI. — THE SYSTEM OF SATURNILUS.

But one Saturnilus,[3] who flourished about the same period with Basilides,[4] but spent his time in Antioch, (a city) of Syria, propounded opinions akin to whatever (tenets) Menander (advanced). He asserts that there is one Father, unknown to all — He who had made angels, archangels, principalities, (and) powers; and that by certain angels, seven (in number), the world was made, and all things that are in it. And (Saturnilus affirms) that man was a work of angels. There had appeared above from (the Being of) absolute sway, a brilliant [5] image; and when (the angels) were not able to detain this, on account of its immediately, he says, returning with rapidity upwards, they exhorted one another, saying, "Let us make man in our likeness and image."[6] And when the figure was formed, and was not, he says, able, owing to the impotence of the angels, to lift up itself, but continued writhing as a worm, the Power above, compassionating him on account of his having been born in its own image, sent forth a scintillation of life, which raised man up, and caused him to have vitality. (Saturnilus) asserts that this scintillation of life rapidly returns after death to those things that are of the same order of existence; and that the rest, from which they have been generated, are resolved into those. And the Saviour [7] he supposed to be unbegotten and incorporeal, and devoid of figure. (Saturnilus,) however, (maintained that Jesus) was manifested as man in appearance only. And he says that the God of the Jews is one of the angels, and, on account of the Father's wishing to deprive of sovereignty all the Archons, that Christ came for the overthrow of the God of the Jews, and for the salvation of those that believe upon Him; and that these have in them the scintillation of life. For he asserted that two kinds of men had been formed by the angels, — one wicked, but the other good. And, since demons from time to time assisted wicked (men, Saturnilus affirms) that the Saviour came for the overthrow of worthless men and demons, but for the salvation of

[1] See Clemens Alexandrinus, *Strom.*, ii. p. 375, ed. Sylburg. [Comp, cap. viii. vol. ii. p. 355, this series.]

[2] Bernays and Bunsen read τὸν Περίπατον, which Abbe Cruice and Duncker consider erroneous, referring us to Eusebius, *Hist. Ecclesiast.*, iv. 7.
[3] See [vol. i. p. 348, this series, where it is *Saturninus*]; Irenæus, i. 24; [vol. iii., this series, p. 649]; Tertullian, *Præscript.*, xlvi.; Epiphanius, *Hær.*, xxiii.; Theodoret, *Hær. Fab.*, i. 3; St. Augustine, *Hær.*, iii. Eusebius styles this heretic Saturninus.
[4] Epiphanius makes Basilides and Saturnilus belong to the same school.
[5] φαεινῆς: Miller reads φωνῆς.
[6] Gen. i. 26.
[7] Miller reads "the Father."

good men. And he affirms that marriage and procreation are from Satan. The majority, however, of those who belong to this (heretic's) school) abstain from animal food likewise, (and) by this affectation of asceticism (make many their dupes). And (they maintain) that the prophecies have been uttered, partly by the world-making angels, and partly by Satan, who is also the very angel whom they suppose to act in antagonism to the cosmical[1] (angels), and especially to the God of the Jews. These, then, are in truth the tenets of Saturnilus.

CHAP. XVII. — MARCION ; HIS DUALISM ; DERIVES HIS SYSTEM FROM EMPEDOCLES ; SKETCH OF THE DOCTRINE OF EMPEDOCLES.

But Marcion,[2] a native of Pontus, far more frantic than these (heretics), omitting the majority of the tenets of the greater number (of speculators), (and) advancing into a doctrine still more unabashed, supposed (the existence of) two originating causes of the universe, alleging one of them to be a certain good (principle), but the other an evil one. And himself imagining that he was introducing some novel (opinion), founded a school full of folly, and attended by men of a sensual mode of life, inasmuch as he himself was one of lustful propensities.[3] This (heretic) having thought that the multitude would forget that he did not happen to be a disciple of Christ, but of Empedocles,[4] who was far anterior to himself, framed and formed the same opinions, — namely, that there are two causes of the universe, discord and friendship. For what does Empedocles say respecting the plan of the world? Even though we have previously spoken (on this subject), yet even now also, for the purpose, at all events, of comparing the heresy of this plagiarist (with its source), we shall not be silent.

This (philosopher) affirms that all the elements out of which the world consists and derives its being, are six : two of them material, (viz.,) earth and water ; and two of them instruments by which material objects are arranged and altered, (viz.,) fire and air ; and two of them, by means of the instruments, operating upon matter and fashioning it, viz., discord and friendship. (Empedocles) expresses himself somehow thus : —

" The four roots of all things hear thou first :
    Brilliant Jove, and life-giving Juno and Aidoneus,
    And Nestis, who with tears bedews the mortal font." [5]

Jupiter is fire, and life-giving Juno earth, which produces fruits for the support of existence ; and Aidoneus air, because although through him we behold all things, yet himself alone we do not see. But Nestis is water, for this is a sole vehicle of (food), and thus becomes a cause of sustenance to all those that are being nourished ; (but) this of itself is not able to afford nutriment to those that are being nourished. For if it did possess the power of affording nutriment, animal life, he says, could never be destroyed by famine, inasmuch as water is always superabundant in the world. For this reason he denominates Nestis water, because, (though indirectly) being a cause of nutriment, it is not (of itself) competent to afford nutriment to those things that are being nourished. These, therefore — to delineate them as by way of outline — are the principles that comprise (Empedocles') entire theory of the world : (viz.,) water and earth, out of which (proceed) generated entities ; fire and spirit, (which are) instruments and efficient (causes), but discord and friendship, which are (principles) artistically fabricating (the universe). And friendship is a certain peace, and unanimity, and love, whose entire effort is, that there should be one finished and complete world. Discord, however, invariably separates that one (world), and subdivides it, or makes many things out of one. Therefore discord is of the entire creation a cause which he styles " oulomenon," that is, destructive. For it is the concern of this (discord), that throughout every age the creation itself should continue to preserve its existing condition. And ruinous discord has been (thus) a fabricator and an efficient cause of the production of all generated entities ; whereas friendship (is the cause) of the eduction, and alteration, and restoration of existing things into one system. And in regard of these (causes), Empedocles asserts that they are two immortal and unbegotten principles, and such as have not as yet received an originating cause of existence. (Empedocles) somewhere or other (expresses himself) in the following manner : —

" For if both once it was, and will be ; never, I think,
    Will be the age eternal void of both of these." [6]

(But) what are these (two) ? Discord and Friendship ; for they did not begin to come into being, but pre-existed and always will exist, because, from the fact of their being unbegotten, they are not able to undergo corruption. But fire, (and water,) and earth, and air, are (entities) that perish and revive. For when these generated (bodies), by reason of Discord, cease to exist, Friendship, laying hold on them, brings them forward, and attaches and associates them

---

[1] Or, " world-making."

[2] See [vol. i. p. 352, this series] ; Irenæus, i. 27 ; [vol. iii., this series especially p. 257], Tertullian, *Adv. Marc.*, and *Præscript.*, xxx. ; Epiphanius, *Hær.*, xlii. ; Theodoret, *Hær. Fab.*, i. 24 ; Eusebius, *Hist. Ecclesiast.*, v. 13, 16 ; and St Augustine, *Hær.*, xxii.

[3] Or, "quarrelsome," or, "frantic."

[4] Hippolytus' discussion respecting the heresy of Marcion is chiefly interesting from the light which it throws on the philosophy of Empedocles.

[5] These are lines 55-57 in Karsten's edition of a collection of the Empedoclean verses.

[6] These are lines 110, 111, in Stein's edition of *Empedocles*.

herself with the universe.   (And this takes place) in order that the Universe may continue one, being always ordered by Friendship in a manner one and the same, and with (uninterrupted) uniformity.

When, however, Friendship makes unity out of plurality, and associates with unity separated entities, Discord, again, forcibly severs them from unity, and makes them many, that is, fire, water, earth, air, (as well as) the animals and plants produced from these, and whatever portions of the world we observe.   And in regard of the form of the world, what sort it is, (as) arranged by Friendship, (Empedocles) expresses himself in the following terms : —

" For not from back two arms arise,
    Not feet, not nimble knees, not genital groin,
    But a globe it was, and equal to itself it is." [1]

An operation of this description Friendship maintains, and makes (one) most beautiful form of the world out of plurality.   Discord, however, the cause of the arrangement of each of the parts (of the universe), forcibly severs and makes many things out of that one (form).   And this is what Empedocles affirms respecting his own generation : —

" Of these I also am from God a wandering exile." [2]

That is, (Empedocles) denominates as God the unity and unification of that (one form) in which (the world) existed antecedent to the separation and production (introduced) by Discord among the majority of those things (that subsisted) in accordance with the disposition (effected) by Discord.   For Empedocles affirms Discord to be a furious, and perturbed, and unstable Demiurge, (thus) denominating Discord the creator of the world.   For this constitutes the condemnation and necessity of souls which Discord forcibly severs from unity, and (which it) fashions and operates upon, (according to Empedocles,) who expresses himself after some such mode as the following : —

" Who perjury piles on sin,
    While demons gain a life prolonged ; " [3]

meaning by demons long-lived souls, because they are immortal, and live for lengthened ages : —

" For thrice ten thousand years banished from bliss ; " [4]

denominating as blissful, those that have been collected by Friendship from the majority of entities into the process of unification (arising out) of the intelligible world.   He asserts that those are exiles, and that

" In lapse of time all sorts of mortal men are born,
    Changing the irksome ways of life." [5]

He asserts the irksome ways to be the alterations and transfigurations of souls into (successive) bodies.   This is what he says : —

" Changing the irksome ways of life."

For souls " change," body after body being altered, and punished by Discord, and not permitted to continue in the one (frame), but that the souls are involved in all descriptions of punishment by Discord being changed from body to body.   He says : —

" Æthereal force to ocean drives the souls,
    And ocean spurts them forth on earth's expanse,
    And earth on beams of blazing sun, who flings
    (The souls) on æther's depths, and each from each
    (A spirit) takes, and all with hatred burn." [6]

This is the punishment which the Demiurge inflicts, just as some brazier moulding (a piece of) iron, and dipping it successively from fire into water.   For fire is the æther whence the Demiurge transfers the souls into the sea ; and land is the earth : whence he uses the words, from water into earth, and from earth into air.   This is what (Empedocles) says : —

" And earth on beams
    Of blazing sun, who flings (the souls)
    On æther's depths, and each from each
    A (spirit) takes, and all with hatred burn."

The souls, then, thus detested, and tormented, and punished in this world, are, according to Empedocles, collected by Friendship as being a certain good (power), and (one) that pities the groaning of these, and the disorderly and wicked device of furious Discord.   And (likewise Friendship is) eager, and toils to lead forth little by little the souls from the world, and to domesticate them with unity, in order that all things, being conducted by herself, may attain unto unification.   Therefore on account of such an arrangement on the part of destructive Discord of this divided world, Empedocles admonishes his disciples to abstain from all sorts of animal food.   For he asserts that the bodies of animals are such as feed on the habitations of punished souls.   And he teaches those who are hearers of such doctrines (as his), to refrain from intercourse with women.   (And he issues this precept) in order that (his disciples) may not co-operate with and assist those works which Discord fabricates, always dissolving and forcibly severing the work of Friendship.   Empedocles asserts that this is the greatest law of the management of the universe, expressing himself somehow thus : —

" There's something swayed by Fate, the ancient,
    Endless law of gods, and sealed by potent oaths." [7]

He thus calls Fate the alteration from unity into plurality, according to Discord, and from plu-

[1] Lines 360–362 (ed. Karst.).
[2] Line 7 (Karsten), 381 (Stein).
[3] Line 4 (Karsten), 372, 373 (Stein).
[4] Line 5 (Karsten), 374 (Stein).
[5] Line 6 (Karsten), 375, 376 (Stein).
[6] Lines 16–19 (Karsten), 377–380 (Stein).
[7] Lines 1, 2 (Karsten), 369, 370 (Stein).

rality into unity, according to Friendship. And, as I stated, (Empedocles asserts) that there are four perishable gods, (viz.,) fire, water, earth, (and) air. (He maintains,) however, that there are two (gods) which are immortal, unbegotten, (and) continually hostile one to the other, (namely) Discord and Friendship. And (he asserts) that Discord always is guilty of injustice and covetousness, and forcible abduction of the things of Friendship, and of appropriation of them to itself. (He alleges,) however, that Friendship, inasmuch as it is always and invariably a certain good (power), and intent on union, recalls and brings towards (itself), and reduces to unity, the parts of the universe that have been forcibly severed, and tormented, and punished in the creation by the Demiurge. Some such system of philosophy as the foregoing is advanced for us by Empedocles concerning the generation of the world, and its destruction, and its constitution, as one consisting of what is good and bad. And he says that there is likewise a certain third power which is cognised by intellect, and that this can be understood from these, (viz., Discord and Friendship,) expressing himself somehow thus : —

" For if, 'neath hearts of oak, these truths you fix,
  And view them kindly in meditations pure,
  Each one of these, in lapse of time, will haunt you,
  And many others, sprung of these, descend.
  For into every habit these will grow, as Nature prompts;
  But if for other things you sigh, which, countless, linger
  Undisguised 'mid men, and blunt the edge of care,
  As years roll on they'll leave you fleetly,
  Since they yearn to reach their own beloved race;
  For know that all possess perception and a share of
    mind." [1]

CHAP. XVIII. — SOURCE OF MARCIONISM ; EMPEDOCLES REASSERTED AS THE SUGGESTER OF THE HERESY.

When, therefore, Marcion or some one of his hounds barks against the Demiurge, and adduces reasons from a comparison of what is good and bad, we ought to say to them, that neither Paul the apostle nor Mark, he of the maimed finger,[2] announced such (tenets). For none of these (doctrines) has been written in the Gospel according to Mark. But (the real author of the system) is Empedocles, son of Meto, a native of Agrigentum. And (Marcion) despoiled this (philosopher), and imagined that up to the

present would pass undetected his transference, under the same expressions, of the arrangement of his entire heresy from Sicily into the evangelical narratives. For bear with me, O Marcion : as you have instituted a comparison of what is good and evil, I also to-day will institute a comparison following up your own tenets, as you suppose them to be. You affirm that the Demiurge of the world is evil — why not hide your countenance in shame, (as thus) teaching to the Church the doctrines of Empedocles? You say that there is a good Deity who destroys the works of the Demiurge : then do not you plainly preach to your pupils, as the good Deity, the Friendship of Empedocles. You forbid marriage, the procreation of children, (and) the abstaining from meats which God has created for participation by the faithful, and those that know the truth.[3] (Thinkest thou, then,) that thou canst escape detection, (while thus) enjoining the purificatory rites of Empedocles? For in point of fact you follow in every respect this (philosopher of paganism), while you instruct your own disciples to refuse meats, in order not to eat any body (that might be) a remnant of a soul which has been punished by the Demiurge. You dissolve marriages that have been cemented by the Deity. And here again you conform to the tenets of Empedocles, in order that for you the work of Friendship may be perpetuated as one (and) indivisible. For, according to Empedocles, matrimony separates unity, and makes (out of it) plurality, as we have proved.

CHAP. XIX. — THE HERESY OF PREPON ; FOLLOWS EMPEDOCLES ; MARCION REJECTS THE GENERATION OF THE SAVIOUR.

The principal heresy of Marcion, and (the one of his) which is most free from admixture (with other heresies), is that which has its system formed out of the theory concerning the good and bad (God). Now this, it has been manifested by us, belongs to Empedocles. But since at present, in our times, a certain follower of Marcion, (namely) Prepon, an Assyrian,[4] has endeavoured to introduce something more novel, and has given an account of his heresy in a work inscribed to Bardesanes, an Armenian, neither of this will I be silent. In alleging that what is just constitutes a third principle, and that it is placed intermediate between what is good and bad, Prepon of course is not able to avoid (the imputation of inculcating) the opinion of Empedocles. For Empedocles asserts that the world is managed by wicked Discord, and that the other

---

[1] The text of these verses, as given by Hippolytus, is obviously corrupt, and therefore obscure. Schneidewin has furnished an emended copy of them (*Philol.*, vi. 166), which the translator has mostly adopted. (See Stein's edition of the *Empedoclean Verses*, line 222 et seq.)

[2] ὁ κολοβοδάκτυλος. Bunsen [*more suo*, vol. i., p. 89] considers this a corrupt reading, and suggests καλῶν λόγων διδάσκαλος, i.e., "a teacher of good words," i.e., an evangelist, which word, as just used, he does not wish to repeat. The Abbe Cruice denies the necessity for any such emendation, and refers us to an article in the *Journal of Classical and Sacred Philology* (Cambridge, March, 1855), the writer of which maintains, on the authority of St. Jerome, that St. Mark had amputated his thumb, in order that he might be considered disqualified for the priesthood.

[3] 1 Tim. iv. 3.

[4] What Hippolytus communicates concerning Prepon is quite new. The only writer who mentions him is Theodoret (*Hær. Fab.*, i. 25) in his article on Apelles.

(world) which (is managed) by Friendship, is cognisable by intellect. And (he asserts) that these are the two different principles of good and evil, and that intermediate between these diverse principles is impartial reason, in accordance with which are united the things that have been separated by Discord, (and which,) in accordance with the influence of Friendship, are accommodated to unity. The impartial reason itself, that which is an auxiliary to Friendship, Empedocles denominates "Musa." And he himself likewise entreats her to assist him, and expresses himself somehow thus : —

> "For if on fleeting mortals, deathless Muse,
> Thy care it be that thoughts our mind engross,
> Calliope, again befriend my present prayer,
> As I disclose a pure account of happy gods." [1]

Marcion, adopting these sentiments, rejected altogether the generation of our Saviour. He considered it to be absurd that under the (category of a) creature fashioned by destructive Discord should have been the Logos that was an auxiliary to Friendship — that is, the Good Deity. (His doctrine,) however, was that, independent of birth, (the Logos) Himself descended from above in the fifteenth year of the reign of Tiberius Cæsar, and that, as being intermediate between the good and bad Deity, He proceeded to give instruction in the synagogues. For if He [2] is a Mediator, He has been, he says, liberated from the entire nature of the Evil Deity. Now, as he affirms, the Demiurge is evil, and his works. For this reason, he affirms, Jesus came down unbegotten, in order that He might be liberated from all (admixture of) evil. And He has, he says, been liberated from the nature of the Good One likewise, in order that He may be a Mediator, as Paul states,[3] and as Himself acknowledges : "Why call ye me good? there is one good." [4] These, then, are the opinions of Marcion, by means of which he made many his dupes, employing the conclusions of Empedocles. And he transferred the philosophy invented by that (ancient speculator) into his own system of thought, and (out of Empedocles) constructed his (own) impious heresy. But I consider that this has been sufficiently refuted by us, and that I have not omitted any opinion of those who purloin their opinions from the Greeks, and act despitefully towards the disciples of Christ, as if they had become teachers to them of these (tenets). But since it seems that we have sufficiently explained the doctrines of this (heretic), let us see what Carpocrates says.

CHAP. XX. — THE HERESY OF CARPOCRATES ; WICKED DOCTRINES CONCERNING JESUS CHRIST ; PRACTISE MAGICAL ARTS ; ADOPT A METEMPSYCHOSIS.

Carpocrates [5] affirms that the world and the things in it were made by angels, far inferior to the unbegotten Father ; and that Jesus was generated of Joseph, and that, having been born similar to (other) men, He was more just than the rest (of the human race). And (Carpocrates asserts) that the soul (of Jesus), inasmuch as it was made vigorous and undefiled, remembered the things seen by it in its converse with the unbegotten God. And (Carpocrates maintains) that on this account there was sent down upon (Jesus) by that (God) a power, in order that through it He might be enabled to escape the world-making (angels). And (he says) that this power, having passed through all, and having obtained liberty in all, again ascended [6] to God (Himself). And (he alleges) that in the same condition with (the soul of Jesus are all the souls) that embrace similar objects of desire with the (power just alluded to). And they assert that the soul of Jesus, (though,) according to law, it was disciplined in Jewish customs, (in reality) despised them. And (he says) that on this account (Jesus) received powers whereby He rendered null and void the passions incidental to men for their punishment. And (he argues), therefore, that the (soul), which, similarly with that soul of Christ, is able to despise the world-making Archons, receives in like manner power for the performance of similar acts. Wherefore, also, (according to Carpocrates, there are persons who) have attained unto such a degree of pride as to affirm some of themselves to be equal to Jesus Himself, whereas others among them to be even still more powerful. But (they also contend) that some enjoy an excellence above the disciples of that (Redeemer), for instance Peter and Paul, and the rest of the Apostles, and that these are in no respect inferior to Jesus. And (Carpocrates asserts) that the souls of these have originated from that supernal power, and that consequently they, as equally despising the world-making (angels), have been deemed worthy of the same power, and (of the privilege) to ascend to the same (place). If, however, any one would despise earthly concerns more than did that (Saviour, Carpocrates says) that such a one would be able to become superior to (Jesus. The followers of this heretic) practise their magical arts and incantations, and spells and volup-

---

[1] Schneidewin gives a restored version of these lines. They are found (at lines 338–341) in Stein's edition of the *Empedoclean Verses*.
[2] Tertullian combats these heretical notions in his *De Carne Christi* [vol. viii. p. 521, this series].
[3] Gal. iii. 19.
[4] Matt. xix. 17; Mark x. 18; Luke xviii. 19.

[5] See [vol. i. p. 350] Irenæus, i. 25; [vol. iii. p. 203] Tertullian, *De Anima*, c. xxiii.-xxv., and *Præscript.*, c. xlviii.; Eusebius, *Hist. Ecclesiast.*, iv. 7. Epiphanius, *Hær.*, xxvii. sec. 2; Theodoret, *Hær. Fab.*, i. 5; and St. Augustine, *Hær.*, c. vii. The entire of this article is taken from Irenæus, and equally coincides with the account given of Carpocrates by Epiphanius.
[6] Or, "came."

tuous feasts. And (they are in the habit of invoking the aid of) subordinate demons and dream-senders, and (of resorting to) the rest of the tricks (of sorcery), alleging that they possess power for now acquiring sway over the Archons and makers of this world, nay, even over all the works that are in it.

(Now these heretics) have themselves been sent forth by Satan, for the purpose of slandering before the Gentiles the divine name of the Church. (And the devil's object is,) that men hearing, now after one fashion and now after another, the doctrines of those (heretics), and thinking that all of us are people of the same stamp, may turn away their ears from the preaching of the truth, or that they also, looking, (without abjuring,) upon all the tenets of those (heretics), may speak hurtfully of us. (The followers of Carpocrates) allege that the souls are transferred from body to body, so far as that they may fill up (the measure of) all their sins. When, however, not one (of these sins) is left, (the Carpocratians affirm that the soul) is then emancipated, and departs unto that God above of the world-making angels, and that in this way all souls will be saved. If, however, some (souls), during the presence of the soul in the body for one life, may by anticipation become involved in the full measure of transgressions, they, (according to these heretics,) no longer undergo metempsychosis. (Souls of this sort,) however, on paying off at once all trespasses, will, (the Carpocratians say,) be emancipated from dwelling any more in a body. Certain, likewise, of these (heretics) brand[1] their own disciples in the back parts of the lobe of the right ear. And they make counterfeit images of Christ, alleging that these were in existence at the time (during which our Lord was on earth, and that they were fashioned) by Pilate.[2]

CHAP. XXI. — THE SYSTEM OF CERINTHUS CONCERNING CHRIST.

But a certain Cerinthus,[3] himself being disciplined in the teaching of the Egyptians, asserted that the world was not made by the primal Deity, but by some virtue which was an offshoot from that Power which is above all things, and which (yet) is ignorant of the God that is above all. And he supposed that Jesus was not generated from a virgin, but that he was born son of Joseph and Mary, just in a manner similar with the rest of men, and that (Jesus) was more just and more

wise (than all the human race). And (Cerinthus alleges) that, after the baptism (of our Lord), Christ in form of a dove came down upon him, from that absolute sovereignty which is above all things. And then, (according to this heretic,) Jesus proceeded to preach the unknown Father,[4] and in attestation (of his mission) to work miracles. It was, however, (the opinion of Cerinthus,) that ultimately Christ departed from Jesus, and that Jesus suffered and rose again ; whereas that Christ, being spiritual,[5] remained beyond the possibility of suffering.

CHAP. XXII. — DOCTRINE OF THE EBIONÆANS.

The Ebionæans,[6] however, acknowledge that the world was made by Him Who is in reality God, but they propound legends concerning the Christ similarly with Cerinthus and Carpocrates. They live conformably to the customs of the Jews, alleging that they are justified according to the law, and saying that Jesus was justified by fulfilling the law. And therefore it was, (according to the Ebionæans,) that (the Saviour) was named (the) Christ of God and Jesus,[7] since not one of the rest (of mankind) had observed completely the law. For if even any other had fulfilled the commandments (contained) in the law, he would have been that Christ. And the (Ebionæans allege) that they themselves also, when in like manner they fulfil (the law), are able to become Christs ; for they assert that our Lord Himself was a man in a like sense with all (the rest of the human family).

CHAP. XXIII. — THE HERESY OF THEODOTUS.

But there was a certain Theodotus,[8] a native of Byzantium, who introduced a novel heresy. He announces tenets concerning the originating cause of the universe, which are partly in keeping with the doctrines of the true Church, in so far as he acknowledges that all things were created by God. Forcibly appropriating, however, (his notions of) Christ from the school of the Gnostics, and of Cerinthus and Ebion, he alleges that (our Lord) appeared in some such manner as I shall now describe. (According to this, Theodotus maintains) that Jesus was a (mere) man, born of a virgin, according to the counsel of the Father, and that after he had lived promiscuously with all men, and had be-

---

[1] Literally, "cauterize."
[2] Epiphanius alludes in the same manner to these images.
[3] See [vol. i. pp. 351, 415] Irenæus, i. 26, iii. 2, 3; [vol. iii. p. 6.1] Tertullian, *Præscript.*, c. xlviii.; Eusebius, *Hist. Ecclesiast.*, iii. 28, vii. 25; Epiphanius, *Hær.*, xxviii.; Theodoret, *Hær. Fab.*, ii. 3; St. Augustine, *Hær.*, c. viii.; and St. Jerome, *Ep.*, lxxxix. We have here, as in the preceding articles, Irenæus in the Greek, as Hippolytus' text corresponds with the Latin version of this portion of Irenæus' work.

[4] Acts xvii. 23.
[5] Or, "paternal."
[6] See [vol. i. p. 352] Irenæus, i. 26; [vol. iii. p. 651] Tertullian, *Præscript.*, c. xlviii.; [vol. iv. p. 429, this series] Origen, *Contr. Cels.*, ii. 1; Eusebius, *Hist. Ecclesiast.*, iii. 27; Epiphanius, *Hær.*, xxx.; and Theodoret, *Hær. Fab.*, ii. 2. Hippolytus is indebted in this article partly to Irenæus, and partly to original sources.
[7] Or, "that the Christ of God was named Jesus" (Bunsen).
[8] See [vol. iii. p. 654, "two Theodoti"] Tertullian, *Præscript.*, c. liii.; Eusebuis, *Hist. Ecclesiast* , v. 27; Epiphanius, *Hær.*, liv.; and Theodoret, *Hær. Fab.*, ii. 5. Clemens Alexandrinus seems to have been greatly indebted to Theodotus, whose system he has explained and commented upon.

come pre-eminently religious, he subsequently at his baptism in Jordan received Christ, who came from above and descended (upon him) in form of a dove. And this was the reason, (according to Theodotus,) why (miraculous) powers did not operate within him prior to the manifestation in him of that Spirit which descended, (and) which proclaims him to be the Christ. But (among the followers of Theodotus) some are disposed (to think) that never was this man made God, (even) at the descent of the Spirit; whereas others (maintain that he was made God) after the resurrection from the dead.

CHAP. XXIV. — THE MELCHISEDECIANS ; THE NICO-LAITANS.

While, however, different questions have arisen among them, a certain (heretic), who himself also was styled Theodotus, and who was by trade a banker,[1] attempted to establish (the doctrine), that a certain Melchisedec constitutes the greatest power, and that this one is greater than Christ. And they allege that Christ happens to be according to the likeness (of this Melchisedec). And they themselves, similarly with those who have been previously spoken of as adherents of Theodotus, assert that Jesus is a (mere) man, and that, in conformity with the same account (already given), Christ descended upon him.

There are, however, among the Gnostics diversities of opinion ; but we have decided that it would not be worth while to enumerate the silly doctrines of these (heretics), inasmuch as they are (too) numerous and devoid of reason, and full of blasphemy. Now, even those (of the heretics) who are of a more serious turn in regard of[2] the Divinity, and have derived their systems of speculation from the Greeks, must stand convicted[3] (of these charges). But Nicolaus[4] has been a cause of the wide-spread combination of these wicked men. He, as one of the seven (that were chosen) for the diaconate,[5] was appointed by the Apostles. (But Nicolaus) departed from correct doctrine, and was in the habit of inculcating indifference of both life and food.[6] And when the disciples (of Nicolaus) continued to offer insult to the Holy Spirit, John reproved them in the Apocalypse as fornicators and eaters of things offered unto idols.[7]

CHAP. XXV. — THE HERESY OF CERDON.

But one Cerdon[8] himself also, taking occasion in like manner from these (heretics) and Simon, affirms that the God preached by Moses and the prophets was not Father of Jesus Christ. For (he contends) that this (Father) had been known, whereas that the Father of Christ[9] was unknown, and that the former was just, but the latter good. And Marcion corroborated the tenet of this (heretic) in the work which he attempted to write, and which he styled *Antitheses.*[10] And he was in the habit, (in this book,) of uttering whatever slanders suggested themselves to his mind against the Creator of the universe. In a similar manner likewise (acted) Lucian,[11] the disciple of this (heretic).

CHAP. XXVI. — THE DOCTRINES OF APELLES ; PHILUMENE, HIS PROPHETESS.

But Apelles,[12] sprung from these, thus expresses himself, (saying) that there is a certain good Deity, as also Marcion supposed, and that he who created all things is just. Now he, (according to Apelles,) was the Demiurge of generated entities. And (this heretic also maintains) that there is a third (Deity), the one who was in the habit of speaking to Moses, and that this (god) was of a fiery nature, and that there was another fourth god, a cause of evils. But these he denominates angels. He utters, however, slanders against law and prophets, by alleging that the things that have been written are (of) human (origin), and are false. And (Apelles) selects from the Gospels or (from the writings of) the Apostle (Paul) whatever pleases himself. But he devotes himself to the discourses of a certain Philumene as to the revelations[13] of a prophetess. He affirms, however, that Christ descended from the power above ; that is, from the good (Deity), and that he is the son of that good (Deity). And (he asserts that Jesus) was not born of a virgin, and that when he did appear he was not devoid of flesh. (He maintains,) however, that (Christ) formed his body by taking portions of it from the substance of the universe : that is, hot and cold, and moist and dry. And (he says that Christ), on receiving in this body cosmical powers, lived for the time he did in (this) world. But (he

---

[1] Concerning the younger Theodotus, see [vol. iii. p. 654] Tertullian, *Præscript.*, c. liii.; Epiphanius, *Hær.*, lv.; and Theodoret, *Hær. Fab.*, ii. 6.

[2] Or, "in reference to" (Bunsen).

[3] Or, "have been adduced" (Miller).

[4] See [*ut supra*] Irenæus, i. 26; [*ut supra*] Tertullian, *Præscript.*, c. xlv.; Epiphanius, *Hær.*, c. xxv.; Eusebius, *Hist. Ecclesinst.*, iii. 29; Theodoret, *Hær. Fab.*, i. 15; and St. Augustine, *Hær.*, c. v. [But see Clement, vol. ii. p. 373, this series.]

[5] [He understands that the seven (Acts vi. 5) were deacons. Bunsen, i. p. 97.]

[6] Or, "knowledge." Bunsen suggests βρώσεως, as translated above.

[7] Rev. ii. 6.

[8] Irenæus, i. 27; Eusebius (who here gives Irenæus' Greek), *Hist. Ecclesiast.*, iv. 2; Epiphanius, c. xli.; Theodoret, *Hær. Fab.*, i. 24; and Philastrius, c. xliv.

[9] Hippolytus follows Irenæus, but introduces some alterations.

[10] 'Αντιθέσεις. This is the emendation proposed by the Abbe Cruice. The textual reading is ἀντιπαραθεσεις (comparisons).

[11] See [*ut supra*, p. 353], Tertullian, *Præscript.*, c. li., and Epiphanius, *Hær.*, c. xliii.

[12] See [vol. iii. p. 257] Tertullian, *Præscript.*, c. xxx.; Eusebius, *Hist. Ecclesiast.*, v. 13; Epiphanius, *Hær.*, c. xliv.; Theodoret, *Hær. Fab.*, i. 25; and St. Augustine, *Hær.*, c. xxiv.

[13] φανερώσεσι. Miller's text reads φανερῶς, the error of which is obvious from Tertullian's *Præscript.*, c. xxx. Cruice considers the word to signify the title of a work written by Apelles.

held that Jesus) was subsequently crucified by the Jews, and expired, and that, being raised up after three days, he appeared to his disciples. And (the Saviour) showed them, (so Apelles taught,) the prints of the nails and (the wound) in his side, desirous of persuading them that he was in truth no phantom, but was present in the flesh. After, says (Apelles), he had shown them his flesh, (the Saviour) restored it to earth, from which substance it was (derived. And this he did because) he coveted nothing that belonged to another. (Though indeed Jesus) might use for the time being (what belonged to another), he yet in due course rendered to each (of the elements) what peculiarly belonged to them. And so it was, that after he had once more loosed the chains of his body, he gave back heat to what is hot, cold to what is cold, moisture to what is moist, (and) dryness to what is dry. And in this condition (our Lord) departed to the good Father, leaving the seed of life in the world for those who through his disciples should believe in him.

It appears to us that these (tenets) have been sufficiently explained. Since, however, we have determined to leave unrefuted not one of those opinions that have been advanced by any (of the heretics), let us see what (system) also has been invented by the Docetæ.

THE REFUTATION OF ALL HERESIES

BOOK VIII.[1]

CHAP. I. — HERESIES HITHERTO REFUTED ; OPINIONS OF THE DOCETÆ.

Since the great body of (the heretics) do not employ the counsel of the Lord, by having the beam in the eye,[4] and announce that they see when in reality labouring under blindness, it seems to us expedient in no wise to be silent concerning the tenets of these. Our object is, that by the refutation accomplished by us, the (heretics), being of themselves ashamed, may be brought to know how the Saviour has advised (men) first to take away the beam, then to behold clearly the mote that is in thy brother's eye. Having therefore adequately and sufficiently explained the doctrines of the majority (of the heretics) in the seven books before this, we shall not now be silent as regards the (heterodox) opinions that follow (from these). We shall by this means exhibit the abundance of the grace of the Holy Spirit ; and we shall refute those (who suppose) that they have acquired stedfastness of doctrine, when it is only in appearance. Now these have styled themselves Docetæ,[5] and propound the following opinions : —

(The Docetæ maintain) that God is the primal (Being), as it were a seed of a fig-tree, which is altogether very diminutive in size, but infinite in power. (This seed constitutes, according to the Docetæ,) a lowly magnitude, incalculable in multitude,[6] (and) labouring under no deficiency as regards generation. (This seed is) a refuge for the terror-stricken, a shelter of the naked, a veil for modesty, (and) the sought-for produce, to which He came in search (for fruit), he says, three times,[7] and did not discover (any). Wherefore, he says, He cursed the fig-tree,[8] because He did not find upon it that sweet fruit — the sought-for produce. And inasmuch as the Deity is, according to them — to express myself briefly — of this description and so great, that is, small and minute, the world, as it seems to them, was made in some such manner as the following : When the branches of the fig-tree became tender, leaves budded (first), as one may (generally) see, and next in succession the fruit. Now, in this (fruit) is pre-

---

[1] Much that we have in this book is quite new. Hippolytus derives his article on Tatian, and in a measure that on the Encratites, from Irenæus. The rest is probably from original sources.

[2] Or, " Noimus."

[3] [Note the honour uniformly rendered to the Holy Scriptures by the Fathers.]

[4] Matt. vii. 3, 4 ; Luke vi. 41, 42.

[5] See [vol. i. p. 526] Irenæus, v. 1 ; Theodoret, *Hær. Fab.*, v. 12 ; and [vol. ii. p. 398, and Elucidation XIV. p. 407] Clemens Alexandrinus (*Strom.*, iii.), who informs us that Julius Cassianus — a pupil of Valentinus — was founder of the Docetic heresy.

[6] Miller's text reads ταπεινὸν (lowly), but this is obviously untenable. Duncker alters it into ἄπειρον (infinite), and joins ταπειν with the word following. He renders the passage thus : " but infin in power — a lowly magnitude." Cruice strikes out the word ταπειν· and renders the passage thus : " but infinite in power, a magnitu incalculable in bulk." The above rendering seems to convey H polytus' meaning.

[7] Or, " the Lord came in search of fruit " (Roeper). The read. followed in the translation agrees with the scriptural account ; see Luke xiii. 7.

[8] Matt. xxi. 19, 20 ; Mark xi. 13, 14, 20, 21.

served treasured the infinite and incalculable seed of the fig-tree. We think, therefore, (say the Docetæ,) that there are three (parts) which are primarily produced by the seed of the fig-tree, (viz.,) stem, which constitutes the fig-tree, leaves, and fruit — the fig itself, as we have previously declared. In this manner, the (Docetic) affirms, have been produced three Æons, which are principles from the primal originating cause of the universe. And Moses has not been silent on this point, when he says, that there are three words of God, "darkness, gloom, tempest, and added no more."[1] For the (Docetic) says, God has made no addition to the three Æons; but these, in every respect, have been sufficient for (the exigencies of) those who have been begotten and are sufficient. God Himself, however, remains with Himself, far separated from the three Æons. When each of these Æons had obtained an originating cause of generation, he grew, as has been declared, by little and little, and (by degrees) was magnified, and (ultimately) became perfect. But they think that that is perfect which is reckoned at ten. When, therefore, the Æons had become equal in number and in perfection, they were, as (the Docetæ) are of opinion, constituted thirty Æons in all, while each of them attains full perfection in a decade. And the three are mutually distinct, and hold one (degree of) honour relatively to one another, differing in position merely, because one of them is first, and the other second, and the other of these third. Position, however, afforded them diversity of power. For he who has obtained a position nearest to the primal Deity — who is, as it were, a seed — possessed a more productive power than the rest, inasmuch as he himself who is the immeasurable one, measured himself tenfold in bulk. He, however, who in position is second to the primal Deity, has, inasmuch as he is the incomprehensible one, comprehended himself sixfold. But he who is now third in position is conveyed to an infinite distance, in consequence of the dilatation of his brethren. (And when this third Æon) had thrice realized himself in thought, he encircled himself with, as it were, some eternal chain of union.

CHAP. II. — DOCETIC NOTION OF THE INCARNATION ; THEIR DOCTRINES OF ÆONS ; THEIR ACCOUNT OF CREATION ; THEIR NOTION OF A FIERY GOD.

And these (heretics) suppose that this is what is spoken by the Saviour : "A sower went forth to sow ; and that which fell on the fair and good ground produced, some a hundred-fold, and some sixty-fold, and some thirty-fold."[2] And for this reason, the (Docetic) says, (that the Saviour) has spoken the words, "He that hath ears to hear, let him hear," because these (truths) are not altogether rumours. All these Æons, both the three and all those infinite (Æons which proceed) from these indefinitely, are hermaphrodite Æons. All these, then, after they had been increased and magnified, and had sprung from that one primary seed, (were actuated by a spirit) of concord and union, and they all coalesced into one Æon. And in this manner they begot of a single virgin, Mary,[3] a joint offspring, who is a Mediator, (that is,) the Saviour of all who are in the (covenant of) mediation. (And this Saviour is,) in every respect, coequal in power with the seed of the fig-tree, with the exception that he was generated. Whereas that primary seed, from whence the fig-tree sprung, is unbegotten. When, therefore, those three Æons were adorned with all virtue and with all sanctity, so these teachers suppose, as well as that only begotten child — for he alone was begotten by those infinite Æons from three immediately concerned in his birth, for three immeasurable Æons being unanimous procreated him ; — (after, I say, the Æons and only Son were thus adorned,) the entire nature, which is cognised by intellect, was fashioned free from deficiency. Now, all those intelligible and eternal (entities) constituted light. Light, however, was not devoid of form, nor inoperative, nor in want, as it were, of the assistance of any (other power). But (light) proportionately with the multitude of those infinite (Æons) indefinitely (generated) in conformity with the exemplar of the fig-tree, possesses in itself infinite species of various animals indigenous to that quarter of creation, and it shone down upon the underlying chaos. And when this (chaos) was simultaneously illuminated, and had form imparted to it by those diversified species from above, it derived (thereby) solidity, and acquired all those supernal species from the third Æon, who had made himself threefold.

This third Æon, however, beholding all his own distinctive attributes laid hold on collectively by the underlying darkness (which was) beneath, and not being ignorant of the power of darkness, and at the same time of the security[4] and profusion of light, did not allow his brilliant attributes (which he derived) from above for any length of time to be snatched away by the darkness beneath. But (he acted in quite a contrary manner), for he subjected (darkness) to the Æons. After, then, he had formed the

---

[1] Deut. v. 22.
[2] Matt. xiii. 3–8; Mark iv. 3–8; Luke viii. 5–8.

[3] The word Mary seems interpolated. Miller's text reads it after ἐν μεσότητι. The passage would then be rendered thus: "that is, Him who through the intervention of Mary (has been born into the world) the Saviour of all."
[4] To ἀσφαλὲς: Cruice reads, on the authority of Bernays, ἀφελὲς, i.e., the simplicity.

firmament over the nether world, " he both divided the darkness from the light, and called the light which was above the firmament day, and the darkness he called night." [1] When all the infinite species, then, as I have said, of the third Æon were intercepted in this the lowest darkness, the figure also of the Æon himself, such as he has been described, was impressed (upon them) along with the rest (of his attributes). (Now this figure is) a life-giving fire, which is generated from light, from whence the Great Archon originated. And respecting this (Archon) Moses observes : " In the beginning God created the heavens and the earth." [2] Moses mentions [3] this fiery God as having spoken from the bush, [4] (batos,) that is, from the darkish air. For the whole of the atmosphere that underlies the darkness is (batos, i.e.,) a medium for the transmission of light. Now Moses has employed, says (the Docetic), the expression batos, because all the species of light pass down from above by means of their having the atmosphere as a medium (batos) of transmission. And in no less degree is capable of being recognised the Word of Jehovah addressed to us from the bush (batos, i.e., an atmospheric medium) ; for voice, as significant (in language) of a meaning, is a reverberation of air, and without this (atmosphere) human speech is incapable of being recognised. And not only the Word (of Jehovah addressed) to us from the bush (batos), that is, the air, legislates and is a fellow-citizen with (us) ; but (it does more than this), for both odours and colours manifest to us, through the medium of air, their own (peculiar) qualities.

CHAP. III. — CHRIST UNDOES THE WORK OF THE DEMIURGE ; DOCETIC ACCOUNT OF THE BAPTISM AND DEATH OF JESUS ; WHY HE LIVED FOR THIRTY YEARS ON EARTH.

This fiery deity, then, after he became fire from light, proceeded to create the world in the manner which Moses describes. He himself, however, as devoid of subsistence, employs the darkness as (his) substance, and perpetually insults those eternal attributes of light which, (being from above, had been laid hold on by (the darkness) beneath. Up to the time, therefore, of the appearance of the Saviour, there prevailed, by reason of the Deity of fiery light, (that is,) the Demiurge, a certain extensive delusion of souls. For the species are styled souls, because they are refrigerations [5] from the (Æons) above, and continue in darkness. But

when (the souls) are altered from bodies to bodies, they remain under the guardianship of the Demiurge. And that these things are so, says (the Docetic), it is possible also to perceive from Job, when he uses the following words : " And I am a wanderer, changing both place after place, and house after house." [6] And (we may learn, according to the Docetæ, the same) from the expressions of the Saviour, " And if ye will receive it, this is Elias that was for to come. He that hath ears to hear, let him hear." [7] But by the instrumentality of the Saviour this transference of souls from body to body was made to cease, and faith is preached for remission of sins. After some such manner, that only-begotten Son, when He gazes upon the forms of the supernal Æons, which were transferred from above into darkish bodies, coming down, wished to descend and deliver them. When (the Son), however, became aware that the Æons, those (that subsist) collectively, are unable to behold the Pleroma of all the Æons, but that in a state of consternation they fear lest they may undergo corruption as being themselves perishable, and that they are overwhelmed by the magnitude and splendour of power ; — (when the Son, I say, perceived this,) He contracted Himself — as it were a very great flash in a very small body, nay, rather as a ray of vision condensed beneath the eyelids, and (in this condition) He advances forth as far as heaven and the effulgent stars. And in this quarter of creation He again collects himself beneath the lids of vision according as He wishes it. Now the light of vision accomplishes the same effect ; for though it is everywhere, and (renders visible) all things, it is yet imperceptible to us. We, however, merely see lids of vision, white corners (of the eye), a tissue which is broad, tortuous, [8] (and) exceedingly fibrous, a membrane of the cornea ; and underneath this, the pupil, which is shaped as a berry, is net-like and round. (And we observe) whatever other membranes there are that belong to the light of the eye, and enveloped in which it lies concealed.

Thus, says (the Docetic), the only-begotten (and) eternal Child from above arrayed Himself in a form to correspond with each individual Æon of the three Æons ; [9] and while he was within the triacontad of Æons, He entered into this world [10] just as we have described Him, un-

---

[1] Gen. i. 4, 5, 7.
[2] Gen. i. 1.
[3] Ex. iii. 2.
[4] The Docetæ here attempted to substantiate their system from Scripture by a play upon words.
[5] The Greek word for soul is derived from the same root as that for refrigeration.

[6] These words are spoken of the wife of Job, as the feminine form, πλανῆτις and λάτρις, proves. They have been added from apocryphal sources to the Greek version (ii. 9), but are absent from the English translation. The passage stands thus: καὶ ἐγὼ πλανῆτις καὶ λάτρις τόπον ἐκ τόπου περιερχομένη καὶ οἰκίαν ἐξ οἰκίας. The Abbe Cruice refers to St. Chrysostom's *Hom. de Statuis* [vol. ii. p. 139, opp. ed Migne. not textually quoted.]
[7] Matt. xi. 14, 15.
[8] Or, " a fleshly membrane."
[9] Miller reads, " of the third Æon."
[10] The Abbe Cruice considers that the mention of the period of our Lord's birth has accidentally dropt out of the MS. here. See book vii. chap. xix.

noticed, unknown, obscure, and disbelieved. In order, therefore, say the Docetæ, that He may be clad in the darkness that is prevalent in more distant quarters of creation — (now by darkness he means) flesh — an angel journeyed with Him from above, and announced the glad tidings to Mary, says (the Docetic), as it has been written. And the (child) from her was born, as it has been written. And He who came from above put on that which was born; and so did He all things, as it has been written (of Him) in the Gospels. He washed in Jordan, and when He was baptized He received a figure and a seal in the water of (another spiritual body beside) the body born of the Virgin. (And the object of this was,) when the Archon condemned his own peculiar figment (of flesh) to death, (that is,) to the cross, that that soul which had been nourished in the body (born of the Virgin) might strip off that body and nail it to the (accursed) tree. (In this way the soul) would triumph by means of this (body) over principalities and powers,[1] and would not be found naked, but would, instead of that flesh, assume the (other) body, which had been represented in the water when he was being baptized. This is, says (the Docetic), what the Saviour affirms: "Except a man be born of water and spirit, he will not enter into the kingdom of heaven, because that which is born of the flesh is flesh."[2] From the thirty Æons, therefore, (the Son) assumed thirty forms. And for this reason that eternal One existed for thirty years on the earth, because each Æon was in a peculiar manner manifested during (his own) year. And the souls are all those forms that have been laid hold on by each of the thirty Æons; and each of these is so constituted as to discern Jesus, who is of a nature (similar to their own). (And it was the nature of this Jesus) which that only-begotten and eternal One assumed from everlasting places. These (places), however, are diverse. Consequently, a proportionate number of heresies, with the utmost emulation, seek Jesus. Now all these heresies have their own peculiar Jesus; but he is seen differently according as the place[3] is different towards which, he says, each soul is borne and hastens. (Now each soul) supposes that (the Jesus seen from its particular place) is alone that (Jesus) who is its own peculiar kinsman and fellow-citizen. And on first beholding (this Jesus, that soul) recognises Him as its own peculiar brother, but the rest as bastards. Those, then, that derive their nature from the places below, are not able to see the forms of the Saviour which are above them. Those, however, he says, who are from

above, from the intermediate decade and the most excellent ogdoad — whence, say (the Docetæ), we are — have themselves known not in part, but entirely, Jesus the Saviour. And those, who are from above, are alone perfect, but all the rest are only partially so.

CHAP. IV. — DOCETIC DOCTRINE DERIVED FROM THE GREEK SOPHISTS.

These (statements), therefore, I consider sufficient to properly-constituted minds for the purpose of attaining unto a knowledge of the complicated and unstable heresy of the Docetæ. (But) those who have propounded attempted arguments about inaccessible and incomprehensible Matter, have styled themselves Docetæ. Now, we consider that some of these are acting foolishly, we will not say in appearance, but in reality. At all events, we have proved that a beam from such matter is carried in the eye, if by any means they may be enabled to perceive it. If, however, they do not (discern it, our object is) that they should not make others blind. But the fact is, that the sophists of the Greeks in ancient times have previously devised, in many particulars, the doctrines of these (Docetæ), as it is possible for my readers (who take the trouble) to ascertain. These, then, are the opinions propounded by the Docetæ. As to what likewise, however, are the tenets of Monoïmus, we shall not be silent.

CHAP. V. — MONOÏMUS; MAN THE UNIVERSE, ACCORDING TO MONOÏMUS; HIS SYSTEM OF THE MONAD.

Monoïmus[4] the Arabian was far removed from the glory of the high-sounding poet. (For Monoïmus) supposes that there is some such man as the poet (calls) Oceanus, expressing himself somehow thus: —

"Oceanus, source of gods and source of men."[5]

Changing these (sentiments) into other words, Monoïmus says that man is the universe. Now the universe is the originating cause of all things, unbegotten, incorruptible, (and) eternal. And (he says) that the son of (the) man previously spoken of is begotten, and subject to passion, (and) that he is generated independently of time, (as well as) undesignedly,[6] (and) without being predestinated. For such, he says, is the power of that man. And he being thus constituted in power, (Monoïmus alleges) that the son was born quicker than thought and volition.

---

[1] Col. ii. 11, 14, 15.
[2] John iii. 5, 6.
[3] Miller's text has "type."

[4] What is given here by Hippolytus respecting Monoïmus is quite new. The only writer that mentions him is Theodoret, *Hær. Fab.*, i. 18. [See Bunsen, vol. i. p. 103.]
[5] *Iliad*, xiv. 201, 246.
[6] Or, "kinglessly," which has no meaning here. Miller therefore alters ἀβασιλεύτως into ἀβουλήτως.

And this, he says, is what has been spoken in the Scriptures, "He was, and was generated."[1] And the meaning of this is: Man, and his son was generated; just as one may say, Fire was, and, independently of time, and undesignedly, and without being predestinated, light was generated simultaneously with the existence of the fire. And this man constitutes a single monad, which is uncompounded and indivisible, (and yet at the same time) compounded (and) divisible. (And this monad is) in all respects friendly (and) in all respects peaceful, in all respects quarrelsome (and) in all respects contentious with itself, dissimilar (and) similar. (This monad is likewise,) as it were, a certain musical harmony, which comprises all things in itself, as many as one may express and may omit when not considering; and it manifests all things, and generates all things. This (is) Mother, this (is) Father—two immortal names. As an illustration, however, consider, he says, as a greatest image of the perfect man, the one jot—that one tittle. And this one tittle is an uncompounded, simple, and pure monad, which derives its composition from nothing at all. (And yet this tittle is likewise) compounded, multiform, branching into many sections, and consisting of many parts. That one indivisible tittle is, he says, one tittle of the (letter) iota, with many faces, and innumerable eyes, and countless names, and this (tittle) is an image of that perfect invisible man.

CHAP. VI. — MONOÏMUS' "IOTA;" HIS NOTION OF THE "SON OF MAN."

The monad, (that is,) the one tittle, is[2] therefore, he says, also a decade. For by the actual power of this one tittle, are produced duad, and triad, and tetrad, and pentad, and hexad, and heptad, and ogdoad, and ennead, up to ten. For these numbers, he says, are capable of many divisions, and they reside in that simple and uncompounded single tittle of the iota. And this is what has been declared: "It pleased (God) that all fulness should dwell in the Son of man bodily."[3] For such compositions of numbers out of the simple and uncompounded one tittle of the iota become, he says, corporeal realities. The Son of man, therefore, he says, has been generated from the perfect man, whom no one knew; every creature who is ignorant of the Son, however, forms an idea of Him as the offspring of a woman. And certain very obscure rays of this Son which approach this world, check and control alteration (and) generation.

And the beauty of that Son of man is up to the present incomprehensible to all men, as many as are deceived in reference to the offspring of the woman. Therefore nothing, he says, of the things that are in our quarter of creation has been produced by that man, nor will aught (of these) ever be (generated from him). All things, however, have been produced, not from the entirety, but from some part of that Son of man. For he says the Son of man is a jot in one tittle, which proceeds from above, is full, and completely replenishes all (rays flowing down from above). And it comprises in itself whatever things the man also possesses (who is) the Father of the Son of man.

CHAP. VII. — MONOÏMUS ON THE SABBATH; ALLEGORIZES THE ROD OF MOSES; NOTION CONCERNING THE DECALOGUE.

The world, then, as Moses says, was made in six days, that is, by six powers, which (are inherent) in the one tittle of the iota. (But) the seventh (day, which is) a rest and Sabbath, has been produced from the Hebdomad, which is over earth, and water, and fire, and air. And from these (elements) the world has been formed by the one tittle. For cubes, and octahedrons, and pyramids, and all figures similar to these, out of which consist fire, air, water, (and) earth, have arisen from numbers which are comprehended in that simple tittle of the iota. And this (tittle) constitutes a perfect son of a perfect man. When, therefore, he says, Moses mentions that the rod was changeably brandished for the (introduction of the) plagues throughout Egypt[4]—now these plagues, he says, are allegorically expressed symbols of the creation[5]—he did not (as a symbol) for more plagues than ten shape the rod. Now this (rod) constitutes one tittle of the iota, and is (both) twofold (and) various. This succession of ten plagues is, he says, the mundane creation. For all things, by being stricken, bring forth and bear fruit, just like vines. Man, he says, bursts forth, and is forcibly separated from man by being severed by a certain stroke. (And this takes place) in order that (man) may be generated, and may declare the law which Moses ordained, who received (it) from God. Conformably[6] with that one tittle, the law constitutes the series of the ten commandments which expresses allegorically the divine mysteries of (those) precepts. For, he says, all knowledge of the universe is contained

---

[1] An allusion is evidently made to the opening chapter of St. John's Gospel. Monoïmus, like Basilides, seems to have formed his system from the prologue to the fourth Gospel.

[2] The iota with a little mark placed above, signifies ten; thus, ί = 10.

[3] Col. i. 19.

[4] Ex. vii., viii.

[5] The plagues, being transformations, were no doubt considered symbols of creation, in accordance with the view of the ancient philosophers, that creation itself brought nothing into existence, but simply altered the disposition of already existing elements. [Gen. i. 2. See Dr. Chalmers' Astronomical Discourses.]

[6] It is very much after this allegorical mode that Philo Judæus interprets the Mosaic law and history.

in what relates to the succession of the ten plagues and the series of the ten commandments. And no one is acquainted with this (knowledge) who is (of the number) of those that are deceived concerning the offspring of the woman. If, however, you say that the Pentateuch constitutes the entire law, it is from the Pentad which is comprehended in the one tittle. But the entire is for those who have not been altogether perfected in understanding a mystery, a new and not antiquated feast, legal, (and) everlasting, a passover of the Lord God kept unto our generations, by those who are able to discern (this mystery), at the commencement of the fourteenth day, which is the beginning of a decade from which, he says, they reckon. For the monad, as far as fourteen, is the summary 'of that one (tittle) of the perfect number. For one, two, three, four, become ten; and this is the one tittle. But from fourteen until one-and-twenty, he asserts that there is an Hebdomad which inheres in the one tittle of the world, and constitutes an unleavened creature in all these. For in what respect, he says, would the one tittle require any substance such as leaven (derived) from without for the Lord's Passover, the eternal feast, which is given for generation upon generation?[1] For the entire world and all causes of creation constitute a passover, (i.e.,) a feast of the Lord. For God rejoices in the conversion of the creation, and this is accomplished by ten strokes of the one tittle. And this (tittle) is Moses' rod, which was given by God into the hand of Moses. And with this (rod Moses) smites the Egyptians, for the purpose of altering bodies, — as, for instance, water into blood; and the rest of (material) things similarly with these, —(as, for example,) the locusts, which is a symbol of grass. And by this he means the alteration of the elements into flesh; "for all flesh," he says, "is grass."[2] These men, nevertheless, receive even the entire law after some such manner; adopting very probably, as I think, the opinions of those of the Greeks who affirm that there are Substance, and Quality, and Quantity, and Relation, and Place, and Time, and Position, and Action, and Possession, and Passion.

CHAP. VIII. — MONOÏMUS EXPLAINS HIS OPINIONS IN A LETTER TO THEOPHRASTUS; WHERE TO FIND GOD; HIS SYSTEM DERIVED FROM PYTHAGORAS.

Monoïmus himself, accordingly, in his letter to Theophrastus, expressly makes the following statement: "Omitting to seek after God, and creation, and things similar to these, seek for Him from (out of) thyself, and learn who it is

that absolutely appropriates (unto Himself) all things in thee, and says, 'My God (is) my mind, my understanding, my soul, my body.' And learn from whence are sorrow, and joy, and love, and hatred, and involuntary wakefulness, and involuntary drowsiness, and involuntary anger, and involuntary affection; and if," he says, "you accurately investigate these (points), you will discover (God) Himself, unity and plurality, in thyself, according to that tittle, and that He finds the outlet (for Deity) to be from thyself." Those (heretics), then, (have made) these (statements). But we are under no necessity of comparing such (doctrines) with what have previously been subjects of meditation on the part of the Greeks, inasmuch as the assertions advanced by these (heretics) evidently derive their origin from geometrical and arithmetical art. The disciples, however, of Pythagoras, expounded this (art) after a more excellent method,[3] as our readers may ascertain by consulting those passages (of our work) in which we have previously furnished expositions of the entire wisdom of the Greeks. But since the heresy of Monoïmus has been sufficiently refuted, let us see what are the fictitious doctrines which the rest also (of these heretics) devise, in their desire to set up for themselves an empty name.

CHAP. IX. — TATIAN.

Tatian,[4] however, although being himself a disciple of Justinus the Martyr, did not entertain similar opinions with his master. But he attempted (to establish) certain novel (tenets), and affirmed that there existed certain invisible Æons. And he framed a legendary account (of them), similarly to those (spoken of) by Valentinus. And similarly with Marcion, he asserts that marriage is destruction. But he alleges that Adam is not saved on account of his having been the author of disobedience. And so far for the doctrines of Tatian.

CHAP. X. — HERMOGENES; ADOPTS THE SOCRATIC PHILOSOPHY; HIS NOTION CONCERNING THE BIRTH AND BODY OF OUR LORD.

But a certain Hermogenes,[5] himself also imagining that he propounded some novel opinion, said that God made all things out of coeval and ungenerated matter. For that it was impossible that God could make generated things out of things that are not. And that God is always

---

[1] [Exod. xii. 17. Comp. 1 Cor. v. 7, 8.]
[2] Isa. xl. 6.

[3] Literally, " nobly born."
[4] See [vol. i. pp. 353, 457. But see his works, vol. ii. p. 61, this series]; Irenæus, i. 28; Eusebius, *Hist. Ecclesiast.*, iv. 16, v. 13; Epiphanius, *Hær.*, xlvi.; Jerome, *Vir. Illustr.*, c. xxix.; and Theodoret, *Hær. Fab.*, i. 20.
[5] See [vol. iii. p. 257, also p. 477] Tertullian, *Præscript*, c. xxx.; [vol. iv. p. 245, this series] Origen, Περὶ ἀρχ., i. 2; Eusebius, *De Præp.*, vii. 8, 9; St. Augustine, *Hær.*, lix.; Theodoret, *Hær. Fab.*, i. 19; and Philastrius, *Hær.*, lv.

Lord, and always Creator, and matter always a subservient (substance), and that which is assuming phases of being — not, however, the whole of it. For when it was being continually moved in a rude and disorderly manner, He reduced (matter) into order by the following expedient. As He gazed (upon matter) in a seething condition, like (the contents of) a pot when a fire is burning underneath, He effected a partial separation. And taking one portion from the whole, He subdued it, but another He allowed to be whirled in a disorderly manner. And he asserts that what was (thus) subdued is the world, but that another portion remains wild, and is denominated chaotic [1] matter. He asserts that this constitutes the substance of all things, as if introducing a novel tenet for his disciples. He does not, however, reflect that this happens to be the Socratic discourse, which (indeed) is worked out more elaborately by Plato than by Hermogenes. He acknowledges, however, that Christ is the Son of the God who created all things; and along with (this admission), he confesses that he was born of a virgin and of (the) Spirit, according to the voice of the Gospels. And (Hermogenes maintains that Christ), after His passion, was raised up in a body, and that He appeared to His disciples, and that as He went up into heaven He left His body in the sun, but that He Himself proceeded on to the Father. Now (Hermogenes) resorts to testimony, thinking to support himself by what is spoken, (viz.,) what the Psalmist David says: "In the sun he hath placed his tabernacle, and himself (is) as a bridegroom coming forth from his nuptial chamber, (and) he will rejoice as a giant to run his course." [2] These, then, are the opinions which also Hermogenes attempted to establish.

CHAP. XI. — THE QUARTODECIMANS.

And certain other (heretics), contentious by nature, (and) wholly uninformed as regards knowledge, as well as in their manner more (than usually) quarrelsome, combine (in maintaining) that Easter should be kept on the fourteenth day [3] of the first month, according to the commandment of the law, on whatever day (of the week) it should occur. (But in this) they only regard what has been written in the law, that he will be accursed who does not so keep (the commandment) as it is enjoined. They do not, however, attend to this (fact), that the legal enactment was made for Jews, who in times to come should kill the real Passover. [4]

And this (paschal sacrifice, in its efficacy,) has spread unto the Gentiles, and is discerned by faith, and not now observed in letter (merely). They attend to this one commandment, and do not look unto what has been spoken by the apostle: "For I testify to every man that is circumcised, that he is a debtor to keep the whole law." [5] In all other respects, however, these consent to all the traditions delivered to the Church by the Apostles.[6]

CHAP. XII. — THE MONTANISTS; PRISCILLA AND MAXIMILLA THEIR PROPHETESSES; SOME OF THEM NOETIANS.

But there are others who themselves are even more heretical in nature (than the foregoing), and are Phrygians [7] by birth. These have been rendered victims of error from being previously captivated by (two) wretched women, called a certain Priscilla and Maximilla, whom they supposed (to be) prophetesses. And they assert that into these the Paraclete Spirit had departed; and antecedently to them, they in like manner consider Montanus as a prophet. And being in possession of an infinite number of their books, (the Phrygians) are overrun with delusion; and they do not judge whatever statements are made by them, according to (the criterion of) reason; nor do they give heed unto those who are competent to decide; but they are heedlessly swept onwards, by the reliance which they place on these (impostors). And they allege that they have learned something more through these, than from law, and prophets, and the Gospels. But they magnify these wretched women above the Apostles and every gift of Grace, so that some of them presume to assert that there is in them a something superior to Christ. These acknowledge God to be the Father of the universe, and Creator of all things, similarly with the Church, and (receive) as many things as the Gospel testifies concerning Christ. They introduce, however, the novelties of fasts,[8] and feasts, and meals of parched food, and repasts of radishes, alleging that they have been instructed by women. And some of these assent to the heresy of the Noetians, and affirm that the Father himself is

---

[1] Literally, "unadorned."
[2] Ps. xix. 4, 5.
[3] They were therefore called "Quartodecimans." (See Eusebius, *Hist. Ecclesiast.*, v. c. xxii. xxv.; Epiphanius, *Hær.*, l.; and Theodoret, *Hær. Fab.*, iii. 4.)
[4] [Bunsen, i. p. 105.] The chapter on the Quartodecimans agrees with the arguments which, we are informed in an extract from

Hippolytus' *Chronicon Paschale*, as preserved in a quotation by Bishop Peter of Alexandria, were employed in his *Treatise against all Heresies*. This would seem irrefragable proof of the authorship of the *Refutation of all Heresies*.
[5] Gal. v. 3.
[6] He regards the Christian Paschal as authorized. 1 Cor. v. 7, 8.
[7] These heretics had several denominations: (1) Phrygians and Cataphrygians, from Phrygia; (2) Pepuzians, from a village in Phrygia of this name; (3) Priscillianists; (4) Quintillists. See Eusebius, *Hist. Ecclesiast.*, iv. 27, v. 16, 18; Epiphanius, *Hær.*, xlviii.; Theodoret, *Hær. Fab.*, iii. 2; Philastrius, xlix.; and St. Augustine, *Hær.*, xxvi. [The "Tertullianists" were a class by themselves, which is a fact going far to encourage the idea that they did not share the worst of these delusions.]
[8] Bunsen thinks that Hippolytus is rather meagre in his details of the heresy of the Phrygians or Montanists, but considers this, with other instances, a proof that parts of *The Refutation* are only abstracts of more extended accounts.

the Son, and that this (one) came under generation, and suffering, and death. Concerning these I shall again offer an explanation, after a more minute manner; for the heresy of these has been an occasion of evils to many. We therefore are of opinion, that the statements made concerning these (heretics) are sufficient, when we shall have briefly proved to all that the majority of their books are silly, and their attempts (at reasoning) weak, and worthy of no consideration. But it is not necessary for those who possess a sound mind to pay attention (either to their volumes or their arguments).

CHAP. XIII. — THE DOCTRINES OF THE ENCRATITES.[1]

Others, however, styling themselves Encratites, acknowledge some things concerning God and Christ in like manner with the Church. In respect, however, of their mode of life, they pass their days inflated with pride. They suppose that by meats they magnify themselves, while abstaining from animal food, (and) being water-drinkers, and forbidding to marry, and devoting themselves during the remainder of life to habits of asceticism. But persons of this description are estimated Cynics rather than Christians, inasmuch as they do not attend unto the words spoken against them through the Apostle Paul. Now he, predicting the novelties that were to be hereafter introduced ineffectually by certain (heretics), made a statement thus: "The Spirit speaketh expressly, In the latter times certain will depart from sound doctrine, giving heed to seducing spirits and doctrines of devils, uttering falsehoods in hypocrisy, having their own conscience seared with a hot iron, forbidding to marry, to abstain from meats, which God has created to be partaken of with thanksgiving by the faithful, and those who know the truth; because every creature of God is good, and nothing to be rejected which is received with thanksgiving; for it is sanctified by the word of God and prayer."[2] This voice, then, of the blessed Paul, is sufficient for the refutation of those who live in this manner, and plume themselves on being just;[3] (and) for the purpose of proving that also, this (tenet of the Encratites) constitutes a heresy. But even though there have been denominated certain other heresies — I mean those of the Cainites,[4] Ophites,[5] or Noachites,[6] and of others of this description — I have not deemed it requisite to explain the things said or done by these, lest on this account they may consider themselves somebody, or deserving of consideration. Since, however, the statements concerning these appear to be sufficient, let us pass on to the cause of evils to all, (viz.,) the heresy of the Noetians. Now, after we have laid bare the root of this (heresy), and stigmatized openly the venom, as it were, lurking within it, let us seek to deter from an error of this description those who have been impelled into it by a violent spirit, as it were by a swollen torrent.

---

[1] [See my Introductory Note to *Hermas*, vol. ii. p. 5, this series.]

[2] 1 Tim. iv. 1-5.

[3] [This, Tertullian should have learned. How happily Keble, in his *Christian Year*, gives it in sacred verse: —

"We need not bid, for cloister'd cell,
Our neighbour and our work farewell,
Nor strive to wind ourselves too high
For sinful man beneath the sky:

"The trivial round, the common task,
Would furnish all we ought to ask;
Room to deny ourselves; a road
To bring us daily nearer God."]

[4] Those did homage to Cain.

[5] The Ophites are not considered, as Hippolytus has already devoted so much of his work to the Naasseni. The former denomination is derived from the Greek, and the latter from the Hebrew, and both signify worshippers of the serpent.

[6] Hippolytus seemingly makes this a synonyme with Ophites. Perhaps it is connected with the Hebrew word נָחָשׁ.

THE REFUTATION OF ALL HERESIES

BOOK IX.

CONTENTS.

THE following are the contents of the ninth book of the *Refutation of all Heresies* : —

What the blasphemous folly is of Noetus, and that he devoted himself to the tenets of Heraclitus the Obscure, not to those of Christ.

And how Callistus, intermingling the heresy of Cleomenes, the disciple of Noetus, with that of Theodotus, constructed another more novel heresy, and what sort the life of this (heretic) was.

What was the recent[1] arrival (at Rome) of the strange spirit Elchasai, and that there served as a concealment of his peculiar errors his apparent adhesion to the law, when in point of fact he devotes himself to the tenets of the Gnostics, or even of the astrologists, and to the arts of sorcery.

What the customs of the Jews are, and how many diversities of opinion there are (amongst them).

CHAP. I. — AN ACCOUNT OF CONTEMPORANEOUS HERESY.[2]

A lengthened conflict, then, having been maintained concerning all heresies by us who, at all events, have not left any unrefuted, the greatest struggle now remains behind, viz., to furnish an account and refutation of those heresies that have sprung up in our own day, by which certain ignorant and presumptuous men have attempted to scatter abroad the Church, and have introduced the greatest confusion[3] among all the faithful throughout the entire world. For it seems expedient that we, making an onslaught upon the opinion which constitutes the prime source of (contemporaneous) evils, should prove what are the originating principles[4] of this (opinion), in order that its offshoots, becoming a matter of general notoriety, may be made the object of universal scorn.

CHAP. II. — SOURCE OF THE HERESY OF NOETUS ; CLEOMENES HIS DISCIPLE ; ITS APPEARANCE AT ROME DURING THE EPISCOPATES OF ZEPHYRINUS AND CALLISTUS ; NOETIANISM OPPOSED AT ROME BY HIPPOLYTUS.

There has appeared one, Noetus[5] by name, *and* by birth a native of Smyrna. This person introduced a heresy from the tenets of Heraclitus.[6] Now a certain man called Epigonus becomes his minister and pupil, and this person during his sojourn at Rome disseminated his godless opinion. But Cleomenes, who had become his disciple, an alien both in way of life and habits from the Church, was wont to corroborate the (Noetian) doctrine. At that time, Zephyrinus imagines that he administers the affairs of the Church[7] — an uninformed and shamefully corrupt man. And he, being persuaded by proffered gain, was accustomed to connive at those who were present for the purpose of becoming disciples of Cleomenes. But (Zephyrinus) himself, being in process of time enticed away, hurried headlong[8] into the same opinions ; and he had Callistus as his adviser, and a fellow-champion of these wicked tenets.[8] But the life of this (Callistus), and the heresy invented by him, I shall after a little explain. The school of these heretics during the succession *of such bishops*, continued to acquire strength and augmentation, from the fact that Zephyrinus and Callistus helped them to prevail.[9] Never at any time, however, have we been guilty of collusion with them ; but we have frequently offered them opposition,[10] and have refuted them, and have forced them reluctantly to acknowledge the truth. And they, abashed and constrained by the truth, have confessed *their errors* for a short period, but after a little, wallow once again in the same mire.[11]

---

[1] Or, "fruitless;" or, "unmeaning."
[2] [Elucidation IV.]
[3] [1 Cor. xi. 19. These terrible confusions were thus foretold. Note the remarkable feeling, the impassioned tone, of the Apostle's warning in Acts xx. 28-31.]
[4] [The *Philosophumena*, therefore, responds to the Apostle's warnings. Col. ii. 8; 1 Tim. vi. 20; Gal. iv. 3, 9; Col. ii. 20.]

[5] See *Fragments of Hippolytus' Works* (p. 235 et seq.), edited by Fabricius; Theodoret, *Hær. Fab.*, iii. 3; Epiphanius, *Hær.*, lvii.; and Philastrius, *Hæret.*, liv. Theodoret mentions Epigonus and Cleomenes, and his account is obviously adopted by Hippolytus.
[6] [See Tatian, vol. ii. p. 66, this series.]
[7] [See note 2, cap. iii. *infra.*, and Elucidation V.]
[8] [See Elucidation VI.]
[9] [Note the emphasis and repeated statement with which our author dwells on this painful charge.]
[10] [Elucidation VI.]
[11] 2 Pet. ii. 22. [See book x. cap xxiii., p. 148, *infra.*]

CHAP. III. — NOETIANISM AN OFFSHOOT FROM THE
HERACLITIC PHILOSOPHY.

But since we have exhibited the succession of
their genealogy, it seems expedient next that we
should also explain the depraved teaching involved in their doctrines. *For this purpose* we
shall first adduce the opinions advanced by Heraclitus " the Obscure," [1] and we shall next make
manifest what are the portions of these *opinions*
that are of Heraclitean origin. *Such parts of
their system* its present champions are not aware
belong to the " Obscure " *philosopher*, but they
imagine [2] them to belong to Christ. But if they
might happen to fall in with the following observations, perhaps they thus might be put out of
countenance, and induced to desist from this
godless blasphemy of theirs. Now, even though
the opinion of Heraclitus has been expounded
by us previously in the *Philosophumena*, it nevertheless seems expedient now also to set down
side by side in contrast *the two systems*, in order
that by this closer refutation they may be evidently instructed. *I mean* the followers of this
(heretic), who imagine [2] themselves to be disciples of Christ, when in reality they are not so, but
of " the Obscure."

CHAP. IV. — AN ACCOUNT OF THE SYSTEM OF
HERACLITUS.

Heraclitus then says that the universe is *one*,[3]
divisible and indivisible ; generated *and* ungenerated ; mortal *and* immortal ; reason, eternity ;
Father, Son, and justice, God.[4] " For those
who hearken not to me, but the doctrine, it is
wise that they acknowledge all things to be one,"
says Heraclitus ; and because all do not know
or confess this, he utters a reproof somewhat in
the following terms : " People do not understand
how what is diverse (nevertheless) coincides
with itself, just like the inverse harmony of a
bow and lyre." [5] But that Reason always exists,
inasmuch as it constitutes the universe, and as it
pervades all things, he affirms in this manner.
" But in regard of this Reason, which always

exists, men are continually devoid of understanding,[6] both before they have heard of it and
in first hearing of it. For though all things take
place according to this Reason, they seem like
persons devoid of any experience regarding it.
Still they attempt both words and works of such
a description as I am giving an account of, by
making a division according to nature, and declaring how things are." And that a Son is the
universe and throughout endless ages an eternal
king of all things, he thus asserts : " A sporting
child, playing at his dice, is eternity ; the kingdom is that of a child." [7] And that the Father
of all things that have been generated is an unbegotten creature who is creator, let us hear
Heraclitus affirming in these words : " Contrariety is a progenitor of all things, and king of
all ; and it exhibited some as gods, but others as
men, and made some slaves, whereas others
free." And (he likewise affirms) that there is " a
harmony, as in a bow and lyre." That obscure
harmony (is better),[8] though unknown and invisible to men, he asserts in these words : " An
obscure harmony is preferable to an obvious
one." He commends and admires before what
is known, that which is unknown and invisible
in regard of its power. And that *harmony* visible to men, and not incapable of being discovered, is better, he asserts in these words :
" Whatever things are objects of vision, hearing,
and intelligence, these I pre-eminently honour,"
he says ; that is, *he prefers* things visible to
those that are invisible. From such expressions
of his it is easy to understand *the spirit of his
philosophy*. " Men," he says, " are deceived in
reference to the knowledge of manifest things
similarly with Homer, who was wiser than all
the Greeks. For even children [9] killing vermin
deceived him, when they said, ' What we have
seen and seized, these we leave behind ; whereas
what we neither have seen nor seized, these we
carry away.' "

CHAP. V. — HERACLITUS' ESTIMATE OF HESIOD ;
PARADOXES OF HERACLITUS ; HIS ESCHATOLOGY ;
THE HERESY OF NOETUS OF HERACLITEAN ORI-
GIN ; NOETUS' VIEW OF THE BIRTH AND PAS-
SION OF OUR LORD.

In this manner Heraclitus assigns to the visible an equality of position and honour with the
invisible, as if what was visible and what was
invisible were confessedly some one thing. For

---

1 ['Ο Σκοτεινός, because he maintained the *darkest* system of
sensual philosophy that ever shed night over the human intellect. —
T. LEWIS in *Plato against the Atheists*, p. 156; Elucidation VII.]
2 [Note the use of this phrase, "*imagine* themselves. etc," as a
specialty of our author's style. See cap. ii. *supra*; Elucidation VIII.]
3 This addition seems necessary from Stobæus' account of Heraclitus. (See *Eclog. Phys.*, i. 47, where we have Heraclitus affirming
that " unity is from plurality, and plurality from unity ; " or, in other
words, " that all things are one.")
4 Dr. Wordsworth for δίκαιον suggests εἰκαῖον, i.e., "but that
the Deity is by chance." Παλίντονος, referring to the shape of the bow,
correct text, and consequently at the meaning of Hippolytus' extracts
from Heraclitus. The Heraclitean philosophy is explained by Stobæus, already mentioned. See likewise Bernays' " Critical Epistle "
in Bunsen's *Analect. Ante-Nicæn.* (vol. iii. p. 331 et seq. of *Hippolytus and his Age*), and Schleiermacher in *Museum der Alter-
thumswissenschaft*, t. i p. 408 et seq.
5 παλίντροπος. Miller suggests παλίντονος, the word used by
Plutarch (*De Isid. et Osirid.*, p. 369, ed. Xyland) in recounting
Heraclitus' opinion. Παλίντονος, referring to the shape of the bow,
means " reflex " or " unstrung," or it may signify " clanging," that
is, as a consequence of its being well bent back to wing a shaft.

6 Compare Aristotle's *Rhet.*, iii. 5, and Sextus Empiricus, *Adv.
Math.*, lib. vii. p. 152, ed. Aurel, 1621.
7 See Lucian, *Vit. Auct.*, vol i. p. 554, ed. Hemsterh.
8 This word seems necessary, see Plutarch, *De Procreat. ani-
mæ*, c. xxvii.
9 This is a well-known anecdote in the life of Homer. See Coleridge's *Greek Poets* — Homer. [The unsavoury story is decently
given by Henry Nelson Coleridge in this work, republished. Bos-
ton · James Munroe & Co., 1842.]

he says, "An obscure harmony is preferable to an obvious one ; " and, "Whatsoever things are objects of vision, hearing, *and* intelligence," that is, of the (corporeal) organs, — " these," he says, " I pre-eminently honour," not (on this occasion, though previously), having pre-eminently honoured invisible things. Therefore neither darkness, nor light, nor evil, nor good, Heraclitus affirms, is different, but one and the same thing. At all events, he censures Hesiod [1] because he knew *not* day and night. For day, he says, and night are one, expressing himself somehow thus : " The teacher, however, of a vast amount of information is Hesiod, and people suppose this *poet* to be possessed of an exceedingly large store of knowledge, and *yet* he did not know (the nature of) day and night, for they are one." As regards both what is good and what is bad, (they are, according to Heraclitus, likewise) one. " Physicians, undoubtedly," says Heraclitus, " when they make incisions and cauterize, *though* in every respect they wickedly torture the sick, complain that they do not receive fitting remuneration from their patients, notwithstanding that they perform these salutary operations upon diseases." And both straight and twisted are, he says, the same. " The way is straight and curved of the carders of wool ; " [2] and the circular movement of an instrument in the fuller's shop called " a screw " is straight and curved, for it revolves up and circularly at the same time. " One and the same," he says, " *are, therefore, straight and curved.*" And upward and downward,[3] he says, are one and the same. " The way up *and the way* down are the same." And he says that what is filthy and what is pure are one and the same, and what is drinkable and unfit for drink are one and the same. " Sea," he says, " is water very pure and very foul, drinkable to fishes no doubt, and salutary *for them*, but not fit to be used as drink by men, and (for them) pernicious." And, confessedly, he asserts that what is immortal is mortal,[4] and that what is mortal is immortal, in the following expressions : " Immortals are mortal, *and* mortals are immortal, *that is*, when the one derive life from death, and the other death from life." And he affirms also that there is a resurrection of this palpable flesh in which we have been born ; and he knows God to be the cause of this resurrection, expressing himself in this manner : " Those that are here [5] *will God enable* to arise and become guardians of quick and dead." And he likewise affirms that a judgment of the world and all things in it takes place by fire, expressing himself thus : " Now, thunder pilots all things," that is, directs *them*, meaning by the thunder everlasting fire. But he also asserts that this fire is endued with intelligence, and a cause of the management of the Universe, and he denominates it craving and satiety. Now craving is, according to him, the arrangement *of the world*, whereas satiety its destruction. " For," says he, " the fire, coming upon *the earth*, will judge and seize all things."

But in this chapter *Heraclitus* simultaneously explains the entire peculiarity of his mode of thinking, but at the same time the (characteristic quality) of the heresy of Noetus. And I have briefly demonstrated *Noetus* to be not a disciple of Christ, but of Heraclitus. For *this philosopher* asserts that the primal world is itself the Demiurge and creator of itself in the following passage : " God is day, night ; winter, summer ; war, peace ; surfeit, famine." All things are contraries — this appears his meaning — " but an alteration takes place, just as [6] if incense were mixed with *other sorts of* incense, but denominated [7] according to the pleasurable sensation produced by each *sort*. Now it is evident to all that the silly successors of Noetus, and the champions of his heresy, even though they have not been hearers of the discourses of Heraclitus, nevertheless, at any rate when they adopt the opinions of Noetus, undisguisedly acknowledge these (Heraclitean) tenets. For they advance statements after this manner — that one and the same God is the Creator and Father of all things ; and that when it pleased Him, He *nevertheless* appeared, (though invisible,) to just men of old. For when He is not seen He is invisible ; *and He is* incomprehensible when He does not wish to be comprehended, but comprehensible when he is comprehended. Wherefore it is that, according to the same account, He is invincible and vincible, unbegotten and begotten, immortal and mortal. How shall not persons holding this description of opinions be proved to be disciples of Heraclitus ? Did not (Heraclitus) the Obscure anticipate *Noetus* in framing a system of philosophy, according to identical modes of expression ?

Now, that *Noetus* affirms that the Son and Father are the same, no one is ignorant. But he makes his statement thus : " When indeed, then,

---

[1] See *Theogon.*, v. 123 et seq., v. 748 et seq.

[2] Γναφέων: some read γναφείῳ, i.e., a fuller's soap. The proper reading, however, is probably γνάφῳ, i.e., a carder's comb. Dr. Wordsworth's text has γραφέων and ἐν τῷ γραφείῳ, and he translates the passage thus: " The path," says he, " of the lines of the machine called the screw is both straight and crooked, and the revolution in the graving-tool is both straight and crooked."

[3] See Diogenes, *Laertius*, ix. 8.

[4] Plato, Clemens Alexandrinus, [vol. ii. p. 384, this series), and Sextus Empiricus notice this doctrine of Heraclitus.

[5] Ἐνθάδε ἐόντας: some read, ἔνθα θεὸν δεῖ, i.e., " God must arise and become the guardian," etc. The rendering in the text is adopted by Bernays and Bunsen.

[6] Or, " as commingled kinds of incense *each* with different names, but denominated," etc.

[7] Dr. Wordsworth reads ὃ νομίζεται, and translates the passage thus: " But they undergo changes, as perfumes do, when whatever is thought agreeable to any individual is mingled with them."

the Father had not been born, He *yet* was justly styled Father; and when it pleased Him to undergo generation, having been begotten, He Himself became His own Son, not another's." For in this manner he thinks to establish the sovereignty *of God*, alleging that Father and Son, *so* called, are one and the same (substance), not one individual produced from a different one, but Himself from Himself; and that He is styled by name Father and Son, according to vicissitude of times.[1] But that He is one who has appeared (amongst us), both having submitted to generation from a virgin, and as a man having held converse among men. And, on account of the birth that had taken place, He confessed Himself to those beholding Him a Son, no doubt; yet He made no secret to those who could comprehend Him of His being a Father. That this person suffered by being fastened to the tree, and that He commended His spirit unto Himself, having died *to appearance*, and not being (in reality) dead. And He raised Himself up the third day, after having been interred in a sepulchre, and wounded with a spear, and perforated with nails. Cleomenes asserts, in common with his band *of followers*, that this person is God and Father of the universe, *and thus* introduces among many an obscurity (of thought) such as we find in the philosophy of Heraclitus.

CHAP. VI. — CONDUCT OF CALLISTUS AND ZEPHYRINUS IN THE MATTER OF NOETIANISM; AVOWED OPINION OF ZEPHYRINUS CONCERNING JESUS CHRIST; DISAPPROVAL OF HIPPOLYTUS; AS A CONTEMPORANEOUS EVENT, HIPPOLYTUS COMPETENT TO EXPLAIN IT.

Callistus attempted to confirm this heresy, — a man cunning in wickedness, and subtle where deceit was concerned, (and) who was impelled by restless ambition to mount the episcopal throne.[2] *Now this man moulded to his purpose* Zephyrinus, an ignorant and illiterate individual, and one unskilled in ecclesiastical definitions.[3] And inasmuch as *Zephyrinus* was accessible to bribes, and covetous, *Callistus*, by luring him through presents, and by illicit demands, was enabled to seduce him into whatever course of action he pleased. And so it was that Callistus succeeded in inducing Zephyrinus to create continually disturbances among the brethren, while he himself took care subsequently, by knavish words, to attach both factions in good-will to himself. And, at one time, to those who entertained true opinions, he would in private[4] allege

that they held similar doctrines (with himself), and thus make them his dupes; while at another time *he would act similarly towards* those (who embraced) the tenets of Sabellius. But *Callistus* perverted *Sabellius* himself, and this, too, though he had the ability of rectifying *this heretic's error*. For (at any time) during our admonition *Sabellius* did not evince obduracy; but as long as he continued alone with Callistus, he was wrought upon to relapse into the system of Cleomenes by this very *Callistus*, who alleges that he entertains similar opinions *to Cleomenes*. *Sabellius*, however, did not then perceive the knavery *of Callistus;* but he afterwards came to be aware of it, as I shall narrate presently.

Now *Callistus* brought forward Zephyrinus himself, and induced him publicly to avow *the following sentiments:* "I know that there is one God, Jesus Christ; nor except Him *do I know* any other that is begotten and amenable to suffering." And on another occasion, when he would make the following statement: "The Father did not die, but the Son." *Zephyrinus* would in this way continue to keep up ceaseless disturbance among the people. And we,[5] becoming aware of his sentiments, did not give place to him, but reproved and withstood him for the truth's sake. And he hurried headlong into folly, from the fact that all consented to his hypocrisy — we,[5] however, *did* not *do so* — and called us worshippers of two gods, disgorging, independent of compulsion,[6] the venom lurking within him. It would seem to us desirable to explain the life of this *heretic*, inasmuch as he was born about the same time with ourselves, in order that, by the exposure of the habits of a person of this description, the heresy attempted to be established by him may be easily known, and may perchance be regarded as silly by those endued with intelligence. This *Callistus* became a "martyr" at the period when Fuscianus was prefect of Rome, and the mode of his "martyrdom" was as follows.[7]

CHAP. VII. — THE PERSONAL HISTORY OF CALLISTUS; HIS OCCUPATION AS A BANKER; FRAUD ON CARPOPHORUS; CALLISTUS ABSCONDS; ATTEMPTED SUICIDE; CONDEMNED TO THE TREADMILL; RE-CONDEMNATION BY ORDER OF THE PREFECT FUSCIANUS; BANISHED TO SARDINIA; RELEASE OF CALLISTUS BY THE INTERFERENCE

---

[1] Hippolytus repeats this opinion in his summary in book x. (See Theodoret, *Hær. Fab.*, iii. 3.)
[2] [Elucidation IX.]
[3] [Elucidation X.]
[4] The MS. reads καθ' ἡδίαν, obviously corrupt. Dr. Wordsworth suggests κατ' ἰδίαν, i.e., "he, under pretext of arguing with them, deluded them."

[5] It is to be noticed how the plural number is observed in this account, as keeping before the reader's mind the episcopal office of him who was thus exercising high ecclesiastical authority. [Elucidation XI.]
[6] Or, "with violence."
[7] Hippolytus is obviously sneering at the martyrdom of Callistus, who did not in reality suffer or die for the truth. Nay, his condemnation before Fuscianus enabled Callistus to succeed entirely in his plans for worldly advancement. [The *martyrdom* of Callistus, so ludicrous in the eyes of our author, is *doctrine* in the Roman system. This heretic figures as a *saint*, and has his festival on the 14th of October. *Maxima veneratione colitur*, says the Roman Breviary.]

Callistus happened to be a domestic of one Carpophorus, a man of the faith belonging to the household of Cæsar. To this *Callistus*, as being of the faith, Carpophorus committed no inconsiderable amount of money, and directed him to bring in profitable returns from the banking business. And he, receiving *the money*, tried (the experiment of) a bank in what is called the *Piscina Publica*.[1] And in process of time were entrusted to him not a few deposits by widows and brethren, under the ostensive cause of *lodging their money with* Carpophorus. *Callistus*, however, made away with all (the moneys committed to him), and became involved in pecuniary difficulties. And after having practised such conduct as this, there was not wanting one to tell Carpophorus, and the latter stated that he would require an account from him. Callistus, perceiving these things, and suspecting danger from his master, escaped away by stealth, directing his flight towards the sea. And finding a vessel in Portus ready for a voyage, he went on board, intending to sail wherever she happened to be bound for. But not even in this way could he avoid detection, for there was not wanting one who conveyed to Carpophorus intelligence of what had taken place. But *Carpophorus*, in accordance with the information he had received, at once repaired to the harbour (Portus), and made an effort to hurry into the vessel *after Callistus*. The boat, however, was anchored in the middle of the harbour; and as the ferryman was slow in his movements, Callistus, who was in the ship, had time to descry his master at a distance. And knowing that himself would be inevitably captured, he became reckless of life; and, considering his affairs to be in a desperate condition, he proceeded to cast himself into the sea. But the sailors leaped into boats and drew him out, unwilling to come, while those on shore were raising a loud cry. And thus *Callistus* was handed over to his master, and brought to Rome, and his master lodged him in the *Pistrinum*.[2]

But as time wore on, as happens to take place *in such cases*, brethren repaired to Carpophorus, and entreated him that he would release the fugitive serf from punishment, on the plea of their alleging that *Callistus* acknowledged himself to have money lying *to his credit* with certain persons. But Carpophorus, as a devout man, said he was indifferent regarding his own *property*, but that he felt a concern for the deposits; for many shed tears as they remarked to him, that they had committed what they had entrusted to Callistus, under the ostensive cause of *lodging the money with* himself.[3] And Carpophorus yielded to their persuasions, and gave directions for the liberation of *Callistus*. The latter, however, having nothing to pay, and not being able again to abscond, from the fact of his being watched, planned an artifice by which he hoped to meet death. Now, pretending that he was repairing as it were to his creditors, he hurried on their Sabbath-day to the synagogue of the Jews, who were congregated, and took his stand, and created a disturbance among them. They, however, being disturbed by him, offered him insult, and inflicted blows upon him, and dragged him before Fuscianus, who was prefect of the city. And (on being asked the cause of such treatment), they replied in the following terms: "Romans have conceded to us[4] the privilege of publicly reading those laws of ours that have been handed down from our fathers. This person, however, by coming into (our place of worship), prevented (us so doing), by creating a disturbance among us, alleging that he is a Christian." And Fuscianus happens at the time to be on the judgment-seat; and on intimating his indignation against Callistus, on account of the statements made by the Jews, there was not wanting one to go and acquaint Carpophorus concerning these transactions. And he, hastening to the judgment-seat of the prefect, exclaimed, "I implore of you, my lord Fuscianus, believe not thou this *fellow;* for he is not a Christian, but seeks occasion of death, having made away with a quantity of my money, as I shall prove." The Jews, however, supposing that this was a stratagem, as if Carpophorus were seeking under this pretext to liberate *Callistus*, with the greater enmity clamoured *against him* in presence of the prefect. *Fuscianus*, however, was swayed by these *Jews*, and having scourged *Callistus*, he gave him *to be sent* to a mine in Sardinia.[5]

But after a time, there being in that place other martyrs, Marcia, a concubine of Commodus, who was a God-loving female, and desirous of performing some good work, invited into her

---

[1] The Latin name is written by Hippolytus in Greek letters, and means "the public fish-market." The *Piscina*, one of the fourteen quarters of Rome, was the resort of money-dealers.
[2] The *Pistrinum* was the domestic treadmill of the Roman slaveholders.

[3] [An instance illustrative of the touching sense of moral obligation given in 2 Kings vi. 5.]
[4] See Josephus, *Antiq.*, xix. 10.
[5] The air of Sardinia was unwholesome, if not pestilential; and for this reason, no doubt, it was selected as a place of exile for martyrs. Hippolytus himself, along with the Roman bishop Pontianus, was banished thither. See Introductory Notice.

presence [1] the blessed Victor, who was at that time a bishop ·of the Church,[2] and inquired of him what martyrs were in Sardinia. And he delivered to her the names of all, but did not give the *name* of Callistus, knowing the *villanous* acts he had ventured upon. Marcia,[3] obtaining her request from Commodus, hands the letter of emancipation to Hyacinthus, a certain eunuch,[4] rather advanced in life. And he, on receiving *it*, sailed away into Sardinia, and having delivered *the letter* to the person who at that time was governor of the territory, he succeeded in having the martyrs released, with the exception of Callistus. But *Callistus* himself, dropping on his knees, and weeping, entreated that he likewise might obtain a release. Hyacinthus, therefore, overcome by *the captive's* importunity, requests the governor *to grant a release*, alleging that permission had been given to himself from Marcia [5] (to liberate Callistus), and that he would make arrangements that there should be no risk *in this* to him. Now (the governor) was persuaded, and liberated Callistus also. And when *the latter* arrived *at Rome*, Victor was very much grieved at what had taken place; but since he was a compassionate man, he took no action in the matter. Guarding, however, against the reproach (uttered) by many, — for the attempts made by *this Callistus* were not distant occurrences, — and because Carpophorus also still continued adverse, *Victor* sends *Callistus* to take up his abode in Antium, having settled on him a certain monthly allowance for food. And after *Victor's death, Zephyrinus, having had Callistus* as a fellow-worker in the management of his clergy, paid him respect to his own damage; and transferring this person from Antium, appointed him over the cemetery.[6]

And Callistus, who was in the habit of always associating with Zephyrinus, and, as I have previously stated, of paying him hypocritical service, disclosed, *by force of contrast, Zephyrinus to be* a person able neither to form a judgment of things said, nor discerning the design of Callistus, who was accustomed to converse with *Zephyrinus* on topics which yielded satisfaction *to the latter*. Thus, after the death of Zephyrinus, supposing

that he had obtained (the position) after which he so eagerly pursued, he excommunicated Sabellius, as not entertaining orthodox opinions. He acted thus from apprehension of me, and imagining that he could in this manner obliterate the charge *against him* among the churches, as if he did not entertain strange opinions.[7] He was then an impostor and knave, and in process of time hurried away many with him. And having even venom imbedded in his heart, and forming no correct opinion on any subject,[8] and yet withal being ashamed to speak the truth, *this Callistus, not only* on account of his publicly saying in the way of reproach to us, "Ye are Ditheists," but also on account of his being frequently accused by Sabellius, as one that had transgressed his first faith, devised some such heresy as the following. *Callistus* alleges that the Logos Himself is Son, and that Himself is Father; and that though denominated by *a different* title, yet that in reality He is one indivisible spirit. *And he maintains* that the Father is not one person and the Son another, but that they are one and the same; and that all things are full of the Divine Spirit, both those above and *those* below. *And he affirms* that the Spirit, which became incarnate in the virgin, is not different from the Father, but one and the same. And *he adds*, that this is what has been declared *by the Saviour:* "Believest thou not that I am in the Father, and the Father in me?"[9] For that which is seen, which is man, *he considers* to be the Son; whereas the Spirit, which was contained in the Son, to be the Father. "For," says (Callistus), "I will not profess belief in two Gods, Father and Son, but in one. For the Father, who subsisted in *the Son* Himself, after He had taken unto Himself our flesh, raised it to the nature of Deity, by bringing it into union with Himself, and made it one; so that Father and Son must be styled one God, and that this Person being one, cannot be two." And in this way *Callistus contends* that the Father suffered along with the Son; for he does not wish to assert that the Father suffered, and is one Person, being careful to avoid blasphemy against the Father. (How careful he is!) senseless and knavish fellow, who improvises blasphemies in every direction, only that he may *not* seem to speak in violation of the truth, and is not abashed at being at one time betrayed into the tenet of Sabellius, whereas at another into the doctrine of Theodotus.

---

[1] Marcia's connection with the emperor would not seem very consistent with the Christian character which Hippolytus gives her. Dr. Wordsworth supposes that Hippolytus speaks ironically in the case of Marcia, as well as of Hyacinthus and Carpophorus. [I do not see the evidence of this. Poor Marcia, afterwards poisoned by the wretch who degraded her, was a heathen who under a little light was awakening to some sense of duty, like the woman of Samaria, John iv. 19.]

[2] [Note this expression in contrast with subsequent claims to be the "Universal Bishop."]

[3] See Dio Cassius, lxxii. 4. [See vol. ii. p. 604, this series.]

[4] Or, "a presbyter, though an eunuch," thus indicating the decay of ecclesiastical discipline.

[5] Or, "that Marcia had been brought up by him." [See what Bunsen has to say (vol. i. pp. 126, 127, and note) upon this subject, about which we know very little.]

[6] The cemetery of Callistus was situated in the *Via Appia.* [The catacombs near the Church of St. Sebastian still bear the name of this unhappy man, and give incidental corroboration to the incident.]

[7] [Here Wordsworth's note is valuable, p. 80. Callistus had doubtless sent letters to announce his consecration to other bishops, as was customary, and had received answers demanding proofs of his orthodoxy. See my note on the intercommunion of primitive bishops, vol. ii. p. 12, note 9: also on the Provincial System, vol. iv. pp. 111, 114. Also Cyprian, this vol. *passim.*]

[8] εὐθέως μηδὲν: Scott reads εὐθέος μηδέν. Dr. Wordsworth translates the words thus: "having no rectitude of mind."

[9] John xiv. 11.

The impostor *Callistus*, having ventured on such opinions, established a school *of theology* in antagonism to the Church, adopting the foregoing system of instruction. And he first invented the device of conniving with men in regard of their indulgence in *sensual* pleasures, saying that all had their sins forgiven by himself.[1] For he who is in the habit of attending the congregation of any one else, and is called a Christian, should he commit any transgression; the sin, they say, is not reckoned unto him, provided only he hurries off *and attaches himself* to the school of Callistus. And many persons were gratified with his regulation, as being stricken in conscience, and at the same time having been rejected by numerous sects; while also some of them, in accordance with our condemnatory sentence, had been by us forcibly ejected from the Church.[2] *Now such disciples as these* passed over to these *followers of Callistus*, and served to crowd his school. This one propounded the opinion, that, if a bishop was guilty of any sin, if even *a sin* unto death,[3] he ought not to be deposed. About the time of this man, bishops, priests, and deacons, who had been twice married, and thrice married, began *to be allowed* to retain their place among the clergy. If also, however, any one who is in holy orders should become married, *Callistus permitted* such a one to continue in holy orders as if he had not sinned.[4] And *in justification*, he alleges that what has been spoken by the Apostle has been declared in reference to this *person:* "Who art thou that judgest another man's servant?"[5] But he asserted that likewise *the* parable of the tares is uttered in reference to this *one:* "Let the tares grow along with the wheat;"[6] or, in other words, let those who in the Church are guilty of sin *remain in it.* But also he affirmed that the ark of Noe was made for a symbol of the Church, in which were both dogs, and wolves, and ravens, and all things clean and unclean; and so he alleges that the case should stand in like manner with the Church. And as many *parts of Scripture* bearing on this *view of the subject* as he could collect, he so interpreted.

And the hearers *of Callistus* being delighted with his tenets, continue with him, *thus* mocking both themselves as well as many *others*, and crowds of these *dupes* stream together into his school. Wherefore also *his pupils* are multiplied, and they plume themselves upon *the* crowds (attending the school) for the sake of pleasures which Christ did not permit. But in contempt of Him, they place restraint on the commission of no sin, alleging that they pardon those who acquiesce (in Callistus' opinions). For even also he permitted females, if they were unwedded,[7] and burned with passion at an age at all events unbecoming, or if they were not disposed to overturn their own dignity through a legal marriage, that they might have whomsoever they would choose as a bedfellow, whether a slave or free, and that *a woman*, though not legally married, might consider such *a companion* as a husband. Whence women, reputed believers, began to resort to drugs[8] for producing sterility, and to gird themselves round, so to expel what was being conceived on account of their not wishing to have a child either by a slave or by any paltry fellow, for the sake of their family and excessive wealth.[9] Behold, into how great impiety that lawless *one* has proceeded, by inculcating adultery and murder at the same time! And withal, after such audacious acts, they, lost to all shame, attempt to call themselves a Catholic Church![10] And some, under the supposition that they will attain prosperity, concur with them. During the *episcopate* of this *one*, second baptism was for the first time presumptuously attempted by them. These, then, (are the practices and opinions which) that most astonishing Callistus established, whose school continues, preserving its customs and tradition, not discerning with whom they ought to communicate, *but* indiscriminately offering communion to all. And from him they have derived the denomination of their *cognomen;* so that, on account of Callistus being a foremost champion of such practices, they should be called Callistians.[11]

CHAP. VIII. — SECT OF THE ELCHASAITES; HIPPOLYTUS' OPPOSITION TO IT.

The doctrine of this *Callistus* having been noised abroad throughout the entire world, a cunning man, and full of desperation, one called Alcibiades, dwelling in Apamea, *a city* of Syria, examined carefully into this business. And considering himself a more formidable character, and more ingenious in *such* tricks, than Callistus, he repaired to Rome; and he brought some book, alleging that a certain just man, Elchasai,[12]

---

1 [Here is a very early precedent for the *Taxa Pœnitentiaria*, of which see Bramhall, vol. i. pp. 56, 180; ii. pp. 445, 446].
2 [Elucidation XII.]
3 1 John v. 16.
4 [Elucidation XIII. And on marriage of the clergy, vol. iv. p. 49, this series.]
5 Rom. xiv. 4.
6 Matt. xiii. 30.

7 This passage, of which there are different readings, has been variously interpreted. The rendering followed above does probably less violence to the text than others proposed. The variety of meaning generally turns on the word ἐναξία in Miller's text. Bunsen alters it into ἐν ἀξίᾳ . . . ἡλικίᾳ, i.e., were inflamed at a proper age. Dr. Wordsworth reads ἡλικιώτῃ . . . ἀναξίῳ, i.e., an unworthy comrade. Roeper reads ἡλικίᾳ . . . ἀναξίου, i.e., in the bloom of youth were enamoured with one undeserving of their choice.
8 Dr. Wordsworth places περιδεσμεῖσθαι in the first sentence, and translates thus: "women began to venture to bandage themselves with ligaments to produce abortion, and to deal with drugs in order to destroy what was conceived."
9 [The prescience of Hermas and Clement is here illustrated. See vol. ii. pp. 9, 32, 279, 597, etc.]
10 [Elucidation XIV.]
11 [Bunsen, i. 115. Elucidation XV.]
12 See Eusebius, *Hist. Ecclesiast.*, vi. 38; Epiphanius, *Hær*, xix.; and Theodoret, *Hær. Fab.*, ii. 7.

had received this from Seræ, a town of Parthia, and that he gave it to one called Sobiaï. *And the contents of this volume*, he alleged, had been revealed by an angel whose height was 24 *schœnoi*, which make 96 miles, and whose breadth is 4 *schœnoi*, and from shoulder to shoulder 6 *schœnoi;* and the tracks of his feet extend to the length of three and a half *schœnoi*, which are *equal to* fourteen miles, while the breadth is one *schœnos* and a half, and the height half a *schœnos*. And *he alleges* that also there is a female with him, whose measurement, he says, is according to the *standards* already mentioned. And *he asserts* that the male (angel) is Son of God, but that the female is called Holy Spirit. By detailing these prodigies he imagines that he confounds fools, *while at the same time* he utters the following sentence : " that there was preached unto men a new remission of sins in the third year of Trajan's reign." And *Elchasai* determines *the nature of* baptism, and even this I shall explain. He alleges, *as to* those who have been involved in every description of lasciviousness, and filthiness, and *in* acts of wickedness, if only any *of them* be a believer, that he determines that such a one, on being converted, and obeying the book, and believing *its contents*, should by baptism receive remission of sins.

Elchasai, however, ventured to continue these knaveries, taking occasion from the aforesaid tenet of which Callistus stood forward as a champion. For, perceiving that many were delighted at this sort of promise, he considered that he could opportunely make the attempt *just alluded to*. And notwithstanding we offered resistance to this, and did not permit many for any length of time to become victims of the delusion.[1] For we carried conviction *to the people, when we affirmed* that this was *the* operation of a spurious spirit, and the invention of a heart inflated with pride, and that this *one* like a wolf had risen up against many wandering sheep, which Callistus, by his *arts of* deception, had scattered abroad. But since we have commenced, we shall not be silent as regards the opinions of this *man*. And, in the first place, we shall expose his life, and we shall prove that his supposed discipline is a mere pretence. And next, I shall adduce the principal heads of his assertions, in order that the reader, looking fixedly on the treatises of this (Elchasai), may be made aware what and what sort is the heresy which has been audaciously attempted by this man.

CHAP. IX. — ELCHASAI DERIVED HIS SYSTEM FROM PYTHAGORAS ; PRACTISED INCANTATIONS.

This *Elchasai* puts forward as a decoy a polity (authorized in the) Law, alleging that believers ought to be circumcised and live according to *the* Law, (while at the same time) he forcibly rends certain *fragments* from the aforesaid heresies. And he asserts that Christ was born a man in the same way as common to all, and that *Christ* was not for the first time *on earth when* born of a virgin, but that both previously and that frequently again He had been born and would be born. *Christ* would thus appear and exist *among us from time to time*, undergoing alterations of birth, and having his soul transferred from body to body. *Now Elchasai* adopted that tenet of pythagoras *to which I have already alluded*. But *the Elchasaites* have reached such an altitude of pride, that even they affirm themselves to be endued with a power of foretelling futurity, using as a starting-point, obviously, *the* measures and numbers of the aforesaid Pythagorean art. These also devote themselves to *the* tenets of mathematicians, and astrologers, and magicians, as if they were true. And *they* resort to these, so as to confuse silly people, *thus led* to suppose that *the heretics* participate in a doctrine of power. And *they* teach certain incantations and formularies for those who have been bitten by dogs, and possessed of demons, and seized with other diseases ; and we shall not be silent respecting even such *practices* of these *heretics*. Having then sufficiently explained their principles, and the causes of their presumptuous attempts, I shall pass on to give an account of their writings, through which my readers will become acquainted with both the trifling and godless efforts of these *Elchasaites*.

CHAP. X. — ELCHASAI'S MODE OF ADMINISTERING BAPTISM ; FORMULARIES.

To those, then, that have been orally instructed by him, he dispenses baptism in this manner, addressing to his dupes some such words as the following : " If, therefore, (my) children,[2] one shall have intercourse with any sort of animal whatsoever, or a male, or a sister, or a daughter, or hath committed adultery, or been guilty of fornication, and is desirous of obtaining remission of sins, from the moment that he hearkens to this book let him be baptized a second time in *the* name of the Great and Most High God, and in *the* name of His Son, the Mighty King. And *by baptism* let him be purified and cleansed, and let him adjure for himself those seven witnesses that have been described in this book — the heaven, and the water, and the holy spirits, and the angels of prayer,[3] and the oil, and the salt, and the earth." These constitute the astonishing mysteries of Elchasai, those ineffable and potent

---

[1] For πλανηθῆναι Dr. Wordsworth reads πλατυνθῆναι, i.e., did not suffer the heresy to spread wide.

[2] Roeper reads τέκνῳ, i.e., if any one is guilty of an unnatural crime.

[3] [Concerning angels of repentance, etc., see Hermas, vol. ii. pp. 19, 24, 26.]

secrets which he delivers to deserving disciples. And with these that lawless *one* is not satisfied, but in the presence of two and three witnesses he puts the seal to his own wicked *practices*. Again expressing himself thus: " Again I say, O adulterers and adulteresses, and false prophets, if you are desirous of being converted, that your sins may be forgiven you, as soon as ever you hearken unto this book, and be baptized a second time along with your garments, shall peace be yours, and *your* portion with the just." But since we have stated that these resort to incantations for those bitten by dogs and for other *mishaps*, we shall explain these. Now *Elchasai* uses the following formulary: " If a dog rabid and furious, in which inheres a spirit of destruction, bite any man, or woman, or youth, or girl, or may worry or touch *them*, in the same hour let such a one run with all their wearing apparel, and go down to a river or to a fountain wherever there is a deep spot. Let (him or her) be dipped with all their wearing apparel, and offer supplication to the Great and Most High God in faith of heart, and then let him *thus* adjure the seven witnesses described in this book: ' Behold, I call to witness the heaven and the water, and the holy spirits, and the angels of prayer, and the oil, and the salt, and the earth. I testify by these seven witnesses that no more shall I sin, nor commit adultery, nor steal, nor be guilty of injustice, nor be covetous, nor be actuated by hatred, nor be scornful, nor shall I take pleasure in any wicked *deeds*.' Having uttered, therefore, these words, let such a one be baptized with the entire of his wearing apparel in *the* name of the Mighty and Most High God."

CHAP. XI. — PRECEPTS OF ELCHASAI.

But in very many other respects he talks folly, inculcating the use of these sentences also for those afflicted with consumption, and that they should be dipped in cold *water* forty times during seven days; and *he prescribes* similar treatment for those possessed of devils. Oh inimitable wisdom and incantations gorged with powers![1] Who will not be astonished at such and such force of words? But since we have stated that they also bring into requisition astrological deceit, we shall prove *this* from their own formularies; for *Elchasai* speaks thus: " There exist wicked stars of impiety. This declaration has been now made by us, O *ye* pious *ones* and disciples: beware of the power of the days *of* the sovereignty of these *stars*, and engage not in the commencement of any undertaking during the *ruling* days of these. And baptize not man or woman during the days of the power of these *stars*, when the moon, (emerging) from among them, courses *the sky*, and travels along with them. Beware of the very day up to that on which *the moon* passes out from these *stars*, and then baptize and enter on every beginning of your works. But, moreover, honour the day of the Sabbath, since that day is one of those during which prevails (the power) of these *stars*. Take care, however, not to commence *your works* the third *day* from a Sabbath, since when three years *of the reign* of the emperor Trajan are again completed from the time that he subjected the Parthians to his own sway, — when, *I say*, three years have been completed, war rages between the impious angels of the northern *constellations; and* on this account all kingdoms of impiety are in a state of confusion."

CHAP. XII. — THE HERESY OF THE ELCHASAITES A DERIVATIVE ONE.

Inasmuch as (Elchasai) considers, then, that it would be an insult to reason that these mighty and ineffable mysteries should be trampled under foot, or that they should be committed to many, he advises that as valuable pearls[2] they should be preserved, expressing himself thus: " Do not recite this account to all men, and guard carefully these precepts, because all men are not faithful, nor are all women straightforward." *Books containing* these (tenets), however, neither the wise men of the Egyptians secreted in shrines, nor did Pythagoras, a sage of the Greeks, conceal *them there*. For if at that time Elchasai had happened to live, what necessity would there be that Pythagoras, or Thales, or Solon, or the wise Plato, or even the rest of the sages of the Greeks, should become disciples of the Egyptian priests, when they could obtain possession of such and such wisdom from Alcibiades, as the most astonishing interpreter of that wretched Elchasai? The statements, therefore, that have been made for the purpose of attaining a knowledge of the madness of these, would seem sufficient for those endued with sound mind. And so it is, that it has not appeared expedient to quote more of their formularies, seeing that these are very numerous and ridiculous. Since, however, we have not omitted those *practices* that have risen up in our own day, and have not been silent as regards those *prevalent* before our time, it seems proper, in order that we may pass through all *their systems*, and leave nothing untold, to state what also are the (customs) of the Jews, and what are the diversities of opinion among them, for I imagine that these as yet remain behind *for our consideration*. Now, when I have broken silence on these points, I shall pass on to the demonstration of the Doctrine of the Truth, in

---

[1] Miller suggests the singular number (δυνάμεως).

[2] Matt. vii. 6.

order that, after the lengthened argumentative struggle against all heresies, we, devoutly pressing forward towards the kingdom's crown, and believing the truth, may not be unsettled.

CHAP. XIII. — THE JEWISH SECTS.

Originally there prevailed but one usage [1] among the Jews; for one teacher was given unto them by God, *namely* Moses, and one law by this *same Moses*. And there *was* one desert region and one Mount Sinai, for one God it was who legislated for these *Jews*. But, again, after they had crossed the river Jordan, and had inherited by lot the conquered country, they in various ways rent in sunder the law of God, each devising *a different interpretation of* the declarations made *by God*. And in this way they raised up for themselves teachers, (and) invented doctrines of an heretical nature, and they continued to advance into (sectarian) divisions. Now it is the diversity of these *Jews* that I at present propose to explain. But though for even a considerable time they have been rent into very numerous sects, yet I intend to elucidate the more principal of them, while those who are of a studious turn will easily become acquainted with the rest. For there is a division amongst them into three sorts; [2] and the adherents of the first are the Pharisees, but of the second the Sadducees, while the rest are Essenes. These practise a more devotional life, being filled with mutual love, and being temperate. And they turn away from every act of inordinate desire, being averse even to hearing *of* things of the sort. And they renounce matrimony, but they take the boys of others, and *thus* have an offspring begotten for them. And they lead *these adopted children* into an observance of their own peculiar customs, and in this way bring them up and impel them to learn the sciences. They do not, however, forbid them to marry, though themselves refraining from matrimony. Women, however, even though they may be disposed to adhere to the same course of life, [3] they do not admit, inasmuch as in no way whatsoever have they confidence in women.

CHAP. XIV. — THE TENETS OF THE ESSENI.

And they despise wealth, and do not turn away from sharing *their goods* with those that are destitute. No one amongst them, however, enjoys a greater amount of riches than another. For a regulation with them is, that an individual coming forward *to join* the sect must sell his possessions, and present *the price of them* to the community. And on receiving *the money*, the head *of the order* distributes it to all according to their necessities. Thus there is no one among them in distress. And they do not use oil, regarding it as a defilement to be anointed. And there are appointed overseers, who take care of all things that belong to them in common, and they all appear always in white clothing.

CHAP. XV. — THE TENETS OF THE ESSENI CONTINUED.

But there is not one city of them, but many of them settle in every *city*. And if any of the adherents of the sect may be present from a strange *place*, they consider that all things are in common for him, and those whom they had not previously known they receive as if they belonged to their own household and kindred. And they traverse their native land, and on each occasion that they go on a journey they carry nothing except arms. And they have also in their cities a president, who expends the *moneys* collected for this *purpose* in procuring clothing and food for them. And their robe and its shape are modest. And they do not own two cloaks, or a double set of shoes; and when those that are in present use become antiquated, then they adopt others. And they neither buy nor sell anything at all; but whatever any one has he gives to him that has not, and that which one has not he receives.

CHAP. XVI. — THE TENETS OF THE ESSENI CONTINUED.

And they continue in an orderly manner, and with perseverance pray from early dawn, and they do not speak a word unless they have praised God in a hymn. And in this way they each go forth and engage in whatever employment they please; and after having worked up to the fifth hour they leave off. Then again they come together into one place, and encircle themselves with linen girdles, for the purpose of concealing their private parts. And in this manner they perform ablutions in cold water; and after being thus cleansed, they repair together into one apartment, — now no one who entertains a different opinion from themselves assembles in the house, — and they proceed to partake of breakfast. And when they have taken their seats in silence, they set down loaves in order, and next some one sort of food to eat along with *the bread*, and each receives from these a sufficient portion. No one, however, tastes these

---

[1] Or, "nation."

[2] See Josephus, *De Bell. Judaic.*, ii. 8, from whom Hippolytus seems to have taken his account of the Jewish sects, except, as Schneidewin remarks, we suppose some other writer whom Josephus and Hippolytus themselves followed. The Abbe Cruice thinks that the author followed by Hippolytus was not Josephus, but a Christian writer of the first century, who derived his materials from the Jewish historian. Hippolytus' text sometimes varies from the text of Josephus, as well as of Porphyry, who has taken excerpts from Josephus' work.

[3] Or "choice."

before the priest utters a blessing,[1] and prays over *the food.* And after breakfast, when he has a second time offered up supplication, as at the beginning, so at the conclusion of their meal they praise God in hymns. Next, after they have laid aside as sacred the garments in which they have been clothed while together taking their repast within *the house* — (now *these garments* are linen) — and having resumed the *clothes which they had left* in the vestibule, they hasten to agreeable occupations until evening. And they partake of supper, doing all things in like manner to those already mentioned. And no one will at any time cry aloud, nor will any other tumultuous voice be heard. But they each converse quietly, and with decorum one concedes the conversation to the other, so that the stillness of those within *the house* appears a sort of mystery to those outside. And they are invariably sober, eating and drinking all things by measure.

CHAP. XVII. — THE TENETS OF THE ESSENI CONTINUED.

All then pay attention to the president; and whatever injunctions he will issue, they obey as law. For they are anxious that mercy and assistance be extended to those that are burdened with toil. And especially they abstain from wrath and anger, and all such *passions*, inasmuch as they consider these to be treacherous to man. And no one amongst them is in the habit of swearing; but whatever any one says, this is regarded more binding than an oath. If, however, one will swear, he is condemned as one unworthy of credence. They are likewise solicitous about the readings of the law and prophets; and moreover also, if there is any treatise of the faithful, *about that likewise.* And they evince the utmost curiosity concerning plants and stones, rather busying themselves as regards the operative powers of these, saying that these *things* were not created in vain.

CHAP. XVIII. — THE TENETS OF THE ESSENI CONTINUED.

But to those who wish to become disciples of the sect, they do not immediately deliver their rules, unless they have previously tried *them.* Now for the space of a year they set before (the candidates) the same food, while the latter continue to live in a different house outside the *Essenes'* own place of meeting. And they give (to the probationists) a hatchet and the linen girdle, and a white robe. When, at the expiration of this period, one affords proof of self-

control, he approaches nearer to the *sect's* method of living, and he is washed more purely than before. Not as yet, however, does he partake of food along with *the Essenes.* For, after having furnished evidence as to whether he is able to acquire self-control, — but for two years the habit of a person of this description is on trial, — and when he has appeared deserving, he is thus reckoned amongst the members *of the sect.* Previous, however, to his being allowed to partake of a repast along with them, he is bound under fearful oaths. First, that he will worship the Divinity; next, that he will observe just *dealings* with men, and that he will in no way injure any one, and that he will not hate a person who injures him, or is hostile to him, but pray for them. He likewise swears that he will always aid the just, *and* keep faith with all, especially those who are rulers. For, *they argue,* a position of authority does not happen to any one without God. And if *the Essene* himself be a ruler, *he swears* that he will not conduct himself at any time arrogantly in *the exercise of* power, nor be prodigal, nor resort to any adornment, or a greater *state of magnificence* than the usage *permits. He likewise swears,* however, to be a lover of truth, and to reprove him that is guilty of falsehood, neither to steal, nor pollute his conscience for the sake of iniquitous gain, nor conceal *aught* from those that are members of his sect, and to divulge nothing to others, though one should be tortured even unto death. And in addition to the foregoing *promises,* he swears to impart to no one a knowledge of the doctrines in a different manner from that in which he has received them himself.

CHAP. XIX. — THE TENETS OF THE ESSENI CONTINUED.

With oaths, then, of this description, they bind those who come forward. If, however, any one may be condemned for any sin, he is expelled from the order; but one that has been *thus* excommunicated sometimes perishes by an awful death. For, inasmuch as he is bound by the oaths and rites *of the sect,* he is not able to partake of the food in use among other people. *Those that are excommunicated,* occasionally, therefore, utterly destroy the body through starvation. And so it is, that when it comes to the last *the Essenes* sometimes pity many *of them* who are at the point of dissolution, inasmuch as they deem a punishment even unto death, *thus inflicted* upon these *culprits,* a sufficient *penalty.*

CHAP. XX. — THE TENETS OF THE ESSENI CONCLUDED.

But as regards judicial decisions, *the Essenes* are most accurate and impartial. And they de-

---

[1] [The Essenes practised many pious and edifying rites; and this became Christian usage, after our Lord's example. Matt. xiv. 19; 1 Tim. iv. 3-5.]

liver their judgments when they have assembled together, *numbering* at the very least one hundred; and the sentence delivered by them is irreversible. And they honour the legislator *next* after God; and if any one is guilty of blasphemy against this *framer of laws*, he is punished. And they are taught to yield obedience to rulers and elders; and if ten occupy seats in the same *room*, one *of them* will not speak unless it will appear expedient to the nine. And they are careful not to spit out into the midst of persons present, and to the right hand. They are more solicitous, however, about abstaining from work on the Sabbath-day than all *other* Jews. For not only do they prepare their victuals for themselves one day previously, so as not (on the Sabbath) to kindle a fire, but not even would they move a utensil from one place to another (on that day), nor ease nature; nay, some would not even rise from a couch. On other days, however, when they wish to relieve nature, they dig a hole a foot long with the mattock, — for of this description is the hatchet, which the president in the first instance gives those who come forward to gain admission as disciples, — and cover (this cavity) on all sides with their garment, alleging that they do not necessarily[1] insult the sunbeams. They then replace the upturned soil into the pit; and this is their practice,[2] choosing the more lonely spots. But after they have performed this operation, immediately they undergo ablution, as if the excrement pollutes them.

CHAP. XXI. — DIFFERENT SECTS OF THE ESSENI.

The Essenes have, however, in the lapse of time, undergone divisions, and they do not preserve their system of training after a similar manner, inasmuch as they have been split up into four parties. For some of them discipline themselves above the requisite *rules of the order*, so that even they would not handle a current coin of the country, saying that they ought not either to carry, or behold, or fashion an image :[3] wherefore no one of those goes into a city, lest (by so doing) he should enter through a gate at which statues are *erected*, regarding it a violation of law to pass beneath images. But the adherents of another party, if they happen to hear any one maintaining a discussion concerning God and His laws — supposing such to be an uncircumcised person, they will closely watch him; and when they meet a person of this description in any place alone, they will threaten to slay him

if he refuses to undergo the rite of circumcision. Now, if the latter does not wish to comply with this request, *an Essene* spares not, but even slaughters. And it is from this occurrence that they have received their appellation, being denominated (by some) Zelotæ, but by others Sicarii. And the adherents of another party call no one Lord except the Deity, even though one should put them to the torture, or even kill them. But there are *others* of a later period, who have to such an extent declined from the discipline (of the order), that, as far as those are concerned who continue in the primitive customs, they would not even touch these. And if they happen to come in contact with them, they immediately resort to ablution, as if they had touched one belonging to an alien tribe. But here also there are very many of them of so great longevity, as even to live longer than a hundred years. They assert, therefore, that a cause of this arises from their extreme devotion to religion, and their condemnation of all excess in regard of what is served up (as food), and from their being temperate and incapable of anger. And so it is that they despise death, rejoicing when they can finish their course with a good conscience. If, however, any one would even put to the torture persons of this description, in order to induce any amongst them either to speak evil of the law, or eat what is offered in sacrifice to an idol, he will not effect his purpose; for *one of this party* submits to death and endures torment rather than violate his conscience.

CHAP. XXII. — BELIEF OF THE ESSENI IN THE RESURRECTION; THEIR SYSTEM A SUGGESTIVE ONE.

Now the doctrine of the resurrection has also derived support among *these;* for they acknowledge both that the flesh will rise again, and that it will be immortal, in the same manner as the soul is already imperishable. *And they maintain* that the soul, when separated in the present life, (departs) into one place, which is well ventilated and lightsome, *where*, they say, *it* rests until judgment. And this locality the Greeks were acquainted with by hearsay, and called it "Isles of the Blessed." And there are other tenets of these which many of the Greeks have appropriated, and thus have from time to time formed their own opinions.[4] For the disciplinary system in regard of the Divinity, according to these (Jewish sects), is of greater antiquity than *that of* all nations. And so it is that the proof is at hand, that all those (Greeks) who

---

[1] [Query, *unnecessarily?* This seems the sense required.]
[2] [Deut. xxiii. 13. The very dogs scratch earth upon their ordure; and this ordinance of decency is in exquisite consistency with the *modesty of nature*, against which Christians should never offend.]
[3] [This zeal for the *letter* of the Second Commandment was not shared by our Lord (Matt. xxii. 20).]

[4] [Important corroborations of Justin and other Fathers, vol. i. p. 286; ii. p. 338, also 81, 117, 148.]

ventured to make assertions concerning God, or concerning the creation of existing things, derived their principles from no other source than from Jewish legislation. And among these *may be particularized* Pythagoras especially, and the Stoics, who derived (their systems) *while resident* among the Egyptians, by having become disciples of these *Jews*.[1] Now they affirm that there will be both a judgment and a conflagration of the universe, and that the wicked will be eternally punished. And among them is cultivated the practice of prophecy, and the prediction of future events.

CHAP. XXIII. — ANOTHER SECT OF THE ESSENI : THE PHARISEES.

There is then another order of the Essenes who use the same customs and prescribed method of living *with the foregoing sects,* but make an alteration from these in one respect, viz., marriage. Now they maintain that those who have abrogated matrimony commit some terrible *offence, which* is for the destruction of life, and that they ought not to cut off the succession of children ; *for,* that if all entertained this opinion, the entire race of men would easily be exterminated. However, they make a trial of their betrothed women for a period of three years ; and when they have been three times purified, with a view of proving their ability of bringing forth children, so then they wed. They do not, however, cohabit with pregnant women, evincing that they marry not from sensual motives, but from the advantage of children. And the women likewise undergo ablution in a similar manner (with their husbands), and are themselves also arrayed in a linen garment, after the mode in which the men *are* with their girdles. These *things,* then, *are the statements which I have to make* respecting the Esseni.

But there are also others who themselves practise the Jewish customs ; and these, both in respect of caste and in respect of the laws, are called Pharisees. Now the greatest part of these is *to be found* in every locality, inasmuch as, though all are styled Jews, yet, on account of the peculiarity of the opinions advanced by them, they have been denominated by titles proper *to each.* These, then, firmly hold the ancient tradition, and continue to pursue in a disputative spirit a close investigation into the things *regarded* according to *the* Law as clean and not clean. And they interpret the *regulations* of the Law, and put forward teachers, *whom they qualify* for *giving instruction in* such *things.* These *Pharisees* affirm the existence of fate, and that

some things are in our power, whereas others are under the control of destiny. In this way *they maintain* that some *actions* depend upon ourselves, whereas others upon fate. But (they assert) that God is a cause of all things, and that nothing is managed or happens without His will. These likewise acknowledge that there is a resurrection of flesh, and that soul is immortal, and that there will be a judgment and conflagration, and that the righteous will be imperishable, but that the wicked will endure everlasting punishment in unqenchable fire.

CHAP. XXIV. — THE SADDUCEES.

These, then, are the opinions even of the Pharisees. The Sadducees, however, are for abolishing fate, and they acknowledge that God does nothing that is wicked, nor exercises providence over (earthly concerns) ; but *they contend* that the choice between good and evil lies within the power of men. And they deny that there is a resurrection not only of flesh, but also they suppose that the soul does not continue *after death. The soul they consider nothing* but mere vitality, and that it is on account of this that man has been created. However, (they maintain) that the notion of the resurrection has been fully realized by the single circumstance, that we close our days after having left children upon earth. But (they still insist) that after death one expects to suffer nothing, either bad or good ; for that there will be a dissolution both of soul and body, and that man passes into non-existence, similarly also with the *material of* the animal creation. But as regards whatever wickedness a man may have committed in life, provided he may have been reconciled *to the injured party*, he has been a gainer (by transgression), inasmuch as he has escaped the punishment (that otherwise would have been inflicted) by men. And whatever acquisitions a man may have made, and (in whatever respect), by becoming wealthy, he may have acquired distinction, he has so far been a gainer. But (they abide by their assertion), that God has no solicitude about the concerns of an individual *here.* And while the Pharisees are full of mutual affection, the Sadducees, on the other hand, are actuated by self-love. This sect had its stronghold especially in *the region* around Samaria. And these also adhere to the customs of the law, saying that one ought so to live, that he may conduct himself virtuously, and leave children behind him on earth. They do not, however, devote attention to prophets, but neither *do they* to any other sages, except to the law of Moses only, *in regard of which,* however, they frame no interpretations. These, then, are the opinions which also the Sadducees choose *to teach.*

---

[1] Thus Plato's " Laws " present many parallels to the writings of Moses. Some have supposed that Plato became acquainted with the Pentateuch through the medium of an ancient Greek version extant prior to that of the Septuagint.

CHAP. XXV. — THE JEWISH RELIGION.

Since, therefore, we have explained even the diversities among the Jews, it seems expedient likewise not to pass over in silence the system of their religion. The doctrine, therefore, among all Jews on the subject of religion is fourfold — theological, natural, moral, *and* ceremonial. And they affirm that there is one God, and that He is Creator and Lord of the universe : that He has formed all these glorious works which had no previous existence ; and this, too, not out of any coeval substance that lay ready at hand, but His Will — the efficient cause — was *to create*, and He did create. And (they maintain) that there are angels, and that these have been brought into being for ministering unto the creation ; but also that there is a sovereign Spirit that always continues beside God, for glory and praise. And that all things in the creation are endued with sensation, and that there is nothing inanimate. And they earnestly aim at serious habits and a temperate life, as one may ascertain from their laws. Now these *matters* have long ago been strictly defined by those who in ancient times have received the divinely-appointed law ;[1] so that the reader will find himself astonished at the amount of temperance, and of diligence, *lavished* on customs legally enacted in reference to man. The ceremonial service, however, which has been adapted to divine *worship* in a manner befitting the dignity *of religion*, has been practised amongst them with the highest degree of elaboration. The superiority of their ritualism it is easy for those who wish it to ascertain, provided they read the book which furnishes information on these points. *They will thus perceive* how that with solemnity and sanctity the *Jewish priests* offer unto God the first-fruits of the gifts bestowed by Him for the use and enjoyment of men ; *how* they fulfil their ministrations with regularity and stedfastness, in obedience to His commandments. There are, however, some (liturgical usages adopted) by these, which the Sadducees refuse to recognise, for they are not disposed to acquiesce in the existence of angels or spirits.

Still all *parties* alike expect Messiah, inasmuch as the Law certainly, and the prophets, preached beforehand that He was about to be present *on earth*. Inasmuch, however, as the Jews were not cognizant of the period of His advent, there remains the supposition that the declarations (of Scripture) concerning His coming have not been fulfilled. And so it is, that up to this day they continue in anticipation of the future coming of *the* Christ, — from the fact of their not discerning Him when He was present *in the world*. And (yet there can be little doubt but) that, on beholding the signs of the times of His having been already amongst us, *the Jews* are troubled ; and that they are ashamed to confess that He has come, since they have with their own hands put Him to death, because they were stung with indignation in being convicted by Himself of not having obeyed the laws. And they affirm that He who was thus sent forth by God is not this Christ (whom they are looking for) ; but they confess that another *Messiah* will come, who as yet has no existence ; and that he will usher in some of the signs which the law and the prophets have shown beforehand, whereas, regarding the rest (of these indications), they suppose that they have fallen into error. For they say that his generation will be from the stock of David, but not from a virgin and *the* Holy Spirit, but from a woman and a man, according as it is a rule for all to be procreated from seed. And they allege that this *Messiah* will be King over them, — a warlike and powerful individual, who, after having gathered together the entire people of the Jews, *and* having done battle with all the nations, will restore for them Jerusalem the royal city. And into this city He will collect together the entire *Hebrew* race, and bring it back once more into the ancient customs, that it may fulfil the regal and sacerdotal functions, and dwell in confidence for periods of time of sufficient duration. *After this repose, it is their opinion* that war would next be waged against them after being thus congregated ; that in this conflict Christ would fall by the edge of the sword ; *and* that, after no long time, would next succeed the termination and conflagration of the universe ; and that in this way their opinions concerning the resurrection would receive completion, and a recompense be rendered to each man according to his works.

CHAP. XXVI. — CONCLUSION TO THE WORK EXPLAINED.

It now seems to us that the tenets of both all the Greeks and barbarians have been sufficiently explained by us, and that nothing has remained unrefuted either of the points about which philosophy has been busied, or of the allegations advanced by the heretics. And from these very explanations the condemnation of the heretics is obvious, for having either purloined their doctrines, or derived contributions to them from some of those tenets elaborately worked out by the Greeks, and for having advanced (these opinions) as if they originated from God. Since, therefore, we have hurriedly passed through all *the systems* of these, and with much labour have, in the nine books, proclaimed all their opinions,

---

[1] Or, "the law not of yesterday," οὐ νεωστὶ τὸν νόμον. Cruice reads θεόκτιστον, as rendered above.

and have left behind us for all men a small viaticum in life, and to those who are our contemporaries have afforded a desire of learning (with) great joy and delight, we have considered it reasonable, as a crowning stroke to the entire *work*, to introduce the discourse (already mentioned) concerning the truth, and to furnish our delineation of this in one book, namely the tenth. *Our object is,* that the reader, not only when made acquainted with the overthrow of those who have presumed to establish heresies, may regard with scorn their idle *fancies*, but also, when brought to know the power of the truth, may be placed in the way of salvation, by reposing that faith in God which He so worthily deserves.

THE REFUTATION OF ALL HERESIES

BOOK X.

CHAP. I. — RECAPITULATION.

After we have, not with violence, burst through the labyrinth [1] of heresies, but have unravelled (their intricacies) through a refutation merely, or, in other words, by the force of truth, we approach the demonstration of the truth *itself.* For then the artificial sophisms of error will be exposed in all their inconsistency, when we shall succeed in establishing whence it is that the definition of the truth *has been derived. The truth* has not taken its principles from the wisdom of the Greeks, nor borrowed its doctrines, as secret mysteries, from the tenets of the Egyptians, which, albeit silly, are regarded amongst them with religious veneration as worthy of reliance. Nor has it been formed out of the fallacies which enunciate the incoherent (conclusions arrived at through the) curiosity of the Chaldeans. Nor does the truth owe its existence to astonishment, through the operations of demons, for the irrational frenzy of the Babylonians. But *its definition* is constituted after the manner in which every true definition is, viz., as simple and unadorned. A definition such as this, provided it is made manifest, will *of itself* refute error. And although we have very frequently propounded demonstrations, and with sufficient fulness elucidated for those willing (to learn) the rule of the truth ; yet even now, after having discussed all the opinions put forward by the Greeks and heretics, we have decided it not to be, at all events, unreasonable to introduce, as a sort of finishing stroke to the (nine) books

preceding, this demonstration throughout the tenth book.

CHAP. II. — SUMMARY OF THE OPINIONS OF PHILOSOPHERS.

Having, therefore, embraced (a consideration of) the tenets of all the wise men among the Greeks in four books, and the doctrines propounded by the heresiarchs in five, we shall now exhibit the doctrine concerning the truth in one, having first presented in a summary the suppositions entertained *severally* by all. For the dogmatists of the Greeks, dividing philosophy into three parts, in this manner devised from time to time their speculative systems ; [2] some denominating their *system* Natural, and others Moral, but others Dialectical *Philosophy.* And *the ancient thinkers who called their science* Natural Philosophy, were those *mentioned in book i.* And the account which they furnished was after this mode : Some of them *derived* all things from one, whereas others from more things *than one.* And of those *who derived all things* from one, some *derived them* from what was devoid of quality, whereas others from what was endued with quality. And among those *who derived all things* from quality, some *derived them* from fire, and some from air, and some from water, and some from earth. And among those *who derived the universe* from more things *than one,* some *derived it* from numerable, but others from infinite quantities. And among those *who derived all things* from numerable quantities, some *derived them* from two, and others from four, and others from five, and others from six. And among those *who derived the universe* from infinite quantities, some *derived entities* from things similar to those generated, whereas others from things dissimilar. And among these some *derived entities* from things incapable of, whereas others from things capable of, passion. From a body devoid of quality and endued with unity, the

---

[1] [This word is an index of authenticity. See on the "Little Labyrinth," Bunsen, i. p. 243, and Wordsworth, pp. 100, 161, and his references to Routh, Lardner, etc.]

[2] Hippolytus in what follows is indebted to Sextus Empiricus. — *Adv. Phys.,* x.

Stoics, then, accounted for the generation of the universe. For, according to them, matter devoid of quality, and in all its parts susceptible of change, constitutes an originating principle of the universe. For, when an alteration of this ensues, there is generated fire, air, water, earth. The followers, however, of Hippasus, and Anaximander, and Thales the Milesian, are disposed *to think* that all things have been generated from one (an entity), endued with quality. Hippasus of Metapontum and Heraclitus the Ephesian declared the origin *of things to be* from fire, whereas Anaximander from air, but Thales from water, and Xenophanes from earth. "For from earth," says he, "are all things, and all things terminate in the earth."[1]

CHAP. III. — SUMMARY OF THE OPINIONS OF PHILOSOPHERS CONTINUED.

But among those *who derive all entities* from more things than one, and from numerable quantities, the poet Homer asserts that the universe consists of two *substances*, namely earth and water; at one time expressing himself thus : —

"The source of gods was Sea and Mother Earth."[2]

And on another occasion *thus :* —

"But indeed ye all might become water and earth."[3]

And Xenophanes of Colophon seems to coincide with him, for he says : —

"We all are sprung from water and from earth."[4]

Euripides, however, (derives the universe) from earth and air, as one may ascertain from the following assertion of his : —

"Mother of all, air and earth, I sing."[5]

But Empedocles *derives the universe* from four principles, expressing himself thus : —

"Four roots of all things hear thou first:
  Brilliant Jove, and life-giving Juno and Aidoneus,
  And Nestis, that with tears bedews the Mortal Font."[6]

Ocellus, however, the Lucanian, and Aristotle, *derive the universe* from five *principles;* for, along with the four elements, they have assumed the *existence of a* fifth, and (that this is) a body with a circular motion; and they say that from this, things celestial have their being. But the disciples of Empedocles supposed the generation of the universe to have proceeded from six *principles.* For in the passage where he says, "Four roots of all things hear thou first," he produces generation out of four *principles.* When, however, he subjoins, —

"Ruinous Strife apart from these, equal in every point,
  And with them Friendship equal in length and breadth,"[7] —

he also delivers six principles of the universe, four of them material — earth, water, fire, *and* air; but two of them formative — Friendship and Discord. The followers, however, of Anaxagoras of Clazomenæ, and of Democritus, and of Epicurus, and multitudes of others, have given it as their opinion that the generation of the universe *proceeds* from infinite *numbers of atoms;* and we have previously made partial mention of these philosophers. But Anaxagoras *derives the universe* from things similar to those that are being produced; whereas the followers of Democritus and Epicurus *derived the universe* from things both dissimilar (to the entities produced), and devoid of passion, that is, from atoms. But the followers of Heraclides of Pontus, and of Asclepiades, *derived the universe* from things dissimilar (to the entities produced), and capable of passion, as if from incongruous corpuscles. But the disciples of Plato affirm that these *entities* are from three principles — God, and Matter, and Exemplar. He divides matter, however, into four principles — fire, water, earth, *and* air. And (he says) that God is the Creator of this (matter), and that Mind is its exemplar.[8]

CHAP. IV. — SUMMARY OF THE OPINIONS OF PHILOSOPHERS CONTINUED.

Persuaded, then, that the principle of physiology is confessedly discovered to be encumbered with difficulties for all these philosophers, we ourselves also shall fearlessly declare concerning the examples of the truth, as to how they are, and *as* we have felt confident *that they are.* But we shall previously furnish an explanation, in the way of epitome, of the tenets of the heresiarchs, in order that, by our having set before our readers the tenets of all made well known by this (plan of treatment), we may exhibit the truth in a plain and familiar (form).

CHAP. V. — THE NAASSENI.

But since it so appears expedient, let us begin first from the public worshippers of the serpent. The Naasseni call the first principle of the universe a Man, and that the same also is a Son of Man; and they divide this *man* into three portions. For they say one part of him is rational, and another psychical, but a third earthly. And they style him Adamas, and suppose that the knowledge *appertaining* to him is *the* originating cause of the capacity of knowing God. And *the Naassene asserts* that all these rational, and

1 See Karst., *Fragm.*, viii. 45.
2 *Iliad*, xiv. 201.
3 *Ibid.*, vii. 99.
4 See Karst., *Fragm.*, ix. p. 46.
5 Fabricius, in his Commentary on Sextus Empiricus, considers that this is a quotation from the Hymns of Euripides.
6 V. 55–57, ed. Karst.
7 V. 106, 107, ed. Karst.
8 [See *De Legibus*, lib. x., and note xii. p. 119, Tayler Lewis' *Plato against the Atheists*.]

psychical, and earthly qualities have retired into Jesus, and that through Him these three substances simultaneously have spoken unto the three genera of the universe. These allege that there are three kinds *of existence* — angelic, psychical, *and* earthly; and that there are three churches — angelic, psychical, *and* earthly; and that the names for these *are* — chosen, called, *and* captive. These are the heads of doctrine advanced by them, as far as one may briefly comprehend them. They affirm that James, the brother of the Lord, delivered these tenets to Mariamne, *by such a statement* belying both.

CHAP. VI. — THE PERATÆ.

The Peratæ, however, viz., Ademes the Carystian, and Euphrates the Peratic, say that there is some one world, — this is the denomination they use, — and affirming that it is divided into three parts. But of the threefold division, according to them, there is one principle, just like an immense fountain, capable of being by reason divided into infinite segments. And the first segment, and the one of more proximity, according to them, is the triad, and is called a perfect good, *and* a paternal magnitude. But the second portion of the triad is a certain multitude of, as it were, infinite powers. The third *part*, however, *is* formal. And the first is unbegotten;[1] whence they expressly affirm that there are three Gods, three Logoi, three minds, (and) three men. For when the division has been accomplished, to each part of the world they assign both Gods, and Logoi, and men, and the rest. But from above, from uncreatedness and the first segment of the world, when afterwards the world had attained to its consummation, *the Peratic affirms* that there came down, in the times of Herod, a certain man with a threefold nature, and a threefold body, and a threefold power, named Christ, and that He possesses from the three parts of the world in Himself all the concretions and capacities of the world. And they are disposed *to think* that this is what has been declared, "in whom dwelleth all the fulness of the Godhead bodily."[2] And *they assert* that from the two worlds situated above — *namely*, both the unbegotten *one* and self-begotten *one* — there were borne down into this world in which we are, germs of all sorts of powers. And (they say) that Christ came down from above from uncreatedness, in order that, by His descent, all things that have been divided into three parts may be saved. For, says *the Peratic*, the things that have been borne down from above will ascend through Him; and the things that have plotted against those that have been borne down

are heedlessly rejected,[3] and sent away to be punished. And *the Peratic* states that there are two parts which are saved — *that is*, those that are situated above — by having been separated from corruption, and that the third is destroyed, which he calls a formal world. These also are the tenets of the Peratæ.

CHAP. VII. — THE SETHIANS.

But to the Sethians it seems that there exist three principles, which have been precisely defined. And each of the principles is fitted by nature for being able to be generated, as in a human soul every art whatsoever *is developed* which is *capable of being* learned. *The result is the same* as when a child, by being long conversant with a musical instrument, becomes a musician; or with geometry a geometrician, or with any *other* art, with a similar result. And the essences of the principles, *the Sethians* say, are light and darkness. And in the midst of these is pure spirit; and the spirit, they say, is that which is placed intermediate between darkness, which is below, and light, which is above. It is not spirit, as a current of wind or a certain gentle breeze which may be felt, but just as if some fragrance of ointment or incense made out of a refined mixture, — a power diffusing itself by some impulse of fragrance which is inconceivable and superior to what one can express. Since, therefore, the light is above and the darkness below, and the spirit is intermediate between these, the light, also, as a ray of sun, shines from above on the underlying darkness. And the fragrance of the spirit is wafted onwards, occupying an intermediate position, and proceeds forth, just as is diffused the odour of incense-offerings (laid) upon the fire. Now the power of the things divided threefold being of this description, the power simultaneously of the spirit and of the light is below, in the darkness that is situated beneath. The darkness, however, they say, is a horrible water, into which the light along with the spirit is absorbed, and *thus* translated into a nature of this description. The darkness being then endued with intelligence, and knowing that when the light has been removed from it the darkness continues desolate, devoid of radiance *and* splendour, power *and* efficiency, as well as impotent, (therefore,) by every effort of reflection and of reason, this makes an exertion to comprise in itself brilliancy, and a scintillation of light, along with the fragrance of the spirit. And of this they introduce the following image, expressing themselves thus: Just as the pupil of the eye appears dark beneath the underlying humours, but is illuminated by the spirit, so the darkness earnestly

---

[1] Cruice supplies from Theodoret: "and the second *which is* good is self-begotten, and the third is generated."
[2] Col. ii. 9.

[3] ἀφίεται εἰκῆ: Bernays proposes ὀφιοειδῆ, i.e., being of the form of the serpent.

strives after the spirit, and has with itself all the powers which wish to retire and return. Now these are indefinitely infinite, from which, when commingled, all things are figured and generated like seals. For just as a seal, when brought into contact with wax, produces a figure, (and yet the seal) itself remains of itself what it was, so also the powers, by coming into communion (one with the other), form all the infinite kinds of animals. *The Sethians assert* that, therefore, from the primary concourse of the three principles was generated an image of *the* great seal, *namely* heaven and earth, having a form like a womb, possessing a navel in the midst. And so that the rest of the figures of all things were, like heaven and earth, fashioned similar to a womb.

And *the Sethians* say that from the water was produced a first-begotten principle, *namely* a vehement and boisterous wind, and that it is a cause of all generation, which creates a sort of heat and motion in the world from the motion of the waters. And *they maintain* that this *wind* is fashioned like the hissing of a serpent into a perfect image. And on this the world gazes and hurries into generation, being inflamed as a womb ; and from thence they are disposed *to think* that the generation of the universe has arisen. And they say that this wind constitutes a spirit, and that a perfect God has arisen from the fragrance of the waters, and that of the spirit, and *from* the brilliant light. And *they affirm* that mind exists after the mode of generation from a female — (meaning by mind) the supernal spark — and that, having been mingled beneath with the compounds of body, it earnestly desires to flee away, that escaping it may depart and not find dissolution on account of the deficiency in the waters. Wherefore it is in the habit of crying aloud from the mixture of the waters, according to the Psalmist, as they say, " For the entire anxiety of the light above is, that it may deliver the spark which is below from the Father beneath," [1] *that is, from* wind. And *the Father* creates heat and disturbance, and produces for Himself a Son, *namely* mind, which, *as* they allege, is not the peculiar *offspring* of Himself. And *these heretics affirm that the Son,* on beholding the perfect Logos of the supernal light, underwent a transformation, and in *the* shape of a serpent entered into a womb, in order that he might be able to recover that Mind *which is* the scintillation from the light. And that this is what has been declared, " Who, being in the form of God, thought it not robbery to be equal with God ; but made Himself of no reputation, and took upon Him the form of a servant." [2]

And the wretched and baneful Sethians are disposed *to think* that this constitutes the servile form *alluded to by the Apostle.* These, then, are the assertions which likewise these *Sethians* advance.

CHAP. VIII. — SIMON MAGUS.

But that very sapient *fellow* Simon makes his statement thus, that there is an indefinite power, *and* that this is the root of the universe. And this indefinite power, he says, which is fire, is in itself not anything which is simple, as the gross bulk *of speculators maintain*, when they assert that there are four incomposite elements, and have supposed fire, *as one of these*, to be uncompounded. *Simon, on the other hand, alleges* that the nature of fire is twofold ; and one portion of this twofold (nature) he calls a something secret, and another (a something) manifest. And *he asserts* that the secret is concealed in the manifest *parts* of the fire, and that the manifest *parts* of the fire have been produced from the secret. And he says that all the parts of the fire, visible and invisible, have been supposed to be in possession of a capacity of perception. The world, therefore, he says, that is begotten, has been produced from the unbegotten fire. And it commenced, he says, to exist thus : The Unbegotten One took six primal roots of the principle of generation from the principle of that fire. For *he maintains* that these roots have been generated in pairs from the fire ; and these he denominates Mind and Intelligence, Voice and Name, Ratiocination and Reflection. And *he asserts* that in the six roots, at the same time, resides the indefinite power, *which* he affirms to be Him that stood, stands, and will stand. And when this *one* has been formed into a figure, He will, *according to this heretic*, exist in the six powers substantially *and* potentially. *And He will be* in magnitude and perfection one and the same with that unbegotten and indefinite power, possessing no attribute in any respect more deficient than that unbegotten, and unalterable, and indefinite power. If, however, *He who stood, stands, and will stand*, continues to exist only potentially in the six powers, and has not assumed any definite figure, He becomes, says *Simon,* utterly evanescent, and perishes. *And this takes place* in the same manner as the grammatical or geometrical capacity, which, though it has been *implanted* in man's soul, *suffers extinction* when it does not obtain (the assistance of) a master of *either of these* arts, who would indoctrinate *that soul into its principles*. Now Simon affirms that he himself is He who stood, stands, *and* will stand, and that He is a power that is above all things. So far, then, for the opinions of Simon like-wise.

---

[1] The commentators refer us to Ps. xxix. 3.
[2] Phil. ii. 6, 7.

CHAP. IX. — VALENTINUS.

Valentinus,[1] however, and the adherents of this school, though they agree in asserting that the originating principle of the universe is *the* Father, still they are impelled into the adoption of a contrary opinion *respecting Him.* For some of them *maintain* that (the Father) is solitary and generative ; whereas others *hold* the impossibility, (in His as in other cases,) of procreation without a female. They therefore add Sige as *the* spouse of this *Father,* and style *the Father* Himself Bythus. From this *Father* and His spouse some *allege* that there have been six projections, — viz., Nous and Aletheia, Logos and Zoe, Anthropos and Ecclesia, — and that this constitutes the procreative Ogdoad. And *the Valentinians* maintain that those *are the first* projections which have taken place within the limit, *and* have been again denominated " *those* within the Pleroma ; " and the second are "those without the Pleroma " ; and the third, "those without the Limit." Now the generation of these constitutes the Hysterema *Acamoth.* And he asserts that what has been generated from an Æon, *that exists* in *the* Hysterema *and* has been projected (beyond the Limit), is the Creator. But *Valentinus* is not disposed *to affirm what is thus generated* to be primal Deity, but speaks in detractive terms both of Him and the things made by Him. And (he asserts) that Christ came down from within the Pleroma for the salvation of the spirit who had erred. This spirit, (according to the Valentinians,) resides in our inner man ; and they say that this *inner man* obtains salvation on account of this indwelling *spirit. Valentinus,* however, (to uphold the doctrine,) determines that the flesh is not saved, and styles it " a leathern tunic," and the perishable *portion of* man. I have (already) declared these tenets in the way of an epitome, inasmuch as in their systems there exists enlarged matter for discussion, and a variety of opinions. In this manner, then, it seems proper also to the school of Valentinus *to propound their opinions.*

CHAP. X. — BASILIDES.

But Basilides also himself affirms that there is a non-existent God, who, being non-existent, has made the non-existent world, that has been formed out of things that are not, by casting down a certain seed, as it were a grain of mustard-seed, having in itself stem, leaves, branches, *and* fruit. Or *this seed is* as a peacock's egg, comprising in itself the varied multitude of colours. And this, say *the Basilidians,* constitutes the seed of the world, from which all things have been produced. For *they maintain* that it com-

prises in itself all things, as it were those that *as yet* are non-existent, and which it has been predetermined to be brought into existence by the non-existent Deity. There was, then, he says, in the seed itself a threefold Sonship, in all respects of the same substance with the non-existent God, which has been begotten from things that are not. And of this Sonship, divided into three parts, one portion of it was refined, and another gross, and another requiring purification. The refined portion, when first the earliest putting down of the seed was accomplished by the non-existent God, immediately burst forth, and ascended upwards, and proceeded towards the non-existent *Deity.* For every nature yearns after that *God* on account of the excess of *His* beauty, but different (creatures desire Him) from different causes. The more gross portion, however, still continues in the seed ; and inasmuch as it is a certain imitative *nature,* it was not able to soar upwards, for it was more gross than the subtle part. *The more gross portion,* however, equipped itself with the Holy Spirit, as it were with wings ; for the Sonship, *thus* arrayed, shows kindness to this *Spirit,* and *in turn* receives kindness. The third Sonship, however, requires purification, *and therefore* this continued in the conglomeration of all germs, and this displays and receives kindness. And (Basilides asserts) that there is something which is called " world," and something else (which is called) supra-mundane ; for *entities* are distributed by him into two primary divisions. And what is intermediate between these he calls " Conterminous Holy Spirit," and (this Spirit) has *in itself* the fragrance of the Sonship.

From the conglomeration of all germs of the cosmical seed burst forth and was begotten the Great Archon, the head of the world, *an Æon* of inexpressible beauty and size. This (Archon) having raised Himself as far as the firmament, supposed that there was not another above Himself. And *accordingly* He became more brilliant and powerful than all the underlying *Æons,* with the exception of the Sonship that had been left beneath, but which He was not aware was more wise than Himself. This one having His attention turned to the creation of the world, first begat a son unto Himself, superior to Himself ; and this *son* He caused to sit on His own right hand, and this these *Basilidians* allege is the Ogdoad. *The Great Archon* Himself, then, produces the entire celestial creation. And another Archon ascended from (the conglomeration of) all the germs, *who was* greater than all the underlying *Æons,* except the Sonship that had been left behind, yet far inferior to the former one. And they style this *second Archon* a Hebdomad. He is Maker, and Creator, and Controller of all things *that are* beneath Him, and

[1] This section differs considerably from what Hippolytus has already stated concerning Valentinus. [" Sige," vol. i. p. 62, note 5.]

this *Archon* produced for Himself a Son more prudent and wiser *than Himself*. Now they assert that all these things exist according to the predetermination of that non-existent *God*, and that there exist also worlds and intervals that are infinite. And *the Basilidians affirm* that upon Jesus, who was born of Mary, came the power of the Gospel, which descended and illuminated the Son both of the Ogdoad and of the Hebdomad. *And this took place* for the purpose of enlightening and distinguishing from the different orders of beings, and purifying the Sonship that had been left behind for conferring benefits on souls, and the receiving benefits in turn. And they say that themselves are sons, who are in the world for this cause, that by teaching they may purify souls, and along with the Sonship may ascend to the Father above, *from* whom proceeded the first Sonship. And they allege that the world endures until the period when all souls may have repaired thither along with the Sonship. These, however, are the opinions which Basilides, who detailed them as prodigies, is not ashamed to advance.

CHAP. XI. — JUSTINUS.

But Justinus also himself attempted to establish similar opinions with these, and expresses himself thus : That there are three unbegotten principles of the universe, two males *and* one female. And of the males one principle is denominated " Good." Now this alone is called after this mode, *and is* endued with a foreknowledge of the universe. And the other *is* Father of all generated entities, *and is* devoid of foreknowledge, and unknown, and invisible, and is called Elohim. The female *principle is* devoid of foreknowledge, passionate, with two minds, *and* with two bodies, as we have minutely detailed in the *previous* discourses concerning this *heretic's system. This female principle*, in her upper parts, as far as the groin, is, *the Justinians say*, a virgin, whereas from the groin downwards a snake. And such is denominated Edem and Israel. *This heretic* alleges that these are the principles of the universe, from which all things have been produced. And *he asserts* that Elohim, without foreknowledge, passed into inordinate desire for the half virgin, and that having had intercourse with her, he begot twelve angels ; and the names of these he states *to be those already given*. And *of these* the paternal ones are connected with the father, and the maternal with the mother. And *Justinus maintains* that these are (the trees of Paradise), concerning which Moses has spoken in an allegorical sense the things written in the law. And *Justinus affirms* that all things were made by Elohim and Edem. And (he says) that animals, with the rest *of the creatures of this kind,* are from the part resembling a beast, whereas man from the parts above the groin. And Edem (is supposed by Justinus) to have deposited in *man* himself the soul, which was her own power, (but Elohim the spirit.) And *Justinus* alleges that this Elohim, after having learned *his origin*, ascended to the Good *Being*, and deserted Edem. And *this heretic asserts that Edem*, enraged on account of such (treatment), concocted all this plot against the spirit of Elohim which he deposited in man. And (Justinus informs us) that for this reason the Father sent Baruch, and issued directions to the prophets, in order that the spirit of Elohim might be delivered, and that all might be seduced away from Edem. But (this heretic) alleges that even Hercules was a prophet, and that he was worsted by Omphale, that is, by Babel ; and *the Justinians* call the latter Venus. And (they say) that afterwards, in the days of Herod, Jesus was born son of Mary and Joseph, to whom he alleges Baruch had spoken. And (Justinus asserts) that Edem plotted against this (Jesus), but could not deceive him ; and for this reason, that she caused him to be crucified. And the spirit of Jesus, (says Justinus,) ascended to the Good *Being*. And (the Justinians maintain) that the spirits of all who thus obey those silly and futile discourses will be saved, and that the body and soul of Edem have been left behind. But the foolish Justinus calls this (Edem) Earth.

CHAP. XII. — THE DOCETÆ.

Now the Docetæ advance assertions of this description : that the primal Deity is as a seed of the fig-tree ; and that from this proceeded three Æons as the stem, and the leaves and the fruit ; and that these projected thirty Æons, each (of them) ten ; and that they were all united in decades, but differed only in positions, as some were before others. And (the Docetæ assert) that infinite Æons were indefinitely projected, and that all these were hermaphrodites. And (they say) that these *Æons* formed a design of simultaneously going together into one Æon, and that from this the intermediate Æon *and* from *the* Virgin Mary they begot a Saviour of all. *And this Redeemer was* like in every respect to the first seed of the fig-tree, but inferior in this respect, from the fact of His having been begotten ; for the seed whence the fig-tree springs is unbegotten. *This*, then, was the great light of the Æons — it was entirely radiance — which receives no adornment, and comprises in itself *the* forms of all animals. And the Docetæ maintain that this *light*, on proceeding into the underlying chaos, afforded a cause (of existence) to the things that were produced, and those actually existing, and that on coming down from above it impressed on chaos beneath the forms of everlasting species. For the third Æon, which had tripled itself, when he perceives that all his characteristic attributes were forcibly drawn off into the nether darkness, and not being ignorant both of the terror of darkness and the simplicity of light, proceeded to create heaven ; and after having rendered firm what intervened, He separated the darkness from the light. As all the species of the third Æon were, he says, overcome by the darkness, the figure even of this *Æon* became a living fire, having been generated by light. And from this (source), they allege, was generated the Great Archon, regarding whom Moses converses, saying that He is a fiery Deity and Demiurge, who also continually alters the forms of all (Æons) into bodies. And the (Docetæ) allege that these are the souls for whose sake the Saviour was begotten, and that He points out the way through which the souls will escape that are (now) overpowered (by darkness). And (the Docetæ maintain) that Jesus arrayed Himself in that only-begotten power, and that for this reason He could not be seen by any, on account of the excessive magnitude of His glory. And they say that all the occurrences took place with Him as it has been written in the Gospels.

CHAP. XIII. — MONOÏMUS.

But the followers of Monoïmus the Arabian assert that the originating principle of the universe is a primal man and son of man ; and that, as Moses states, the things that have been produced were produced not by the primal man, but by the Son of that primal man, *yet* not by the entire *Son*, but by part of Him. And (Monoïmus asserts) that the Son of man is iota, which stands for ten, the principal number in which is (inherent) the subsistence of all number (in general, and) through which every number (in particular) consists, as well as the generation of the universe, fire, air, water, *and* earth. But inasmuch as this is one iota and one tittle, *and* what is perfect (emanates) from what is perfect, *or, in other words*, a tittle flows down from above, containing all things in itself ; (therefore,) whatsoever things also the man possesses, the Father of the Son of man *possesses likewise*. Moses, therefore, says that the world was made in six days, that is, by six powers, out of which the world was made by the one tittle. For cubes, and octahedrons, and pyramids, and all figures similar to these, having equal superficies, out of which consist fire, air, water, *and* earth, have been produced from numbers comprehended in that simple tittle of the iota, which is Son of man. When, therefore, says (Monoïmus), Moses mentions the rod's being brandished for the purpose *of bringing* the plagues upon Egypt, he alludes allegorically to the (alterations of the) world of iota ; nor did he frame more than ten

plagues. If, however, says he, you wish to become acquainted with the universe, search within yourself who is it that says, " My soul, my flesh, *and* my mind," and who is it that appropriates each one thing unto himself, as another (would do) for himself. Understand that this is a perfect *one* arising from (one that is) perfect, and that he considers as his own all so-called non-entities and all entities. These, then, are the opinions of Monoïmus also.

CHAP. XIV. — TATIAN.

Tatian, however, similarly with Valentinus and the others, says that there are certain invisible Æons, and that by some one of these the world below has been created, and the things existing in *it*. And he habituates himself to a very cynical [1] mode of life, and almost in nothing differs from Marcion, as appertaining both to his slanders, and the regulations enacted concerning marriage.

CHAP. XV. — MARCION AND CERDO.

But Marcion, of Pontus, and Cerdon, [2] his preceptor, themselves also lay down that there are three principles of the universe — good, just, *and* matter. Some disciples, however, of these add *a fourth*, saying, good, just, evil, *and* matter. But they all affirm that the good (Being) has made nothing at all, though some denominate the just one *likewise* evil, whereas others that his only title is that of just. And they allege that (the just Being) made all things out of subjacent matter, for that he made them not well, but irrationally. For it is requisite that the things made should be similar to the maker ; wherefore also they thus employ the evangelical parables, saying, " A good tree cannot bring forth evil fruit," [3] and the rest of the passage. *Now Marcion* alleges that the conceptions badly devised by the (just one) himself constituted the allusion in this passage. And (he says) that Christ is the Son of the good Being, and was sent for the salvation of souls by him whom he styles the inner man. And he asserts that he appeared as a man *though* not being a man, and as incarnate *though* not being incarnate. *And he maintains* that his manifestation was only phantastic, and that he underwent neither generation nor passion except in appearance. And he will not allow that flesh rises again ; but in affirming marriage to be destruction, he leads his disciples towards a very cynical life. And by these *means* he imagines that he annoys the Creator, if he should abstain from the things that are made or appointed by Him.

---

[1] The allusion here is to the shamelessness of the Cynics in regard to sexual intercourse.
[2] The account here given of Cerdon and Marcion does not accurately correspond with that already furnished by Hippolytus of these heretics.
[3] Matt. vii. 18.

CHAP. XVI. — APELLES.

But Apelles, a disciple of this *heretic*, was displeased at the statements advanced by his preceptor, as we have previously declared, and by another theory supposed that there are four gods. And the first of these he alleges to be the "Good Being," whom the prophets did not know, and Christ to be His Son. And the second *God, he affirms* to be the Creator of the universe, and Him he does not wish to be a God. And the third *God, he states* to be the fiery one that was manifested; and the fourth to be an evil one. And *Apelles* calls these angels; and by adding (to their number) Christ likewise, he will assert Him to be a fifth *God*. But *this heretic* is in the habit of devoting his attention to a book which he calls "Revelations" of a certain Philumene, whom he considers a prophetess. And he affirms that Christ did not receive his flesh from the Virgin, but from the adjacent substance of the world. In this manner he composed his treatises against the law and the prophets, and attempts to abolish them as if they had spoken falsehoods, and had not known God. And *Apelles*, similarly with Marcion, affirms that the different sorts of flesh are destroyed.

CHAP. XVII. — CERINTHUS.

Cerinthus, however, himself having been trained in Egypt, determined that the world was not made by the first God, but by a certain angelic power. *And this power was* far separated and distant from that sovereignty which is above the entire circle of existence, and it knows not *the* God (that is) above all things. And he says that Jesus was not born of a virgin, but that He sprang from Joseph and Mary *as their* son, similar to the rest of men; and that He excelled in justice, and prudence, and understanding above all the rest *of mankind*. And *Cerinthus maintains* that, after Jesus' baptism, Christ came down in the form of a dove upon Him from the sovereignty that is above the whole circle of existence, and that then He proceeded to preach the unknown Father, and to work miracles. And *he asserts* that, at the conclusion of the passion, Christ flew away from Jesus,[1] but that Jesus suffered, and that Christ remained incapable of suffering, being a spirit of *the* Lord.

CHAP. XVIII. — THE EBIONÆANS.

But the Ebionæans assert that the world is made by the true God, and *they speak of* Christ in a similar manner with Cerinthus. They live, however, in all respects according to the law of Moses, alleging that they are thus justified.

CHAP. XIX. — THEODOTUS.[2]

But Theodotus of Byzantium introduced a heresy of the following description, alleging that all things were created by the true God; whereas that Christ, he states, in a manner similar to that advocated by the Gnostics already mentioned, made His appearance according to some mode of this description. And *Theodotus affirms* that Christ is a man of a kindred nature with all *men*, but that He surpasses them in this respect, that, according to the counsel of God, He had been born of a virgin, and the Holy Ghost had overshadowed *His mother*. This *heretic*, however, *maintained that Jesus* had not assumed flesh in *the womb of* the Virgin, but that afterwards Christ descended upon Jesus at His baptism in form of a dove. And from this circumstance, *the followers of Theodotus* affirm that at first miraculous powers did not acquire operating energy in *the Saviour* Himself. *Theodotus*, however, determines to deny the divinity of Christ. Now, opinions of this description were advanced by Theodotus.

CHAP. XX. — MELCHISEDECIANS.

And others also make all their assertions similarly with those which have been already specified, introducing one only alteration, viz., in respect of regarding Melchisedec as a certain power. But they allege that *Melchisedec* himself is superior to all powers; and according to his image, they are desirous of *maintaining* that Christ likewise is *generated*.

CHAP. XXI. — THE PHRYGIANS OR MONTANISTS.

The Phrygians, however, derive the principles of their heresy from a certain Montanus, and Priscilla, and Maximilla, and regard these wretched women as prophetesses, and Montanus as a prophet. In respect, however, of what appertains to the origin and creation of the universe, *the Phrygians* are supposed to express themselves correctly; while in the tenets which they enunciate respecting Christ, they have not irrelevantly formed their opinions. But they are seduced into error in common with *the heretics* previously alluded to, and devote their attention to the discourses of these above the Gospels, thus laying down regulations concerning novel and strange fasts.[3]

CHAP. XXII. — THE PHRYGIANS OR MONTANISTS CONTINUED.

But others of them, being attached to the heresy of the Noetians, entertain similar opin-

---

[1] Or, "the Son;" or, "the Son of Mary" (Cruice).

[2] [Vol. iii. p. 654, this series, where it should have been noted that the *Appendix* to Tertullian is supposed by Waterland to be "little else but an extract from Hippolytus." He pronounces it "ancient and of good value." See Wordsworth's remarks on the *biblidarion*, p. 59.]

[3] The MS. has the obviously corrupt reading παραδόσεις, which Duncker alters into παραδόξους (strange).

ions to those relating to the silly women *of the Phrygians*, and to Montanus. As regards, however, the truths appertaining to the Father of the entire of existing things, they are guilty of blasphemy, because they assert that He is Son and Father, visible and invisible, begotten and unbegotten, mortal and immortal. These have taken occasion from a certain Noetus *to put forward their heresy.*

CHAP. XXIII. — NOETUS AND CALLISTUS.

But in like manner, also, Noetus, being by birth a native of Smyrna, and a fellow addicted to reckless babbling, as well as crafty withal, introduced (among us) this heresy which originated from one Epigonus. It reached *Rome,* and was adopted by Cleomenes, and so has continued to this day among his successors. *Noetus* asserts that there is one Father and God of the universe, and that He made all things, and was imperceptible to those that exist when He might *so* desire. *Noetus maintained that the Father* then appeared when He wished ; and He is invisible when He is not seen, but visible when He is seen. And *this heretic also alleges that the Father* is unbegotten when He is not generated, but begotten when He is born of a virgin ; as also that He is not subject to suffering, and is immortal when He does not suffer or die. When, however, His passion [1] came upon Him, *Noetus allows that the Father* suffers and dies. And *the Noetians* suppose that this Father Himself is called Son, (and *vice versa*,) in reference to the events which at their own proper periods happen to them severally.

Callistus corroborated the heresy of these *Noetians,* but we have *already* carefully explained the details of his life. And *Callistus* himself produced likewise a heresy, and derived its starting-points from these *Noetians,* — namely, so far as he acknowledges that there is one Father and God, viz., the Creator of the universe, and that this (God) is spoken of, and called by the name of Son, yet that in substance He is one Spirit. For Spirit, *as* the Deity, is, he says, not any *being* different from the Logos, or the Logos from the Deity ; therefore this one person, (according to Callistus,) is divided nominally, but substantially not so. He supposes this one Logos to be God, and affirms that there was *in the case of the Word* an incarnation. And he is disposed (to maintain), that He who was seen in the flesh and was crucified [2] is Son, but that

the Father it is who dwells in Him. *Callistus thus* at one time branches off into the opinion of Noetus, but at another into that of Theodotus, and holds no sure doctrine. These, then, are the opinions of Callistus.

CHAP. XXIV. — HERMOGENES.

But one Hermogenes himself also being desirous of saying something, asserted that God made all things out of matter coeval *with Himself,* and subject *to His design.* For *Hermogenes* [3] held it to be an impossibility that God should make the things that were made, except out of existent things.

CHAP. XXV. — THE ELCHASAITES.

But certain others, introducing as it were some novel *tenet,* appropriated *parts of their system* from all heresies, and procured a strange volume, which bore on the titlepage the name of one Elchasaï. These, in like manner, acknowledge that the principles of the universe were originated by the Deity. They do not, however, confess that there is but one Christ, but that there is one that is superior *to the rest,* and that He is transfused into many bodies frequently, and was now in Jesus. And, in like manner, *these heretics maintain* that at one time *Christ* was begotten of God, and at another time became the Spirit, and at another time *was born* of a virgin, and at another time not so. And *they affirm* that likewise this Jesus afterwards was continually being transfused into bodies, and was manifested in many (different bodies) at *different* times. And they resort to incantations and baptisms in their confession of elements. And they occupy themselves with bustling activity in regard of astrological and mathematical science, and of the arts of sorcery. But *also* they allege themselves to have powers of prescience.

CHAP. XXVI. — JEWISH CHRONOLOGY.

. . . From Haran, a city of Mesopotamia, (Abraham, by the command) [4] of God, transfers his residence into the country which is now called Palestine and Judea, but then the region of Canaan. Now, concerning this territory, we have in part, but still not negligently, rendered an account in other discourses. From the circumstance, then, (of this migration) is traceable the beginning of an increase (of population) in

---

[1] Cruice suggests the addition of the words "and death," in order to correspond with the remainder of the sentence. The punctuation followed above is conjectural, but gives substantially the meaning of the text as settled by Duncker.

[2] σταυρούμενον. The MS. reads κρατούμενον, which would mean seized or vanquished. The former yields no meaning, and the latter conveys an erroneous conception regarding the Blessed Lord, who, in yielding to suffering and death, showed Himself more than conqueror of both (John x. 17, 18).

[3] Cruice considers that Theodoret has taken his account (*Hær. Fab.,* i. 19) from this tenth book of *The Refutation.*

[4] There is here a hiatus, which Abbe Cruice thinks is caused by those portions of the MS. being lost, in which Hippolytus furnishes his Summary of the Jewish Sects. The object of introducing these genealogical and ethnic remarks might at first seem irrelevant; but they are intended to be subservient to Hippolytus' *Demonstration of the Truth,* by proving the superior antiquity, as coming down from Abraham, of revelation above all pagan philosophy. [See, cap. xxvii. *infra*] Abbe Cruice refers us to his work (pp. 72-77), *Études sur de Nouveaux Documents Historiques empruntés à L'Ouvrage des φιλοσοφούμενα,* Paris; 1853.

Judea, which obtained its name from Judah, fourth son of Jacob, whose *name* was also called *Israel*, from the fact that a race of kings would be descended from him.[1] Abraham removes from Mesopotamia (when 75 years old, and) when 100 years old he begat Isaac. But Isaac, when 60 years of age, begat Jacob. And Jacob, when 86 years old, begat Levi; and Levi, at 40 years of age, begat Caath;[2] and Caath was four years of age when he went down with Jacob into Egypt. Therefore the entire period during which Abraham sojourned, and the entire family descended from him by Isaac, in the country then called Canaanitis, was 215 years. But the father of this *Abraham* is Thare,[3] and of this *Thare the father is* Nachor, and of this *Nachor the father is* Serag, *and of this Serag the father is Reu, and of this Reu the father is Peleg, and of this Peleg*[4] *the father is Heber.* And so it comes to pass that *the Jews* are denominated by the name of Hebrews. *In the time of Phaleg,*[5] *however, arose the dispersion of nations.* Now these nations were 72,[6] *corresponding with the number of Abraham's children.* And the names of these *nations* we have likewise set down in other books, not even omitting this *point* in its own proper place. *And the reason of our particularity* is our desire to manifest to those which are of a studious disposition the love which we cherish towards the Divinity, and the indubitable knowledge respecting the Truth, which in the course of our labours[7] we have acquired possession of. But of this Heber the father is Salah; and of this *Salah the father is* Caïnan; and of this *Caïnan the father is* Arphaxad, whose *father* is Shem; and of this *Shem the father is* Noah. And in *Noah's* time there occurred a flood throughout the entire world, which neither Egyptians, nor Chaldeans, nor Greeks recollect; for the inundations which took place in the age of Ogyges and Deucalion prevailed only in the localities where these dwelt.[8] There are, then, in the

case of these (patriarchs — that is, from Noah to Heber inclusive) — 5 generations, *and* 495 years.[9] This *Noah*, inasmuch as he was a most religious and God-loving man, alone, with wife and children, and the three wives of these, escaped the flood that ensued. And he owed his preservation to an ark; and both the dimensions and relics of this *ark* are, as we have explained, shown to this day in the mountains called Ararat, which are situated in the direction of the country of the Adiabeni.[10] It is then possible for those who are disposed to investigate the subject industriously, to perceive how clearly has been demonstrated *the existence of* a nation of worshippers of *the true* God, more ancient than all *the* Chaldeans, Egyptians, *and* Greeks. What necessity, however, is there at present to specify those who, anterior to Noah, were both devout men, and permitted to hold converse with *the true* God, inasmuch as, so far as the subject taken in hand is concerned, this testimony in regard of the antiquity *of the people of God* is sufficient?

CHAP. XXVII. — JEWISH CHRONOLOGY CONTINUED.

But since it does not seem irrational to prove that these nations that had their attention engrossed with *the speculations* of philosophy are of more modern date than those that had habitually worshipped *the true* God,[11] it is reasonable that we should state both whence the family of these *latter originated;* and that when they took up their abode in these countries, they did not receive a name from the actual localities, but claimed for themselves *names* from those who were primarily born, and had inhabited these. Noah had three sons — Shem, Ham, *and* Japheth. From these the entire family of man was multiplied, and every quarter *of the earth* owes its inhabitants *in the first instance to these.* For the word of God to them prevailed, when *the Lord* said, "Be fruitful, and multiply, and replenish the earth." So great efficacy had *that* one word *that* from the three *sons of Noah* are begotten in *the* family 72 children, — (viz.,) from Shem, 25; from Japheth, 15; *and* from Ham, 32. Unto Ham, however, these 32 children are born in accordance with previous declarations. *And among Ham's children are:* Canaan,[12] from whom came the Canaanites; Mizraim, from whom the Egyptians; Cush, from whom the Ethiopians; *and* Phut, from whom the Libyans. These, according to the language *prevalent* among them, are up to the present day styled by the appellation of their ancestors; nay, even in the Greek tongue they are called by the names by which

---

1　[Vol. ii. p. 306, this series.]
2　That is, Kohath (see Gen. xlvi. 11).
3　That is, Tera (see Gen. xi. 26).
4　Gen. xi. 16.
5　[Possibly a *physical* catastrophe. Gen. x. 25, and 1 Chron. i. 19.]
6　The system of seventy-two nations here adopted by Hippolytus is that advanced by Jewish writers generally, and has been probably deduced from the tenth chapter of Genesis　Another historian of the heresies of the Church adopts it — Epiphanius. A chronographer, however, contemporary with Hippolytus — Julius Africanus — discarded this number, as is proved by the fragments of his work preserved by Eusebius and Syncellus.
7　The allusion here made constitutes a strong reason for ascribing *The Refutation* to Hippolytus, the author of which here states that he had written a *Chronicle.* But the fragment in our text corresponds with a Latin translation of a *Chronicon* given by Fabricius, and bearing the name of Hippolytus. The terms in which Hippolytus delivers himself above imply that he was the inventor of a chronological system, thus harmonizing with the fact that the Paschal Cycle, though ever so faulty, was selected out of all his writings for being inscribed on Hippolytus' statue, dug up on the road to Tivoli A D. 1551, in the vicinity of Rome, near the Church of St. Lorenzo. [This modest note is of no slight importance to the case, as elucidated by Bunsen and Wordsworth.]
8　[Hippolytus does not call in the Greek fables to support the biblical story: he dismisses them with indifference. Yet the *universality* of such traditions is unaccountable save as derived from the history of Noah.]

9　Cruice has 435 years.
10　[That such relics were exhibited need not be doubted if the account of Berosus is credited. We may doubt as to their genuineness, of course.]
11　[See note 4, p. 148, *supra.*]
12　[The only son of Ham who did *not* go to Africa, vol. iii. p. 3.]

they have been now denominated. But even supposing that neither these localities had been previously inhabited, nor that it could be proved that a race of men from the beginning existed there, nevertheless these sons of Noah, a worshipper of God, are *quite sufficient to prove the point at issue. For it is evident that Noah* himself must have been a disciple of devout people, for which reason he escaped the tremendous, though transient, threat of water.

How, then, should not the worshippers of *the true* God be of greater antiquity than all Chaldeans, Egyptians, *and* Greeks, for we must bear in mind that the father of these *Gentiles* was born from this Japheth,[1] and received the name Javan, and became the progenitor of Greeks and Ionians? Now, if the nations that devoted themselves to questions concerning philosophy are shown to belong to a period altogether more recent than the race of the worshippers of God as well as *the time of* the deluge, how would not the nations of the barbarians, and as many *tribes* as in the world are known and unknown, appear to belong to a more modern epoch than these? Therefore ye Greeks, Egyptians, Chaldeans, and the entire race of men, become adepts in this doctrine, and learn from us, who are the friends of God, what the nature of God is, and what His well-arranged creation. And we have cultivated this *system*, not expressing ourselves in mere pompous language, but executing our treatises in *terms that prove our* knowledge of truth and our practice of good sense, our object being the demonstration of His *Truth*.[2]

CHAP. XXVIII. — THE DOCTRINE OF THE TRUTH.

The first and only (one God),[3] both Creator and Lord of all, had nothing coeval *with Himself*, not infinite chaos, nor measureless water, nor solid earth, nor dense air, not warm fire, nor refined spirit, nor the azure canopy[4] of the stupendous firmament. But He was One, alone in Himself. By an exercise of His will He created things that are, which antecedently had no existence, except that He willed to make them. For He is fully acquainted with whatever is about to take place, for foreknowledge also is present to Him. The different principles, how-

ever, of what will come into existence, He first fabricated, viz., fire and spirit, water and earth, from which diverse *elements* He proceeded to form His own creation. And some objects He formed of one essence, but others He compounded from two, and others from three, and others from four. And those *formed* of one *substance* were immortal, for *in their case* dissolution does not follow, for what is one will never be dissolved. Those, on the other hand, which are formed out of two, or three, or four *substances*, are dissoluble; wherefore also are they named mortal. For this has been denominated death, namely, the dissolution of *substances* connected. I now therefore think that I have sufficiently answered those endued with a sound mind, who, if they are desirous of additional instruction, and are disposed accurately to investigate the substances of these things, and the causes of the entire creation, will become acquainted with these points should they peruse a work of ours comprised (under the title), *Concerning the Substance of the Universe*.[5] I consider, however, that at present it is enough to elucidate those causes of which the Greeks, not being aware, glorified, in pompous phraseology, the parts of creation, while they remained ignorant of the Creator. And from these the heresiarchs have taken occasion, and have transformed the statements previously made by those *Greeks* into similar doctrines, and thus have framed ridiculous heresies.

CHAP. XXIX. — THE DOCTRINE OF THE TRUTH CONTINUED.

Therefore this solitary and supreme Deity, by an exercise of reflection, brought forth the Logos first; not the word in the sense *of being articulated by* voice, but as a ratiocination of the universe, conceived and residing *in the divine mind*. Him alone He produced from existing things; for the Father Himself constituted existence, and the being born from Him was the cause of all things that are produced.[6] The Logos was in *the Father* Himself, bearing the will of His progenitor, and not being unacquainted

---

[1] [The fable of Iapetus cannot be explained away as a corroboration of the biblical narrative. Hor., *Od.*, i. 3, 27.]

[2] [Here the Edinburgh has "nature." The context seems to require the more comprehensive word "Truth."]

[3] The margin of the MS. has the words "Origen and Origen's opinion." This seemed to confirm the criticism which ascribes *The Refutation* to Origen. But even supposing Origen not the author, the copyer of the MS. might have written Origen's name on the margin, as indicating the transcriber's opinion concerning the coincidence of creed between Origen and the author of *The Refutation*. The fact, however, is, that the doctrine of eternal punishment, asserted in the concluding chapter of *The Refutation*, was actually controverted by Origen. See translator's Introductory Notice. [See also Wordsworth (a lucid exposition), p. 20, etc., and *infra*, cap. xxix. note 5.]

[4] ὀροφήν (Scott). The MS. has μορφήν.

[5] Here we have another reference intimately bearing on the authorship of *The Refutation*. What follows corresponds with a fragment having a similar title to that stated above, first published by Le Moyne, and inserted in Fabricius (i. pp. 220–222) as the work of Hippolytus. Photius mentions this work, and gives an extract from it corresponding with what is furnished by Hippolytus. Photius, however, mentions that the book *On the Substance of the Universe* was said to be written by Josephus, but discovers in marginal notes the ascription of it to Caius. But Caius cannot be the writer, since Photius states that the author of *The Labyrinth* affirmed that he had written *On the Substance of the Universe*. Now Hippolytus informs us that he is author of *The Labyrinth*. Hippolytus thus refers to three of his works in *The Refutation*: (1) ετεραι βιβλοι, i.e., on Chronology; (2) *Concerning the Substance of the Universe*; (3) *Little Labyrinth*. Except Hippolytus and Photius refer to different works in speaking of *The Labyrinth*, the foregoing settles the question of the authorship of *The Refutation*. [See the case of Caius stated, Wordsworth, cap. iv. p. 27, etc.]

[6] [Elucidation XVI.]

with the mind of the Father. For simultaneously [1] with His procession from His Progenitor, inasmuch as He is this *Progenitor's* first-born, He has, as a voice in Himself, the ideas conceived in the Father. And so it was, that when the Father ordered the world to come into existence, the Logos one by one completed *each object of creation, thus* pleasing God. And some things which multiply by generation [2] He formed male and female ; but whatsoever beings were *designed* for service and ministration *He made* either male, or not requiring females, or neither male nor female. For even the primary substances of these, which were formed out of nonentities, viz., fire and spirit, water and earth, are neither male nor female ; nor could male or female proceed from any one of these, were it not that God, who is the source of all authority, wished that *the* Logos might render assistance [3] *in accomplishing a production of this kind*. I confess that angels are of fire, and I maintain that female spirits are not present with them. And I am of opinion that sun and moon and stars, in like manner, *are produced* from fire and spirit, and are neither male nor female. And the will of the Creator is, that swimming and winged animals are from water, male and female. For so God, whose will it was, ordered that there should exist a moist substance, endued with productive power. And in like manner *God commanded*, that from earth should arise reptiles and beasts, as well males and females of all sorts of animals ; for so the nature of the things produced admitted. For as many things as He willed, God made from time to time. These things He created through *the* Logos, it not being possible for things to be generated otherwise than as they were produced. But when, according as He willed, He also formed (objects), He called them by names, and thus notified *His creative effort*.[4] And *making* these, He formed the ruler of all, and fashioned him out of all composite substances.[5] *The Creator* did not wish to make him a god, and failed in His aim ; nor an angel, — be not deceived, — but a man. For if He had willed to make thee a god, He could have done so. Thou hast the example of the Logos. His will, however, was, that you should be a man, *and* He has made thee a man. But if thou art desirous of also becoming a god, obey Him that has created thee, and resist not now, in order

that, being found faithful in that which is small, you may be enabled to have entrusted to you also that which is great.[6]

The Logos alone of this *God* is from *God* himself ; wherefore also *the Logos* is God, being *the* substance of God.[7] Now the world was made from nothing ; wherefore *it* is not God ; *as also because* this *world* admits of dissolution whenever the Creator so wishes it. But God, who created *it*, did not, nor does not, make evil. He makes what is glorious and excellent ; for He who makes *it* is good. Now man, that was brought into existence, was a creature endued with a capacity of self-determination,[8] yet not possessing a sovereign intellect,[9] nor holding sway over all things by reflection, and authority, and power, but a slave *to his passions*, and comprising all *sorts of* contrarieties in himself. But man, from the fact of his possessing a capacity of self-determination, brings forth what is evil,[10] that is, accidentally ; which *evil* is not consummated except you actually commit some piece of wickedness. For it is in regard of our desiring anything that is wicked, or our meditating upon it, that what is evil is *so* denominated. Evil had no existence from the beginning, but came into being subsequently.[11] Since man has free will, a law has been defined *for his guidance* by the Deity, not without answering a good purpose. For if man did not possess the power to will and not to will, why should a law be established ? For a law will not be laid down for an animal devoid of reason, but a bridle and a whip ; [12] whereas to man has been given a precept and penalty to perform, or for not carrying into execution what has been enjoined. For man thus constituted has a law been enacted by just men in primitive ages. Nearer our own day was there established a law, full of gravity and justice, by Moses, to whom allusion has been already made, a devout man, and one beloved of God.

Now the Logos of God controls all these ; the first begotten Child of the Father, the voice of the Dawn antecedent to the Morning Star.[13] Afterwards just men were born, friends of God ;

---

[1] This passage is differently rendered, according as we read φωνή with Bunsen, or φωνήν with Dr. Wordsworth. The latter also alters the reading of the MS. (at the end of the next sentence), ἀπετελειτο αρέσκιον νιεῳ into ἀπετελεῖ τὸ ἀρέσκον, "he carried into effect what was pleasing to the Deity."

[2] Dr. Wordsworth suggests for γενέσει, ἐπιγενέσει, i.e., a continuous series of procreation.

[3] See Origen, *in Joann.*, tom. ii. sec. 8.

[4] [Rather, *His will*.]

[5] Compare Origen, *in Joann.*, sec. 2, where we have a similar opinion stated. A certain parallel in this and other portions of Hippolytus' concluding remarks, induces the transcriber, no doubt, to write "Origen's opinion" in the margin.

[6] Matt. xxv. 21, 23 ; Luke xvi. 10, 11, 12. [Also 2 Pet. i. 4, one of the king-texts of the inspired oracles.]

[7] [Nicene doctrine, ruling out all conditions of time from the idea of the generation of the Logos.]

[8] αυτεξούσιος. Hippolytus here follows his master Irenæus (*Hær.*, iv. 9), and in doing so enunciates an opinion, and uses an expression adopted universally by patristic writers, up to the period of St. Augustine. This great philosopher and divine, however, shook the entire fabric of existing theology respecting the will, and started difficulties, speculative ones at least, which admit of no solution short of the annihilation of finite thought and volition. See translator's *Treatise on Metaphysics*, chap. x. [Also compare Irenæus, vol. i. p. 518, and Clement, vol. ii. pp. 319 *passim* to 525; also vol. iii. 301, and vol. iv. Tertull. and Origen. See *Indexes* on *Free-will*.]

[9] Dr. Wordsworth translates the passage thus: "Endued with free will, but not dominant; having reason, but not able to govern," etc.

[10] [One of the most pithy of all statements as to the origin of *subjective* evil, i.e., evil in humanity.]

[11] See Origen, *in Joann.*, tom. ii. sec. 7.

[12] Ps. xxxii. 9.

[13] Ps. cx. 3 ; 2 Pet. i. 18, 19.

and these have been styled prophets,[1] on account of their foreshowing future events. And the word *of prophecy*[2] was committed unto them, not for one age *only;* but also the utterances of events predicted throughout all generations, were vouchsafed in perfect clearness. And this, too, not at the time merely when *seers* furnished a reply to those present;[3] but also events that would happen throughout all ages, have been manifested beforehand; because, in speaking of incidents gone by, *the prophets* brought them back to the recollection of humanity; whereas, in showing forth present occurrences, they endeavoured to persuade men not to be remiss; while, by foretelling future events, they have rendered each one of us terrified on beholding events that had been predicted long before, *and* on expecting likewise those events *predicted as* still future. Such is our faith, O all ye men, — *ours, I say*, who are not persuaded by empty expressions, nor caught away by sudden impulses of *the* heart, nor beguiled by the plausibility of eloquent discourses, yet who do not refuse to obey words that have been uttered by divine power. And these injunctions has God given to the Word. But the Word, by declaring them, promulgated the divine commandments, thereby turning man from disobedience, not bringing him into servitude by force of necessity, but summoning him to liberty through a choice involving spontaneity.

This Logos the Father in the latter *days* sent forth, no longer to speak by a prophet, and not wishing that *the Word*, being obscurely proclaimed, should be made the subject of mere conjecture, but that He should be manifested, so that we could see Him with our own eyes. This *Logos*, I say, the Father sent forth, in order that *the* world, on beholding Him, might reverence Him who was delivering precepts not by *the* person of prophets, nor terrifying the soul by an angel, but who was Himself — He that had spoken — *corporally* present *amongst us*. This *Logos* we know to have received a body from a virgin, *and* to have remodelled the old man[4] by a new creation. *And we believe the Logos* to

have passed through every period in *this* life, in order that He Himself might serve as a law for every age,[5] and that, by being present (amongst) us, He might exhibit His own manhood as an aim for all men. And that by Himself *in person* He might prove that God made nothing evil, and that man possesses the capacity of self-determination, inasmuch as he is able to will and not to will, *and* is endued with power to do both.[6] This *Man* we know to have been made out of the compound *of our humanity*. For if He were not of the same *nature with ourselves*, in vain does He ordain that we should imitate the Teacher. For if that Man happened to be of a different substance *from us*, why does He lay injunctions similar *to those He has received* on myself, who am born weak; and how is this *the act of one that is* good and just? In order, however, that He might not be supposed to be different *from us*, He even underwent toil, and was willing to endure hunger, and did not refuse to feel thirst, and sunk into the quietude of slumber. He did not protest against His Passion, but became obedient unto death, and manifested His resurrection. Now in all these *acts* He offered up, as the first-fruits, His own manhood, in order that thou, when thou art in tribulation, mayest not be disheartened, but, confessing thyself to be a man (of like *nature* with the Redeemer), mayest dwell in expectation of also receiving what *the Father* has granted unto this *Son*.[7]

CHAP. XXX. — THE AUTHOR'S CONCLUDING ADDRESS.

Such is the true doctrine in regard of the divine nature, O ye men, Greeks and Barbarians, Chaldeans and Assyrians, Egyptians and Libyans, Indians and Ethiopians, Celts, and ye Latins, who lead armies, and all ye that inhabit Europe, and Asia, and Libya.[8] And to you I am become an adviser, inasmuch as I am a disciple of *the* benevolent Logos, and *hence* humane, in order that you may hasten and by us may be taught who the true God is, and *what* is His well-ordered creation. Do not devote your attention to the fallacies of artificial discourses, nor the vain promises of plagiarizing heretics,[9] but to the venerable simplicity of unassuming

---

[1] In making the Logos a living principle in the prophets, and as speaking through them to the Church of God in all ages, Hippolytus agrees with Origen. This constitutes another reason for the marginal note "Origen's opinion," already mentioned. (See Origen, Περὶ Ἀρχῶν, i. 1.)

[2] Hippolytus expresses similar opinions respecting the economy of the prophets, in his work, *De Antichristo*, sec. 2.

[3] Hippolytus here compares the ancient prophets with the oracles of the Gentiles. The heathen seers did not give forth their vaticinations spontaneously, but furnished responses to those only who made inquiries after them, says Dr. Wordsworth.

[4] πεφυρακότα. This is the reading adopted by Cruice and Wordsworth. The translator has followed Cruice's rendering, *refinxisse*, while Dr. Wordsworth construes the word "fashioned." The latter is more literal, as φυράω means to knead, though the sense imparted to it by Cruice would seem more coincident with the scriptural account (1 Cor. v. 7; 2 Cor. v. 17; Gal. vi. 15). Bunsen does not alter πεφορηκότα, the reading of the MS., and translates it, "to have put on the old man through a new formation." Sauppe reads πεφυρηκότα. See Hippolytus, *De Antichristo*, sec. 26, *in Danielem* (p. 205, Mai); and Irenæus, v. 6.

[5] [See Irenæus (a very beautiful passage), vol. i. p. 391.]

[6] [See vol. iv. pp. 255 and 383.]

[7] This is the reading adopted by Cruice and Bunsen. Dr. Wordsworth translates the passage thus: "acknowledging thyself a man of like nature with Christ, and thou also waiting for the appearance of what thou gavest Him." The source of consolation to man which Hippolytus, according to Dr. Wordsworth, is here anxious to indicate, is the glorification of human nature in the person of the Lord Jesus Christ. Dr. Wordsworth therefore objects to Bunsen's rendering, as it gives to the passage a meaning different from this.

[8] [The translator's excessive interpolations sometimes needlessly dilute the terse characteristics of the author. Thus, with confusing brackets, the Edinburgh reads: "who so often lead your armies to victory." This is not Hippolytus, and, in such instances, I feel bound to reduce a plethoric text.]

[9] [Here the practical idea of the *Philosophumena* comes out; and compare vol. iv. pp. 469 and 570.]

truth. And by means of this knowledge you shall escape the approaching threat of *the* fire of judgment, and the rayless scenery of gloomy Tartarus,[1] where never shines a beam from the irradiating voice of the Word !

You shall escape the boiling flood of hell's[2] eternal lake of fire, and the eye ever fixed in menacing glare of *fallen* angels chained in Tartarus as punishment for their sins ; *and you shall escape* the worm that ceaselessly coils for food around the body whose scum[3] has bred *it*. Now such (torments) as these shalt thou avoid by being instructed in a knowledge of the true God. And thou shalt possess an immortal body, even one placed beyond the possibility of corruption, just like the soul. And thou shalt receive the kingdom of heaven, thou who, whilst thou didst sojourn in *this* life, didst know the Celestial King. And thou shalt be a companion of the Deity, and a co-heir with Christ, no longer enslaved by lusts or passions, and *never again* wasted by disease. For thou hast become God :[4] for whatever sufferings thou didst undergo while being a man, these He gave to thee, because thou wast of mortal mould, but whatever it is

consistent with God *to impart*, these God has promised to bestow upon thee, because thou hast been deified, and begotten unto immortality.[5] This constitutes *the import of the proverb,* " Know thyself ; " i.e., discover God *within thyself, for* He has formed thee *after His own image.* For with the knowledge of self is conjoined the being an object of God's knowledge, for thou art called by *the Deity* Himself. Be not therefore inflamed, O ye men, with enmity one towards another, nor hesitate to retrace[6] with all speed your steps. For Christ is the God above all, and He has arranged to wash away sin from human beings,[7] rendering regenerate the old man. And God called man His likeness from the beginning, and has evinced in a figure His love towards thee. And provided thou obeyest His solemn injunctions, and becomest a faithful follower of Him who is good, thou shalt resemble Him, inasmuch as thou shalt have honour conferred upon thee by Him. For the Deity, (by condescension,) does not diminish aught of the dignity of His divine[8] perfection ; having made thee even God unto His glory ![9]

---

[1] Dr. Wordsworth justifies Hippolytus' use of the pagan word " Tartarus," by citing the passage (2 Pet ii. 4), " For if God spared not the angels that sinned, but cast them down to hell, and delivered them into chains of darkness (σειραις ζόφου ταρταρώσας), to be reserved unto judgment," etc. [Elucidation XVII. and vol. iv. 140.]

[2] Schneidewin suggests a comparison of this passage with Hippolytus' fragment, *Against Plato, concerning the Cause of the Universe* (p. 220, ed. Fabricii; p. 68, ed. de Lagarde).

[3] The different renderings of this passage, according to different readings, are as follow: " And the worm the scum of the body, turning to the Body that foamed it forth as to that which nourisheth it " (Wordsworth). " The worm which winds itself without rest round the mouldering body, to feed upon it " (Bunsen and Scott). " The worm wriggling as over the filth of the (putrescent) flesh towards the exhaling body " (Roeper). " The worm turning itself towards the substance of the body, towards, (I say,) the exhalations of the decaying frame, as to food " (Schneidewin). The words chiefly altered are: ἀπουσίαν, into (1) ἐπ' οὐσίαν, (2) ἐπ' ἀλουσίᾳ (3) ἀπαύστως; and ἐπιστρεφόμενον into (1) ἐπιστρέφον, (2) ἐπὶ τροφήν.

[4] [This startling expression is justified by such texts as 2 Pet. i. 4 compared with John xvii. 22, 23, and Rev. iii. 21. Thus, Christ overrules the Tempter (Gen. iii. 5), and gives more than was offered by the " Father of Lies."]

[5] [Compare John x. 34 with Rev. v. 10. Kings of the earth may be called " gods," in a sense; *ergo*, etc.]

[6] Bunsen translates thus: " Doubt not that you will exist again," —a rendering which Dr. Wordsworth controverts in favour of the one adopted above.

[7] Bunsen translates thus: " For Christ is He whom the God of all has ordered to wash away the sins," etc. Dr. Wordsworth severely censures this rendering in a lengthened note.

[8] πτωχεύει. Bunsen translates, " for God acts the beggar towards thee," which is literal, though rather unintelligible. Dr. Wordsworth renders the word thus: " God has a longing for thee."

[9] Hippolytus, by his argument, recognises the duty not merely of overthrowing error but substantiating truth, or in other words, the negative and positive aspect of theology. His brief statement (chap. xxviii.-xxx.) in the latter department, along with being eminently reflective, constitutes a noble specimen of patristic eloquence. [This is most just; and it must be observed, that having summed up his argument against the heresies derived from carnal and inferior sources, and shown the primal truth, he advances (in chap. xxviii.) to the Nicene position, and proves himself one of the witnesses on whose traditive testimony that sublime formulary was given to the whole Church as the κτῆμα ἐς ἀεὶ of Christendom, — a formal countersign of apostolic doctrine.]

ELUCIDATIONS.

I.

(Who first propounded these heresies, p. 11.)

HIPPOLYTUS seems to me to have felt the perils to the pure Gospel of many admissions made by Clement and other Alexandrian doctors as to the merits of some of the philosophers of the Gentiles. Very gently, but with prescient genius, he adopts this plan of tracing the origin and all the force of heresies to " philosophy falsely so called." The existence of this " cloud of locusts " is (1) evidence of the antagonism of Satan ; (2) of the prophetic spirit of the apostles ; (3) of the tremendous ferment produced by the Gospel leaven as soon as it was hid in the " three measures of meal " by " the Elect Lady," the *Ecclesia Dei ;* (4) of the fidelity of the witnesses, — that grand, heroic glory of the Ante-Nicene Fathers, — who never suffered these heresies to be mistaken for the faith, or to corrupt the Scriptures; and (5) finally of the power of the Holy Spirit, who gave them victory over errors, and enabled them to define truth in all the crystalline beauty of that "Mountain of Light," that true Koh-i-noor, the Nicene Symbol. Thus, also, Christ's promises were fulfilled.

II.

(Caulacau, p. 52.)

See Irenæus, p. 350, vol. i., this series, where I have explained this jargon of heresy. But I think it worth while to make use here of two notes on the subject, which I made in 1845,[1] with little foresight of these tasks in 1885.

Fleury (tom. ii.) makes this statement: "Les Nicolaites donnaient une infinité de noms barbares aux princes et aux puissances qu'ils mettaient en chaque ciel. Ils en nommaient un *caulaucauch*, abusant d'un passage d'Isaie, où se lisent ces mots hebreux: *cau-la-cau, cau-la-cau*, pour representer l'insolence avec laquelle les impies se moquaient du prophète, en répétant plusieurs fois quelques-unes de ses paroles." Compare Guerricus, thus: "Vox illa tædii et desperationis, quæ apud Isaiam (xxviii. 13) legitur, quia, viz., moram faciente Domino, frequentibus nuntiis ejus increduli et illusores insultare videntur: *manda remanda*," etc. See the spurious *Bernardina*, "de Adventu Dom., serm. i.," S. Bernard., opp. Paris (ed. Mabillon), vol. ii. p. 1799.

III.

(The Phrygians call Papa, p. 54.)

Hippolytus had little idea, when he wrote this, what the word *Papa* was destined to signify in mediæval Rome. The *Abba* of Holy Writ has its equivalent in many Oriental languages, as well as in the Greek and Latin, through which it has passed into all the dialects of Europe. It was originally given to all *presbyters*, as implied in their name of *elders*, and was a title of humility when it became peculiar to the bishops, as (1 Pet. v. 3) *non Domini sed patres*. St. Paul (1 Cor. iv. 15) shows that "in Christ" — that is, under Him — we may have such "fathers;" and thus, while he indicates the true sense of the precept, he leads us to recognise a *prophetic force* and admonition in our Saviour's words (Matt. xxiii.), "Call no man your father upon the earth." Thus interpreted, these words seem to be a warning against the sense to which this name, *Papa*, became, long afterwards, restricted, in Western Europe: *Notre St. Père, le Pape*, as they say in France. This was done by the decree of the ambitious Hildebrand, Gregory VII. (who died A.D. 1085), when, in a synod held at Rome, he defined that "the title *Pope* should be peculiar to one only in the Christian world." The Easterns, of course, never paid any respect to this novelty and dictation, and to this day their patriarchs are popes; and not only so, for the parish priests of the Greek churches are called by the same name. I was once cordially invited to take a repast "with the *pope*," on visiting a Greek church on the shores of the Adriatic. It is said, however, that a distinction is made between the words πάπας and παπᾶς; the latter being peculiar to inferiors, according to the refinements of Goar, a Western critic. *Valeat quantum*. But I must here note, that as "words are things," and as infinite damage has been done to history and to Christian truth by tolerating this empiricism of Rome, I have restored scientific accuracy, in this series, whenever reference is made to the primitive bishops of Rome, who were no more "Popes" than Cincinnatus was an emperor. It is time that theological science should accept, like other sciences, the language of truth and the terminology of demonstrated fact. The early bishops of Rome were geographically important, and were honoured as sitting in the only apostolic see of

---

[1] I venture to state this to encourage young students to keep pen in hand in all their researches, and always to make notes.

the West ; but they were almost inconsiderable in the structural work of the ante-Nicene ages, and have left no appreciable impress on its theology. After the Council of Nice they were recognised as patriarchs, though equals among brethren, and nothing more. The ambition of Boniface III. led him to name himself "universal bishop." This was at first a mere name " of intolerable pride," as his predecessor Gregory had called it , but Nicholas I. (A.D. 858) tried to make it real, and, by means of the false decretals, created himself the first " Pope " in the modern sense, imposing his despotism on the West, and identifying it with the polity of Western churches, which alone submitted to it. Thus, it was never Catholic, and came into existence only by nullifying the Nicene Constitutions, and breaking away from Catholic communion with the parent churches of the East. Compare Casaubon (*Exercit.*, xiv. p. 280, etc.) in his comments on Baronius. I have thus stated with scientific precision what all candid critics and historians, even the Gallicans included, enable us to prove. Why, then, keep up the language of fiction and imposture,[1] so confusing to young students? I believe the youthful Oxonians whom our modern Tertullian carried with him into the papal schism, could never have been made dupes but for the persistent empiricism of orthodox writers who practically adopt in words what they refute in argument, calling all bishops of Rome " Popes," and even including St. Peter's blessed name in this fallacious designation.[2] In this series I adhere to the logic of facts, calling (1) all the bishops of Rome from Linus to Sylvester simply bishops ; and (2) all their successors to Nicholas I. " patriarchs " under the Nicene Constitutions, which they *professed* to honour, though, after Gregory the Great, they were ever vying with Constantinople to make themselves greater. (3) Nicholas, who trampled on the Nicene Constitutions, and made the false decretals the canon law of the Western churches, was therefore the first " Pope" who answers to the Tridentine definitions. Even these, however, were never able to make dogmatic[3] the claim of " supremacy," which was first done by Pius IX. in our days. A canonical *Primacy* is one thing : a self-asserted *Supremacy* is quite another, as the French doctors have abundantly demonstrated.

IV.

(Contemporaneous heresy, p. 125.)

Here begins that " duplicating of our knowledge " of primitive Rome of which Bunsen speaks so justly. A thorough mastery of this book will prepare us to understand the great Cyprian in all his relations with the Roman Province, and not less to comprehend the affairs of Novatian.

Bunsen, with all respect, does not comprehend the primitive system, and *reads it backward*, from the modern system, which travesties antiquity even in its *apparent* conformities. These conformities are only the borrowing of old names for new contrivances. Thus, he reads the cardinals of the eleventh century into the simple presbytery of comprovincial bishops of the third century,[4] just as he elsewhere lugs in the *Ave Maria* of modern Italy to expound the *Evening Hymn to the Trinity*.[5] In a professed Romanist, like De Maistre, this would be resented as jugglery. But let us come to facts. Bunsen's preliminary remarks[6] are excellent. But when he comes to note an " exceptional system " in the Roman " presbytery," he certainly confuses all things. Let us recur to Tertullian.[7] See how much was already established in his day, which the

---

[1] Pompey and others were called *imperatores* before the Cæsars , but who includes them with the Roman emperors?

[2] How St. Peter would regard it, see 1 Pet. v. 1–3. I am sorry to find Dr. Schaff, in his useful compilation, *History of the Christian Church*, vol. ii. p 166, dropping into the old ruts of fable, after sufficiently proving just before, what I have maintained. He speaks of " the insignificance of *the first Popes*," — meaning the early Bishops of Rome, men who minded their own business, but could not have been " insignificant" had they even imagined themselves " Popes."

[3] See Bossuet, *passim*, and all the Gallican doctors down to our own times. In England the " supremacy " was never acknowledged, nor in France, until now.

[4] See his Hippol., vol. i. pp. 209, 311.

[5] See vol. ii. p. 298, this series.

[6] p. 207.

[7] Vol. iv p 114, Elucidation II., this series.

Council of Nicæa recognised a century later as (τὰ ἀρχαῖα ἔθη) old primitive institutions. In all things the Greek churches were the exemplar and the model for other churches to follow. "Throughout *the provinces of Greece,*" he says, "there are held, in definite localities, those councils," etc. "If we also, in *our* diverse *provinces,* observe," etc. Now, these councils, or "meetings," in spite of the emperors or the senate who issued mandates against them, as appears from the same passage, were, in the Roman Province, made up of the comprovincial bishops: and their gatherings seem to have been called "the Roman presbytery;" for, as is evident, the bishops and elders were alike called "presbyters," the word being as common to both orders as the word *pastors* or *clergymen* in our days. According to the thirty-fourth of the "Canons Apostolical," as Bunsen remarks, "the bishops of the suburban towns, including Portus, also formed at that time an integral part of the Roman presbytery." This word *also* refers to all the presbyters of the diocese of Rome itself; and I doubt not originally the laity had their place, as they did in Carthage: "the apostles, elders, and brethren" being the formula of Scripture; or, "with the whole Church," which includes them, — *omni plebe adstante.*[1] Now, all this accounts, as Bunsen justly observes, for the fact that one of the "presbytery" should be thus repeatedly called presbyter and "at the same time have the charge of the church at Portus, for which (office) there was no other title than the old one of *bishop;* for such was the title of every man who presided *over the congregation* in any city, — at Ostia, at Tusculum, or in the other suburban cities.

Now let us turn to the thirty-fourth[2] "Apostolical Canon" (so called), and note as follows: "It is necessary that the bishops of every nation should know who is chief among them, and should recognise him as their head by doing nothing of great moment without his consent; and that each of them should do such things only as pertain to his own parish and *the districts under him. And neither let him do any thing* without the consent of all, for thus shall there be unity of heart, and thus shall God be glorified through our Lord Jesus Christ." I do not pause to expound this word *parish,* for I am elucidating Hippolytus by Bunsen's aid, and do not intend to interpolate my own theory of the primitive episcopate.

Let the "Apostolical Constitutions" go for what they are worth:[3] I refer to them only under lead of Dr. Bunsen. But now turn to the Nicene Council (Canon VI.) as follows: "*Let the ancient customs prevail* in Egypt, Libya, and Pentapolis, so that the Bishop of Alexandria have jurisdiction in all these provinces, *since the like is customary in Rome also.* Likewise in Antioch and *the other provinces,* let the churches retain their privileges." Here the Province of Rome is recognised as an *ancient* institution, while its jurisdiction and privileges are equalized with those of other churches. Now, Rufinus, interpreting this canon, says it means, "the ancient custom of Alexandria and Rome shall still be observed; that the one shall have the care or government of the Egyptian, and the other that of the *suburbicary churches.*" Bunsen refers us to Bingham, and from him we learn that *the suburbicary region,* as known to the Roman magistrates, included only "a hundred miles about Rome."[4] This seems to have been canonically extended even to Sicily on the south, but certainly not to Milan on the north. Suffice it, Hippolytus was one of those *suburbicarian bishops* who sat in the Provincial Council of Rome; without consent of which the Bishop of Rome could not, canonically, do anything of importance, as the canon above cited ordains. Such are the facts necessary to a comprehension of conflicts excited by "the contemporaneous heresy," here noted.

V.

(Affairs of the Church, p. 125.)

"Zephyrinus *imagines* that he administers the affairs of the Church — an uninformed and shamefully corrupt man." This word *imagines* is common with Hippolytus in like cases, and

---

[1] Even Quinet notes this. See his *Ultramontanism,* p. 40, ed. 1845.
[2] Bunsen gives it as the thirty-fifth, vol. i. p. 311.
[3] Of which we shall learn in vol. viii., this series.
[4] See Bingham, book ix. cap. i. sec. 9.

Dr. Wordsworth gives an ingenious explanation of this usage. But it seems to me to be based upon the relations of Hippolytus as one of the synod or "presbytery," without consent of which the bishop could do nothing important. Zephyrinus, on the contrary, *imagined* himself competent to decide as to the orthodoxy of a tenet or of a teacher, without his comprovincials. This, too, relieves our author from the charge of *egotism* when he exults in the defeat of such a bishop.[1] He says, it is true, "Callistus threw off Sabellius through fear of *me*," and we may readily believe that; but he certainly means to give honour to others in the Province when he says, "*We* resisted Zephyrinus and Callistus;" "*We* nearly converted Sabellius;" "All were carried away by the hypocrisy of Callistus, except *ourselves*." This man cried out to his episcopal brethren, "*Ye* are Ditheists," apparently in open council. His council prevailed over him by the wise leadership of Hippolytus, however; and he says of the two guilty bishops, "Never, at any time, *have we been guilty of collusion with them*." They only *imagined*, therefore, that they were managing the "affairs of the Church." The fidelity of their comprovincials preserved the faith of the Apostles in apostolic Rome.

VI.

(We offered them opposition, p. 125.)

Here we see that Hippolytus had no idea of the sense some put upon the *convenire* of his master Irenæus.[2] It was not "necessary" for them to *conform* their doctrines to that of the *Bishop* of Rome, evidently; nor to "the Church of Rome" as represented by him. To the church which presided over a province, indeed, recourse was to be had by all belonging to that province; but it is our author's grateful testimony, that to the *council of comprovincials*, and not to any one bishop therein, Rome owed its own adhesion to orthodoxy at this crisis.

All this illustrates the position of Tertullian, who never thinks of ascribing to Rome any other jurisdiction than that belonging to other provinces. As seats of testimony, the apostolic sees, indeed, are *all to be honoured*. "In Greece, go to Corinth; in Asia Minor, to Ephesus; if you are adjacent to Italy, you have Rome; whence also (an apostolic) authority is at hand for us in Africa." Such is his view of "contemporaneous affairs."

VII.

(Heraclitus the Obscure, p. 126.)

"Well might he weep," says Tayler Lewis, "as Lucian represents him, over his overflowing universe of perishing phenomena, where *nothing stood;* . . . nothing was fixed, but, as in a mixture, all things were confounded." He was "the weeping philosopher."

Here let me add Henry Nelson Coleridge's remarks on the Greek seed-plot of those philosophies which were begotten of the Egyptian mysteries, and which our author regards as, in turn, engendering "all heresies," when once their leaders felt, like Simon Magus, a power in the Gospel of which they were jealous, and of which they wished to make use without submitting to its yoke. "Bishop Warburton," says Henry Nelson Coleridge, "discovered, perhaps, more ingenuity than sound judgment in his views of the nature of the Greek mysteries; entertaining a general opinion that their ultimate object was to teach the initiated a pure theism, and to inculcate the certainty and the importance of a future state of rewards and punishments. I am led by the arguments of Villoison and Ste. Croix to doubt the accuracy of this." In short, he supposes a "pure pantheism," or *Spinosism*, the substance of their teaching.[3]

---

[1] Wordsworth, chap. viii. p. 93.   [2] See vol. i. pp. 415, 460, this series.   [3] *Introduction to Greek Classics*, p. 228.

VIII.

(Imagine themselves to be disciples of Christ, p. 126.)

This and the foregoing chapter offer us a most overwhelming testimony to the independence of councils. In the late " Council of Sacristans " at the Vatican, where truth perished, Pius IX. refused to all the bishops of what he accounted " the Catholic universe " what the seven suburbicarian bishops were able to enforce as a right, in the primitive age, against two successive Bishops of Rome, who were patrons of heresy. These heretical prelates persisted ; but the Province remained in communion with the other apostolic provinces, while rejecting all communion with them. All this will help us in studying Cyprian's treatise *On Unity*, and it justifies his own conduct.

IX.

(The episcopal throne, p. 128.)

The simple primitive *cathedra*,[1] of which we may learn something from the statue of Hippolytus, was, no doubt, " a throne " in the eyes of an ambitious man. Callistus is here charged, by one who knew him and his history, with obtaining this position by knavish words and practices. The question may well arise, in our Christian love for antiquity, How could such things be, even in the age of martyrdoms? Let us recollect, that under the good Bishop Pius, when his brother wrote the *Hermas*, the peril of wealth and love of money began to be imminent at Rome. Tertullian testifies to the lax discipline of that see when he was there. Minucius Felix lets us into the impressions made by the Roman Christians upon surrounding heathen : they were a set of conies burrowing in the earth ; a " light-shunning people," lurking in the catacombs. And yet, while this fact shows plainly that good men were not ambitious to come forth from these places of exile and suffering, and expose themselves needlessly to death, it leads us to comprehend how ambitious men, *studiosi novarum rerum*, could remain above ground, conforming very little to the discipline of Christ, making friends with the world, and yet using their nominal religion on the principle that " gain is godliness." There were some wealthy Christians ; there were others, like Marcia in the palace, sufficiently awakened to perceive their own wickedness, and anxious to do favours to the persecuted flock, by way, perhaps, of compounding for sins not renounced. And when we come to the Epistles of Cyprian,[2] we shall see what opportunities were given to desperate men to make themselves a sort of brokers to the Christian community ; for selfish ends helping them in times of peril, and rendering themselves, to the less conscientious, a medium for keeping on good terms with the magistrates. Such a character was Callistus, one of " the grievous wolves " foreseen by St. Paul when he exhorted his brethren night and day, with tears, to beware of them. How he made himself Bishop of Rome, the holy Hippolytus sufficiently explains.

X.

(Unskilled in ecclesiastical definitions, p. 128.)

It has been sufficiently demonstrated by the learned Döllinger, than whom a more competent and qualified witness could not be named, that the late pontiff, Pius IX., was in this respect, as a bishop, very much like Callistus. Moreover, his chief adviser and prime minister, Antonelli, was notoriously Callistus over again ; standing towards him in the same relations which Callistus bore to Zephyrinus. Yet, by the bull *Ineffabilis*, that pontiff has retrospectively clothed the definitions of Zephyrinus and Callistus with *infallibility ;* thus making himself also a partaker in their heresies, and exposing himself to the *anathemas* with which the Catholic councils overwhelmed his predecessor Honorius and others. That at such a crisis the testimony of Hippolytus

---

[1] See vol. ii. p. 12, also iv. 210.   [2] See *Treatise on the Lapsed*, infra.

should come to light, and supply a *reductio ad absurdum* to the late papal definitions, may well excite such a recognition of divine providence as Dr. Bunsen repeatedly suggests.

XI.

(All consented — we did not, p. 128.)

The Edinburgh editor supposes that the use of the plural *we*, in this place, is the official plural of a bishop. It has been already explained, however, that he is speaking of the provincial bishops with whom he withstood Callistus when the *plebs* were carried away by his hypocrisy. In England, bishops in certain cases, are a "corporation sole;" and, as such, the plural is legal phraseology. All bishops, however, use the plural in certain documents, as identifying themselves with the universal episcopate, on the Cyprianic principle — *Episcopatus unus est*, etc.

In Acts v. 13 is a passage which may be somewhat explained, perhaps, by this : "*All* consented . . . *we* did not." The *plebs* joined themselves to the apostles ; "but *of the rest* durst no man join himself to them : howbeit, the *plebs* magnified them, and believers were added," etc. "The rest" (τῶν δὲ λοιπῶν) here means the priests, the Pharisees, and Sadducees, the classes who were not the *plebs*, as appears by what immediately follows.[1]

XII.

(Our condemnatory sentence, p. 131.)

Again : Hippolytus refers to the action of the *suburbicarian* bishops in provincial council. And here is the place to express dissatisfaction with the apologetic tone of some writers, who seem to think Hippolytus too severe, etc. As if, in dealing with such "wolves in sheep's clothing," this faithful leader could show himself a true shepherd without emphasis and words of abhorrence. Hippolytus has left to the Church the impress of his character[2] as "superlatively sweet and amiable." Such was St. John, the beloved disciple ; but he was not less a "son of thunder." Our Divine Master was "the Lamb," and "the Lion ;" the author of the *Beatitudes*, and the author of those terrific *woes;* the "meek and gentle friend of publicans and sinners," and the "lash of small cords" upon the backs of those who made His Father's house a "den of thieves." Such was Chrysostom, such was Athanasius, such was St. Paul, and such have ever been the noblest of mankind ; tender and considerate, gentle and full of compassion ; but not less resolute, in the *crises* of history, in withstanding iniquity in the persons of arch-enemies of truth, and setting the brand upon their foreheads. Good men, who hate strife, and love study and quiet, and to be friendly with others ; men who never permit themselves to indulge a personal enmity, or to resent a personal affront ; men who forgive injuries to the last farthing when they only are concerned, — may yet crucify their natures in withstanding evil when they are protecting Christ's flock, or fulfilling the command to "contend earnestly for the faith once delivered to the saints." What the Christian Church owes to the loving spirit of Hippolytus in the awful emergencies of his times, protecting the poor sheep, and grappling with wolves for their sake, the Last Day will fully declare. But let us who know nothing of such warfare concede nothing, in judging of his spirit, to the spirit of our unbelieving age, which has no censures except for the defenders of truth : —

> "Eternal smiles its emptiness betray,
> As shallow streams run dimpling all the way."

Bon Dieu, bon diable, as the French say, is the creed of the times. Every one who insults the faith of Christians, who betrays truths he was sworn to defend, who washes his hands but

---

[1] Ver. 17.　　　　　[2] See p. v. *supra*.

then gives Christ over to be crucified, must be treated with especial favour. Christ is good : so is Pilate ; and Judas must not be censured. My soul be with Hippolytus when the great Judge holds his assize. His eulogy is in the psalm : [1] "Then stood up Phinehas, and executed judgment : and *so* the plague was stayed. And that was counted unto him for righteousness unto all generations, for evermore."

XIII.

(As if he had not sinned, p. 131.)

There is an ambiguity in the facts as given in the Edinburgh edition, of which it is hard to relieve the text. The word καθίστασθαι is rendered *to retain* (their places) in the first instance, as if the case were all one with the second instance, where μένειν is justly rendered *to continue*. The second case seems, then, to cover all the ground. What need to speak of men "twice or thrice married," if a man *once* married, after ordination is not to be retained? The word *retained* is questionable in the first instance ; and I have adopted Wordsworth's reading, *to be enrolled*, which is doubtless the sense.

This statement of our author lends apparent countenance to the antiquity of the "Apostolic Constitutions," so called. Perhaps Hippolytus really supposed them to be apostolic. By Canon XVII. of that collection, a man twice married, after baptism cannot be "on the sacerdotal list at all." By Canon XXVI., an unmarried person once admitted to the clergy cannot be permitted to marry. These are the two cases referred to by our author. In the Greek churches this rule holds to this day ; and the Council of Nice refused to prohibit the married clergy to live in that holy estate, while allowing the *traditional discipline* which Hippolytus had in view in speaking of a violation of the twenty-sixth *traditional* canon as a sin. As Bingham has remarked, however, canons of discipline may be relaxed when not resting on fundamental and scriptural laws.

XIV.

(Attempt to call themselves a Catholic Church, p. 131)

The *Callistians*, it seems, became a heretical sect, and yet presumed to call themselves a "Catholic Church." Yet this sect, while Callistus lived, was in full communion with the Bishop of Rome. Such communion, then, was no test of Catholicity. Observe the enormous crimes of which this *lawless one* was guilty ; he seems to antedate the age of Theodora's popes and Marozia's, and what Hippolytus would have said of them is not doubtful. It is remarkable that he employed St. Paul's expression, however, ὁ ἄνομος,[2] "that wicked" or that "lawless one," seeing, in such a bishop, what St. Gregory did in another, — "a forerunner of the Antichrist."

XV.

(Callistians, p. 131.)

Bunsen remarks that Theodoret speaks of this sect [3] under the head of the "Noetians." Wordsworth quotes as follows : "Callistus *took the lead* in propagating this heresy after Noetus, and *devised certain additions* to the impiety of the doctrine." In other words, he was not merely a heretic, but himself a *heresiarch*. He gives the whole passage textually,[4] and institutes interesting parallelisms between the *Philosophumena* and Theodoret, who used our author, and boldly borrowed from him.

---

[1] Ps. cvi. 30-31.
[2] 2 Thess. ii. 8.
[3] Bunsen, p. 134; Theodor., tom. iv. pt. i. p. 343, ed. Hal. 1772.
[4] *St. Hippol.*, p 315.

XVI.

(The cause of all things, p. 150.)

When one looks at the infinite variety of opinions, phrases, ideas, and the like, with which the heresies of three centuries threatened to obscure, defile, and destroy the revelations of Holy Scripture, who can but wonder at the miracle of orthodoxy? Note with what fidelity the good fight of faith was maintained, the *depositum* preserved, and the Gospel epitomized at last in the Nicæno-Constantinopolitan definitions, which Professor Shedd, as I have previously noted, declares to be the accepted confession of all the reformed, reputed orthodox, as well as of Greeks and Latins. Let us not be surprised, that, during these conflicts, truth on such mysterious subjects was reflected from good men's minds with slight variations of expression. Rather behold the *miracle* of their essential agreement, and of their entire harmony in the *Great Symbol*, universally accepted as the testimony of the ante-Nicene witnesses. The Word was Himself the cause of all created things; Himself increate; His eternal generation implied in the eternity of His existence and His distinct personality.

XVII.

(Tartarus, p. 153.)

I am a little surprised at the innocent statement of the learned translator, that " Dr. Wordsworth justifies Hippolytus' use of this word." It must have occurred to every student of the Greek Testament that *St. Peter* justifies this use in the passage quoted by Wordsworth, which one would think must be self-suggested to any theologian reading our author's text. In short, Hippolytus *quotes* the second Epistle of St. Peter [1] (ii. 4) when he uses this otherwise startling word. Josephus also employs it; [2] it was familiar to the Jews, and the apostle had no scruple in adopting a word which proves the Gentile world acquainted with a Gehenna as well as a Sheol.

XVIII.

(For Christ is the God, p. 153.)

Dr. Wordsworth justly censures Bunsen for his rendering of this passage, [3] also for manufacturing for Hippolytus a "Confession of Faith" out of his tenth book. [4] I must refer the student to that all-important chapter in Dr. Wordsworth's work (cap. xi.) on the "Development of Christian Doctrine." It is masterly, as against Dr. Newman, as well; and the respectful justice which he renders at the same time to Dr. Bunsen is worthy of all admiration. Let it be noted, that, while one must be surprised by the ready command of literary and theological materials which the learned doctor and chevalier brings into instantaneous use for his work, it is hardly less surprising, in spite of all that, that he was willing to throw off his theories and strictures, without any delay, during the confusions of that memorable year 1851, when I had the honour of meeting him among London notabilities. He says to his " dearest friend, Archdeacon Hare, . . . Dr. Tregelles informed me *last week* of the appearance of the work (of Hippolytus). . . . I procured a copy in consequence, and perused it *as soon as I could;* and I have already arrived at conclusions which seem to me so evident that I feel no hesitation in expressing them to you at

---

[1] ταρταρώσας, 2 Pet. ii. 4. A sufficient answer to Dr. Bunsen, vol. iv. p. 33, who says this Epistle was not known to the primitive Church.

[2] See *Speaker's Comm., ad loc.*

[3] *St. Hippol.*, p. 301, with original text.

[4] Vol. i. p. 141, etc.

once." These conclusions were creditable to his *acumen* and learning in general; eminently so. But the theories he had so hastily conceived, in other particulars, crop out in so many crudities of theological caprice, that nobody should try to study his theoretical opinions without the aid of that calm reviewal they have received from Dr. Wordsworth's ripe and sober scholarship and well-balanced intellect.

GENERAL NOTE.

I avail myself of a little spare space to add, from Michelet's friend, E. Quinet,[1] the passage to which I have made a reference on p. 156. Let me say, however, that Quinet and Michelet are specimens of that intellectual revolt against Roman dogma which is all but universal in Europe in our day, and of which the history of M. Renan is a melancholy exposition. To Quinet, with all his faults, belongs the credit of having more thoroughly understood than any theological writer the absolute revolution created by the Council of Trent; and he justly remarks that the Jesuits showed their address " in making this revolution, *without anywhere speaking of it.*" Hence a dull world has not observed it. Contrasting this pseudo-council with the free councils of antiquity, M. Quinet says : " The Council of Trent has not its roots in all nations ; it does not assemble about it the representatives of all nations . . . *omni plebe adstante,* according to the ancient formula. . . . The East and the North are, almost equally, wanting ; and *this is why the king of France refused it the title of a council.*" He quotes noble passages from Bossuet.[2]

---

[1] A translation of Quinet, on *Ultramontanism*, appeared in London in a semi-infidel series, 1845.   [2] See pp. 40, 47.

THE EXTANT WORKS AND FRAGMENTS

OF

HIPPOLYTUS.

[TRANSLATED BY THE REV. S. D. F. SALMOND.]

PART I.—EXEGETICAL.

FRAGMENTS FROM COMMENTARIES ON VARIOUS BOOKS OF SCRIPTURE.

ON THE HEXAËMERON,[1] OR SIX DAYS' WORK.

Now these things we are under the necessity of setting forth at length, in order to disprove the supposition of others. For some choose to maintain that paradise is in heaven, and forms no part of the system of creation. But since we see with our eyes the rivers that go forth from it, which are open, indeed, even in our day, to the inspection of any who choose, let every one conclude from this that it did not belong to heaven, but was in reality planted in the created system. And, in truth, it is a locality in the east, and a place select.

ON GENESIS.[2]

GEN. I. 5. And it was evening, and it was morning, one day.

HIPPOLYTUS. He did not say[3] "night and day," but "one day," with reference to the name of the light. He did not say the "first day;" for if he had said the "first" day, he would also have had to say that the "second" day was made. But it was right to speak not of the "first day," but of "one day," in order that by saying "one," he might show that it returns on its orbit, and, while it remains one, makes up the week.

GEN. I. 6. And God said, Let there be a firmament in the midst of the water.

HIPP. On the first day God made what He made out of nothing. But on the other days He did not make out of nothing, but out of what He had made on the first day, by moulding it according to His pleasure.

GEN. I. 6, 7. And let it divide between water and water: and it was so. And God made the firmament; and God divided between the water which was under the firmament, and the water above the firmament: and it was so.

HIPP. As the excessive volume of water bore along over the face of the earth, the earth was by reason thereof "invisible" and "formless." When the Lord of all designed to make the invisible visible, He fixed then a third part of the waters in the midst; and another third part He set by itself on high, raising it together with the firmament by His own power; and the remaining third He left beneath, for the use and benefit of men. Now at[4] this point we have an asterisk. The words are found in the Hebrew, but do not occur in the Septuagint.

GEN. III. 8. And they heard the voice of the Lord God walking in the garden at even.

HIPP. Rather they discerned the approach of the Lord by a certain breeze. As soon, therefore, as they had sinned, God appeared to them, producing consciousness of their sin, and calling them to repentance.

GEN. XLIX. 3. Reuben, my first-born, thou art my strength, and the first of my children; hard to bear with, and hard and self-willed: thou hast waxed wanton as water; boil not over.[5]

---

[1] In John Damasc., *Sacr. Parall.*, *Works*, ii. p. 787. That Hippolytus wrote on the *Hexaëmeron* is noticed by Eusebius, *Hist. Eccl.*, vi. 22, and by Jerome, Syncellus, Honorius, etc.

[2] These fragments are excerpts from a *Commentary on Genesis*, compiled from eighty-eight fathers, which is extant in manuscript in the Vienna Library. They are found also in a *Catena* on Matthew, issued at Leipsic in 1772.

[3] i.e., νυχθήμερον.

[4] This must refer, I suppose, to the words, "And it was so."

[5] μὴ ἐκζέσῃς.

AQUILA. Reuben, my first-born, thou art my strength, and the sum of my sorrow: excelling in dignity and excelling in might: thou hast been insensate as water; excel not.[1]

SYMMACHUS. Reuben, my first-born, and beginning of my [2] pain: above measure grasping, and above measure hot as water, thou shalt not more excel.[3]

HIPP. For there was a great display of strength made by God in behalf of His first-born people from Egypt. For in very many ways was the land of the Egyptians chastised. That first people of the circumcision is meant by "my strength, and the first of my children:" even as God gave the promise to Abraham and to his seed. But "hard to bear with," because the people hardened itself against the obedience of God. And "hard, self-willed," because it was not only hard against the obedience of God, but also self-willed so as to set upon the Lord. "Thou hast waxed wanton," because in the instance of our Lord Jesus Christ the people waxed wanton against the Father. But "boil not over," says the Spirit, by way of comfort, that it might not, by boiling utterly over, be spilt abroad, — giving it hope of salvation. For what has boiled over and been spilt is lost.

GEN. XLIX. 4. For thou wentest up to thy father's bed.

HIPP. First he mentions the event, — that in the last days the people will assault the bed of the Father, that is, the bride,[4] the Church, with intent to corrupt her; which thing, indeed, it does even at this present day, assaulting her by blasphemies.

GEN. XLIX. 5. Simeon and Levi, brethren.

HIPP. Since from Simeon sprang the scribes, and from Levi the priests. For the scribes and priests fulfilled iniquity[5] of their own choice, and with one mind they slew the Lord.

GEN. XLIX. 5. Simeon and Levi, brethren, fulfilled iniquity of their own choice. Into their counsel let not my soul enter, and in their assembly let not my heart contend; for in their anger they slew men, and in their passion they houghed a bull.

HIPP. This he says regarding the conspiracy into which they were to enter against the Lord. And that he means this conspiracy, is evident to us. For the blessed David sings, "Rulers have taken counsel together against the Lord,"[6] and so forth. And of this conspiracy the Spirit prophesied, saying, "Let not my soul contend," desiring to draw them off, if possible, so that

that future crime might not happen through them. "They slew men, and houghed the bull;" by the "strong bull" he means Christ. And "they houghed," since, when He was suspended on the tree, they pierced through His sinews. Again, "in their anger they houghed a bull." And mark the nicety of the expression: for "they slew men, and houghed a bull." For they killed the saints, and they remain dead, awaiting the time of the resurrection. But as a young bull, so to speak, when houghed, sinks down to the ground, such was Christ in submitting voluntarily to the death of the flesh; but He was not overcome of death. But though as man He became one of the dead, He remained alive in the nature of divinity. For Christ is the bull, — an animal, above all, strong and neat and devoted to sacred use. And the Son is Lord of all power, who did no sin, but rather offered Himself for us, a savour of a sweet smell to His God and Father. Therefore let those hear who houghed this august bull: "Cursed be their anger, for it was stubborn; and their wrath, for it was hardened." [7] But this people of the Jews dared to boast of houghing the bull: "Our hands shed this." [8] For this is nothing different, I think, from the word of folly: "His blood" (be upon us), and so forth.[9] Moses recalls [10] the curse against Levi, or, rather converts it into a blessing, on account of the subsequent zeal of the tribe, and of Phinehas in particular, in behalf of God. But that against Simeon he did not recall. Wherefore it also was fulfilled in deed.[11] For Simeon did not obtain an inheritance like the other tribes, for he dwelt in the midst of Judah. Yet his tribe was preserved, although it was small in number.[12]

GEN. XLIX. 11. Binding his foal unto the vine, and his ass's colt to the choice vine, — the tendril of the vine, — he will wash his garment in wine, and his clothes in the blood of the grape.

HIPP. By the "foal" he means the calling of the Gentiles; by the other, that of the circumcision: "one ass," moreover, that is to signify that the two colts are of one faith; in other words, the two callings. And one colt is bound to the "vine," and the other to the "vine tendril," which means that the Church of the Gentiles is bound to the Lord, but he who is of the circumcision to the oldness of the law. "He will wash his garment in wine;" that is, by the

---

[1] μὴ περισσεύῃς.
[2] "My" (μου) is wanting in Origen's *Hexapla*.
[3] οὐκ ἔσῃ περισσότερος.
[4] [He makes the curse of Reuben applicable to all who corrupt the Church's truth and purity.]
[5] ἐξαιρέσεως αὐτῶν, "of set purpose."
[6] Ps. ii. 2.

[7] Gen. xlix. 7.
[8] After "this" (τοῦτο) the word "blood" (τὸ αἷμα) seems to have been dropped.
[9] Matt. xxvii. 25.
[10] Deut. xxxiii. 8.
[11] [By the sin of Annas and Caiaphas, with others, the tribe of Levi became *formally* subject to this curse again, and with Simeon (absorbed into Judah) inherited it. But compare Acts iv. 36 and vi. 7.]
[12] [Luke ii. 25.]

Holy Spirit and the word of truth, he will cleanse the flesh, which is meant by the garment. And "in the blood of the grape," trodden and giving forth blood, which means the flesh of the Lord, he cleanses the whole calling of the Gentiles.

GEN. XLIX. 12–15. His eyes are gladsome with wine, and his teeth white as milk. Zabulun shall dwell by the sea, and he shall be by a haven of ships, and he shall extend to Sidon. Issachar desired the good part, resting in the midst of the lots. And seeing that rest was good, and that the land was fat, he set his shoulder to toil, and became a husbandman.

HIPP. That is, his eyes are brilliant as with the word of truth; for they regard all who believe upon him. And his teeth are white as milk; — that denotes the luminous power of his words: for this reason he calls them white, and compares them to milk, as that which nourishes the flesh and the soul. And Zabulun is, by interpretation, "*fragrance*" and "*blessing*."

Then, after something from Cyril: —

HIPP. Again, I think, it mystically signifies the [1] sacraments of the New Testament of our Saviour; and the words, "his teeth are white as milk," denote the excellency and purity of the sacramental food. And again, these words, "his teeth are white as milk," we take in the sense that His words give light to those who believe on Him.

And in saying, moreover, that Zabulun will dwell by the sea, he speaks prophetically of his territory as bordering on the sea, and of Israel as mingling with the Gentiles, the two nations being brought as it were into one flock. And this is manifest in the Gospel. "The land of Zabulun, and the land of Nephthalim," etc. And you will mark more fully the richness of his lot as having both inland territory and seaboard.

"And he is by a haven of ships;" that is, as in a safe anchorage, referring to Christ, the anchor of hope. And this denotes the calling of the Gentiles — that the grace of Christ shall go forth to the whole earth and sea. For he says, "And (he is) by a haven of ships, and shall extend as far as Sidon." And that this is said prophetically of the Church of the Gentiles, is made apparent to us in the Gospel: "The land of Zabulun, and the land of Nephthalim, by the way of the sea, beyond Jordan, Galilee of the Gentiles; the people which sat in darkness saw great light." [2] In saying, then, that he, namely Zabulun, would inhabit a territory bordering on the sea, he plainly confirmed that, just as if he had said that in the future

Israel would mingle with the Gentiles, the two peoples being brought together into one fold and under the hand of one chief Shepherd, the good (Shepherd) by nature, that is, Christ. In blessing him Moses said, "Zabulun shall rejoice." [3] And Moses prophesies, that in the allocation of the land he should have abundance ministered of the good things both of land and sea, under the hand of One. "By a haven of ships;" that is, as in an anchorage that proves safe, referring to Christ, the anchor of hope. For by His grace he shall come forth out of many a tempest, and shall be brought hereafter to land, like ships secure in harbours. Besides, he said that "he extends as far even as Sidon," indicating, as it seems, that so complete a unity will be effected in the spirit's course between the two peoples, that those of the blood of Israel shall occupy those very cities which once were exceeding guilty in the sight of God. [4]

After something from Cyril: —

HIPP. And "that the land was fat;" that is, the flesh of our Lord: "fat," that is, "rich;" for it flows with honey and milk. The parts of the land are marked off for an inheritance and possession to him — that means the doctrine of the Lord. For this is a pleasant rest, as He says Himself: "Come unto me, all ye that labour and are heavy laden," [5] etc. For they who keep the commandments, and do not disclaim the ordinances of the law, enjoy rest both in them and in the doctrine of our Lord; and that is the meaning of "in the midst of the lots." As the Lord says, "I am not come to destroy the law and the prophets, but to fulfil them." [6] For even our Lord, in the fact that He keeps the commandments, does not destroy the law and the prophets, but fulfils them, as He says in the Gospels. "He set his shoulder to toil, and became a husbandman." This the apostles did. Having received power from God, and having set themselves to labour, they became husbandmen of the Lord, cultivating the earth — that is, the human race — with the preaching of our Lord.

GEN. XLIX. 16–20. Dan shall judge his people, as himself also one tribe in Israel. And let Dan become a serpent by the way, lying on the path, stinging the horse's heel; and the horseman shall fall backward, waiting for the salvation of the Lord. Gad — a robber's troop shall rob him; and he shall spoil it [7] at the heels. Aser — his bread shall be fat, and he shall furnish dainties to princes.

---

[1] τὰ μυστήρια.
[2] Matt. iv. 15, 16.
[3] Deut. xxxiii. 18.
[4] [In thus spiritualizing, the Fathers do not deny a literal sense also, as in "Aser," p. 166, *infra ;* only they think that geography, history, etc., should pay tribute to a higher meaning.]
[5] Matt. xi. 28.
[6] Matt. v. 17.
[7] κατὰ πόδας, "quickly," "following close."

After something from Cyril, Apollinaris, and Diodorus : —

Hipp. The Lord is represented to us as a horseman ; and the " heel " points us to the " last times." And His " falling " denotes His death ; as it is written in the Gospel : " Behold, this (child) is set for the fall and rising again of many." [1] We take the " robber " to be the traitor. Nor was there any other traitor to the Lord save the (Jewish) people. " Shall rob him," i.e., shall plot against him. At the heels : that refers to the help of the Lord against those who lie in wait against Him. And again, the words " at the heels " denote that the Lord will take vengeance swiftly. He shall be well armed in the foot [2] (heel), and shall overtake and rob the robber's troop.

Aquila. " Girded, he shall gird himself ;" that means that as a man of arms and war he shall arm himself. " And he shall be armed in the heel : " he means this rather, that Gad shall follow behind his brethren in arms. For though his lot was beyond Jordan, yet they (the men of that tribe) were enjoined to follow their brethren in arms until they too got their lots. Or perhaps he meant this, that Gad's tribesmen were to live in the manner of robbers, and that he was to take up a confederacy of freebooters, which is just a " robber's troop," and to follow them, practising piracy, which is robbery, along with them.

Whereas, on the abolition of the shadow in the law, and the introduction of the worship in spirit and truth, the world had need of greater light, at last, with this object, the inspired disciples were called, and put in possession of the lot of the teachers of the law. For thus did God speak with regard to the mother of the Jews — that is to say, Jerusalem — by the voice of the Psalmist : " Instead of thy fathers were thy sons ; " [3] that is, to those called thy sons was given the position of fathers. And with regard to our Lord Jesus Christ in particular : " Thou wilt appoint them rulers over all the earth." Yet presently their authority will not be by any means void of trouble to them. Nay rather, they were to experience unnumbered ills and they were to be in perplexity ; and the course of their apostleship they were by no means to find free of peril, as he intimated indeed by way of an example, when he said, " Let (Dan) be," meaning by that, that there shall be a multitude of persecutors in Dan like a " serpent lying by the way on the path, stinging the horse's heel," i.e., giving fierce and dangerous bites ; for the bites of snakes are generally very dangerous. And they were " in the heel " in particular : for " he shall bruise thy head, and thou shalt bruise his heel." [4] And some did persecute the holy apostles in this way even to the death of the flesh. And thus we may say that their position was something like that when a horse stumbles and flings out his heels. For in such a case the horseman will be thrown, and, falling to the ground, I suppose, he waits [5] thus for some one alive. And thus, too, the inspired apostles survive and wait for the time of their redemption, when they shall be called into a kingdom which cannot be moved, when Christ addresses them

with the word, " Come, ye blessed of my Father,' [6] etc.

And again, if any one will take the words as meaning, not that there will be some lying in wait against Dan like serpents, but that this Dan himself lies in wait against others, we may say that those meant thereby are the scribes and Pharisees, hypocrites who, while in possession of the power of judgment and instruction among the people, fastened like snakes upon Christ, and strove impiously to compass His fall, vexing Him with their stings as He held on in His lofty and gentle course. But if that horseman did indeed fall, He fell at least of His own will, voluntarily enduring the death of the flesh. And, moreover, it was destined that He should come to life again, having the Father as His helper and conductor. For the Son, being the power of God the Father, endued the temple of His own body again with life. Thus is He said to have been saved by the Father, as He stood in peril as a man, though by nature He is God, and Himself maintains the whole creation, visible and invisible, in a state of wellbeing. In this sense, also, the inspired Paul says of Him : " Though He was crucified in weakness, yet He liveth by the power of God." [7]

Aser obtained the parts about Ptolemais and Sidon. Wherefore he says, " His bread shall be fat, and he shall furnish dainties to princes." This we take to be a figure of our calling ; for " fat " means " rich." And whose bread is rich, if not ours ? For the Lord is our bread, as He says Himself : " I am the bread of life." [8] And who else will furnish dainties to princes but our Lord Jesus Christ ? — not only to the believing among the Gentiles, but also to those of the circumcision, who are first in the faith, to wit, to the fathers, and the patriarchs, and the prophets, and to all who believe in His name and passion.

Gen. xlix. 21–26. Nephthalim is a slender [9] trunk, showing beauty in the shoot. Joseph is a goodly son ; my goodly, envied son ; my youngest son. Turn back to me. Against him the archers took counsel together, and reviled him, and pressed him sore. And their bows were broken with might, and the sinews of the arms of their hands were relaxed by the hand of the Mighty One of Jacob. Thence is he who strengthened Israel from the God of thy father. And my God helped thee, and blessed thee with the blessing of heaven above, and with the blessing of the earth which possesseth all things, with the blessing of the breasts and womb, with the blessing of thy father and thy mother. It prevailed above the blessings of abiding mountains, and above the blessings of everlasting hills ; which (blessings) shall be upon the head of Joseph, and upon the temples of his brothers, whose chief he was.

Hipp. Who is the son goodly and envied, even to this day, but our Lord Jesus Christ ? An object of envy is He indeed to those who choose to hate Him, yet He is not by any means to be overcome. For though He endured the cross, yet as God He returned to life, having trampled

---

[1] Luke ii. 34.
[2] [An important hint that by "heel," in Gen. iii. 15, the "foot" is understood, by rhetorical figure.]
[3] Ps. xliv. 17 (English, xlv. 16).
[4] Gen. iii 15. [The rhetoric here puts the heel for the foot to emphasize the other part of the prophecy, i.e., the wounded heel coming down on the biter's head.]
[5] περιμένει τὸν ζῶντα.

[6] Matt. xxv. 34.
[7] 2 Cor. xiii. 4.
[8] John vi. 35.
[9] στέλεχος ἀνειμένον.

upon death, as His God and Father addresses Him, and says, "Sit Thou at my right hand." [1] And that even those are brought to nought who strive with the utmost possible madness against Him, he has taught us, when he says, "Against Him the archers took counsel together, and reviled Him." For the "archers"—that is, the leaders of the people—did convene their assemblies, and take bitter counsel. "But their bows were broken, and the sinews of their arms were relaxed, by the hand of the Mighty One of Jacob," that is to say, by God the Father, who is the Lord of power, who also made His Son blessed in heaven and on earth. And he (Naphtali) is adopted as a figure of things pertaining to us, as the Gospel shows: "The land of Zabulun, and the land of Nephthalim, by the way of the sea, beyond Jordan," [2] etc.; and, "To them that sat in darkness light has arisen." [3] And what other light was this but the calling of the Gentiles, which is the trunk, i.e., the tree of the Lord, in whom engrafted it bears fruit? And the word, "giving increase of beauty in the case of the shoot," expresses the excellency of our calling. And if the words, "giving increase of beauty in the case of the shoot," are understood, as perhaps they may, with reference to us, the clause is still quite intelligible. For, by progressing in virtue, and attaining to better things, "reaching forth to those things which are before," [4] according to the word of the blessed Paul, we rise ever to the higher beauty. I mean, however, of course, spiritual beauty, so that to us too it may be said hereafter, "The King greatly desired thy beauty." [5]

After something from Apollinaris:—

Hipp. The word of prophecy passes again to Immanuel Himself. For, in my opinion, what is intended by it is just what has been already stated in the words, "giving increase of beauty in the case of the shoot." For he means that He increased and grew up into that which He had been from the beginning, and indicates the return to the glory which He had by nature. [6] This, if we apprehend it correctly, is (we should say) just "restored" to Him. For [7] as the only begotten Word of God, being God of God, [8] emptied Himself, according to the Scriptures, humbling Himself of His own will to that which He was not before, and took unto Himself this

vile flesh, and appeared [9] in the "form of a servant," and "became obedient to God the Father, even unto death," so hereafter He is said to be "highly exalted;" and as if well-nigh He had it not by reason of His humanity, and as if it were in the way of grace, He "receives the name which is above every name," [10] according to the word of the blessed Paul. But the matter, in truth, was not a "giving," as for the first time, of what He had not by nature; far otherwise. But rather we must understand a return and restoration to that which existed in Him at the beginning, essentially and inseparably. And it is for this reason that, when He had assumed, by divine arrangement, [11] the lowly estate of humanity, He said, "Father, glorify me with the glory which I had," [12] etc. For He who was co-existent with His Father before all time, and before the foundation of the world, always had the glory proper to Godhead. "He" too may very well be understood as the "youngest (son)." For He appeared in the last times, after the glorious and honourable company of the holy prophets, and simply once, after all those who, previous to the time of His sojourn, were reckoned in the number of sons by reason of excellence. That Immanuel, however, was an "object of envy," [13] is a somewhat doubtful phrase. Yet He is an "object of envy" or "emulation" to the saints, who aspire to follow His footsteps, and conform themselves to His divine beauty, and make Him the pattern of their conduct, and win thereby their highest glory. And again, He is an "object of envy" in another sense,—an "object of ill-will," namely, to those who are declared not to love Him. I refer to the leading parties among the Jews,—the scribes, in sooth, and the Pharisees,—who travailed with bitter envy against Him, and made the glory of which He could not be spoiled the ground of their slander, and assailed Him in many ways. For Christ indeed raised the dead to life again, when they already stank and were corrupt; and He displayed other signs of divinity. And these should have filled them with wonder, and have made them ready to believe, and to doubt no longer. Yet this was not the case with them; but they were consumed with ill-will, and nursed its bitter pangs in their mind.

After something from Cyril:—

Hipp. Who else is this than as is shown us by the apostle, "the second man, the Lord from heaven?" [14] And in the Gospel, [15] He said that he who did the will of the Father was "the

---

[1] Ps. cx. 1.
[2] Matt. iv. 15.
[3] Matt. iv. 17.
[4] Phil. iii. 15.
[5] Ps. xlv. 11.
[6] The text is τοῦτο πάντως κατάγεται ὀρθῶς ἔχειν ὑπειλημμένον.
[7] This passage, down to the word "inseparably," was transcribed by Isaac Vossius at Rome, and first edited by Grabe in the *Annotations to Bull's Defens. fid. Nic.*, p. 103.
[8] "God of God," Θεὸς ὑπάρχων ἐκ Θεοῦ. Hippolytus uses here the exact phrase of the Nicene Council. So, too, in his *Contra Noetum*, chap. x., he has the exact phrase, "light of light" (φῶς ἐκ φωτός). [See my concluding remarks (note 9) on the last chapters of the *Philosophumena*, p. 153, *supra.*]

[9] The words from "and appeared" down to "so hereafter" are given by Grabe, but omitted in Fabricius.
[10] Phil. ii. 7–9.
[11] οἰκονομικῶς.
[12] John xvii. 5.
[13] ζηλωτός.
[14] 1 Cor. xv. 47.
[15] Matt. xxi. 31.

last." [1] And by the words, "Turn back to me,"
is meant His ascension to His Father in heaven
after His passion. And in the phrase, "Against
Him they took counsel together, and reviled
Him," who are intended but just the people in
their opposition to our Lord? And as to the
words, "they pressed Him sore," who pressed
Him, and to this day still press Him sore?
Those — these "archers," namely — who think
to contend against the Lord. But though they
prevailed to put Him to death, yet "their bows
were broken with might." This plainly means,
that "after the resurrection" their bows were
broken with might. And those intended are the
leaders of the people, who set themselves in
array against Him, and, as it were, sharpened
the points of their weapons. But they failed to
transfix Him, though they did what was unlawful, and dared to assail Him even in the manner
of wild beasts.

"Thou didst prevail above the blessings of
abiding mountains." By "eternal and abiding
mountains and everlasting hills," he means the
saints, because they are lifted above the earth,
and make no account of the things that perish,
but seek the things that are above, and aspire
earnestly to rise to the highest virtues. After
the glory of Christ, therefore, are those of the
Fathers who were most illustrious, and reached
the greatest elevation in virtue. These, however, were but servants; but the Lord, the Son,
supplied them with the means by which they
became illustrious. Wherefore also they acknowledge (the truth of this word), "Out of His
fulness have all we received." [2]

"And my God helped thee." This indicates
clearly that the aid and support of the Son came
from no one else but our God and Father in
heaven. And by the word "my God," is meant
that the Spirit speaks by Jacob.[3]

EUSEB. "The sinews of the arms." He could not
say, of "the hands" or "shoulders;" but since the
broad central parts of the bow are termed "arms," he
says appropriately "arms."

HIPP. "Blessings of the breasts and womb."
By this is meant that the true blessing from
heaven is the Spirit descending through the
Word upon flesh. And by "breasts and womb"
he means the blessings of the Virgin. And by

that of "thy father and thy mother," [4] he means
also the blessing of the Father which we have received in the Church through our Lord Jesus
Christ.

GEN. XLIX. 27. "Benjamin is a ravening
wolf; in the morning he shall devour still, and
till evening he apportions food."

HIPP. This thoroughly suits Paul, who was of
the tribe of Benjamin. For when he was young,
he was a ravening wolf; but when he believed,
he "apportioned" food. This also is shown us
by the grace of our Lord Jesus Christ, that the
tribe of Benjamin is among the first persecutors,
which is the sense of "in the morning." For
Saul, who was of the tribe of Benjamin, persecuted David, who was appointed to be a type of
the Lord.

II.

From the Commentary of the holy Hippolytus of Rome upon
Genesis.[5]

GEN. II. 7. "And God formed man of the
dust of the ground." And what does this import? Are we to say, according to the opinion
of some, that there were three men made, one
spiritual, one animal, and one earthy? Not such
is the case, but the whole narrative is of one
man. For the word, "Let us make," is about
the man that was to be; and then comes the
word, "God made man of the dust of the ground,"
so that the narrative is of one and the same man.
For then He says, "Let him be made," and now
He "makes him," and the narrative tells "how"
He makes him.

III.

Quoted in Jerome, epist. 36, *ad Damasum*, Num. xviii. (from
Galland).

[6] Isaac conveys a figure of God the Father;
Rebecca of the Holy Spirit; Esau of the first
people and the devil; Jacob of the Church, or
of Christ. That Isaac was *old*, points to the end
of the world; that his eyes were dim, denotes
that faith had perished from the world, and that
the light of religion was neglected before him;
that the elder son is called, expresses the Jews'
possession of the law; that the father loves his

<hr>

[1] ὁ ἔσχατος. Several manuscripts and versions and Fathers read
ἔσχατος with Hippolytus instead of πρῶτος. Jerome *in loc.* remarks
on the fact, and observes that with that reading the interpretation
would be quite intelligible; the sense then being, that "the Jews
understand the truth indeed, but evade it, and refuse to acknowledge
what they perceive." Wetstein, in his *New Test.*, i. p. 467, also cites
this reading, and adds the conjecture, that "some, remembering what
is said in Matt. xx. 16, viz., 'the last shall be first,' thought that
the 'publicans' would be called more properly 'the last,' and that
then some one carried out this emendation so far as to transpose the
replies too."
[2] John i. 16.
[3] Gen. xlviii. 3, 4.

[4] Grabe adduces another fragment of the comments of Hippolytus on this passage, found in some leaves deciphered at Rome. It is
to this effect: Plainly and evidently the generation of the Only-begotten, which is at once from God the Father, and through the holy
Virgin, is signified, even as He is believed and manifested to be a
man. For being by nature and in truth the Son of God the Father,
on our account He submitted to birth by woman and the womb, and
sucked the breast. For He did not, as some fancy, become man only
in appearance, but He manifested Himself as in reality that which
we are who follow the laws of nature, and supported Himself by food,
though Himself giving life to the world.
[5] From the Second Book of the *Res Sacræ* of Leontius and Joannes, in Mai, *Script. vet.*, vii. p. 84.
[6] Jerome introduces this citation from the Commentary of Hippolytus on Genesis in these terms: "Since, then, we promised to add
what that (concerning Isaac and Rebecca, Gen. xxvii.) signifies figuratively, we may adduce the words of the martyr Hippolytus, with
whom our Victorinus very much agrees: not that he has made out
everything quite fully, but that he may give the reader the means for
a broader understanding of the passage."

meat and venison, denotes the saving of men from error, whom every righteous man seeks to gain (lit. *hunt for*) by doctrine. The word of God here is the promise anew of the blessing and the hope of a kingdom to come, in which the saints shall reign with Christ, and keep the true Sabbath. Rebecca is full of the Holy Spirit, as understanding the word which she heard before she gave birth, " For the elder shall serve the younger." [1] As a figure of the Holy Spirit, moreover, she cares for Jacob in preference. She says to her younger son, "Go to the flock and fetch me two kids," [2] prefiguring the Saviour's advent in the flesh to work a mighty deliverance for them who were held liable to the punishment of sin ; for indeed in all the Scriptures kids are taken for emblems of sinners. His being charged to bring " two," denotes the reception of two peoples : by the "tender and good," are meant teachable and innocent souls. The robe or raiment of Esau denotes the faith and Scriptures of the Hebrews, with which the people of the Gentiles were endowed. The skins which were put upon his arms are the sins of both peoples, which Christ, when His hands were stretched forth on the cross, fastened to it along with Himself. In that Isaac asks of Jacob why he came so soon,[3] we take him as admiring the quick faith of them that believe. That savoury meats are offered, denotes an offering pleasing to God, the salvation of sinners. After the eating follows the blessing, and he delights in his smell. He announces with clear voice the perfection of the resurrection and the kingdom, and also how his brethren who believe in Israel adore him and serve him. Because iniquity is opposed to righteousness, Esau is excited to strife, and meditates death deceitfully, saying in his heart, " Let the days of the mourning for my father come on, and I will slay my brother Jacob." [4] The devil, who previously exhibited the fratricidal Jews by anticipation in Cain, makes the most manifest disclosure of them now in Esau, showing also the time of the murder : " Let the days," says he, " of the mourning for my father come on, that I may slay my brother." Wherefore Rebecca — that is, patience — told her husband of the brother's plot : who, summoning Jacob, bade him go to Mesopotamia and thence take a wife of the family of Laban the Syrian, his mother's brother. As therefore Jacob, to escape his brother's evil designs, proceeds to Mesopotamia, so Christ, too, constrained by the unbelief of the Jews, goes into Galilee, to take from thence to Himself a bride from the Gentiles, His Church.

[1] Gen. xxv. 23.
[2] Gen. xxvii. 9.
[3] Gen. xxvii. 20.
[4] Gen. xxvii. 41.

ON NUMBERS.

By the holy bishop and martyr Hippolytus, from *Balaam's Blessings.*[5]

Now, in order that He might be shown to have together in Himself at once the nature of God and that of man, — as the apostle, too, says : " Mediator between God and men, the man Christ Jesus.[6] Now a mediator is not of one man,[7] but two," [8] — it was therefore necessary that Christ, in becoming the Mediator between God and men, should receive from both an earnest of some kind, that He might appear as the Mediator between two distinct persons.

ON KINGS.[9]

The question is raised, whether Samuel rose by the hand of the sorceress or not. And if, indeed, we were to allow that he did rise, we should be propounding what is false. For how could a demon call back the soul, I say not of a righteous man merely, but of any one whatever, when it had gone, and was tarrying one knew not where? But he says, how then was the woman dismayed, and how did she see in an extraordinary way men ascending? For if her vision had not been of an extraordinary kind, she would not have said, " I see gods [10] ascending out of the earth." She invoked one, and how did there ascend many? What then? Shall we say that the souls of all who appeared ascended, and those, too, not invoked by the woman ; [11] or that what was seen was merely phantasms of them? Even this, however, will not suffice. How, he urges further, did Saul recognise (what appeared), and do obeisance? Well, Saul did not actually see, but only, on being told by the woman that the figure of one of those who ascended was the figure he desired, and taking it to be Samuel, he consulted it as such, and did it obeisance. And it could be no difficult matter for the demon to conjure up the form of Samuel, as it was known to him. How then, says he, did he foretell the calamities that were to befall Saul and Jonathan at the same time? He did foretell indeed the end of the war, and how Saul would be overcome, drawing that as an inference from the wrath of God against him. Just as a physician, who has no exact knowledge

[5] In Leontius Byzant., book i. *Against Nestorius and Eutyches* (from Galland). The same fragment is found in Mai, *Script. vet.*, vii. p. 134. [Galland was a French Orientalist, A.D. 1646–1715.]
[6] 1 Tim. ii. 5.
[7] This word " man " agrees ill, not only with the text in Galatians, but even with the meaning of the writer here; for he is treating, not of a mediator between " two " men, but between " God and men." — MIGNE.
[8] Gal. iii. 20.
[9] A fragment from the tractate of Hippolytus, *On the Sorceress* (*ventriloquist*), or *On Saul and the Witch*, 1 Sam. xxviii. From the Vatican MS. cccxxx. in Allat., *De Engastr.*, edited by Simon, in the *Acts of the Martyrs of Ostia*, p. 160, Rome, 1795.
[10] [Rather " god," the plural of excellence, Elohim.]
[11] [This passage is the scandal of commentators. As I read it, *the Lord interfered*, surprising the woman and horrifying her. The soul of the prophet came back from Sheol, and prophesied by the power of God. Our author misunderstands the Hebrew plural.]

of the science, might yet, seeing a patient past cure, tell of his death, though he made an error as to the hour, so, too, the demon, knowing the wrath of God by Saul's deeds, and by this very attempt to consult the sorceress, foretells his defeat and his death at the same time, though in error as to the day of his death.

ON THE PSALMS.

The argument prefixed by Hippolytus, bishop of Rome, to his Exposition of the Psalms.[1]

The book of Psalms contains new doctrine after the law of Moses. And after the writing of Moses, it is the second book of doctrine. Now, after the death of Moses and Joshua, and after the judges, arose David, who was deemed worthy of bearing the name of father of the Saviour himself; and he first gave to the Hebrews a new style of psalmody, by which he abrogates the ordinances established by Moses with respect to sacrifices, and introduces the new hymn and a new style of jubilant praise in the worship of God; and throughout his whole ministry he teaches very many other things that went beyond the law of Moses.[2]

ON PSALM II.[3]

From the exposition of the second Psalm, by the holy bishop Hippolytus.

When he came into the world, He was manifested as God and man. And it is easy to perceive the man in Him, when He hungers and shows exhaustion, and is weary and athirst, and withdraws in fear, and is in prayer and in grief, and sleeps on a boat's pillow, and entreats the removal of the cup of suffering, and sweats in an agony, and is strengthened by an angel, and betrayed by a Judas, and mocked by Caiaphas, and set at nought by Herod, and scourged by Pilate, and derided by the soldiers, and nailed to the tree by the Jews, and with a cry commits His spirit to His Father, and drops His head and gives up the ghost, and has His side pierced with a spear, and is wrapped in linen and laid in a tomb, and is raised by the Father on the third day. And the divine in Him, on the other hand, is equally manifest, when He is worshipped by angels, and seen by shepherds, and waited for by Simeon, and testified of by Anna, and inquired after by wise men, and pointed out by a star, and at a marriage makes wine of water, and chides the sea when tossed by the violence of winds, and walks upon the deep, and makes one see who was blind from birth, and raises Laza-

rus when dead for four days, and works many wonders, and forgives sins, and grants power to His disciples.

ON PSALM XXII. OR XXIII.

From the Commentary by the holy bishop and martyr Hippolytus, on " The Lord is my Shepherd."[4]

And, moreover, the ark made of imperishable wood was the Saviour Himself. For by this was signified the imperishable and incorruptible tabernacle of (the Lord) Himself, which gendered no corruption of sin. For the sinner, indeed, makes this confession : " My wounds stank, and were corrupt, because of my foolishness."[5] But the Lord was without sin, made of imperishable wood, as regards His humanity ; that is, of the virgin and the Holy Ghost inwardly, and outwardly of the word of God, like an ark overlaid with purest gold.

ON PSALM XXIII. OR XXIV.

From the Commentary by the same, on Ps. xxiii.[6]

He comes to the heavenly gates : angels accompany Him : and the gates of heaven were closed. For He has not yet ascended into heaven. Now first does He appear to the powers of heaven as flesh ascending. Therefore to these powers it is said by the angels, who are the couriers of the Saviour and Lord : " Lift up your gates, ye princes ; and be lifted up, ye everlasting doors : and the King of glory shall come in.[7]

ON PSALM CIX. OR CX.

From the Commentary by the same on the great Song.[8]

1. He who delivered from the lowest hell the man first made of earth, when lost and bound by the chains of death ; He who came down from above, and exalted earth-born man on high ; He who is become the preacher of the Gospel to the dead, the redeemer of souls, and the resurrection of the buried ; — He became the helper of man in his defeat, and appeared in his likeness, the first-born Word, and took upon Himself the first Adam in the Virgin ; and though spiritual Himself, He made acquaintance with the earthy in the womb ; though Himself the ever-living One, He made acquaintance with the dead in transgressions ; Himself the heavenly One, He bore the terrestrial on high ; Himself of lofty extraction, He chose, by His own subjection, to set the slave free ; and making man, who turns to dust, and forms food for the serpent, unconquerable as adamant, and that, too, when hung upon the tree, He declared him lord over his victor, and is thus Himself proved conqueror by the tree.

---

[1] From Gallandi.
[2] [i.e., Samuel prepares for the Christian era, introducing the "schools of the prophets" and the synagogue service, which God raised up David to complete, by furnishing the Psalter. Compare Acts iii. 24, where Samuel's position in the " goodly fellowship " is marked. See Payne Smith's *Prophecy a Preparation for Christ.*]
[3] i.e., in our version the third. From Theodoret, Dialogue Second, entitled Ἀσύγχυτος, p. 167.

[4] Theodoret, in his First Dialogue.
[5] Ps. xxxviii. 6.
[6] Theodoret, in his First Dialogue.
[7] Ps. xxiv. 7.
[8] Theodoret, in his Second Dialogue.

2. Those, indeed, who do not acknowledge the incarnate Son of God now, shall have to acknowledge Him as Judge, when He who is now despised in His inglorious body, comes in His glory.

3. And when the apostles came to the sepulchre on the third day, they did not find the body of Jesus; just as the children of Israel went up the mount to seek the tomb of Moses, and did not find it.

ON PSALM LXXVII. OR LXXVIII.[1]

45. He sent the dog-fly among them, and consumed them; and the frog, and destroyed them.

46. He gave also their fruits to the mildew, and their labours to the locust.

47. He destroyed their vine with hail, and their sycamines with frost.

Now, just as, in consequence of an irregular mode of living, a deadly bilious humour may be formed in the inwards, which the physician by his art may bring on to be a sick-vomiting, without being himself chargeable with producing the sick humour in the man's body; for excess in diet was what produced it, while the physician's science only made it show itself; so, although it may be said that the painful retribution that falls upon those who are by choice wicked comes from God, it would be only in accordance with right reason, to think that ills of that kind find both their beginnings and their causes in ourselves. For to one who lives without sin there is no darkness, no worm, no hell (Gehenna), no fire, nor any other of these words or things of terror; just as the plagues of Egypt were not for the Hebrews, — those fine lice annoying with invisible bites, the dog-fly fastening on the body with its painful sting, the hurricanes from heaven falling upon them with hailstones, the husbandman's labours devoured by the locusts, the darkened sky, and the rest. It is God's counsel, indeed, to tend the true vine, and to destroy the Egyptian, while sparing those who are to "eat the grape of gall, and drink the deadly venom of asps."[2] And the sycamine of Egypt is utterly destroyed; not, however, that one which Zaccheus climbed that he might be able to see my Lord. And the fruits of Egypt are wasted, that is, the works of the flesh, but not the fruit of the Spirit, love, joy, and peace.[3]

48. He gave up their cattle also to the hail, and their substance to the fire.

Symmachus renders it: "Who gave up their cattle to the plague, and their possessions to birds." For, having met an overwhelming over-throw, they became a prey for carnivorous birds. But, according to the Seventy, the sense is not that the hail destroyed their cattle, and the fire the rest of their substance, but that hail, falling in an extraordinary manner along with fire, destroyed utterly their vines and sycamines first of all, which were entirely unable to stand out against the first attack; then the cattle which grazed on the plains; and then every herb and tree, which the fire accompanying the hail consumed; and the affair was altogether portentous, as fire ran with the water, and was commingled with it. "For fire ran in the hail," he says; and it was thus hail, and fire burning in the hail. David also calls the cattle and the fruit of the trees "substance," or "riches." And it should be observed that, though the hail is recorded to have destroyed every herb and every tree, yet there were left some which the locust, as it came upon them after the fiery hail, consumed; of which it is said, that it eats up every herb, and all the fruit of the trees which the hail left behind it. Now, in a spiritual sense, there are some sheep belonging to Christ, and others belonging to the Egyptians. Those, however, which once belonged to others may become His, as the sheep of Laban became Jacob's; and contrariwise. Whichever of the sheep, moreover, Jacob rejected, he made over to Esau. Beware, then, lest, being found in the flock of Jesus, you be set apart when gifts are sent to Esau, and be given over to Esau as reprobate and unworthy of the spiritual Jacob. The single-minded are the sheep of Christ, and these God saves according to the word: "O Lord, Thou preservest man and beast."[4] They who in their folly attach themselves to godless doctrine, are the sheep of the Egyptians, and these, too, are destroyed by the hail. And whatsoever the Egyptians possess is given over to the fire, but Abraham's substance is given to Isaac.

49. He discharged upon them the wrath of His anger; — anger, and wrath, and tribulation, a visitation by evil angels.

Under anger, wrath, and tribulation, he intended bitter punishments; for God is without passion. And by anger you will understand the lesser penalties, and by wrath the greater, and by tribulation the greatest. [5] The angels also are called evil, not because they are so in their nature, or by their own will, but because they have this office, and are appointed to produce pains and sufferings, — being so called, therefore, with reference to the disposition of those who endure such things; just as the day of judgment is called the evil day, as being laden with miseries and

---

[1] Bandini, *Catalog. Codd. Græc. Biblioth. Mediceo-Laurent.*, i. p. 91.
[2] Deut. xxxii. 33.
[3] Gal. v. 22.

[4] Ps. xxxvi. 6.
[5] Theodoret also, following Hippolytus, understood by "evil angels" here, not "demons," but the ministers of temporal punishment. See on Ps. lxxviii. 54, and on Jer. xlix. 14. So, too, others, as may be seen in Poli *Synops.*, ii. col. 1113.

pains for sinners. To the same effect is the word of Isaiah, " I, the Lord, make peace, and create evil ; "[1] meaning by that, I maintain peace, and permit war.

ON PROVERBS.

From the Commentary of St. Hippolytus on Proverbs.[2]

Proverbs, therefore, are words of exhortation serviceable for the whole path of life ; for to those who seek their way to God, these serve as guides and signs to revive them when wearied with the length of the road. These, moreover, are the proverbs of " Solomon," that is to say, the " peacemaker," who, in truth, is Christ the Saviour. And since we understand the words of the Lord without offence, as being the words of the Lord, that no one may mislead us by likeness of name, he tells us who wrote these things, and of what people he was king, in order that the credit of the speaker may make the discourse acceptable and the hearers attentive ; for they are the words of that Solomon to whom the Lord said : " I will give thee a wise and an understanding heart ; so that there has been none like thee upon the earth, and after thee there shall not arise any like unto thee,"[3] and as follows in what is written of him. Now he was the wise son of a wise father ; wherefore there is added the name of David, by whom Solomon was begotten. From a child he was instructed in the sacred Scriptures, and obtained his dominion not by lot, nor by force, but by the judgment of the Spirit and the decree of God.

" To know wisdom and instruction." He who knows the wisdom of God, receives from Him also instruction, and learns by it the mysteries of the Word ; and they who know the true heavenly wisdom will easily understand the words of these mysteries. Wherefore he says : " To understand the difficulties of words ; "[4] for things spoken in strange language by the Holy Spirit become intelligible to those who have their hearts right with God.

[5] These things he understands of the people of the Jews, and their guilt in the blood of Christ ; for they thought that He had His conversation (citizenship) on earth only.

[6] They will not simply obtain, but inherit. The wicked, again, even though they are exalted, are exalted only so as to have greater dishonour. For as one does not honour an ugly and misshapen fellow, if he exalts him, but only dishonours him the more, by making his shame manifest to a larger number ; so also God exalts the wicked, in order that He may make their disgrace patent. For Pharaoh was exalted, but only to have the world as his accuser.

[7] It must be noted, that he names the law a good gift, on account of the man who takes gifts into his bosom unrighteously. And he forsakes the law who transgresses it ; the law, namely, of which he speaks, or which he has kept.

[8] And what is meant by " exalt (fortify) her ? " Surround her with holy thoughts ; for you have need of large defence, since there are many things to imperil such a possession. But if it is in our power to fortify her, and if there are virtues in our power which exalt the knowledge of God, these will be her bulwarks, — as, for example, practice, study, and the whole chain of other virtues ; and the man who observes these, honours wisdom ; and the reward is, to be exalted to be with her, and to be embraced by her in the chamber of heaven.

[9] The heterodox are the " wicked," and the transgressors of the law are " evil men," whose " ways " — that is to say, their deeds — he bids us not enter.

[10] He " looks right on " who has thoughts free of passion ; and he has true judgments, who is not in a state of excitement about external appearances. When he says, " Let thine eyes look right on," he means the vision of the soul ; and when he gives the exhortation, " Eat honey, my son, that it may be sweet to thy palate," he uses " honey " figuratively, meaning divine doctrine, which restores the spiritual knowledge of the soul. But wisdom embraces the soul also ; for, says he, " love her, that she may embrace thee." And the soul, by her embrace being made one with wisdom, is filled with holiness and purity. Yea more, the fragrant ointments of Christ are laid hold of by the soul's sense of smell.

[11] Virtue occupies the middle position ; whence also he says, that manly courage is the mean between boldness and cowardice. And now he mentions the " right," not meaning thereby things which are right by nature, such as the virtues, but things which seem to thee to be right on account of their pleasures. Now pleasures are not simply sensual enjoyments, but also riches and luxury. And the " left " indicates envy, robberies, and the like. For " Boreas," says he, " is a bitter wind, and yet is called by name right."[12] For, symbolically, under Boreas he designates the wicked devil by whom every flame of evil is kindled in the earth. And this has the name " right," because an angel is called by a right (propitious) name. Do thou,

---

[1] Isa. xlv. 7.
[2] Mai, *Bibliotheca nova Patrum*, vii. ii. 71, Rome, 1854.
[3] 1 Kings iii. 12.
[4] Prov. i. 3.
[5] Ch. i. 11.
[6] Ch. iii. 35.

[7] Prov. iv. 2.
[8] Ch. iv. 8.
[9] Ch. iv. 14.
[10] Ch. iv. 25.
[11] Ch. iv. 27.
[12] This is the Septuagint translation of ch. xxvii. 16.

says he, turn aside from evil, and God will take care of thine end; for He will go before thee, scattering thine enemies, that thou mayest go in peace.

[1] He shows also, by the mention of the creature (the hind), the purity of that pleasure; and by the roe he intimates the quick responsive affection of the wife. And whereas he knows many things to excite, he secures them against these, and puts upon them the indissoluble bond of affection, setting constancy before them. And as for the rest, wisdom, figuratively speaking, like a stag, can repel and crush the snaky doctrines of the heterodox. Let her therefore, says he, be with thee, like a roe, to keep all virtue fresh. And whereas a wife and wisdom are not in this respect the same, let her rather lead thee; for thus thou shalt conceive good thoughts.

[2] That thou mayest not say, What harm is there in the eyes, when there is no necessity that he should be perverted who looks? he shows thee that desire is a fire, and the flesh is like a garment. The latter is an easy prey, and the former is a tyrant. And when anything harmful is not only taken within, but also held fast, it will not go forth again until it has made an exit for itself. For he who looks upon a woman, even though he escape the temptation, does not come away pure of all lust. And why should one have trouble, if he can be chaste and free of trouble? See what Job says: "I made a covenant with mine eyes, that I should not think of another's wife." [3] Thus well does he know the power of abuse. And Paul for this reason kept "under his body, and brought it into subjection." And, figuratively speaking, he keeps a fire in his breast who permits an impure thought to dwell in his heart. And he walks upon coals who, by sinning in act, destroys his own soul.

The "cemphus" [4] is a kind of wild sea-bird, which has so immoderate an impulse to sexual enjoyment, that its eyes seem to fill with blood in coition; and it often blindly falls into snares, or into the hands of men.[5] To this, therefore, he compares the man who gives himself up to the harlot on account of his immoderate lust; or else on account of the insensate folly of the creature, for he, too, pursues his object like one senseless. And they say that this bird is so much pleased with foam, that if one should hold foam in his hand as he sails, it will sit upon his hand. And it also brings forth with pain.

[6] You have seen her mischief. Wait not to admit the rising of lust; for her death is everlasting. And for the rest, by her words, her arguments in sooth, she wounds, and by her sins she kills those who yield to her. For many are the forms of wickedness that lead the foolish down to hell. And the chambers [7] of death mean either its depths or its treasure. How, then, is escape possible?

[8] He intends the new Jerusalem, or the sanctified flesh. By the seven pillars he means the sevenfold unity of the Holy Spirit resting upon it; as Isaiah testifies, saying, "She has slain" her "victims."

[9] Observe that the wise man must be useful to many; so that he who is useful only to himself cannot be wise. For great is the condemnation of wisdom if she reserves her power simply for the one possessing her. But as poison is not injurious to another body, but only to that one which takes it, so also the man who turns out wicked will injure himself, and not another. For no man of real virtue is injured by a wicked man.

[10] The fruit of righteousness and the tree of life is Christ. He alone, as man, fulfilled all righteousness. And with His own underived life [11] He has brought forth the fruits of knowledge and virtue like a tree, whereof they that eat shall receive eternal life, and shall enjoy the tree of life in paradise, with Adam and all the righteous. But the souls of the unrighteous meet an untimely expulsion from the presence of God, by whom they shall be left to remain in the flame of torment.

[12] Not from men, but with the Lord, will he obtain favour.

[13] He asks of wisdom, who seeks to know what is the will of God. And he will show himself prudent who is sparing of his words on that which he has come to learn. If one inquires about wisdom, desiring to learn something about wisdom, while another asks nothing of wisdom, as not only wishing to learn nothing about wisdom himself, but even keeping back his neighbours from so doing, the former certainly is deemed to be more prudent than the latter.

[14] As to the horse-leech. There were three daughters fondly loved by sin — fornication, murder,[15] and idolatry. These three did not satisfy her, for she is not to be satisfied. In

---

[1] Prov. v. 19.
[2] Ch. vi. 27.
[3] Job xxxi. 1.
[4] Prov. vii. 22. The Hebrew word, rendered "straightway" in our version, is translated κεπφωθείς in the Septuagint, i.e., "ensnared like a cepphus." [Quasi agnus lasciviens, according to the Vulgate.]
[5] [If the "cemphus" of the text equals "cepphus" of note, then "cepphus" equals "cebus" or "cepus," which equals κῆβος, a sort of monkey. The "Kophim" of 1 Kings x. 22 seems to supply the root of the word. The κέπφος, however, is said to be a sea-bird "driven about by every wind," so that it is equal to a fool. So used by Aristophanes.]

[6] Prov. vii. 26.
[7] ταμεῖα, "magazines."
[8] Ch. ix. 1.
[9] Ch. ix. 12.
[10] Ch. xi. 30.
[11] ὡς αὐτοζωή.
[12] Ch. xii. 2.
[13] Ch. xvii. 27.
[14] Ch. xxx. 15.
[15] Other reading (φθόνος) = "envy."

destroying man by these actions, sin never varies, but only grows continually. For the fourth, he continues, is never content to say "enough," meaning that it is universal lust. In naming the "fourth," he intends lust in the universal. For as the body is one, and yet has many members; so also sin, being one, contains within it many various lusts by which it lays its snares for men. Wherefore, in order to teach us this, he uses the examples of Sheol (Hades), and the love of women, and hell[1] (Tartarus), and the earth that is not filled with water. And water and fire, indeed, will never say, "It is enough." And the grave[2] (Hades) in no wise ceases to receive the souls of unrighteous men ; nor does the love of sin, in the instance of the love of women, cease to be given to fornication, and it becomes the betrayer of the soul. And as Tartarus, which is situated in a doleful and dark locality, is not touched by a ray of light, so is every one who is the slave of sin in all the passions of the flesh. Like the earth not filled with water, he is never able to come to confession, and to the laver of regeneration, and like water and fire, never says, "It is enough."

[3] For as a serpent cannot mark its track upon a rock, so the devil could not find sin in the body of Christ. For the Lord says, "Behold, the prince of this world cometh, and will find nothing in me."[4] — For as a ship, sailing in the sea, leaves no traces of her way behind her, so neither does the Church, which is situate in the world as in a sea, leave her hope upon the earth, because she has her life reserved in heaven ; and as she holds her way here only for a short time, it is not possible to trace out her course. — As the Church does not leave her hope behind in the world, her hope in the incarnation of Christ which bears us all good, she did not leave the track of death in Hades. — Of whom but of Him who is born of the Holy Spirit and the Virgin? — who, in renewing the perfect man in the world, works miracles, beginning from the baptism of John, as the Evangelist also testifies : And Jesus was then beginning to be about thirty years of age. This, then, was the youthful and blooming period of the age of Him who, in journeying among the cities and districts, healed the diseases and infirmities of men.

[5] "The eye that mocketh at his father, and dishonours the old age of his mother." That is to say, one that blasphemes God and despises the mother of Christ, the wisdom of God, — his eyes may ravens from the caves tear out, i.e., him may unclean and wicked spirits deprive of the clear eye of gladness ; and may the young eagles devour him : and such shall be trodden under the feet of the saints.

[6] "There be three things which I cannot understand, and the fourth I know not : the tracks of an eagle flying," i.e., Christ's ascension ; "and the ways of a serpent upon a rock," i.e., that the devil did not find a trace of sin in the body of Christ ; "and the ways of a ship crossing the sea," i.e., the ways of the Church, which is in this life as in a sea, and which is directed by her hope in Christ through the cross ; "and the ways of a man in youth,"[7] — the ways of Him, namely, who is born of the Holy Spirit and the Virgin. For behold, says the Scripture, a man whose name is the Rising.[8]

[9] "Such is the way of an adulterous woman, who, when she has done the deed of sin, wipeth herself, and will say that no wickedness has been done." Such is the conduct of the Church that believes on Christ, when, after committing fornication with idols, she renounces these and the devil, and is cleansed of her sins and receives forgiveness, and then asserts that she has done no wickedness.

[10] "By three things the earth is moved," viz., by the Father, the Son, and the Holy Ghost. "And the fourth it cannot bear," viz., the last appearing of Christ. "When a servant reigneth : " Israel was a slave in Egypt, and in the land of promise became a ruler. "And a fool when he is filled with meat : " i.e., getting the land in possession readily, and eating its fruit, and being filled, it (the people) kicked. "And a handmaid when she casts out her mistress : " i.e., the synagogue which took the life of the Lord, and crucified the flesh of Christ.

[11] "There be four things which are least upon the earth, and these are wiser than the wise : The ants have no strength, yet they prepare their meat in the summer." And in like manner, the Gentiles by faith in Christ prepare for themselves eternal life through good works. "And the conies,[12] a feeble folk, have made their houses in the rocks." The Gentiles, that is to say, are built upon Christ, the spiritual rock, which is become the head of the corner. "The spider,[13] that supports itself upon its hands, and is easily caught, dwells in the strongholds of kings." That is, the thief with his hands extended (on the cross), rests on the cross of Christ and dwells in Paradise, the stronghold of the three Kings — Father, Son, and Holy Ghost.

---

[1] [The place of torment (2 Pet. ii. 4). Vol. iv. 140.]
[2] [*Sheol*, rather, — the receptacle of departed spirits. See vol. iii. pp. 59 and 595; also vol. iv. p. 194.]
[3] Prov. xxx. 19.
[4] John xiv. 30.
[5] Ch. xxx. 17.

[6] Prov. xxx. 18, 19.
[7] [The Authorized Version reads very differently; but our author follows the Sept., with which agrees the Vulgate.]
[8] The reference probably is to Zech vi. 12, where the word is rendered " Branch." The word in the text is ἀνατολή.
[9] Ch. xxx. 20.
[10] Ch. xxx. 21–23.
[11] Ch. xxx. 24–28.
[12] χοιρογρύλλοι, i.e., " grunting hogs."
[13] ἀσκαλαβώτης, i.e., a " lizard."

"The locust has no king, and yet marches out in array as by one command." The Gentiles had no king, for they were ruled by sin; but now, believing God, they engage in the heavenly warfare.

[1]"There be three things which go well,[1] and the fourth which is comely in going;" that is, the angels in heaven, the saints upon earth, and the souls of the righteous under the earth. And the fourth, viz., God, the Word Incarnate, passed in honour through the Virgin's womb; and creating our Adam anew, he passed through the gates of heaven, and became the first-fruits of the resurrection and of the ascension for all.

"The whelp of the lion is stronger than the beasts:" i.e., Christ as prophesied of by Jacob in the person of Judah. "A cock walking with high spirit among his dames:" such was Paul, when preaching boldly among the churches the word of the Christ of God. "A goat heading the herd:" such is He who was offered for the sins of the world. "And a king speaking among the people:" so Christ reigns over the nations, and speaks by prophets and apostles the word of truth.

[2]That is one confirmed in wickedness.[2] The apostle, too, says, "Them that sin, rebuke before all;"[3] that is to say, all but reprobate. Who are meant by the "conies,"[4] but we ourselves, who once were like hogs, walking in all the filthiness of the world; but now, believing in Christ, we build our houses upon the holy flesh of Christ as upon a rock?

[5]The shaking (of the earth) signifies the change of things upon earth.—Sin, then, which in its own nature is a slave, has reigned in the mortal body of men: once, indeed, at the time of the flood; and again in the time of the Sodomites, who, not satisfied with what the land yielded, offered violence to strangers; and a third time in the case of hateful Egypt, which, though it obtained in Joseph a man who distributed food to all, that they might not perish of famine, yet did not take well with his prosperity, but persecuted the children of Israel. "The handmaid casting out her mistress:" i.e., the Church of the Gentiles, which, though itself a slave and a stranger to the promises, cast out the free-born and lordly synagogue, and became the wife and bride of Christ. By Father, Son, and Holy Spirit, the whole earth is moved. The "fourth it cannot bear:" for He came first by lawgivers, and secondly by prophets, and thirdly

by the Gospel, manifesting Himself openly; and in the fourth instance He shall come as the Judge of the living and the dead, whose glory the whole creation will not be able to endure.

ANOTHER FRAGMENT.[6]

St. Hippolytus[7] on Prov. ix. 1, "Wisdom hath builded her house."

Christ, he means, the wisdom and power of God the Father, hath builded His house, i.e., His nature in the flesh derived from the Virgin, even as he (John) hath said beforetime, "The Word became flesh, and dwelt among us."[8] As likewise the wise prophet[9] testifies: Wisdom that was before the world, and is the source of life, the infinite "Wisdom of God, hath builded her house" by a mother who knew no man, — to wit, as He assumed the temple of the body. "And hath raised[10] her seven pillars;" that is, the fragrant grace of the all-holy Spirit, as Isaiah says: "And the seven spirits of God shall rest upon Him."[11] But others say that the seven pillars are the seven divine orders which sustain the creation by His holy and inspired teaching; to wit, the prophets, the apostles, the martyrs, the hierarchs, the hermits, the saints, and the righteous. And the phrase, "She hath killed her beasts," denotes the prophets and martyrs who in every city and country are slain like sheep every day by the unbelieving, in behalf of the truth, and cry aloud, "For thy sake we are killed all the day long, we were counted as sheep for the slaughter."[12] And again, "She hath mingled her wine" in the bowl, by which is meant, that the Saviour, uniting his Godhead, like pure wine, with the flesh in the Virgin, was born of her at once God and man without confusion of the one in the other. "And she hath furnished her table:" that denotes the promised knowledge of the Holy Trinity; it also refers to His honoured and undefiled body and blood, which day by day are administered and offered sacrificially at the spiritual divine table, as a memorial of that first and ever-memorable table of the spiritual divine supper. And again, "She hath sent forth her servants:" Wisdom, that is to say, has done so — Christ, to wit — summoning them with lofty announcement. "Whoso is simple, let him turn to me," she says, alluding manifestly to the holy apostles, who traversed the whole

---

[1] Prov. xxx. 29, etc. [As in Vulgate.]
[2] Cf. xxvii. 22, the Septuagint rendering being: "Though thou shouldest disgrace and scourge a fool in the midst of the council, thou wilt not strip him of his folly." [What version did our author use?]
[3] 1 Tim. v. 30.
[4] Literally, "grunting hogs."
[5] Ch. xxx. 21, etc. [As to version, see Burgon, *Lett. from Rome*, p. 34.]

[6] From Gallandi.
[7] [I omit here the suffix "Pope of Rome," for obvious reasons. He was *papa* of Portus at a time when all bishops were so called· but this is a misleading absurdity, borrowed from the Galland MS., where it could hardly have been placed earlier. A mere mediæval blunder.]
[8] John i. 14.
[9] i.e., Solomon.
[10] Other reading, "hewn out."
[11] Isa. xi. 2.
[12] Ps. xliv. 2; Rom. viii. 36.

world, and called the nations to the knowledge of Him in truth, with their lofty and divine preaching. And again, "And to those that want understanding she said" — that is, to those who have not yet obtained the power of the Holy Ghost — "Come, eat of my bread, and drink of the wine which I have mingled for you;" by which is meant, that He gave His divine flesh and honoured blood to us, to eat and to drink it for the remission of sins.

ON THE SONG OF SONGS.[1]

1. Arise, O north wind, and come, thou south; blow upon my garden, that the spices thereof may flow out (Canticles iv. 16). As Joseph was delighted with these spices, he is designated the King's son by God; as the Virgin Mary was anointed with them, she conceived the Word: then new secrets, and new truth, and a new kingdom, and also great and inexplicable mysteries, are made manifest.

2. And where is all this rich knowledge? and where are these mysteries? and where are the books? For the only ones extant are Proverbs, and Wisdom, and Ecclesiastes, and the Song of Songs. What then? Does the Scripture speak falsely? God forbid. But the matter of his writings was various, as is shown in the phrase "Song of Songs;" for that indicates that in this one book he digested the contents of the 5,000 songs.[2] In the days moreover of Hezekiah, there were some of the books selected for use, and others set aside. Whence the Scripture says, "These are the mixed[3] Proverbs of Solomon, which the friends of Hezekiah the king copied out."[4] And whence did they take them, but out of the books containing the 3,000 parables and the 5,000 songs? Out of these, then, the wise friends of Hezekiah took those portions which bore upon the edification of the Church. And the books of Solomon on the "Parables" and "Songs," in which he wrote of the physiology of plants, and all kinds of animals belonging to the dry land, and the air, and the sea, and of the cures of disease, Hezekiah did away with, because the people looked to these for the remedies for their diseases, and neglected to seek their healing from God.[5]

---

1 Simon de Magistris, in his *Acta Martyr. Ostiens.*, p. 274, adduces the following fragment in Latin and Syriac, from a Vatican codex, and prefaces it with these words: Hippolytus wrote on the Song of Solomon, and showed that early did God the Word seek His pleasure in the Church gathered from among the Gentiles, and especially in His most holy mother the Virgin; and thus the Syrians, who boasted that the Virgin was born among them, translated the Commentary of Hippolytus at a very early period from the Greek into their own tongue, of which some fragments still remain, — as, for example, one to this effect on the above words.
2 1 Kings iv. 32.
3 ἀδιάκριτοι, "mixed," or "dark."
4 Prov. xxv. 1.
5 In Gallandi, from *Anastasius Sinaita*, quæst. 41, p 320.

ON THE PROPHET ISAIAH.[6]

I.

Hippolytus, (Bishop) of Rome, on Hezekiah.[7]

When Hezekiah, king of Judah, was still sick and weeping, there came an angel, and said to him: "I have seen thy tears, and I have heard thy voice. Behold, I add unto thy time fifteen years. And this shall be a sign to thee from the Lord: Behold, I turn back the shadow of the degrees of the house of thy father, by which the sun has gone down, the ten degrees by which the shadow has gone down,"[8] so that that day be a day of thirty-two hours. For when the sun had run its course to the tenth hour, it returned again. And again, when Joshua the son of Nun was fighting against the Amorites, when the sun was now inclining to its setting, and the battle was being pressed closely, Joshua, being anxious lest the heathen host should escape on the descent of night, cried out, saying, "Sun, stand thou still in Gibeon; and thou moon, in the valley of Ajalon,"[9] until I vanquish this people. And the sun stood still, and the moon, in their places, so that that day was one of twenty-four hours. And in the time of Hezekiah the moon also turned back along with the sun, that there might be no collision between the two elemental bodies, by their bearing against each other in defiance of law. And Merodach the Chaldean, king of Babylon, being struck with amazement at that time — for he studied the science of astrology, and measured the courses of these bodies carefully — on learning the cause, sent a letter and gifts to Hezekiah, just as also the wise men from the east did to Christ.

II.

From the Discourse of St. Hippolytus on the beginning of Isaiah.[10]

Under Egypt he meant the world, and under things made with hands its idolatry, and under the shaking its subversion and dissolution. [11]"And the Lord, the Word, he represented as upon a light cloud, referring to that most pure tabernacle, in which setting up His throne, our Lord Jesus Christ came into the world to shake error.

III.

We find in the commentaries, written by our predecessors, that that day had thirty-two hours.

---

6 In Gallandi, from a codex of the Coislin Library, Num. 193, fol. 36.
7 [Here we have the blunder (noted *supra*, p. 175) repeated as to Rome, which must be here taken as meaning the *Roman Province*, not the See. The word "Bishop," which avoids the ambiguity above noted, I have therefore put into parenthesis.]
8 Isa. xxxviii. 5, 7, 8.
9 Josh. x. 12.
10 [Theodoret, in his First Dialogue.]
11 The text is evidently corrupt: Κύριον δὲ τὸν Λόγον, νεφέλην δὲ κούφην τὸ καθαρώτατον σκῆνος, etc. The reference must be to ch. xix. 1.

For when the sun had run its course, and reached the tenth hour, and the shadow had gone down by the ten degrees in the house of the temple, the sun turned back again by the ten degrees, according to the word of the Lord, and there were thus twenty hours. And again, the sun accomplished its own proper course, according to the common law, and reached its setting. And thus there were thirty-two hours.[1]

ON JEREMIAH AND EZEKIEL.[2]

What were the dimensions, then, of the temple of Solomon? Its length was sixty cubits, and its breadth twenty. And it was not turned to the east, that the worshippers might not worship the rising sun, but the Lord of the sun. And let no one marvel if, when the Scripture gives the length at forty cubits, I have said sixty. For a little after it mentions the other twenty, in describing the holy of holies, which it also names Dabir. Thus the holy place was forty cubits, and the holy of holies other twenty. And Josephus says that the temple had two storeys,[3] and that the whole height was one hundred and twenty cubits. For so also the book of Chronicles indicates, saying, "And Solomon began to build the house of God. In length its first measure was sixty cubits, and its breadth twenty cubits, and its height one hundred and twenty; and he overlaid it within with pure gold."[4]

ON DANIEL.

I.

Preface by the most holy Hippolytus, (Bishop) of Rome.[5]

As I wish to give an accurate account of the times of the captivity of the children of Israel in Babylon, and to discuss the prophecies contained in the visions of the blessed Daniel, (as well as) his manner of life from his boyhood in Babylon, I too shall proceed to bear my testimony to that holy and righteous man, a prophet and witness of Christ, who not only declared the visions of Nebuchadnezzar the king in those times, but also trained youths of like mind with himself, and raised up faithful witnesses in the world. He is born, then, in the time of the prophetic ministry of the blessed Jeremiah, and in the reign of Jehoiakim or Eliakim. Along with

the other captives, he is carried off a prisoner to Babylon. Now there are born to the blessed Josiah these five sons — Jehoahaz, Eliakim, Johanan, Zedekiah, or Jeconiah, and Sadum.[6] And on his father's death, Jehoahaz is anointed as king by the people at the age of twenty-three years. Against him comes up Pharaoh-Necho, in the third month of his reign; and he takes him (Jehoahaz) prisoner, and carries him into Egypt, and imposes tribute on the land to the extent of one hundred talents of silver and ten talents of gold. And in his stead he sets up his brother Eliakim as king over the land, whose name also he changed to Jehoiakim, and who was then eleven years old. Against him came up Nebuchadnezzar king of Babylon,[7] and carries him off prisoner to Babylon, taking with him also some of the vessels of the house in Jerusalem. Thrown into prison as a friend of Pharaoh, and as one set up by him over the kingdom,[8] he is released at length in the thirty-seventh year by Evil-Merodach king of Babylon; and he cut his hair short, and was counsellor to him, and ate at his table until the day that he died. On his removal, his son Jehoiakim[9] reigns three years.[10] And against him came up Nebuchadnezzar, and transports him and ten thousand of the men of his people to Babylon, and sets up in his stead his father's brother, whose name he changed also to Zedekiah; and after making agreement with him by oath and treaty, he returns to Babylon. This (Zedekiah), after a reign of eleven years, revolted from him and went over to Pharaoh king of Egypt. And in the tenth year Nebuchadnezzar came against him from the land of the Chaldeans, and surrounded the city with a stockade, and environed it all round, and completely shut it up. In this way the larger number of them perished by famine, and others perished by the sword, and some were taken prisoners, and the city was burned with fire, and the temple and the wall were destroyed. And the army of the Chaldeans seized all the treasure that was found in the house of the Lord, and all the vessels of gold and silver; and all the brass, Nebuzaradan, chief of the slaughterers,[11] stripped off, and carried it to Babylon. And the army of the Chaldeans pursued Zedekiah himself as he fled by night along with seven hundred men, and surprised him in Jericho, and brought him to the king of Babylon at Reblatha. And the king pronounced judgment upon him in wrath, because he had violated the oath of the Lord, and the agreement he had made with him; and he

---

[1] Hippolytus wrote on Isaiah with the view of making the most of the favourable disposition entertained by the Emperor Alexander Severus towards the Christians, and particularly on that part where the retrogression of the sun is recorded as a sign of an extension of life to Hezekiah.

[2] That Hippolytus wrote on Jeremiah is recorded, so far as I know, by none of the ancients; for the quotation given in the *Catena* of Greek fathers on Jer. xvii. 11 is taken from his book *On Antichrist*, chap. lv. Rufinus mentions that Hippolytus wrote on a certain part of the prophet Ezekiel, viz., on those chapters which contain the description of the temple of Jerusalem; and of that commentary the following fragments are preserved. — *De Magistris.*

[3] διόροφον.

[4] 2 Chron. iii. 1, 3, 4.

[5] Simon de Magistris, *Daniel secundum Septuaginta*, from the *Codex Chisianus*, Rome, 1772; and Mai, *Script. vet. collectio nova*, i. iii. ed. 1831, pp. 29–56.

[6] Shallum. See 1 Chron. iii. 15.

[7] 2 Kings xxiv. 10.

[8] 2 Kings xxv. 27. Note the confusion between Jehoiakim and Jehoiachin in what follows.

[9] i.e., Jehoiachin.

[10] Others τριμήνιον = three months.

[11] ἀρχιμάγειρος, "chief cook."

slew his sons before his face, and put out Zedekiah's eyes. And he cast him into chains of iron, and carried him to Babylon; and there he remained grinding at the mill until the day of his death. And when he died, they took his body and cast it behind the wall of Nineveh. In his case is fulfilled the prophecy of Jeremiah, saying, "(As) I live, saith the Lord, though Jeconiah son of Jehoiakim king of Judah should become the signet upon my right hand, yet will I pluck thee thence; and I will give thee into the hands of them that seek thy life, of them whose face thou fearest, even into the hands of the Chaldeans. And I will cast thee out, and thy mother that bare thee, into a country where thou wast not born; and there ye shall die. But to the land which they desire in their souls, I will not send thee back. Dishonoured is Jeconias, like an unserviceable vessel, of which there is no use, since he is cast out and expelled into a land which he knew not. O earth, hear the word of the Lord. Write this man, a man excommunicate; for no man of his seed shall prosper (grow up), sitting upon the throne of David, ruling any more in Judah."[1] Thus the captivity in Babylon befell them after the exodus from Egypt. When the whole people, then, was transported, and the city made desolate, and the sanctuary destroyed, that the word of the Lord might be fulfilled which He spake by the mouth of the prophet Jeremiah, saying, "The sanctuary shall be desolate seventy years;"[2] then we find that the blessed Daniel prophesied in Babylon, and appeared as the vindicator of Susanna.

II.

The interpretation by Hippolytus, (bishop) of Rome, of the visions of Daniel and Nebuchadnezzar, taken in conjunction.[3]

1. In speaking of a "lioness from the sea,"[4] he meant the rising of the kingdom of Babylon, and that this was the "golden head of the image." And in speaking of its "eagle wings," he meant that king Nebuchadnezzar was exalted, and that his glory was lifted up against God. Then he says "its wings were plucked off," i.e., that his glory was destroyed; for he was driven out of his kingdom. And the words, "A man's heart was given it, and it was made stand upon the feet of a man," mean that he came to himself again, and recognised that he was but a man, and gave the glory to God. Then after the lioness he sees a second beast, "like a bear," which

signified the Persians. For after the Babylonians the Persians obtained the power. And in saying that "it had three ribs in its mouth," he pointed to the three nations, Persians, Medes, and Babylonians, which were expressed in the image by the silver after the gold. Then comes the third beast, "a leopard," which means the Greeks; for after the Persians, Alexander of Macedon had the power, when Darius was overthrown, which was also indicated by the brass in the image. And in saying that the beast "had four wings of a fowl, and four heads," he showed most clearly how the kingdom of Alexander was parted into four divisions. For in speaking of four heads, he meant the four kings that arose out of it. For Alexander, when dying, divided his kingdom into four parts. Then he says, "The fourth beast (was) dreadful and terrible: it had iron teeth, and claws of brass." Who, then, are meant by this but the Romans, whose kingdom, the kingdom that still stands, is expressed by the iron? "for," says he, "its legs are of iron."

2. After this, then, what remains, beloved, but the toes of the feet of the image, in which "part shall be of iron and part of clay mixed together?" By the toes of the feet he meant, mystically, the ten kings that rise out of that kingdom. As Daniel says, "I considered the beast; and, lo, (there were) ten horns behind, among which shall come up another little horn springing from them;" by which none other is meant than the antichrist that is to rise; and he shall set up the kingdom of Judah. And in saying that "three horns" were "plucked up by the roots" by this one, he indicates the three kings of Egypt, Libya, and Ethiopia, whom this one will slay in the array of war. And when he has conquered all, he will prove himself a terrible and savage tyrant, and will cause tribulation and persecution to the saints, exalting himself against them. And after him, it remains that "the stone" shall come from heaven which "smote the image" and shivered it, and subverted all the kingdoms, and gave the kingdom to the saints of the Most High. This "became a great mountain, and filled the whole earth."

3. As these things, then, are destined to come to pass, and as the toes of the image turn out to be democracies,[5] and the ten horns of the beast are distributed among ten kings, let us look at what is before us more carefully, and scan it, as it were, with open eye. The "golden head of the image" is identical with the "lioness," by which the Babylonians were represented. "The golden shoulders and the arms of silver" are the same with the "bear," by which the Persians and Medes are meant. "The belly and

---

[1] Jer. xxii. 24, etc.
[2] Jer. xxv. 11.
[3] The same method of explaining the two visions is also adopted by Jacobus Nisibenus, serm. v., and by his illustrious disciple Ephraem Syrus on Dan. vii. 4. [Let me again refer to Dr. Pusey's work on Daniel, as invaluable in this connection. The comments of our author on this book and on "the Antichrist," *infra*, deserve special attention, as from a disciple of the disciples of St. John himself.]
[4] Dan. vii.

[5] [True in A.D. 1885. A very pregnant testimony to our own times.]

thighs of brass" are the "leopard," by which the Greeks who ruled from Alexander onwards are intended. The "legs of iron" are the "dreadful and terrible beast," by which the Romans who hold the empire now are meant. The "toes of clay and iron" are the "ten horns" which are to be. The "one other little horn springing up in their midst" is the "antichrist." The stone that "smites the image and breaks it in pieces," and that filled the whole earth, is Christ, who comes from heaven and brings judgment on the world.

4. But that we may not leave our subject at this point undemonstrated, we are obliged to discuss the matter of the times, of which a man should not speak hastily, because they are a light to him. For as the times are noted from the foundation of the world, and reckoned from Adam, they set clearly before us the matter with which our inquiry deals. For the first appearance of our Lord in the flesh took place in Bethlehem, under Augustus, in the year 5500; and He suffered in the thirty-third year. And 6,000 years must needs be accomplished, in order that the Sabbath may come, the rest, the holy day "on which God rested from all His works." [1] For the Sabbath is the type and emblem of the future kingdom of the saints, when they "shall reign with Christ," when He comes from heaven, as John says in his Apocalypse: for "a day with the Lord is as a thousand years." [2] Since, then, in SIX days God made all things, it follows that 6,000 years must be fulfilled. And they are not yet fulfilled, as John says: "five are fallen; one is," that is, the sixth; "the other is not yet come." [3]

5. In mentioning the "other," moreover, he specifies the seventh, in which there is rest. But some one may be ready to say, How will you prove to me that the Saviour was born in the year 5500? Learn that easily, O man; for the things that took place of old in the wilderness, under Moses, in the case of the tabernacle, were constituted types and emblems of spiritual mysteries, in order that, when the truth came in Christ in these last days, you might be able to perceive that these things were fulfilled. For He says to him, "And thou shalt make the ark of imperishable wood, and shalt overlay it with pure gold within and without; and thou shalt make the length of it two cubits and a half, and the breadth thereof one cubit and a half, and a cubit and a half the height;" [4] which measures, when summed up together, make five cubits and

a half, so that the 5500 years might be signified thereby.

6. At that time, then, the Saviour appeared and showed His own body to the world, (born) of the Virgin, who was the "ark overlaid with pure gold," with the Word within and the Holy Spirit without; so that the truth is demonstrated, and the "ark" made manifest. From the birth of Christ, then, we must reckon the 500 years that remain to make up the 6000, and thus the end shall be. And that the Saviour appeared in the world, bearing the imperishable ark, His own body, at a time which was the fifth and half, John declares: "Now it was the sixth hour," [5] he says, intimating by that, one-half of the day. But a day with the Lord is 1000 years; and the half of that, therefore, is 500 years. For it was not meet that He should appear earlier, for the burden of the law still endured, nor yet when the sixth day was fulfilled (for the baptism is changed), but on the fifth and half, in order that in the remaining half time the gospel might be preached to the whole world, and that when the sixth day was completed He might end the present life.

7. Since, then, the Persians held the mastery for 330 years, [6] and after them the Greeks, who were yet more glorious, held it for 300 years, of necessity the fourth beast, as being strong and mightier than all that were before it, will reign 500 years. When the times are fulfilled, and the ten horns spring from the beast in the last (times), then Antichrist will appear among them. When he makes war against the saints, and persecutes them, then may we expect the manifestation of the Lord from heaven.

8. The prophet having thus instructed us with all exactness as to the certainty of the things that are to be, broke off from his present subject, and passed again to the kingdom of the Persians and Greeks, recounting to us another vision which took place, and was fulfilled in its proper time; in order that, by establishing our belief in this, he might be able to present us to God as readier believers in the things that are to be. Accordingly, what he had narrated in the first vision, he again recounts in detail for the edification of the faithful. For by the "ram pushing westward, and northward, and southward," he means Darius, the king of the Persians, who overcame all the nations; "for," says he, "these beasts shall not stand before him." And by the "he-goat that came from the west," he means Alexander the Macedonian,

---

[1] This is what Photius condemned in Hippolytus. Irenæus, however, held the same opinion (book v. c. 28 and 29). The same view is expressed yet earlier in the Epistle of Barnabas (sec. 15). It was an opinion adopted from the rabbis.
[2] Ps. xc. 4.
[3] Apoc. xvii. 10.
[4] Ex. xxv. 10.

[5] John xix. 14.
[6] Migne thinks we should read διακόσια τριάκοντα, i.e., 230, as it is also in Julius Africanus, who was contemporary with Hippolytus. As to the duration of the Greek empire, Hippolytus and Africanus make it both 300 years, if we follow Jerome's version of the latter in his comment on Dan. ix. 24. Eusebius makes it seventy years longer in his *Demonstr. Evang.*, viii. 2.

the king of the Greeks; and in that he " came against that very ram, and was moved with choler, and smote him upon the face, and shivered him, and cast him upon the ground, and stamped upon him," this expresses just what has happened.

9. For Alexander waged war against Darius, and overcame him, and made himself master of the whole sovereignty, after routing and destroying his camp. Then, after the exaltation of the he-goat, his horn — the great one, namely — was broken; and there arose four horns under it, toward the four winds of heaven. For, when Alexander had made himself master of all the land of Persia, and had reduced its people into subjection, he thereupon died, after dividing his kingdom into four principalities, as has been shown above. And from that time " one horn was exalted, and waxed great, even to the power of heaven; and by him the sacrifice," he says, " was disturbed, and righteousness cast down to the ground."

10. For Antiochus arose, surnamed Epiphanes, who was of the line of Alexander. And after he had reigned in Syria, and brought under him all Egypt, he went up to Jerusalem, and entered the sanctuary, and seized all the treasures in the house of the Lord, and the golden candlestick, and the table, and the altar, and made a great slaughter in the land; even as it is written: " And the sanctuary shall be trodden under foot, unto evening and unto morning, a thousand and three hundred days." For it happened that the sanctuary remained desolate during that period, three years and a half, that the thousand and three hundred days might be fulfilled; until Judas Maccabæus arose after the death of his father Matthias, and withstood him, and destroyed the encampment of Antiochus, and delivered the city, and recovered the sanctuary, and restored it in strict accordance with the law.

11. Since, then, the angel Gabriel also recounted these things to the prophet, as they have been understood by us, as they have also taken place, and as they have been all clearly described in the books of the Maccabees, let us see further what he says on the other weeks. For when he read the book of Jeremiah the prophet, in which it was written that the sanctuary would be desolate seventy years, he made confession with fastings and supplications, and prayed that the people might return sooner from their captivity to the city Jerusalem. Thus, then, he speaks in his account: " In the first year of Darius the son of Ahasuerus, of the seed of the Medes, who was king over the realm of the Chaldeans, I Daniel understood in the books the number of the years, as the word of the Lord had come to Jeremiah the prophet, for

the accomplishment of the desolation of Jerusalem in seventy years," etc.

12. After his confession and supplication, the angel says to him, " Thou art a man [1] greatly beloved: " for thou desirest to see things of which thou shalt be informed by me; and in their own time these things will be fulfilled; and he touched me, saying, " Seventy weeks are determined upon thy people, and upon the holy city, to seal up sins and to blot out transgressions, and to seal up vision and prophet, and to anoint the Most Holy; and thou shalt know and understand, that from the going forth of words for the answer, and for the building of Jerusalem, unto Christ the Prince, shall be seven weeks, and threescore and two weeks."

13. Having mentioned therefore seventy weeks, and having divided them into two parts, in order that what was spoken by him to the prophet might be better understood, he proceeds thus, " Unto Christ the Prince shall be seven weeks," which make forty-nine years. It was in the twenty-first year that Daniel saw these things in Babylon. Hence, the forty-nine years added to the twenty-one, make up the seventy years, of which the blessed Jeremiah spake: " The sanctuary shall be desolate seventy years from the captivity that befell them under Nebuchadnezzar; and after these things the people will return, and sacrifice and offering will be presented, when Christ is their Prince." [2]

14. Now of what Christ does he speak, but of Jesus the son of Josedech, who returned at that time along with the people, and offered sacrifice according to the law, in the seventieth year, when the sanctuary was built? For all the kings and priests were styled Christs, because they were anointed with the holy oil, which Moses of old prepared. These, then, bore the name of the Lord in their own persons, showing aforetime the type, and presenting the image until the perfect King and Priest appeared from heaven, who alone did the will of the Father; as also it is written in Kings: " And I will raise me up a faithful priest, that shall do all things according to my heart." [3]

15. In order, then, to show the time when He is to come whom the blessed Daniel desired to see, he says, " And after seven weeks there are other threescore and two weeks," which period embraces the space of 434 years. For after the return of the people from Babylon under the leadership of Jesus the son of Josedech, and Ezra the scribe, and Zerubbabel the son of Salathiel, of the tribe of David, there were 434 years unto the coming of Christ, in order that the Priest of priests might be manifested in

---

[1] Literally, "a man of *desires*." [Our author plays on this word, as if the desire of knowledge were referred to. Our Authorized Version is better, and the rendering might be " a man of loves."]
[2] Jer. xxv. 11.
[3] 1 Sam. ii. 35.

the world, and that He who taketh away the sins of the world might be evidently set forth, as John speaks concerning Him: "Behold the Lamb of God, that taketh away the sin of the world!"[1] And in like manner Gabriel says: "To blot out transgressions, and make reconciliation for sins." But who has blotted out our transgressions? Paul the apostle teaches us, saying, "He is our peace who made both one;"[2] and then, "Blotting out the handwriting of sins that was against us."[3]

16. That transgressions, therefore, are blotted out, and that reconciliation is made for sins, is shown by this. But who are they who have reconciliation made for their sins, but they who believe on His name, and propitiate His countenance by good works? And that after the return of the people from Babylon there was a space of 434 years, until the time of the birth of Christ, may be easily understood. For, since the first covenant was given to the children of Israel after a period of 434 years, it follows that the second covenant also should be defined by the same space of time, in order that it might be expected by the people and easily recognised by the faithful.

17. And for this reason Gabriel says: "And to anoint the Most Holy." And the Most Holy is none else but the Son of God alone, who, when He came and manifested Himself, said to them, "The Spirit of the Lord is upon me, because He has anointed me;"[4] and so forth. Whosoever, therefore, believed on the heavenly Priest, were cleansed by that same Priest, and their sins were blotted out. And whosoever believed not on Him, despising Him as a man, had their sins sealed, as those which could not be taken away; whence the angel, foreseeing that not all should believe on Him, said, "To finish sins, and to seal up sins." For as many as continued to disbelieve Him, even to the end, had their sins not finished, but sealed to be kept for judgment. But as many as will believe on Him as One able to remit sins, have their sins blotted out. Wherefore he says: "And to seal up vision and prophet."

18. For when He came who is the fulfilling of the law and of the prophets (for the law and the prophets were till John), it was necessary that the things spoken by them should be confirmed (sealed), in order that at the coming of the Lord all things loosed should be brought to light, and that things bound of old should now be loosed by Him, as the Lord said Himself to the rulers of the people, when they were indignant at the cure on the Sabbath-day: "Ye hypo-crites, doth not each one of you loose his ox or his ass from the stall, and lead him away to watering? and ought not this woman, being a daughter of Abraham, whom Satan hath bound these eighteen years, be loosed on the Sabbath-day?"[5] Whomsoever, therefore, Satan bound in chains, these did the Lord on His coming loose from the bonds of death, having bound our strong adversary and delivered humanity. As also Isaiah says: "Then will He say to those in chains, Go forth; and to them that are in darkness, Show yourselves."[6]

19. And that the things spoken of old by the law and the prophets were all sealed, and that they were unknown to men, Isaiah declares when he says: "And they will deliver the book that is sealed to one that is learned, and will say to him, Read this; and he will say, I cannot read it, for it is sealed."[7] It was meet and necessary that the things spoken of old by the prophets should be sealed to the unbelieving Pharisees, who thought that they understood the letter of the law, and be opened to the believing. The things, therefore, which of old were sealed, are now by the grace of God the Lord all open to the saints.

20. For He was Himself the perfect Seal, and the Church is the key: "He who openeth, and no man shutteth; and shutteth, and no man openeth,"[8] as John says. And again, the same says: "And I saw, on the right hand of Him that sat on the throne, a book written within and without, sealed with seven seals; and I saw an angel proclaiming with a loud voice, Who is worthy to open the book, and to loose the seals thereof?" and so forth. "And I beheld in the midst of the throne, and of the four beasts, a Lamb standing slain, having seven horns, and seven eyes, which are the seven Spirits of God sent forth into all the earth. And He came and took the book out of the right hand of Him that sat upon the throne. And when He had taken the book, the four beasts and four-and-twenty elders fell down before the Lamb, having harps and golden vials full of incense, which is the prayers of the saints. And they sing a new song, saying, Thou art worthy to take the book, and to open the seals thereof: for Thou wast slain, and hast redeemed us to God by Thy blood."[9] He took the book, therefore, and loosed it, in order that the things spoken concerning Him of old in secret, might now be proclaimed with boldness upon the house-tops.[10]

21. For this reason, then, the angel says to Daniel, "Seal the words, for the vision is until

[1] John i. 29.
[2] Eph. ii. 14.
[3] Col. ii. 14.
[4] Isa. lxi. 1; Luke iv. 18.

[5] Luke xiii. 15, 16.
[6] Isa. xlix. 9.
[7] Isa. xxix. 11.
[8] Apoc. iii. 7.
[9] Apoc. v.
[10] Cf. Matt. x. 27.

the end of the time." But to Christ it was not said "seal," but "loose" the things bound of old; in order that, by His grace, we might know the will of the Father, and believe upon Him whom He has sent for the salvation of men, Jesus our Lord. He says, therefore, "They shall return, and the street shall be built, and the wall;" which in reality took place. For the people returned and built the city, and the temple, and the wall round about. Then he says: "After threescore and two weeks the times will be fulfilled, and one week will make a covenant with many; and in the midst (half) of the week sacrifice and oblation will be removed, and in the temple will be the abomination of desolations."

22. For when the threescore and two weeks are fulfilled, and Christ is come, and the Gospel is preached in every place, the times being then accomplished, there will remain only one week, the last, in which Elias will appear, and Enoch, and in the midst of it the abomination of desolation will be manifested,[1] viz., Antichrist, announcing desolation to the world. And when he comes, the sacrifice and oblation will be removed, which now are offered to God in every place by the nations. These things being thus recounted, the prophet again describes another vision to us. For he had no other care save to be accurately instructed in all things that are to be, and to prove himself an instructor in such.

23. He says then: "In the third year of Cyrus king of Persia, a word was revealed unto Daniel, whose name was Belshazzar; and the word was true, and great power and understanding were given him in the vision. In those days, I Daniel was mourning three weeks of days. I ate no pleasant bread, neither came flesh nor wine into my mouth, neither did I anoint myself at all, till three weeks of days were fulfilled. On the fourth day of the first month I humbled myself," says he, "one and twenty days," praying to the living God, and asking of Him the revelation of the mystery. And the Father in truth heard me, and sent His own Word, to show what should happen by Him. And that took place, indeed, by the great river. For it was meet that the Son should be manifested there, where also He was to remove sins.

24. "And I lifted up mine eyes," he says, "and, behold, a man clothed in linen."[2] In the first vision he says, "Behold, the angel Gabriel (was) sent." Here, however, it is not so; but he sees the Lord, not yet indeed as perfect man, but with the appearance and form of man, as he says: "And, behold, a man clothed in linen." For in being clothed in a various-col-

oured coat, he indicated mystically[3] the variety of the graces of our calling. For the priestly coat was made up of different colours, as various nations waited for Christ's coming, in order that we might be made up (as one body) of many colours. "And his loins were girded with the gold of Ophaz."

25. Now the word "Ophaz," which is a word transferred from Hebrew to Greek, denotes pure gold. With a pure girdle, therefore, he was girded round the loins. For the Word was to bear us all, binding us like a girdle round His body, in His own love. The complete body was His,[4] but we are members in His body, united together, and sustained by the Word Himself. "And his body was like Tharses."[5] Now "Tharses," by interpretation, is "Ethiopians." For that it would be difficult to recognise Him, the prophet had thus already announced beforehand, intimating that He would be manifested in the flesh in the world, but that many would find it difficult to recognise Him. "And his face as lightning, and his eyes as lamps of fire;" for it was meet that the fiery and judicial power of the Word should be signified aforetime, in the exercise of which He will cause the fire (of His judgment) to light with justice upon the impious, and consume them.

26. He added also these words: "And his arms and his feet like polished brass;" to denote the first calling of men, and the second calling like unto it, viz., of the Gentiles. [6] "For the last shall be as the first; for I will set thy rulers as at the beginning, and thy leaders as before. And His voice was as the voice of a great multitude."[7] For all we who believe on Him in these days utter things oracular, as speaking by His mouth the things appointed by Him.

27. And after a little He says to him: "Knowest thou wherefore I come unto thee? And now will I return to fight with the prince of Persia. But I will show thee that which is noted in the Scripture of truth: and there is none that holdeth with me in these things but Michael your prince, and I left him there. For from the day that thou didst give thy countenance to be afflicted before the Lord thy God, thy prayer was heard, and I was sent to fight with the prince of Persia:" for a certain counsel was formed not to send the people away: "that therefore thy prayer might be speedily granted, I withstood him, and left Michael there."

---

[1] In the text, the word ἕως, "until," is introduced, which seems spurious.
[2] βαδδίν.

[3] In the text, μυστηρίων (of "mysteries"), for which μυστηριω-δῶς or μυστικῶς, "mystically," is proposed.
[4] The Latin translation renders: His body was perfect.
[5] "Tharses" (Θαρσείς) in Hippolytus. The Septuagint gives Θαρσίς as the translation of the Hebrew תַּרְשִׁישׁ, rendered in our version as "beryl" (Dan. x. 6).
[6] Isa. i. 26.
[7] Apoc. xix. 6.

28. And who was he that spake, but the angel who was given to the people, as he says in the law of Moses : " I will not go with you, because the people is stiff-necked ; but my angel shall go before along with you ? " [1] This (angel) withstood Moses at the inn, when he was bringing the child uncircumcised into Egypt. For it was not allowed Moses, who was the elder (or legate) and mediator of the law, and who proclaimed the covenant of the fathers, to introduce a child uncircumcised, lest he should be deemed a false prophet and deceiver by the people. " And now," says he, " will I show the truth to thee." Could the Truth have shown anything else but the truth ?

29. He says therefore to him : " Behold, there shall stand up three kings in Persia : and the fourth shall be far richer than they all ; and when he has got possession of his riches, he shall stand up against all the realms of Grecia. And a mighty king shall stand up, and shall rule with great dominion, and do according to his will ; and when his kingdom stands, it shall be broken, and shall be divided toward the four winds of heaven." These things we have already discussed above, when we discoursed upon the four beasts. But since Scripture now again sets them forth explicitly, we must also discourse upon them a second time, that we may not leave Scripture unused and unexplained.

30. " There shall stand up yet three kings," he says, " in Persia ; and the fourth shall be far richer than they all." This has been fulfilled. For after Cyrus arose Darius, and then Artaxerxes. These were the three kings ; (and) the Scripture is fulfilled. " And the fourth shall be far richer than they all." Who is that but Darius, who reigned and made himself glorious, — who was rich, and assailed all the realms of Greece ? Against him rose Alexander of Macedon, who destroyed his kingdom ; and after he had reduced the Persians, his own kingdom was divided toward the four winds of heaven. For Alexander at his death divided his kingdom into four principalities. " And a king shall stand up, and shall enter into the fortress of the king of Egypt."

31. For Antiochus became king of Syria. He held the sovereignty in the 107th year of the kingdom of the Greeks. And in those same times indeed he made war against Ptolemy king of Egypt, and conquered him, and won the power. On returning from Egypt he went up to Jerusalem, in the 103d year, and carrying off with him all the treasures of the Lord's house, he marched to Antioch. And after two years of days the king sent his raiser of taxes [2] into the cities of Judea, to compel the Jews to for-

sake the laws of their fathers, and submit to the decrees of the king. And he came, and tried to compel them, saying, " Come forth, and do the commandment of the king, and ye shall live."

32. But they said, " We will not come forth, neither will we do the king's commandment ; we will die in our innocency : and he slew of them a thousand souls." [3] The things, therefore, which were spoken to the blessed Daniel are fulfilled : " And my servants shall be afflicted, and shall fall by famine, and by sword, and by captivity." [4] Daniel, however, adds : " And they shall be holpen with a little help." For at that time Matthias arose, and Judas Maccabæus, and helped them, and delivered them from the hand of the Greeks.

33. That therefore was fulfilled which was spoken in the Scripture. He proceeds then thus : " And the (king's) daughter of the South shall come to the king of the North to make an agreement with him ; and the arms of him that bringeth her shall not stand ; and she, too, shall be smitten, and shall fall, and he that bringeth her." For this was a certain Ptolemaïs,[5] queen of Egypt. At that time indeed she went forth with her two sons, Ptolemy and Philometor, to make an agreement with Antiochus king of Syria ; and when she came to Scythopolis, she was slain there. For he who brought her betrayed her. At that same time, the two brothers made war against each other, and Philometor was slain, and Ptolemy gained the power.

34. War, then, was again made by Ptolemy against Antiochus, (and) Antiochus met him. For thus saith the Scripture : " And the king of the South shall stand up against the king of the North, and her seed shall stand up against him." And what seed but Ptolemy, who made war with Antiochus ? And Antiochus having gone forth against him, and having failed to overcome him, had to flee, and returned to Antioch, and collected a larger host. Ptolemy accordingly took his whole equipment, and carried it into Egypt. And the Scripture is fulfilled, as Daniel says : And he shall carry off into Egypt their gods, and their cast-works, and all their precious (vessels of) gold.

35. And after these things Antiochus went forth a second time to make war against him, and overcome Ptolemy. And after these events Antiochus commenced hostilities again against the children of Israel, and despatched one Nicanor with a large army to subdue the Jews, at the time when Judas, after the death of Matthias, ruled the people ; and so forth, as is written in

---

[1] Ex. xxxii. 4, xxxiii. 3.
[2] φορολόγον.

[3] 1 Macc. ii. 33.
[4] Dan. xi. 33.
[5] He seems to refer to Cleopatra, wife and niece of Physco. For Lathyrus was sometimes called Philometor in ridicule (ἐπὶ χλευασμῴ), as Pausanias says in the *Attica*.

the Maccabees. These events having taken place, the Scripture says again : " And there shall stand up another king, and he shall prevail upon the earth ; and the king of the South shall stand up, and he shall obtain his daughter to wife."

36. For it happened that there arose a certain Alexander,[1] son of Philip. He withstood Antiochus[2] at that time, and made war upon him, and cut him off, and gained possession of the kingdom. Then he sent to Ptolemy king of Egypt, saying, Give me thy daughter Cleopatra to wife. And he gave her to Alexander to wife. And thus the Scripture is fulfilled, when it says : "And he shall obtain his daughter to wife." And it says further : "And he shall corrupt her, and she shall not be his wife." This also has been truly fulfilled. For after Ptolemy had given him his daughter, he returned, and saw the mighty and glorious kingdom of Alexander. And coveting its possession, he spoke falsely to Alexander, as the Scripture says : "And the two kings shall speak lies at (one) table." And, in sooth, Ptolemy betook himself to Egypt, and collected a great army, and attacked the city at the time when Alexander had marched into Cilicia.

37. Ptolemy then invaded the country, and established garrisons throughout the cities ; and on making himself master of Judea, set out for his daughter, and sent letters to Demetrius in the islands, saying, Come and meet me here, and I will give thee my daughter Cleopatra to wife, for Alexander has sought to kill me. Demetrius came accordingly, and Ptolemy received him, and gave him her who had been destined for Alexander. Thus is fulfilled that which is written : "And he shall corrupt her, and she shall not be his wife." Alexander was slain. Then Ptolemy wore two crowns, that of Syria and that of Egypt, and died the third day after he had assumed them. Thus is fulfilled that which is written in Scripture : "And they shall not give him the glory of the kingdom." For he died, and received not honour from all as king.

38. The prophet then, after thus recounting the things which have taken place already, and been fulfilled in their times, declares yet another mystery to us, while he points out the last times. For he says : "And there shall rise up another shameless king ; and he shall exalt himself above every god, and shall magnify himself, and shall speak marvellous things, and shall prosper till

the indignation be accomplished ; " and so forth. "And these shall escape out of his hand, Edom, and Moab, and the chief (or principality) of the children of Ammon. And he shall stretch forth his hand upon the land ; and the land of Egypt shall not escape. And he shall have power over the secret treasures of gold and silver, and over all the precious things of Egypt and of the Libyans, and the Ethiopians in their strongholds."

39. Thus, then, does the prophet set forth these things concerning the Antichrist, who shall be shameless, a war-maker, and despot, who, exalting himself above all kings and above every god, shall build the city of Jerusalem, and restore the sanctuary. Him the impious will worship as God, and will bend to him the knee, thinking him to be the Christ. He shall cut off the two witnesses and forerunners of Christ, who proclaim His glorious kingdom from heaven, as it is said : "And I will give (power) unto my two witnesses, and they shall prophesy a thousand two hundred and threescore days, clothed in sackcloth."[3] As also it was announced to Daniel : "And one week shall confirm a covenant with many ; and in the midst of the week it shall be that the sacrifice and oblation shall be removed " — that the one week might be shown to be divided into two. The two witnesses, then, shall preach three years and a half ; and Antichrist shall make war upon the saints during the rest of the week, and desolate the world, that what is written may be fulfilled : "And they shall make the abomination of desolation for a thousand two hundred and ninety days."

40. Daniel has spoken, therefore, of two abominations ; the one of destruction, and the other of desolation. What is that of destruction, but that which Antiochus established there at the time ? And what is that of desolation, but that which shall be universal when Antichrist comes ? "And there shall escape out of his hand, Edom, and Moab, and the chief of the children of Ammon." For these are they who ally themselves with him on account of their kinship, and first address him as king. Those of Edom are the sons of Esau, who inhabit Mount Seir. And Moab and Ammon are they who are descended from his two daughters, as Isaiah also says : "And they shall fly (extend themselves) in the ships of strangers, and they shall also plunder the sea ; and those from the east, and from the west, and the north, shall give them honour : and the children of Ammon shall first obey them."[4] He shall be proclaimed king by them, and shall be magnified by all, and shall prove himself an abomination of desolation to the world, and shall reign for a thousand two hun-

---

[1] He refers to Alexander I. king of Syria, of whom we read in 1 Macc. x. He pretended to be the son of Antiochus Epiphanes, and even gained a decree of the senate of Rome in his favour as such. Yet he was a person of unknown origin, as indeed he acknowledged himself in his choice of the designation *Theopator*. Livy calls him " a man unknown, and of uncertain parentage" (*homo ignotus et incertæ stirpis*). So Hippolytus calls him here, " a certain Alexander" (τινα). He had also other surnames, e.g., Euergetes, Balas, etc.

[2] For "Antiochus" in the text, read "Demetrius."

[3] Apoc. xi. 3.
[4] Isa. xi. 14.

dred and ninety days. "Blessed is he that waiteth, and cometh to the thousand three hundred and five and thirty days;" for when the abomination cometh and makes war upon the saints, whosoever shall survive his days, and reach the forty-five days, while the other period of fifty days advances, to him the kingdom of heaven comes. Antichrist, indeed, enters even into part of the fifty days, but the saints shall inherit the kingdom along with Christ.

41. These things being thus narrated, Daniel proceeds: "And, behold, there stood two men, the one on this side of the bank of the river, and the other on that side; and they made answer to the man that stood upon the bank of the river, and said to him, How long shall it be to the end of these wonderful words which thou hast spoken? And I heard the man clothed in linen, who was upon the water of the river; and he lifted up his right hand and his left hand unto heaven, and sware by Him that liveth for ever, that it shall be for a time, times, and an half; and they shall know all these things when the dispersion is accomplished."

42. Who, then, were the two men who stood on the bank of the river, but the law and the prophets? And who was he who stood upon the water, but He concerning whom they prophesied of old, who in the last times was to be borne witness to by the Father at the Jordan, and to be declared to the people boldly by John, "who wore the casty[1] of the scribe about his loins, and was clothed with a linen coat of various colours?" These, therefore, interrogate Him, knowing that to Him were given all government and power, in order to learn accurately of Him when He will bring the judgment on the world, and when the things spoken by Him will be fulfilled. And He, desiring by all means to convince them, lifted His right hand and His left hand to heaven, and sware by Him that liveth for ever. Who is He that swore, and by whom sware He? Manifestly the Son by the Father, saying, The Father liveth for ever, but in a time, and times, and an half, when the dispersion is accomplished, they shall know all these things.

43. By the stretching forth of His two hands He signified His passion; and by mentioning "a time, and times, and an half, when the dispersion is accomplished," He indicated the three years and a half of Antichrist. For by "a time" He means a year, and by "times" two years, and by an "half time" half a year. These are the thousand two hundred and ninety days of which Daniel prophesied for the finishing of the passion, and the accomplishment of the dispersion when Antichrist comes. In those days they shall know all these things. And from the time of the removal of the continuous sacrifice there are also reckoned one thousand two hundred and ninety days. (Then) iniquity shall abound, as the Lord also says: "Because iniquity shall abound, the love of many shall wax cold."[2]

44. And that divisions will arise when the falling away takes place, is without doubt. And when divisions arise, love is chilled. The words, "Blessed is he that waiteth and cometh to the thousand three hundred and five and thirty days," have also their value, as the Lord said: "But he that shall endure unto the end, the same shall be saved." Wherefore let us by no means admit the falling away, lest iniquity abound, and the abomination of desolation—that is, the adversary—overtake us. And He said to him, "unto evening"—that is, unto the consummation—"and morning." What is "morning?" The day of resurrection. For that is the beginning of another age, as the morning is the beginning of the day. And the thousand and four hundred days are the light of the world. For on the appearing of the light in the world (as He says, "I am the light of the world"), the sanctuary shall be purged, as he said,[3] (of) the adversary. For it cannot by any means be purged but by his destruction.

III.

SCHOLIA ON DANIEL.[4]

CHAP. I. I. "In the third year of the reign of Jehoiakim." The Scripture narrates these things, with the purpose of intimating the second captivity of the people, when Jehoiakim and the three youths with him, together with Daniel, were taken captive and carried off.

2. "And the Lord gave," etc. These words, "and the Lord gave," are written, that no one, in reading the introduction to the book, may attribute their capture to the strength of the captors and the slackness of their chief. And it is well said, "with part," for the deportation was for the correction, not the ruin, of the whole nation, that there might be no misapplication of the cause.

8. "And Daniel purposed in his heart." Oh, blessed are they who thus kept the covenant of the fathers, and transgressed not the law given by Moses, but feared the God proclaimed by him. These, though captives in a strange land, were not seduced by delicate meats, nor were they slaves to the pleasures of wine, nor were they caught by the bait of princely glory. But they kept their mouth holy and pure, that pure speech might proceed from pure mouths, and praise with such (mouths) the heavenly Father.

---

[1] Girdle.

[2] Matt. xxiv. 12.
[3] The text gives ὁ ἀντικείμενος, which is corrupt.
[4] Mai, *Script. vet. collectio nova*, i. p. iii. pp. 29-56.

12. "Prove now thy servants." They teach that it is not earthly meats that give to men their beauty and strength, but the grace of God bestowed by the Word. "And after a little." Thou hast seen the incorruptible faith of the youths, and the unalterable fear of God. They asked an interval of ten days, to prove therein that man cannot otherwise find grace with God than by believing the word preached by the Lord.

19. "And among them all, was found none like Daniel." These men, who were proved faithful witnesses in Babylon, were led by the Word in all wisdom, that by their means the idols of the Babylonians should be put to shame, and that Nebuchadnezzar should be overcome by three youths, and that by their faith the fire in the furnace should be kept at bay, and the desire of the wicked elders (or chiefs) proved vain.

CHAP. II. 3. "I have dreamed a dream." The dream, then, which was seen by the king was not an earthly dream, so that it might be interpreted by the wise of the world; but it was a heavenly dream, fulfilled in its proper times, according to the counsel and foreknowledge of God. And for this reason it was kept secret from men who think of earthly things, that to those who seek after heavenly things heavenly mysteries might be revealed. And, indeed, there was a similar case in Egypt in the time of Pharaoh and Joseph.

5. "The thing is gone from me." For this purpose was the vision concealed from the king, that he who was chosen of God., viz., Daniel, might be shown to be a prophet. For when things concealed from some are revealed by another, he who tells them is of necessity shown to be a prophet.

10. "And they say, There is not a man." Whereas, therefore, they declared it to be impossible that what was asked by the king should be told by man; God showed them, that what is impossible with man is possible with God.

14. "Arioch, the captain of the king's guard" (literally, "the chief slaughterer or cook"). For as the cook slays all animals and cooks them, of a similar nature was his occupation. And the rulers of the world slay men, butchering them like brute beasts.

23. "Because Thou hast given me wisdom and might." We ought therefore to mark the goodness of God, how He straightway reveals and shows (Himself) to the worthy, and to those that fear Him, fulfilling their prayers and supplications, as the prophet says: "Who is wise, and he shall understand these things? and prudent, and he shall know them?" [1]

27. "Cannot the wise men, the magicians." He instructs the king not to seek an explanation of heavenly mysteries from earthly men, for they shall be accomplished in their due time by God.

29. "As for thee, O king, thy thoughts." For the king, on making himself master of the land of Egypt, and getting hold of the country of Judea, and carrying off the people, thought upon his bed what should be after these things; and He who knows the secrets of all, and searcheth the thoughts of the hearts, revealed to him by means of the image the things that were to be. And He hid from him the vision, in order that the counsels of God might not be interpreted by the wise men of Babylon, but that by the blessed Daniel, as a prophet of God, things kept secret from all might be made manifest.

31. "Behold a great image." How, then, should we not mark the things prophesied of old in Babylon by Daniel, and now yet in the course of fulfilment in the world? For the image shown at that time to Nebuchadnezzar furnished a type of the whole world. In these times the Babylonians were sovereign over all, and these were the golden head of the image. And then, after them, the Persians held the supremacy for 245 years, and they were represented by the silver. Then the Greeks had the supremacy, beginning with Alexander of Macedon, for 300 years, so that they were the brass. After them came the Romans, who were the iron legs of the image, for they were strong as iron. Then (we have) the toes of clay and iron, to signify the democracies that were subsequently to rise, partitioned among the ten toes of the image, in which shall be iron mixed with clay.

31. "Thou sawest," etc. Apollinaris on this: He looked, and behold, as it were, an image. For it did not appear to him as an actual object, presented to the view of an onlooker, but as an image or semblance. And while it contains in it many things together, that is in such a way that it is not really one, but manifold. For it comprised a summary of all kingdoms; and its exceeding splendour was on account of the glory of the kings, and its terrible appearance on account of their power. Eusebius Pamphili, and Hippolytus the most holy bishop of Rome, compare the dream of Nebuchadnezzar now in question with the vision of the prophet Daniel. Since these have given a different interpretation of this vision now before us in their expositions, I deemed it necessary to transcribe what is said by Eusebius of Cæsarea, who bears the surname Pamphili, in the 15th book of his *Gospel Demonstration;* [2] for he expounds the whole vision in these terms: "I think that this (i.e., the vision of Nebuchadnezzar) differs in nothing

---

[1] Hos. xiv. 9.

[2] This book is not now extant, the first ten alone having reached our time.

from the vision of the prophet. For as the prophet saw a great sea, so the king saw a great image. And again, as the prophet saw four beasts, which he interpreted as four kingdoms, so the king was given to understand four kingdoms under the gold, and silver, and brass, and iron. And again, as the prophet saw the division of the ten horns of the last beast, and three horns broken by one ; so the king, in like manner, saw in the extremities of the image one part iron and another clay. And besides this, as the prophet, after the vision of the four kingdoms, saw the Son of man receive dominion, and power, and a kingdom ; so also the king thought he saw a stone smite the whole image, and become a great mountain and fill the sea. And rightly so. For it was quite consistent in the king, whose view of the spectacle of life was so false, and who admired the beauty of the mere sensible colours, so to speak, in the picture set up to view, to liken the life of all men to a great image ; but (it became) the prophet to compare the great and mighty tumult of life to a mighty sea. And it was fitting that the king, who prized the substances deemed precious among men, gold, and silver, and brass, and iron, should liken to these substances the kingdoms that held the sovereignty at different times in the life of men ; but that the prophet should describe these same kingdoms under the likeness of beasts, in accordance with the manner of their rule. And again, the king — who was puffed up, as it seems, in his own conceit, and plumed himself on the power of his ancestors — is shown the vicissitude to which affairs are subject, and the end destined for all the kingdoms of earth, with the view of teaching him to lay aside his pride in himself, and understand that there is nothing stable among men, but only that which is the appointed end of all things — the kingdom of God. For after the first kingdom of the Assyrians, which was denoted by the gold, there will be the second kingdom of the Persians, expressed by the silver ; and then the third kingdom of the Macedonians, signified by the brass ; and after it, the fourth kingdom of the Romans will succeed, more powerful than those that went before it ; for which reason also it was likened to iron. For of it it is said : "And the fourth kingdom shall be strong as iron ; as iron breaketh and subdueth all things, so shall it break and subdue all things." And after all these kingdoms which have been mentioned, the kingdom of God is represented by the stone that breaks the whole image. And the prophet, in conformity with this, does not see the kingdom which comes at the end of all these things, until he has in order described the four dominions mentioned under the four beasts. And I think that the visions shown, both to the king and to the prophet,

were visions of these four kingdoms alone, and of none others, because by these the nation of the Jews was held in bondage from the times of the prophet."

33. "His feet," etc. Hippolytus : In the vision of the prophet, the ten horns are the things that are yet to be.

34. "Thou sawest till that a stone was cut." Thou sawest, as it were, a stone cut without hands, and smiting the image upon its feet. For the human kingdom was decisively separated from the divine ; with reference to which it is written, "as it were cut." The stroke, however, smites the extremities, and in these it broke all dominion that is upon earth.

45. "And the dream is certain," That no one, therefore, may have any doubt whether the things announced shall turn out so or not, the prophet has confirmed them with the words, "And the dream is certain, and the interpretation thereof sure ;" I have not erred in the interpretation of the vision.

46. "Then king Nebuchadnezzar fell upon his face." Nebuchadnezzar hearing these things, and being put in remembrance of his vision, knew that what was spoken by Daniel was true. How great is the power of the grace of God, beloved, that one who a little before was doomed to death with the other wise men of Babylon, should now be worshipped by the king, not as man, but as God ! "He commanded that they should offer manaa"[1] (i.e., in Chaldee, "oblation") "and sweet odours unto him." Of old, too, the Lord made a similar announcement to Moses, saying, "See, I have made thee a god to Pharaoh ;"[2] in order that, on account of the signs wrought by him in the land of Egypt, Moses might no longer be reckoned a man, but be worshipped as a god by the Egyptians.

48. "Then the king made Daniel a great man." For as he had humbled himself, and presented himself as the least among all men, God made him great, and the king established him as ruler over the whole land of Babylon. Just as also Pharaoh did to Joseph, appointing him then to be ruler over the whole land of Egypt.

49. "And Daniel requested," etc. For as they had united with Daniel in prayer to God that the vision might be revealed to him, so Daniel, when he obtained great honour from the king, made mention of them, explaining to the king what had been done by them, in order that they also should be deemed worthy of some honour as fellow-seers and worshippers of God. For when they asked heavenly things from the Lord, they received also earthly things from the king.

---

[1] [The *minchah*, that is.]
[2] Ex. vii. 1.

Chap. iii. 1. " In the eighteenth year," etc. (These words are wanting in the Vulgate, etc.) A considerable space of time having elapsed, therefore, and the eighteenth year being now in its course, the king, calling to mind his vision, " made an image of gold, whose height was threescore cubits, and the breadth thereof six cubits." For as the blessed Daniel, in interpreting the vision, had answered the king, saying, " Thou art this head of gold in the image," the king, being puffed up with this address, and elated in heart, made a copy of this image, in order that he might be worshipped by all as God.

7. " All the people fell." Some (did so) because they feared the king himself; but all (or " most "), because they were idolaters, obeyed the word commanded by the king.

16. " Shadrach, Meshach, and Abednego answered," etc. These three youths are become an example to all faithful men, inasmuch as they did not fear the crowd of satraps, neither did they tremble when they heard the king's words, nor did they shrink when they saw the flame of the blazing furnace, but deemed all men and the whole world as nought, and kept the fear of God alone before their eyes. Daniel, though he stood at a distance and kept silence, encouraged them to be of good cheer as he smiled to them. And he rejoiced also himself at the witness they bore, understanding, as he did, that the three youths would receive a crown in triumph over the devil.

19. " And commanded that they should heat the furnace one seven times more." He bids the vast furnace be heated one seven times more, as if he were already overcome by them. In earthly things, then, the king was superior; but in faith toward God the three youths were superior. Tell me, Nebuchadnezzar, with what purpose you order them to be cast into the fire bound? Is it lest they might escape, if they should have their feet unbound, and thus be able to extinguish the fire? But thou doest not these things of thyself, but there is another who worketh these things by thy means.

47.[1] " And the flame streamed forth." The fire, he means, was driven from within by the angel, and burst forth outwardly. See how even the fire appears intelligent, as if it recognised and punished the guilty. For it did not touch the servants of God, but it consumed the unbelieving and impious Chaldeans. Those who were within were besprinkled with a (cooling) dew by the angel, while those who thought they stood in safety outside the furnace were destroyed by the fire. The men who cast in the youths were burned by the flame, which caught them on all

sides, as I suppose, when they went to bind the youths.

92 (i.e., 25). " And the form of the fourth is like the Son of God." Tell me, Nebuchadnezzar, when didst thou see the Son of God, that thou shouldst confess that this is the Son of God? And who pricked thy heart, that thou shouldst utter such a word? And with what eyes wert thou able to look into this light? And why was this manifested to thee alone, and to none of the satraps about thee? But, as it is written, " The heart of a king is in the hand of God : " the hand of God is here, whereby the Word pricked his heart, so that he might recognise Him in the furnace, and glorify Him. And this idea of ours is not without good ground. For as the children of Israel were destined to see God in the world, and yet not to believe on Him, the Scripture showed beforehand that the Gentiles would recognise Him, whom, while not incarnate, Nebuchadnezzar saw and recognised of old in the furnace, and acknowledged to be the Son of God.

93 (i.e., 26). " And he said, Shadrach, Meshach, and Abednego." The three youths he thus called by name. But he found no name by which to call the fourth. For He was not yet that Jesus born of the Virgin.

97 (i.e., 30). " Then the king promoted," etc. For as they honoured God by giving themselves up to death, so, too, they were themselves honoured not only by God, but also by the king. And they taught strange and foreign nations also to worship God.

Chap. vii. 1. " And he wrote the dream." The things, therefore, which were revealed to the blessed prophet by the Spirit in visions, these he also recounted fully for others, that he might not appear to prophesy of the future to himself alone, but might be proved a prophet to others also, who wish to search the divine Scriptures.

2. " And behold the four winds." He means created existence in its fourfold division.

3. " And four great beasts." As various beasts then were shown to the blessed Daniel, and these different from each other, we should understand that the truth of the narrative deals not with certain beasts, but, under the type and image of different beasts, exhibits the kingdoms that have risen in this world in power over the race of man. For by the great sea he means the whole world.

4. " Till the wings thereof were plucked." For this happened in reality in the time of Nebuchadnezzar, as has been shown in the preceding book. And he bears witness directly that this very thing was fulfilled in himself; for he was driven out of the kingdom, and stripped of his glory, and of the greatness which he formerly possessed. " And after a little : " the words, " It

---

[1] The verses are numbered according to the Greek translation, which incorporates the apocryphal " song of the three holy children."

was made stand upon the feet as a man, and a man's heart was given to it," signify that Nebuchadnezzar, when he humbled himself, and acknowledged that he was but a man, in subjection under the power of God, and made supplication to the Lord, found mercy with Him, and was restored to his own kingdom and honour.

5. "A second beast like to a bear." To represent the kingdom of the Persians. "And it had three ribs." The three nations he calls three ribs. The meaning, therefore, is this : that beast had the dominion, and these others under it were the Medes, Assyrians, and Babylonians. "And they said thus to it, Arise, devour." For the Persians arising in these times, devastated every land, and made many men subject to them, and slew them. For as this beast, the bear, is a foul animal, and carnivorous, tearing with claws and teeth, such also was the kingdom of the Persians, who held the supremacy for two hundred and thirty years.

6. "And, lo, another beast like a leopard." In mentioning a leopard, he means the kingdom of the Greeks, over whom Alexander of Macedon was king. And he likened them to a leopard, because they were quick and inventive in thought, and bitter in heart, just as that animal is many-coloured in appearance, and quick in wounding and in drinking man's blood.

"The beast had also four heads." When the kingdom of Alexander was exalted, and grew, and acquired a name over the whole world, his kingdom was divided into four principalities. For Alexander, when near his end, partitioned his kingdom among his four comrades of the same race, viz., "Seleucus, Demetrius, Ptolemy, and Philip ; " and all these assumed crowns, as Daniel prophesies, and as it is written in the first book of Maccabees.

7. "And behold a fourth beast." Now, that there has arisen no other kingdom after that of the Greeks except that which stands sovereign at present, is manifest to all. This one has iron teeth, because it subdues and reduces all by its strength, just as iron does. And the rest it did tread with its feet, for there is no other kingdom remaining after this one, but from it will spring ten horns.

"And it had ten horns." For as the prophet said already of the leopard, that the beast had four heads, and that was fulfilled, and Alexander's kingdom was divided into four principalities, so also now we ought to look for the ten horns which are to spring from it, when the time of the beast shall be fulfilled, and the little horn, which is Antichrist, shall appear suddenly in their midst, and righteousness shall be banished from the earth, and the whole world shall reach its consummation. So that we ought not to anticipate the counsel of God, but exercise pa-

tience and prayer, that we fall not on such times. We should not, however, refuse to believe that these things will come to pass. For if the things which the prophets predicted in former times have not been realized, then we need not look for these things. But if those former things did happen in their proper seasons, as was foretold, these things also shall certainly be fulfilled.

8. "I considered the horns." That is to say, I looked intently at the beast, and was astonished at everything about it, but especially at the number of the horns. For the appearance of this beast differed from that of the other beasts in kind.

13. "And came to the Ancient of days." By the Ancient of days he means none other than the Lord and God and Ruler of all, and even of Christ Himself, who maketh the days old, and yet becometh not old Himself by times and days.

14. "His dominion is an everlasting dominion." The Father, having put all things in subjection to His own Son, both things in heaven and things on earth, showed Him forth by all as the first-begotten of God, in order that, along with the Father, He might be approved the Son of God before angels, and be manifested as the Lord also of angels : (He showed Him forth also as) the first-begotten of a virgin, that He might be seen to be in Himself the Creator anew of the first-formed Adam, (and) as the first-begotten from the dead, that He might become Himself the first-fruits of our resurrection.

"Which shall not pass away." He exhibited all the dominion given by the Father to His own Son, who is manifested as King of all in heaven and on earth, and under the earth, and as Judge of all : of all in heaven, because He was born the Word, of the heart of the Father before all ; and of all in earth, because He was made man, and created Adam anew of Himself ; and of all under the earth, because He was also numbered among the dead, and preached to the souls of the saints, (and) by death overcame death.

17. "Which shall arise." For when the three beasts have finished their course, and been removed, and the one still stands in vigour, — if this one, too, is removed, then finally earthly things (shall) end, and heavenly things begin ; that the indissoluble and everlasting kingdom of the saints may be brought to view, and the heavenly King manifested to all, no longer in figure, like one seen in vision, or revealed in a pillar of cloud upon the top of a mountain, but amid the powers and armies of angels, as God incarnate and man, Son of God and Son of man — coming from heaven as the world's Judge.

19. "And I inquired about the fourth beast." It is to the fourth kingdom, of which we have already spoken, that he here refers: that kingdom, than which no greater kingdom of like nature has arisen upon the earth; from which also ten horns are to spring, and to be apportioned among ten crowns. And amid these another little horn shall rise, which is that of Antichrist. And it shall pluck by the roots the three others before it; that is to say, he shall subvert the three kings of Egypt, Libya, and Ethiopia, with the view of acquiring for himself universal dominion. And after conquering the remaining seven horns, he will at last begin, inflated by a strange and wicked spirit, to stir up war against the saints, and to persecute all everywhere, with the aim of being glorified by all, and being worshipped as God.

22. "Until the Ancient of days come." That is, when at length the Judge of judges and the King of kings comes from heaven, who shall subvert the whole dominion and power of the adversary, and shall consume all with the eternal fire of punishment. But to His servants, and prophets, and martyrs, and to all who fear Him, He will give an everlasting kingdom; that is, they shall possess the endless enjoyment of good.

25. "Until a time, and times, and the dividing of time." This denotes three years and a half.

CHAP. IX. 21. "And, behold, the man Gabriel . . . flying." You see how the prophet likens the speed of the angels to a winged bird, on account of the light and rapid motion with which these spirits fly so quickly in discharge of orders.

CHAP. X. 6. "And the voice of His words." For all we who now believe on Him declare the words of Christ, as if we spake by His mouth the things enjoined by Him.

7. "And I saw," etc. For it is to His saints that fear Him, and to them alone, that He reveals Himself. For if any one seems to be living now in the Church, and yet has not the fear of God, his companionship with the saints will avail him nothing.

12. "Thy words were heard." Behold how much the piety of a righteous man availeth, that to him alone, as to one worthy, things not yet to be manifested in the world should be revealed.

13. "And lo, Michael." Who is Michael but the angel assigned to the people? As (God) says to Moses, "I will not go with you in the way, because the people are stiff-necked; but my angel shall go with you."

16. "My inwards are turned" (A. V., "my sorrows are turned upon me"). For it was meet that, at the appearing of the Lord, what was above should be turned beneath, in order that also what was beneath might come above. —I require time, he says, to recover myself, and to be able to endure the words and to make reply to what is said.—But while I was in this position, he continues, I was strengthened beyond my hope. For one unseen touched me, and straightway my weakness was removed, and I was restored to my former strength. For whenever all the strength of our life and its glory pass from us, then are we strengthened by Christ, who stretches forth His hand and raises the living from among the dead, and as it were from Hades itself, to the resurrection of life.

18. "And he strengthened me." For whenever the Word has made us of good hope with regard to the future, we are able also readily to hear His voice.

20. "To fight with the prince of Persia." For from the day that thou didst humble thyself before the Lord thy God thy prayer was heard, and I was sent "to fight with the prince of Persia." For there was a design not to let the people go. Therefore, that thy prayer might be speedily answered, "I stood up against him."

CHAP. XII. 1. "There shall be a time of trouble." For at that time there shall be great trouble, such as has not been from the foundation of the world, when some in one way, and others in another, shall be sent through every city and country to destroy the faithful; and the saints shall travel from the west to the east, and shall be driven in persecution from the east to the south, while others shall conceal themselves in the mountains and caves; and the abomination shall war against them everywhere, and shall cut them off by sea and by land by his decree, and shall endeavour by every means to destroy them out of the world; and they shall not be able any longer to sell their own property, nor to buy from strangers, unless one keeps and carries with him the name of the beast, or bears its mark upon his forehead. For then they shall all be driven out from every place, and dragged from their own homes and haled into prison, and punished with all manner of punishment, and cast out from the whole world.

2. "These shall awake to everlasting life." That is, those who have believed in the true life, and who have their names written in the book of life. "And these to shame." That is, those who are attached to Antichrist, and who are cast with him into everlasting punishment.

3. "And they that be wise shall shine." And the Lord has said the same thing in the Gospel: "Then shall the righteous shine forth as the sun." [1]

7. "For a time, times, and an half." By this he indicated the three and a half years of Antichrist. For by a time he means a year; and by times, two years; and by an half time, half a year.

---

[1] Matt. xiii. 43.

These are the "one thousand two hundred and ninety days" of which Daniel prophesied.

9. "The words are closed up and sealed." For as a man cannot tell what God has prepared for the saints; for neither has eye seen nor ear heard, nor has it entered into the heart of man (to conceive) these things, into which even the saints, too, shall then eagerly desire to look; so He said to him, "For the words are sealed until the time of the end; until many shall be chosen and tried with fire." And who are they who are chosen, but those who believe the word of truth, so as to be made white thereby, and to cast off the filth of sin, and put on the heavenly, pure, and glorious Holy Spirit, in order that, when the Bridegroom comes, they may go in straightway with Him?

11. "The abomination of desolation shall be given (set up)." Daniel speaks, therefore, of two abominations: the one of destruction, which Antiochus set up in its appointed time, and which bears a relation to that of desolation, and the other universal, when Antichrist shall come. For, as Daniel says, he too shall be set up for the destruction of many.[1]

IV.

OTHER FRAGMENTS ON DANIEL.[2]

For when the iron legs that now hold the sovereignty have given place to the feet and the toes, in accordance with the representation of the terrible beast, as has also been signified in the former times, then from heaven will come the stone that smites the image, and breaks it; and it will subvert all the kingdoms, and give the kingdom to the saints of the Most High. This is the stone which becomes a great mountain, and fills the earth, and of which it is written: "I saw in the night-visions, and, behold, one like the Son of man came with the clouds of heaven, and came to the Ancient of days. And there was given Him dominion, and glory, and a kingdom; and all peoples, nations, and languages shall serve Him: His power is an everlasting power, which shall not pass away, and His kingdom shall not be destroyed."[3]

V.

ON THE SONG OF THE THREE CHILDREN.[4]

"O Ananias, Azarias, and Misael, bless ye the Lord; O ye apostles, prophets, and martyrs of the Lord, bless ye the Lord: praise Him, and exalt Him above all, for ever."

We may well marvel at the words of the three youths in the furnace, how they enumerated all created things, so that not one of them might be reckoned free and independent in itself; but, summing up and naming them all together, both things in heaven, and things in earth, and things under the earth, they showed them to be all the servants of God, who created all things by the Word, that no one should boast that any of the creatures was without birth and beginning.

VI.

ON SUSANNAH.[5]

What is narrated here, happened at a later time, although it is placed before the first book (at the beginning of the book). For it was a custom with the writers to narrate many things in an inverted order in their writings. For we find also in the prophets some visions recorded among the first and fulfilled among the last; and again, on the other hand, some recorded among the last and fulfilled first. And this was done by the disposition of the Spirit, that the devil might not understand the things spoken in parables by the prophets, and might not a second time lay his snares and ruin man.

VER. 1. "Called Joacim." This Joacim, being a stranger in Babylon, obtains Susannah in marriage. And she was the daughter of Chelcias the priest,[6] who found the book of the law in the house of the Lord, when Josiah the king commanded him to purify the holy of holies. His brother was Jeremiah the prophet, who was carried, with the remnant that was left after the deportation of the people to Babylon, into Egypt, and dwelt in Taphnæ;[7] and, while prophesying there, he was stoned to death by the people.

"A very fair woman, and one that feared the Lord," etc. For by the fruit produced, the tree also is easily known. For men who are pious and zealous for the law, bring into the world children worthy of God; such as he was who became a prophet and witness of Christ, and she who was found chaste and faithful in Babylon, whose honour and chastity were the occasion of the manifestation of the blessed Daniel as a prophet.

4. "Now Joacim was a great rich man," etc. We must therefore seek the explanation of this. For how could those who were captives, and had been made subject to the Babylonians, meet together in the same place, as if they were their own masters? In this matter, therefore, we should observe that Nebuchadnezzar, after their

---

[1] " By the most holy Hippolytus, (bishop) of Rome: The Exact Account of the Times," etc. From Gallandi. This fragment seems to have belonged to the beginning or introduction to the commentary of Hippolytus on Daniel.
[2] In *Anastasius Sinaita*, quæst. xlviii. p. 327.
[3] Dan. vii. 13.
[4] From the *Catena Patrum in Psalmos et Cantica*, vol. iii. ed. Corderianæ, pp. 951, ad v. 87.

[5] This apocryphal story of Susannah is found in the Greek texts of the LXX. and Theodotion, in the old Latin and Vulgate, and in the Syriac and Arabic versions. But there is no evidence that it ever formed part of the Hebrew, or of the original Syriac text. It is generally placed at the beginning of the book, as in the Greek MSS. and the old Latin, but is also sometimes set at the end, as in the Vulgate, ed. Compl.
[6] 2 Kings xxii. 8.
[7] Jer. xliii. 8.

deportation, treated them kindly, and permitted them to meet together, and do all things according to the law.

7. "And at noon Susannah went into (her husband's garden)." Susannah prefigured the Church; and Joacim, her husband, Christ; and the garden, the calling of the saints, who are planted like fruitful trees in the Church. And Babylon is the world; and the two elders are set forth as a figure of the two peoples that plot against the Church — the one, namely, of the circumcision, and the other of the Gentiles. For the words, "were appointed rulers of the people and judges," (mean) that in this world they exercise authority and rule, judging the righteous unrighteously.

8. "And the two elders saw her." These things the rulers of the Jews wish now to expunge from the book, and assert that these things did not happen in Babylon, because they are ashamed of what was done then by the elders.

9. "And they perverted their own mind." For how, indeed, can those who have been the enemies and corruptors of the Church judge righteously, or look up to heaven with pure heart, when they have become the slaves of the prince of this world?

10. "And they were both wounded with her (love)." This word is to be taken in truth; for always the two peoples, being wounded (instigated) by Satan working in them, strive to raise persecutions and afflictions against the Church, and seek how they may corrupt her, though they do not agreè with each other.

12. "And they watched diligently." And this, too, is to be noted. For up to the present time both the Gentiles and the Jews of the circumcision watch and busy themselves with the dealings of the Church, desiring to suborn false witnesses against us, as the apostle says: "And that because of false brethren unawares brought in, who came in privily to spy out our liberty which we have in Christ Jesus." [1]

It is a kind of sin to be anxious to give the mind to women.

14. "And when they were gone out, they parted the one from the other." As to their parting the one from the other at the hour of dinner (luncheon), this signifies that in the matter of earthly meats the Jews and the Gentiles are not at one; but in their views, and in all worldly matters, they are of one mind, and can meet each other.

14. "And asking one another, they acknowledged their lust." Thus, in revealing themselves to each other, they foreshadow the time when they shall be proved by their thoughts, and shall

have to give account to God for all the sin which they have done, as Solomon says: "And scrutiny shall destroy the ungodly." [2] For these are convicted by the scrutiny.

15. "As they watched a fit time." What fit time but that of the passover, at which the laver is prepared in the garden for those who burn, and Susannah washes herself, and is presented as a pure bride to God?

"With two maids only." For when the Church desires to take the laver according to use, she must of necessity have two handmaids to accompany her. For it is by faith on Christ and love to God that the Church confesses and receives the laver.

18. "And she said to her maids, Bring me oil." For faith and love prepare oil and unguents to those who are washed. But what were these unguents, but the commandments of the holy Word? And what was the oil, but the power of the Holy Spirit, with which believers are anointed as with ointment after the laver of washing? All these things were figuratively represented in the blessed Susannah, for our sakes, that we who now believe on God might not regard the things that are done now in the Church as strange, but believe them all to have been set forth in figure by the patriarchs of old, as the apostle also says: "Now these things happened unto them for ensamples: and they were written for our instruction, on whom the ends of the world are come." [3]

18. "And they went out at privy doors;" showing thus by anticipation, that he who desires to partake of the water in the garden must renounce the broad gate, and enter by the strait and narrow. [4]

"And they saw not the elders." For as of old the devil was concealed in the serpent in the garden, so now too, concealed in the elders, he fired them with his own lust, that he might again a second time corrupt Eve.

20. "Behold, the garden doors are shut." O wicked rulers, and filled with the workings of the devil, did Moses deliver these things to you? And while ye read the law yourselves, do ye teach others thus? Thou that sayest, "Thou shalt not kill," dost thou kill? Thou that sayest, "Thou shall not covet," dost thou desire to corrupt the wife of thy neighbour?

"And we are in love with thee." Why, ye lawless, do ye strive to gain over a chaste and guileless soul by deceitful words, in order to satisfy your own lust?

21. "If thou wilt not, we will bear witness against thee." This wicked audacity with which

---

[1] Gal. ii. 4.

[2] Prov. i. 32; in our version given as, "The prosperity of fools shall destroy them."
[3] 1 Cor. x. 11.
[4] Matt. vii. 13, 14.

you begin, comes of the deceitfulness that lurks in you from the beginning And there was in reality a young man with her, that one [1] of yours ; one from heaven, not to have intercourse with her, but to bear witness to her truth.

22. "And Susannah sighed." The blessed Susannah, then, when she heard these words, was troubled in her heart, and set a watch upon her mouth, not wishing to be defiled by the wicked elders. Now it is in our power also to apprehend the real meaning of all that befell Susannah. For you may find this also fulfilled in the present condition of the Church. For when the two peoples conspire to destroy any of the saints, they watch for a fit time, and enter the house of God while all there are praying and praising God, and seize some of them, and carry them off, and keep hold of them, saying, Come, consent with us, and worship our Gods ; and if not, we will bear witness against you. And when they refuse, they drag them before the court and accuse them of acting contrary to the decrees of Cæsar, and condemn them to death.

"I am straitened on every side." Behold the words of a chaste woman, and one dear to God : "I am straitened on every side." For the Church is afflicted and straitened, not only by the Jews, but also by the Gentiles, and by those who are called Christians, but are not such in reality. For they, observing her chaste and happy life, strive to ruin her.

"For if I do this thing, it is death to me." For to be disobedient to God, and obedient to men, works eternal death and punishment.

"And if I do it not, I cannot escape your hands." And this indeed is said with truth. For they who are brought into judgment for the sake of God's name, if they do what is commanded them by men, die to God, and shall live in the world. But if they refuse to do what is commanded them by men, they escape not the hands of their judges, but are condemned by them.

23. "It is better for me not to do it." For it is better to die by the hand of wicked men and live with God, than, by consenting to them, to be delivered from them and fall into the hands of God.

24. "And Susannah cried with a loud voice." And to whom did Susannah cry but to God? as Isaiah says : "Then shalt thou call, and the Lord shall answer thee ; whilst thou art yet speaking, He shall say, Lo, here I am." [2]

"And the two elders cried out against her." For the wicked never cease to cry out against us, and to say : Away with such from off the earth, for it is not fit that they should live. In an evangelical sense, Susannah despised them

who kill the body, in order that she might save her soul from death. Now sin is the death of the soul, and especially (the sin of) adultery. For when the soul that is united with Christ forsakes its faith, it is given over to perpetual death, viz., eternal punishment. And in confirmation of this, in the case of the transgression and violation of marriage unions in the flesh, the law has decreed the penalty of death.

25. "Then ran the one and opened the gates ;" pointing to the broad and spacious way on which they who follow such persons perish.

31. "Now Susannah was a very delicate woman." Not that she had meretricious adornments about her person, as Jezebel had, or eyes painted with divers colours ; but that she had the adornment of faith, and chastity, and sanctity.

34. "And laid their hands upon her head ;" that at least by touching her they might satisfy their lust.

35. "And she was weeping." For by her tears she attracted the (regard of) the Word from heaven, who was with tears to raise the dead Lazarus.

41. "Then the assembly believed them." It becomes us, then, to be stedfast in every duty, and to give no heed to lies, and to yield no obsequious obedience to the persons of rulers, knowing that we have to give account to God ; but if we follow the truth, and aim at the exact rule of faith, we shall be well-pleasing to God.

44. "And the Lord heard her voice." For those who call upon Him from a pure heart, God heareth. But from those who (call upon Him) in deceit and hypocrisy, God turneth away His face.

52. "O thou that art waxen old in wickedness." Now, since at the outset, in the introduction, we explained that the two elders are to be taken as a type of the two peoples, that of the circumcision and that of the Gentiles, which are always enemies of the Church ; let us mark the words of Daniel, and learn that the Scripture deals falsely with us in nothing. For, addressing the first elder, he censures him as one instructed in the law ; while he addresses the other as a Gentile, calling him "the seed of Chanaan," although he was then among the circumcision.

55. "For even now the angel of God." He shows also, that when Susannah prayed to God, and was heard, the angel was sent then to help her, just as was the case in the instance of Tobias [3] and Sara. For when they prayed, the supplication of both of them was heard in the same day and the same hour, and the angel Raphael was sent to heal them both.

61. "And they arose against the two elders ;" that the saying might be fulfilled, "Whoso diggeth a pit for his neighbour, shall fall therein." [4]

---

[1] That is, Daniel, present in the spirit of prophecy. — COMBEF.
[2] Isa. lviii. 9.
[3] Tobit iii. 17.
[4] Prov. xxvi. 27.

To all these things, therefore, we ought to give heed, beloved, fearing lest any one be overtaken in any transgression, and risk the loss of his soul, knowing as we do that God is the Judge of all; and the Word[1] Himself is the Eye which nothing that is done in the world escapes. Therefore, always watchful in heart and pure in life, let us imitate Susannah.

ON MATTHEW.[2]

Matt. vi. 11.[3]

For this reason we are enjoined to ask what is sufficient for the preservation of the substance of the body: not luxury, but food, which restores what the body loses, and prevents death by hunger; not tables to inflame and drive on to pleasures, nor such things as make the body wax wanton against the soul; but bread, and that, too, not for a great number of years, but what is sufficient for us to-day.

ON LUKE.[4]

CHAP. II. 7. And if you please, we say that the Word was the first-born of God, who came down from heaven to the blessed Mary, and was made a first-born man in her womb, in order that the first-born of God might be manifested in union with a first-born man.

22. When they brought Him to the temple to present Him to the Lord, they offered the oblations of purification. For if the gifts of purification according to the law were offered for Him, in this indeed He was made under the law. But the Word was not subject to the law in such wise as the sycophants[5] fancy, since He is the law Himself; neither did God need sacrifices of purification, for He purifieth and sanctifieth all things at once in a moment. But though He took to Himself the frame of man as He received it from the Virgin, and was made under the law, and was thus purified after the manner of the first-born, it was not because He needed this ceremonial that He underwent its services, but only for the purpose of redeeming from the bondage of the law those who were sold under the judgment of the curse.

CHAP. XXIII. For this reason the warders of Hades trembled when they saw Him; and the gates of brass and the bolts of iron were broken. For, lo, the Only-begotten entered, a soul among souls, God the Word with a (human) soul. For His body lay in the tomb, not emptied of divinity; but as, while in Hades, He was in essential being with His Father, so was He also in the

body and in Hades.[6] For the Son is not contained in space, just as the Father; and He comprehends all things in Himself. But of His own will he dwelt in a body animated by a soul, in order that with His soul He might enter Hades, and not with His pure divinity.

DOUBTFUL FRAGMENTS ON THE PENTATEUCH.[7]

PREFACE.

In the name of the Father, and the Son, and the Holy Spirit, one God. This is a transcript of the excellent law. But before beginning to give the transcript of the book of the law, it will be worth while to instruct you, O brother, as to its excellence, and the dignity of its disposition. Its first excellence is, that God delivered it by the hand of our most blessed ruler, the chief of the prophets, and first of the apostles, or those who were sent to the children of Israel, viz., Moses the son of Amram, the son of Kohath, of the sons of Levi. Now he was adorned with all manner of wisdom, and endowed with the best genius. Illustrious in dignity, remarkable for the integrity of his disposition, distinguished for power of reason, he talked with God. And He chose him as an instrument of value. By His leader and prophet, God Most High sent it down to us, and committed it to us (blessed be His name) in the Syriac tongue of the Targum, which the Seventy translated into the Hebrew tongue, to wit, into the tongue of the nation, and the idiom of the common people. Moses, therefore, received it from the eternal Lord, and was the first to whom it was entrusted, and who obeyed its rules and ordinances. Then he taught it to the children of Israel, who also embraced it. And he explained to them its profound mysteries and dark places. And he expounded to them those things which were less easy, as God permitted him, and concealed from them those secrets of the law, as God forbade him (to reveal them). Nor did there rise among them one who was better practised in His judgments and decrees, and who communicated more clearly the mysteries of His doctrine, until God translated him to Himself, after He had made him perfect by forty whole years in the wilderness.

And these following are the names of the teachers who handed down the law in continuous succession after Moses the prophet, until the advent of Messiah:—

Know, then, my brother, whom may God bless, that God delivered the most excellent law into the hands of Moses the prophet, the son of Amram.

---

[1] Cotelerius reads ὅλος instead of ὁ λόγος, and so = and He is Himself the whole or universal eye.
[2] De Magistris, *Acta Martyrum Ostiens.*, p. 405.
[3] He is giving his opinion on the ἐπιούσιον, i.e., the "daily bread."
[4] Mai, *Script. vet. collectio nova*, vol ix. p. 645, Rome, 1837.
[5] οἱ συκοφάνται.

[6] Pearson *On the Creed*, art. iv. p. 355.
[7] These are edited in Arabic and Latin by Fabricius, *Opp. Hippol.*, ii. 33. That these are spurious is now generally agreed. The translation is from the Latin version, which alone is given by Migne.

And Moses delivered it to Joshua the son of Nun.

And Joshua the son of Nun delivered it to Anathal.

And Anathal delivered it to Jehud.

And Jehud delivered it to Samgar.

And Samgar delivered it to Baruk.

And Baruk delivered it to Gideon.

And Gideon delivered it to Abimelech.

And Abimelech delivered it to Taleg.

And Taleg delivered it to Babin the Gileadite.

And Babin delivered it to Jiphtach.

And Jiphtach delivered it to Ephran.

And Ephran delivered it to Elul of the tribe Zebulon.

And Elul delivered it to Abdan.

And Abdan delivered it to Shimshon the brave.

And Shimshon delivered it to Helkanah, the son of Jerachmu, the son of Jehud. Moreover, he was the father of Samuel the prophet. Of this Helkanah mention is made in the beginning of the first book of Kings (Samuel).

And Helkanah delivered it to Eli the priest.

And Eli delivered it to Samuel the prophet.

And Samuel delivered it to Nathan the prophet.

And Nathan delivered it to Gad the prophet.

And Gad the prophet delivered it to Shemaiah the teacher.

And Shemaiah delivered it to Iddo the teacher.

And Iddo delivered it to Achia.

And Achia delivered it to Abihu.

And Abihu delivered it to Elias the prophet.

And Elias delivered it to his disciple Elisaeus.

And Elisaeus delivered it to Malachia the prophet.

And Malachia delivered it to Abdiahu.

And Abdiahu delivered it to Jehuda.

And Jehuda delivered it to Zacharias the teacher.

In those days came Bachthansar king of Babel, and laid waste the house of the sanctuary, and carried the children of Israel into captivity to Babel.

And after the captivity of Babel, Zacharia the teacher delivered it to Esaia the prophet, the son of Amos.

And Esaia delivered it to Jeremia the prophet.

And Jeremia the prophet delivered it to Chizkiel.

And Chizkiel the prophet delivered it to Hosea the prophet, the son of Bazi.

And Hosea delivered it to Joiel the prophet.

And Joiel delivered it to Amos the prophet.

And Amos delivered it to Obadia.

And Obadia delivered it to Jonan the prophet, the son of Mathi, the son of Armelah, who was the brother of Elias the prophet.

And Jonan delivered it to Micha the Morasthite, who delivered it to Nachum the Alcusite.

And Nachum delivered it to Chabakuk the prophet.

And Chabakuk delivered it to Sophonia the prophet.

And Sophonia delivered it to Chaggaeus the prophet.

And Chaggaeus delivered it to Zecharia the prophet, the son of Bershia.

And Zecharia, when in captivity, delivered it to Malachia.

And Malachia delivered it to Ezra the teacher.

[1] And Ezra delivered it to Shamai the chief priest, and Jadua to Samean, (and) Samean delivered it to Antigonus.

And Antigonus delivered it to Joseph the son of Johezer, (and) Joseph the son of Gjuchanan.

And Joseph delivered it to Jehosua, the son of Barachia.

And Jehosua delivered it to Nathan the Arbelite.

And Nathan delivered it to Shimeon, the elder son of Shebach. This is he who carried the Messias in his arms.

Simeon delivered it to Jehuda.

Jehuda delivered it to Zecharia the priest.

And Zecharia the priest, the father of John the Baptist, delivered it to Joseph, a teacher of his own tribe.

And Joseph delivered it to Hanan and Caiaphas. Moreover, from them were taken away the priestly, and kingly, and prophetic offices.

These were teachers at the advent of Messias; and they were both priests of the children of Israel. Therefore the whole number of venerable and honourable priests put in trust of this most excellent law was fifty-six, Hanan (i.e., Annas) and Caiaphas being excepted.

And those are they who delivered it in the last days to the state of the children of Israel; nor did there arise any priests after them.

This is the account of what took place with regard to the most excellent law.

Armius, author of the book of *Times*, has said: In the nineteenth year of the reign of King Ptolemy, he ordered the elders of the children of Israel to be assembled, in order that they might put into his hands a copy of the law, and that they might each be at hand to explain its meaning.

The elders accordingly came, bringing with them the most excellent law. Then he commanded that every one of them should interpret the book of the law to him.

But he dissented from the interpretation which the elders had given. And he ordered the elders to be thrust into prison and chains. And seizing the book of the law, he threw it into a deep ditch, and cast fire and hot ashes upon it for

[1] See Tsemach David, and Maimon. Præfat. ad Seder Zeraim, in Pocockii *Porta Moses*, p. 36.

seven days. Then afterwards he ordered them to throw the filth of the city into that ditch in which was the book of the law. And the ditch was filled to the very top.

The law remained seventy years under the filth in that ditch, yet did not perish, nor was there even a single leaf of it spoilt.

In the twenty-first year of the reign of King Apianutus they took the book of the law out of the ditch, and not one leaf thereof was spoilt.

And after the ascension of Christ into heaven, came King Titus, son of Aspasianus king of Rome, to Jerusalem, and besieged and took it. And he destroyed the edifice of the second house, which the children of Israel had built. Titus the king destroyed the house of the sanctuary, and slew all the Jews who were in it, and built Tsion (*sic*) in their blood. And after that deportation the Jews were scattered abroad in slavery. Nor did they assemble any more in the city of Jerusalem, nor is there hope anywhere of their returning.

After Jerusalem was laid waste, therefore, Shemaia and Antalia (Abtalion) delivered the law, — kings of Baalbach,[1] a city which Soliman, son of King David, had built of old, and which was restored anew in the days of King Menasse, who sawed Esaia the prophet asunder.

King Adrian, of the children of Edom, besieged Baalbach, and took it, and slew all the Jews who were in it, (and) as many as were of the family of David he reduced to slavery. And the Jews were dispersed over the whole earth, as God Most High had foretold : " And I will scatter you among the Gentiles, and disperse you among the nations."

And these are the things which have reached us as to the history of that most excellent book. The Preface is ended.

THE LAW.

In the name of God eternal, everlasting, most mighty, merciful, compassionate.

By the help of God we begin to describe the book of the law, and its interpretation, as the holy, learned, and most excellent fathers have interpreted it.

The following, therefore, is the interpretation of the first book, which indeed is the book of the creation (and) of created beings.

SECTION I.

Of the creation of heaven and earth. " In the beginning God created," etc.

An exposition of that which God said.

And the blessed prophet, indeed, the great Moses, wrote this book, and designated and marked it with the title, *The Book of Being*, i.e., " of created beings," etc.

---

[1] Heliopolis of Syria.

SECTIONS II., III.

And the Lord said : " And I will bring the waters of the flood upon the earth to destroy all flesh," etc.

Hippolytus, the Targumist expositor, said : The names of the wives of the sons of Noah are these : the name of the wife of Sem, Nahalath Mahnuk ; and the name of the wife of Cham, Zedkat Nabu ; and the name of the wife of Japheth, Arathka. These, moreover, are their names in the Syriac Targum.[2] The name of the wife of Sem was Nahalath Mahnuk ; the name of the wife of Cham, Zedkat Nabu ; the name of the wife of Japheth, Arathka.

Therefore God gave intimation to Noah, and informed him of the coming of the flood, and of the destruction of the ruined (wicked).

And God Most High ordered him to descend from the holy mount, him and his sons, and the wives of his sons, and to build a ship of three storeys. The lower storey was for fierce, wild, and dangerous beasts. Between them there were stakes or wooden beams, to separate them from each other, and prevent them from having intercourse with each other. The middle storey was for birds, and their different genera. Then the upper storey was for Noah himself and his sons — for his own wife and his sons' wives.

Noah also made a door in the ship, on the east side. He also constructed tanks of water, and store-rooms of provisions.

When he had made an end, accordingly, of building the ship, Noah, with his sons, Sem, Cham, and Japheth, entered the cave of deposits.[3]

And on their first approach, indeed, they happily found the bodies of the fathers, Adam, Seth, Enosh, Kainan, Mahaliel, Jared, Mathusalach, and Lamech. Those eight bodies were in the place of deposits, viz., those of Adam, Seth, Enosh, Kainan, Mahaliel, Jared, Mathusalach, and Lamech.

Noah, moreover, took the body of Adam. And his sons took with them offerings. Sem carried gold, Cham myrrh, and Japheth frankincense. Then, leaving the cave of deposits, they transferred the offerings and the body of Adam to the holy mount.[3]

And when they sat down by the body of Adam, over against paradise, they began to lament and weep for the loss of paradise.

Then, descending from the holy mount, and lifting up their eyes towards paradise, they renewed their weeping and wailing, (and) uttered an eternal farewell in these terms : Farewell ! peace to thee, O paradise of God ! Farewell, O habitation of religion and purity ! Farewell, O seat of pleasure and delight !

---

[2] What follows was thus expressed probably in Syriac in some Syriac version.

[3] Cavernam thesaurorum. [Cant. iv. 6, i.e., Paradise.]

Then they embraced the stones and trees of the holy mount, and wept, and said : Farewell, O habitation of the good ! Farewell, O abode of holy bodies !

Then, after three days, Noah, with his sons and his sons' wives, came down from the holy mount to the base of the holy mount, to the ship's place. For the (ark) was under the projecting edge of the holy mount.

And Noah entered the ship, and deposited the body of Adam, and the offerings, in the middle of the ship, upon a bier of wood, which he had prepared for the reception of the body.

And God charged Noah, saying : Make for thyself rattles [1] of boxwood (or cypress). Now שמשאר is the wood called Sagh, i.e., Indian plane.

Make also the hammer (bell) thereof of the same wood. And the length of the rattle shall be three whole cubits, and its breadth one and a half cubit.

And God enjoined him to strike the rattles three times every day, to wit, for the first time at early dawn, for the second time at mid-day, and for the third time at sunset.

And it happened that, as soon as Noah had struck the rattles, the sons of Cain and the sons of Vahim ran up straightway to him, and he warned and alarmed them by telling of the immediate approach of the flood, and of the destruction already hasting on and impending.

Thus, moreover, was the pity of God toward them displayed, that they might be converted and come to themselves again. But the sons of Cain did not comply with what Noah proclaimed to them. And Noah brought together pairs, male and female, of all birds of every kind ; and thus also of all beasts, tame and wild alike, pair and pair.

SECTION IV.

On Gen. vii. 6.

Hippolytus, the Syrian expositor of the Targum, has said : We find in an ancient Hebrew copy that God commanded Noah to range the wild beasts in order in the lower floor or storey, and to separate the males from the females by putting wooden stakes between them.

And thus, too, he did with all the cattle, and also with the birds in the middle storey. And God ordered the males thus to be separated from the females for the sake of decency and purity, lest they should perchance get intermingled with each other.

Moreover, God said to Moses : Provide victuals for yourself and your children. And let them be of wheat, ground, pounded, kneaded with water, and dried. And Noah there and then bade his wife, and his sons' wives, diligently attend to kneading dough and laying it in the oven. They kneaded dough accordingly, and prepared just about as much as might be sufficient for them, so that nothing should remain over but the very least.

And God charged Noah, saying to him : Whosoever shall first announce to you the approach of the deluge, him you shall destroy that very moment. In the meantime, moreover, the wife of Cham was standing by, about to put a large piece of bread into the oven. And suddenly, according to the word of the Lord, water rushed forth from the oven, and the flow of water penetrated and destroyed the bread. Therefore the wife of Cham exclaimed, addressing herself to Noah : Oh, sir, the word of God is come good : " that which God foretold is come to pass ; " execute, therefore, that which the Lord commanded. And when Noah heard the words of the wife of Cham, he said to her : Is then the flood already come ? The wife of Cham said to him : Thou hast said it. God, however, suddenly charged Noah, saying : Destroy not the wife of Cham ; for from thy mouth is the beginning of destruction — " thou didst first say, The flood is come." At the voice of Noah the flood came, and suddenly the water destroyed that bread. And the floodgates of heaven were opened, and the rains broke upon the earth. And that same voice, in sooth, which had said of old, " Let the waters be gathered together into one place, and let the dry land appear," [2] gave permission to the fountain of waters and the floods of the seas to break forth of their own accord, and brought out the waters.

Consider what God said about the world : Let all its high places be brought low, and they were brought low ; and let its low places be raised from its depths.

And the earth was made bare and empty of all existence, as it was at the beginning.

And the rain descended from above, and the earth burst open beneath. And the frame of the earth was destroyed, and its primitive order was broken. And the world became such as it was when desolated at the beginning by the waters which flowed over it. Nor was any one of the existences upon it left in its integrity.

Its former structure went to wreck, and the earth was disfigured by the flood of waters that burst upon it, and by the magnitude of its inundations, and the multitude of showers, and the eruption from its depths, as the waters continually broke forth. In fine, it was left such as it was formerly. [2]

---

[1] Crepitacula.

[2] Gen. i. 9.

SECTION V.
On Gen. viii. 1.

Hippolytus, the expositor of the Targum, and my master, Jacobus Rohaviensis, have said: On the twenty-seventh day of the month Jiar, which is the second Hebrew month, the ark rose from the base of the holy mount; and already the waters bore it, and it was carried upon them round about towards the four cardinal points of the world. The ark accordingly held off from the holy mount towards the east, then returned towards the west, then turned to the south, and finally, bearing off eastwards, neared Mount Kardu on the first day of the tenth month. And that is the second month Kanun.

And Noah came out of the ark on the twenty-seventh day of the month Jiar, in the second year: for the ark continued sailing five whole months, and moved to and fro upon the waters, and in a period of fifty-one days neared the land. Nor thereafter did it float about any longer. But it only moved successively toward the four cardinal points of the earth, and again finally stood toward the east. We say, moreover, that that was a sign of the cross. And the ark was a symbol of the Christ who was expected. For that ark was the means of the salvation of Noah and his sons, and also of the cattle, the wild beasts, and the birds. And Christ, too, when He suffered on the cross, delivered us from accusations and sins, and washed us in His own blood most pure.

And just as the ark returned to the east, and neared Mount Kardu, so also Christ, when the work was accomplished and finished which He had proposed to Himself, returned to heaven to the bosom of His Father, and sat down upon the throne of His glory at the Father's right hand.

As to Mount Kardu, it is in the east, in the land of the sons of Raban, and the Orientals call it Mount Godash;[1] the Arabians and Persians call it Ararat.[2]

And there is a town of the name Kardu, and that hill is called after it, which is indeed very lofty and inaccessible, whose summit no one has ever been able to reach, on account of the violence of the winds and the storms which always prevail there. And if any one attempts to ascend it, there are demons that rush upon him, and cast him down headlong from the ridge of the mountain into the plain, so that he dies. No one, moreover, knows what there is on the top of the mountain, except that certain relics of the wood of the ark still lie there on the surface of the top of the mountain.[3]

SECTION X.
On Deut. xxxiii. 11.

Hippolytus, the expositor of the Targum, has said that Moses, when he had finished this prophecy, also pronounced a blessing upon all the children of Israel, by their several tribes, and prayed for them. Then God charged Moses, saying to him, Go up to Mount Nebo, which indeed is known by the name of the mount of the Hebrews, which is in the land of Moab over against Jericho.

And He said to him: View the land of Chanaan, which I am to give to the children of Israel for an inheritance. Thou, however, shalt never enter it; wherefore view it well from afar off. When Moses therefore viewed it, he saw that land, — a land green, and abounding with all plenty and fertility, planted thickly with trees; and Moses was greatly moved, and wept.

And when Moses descended from Mount Nebo, he called for Joshua the son of Nun, and said to him before the children of Israel: Prevail, and be strong; for thou art to bring the children of Israel into the land which God promised to their fathers that He would give them for an inheritance. Fear not, therefore, the people, neither be afraid of the nations: for God will be with thee.

And Moses wrote that Senna[4] (Hebr. משנה = "secondary law," or "Deuteronomy"), and gave it to the priests the sons of Levi, and commanded them, saying: For seven years keep this Senna hid, and show it not within the entire course of seven years. ("And then") in the feast of tabernacles, the priests the sons of Levi will read this law before the children of Israel, that the whole people, men and women alike, may observe the words of God: Command them to keep the word of God, which is in that law. And whosoever shall violate one of its precepts, let him be accursed.

Accordingly, when Moses had finished the writing of the law, he gave it to Joshua the son of Nun, and enjoined him to give it to the sons of Levi, the priests. Moses also enjoined and charged them to place the book of the law again within the ark of the covenant of the Lord, that it might remain there for a testimony for ever.

And when Moses had made an end of his injunctions, God bade him go up Mount Nebo, which is over against Jericho. The Lord showed him the whole land of promise in its four quarters, from the wilderness to the sea, and from sea to sea. And the Lord said to him, Thou hast seen it indeed with thine eyes, but thou shalt never enter it. There accordingly Moses died, the servant of God, by the command of

---

1 Gordyæum.
2 See Fuller, *Misc. Sacr.*, i. 4: and Bochart, *Phaleg.*, p. 22.
3 [See p. 149, note 10, *supra.*]

---

4 That is the name the Mohammedans give to their *Traditions.*

God. And the angels buried him on Mount Nebo, which is over against Beth-Phegor. And no one knows of his sepulchre, even to this day. For God concealed his grave.

And Moses lived 120 years; nor was his eye dim, nor was the skin of his face wrinkled.

Moses died on a certain day, at the third hour of the day, on the seventh day of the second month, which is the month Jiar.

And the children of Israel wept for him in the plains of Moab three days.

And Joshua the sun of Nun was filled with the spirit of wisdom; for Moses had laid his hand upon him. And all the children of Israel obeyed him. And God charged Joshua the son of Nun on a certain day, — namely, the seventh day of the month Nisan.

And Joshua the son of Nun lived 110 years, and died on the fourth day, which was the first day of the month Elul. And they buried him in the city Thamnatserach, on Mount Ephraim.

Praise be to God for the completion *of the work.*

ON THE PSALMS.[1]

I.

The argument of the exposition of the Psalms by Hippolytus, (bishop) of Rome.

1. The book of Psalms contains new doctrine after the law which was given by Moses; and thus it is the second book of doctrine after the Scripture of Moses. After the death, then of Moses and Joshua, and after the judges, David arose, one deemed worthy to be called the father of the Saviour, and he was the first to give the Hebrews a new style of psalmody, by which he did away with the ordinances established by Moses with respect to sacrifice, and introduced a new mode of the worship of God by hymns and acclamations; and many other things also beyond the law of Moses he taught through his whole ministry. And this is the sacredness of the book, and its utility. And the account to be given of its inscription is this : (for) as most of the brethren who believe in Christ think that this book is David's, and inscribe it " Psalms of David," we must state what has reached us with respect to it. The Hebrews give the book the title " Sephra Thelim,"[2] and in the " Acts of the Apostles " it is called the " Book of Psalms " (the words are these, " as it is written in the Book of Psalms "), but the name (of the author) in the inscription of the book is not found there. And the reason of that is, that the words written there are not the words of one man, but those of several together; Esdra, as tradition says,

having collected in one volume, after the captivity, the psalms of several, or rather their words, as they are not all psalms. Thus the name of David is prefixed in the case of some, and that of Solomon in others, and that of Asaph in others. There are some also that belong to Idithum (Jeduthun) ; and besides these there are others that belong to the sons of Core (Korah), and even to Moses. As they are therefore the words of so many thus collected together, they could not be said by any one who understands the matter to be by David alone.

2. As regards those which have no inscription, we must also inquire to whom we ought to ascribe them. For why is it that even the simplest inscription is wanting in them — such as the one which runs thus, " A psalm of David," or " Of David," without any addition? Now, my idea is, that wherever this inscription occurs alone, what is written is neither a psalm nor a song, but some sort of utterance under guidance of the Holy Spirit, recorded for the behoof of him who is able to understand it. But the opinion of a certain Hebrew on these last matters has reached me, who held that, when there were many without any inscription, but preceded by one with the inscription " Of David," all these should be reckoned also to be by David. And if this be the case, it follows that those without any inscription are by those (writers) who are rightly reckoned, according to the titles, to be the authors of the psalms preceding these. This book of Psalms before us has also been called by the prophet the " Psalter," because, as they say, the psaltery alone among musical instruments gives back the sound from above when the brass is struck, and not from beneath, after the manner of others. In order, therefore, that those who understand it may be zealous to carry out the analogy of such an appellation, and may also look above, from which direction its melody comes — for this reason he has styled it the Psalter. For it is entirely the voice and utterance of the most Holy Spirit.

3. Let us inquire, further, why there are one hundred and fifty psalms. That the number fifty is sacred, is manifest from the days of the celebrated festival of Pentecost, which indicates release from labours, and (the possession of) joy. For which reason neither fasting nor bending the knee is decreed for those days.[3] For this is a symbol of the great assembly that is reserved for future times. Of which times there was a shadow in the land of Israel in the year called among the Hebrews " Jobel " (Jubilee), which is the fiftieth year in number, and brings with it liberty for the slave, and release from debt, and the like. And the holy Gospel knows

---

[1] Simon de Magistris, *Acta Martyrum Ostiensium*, Append., p. 439.
[2] That is an attempt to express in Greek letters the Hebrew title, viz., סֵפֶר תְּהִלִּים = Book of Praises.

[3] [See vol. iii. pp. 94, 103.]

also the remission of the number fifty, and of that number which is cognate with it, and stands by it, viz., five hundred;[1] for it is not without a purpose that we have given us there the remission of fifty pence and of five hundred. Thus, then, it was also meet that the hymns to God on account of the destruction of enemies, and in thanksgiving for the goodness of God, should contain not simply one set of fifty, but three such, for the name of Father, and Son, and Holy Spirit.

4. The number fifty, moreover, contains seven sevens, or a Sabbath of Sabbaths; and also over and above these full Sabbaths, a new beginning, in the eight, of a really new rest that remains above the Sabbaths. And let any one who is able, observe this (as it is carried out) in the Psalms with more, indeed, than human accuracy, so as to find out the reasons in each case, as we shall set them forth. Thus, for instance, it is not without a purpose that the eighth psalm has the inscription, "On the wine-presses," as it comprehends the perfection of fruits in the eight; for the time for the enjoyment of the fruits of the true vine could not be before the eight. And again, the second psalm inscribed "On the wine-presses," is the eightieth, containing another eighth number, viz., in the tenth multiple. The eighty-third, again, is made up by the union of two holy numbers, viz., the eight in the tenth multiple, and the three in the first multiple. And the fiftieth psalm is a prayer for the remission of sins, and a confession. For as, according to the Gospel, the fiftieth obtained remission, confirming thereby that understanding of the jubilee, so he who offers up such petitions in full confession hopes to gain remission in no other number than the fiftieth. And again, there are also certain others which are called "Songs of degrees," in number fifteen, as was also the number of the steps of the temple, and which show thereby, perhaps, that the "steps" (or "degrees") are comprehended within the number seven and the number eight. And these songs of degrees begin after the one hundred and twentieth psalm, which is called simply "a psalm," as the more accurate copies give it. And this is the number[2] of the perfection of the life of man. And the hundredth[3] psalm, which begins thus, "I will sing of mercy and judgment, O Lord," embraces the life of the saint in fellowship with God. And the one hundred and fiftieth ends with these words, "Let every thing that hath breath praise the Lord."

5. But since, as we have already said, to do this in the case of each, and to find out the reasons, is very difficult, and too much for human nature to accomplish, we shall content ourselves with these things by way of an outline. Only let us add this, that the psalms which deal with historical matter are not found in regular historical order. And the only reason for this is to be found in the numbers according to which the psalms are arranged. For instance, the history in the fifty-first is antecedent to the history in the fiftieth. For everybody acknowledges that the matter of Doeg the Idumean calumniating David to Saul is antecedent to the sin with the wife of Urias; yet it is not without good reason that the history which should be second is placed first, since, as we have before said, the place regarding remission has an affinity with the number fifty. He, therefore, who is not worthy of remission, passes the number fifty, as Doeg the Idumean. For the fifty-first is the psalm that treats of him. And, moreover, the third is in the same position, since it was written when David fled from the face of Absalom his son; and thus, as all know who read the books of Kings, it should come properly after the fifty-first and the fiftieth. And if any one desires to give further attention to these and such like matters, he will find more exact explanations of the history for himself, as well as of the inscriptions and the order of the psalms.

6. It is likely, also, that a similar account is to be given of the fact, that David alone of the prophets prophesied with an instrument, called by the Greeks the "psaltery,"[4] and by the Hebrews the "nabla," which is the only musical instrument that is quite straight, and has no curve. And the sound does not come from the lower parts, as is the case with the lute and certain other instruments, but from the upper. For in the lute and the lyre the brass when struck gives back the sound from beneath. But this psaltery has the source of its musical numbers above, in order that we, too, may practise seeking things above, and not suffer ourselves to be borne down by the pleasure of melody to the passions of the flesh. And I think that this truth, too, was signified deeply and clearly to us in a prophetic way in the construction of the instrument, viz., that those who have souls well-ordered and trained, have the way ready to things above. And again, an instrument having the source of its melodious sound in its upper parts, may be taken as like the body of Christ and His saints — the only instrument that maintains rectitude; "for He did no sin, neither was guile found in his mouth."[5] This is indeed an instrument, harmonious, melodious, well-ordered, that took in no human discord, and did nothing out of measure, but maintained in all things, as

---

[1] Luke vii. 41. [Dan. viii. 13, (*Margin.*) "Palmoni," etc.]
[2] Gen. vi. 3.
[3] i.e., in our version the 101st.

[4] [See learned remarks of Pusey, p. 27 of his *Lectures on Daniel.*]
[5] Isa. liii. 9. [Vol. i. cap. iv. p. 50.]

it were, harmony towards the Father; for, as He says: "He that is of the earth is earthly, and speaketh of the earth: He that cometh from heaven, testifies of what He has seen and heard." [1]

7. As there are "psalms," and "songs," and "psalms of song," and "songs of psalmody," [2] it remains that we discuss the difference between these. We think, then, that the "psalms" are those which are simply played to an instrument, without the accompaniment of the voice, and (which are composed) for the musical melody of the instrument; and that those are called "songs" which are rendered by the voice in concert with the music; and that they are called "psalms of song" when the voice takes the lead, while the appropriate sound is also made to accompany it, rendered harmoniously by the instruments; and "songs of psalmody," when the instrument takes the lead, while the voice has the second place, and accompanies the music of the strings. And thus much as to the letter of what is signified by these terms. But as to the mystical interpretation, it would be a "psalm" when, by smiting the instrument, viz., the body, with good deeds we succeed in good action, though not wholly proficient in speculation; and a "song," when, by revolving the mysteries of the truth, apart from the practical, and assenting fully to them, we have the noblest thoughts of God and His oracles, while knowledge enlightens us, and wisdom shines brightly in our souls; and a "song of psalmody," when, while good action takes the lead, according to the word, "If thou desire wisdom, keep the commandments, and the Lord shall give her unto thee," [3] we understand wisdom at the same time, and are deemed worthy by God to know the truth of things, till now kept hid from us; and a "psalm of song," when, by revolving with the light of wisdom some of the more abstruse questions pertaining to morals, we first become prudent in action, and then also able to tell what, and when, and how action is to be taken. And perhaps this is the reason why the first inscriptions nowhere contain the word "songs," but only "psalm" or "psalms;" for the saint does not begin with speculation; but when he has become in a simple way a believer, according to orthodoxy, he devotes himself to the actions that are to be done. For this reason, also, are there many "songs" at the end; and wherever there is the word "degrees," there we do not find the word "psalm," whether by itself alone or with any addition, but only "songs." For in the "degrees" (or "ascents"), the saints will be engaged in nothing but in speculation alone. And let the account which we have offered, following the indications given in the interpretation of the Seventy, suffice for this subject in general.

8. But again, as we found in the Seventy, and in Theodotion, and in Symmachus, in some psalms, and these not a few, the word διάψαλμα inserted, [4] we endeavoured to make out whether those who placed it there meant to mark a change at those places in rhythm or melody, or any alteration in the mode of instruction, or in thought, or in force of language. It is found, however, neither in Aquila nor in the Hebrew; but there, instead of διάψαλμα (= an intervening musical symphony), we find the word ἀεί (= ever). And further, let not this fact escape thee, O man of learning, that the Hebrews also divided the Psalter into five books, so that it might be another Pentateuch. For from Ps. i. to xl. they reckoned one book; and from xli. to lxxi. they reckoned a second; and from lxxii. to lxxxviii. they counted a third book; and from lxxxix. to cv. a fourth; and from cvi. to cl. they made up the fifth. For they judged that each psalm closing with the words, "Blessed be the Lord, Amen, amen," formed the conclusion of a book. And in them we have "prayer," viz., supplication offered to God for anything requisite; and the "vow," i.e., engagement; and the "hymn," which is the song of blessing to God for benefits enjoyed; and "praise" or "extolling," which is the laudation of the wonders of God. For laudation is nothing else but just the superlative of praise.

9. However it may be with the "time when and the manner" in which this idea of the Psalms was hit upon by the inspired David, he at least seems to have been the first, and indeed the only one, concerned in it, and that, too, at the earliest period, when he taught his fingers to tune the psaltery. For if any other before him showed the use of the psaltery and lute, it was at any rate in a very different way that such an one did it, only putting together some rude and clumsy contrivance, or simply employing the instrument, without singing either to melody or to words, but only amusing himself with a rude sort of pleasure. But after such he was the first to reduce the affair to rhythm, and order, and art, and also to wed the singing of the song with the melody. And, what is of greater importance, this most inspired of men sang to God, or of God, beginning in this wise even at the period when he was among the shepherds and youths in a simpler and humbler style, and afterwards when he became a man and a king, attempting something loftier and of more public interest. And he is said to have made this advance, especially after

[1] John iii. 31.
[2] The Greek is: ὄντων ψαλμῶν, καὶ οὐσῶν ᾠδῶν, καὶ ψαλμῶν ᾠδῆς, καὶ ᾠδῶν ψαλμοῦ.
[3] Ecclus. i. 26.
[4] [Our author throws no great light on this vexed word, but the article Selah in Smith's Dict. of the Bible is truly valuable.]

he had brought back the ark into the city. At that time he often danced before the ark, and often sang songs of thanksgiving, and songs to celebrate its recovery. And then by and by, allocating the whole tribe of the Levites to the duty, he appointed four leaders of the choirs, viz., Asaph, Aman (Heman), Ethan, and Idithum (Jeduthun), inasmuch as there are also in all things visible four primal principles. And he then formed choirs of men, selected from the rest. And he fixed their number at seventy-two, having respect, I think, to the number of the tongues that were confused, or rather divided, at the time of the building of the tower. And what was typified by this, but that hereafter all tongues shall again unite in one common confession, when the Word takes possession of the whole world?

OTHER FRAGMENTS ON THE PSALMS.[1]

II.

On Psalm xxxi. 22. Of the triumph of the Christian faith.

The mercy of God is not so "marvellous" when it is shown in humbler cities as when it is shown in "a strong city,"[2] and for this reason "God is to be blessed."

III.

On Psalm lv. 15.

One of old used to say that those only descend alive into Hades who are instructed in the knowledge of things divine; for he who has not tasted of the words of life is dead.

IV.

On Psalm lviii. 11.

But since there is a time when the righteous shall rejoice, and sinners shall meet the end foretold for them, we must with all reason fully acknowledge and declare that God is inspector and overseer of all that is done among men, and judges all who dwell upon earth. It is proper further to inquire whether the prophecy in hand, which quite corresponds and fits in with those preceding it, may describe the end.

When Hippolytus dictated these words,[3] the grammarian asked him why he hesitated about that prophecy, as if he mistrusted the divine power in that calamity of exile.

The learned man calls attention to the question why the word διαγράφῃ (= may describe) was used by me in the subjunctive mood, as if silently indicating doubt.

Hippolytus accordingly replied: —

You know indeed quite well, that words of that form are used as conveying by implication a re-

buke to those who study the prophecies about Christ, and talk righteousness with the mouth, while they do not admit His coming, nor listen to His voice when He calls to them, and says, "He that hath ears to hear, let him hear;" who who have made themselves like the serpent, and have made their ears like those of a deaf viper, and so forth. God then does, in truth, take care of the righteous, and judges their cause when injured on the earth; and He punishes those who dare to injure them.

V.

On Psalm lix. 11. Concerning the Jews.

For this reason, even up to our day, though they see the boundaries (of their country), and go round about them, they stand afar off. And therefore have they no longer king or high priest or prophet, nor even scribes and Pharisees and Sadducees among them. He does not, however, say that they are to be cut off; wherefore their race still subsists, and the succession of their children is continued. For they have not been cut off nor consumed from among men — but they are and exist still — yet only as those who have been rejected and cast down from the honour of which of old they were deemed worthy by God. But again, "Scatter them," he says, "by Thy power;" which word has also come to pass. For they are scattered throughout the whole earth, in servitude everywhere, and engaging in the lowest and most servile occupations, and doing any unseemly work for hunger's sake.

For if they were destroyed from among men, and remained nowhere among the living, they could not see my people, he means, nor know my Church in its prosperity. Therefore "scatter" them everywhere on earth, where my Church is to be established, in order that when they see the Church founded by me, they may be roused to emulate it in piety. And these things did the Saviour also ask on their behalf.

VI.

On Psalm lxii. 6.

Aliens (μετανάσται) properly so called are those who have been despoiled by some enemies or adversaries, and have then become wanderers; a thing which we indeed also endured formerly at the hand of the demons. But from the time that Christ took us up by faith in Him, we are no longer aliens from the true country — the Jerusalem which is above — nor have we to bear alienation in error from the truth.

VII.

On Psalm lxviii. 18. Of the enlargement of the Church.

And the unbelieving, too, He sometimes draws by means of sickness and outward circumstances;

---

[1] De Magistris, *Acta Martyrum Ostien.*, p. 256.
[2] The allusion probably is to the seat of imperial power itself.
[3] He is addressing his amanuensis, a man not without learning, as it seems. Hippolytus dictates these words.

yea, many also by means of visions have come to make their abode with Jesus.

VIII.

On Psalm lxxxix. 4. Of the Gentiles.

And around us are the wise men of the Greeks, mocking and jeering us, as those who believe without inquiry, and foolishly.

IX.

On the words in Psalm xcvi. 11: "Let the sea roar (be moved), and the fulness thereof."

By these words it is signified that the preaching of the Gospel will be spread abroad over the seas and the islands in the ocean, and among the people dwelling therein, who are here called "the fulness thereof." And that word has been made good. For churches of Christ fill all the islands, and are being multiplied every day, and the teaching of the Word of salvation is gaining accessions.

X.

On Psalm cxix. 30-32.

He who loves truth, and never utters a false word with his mouth, may say, "I have chosen the way of truth." Moreover, he who always sets the judgments of God before his eyes, and remembers them in every action, will say, "Thy judgments have I not forgotten." And how is our heart enlarged by trials and afflictions! For these pluck out the thorns of anxious thoughts within us, and enlarge the heart for the reception of the divine laws. For, says he, "in affliction Thou hast enlarged me." Then do we walk in the way of God's commandments, well prepared for it by the endurance of trials.

XI.

On the words in Psalm cxxvii. 7: "On the wrath of mine enemies," etc.

Hast thou [1] seen that the power (of God) is most mighty on every side? For (says he) Thou wilt be able to save me when in the midst of troubles, and to keep them in check when they rage, and rave, and breathe fire.

XII.

On the words in Psalm cxxxix. 15: "My substance or (bones) was not hid from Thee, which Thou madest in secret."

It is said also by those who treat of the nature and generation of animals, that the change of the blood into bone is something invisible and intangible, although in the case of other parts, I mean the flesh and nerves, the mode of their formation may be seen. And the Scripture also, in Ecclesiastes, adduces this, saying, "As thou knowest not the bones in the womb of her that is with child, so thou shalt not know the works of God." [2] But from Thee was not hid even my substance, as it was originally in the lowest parts of the earth.

[1] To his amanuensis.
[2] Eccles. xi. 5.

THE EXTANT WORKS AND FRAGMENTS

OF

HIPPOLYTUS.

PART II.—DOGMATICAL AND HISTORICAL.

TREATISE ON CHRIST AND ANTICHRIST.[1]

1. As it was your desire, my beloved brother Theophilus,[2] to be thoroughly informed on those topics which I put summarily before you, I have thought it right to set these matters of inquiry clearly forth to your view, drawing largely from the Holy Scriptures themselves as from a holy fountain, in order that you may not only have the pleasure of hearing them on the testimony of men,[3] but may also be able, by surveying them in the light of (divine) authority, to glorify God in all. For this will be as a sure supply furnished you by us for your journey in this present life, so that by ready argument applying things ill understood and apprehended by most, you may sow them in the ground of your heart, as in a rich and clean soil.[4] By these, too, you will be able to silence those who oppose and gainsay the word of salvation. Only see that you do not give these things over to unbelieving and blasphemous tongues, for that is no common danger. But impart them to pious and faithful men, who desire to live holily and righteously with fear. For it is not to no purpose that the blessed apostle exhorts Timothy, and says, "O Timothy, keep that which is committed to thy trust, avoiding profane and vain babblings, and oppositions of science falsely so called ; which some professing have erred concerning the faith."[5] And again, "Thou therefore, my son, be strong in the grace that is in Christ Jesus. And the things that thou hast heard of me in many exhortations, the same commit thou to faithful men,[6] who shall be able to teach others also."[7] If, then, the blessed (apostle) delivered these things with a pious caution, which could be easily known by all, as he perceived in the spirit that "all men have not faith,"[8] how much greater will be our danger, if, rashly and without thought, we commit the revelations of God to profane and unworthy men?

2. For as the blessed prophets were made, so to speak, eyes for us, they foresaw through faith the mysteries of the word, and became ministers of these[9] things also to succeeding generations, not only reporting the past, but also announcing the present and the future, so that the prophet might not appear to be one only for the time being, but might also predict the future for all generations, and so be reckoned a (true) prophet. For these fathers were furnished with the Spirit, and largely honoured by the Word Himself ; and just as it is with instruments of music, so had they the Word always, like the plectrum,[10] in union with them, and when moved by Him the prophets announced what God willed. For they spake not of their own power[11] (let there be no mistake as to that[12]), neither did they declare what pleased themselves. But first of all they were endowed with wisdom by the Word, and then again were rightly instructed

---

[1] Gallandi, *Bibl. vet. Patr.*, ii. p. 417, Venice, 1765.
[2] Perhaps the same Theophilus whom Methodius, a contemporary of Hippolytus, addresses as Epiphanius. [See vol. vi., this series.] From this introduction, too, it is clear that they are in error who take this book to be a homily. (Fabricius.)
[3] In the text the reading is τῶν ὄντων, for which τῶν ὤτων = *of the ears*, is proposed by some, and ἀνθρώπων = *of men*, by others. In the manuscripts the abbreviation ανων is often found for ἀνθρώπων.
[4] In the text we find ὡς πίων καθαρᾷ γῇ, for which grammar requires ὡς πίονι καθαρᾷ γῇ. Combefisius proposes ὥσπερ οὖν καθαρᾷ γῇ = *as in clean ground*. Others would read ὡς πυρόν, etc., = *like grain in clean ground*.
[5] 1 Tim. vi. 20, 21.

[6] This reading, παρακλήσεων for μαρτύρων (= witnesses), which is peculiar to Hippolytus alone, is all the more remarkable as so thoroughly suiting Paul's meaning in the passage.
[7] 2 Tim. ii. 1, 2.
[8] 2 Thess. iii. 2.
[9] The text reads ἅτινα = which. Gudius proposes τινά = some.
[10] The plectrum was the instrument with which the lyre was struck. The text is in confusion here. Combefisius corrects it, as we render it, ὀργάνων δίκην ἡνωμένον ἔχοντες ἐν ἑαυτοῖς.
[11] 2 Pet. i. 21.
[12] The text reads μὴ πλανῶ (= that I may not deceive). Some propose ὡς πλάνοι = as deceivers.

in the future by means of visions. And then, when thus themselves fully convinced, they spake those things which [1] were revealed by God to them alone, and concealed from all others. For with what reason should the prophet be called a prophet, unless he in spirit foresaw the future? For if the prophet spake of any chance event, he would not be a prophet then in speaking of things which were under the eye of all. But one who sets forth in detail things yet to be, was rightly judged a prophet. Wherefore prophets were with good reason called from the very first "seers."[2] And hence we, too, who are rightly instructed in what was declared aforetime by them, speak not of our own capacity. For we do not attempt to made any change one way or another among ourselves in the words that were spoken of old by them, but we make the Scriptures in which these are written public, and read them to those who can believe rightly; for that is a common benefit for both parties: for him who speaks, in holding in memory and setting forth correctly things uttered of old;[3] and for him who hears, in giving attention to the things spoken. Since, then, in this there is a work assigned to both parties together, viz., to him who speaks, that he speak forth faithfully without regard to risk,[4] and to him who hears, that he hear and receive in faith that which is spoken, I beseech you to strive together with me in prayer to God.

3. Do you wish then to know in what manner the Word of God, who was again the Son of God,[5] as He was of old the Word, communicated His revelations to the blessed prophets in former times? Well, as the Word shows His compassion and His denial of all respect of persons by all the saints, He enlightens them[6] and adapts them to that which is advantageous for us, like a skilful physician, understanding the weakness of men. And the ignorant He loves to teach, and the erring He turns again to His own true way. And by those who live by faith He is easily found; and to those of pure eye and holy heart, who desire to knock at the door, He opens immediately. For He casts away none of His servants as unworthy of the divine mysteries. He does not esteem the rich man more highly than the poor, nor does He despise the poor man for his poverty. He does not disdain the barbarian, nor does He set the eunuch aside as no man.[7] He does not hate the female on ac-

count of the woman's act of disobedience in the beginning, nor does He reject the male on account of the man's transgression. But He seeks all, and desires to save all, wishing to make all the children of God, and calling all the saints unto one perfect man. For there is also one Son (or Servant) of God, by whom we too, receiving the regeneration through the Holy Spirit, desire to come all unto one perfect and heavenly man.[8]

4. For whereas the Word of God was without flesh,[9] He took upon Himself the holy flesh by the holy Virgin, and prepared a robe which He wove for Himself, like a bridegroom, in the sufferings of the cross, in order that by uniting His own power with our motal body, and by mixing[10] the incorruptible with the corruptible, and the strong with the weak, He might save perishing man. The web-beam, therefore, is the passion of the Lord upon the cross, and the warp on it is the power of the Holy Spirit, and the woof is the holy flesh wrought (woven) by the Spirit, and the thread is the grace which by the love of Christ binds and unites the two in one, and the combs or (rods) are the Word; and the workers are the patriarchs and prophets who weave the fair, long, perfect tunic for Christ; and the Word passing through these, like the combs or (rods), completes through them that which His Father willeth.[10]

5. But as time now presses for the consideration of the question immediately in hand, and as what has been already said in the introduction with regard to the glory of God, may suffice, it is proper that we take the Holy Scriptures themselves in hand, and find out from them what, and of what manner, the coming of Antichrist is; on what occasion and at what time that impious one shall be revealed; and whence and from what tribe (he shall come); and what his name is, which is indicated by the number in the Scripture; and how he shall work error among the people, gathering them from the ends of the earth; and (how) he shall stir up tribulation and persecution against the saints; and how he shall glorify himself as God; and what his end shall be; and how the sudden appearing of the Lord shall be revealed from heaven; and what the conflagration of the whole world shall be; and what the glorious and heavenly kingdom of the saints is to be, when they reign together with Christ; and what the punishment of the wicked by fire.

---

[1] This is according to the emendation of Combefisius. [And note this primitive theory of inspiration as illustrating the words, " who spake by the prophets," in the Nicene Symbol.]

[2] 1 Sam. ix. 9.

[3] In the text it is προκείμενα (= things before us or proposed to us), for which Combefisius proposes, as in our rendering, προειρημένα.

[4] The original is ἀκινδύνον.

[5] Isa. xlii 1; Matt. xii. 18. The text is αὐτὸς πάλιν ὁ τοῦ Θεοῦ παῖς. See Macarius, *Divinitas D. N. S. C.*, book iv. ch. xiii. p. 460, and Grabe on Bull's *Defens. Fid. Nic.*, p. 101.

[6] Reading αὐτούς for αὐτόν.

[7] [Isa. lvi. 3, 4.]

[8] Eph. iv. 13.

[9] The text has ὢν = being, for which read ἦν = was.

[10] μίξας. Thomassin, *De Incarnatione Verbi*, iii. 5, cites the most distinguished of the Greek and Latin Fathers, who taught that a mingling (*commistio*), without confusion indeed, but yet most thorough, of the two natures, is the bond and nexus of the personal unity.

[11] [This analogy of weaving is powerfully employed by Gray (" Weave the warp, and weave the woof," etc.). See his Pindaric ode, *The Bard*.]

6. Now, as our Lord Jesus Christ, who is also God, was prophesied of under the figure of a lion,[1] on account of His royalty and glory, in the same way have the Scriptures also aforetime spoken of Antichrist as a lion, on account of his tyranny and violence. For the deceiver seeks to liken himself in all things to the Son of God. Christ is a lion, so Antichrist is also a lion; Christ is a king,[2] so Antichrist is also a king. The Saviour was manifested as a lamb;[3] so he too, in like manner, will appear as a lamb, though within he is a wolf. The Saviour came into the world in the circumcision, and he will come in the same manner. The Lord sent apostles among all the nations, and he in like manner will send false apostles. The Saviour gathered together the sheep that were scattered abroad,[4] and he in like manner will bring together a people that is scattered abroad. The Lord gave a seal to those who believed on Him, and he will give one in like manner. The Saviour appeared in the form of man, and he too will come in the form of a man. The Saviour raised up and showed His holy flesh like a temple,[5] and he will raise a temple of stone in Jerusalem. And his seductive arts we shall exhibit in what follows. But for the present let us turn to the question in hand.

7. Now the blessed Jacob speaks to the following effect in his benedictions, testifying prophetically of our Lord and Saviour: "Judah, let thy brethren praise thee: thy hand shall be on the neck of thine enemies; thy father's children shall bow down before thee. Judah is a lion's whelp: from the shoot, my son, thou art gone up: he stooped down, he couched as a lion, and as a lion's whelp; who shall rouse him up? A ruler shall not depart from Judah, nor a leader from his thighs, until he come for whom it is reserved; and he shall be the expectation of the nations. Binding his ass to a vine, and his ass's colt to the vine tendril; he shall wash his garment in wine, and his clothes in the blood of the grapes. His eyes shall be gladsome as with wine, and his teeth shall be whiter than milk."[6]

8. Knowing, then, as I do, how to explain these things in detail, I deem it right at present to quote the words themselves. But since the expressions themselves urge us to speak of them, I shall not omit to do so. For these are truly divine and glorious things, and things well calculated to benefit the soul. The prophet, in using the expression, *a lion's whelp*, means him who sprang from Judah and David according to the flesh, who was not made indeed of the seed of David, but was conceived by the (power of the) Holy Ghost, and came forth[7] from the holy shoot of earth. For Isaiah says, "There shall come forth a rod out of the root of Jesse, and a flower shall grow up out of it."[8] That which is called by Isaiah a *flower*, Jacob calls a shoot. For first he shot forth, and then he flourished in the world. And the expression, "he stooped down, he couched as a lion, and as a lion's whelp," refers to the three days' sleep (death, couching) of Christ; as also Isaiah says, "How is faithful Sion become an harlot! it was full of judgment; in which righteousness lodged (couched); but now murderers."[9] And David says to the same effect, "I laid me down (couched) and slept; I awaked: for the Lord will sustain me;"[10] in which words he points to the fact of his sleep and rising again. And Jacob says, "Who shall rouse him up?" And that is just what David and Paul both refer to, as when Paul says, "and God the Father, who raised Him from the dead."[11]

9. And in saying, "A ruler shall not depart from Judah, nor a leader from his thighs, until he come for whom it is reserved; and he shall be the expectation of the nations," he referred the fulfilment (of that prophecy) to Christ. For He is our expectation. For we expect Him, (and) by faith we behold Him as He comes from heaven with power.

10. "Binding his ass to a vine:" that means that He unites His people of the circumcision with His own calling (vocation). For He was the vine.[12] "And his ass's colt to the vine-tendril:" that denotes the people of the Gentiles, as He calls the circumcision and the uncircumcision unto one faith.

11. "He shall wash his garment in wine," that is, according to that voice of His Father which came down by the Holy Ghost at the Jordan.[13] "And his clothes in the blood of the grape." In the blood of what grape, then, but just His own flesh, which hung upon the tree like a cluster of grapes? — from whose side also flowed two streams, of blood and water, in which the nations are washed and purified, which (nations) He may be supposed to have as a robe about Him.[14]

---

[1] Rev. v. 5; [also Gen. xlix. 8. See below, 7, 8].
[2] John xviii. 37.
[3] John i. 29.
[4] John xi. 52.
[5] John ii. 19.
[6] Gen. xlix. 8–12.

[7] The text has τούτου — προερχομένου, for which we read, with Combefisius, προερχόμενον.
[8] Isa. xi. 1.
[9] Isa. i. 21.
[10] Ps. iii. 5.
[11] Gal. i. 1.
[12] John xv. 1.
[13] The text gives simply, τὴν τοῦ ἁγίου, etc., = the *paternal voice of the Holy Ghost*, etc. As this would seem to represent the Holy Ghost as the Father of Christ, Combefisius proposes, as in our rendering, κατὰ τὴν διὰ τοῦ ἁγίου, etc. The *wine*, therefore, is taken as a figure of His *deity*, and the garment as a figure of His *humanity;* and the sense would be, that He has the latter imbued with the former in a way peculiar to Himself — even as the voice at the Jordan declared Him to be the Father's Son, not His Son by adoption, but His *own* Son, anointed as man with divinity itself.
[14] The nations are compared to a robe about Christ, as something foreign to Himself, and deriving all their gifts from Him.

12. "His eyes gladsome with wine." And what are the eyes of Christ but the blessed prophets, who foresaw in the Spirit, and announced beforehand, the sufferings that were to befall Him, and rejoiced in seeing Him in power with spiritual eyes, being furnished (for their vocation) by the word Himself and His grace?

13. And in saying, "And his teeth (shall be) whiter than milk," he referred to the commandments that proceed from the holy mouth of Christ, and which are pure (purify) as milk.

14. Thus did the Scriptures preach beforetime of this lion and lion's whelp. And in like manner also we find it written regarding Antichrist. For Moses speaks thus :· "Dan is a lion's whelp, and he shall leap from Bashan." [1] But that no one may err by supposing that this is said of the Saviour, let him attend carefully to the matter. "Dan," he says, "is a lion's whelp ; " and in naming the tribe of Dan, he declared clearly the tribe from which Antichrist is destined to spring. For as Christ springs from the tribe of Judah, so Antichrist is to spring from the tribe of Dan.[2] And that the case stands thus, we see also from the words of Jacob: "Let Dan be a serpent, lying upon the ground, biting the horse's heel." [3] What, then, is meant by the serpent but Antichrist, that deceiver who is mentioned in Genesis,[4] who deceived Eve and supplanted Adam ($\pi\tau\epsilon\rho\nu\acute{\iota}\sigma\alpha\varsigma$, bruised Adam's heel)? But since it is necessary to prove this assertion by sufficient testimony, we shall not shrink from the task.

15. That it is in reality out of the tribe of Dan, then, that that tyrant and king, that dread judge, that son of the devil, is destined to spring and arise, the prophet testifies when he says, "Dan shall judge his people, as (he is) also one tribe in Israel." [5] But some one may say that this refers to Samson, who sprang from the tribe of Dan, and judged the people twenty years. Well, the prophecy had its partial fulfilment in Samson, but its complete fulfilment is reserved for Antichrist. For Jeremiah also speaks to this effect : " From Dan we are to hear the sound of the swiftness of his horses : the whole land trembled *at the sound of the neighing, of the driving of his horses.*" [6] And another prophet says : " He shall gather together all his strength, from the east even to the west. They whom he calls, and they whom he calls not, shall go with him. He shall make the sea white with the sails of his ships, and the plain black with the shields

of his armaments. And whosoever shall oppose him in war shall fall by the sword." [7] That these things, then, are said of no one else but that tyrant, and shameless one, and adversary of God, we shall show in what follows.

16. But Isaiah also speaks thus : "And it shall come to pass, that when the Lord hath performed His whole work upon Mount Zion and on Jerusalem, He will punish (visit) the stout mind, the king of Assyria, and the greatness (height) of the glory of his eyes. For he said, By my strength will I do it, and by the wisdom of my understanding I will remove the bounds of the peoples, and will rob them of their strength : and I will make the inhabited cities tremble, and will gather the whole world in my hand like a nest, and I will lift it up like eggs that are left. And there is no one that shall escape or gainsay me, *and open the mouth and chatter. Shall the axe boast itself without him that heweth therewith ? or shall the saw magnify itself without him that shaketh (draweth) it ? As if one should raise a rod or a staff, and the staff should lift itself up :* and not thus. But the Lord shall send dishonour unto thy honour ; and into thy glory a burning fire shall burn. And the light of Israel shall be a fire, and shall sanctify him in flame, and shall consume the forest like grass." [8]

17. And again he says in another place : "How hath the exactor ceased, and how hath the oppressor ceased ! [9] God hath broken the yoke of the rulers of sinners, He who smote the people in wrath, and with an incurable stroke : He that strikes the people with an incurable stroke, which He did not spare. He ceased (rested) confidently : the whole earth shouts with rejoicing. The trees of Lebanon rejoiced at thee, and the cedar of Lebanon, (saying), Since thou art laid down, no feller is come up against us. Hell from beneath is moved at meeting thee : all the mighty ones, the rulers of the earth, are gathered together — the lords from their thrones. All the kings of the nations, all they shall answer together, and shall say, And thou, too, art taken as we ; and thou art reckoned among us. Thy pomp is brought down to earth, thy great rejoicing : they will spread decay under thee ; and the worm shall be thy covering.[10] How art thou fallen from heaven, O Lucifer, son of the morning ! [11] He is cast down to the ground who sends off to all the nations. And thou didst say in thy mind, I will ascend into heaven, I will set my throne above the stars of heaven : I will sit down upon the lofty mountains towards the north : I will

---

[1] Deut. xxxiii. 22.
[2] [See Irenæus, vol. i. p. 559. Dan's name is excepted in Rev. vii., and this was always assigned as the reason. The learned Calmet (*sub voce* Dan) makes a prudent reflection on this idea. The history given in Judg. xviii. is more to the purpose.]
[3] Gen. xlix. 17.
[4] Gen. iii. 1.
[5] Gen. xlix. 16.
[6] Jer. viii. 16.

[7] Perhaps from an apocryphal book, as also below in ch. liv.
[8] Isa. x. 12-17.
[9] $\epsilon\pi\iota\sigma\pi\sigma\upsilon\delta\alpha\sigma\tau\acute{\eta}\varsigma$.
[10] $\kappa\alpha\tau\alpha\kappa\acute{\alpha}\lambda\upsilon\mu\mu\alpha$; other reading, $\varkappa\alpha\tau\acute{\alpha}\lambda\epsilon\iota\mu\mu\alpha$ = remains.
[11] Lit., that risest early.

208 TREATISE ON CHRIST AND ANTICHRIST.

ascend above the clouds : I will be like the Most High. Yet now thou shalt be brought down to hell, and to the foundations of the earth ! They that see thee shall wonder at thee, and shall say, This is the man that excited the earth, that did shake kings, that made the whole world a wilderness, and destroyed the cities, that released not those in prison.[1] All the kings of the earth did lie in honour, every one in his own house ; but thou shalt be cast out on the mountains like a loathsome carcase, with many who fall, pierced through with the sword, and going down to hell. As a garment stained with blood is not pure, so neither shalt thou be comely (or clean) ; because thou hast destroyed my land, and slain my people. Thou shalt not abide, enduring for ever, a wicked seed. Prepare thy children for slaughter, for the sins of thy father, that they rise not, neither possess my land."[2]

18. Ezekiel also speaks of him to the same effect, thus : "Thus saith the Lord God, Because thine heart is lifted up, and thou hast said, I am God, I sit in the seat of God, in the midst of the sea ; yet art thou a man, and not God, (though) thou hast set thine heart as the heart of God. Art thou wiser than Daniel? Have the wise not instructed thee in their wisdom? With thy wisdom or with thine understanding hast thou gotten thee power, and gold and silver in thy treasures? By thy great wisdom and by thy traffic[3] hast thou increased thy power? Thy heart is lifted up in thy power. Therefore thus saith the Lord God : Because thou hast set thine heart as the heart of God : behold, therefore I will bring strangers[4] upon thee, plagues from the nations : and they shall draw their swords against thee, and against the beauty of thy wisdom ; and they shall level thy beauty to destruction ; and they shall bring thee down ; and thou shalt die by the death of the wounded in the midst of the sea. Wilt thou yet say *before them that slay thee, I am God? But thou art a man, and no God, in the hand of them that wound thee. Thou shalt die the deaths of the uncircumcised by the hand of* strangers : for I have spoken it, saith the Lord."[5]

19. These words then being thus presented, let us observe somewhat in detail what Daniel says in his visions. For in distinguishing the kingdoms that are to rise after these things, he showed also the coming of Antichrist in the last times, and the consummation of the whole world. In expounding the vision of Nebuchadnezzar, then, he speaks thus : "Thou, O king, sawest, and behold a great image standing before thy face : the head of which was of fine gold, its arms and shoulders of silver, its belly and its thighs of brass, and its legs of iron, (and) its feet part of iron and part of clay. Thou sawest, then, till that a stone was cut out without hands, and smote the image upon the feet that were of iron and clay, and brake them to an end. Then were the clay, the iron, the brass, the silver, (and) the gold broken, and became like the chaff from the summer threshing-floor ; and the strength (fulness) of the wind carried them away, and there was no place found for them. And the stone that smote the image became a great mountain, and filled the whole earth."[6]

20. Now if we set Daniel's own visions also side by side with this, we shall have one exposition to give of the two together, and shall (be able to) show how concordant with each other they are, and how true. For he speaks thus : " I Daniel saw, and behold the four winds of the heaven strove upon the great sea. And four great beasts came up from the sea, diverse one from another. The first (was) like a lioness, and had wings as of an eagle. I beheld till the wings thereof were plucked, and it was lifted up from the earth, and made stand upon the feet as a man, and a man's heart was given to it. And behold a second beast like to a bear, and it was made stand on one part, and it had three ribs in the mouth of it.[7] I beheld, and lo a beast like a leopard, and it had upon the back of it four wings of a fowl, and the beast had four heads. After this I saw, and behold a fourth beast, dreadful and terrible, and strong exceedingly ; it had iron teeth *and claws of brass*,[8] which devoured and brake in pieces, and it stamped the residue with the feet of it ; and it was diverse from all the beasts that were before it, and it had ten horns. I considered its horns, and behold there came up among them another little horn, and before it there were three of the first horns plucked up by the roots ; and behold in this horn were eyes like the eyes of man, and a mouth speaking great things."[9]

21. " I beheld till the thrones were set, and the Ancient of days did sit : and His garment was white as snow, and the hair of His head like pure wool : His throne was a flame of fire, His wheels were a burning fire. A stream of fire flowed before Him. Thousand thousands ministered unto Him, and ten thousand times ten thousand stood around Him : the judgment was set, and the books were opened. I beheld then, because of the voice of the great words which the horn spake, till the beast was slain and per-

---

[1] The text gives ἐπαγωγῇ. Combefisius prefers ἀπαγωγῇ = *trial.*
[2] Isa. xiv. 4-21.
[3] i.e., according to the reading, ἐμπορίᾳ. The text is ἐμπειρίᾳ = *experience.*
[4] There is another reading, λιμοὺς (=*famines*) τῶν ἐθνῶν.
[5] Ezek. xxviii. 2-10.
[6] Dan. ii. 31-35.
[7] Combefisius adds, "between the teeth of it: and they said thus to it, Arise, devour much flesh."
[8] Combefisius inserted these words, because he thought that they must have been in the vision, as they occur subsequently in the explanation of the vision (v. 19).
[9] Dan. vii. 2-8.

ished, and his body given to the burning of fire. And the dominion of the other beasts was taken away." [1]

22. "I saw in the night vision, and, behold, one like the Son of man was coming with the clouds of heaven, and came to the Ancient of days, and was brought near before Him. And there was given Him dominion, and honour, and the kingdom; and all peoples, tribes, and tongues shall serve Him: His dominion is an everlasting dominion, which shall not pass away, and His kingdom shall not be destroyed." [2]

23. Now since these things, spoken as they are with a mystical meaning, may seem to some hard to understand, we shall keep back nothing fitted to impart an intelligent apprehension of them to those who are possessed of a sound mind. He said, then, that a "lioness came up from the sea," and by that he meant the kingdom of the Babylonians in the world, which also was the head of gold on the image. In saying that "it had wings as of an eagle," he meant that Nebuchadnezzar the king was lifted up and was exalted against God. Then he says, "the wings thereof were plucked," that is to say, his glory was destroyed; for he was driven out of his kingdom. And the words, "a man's heart was given to it, and it was made stand upon the feet as a man," refer to the fact that he repented and recognised himself to be only a man, and gave the glory to God.

24. Then, after the lioness, he sees a "second beast like a bear," and that denoted the Persians. For after the Babylonians, the Persians held the sovereign power. And in saying that there were "three ribs in the mouth of it," he pointed to three nations, viz., the Persians, and the Medes, and the Babylonians; which were also represented on the image by the silver after the gold. Then (there was) "the third beast, a leopard," which meant the Greeks. For after the Persians, Alexander of Macedon obtained the sovereign power on subverting Darius, as is also shown by the brass on the image. And in saying that it had "four wings of a fowl," he taught us most clearly how the kingdom of Alexander was partitioned. For in speaking of "four heads," he made mention of four kings, viz., those who arose out of that (kingdom).[3] For Alexander, when dying, partitioned out his kingdom into four divisions.

25. Then he says: "A fourth beast, dreadful and terrible; it had iron teeth and claws of brass." And who are these but the Romans? which (kingdom) is meant by the iron — the kingdom which is now established; for the legs

of that (image) were of iron. And after this, what remains, beloved, but the toes of the feet of the image, in which part is iron and part clay, mixed together? And mystically by the toes of the feet he meant the kings who are to arise from among them; as Daniel also says (in the words), "I considered the beast, and lo there were ten horns behind it, among which shall rise another (horn), an offshoot, and shall pluck up by the roots the three (that were) before it." And under this was signified none other than Antichrist, who is also himself to raise the kingdom of the Jews. He says that three horns are plucked up by the root by him, viz., the three kings of Egypt, and Libya, and Ethiopia, whom he cuts off in the array of battle. And he, after gaining terrible power over all, being nevertheless a tyrant,[4] shall stir up tribulation and persecution against men, exalting himself against them. For Daniel says: "I considered the horn, and behold that horn made war with the saints, and prevailed against them, till the beast was slain and perished, and its body was given to the burning of fire." [5]

26. After a little space the stone [6] will come from heaven which smites the image and breaks it in pieces, and subverts all the kingdoms, and gives the kingdom to the saints of the Most High. This is the stone which becomes a great mountain, and fills the whole earth, of which Daniel says: "I saw in the night visions, and behold one like the Son of man came with the clouds of heaven, and came to the Ancient of days, and was brought near before Him. And there was given Him dominion, and glory, and a kingdom; and all peoples, tribes, and languages shall serve Him: and His dominion is an everlasting dominion, which shall not pass away, and His kingdom shall not be destroyed." [7] He showed all power given by the Father to the Son,[8] who is ordained Lord of things in heaven, and things on earth, and things under the earth, and Judge of all: [9] of things in heaven, because He was born, the Word of God, before all (ages); and of things on earth, because He became man in the midst of men, to re-create our Adam through Himself; and of things under the earth, because He was also reckoned among the dead, preaching the Gospel to the souls of the saints,[10] (and) by death overcoming death.

27. As these things, then, are in the future, and as the ten toes of the image are equivalent to (so many) democracies,[11] and the ten horns of

---

[1] Dan vii. 9–12.
[2] Dan. vii. 13, 14.
[3] See Curtius, x. 10. That Alexander himself divided his kingdom is asserted by Josephus Gorionides (iii.) and Cyril of Jerusalem (*Catech.*, 4, *De Sacra Scriptura*), and others.

[4] For ὅμως = *nevertheless*, Gudius suggests ὠμός = *savage*.
[5] Dan. vii. 21, 11.
[6] Dan. ii. 34, 45.
[7] Dan. vii. 13, 14.
[8] Matt. xxviii. 18.
[9] Phil. ii. 10.
[10] 1 Pet. iii. 19.
[11] [Deserving of especial note. Who could have foreseen the universal spirit of democracy in this century save by the light of this prophecy? Comp. 2 Tim. iii. 1–3.]

the fourth beast are distributed over ten kingdoms, let us look at the subject a little more
closely, and consider these matters as in the clear
light of a personal survey.[1]

28. The golden head of the image and the
lioness denoted the Babylonians; the shoulders
and arms of silver, and the bear, represented the
Persians and Medes; the belly and thighs of
brass, and the leopard, meant the Greeks, who
held the sovereignty from Alexander's time; the
legs of iron, and the beast dreadful and terrible,
expressed the Romans, who hold the sovereignty
at present; the toes of the feet which were part
clay and part iron, and the ten horns, were emblems of the kingdoms that are yet to rise; the
other little horn that grows up among them meant
the Antichrist in their midst; the stone that
smites the earth and brings judgment upon the
world was Christ.

29. These things, beloved, we impart to you
with fear, and yet readily, on account of the love
of Christ, which surpasseth all. For if the blessed
prophets who preceded us did not choose to
proclaim these things, though they knew them,
openly and boldly, lest they should disquiet the
souls of men, but recounted them mystically in
parables and dark sayings, speaking thus, "Here
is the mind which hath wisdom,"[2] how much
greater risk shall we run in venturing to declare
openly things spoken by them in obscure terms!
Let us look, therefore, at the things which are to
befall this unclean harlot in the last days; and
(let us consider) what and what manner of tribulation is destined to visit her in the wrath of God
before the judgment as an earnest of her doom.

30. Come, then, O blessed Isaiah; arise, tell us
clearly what thou didst prophesy with respect to
the mighty Babylon. For thou didst speak also
of Jerusalem, and thy word is accomplished.
For thou didst speak boldly and openly: "Your
country is desolate, your cities are burned with
fire; your land, strangers devour it in your presence, and it is desolate as overthrown by many
strangers.[3] The daughter of Sion shall be left as
a cottage in a vineyard, and as a lodge in a
garden of cucumbers, as a besieged city."[4] What
then? Are not these things come to pass? Are
not the things announced by thee fulfilled? Is
not their country, Judea, desolate? Is not the
holy place burned with fire? Are not their walls
cast down? Are not their cities destroyed?
Their land, do not strangers devour it? Do not
the Romans rule the country? And indeed
these impious people hated thee, and did saw
thee asunder, and they crucified Christ. Thou
art dead in the world, but thou livest in Christ.

31. Which of you, then, shall I esteem more
than thee? Yet Jeremiah, too, is stoned. But
if I should esteem Jeremiah most, yet Daniel
too has his testimony. Daniel, I commend thee
above all; yet John too gives no false witness.
With how many mouths and tongues would I
praise you; or rather the Word who spake in
you! Ye died with Christ; and ye will live
with Christ. Hear ye, and rejoice; behold the
things announced by you have been fulfilled in
their time. For ye saw these things yourselves
first, and then ye proclaimed them to all generations. Ye ministered the oracles of God to all
generations. Ye prophets were called, that ye
might be able to save all. For then is one a
prophet indeed, when, having announced beforetime things about to be, he can afterwards
show that they have actually happened. Ye
were the disciples of a good Master. These
words I address to you as if alive, and with
propriety. For ye hold already the crown of
life and immortality which is laid up for you in
heaven.[5]

32. Speak with me, O blessed Daniel. Give
me full assurance, I beseech thee. Thou dost
prophesy concerning the lioness in Babylon;[6]
for thou wast a captive there. Thou hast unfolded the future regarding the bear; for thou
wast still in the world, and didst see the things
come to pass. Then thou speakest to me of
the leopard; and whence canst thou know this,
for thou art already gone to thy rest? Who
instructed thee to announce these things, but
He who formed[7] thee in (from) thy mother's
womb?[8] That is God, thou sayest. Thou hast
spoken indeed, and that not falsely. The leopard has arisen; the he-goat is come; he hath
smitten the ram; he hath broken his horns in
pieces; he hath stamped upon him with his
feet. He has been exalted by his fall; (the)
four horns have come up from under that one.[9]
Rejoice, blessed Daniel! thou hast not been in
error: all these things have come to pass.

33. After this again thou hast told me of the
beast dreadful and terrible. "It had iron teeth
and claws of brass: it devoured and brake in
pieces, and stamped the residue with the feet
of it."[10] Already the iron rules; already it subdues and breaks all in pieces; already it brings
all the unwilling into subjection; already we see
these things ourselves. Now we glorify God,
being instructed by thee.

34. But as the task before us was to speak of
the harlot, be thou with us, O blessed Isaiah.

---

[1] ὀφθαλμοφανῶς.
[2] Rev. xvii. 9.
[3] For ὑπὸ πολλῶν Combefisius has ὑπὸ λαῶν = by peoples.
[4] Isa. i. 7, 8.

[5] 2 Tim. iv. 8.
[6] Dan. vii. 4.
[7] For πλάσας Gudius proposes ἁγιάσας (sanctified) or καλέσας
(called).
[8] Jer. i. 5.
[9] Dan. viii. 2-8.
[10] Dan. vii. 6.

Let us mark what thou sayest about Babylon. "Come down, sit upon the ground, O virgin daughter of Babylon; sit, O daughter of the Chaldeans; thou shalt no longer be called tender and delicate. Take the millstone, grind meal, draw aside thy veil,[1] shave the grey hairs, make bare the legs, pass over the rivers. Thy shame shall be uncovered, thy reproach shall be seen: I will take justice of thee, I will no more give thee over to men. As for thy Redeemer, (He is) the Lord of hosts, the Holy One of Israel is his name. Sit thou in compunction, get thee into darkness, O daughter of the Chaldeans: thou shalt no longer be called the strength of the kingdom.

35. "I was wroth with my people; I have polluted mine inheritance, I have given them into thine hand: and thou didst show them no mercy; but upon the ancient (the elders) thou hast very heavily laid thy yoke. And thou saidst, I shall be a princess for ever: thou didst not lay these things to thy heart, neither didst remember thy latter end. Therefore hear now this, thou that art delicate; that sittest, that art confident, that sayest in thine heart, I am, and there is none else; I shall not sit as a widow, neither shall I know the loss of children. But now these two things shall come upon thee in one day, widowhood and the loss of children: they shall come upon thee suddenly in thy sorcery, in the strength of thine enchantments mightily, in the hope of thy fornication. For thou hast said, I am, and there is none else. And thy fornication shall be thy shame, because thou hast said in thy heart, I am. And destruction shall come upon thee, and thou shalt not know it. (*And there shall be*) *a pit, and thou shalt fall into it; and misery shall fall upon thee, and thou shalt not be able to be made clean; and destruction shall come upon thee, and thou shalt not know it.* Stand now with thy enchantments, and with the multitude of thy sorceries, which thou hast learned from thy youth; if so be thou shalt be able to be profited. Thou art wearied in thy counsels. Let the astrologers of the heavens stand and save thee; let the star-gazers announce to thee what shall come upon thee. Behold, they shall all be as sticks for the fire; so shall they be burned, and they shall not deliver their soul from the flame. Because thou hast coals of fire, sit upon them; so shall it be for thy help. Thou art wearied with change from thy youth. Man has gone astray (each one) by himself; and there shall be no salvation for thee."[2] These things does Isaiah prophesy for thee. Let us see now whether John has spoken to the same effect.

36. For he sees, when in the isle Patmos, a revelation of awful mysteries, which he recounts freely, and makes known to others. Tell me, blessed John, apostle and disciple of the Lord, what didst thou see and hear concerning Babylon? Arise, and speak; for it sent thee also into banishment.[3] "And there came one of the seven angels which had the seven vials, and talked with me, saying unto me, Come hither; I will show unto thee the judgment of the great whore that sitteth upon many waters; with whom the kings of the earth have committed fornication, and the inhabitants of the earth have been made drunk with the wine of her fornication. And he carried me away in the spirit into the wilderness: and I saw a woman sit upon a scarlet-coloured beast, full of names of blasphemy, having seven heads and ten horns. And the woman was arrayed in purple and scarlet colour, and decked with gold, and precious stone,[4] and pearls, having a golden cup in her hand, full of abominations and filthiness [5] of the fornication of the earth. Upon her forehead was a name written, Mystery, Babylon the Great, the Mother of Harlots and Abominations of the Earth.

37. "And I saw the woman drunken with the blood of the saints, and with the blood of the martyrs of Jesus: and when I saw her, I wondered with great admiration. And the angel said unto me, Wherefore didst thou marvel? I will tell thee the mystery of the woman, and of the beast that carrieth her, which hath the seven heads and the ten horns. The beast that thou sawest was, and is not; and shall ascend out of the bottomless pit, and go into perdition: and they that dwell on the earth shall wonder (whose name was not written in the book of life from the foundation of the world) when they behold the beast that was, and is not, and yet shall be.[6]

38. "And here is the mind that has wisdom. The seven heads are seven mountains, on which the woman sitteth. And there are seven kings: five are fallen, and one is, and the other is not yet come; and when he cometh, he must continue a short space. And the beast that was *and* is not, (even he is the eighth,) and is of the seven, and goeth into perdition. And the ten horns which thou sawest are ten kings, which have received no kingdom as yet; but receive power as kings one hour with the beast. These have one mind, and shall give their power and strength unto the beast. These shall make war with the Lamb, and the Lamb shall overcome them: for he is Lord of lords, and King of

---

[1] For ἀναξύρισον others read ἀνακάλυψαι = uncover.
[2] Isa. xlvii. 1-15.

[3] [Note this token, that, with all his prudence, he identifies "Babylon" with Rome.]
[4] "Stones," rather.
[5] τὰ ἀκάθαρτα, for the received ἀκαθαρτότητος.
[6] καὶ παρέσται, for the received καίπερ ἐστί.

kings; and they that are with Him are called, and chosen, and faithful.

39. "And he saith to me, The waters which thou sawest, where the whore sitteth, are peoples, and multitudes, and nations, and tongues. And the ten horns which thou sawest, and [1] the beast, these shall hate the whore, and shall make her desolate and naked, and shall eat her flesh, and burn her with fire. For God hath put in their hearts to fulfil His will, and to agree, and give their kingdom unto the beast, until the words of God shall be fulfilled. And the woman which thou sawest is that great city, which reigneth over the kings of the earth.

40. "After these things I saw another angel come down from heaven, having great power; and the earth was lightened with his glory. And he cried mightily [2] with a strong voice, saying, Babylon the great is fallen, is fallen, and is become the habitation of devils, and the hold of every foul spirit, *and a cage of every unclean* and hateful bird. For all nations have drunk of the wine of the wrath of her fornication, and the kings of the earth have committed fornication with her, and the merchants of the earth are waxed rich through the abundance of her delicacies. And I heard another voice from heaven, saying, Come out of her, my people, that ye be not partakers of her sins, and that ye receive not of her plagues: for her sins did cleave even unto heaven,[3] and God hath remembered her iniquities.

41. "Reward her even as she rewarded (you), and double unto her double, according to her works: in the cup which she hath filled, fill to her double. How much she hath glorified herself, and lived deliciously, so much torment and sorrow give her: for she saith in her heart, I sit a queen, and am no widow, and shall see no sorrow. Therefore shall her plagues come in one day, death, and mourning, and famine; and she shall be utterly burned with fire: for strong is the Lord God who judgeth her. And the kings of the earth, who have committed fornication, and lived deliciously with her, shall bewail her, and lament for her, when they shall see the smoke of her burning, standing afar off for the fear of her torment, saying, Alas, alas! that great city Babylon, that mighty city! for in one hour is thy judgment come. And the merchants of the earth shall weep and mourn over her; for no man shall buy their merchandise [4] any more. The merchandise of gold, and silver, and precious stones, and of pearls, and fine linen, and purple, and silk, and scarlet, and all thyine wood, and all manner vessels of ivory, and all manner

vessels of most precious wood, and of brass, and iron, and marble, and cinnamon, and spices,[5] and odours, and ointments, and frankincense, and wine, and oil, and fine flour, and wheat, and beasts, and sheep, and goats,[6] and horses, and chariots, and slaves (bodies), and souls of men. And the fruits that thy soul lusted after are departed from thee, and all things which were dainty and goodly have perished [7] from thee, and thou shalt find them no more at all. The merchants of these things, which were made rich [8] by her, shall stand afar off for the fear of her torment, weeping and wailing, and saying, Alas, alas! that great city, that was clothed in fine linen, and purple, and scarlet, and decked with gold, and precious stones, and pearls! for in one hour so great riches is come to nought. And every shipmaster, and all the company in ships, and sailors, and as many as trade by sea, stood afar off, and cried, when they saw the smoke of her burning, saying, What city is like unto this great city? And they cast dust on their heads, and cried, weeping and wailing, saying, Alas, alas! that great city, wherein were made rich all that had ships in the sea by reason of her fatness! [9] for in one hour is she made desolate.

42. "Rejoice over her, thou heaven, and ye angels,[10] and apostles, and prophets; for God hath avenged you on her. And a mighty angel took up a stone like a great millstone, and cast it into the sea, saying, Thus with violence shall that great city Babylon be thrown down, and shall be found no more at all. And the voice of harpers and musicians, and of pipers and trumpeters, shall be heard no more at all in thee; and no craftsman, of whatsoever craft he be, shall be found any more in thee; and the sound of a millstone shall be heard no more at all in thee; and the light of a candle shall shine no more at all in thee; and the voice of the bridegroom and of the bride shall be heard no more at all in thee: for thy merchants were the great men of the earth; for by thy sorceries were all nations deceived. And in her was found the blood of prophets and of saints, and of all that were slain upon the earth." [11]

43. With respect, then, to the particular judgment in the torments that are to come upon it in the last times by the hand of the tyrants who shall arise then, the clearest statement has been given in these passages. But it becomes us further diligently to examine and set forth the period at which these things shall come to pass, and how the little horn shall spring up in their midst. For

---

1 καί, for the received ἐπί.
2 ἰσχυρᾷ for ἐν ἰσχύϊ.
3 ἐκολλήθησαν, for the received ἠκολούθησαν.
4 ἀγοράσει, for the received ἀγοράζει.

5 ἄμωμον, omitted in the received text.
6 καὶ τράγους, omitted in the received text.
7 ἀπώλετο, for the received ἀπῆλθεν.
8 πλουτίσαντες, for the received πλουτήσαντες.
9 πιότητος, for the received τιμιότητος.
10 καὶ οἱ ἄγγελοι, which the received omits.
11 Rev. xvii., xviii.

when the legs of iron have issued in the feet and toes, according to the similitude of the image and that of the terrible beast, as has been shown in the above, (then shall be the time) when the iron and the clay shall be mingled together. Now Daniel will set forth this subject to us. For he says, "And one week will make [1] a covenant with many, and it shall be that in the midst (half) of the week my sacrifice and oblation shall cease." [2] By one week, therefore, he meant the last week which is to be at the end of the whole world; of which week the two prophets Enoch and Elias will take up the half. For they will preach 1,260 days clothed in sackcloth, proclaiming repentance to the people and to all the nations.

44. For as two advents of our Lord and Saviour are indicated in the Scriptures, the one being His first advent in the flesh, which took place without honour by reason of His being set at nought, as Isaiah spake of Him aforetime, saying, "We saw Him, and He had no form nor comeliness, but His form was despised (and) rejected (lit. = deficient) above all men; a man smitten and familiar with bearing infirmity, (for His face was turned away); He was despised, and esteemed not." [3] But His second advent is announced as glorious, when He shall come from heaven with the host of angels, and the glory of His Father, as the prophet saith, "Ye shall see the King in glory;" [4] and, "I saw one like the Son of man coming with the clouds of heaven; and he came to the Ancient of days, and he was brought to Him. And there were given Him dominion, and honour, and glory, and the kingdom; all tribes and languages shall serve Him: His dominion is an everlasting dominion, which shall not pass away." [5] Thus also two forerunners were indicated. The first was John the son of Zacharias, who appeared in all things a forerunner and herald of our Saviour, preaching of the heavenly light that had appeared in the world. He first fulfilled the course of forerunner, and that from his mother's womb, being conceived by Elisabeth, in order that to those, too, who are children from their mother's womb he might declare the new birth that was to take place for their sakes by the Holy Ghost and the Virgin.

45. He, on hearing the salutation addressed to Elisabeth, leaped with joy in his mother's womb, recognising God the Word conceived in the womb of the Virgin. Thereafter he came forward preaching in the wilderness, proclaiming the baptism of repentance to the people, (and thus) announcing prophetically salvation to the nations living in the wilderness of the world.

After this, at the Jordan, seeing the Saviour with his own eye, he points Him out, and says, "Behold the Lamb of God, that taketh away the sin of the world!" [6] He also first preached to those in Hades,[7] becoming a forerunner there when he was put to death by Herod, that there too he might intimate that the Saviour would descend to ransom the souls of the saints from the hand of death.

46. But since the Saviour was the beginning of the resurrection of all men, it was meet that the Lord alone should rise from the dead, by whom too the judgment is to enter for the whole world, that they who have wrestled worthily may be also crowned worthily by Him, by the illustrious Arbiter, to wit, who Himself first accomplished the course, and was received into the heavens, and was set down on the right hand of God the Father, and is to be manifested again at the end of the world as Judge. It is a matter of course that His forerunners must appear first, as He says by Malachi and the angel,[8] "I will send to you Elias the Tishbite before the day of the Lord, the great and notable day, comes; and he shall turn the hearts of the fathers to the children, and the disobedient to the wisdom of the just, lest I come and smite the earth utterly." [9] These, then, shall come and proclaim the manifestation of Christ that is to be from heaven; and they shall also perform signs and wonders, in order that men may be put to shame and turned to repentance for their surpassing wickedness and impiety.

47. For John says, "And I will give power unto my two witnesses, and they shall prophesy a thousand two hundred and threescore days, clothed in sackcloth." [10] That is the half of the week whereof Daniel spake. "These are the two olive trees and the two candlesticks standing before the Lord of the earth. And if any man will hurt them, fire will proceed out of their mouth, and devour their enemies; and if any man will hurt them, he must in this manner be killed. These have power to shut heaven, that it rain not in the days of their prophecy; and have power over waters, to turn them to blood, and to smite the earth with all plagues as often as *they will*. *And when* they shall have finished their course and their testimony," what saith the prophet? "the beast that ascendeth out of the bottomless pit shall make war against them, and

---

[1] διαθήσει = will *make;* others, δυναμώσει = will *confirm.*
[2] Dan. ix. 27.
[3] Isa. liii. 2–5.
[4] Isa. xxxiii. 17.
[5] Dan. vii. 13, 14.

[6] John i. 29.
[7] It was a common opinion among the Greeks, that the Baptist was Christ's forerunner also among the dead. See Leo Allatius, *De libris Eccles. Græcorum*, p. 303.
[8] Or it may be, "Malachi, even the messenger." Ἀγγέλου is the reading restored by Combefisius instead of Ἀγγαίου. The words of the angel in Luke i. 17 ("and the disobedient to the wisdom of the just") are thus inserted in the citation from Malachi; and to that Hippolytus may refer in the addition "and the angel." Or perhaps, as Combefisius rather thinks, the addition simply refers to the meaning of the name Malachi, viz., messenger.
[9] Mal. iv. 5, 6.
[10] Rev. xi. 3.

shall overcome them, and kill them,"[1] because they will not give glory to Antichrist. For this is meant by the little horn that grows up. He, being now elated in heart, begins to exalt himself, and to glorify himself as God, persecuting the saints and blaspheming Christ, even as Daniel says, " I considered the horn, and, behold, in the horn were eyes like the eyes of man, and a mouth speaking great things; and he opened his mouth to blaspheme God. And that horn made war against the saints, and prevailed against them until the beast was slain, and perished, and his body was given to be burned."[2]

48. But as it is incumbent on us to discuss this matter of the beast more exactly, and in particular the question how the Holy Spirit has also mystically indicated his name by means of a number, we shall proceed to state more clearly what bears upon him. John then speaks thus: " And I beheld another beast coming up out of the earth; and he had two horns, like a lamb, and he spake as a dragon. And he exercised all the power of the first beast before him; and he made the earth and them which dwell therein to worship the first beast, whose deadly wound was healed. And he did great wonders, so that he maketh fire come down from heaven on the earth in the sight of men, and deceiveth them that dwell on the earth by means of those miracles which he had power to do in the sight of the beast, saying to them that dwell on the earth, that they should make an image to the beast which had the wound by a sword and did live. And he had power to give life unto the image of the beast, *that the image of the beast should both speak*, and cause that as many as would not worship the image of the beast should be killed. And he caused all, both small and great, rich and poor, free and bond, to receive a mark in their right hand or in their forehead; and that no man might buy or sell, save he that had the mark, the name of the beast, or the number of his name. Here is wisdom. Let him that hath understanding count the number of the beast; for it is the number of a man, and his number is six hundred threescore and six."[3]

49. By the beast, then, coming up out of the earth, he means the kingdom of Antichrist; and by the two horns he means him and the false prophet after him.[4] And in speaking of "the horns being like a lamb," he means that he will make himself like the Son of God, and set himself forward as king. And the terms, " he spake like a dragon," mean that he is a deceiver, and not truthful. And the words, " he exercised all

the power of the first beast before him, and caused the earth and them which dwell therein to worship the first beast, whose deadly wound was healed," signify that, after the manner of the law of Augustus, by whom the empire of Rome was established, he too will rule and govern, sanctioning everything by it, and taking greater glory to himself. For this is the fourth beast, whose head was wounded and healed again, in its being broken up or even dishonoured, and partitioned into four crowns; and he then (Antichrist) shall with knavish skill heal it, as it were, and restore it. For this is what is meant by the prophet when he says, " He will give life unto the image, and the image of the beast will speak." For he will act with vigour again, and prove strong by reason of the laws established by him; and he will cause all those who will not worship the image of the beast to be put to death. Here the faith and the patience of the saints will appear, for he says: " And he will cause all, both small and great, rich and poor, free and bond, to receive a mark in their right hand or in their forehead; that no man might buy or sell, save he that had the mark, the name of the beast, or the number of his name." For, being full of guile, and exalting himself against the servants of God, with the wish to afflict them and persecute them out of the world, because they give not glory to him, he will order incense-pans[5] to be set up by all everywhere, that no man among the saints may be able to buy or sell without first sacrificing; for this is what is meant by the mark received upon the right hand. And the word—" in their forehead " —indicates that all are crowned, and put on a crown of fire, and not of life, but of death. For in this wise, too, did Antiochus Epiphanes the king of Syria, the descendant of Alexander of Macedon, devise measures against the Jews. He, too, in the exaltation of his heart, issued a decree in those times, that " all should set up shrines before their doors, and sacrifice, and that they should march in procession to the honour of Dionysus, waving chaplets of ivy;" and that those who refused obedience should be put to death by strangulation and torture. But he also met his due recompense at the hand of the Lord, the righteous Judge and all-searching God; for he died eaten up of worms. And if one desires to inquire into that more accurately, he will find it recorded in the books of the Maccabees.[6]

50. But now we shall speak of what is before us. For such measures will he, too, devise, seeking to afflict the saints in every way. For

---

[1] Rev. xi. 4–6.
[2] Dan. vii. 8, 9.
[3] Rev. xiii. 11–18.
[4] The text is simply καὶ τὸν μετ' αὐτόν = the false prophet after him. Gudius and Combefisius propose as above, καὶ αὐτόν τε καὶ τὸν μετ' αὐτόν, or μετ' αὐτοῦ = him and the false prophet *with* him.

[5] πυρεῖα = censers, incense-pans, or sacrificial tripods. This offering of incense was a test very commonly proposed by the pagans to those whose religion they suspected.
[6] [Not referred to as Scripture, but as authentic history.]

the prophet and apostle says : " Here is wisdom, Let him that hath understanding count the number of the beast ; for it is the number of a man, and his number is six hundred threescore and six." With respect to his name, it is not in our power to explain it exactly, as the blessed John understood it and was instructed about it, but only to give a conjectural account of it ; [1] for when he appears, the blessed one will show us what we seek to know. Yet as far as our doubtful apprehension of the matter goes, we may speak. Many names indeed we find,[2] the letters of which are the equivalent of this number : such as, for instance, the word Titan,[3] an ancient and notable name ; or Evanthas,[4] for it too makes up the same number ; and many others which might be found. But, as we have already said,[5] the wound of the first beast was healed, and he (the second beast) was to make the image speak,[6] that is to say, he should be powerful ; and it is manifest to all that those who at present still hold the power are Latins. If, then, we take the name as the name of a single man, it becomes *Latinus*. Wherefore we ought neither to give it out as if this were certainly his name, nor again ignore the fact that he may not be otherwise designated. But having the mystery of God in our heart, we ought in fear to keep faithfully what has been told us by the blessed prophets, in order that when those things come to pass, we may be prepared for them, and not deceived. For when the times advance, he too, of whom these thing are said, will be manifested.[7]

51. But not to confine ourselves to these words and arguments alone, for the purpose of convincing those who love to study the oracles of God, we shall demonstrate the matter by many other proofs. For Daniel says, "And these shall escape out of his hand, even Edom, and Moab, and the chief of the children of Ammon."[8] Ammon and Moab[9] are the children born to Lot by his daughters, and their race survives even now. And Isaiah says : " And they shall fly in the boats of strangers, plundering the sea together, and (they shall spoil) them of the east : and they shall lay hands upon Moab first ; and the children of Ammon shall first obey them."[10]

52. In those times, then, he shall arise and meet them. And when he has overmastered three horns out of the ten in the array of war, and has rooted these out, viz., Egypt, and Libya, and Ethiopia, and has got their spoils and trappings, and has brought the remaining horns which suffer into subjection, he will begin to be lifted up in heart, and to exalt himself against God as master of the whole world. And his first expedition will be against Tyre and Berytus, and the circumjacent territory. For by storming these cities first he will strike terror into the others, as Isaiah says, " Be thou ashamed, O Sidon ; the sea hath spoken, even the strength of the sea hath spoken, saying, I travailed not, nor brought forth children ; neither did I nurse up young men, nor bring up virgins. But when the report comes to Egypt, pain shall seize them for Tyre." [11]

53. These things, then, shall be in the future, beloved ; and when the three horns are cut off, he will begin to show himself as God, as Ezekiel has said aforetime : " Because thy heart has been lifted up, and thou hast said, I am God." [12] And to the like effect Isaiah says : " For thou hast said in thine heart, I will ascend into heaven, I will exalt my throne above the stars of heaven : I will be like the Most High. Yet now thou shall be brought down to hell (Hades), to the foundations of the earth." [13] In like manner also Ezekiel : " Wilt thou yet say to those who slay thee, I am God ? But thou (shalt be) a man, and no God." [14]

54. As his tribe, then, and his manifestation, and his destruction, have been set forth in these words, and as his name has also been indicated mystically, let us look also at his action. For he will call together all the people to himself, out of every country of the dispersion, making them his own, as though they were his own children, and promising to restore their country, and establish again their kingdom and nation, in order that he may be worshipped by them as God, as the prophet says : " He will collect his whole kingdom, from the rising of the sun even to its setting : they whom he summons and they whom he does not summon shall march with him." [15] And Jeremiah speaks of him thus in a parable : " The partridge cried, (and) gathered what he did not hatch, making himself riches without judgment : in the midst of his days they shall leave him, and at his end he shall be a fool." [16]

55. It will not be detrimental, therefore, to the course of our present argument, if we explain

---

[1] ὅσον μόνον ὑπονοῆσαι.
[2] ἰσόψηφα.
[3] Τειτάν. Hippolytus here follows his master Irenæus, who in his *Contra Hæres.*, v. 30, § 3, has the words, " *Titan . . . et antiquum et fide dignum et regale . . . nomen*" = Titan . . . both an ancient and good and royal . . . name. [See this series, vol. i, p 559.]
[4] Εὐάνθας, mentioned also by Irenæus in the passage already referred to.
[5] προεφθημεν, the reading proposed by Fabricius instead of προέφημεν.
[6] ποιήσει, Combef. ἐποίησε.
[7] [Let us imitate the wisdom of our author, whose modest commentary upon his master Irenæus cannot be too much applauded. The mystery, however, does seem to turn upon something in the Latin race and its destiny.]
[8] Dan. xi. 41.
[9] Gen. xix. 37, 38.
[10] Isa. xi. 14.

[11] Isa. xxiii. 4, 5.
[12] Ezek. xxviii. 2.
[13] Isa. xiv. 13-15.
[14] Ezek. xxviii. 9.
[15] Quoted already in chap. xv. as from one of the prophets.
[16] Jer. xvii. 11.

the art of that creature, and show that the prophet has not spoken[1] without a purpose in using the parable (or similitude) of the creature. For as the partridge is a vainglorious creature, when it sees near at hand the nest of another partridge with young in it, and with the parent-bird away on the wing in quest of food, it imitates the cry of the other bird, and calls the young to itself; and they, taking it to be their own parent, run to it. And it delights itself proudly in the alien pullets as in its own. But when the real parent-bird returns, and calls them with its own familiar cry, the young recognise it, and forsake the deceiver, and betake themselves to the real parent. This thing, then, the prophet has adopted as a simile, applying it in a similar manner to Antichrist. For he will allure mankind to himself, wishing to gain possession of those who are not his own, and promising deliverance to all, while he is unable to save himself.

56. He then, having gathered to himself the unbelieving everywhere throughout the world, comes at their call to persecute the saints, their enemies and antagonists, as the apostle and evangelist says: "There was in a city a judge, which feared not God, neither regarded man: and there was a widow in that city, who came unto him, saying, Avenge me of mine adversary. And he would not for a while: but afterward he said within himself, Though I fear not God, nor regard man; yet because this widow troubleth me, I will avenge her."[2]

57. By the unrighteous judge, who fears not God, neither regards man, he means without doubt Antichrist, as he is a son of the devil and a vessel of Satan. For when he has the power, he will begin to exalt himself against God, neither in truth fearing God, nor regarding the Son of God, who is the Judge of all. And in saying that there was a widow in the city, he refers to Jerusalem itself, which is a widow indeed, forsaken of her perfect, heavenly spouse, God. She calls Him her adversary, and not her Saviour; for she does not understand that which was said by the prophet Jeremiah: "Because they obeyed not the truth, a spirit of error shall speak then to this people and to Jerusalem."[3] And Isaiah also to the like effect: "Forasmuch as the people refuseth to drink the water of Siloam that goeth softly, but chooseth to have Rasin and Romeliah's son as king over you: therefore, lo, the Lord bringeth up upon you the water of the river, strong and full, even the king of Assyria."[4] By the king he means metaphorically Antichrist, as also another prophet saith: "And this man shall be the peace from me,

when the Assyrian shall come up into your land, and when he shall tread in your mountains."[5]

58. And in like manner Moses, knowing beforehand that the people would reject and disown the true Saviour of the world, and take part with error, and choose an earthly king, and set the heavenly King at nought, says: "Is not this laid up in store with me, and sealed up among my treasures? In the day of vengeance I will recompense (them), and in the time when their foot shall slide."[6] They did slide, therefore, in all things, as they were found to be in harmony with the truth in nothing: neither as concerns the law, because they became transgressors; nor as concerns the prophets, because they cut off even the prophets themselves; nor as concerns the voice of the Gospels, because they crucified the Saviour Himself; nor in believing the apostles, because they persecuted them. At all times they showed themselves enemies and betrayers of the truth, and were found to be haters of God, and not lovers of Him; and such they shall be then when they find opportunity: for, rousing themselves against the servants of God, they will seek to obtain vengeance by the hand of a mortal man. And he, being puffed up with pride by their subserviency, will begin to despatch missives against the saints, commanding to cut them all off everywhere, on the ground of their refusal to reverence and worship him as God, according to the word of Esaias: "Woe to the wings of the vessels of the land,[7] beyond the rivers of Ethiopia: (woe to him) who sendeth sureties by the sea, and letters of papyrus (upon the water; for nimble messengers will go) to a nation[8] anxious and expectant, and a people strange and bitter against them; a nation hopeless and trodden down."[9]

59. But we who hope for the Son of God are persecuted and trodden down by those unbelievers. For the *wings of the vessels* are the churches; and the sea is the world, in which the Church is set, like a ship tossed in the deep, but not destroyed; for she has with her the skilled Pilot, Christ. And she bears in her midst also the trophy (which is erected) over death; for she carries with her the cross of the Lord.[10] For her prow is the east, and her stern is the west, and her hold[11] is the south, and her

---

[1] Reading ἀπεφήνατο for ἀπεκρίνατο.
[2] Luke xviii. 2-5.
[3] Jer. iv. 11.
[4] Isa. viii. 6, 7.

[5] Mic. v. 5. The Septuagint reads αὐτῇ = And (he) shall be the peace to it. Hippolytus follows the Hebrew, but makes the pronoun feminine, αὐτη referring to the peace. Again Hippolytus reads ὄρη = mountains, where the Septuagint has χώραν = land, and where the Hebrew word = fortresses or palaces. [He must mean that "the Assyrian" = Antichrist. "The peace" is attributable only to the "Prince of peace." So the Fathers generally.]
[6] Deut. xxxii. 34, 35.
[7] οὐαὶ γῆς πλοίων πτέρυγες.
[8] μετεώρον.
[9] Isa. xviii. 1, 2.
[10] Wordsworth, reading ὡς ἱστὸν for ὡς τὸν, would add, *like a mast*. See his Commentary on Acts xxvii. 40.
[11] κύτος, a conjecture of Combefisius for κύκλον.

tillers are the two Testaments; and the ropes that stretch around her are the love of Christ, which binds the Church; and the net[1] which she bears with her is the laver of the regeneration which renews the believing, whence too are these glories. As the wind the Spirit from heaven is present, by whom those who believe are sealed : she has also anchors of iron accompanying her, viz., the holy commandments of Christ Himself, which are strong as iron. She has also mariners on the right and on the left, assessors like the holy angels, by whom the Church is always governed and defended. The ladder in her leading up to the sailyard is an emblem of the passion of Christ, which brings the faithful to the ascent of heaven. And the top-sails[2] aloft[3] upon the yard are the company of prophets, martyrs, and apostles, who have entered into their rest in the kingdom of Christ.

60. Now, concerning the tribulation of the persecution which is to fall upon the Church from the adversary, John also speaks thus : " And I saw a great and wondrous sign in heaven ; a woman clothed with the sun, and the moon under her feet, and upon her head a crown of twelve stars. And she, being with child, cries, travailing in birth, and pained to be delivered. And the dragon stood before the woman which was ready to be delivered, for to devour her child as soon as it was born. And she brought forth a man-child, who is to rule all the nations : and the child was caught up unto God and to His throne. And the woman fled into the wilderness, where she hath the place prepared of God, that they should feed her there a thousand two hundred and threescore days. And then when the dragon saw it, he persecuted the woman which brought forth the man-child. And to the woman were given two wings of the great eagle, that she might fly into the wilderness, where she is nourished for a time, and times, and half a time, from the face of the serpent. And the serpent cast (out of his mouth water as a flood after the woman, that he might cause her to be carried away of the flood. And the earth helped the woman, and opened her mouth, and swallowed up the flood which the dragon cast) out of his mouth. And the dragon was wroth with the woman, and went to make war with the saints of her seed, which keep the commandments of God, and have the testimony of Jesus."[4]

61. By the " woman then clothed with the sun," he meant most manifestly the Church, endued wth the Father's word,[5] whose brightness is above the sun. And by " the moon under her feet " he referred to her being adorned, like the moon, with heavenly glory. And the words, " upon her head a crown of twelve stars," refer to the twelve apostles by whom the Church was founded. And those, " she, being with child, cries, travailing in birth, and pained to be delivered," mean that the Church will not cease to bear from her heart[6] the Word that is persecuted by the unbelieving in the world. " And she brought forth," he says, " a man-child, who is to rule all the nations ; " by which is meant that the Church, always bringing forth Christ, the perfect man-child of God, who is declared to be God and man, becomes the instructor of all the nations. And the words, " her child was caught up unto God and to His throne," signify that he who is always born of her is a heavenly king, and not an earthly ; even as David also declared of old when he said, " The Lord said unto my Lord, Sit Thou at my right hand, until I make Thine enemies Thy footstool."[7] " And the dragon," he says, " saw and persecuted the woman which brought forth the man-child. And to the woman were given two wings of the great eagle, that she might fly into the wilderness, where she is nourished for a time, and times, and half a time, from the face of the serpent."[8] That refers to the one thousand two hundred and threescore days (the half of the week) during which the tyrant is to reign and persecute the Church,[9] which flees from city to city, and seeks concealment in the wilderness among the mountains, possessed of no other defence than the two wings of the great eagle, that is to say, the faith of Jesus Christ, who, in stretching forth His holy hands on the holy tree, unfolded two wings, the right and the left, and called to Him all who believed upon Him, and covered them as a hen her chickens. For by the mouth of Malachi also He speaks thus : " And unto you that fear my name shall the Sun of righteousness arise with healing in His wings."[10]

62. The Lord also says, " When ye shall see the abomination of desolation stand in the holy place (whoso readeth, let him understand), then let them which be in Judea flee into the mountains, and let him which is on the housetop not come down to take his clothes ; neither let him which is in the field return back to take anything out of his house. And woe unto them that are with child, and to them that give suck, in those days ! for then shall be great tribulation, such as was not since the beginning of the world. And except those days should be shortened, there

---

[1] λίνον, proposed by the same for πλοῖον, boat.
[2] ψηφαροί, a term of doubtful meaning. May it refer to the καρχήσια?
[3] The text reads here αἰνούμενοι, for which αἱρούμενοι is proposed, or better, ἠωρούμενοι.
[4] Rev. xii. 1-6, etc.
[5] τὸν Λόγον τὸν Πατρῷον.

[6] γεννῶσα ἐκ καρδίας.
[7] Ps. cx. 1.
[8] Rev. xi. 3.
[9] [Concerning Antichrist, two advents, etc., see vol. iv. p. 219, this series]
[10] Mal. iv. 2.

should no flesh be saved."[1] And Daniel says, "And they shall place the abomination of desolation a thousand two hundred and ninety days. Blessed is he that waiteth, and cometh to the thousand two hundred and ninety-five days."[2]

63. And the blessed Apostle Paul, writing to the Thessalonians, says: "Now we beseech you, brethren, concerning the coming of our Lord Jesus Christ, and our gathering together at it,[3] that ye be not soon shaken in mind, or be troubled, neither by spirit, nor by word, nor by letters as from us, as that the day of the Lord is at hand. Let no man deceive you by any means; for (that day shall not come) except there come the falling away first, and that man of sin be revealed, the son of perdition, who opposeth and exalteth himself above all that is called God, or that is worshipped: so that he sitteth in the temple of God, showing himself that he is God. Remember ye not, that when I was yet with you, I told you these things? And now ye know what withholdeth, that he might be revealed in his time. For the mystery of iniquity doth already work; only he who now letteth (will let), until he be taken out of the way. And then shall that wicked be revealed, whom the Lord Jesus shall consume with the Spirit of His mouth, and shall destroy with the brightness of His coming: (even him) whose coming is after the working of Satan, with all power, and signs, and lying wonders, and with all deceivableness of unrighteousness in them that perish; because they received not the love of the truth. And for this cause God shall send them strong delusion, that they should believe a lie: that they all might be damned who believed not the truth, but had pleasure in unrighteousness."[4] And Esaias says, "Let the wicked be cut off, that he behold not the glory of the Lord."[5]

64. These things, then, being to come to pass, beloved, and the one week being divided into two parts, and the abomination of desolation being manifested then, and the two prophets and forerunners of the Lord having finished their course, and the whole world finally approaching the consummation, what remains but the coming of our Lord and Saviour Jesus Christ from heaven, for whom we have looked in hope? who shall bring the conflagration and just judgment upon all who have refused to believe on Him. For the Lord says, "And when these things begin to come to pass, then look up, and lift up your heads; for your redemption draweth nigh."[6] "And there shall not a hair of your

head perish."[7] "For as the lightning cometh out of the east, and shineth even unto the west, so shall also the coming of the Son of man be. For wheresoever the carcase is, there will the eagles be gathered together."[8] Now the fall[9] took place in paradise; for Adam fell there. And He says again, "Then shall the Son of man send His angels, and they shall gather together His elect from the four winds of heaven."[10] And David also, in announcing prophetically the judgment and coming of the Lord, says, "His going forth is from the end of the heaven, and His circuit unto the end of the heaven: and there is no one hid from the heat thereof."[11] By the heat he means the conflagration. And Esaias speaks thus: "Come, my people, enter thou into thy chamber, (and) shut thy door: hide thyself as it were for a little moment, until the indignation of the Lord be overpast."[12] And Paul in like manner: "For the wrath of God is revealed from heaven against all ungodliness and unrighteousness of men, who hold the truth of God in unrighteousness."[13]

65. Moreover, concerning the resurrection and the kingdom of the saints, Daniel says, "And many of them that sleep in the dust of the earth shall arise, some to everlasting life, (and some to shame and everlasting contempt)."[14] Esaias says, "The dead men shall arise, and they that are in their tombs shall awake; for the dew from thee is healing to them."[15] The Lord says, "Many in that day shall hear the voice of the Son of God, and they that hear shall live."[16] And the prophet says, "Awake, thou that sleepest, and arise from the dead, and Christ shall give thee light."[17] And John says, "Blessed and holy is he that hath part in the first resurrection: on such the second death hath no power."[18] For the second death is the lake of fire that burneth. And again the Lord says, "Then shall the righteous shine forth as the sun shineth in his glory."[19] And to the saints He will say, "Come, ye blessed of my Father, inherit the kingdom prepared for you from the foundation of the world."[20] But what saith He to the wicked? "Depart from me, ye cursed, into everlasting fire, prepared for the devil and his angels, which my Father hath

---

[1] Matt. xxiv. 15–22; Mark xiii. 14–20; Luke xxi. 20–23.
[2] Dan. xi. 31, xii. 11, 12. The Hebrew has 1,335 as the number in the second verse.
[3] Hippolytus reads here ἐπ' αὐτῆς instead of ἐπ' αὐτόν, and makes the pronoun therefore refer to the coming.
[4] 2 Thess. ii. 1–11.
[5] Isa. xxvi. 10.
[6] Luke xxi. 28.

[7] Luke xxi. 18.
[8] Matt. xxiv. 27, 28.
[9] The word πτῶμα, used in the Greek as = carcase, is thus interpreted by Hippolytus as = fall, which is its literal sense.
[10] Matt. xxiv. 31.
[11] Ps. xix. 6.
[12] Isa. xxvi. 20.
[13] Rom. i. 17.
[14] Dan. xii. 2.
[15] Isa. xxvi. 19.
[16] John v. 25.
[17] Eph. v. 14. Epiphanius and others suppose that the words thus cited by Paul are taken from the apocryphal writings of Jeremiah; others that they are a free version of Isa. lx. 1. [But their metrical form justifies the criticism that they are a quotation from a hymn of the Church, based, very likely, on the passage from Isaiah.]
[18] Rev. xx. 6.
[19] Matt. xiii. 43.
[20] Matt. xxv. 34.

prepared." And John says, "Without are dogs, and sorcerers, and whoremongers, and murderers, and idolaters, and whosoever maketh and loveth a lie; for your part is in the hell of fire." [1] And in like manner also Esaias: "And they shall go forth and look upon the carcases of the men that have transgressed against me. And their worm shall not die, neither shall their fire be quenched; and they shall be for a spectacle to all flesh." [2]

66. Concerning the resurrection of the righteous, Paul also speaks thus in writing to the Thessalonians: "We would not have you to be ignorant concerning them which are asleep, that ye sorrow not even as others which have no hope. For if we believe that Jesus died and rose again, even so them also which sleep in Jesus will God bring with Him. For this we say unto you by the word of the Lord, that we which are alive (and) remain unto the coming of the Lord, shall not prevent them which are asleep. For the Lord Himself shall descend from heaven with a shout, with the voice and trump of God, and the dead in Christ shall rise first. Then we which are alive (and) remain shall be caught up together with them in the clouds to meet the Lord in the air; and so shall we ever be with the Lord." [3]

67. These things, then, I have set shortly before thee, O Theophilus, drawing them *from Scripture itself,*[4] in order that, maintaining in faith what is written, and anticipating the things that are to be, thou mayest keep thyself void of offence both toward God and toward men, "looking for that blessed hope and appearing of our God and Saviour," [5] when, having raised the saints among us, He will rejoice with them, glorifying the Father. To Him be the glory unto the endless ages of the ages. Amen.

[1] Rev. xxii. 15.
[2] Isa. lxvi. 24.
[3] 1 Thess. iv. 12.
[4] [The immense value of these quotations, authenticating the Revelations and other Scriptures, must be apparent. Is not this treatise a voice to our own times of vast significance?]
[5] Tit. ii. 13.

EXPOSITORY TREATISE AGAINST THE JEWS.

1. Now, then, incline thine ear to me, and hear my words, and give heed, thou Jew. Many a time dost thou boast thyself, in that thou didst condemn Jesus of Nazareth to death, and didst give Him vinegar and gall to drink; and thou dost vaunt thyself because of this. Come therefore, and let us consider together whether perchance thou dost not boast unrighteously, O Israel, (and) whether that small portion of vinegar and gall has not brought down this fearful threatening upon thee, (and) whether this is not the cause of thy present condition involved in these myriad troubles.

2. Let him then be introduced before us who speaketh by the Holy Spirit, and saith truth — David the son of Jesse. He, singing a certain strain with prophetic reference to the true Christ, celebrated our God by the Holy Spirit, (and) declared clearly all that befell Him by the hands of the Jews in His passion; in which (strain) the Christ who humbled Himself and took unto Himself the form of the servant Adam, calls upon God the Father in heaven as it were in our person, and speaks thus in the sixty-ninth Psalm: "Save me, O God; for the waters are come in unto my soul. I am sunk in the mire of the abyss," that is to say, in the corruption of Hades, on account of the transgression in paradise; and "there is no substance," that is, help. "My eyes failed while I hoped (or, from my hoping) upon my God; when will He come and save me?" [1]

3. Then, in what next follows, Christ speaks, as it were, in His own person: "Then I restored that," says He, "which I took not away;" that is, on account of the sin of Adam I endured the death which was not mine by sinning. "For, O God, Thou knowest my foolishness; and my sins are not hid from Thee," that is, "for I did not sin," as He means it; and for this reason (it is added), "Let not them be ashamed who want to see" my resurrection on the third day, to wit, the apostles. "Because for Thy sake," that is, for the sake of obeying Thee, "I have borne reproach," namely the cross, when "they covered my face with shame," that is to say, the Jews; when "I became a stranger unto my brethren after the flesh, and an alien unto my mother's children," meaning (by the mother) the synagogue. "For the zeal of Thine house, Father, hath eaten me up; and the reproaches of them that reproached Thee are fallen on me," and of them that sacrificed to idols. Wherefore "they that sit in the gate spoke against me," for they crucified me without the gate. "And they that drink sang against me," that is, (they) who drink wine) at the feast of the passover. "But as for me, in my prayer unto Thee, O

[1] Ps. lxix. 1 ff.

Lord, I said, Father, forgive them," namely the Gentiles, because it is the time for favour with Gentiles. " Let not then the hurricane (of temptations) overwhelm me, neither let the deep (that is, Hades) swallow me up : for Thou wilt not leave my soul in hell (Hades) ; neither let the pit shut her mouth upon me,"[1] that is, the sepulchre. " By reason of mine enemies, deliver me," that the Jews may not boast, saying, Let us consume him.

4. Now Christ prayed all this economically[2] as man ; being, however, true God. But, as I have already said, it was the " form of the servant "[3] that spake and suffered these things. Wherefore He added, " My soul looked for reproach and trouble," that is, I suffered of my own will, (and) not by any compulsion. Yet " I waited for one to mourn with me, and there was none," for all my disciples forsook me and fled ; and for a " comforter, and I found none."

5. Listen with understanding, O Jew, to what the Christ says : " They gave me gall for my meat ; and in my thirst they gave me vinegar to drink." And these things He did indeed endure from you. Hear the Holy Ghost tell you also what return He made to you for that little portion of vinegar. For the prophet says, as in the person of God, " Let their table become a snare and retribution." Of what retribution does He speak ? Manifestly, of the misery which has now got hold of thee.

6. And then hear what follows : " Let their eyes be darkened, that they see not." And surely ye have been darkened in the eyes of your soul with a darkness utter and everlasting. For now that the true light has arisen, ye wander as in the night, and stumble on places with no roads, and fall headlong, as having forsaken the way that saith, " I am the way."[4] Furthermore, hear this yet more serious word : " And their back do thou bend always ;" that means, in order that they may be slaves to the nations, not four hundred and thirty years as in Egypt, nor seventy as in Babylon, but bend them to servitude, he says, " always." In fine, then, how dost thou indulge vain hopes, expecting to be delivered from the misery which holdeth thee ? For that is somewhat strange. And not unjustly has he imprecated this blindness of eyes upon thee. But because thou didst cover the eyes of Christ, (and[5]) thus thou didst beat Him, for this reason, too, bend thou thy back for servitude always. And whereas thou didst pour out His blood in indignation, hear what thy recompense shall be : " Pour out Thine indignation upon

them, and let Thy wrathful anger take hold of them ;" and, " Let their habitation be desolate," to wit, their celebrated temple.

7. But why, O prophet, tell us, and for what reason, was the temple made desolate ? Was it on account of that ancient fabrication of the calf ? Was it on account of the idolatry of the people ? Was it for the blood of the prophets ? Was it for the adultery and fornication of Israel ? By no means, he says ; for in all these transgressions they always found pardon open to them, and benignity ; but it was because they killed the Son of their Benefactor, for He is co-eternal with the Father. Whence He saith, " Father, let their temple be made desolate ;[6] for they have persecuted Him whom Thou didst of Thine own will smite for the salvation of the world ; " that is, they have persecuted me with a violent and unjust death, " and they have added to the pain of my wounds." In former time, as the Lover of man, I had pain on account of the straying of the Gentiles ; but to this pain they have added another, by going also themselves astray. Wherefore " add iniquity to their iniquity, and tribulation to tribulation, and let them not enter into Thy righteousness," that is, into Thy kingdom ; but " let them be blotted out of the book of the living, and not be written with the righteous," that is, with their holy fathers and patriarchs.

8. What sayest thou to this, O Jew ? It is neither Matthew nor Paul that saith these things, but David, thine anointed, who awards and declares these terrible sentences on account of Christ. And like the great Job, addressing you who speak against the righteous and true, he says, " Thou didst barter the Christ like a slave, thou didst go to Him like a robber in the garden."

9. I produce now the prophecy of Solomon, which speaketh of Christ, and announces clearly and perspicuously things concerning the Jews ; and those which not only are befalling them at the present time, but those, too, which shall befall them in the future age, on account of the contumacy and audacity which they exhibited toward the Prince of Life ; for the prophet says, " The ungodly said, reasoning with themselves, but not aright," that is, about Christ, " Let us lie in wait for the righteous, because he is not for our turn, and he is clean contrary to our doings and words, and upbraideth us with our offending the law, and professeth to have knowledge of God ; and he calleth himself the Child of God."[7] And then he says, " He is grievous to us even to behold ; for his life is not like other men's, and his ways are of another fashion. We are esteemed of him as counterfeits, and he

---

[1] Ps. xvi. 10.
[2] οἰκονομικῶς. [The Fathers find Christ everywhere in Scripture, and often understand the expressions of David to be those of our Lord's humanity, by *economy*.]
[3] Phil. ii. 7.
[4] John xiv. 6.
[5] The text is οὕτως, for which read perhaps ὅτε = when.

[6] Cf. Matt. xxiii. 38.
[7] Wisd. ii. 1, 12, 13.

abstaineth from our ways as from filthiness, and pronounceth the end of the just to be blessed." [1] And again, listen to this, O Jew! None of the righteous or prophets called himself the Son of God. And therefore, as in the person of the Jews, Solomon speaks again of this righteous one, who is Christ, thus: "He was made to reprove our thoughts, and he maketh his boast that God is his Father. Let us see, then, if his words be true, and let us prove what shall happen in the end of him; for if the just man be the Son of God, He will help him, and deliver him from the hand of his enemies. Let us condemn him with a shameful death, for by his own saying he shall be respected." [2]

10. And again David, in the Psalms, says with respect to the future age, "Then shall He " (namely Christ) "speak unto them in His wrath, and vex them in His sore displeasure." [3] And again Solomon says concerning Christ and the

Jews, that "when the righteous shall stand in great boldness before the face of such as have afflicted Him, and made no account of His words, when they see it they shall be troubled with terrible fear, and shall be amazed at the strangeness of His salvation; and they, repenting and groaning for anguish of spirit, shall say within themselves, This is He whom we had sometimes in derision and a proverb of reproach; we fools accounted His life madness, and His end to be without honour. How is He numbered among the children of God, and His lot is among the saints? Therefore have we erred from the way of truth, and the light of righteousness hath not shined unto us, and the sun of righteousness rose not on us. We wearied ourselves in the way of wickedness and destruction; we have gone through deserts where there lay no way: but as for the way of the Lord, we have not known it. What hath our pride profited us? all those things are passed away like a shadow." [4]

THE CONCLUSION IS WANTING.[5]

---

[1] Wisd. ii. 15, 16.
[2] Wisd. ii. 14, 16, 17, 20. [The argument is *ad hominem*. The Jews valued this book, but did not account it to be Scripture; yet this quotation is a very remarkable comment on what ancient Jews understood concerning the Just One. Comp. Acts iii. 14, vii. 52, and xxii. 14.]
[3] Ps. ii. 5.

[4] Wisd. v. 1–9.
[5] [Compare Justin, vol. i. p. 194; Clement, vol. ii. pp. 334–343; Tertullian, vol. iii. p. 151; Origen, vol. iv. p. 402, etc.; and Cyprian, vol. v., this series.]

AGAINST PLATO, ON THE CAUSE OF THE UNIVERSE.[1]

1. And this is the passage regarding demons.[2] But now we must speak of Hades, in which the souls both of the righteous and the unrighteous are detained. Hades is a place in the created system, rude,[3] a locality beneath the earth, in which the light of the world does not shine; and as the sun does not shine in this locality, there must necessarily be perpetual darkness there. This locality has been destined to be as it were a guard-house for souls, at which the angels are stationed as guards, distributing according to each one's deeds the temporary[4] punishments for (different) characters. And in this locality there is a certain place[5] set apart by itself, a lake of unquenchable fire, into which we suppose no one has ever yet been cast; for it is prepared against the day determined by God, in which one sentence of righteous judgment shall be

justly applied to all. And the unrighteous, and those who believed not God, who have honoured as God the vain works of the hands of men, idols fashioned (by themselves), shall be sentenced to this endless punishment. But the righteous shall obtain the incorruptible and unfading kingdom, who indeed are at present detained in Hades,[6] but not in the same place with the unrighteous. For to this locality there is one descent, at the gate whereof we believe an archangel is stationed with a host. And when those who are conducted by the angels[7] appointed unto the souls have passed through this gate, they do not proceed on one and the same way; but the righteous, being conducted in the light toward the right, and being hymned by the angels stationed at the place, are brought to a

---

[1] Gallandi, *Vet. Patr.*, ii. 451. Two fragments of this discourse are extant also in the *Parallela Damascenica Rupefucaldina*, pp. 755, 789. [Compare Justin, vol. i. p. 273; Tatian, ii. 65; Athenagoras, 130, and Clement *passim*; vol. iii. Tertullian, 129; Origen, iv. p. 412. This is a fragment from Hippol. *Against the Greeks*.]
[2] The reading in the text is ὁ περὶ δαιμόνων τόπος; others read λόγος for τόπος = thus far the discussion on demons.
[3] ἀκατασκεύαστος.
[4] Or it may be "seasonable," προσκαροίυς.
[5] τρόπων. There is another reading, τόπων = of the places.

[6] Hades, in the view of the ancients, was the general receptacle of souls after their separation from the body, where the good abode happily in a place of light (φωτεινῷ), and the evil all in a place of darkness (σκοτωτέρῳ). See Colomesii Κειμήλια *litteraria*, 28, and Suicer on ᾅδης. Hence Abraham's bosom and paradise were placed in Hades. See Olympiodorus on *Eccles.*, iii. p. 264. The Macedonians, on the authority of Hugo Broughton, prayed in the Lord's words, "Our Father who art in Hades (Πατὴρ ἡμῶν ὁ ἐν ᾅδῃ) (Fabricius). [Hippolytus is singular in assigning the *ultimate* receptacle of lost spirits to this Hades. But compare vol. iii. p. 428, and vol. iv. pp. 293, 495, 541, etc.]
[7] Cf. *Constitut. Apostol.*, viii. 41.

locality full of light. And there the righteous from the beginning[1] dwell, not ruled by necessity, but enjoying always the contemplation of the blessings which are in their view, and delighting themselves with the expectation of others ever new, and deeming those ever better than these. And that place brings no toils to them. There, there is neither fierce heat, nor cold, nor thorn;[2] but the face of the fathers and the righteous is seen to be always smiling, as they wait for the rest and eternal revival in heaven which succeed this location. And we call it by the name *Abraham's bosom*. But the unrighteous are dragged toward the left by angels who are ministers of punishment, and they go of their own accord no longer, but are dragged by force as prisoners. And the angels appointed over them send them along,[3] reproaching them and threatening them with an eye of terror, forcing them down into the lower parts. And when they are brought there, those appointed to that service drag them on to the confines of hell.[4] And those who are so near hear incessantly the agitation, and feel the hot smoke. And when that vision is so near, as they see the terrible and excessively glowing[5] spectacle of the fire, they shudder in horror at the expectation of the future judgment, (as if they were) already feeling the power of their punishment. And again, where they see the place of the fathers and the righteous,[6] they are also punished there. For a deep and vast abyss is set there in the midst, so that neither can any of the righteous in sympathy think to pass it, nor any of the unrighteous dare to cross it.

2. Thus far, then, on the subject of Hades, in which the souls of all are detained until the time which God has determined; and then[7] He will accomplish a resurrection of all, not by transferring souls into other bodies,[8] but by raising the bodies themselves. And if, O Greeks, ye refuse credit to this because ye see these (bodies) in their dissolution, learn not to be incredulous. For if ye believe that the soul is originated and is made immortal by God, according to the opinion of Plato,[9] in time, ye ought not to refuse to believe that God is able also to raise the body, which is composed of the same elements, and make it immortal.[10] To be able in one thing, and to be unable in another, is a word which cannot be said of God. We therefore believe that the body also is raised. For if it become corrupt, it is not at least destroyed. For the earth receiving its remains preserves them, and they, becoming as it were seed, and being wrapped up with the richer part of earth, spring up and bloom. And that which is sown is sown indeed bare grain; but at the command of God the Artificer it buds, and is raised arrayed and glorious, but not until it has first died, and been dissolved, and mingled with earth. Not, therefore, without good reason do we believe in the resurrection of the body. Moreover, if it is dissolved in its season on account of the primeval transgression, and is committed to the earth as to a furnace, to be moulded again anew, it is not raised the same thing as it is now, but pure and no longer corruptible. And to every body its own proper soul will be given again; and the soul, being endued again with it, shall not be grieved, but shall rejoice together with it, abiding itself pure with it also pure. And as it now sojourns with it in the world righteously, and finds it in nothing now a traitor, it will receive it again (the body) with great joy. But the unrighteous will receive their bodies unchanged, and unransomed from suffering and disease, and unglorified, and still with all the ills in which they died. And whatever manner of persons they (were when they) lived without faith, as such they shall be faithfully judged.[11]

3.[12] For all, the righteous and the unrighteous alike, shall be brought before God the Word. For the Father hath committed all judgment to Him; and in fulfilment of the Father's counsel, He cometh as Judge whom we call Christ. For it is not Minos and Rhadamanthys that are to judge (the world), as ye fancy, O Greeks, but He whom God the Father hath glorified, of whom we have spoken elsewhere more in particular, for the profit of those who seek the truth. He, in administering the righteous judgment of the Father to all, assigns to each what is righteous according to his works. And being present at His judicial decision, all, both men and angels and demons, shall utter one voice, saying, "Righteous is Thy judgment."[13] Of which voice the justification will be seen in the awarding to each that which is just; since to those who have done well shall be assigned righteously eternal bliss, and to the lovers of iniquity shall be given eternal punishment. And the fire which is unquenchable and without end awaits these latter, and a certain fiery worm which dieth not, and

---

[1] [They do not pass into an intermediate *purgatory*, nor require prayers for "the repose of their souls."]

[2] τρίβολος. [Also the Pindaric citation in my note, vol. i. 74.]

[3] In the *Parallela* is inserted here the word ἐπιγελῶντες, *deriding* them.

[4] γέεννα.

[5] According to the reading in *Parallela*, which inserts ξανθὴν = red.

[6] The text reads καὶ οὖ, and *where*. But in *Parallela* it is καὶ οὗτοι = and these see, etc. In the same we find ὡς μήτε for καὶ τοὺς δικαίους.

[7] [It would be hard to frame a system of belief concerning the state of the dead more entirely exclusive of *purgatory*, i.e., a place where the souls *of the faithful* are detained till (by Masses and the like) they are relieved and admitted to glory, before the resurrection. See vol. iii. p. 706.]

[8] μετενσωμάτων, in opposition to the dogma of metempsychosis.

[9] In the *Timæus*.

[10] The first of the two fragments in the *Parallela* ends here.

[11] [The text Eccles. xi. 3 may be accommodated to this truth, but seems to have no force as proof.]

[12] The second fragment extant in the *Parallela* begins here.

[13] Ps. cxix. 137.

which does not waste the body, but continues bursting forth from the body with unending pain. No sleep will give them rest; no night will soothe them; no death will deliver them from punishment; no voice of interceding friends will profit them.[1] For neither are the righteous seen by them any longer, nor are they worthy of remembrance. But the righteous will remember only the righteous deeds by which they reached the heavenly kingdom, in which there is neither sleep, nor pain, nor corruption, nor care,[2] nor night, nor day measured by time; nor sun traversing in necessary course the circle of heaven, which marks the limits of seasons, or the points measured out for the life of man so easily read; nor moon waning or waxing, or inducing the changes of seasons, or moistening the earth; no burning sun, no changeful Bear, no Orion coming forth, no numerous wandering of stars, no pain-

fully-trodden earth, no abode of paradise hard to find; no furious roaring of the sea, forbidding one to touch or traverse it; but this too will be readily passable for the righteous, although it lacks no water. There will be no heaven inaccessible to men, nor will the way of its ascent be one impossible to find; and there will be no earth unwrought, or toilsome for men, but one producing fruit spontaneously in beauty and order; nor will there be generation of wild beasts again, nor the bursting[3] substance of other creatures. Neither with man will there be generation again, but the number of the righteous remains indefectible with the righteous angels and spirits. Ye who believe these words, O men, will be partakers with the righteous, and will have part in these future blessings, which "eye hath not seen nor ear heard, neither have entered into the heart of man the things which God hath prepared for them that love Him."[4] To Him be the glory and the power, for ever and ever. Amen.

---

[1] [It is not the unrighteous, be it remembered, who go to "purgatory," according to the Trent theology, but only true Christians, dying in full communion with the Church. Hippolytus is here speaking of the *ultimate* doom of the wicked, but bears in mind the imagery of Luke xvi. 24 and the appeal to Abraham.]
[2] The second fragment in the *Parallela* ends here.

[3] ἐκβρασσομένη.
[4] 1 Cor. ii. 9.

AGAINST THE HERESY OF ONE NOETUS.[1]

1. Some others are secretly introducing another doctrine, who have become disciples of one Noetus, who was a native of Smyrna,[2] (and) lived not very long ago.[3] This person was greatly puffed up and inflated with pride, being inspired by the conceit of a strange spirit. He alleged that Christ was the Father Himself, and that the Father Himself was born, and suffered, and died. Ye see what pride of heart and what a strange inflated spirit had insinuated themselves into him. From his other actions, then, the proof is already given us that he spoke not with a pure spirit; for he who blasphemes against the Holy Ghost is cast out from the holy inheritance. He alleged that he was himself Moses, and that Aaron was his brother.[4] When the blessed presbyters heard this, they summoned him before the Church, and examined him. But he denied

at first that he held such opinions. Afterwards, however, taking shelter among some, and having gathered round him some others[5] who had embraced the same error, he wished thereafter to uphold his dogma openly as correct. And the blessed presbyters called him again before them, and examined him. But he stood out against them, saying, "What evil, then, am I doing in glorifying Christ?" And the presbyters replied to him, "We too know in truth one God;[6] we know Christ; we know that the Son suffered even as He suffered, and died even as He died, and rose again on the third day, and is at the right hand of the Father, and cometh to judge the living and the dead. And these things which we have learned we allege." Then, after examining him, they expelled him from the Church. And he was carried to such a pitch of pride, that he established a school.

2. Now they seek to exhibit the foundation for their dogma by citing the word in the law, "I am the God of your fathers: ye shall have no other gods beside me;"[7] and again in another passage, "I am the first," He saith, "and the

---

[1] Gallandi, p. 454.
[2] That Noetus was a native of Smyrna is mentioned also by Theodoret, book iii. *Hæret. Fab.*, c. iii., and Damascenus, sec. lvii. (who is accustomed to follow Epiphanius); and yet in Epiphanius, *Hæres.*, 57, we read that Noetus was an Asian of the city of Ephesus (Ἀσιανὸν τῆς Ἐφέσου πόλεως). (Fabricius.)
[3] Epiphanius says that Noetus made his heresy public about 130 years before his time (οὐ πρὸ ἐτῶν πλειόνων ἀλλ᾽ ὡς πρὸ χρόνου τῶν τούτων ἑκατὸν τριάκοντα, πλείω ἢ ἐλάσσω); and as Epiphanius wrote in the year 375, that would make the date of Noetus about 245. He says also that Noetus died *soon after* (ἔναγχος), along with his brother. (Fabricius.)
[4] So also Epiphanius and Damascenus. But Philastrius, *Heresy*, 53, puts Elijah for Aaron: hic etiam dicebat se Moysem esse, et fratrem suum Eliam prophetam.

[5] Epiphanius remarks that they were but ten in number.
[6] The following words are the words of the *Symbolum*, as it is extant in Irenæus, i. 10, etc., and iii. 4; and in Tertullian, *Contra Praxeam*, ch. ii., and *De Præscript.*, ch. xiii., and *De virginibus velandis*, ch. i. [See vol. iii., this series.]
[7] Ex. iii. 6 and xx. 3.

last; and beside me there is none other." [1] Thus they say they prove that God is one. And then they answer in this manner: "If therefore I acknowledge Christ to be God, He is the Father Himself, if He is indeed God; and Christ suffered, being Himself God; and consequently the Father suffered, for He was the Father Himself." But the case stands not thus; for the Scriptures do not set forth the matter in this manner. But they make use also of other testimonies, and say, Thus it is written: "This is our God, and there shall none other be accounted of in comparison of Him. He hath found out all the way of knowledge, and hath given it unto Jacob His servant (son), and to Israel His beloved. Afterward did He show Himself upon earth, and conversed with men." [2] You see, then, he says, that this is God, who is the only One, and who afterwards did show Himself, and conversed with men." And in another place he says, "Egypt hath laboured; and the merchandise of Ethiopia and the Sabeans, men of stature, shall come over unto thee, (and they shall be slaves to thee); and they shall come after thee bound with manacles, and they shall fall down unto thee, because God is in thee; and they shall make supplication unto thee: and there is no God beside thee. For Thou art God, and we knew not; God of Israel, the Saviour." [3] Do you see, he says, how the Scriptures proclaim one God? And as this is clearly exhibited, and these passages are testimonies to it, I am under necessity, he says, since one is acknowledged, to make this One the subject of suffering. For Christ was God, and suffered on account of us, being Himself the Father, that He might be able also to save us. And we cannot express ourselves otherwise, he says; for the apostle also acknowledges one God, when he says, "Whose are the fathers, (and) of whom as concerning the flesh Christ came, who is over all, God blessed for ever." [4]

8. In this way, then, they choose to set forth these things, and they make use only of one class of passages; [5] just in the same one-sided manner that Theodotus employed when he sought to prove that Christ was a mere man. But neither has the one party nor the other

understood the matter rightly, as the Scriptures themselves confute their senselessness, and attest the truth. See, brethren, what a rash and audacious dogma they have introduced, when they say without shame, the Father is Himself Christ, Himself the Son, Himself was born, Himself suffered, Himself raised Himself. But it is not so. The Scriptures speak what is right; but Noetus is of a different mind from them. Yet, though Noetus does not understand the truth, the Scriptures are not at once to be repudiated. For who will not say that there is one God? Yet he will not on that account deny the economy (i.e., the number and disposition of persons in the Trinity). The proper way, therefore, to deal with the question is first of all to refute the interpretation put upon these passages by these men, and then to explain their real meaning. For it is right, in the first place, to expound the truth that the Father is one God, "of whom is every family," [6] "by whom are all things, of whom are all things, and we in Him." [7]

4. Let us, as I said, see how he is confuted, and then let us set forth the truth. Now he quotes the words, "Egypt has laboured, and the merchandise of Ethiopia and the Sabeans," and so forth on to the words, "For Thou art the God of Israel, the Saviour." And these words he cites without understanding what precedes them. For whenever they wish to attempt anything underhand, they mutilate the Scriptures. But let him quote the passage as a whole, and he will discover the reason kept in view in writing it. For we have the beginning of the section a little above; and we ought, of course, to commence there in showing to whom and about whom the passage speaks. For above, the beginning of the section stands thus: "Ask me concerning my sons and my daughters, and concerning the work of my hands command ye me. I have made the earth, and man upon it: I with my hand have stablished the heaven; I have commanded all the stars. I have raised him up, and all his ways are straight. He shall build my city, and he shall turn back the captivity; not for price nor reward, said the Lord of hosts. Thus said the Lord of hosts, Egypt hath laboured, and the merchandise of Ethiopia and the Sabeans, men of stature, shall come over unto thee, and they shall be slaves to thee: and they shall come after thee bound with manacles, and they shall fall down unto thee; and they shall make supplication unto thee, because God is in thee; and there is no God beside thee. For Thou art God, and we knew not; the God of Israel, the Saviour." [8] "In thee, therefore," says he, "God is." But in whom is God except

---

[1] Isa. xliv. 6.

[2] Baruch iii. 35-38. [Based on Prov. viii., but so remarkable that Grotius presumptuously declared it an interpolation. It reflects canonical Scripture, but has no canonical value otherwise.]

[3] Isa. xlv. 14.

[4] Rom. ix. 5.

[5] καὶ αὐτοῖς μονοκῶλα χρώμενοι, etc. The word μονοκῶλα appears to be used adverbially, instead of μονοκώλως and μονοτύπως, which are the terms employed by Epiphanius (p. 481). The meaning is, that the Noetians, in explaining the words of Scripture concerning Christ, looked only to one side of the question — namely, to the divine nature; just as Theodotus, on his part going to the opposite extreme, kept by the human nature exclusively, and held that Christ was a mere man. Besides others, the presbyter Timotheus, in *Cotelerii Monument*, vol. iii. p. 389, mentions Theodotus in these terms: "They say that this Theodotus was the leader and father of the heresy of the Samosatan, having first alleged that Christ was a mere man." [See vol. iii. p. 654, this series.]

[6] Eph. iii. 15.

[7] 1 Cor. viii. 6.

[8] Isa. xlv. 11-15.

in Christ Jesus, the Father's Word, and the mystery of the economy?[1] And again, exhibiting the truth regarding Him, he points to the fact of His being in the flesh when He says, " I have raised Him up in righteousness, and all His ways are straight." For what is this? Of whom does the Father thus testify? It is of the Son that the Father says, " I have raised Him up in righteousness." And that the Father did raise up His Son in righteousness, the Apostle Paul bears witness, saying, " But if the Spirit of Him that raised up Christ Jesus from the dead dwell in you, He that raised up Christ Jesus from the dead shall also quicken your mortal bodies by His Spirit that dwelleth in you."[2] Behold, the word spoken by the prophet is thus made good, " I have raised Him up in righteousness." And in saying, " God is in thee," he referred to the mystery of the economy, because when the Word was made incarnate and became man, the Father was in the Son, and the Son in the Father, while the Son was living among men. This, therefore, was signified, brethren, that in reality the mystery of the economy by the Holy Ghost and the Virgin was this Word, constituting yet one Son to God.[3] And it is not simply that I say this, but He Himself attests it who came down from heaven; for He speaketh thus: " No man hath ascended up to heaven, but He that came down from heaven, even the Son of man which is in heaven."[4] What then can he seek beside what is thus written? Will he say, forsooth, that flesh was in heaven? Yet there is the flesh which was presented by the Father's Word as an offering, — the flesh that came by the Spirit and the Virgin, (and was) demonstrated to be the perfect Son of God. It is evident, therefore, that He offered Himself to the Father. And before this there was no flesh in heaven. Who, then, was in heaven[5] but the Word unincarnate, who was despatched to show that He was upon earth and was also in heaven? For He was Word, He was Spirit, He was Power. The same took to Himself the name common and current among men, and was called from the beginning the Son of man on account of what He was to be, although He was not yet man, as Daniel testifies when he says, " I saw, and behold one like the Son of man came on the clouds of heaven."[6] Rightly, then, did he say that He who was in heaven was called from the beginning by this name, the Word of God, as being that from the beginning.

5. But what is meant, says he, in the other passage : " This is God, and there shall none other be accounted of in comparison of Him ? "[7] That said he rightly. For in comparison of the Father who shall be accounted of? But he says : " This is our God ; there shall none other be accounted of in comparison of Him. He hath found out all the way of knowledge, and hath given it unto Jacob His servant, and to Israel His beloved." He saith well. For who is Jacob His servant, Israel His beloved, but He of whom He crieth, saying, " This is my beloved Son, in whom I am well pleased : hear ye Him ? "[8] Having received, then, all knowledge from the Father, the perfect Israel, the true Jacob, afterward did show Himself upon earth, and conversed with men. And who, again, is meant by Israel[9] but *a man who sees God ?* and there is no one who sees God except the Son alone, the perfect man who alone declares the will of the Father. For John also says, " No man hath seen God at any time ; the only-begotten Son, which is in the bosom of the Father, He hath declared[10] Him."[11] And again : " He who came down from heaven testifieth what He hath heard and seen."[12] This, then, is He to whom the Father hath given all knowledge, who did show Himself upon earth, and conversed with men.

6. Let us look next at the apostle's word : " Whose are the fathers, of whom as concerning the flesh Christ came, who is over all, God blessed for ever."[13] This word declares the mystery of the truth rightly and clearly. He who is over all is God ; for thus He speaks boldly, " All things are delivered unto me of my Father."[14] He who is over all, God blessed, has been born ; and having been made man, He is (yet) God for ever. For to this effect John also has said, " Which is, and which was, and which is to come, the Almighty."[15] And well has he named Christ the Almighty. For in this he has said only what Christ testifies of Himself. For Christ gave this testimony, and said, " All things are delivered unto me of my Father ; "[16] and Christ rules all things, and has been appointed[17]

---

1 [Bull, *Opp.*, v. pp. 367, 734, 740-743, 753-756.]
2 Rom. viii. 11.
3 Turrian has the following note: " The Word of God constituted (operatum est) one Son to God; i.e., the Word of God effected, that He who was the one Son of God was also one Son of man, because as His hypostasis He assumed the flesh. For thus was the Word made flesh."
4 John iii. 13.
5 [John iii. 13.]
6 Dan. vii. 13.

7 Baruch iii. 36, etc.
8 Matt. xvii. 5.
9 The word *Israel* is explained by Philo, *De præmiis et pœnis*, p. 710, and elsewhere, as = *a man seeing God*, ὁρῶν Θεόν, i.e., אִישׁ רֹאֶה אֵל. So also in the *Constitutiones Apostol.*, vii. 37, viii. 15; Eusebius, *Præparat.*, xi. 6, p. 519, and in many others. To the same class may be referred those who make Israel = ὁρατικὸς ἀνὴρ καὶ θεωρητικὸς, *a man apt to see and speculate*, as Eusebius, *Præparat.*, p. 310, or = νοῦς ὁρῶν Θεόν, as Optatus in the end of the second book; Didymus in Jerome, and Jerome himself in various passages; Maximus, i. p. 284; Olympiodorus on Ecclesiastes, ch. i.; Leontius, *De Sectis*, p. 392; Theophanes, *Ceram. homil.*, iv. p. 22, etc. Justin Martyr, *Dialog. cum Tryph.* [see vol. i. pp. 226, 262], adduces another etymology, ἄνθρωπος νικῶν δύναμιν.
10 Hippolytus reads διηγήσατο for ἐξηγήσατο.
11 John i. 18.
12 John iii. 11, 13.
13 Rom. ix. 5.
14 Matt. xi. 27.
15 Apoc. i. 8.
16 Matt. xi. 27. [Compare John v. 22.]
17 [Strictly scriptural as to the humanity of Messiah, Heb. i. 9.]

Almighty by the Father. And in like manner Paul also, in setting forth the truth that all things are delivered unto Him, said, "Christ the first-fruits; afterwards they that are Christ's at His coming. Then cometh the end, when He shall have delivered up the kingdom to God, even the Father; when He shall have put down all rule, and all authority, and power. For He must reign, till He hath put all enemies under His feet. The last enemy that shall be destroyed is death. For all things are put under Him. But when He saith, All things are put under Him, it is manifest that He is excepted which did put all things under Him. Then shall He also Himself be subject to Him who put all things under Him, that God may be all in all." [1] If, therefore, all things are put under Him with the exception of Him who put them under Him, He is Lord of all, and the Father is Lord of Him, that in all there might be manifested one God, to whom all things are made subject together with Christ, to whom the Father hath made all things subject, with the exception of Himself. And this, indeed, is said by Christ Himself, as when in the Gospel He confessed Him to be His Father and His God. For He speaks thus: "I go to my Father and your Father, and to my God and your God." [2] If, then, Noetus ventures to say that He is the Father Himself, to what father will he say Christ goes away according to the word of the Gospel? But if he will have us abandon the Gospel and give credence to his senselessness, he expends his labour in vain; for "we ought to obey God rather than men." [3]

7. If, again, he allege His own word when He said, "I and the Father are one," [4] let him attend to the fact, and understand that He did not say, "I and the Father *am one*, but *are one*." [5] For the word *are* [6] is not said of one person, but it refers to *two persons*, and one power. [7] He has Himself made this clear, when He spake to His Father concerning the disciples, "The glory which Thou gavest me I have given them; that they may be one, even as we are one : I in them, and Thou in me, that they may be made perfect in one; that the world may know that Thou hast sent me." [8] What have the Noetians to say to these things? Are all one body in respect of substance, or is it that we become one in the power and disposition of unity of mind? [9] In the same manner the Son, who was sent and was not known of those who are in the world, confessed that He was in the Father

in power and disposition. For the Son is the one mind of the Father. We who have the Father's mind believe so (in Him) ; but they who have it not have denied the Son. And if, again, they choose to allege the fact that Philip inquired about the Father, saying, "Show us the Father, and it sufficeth us," to whom the Lord made answer in these terms : "Have I been so long time with you, and yet hast thou not known me, Philip? He that hath seen me hath seen the Father. Believest thou not that I am in the Father, and the Father in me?" [10] and if they choose to maintain that their dogma is ratified by this passage, as if He owned Himself to be the Father, let them know that it is decidedly against them, and that they are confuted by this very word. For though Christ had spoken of Himself, and showed Himself among all as the Son, they had not yet recognised Him to be such, neither had they been able to apprehend or contemplate His real power. And Philip, not having been able to receive this, as far as it was possible to see it, requested to behold the Father. To whom then the Lord said, "Philip, have I been so long time with you, and yet hast thou not known me? He that hath seen me hath seen the Father." By which He means, If thou hast seen me, thou mayest know the Father through me. For through the image, which is like (the original), the Father is made readily known. But if thou hast not known the image, which is the Son, how dost thou seek to see the Father? And that this is the case is made clear by the rest of the chapter, which signifies that the Son who "has been set forth [11] was sent from the Father, [12] and goeth to the Father." [13]

8. Many other passages, or rather all of them, attest the truth. A man, therefore, even though he will it not, is compelled to acknowledge God the Father Almighty, and Christ Jesus the Son of God, who, being God, became man, to whom also the Father made all things subject, Himself excepted, and the Holy Spirit ; and that these, therefore, are three. But if he desires to learn how it is shown still that there is one God, let him know that His power [14] is one. As far as regards the power, therefore, God is one. But as far as regards the economy there is a threefold manifestation, as shall be proved afterwards when we give account of the true doctrine. In these things, however, which are thus set forth by us, we are at one. For there is one God in whom we must believe, but unoriginated, impassible, immortal, doing all things as He wills, in the way He wills, and when He wills. What,

---

[1] 1 Cor. xv. 23–28.
[2] John xx. 17.
[3] Acts v. 29, iv. 19.
[4] John x. 30.
[5] ἐγὼ καὶ ὁ πατὴρ — ἕν ἐσμεν, not ἕν εἰμι.
[6] ἐσμέν.
[7] δύναμιν.
[8] John xvii. 22, 23.
[9] ἢ τῇ δυνάμει καὶ τῇ διαθέσει τῆς ὁμοφρονίας ἐν γινόμεθα.

[10] John xiv. 8, 9.
[11] Rom. iii. 25.
[12] John v. 30, vi. 29, viii. 16, 18, etc.
[13] John xiii. 1, xiv. 12.
[14] δύναμις.

then, will this Noetus, who knows[1] nothing of the truth, dare to say to these things? And now, as Noetus has been confuted, let us turn to the exhibition of the truth itself, that we may establish the truth, against which all these mighty heresies[2] have arisen without being able to state anything to the purpose.

9. There is, brethren, one God, the knowledge of whom we gain from the Holy Scriptures, and from no other source. For just as a man, if he wishes to be skilled in the wisdom of this world, will find himself unable to get at it in any other way than by mastering the dogmas of philosophers, so all of us who wish to practise piety will be unable to learn its practice from any other quarter than the oracles of God.[3] Whatever things, then, the Holy Scriptures declare, at these let us look; and whatsoever things they teach, these let us learn; and as the Father wills our belief to be, let us believe; and as He wills the Son to be glorified, let us glorify Him; and as He wills the Holy Spirit to be bestowed, let us receive Him. Not according to our own will, nor according to our own mind, nor yet as using violently those things which are given by God, but even as He has chosen to teach them by the Holy Scriptures, so let us discern them.

10. God, subsisting alone, and having nothing contemporaneous with Himself, determined to create the world. And conceiving the world in mind, and willing and uttering the word, He made it; and straightway it appeared, formed as it had pleased Him. For us, then, it is sufficient simply to know that there was nothing contemporaneous with God. Beside Him there was nothing; but[4] He, while existing alone, yet existed in plurality.[5] For He was neither without reason, nor wisdom, nor power, nor counsel.[6] And all things were in Him, and He was the All. When He willed, and as He willed,[7] He manifested His word in the times determined by Him, and by Him He made all things. When He wills, He does; and when He thinks, He executes; and when He speaks, He manifests; when He fashions, He contrives in wisdom. For all things that are made He forms by reason and wisdom — creating them in reason, and arranging them in wisdom. He made them, then, as He pleased, for He was God. And as the

Author, and fellow-Counsellor, and Framer[8] of the things that are in formation, He begat[9] the Word; and as He bears this Word in Himself, and that, too, as (yet) invisible to the world which is created, He makes Him visible; (and) uttering the voice first, and begetting Him as Light of Light,[10] He set Him forth to the world as its Lord, (and) His own mind;[11] and whereas He was visible formerly to Himself alone, and invisible to the world which is made, He makes Him visible in order that the world might see Him in His manifestation, and be capable of being saved.

11. And thus there appeared another beside Himself. But when I say *another*,[12] I do not mean that there are two Gods, but that it is only as light of light, or as water from a fountain, or as a ray from the sun. For there is but one power, which is from the All;[13] and the Father is the All, from whom cometh this Power, the Word. And this is the mind[14] which came forth into the world, and was manifested as the Son[15] of God. All things, then, are by Him, and He alone is of the Father. Who then adduces a multitude of gods brought in, time after time? For all are shut up, however unwillingly, to admit this fact, that the All runs up into one. If, then, all things run up into one, even according to Valentinus, and Marcion, and Cerinthus, and all their fooleries, they are also reduced, however unwillingly, to this position, that they must acknowledge that the One is the cause of all things. Thus, then, these too, though they wish it not, fall in with the truth, and admit that one God made all things according to His good pleasure. And He gave the law and the prophets; and in giving them, He made them speak by the Holy Ghost, in order that, being gifted with the inspiration of the Father's power, they might declare the Father's counsel and will.

12. Acting then in these (prophets), the Word spoke of Himself. For already He became His own herald, and showed that the Word would

---

[1] There is perhaps a play on the words here — Νόητος μὴ νοῶν.

[2] i.e., the other thirty-one heresies, which Hippolytus had already attacked. From these words it is apparent also that this treatise was the closing portion of a book against the heresies (Fabricius).

[3] [This emphatic testimony of our author to the sufficiency of the Scriptures is entirely in keeping with the entire system of the Ante-Nicene Fathers. Note our teeming indexes of Scripture texts.]

[4] See, on this passage, Bull's *Defens. Fid. Nic.*, sec. iii. cap. viii. § 2, p. 219.

[5] πολὺς ἦν.

[6] ἄλογος, ἄσοφος, ἀδύνατος, ἀβούλευτος.

[7] On these words see Bossuet's explanation and defence, *Avertiss.*, vi. § 68, *sur les lettres de M. Jurieu.*

[8] ἀρχηγόν, καὶ σύμβουλον, καὶ ἐργάτην.

[9] The "begetting" of which Hippolytus speaks here is not the generation, properly so called, but that manifestation and bringing forth of the Word co-existing from eternity with the Father, which referred to the creation of the world. So at least Bull and Bossuet, as cited above; also Maranus, *De Divinit. J. C.*, lib. iv. cap. xiii. § 3, p. 458.

[10] φῶς ἐκ φωτός. This phrase, adopted by the Nicene Fathers, occurs before their time not only here, but also in Justin Martyr, Tatian, and Athenagoras, as is noticed by Grabe, *ad Irenæum*, lib. ii. c. xxiii. Methodius also, in his *Homily on Simeon and Anna*, p. 152, has the expression, σὺ εἶ φῶς ἀληθινὸν ἐκ φωτὸς ἀληθινοῦ Θεὸς ἀληθινὸς ἐκ Θεοῦ ἀληθινοῦ. Athanasius himself also uses the phrase λύχνον ἐκ λύχνου, vol. i. p. 881, ed. Lips. [Illustrating my remarks (p. v. of this volume), in the preface, as to the study of Nicene theology in Ante-Nicene authors.]

[11] νοῦν.

[12] Justin Martyr also says that the Son is ἕτερόν τι, *something other*, from the Father; and Tertullian affirms, *Filium et Patrem esse aliud ab alio*, with the same intent as Hippolytus here, viz., to express the distinction of persons. [See vol. i. pp. 170, 216, 263, and vol. iii. p. 604.]

[13] ἐκ τοῦ παντός.

[14] Or reason.

[15] παῖς.

be manifested among men. And for this reason He cried thus : " I am made manifest to them that sought me not ; I am found of them that asked not for me." [1] And who is He that is made manifest but the Word of the Father?— whom the Father sent, and in whom He showed to men the power proceeding from Him. Thus, then, was the Word made manifest, even as the blessed John says. For he sums up the things that were said by the prophets, and shows that this is the Word, by whom all things were made. For he speaks to this effect : " In the beginning was the Word, and the Word was with God, and the Word was God. All things were made by Him, and without Him was not anything made." [2] And beneath He says, " The world was made by Him, and the world knew Him not ; He came unto His own, and His own received Him not." [3] If, then, said he, the world was made by Him, according to the word of the prophet, " By the Word of the Lord were the heavens made," [4] then this is the Word that was also made manifest. We accordingly see the Word incarnate, and we know the Father by Him, and we believe in the Son, (and) we worship the Holy Spirit. Let us then look at the testimony of Scripture. with respect to the announcement of the future manifestation of the Word.

13. Now Jeremiah says, " Who hath stood in the counsel [5] of the Lord, and hath perceived His Word ? " [6] But the Word of God alone is visible, while the word of man is audible. When he speaks of seeing the Word, I must believe that this visible (Word) has been sent. And there was none other (sent) but the Word. And that He was sent Peter testifies, when he says to the centurion Cornelius : " God sent His Word unto the children of Israel by the preach-ing of Jesus Christ. This is the God who is Lord of all." [7] If, then, the Word is sent by Jesus Christ, the will [8] of the Father is Jesus Christ.

14. These things then, brethren, are declared by the Scriptures. And the blessed John, in the testimony of his Gospel, gives us an account of this economy (disposition) and acknowledges this Word as God, when he says, " In the begin-ning was the Word, and the Word was with God, and the Word was God." If, then, the Word was with God, and was also God, what follows? Would one say that he speaks of two Gods? [9] I shall not indeed speak of two Gods, but of one ; of two Persons however, and of a third economy (disposition), viz., the grace of the Holy Ghost. For the Father indeed is One, but there are two Persons, because there is also the Son ; and then there is the third, the Holy Spirit. The Father decrees, the Word executes, and the Son is manifested, through whom the Father is believed on. The economy [10] of har-mony is led back to one God ; for God is One. It is the Father who commands, [11] and the Son who obeys, and the Holy Spirit who gives un-derstanding : [12] the Father who is *above all*, [13] and the Son who is *through all*, and the Holy Spirit who is *in all*. And we cannot otherwise think of one God, [14] but by believing in truth in Father and Son and Holy Spirit. For the Jews glorified (or gloried in) the Father, but gave Him not thanks, for they did not recognise the Son. The disciples recognised the Son, but not in the Holy Ghost ; wherefore they also denied Him. [15] The Father's Word, therefore, knowing the economy (disposition) and the will of the Father, to wit, that the Father seeks to be worshipped in none other way than this, gave this charge to the dis-ciples after He rose from the dead : " Go ye and teach all nations, baptizing them in the name of the Father, and of the Son, and of the Holy Ghost." [16] And by this He showed, that whosoever omitted any one of these, failed in glorifying God perfectly. For it is through this Trinity [17] that the Father is glorified. For the Father willed, the Son did, the Spirit manifested. The whole Scriptures, then, proclaim this truth.

---

[1] Isa. lxv. 1.
[2] John i. 1-3. Hippolytus evidently puts the full stop at the οὐδὲ ἕν, attaching the ὃ γέγονεν to the following. So also Irenæus, Clemens Alex., Origen, Theophilus of Antioch, and Eusebius, in several places; so, too, of the Latin Fathers — Tertullian, Lactantius, Victorinus, Augustine; and long after these, Honorius Augusto-dunensis, in his *De imagine Mundi*. This punctuation was also adopted by the heretics Valentinus, Heracleon, Theodotus, and the Macedonians and Eunomians; and hence it is rejected by Epiphanius, ii. p. 80, and Chrysostom. (Fabricius.)
[3] John i. 10, 11.
[4] Ps. xxxiii. 6.
[5] ὑποστήματι, foundation. Victor reads ἐν τῇ ὑποστάσει, in the substance, nature; Symmachus has ἐν τῇ ὁμιλίᾳ, in the fellowship.
[6] Jer. xxiii. 18.
[7] Acts x. 36.
[8] τὸ θέλημα. Many of the patristic theologians called the Son the Father's βούλησις or θέλημα. See the passages in Petavius, *De S. S. Trinitate*, lib. vi. c. 8, § 21, and vii. 12, § 12. [Dubious.]

[9] From this passage it is clear that Hippolytus taught the doc-trine of one God alone and three Persons. A little before, in the eighth chapter, he said that there is one God, according to substance or divine essence, which one substance is in three Persons; and that, according to disposition or economy, there are three Persons mani-fested. By the term *economy*, therefore, he understands, with Ter-tullian, *adversus Praxeam*, ch. iii., the number and disposition of the Trinity (*numerum et dispositionem Trinitatis*). Here he also calls the grace of the Holy Spirit the *third economy*, but in the same way as Tertullian, who calls the Holy Spirit the *third grade* (*tertium gradum*). For the terms *gradus*, *forma*, *species*, *dis-positio*, and *œconomia* mean the same in Tertullian. (Maranus.) [Another proof that the Nicene Creed was a *compilation* from Ante-Nicene theologians.]
[10] οἰκονομία συμφωνίας συνάγεται εἰς ἕνα Θεόν, perhaps = the economy as being one of harmony, leads to one God.
[11] This mode of speaking of the Father's *commanding* and the Son's *obeying*, was used without any offence, not only by Irenæus, Hippolytus, Origen, and others before the Council of Nicæa, but also after that council by the keenest opponents of the Arian heresy — Athanasius, Basil, Marius Victorinus, Hilary, Prosper, and others. See Petavius, *De Trin.*, i. 7, § 7; and Bull, *Defens Fid. Nic.*, pp. 138, 164, 167, 170. (Fabricius.)
[12] συνετίζον.
[13] Referring probably to Eph. iv. 6.
[14] The Christian doctrine, Maranus remarks, could not be set forth more accurately; for he contends not only that the number of Per-sons in no manner detracts from the unity of God, but that the unity of God itself can neither consist nor be adored without this number of Persons.
[15] This is said probably with reference to Peter's denial.
[16] Matt. xxviii. 19.
[17] Τριάδος. [See Theophilus, vol. ii. p. 101, note.]

15. But some one will say to me, You adduce a thing strange to me, when you call the Son the Word. For John indeed speaks of the Word, but it is by a figure of speech. *Nay, it is by no figure of speech.*[1] For while thus presenting this Word that was from the beginning, and has now been sent forth, he said below in the Apocalypse, "And I saw heaven opened, and behold a white horse ; and He that sat upon him (was) Faithful and True ; and in righteousness He doth judge and make war. And His eyes (were) as flame of fire, and on His head were many crowns ; and He had a name written that no man knew but He Himself. And He (was) clothed in a vesture dipped in blood : and His name is called the Word of God."[2] See then, brethren, how the vesture sprinkled with blood denoted in symbol the flesh, through which the impassible Word of God came under suffering, as also the prophets testify to me. For thus speaks the blessed Micah : "The house of Jacob provoked the Spirit of the Lord to anger. These are their pursuits. Are not His words good with them, and do they walk rightly? And they have risen up in enmity against His countenance of peace, and they have stripped off His glory."[3] That means His suffering in the flesh. And in like manner also the blessed Paul says, "For what the law could not do, in that it was weak, God, sending His own Son in the likeness of sinful flesh, condemned sin in the flesh, that the righteousness of the law might be shown in us, who walk not after the flesh, but after the Spirit."[4] What Son of His own, then, did God send through the flesh but the Word,[5] whom He addressed as Son because He was to become such (or be begotten) in the future? And He takes the common name for tender affection among men in being called the Son. For neither was the Word, prior to incarnation and when by Himself,[6] yet perfect Son, although He was perfect Word, only-begotten. Nor could the flesh subsist by itself apart from the Word, because it has its subsistence[7] in the Word.[8] Thus, then, one perfect Son of God was manifested.

16. And these indeed are testimonies bearing on the incarnation of the Word ; and there are also very many others. But let us also look at the subject in hand, — namely, the question, brethren, that in reality the Father's power, which is the Word, came down from heaven, and not the Father Himself. For thus He speaks : "I came forth from the Father, and am come."[9] Now what subject is meant in this sentence, "I came forth from the Father,"[10] but just the Word? And what is it that is begotten of Him, but just the Spirit,[11] that is to say, the Word? But you will say to me, How is He begotten? In your own case you can give no explanation of the way in which you were begotten, although you see every day the cause according to man ; neither can you tell with accuracy the economy in His case.[12] For you have it not in your power to acquaint yourself with the practised and indescribable art[13] (method) of the Maker, but only to see, and understand, and believe that man is God's work. Moreover, you are asking an account of the generation of the Word, whom God the Father in His good pleasure begat as He willed. Is it not enough for you to learn that God made the world, but do you also venture to ask whence He made it? Is it not enough for you to learn that the Son of God has been manifested to you for salvation if you believe, but do you also inquire curiously how He was begotten after the Spirit? No more than two,[14] in sooth, have been put in trust to give the account of His generation after the flesh ; and are you then so bold as to seek the account (of His generation) after the Spirit, which the Father keeps with Himself, intending to reveal it then to the holy ones and those worthy of seeing His face? Rest satisfied with the word spoken by Christ, viz., "That which is born of the Spirit is spirit,"[15] just as, speaking by the prophet of the generation of the Word, He shows the fact that He is begotten, but reserves the question of the manner and means, to reveal it only in the time determined by Himself. For He speaks thus : "From the womb, before the morning star, I have begotten Thee."[16]

---

[1] ἀλλ᾽ ἄλλως ἀλληγορεῖ. The words in Italics are given only in the Latin. They may have dropped from the Greek text. At any rate, some such addition seems necessary for the sense.
[2] Apoc. xix. 11-13.
[3] Mic. ii. 7, 8. δόξαν: In the present text of the Septuagint it is δοράν, skin.
[4] Hippolytus omits the words διὰ τῆς σαρκός and καὶ περὶ ἁμαρτίας, and reads φανερωθῇ for πληρωθῇ.
[5] ὃν Υἱὸν προσηγόρευε διὰ τὸ μέλλειν αὐτὸν γενέσθαι.
[6] Hippolytus thus gives more definite expression to this temporality of the Sonship, as Dorner remarks, than even Tertullian. See Dorner's *Doctrine of the Person of Christ* (T. & T. Clark), div. i. vol. ii. p. 88, etc. [Pearson *On the Creed*, art. ii. p. 199 et seqq. The patristic citations are sufficient, and Hippolytus may be harmonized with them.]
[7] τὴν σύστασιν.
[8] "Σύστασις," says Dorner, "be it observed, is not yet equivalent to personality. The sense is, it had its subsistence in the Logos; He was the connective and vehicular force. This is thoroughly unobjectionable. He does not thus necessarily pronounce the humanity of Christ impersonal; although in view of what has preceded, and what remains to be adduced, there can be no doubt [?] that Hippol-

ytus would have defended the impersonality, had the question been agitated at the period at which he lived." See Dorner, as above, i. 95. [But compare Burton, *Testimonies of the Ante-Nicene Fathers*, etc., pp. 60-87, where Tertullian and Hippolytus speak for themselves. Note also what he says of the latter, and his variations of expression, p. 87.]
[9] John xvi. 28.
[10] Reading ἐξῆλθον. The Latin interpreter seems to read ἐξελθόν = what is this that came forth.
[11] πνεῦμα. The divine in Christ is thus designated in the Ante-Nicene Fathers generally. See Grotius on Mark ii. 8; and for a full history of the term in this use, Dorner's *Person of Christ*, i. p. 390, etc. (Clark).
[12] τὴν περὶ τοῦτον οἰκονομίαν.
[13] τὴν τοῦ δημιουργήσαντος ἔμπειρον καὶ ἀνεκδιήγητου τέχνην.
[14] i.e., Matthew and Luke in their Gospels.
[15] John iii. 6.
[16] Ps. cx. 3.

17. These testimonies are sufficient for the believing who study truth, and the unbelieving credit no testimony.[1] For the Holy Spirit, indeed, in the person of the apostles, has testified to this, saying, " And who has believed our report? "[2] Therefore let us not prove ourselves unbelieving, lest the word spoken be fulfilled in us. Let us believe then, dear[3] brethren, according to the tradition of the apostles, that God the Word came down from heaven, (and entered) into the holy Virgin Mary, in order that, taking the flesh from her, and assuming also a human, by which I mean a rational soul, and becoming thus all that man is with the exception of sin, He might save fallen man, and confer immortality on men who believe on His name. In all, therefore, the word of truth is demonstrated to us, to wit, that the Father is One, whose word is present (with Him), by whom He made all things; whom also, as we have said above, the Father sent forth in later times for the salvation of men. This (Word) was preached by the law and the prophets as destined to come into the world. And even as He was preached then, in the same manner also did He come and manifest Himself, being by the Virgin and the Holy Spirit made a new man; for in that He had the heavenly (nature) of the Father, as the Word and the earthly (nature), as taking to Himself the flesh from the old Adam by the medium of the Virgin, He now, coming forth into the world, was manifested as God in a body, coming forth too as a perfect man. For it was not in mere appearance or by conversion,[4] but in truth, that He became man.

18. [5] Thus then, too, though demonstrated as God, He does not refuse the conditions proper to Him as man,[6] since He hungers and toils and thirsts in weariness, and flees in fear, and prays in trouble. And He who as God has a sleepless nature, slumbers on a pillow. And He who for this end came into the world, begs off from the cup of suffering. And in an agony He sweats blood, and is strengthened by an angel, who Himself strengthens those who believe on Him, and taught men to despise death by His work.[7] And He who knew what manner of man Judas was, is betrayed by Judas. And He, who formerly was honoured by him as God, is con-

temned by Caiaphas.[8] And He is set at nought by Herod, who is Himself to judge the whole earth. And He is scourged by Pilate, who took upon Himself our infirmities. And by the soldiers He is mocked, at whose behest stand thousands of thousands and myriads of myriads of angels and archangels. And He who fixed the heavens like a vault is fastened to the cross by the Jews. And He who is inseparable from the Father cries to the Father, and commends to Him His spirit; and bowing His head, He gives up the ghost, who said, " I have power to lay down my life, and I have power to take it again; "[9] and because He was not overmastered by death, as being Himself Life, He said this: " I lay it down of myself."[9] And He who gives life bountifully to all, has His side pierced with a spear. And He who raises the dead is wrapped in linen and laid in a sepulchre, and on the third day He is raised again by the Father, though Himself the Resurrection and the Life. For all these things has He finished for us, who for our sakes was made as we are. For " Himself hath borne our infirmities, and carried our diseases; and for our sakes He was afflicted,"[10] as Isaiah the prophet has said. This is He who was hymned by the angels, and seen by the shepherds, and waited for by Simeon, and witnessed to by Anna. This is He who was inquired after by the wise men, and indicated by the star; He who was engaged in His Father's house, and pointed to by John, and witnessed to by the Father from above in the voice, " This is my beloved Son; hear ye Him."[11] He is crowned victor against the devil.[12] This is Jesus of Nazareth, who was invited to the marriage-feast in Cana, and turned the water into wine, and rebuked the sea when agitated by the violence of the winds, and walked on the deep as on dry land, and caused the blind man from birth to see, and raised Lazarus to life after he had been dead four days, and did many mighty works, and forgave sins, and conferred power on the disciples, and had blood and water flowing from His sacred side when pierced with the spear. For His sake the sun is darkened, the day has no light, the rocks are shattered, the veil is rent, the foundations of the earth are shaken, the graves are opened, and the dead are raised, and the rulers are ashamed when they see the Director of the universe upon the cross closing His eye and giving up the ghost. Creation saw, and was troubled; and, unable to bear the sight of His exceeding glory, shrouded itself in dark-

---

[1] [A noble aphorism. See Shedd, *Hist. of Theol.*, i. pp. 300, 301, and tribute to Pearson, p. 319, note. The loving spirit of Auberlen, on the defeat of rationalism, may be noted with profit in his *Divine Revelations*, translation, Clark's ed., 1867.]

[2] Isa. liii. 1.

[3] μακάριοι.

[4] κατὰ φαντασίαν ἢ τροπήν.

[5] [The sublimity of this concluding chapter marks our author's place among the most eloquent of Ante-Nicene Fathers.]

[6] The following passage agrees almost word for word with what is cited as from the *Memoria hæresium* of Hippolytus by Gelasius, in the *De duabus naturis Christi*, vol. viii. *Bibl. Patr.*, edit. Lugd. p. 704. [Compare St. Ignatius, vol. i. cap. vii. p. 52, this series; and for the crucial point (γεννητὸς καὶ ἀγέννητος) see Jacobson, ii. p. 278.]

[7] Or, by deed, ἔργῳ.

[8] ἱερατευόμενος, referring to John xi. 51, 52.

[9] John x. 18.

[10] Isa. liii. 4.

[11] Matt. xvii. 5. [It may be convenient for some to turn to the Oxford translation of Bishop Bull's *Defensio*, part i. pp. 193-216, where Tertullian and Hippolytus are nobly vindicated on Nicene grounds. The notes are also valuable.]

[12] Matt. xxvii. 29. στεφανοῦται κατὰ διαβόλου, [i.e., with thorns].

ness.[1] This (is He who) breathes upon the disciples, and gives them the Spirit, and comes in among them when the doors are shut, and is taken up by a cloud into the heavens while the disciples gaze at Him, and is set down on the right hand of the Father, and comes again as the Judge of the living and the dead. This is the God who for our sakes became man, to whom also the Father hath put all things in subjection. To Him be the glory and the power, with the Father and the Holy Spirit, in the holy Church both now and ever, and even for evermore. Amen.

---

[1] [Hippolytus confirms Tertullian's testimony. Compare vol. iii. pp. 35 and 58.]

AGAINST BERON AND HELIX.

FRAGMENTS OF A DISCOURSE, ALPHABETICALLY DIVIDED,[1] ON THE DIVINE NATURE[2] AND THE INCARNATION, AGAINST THE HERETICS BERON AND HELIX,[3] THE BEGINNING OF WHICH WAS IN THESE WORDS, "HOLY, HOLY, HOLY, LORD GOD OF SABAOTH, WITH VOICE NEVER SILENT THE SERAPHIM EXCLAIM AND GLORIFY GOD."

FRAGMENT I.

By the omnipotent will of God all things are made, and the things that are made are also preserved, being maintained according to their several principles in perfect harmony by Him who is in His nature the omnipotent God and maker of all things,[4] His divine will remaining unalterable by which He has made and moves all things, sustained as they severally are by their own natural laws.[5] For the infinite cannot in any manner or by any account be susceptible of movement, inasmuch as it has nothing towards which and nothing around which it shall be moved. For in the case of that which is in its nature infinite, and so incapable of being moved, movement would be conversion.[6] Wherefore also the Word of God being made truly man in our manner, yet without sin, and acting and enduring in man's way such sinless things as are proper to our nature, and assuming the circumscription of the flesh of our nature on our behalf, sustained no conversion in that aspect in which He is one with the Father, being made in no respect one with the flesh through the exinanition.[7] But as He was without flesh,[8] He remained without any circumscription. And through the flesh He wrought divinely[9] those things which are proper to divinity, showing Himself to have both those natures in both of which He wrought, I mean the divine and the human, according to that veritable and real and natural subsistence,[10] (showing Himself thus) as both being in reality and as being understood to be at one and the same time infinite God and finite man, having the nature[11] of each in perfection, with the same activity,[12] that is to say, the same natural properties;[13] whence we know that their distinction abides always according to the nature of each, and without conversion. But it is not (i.e., the distinction between deity and humanity), as some say, a merely comparative (or relative) matter,[14] that we may not speak in an unwarrantable manner of a greater and a less in one who is ever the same in Himself.[15] For comparisons can be instituted only between objects of like nature, and not between objects of unlike nature. But between God the Maker of all things and that which is made, between the infinite and the finite, between infinitude and finitude, there can be no kind of comparison, since these differ from each other not in mere comparison (or relatively), but absolutely in essence. And yet at the same time there has been effected a certain inexpressible and irrefragable union of the two into one substance,[16] which entirely passes the understanding of anything that is made.

---

[1] κατὰ στοιχεῖον. The Latin title in the version of Anastasius renders it "ex sermone qui est per elementum."

[2] περὶ θεολογίας.

[3] For Ἡλικος the Codex Regius et Colbertinus of Nicephorus prefers Ἡλικίωνος. Fabricius conjectures that we should read ἡλικιωτῶ αἱρετικῶν, so that the title would be, Against Beron and his fellow-heretics. [N.B. Beron = Vero.]

[4] αὐτῷ τῷ . . . Θεῷ.

[5] τοῖς ἔκαστα φυσικοῖς διεξαγόμενα νόμοις. Anastasius makes it naturalibus producta legibus; Capperonnier, suis quæque legibus temperata vel ordinata.

[6] τροπὴ γὰρ τοῦ κατὰ φύσιν ἀπείρου, κινεῖσθαι μὴ πεφυκότος, ἡ κίνησις; or may the sense be, "for a change in that which is in its nature infinite would just be the moving of that which is incapable of movement?"

[7] μηδ᾽ ἐνὶ παντελῶς ὁ ταυτόν ἐστι τῷ Πατρὶ γενόμενος ταυτὸν τῇ σαρκὶ διὰ τὴν κένωσιν. Thus in effect Combefisius, correcting the Latin version of Anastasius. Baunius adopts the reading in the Greek Codex Nicephori, viz., ἕνωσιν for κένωσιν, and renders it, "In nothing was the Word, who is the same with the Father, made the same with the flesh through the union:" nulla re Verbum quod idem est cum Patre factum est idem cum carne propter unionem.

[8] δίχα σαρκὸς, i.e., what He was before assuming the flesh, that He continued to be in Himself, viz., independent of limitation.

[9] θεϊκῶς.

[10] Or existence, ὕπαρξιν. Anastasius makes it substantia.

[11] οὐσίαν.

[12] ἐνεργείας.

[13] φυσικῆς ἰδιότητος.

[14] κατὰ σύγκρισιν. Migne follows Capperonnier in taking σύγκρισις in this passage to mean not "comparison" or "relation," but "commixture," the "concretion and commixture" of the divine and human, which was the error of Apollinaris and Eutyches in their doctrine of the incarnation, and which had been already refuted by Tertullian, Contra Praxeam, c. xxvii.

[15] Or, "for that would be to speak of the same being as greater and less than Himself."

[16] ὑπόστασιν.

For the divine is just the same after the incarnation that it was before the incarnation; in its essence infinite, illimitable, impassible, incomparable, unchangeable, inconvertible, self-potent,[1] and, in short, subsisting in essence alone the infinitely worthy good.

FRAGMENT II.

The God of all things therefore became truly, according to the Scriptures, without conversion, sinless man, and that in a manner known to Himself alone, as He is the natural Artificer of things which are above our comprehension. And by that same saving act of the incarnation[2] He introduced into the flesh the activity of His proper divinity, yet without having it (that activity) either circumscribed by the flesh through the exinanition, or growing naturally out of the flesh as it grew out of His divinity,[3] but manifested through it in the things which He wrought in a divine manner in His incarnate state. For the flesh did not become divinity in nature by a transmutation of nature, as though it became essentially flesh of divinity. But what it was before, that also it continued to be in nature and activity when united with divinity, even as the Saviour said, "The spirit indeed is willing, but the flesh is weak."[4] And working and enduring in the flesh things which were proper to sinless flesh, He proved the evacuation of divinity (to be) for our sakes, confirmed as it was by wonders and by sufferings of the flesh naturally. For with this purpose did the God of all things become man, viz., in order that by suffering in the flesh, which is susceptible of suffering, He might redeem our whole race, which was sold to death; and that by working wondrous things by His divinity, which is unsusceptible of suffering, through the medium of the flesh He might restore it to that incorruptible and blessed life from which it fell away by yielding to the devil; and that He might establish the holy orders of intelligent existences in the heavens in immutability by the mystery of His incarnation,[5] the doing of which is the recapitulation of all things in himself.[6] He remained therefore, also, after His incarnation, according to nature, God infinite, and more,[7] having the activity proper and suitable to Himself, — an activity growing out of His divinity essentially, and manifested through His perfectly holy flesh by wondrous acts economically, to the intent that He might be believed in as God, while working out of Himself[8] by the flesh, which by nature is weak, the salvation of the universe.

FRAGMENT III.

Now, with the view of explaining, by means of an illustration, what has been said concerning the Saviour, (I may say that) the power of thought[9] which I have by nature is proper and suitable to me, as being possessed of a rational and intelligent soul; and to this soul there pertains, according to nature, a self-moved energy and first power, ever-moving, to wit, the thought that streams from it naturally. This thought I utter, when there is occasion, by fitting it to words, and expressing it rightly in signs, using the tongue as an organ, or artificial characters, showing that it is heard, though it comes into actuality by means of objects foreign to itself, and yet is not changed itself by those foreign objects.[10] For my natural thought does not belong to the tongue or the letters, although I effect its utterance by means of these; but it belongs to me, who speak according to my nature, and by means of both these express it as my own, streaming as it does always from my intelligent soul according to its nature, and uttered by means of my bodily tongue organically, as I have said, when there is occasion. Now, to institute a comparison with that which is utterly beyond comparison, just as in us the power of thought that belongs by nature to the soul is brought to utterance by means of our bodily tongue without any change in itself, so, too, in the wondrous incarnation[11] of God is the omnipotent and all-creating energy of the entire deity[12] manifested without mutation in itself, by means of His perfectly holy flesh, and in the works which He wrought after a divine manner, (that energy of the deity) remaining in its essence free from all circumscription, although it shone through the flesh, which is itself essentially limited. For that which is in its nature unoriginated cannot be circumscribed by an originated nature, although this latter may have grown into one with it[13] by a conception which circumscribes all understanding:[14] nor can this be ever brought into the same nature and natural activity with that, so long as they remain each within its own proper and inconvertible nature.[15] For it is only in objects of the same nature that there is the motion that works the same works,

---

[1] αὐτοσθενές.
[2] σωτήριον σάρκωσιν.
[3] οὐδ᾽ ὥσπερ τῆς αὐτοῦ θεότητος οὕτω καὶ αὐτῆς φυσικῶς ἐκφυομένην.
[4] Matt. xxvi. 41.
[5] σωματώσεως.
[6] Referring probably to Eph. i. 10.
[7] ὑπεράπειρος.
[8] αὐτουργῶν.
[9] λόγος.
[10] The text is, διὰ τῶν ἀνομοίων μὲν ὑπάρχοντα. Anastasius reads μὴ for μέν.
[11] σωματώσεως.
[12] τῆς ὅλης θεότητος.
[13] συνέφυ.
[14] Κατὰ σύλληψιν πάντα περιγράφουσαν νοῦν.
[15] οὔτε μὴν εἰς τ᾽ αὐτὸν αὐτῷ φέρεσθαι φύσεώς ποτε καὶ φυσικῆς ἐνεργείας, ἕως ἂν ἑκάτερον τῆς ἰδίας ἐντὸς μένει φυσικῆς ἀτρεψίας. Τὸ φέρεσθαι we supply again πέφυκε.

showing that the being [1] whose power is natural is incapable in any manner of being or becoming the possession of a being of a different nature without mutation.[2]

FRAGMENT IV.

For, in the view of apostles and prophets and teachers, the mystery of the divine incarnation has been distinguished as having two points of contemplation natural to it,[3] distinct in all things, inasmuch as on the one hand it is the subsistence of perfect deity, and on the other is demonstrative of full humanity. As long, therefore,[4] as the Word is acknowledged to be in substance one, of one energy, there shall never in any way be known a movement [5] in the two. For while God, who is essentially ever-existent, became by His infinite power, according to His will, sinless man, He is what He was, in all wherein God is known; and what He became, He is in all wherein man is known and can be recognised. In both aspects of Himself He never falls out of Himself,[6] in His divine activities and in His human alike, preserving in both relations His own essentially unchangeable perfection.

FRAGMENT V.

For lately a certain person, Beron, along with some others, forsook the delusion of Valentinus, only to involve themselves in deeper error, affirming that the flesh assumed to Himself by the Word became capable of working like works with the deity [7] by virtue of its assumption, and that the deity became susceptible of suffering in the same way with the flesh [8] by virtue of the exinanition; [9] and thus they assert the doctrine that there was at the same time a conversion and a mixing and a fusing [10] of the two aspects one with the other. For if the flesh that was assumed became capable of working like works with the deity, it is evident that it also became God in essence in all wherein God is essentially known. And if the deity by the exinanition became susceptible of the same sufferings with the flesh, it is evident that it also became in essence flesh in all wherein flesh essentially can be known.

For objects that act in like manner,[11] and work like works, and are altogether of like kind, and are susceptible of like suffering with each other, admit of no difference of nature; and if the natures are fused together,[12] Christ will be a duality; [13] and if the persons [14] are separated, there will be a quaternity,[15] — a thing which is altogether to be avoided. And how will they conceive of the one and the same Christ, who is at once God and man by nature? And what manner of existence will He have according to them, if He has become man by a conversion of the deity, and if he has become God by a change of the flesh? For the mutation [16] of these, the one into the other, is a complete subversion of both. Let the discussion, then, be considered by us again in a different way.

FRAGMENT VI.

Among Christians it is settled as the doctrine of piety, that, according to nature itself, and to the activity and to whatever else pertains thereunto, God is equal and the same with Himself,[17] having nothing that is His unequal to Himself at all and heterogeneous.[18] If, then, according to Beron, the flesh that He assumed to Himself became possessed of the like natural energy with them, it is evident that it also became possessed of the like nature with Him in all wherein that nature consists, — to wit, non-origination, non-generation, infinitude, eternity, incomprehensibility, and whatever else in the way of the transcendent the theological mind discerns in deity; and thus they both underwent conversion, neither the one nor the other preserving any more the substantial relation of its own proper nature.[19] For he who recognises an identical operation [20] in things of unlike nature, introduces at the same time a fusion of natures and a separation of persons,[21] their natural existence [22] being made entirely undistinguishable by the transference of properties.[23]

FRAGMENT VII.

But if it (the flesh) did not become of like nature with that (the deity), neither shall it ever become of like natural energy with that; that He may not be shown to have His energy unequal with His nature, and heterogeneous, and, through all that pertains to Himself, to have

---

[1] οὐσίαν.
[2] The sense is extremely doubtful here. The text runs thus: ὁμοφυῶν γὰρ μόνων ἡ ταυτουργός ἐστι κίνησις σημαίνουσα τὴν οὐσίαν, ἧς φυσικὴ καθέστηκε δύναμις, ἑτεροφυοῦς ἰδιότητος οὐσίας εἶναι κατ᾽ οὐδένα λόγον, ἢ γενέσθαι δίχα τροπῆς δυναμένην. Anastasius renders it: Connaturalium enim tantum per se operans est motus, manifestans substantiam, cujus naturalem constat esse virtutem: diversæ naturæ proprietatis substantia nulla naturæ esse vel fieri sine convertibilitate valente.
[3] διττὴν καὶ διαφορὰν ἔχον διέγνωσται τὴν ἐν πᾶσι φυσικὴν θεωρίαν.
[4] The text goes, ἕως ἂν οὐχ, which is adopted by Combefisius. But Capperonnier and Migne read οὖν for οὐχ, as we have rendered it.
[5] Change, κίνησις.
[6] μένει ἀνέκπτωτος.
[7] γενέσθαι ταυτουργὸν τῇ θεότητι.
[8] ταυτοπαθῇ τῇ σαρκί.
[9] κένωσιν.
[10] σύγχυσιν.

[11] ὁμοεργῆ.
[12] συγκεχυμένων. [Vol. iii. p. 623].
[13] δυάς.
[14] προσώπων.
[15] τετράς, i.e., instead of Trinity [the Τριὰς].
[16] μετάπτωσις. [Compare the Athanasian Confession].
[17] ἴσον ἑαυτῷ καὶ ταυτόν.
[18] ἀκατάλληλον.
[19] τῆς ἰδίας φύσεως οὐσιώδη λόγον.
[20] ταυτουργίαν.
[21] διαίρεσιν προσωπικήν.
[22] ὑπάρξεως.
[23] ἰδιωμάτων.

entered on an existence outside of His natural equality and identity,[1] which is an impious supposition.

FRAGMENT VIII.

Into this error, then, have they been carried, by believing, unhappily, that that divine energy was made the property of the flesh which was only manifested through the flesh in His miraculous actions; by which energy Christ, in so far as He is apprehended as God, gave existence to the universe, and now maintains and governs it. For they did not perceive that it is impossible for the energy of the divine nature to become the property[2] of a being of a different nature[3] apart from conversion; nor did they understand that that is not by any means the property of the flesh which is only manifested through it, and does not spring out of it according to nature; and yet the proof thereof was clear and evident to them. For I, by speaking with the tongue and writing with the hand, reveal through both these one and the same thought of my intelligent soul, its energy (or operation) being natural; in no way showing it as springing naturally out of tongue or hand; nor yet (showing) even the spoken thought as made to belong to them in virtue of its revelation by their means. For no intelligent person ever recognised tongue or hand as capable of thought, just as also no one ever recognised the perfectly holy flesh of God, in virtue of its assumption, and in virtue of the revelation of the divine energy through its medium, as becoming in nature creative.[4] But the pious confession of the believer is that, with a view to our salvation, and in order to connect

the universe with unchangeableness, the Creator of all things incorporated with Himself[5] a rational soul and a sensible[6] body from the all-holy Mary, ever-virgin, by an undefiled conception, without conversion, and was made man in nature, but separate from wickedness: the same was perfect God, and the same was perfect man; the same was in nature at once perfect God and man. In His deity He wrought divine things through His all-holy flesh, — such things, namely, as did not pertain to the flesh by nature; and in His humanity He suffered human things, — such things, namely, as did not pertain to deity by nature, by the upbearing of the deity.[7] He wrought nothing divine without the body;[8] nor did the same do anything human without the participation of deity.[9] Thus He preserved for Himself a new and fitting method[10] by which He wrought (according to the manner of) both, while that which was natural to both remained unchanged;[11] to the accrediting[12] of His perfect incarnation,[13] which is really genuine, and has nothing lacking in it.[14] Beron, therefore, since the case stands with him as I have already stated, confounding together in nature the deity and the humanity of Christ in a single energy,[15] and again separating them in person, subverts the life, not knowing that identical operation[16] is indicative of the connatural identity only of connatural persons.[17]

---

[1] φυσικῆς ἔξω γεγονὼς ἰσότητος καὶ ταυτότητος.
[2] ἰδίωμα.
[3] ἑτεροφανοῦς οὐσίας.
[4] δημιουργόν.

[5] ἐνουσιώσας.
[6] Or sensitive, αἰσθητικοῦ.
[7] ἀνοχῇ πάσχων θεότητος.
[8] γυμνὸν σώματος.
[9] ἄμοιρον δράσας θεότητος.
[10] καινοπρεπῆ τρόπον.
[11] τὸ κατ' ἄμφω φυσικῶς ἀναλλοίωτον.
[12] εἰς πίστωσιν.
[13] ἐνανθρωπήσεως. [See Athanasian Creed, in Dutch Hymnal.]
[14] μηδὲν ἐχούσης φαυλότητος.
[15] ἐνεργείας μονάδι.
[16] ταυτουργίαν.
[17] μόνης τῆς τῶν ὁμοφυῶν προσώπων ὁμοφυοῦς ταυτότητος.

THE DISCOURSE ON THE HOLY THEOPHANY.

1. Good, yea, very good, are all the works of our God and Saviour — all of them that eye seeth and mind perceiveth, all that reason interprets and hand handles, all that intellect comprehends and human nature understands. For what richer beauty can there be than that of the circle[1] of heaven? And what form of more blooming fairness than that of earth's surface? And what is there swifter in the course than the chariot of the sun? And what more graceful car than the lunar orb?[2] And what work more

wonderful than the compact mosaic of the stars?[3] And what more productive of supplies than the seasonable winds? And what more spotless mirror than the light of day? And what creature more excellent than man? Very good, then, are all the works of our God and Saviour. And what more requisite gift, again, is there than the element[4] of water? For with water all things are washed and nourished, and cleansed and bedewed. Water bears the earth, water produces the dew, water exhilarates the vine; water ma-

---

[1] δίσκου.
[2] σεληνιακοῦ στοιχείου.

[3] πολυπηγήτου τῶν ἄστρων μουσίου.
[4] φύσεως.

tures the corn in the ear, water ripens the grape-cluster, water softens the olive, water sweetens the palm-date, water reddens the rose and decks the violet, water makes the lily bloom with its brilliant cups. And why should I speak at length? Without the element of water, none of the present order of things can subsist. So necessary is the element of water; for the other elements [1] took their places beneath the highest vault of the heavens, but the nature of water obtained a seat also above the heavens. And to this the prophet himself is a witness, when he exclaims, " Praise the Lord, ye heavens of heavens, and the water that is above the heavens." [2]

2. Nor is this the only thing that proves the dignity [3] of the water. But there is also that which is more honourable than all — the fact that Christ, the Maker of all, came down as the rain, [4] and was known as a spring, [5] and diffused Himself as a river, [6] and was baptized in the Jordan. [7] For you have just heard how Jesus came to John, and was baptized by him in the Jordan. Oh things strange beyond compare! How should the boundless River [8] that makes glad the city of God have been dipped in a little water! The illimitable Spring that bears life to all men, and has no end, was covered by poor and temporary waters! He who is present everywhere, and absent nowhere — who is incomprehensible to angels and invisible to men — comes to the baptism according to His own good pleasure. When you hear these things, beloved, take them not as if spoken literally, but accept them as presented in a figure. [9] Whence also the Lord was not unnoticed by the watery element in what He did in secret, in the kindness of His condescension to man. " For the waters saw Him, and were afraid." [10] They wellnigh broke from their place, and burst away from their boundary. Hence the prophet, having this in his view many generations ago, puts the question, " What aileth thee, O sea, that thou fleddest; and thou, Jordan, that thou wast driven back?" [11] And they in reply said, We have seen the Creator of all things in the " form of a servant," [12] and being ignorant of the mystery of the economy, we were lashed with fear.

3. But we, who know the economy, adore His mercy, because He hath come to save and not to judge the world. Wherefore John, the forerunner of the Lord, who before knew not this mystery, on learning that He is Lord in truth, cried out, and spake to those who came to be baptized of him, " O generation of vipers," [13] why look ye so earnestly at me? " I am not the Christ;" [14] I am the servant, and not the lord; I am the subject, and not the king; I am the sheep, and not the shepherd; I am a man, and not God. By my birth I loosed the barrenness of my mother; I did not make virginity barren. [15] I was brought up from beneath; I did not come down from above. I bound the tongue of my father; [16] I did not unfold divine grace. I was known by my mother, and I was not announced by a star. [17] I am worthless, and the least; but " after me there comes One who is before me " [18] — after me, indeed, in time, but before me by reason of the inaccessible and unutterable light of divinity. "There comes One mightier than I, whose shoes I am not worthy to bear: He shall baptize you with the Holy Ghost, and with fire." [19] I am subject to authority, but He has authority in Himself. I am bound by sins, but He is the Remover of sins. I apply [20] the law, but He bringeth grace to light. I teach as a slave, but He judgeth as the Master. I have the earth as my couch, but He possesses heaven. I baptize with the baptism of repentance, but He confers the gift of adoption: " He shall baptize you with the Holy Ghost, and with fire." Why give ye attention to me? I am not the Christ.

4. As John says these things to the multitude, and as the people watch in eager expectation of seeing some strange spectacle with their bodily eyes, and the devil [21] is struck with amazement at such a testimony from John, lo, the Lord appears, plain, solitary, uncovered, [22] without escort, [23] having on Him the body of man like a garment, and hiding the dignity of the Divinity, that He may elude the snares of the dragon. And not only did He approach John as Lord without royal retinue; but even like a mere man, and one involved in sin, He bent His head to be baptized by John. Wherefore John, on seeing so great a humbling of Himself, was struck with astonishment at the affair, and began to prevent Him, saying, as ye have just heard, " I have need to be baptized of Thee, and comest Thou

---

[1] στοιχεῖα.
[2] Ps. cxlviii. 4. [Pindar (Ἄριστον μὲν ὕδωρ, Olymp., i. 1), is here expounded and then transcended.]
[3] ἀξιοπιστίαν.
[4] Hos. vi. 3.
[5] John iv. 14.
[6] John vii. 38.
[7] Matt. iii. 13.
[8] Ps. xlvi. 4.
[9] Economically.
[10] Ps. lxxvii. 16.
[11] Ps. cxiv. 5.
[12] Phil. ii. 7.

[13] Matt. iii. 7.
[14] John i. 20.
[15] οὐ παρθενίαν ἐστείρωσα. So Gregory Thaumaturgus, Sancta Theophania, p. 106, edit. Vossii: " Thou, when born of the Virgin Mary, . . . didst not loose her virginity; but didst preserve it, and gifted her with the name of mother."
[16] Luke i. 20.
[17] Matt. ii. 9.
[18] John i. 27.
[19] Matt. iii. 11.
[20] παράπτω.
[21] It was a common opinion among the ancient theologians that the devil was ignorant of the mystery of the economy, founding on such passages as Matt. iv. 3, 1 Cor. ii. 8. (Fabricius.) [See Ignatius, vol. i. p. 57, this series.]
[22] γυμνός.
[23] ἀπροστάτευτος.

to me?"[1] What doest Thou, O Lord? Thou teachest things not according to rule.[2] I have preached one thing (regarding Thee), and Thou performest another; the devil has heard one thing, and perceives another. Baptize me with the fire of Divinity; why waitest Thou for water? Enlighten me with the Spirit; why dost Thou attend upon a creature? Baptize me, the Baptist, that Thy pre-eminence may be known. I, O Lord, baptize with the baptism of repentance, and I cannot baptize those who come to me unless they first confess fully their sins. Be it so then that I baptize Thee, what hast Thou to confess? Thou art the Remover of sins, and wilt Thou be baptized with the baptism of repentance? Though I should venture to baptize Thee, the Jordan dares not to come near Thee. "I have need to be baptized of Thee, and comest Thou to me?"

5. And what saith the Lord to him? "Suffer it to be so now, for thus it becometh us to fulfil all righteousness."[3] "Suffer it to be so now," John; thou art not wiser than I. Thou seest as man; I foreknow as God. It becomes me to do this first, and thus to teach. I engage in nothing unbecoming, for I am invested with honour. Dost thou marvel, O John, that I am not come in my dignity? The purple robe of kings suits not one in private station, but military splendour suits a king: am I come to a prince, and not to a friend? "Suffer it to be so now, for thus it becometh us to fulfil all righteousness:" I am the Fulfiller of the law; I seek to leave nothing wanting to its whole fulfilment, that so after me Paul may exclaim, "Christ is the fulfilling of the law for righteousness to every one that believeth."[4] "Suffer it to be so now, for thus it becometh us to fulfil all righteousness." Baptize me, John, in order that no one may despise baptism. I am baptized by thee, the servant, that no one among kings or dignitaries may scorn to be baptized by the hand of a poor priest. Suffer me to go down into the Jordan, in order that they may hear my Father's testimony, and recognise the power of the Son. "Suffer it to be so now, for thus it becometh us to fulfil all righteousness." Then at length John suffers Him. "And Jesus, when He was baptized, went up straightway out of the water: and the heavens were opened unto Him; and, lo, the Spirit of God descended like a dove, and rested upon Him. And a voice (came) from heaven, saying, This is my beloved Son, in whom I am well pleased."[5]

6. Do you see, beloved, how many and how great blessings we would have lost, if the Lord had yielded to the exhortation of John, and declined baptism? For the heavens were shut before this; the region above was inaccessible. We would in that case descend to the lower parts, but we would not ascend to the upper. But was it only that the Lord was baptized? He also renewed the old man, and committed to him again the sceptre of adoption. For straightway "the heavens were opened to Him." A reconciliation took place of the visible with the invisible; the celestial orders were filled with joy; the diseases of earth were healed; secret things were made known; those at enmity were restored to amity. For you have heard the word of the evangelist, saying, "The heavens were opened to Him," on account of three wonders. For when Christ the Bridegroom was baptized, it was meet that the bridal-chamber of heaven should open its brilliant gates. And in like manner also, when the Holy Spirit descended in the form of a dove, and the Father's voice spread everywhere, it was meet that "the gates of heaven should be lifted up."[6] "And, lo, the heavens were opened to Him; and a voice was heard, saying, This is my beloved Son, in whom I am well pleased."

7. The beloved generates love, and the light immaterial the light inaccessible.[7] "This is my beloved Son," He who, being manifested on earth and yet unseparated from the Father's bosom, was manifested, and yet did not appear.[8] For the appearing is a different thing, since in appearance the baptizer here is superior to the baptized. For this reason did the Father send down the Holy Spirit from heaven upon Him who was baptized. For as in the ark of Noah the love of God toward man is signified by the dove, so also now the Spirit, descending in the form of a dove, bearing as it were the fruit of the olive, rested on Him to whom the witness was borne. For what reason? That the faithfulness of the Father's voice might be made known, and that the prophetic utterance of a long time past might be ratified. And what utterance is this? "The voice of the Lord (is) on the waters, the God of glory thundered; the Lord (is) upon many waters."[9] And what voice? "This is my beloved Son, in whom I am well pleased." This is He who is named the son of Joseph, and (who is) according to the divine essence my Only-begotten. "This is my beloved Son"—He who is hungry, and yet maintains myriads; who is weary, and yet gives rest to the weary; who has not where to

---

[1] Matt. iii. 14.
[2] ἀκανόνιστα δογματίζεις.
[3] Matt. iii. 15.
[4] Rom. x. 4.
[5] Matt. iii. 16, 17.

[6] Ps. xxiv. 7.
[7] φῶς ἄϋλον γεννᾷ φῶς ἀπρόσιτον. The Son is called "Light of Light" in the Discourse against Noetus, ch. x. [See p. 227 supra.] In φῶς ἀπρόσιτον the reference is to 1 Tim. vi. 16.
[8] ἐπεφάνη οὐκ ἐφάνη. See Dorner's Doctrine of the Person of Christ, div. i. vol. ii. p. 97 (Clark).
[9] Ps. xxix. 3.

lay His head,[1] and yet bears up all things in His hand; who suffers, and yet heals sufferings; who is smitten,[2] and yet confers liberty on the world; [3] who is pierced in the side,[4] and yet repairs the side of Adam.[5]

8. But give me now your best attention, I pray you, for I wish to go back to the fountain of life, and to view the fountain that gushes with healing. The Father of immortality sent the immortal Son and Word into the world, who came to man in order to wash him with water and the Spirit; and He, begetting us again to incorruption of soul and body, breathed into us the breath (spirit) of life, and endued us with an incorruptible panoply. If, therefore, man has become immortal, he will also be God.[6] And if he is made God by water and the Holy Spirit after the regeneration of the laver[7] he is found to be also joint-heir with Christ[8] after the resurrection from the dead. Wherefore I preach to this effect: Come, all ye kindreds of the nations, to the immortality of the baptism. I bring good tidings of life to you who tarry in the darkness of ignorance. Come into liberty from slavery, into a kingdom from tyranny, into incorruption from corruption. And how, saith one, shall we come? How? By water and the Holy Ghost. This is the water in conjunction with the Spirit, by which paradise is watered, by which the earth is enriched, by which plants grow, by which animals multiply, and (to sum up the whole in a single word) by which man is begotten again and endued with life, in which also Christ was baptized, and in which the Spirit descended in the form of a dove.

9. This is the Spirit that at the beginning "moved upon the face of the waters;"[9] by whom the world moves; by whom creation consists, and all things have life; who also wrought mightily in the prophets,[10] and descended in flight upon Christ.[11] This is the Spirit that was given to the apostles in the form of fiery tongues.[12] This is the Spirit that David sought when he said, "Create in me a clean heart, O God, and renew a right spirit within me." [13] Of this Spirit Gabriel also spoke to the Virgin, "The Holy Ghost shall come upon thee, and the power of the Highest shall overshadow thee." [14] By this Spirit Peter spake that blessed word, "Thou art the Christ, the Son of the living God." [15] By this Spirit the rock of the Church was stablished.[16] This is the Spirit, the Comforter, that is sent because of thee,[17] that He may show thee to be the Son [18] of God.

10. Come then, be begotten again, O man, into the adoption of God. And how? says one. If thou practisest adultery no more, and committest not murder, and servest not idols; if thou art not overmastered by pleasure; if thou dost not suffer the feeling of pride to rule thee; if thou cleanest off the filthiness of impurity, and puttest off the burden of sin; if thou castest off the armour of the devil, and puttest on the breastplate of faith, even as Isaiah saith, "Wash you, and seek judgment, relieve the oppressed, judge the fatherless, and plead for the widow. And come and let us reason together, saith the Lord. Though your sins be as scarlet, I shall make them white as snow; and though they be like crimson, I shall make them white as wool. And if ye be willing, and hear my voice, ye shall eat the good of the land." [19] Do you see, beloved, how the prophet spake beforetime of the purifying power of baptism? For he who comes down in faith to the laver of regeneration, and renounces the devil, and joins himself to Christ; who denies the enemy, and makes the confession that Christ is God; who puts off the bondage, and puts on the adoption, — he comes up from the baptism brilliant as the sun,[20] flashing forth beams of righteousness, and, which is indeed the chief thing, he returns a son of God and joint-heir with Christ. To Him be the glory and the power, together with His most holy, and good, and quickening Spirit, now and ever, and to all the ages of the ages. Amen.

---

[1] Luke ix. 5. [Compare the *Paradoxes*, attributed to Bacon, in his Works, vol. xiv. p. 143; also the *Appendix*, pp. 139–142.]
[2] ῥαπιζόμενος, referring to the slap in the process of manumitting slaves.
[3] Heb. i. 3.
[4] Matt. xxvi. 67. [From which proceeds His Church.]
[5] That is, the sin introduced by Eve, who was formed by God out of Adam's side. (Fabricius.)
[6] ἔσται καὶ Θεός, referring probably to 2 Pet. i. 4, ἵνα διὰ τούτων γένησθε θείας κοινωνοὶ φύσεως, "that by these ye might be partakers of the divine nature." [See vol. iii. p. 317, note 11. Tertullian anticipates the language of the "Athanasian Confession," — "taking the manhood into God;" applicable, through Christ, to our redeemed humanity. Eph. ii. 6.; Rev. iii. 21.]
[7] κολυμβήθρας.
[8] Rom. viii. 17.
[9] Gen. i. 2.
[10] Acts xxviii. 25.
[11] Matt. iii. 16.

[12] Acts ii. 3.
[13] Ps. li. 10.
[14] Luke i. 35.
[15] Matt. xvi. 16.
[16] Matt. xvi. 18.
[17] John xvi. 26.
[18] τέκνον.
[19] Isa. i. 16–19.
[20] This seems to refer to what the poets sing as to the sun rising out of the waves of ocean. (Fabricius.) [Note, this is not said of such as Simon Magus, but of one who *puts off the bondage*, i.e., of corruption. Our author's *perorations* are habitually sublime.]

FRAGMENTS OF DISCOURSES OR HOMILIES.

I.[1]

From the Discourse of Hippolytus, Bishop of Rome, on the Resurrection and Incorruption.

Men, he says, " in the resurrection will be like the angels of God," [2] to wit, in incorruption, and immortality, and incapacity of loss.[3] For the incorruptible nature is not the subject of generation ; [4] it grows not, sleeps not, hungers not, thirsts not, is not wearied, suffers not, dies not, is not pierced by nails and spear, sweats not, drops not with blood. Of such kind are the natures of the angels and of souls released from the body. For both these are of another kind, and different from these creatures of our world, which are visible and perishing.

II.[5]

From the Discourse of St. Hippolytus, Bishop and Martyr, on the Divine Nature.[6]

God is capable of willing, but not of not willing,[7] for that pertains only to one that changes and makes choice ; [8] for things that are being made follow the eternal will of God, by which also things that are made abide sustained.

III.[9]

St. Hippolytus, Bishop and Martyr, in his Homily on the Paschal Supper.

He was altogether [10] in all, and everywhere ; and though He filleth the universe up to all the principalities of the air, He stripped Himself again. And for a brief space He cries that the cup might pass from Him, with a view to show truly that He was also man.[11] But remembering, too, the purpose for which He was sent, He fulfils the dispensation (economy) for which He was sent, and exclaims, " Father, not my will," [12] and, " The spirit is willing, but the flesh is weak." [13]

IV.[14]

1. Take me, O Samuel, the heifer brought to Bethlehem, in order to show the king begotten of David, and him who is anointed to be king and priest by the Father.

2. Tell me, O blessed Mary, what that was that was conceived by thee in the womb, and what that was that was born by thee in thy virgin matrix. For it was the first-born Word of God that descended to thee from heaven, and was formed as a first-born man in the womb, in order that the first-born Word of God might be shown to be united with a first-born man.

3. And in the second (form), — to wit, by the prophets, as by Samuel, calling back and delivering the people from the slavery of the aliens. And in the third (form), that in which He was incarnate, taking to Himself humanity from the Virgin, in which character also He saw the city, and wept over it.

V.[15]

And for this reason three seasons of the year prefigured the Saviour Himself, so that He should fulfil the mysteries prophesied of Him. In the Passover season, so as to exhibit Himself as one destined to be sacrificed like a sheep, and to prove Himself the true Paschal-lamb, even as the apostle says, " Even Christ," who is God, " our passover was sacrificed for us." [16] And at Pentecost so as to presignify the kingdom of heaven, as He Himself first ascended to heaven and brought man as a gift to God.[17]

VI.[18]

And an ark of imperishable wood was the Saviour Himself. For by this was signified the imperishable and incorruptible tabernacle (of His body), which engendered no corruption of sin. For the man who has sinned also has this confession to make : " My wounds stank, and were corrupt, because of my foolishness." [19] But the Lord was without sin, being of imperishable wood in respect of His humanity, — that is

---

[1] From a Discourse on the Resurrection, in Anastasius Sinaita, Hodegus, p. 350. This treatise is mentioned in the list of his works given on the statue, and also by Jerome, Sophronius, Nicephorus, Honorius, etc.

[2] Matt. xxii. 30.

[3] ἀφευσία.

[4] γεννᾶται.

[5] From the Discourse on the Theology or the Doctrine of Christ's Divine Nature, extant in the *Acts of the Lateran Council*, under Martinus I., ann. 649, secret. v. p. 287, vol. vii. edit. Veneto-Labb.

[6] περὶ θεολογίας.

[7] οὐ τὸ μὴ θέλειν.

[8] τρεπτοῦ καὶ προαιρετοῦ.

[9] From a Homily on the Lord's Paschal Supper, *ibid.*, p. 293.

[10] ὅλος.

[11] καὶ ἄνθρωπος, *also* man. See Grabe, Bull's *Defens. Fid. Nic.*, p. 103.

[12] Luke xxii. 42.

[13] Matt. xxvi. 41.

[14] From a Discourse on Elkanah and Hannah. In Theodoret, Dial. I., bearing the title " Unchangeable " (ἄτρεπτος); *Works*, vol. iv. p. 36.

[15] From the same Discourse. From Theodoret's Second Dialogue, bearing the title " Unmixed," ἀσύγχυτος; *Works*, vol. iv. p. 88.

[16] 1 Cor. v. 7.

[17] [Man's nature was never before in heaven. John iii. 13; Acts ii. 34.]

[18] From an Oration on " The Lord is my Shepherd." In Theodoret, Dial. I. p. 36.

[19] Ps. xxxviii. 5.

to say, being of the Virgin and the Holy Spirit, covered, as it were, within and without with the purest gold of the Word of God.

VII.[1]

1. He who rescued from the lowest hell the first-formed man of earth when he was lost and bound with the chains of death; He who came down from above, and raised the earthy on high;[2] He who became the evangelist of the dead, and the redeemer of the souls, and the resurrection of the buried, — He was constituted the helper of vanquished man, being made like him Himself, (so that) the first-born Word acquainted Himself with the first-formed Adam in the Virgin; He who is spiritual sought out the earthy in the womb; He who is the ever-living One sought out him who, through disobedience, is subject to death; He who is heavenly called the terrene to the things that are above; He who is the nobly-born sought, by means of His own subjection, to declare the slave free; He transformed the man into adamant who was dissolved into dust and made the food of the serpent, and declared Him who hung on the tree to be Lord over the conqueror, and thus through the tree He is found victor.

2. For they who know not now the Son of God incarnate, shall know in Him who comes as Judge in glory, Him who is now despised in the body of His humiliation.

3. And the apostles, when they came to the sepulchre on the third day, did not find the body of Jesus; just as the children of Israel went up the mount and sought for the tomb of Moses, but did not find it.

VIII.[3]

Under the figure of Egypt he described the world; and under things made with hands, idolatry; and under the earthquake, the subversion and dissolution of the earth itself. And he represented the Lord the Word as a light cloud, the purest tabernacle, enthroned on which our Lord Jesus Christ entered into this life in order to subvert error.

IX.[4]

Now Hippolytus, the martyr and bishop of [the Province of] Rome, in his second discourse on Daniel, speaks thus: —

Then indeed Azarias, standing along with the others, made their acknowledgments to God with song and prayer in the midst of the furnace. Beginning thus with His holy and glorious and honourable name, they came to the works of the Lord themselves, and named first of all those of heaven, and glorified Him, saying, "Bless the Lord, all ye works of the Lord." Then they passed to the sons of men, and taking up their hymn in order, they then named the spirits [that people Tartarus[5] beneath the earth,] and the souls of the righteous, in order that they might praise God together with them.

X.[6]

Now a person might say that these men, and those who hold a different opinion, are yet near neighbours, being involved in like error. For those men, indeed, either profess that Christ came into our life a mere man, and deny the talent of His divinity, or else, acknowledging Him to be God, they deny, on the other hand, His humanity, and teach that His appearances to those who saw Him as man were illusory, inasmuch as He did not bear with Him true manhood, but was rather a kind of phantom manifestation. Of this class are, for example, Marcion and Valentinus, and the Gnostics, who sunder the Word from the flesh, and thus set aside the one talent, viz., the incarnation.

XI.[7]

1. The body of the Lord presented both these to the world, the sacred blood and the holy water.

2. And His body, though dead after the manner of man, possesses in it great power of life. For streams which flow not from dead bodies flowed forth from Him, viz., blood and water; in order that we might know what power for life is held by the virtue that dwelt in His body, so as that it appears not to be dead like others, and is able to shed forth for us the springs of life.

3. And not a bone of the Holy Lamb is broken, this figure showing us that suffering toucheth not His strength. For the bones are the strength of the body.

---

[1] From a Discourse on the "Great Song" [i.e., Ps. xc. See Bunsen, i. p. 285. Some suppose it Ps. cxix.] In Theodoret, Dial. ll. pp. 88, 89.
[2] τὸν κάτω εἰς τὰ ἄνω. [See p. 238, note 17, *supra*.]
[3] From a Discourse on the beginning of Isaiah. In Theodoret, Dial. I. p. 36.
[4] From a second Oration on Daniel. In the tractate of Eustratius, a presbyter of the Church of Constantinople, "Against those who

allege that souls, as soon as they are released from the body, cease to act," ch. xix., as edited by Allatius in his work on the *Continuous Harmony of the Western and the Eastern Church on the Dogma of Purgatory*, p. 432. [Conf. Macaire, *Theol. Orthod.*, ii. p. 725.]
[5] [Nothing of this in the hymn: hence my brackets.]
[6] From an Oration on the Distribution of Talents. In Theodoret, Dial. II. p. 88.
[7] From a Discourse on "The two Robbers." In Theodoret's Third Dialogue, bearing the title "Impassible" (ἀπαθής), p. 156.

FRAGMENTS FROM OTHER WRITINGS OF HIPPOLYTUS.[1]

I.

Now Hippolytus, a martyr for piety, who was bishop of the place called Portus, near Rome, in his book *Against all Heresies*, wrote in these terms : —

I perceive, then, that the matter is one of contention. For he[2] speaks thus : Christ kept the supper, then, on that day, and then suffered ; whence it is needful that I, too, should keep it in the same manner as the Lord did. But he has fallen into error by not perceiving that at the time when Christ suffered He did not eat the passover of the law.[3] For He was the passover that had been of old proclaimed, and that was fulfilled on that determinate day.

II.

From the same.

And again the same (authority), in the first book of his treatise on the Holy Supper, speaks thus : —

Now that neither in the first nor in the last there was anything false is evident ; for he who said of old, " I will not any more eat the passover,"[4] probably partook of supper before the passover. But the passover He did not eat, but He suffered ; for it was not the time for Him to eat.

III.[5]

Hippolytus, Bishop and Martyr, in a letter to a certain queen.[6]

1. He calls Him, then, " the first-fruits of them that sleep,"[7] as the " first-begotten of the dead."[8] For He, having risen, and being desirous to show that that same (body) had been raised which had also died, when His disciples were in doubt, called Thomas to Him, and said, " Reach hither ; handle me, and see : for a spirit hath not bone and flesh, as ye see me have."[9]

2. In calling Him *the first-fruits*, he testified to that which we have said, viz., that the Saviour, taking to Himself the flesh out of the same lump, raised this same flesh, and made it the first-fruits of the flesh of the righteous, in order that all we who have believed in the hope of the Risen One may have the resurrection in expectation.

THE STORY OF A MAIDEN OF CORINTH, AND A CERTAIN MAGISTRIANUS.

The account given by Hippolytus, the friend of the apostles [10]

In another little book bearing the name of Hippolytus, the friend of the apostles, I found a story of the following nature : —

There lived a certain most noble and beautiful maiden[11] in the city of Corinth, in the careful exercise of a virtuous life. At that time some persons falsely charged her before the judge there, who was a Greek, with cursing the times, and the princes, and the images. Now those who trafficked in such things, brought her beauty under the notice of the impious judge, who lusted after women. And he gladly received the accusation with his equine ears and lascivious thoughts. And when she was brought before the bloodstained (judge), he was driven still more frantic with profligate passion. But when, after bringing every device to bear upon her, the profane man could not gain over this woman of God, he subjected the noble maiden to various outrages. And when he failed in these too, and was unable to seduce her from her confession of Christ, the cruel judge became furious against her, and gave her over to a punishment of the following nature : Placing the chaste maiden in a brothel, he charged the manager, saying, Take this woman, and bring me three nummi by her every day. And the man, exacting the money from her by her dishonour, gave her up to any who sought her in the brothel. And when the women-hunters knew that, they came to the brothel, and, paying the price put upon their iniquity, sought to seduce her. But this most honourable maiden, taking counsel with herself to deceive them, called them to her, and earnestly besought them, saying : I have a certain ulceration of the *pudenda*, which has an extremely hateful stench ; and I am afraid that ye might come to hate me on account of the abominable sore. Grant me therefore a few days, and then ye may have me even for nothing. With these words the blessed maiden gained over the profligates, and dismissed them for a time.[12] And with most fitting prayers she impor-

---

[1] Preserved by the author of the *Chronicon Paschale*, ex ed. Cangii, p. 6.
[2] i.e., the opponent of Hippolytus, one of the forerunners of the Quartodecimans.
[3] [For *pro & con* see *Speaker's Com.*, note to Matt. xxvi.]
[4] Luke xxii. 16.
[5] From a Letter of Hippolytus to a certain queen. In Theodoret's Dial. II., bearing the title " Unmixed " (ἀσύγχυτος). and Dial. III., entitled " Impassible " (ἀπαθής) [pp. 238-239 *supra*].
[6] On the question as to who this queen was, see Stephen le Moyne, in notes to the *Varia Sacra*, pp. 1103, 1112. In the marble monument mention is made of a letter of Hippolytus to Severina. [Bunsen decides that she was only a princess, a daughter of Alexander Severus. See his *Hippolytus*, i. p. 276.]
[7] 1 Cor. xv. 20.
[8] Col. i. 18.
[9] John xx. 27; Luke xxiv. 39.

[10] Extract in Palladius, *Historia Lausiaca*, chap. cxlviii.; Gallandi, *Biblioth.*, ii. 513.
[11] Nicephorus also mentions her in his *Hist. Eccl.*, vii. 13.
[12] [On the morality of this, see vol. ii. pp. 538, 556.]

tuned God, and with contrite supplications she sought to turn Him to compassion. God, therefore, who knew her thoughts, and understood how the chaste maiden was distressed in heart for her purity, gave ear to her; and the Guardian of the safety of all men in those days interposed with His arrangements in the following manner: —

Of a certain person Magistrianus.[1]

There was a certain young man, Magistrianus,[2] comely in his personal appearance, and of a pious mind, whom God had inspired with such a burning spiritual zeal, that he despised even death itself. He, coming under the guise of profligacy, goes in, when the evening was far gone, to the fellow who kept the women, and pays him five nummi, and says to him, Permit me to spend this night with this damsel. Entering then with her into the private apartment, he says to her, Rise, save thyself. And taking off her garments, and dressing her in his own attire,

---

[1] From the same, chap. cxlix.
[2] Nicephorus gives this story also, *Hist. Eccl.*, vii. 13.

his night-gown, his cloak, and all the habiliments of a man, he says to her, Wrap yourself up with the top of your cloak, and go out; and doing so, and signing herself entirely with the mystery of the cross, she went forth uncorrupted from that place, and was preserved perfectly stainless by the grace of Christ, and by the instrumentality of the young man, who by his own blood delivered her from dishonour. And on the following day the matter became known, and Magistrianus was brought before the infuriated judge. And when the cruel tyrant had examined the noble champion of Christ, and had learned all, he ordered him to be thrown to the wild beasts, — that in this, too, the honour-hating demon might be put to shame. For, whereas he thought to involve the noble youth in an unhallowed punishment, he exhibited him as a double martyr for Christ, inasmuch as he had both striven nobly for his own immortal soul, and persevered manfully in labours also in behalf of that noble and blessed maiden. Wherefore also he was deemed worthy of double honour with Christ, and of the illustrious and blessed crowns by His goodness.

ELUCIDATION.

THE conduct of Father Abraham, although not approved of by Inspiration, but simply recorded (Gen. xxvi. 7), gave early Christians an opinion that the wicked may be justly foiled, by equivocation and deception, for the preservation of innocence or the life of the innocent. In such case the person deceived, they might argue, is not injured, but benefited (Gen. xxvi. 10), being saved from committing violence and murder. The Corinthian maiden was accustomed to be veiled (as Tertullian intimates), and was taught alike to cherish her own purity and to have no share in affording occasion of sin to others. See vol. iv. pp. 32, 33. Let us call this narrative "The Story of Corinthia and Magistrianus."

APPENDIX TO THE WORKS OF HIPPOLYTUS.

CONTAINING DUBIOUS AND SPURIOUS PIECES.

A DISCOURSE[1] BY THE MOST BLESSED HIPPOLYTUS, BISHOP AND MARTYR, ON THE END OF THE WORLD, AND ON ANTICHRIST, AND ON THE SECOND COMING OF OUR LORD JESUS CHRIST.

I.

SINCE, then, the blessed prophets have been eyes to us, setting forth for our behoof the clear declaration of things secret, both through life, and through declaration, and through inspiration[2] of the Holy Spirit, and discoursing, too, of things not yet come to pass,[3] in this way also[4] to all generations they have pictured forth the grandest subjects for contemplation and for action. Thus, too, they preached of the advent of God[5] in the flesh to the world, His advent by the spotless and God-bearing[6] Mary in the way of birth and growth, and the manner of His life and conversation with men, and His manifestation by baptism, and the new birth that was to be to all men, and the regeneration by the laver; and the multitude of His miracles, and His blessed passion on the cross, and the insults which He bore at the hands of the Jews, and His burial, and His descent to Hades, and His ascent again, and redemption of the spirits that were of old,[7] and the destruction of death, and His life-giving awaking from the dead, and His re-creation of the whole world, and His assumption and return to heaven, and His reception of the Spirit, of which the apostles were deemed worthy, and again the second coming, that is destined to declare all things. For as being designated *seers*,[8] they of necessity signified and spake of these things beforetime.

II.

Hence, too, they indicated the day of the consummation to us, and signified beforehand the day of the apostate that is to appear and deceive men at the last times, and the beginning and end of his kingdom, and the advent of the Judge, and the life of the righteous, and the punishment of the sinners, in order that we all, bearing these things in mind day by day and hour by hour, as children of the Church, might know that "not one jot nor one tittle of these things shall fail,"[9] as the Saviour's own word announced. Let all of you, then, of necessity, open the eyes of your hearts and the ears of your soul, and receive the word which we are about to speak. For I shall unfold to you to-day a narration full of horror and fear, to wit, the account of the consummation, and in particular, of the seduction of the whole world by the enemy and devil; and after these things, the second coming of our Lord Jesus Christ.

III.

Where, then, ye friends of Christ, shall I begin? and with what shall I make my commencement, or what shall I expound? and what witness shall I adduce for the things spoken? But let us take those (viz., the prophets) with whom we began this discourse, and adduce them as credible witnesses, to confirm our exposition of the matters discussed; and after them the teaching, or rather the prophecy, of the apostles, (so as to see) how throughout the whole world they herald the day of the consummation. Since these, then, have also shown beforetime things not yet come to pass, and have declared the devices and deceits of wicked men, who are destined to be made manifest, come and let us bring forward Isaiah as our first witness, inasmuch as he instructs us in the times of the con-

---

[1] This discourse seems to have been a homily addressed to the people. Fabricius, *Works of Hippolytus*, vol. ii.
[2] ἐπιφοιτήσεως
[3] γεγονότα. Codex Baroccianus gives εὑρηκότα.
[4] ὅθεν καί, etc.
[5] Others, τοῦ υἱοῦ τοῦ Θεοῦ, of the Son of God.
[6] θεοτόκου. [The epithet applied to the Blessed Virgin by the "Council of Ephesus," against Nestorius, A.D. 431. Elucidation, p. 259.] This is one of those terms which some allege not to have been yet in use in the time of Hippolytus. But, as Migne observes, if there were no other argument than this against the genuineness of this discourse, this would not avail much, as the term is certainly used by Origen, Methodius, and Dionysius Alex., who were nearly coeval with Hippolytus.
[7] ἀπ' αἰώνων.
[8] βλέποντες.

[9] Matt. v. 18.

summation. What, then, does he say? "Your country is desolate, your cities are burned with fire : your land, strangers devour it in your presence : the daughter of Zion shall be left as a cottage in a vineyard, and as a lodge in a garden of cucumbers, as a besieged city."[1] You see, beloved, the prophet's illumination, whereby he announced that time so many generations before. For it is not of the Jews that he spake this word of old, nor of the city of Zion, but of the Church. For all the prophets have declared Sion to be the bride brought from the nations.

IV.

Wherefore let us direct our discourse to a second witness. And of what sort is this one? Listen to Osea, as he speaks thus grandly : " In those days the Lord shall bring on a burning wind from the desert against them, and shall make their veins dry, and shall make their springs desolate ; and all their goodly vessels shall be spoiled. Because they rose up against God, they shall fall by the sword, and their women with child shall be ripped up."[2] And what else is this burning wind from the east, than the Antichrist that is to destroy and dry up the veins of the waters and the fruits of the trees in his times, because men set their hearts on his works? For which reason he shall indeed destroy them, and they shall serve him in his pollution.

V.

Mark the agreement of prophet with prophet. Acquaint yourself also with another prophet who expresses himself in like manner. For Amos prophesied of the same things in a manner quite in accordance : "Thus saith the Lord, Forasmuch therefore as ye have beaten the poor with the fist,[3] and taken choice gifts from him : ye have built houses, but ye shall not dwell in them : ye have planted pleasant vineyards, but ye shall not drink wine of them. For I know your manifold transgressions, in trampling justice beneath your foot, and taking a bribe, and turning aside the poor in the gate from their right. Therefore the prudent shall keep silence in that time, for it is an evil time."[4] Learn, beloved, the wickedness of the men of that time, how they spoil houses and fields, and take even justice from the just ; for when these things come to pass, ye may know that it is the end. For this reason art thou instructed in the wisdom of the prophet, and the revelation that is to be in those days. And all the prophets, as we have already said, have clearly signified the things that are to come to pass in the last times, just as they also have declared things of old.

VI.

But not to expend our argument entirely in going over the words of all the prophets,[5] after citing one other, let us revert to the matter in hand. What is it, then, that Micah says in his prophecy? "Thus saith the Lord concerning the prophets that make my people err, that bite with their teeth, and cry to him, Peace ; and if it was not put into their mouth,[6] they prepared[7] war against him. Therefore night shall be unto you, that ye shall not have a vision ;[8] and it shall be dark unto you, that ye shall not divine ; and the sun shall not go down over the prophets, and the day shall be dark over them. And the seers shall be ashamed, and the diviners confounded."[9] These things we have recounted beforehand, in order that ye may know the pain that is to be in the last times, and the perturbation, and the manner of life on the part of all men toward each other,[10] and their envy, and hate, and strife, and the negligence of the shepherds toward the sheep, and the unruly disposition of the people toward the priests.[11]

VII.

Wherefore all shall walk after their own will. And the children will lay hands on their parents. The wife will give up her own husband to death, and the husband will bring his own wife to judgment like a criminal. Masters will lord it over their servants savagely,[12] and servants will assume an unruly demeanour toward their masters. None will reverence the grey hairs of the elderly, and none will have pity upon the comeliness of the youthful. The temples of God will be like houses, and there will be overturnings of the churches everywhere. The Scriptures will be despised, and everywhere they will sing the songs of the adversary.[13] Fornications, and adulteries, and perjuries will fill the land ; sorceries, and incantations, and divinations will follow after these with all force and zeal. And, on the whole, from among those who profess to be Christians will rise up then false prophets, false

---

[1] Isa. i. 7.
[2] Hos. xiii. 15.
[3] κατηγκονδυλίσετε in the text, for which read κατεκονδυλίσατε.
[4] Amos v. 11, 12, 13.

[5] Manuscript E gives the better reading, λόγον ἅπαντα τοῖς τῶν προφητῶν ῥήμασι, " our whole argument on the words of the prophets."
[6] εἰ οὐκ ἐδόθη. Manuscript B omits εἰ = and it was not put into their mouth.
[7] The text reads ἡγίασαν. Manuscript B reads ἥγγισαν. Migne suggests ἥγειραν.
[8] ἐξ ὁράσεως.
[9] Mic. iii. 5-7.
[10] For τὴν πρὸς ἀλλήλους ἀναστροφήν, Codex B reads διαστροφὴν καὶ φθοράν.
[11] For ἀνυπότακτον διάθεσιν, Codex B reads ἀταξίαν = unruliness, and adds, καὶ γονεῖς τὰ τέκνα μισήσουσι, καὶ τέκνα τοῖς γονεῦσιν ἐπιβάλλονται χεῖρας, " and parents shall hate their children, and children lay hands on their parents."
[12] For εἰς τοὺς δούλους ἀπάνθρωποι αὐθεντήσονται, Codex B reads, πρὸς τοὺς δούλους ἀπανθρωπίαν κτήσονται.
[13] For ἐχθροῦ, Codex B reads, διαβόλου, the devil.

apostles, impostors, mischief-makers, evil-doers, liars against each other, adulterers, fornicators, robbers, grasping, perjured, mendacious, hating each other. The shepherds will be like wolves; the priests will embrace falsehood; the monks[1] will lust after the things of the world; the rich will assume hardness of heart; the rulers will not help the poor; the powerful will cast off all pity; the judges will remove justice from the just, and, blinded with bribes, they will call in unrighteousness.

VIII.

And what am I to say with respect to men,[2] when the very elements themselves will disown their order? There will be earthquakes in every city, and plagues in every country; and monstrous[3] thunderings and frightful lightnings will burn up both houses and fields. Storms of winds will disturb both sea and land excessively; and there will be unfruitfulness on the earth, and a roaring in the sea, and an intolerable agitation on account of souls and the destruction of men.[4] There will be signs in the sun, and signs in the moon, deflections in the stars, distresses of nations, intemperateness in the atmosphere, discharges of hail upon the face of the earth, winters of excessive severity, different[5] frosts, inexorable scorching winds, unexpected thunderings, unlooked-for conflagrations; and in general, lamentation and mourning in the whole earth, without consolation. For, "because iniquity shall abound, the love of many shall wax cold."[6] By reason of the agitation and confusion of all these, the Lord of the universe cries in the Gospel, saying, "Take heed that ye be not deceived; for many shall come in my name, saying, I am Christ, and the time draweth near: go ye not therefore after them. But when ye shall hear of wars and commotions, be not terrified: for these things must first come to pass; but the end is not yet by and by."[7] Let us observe the word of the Saviour, how He always admonished us with a view to our security: "Take heed that ye be not deceived: for many shall come in my name, saying, I am Christ."

IX.

Now after He was taken up again to the Father, there arose some, saying, "I am Christ," like Simon Magus and the rest, whose names we have not time at present to mention. Where-

fore also in the last day of the consummation, it must needs be that false Christs will arise again, saying, "I am Christ," and they will deceive many. And multitudes of men will run from the east even to the west, and from the north even to the sea, saying, Where is Christ here? where is Christ there? But being possessed of a vain conceit, and failing to read the Scriptures carefully, and not being of an upright mind, they will seek for a name which they shall be unable to find. For these things must first be; and thus the son of perdition — that is to say, the devil — must be seen.

X.

And the apostles, who speak of God,[8] in establishing the truth of the advent of the Lord Jesus Christ, have each of them indicated the appearing of these abominable and ruin-working men, and have openly announced their lawless deeds. First of all Peter, the rock of the faith, whom Christ our God called blessed, the teacher of the Church, the first disciple, he who has the keys of the kingdom, has instructed us to this effect: "Know this first, children, that there shall come in the last days scoffers, walking after their own lusts.[9] And there shall be false teachers among you, who privily shall bring in damnable heresies."[10] After him, John the theologian,[11] and the beloved of Christ, in harmony with him, cries, "The children of the devil are manifest;[12] and even now are there many antichrists;[13] but go not after them.[14] Believe not every spirit, because many false prophets are gone out into the world."[15] And then Jude, the brother of James, speaks in like manner: "In the last times there shall be mockers, walking after their own ungodly lusts. There be they who, without fear, feed[16] themselves."[17] You have observed the concord of the theologians and apostles, and the harmony of their doctrine.

XI.

Finally, hear Paul as he speaks boldly, and mark how clearly he discovers these: "Beware of evil workers, beware of the concision.[18] Beware lest any man spoil you through philosophy and vain deceit.[19] See that ye walk circumspectly, because the days are evil."[20] In fine, then, what man shall have any excuse who hears these

---

[1] This does not agree with the age of Hippolytus.
[2] περι ἀνθρώπων, which is the reading of Codex B, instead of ἀπὸ ἀνθρώπων.
[3] ἄμετροι, the reading of Codex B instead of ἄνεμοι.
[4] The text is, ἀπὸ ψυχων καὶ ἀπωλείας ἀνθρώπων. We may suggest some such correction as ἀποψυχόντων κατ᾽ ἀπωλείας ἀνθρώπων = "men's hearts failing them concerning the destruction."
[5] διάφοροι. Better with B, ἀδιάφοροι = *promiscuous, without distinction*, and so perhaps *continuous* or *unseasonable*.
[6] Matt. xxiv. 12.
[7] Luke xxi. 8, 9.

[8] θεηγόροι. Codex B gives θεολόγοι.
[9] 2 Pet. iii. 3.
[10] 2 Pet. ii. 1.
[11] θεολόγος.
[12] 1 John iii. 10.
[13] 1 John ii. 18.
[14] Luke xxi. 8.
[15] 1 John iv. 1.
[16] οἱ ἀφόβως ἑαυτοὺς ποιμαίνοντες, instead of the received οἱ ἀποδιορίζοντες ἑαυτούς.
[17] Jude 18, 19.
[18] Phil. iii. 2.
[19] Col. ii. 8.
[20] Eph. v. 15, 16.

things in the Church from prophets and apostles, and from the Lord Himself, and yet will give no heed to the care of his soul, and to the time of the consummation, and to that approaching hour when we shall have to stand at the judgment-seat of Christ?

XII.

But having now done with this account of the consummation, we shall turn our exposition to those matters which fall to be stated by us next in order. I adduce, therefore, a witness altogether worthy of credit, — namely, the prophet Daniel, who interpreted the vision of Nabuchodonosor, and from the beginning of the kings down to their end indicated the right [1] way to those who seek to walk therein — to wit, the manifestation of the truth. For what saith the prophet? He presignified the matter clearly to Nabuchodonosor in the following terms: "Thou, O king, sawest, and behold a great image standing before thee, whose head was of gold, its arms and shoulders of silver, its belly and thighs of brass, its legs of iron, its feet part of iron and part of clay. Thou sawest till that a stone was cut out without hand; and it smote the image upon its feet, which were part of iron and part of clay, and brake them to pieces. Then was the clay, and the iron, and the brass, and the silver, and the gold broken to pieces together, and became like the chaff of the summer threshing-floor; and the stone that smote the image became a great mountain, and filled the whole earth." [2]

XIII.

Wherefore, bringing the visions of Daniel into conjunction with these, we shall make one narrative of the two, and show how true and consistent were the things seen in vision by the prophet with those which Nabuchodonosor saw beforehand. For the prophet speaks thus: "I Daniel saw, and, behold, the four winds of the heaven strove upon the great sea. And four great beasts came up from the sea, diverse one from another. The first was like a lioness, and had eagle's wings: I beheld till the wings thereof were plucked, and it was lifted up from the earth, and made stand upon the feet as a man, and a man's heart was given it. And behold a second beast, like to a bear, and it raised up itself on one side, and it had three ribs in the mouth of it between the teeth of it: and they said thus unto it, Arise, devour much flesh. After this I beheld, and lo a third beast, like a leopard, which had upon the back of it four wings of a fowl: the beast had also four heads. After this I saw, and behold a fourth beast, dreadful and terrible, and strong

exceedingly; its great iron teeth and its claws of brass [3] devoured and brake in pieces, and it stamped the residue with the feet of it: and it was diverse exceedingly from all the beasts that were before it; and it had ten horns. I considered its horns, and, behold, there came up among them a little horn, and before it there were three of the first horns plucked up by the roots: and, behold, in this horn were eyes like the eyes of man, and a mouth speaking great things." [4]

XIV.

Now, since these things which are thus spoken mystically by the prophet seem to all to be hard to understand, we shall conceal none of them from those who are possessed of sound mind. By mentioning the first beast, namely the *lioness* that comes up out of the sea, Daniel means the kingdom of the Babylonians which was set up in the world; and that same is also the "golden head" of this image. And by speaking of its "wings like an eagle," he shows that king Nabuchodonosor was elevated and exalted himself against God. Then he says that its "wings were plucked out," and means by this that his glory was subverted: for he was driven from his kingdom. And in stating that a "man's heart was given it, and it was made stand upon the feet like a man," he means that he repented, and acknowledged that he was himself but a man, and gave the glory to God. Lo, I have thus unfolded the similitude of the first beast.

XV.

Then after the lioness, the prophet sees a second beast like a bear, which denoted the Persians; for after the Babylonians the Persians had the sovereignty. And in saying, "I saw three ribs in the mouth of it," he referred to three nations, the Persians, Medes, and Babylonians, which were also expressed by the silver that came after the gold in the image. Behold, we have explained the second beast too. Then the third was the leopard, by which were meant the Greeks. For after the Persians, Alexander king of the Macedonians held the sovereignty, when he had destroyed Darius; and this is expressed by the brass in the image. And in speaking of "four wings of a fowl, and four heads in the beast," he showed most clearly how the kingdom of Alexander was divided into four parts. For it had four heads, — namely, the four kings that rose out of it. For on his death-bed [5] Alexander divided his kingdom into four parts. Behold, we have discussed the third also.

---

[1] Unchangeable, ἀπαράτροπον.
[2] Dan. ii. 31-35.

[3] These words, καὶ οἱ ὄνυχες αὐτοῦ χαλκοῖ, are strange both to the Greek and the Hebrew text of Daniel.
[4] Dan. vii. 2-8.
[5] See Hippolytus on Antichrist, ch. xxiv. p. 209, *supra*.

XVI.

Next he tells us of the " fourth beast, dreadful and terrible ; its teeth were of iron, and its claws of brass." And what is meant by these but the kingdom of the Romans, which also is meant by the iron, by which it will crush all the seats of empire that were before it, and will lord it over the whole earth? After this, then, what is left for us to interpret of all that the prophet saw, but the " toes of the image, in which part was of iron and part of clay, mingled together in one?" For by the ten toes of the image he meant figuratively the ten kings who sprang out of it, as Daniel also interpreted the matter. For he says, " I considered the beast, namely the fourth ; and behold ten horns after it, among which another horn arose like an offshoot ; and it will pluck up by the root three of those before it." And by this offshoot horn none other is signified than the Antichrist that is to restore the kingdom of the Jews. And the three horns which are to be rooted out by it signify three kings, namely those of Egypt, Libya, and Ethiopia, whom he will destroy in the array of war ; *and* when he has vanquished them all, being a savage tyrant, he will raise tribulation and persecution against the saints, exalting himself against them.

XVII.

You see how Daniel interpreted to Nabuchodonosor the dominion of the kingdoms ; you see how he explained the form of the image in all its parts ;[1] you have observed how he indicated prophetically the meaning of the coming up of the four beasts out of the sea. It remains that we open up to you the things done by the Antichrist in particular ; and, as far as in our power, declare to you by means of the Scriptures and the prophets, his wandering over the whole earth, and his lawless advent.

XVIII.

As the Lord Jesus Christ made His sojourn with us in the flesh (which He received) from the holy, immaculate Virgin, and took to Himself the tribe of Judah, and came forth from it, the Scripture declared His royal lineage in the word of Jacob, when in his benediction he addressed himself to his son in these terms : " Judah, thou art he whom thy brethren shall praise : thy hands shall be on the neck of thine enemies ; thy father's children shall bow down before thee. Judah is a lion's whelp ; from a sprout,[2] my son, thou art gone up : he stooped down, he couched as a lion, and as a lion's whelp :[3] who shall rouse him up? A ruler[4] shall not depart from Judah, nor a leader[5] from his thighs,[6] until what is in store for him[7] shall come, and he is the expectation[8] of the nations."[9] Mark these words of Jacob which were spoken to Judah, and are fulfilled in the Lord. To the same effect, moreover, does the patriarch express himself regarding Antichrist. Wherefore, as he prophesied with respect to Judah, so did he also with respect to his son Dan. For Judah was his fourth son ; and Dan, again, was his seventh son. And what, then, did he say of him? " Let Dan be a serpent sitting by the way, that biteth the horse's heel?"[10] And what serpent was there but the deceiver from the beginning, he who is named in Genesis, he who deceived Eve, and bruised Adam in the heel?[11]

XIX.

But seeing now that we must make proof of what is alleged at greater length, we shall not shrink from the task. For it is certain that he is destined to spring from the tribe of Dan,[12] and to range himself in opposition like a princely tyrant, a terrible judge and accuser,[13] as the prophet testifies when he says, " Dan shall judge his people, as one tribe in Israel."[14] But some one may say that this was meant of Samson, who sprang from the tribe of Dan, and judged his people for twenty years. That, however, was only partially made good in the case of Samson ; but this shall be fulfilled completely in the case of Antichrist. For Jeremiah, too, speaks in this manner : " From Dan we shall hear the sound of the sharpness[15] of his horses ; at the sound of the neighing[16] of his horses the whole land trembled."[17] And again, Moses says : " Dan is a lion's whelp, and he shall leap from Bashan."[18] And that no one may fall into the mistake of thinking that this is spoken of the Saviour, let him attend to this. " Dan," says he, " is a lion's whelp ; " and by thus naming the tribe of Dan as the one whence the accuser is destined to spring, he made the matter in hand quite clear. For as Christ is born of the tribe of Judah, so Antichrist shall be born of the tribe of Dan. And as our Lord and Saviour Jesus Christ, the

---

[1] πᾶσι τοῖς πέρασιν.
[2] βλαστοῦ.
[3] σκύμνος.
[4] ἄρχων.
[5] ἡγούμενος.
[6] ἐκ τῶν μηρῶν.
[7] τὰ ἀποκείμενα.
[8] καὶ αὐτὸς προσδοκία.
[9] Gen. xlix. 8–10.
[10] 2 Gen. xlix. 17.
[11] πτερνίσας.
[12] After Irenæus, book v. ch. xxx. [vol. i. p. 559, this series], many of the ancients express this opinion. See too Bellarmine, *De Pontifice Rom.*, iii. 12.
[13] διάβολος.
[14] Gen. xlix. 16.
[15] φωνὴν ὀξύτητος. There is another reading, σπουδήν = haste.
[16] χρεμετισμοῦ. [Conf. p. 207, *supra*.]
[17] Jer. viii. 16.
[18] Deut. xxxiii. 22.

Son of God, was spoken of in prophecy as a *lion* on account of His royalty and glory, in the same manner also has the Scripture prophetically described the accuser as a lion, on account of his tyranny and violence.

XX.

For in every respect that deceiver seeks to make himself appear like the Son of God. Christ is a lion, and Antichrist is a lion. Christ is King of things celestial and things terrestrial, and Antichrist will be king upon earth. The Saviour was manifested as a lamb; and he, too, will appear as a lamb, while he is a wolf within. The Saviour was circumcised, and he in like manner will appear in circumcision. The Saviour sent the apostles unto all the nations, and he in like manner will send false apostles. Christ gathered together the dispersed sheep, and he in like manner will gather together the dispersed people of the Hebrews. Christ gave to those who believed on Him the honourable and life-giving cross, and he in like manner will give his own sign. Christ appeared in the form of man, and he in like manner will come forth in the form of man. Christ arose from among the Hebrews, and he will spring from among the Jews. Christ displayed His flesh like a temple, and raised it up on the third day; and he too will raise up again the temple of stone in Jerusalem. And these deceits fabricated by him will become quite intelligible to those who listen to us attentively, from what shall be set forth next in order.

XXI.

For through the Scriptures we are instructed in two advents of the Christ and Saviour. And the first after the flesh was in humiliation, because He was manifested in lowly estate. So then His second advent is declared to be in glory; for He comes from heaven with power, and angels, and the glory of His Father. His first advent had John the Baptist as its forerunner; and His second, in which He is to come in glory, will exhibit Enoch, and Elias, and John the Divine.[1] Behold, too, the Lord's kindness to man; how even in the last times He shows His care for mortals, and pities them. For He will not leave us even then without prophets, but will send them to us for our instruction and assurance, and to make us give heed to the

advent of the adversary, as He intimated also of old in this Daniel. For he says, "I shall make a covenant of one week, and in the midst of the week my sacrifice and libation will be removed." For by one week he indicates the showing forth of the seven years which shall be in the last times.[2] And the half of the week the two prophets, along with John, will take for the purpose of proclaiming to all the world the advent of Antichrist, that is to say, for a "thousand two hundred and sixty days clothed in sackcloth;"[3] and they will work signs and wonders with the object of making men ashamed and repentant, even by these means, on account of their surpassing lawlessness and impiety. "And if any man will hurt them, fire will proceed out of their mouth, and devour their enemies. These have power to shut heaven, that it rain not in the days of the advent of Antichrist, and to turn waters into blood, and to smite the earth with all plagues as often as they will."[4] And when they have proclaimed all these things they will fall on the sword, cut off by the accuser.[5] And they will fulfil their testimony, as Daniel also says; for he foresaw that the beast that came up out of the abyss would make war with them, namely with Enoch, Elias, and John, and would overcome them, and kill them, because of their refusal to give glory to the accuser. that is the little horn that sprang up.[6] And he, being lifted up in heart, begins in the end to, exalt himself and glorify himself as God, persecuting the saints and blaspheming Christ.

XXII.

But as, in accordance with the train of our discussion, we have been constrained to come to the matter of the days of the dominion of the adversary, it is necessary to state in the first place what concerns his nativity and growth; and then we must turn our discourse, as we have said before, to the expounding of this matter, viz., that in all respects the accuser and son of lawlessness[7] is to make himself like our Saviour. Thus also the demonstration makes the matter clear to us. Since the Saviour of the world, with the purpose of saving the race of men, was born of the immaculate and virgin Mary,[8] and in the form of the flesh trod the enemy under foot, in the exercise of the power of His own proper divinity; in the same manner also will the accuser come forth from an impure woman upon the earth, but shall be born of a virgin

---

[1] Or, the theologian. The Apocalypse (xi. 3) mentions only two witnesses, who are understood by the ancients in general as Enoch and Elias. The author of the *Chronicon Paschale*, p. 21, on Enoch, says: "This is he who, along with Elias, is to withstand Antichrist in the last days, and to confute his deceit, according to the tradition of the Church." This addition as to the return of John the Evangelist is somewhat more uncommon. And yet Ephraem of Antioch, in Photius, cod. ccxxix., states that this too is supported by ancient ecclesiastical tradition, Christ's saying in John xxi. 22 being understood to that effect. See also Hippolytus, *De Antichristo*, ch. l. p. 213, *supra*. — MIGNE. [Enoch and Elias are not dead. But see Heb. ix. 27.]

[2] Dan. ix. 27. [Note our author's adoption of the plan of a year for a day, Ezek. iv. 6. See Pusey, *Daniel*, p. 165.]
[3] Rev. xi. 3.
[4] Rev. xi. 6; [1 Kings xvii. 1; Ecclus. xlviii. 3].
[5] παρὰ τοῦ διαβόλου. [That is, by the devil.]
[6] ἀναφανέν. But Cod. B reads ἀναφυέν.
[7] ἀνομίας. Cod. B gives ἀπωλείας, perdition: and for μέλλει = is to, it reads θέλει = wishes. [2 Thess. ii. 3, 4–3.]
[8] Cod. B gives ἀειπαρθένου, ever-virgin.

spuriously.[1] For our God sojourned with us in the flesh, after that very flesh of ours which He made for Adam and all Adam's posterity, yet without sin. But the accuser, though he take up the flesh, will do it only in appearance; for how should we wear that flesh which he did not make himself, but against which he warreth daily? And it is my opinion, beloved, that he will assume this phenomenal kind of flesh[2] as an instrument.[3] For this reason also is he *to be* born of a virgin, as if a spirit, and then to the rest he will be manifested as flesh. For as to a virgin bearing, this we have known only in the case of the all-holy *Virgin*, who bore the Saviour verily clothed in flesh.[4] For Moses says, "Every male that openeth the womb shall be called holy unto the Lord."[5] This is by no means the case with him;[6] but as the adversary will not open the womb, so neither will he take to himself real flesh, and be circumcised as Christ was circumcised. And even as Christ chose His apostles, so will he too assume a whole people of disciples like himself in wickedness.

XXIII.

Above all, moreover, he will love the nation of the Jews. And with all these he will work signs and terrible wonders, false wonders and not true, in order to deceive his impious equals. For if it were possible, he would seduce even the elect[7] from the love of Christ. But in his first steps he will be gentle, loveable, quiet, pious, pacific, hating injustice, detesting gifts, not allowing idolatry; loving, says he, the Scriptures, reverencing priests, honouring his elders, repudiating fornication, detesting adultery, giving no heed to slanders, not admitting oaths, kind to strangers, kind to the poor, compassionate. And then he will work wonders, cleansing lepers, raising paralytics, expelling demons, proclaiming things remote just as things present, raising the dead, helping widows, defending orphans, loving all, reconciling in love men who contend, and saying to such, " Let not the sun go down upon your wrath;"[8] and he will not acquire gold, nor love silver, nor seek riches.

XXIV.

And all this he will do corruptly and deceitfully, and with the purpose of deluding all to make him king. For when the peoples and tribes see so great virtues and so great powers in him, they will all with one mind meet together to make him king. And above all others shall the nation of the Hebrews be dear to the tyrant himself, while they say one to another, Is there found indeed in our generation such a man, so good and just? That shall be the way with the race of the Jews pre-eminently, as I said before, who, thinking, as they do, that they shall behold the king himself in such power, will approach him to say, We all confide in thee, and acknowledge thee to be just upon the whole earth; we all hope to be saved by thee; and by thy mouth we have received just and incorruptible judgment.

XXV.

And at first, indeed, that deceitful and lawless one, with crafty deceitfulness, will refuse such glory; but the men persisting, and holding by him, will declare him king. And thereafter he will be lifted up in heart, and he who was formerly gentle will become violent, and he who pursued love will become pitiless, and the humble in heart will become haughty and inhuman, and the hater of unrighteousness will persecute the righteous. Then, when he is elevated to his kingdom, he will marshal war; and in his wrath he will smite three mighty kings,—those, namely, of Egypt, Libya, and Ethiopia. And after that he will build the temple in Jerusalem, and will restore it again speedily, and give it over to the Jews. And then he will be lifted up in heart against every man; yea, he will speak blasphemy also against God, thinking in his deceit that he shall be king upon the earth hereafter for ever; not knowing, miserable wretch, that his kingdom is to be quickly brought to nought, and that he will quickly have to meet the fire which is prepared for him, along with all who trust him and serve him. For when Daniel said, " I shall make my covenant for one week,"[9] he indicated seven years; and the one half of the week is for the preaching of the prophets, and for the other half of the week — that is to say, for three years and a half — Antichrist will reign upon the earth. And after this his kingdom and his glory shall be taken away. Behold, ye who love God, what manner of tribulation there shall rise in those days, such as has not been from the foundation of the world, no, nor ever shall be, except in those days alone. Then the lawless one, being lifted up in heart, will gather together his demons in man's form, and will abominate those who call him to the kingdom, and will pollute many souls.

---

[1] ἐν πλάνῃ. Cod. B reads ἀκριβῶς, exactly. Many of the ancients hold that Antichrist will be a demon in human figure. See Augustine, Sulpicius Severus, in Dialogue II., and Philippus Dioptra, iii. 11, etc.
[2] φανταστικὴν τῆς σαρκὸς αὐτοῦ οὐσίαν.
[3] Organ, ὄργανον.
[4] Cod. B reads τὴν θεοτόκον ἔγνωμεν σαρκικῶς καὶ ἀπλανῶς, instead of the text, σαρκοφόρον ἀπλανῶς, etc. [Conf. vol. iii. p. 523.]
[5] Ex. xxxiv. 19; Num. viii. 16; Luke ii. 23.
[6] οὐ μὴν οὐδαμῶς.
[7] Matt. xxiv. 24.
[8] Eph. iv. 26.

[9] Dan. ix. 27. [The ἀνομία which more and more prevails in our age in all nations, makes all this very significant to us, of "the last days."]

XXVI.

For he will appoint princes over them from among the demons. And he will no longer seem to be pious, but altogether and in all things he will be harsh, severe, passionate, wrathful, terrible, inconstant, dread, morose, hateful, abominable, savage, vengeful, iniquitous. And, bent on casting the whole race of men into the pit of perdition, he will multiply false signs. For when all the people greet him with their acclamations at his displays, he will shout with a strong voice, so that the place shall be shaken in which the multitudes stand by him : " Ye peoples, and tribes, and nations, acquaint yourselves with my mighty authority and power, and the strength of my kingdom. What prince is there so great as I am? What great God is there but I? Who will stand up against my authority?" Under the eye of the spectators he will remove mountains from their places, he will walk on the sea with dry feet, he will bring down fire from heaven, he will turn the day into darkness and the night into day, he will turn the sun about wheresoever he pleases ; and, in short, in presence of those who behold him, he will show all the elements of earth and sea to be subject to him in the power of his specious manifestation. For if, while as yet he does not exhibit himself as the son of perdition, he raises and excites against us open war even to battles and slaughters, at that time when he shall come in his own proper person, and men shall see him as he is in reality, what machinations and deceits and delusions will he not bring into play, with the purpose of seducing all men, and leading them off from the way of truth, and from the gate of the kingdom?

XXVII.

Then, after all these things, the heavens will not give their dew, the clouds will not give their rain, the earth will refuse to yield its fruits, the sea shall be filled with stench, the rivers shall be dried up, the fish of the sea shall die, men shall perish of hunger and thirst ; and father embracing son, and mother embracing daughter, will die together, and there will be none to bury them. But the whole earth will be filled with the stench arising from the dead bodies cast forth. And the sea, not receiving the floods of the rivers, will become like mire, and will be filled with an unlimited smell and stench. Then there will be a mighty pestilence upon the whole earth, and then, too, inconsolable lamentation, and measureless weeping, and unceasing mourning Then men will deem those happy who are dead before them, and will say to them, " Open your sepulchres, and take us miserable beings in ; open your receptacles for the reception of your wretched kinsmen and acquaintances.

Happy are ye, in that ye have not seen our days. Happy are ye, in that ye have not had to witness this painful life of ours, nor this irremediable pestilence, nor these straits that possess our souls."

XXVIII.

Then that abominable one will send his commands throughout every government by the hand at once of demons and of visible men, who shall say, " A mighty king has arisen upon the earth ; come ye all to worship him ; come ye all to see the strength of his kingdom : for, behold, he will give you corn ; and he will bestow upon you wine, and great riches, and lofty honours. For the whole earth and sea obeys his command. Come ye all to him." And by reason of the scarcity of food, all will go to him and worship him ; and he will put his mark on their right hand and on their forehead, that no one may put the sign of the honourable cross upon his forehead with his right hand ; but his hand is bound. And from that time he shall not have power to seal any one of his members, but he shall be attached to the deceiver, and shall serve him ; and in him there is no repentance. But such an one is lost at once to God and to men, and the deceiver will give them scanty food by reason of his abominable seal. And his seal upon the forehead and upon the right hand is the number, " Six hundred threescore and six.".[1] And I have an opinion as to this number, though I do not know the matter for certain ; for many names have been found in this number when it is expressed in writing.[2] Still we say that perhaps the scription of this same seal will give us the word *I deny.*[3] For even in recent days, by means of his ministers — that is to say, the idolaters — that bitter adversary took up the word *deny*, when the lawless pressed upon the witnesses of Christ, with the adjuration, " Deny thy God, the crucified One."[4]

XXIX.

Of such kind, in the time of that hater of all good, will be the seal, the tenor of which will be this : I deny the Maker of heaven and earth, I deny the baptism, I deny my (former) service, and attach myself to thee, and I believe in thee. For this is what the prophets Enoch and Elias will preach : Believe not the enemy who is to come and be seen ; for he is an adversary[5] and corrupter and son of perdition, and deceives

---

[1] Rev. xiii. 18.
[2] ἐν τῇ γραφῇ.
[3] ἀρνοῦμαι. But the letters of the word ἀρνοῦμαι in their numerical value will not give the number 666 unless it is written ἀρνούμε. See Haymo on the Apocalypse, book iv.
[4] The text is in confusion: ἐπειδὴ καὶ πρῴην διὰ τῶν ὑπηρετῶν αὐτοῦ ὁ ἀντίδικος ἐχθρὸς, ἢ γοῦν τῶν εἰδωλολατρῶν, τοῖς μάρτυσι τοῦ Χριστοῦ προέτρεπον οἱ ἄνομοι, etc.
[5] ἀντίδικος. In B, πλάνος = deceiver.

you;[1] and for this reason he will kill you, and smite them with the sword. Behold the deceit of the enemy, know the machinations of the beguiler, how he seeks to darken the mind of men utterly. For he will show forth his demons brilliant like angels, and he will bring in hosts of the incorporeal without number. And in the presence of all he exhibits himself as taken up into heaven with trumpets and sounds, and the mighty shouting of those who hail him with indescribable hymns; the heir of darkness himself shining like light, and at one time soaring to the heavens, and at another descending to the earth with great glory, and again charging the demons, like angels, to execute his behests with much fear and trembling. Then will he send the cohorts of the demons among mountains and caves and dens of the earth, to track out those who have been concealed from his eyes, and to bring them forward to worship him. And those who yield to him he will seal with his seal; but those who refuse to submit to him he will consume with incomparable pains and bitterest torments and machinations, such as never have been, nor have reached the ear of man, nor have been seen by the eye of mortals.

XXX.

Blessed shall they be who overcome the tyrant then. For they shall be set forth as more illustrious and loftier than the first witnesses; for the former witnesses overcame his minions only, but these overthrow and conquer the accuser himself, the son of perdition. With what eulogies and crowns, therefore, will they not be adorned by our King, Jesus Christ!

XXXI.

But let us revert to the matter in hand. When men have received the seal, then, and find neither food nor water, they *will* approach him with a voice of anguish, saying, Give us to eat and drink, for we all faint with hunger and all manner of straits;[2] and bid the heavens yield us water, and drive off from us the beasts that devour men. Then will that crafty one make answer, mocking them with absolute inhumanity, and saying, The heavens refuse to give rain, the earth yields not again its fruits; whence then can I give you food? Then, on hearing the words of this deceiver, these miserable men will perceive that this is the wicked accuser, and will mourn in anguish, and weep vehemently, and beat their face with their hands, and tear their hair, and lacerate their cheeks with their nails, while they say to each other: Woe for the calamity! woe for the bitter contract! woe for the deceitful covenant! woe for the mighty mis-

chance! How have we been beguiled by the deceiver! how have we been joined to him! how have we been caught in his toils! how have we been taken in his abominable net! how have we heard the Scriptures, and understood them not! For truly those who are engrossed with the affairs of life, and with the lust of this world, will be easily brought over to the accuser then, and sealed by him.

XXXII.

But many who are hearers of the divine Scriptures,[3] and have them in their hand, and keep them in mind with understanding, will escape his imposture. For they will see clearly through his insidious appearance and his deceitful imposture, and will flee from his hands, and betake themselves to the mountains, and hide themselves in the caves of the earth; and they will seek after the Friend of man with tears and a contrite heart; and He will deliver them out of his toils, and with His right hand He will save those from his snares who in a worthy and righteous manner make their supplication to Him.

XXXIII.

You see in what manner of fasting and prayer the saints will exercise themselves at that time. Observe, also, how hard the season and the times will be that are to come upon those in city and country alike. At that time they will be brought from the east even unto the west; and they will come up from the west even unto the east, and will weep greatly and wail vehemently. And when the day begins to dawn they will long for the night, in order that they may find rest from their labours; and when the night descends upon them, by reason of the continuous earthquakes and the tempests in the air, they will desire even to behold the light of the day, and will seek how they may hereafter meet a bitter death.[4] At that time the whole earth will bewail the life of anguish, and the sea and air in like manner will bewail it; and the sun, too, will wail; and the wild beasts, together with the fowls, will wail; mountains and hills, and the trees of the plain, will wail on account of the race of man, because all have turned aside from the holy God, and obeyed the deceiver, and received the mark of that abominable one, the enemy of God, instead of the quickening cross of the Saviour.

XXXIV.

And the churches, too, will wail with a mighty lamentation, because neither "oblation nor in-

---

[1] B reads τὸν κόσμον, the world.
[2] B reads ὀδύνης, pain.

[3] [Note this. The faithful are to have the Holy Scriptures *in their hand*. But this has been condemned by repeated bulls and anathemas of Roman pontiffs; e.g., by Clement XI., A.D 1713: and no Bible in the vulgar tongue ever appeared in Rome till A.D. 1870, on the overthrow of the papal kingdom.]
[4] [Deut. xxviii. 66, 67.]

cense" is attended to, nor a service acceptable to God;[1] but the sanctuaries of the churches will become like a garden-watcher's hut,[2] and the holy body and blood of Christ will not be shown in those days. The public service of God shall be extinguished, psalmody shall cease, the reading of the Scriptures shall not be heard;[3] but for men there shall be darkness, and lamentation on lamentation, and woe on woe. At that time silver and gold shall be cast out in the streets, and none shall gather them; but all things shall be held an offence. For all shall be eager to escape and to hide themselves, and they shall not be able anywhere to find concealment from the woes[4] of the adversary; but as they carry his mark about them, they shall be readily recognised and declared to be his. Without there shall be fear, and within trembling, both by night and by day. In the street and in the houses there shall be the dead; in the streets and in the houses there shall be hunger and thirst; in the streets there shall be tumults, and in the houses lamentations. And beauty of countenance shall be withered, for their forms shall be like those of the dead; and the beauty of women shall fade, and the desire of all men shall vanish.

XXXV.

Notwithstanding, not even then will the merciful and benignant God leave the race of men without all comfort; but He will shorten even those days and the period of three years and a half, and He will curtail those times on account of the remnant of those who hide themselves in the mountains and caves, that the phalanx of all those saints fail not utterly. But these days shall run their course rapidly; and the kingdom of the deceiver and Antichrist shall be speedily removed. And then, in fine, in the glance of an eye shall the fashion of this world pass away, and the power of men[5] shall be brought to nought, and all these visible things shall be destroyed.

XXXVI.

As these things, therefore, of which we have spoken before are in the future, beloved, when the one week is divided into parts, and the abomination of desolation has arisen then, and the forerunners of the Lord have finished their proper course, and the whole world, in fine, comes to the consummation, what remains but the manifestation[6] of our Lord and Saviour Jesus Christ, the Son of God, from heaven, for whom

we have hoped; who shall bring forth fire and all just judgment against those who have refused to believe in Him? For the Lord says, "For as the lightning cometh out of the east, and shineth even unto the west, so shall also the coming of the Son of man be; for wheresoever the carcase is, there will the eagles be gathered together."[7] For the sign of the cross[8] shall arise from the east even unto the west, in brightness exceeding that of the sun, and shall announce the advent and manifestation of the Judge, to give to every one according to his works. For concerning the general resurrection and the kingdom of the saints, Daniel says: "And many of them that sleep in the dust of the earth shall awake, some to everlasting life, and some to shame and everlasting contempt."[9] And Isaiah says: "The dead shall rise, and those in the tombs shall awake, and those in the earth shall rejoice."[10] And our Lord says: "Many[11] in that day shall hear the voice of the Son of God, and they that hear shall live."[12]

XXXVII.

For at that time the trumpet shall sound,[13] and awake those that sleep from the lowest parts of the earth, righteous and sinners alike. And every kindred, and tongue, and nation, and tribe shall be raised in the twinkling of an eye;[14] and they shall stand upon the face of the earth, waiting for the coming of the righteous and terrible Judge, in fear and trembling unutterable. For the river of fire shall come forth in fury like an angry sea, and shall burn up mountains and hills, and shall make the sea vanish, and shall dissolve the atmosphere with its heat like wax.[15] The stars of heaven shall fall,[16] the sun shall be turned into darkness, and the moon into blood.[17] The heaven shall be rolled together like a scroll:[18] the whole earth shall be burnt up by reason of the deeds done in it, which men did corruptly,[19] in fornications, in adulteries, and in lies and uncleanness, and in idolatries, and in murders, and in battles. For there shall be the new heaven and the new earth.[20]

XXXVIII.

Then shall the holy angels run on their commission to gather together all the nations, whom

---

1 [The reference is to Mal. i. 11, and *incense* is expounded spiritually by the Ante-Nicene Fathers generally See Irenæus, vol. i. p. 574, Tertullian, iii. p. 346 and *passim*.]
2 [Isa. i. 8.]
3 [The public reading of Scripture-lessons is implied, Acts xv. 21. See Hooker, *Eccl. Pol.*, book v. cap. xix.]
4 παθῶν. B reads παγίδων, snares.
5 B reads δαιμόνων, demons.
6 ἐπιφάνεια.

7 Matt. xxiv. 27, 28.
8 See Jo. Voss, *Theses Theolog.*, p. 228. [And compare, concerning Constantine's vision, Robertson and his notes, *Hist.*, vol. i. p. 186, and Newman's characteristic argument in his *Essay on Miracles*, prefixed to the third volume of his *Fleury*, pp. 133-143.]
9 Dan. xii. 2.
10 Isa. xxvi. 19.
11 πολλοί, for the received οἱ νεκροί.
12 John v. 25.
13 1 Thess. iv. 16.
14 1 Cor. xv. 52.
15 2 Pet. iii. 12.
16 Matt. xxiv. 29.
17 Acts ii. 20.
18 Rev. vi. 14.
19 διέφθειραν. B reads ἔκραξαν.
20 Rev. xxi. 1.

that terrible voice of the trumpet shall awake out of sleep. And before the judgment-seat of Christ shall stand those who once were kings and rulers, chief priests and priests; and they shall give an account of their administration, and of the fold, whoever of them through their negligence have lost one sheep out of the flock. And then shall be brought forward soldiers who were not content with their provision,[1] but oppressed widows and orphans and beggars. Then shall be arraigned the collectors of tribute, who despoil the poor man of more than is ordered, and who make real gold like adulterate, in order to mulct the needy, in fields and in houses and in the churches. Then shall rise up the lewd with shame, who have not kept their bed undefiled, but have been ensnared by all manner of fleshly beauty, and have gone in the way of their own lusts. Then shall rise up those who have not kept the love of the Lord, mute and gloomy, because they contemned the light commandment of the Saviour, which says, Thou shalt love thy neighbour as thyself. Then they, too, shall weep who have possessed the unjust balance, and unjust weights and measures, and dry measures, as they wait for the righteous Judge.

XXXIX.

And why should we add many words concerning those who are sisted before the bar? Then the righteous shall shine forth like the sun, while the wicked shall be shown to be mute and gloomy. For both the righteous and the wicked shall be raised incorruptible: the righteous, to be honoured eternally, and to taste immortal joys; and the wicked, to be punished in judgment eternally. Each ponders[2] the question as to what answer he shall give to the righteous Judge for his deeds, whether good or bad. With all men each one's actions shall environ him, whether he be good or evil. For the powers of the heavens shall be shaken,[3] and fear and trembling shall consume all things, both heaven and earth and things under the earth. And every tongue shall confess Him openly,[4] and shall confess Him who comes to judge righteous judgment, the mighty God and Maker of all things. Then with fear and astonishment shall come angels, thrones, powers, principalities, dominions,[5] and the cherubim and seraphim with their many eyes and six wings, all crying aloud with a mighty voice, "Holy, holy, holy is the Lord of hosts, omnipotent; the heaven and the earth are full of Thy glory."[6] And the King of kings and Lord of lords, the Judge who accepts no man's person,

and the Jurist who distributes justice to every man, shall be revealed upon His dread and lofty throne; and all the flesh of mortals shall see His face with great fear and trembling, both the righteous and the sinner.

XL.

Then shall the son of perdition be brought forward, to wit, the accuser, with his demons and with his servants, by angels stern and inexorable. And they shall be given over to the fire that is never quenched, and to the worm that never sleepeth, and to the outer darkness. For the people of the Hebrews shall see Him in human form, as He appeared to them *when He came* by the holy Virgin in the flesh, and as they crucified Him. And He will show them the *prints of the* nails in His hands and feet, and His side pierced with the spear, and His head crowned with thorns, and His honourable cross. And once for all shall the people of the Hebrews see all these things, and they shall mourn and weep, as the prophet exclaims, "They shall look on Him whom they have pierced;"[7] and there shall be none to help them or to pity them, because they repented not, neither turned aside from the wicked way. And these shall go away into everlasting punishment with the demons and the accuser.

XLI.

Then He shall gather together all nations, as the holy Gospel so strikingly declares. For what says Matthew the evangelist, or rather the Lord Himself, in the Gospel? "When the Son of man shall come in His glory, and all the holy angels with Him, then shall He sit upon the throne of His glory: and before Him shall be gathered all nations; and He shall separate them one from another, as a shepherd divideth his sheep from the goats: and He shall set the sheep on His right hand, but the goats on the left. Then shall the King say unto them on His right hand, Come, ye blessed of my Father, inherit the kingdom prepared for you from the foundation of the world."[8] Come, ye prophets, who were cast out for my name's sake. Come, ye patriarchs, who before my advent were obedient to me, and longed for my kingdom. Come, ye apostles, who were my fellows in my sufferings in my incarnation, *and suffered with me* in the Gospel. Come, ye martyrs, who confessed me before despots, and endured many torments and pains. Come, ye hierarchs, who did me sacred service blamelessly day and night, and made the oblation of my honourable body and blood daily.[9]

---

[1] Luke iii. 14.
[2] The text gives ἐνθυμηθεῖ τε, for which B reads ἐνθυμεῖται.
[3] Matt. xxiv. 29.
[4] Phil. ii. 11.
[5] Col. i. 16.
[6] Isa. vi. 3.

[7] Zech. xii. 10; John xix. 37.
[8] Matt. xxv. 31–34.
[9] [All this is in the manner of Hippolytus; and here is a striking testimony to a daily Eucharist, if this be genuine.]

XLII.

Come, ye saints, who disciplined yourselves in mountains and caves and dens of the earth, who honoured my name by continence and prayer and virginity. Come, ye maidens, who desired my bride-chamber, and loved no other bridegroom than me, who by your testimony and habit of life were wedded to me, the immortal and incorruptible Bridegroom. Come, ye friends of the poor and the stranger. Come, ye who kept my love, as I am love. Come, ye who possess peace, for I own that peace. Come, ye blessed of my Father, inherit the kingdom prepared for you, ye who esteemed not riches, ye who had compassion on the poor, who aided the orphans, who helped the widows, who gave drink to the thirsty, who fed the hungry, who received strangers, who clothed the naked, who visited the sick, who comforted those in prison, who helped the blind, who kept the seal of the faith inviolate, who assembled yourselves together in the churches, who listened to my Scriptures, who longed for my words, who observed my law day and night, who endured hardness with me like good soldiers, seeking to please me, your heavenly King. Come, inherit the kingdom prepared for you from the foundation of the world. Behold, my kingdom is made ready; behold, paradise is opened; behold, my immortality is shown in its beauty.[1] Come all, inherit the kingdom prepared for you from the foundation of the world.

XLIII.

Then shall the righteous answer, astonished at the mighty and wondrous fact that He, whom the hosts of angels cannot look upon openly, addresses them as friends, and shall cry out to Him, Lord, when saw we Thee an hungered, and fed Thee? Master,[2] when saw we Thee thirsty, and gave Thee drink? Thou Terrible One,[3] when saw we Thee naked, and clothed Thee? Immortal,[4] when saw we Thee a stranger, and took Thee in? Thou Friend of man,[5] when saw we Thee sick or in prison, and came unto Thee?[6] Thou art the ever-living One. Thou art without beginning, like the Father,[7] and co-eternal with the Spirit. Thou art He who made all things out of nothing. Thou art the prince of the angels. Thou art He at whom the depths tremble.[8] Thou art He who is covered with light as with a garment.[9] Thou art He who made us, and fashioned us of earth. Thou art He who formed[10]

---

[1] κεκαλλώπισται. [Isa. xxxiii. 17.]
[2] δέσποτα.
[3] φοβερέ.
[4] ἀθάνατε.
[5] φιλάνθρώπε.
[6] Matt. xxv. 37, etc.
[7] συνάναρχος.
[8] 4 Esdr. iii. 8.
[9] Ps. civ. 2.
[10] δημιουργήσας.

things invisible.[11] From Thy presence the whole earth fleeth away,[12] and how have we received hospitably Thy kingly power and lordship?

XLIV.

Then shall the King of kings make answer again, and say to them, Inasmuch as ye have done it unto one of the least of these my brethren, ye have done it unto me. Inasmuch as ye have received those of whom I have already spoken to you, and clothed them, and fed them, and gave them to drink, I mean the poor who are my members, ye have done it unto me. But come ye into the kingdom prepared for you from the foundation of the world; enjoy for ever and ever that which is given you by my Father in heaven, and the holy and quickening Spirit. And what mouth then will be able to tell out those blessings which eye hath not seen, nor ear heard, neither have entered into the heart of man, the things which God hath prepared for them that love Him?[13]

XLV.

Ye have heard of the ceaseless joy, ye have heard of the immoveable kingdom, ye have heard of the feast of blessings without end. Learn now, then, also the address of anguish with which the just Judge and the benignant God shall speak to those on the left hand in unmeasured anger and wrath, Depart from me, ye cursed, into everlasting fire, prepared for the devil and his angels. Ye have prepared these things for yourselves; take to yourselves also the enjoyment of them. Depart from me, ye cursed, into the outer darkness, and into the unquenchable fire, prepared for the devil and his angels. I made you, and ye gave yourselves to another. I am He who brought you forth from your mother's womb, and ye rejected me. I am He who fashioned you of earth by my word of command, and ye gave yourselves to another. I am He who nurtured you, and ye served another. I ordained the earth and the sea for your maintenance and the bound[14] of your life, and ye listened not to my commandments. I made the light for you, that ye might enjoy the day, and the night also, that ye might have rest; and ye vexed me, and set me at nought with your wicked words, and opened the door to the passions. Depart from me, ye workers of iniquity. I know you not, I recognise you not: ye made yourselves the workmen of another lord — namely, the devil. With him inherit ye the darkness, and the fire that is not quenched, and the worm that sleepeth not, and the gnashing of teeth.

---

[11] Col. i. 16.
[12] Rev. xx. 11.
[13] Isa. lxiv. 4; 1 Cor. ii. 9.
[14] συμπέρασμα.

XLVI.

For I was an hungered, and ye gave me no meat: I was thirsty, and ye gave me no drink: I was a stranger, and ye took me not in; naked, and ye clothed me not; sick, and ye visited me not: I was in prison, and ye came not unto me. I made your ears that ye might hear the Scriptures; and ye prepared them for the songs of demons, and lyres, and jesting. I made your eyes that you might see the light of my commandments, and keep them; and ye called in fornication and wantonness, and opened them to all other manner of uncleanness. I prepared your mouth for the utterance of adoration, and praise, and psalms, and spiritual odes, and for the exercise of continuous reading; and ye fitted it to railing, and swearing, and blasphemies, while ye sat and spake evil of your neighbours. I made your hands that ye might stretch them forth in prayers and supplications, and ye put them forth to robberies, and murders, and the killing of each other. I ordained your feet to walk in the preparation of the Gospel of peace, both in the churches and the houses of my saints; and ye taught them to run to adulteries, and fornications, and theatres, and dancings, and elevations.[1]

XLVII.

At last the assembly is dissolved, the spectacle of this life ceaseth: its deceit and its semblance are passed away. Cleave to me, to whom every knee boweth, of things in heaven, and things on earth, and things under the earth. For all who have been negligent, and have not shown pity in well-doing there, have nothing else due them than the unquenchable fire. For I am the friend of man, but yet also a righteous Judge to all. For I shall award the recompense according to desert; I shall give the reward to all, according to each man's labour; I shall make return to all, according to each man's conflict. I wish to have pity, but I see no oil in your vessels. I desire to have mercy, but ye have passed through life entirely without mercy. I long to have compassion, but your lamps are dark by reason of your hardness of heart. Depart from me. For judgment is without mercy to him that hath showed no mercy.[2]

XLVIII.

Then shall they also make answer to the dread Judge, who accepteth no man's person: Lord, when saw we Thee an hungered, or athirst, or a stranger, or naked, or sick, or in prison, and ministered not unto Thee? Lord, dost Thou know us not? Thou didst form us, Thou didst fashion us, Thou didst make us of four elements,

Thou didst give us spirit and soul. On Thee we believed; Thy seal we received, Thy baptism we obtained; we acknowledged Thee to be God, we knew Thee to be Creator; in Thee we wrought signs, through Thee we cast out demons, for Thee we mortified the flesh, for Thee we preserved virginity, for Thee we practised chastity, for Thee we became strangers on the earth; and Thou sayest, I know you not, depart from me! Then shall He make answer to them, and say, Ye acknowledged me as Lord, but ye kept not my words. Ye were marked with the seal of my cross, but ye deleted it by your hardness of heart. Ye obtained my baptism, but ye observed not my commandments. Ye subdued your body to virginity, but ye kept not mercy, but ye did not cast the hatred of your brother out of your souls. For not every one that saith to me, Lord, Lord, shall be saved, but he that doeth my will.[3] And these shall go away into everlasting punishment, but the righteous into life eternal.[4]

XLIX.

"Be thou faithful unto death, and I will give thee the crown of life."

Ye have heard, beloved, the answer of the Lord; ye have learned the sentence of the Judge; ye have been given to understand what kind of awful scrutiny awaits us, and what day and what hour are before us. Let us therefore ponder this every day; let us meditate on this both day and night, both in the house, and by the way, and in the churches, that we may not stand forth at that dread and impartial judgment condemned, abased, and sad, but with purity of action, life, conversation, and confession; so that to us also the merciful and benignant God may say, "Thy faith hath saved thee, go in peace;"[5] and again, "Well done, good and faithful servant; thou hast been faithful over a few things, I will make thee the ruler over many things: enter thou into the joy of thy Lord."[6] Which joy may it be ours to reach, by the grace and kindness of our Lord Jesus Christ, to whom pertain glory, honour, and adoration, with His Father, who is without beginning, and His holy, and good, and quickening Spirit, now and ever, and to the ages of the ages. Amen.[7]

HIPPOLYTUS ON THE TWELVE APOSTLES·

WHERE EACH OF THEM PREACHED, AND WHERE HE MET HIS END.

1. Peter preached the Gospel in Pontus, and Galatia, and Cappadocia, and Betania, and Italy, and Asia, and was afterwards crucified by Nero

---

[1] Tossings, μετεωρισμούς. ["Tossings," etc. Does it refer to the somersaults of harlequins?]
[2] Jas. ii. 13.

[3] Matt. vii. 23.
[4] Matt. xxv. 46.
[5] Luke vii. 50.
[6] Matt. xxv. 23.
[7] [Here follows the text, Apoc. ii. 10, transposed above.]

in Rome with his head downward, as he had himself desired to suffer in that manner.

2. Andrew preached to the Scythians and Thracians, and was crucified, suspended on an olive tree, at Patræ, *a town* of Achaia ; and there too he was buried.

3. John, again, in Asia, was banished by Domitian the king to the isle of Patmos, in which also he wrote his Gospel and saw the apocalyptic vision ; and in Trajan's time he fell asleep at Ephesus, where his remains were sought for, but could not be found.

4. James, his brother, when preaching in Judea, was cut off with the sword by Herod the tetrarch, and was buried there.

5. Philip preached in Phrygia, and was crucified in Hierapolis with his head downward in the time of Domitian, and was buried there.

6. Bartholomew, again, *preached* to the Indians, to whom he also gave the Gospel according to Matthew, *and* was crucified with his head downward, and was buried in Allanum,[1] *a town* of the great Armenia.[2]

7. And Matthew wrote the Gospel in the Hebrew tongue,[3] and published it at Jerusalem, and fell asleep at Hierees, *a town* of Parthia.

8. And Thomas preached to the Parthians, Medes, Persians, Hyrcanians, Bactrians, and Margians,[4] and was thrust through in the four members of his body with a pine spear[5] at Calamene,[6] the city of India, and was buried there.

9. And James the son of Alphæus, when preaching in Jerusalem, was stoned to death by the Jews, and was buried there beside the temple.

10. Jude, who is also *called* Lebbæus, preached to the people of Edessa,[7] and to all Mesopotamia, and fell asleep at Berytus, and was buried there.

11. Simon the Zealot,[8] the son of Clopas, who is also *called* Jude, became bishop of Jerusalem after James the Just, and fell asleep and was buried there at the age of 120 years.

12. And Matthias, who was one of the seventy, was numbered along with the eleven apostles, and preached in Jerusalem, and fell asleep and was buried there.

13. And Paul entered into the apostleship a year after the assumption of Christ ; and beginning at Jerusalem, he advanced as far as Illyricum, and Italy, and Spain, preaching the Gospel for five-and-thirty years. And in the time of Nero he was beheaded at Rome, and was buried there.

THE SAME HIPPOLYTUS ON THE SEVENTY APOSTLES.[9]

1. James the Lord's brother,[10] bishop of Jerusalem.

2. Cleopas, bishop of Jerusalem.

3. Matthias, who supplied the vacant place in the number of the twelve apostles.

4. Thaddeus, who conveyed the epistle to Augarus.

5. Ananias, who baptized Paul, *and was* bishop of Damascus.

6. Stephen, the first martyr.

7. Philip, who baptized the eunuch.

8. Prochorus, bishop of Nicomedia, who also was the first that departed,[11] believing together with his daughters.

9. Nicanor died when Stephen was martyred.

10. Timon, bishop of Bostra.

11. Parmenas, bishop of Soli.

12. Nicolaus, bishop of Samaria.

13. Barnabas, bishop of Milan.

14. Mark the evangelist, bishop of Alexandria.

15. Luke the evangelist.

These two belonged to the seventy disciples who were scattered[12] by the offence of the word which Christ spake, "Except a man eat my flesh, and drink my blood, he is not worthy of me."[13] But the one being induced to return to the Lord by Peter's instrumentality, and the other by Paul's, they were honoured to preach that Gospel[14] on account of which they also suffered martyrdom, the one being burned, and the other being crucified on an olive tree.

16. Silas, bishop of Corinth.

17. Silvanus, bishop of Thessalonica.

18. Crisces (Crescens), bishop of Carchedon in Gaul.

19. Epænetus, bishop of Carthage.

20. Andronicus, bishop of Pannonia.

21. Amplias, bishop of Odyssus.

22. Urban, bishop of Macedonia.

23. Stachys, bishop of Byzantium.

24. Barnabas, bishop of Heraclea.

25. Phygellus, bishop of Ephesus. He was of the party also of Simon.[15]

26. Hermogenes. He, too, was of the same mind with the former.

---

[1] Or Albanum.

[2] [The general tradition is, that he was flayed alive, and then crucified.]

[3] [See Scrivener, *Introduction*, p. 282, note 1, and Lardner, *Credib.*, ii. 494, etc.]

[4] Μάργοις. Combefisius proposes Μάρδοις. Jerome has "Magis."

[5] The text is ἐλακήδη ἐλογχιάσθη, ἐλακήδη being probably for ἐλάτῃ.

[6] Καλαμήνῃ. Steph. le Moyne reads Καραμήνῃ.

[7] Αἰδεσινοῖς.

[8] ὁ Κανανίτης.

[9] In the Codex Baroccian. 206. This is found also, along with the former piece, *On the Twelve Apostles*, in two codices of the Coislinian or Seguierian Library, as Montfaucon states in his recension of the Greek manuscripts of that library. He mentions also a third codex of Hippolytus, *On the Twelve Apostles*. [Probably spurious, but yet antique.]

[10] ἀδελφόθεος.

[11] ἐξελθών.

[12] The text is, οὗτοι οἱ β' τῶν ὁ τυγχανόντων διασκορπισθέντων. It may be meant for, "these two of the seventy were scattered," etc.

[13] John vi. 53, 66.

[14] εὐαγγελίζεσθαι, perhaps = *write* of that Gospel, as the Latin version puts it. [But St. Mark's body is *said to be* in Venice.]

[15] *Magus.*

27. Demas, who also became a priest of idols.
28. Apelles, bishop of Smyrna.
29. Aristobulus, bishop of Britain.
30. Narcissus, bishop of Athens.
31. Herodion, bishop of Tarsus.
32. Agabus the prophet.
33. Rufus, bishop of Thebes.
34. Asyncritus, bishop of Hyrcania.
35. Phlegon, bishop of Marathon.
36. Hermes, bishop of Dalmatia.
37. Patrobulus,[1] bishop of Puteoli.
38. Hermas, bishop of Philippi.
39. Linus, bishop of Rome.
40. Caius, bishop of Ephesus.
41. Philologus, bishop of Sinope.
42, 43. Olympus and Rhodion were martyred in Rome.
44. Lucius, bishop of Laodicea in Syria.
45. Jason, bishop of Tarsus.
46. Sosipater, bishop of Iconium.
47. Tertius, bishop of Iconium.
48. Erastus, bishop of Panellas.
49. Quartus, bishop of Berytus.
50. Apollo, bishop of Cæsarea.
51. Cephas.[2]
52. Sosthenes, bishop of Colophonia.
53. Tychicus, bishop of Colophonia.
54. Epaphroditus, bishop of Andriace.
55. Cæsar, bishop of Dyrrachium.
56. Mark, cousin to Barnabas, bishop of Apollonia.
57. Justus, bishop of Eleutheropolis.
58. Artemas, bishop of Lystra.
59. Clement, bishop of Sardinia.
60. Onesiphorus, bishop of Corone.
61. Tychicus, bishop of Chalcedon.
62. Carpus, bishop of Berytus in Thrace.
63. Evodus, bishop of Antioch.
64. Aristarchus, bishop of Apamea.
65. Mark, who is also John, bishop of Bibloupolis.
66. Zenas, bishop of Diospolis.
67. Philemon, bishop of Gaza.
68, 69. Aristarchus and Pudes.
70. Trophimus, who was martyred along with Paul.

HEADS OF THE CANONS OF ABULIDES OR HIPPOLYTUS,

WHICH ARE USED BY THE ÆTHIOPIAN CHRISTIANS.[3]

1. Of the holy faith of Jesus Christ.[4]
2. Of bishops.[5]

3. Of prayers spoken on the ordination of bishops, and of the order of the *Missa*.[6]
4. Of the ordination of presbyters.
5. Of the ordination of deacons.
6. Of those who suffer persecution for the faith.[7]
7. Of the election of reader and sub-deacon.[8]
8. Of the gift of healing.[9]
9. Of the presbyter who abides in a place inconvenient for his office.[10]
10. Of those who are converted to the Christian religion.
11. Of him who makes idols.[10]
12. Various pursuits[11] are enumerated, the followers of which are not to be admitted to the Christian religion until repentance is exhibited.[10]
13. Of the place which the highest kings or princes shall occupy in the temple.[12]
14. That it is not meet for Christians to bear arms.[13]
15. Of works which are unlawful to Christians.[13]
16. Of the Christian who marries a slave-woman.[13]
17. Of the free woman.[13]
18. Of the midwife; and that the women ought to be separate from the men in prayer.[14]
19. Of the catechumen who suffers martyrdom before baptism.[15]
20. Of the fast of the fourth and sixth holiday; and of Lent.[16]
21. That presbyters should assemble daily with the people in church.[17]
22. Of the week of the Jews' passover; and of him who knows not passover (Easter).[18]
23. That every one be held to learn doctrine.[19]
24. Of the care of the bishop over the sick.[20]
25. Of him on whom the care of the sick is enjoined; and of the time at which prayers are to be made.[21]
26. Of the time at which exhortations are to be heard.[13]
27. Of him who frequents the temple every day.[22]
28. That the faithful ought to eat nothing before the holy communion.[23]

---

[1] Rom. xvi. 14, Πατρόβας.
[2] In the manuscript there is a *lacuna* here.
[3] These were first published in French by Jo. Michael Wanslebius in his book *De Ecclesia Alexandrina*, Paris, 1677, p. 12; then in Latin, by Job Ludolfus, in his *Commentar. ad historiam Æthiopicam*, Frankfort, 1691, p. 333; and by William Whiston, in vol. iii. of his *Primitive Christianity Revived*, published in English at London, 1711, p. 543. He has also noted the passages in the *Constitutiones Apostolicæ*, treating the same matters.
[4] *Constit. Apostol.*, lib. vi. ch. 11, etc.
[5] Lib. vii. ch. 41.

[6] Lib. vii. ch. 4, 5, 10. [The service of the faithful, *Missa Fidelium*, not the modern Mass. See Bingham, book xv. The *Missa* was an innocent word for the *dismission* of those not about to receive the Communion. See Guettée, *Exposition*, etc., p. 433.]
[7] Lib. viii. ch. 17, 18, 19, 20, 23, 45.
[8] Lib. viii. ch. 21, 22.
[9] Lib. viii. ch. 1, 2.
[10] Lib. viii. ch. 46, 32.
[11] *Studia*.
[12] Wanting.
[13] Lib. viii. ch. 32.
[14] Lib. ii. ch. 57.
[15] Lib. v. ch. 6.
[16] Lib. v. ch. 13, 15.
[17] Lib. ii. ch. 36.
[18] Lib. v. ch. 15, etc.
[19] Lib. vii. ch. 39, 40, 41.
[20] Lib. iv. ch. 2.
[21] Lib. iii. ch. 19, viii. ch. 34.
[22] Lib. ii. ch. 59.
[23] Wanting.

29. That care is to be well taken that nothing fall from the chalice to the ground.[1]

30. Of catechumens.[2]

31. That a deacon may dispense the Eucharist to the people with permission of a bishop or presbyter.[3]

32. That widows and virgins ought to pray constantly.[4]

33. That commemoration should be made of the faithful dead every day, with the exception of the Lord's day.[5]

34. Of the sober behaviour of the secular[6] in church.[7]

35. That deacons may pronounce the benediction and thanksgiving at the love-feasts when a bishop is not present.[8]

36. Of the first-fruits of the earth, and of vows.[9]

37. When a bishop celebrates the holy communion (Synaxis),[10] the presbyters who stand by him should be clothed in white.[11]

38. That no one ought to sleep on the night of the resurrection of our Lord Jesus Christ.[12]

CANONS OF THE CHURCH OF ALEXANDRIA.

WRONGLY ASCRIBED TO HIPPOLYTUS.[13]

In the name of the Father, and the Son, and the Holy Spirit, Amen. Those are the canons of the Church, ordinances which Hippolytus wrote, by whom *the Church* speaketh; and the number of them is thirty-eight canons. Greeting from the Lord.

Canon First. Of the Catholic faith. Before all things should we speak of the faith, holy and right, regarding our Lord Jesus Christ, the Son of the living God; and we have *consequently* placed that canon in the faith (the symbol); and we agree in this with all reasonable certitude, that the Trinity is equal perfectly in honour, and equal in glory, and has neither beginning nor end. The Word *is* the Son of God, and is Himself the Creator of every creature, of things visible and invisible. This we lay down with one accord, in opposition to those who have said boldly, that it is not right *to speak* of the Word of God as our Lord Jesus Christ spake. We come together chiefly to bring out the holy truth[14] regarding God; and we have separated

them, because they do not agree with the Church in theology, nor with us the sons of the Scriptures. On this account we have sundered them from the Church, and have left what concerns them to God, who will judge His creatures with justice.[15] To those, moreover, who are not cognisant of them, we make this known without ill-will, in order that they may not rush into an evil death, like heretics, but may gain eternal life, and teach their sons and their posterity this one true faith.

Canon Second. Of bishops. A bishop should be elected by all the people, and he should be unimpeachable, as it is written of him in the apostle; in the week in which he is ordained, the whole people should also say, We desire him; and there should be silence in the whole hall, and they should all pray in his behalf, and say, O God, stablish him whom Thou hast prepared for us, etc.

Canon Third. Prayer in behalf of him who is made bishop, and the ordinance of the Missa.[16] O God, the Father of our Lord Jesus Christ, the Father of mercies, and the God of all consolation, etc.

Canon Fourth. Of the ordination of a presbyter.

Canon Fifth. Of the constituting a deacon.

Canon Sixth. Of those who have suffered for the faith.

Canon Seventh. Of him who is elected reader and sub-deacon.

Canon Eighth. Of the gift of healings.

Canon Ninth. That a presbyter should not dwell in unbefitting places; and of the honour of widows.

Canon Tenth. Of those who wish to become Nazarenes (Christians).

Canon Eleventh. Of him who makes idols and images, or the artificer.

Canon Twelfth. Of the prohibition of those works, the authors of which are not to be received but on the exhibition of repentance.

Canon Thirteenth. Of a prince or a soldier, that they be not received indiscriminately.

Canon Fourteenth. That a Nazarene may not become a soldier unless by order.

Canon Fifteenth. Enumeration of works which are unlawful.

Canon Sixteenth. Of him who has a lawful wife, and takes another beside her.

Canon Seventeenth. Of a free-born woman, and her duties. Of midwives, and of the separation of men from women. Of virgins, that they should cover their faces and their heads.

Canon Eighteenth. Of women in childbed, and of midwives again.

Canon Nineteenth. Of catechumens, and the ordinance of Baptism and the Missa.

---

[1] Wanting.
[2] Lib. vii. ch. 39, etc.
[3] Lib. viii. ch. 28.
[4] Lib. iii. ch. 6, 7, 13.
[5] Lib iv. ch. 14, viii. ch. 41–44.
[6] i.e., laymen.
[7] Lib. ii. ch. 57.
[8] Wanting.
[9] Or offerings. Lib. ii. ch. 25.
[10] [Synaxis. Elucidation II.]
[11] Lib. vii. ch. 29, viii. 30, 31. [See the whole history of ecclesiastical antiquity, on this point, in the learned work of Wharton B. Marriott, *Vestiarium Christianum*, London, Rivingtons, 1868.]
[12] Lib. viii. ch. 12, v. ch. 19.
[13] *De Magistris, Acta Martyrum ad Ostia Tiberina*, Rome, 1795, fol. Append., p. 478. [Bunsen, vol. ii. p. 302.]
[14] [*Ad proferendum sancte.* A very primitive token.]

[15] [Note this mild excommunication of primitive ages.]
[16] *Ordinatio missæ.* [Missa. See note 6, p. 256, *supra.*]

Canon Twentieth. Of the fast *the six days,* and of that of Lent.

Canon Twenty-first. Of the daily assembling of priests and people in the church.

Canon Twenty-second. Of the week of the Jews' passover, wherein joy shall be put away, and of what is eaten therein ; and of him who, being brought up abroad, is ignorant of the Calendar.[1]

Canon Twenty-third. Of doctrine, that it should be continuous, *greater than the sea,* and that its words ought to be fulfilled by deeds.

Canon Twenty-fourth. Of the bishop's visitation of the sick ; and that if an infirm man has prayed in the church, and has a house, he should go to him.

Canon Twenty-fifth. Of the procurator appointed for the sick, and of the bishop, and the times of prayer.

Canon Twenty-sixth. Of the hearing of the word in church, and of praying in it.

Canon Twenty-seventh. Of him who does not come to church daily, — let him read books ; and of prayer at midnight and cock-crowing, and of the washing of hands at the time of any prayer.

Canon Twenty-eighth. That none of the believers should taste anything, but after he has taken the sacred mysteries, especially in the days of fasting.

Canon Twenty-ninth. Of the keeping of oblations which are laid upon the altar, — that nothing fall into the sacred chalice, and that nothing fall from the priests, nor from the boys when they take communion ; that an evil spirit rule them not, and that no one speak in the protection,[2] except in prayer ; and when the oblations of the people cease, let psalms be read with all attention, even to the signal of the bell ; and of the sign of the cross, and the casting of the dust of the altar into the pool.[3]

Canon Thirtieth. Of catechumens and the like.

Canon Thirty-first. Of the bishop and presbyter bidding the deacons present the communion.

Canon Thirty-second. Of virgins and widows, that they should pray and fast in the church. Let those who are given to the clerical order pray according to their judgment. Let not a bishop be bound to fasting but with the clergy. And on account of a feast or supper, let him prepare for the poor.[4]

Canon Thirty-third. Of the *Atalmsas* (the oblation), which they shall present for those who are dead, that it be not done on the Lord's day.

Canon Thirty-fourth. That no one speak much, nor make a clamour ; and of the entrance of the saints into the mansions of the faithful.

Canon Thirty-fifth. Of a deacon present at a feast at which there is a presbyter present, — let him do his part in prayer and the breaking of bread for a blessing, and not for the body ; and of the discharge of widows.

Canon Thirty-sixth. Of the first-fruits of the earth, and the first dedication of them ; and of presses, oil, honey, milk, wool, and the like, which may be offered to the bishop for his blessing.

Canon Thirty-seventh. As often as a bishop takes of the sacred mysteries, let the deacons and presbyters be gathered together, clothed in white robes, brilliant in the view of all the people ; and in like manner with a reader.

Canon Thirty-eighth. Of the night on which our Lord Jesus Christ rose. That no one shall sleep on that night, and wash himself with water ; and a declaration concerning such a one ; and a declaration concerning him who sins after baptism, and of things lawful and unlawful.

The sacred canons of the holy patriarch Hippolytus, the first patriarch of the great city of Rome,[5] which he composed, are ended ; and the number of them is thirty-eight canons. May the Lord help us to keep them. And to God be glory for ever, and on us be His mercy for ever. Amen.

---

[1] Connection, *textum*
[2] Sanctuary [Guettée, p. 424. Within the chancel-rails].
[3] [Bells first used in the fourth century by Paulinus in Campania.]

[4] And of the preparing a table for the poor.
[5] [A very strange title in many respects. But see p. 239, *supra.*]

ELUCIDATIONS.

I.

(The God-bearing Mary, p. 242.)

" THIS name " (θεοτόκος), says Pearson, " was first in use in the Greek Church, which, delight-ing in the happy compositions of that language, so called the Blessed Virgin ; from which the Latins, in imitation, styled her *Virginem Deiparam*," etc. . . . Yet those ancient Greeks which call the Virgin θεοτόκος, did not call her μητέρα τοῦ Θεοῦ, " Mother of God." This was very different to a pious ear, and rests on no synodical authority. The very learned notes of Pearson, *On the Creed*, pp. 297, 299, should by all means be consulted. Leo of Rome, called " the Great," seems to have coined the less orthodox expression, relying on Holy Scripture, indeed, in the salutation of Elisabeth (Luke i. 43). This term has been sadly abused for Mariolatry.

II.

(Synaxis, p. 257.)

It seems to me worth while to quote a few words from the new and critical edition of Leighton's *Works*, which should be consulted for fuller information.[1] The editor says : " Leighton uses a word for the Holy Communion which is worth noting, because it is rarely used by *Western theo-logians*." The word *Synaxis* is but a Christianized form of the word *Synagogue;* but, like the word κοινωνία, it points to Christ's mystical body, — " gathering together in one the children of God." *Synaxis* = συνάγει εἰς ἕν. It sums up the idea, " We, being many, are one Bread and one Body, for we are all partakers of that one Bread." Compare John xi. 52 and 1 Cor. x. 15.

St. Chrysostom calls the *Synaxis* φρικωδεστάτη, which is a very different thing from *maxime tremenda*, as applied to the modern " Mass," in behalf of which it is quoted. For Chrysostom applies it to the *participation* of the " Synaxis," and not to the " oblation," much less to the " Host " as an object of adoration, of which he never heard or dreamed. He calls " the Synaxis " *Shudderful* (to borrow a word from the Germans), because the unworthy recipient, in the *Synaxis*, eats and drinks his own condemnation.[2] One must ever be on his guard against the subtlety which reads into the Fathers *modern ideas* under ancient phrases.[3] Precisely so Holy Scripture itself is paraphrased into Trent doctrine, as in Acts xiii. 2 the Louvain versionists rendered the text, " And while *they offered the sacrifice of the Mass* and fasted."

---

[1] Leighton, *Works*, edited by West, of Nairn, vol. vi. p. 243, note. London, Longmans, 1870.

[2] 1 Cor. xi. 29-34. Chrysostom evidently has in view the apostle's argument, based on the Communion as a *Synaxis*, and not on its *hierurgic* aspects.

[3] Mendham's *Literary Policy of the Church of Rome* (*passim*), and also the old work of James, *On the Corruptions of Scripture, Councils, and Fathers*, a new edition. London: Parker, 1843.

CYPRIAN

[TRANSLATED BY THE REV. ERNEST WALLIS, PH.D.]

INTRODUCTORY NOTICE TO CYPRIAN

[A.D. 200–258.] If Hippolytus reflects the spirit of Irenæus in all his writings, it is not remarkable. He was the spiritual son of the great Bishop of Lyons, and deeply imbued with the family character imparted to his disciples by the blessed presbyter of Patmos and Ephesus. But while Cyprian is the spiritual son and pupil of Tertullian, we must seek his characteristics and the key to his whole ministry in the far-off See and city where the disciples were first called Christians. Cyprian is the Ignatius of the West. We see in his works how truly historical are the writings of Ignatius, and how diffused was his simple and elementary system of organic unity. It embodies no hierarchical assumption, no "lordship over God's heritage," but is conceived in the spirit of St. Peter when he disclaimed all this, and said, "The *presbyters* who are among you I exhort, who am also a *presbyter*." Cyprian was indeed a strenuous asserter of the responsibilities of his office ; but he built upon that system universally recognised by the Great Councils, which the popes and their adherents have ever laboured to destroy. Nothing can be more delusive than the idea that the mediæval system derives any support from Cyprian's theory of the episcopate or of Church organization. His was the system of the universal parity and community of bishops. In his scheme the apostolate was perpetuated in the episcopate, and the *presbyterate* was an apostolic institution, by which others were associated with bishops in all their functions as *co-presbyters*, but not in those reserved to the presidency of the churches. Feudal ideas imposed a very different system upon the simple framework of original Catholicity. But a careful study of that primitive framework, and of the history of papal development, makes evident the following propositions : —

1. That Cyprian's maxim, *Ecclesia in Episcopo*, whatever else he may have meant by it, is an aphoristic statement of the Nicene Constitutions. These were embedded in the Ignatian theory of an episcopate without a trace of a papacy; and Cyprian's maxims had to be practically destroyed in the West before it was possible to raise the portentous figure of a supreme pontiff, and to subject the Latin churches to the entirely novel principle of *Ecclesia in Papa*. To this novelty Cyprian's system is essentially antagonistic.

2. It will be seen that Cyprian, far from being the patron of ecclesiastical despotism, is the expounder of early canons and constitutions, in the spirit of order and discipline, indeed, but with the largest exemplification of that "liberty" which is manifested wherever "the Spirit of the Lord" is operative. Cyprian is the patron and defender of the presbytery and of lay co-operation, as well as of the regimen of the episcopate. His letters illustrate the Catholic system as it was known to the Nicene Fathers ; but, of all the Christian Fathers, he is the most clear and comprehensive in his conception of the body of Christ as an organic whole, in which every member has an honourable function.[1] Popular government and representative government, the legitimate power and place of the laity, the organization of the Christian *plebs* into their faculty as the ἀντιλήψεις of St. Paul,[2] the development of synods, *omni plebe adstante*, — all this is embodied in the Catholic system as Cyprian understood it.

---

[1] Eph. iv. 15, 16; 1 Cor. xii. 12–30. I have little doubt that our author's theory was guided by his conceptions of this passage, and by Ignatian traditions.

[2] 1 Cor. xii. 28.

3. The Orientals [1] in large degree, even under their yoke of bondage and the superstitions engendered by their decay, have ever adhered to this Ignatian theory, of which Cyprian was the great expounder in the West; while the terrible schism of the ninth century, which removed the West from the Nicene basis, and placed the Latin churches upon the foundation of the forged Decretals,[2] was effected by ignoring the Cyprianic maxims, and then by a practical pulverizing of their fundamental principle of unity. This change involved a subversion of the primitive episcopate, an annihilation of the rights of the presbytery, and a total abasement of the laity; in a word, the destruction of synodical constitutions and of constitutional freedom.

4. The constitutional *primacy*, of which Cyprian was an early promotor, had to be entirely destroyed by decretalism before the papacy could exist. Gregory the Great stood upon the Cyprianic base when he pronounced the author of a scheme for a "universal bishopric" to be a forerunner of Antichrist. It was the spirit of the Decretals to substitute the fictitious idea of a divine supremacy in one bishop and one See, for the canonical presidency of a bishop who was only *primus inter pares*.

5. Hence the Cyprianic system has ever been the great resource of the "Gallicans against the Ultramontanes" in the cruel but most interesting history of the West. From the Council of Frankfort to our own times Cyprian's spirit is reflected in Hincmar, in Gerbert, in the Gallican canonists, in De Marca, in Bossuet, in Launoy, in Dupin, in Pascal, in the Jansenists (Augustinians), and by the Old Catholics in their late uprising against the dogmatic triumph of Ultramontanism. Nobody can understand the history of Latin Christianity without mastering the system of Cyprian, and comprehending the entirely hostile and uncatholic system of the Decretals.

6. I am not anxious to conceal the fact that I profoundly sympathize with the free spirit, the true benignity, and the moral purity which are everywhere reflected in the writings of Cyprian. If ever American Romanism becomes sufficiently enlightened and purified to comprehend this great Carthaginian Father, and to speak in his tones to the Bishop of Rome, a glorious reformation of this alien religion will be the result; and then we may comprehend the mysterious Providence which has transferred to these shores so many subjects of the despotism of the Vatican. Meanwhile the student of the *Ante-Nicene Fathers* will not be slow to perceive that he has, in the eight volumes of this series, all that is needful to disarm Romanism, to refute its pretensions, and to direct honest and truth-loving spirits in the Roman Obedience to the door of escape opened by Döllinger and his associates in the "Old Catholic" effort for the restoration of the Latin churches. Let us "speak the truth in love," and pray the Lord to bless this and every endeavour to promote and to sanctify the spirit of enlightened research after the "pattern in the mount." For "thus saith the Lord, Stand ye in the ways, and see and ask for the old paths:" τὰ ἀρχαῖα ἔθη. The following Introduction, from the Edinburgh editor, supplies further answers to inquiry, and suffices to elucidate the subjoined narrative of Pontius.

Little is known of the early history of Thascius Cyprian (born probably about 200 A.D.) until the period of his intimacy with the Carthaginian presbyter Cæcilius, which led to his conversion A.D 246. That he was born of respectable parentage, and highly educated for the profession of a rhetorician, is all that can be said with any degree of certainty. At his baptism he assumed the name of his friend Cæcilius, and devoted himself, with all the energies of an ardent and vigorous mind, to the study and practice of Christianity.

His ordination and his elevation to the episcopate rapidly followed his conversion. With some resistance on his own part, and not without great objections on the part of older presbyters, who saw themselves superseded by his promotion, the popular urgency constrained him to accept the office of Bishop of Carthage (A.D. 248), which he held until his martyrdom (A.D. 258).

---

[1] See Guettée's Exposition, p. 93.   [2] Of which, hereafter, in an elucidation. See Guettée, p. 383.

The writings of Cyprian, apart from their intrinsic worth, have a very considerable historical interest and value, as illustrating the social and religious feelings and usages that then prevailed among the members of the Christian community. Nothing can enable us more vividly to realize the intense convictions — the high-strained enthusiasm — which formed the common level of the Christian experience, than does the indignation with which the prelate denounces the evasions of those who dared not confess, or the lapses of those who shrank from martyrdom. Living in the atmosphere of persecution, and often in the immediate presence of a lingering death, the professors of Christianity were nerved up to a wonderful contempt of suffering and of worldly enjoyment, and saw every event that occurred around them in the glow of their excited imagination ; so that many circumstances were sincerely believed and honestly recorded, which will not be for a moment received as true by the calm and critical reader. The account given by Cyprian in his treatise on the Lapsed [1] may serve as an illustration. Of this Dean Milman observes : " In what a high-wrought state of enthusiasm must men have been, who could relate and believe such statements as miraculous ! " [2]

Before being advanced to the episcopate, Cyprian had written his Epistle to Donatus shortly after his baptism (A.D. 246) ; his treatise, or fragment of a treatise, on the Vanity of Idols ; and his three books of Testimonies against the Jews. In the following translation the order of Migne has been adopted, which places the letter to Donatus, as seems most natural, first among the Epistles, instead of with the Treatises.

The breaking out of the Decian persecution (A.D. 250) induced Cyprian to retire into concealment for a time ; and his retreat gave occasion to a sharp attack upon his conduct, in a letter from the Roman to the Carthaginian clergy.[3] During this year he wrote many letters from his place of concealment to the clergy and others at Rome and at Carthage, controlling, warning, directing, and exhorting, and in every way maintaining his episcopal superintendence in his absence, in all matters connected with the well-being of the Church.

The first 39 of the epistles, excepting the one to Donatus, were probably written during the period of Cyprian's retirement. He appears to have returned to his public duties early in June, 251. Then follow many letters beween himself and Cornelius bishop of Rome, and others, on subjects connected with the schisms of Novatian, Novatus, and Felicissimus, and with the condition of those who had been perverted by them. The question proposed in Epistle 52 was settled in the Council that was held in May, 252 ; and the reference to that anticipated decision limits the date of the letter to about April in the same year. In the 53d Epistle, Cyprian is alluding to the impending persecution of Gallus, under which Cornelius was banished in July, 252. The 56th Epistle was a letter of congratulation to Cornelius on his banishment ; and therefore it must have been written before September 14th in that year, the date of the death of Cornelius. Lucius, his successor, was also banished, and was congratulated on his return by Cyprian in Epistle 57, which therefore must have been written about the end of November, 252. The 59th Epistle is referred by Bishop Pearson to the beginning of the year 253.

There seems nothing to suggest the date of Epistles 60 and 61, except the probability that they were written during a time of peace ; and for this reason they are referred to the beginning of Cyprian's episcopate, before the outbreak of the Decian persecution, A.D. 249. It is usual to assign Epistle 64 to the same year, or at least to a very early period of Cyprian's official life ; but it seems scarcely likely that his episcopal counsel should have been sought by a brother bishop in a matter of practice, until he had had some experience ; and as it was probably written at a time of peace, when discipline had become relaxed, the date 253 seems preferable. The 68th Epistle is easily dated by the reference, on page 246, to an episcopate of six years' duration ; and it must therefore have been written in A.D. 254. On the 14th September, Cyprian was banished to Curubis by the Emperor Valerian. From his place of exile he wrote Epistle 76, which was replied to in

---

[1] P. 368, vol. i. Edin. edition.   [2] Milman's *History of Christianity*, vol. ii. p. 190, note *b*. See note, p. 266.   [3] Epistle ii.

Epistles 77, 78, and 79.   Doubts are entertained as to the date of Epistle 80, whether it should be referred to A.D. 250 or 257.   Pamelius prefers the latter date, on the ground that the Rogatianus to whom it is inscribed was one who survived the Decian persecution, and a younger man than the one who, as he supposes, was declared to have suffered martyrdom at the date of this Epistle.[1] This, however, seems very unsatisfactory ; and the weight of authority is in favour of the earlier date.   The remaining Epistles are easily limited by their contents to the period immediately preceding Cyprian's martyrdom.

For the sake of uniformity, it has been thought well to adhere to the arrangement of Migne, in the order of the Epistles as well as in their divisions.   For the convenience of reference, however, the number of each Epistle in the Oxford edition is appended in a note.   For a similar reason, the general form of Migne's text has been used in the following translation ; but the use of other texts and of preceding translations has not been rejected in the endeavour to approximate to the sense of the author.   Moreover, such various readings as might suggest different shades of meaning in doubtful passages have been given.

The Translator has only to add, that, as a rule, an exact rendering has been sought after, sometimes in preference to a version in fluent English.   But, except in cases where the corruption or obscurity of the text seems insurmountable, the meaning of the writer is believed to be given fairly and intelligibly.   The style of Cyprian, like that of his master Tertullian, is marked much more by vehemence than perspicuity, and it is often no easy matter to give exact expression in another language to the idea contained in the original text.   Cyprian's Life, as written by his own deacon Pontius, is subjoined.

NOTE BY THE AMERICAN EDITOR.[2]

IT is easy to speak with ridicule of such instances as Dean Milman here treats so philosophically.   But, lest believers should be charged with exceptional credulity, let us recall what the father of English Deism relates of his own experiences, in the conclusion of his Autobiography : " I had no sooner spoken these words (of prayer to the Deist's deity) but a loud though yet a gentle noise came from the heavens, for it was like nothing on earth, which did so comfort and cheer me, that I took my petition as granted, and that I had the sign I demanded. . . . This, how strange soever it may seem, I protest, before the eternal God, is true," etc.   *Life of Herbert,* p. 52, *Popular Authors* (no date).   London.   From Horace Walpole's edition.

---

[1] P. 328, Ed. Edinburgh.   [2] See p. 265.

THE LIFE AND PASSION

OF

CYPRIAN, BISHOP AND MARTYR

BY PONTIUS THE DEACON.

1. ALTHOUGH Cyprian, the devout priest [1] and glorious witness of God, composed many writings whereby the memory of his worthy name survives ; and although the profuse fertility of his eloquence and of God's grace so expands itself in the exuberance and richness of his discourse, that he will probably never cease to speak even to the end of the world ; yet, since to his works and deserts it is justly due that his example should be recorded in writing, I have thought it well to prepare this brief and compendious narrative. Not that the life of so great a man can be unknown to any even of the heathen nations, but that to our posterity also this incomparable and lofty pattern may be prolonged into immortal remembrance. It would assuredly be hard that, when our fathers have given such honour even to lay-people and catechumens who have obtained martyrdom, for reverence of their very martyrdom, as to record many, or I had nearly said, well nigh all, of the circumstances of their sufferings, so that they might be brought to our knowledge also who as yet were not born, the passion of such a priest and such a martyr as Cyprian should be passed over, who, independently of his martyrdom, had much to teach, and that what he did while he lived should be hidden from the world. And, indeed, these doings of his were such, and so great, and so admirable, that I am deterred by the contemplation of their greatness, and confess myself incompetent to discourse in a way that shall be worthy of the honour of his deserts, and unable to relate such noble deeds in such a way that they may appear as great as in fact they are, except that the multitude of his glories is itself sufficient for itself, and needs no other heraldry. It enhances my difficulty, that you also are anxious to hear very much, or if it be possible every thing, about him, longing with eager warmth at least to become acquainted with his deeds, although now his living words are silent. And in this behalf, if I should say that the powers of eloquence fail me, I should say too little. For eloquence itself fails of suitable powers fully to satisfy your desire. And thus I am sorely pressed on both sides, since he burdens me with his virtues, and you press me hard with your entreaties.

2. At what point, then, shall I begin, — from what direction shall I approach the description of his goodness, except from the beginning of his faith and from his heavenly birth? inasmuch as the doings of a man of God should not be reckoned from any point except from the time that he was born of God. He may have had pursuits previously, and liberal arts may have imbued his mind while engaged therein ; but these things I pass over ; for as yet they had nothing to do with anything but his secular advantage. But when he had learned sacred knowledge, and breaking through the clouds of this world had emerged into the light of spiritual wisdom, if I was with him in any of his doings, if I have discerned any of his more illustrious labours, I will speak of them ; only asking meanwhile for this indulgence, that whatever I shall say too little (for too little I must needs say) may rather be attributed to my ignorance than subtracted from his glory. While his faith was in its first rudiments, he believed that before God nothing was worthy in comparison of the observance of continency. For he thought that the heart might then become what it ought to be, and the mind attain to the full capacity of truth, if he trod under foot the lust of the flesh with the robust and healthy vigour of holiness. Who has ever recorded such a marvel? His second birth had not yet enlightened the new man with the entire splendour of the divine light, yet he

1 [Here put for the chief in the sacerdocy. See p. 268, *infra*.]

was already overcoming the ancient and pristine darkness by the mere dawning of the light. Then — what is even greater — when he had learned from the reading of Scripture certain things not according to the condition of his noviciate, but in proportion to the earliness of his faith, he immediately laid hold of what he had discovered, for his own advantage in deserving well of God.[1] By distributing his means for the relief of the indigence of the poor, by dispensing the purchase-money of entire estates, he at once realized two benefits, — the contempt of this world's ambition, than which nothing is more pernicious, and the observance of that mercy which God has preferred even to His sacrifices, and which even he did not maintain who said that he had kept all the commandments of the law; whereby with premature swiftness of piety he almost began to be perfect before he had learnt the way to be perfect. Who of the ancients, I pray, has done this? Who of the most celebrated veterans in the faith, whose hearts and ears have throbbed to the divine words for many years, has attempted any such thing, as this man — of faith yet unskilled, and whom, perhaps, as yet nobody trusted — surpassing the age of antiquity, accomplished by his glorious and admirable labours? No one reaps immediately upon his sowing; no one presses out the vintage harvest from the trenches just formed; no one ever yet sought for ripened fruit from newly planted slips. But in him all incredible things concurred. In him the threshing preceded (if it may be said, for the thing is beyond belief) — preceded the sowing, the vintage the shoots, the fruit the root.

3. The apostle's epistle says[2] that novices should be passed over, lest by the stupor of heathenism that yet clings to their unconfirmed minds, their untaught inexperience should in any respect sin against God. He first, and I think he alone, furnished an illustration that greater progress is made by faith than by time. For although in the Acts of the Apostles[3] the eunuch is described as at once baptized by Philip, because he believed with his whole heart, this is not a fair parallel. For he was a Jew,[4] and as he came from the temple of the Lord he was reading the prophet Isaiah, and he hoped in Christ, although as yet he did not believe that He had come; while the other, coming from the ignorant heathens, began with a faith as mature as that with which few perhaps have finished their course. In short, in respect of God's grace, there was no delay, no postponement, — I have said but little, — he immediately received the

presbyterate and the priesthood.[5] For who is there that would not entrust every grade of honour to one who believed with such a disposition? There are many things which he did while still a layman, and many things which now as a presbyter he did — many things which, after the examples of righteous men of old, and following them with a close imitation, he accomplished with the obedience of entire consecration — that deserved well of the Lord.[6] For his discourse concerning this was usually, that if he had read of any one being set forth with the praise of God, he would persuade us to inquire on account of what doings he had pleased God. If Job, glorious by God's testimony, was called a true worshipper of God, and one to whom there was none upon earth to be compared, he taught that we should do whatever Job had previously done, so that while we are doing like things we may call forth a similar testimony of God for ourselves. He, contemning the loss of his estate, gained such advantage by his virtue thus tried, that he had no perception of the temporal losses even of his affection. Neither poverty nor pain broke him down; the persuasion of his wife did not influence him; the dreadful suffering of his own body did not shake his firmness. His virtue remained established in its own home, and his devotion, founded upon deep roots, gave way under no onset of the devil tempting him to abstain from blessing his God with a grateful faith even in his adversity. His house was open to every comer. No widow returned from him with an empty lap; no blind man was unguided by him as a companion; none faltering in step was unsupported by him for a staff; none stripped of help by the hand of the mighty was not protected by him as a defender. Such things ought they to do, he was accustomed to say, who desire to please God. And thus running through the examples of all good men, by always imitating those who were better than others he made himself also worthy of imitation.

4. He had a close association among us with a just man, and of praiseworthy memory, by name Cæcilius, and in age as well as in honour a presbyter, who had converted him from his worldly errors to the acknowledgment of the true divinity. This man he loved with entire honour and all observance, regarding him with an obedient veneration, not only as the friend and comrade of his soul, but as the parent of his new life. And at length he, influenced by his attentions, was, as well he might be, stimulated to such a pitch of excessive love, that when he was departing from this world, and his summons was at hand, he commended to him his wife and children; so that him whom he had

---

[1] [St. Luke xx. 35. Creature-*merit* is not implied, but, through grace, the desert of Matt. xxv. 21.]
[2] 1 Tim. iii. 6.
[3] Acts viii. 37.
[4] [A proselyte rather, known in legends as Indich. Vol. i. p. 433.]

[5] [Elucidation I.]
[6] [See above note 1, this page.]

made a partner in the fellowship of his way of life, he afterwards made the heir of his affection.

5. It would be tedious to go through individual circumstances, it would be laborious to enumerate all his doings. For the proof of his good works I think that this one thing is enough, that by the judgment of God and the favour of the people, he was chosen to the office of the priesthood and the degree of the episcopate while still a neophyte, and, as it was considered, a novice. Although still in the early days of his faith, and in the untaught season of his spiritual life, a generous disposition so shone forth in him, that although not yet resplendent with the glitter of office, but only of hope, he gave promise of entire trustworthiness for the priesthood that was coming upon him. Moreover, I will not pass over that remarkable fact, of the way in which, when the entire people by God's inspiration leapt forward in his love and honour, he humbly withdrew, giving place to men of older standing, and thinking himself unworthy of a claim to so great honour, so that he thus became more worthy. For he is made more worthy who dispenses with what he deserves. And with this excitement were the eager people at that time inflamed, desiring with a spiritual longing, as the event proved, not only a bishop, — for in him whom then with a latent foreboding of divinity they were in such wise demanding, they were seeking not only a priest, — but moreover a future martyr. A crowded fraternity was besieging the doors of the house, and throughout all the avenues of access an anxious love was circulating. Possibly that apostolic experience might then have happened to him, as he desired, of being let down through a window, had he also been equal to the apostle in the honour of ordination.[1] It was plain to be seen that all the rest were expecting his coming with an anxious spirit of suspense, and received him when he came with excessive joy. I speak unwillingly, but I must needs speak. Some resisted him, even that he might overcome them; yet with what gentleness, how patiently, how benevolently he gave them indulgence! how mercifully he forgave them, reckoning them afterwards, to the astonishment of many, among his closest and most intimate friends! For who would not be amazed at the forgetfulness of a mind so retentive?

6. Henceforth who is sufficient to relate the manner in which he bore himself? — what pity was his? what vigour? how great his mercy? how great his strictness? So much sanctity and grace beamed from his face that it confounded the minds of the beholders. His countenance was grave and joyous. Neither was his severity gloomy, nor his affability excessive, but a mingled tempering of both; so that it might be doubted whether he most deserved to be revered or to be loved, except that he deserved both to be revered and to be loved. And his dress was not out of harmony with his countenance, being itself also subdued to a fitting mean. The pride of the world did not inflame him, nor yet did an excessively affected penury make him sordid, because this latter kind of attire arises no less from boastfulness, than does such an ambitious frugality from ostentation. But what did he as bishop in respect of the poor, whom as a catechumen he had loved? Let the priests of piety consider, or those whom the teaching of their very rank has trained to the duty of good works, or those whom the common obligation of the Sacrament has bound to the duty of manifesting love. Cyprian the bishop's *cathedra* received such as he had been before, — it did not make him so.[2]

7. And therefore for such merits he at once obtained the glory of proscription also. For nothing else was proper than that he who in the secret recesses of his conscience was rich in the full honour of religion and faith, should moreover be renowned in the publicly diffused report of the Gentiles. He might, indeed, at that time, in accordance with the rapidity wherewith he always attained everything, have hastened to the crown of martyrdom appointed for him, especially when with repeated calls he was frequently demanded for the lions, had it not been needful for him to pass through all the grades of glory, and thus to arrive at the highest, and had not the impending desolation needed the aid of so fertile a mind. For conceive of him as being at that time taken away by the dignity of martyrdom. Who was there to show the advantage of grace, advancing by faith? Who was there to restrain virgins to the fitting discipline of modesty and a dress worthy of holiness, as if with a kind of bridle of the lessons of the Lord? Who was there to teach penitence to the lapsed, truth to heretics, unity to schismatics, peacefulness and the law of evangelical prayer to the sons of God? By whom were the blaspheming Gentiles to be overcome by retorting upon themselves the accusations which they heap upon us? By whom were Christians of too tender an affection, or, what is of more importance, of a too feeble faith in respect of the loss of their friends, to be consoled with the hope of futurity? Whence should we so learn mercy? whence patience? Who was there to restrain the ill blood arising from the envenomed malignity of envy, with the·sweetness of a wholesome remedy? Who was there to raise up such great

[1] [The *charismata* of a higher ministry.]

[2] [Nor does it make any one so. But the Fathers seem to have thought it made good men more humble.]

martyrs by the exhortation of his divine discourse? Who was there, in short, to animate so many confessors sealed with a second inscription on their distinguished brows, and reserved alive for an example of martyrdom, kindling their ardour with a heavenly trumpet? Fortunately, fortunately it occurred then, and truly by the Spirit's direction, that the man who was needed for so many and so excellent purposes was withheld from the consummation of martyrdom. Do you wish to be assured that the cause of his withdrawal was not fear? to allege nothing else, he did suffer subsequently, and this suffering he assuredly would have evaded as usual, if he had evaded it before. It was indeed that fear — and rightly so — that fear which would dread to offend the Lord — that fear which prefers to obey God's commands rather than to be crowned in disobedience. For a mind dedicated in all things to God, and thus enslaved to the divine admonitions, believed that even in suffering itself it would sin, unless it had obeyed the Lord, who then bade *him seek* the place of concealment.

8. Moreover, I think that something may here be said about the benefit of the delay, although I have already touched slightly on the matter. By what appears subsequently to have occurred, it follows that we may prove that that withdrawal was not conceived by human pusillanimity, but, as indeed is the case, was truly divine. The unusual and violent rage of a cruel persecution had laid waste God's people; and since the artful enemy could not deceive all by one fraud, wherever the incautious soldier laid bare his side, there in various manifestations of rage he had destroyed individuals with different kinds of overthrow. There needed some one who could, when men were wounded and hurt by the various arts of the attacking enemy, use the remedy of the celestial medicine according to the nature of the wound, either for cutting or for cherishing them. *Thus* was preserved a man of an intelligence, besides other excellences, also spiritually trained, who between the resounding waves of the opposing schisms could steer the middle course of the Church in a steady path. Are not such plans, I ask, divine? Could this have been done without God? Let them consider who think that such things as these can happen by chance. To them the Church replies with clear voice, saying, "I do not allow and do not believe that such needful men are reserved without the decree of God."

9. Still, if it seem well, let me glance at the rest. Afterwards there broke out a dreadful plague, and excessive destruction of a hateful disease invaded every house in succession of the trembling populace, carrying off day by day with abrupt attack numberless people, every one from his own house. All were shuddering, fleeing, shunning the contagion, impiously exposing their own friends, as if with the exclusion of the person who was sure to die of the plague, one could exclude death itself also. There lay about the meanwhile, over the whole city, no longer bodies, but the carcases of many, and, by the contemplation of a lot which in their turn would be theirs, demanded the pity of the passers-by for themselves. No one regarded anything besides his cruel gains. No one trembled at the remembrance of a similar event. No one did to another what he himself wished to experience. In these circumstances, it would be a wrong to pass over what the pontiff[1] of Christ did, who excelled the pontiffs of the world as much in kindly affection as he did in truth of religion. On the people assembled together in one place he first of all urged the benefits of mercy, teaching by examples from divine lessons, how greatly the duties of benevolence avail to deserve well of God. Then afterwards he subjoined, that there was nothing wonderful in our cherishing our own people only with the needed attentions of love, but that he might become perfect who would do something more than the publican or the heathen, who, overcoming evil with good, and practising a clemency which was like the divine clemency, loved even his enemies, who would pray for the salvation of those that persecute him, as the Lord admonishes and exhorts. God continually makes His sun to rise, and from time to time gives showers to nourish the seed, exhibiting all these kindnesses not only to His people, but to aliens also. And if a man professes to be a son of God, why does not he imitate the example of his Father? "It becomes us," said he, "to answer to our birth; and it is not fitting that those who are evidently born of God should be degenerate, but rather that the propagation of a good Father should be proved in His offspring by the emulation of His goodness."

10. I omit many other matters, and, indeed, many important ones, which the necessity of a limited space does not permit to be detailed in more lengthened discourse, and concerning which this much is sufficient to have been said. But if the Gentiles could have heard these things as they stood before the rostrum, they would probably at once have believed. What, then, should a Christian people do, whose very name proceeds from faith? Thus the ministrations are constantly distributed according to the quality of the men and their degrees. Many who, by the straitness of poverty, were unable to manifest the kindness of wealth, manifested more than wealth, making up by their own labour a service dearer than all riches. And under such

---

[1] [This heathen word thus comes into use as applicable to all bishops. It was used derisively by Tertullian, vol. iv. p. 74.]

a teacher, who would not press forward to be found in some part of such a warfare, whereby he might please both God the Father, and Christ the Judge, and for the present so excellent a priest? Thus what is good was done in the liberality of overflowing works to all men, not to those only who are of the household of faith. Something more was done than is recorded of the incomparable benevolence of Tobias. He must forgive, and forgive again, and frequently forgive; or, to speak more truly, he must of right concede that, although very much might be done before Christ, yet that something more might be done after Christ, since to His times all fulness is attributed. Tobias collected together those who were slain by the king and cast out, of his own race only.

11. Banishment followed these actions, so good and so benevolent. For impiety always makes this return, that it repays the better with the worse. And what God's priest replied to the interrogation of the proconsul, there are Acts which relate. In the meantime, he is excluded from the city who had done some good for the city's safety; he who had striven that the eyes of the living should not suffer the horrors of the infernal abode; he, I say, who, vigilant in the watches of benevolence, had provided — oh wickedness! with unacknowledged goodness — that when all were forsaking the desolate appearance of the city, a destitute state and a deserted country should not perceive its many exiles. But let the world look to this, which accounts banishment a penalty. To them, their country is too dear, and they have the same name as their parents; but we abhor even our parents themselves if they would persuade us against God. To them, it is a severe punishment to live outside their own city; to the Christian, the whole of this world is one home. Wherefore, though he were banished into a hidden and secret place, yet, associated with the affairs of his God, he cannot regard it as an exile. In addition, while honestly serving God, he is a stranger even in his own city. For while the continency of the Holy Spirit restrains him from carnal desires, he lays aside the conversation of the former man, and even among his fellow-citizens, or, I might almost say, among the parents themselves of his earthly life, he is a stranger. Besides, although this might otherwise appear to be a punishment, yet in causes and sentences of this kind, which we suffer for the trial of the proof of our virtue, it is not a punishment, because it is a glory. But, indeed, suppose banishment not to be a punishment to us, yet the witness of their own conscience may still attribute the last and worst wickedness to those who can lay upon the innocent what they think to be a punishment. I will not now de-

scribe a charming place; and, for the present, I pass over the addition of all possible delights. Let us conceive of the place, filthy in situation, squalid in appearance, having no wholesome water, no pleasantness of verdure, no neighbouring shore, but vast wooded rocks between the inhospitable jaws of a totally deserted solitude, far removed in the pathless regions of the world. Such a place might have borne the name of exile, if Cyprian, the priest of God, had come thither; although to him, if the ministrations of men had been wanting, either birds, as in the case of Elias, or angels, as in that of Daniel, would have ministered. Away, away with the belief that anything would be wanting to the least of us, so long as he stands for the confession of the name. So far was God's pontiff, who had always been urgent in merciful works, from needing the assistance of all these things.

12. And now let us return with thankfulness to what I had suggested in the second place, that for the soul of such a man there was divinely provided a sunny and suitable spot, a dwelling, secret as he wished, and all that has before been promised to be added to those who seek the kingdom and righteousness of God. And, not to mention the number of the brethren who visited him, and then the kindness of the citizens themselves, which supplied to him everything whereof he appeared to be deprived, I will not pass over God's wonderful visitation, whereby He wished His priest in exile to be so certain of his passion that was to follow, that in his full confidence of the threatening martyrdom, Curubis possessed not only an exile, but a martyr too. For on that day whereon we first abode in the place of banishment (for the condescension of his love had chosen me among his household companions to a voluntary exile: would that he could also have chosen me to share his passion!),[1] "there appeared to me," said he, "ere yet I was sunk in the repose of slumber, a young man of unusual stature, who, as it were, led me to the prætorium, where I seemed to myself to be led before the tribunal of the proconsul, then sitting. When he looked upon me, he began at once to note down a sentence on his tablet, which I knew not, for he had asked nothing of me with the accustomed interrogation. But the youth, who was standing at his back, very anxiously read what had been noted down. And because he could not then declare it in words, he showed me by an intelligible sign what was contained in the writing of that tablet. For, with hand expanded and flattened like a blade, he imitated the stroke of the accustomed punishment, and expressed what he wished to be understood as clearly as by speech, — I understood the future

---

[1] [Pontius is said to have followed his beloved bishop, A.D. 258 dying a martyr.]

sentence of my passion. I began to ask and to beg immediately that a delay of at least one day should be accorded me, until I should have arranged my property in some reasonable order. And when I had urgently repeated my entreaty, he began again to note down, I know not what, on his tablet. But I perceived from the calmness of his countenance that the judge's mind was moved by my petition, as being a just one. Moreover, that youth, who already had disclosed to me the intelligence of my passion by gesture rather than by words, hastened to signify repeatedly by secret signal that the delay was granted which had been asked for until the morrow, twisting his fingers one behind the other. And I, although the sentence had not been read, although I rejoiced with very glad heart with joy at the delay accorded, yet trembled so with fear of the uncertainty of the interpretation, that the remains of fear still set my exulting heart beating with excessive agitation."

13. What could be more plain than this revelation? What could be more blessed than this condescension? Everything was foretold to him beforehand which subsequently followed. Nothing was diminished of the words of God, nothing was mutilated of so sacred a promise. Carefully consider each particular in accordance with its announcement. He asks for delay till the morrow, when the sentence of his passion was under deliberation, begging that he might arrange his affairs on the day which he had thus obtained. This one day signified a year, which he was about to pass in the world after his vision. For, to speak more plainly, after the year was expired, he was crowned, on that day on which, at the commencement of the year, the fact had been announced to him. For although we do not read of the day of the Lord as a year in sacred Scripture, yet we regard that space of time as due in making promise of future things.[1] Whence is it of no consequence if, in this case, under the ordinary expression of a day, it is only a year that in this place is implied, because that which is the greater ought to be fuller in meaning. Moreover, that it was explained rather by signs than by speech, was because the utterance of speech was reserved for the manifestation of the time itself. For anything is usually set forth in words, whenever what is set forth is accomplished. For, indeed, no one knew why this had been shown to him, until afterwards, when, on the very day on which he had seen it, he was crowned. Nevertheless, in the meantime, his impending suffering was certainly known by all, but the exact day of his passion was not spoken of by any of the same, just as if they were ignorant of it. And, indeed, I find something simi-

lar in the Scriptures. For Zacharias the priest, because he did not believe the promise of a son, made to him by the angel, became dumb; so that he asked for tablets by a sign, being about to write his son's name rather than utter it. With reason, also in this case, where God's messenger declared the impending passion of His priest rather by signs, he both admonished his faith and fortified His priest. Moreover, the ground of asking for delay arose out of his wish to arrange his affairs and settle his will. Yet what affairs or what will had he to arrange, except ecclesiastical concerns? And thus that last delay was received, in order that whatever had to be disposed of by his final decision concerning the care of cherishing the poor might be arranged. And I think that for no other reason, and indeed for this reason only, indulgence was granted to him even by those very persons who had ejected and were about to slay him, that, being at hand, he might relieve the poor also who were before him with the final or, to speak more accurately, with the entire outlay of his last stewardship. And therefore, having so benevolently ordered matters, and so arranged them according to his will, the morrow drew near.

14. Now also a messenger came to him from the city from Xistus, the good and peace-making priest, and on that account most blessed martyr. The coming executioner was instantly looked for who should strike through that devoted neck of the most sacred victim ; and thus, in the daily expectation of dying, every day was to him as if the crown might be attributed to each. In the meantime, there assembled to him many eminent people, and people of most illustrious rank and family, and noble with the world's distinctions, who, on account of ancient friendship with him, repeatedly urged his withdrawal ; and, that their urgency might not be in some sort hollow, they also offered places to which he might retire. But he had now set the world aside, having his mind suspended upon heaven, and did not consent to their tempting persuasions. He would perhaps even then have done what was asked for by so many and faithful friends, if it had been bidden him by divine command. But that lofty glory of so great a man must not be passed over without announcement, that now, when the world was swelling, and of its trust in its princes breathing out hatred of the name, he was instructing God's servants, as opportunity was given, in the exhortations of the Lord, and was animating them to tread under foot the sufferings of this present time by the contemplation of a glory to come hereafter. Indeed, such was his love of sacred discourse, that he wished that his prayers in regard to his suffering might be so answered, that he would be put to death in the very act of speaking about God.

---

[1] [See Origen, "weeks of years," vol. iv. p. 353.]

15. And these were the daily acts of a priest destined for a pleasing sacrifice to God, when, behold, at the bidding of the proconsul, the officer with his soldiers on a sudden came unexpectedly on him, — or rather, to speak more truly, thought that he had come unexpectedly on him, at his gardens, — at his gardens, I say, which at the beginning of his faith he had sold, and which, being restored by God's mercy, he would assuredly have sold again for the use of the poor, if he had not wished to avoid ill-will from the persecutors. But when could a mind ever prepared be taken unawares, as if by an unforeseen attack? Therefore now he went forward, certain that what had been long delayed would be settled. He went forward with a lofty and elevated mien, manifesting cheerfulness in his look and courage in his heart. But being delayed to the morrow, he returned from the prætorium to the officer's house, when on a sudden a scattered rumour prevailed throughout all Carthage, that now Thascius was brought forward, whom there was nobody who did not know as well for his illustrious fame in the honourable opinion of all, as on account of the recollection of his most renowned work. On all sides all men were flocking together to a spectacle, to us glorious from the devotion of faith, and to be mourned over even by the Gentiles. A gentle custody, however, had him in charge when taken and placed for one night in the officer's house; so that we, his associates and friends, were as usual in his company. The whole people in the meantime, in anxiety that nothing should be done throughout the night without their knowledge, kept watch before the officer's door. The goodness of God granted him at that time, so truly worthy of it, that even God's people should watch on the passion of the priest. Yet, perhaps, some one may ask what was the reason of his returning from the prætorium to the officer. And some think that this arose from the fact, that for his own part the proconsul was then unwilling. Far be it from me to complain, in matters divinely ordered, of slothfulness or aversion in the proconsul. Far be it from me to admit such an evil into the consciousness of a religious mind, as that the fancy of man should decide the fate of so blessed a martyr. But the morrow, which a year before the divine condescension had foretold, required to be literally the morrow.[1]

16. At last that other day dawned — that destined, that promised, that divine day — which, if even the tyrant himself had wished to put off, he would not have had any power to do so; the day rejoicing at the consciousness of the future martyr; and, the clouds being scattered throughout the circuit of the world, the day shone upon them with a brilliant sun. He went out from the house of the officer, though he was the officer of Christ and God, and was walled in on all sides by the ranks of a mingled multitude. And such a numberless army hung upon his company, as if they had come with an assembled troop to assault death itself. Now, as he went, he had to pass by the race-course. And rightly, and as if it had been contrived on purpose, he had to pass by the place of a corresponding struggle, who, having finished his contest, was running to the crown of righteousness. But when he had come to the prætorium, as the proconsul had not yet come forth, a place of retirement was accorded him. There, as he sat moistened after his long journey with excessive perspiration (the seat was by chance covered with linen, so that even in the very moment of his passion he might enjoy the honour of the episcopate),[2] one of the officers ("Tesserarius"), who had formerly been a Christian, offered him his clothes, as if he might wish to change his moistened garments for drier ones; and he doubtless coveted nothing further in respect of his proffered kindness than to possess the now blood-stained sweat of the martyr going to God. He made reply to him, and said, "We apply medicines to annoyances which probably to-day will no longer exist." Is it any wonder that he despised suffering in body who had despised death in soul? Why should we say more? He was suddenly announced to the proconsul; he is brought forward; he is placed before him; he is interrogated as to his name. He answers who he is, and nothing more.

17. And thus, therefore, the judge reads from his tablet the sentence which lately in the vision he had not read, — a spiritual sentence, not rashly to be spoken, — a sentence worthy of such a bishop and such a witness; a glorious sentence, wherein he was called a standard-bearer of the sect, and an enemy of the gods, and one who was to be an example to his people; and that with his blood discipline would begin to be established. Nothing could be more complete, nothing more true, than this sentence. For all the things which were said, although said by a heathen, are divine. Nor is it indeed to be wondered at, since priests are accustomed to prophesy of the passion. He had been a standard-bearer, who was accustomed to teach concerning the bearing of Christ's standard; he had been an enemy of the gods, who commanded the idols to be destroyed. Moreover, he gave example to his friends, since, when many were about to follow in a similar manner, he was the first in the province to consecrate the first-fruits

---

[1] That is, Providence ensured the respite, to fulfil the promise.

[2] [See note at end of this memoir]

of martyrdom. And by his blood discipline began to be established ; but it was the discipline of martyrs, who, emulating their teacher, in the imitation of a glory like his own, themselves also gave a confirmation to discipline by the very blood of their own example.

18. And when he left the doors of the prætorium, a crowd of soldiery accompanied him ; and that nothing might be wanting in his passion, centurions and tribunes guarded his side. Now the place itself where he was about to suffer is level, so that it affords a noble spectacle, with its trees thickly planted on all sides. But as, by the extent of the space beyond, the view was not attainable to the confused crowd, persons who favoured him had climbed up into the branches of the trees, that there might not even be wanting to him (what happened in the case of Zacchæus), that he was gazed upon from the trees. And now, having with his own hands bound his eyes, he tried to hasten the slowness of the executioner, whose office was *to wield* the sword, and who with difficulty clasped the blade in his failing right hand with trembling fingers, until the mature hour of glorification strengthened the hand of the centurion with power granted from above to accomplish the death of the excellent man, and at length supplied him with the permitted strength. O blessed people of the Church, who as well in sight as in feeling, and, what is more, in outspoken words, suffered with such a bishop as theirs ; and, as they had ever heard him in his own discourses, were crowned by God the Judge ! For although that which the general wish desired could not occur, viz., that the entire congregation should suffer at once in the fellowship of a like glory, yet whoever under the eyes of Christ beholding, and in the hearing of the priest, eagerly desired to suffer, by the sufficient testimony of that desire did in some sort send a missive to God, as his ambassador.

19. His passion being thus accomplished, it resulted that Cyprian, who had been an example to all good men, was also the first who in Africa imbued his priestly crown [1] *with blood of martyrdom*, because he was the first who began to be such after the apostles. For from the time at which the episcopal order is enumerated at Carthage, not one is ever recorded, even of good men and priests, to have come to suffering. Although devotion surrendered to God is always in consecrated men reckoned instead of martyrdom ; yet Cyprian attained even to the perfect crown by the consummation of the Lord ; so that in that very city in which he had in such wise lived, and in which he had been the first to do many noble deeds, he also was the first to decorate the insignia [2] of his heavenly priesthood with glorious gore. What shall I do now? Between joy at his passion, and grief at still remaining, my mind is divided in different directions, and twofold affections are burdening a heart too limited for them. Shall I grieve that I was not his associate? But yet I must triumph in his victory. Shall I triumph at his victory? Still I grieve that I am not his companion. Yet still to you I must in simplicity confess, what you also are aware of, that it was my intention to be his companion. Much and excessively I exult at his glory ; but still more do I grieve that I remained behind.

---

[1] [He was the first of the *province*, that is. See p 273, *supra.*]
[2] [The simple attire of Hippolytus, as seen in his statue, was doubtless what is here meant by *insignia*. But see Hermas, vol. ii. p. 12.]

THE EPISTLES OF CYPRIAN

EPISTLE I.[1]

TO DONATUS.

ARGUMENT. — CYPRIAN HAD PROMISED DONATUS THAT HE WOULD HAVE A DISCOURSE WITH HIM CONCERNING THINGS DIVINE, AND NOW BEING REMINDED OF HIS PROMISE, HE FULFILS IT. COMMENDING AT LENGTH THE GRACE OF GOD CONFERRED IN BAPTISM, HE DECLARES HOW HE HAD BEEN CHANGED THEREBY; AND, FINALLY, POINTING OUT THE ERRORS OF THE WORLD, HE EXHORTS TO CONTEMPT OF IT, AND TO READING AND PRAYER.

1. CÆCILIUS CYPRIAN to Donatus sends, greeting. You rightly remind me, dearest Donatus; for I not only remember my promise, but I confess that this is the appropriate time for its fulfilment, when the vintage festival invites the mind to unbend in repose, and to enjoy the annual and appointed respite of the declining year.[2] Moreover, the place is in accord with the season, and the pleasant aspect of the gardens harmonizes with the gentle breezes of a mild autumn in soothing and cheering the senses. In such a place as this it is delightful to pass the day in discourse, and, by the (study of the sacred) parables,[3] to train the conscience of the breast to the apprehension of the divine precepts. And that no profane intruder may interrupt our converse, nor any unrestrained clatter of a noisy household disturb it, let us seek this bower.[4] The neighbouring thickets ensure us solitude, and the vagrant trailings of the vine branches creeping in pendent mazes among the reeds that support them have made for us a porch of vines and a leafy shelter. Pleasantly here we clothe our thoughts in words; and while we gratify our eyes with the agreeable outlook upon trees and vines, the mind is at once instructed by what we hear, and nourished by what we see, although at the present time your only pleasure and your only interest is in our discourse. Despising the pleasures of sight, your eye is now fixed on me. With your mind as well as your ears you are altogether a listener; and a listener, too, with an eagerness proportioned to your affection.

2. And yet, of what kind or of what amount is anything that my mind is likely to communicate to yours? The poor mediocrity of my shallow understanding produces a very limited harvest, and enriches the soil with no fruitful deposits. Nevertheless, with such powers as I have, I will set about the matter; for the subject itself on which I am about to speak will assist me. In courts of justice, in the public assembly, in political debate, a copious eloquence may be the glory of a voluble ambition; but in speaking of the Lord God, a chaste simplicity of expression strives for the conviction of faith rather with the substance, than with the powers, of eloquence. Therefore accept from me things, not clever but weighty, words, not decked up to charm a popular audience with cultivated rhetoric, but simple and fitted by their unvarnished truthfulness for the proclamation of the divine mercy. Accept what is felt before it is spoken, what has not been accumulated with tardy painstaking during the lapse of years, but has been inhaled in one breath of ripening grace.

3. While I was still lying in darkness and gloomy night, wavering hither and thither, tossed about on the foam of this boastful age, and uncertain of my wandering steps, knowing nothing of my real life, and remote from truth and light, I used to regard it as a difficult matter, and especially as difficult in respect of my character at that time, that a man should be capable of being born again[5] — a truth which the divine mercy had announced for my salvation, — and that a man quickened to a new life in the laver of saving water should be able to put off what he had previously been; and, although retaining all his bodily structure, should be himself changed in heart and soul. "How," said I, "is such a conversion possible, that there should be a sudden and rapid divestment of all which, either innate in us has hardened in the corruption of our material nature, or acquired by us has be-

---

[1] In the Oxford edition this epistle is given among the treatises.
[2] Wearying, *scil.* "fatigantis."
[3] "Fabulis." [Our "Thanksgiving Day" = the "Vindemia."]
[4] [A lover of gardens and of nature. The religion of Christ gave a new and loftier impulse to such tastes universally. Vol. ii. p. 9.]

[5] [Another Nicodemus, John iii.]

come inveterate by long accustomed use? These things have become deeply and radically engrained within us. When does he learn thrift who has been used to liberal banquets and sumptuous feasts? And he who has been glittering in gold and purple, and has been celebrated for his costly attire, when does he reduce himself to ordinary and simple clothing? One who has felt the charm of the fasces and of civic honours shrinks from becoming a mere private and inglorious citizen. The man who is attended by crowds of clients, and dignified by the numerous association of an officious train, regards it as a punishment when he is alone. It is inevitable, as it ever has been, that the love of wine should entice, pride inflate, anger inflame, covetousness disquiet, cruelty stimulate, ambition delight, lust hasten to ruin, with allurements that will not let go their hold."

4. These were my frequent thoughts. For as I myself was held in bonds by the innumerable errors of my previous life, from which I did not believe that I could by possibility be delivered, so I was disposed to acquiesce in my clinging vices; and because I despaired of better things, I used to indulge my sins as if they were actually parts of me, and indigenous to me. But after that, by the help of the water of new birth, the stain of former years had been washed away, and a light from above, serene and pure, had been infused into my reconciled heart, — after that, by the agency of the Spirit breathed from heaven, a second birth had restored me to a new man; — then, in a wondrous manner, doubtful things at once began to assure themselves to me, hidden things to be revealed, dark things to be enlightened, what before had seemed difficult began to suggest a means of accomplishment, what had been thought impossible, to be capable of being achieved; so that I was enabled to acknowledge that what previously, being born of the flesh, had been living in the practice of sins, was of the earth earthly, but had now begun to be of God, and was animated by the Spirit of holiness. You yourself assuredly know and recollect as well as I do what was taken away from us, and what was given to us by that death of evil, and that life of virtue. You yourself know this without my information. Anything like boasting in one's own praise is hateful, although we cannot *in reality* boast but only be grateful for whatever we do not ascribe to man's virtue but declare to be the gift of God; so that now we sin not is the beginning of the work of faith, whereas that we sinned before was the result of human error. All our power is of God; I say, of God. From Him we have life, from Him we have strength, by power derived and conceived from Him we do, while yet in this world, foreknow the indications of things to come. Only

let fear be the keeper of innocence, that the Lord, who of His mercy has flowed [1] into our hearts in the access of celestial grace, may be kept by righteous submissiveness in the hostelry of a grateful mind, that the assurance we have gained may not beget carelessness, and so the old enemy creep upon us again.

5. But if you keep the way of innocence, the way of righteousness, if you walk with a firm and steady step, if, depending on God with your whole strength and with your whole heart, you only *be* what you have begun to be, liberty and power to do is given you in proportion to the increase of your spiritual grace. For there is not, as is the case with earthly benefits, any measure or stint in the dispensing of the heavenly gift. The Spirit freely flowing forth is restrained by no limits, is checked by no closed barriers within certain bounded spaces; it flows perpetually, it is exuberant in its affluence. Let our heart only be athirst, and be ready to receive: in the degree in which we bring to it a capacious faith, in that measure we draw from it an overflowing grace. Thence is given power, with modest chastity, with a sound mind, with a simple voice, with unblemished virtue, that is able to quench the virus of poisons for the healing of the sick, to purge out the stains of foolish souls by restored health, to bid peace to those that are at enmity, repose to the violent, gentleness to the unruly, — by startling threats to force to avow themselves the impure and vagrant spirits that have betaken themselves into the bodies of men whom they purpose to destroy, to drive them with heavy blows to come out of them, to stretch them out struggling, howling, groaning with increase of constantly renewing pain, to beat them with scourges, to roast them with fire: the matter is carried on there, but is not seen; the strokes inflicted are hidden, but the penalty is manifest. Thus, in respect of what we have already begun to be, the Spirit that we have received possesses its own liberty of action; while in that we have not yet changed our body and members, the carnal view is still darkened by the clouds of this world. How great is this empire of the mind, and what a power it has, not alone that itself is withdrawn from the mischievous associations of the world, as one who is purged and pure can suffer no stain of a hostile irruption, but that it becomes still greater and stronger in its might, so that it can rule over all the imperious host of the attacking adversary with its sway!

6. But in order that the characteristics of the divine may shine more brightly by the development of the truth, I will give you light to apprehend it, the obscurity caused by sin being wiped

---

[1] Or, "shone," "infulsit."

away. I will draw away the veil from the darkness of this hidden world. For a brief space conceive yourself to be transported to one of the loftiest peaks of some inaccessible mountain, thence gaze on the appearances of things lying below you, and with eyes turned in various directions look upon the eddies of the billowy world, while you yourself are removed from earthly contacts, — you will at once begin to feel compassion for the world, aud with self-recollection and increasing gratitude to God, you will rejoice with all the greater joy that you have escaped it. Consider the roads blocked up by robbers, the seas beset with pirates, wars scattered all over the earth with the bloody horror of camps. The whole world is wet with mutual blood; and murder, which in the case of an individual is admitted to be a crime, is called a virtue when it is committed wholesale. Impunity is claimed for the wicked deeds, not on the plea that they are guiltless, but because the cruelty is perpetrated on a grand scale.

7. And now, if you turn your eyes and your regards to the cities themselves, you will behold a concourse more fraught with sadness than any solitude. The gladiatorial games are prepared, that blood may gladden the lust of cruel eyes. The body is fed up with stronger food, and the vigorous mass of limbs is enriched with brawn and muscle, that the wretch fattened for punishment may die a harder death. Man is slaughtered that man may be gratified, and the skill that is best able to kill is an exercise and an art. Crime is not only committed, but it is taught. What can be said more inhuman, — what more repulsive? Training is undergone to acquire the power to murder, and the achievement of murder is its glory. What state of things, I pray you, can that be, and what can it be like, in which men, whom none have condemned, offer themselves to the wild beasts — men of ripe age, of sufficiently beautiful person, clad in costly garments? Living men, they are adorned for a voluntary death; wretched men, they boast of their own miseries. They fight with beasts, not for their crime, but for their madness. Fathers look on their own sons; a brother is in the arena, and his sister is hard by; and although a grander display of pomp increases the price of the exhibition, yet, oh shame! even the mother will pay the increase in order that she may be present at her own miseries. And in looking upon scenes so frightful and so impious and so deadly, they do not seem to be aware that they are parricides with their eyes.

8. Hence turn your looks to the abominations, not less to be deplored, of another kind of spectacle.[1] In the theatres also you will behold what may well cause you grief and shame. It is the tragic buskin which relates in verse the crimes of ancient days. The old horrors[2] of parricide and incest are unfolded in action calculated to express the image of the truth, so that, as the ages pass by, any crime that was formerly committed may not be forgotten. Each generation is reminded by what it hears, that whatever has once been done may be done again. Crimes never die out by the lapse of ages; wickedness is never abolished by process of time; impiety is never buried in oblivion. Things which have now ceased to be actual deeds of vice become examples. In the mimes, moreover, by the teaching of infamies, the spectator is attracted either to reconsider what he may have done in secret, or to hear what he may do. Adultery is learnt while it is seen; and while the mischief having public authority panders to vices, the matron, who perchance had gone to the spectacle a modest woman, returns from it immodest. Still further, what a degradation of morals it is, what a stimulus to abominable deeds, what food for vice, to be polluted by histrionic gestures, against the covenant and law of one's birth, to gaze in detail upon the endurance of incestuous abominations! Men are emasculated, and all the pride and vigour of their sex is effeminated in the disgrace of their enervated body; and he is most pleasing there who has most completely broken down the man into the woman. He grows into praise by virtue of his crime; and the more he is degraded, the more skilful he is considered to be. Such a one is looked upon — oh shame! and looked upon with pleasure. And what cannot such a creature suggest? He inflames the senses, he flatters the affections, he drives out the more vigorous conscience of a virtuous breast; nor is there wanting authority for the enticing abomination, that the mischief may creep upon people with a less perceptible approach. They picture Venus immodest, Mars adulterous; and that Jupiter of theirs not more supreme in dominion than in vice, inflamed with earthly love in the midst of his own thunders, now growing white in the feathers of a swan, now pouring down in a golden shower, now breaking forth by the help of birds to violate the purity of boys. And now put the question, Can he who looks upon such things be healthy-minded or modest? Men imitate the gods whom they adore, and to such miserable beings their crimes become their religion.[3]

9. Oh, if placed on that lofty watch-tower you could gaze into the secret places — if you could open the closed doors of sleeping chambers, and recall their dark recesses to the perception of sight, — you would behold things

---

[1] [Alas, that in the modern theatre and opera all this has been reproduced, and Christians applaud!]

[2] Errors, *v. l.*

[3] [Compare Tertullian, vol. iii. pp. 87 et seqq.]

done by immodest persons which no chaste eye could look upon ; you would see what even to see is a crime ; you would see what people embruted with the madness of vice deny that they have done, and yet hasten to do, — men with frenzied lusts rushing upon men, doing things which afford no gratification even to those who do them. I am deceived if the man who is guilty of such things as these does not accuse others of them. The depraved maligns the depraved, and thinks that he himself, though conscious of the guilt, has escaped, as if consciousness were not a sufficient condemnation. The same people who are accusers in public are criminals in private, condemning themselves at the same time as they condemn the culprits ; they denounce abroad what they commit at home, willingly doing what, when they have done, they accuse, — a daring which assuredly is fitly mated with vice, and an impudence quite in accordance with shameless people. And I beg you not to wonder at the things that persons of this kind speak : the offence of their mouths in words is the least of which they are guilty.[1]

10. But after considering the public roads full of pitfalls, after battles of many kinds scattered abroad over the whole world, after exhibitions either bloody or infamous, after the abominations of lust, whether exposed for sale in brothels or hidden within the domestic walls — abominations, the audacity of which is greater in proportion to the secrecy of the crime, — possibly you may think that the Forum at least is free from such things, that it is neither exposed to exasperating wrongs, nor polluted by the association of criminals. Then turn your gaze in that direction : there you will discover things more odious than ever, so that thence you will be more desirous of turning away your eyes, although the laws are carved on twelve tables, and the statutes are publicly prescribed on brazen tablets. Yet wrong is done in the midst of the laws themselves ; wickedness is committed in the very face of the statutes ; innocence is not preserved even in the place where it is defended. By turns the rancour of disputants rages ; and when peace is broken among the togas,[2] the Forum echoes with the madness of strife. There close at hand is the spear and the sword, and the executioner also ; there is the claw that tears, the rack that stretches, the fire that burns up, — more tortures for one poor human body than it has limbs. And in such cases who is there to help? One's patron? He makes a feint, and deceives. The judge? But he sells his sentence. He who sits to avenge crimes commits them, and the judge becomes

the culprit, in order that the accused may perish innocently. Crimes are everywhere common ; and everywhere in the multiform character of sin, the pernicious poison acts by means of degraded minds. One man forges a will, another by a capital fraud makes a false deposition ; on the one hand, children are cheated of their inheritances, on the other, strangers are endowed with their estates. The opponent makes his charge, the false accuser attacks, the witness defames, on all sides the venal impudence of hired voices sets about the falsification of charges, while in the meantime the guilty do not even perish with the innocent. There is no fear about the laws ; no concern for either inquisitor or judge ; when the sentence can be bought off for money, it is not cared for. It is a crime now among the guilty to be innocent ; whoever does not imitate the wicked is an offence to them. The laws have come to terms with crimes, and whatever is public has begun to be allowed. What can be the modesty, what can be the integrity, that prevails there, when there are none to condemn the wicked, and one only meets with those who ought themselves to be condemned?

11. But that we may not perchance appear as if we were picking out extreme cases, and with the view of disparagement were seeking to attract your attention to those things whereof the sad and revolting view may offend the gaze of a better conscience, I will now direct you to such things as the world in its ignorance accounts good. Among these also you will behold things that will shock you. In respect of what you regard as honours, of what you consider the fasces, what you count affluence in riches, what you think power in the camp, the glory of the purple in the magisterial office, the power of licence in the chief command, — there is hidden the virus of ensnaring mischief, and an appearance of smiling wickedness, joyous indeed, but the treacherous deception of hidden calamity. Just as some poison, in which the flavour having been medicated with sweetness, craftily mingled in its deadly juices, seems, when taken, to be an ordinary draught, but when it is drunk up, the destruction that you have swallowed assails you. You see, forsooth, that man distinguished by his brilliant dress, glittering, as he thinks, in his purple. Yet with what baseness has he purchased this glitter ! What contempts of the proud has he had first to submit to ! what haughty thresholds has he, as an early courtier, besieged ! How many scornful footsteps of arrogant great men has he had to precede, thronged in the crowd of clients, that by and by a similar procession might attend and precede him with salutations, — a train waiting not upon his person, but upon his power ! for he has no claim to be regarded for his character, but for his fasces. Of these,

[1] [Rom. i. 26, 27. The enormous extent of this diabolical form of lust is implied in all these patristic rebukes.]
[2] The dresses of peace.

finally, you may see the degrading end, when the time-serving sycophant has departed, and the hanger-on, deserting them, has defiled the exposed side of the man who has retired into a private condition.[1] It is then that the mischiefs done to the squandered family-estate smite upon the conscience, then the losses that have exhausted the fortune are known, — expenses by which the favour of the populace was bought, and the people's breath asked for with fickle and empty entreaties. Assuredly, it was a vain and foolish boastfulness to have desired to set forth in the gratification of a disappointing spectacle, what the people would not receive, and what would ruin the magistrates.

12. But those, moreover, whom you consider rich, who add forests to forests, and who, excluding the poor from their neighbourhood, stretch out their fields far and wide into space without any limits, who possess immense heaps of silver and gold and mighty sums of money, either in built-up heaps or in buried stores, — even in the midst of their riches those are torn to pieces by the anxiety of vague thought, lest the robber should spoil, lest the murderer should attack, lest the envy of some wealthier neighbour should become hostile, and harass them with malicious lawsuits. Such a one enjoys no security either in his food or in his sleep. In the midst of the banquet he sighs, although he drinks from a jewelled goblet; and when his luxurious bed has enfolded his body, languid with feasting, in its yielding bosom, he lies wakeful in the midst of the down; nor does he perceive, poor wretch, that these things are merely gilded torments, that he is held in bondage by his gold, and that he is the slave of his luxury and wealth rather than their master. And oh, the odious blindness of perception, and the deep darkness of senseless greed! although he might disburden himself and get rid of the load, he rather continues to brood over his vexing wealth, — he goes on obstinately clinging to his tormenting hoards. From him there is no liberality to dependents, no communication to the poor. And yet such people call that their own money, which they guard with jealous labour, shut up at home as if it were another's, and from which they derive no benefit either for their friends, for their children, or, in fine, for themselves. Their possession amounts to this only, that they can keep others from possessing it; and oh, what a marvellous perversion of names! they call those things *goods*, which they absolutely put to none but *bad* uses.

13. Or think you that even those are secure, — that those at least are safe with some stable permanence among the chaplets of honour and vast wealth, whom, in the glitter of royal palaces,

the safeguard of watchful arms surrounds? They have greater fear than others. A man is constrained to dread no less than he is dreaded. Exaltation exacts its penalties equally from the more powerful, although he may be hedged in with bands of satellites, and may guard his person with the enclosure and protection of a numerous retinue. Even as he does not allow his inferiors to feel security, it is inevitable that he himself should want the sense of security. The power of those whom power makes terrible to others, is, first of all, terrible to themselves. It smiles to rage, it cajoles to deceive, it entices to slay, it lifts up to cast down. With a certain usury of mischief, the greater the height of dignity and honours attained, the greater is the interest of penalty required.

14. Hence, then, the one peaceful and trustworthy tranquillity, the one solid and firm and constant security, is this, for a man to withdraw from these eddies of a distracting world, and, anchored on the ground of the harbour of salvation, to lift his eyes from earth to heaven; and having been admitted to the gift of God, and being already very near to his God in mind, he may boast, that whatever in human affairs others esteem lofty and grand, lies altogether beneath his consciousness. He who is actually greater than the world can crave nothing, can desire nothing, from the world. How stable, how free from all shocks is that safeguard; how heavenly the protection in its perennial blessings, — to be loosed from the snares of this entangling world, and to be purged from earthly dregs, and fitted for the light of eternal immortality! He will see what crafty mischief of the foe that previously attacked us has been in progress against us. We are constrained to have more love for what we shall be, by being allowed to know and to condemn what we were. Neither for this purpose is it necessary to pay a price either in the way of bribery or of labour; so that man's elevation or dignity or power should be begotten in him with elaborate effort; but it is a gratuitous gift from God, and it is accessible to all. As the sun shines spontaneously, as the day gives light, as the fountain flows, as the shower yields moisture, so does the heavenly Spirit infuse itself into us. When the soul, in its gaze into heaven, has recognised its Author, it rises higher than the sun, and far transcends all this earthly power, and begins to be that which it believes itself to be.[2]

15. Do you, however, whom the celestial warfare has enlisted in the spiritual camp, only observe a discipline uncorrupted and chastened in the virtues of religion. Be constant as well

---

[1] [Confirmed by all the Roman satirists, as will be recalled by the reader. Conf. Horace, *Sat.*, vi. book i.]

[2] [What a testimony to regeneration! Cyprian speaks from heathen experience, then from the experience of a new birth. Few specimens of simple eloquence surpass this.]

in prayer as in reading; now speak with God, now let God speak with you, let Him instruct you in His precepts, let Him direct you. Whom He has made rich, none shall make poor; for, in fact, there can be no poverty to him whose breast has once been supplied with heavenly food. Ceilings enriched with gold, and houses adorned with mosaics of costly marble, will seem mean to you, now when you know that it is you yourself who are rather to be perfected, you who are rather to be adorned, and that that dwelling in which God has dwelt as in a temple, in which the Holy Spirit has begun to make His abode, is of more importance than all others. Let us embellish this house with the colours of innocence, let us enlighten it with the light of justice : this will never fall into decay with the wear of age, nor shall it be defiled by the tarnishing of the colours of its walls, nor of its gold. Whatever is artificially beautified is perishing; and such things as contain not the reality of possession afford no abiding assurance to their possessors. But this remains in a beauty perpetually vivid, in perfect honour, in permanent splendour. It can neither decay nor be destroyed; it can only be fashioned into greater perfection when the body returns to it.

16. These things, dearest Donatus, briefly for the present. For although what you profitably hear delights your patience, indulgent in its goodness, your well-balanced mind, and your assured faith — and nothing is so pleasant to your ears as what is pleasant to you in God, — yet, as we are associated as neighbours, and are likely to talk together frequently, we ought to have some moderation in our conversation; and since this is a holiday rest, and a time of leisure, whatever remains of the day, now that the sun is sloping towards the evening,[1] let us spend it in gladness, nor let even the hour of repast be without heavenly grace. Let the temperate meal resound with psalms;[2] and as your memory is tenacious and your voice musical, undertake this office, as is your wont. You will provide a better entertainment for your dearest friends, if, while we have something spiritual to listen to, the sweetness of religious music charm our ears.

EPISTLE II.[3]

FROM THE ROMAN CLERGY TO THE CARTHAGINIAN CLERGY, ABOUT THE RETIREMENT OF THE BLESSED CYPRIAN.

ARGUMENT. — THE ROMAN CLERGY HAD LEARNT FROM CREMENTIUS THE SUB-DEACON, THAT IN THE TIME OF PERSECUTION CYPRIAN HAD WITHDRAWN HIMSELF. THEREFORE, WITH THEIR AC-CUSTOMED ZEAL FOR THE FAITH, THEY REMIND THE CARTHAGINIAN CLERGY OF THEIR DUTY, AND INSTRUCT THEM WHAT TO DO IN THE CASE OF THE LAPSED, DURING THE INTERVAL OF THE BISHOP'S ABSENCE.

1. We have been informed by Crementius the sub-deacon, who came to us from you, that the blessed father[4] Cyprian has for a certain reason withdrawn; "in doing which he acted quite rightly, because he is a person of eminence, and because a conflict is impending," which God has allowed in the world, for the sake of co-operating with His servants in their struggle against the adversary, and was, moreover, willing that this conflict should show to angels and to men that the victor shall be crowned, while the vanquished shall in himself receive the doom which has been made manifest to us. Since, moreover, it devolves upon us who appear to be placed on high, in the place of a shepherd,[5] to keep watch over the flock; if we be found neglectful, it will be said to us, as it was said to our predecessors also, who in such wise negligent had been placed in charge, that "we have not sought for that which was lost, and have not corrected the wanderer, and have not bound up that which was broken, but have eaten their milk, and been clothed with their wool;"[6] and then also the Lord Himself, fulfilling what had been written in the law and the prophets, teaches, saying, "I am the good shepherd, who lay down my life for the sheep. But the hireling, whose own the sheep are not, seeth the wolf coming, and leaveth the sheep, and fleeth, and the wolf scattereth them."[7] To Simon, too, He speaks thus : "Lovest thou me? He answered, I do love Thee. He saith to him, Feed my sheep."[8] We know that this saying arose out of the very circumstance of his withdrawal, and the rest of the disciples did likewise.[9]

2. We are unwilling, therefore, beloved brethren, that you should be found hirelings, but we desire you to be good shepherds, since you are aware that no slight danger threatens you if you do not exhort our brethren to stand stedfast in the faith, so that the brotherhood be not absolutely rooted out, as being of those who rush headlong into idolatry. Neither is it in words only that we exhort you to this; but you will be

---

[1] [See Cowper, on "the Sabine bard," *Task*, b. iv. But compare even the best of Horatian epistles with this : " O noctes cœnæque Deum," etc. What a blessed contrast in Christian society !]
[2] [Here recall the *Evening Hymn*, vol. ii. p. 298.]
[3] Oxford ed.: Ep. viii.

[4] Papam. [The Roman clergy give this title to Cyprian.]
[5] [This exercise of *jurisdictiou, vice episcopi*, is to be noted.]
[6] Ezek. xxxiv. 3, 4.
[7] John x. 11, 12.
[8] John xxi. 17.
[9] This is a very obscure passage, and is variously understood. It seems most probable that the allusion is to Peter's denial of his Lord, and following Him afar off; and is intended to bear upon Cyprian's retirement. There seems no meaning in interpreting the passage as a reference to Peter's death. [It seems, in a slight degree, to reflect on Cyprian's withdrawal. But note, it asserts that the *pasce oves meas* was a reproach to St. Peter, and was understood to be so by his fellow-apostles. In other words, our Lord, so these clergy argue, bade St. Peter not again to forsake the brethren whom he should strengthen. Luke xxii. 32.]

able to ascertain from very many who come to you from us, that, God blessing us, we both have done and still do all these things ourselves with all anxiety and worldly risk, having before our eyes rather the fear of God and eternal sufferings than the fear of men and a short-lived discomfort, not forsaking the brethren, but exhorting them to stand firm in the faith, and to be ready to go with the Lord. And we have even recalled those who were ascending [1] to do that to which they were constrained. The Church stands in faith, notwithstanding that some have been driven to fall by very terror, whether that they were persons of eminence, or that they were afraid, when seized, with the fear of man : these, however, we did not abandon, although they were separated from us, but exhorted them, and do exhort them, to repent, if in any way they may receive pardon from Him who is able to grant it ; lest, haply, if they should be deserted by us, they should become worse.

3. You see, then, brethren, that you also ought to do the like, so that even those who have fallen may amend their minds by your exhortation ; and if they should be seized once more, may confess, and may so make amends for their previous sin. And there are other matters which are incumbent on you, which also we have here added, as that if any who may have fallen into this temptation begin to be taken with sickness, and repent of what they have done, and desire communion, it should in any wise be granted them. Or if you have widows or bedridden people [2] who are unable to maintain themselves, or those who are in prisons or are excluded from their own dwellings, these ought in all cases to have some to minister to them. Moreover, catechumens when seized with sickness ought not to be deceived,[3] but help is to be afforded them. And, as matter of the greatest importance, if the bodies of the martyrs and others be not buried, a considerable risk is incurred by those whose duty it is to do this office. By whomsoever of you, then, and on whatever occasion this duty may have been performed, we are sure that he is regarded as a good servant, — as one who has been faithful in the least, and will be appointed ruler over ten cities. May God, however, who gives all things to them that hope in Him, grant to us that we may all be found in these works. The brethren who are in bonds greet you, as do the elders, and the whole Church, which itself also with the deepest anxiety keeps watch over all who call on the name of the Lord. And we likewise beg you in your turn to have us in remembrance. Know, moreover, that Bassianus has come to us ; and we request of you who

have a zeal for God, to send a copy of this letter to whomsoever you are able, as occasions may serve, or make your own opportunities, or send a message, that they may stand firm and stedfast in the faith. We bid you, beloved brethren, ever heartily farewell.

EPISTLE III.[4]

TO THE PRESBYTERS AND DEACONS ABIDING AT ROME. A.D. 250.

ARGUMENT. — THIS IS A FAMILIAR AND FRIENDLY EPISTLE ; SO THAT IT REQUIRES NO FORMAL ARGUMENT, ESPECIALLY AS IT CAN BE SUFFICIENTLY GATHERED FROM THE TITLE ITSELF. THE LETTER OF THE ROMAN CLERGY, TO WHICH CYPRIAN IS REPLYING, IS MISSING.

1. Cyprian to the elders and deacons, brethren abiding at Rome, sends, greeting. When the report of the departure of the excellent man, my colleague,[5] was still uncertain among us, my beloved brethren, and I was wavering doubtfully in my opinion on the matter, I received a letter sent to me from you by Crementius the sub-deacon, in which I was most abundantly informed of his glorious end,; and I rejoiced greatly that, in harmony with the integrity of his administration, an honourable consummation also attended him. Wherein, moreover, I greatly congratulate you, that you honour his memory with a testimony so public and so illustrious, so that by your means is made known to me, not only what is glorious to you in connection with the memory of your bishop, but what ought to afford to me also an example of faith and virtue. For in proportion as the fall of a bishop is an event which tends ruinously to the fall of his followers, so on the other hand it is a useful and helpful thing when a bishop, by the firmness of his faith, sets himself forth to his brethren as an object of imitation.

2. I have, moreover, read another epistle,[6] in which neither the person who wrote nor the persons to whom it was written were plainly declared ; and inasmuch as in the same letter both the writing and the matter, and even the paper itself, gave me the idea that something had been taken away, or had been changed from the original, I have sent you back the epistle as it actually came to hand, that you may examine whether it is the very same which you gave to Crementius the sub-deacon, to carry. For it is a very serious thing if the truth of a clerical letter is corrupted by any falsehood or deceit. In order, then, that we may know this, ascertain whether

---

[1] That is to say, " to the Capitol to sacrifice."
[2] Clinomeni.
[3] i.e., as to the implied promise of their preparation for baptism.

[4] Oxford ed.: Ep. ix.
[5] Fabian, bishop of Rome. [Cyprian's " colleague," but their bishop. See Greek of Philip. ii. 25. He is an example to his brethren : such the simple position of a primitive Bishop of Rome.]
[6] The foregoing letter, Ep. ii.

the writing and subscription are yours, and write me again what is the truth of the matter. I bid you, dearest brethren, ever heartily farewell.

EPISTLE IV.[1]

TO THE PRESBYTERS AND DEACONS.

ARGUMENT. — CYPRIAN EXHORTS HIS CLERGY FROM HIS PLACE OF RETIREMENT, THAT IN HIS AB-SENCE THEY SHOULD BE UNITED; THAT NOTHING SHOULD BE WANTING TO PRISONERS OR TO THE REST OF THE POOR; AND FURTHER, THAT THEY SHOULD KEEP THE PEOPLE IN QUIET, LEST, IF THEY SHOULD RUSH IN CROWDS TO VISIT THE MARTYRS IN PRISON, THIS PRIVILEGE SHOULD AT LENGTH BE FORBIDDEN THEM. A.D. 250.

1. Cyprian to the presbyters and deacons, his beloved brethren, greeting. Being by the grace of God in safety, dearest brethren, I salute you, rejoicing that I am informed of the prosperity of all things in respect of your safety also; and as the condition of the place[2] does not permit me to be with you now, I beg you, by your faith and your religion, to discharge there both your own office and mine, that there may be nothing want-ing either to discipline or diligence. In respect of means, moreover, for meeting the expenses, whether for those who, having confessed their Lord with a glorious voice, have been put in prison, or for those who are labouring in poverty and want, and still stand fast in the Lord, I en-treat that nothing be wanting, since the whole of the small sum which was collected there was distributed among the clergy for cases of that kind, that many might have means whence they could assist the necessities and burthens of in-dividuals.

2. I beg also that there may be no lack, on your parts, of wisdom and carefulness to preserve peace. For although from their affection the brethren are eager to approach and to visit those good confessors, on whom by their glorious be-ginnings the divine consideration has already shed a brightness, yet I think that this eagerness must be cautiously indulged, and not in crowds, — not in numbers collected together at once, lest from this very thing ill-will be aroused, and the means of access be denied, and thus, while we insatiably wish for all, we lose all. Take counsel, therefore, and see that this may be more safely managed with moderation, so that the presbyters also, who there offer[3] with the confessors, may one by one take turns with the deacons individually; because, by thus chan-ging the persons and varying the people that come together, suspicion is diminished. For,

---

[1] Oxford ed.: Ep. v.
[2] *Scil.* Carthage, where the populace had already demanded Cyp-rian's blood.
[3] "Qui illic apud confessores offerunt," *scil.* "the oblation" (προσφορά, Rom. xv. 16), i.e., "who celebrate the Eucharist."

meek and humble in all things, as befits the ser-vants of God, we ought to accommodate our-selves to the times, and to provide for quietness, and to have regard to the people. I bid you, brethren, beloved and dearly longed-for, always heartily farewell; and have me in remembrance. Greet all the brotherhood. Victor the deacon, and those who are with me, greet you. Fare-well!

EPISTLE V.[4]

TO THE PRESBYTERS AND DEACONS.

ARGUMENT. — THE ARGUMENT OF THIS LETTER IS NEARLY THE SAME AS THAT OF THE PRECED-ING ONE, EXCEPT THAT THE WRITER DIRECTS THE CONFESSORS ALSO TO BE ADMONISHED BY THE CLERGY OF THEIR DUTY, TO GIVE ATTEN-TION TO HUMILITY, AND OBEY THE PRESBYTERS AND DEACONS. HIS OWN RETIREMENT INCI-DENTALLY FURNISHES AN OCCASION FOR THIS.

1. Cyprian to the presbyters and deacons, his brethren, greeting. I had wished indeed, be-loved brethren, with this my letter to greet the whole of my clergy in health and safety. But since the stormy time which has in a great measure overwhelmed my people, has, moreover, added this enhancement to my sorrows, that it has touched even a portion of the clergy, I pray the Lord that, by the divine mercy, I may hereafter greet you at all events as safe, who, as I have learned, stand fast both in faith and virtue. And although some reasons might appear to urge me to the duty of myself hastening to come to you, firstly, for instance, because of my eagerness and desire for you, which is the chief consideration in my prayers, and then, that we might be able to consult to-gether on those matters which are required by the general advantage, in respect of the govern-ment of the Church, and having carefully ex-amined them with abundant counsel, might wisely arrange them; — yet it seemed to me better, still to preserve my retreat and my quiet for a while, with a view to other advantages con-nected with the peace and safety of us all: — of which advantages an account will be given you by our beloved brother Tertullus, who, besides his other care which he zealously bestows on divine labours, was, moreover, the author of this counsel; that I should be cautious and moder-ate, and not rashly trust myself into the sight of the public; and especially that I should beware of that place where I had been so often inquired for and sought after.

2. Relying, therefore, upon your love and your piety, which I have abundantly known, in this letter I both exhort and command you, that those of you whose presence there is least sus-picious and least perilous, should in my stead

---

[4] Oxford ed.: Ep. xiv. A D. 250.

discharge my duty, in respect of doing those things which are required for the religious administration. In the meantime let the poor be taken care of as much and as well as possible; but especially those who have stood with unshaken faith and have not forsaken Christ's flock, that, by your diligence, means be supplied to them to enable them to bear their poverty, so that what the troublous time has not effected in respect of their faith, may not be accomplished by want in respect of their afflictions. Let a more earnest care, moreover, be bestowed upon the glorious confessors. And although I know that very many of those have been maintained by the vow [1] and by the love of the brethren, yet if there be any who are in want either of clothing or maintenance, let them be supplied with whatever things are necessary, as I formerly wrote to you, while they were still kept in prison, — only let them know from you and be instructed, and learn what, according to the authority of Scripture, the discipline of the Church requires of them, that they ought to be humble and modest and peaceable, that they should maintain the honour of their name, so that those who have achieved glory by what they have testified, may achieve glory also by their characters, and in all things seeking the Lord's approval, may show themselves worthy, in consummation of their praise, to attain a heavenly crown. For there remains more than what is yet seen to be accomplished, since it is written, "Praise not any man before his death;"[2] and again, "Be thou faithful unto death, and I will give thee a crown of life."[3] And the Lord also says, "He that endureth to the end, the same shall be saved."[4] Let them imitate the Lord, who at the very time of His passion was not more proud, but more humble. For then He washed His disciples' feet, saying, "If I, your Lord and Master, have washed your feet, ye ought also to wash one another's feet. For I have given you an example, that ye should do as I have done to you."[5] Let them also follow the example of the Apostle Paul, who, after often-repeated imprisonment, after scourging, after exposures to wild beasts, in everything continued meek and humble; and even after his rapture to the third heaven and paradise, he did not proudly arrogate anything to himself when he said, "Neither did we eat any man's bread for nought, but wrought with labour and travail night and day, that we might not be chargeable to any of you."[6]

3. These several matters, I pray you, suggest to our brethren. And as "he who humbleth himself shall be exalted,"[7] now is the time when they should rather fear the ensnaring adversary, who more eagerly attacks the man that is strongest, and becoming more virulent, for the very reason that he is conquered, strives to overcome his conqueror. The Lord grant that I may soon both see them again, and by salutary exhortation may establish their minds to preserve their glory. For I am grieved when I hear that some of them run about wickedly and proudly, and give themselves up to follies or to discords; that members of Christ, and even members that have confessed Christ, are defiled by unlawful concubinage, and cannot be ruled either by deacons or by presbyters, but cause that, by the wicked and evil characters of a few,[8] the honourable glories of many and good confessors are tarnished;[9] whom they ought to fear, lest, being condemned by their testimony and judgment, they be excluded from their fellowship. That, finally, is the illustrious and true confessor, concerning whom afterwards the Church does not blush, but boasts.

4. In respect of that which our fellow-presbyters, Donatus and Fortunatus, Novatus and Gordius, wrote to me, I have not been able to reply by myself, since, from the first commencement of my episcopacy, I made up my mind to do nothing on my own private opinion, without your advice and without the consent of the people.[10] But as soon as, by the grace of God, I shall have come to you, then we will discuss in common, as our respective dignity requires, those things which either have been or are to be done. I bid you, brethren beloved and dearly longed-for, ever heartily farewell, and be mindful of me. Greet the brotherhood that is with you earnestly from me, and tell them to remember me. Farewell.

EPISTLE VI.[11]

TO ROGATIANUS THE PRESBYTER, AND THE OTHER CONFESSORS. A.D. 250.

ARGUMENT.—HE EXHORTS ROGATIANUS AND THE OTHER CONFESSORS TO MAINTAIN DISCIPLINE, THAT NONE WHO HAD CONFESSED CHRIST IN WORD SHOULD SEEM TO DENY HIM IN DEED; CASUALLY REBUKING SOME OF THEM, WHO, BEING EXILED ON ACCOUNT OF THE FAITH, WERE NOT AFRAID TO RETURN UNBIDDEN INTO THEIR COUNTRY.

1. Cyprian to the presbyter Rogatianus, and to the other confessors, his brethren, greeting. I

---

[1] It is thought that Cyprian here speaks of an order of men called "Parabolani," who systematically devoted themselves to the service of the sick and poor and imprisoned. [Acts iv. 6, οἱ νεώτεροι.]
[2] Ecclus. xi. 28. [Conf. Solon, Herod., i. 86.]
[3] Apoc. ii. 10.
[4] Matt. x. 22.
[5] John xiii. 14, 15. [The parabolani were so called circa A.D. 415.]
[6] 2 Thess. iii. 8.

[7] Luke xiv. 11.
[8] [Strange, indeed, that such should be found amid the persecuted sheep of Christ; but it illustrates the history of Callistus at Rome, and the possibility of such characters enlisting in the Church.]
[9] ["Whence hath it tares?" Ans.: "An enemy hath done this." See Matt. xiii. 27; Acts xx. 29-31.]
[10] [Elucidation II. This was the canonical duty neglected by Callistus and his predecessor, who "imagined," etc. See p. 156, supra.]
[11] Oxford ed.: Ep. xiii. [Rogatian was a bishop afterwards.]

had both heretofore, dearly beloved and bravest brethren, sent you a letter, in which I congratulated your faith and virtue with exulting words, and now my voice has no other object, first of all, than with joyous mind, repeatedly and always to announce the glory of your name. For what can I wish greater or better in my prayers than to see the flock of Christ enlightened by the honour of your confession? For although all the brethren ought to rejoice in this, yet, in the common gladness, the share of the bishop is the greatest. For the glory of the Church is the glory of the bishop.[1] In proportion as we grieve over those whom a hostile persecution has cast down, in the same proportion we rejoice over you whom the devil has not been able to overcome.

2. Yet I exhort you by our common faith, by the true and simple love of my heart towards you, that, having overcome the adversary in this first encounter, you should hold fast your glory with a brave and persevering virtue. We are still in the world; we are still placed in the battle-field; we fight daily for our lives. Care must be taken, that after such beginnings as these there should also come an increase, and that what you have begun to be with such a blessed commencement should be consummated in you. It is a slight thing to have been able to attain anything; it is more to be able to keep what you have attained; even as faith itself and saving birth makes alive, not by being received, but by being preserved. Nor is it actually the attainment, but the perfecting, that keeps a man for God. The Lord taught this in His instruction when He said, "Behold, thou art made whole; sin no more, lest a worse thing come unto thee."[2] Conceive of Him as saying this also to His confessor, "Lo thou art made a confessor; sin no more, lest a worse thing come unto thee." Solomon also, and Saul, and many others, so long as they walked in the Lord's ways, were able to keep the grace given to them. When the discipline of the Lord was forsaken by them, grace also forsook them.

3. We must persevere in the straight and narrow road of praise and glory; and since peacefulness and humility and the tranquillity of a good life is fitting for all Christians, according to the word of the Lord, who looks to none other man than "to him that is poor and of a contrite spirit, and that trembleth at"[3] His word, it the more behoves you confessors, who have been made an example to the rest of the brethren, to observe and fulfil this, as being those whose characters should provoke to imitation the life and conduct of all. For as the Jews were alienated from God, as those on whose account "the name of God is blasphemed among the Gentiles,"[4] so on the other hand those are dear to God through whose conformity to discipline the name of God is declared with a testimony of praise, as it is written, the Lord Himself forewarning and saying, "Let your light so shine before men that they may see your good works and glorify your Father which is in heaven."[5] And Paul the apostle says, "Shine as lights in the world."[6] And similarly Peter exhorts: "As strangers," says he, "and pilgrims, abstain from fleshly lusts, which war against the soul, having your conversation honest among the Gentiles; that whereas they speak against you as evil-doers, they may by your good works, which they shall behold, glorify the Lord."[7] This, indeed, the greatest part of you, I rejoice to say, are careful for; and, made better by the honour of your confession itself, guard and preserve its glory by tranquil and virtuous lives.

4. But I hear that some infect your number, and destroy the praise of a distinguished name by their corrupt conversation; whom you yourselves, even as being lovers and guardians of your own praise, should rebuke and check and correct. For what a disgrace is suffered by your name, when one spends his days in intoxication and debauchery,[8] another returns to that country whence he was banished, to perish when arrested, not now as being a Christian, but as being a criminal![9] I hear that some are puffed up and are arrogant, although it is written, "Be not highminded, but fear: for if God spared not the natural branches, take heed lest He also spare not thee."[10] Our Lord "was led as a sheep to the slaughter; and as a lamb before her shearers is dumb, so He opened not His mouth."[11] "I am not rebellious," says He, "neither do I gainsay. I gave my back to the smiters, and my cheeks to the palms of their hands. I hid not my face from the filthiness of spitting."[12] And dares any one now, who lives by and in this very One, lift up himself and be haughty, forgetful, as well of the deeds which He did, as of the commands which He left to us either by Himself or by His apostles? But if "the servant is not greater than his Lord."[13] let those who follow

---

1 [A beautiful aphorism. See below, note 8, this page.]
2 John v. 14.
3 Isa. lxvi. 2.

4 Rom. ii. 24.
5 Matt. v. 16.
6 Phil. ii. 15.
7 1 Pet. ii. 11, 12.
8 [The *shame* of the Church is the *shame* of the bishop. See above, note 1; also 1 Tim. v. 22.]
9 Either as criminals having returned from banishment without authority, or as having committed some crime for which they became amenable to punishment. See 1 Pet. iv. 15: "But let none of you suffer as a murderer, or as a thief, or as an evil-doer."
10 Rom. xi. 20, 21. [How significant this warning to Rome!]
11 Isa. liii. 7.
12 Isa. l. 5. 6.
13 John xiii., 16.

the Lord humbly and peacefully and silently tread in His steps, since the lower one is, the more exalted he may become ; as says the Lord, " He that is least among you, the same shall be great." [1]

5. What, then, is that — how execrable should it appear to you — which I have learnt with extreme anguish and grief of mind, to wit, that there are not wanting those who defile the temples of God, and the members sanctified after confession and made glorious,[2] with a disgraceful and infamous concubinage, associating their beds promiscuously with women's ! In which, even if there be no pollution of their conscience, there is a great guilt in this very thing, that by their offence originate examples for the ruin of others.[3] There ought also to be no contentions and emulations among you, since the Lord left to us His peace, and it is written, " Thou shalt love thy neighbour as thyself." [4] " But if ye bite and find fault with one another, take heed that ye be not consumed one of another." [5] From abuse and revilings also I entreat you to abstain, for " revilers do not attain the kingdom of God ; " [6] and the tongue which has confessed Christ should be preserved sound and pure with its honour. For he who, according to Christ's precept, speaks things peaceable and good and just, daily confesses Christ. We had renounced the world when we were baptized ; but we have now indeed renounced the world when tried and approved by God, we leave all that we have, and have followed the Lord, and stand and live in His faith and fear.

6. Let us confirm one another by mutual exhortations, and let us more and more go forward in the Lord ; so that when of His mercy He shall have made that peace which He promises to give, we may return to the Church new and almost changed men, and may be received, whether by our brethren or by the heathen, in all things corrected and renewed for the better ; and those who formerly admired our glory in our courage may now admire the discipline in our lives.[7] I bid you, beloved brethren, ever heartily farewell ; and be mindful of me.

---

[1] Luke ix. 48.
[2] " Illustrata." The Oxford translation has " bathed in light."
[3] [That is, if they have not actually committed the great sin themselves, yet, etc. See vol. ii. p. 57.]
[4] Lev. xix. 18.
[5] Matt. xxii. 39.
[6] Gal. v. 15. [See note 9, *infra*.]
[7] The following is found only in one MS. Its genuineness is therefore doubted by some: " And although I have most fully written to our clergy, both lately when you were still kept in prison, and now also again, to supply whatever was needful, either for your clothing or for your food, yet I myself have also sent you from the small means of my own which I had with me, 250 pieces; and another 250 I had also sent before. Victor also, who from a reader has become a deacon, and is with me, sent you 175. But I rejoice when I know that very many of our brethren of their love are striving with each other, and are aiding your necessities with their contributions."

EPISTLE VII.[8]

TO THE CLERGY, CONCERNING PRAYER TO GOD.

ARGUMENT. — THE ARGUMENT OF THE PRESENT EPISTLE IS NEARLY THE SAME AS THAT OF THE TWO PRECEDING, EXCEPT THAT HE EXHORTS IN THIS TO DILIGENT PRAYER.

1. Cyprian to the presbyters and deacons, his brethren, greeting. Although I know, brethren beloved, that from the fear which we all of us owe to God, you also are instantly urgent in continual petitions and earnest prayers to Him, still I myself remind your religious anxiety, that in order to appease and entreat the Lord, we must lament not only in words, but also with fastings and with tears, and with every kind of urgency. For we must perceive and confess that the so disordered ruin arising from that affliction, which has in a great measure laid waste, and is even still laying waste, our flock, has visited us according to our sins, in that we do not keep the way of the Lord, nor observe the heavenly commandments given to us for our salvation. Our Lord did the will of His Father, and we do not do the will of our Lord ; eager about our patrimony and our gain, seeking to satisfy our pride, yielding ourselves wholly to emulation and to strife, careless of simplicity and faith, renouncing the world in words only, and not in deeds, every one of us pleasing himself, and displeasing all others,[9] — therefore we are smitten as we deserve, since it is written : " And that servant, which knoweth his master's will, and has not obeyed his will, shall be beaten with many stripes." [10] But what stripes, what blows, do we not deserve, when even confessors, who ought to be an example of virtuous life to others, do not maintain discipline? Therefore, while an inflated and immodest boastfulness about their own confession excessively elates some, tortures come upon them, and tortures without any cessation of the tormentor, without any end of condemnation, without any comfort of death, — tortures which do not easily let them pass to the crown, but wrench them on the rack until they cause them to abandon their faith, unless some one taken away by the divine compassion should depart in the very midst of the torments, gaining glory, not by the cessation of his torture, but by the quickness of his death.

2. These things we suffer by our own fault and our own deserving, even as the divine judgment has forewarned us, saying, " If they forsake my

---

[8] Oxford ed.: Ep. xi. A.D. 250.
[9] [Compare, in former letters, similar complaints, to which brief notes are subjoined. And mark the honest simplicity of these confessions. 2 Peter ii. 13, 14, 15.]
[10] Luke xii. 47.

law and walk not in my judgments, if they profane my statutes and keep not my commandments, then will I visit their transgressions with the rod, and their iniquities with stripes." [1] It is for this reason that we feel the rods and the stripes, because we neither please God with good deeds nor atone [2] for our sins. Let us of our inmost heart and of our entire mind ask for God's mercy, because He Himself also adds, saying, "Nevertheless my loving-kindness will I not scatter away from them." [3] Let us ask, and we shall receive ; and if there be delay and tardiness in our receiving, since we have grievously offended, let us knock, because "to him that knocketh also it shall be opened," [4] if only our prayers, our groanings, and our tears, knock at the door ; and with these we must be urgent and persevering, even although prayer be offered with one mind. [5]

3. For, — which the more induced and constrained me to write this letter to you, — you ought to know (since the Lord has condescended to show and to reveal it) that it was said in a vision, "Ask, and ye shall obtain." Then, afterwards, that the attending people were bidden to pray for certain persons pointed out to them, but that in their petitions there were dissonant voices, and wills disagreeing, and that this excessively displeased Him who had said, "Ask, and ye shall obtain," because the disagreement of the people was out of harmony, and there was not a consent of the brethren one and simple, and a united concord ; since it is written, "God who maketh men to be of one mind in a house ; " [6] and we read in the Acts of the Apostles, "And the multitude of them that believed were of one heart and of one soul." [7] And the Lord has bidden us with His own voice, saying, "This is my command, that ye love one another." [8] And again, "I say unto you, that if two of you shall agree on earth as touching anything that you shall ask, it shall be done for you of my Father which is in heaven." [9] But if two of one mind can do so much, what might be effected if the unanimity prevailed among all? But if, according to the peace which our Lord gave us, there were agreement among all brethren, we should before this have obtained from the divine mercy what we seek ; nor should we be wavering so long in this peril of our salvation and our faith. Yes, truly, and these evils would not have come upon the brethren, if the brotherhood had been animated with one spirit.

4. For there also was shown that there sate the father of a family, a young man also being seated at his right hand, who, anxious and somewhat sad with a kind of indignation, holding his chin in his right hand, occupied his place with a sorrowful look. But another standing on the left hand, bore a net, which he threatened to throw, in order to catch the people standing round. [10] And when he who saw marvelled what this could be, it was told him that the youth who was thus sitting on the right hand was saddened and grieved because his commandments were not observed ; but that he on the left was exultant because an opportunity was afforded him of receiving from the father of the family the power of destroying. This was shown long before the tempest of this devastation arose. And we have seen that which had been shown fulfilled ; that while we despise the commandments of the Lord, while we do not keep the salutary ordinances of the law that He has given, the enemy was receiving a power of doing mischief, and was overwhelming, by the cast of his net, those who were imperfectly armed and too careless to resist.

5. Let us urgently pray and groan with continual petitions. For know, beloved brethren, that I was not long ago reproached with this also in a vision, that we were sleepy in our prayers, and did not pray with watchfulness ; and undoubtedly God, who "rebukes whom He loves," [11] when He rebukes, rebukes that He may amend, amends that He may preserve. Let us therefore strike off and break away from the bonds of sleep, and pray with urgency and watchfulness, as the Apostle Paul bids us, saying, "Continue in prayer, and watch in the same." [12] For the apostles also ceased not to pray day and night ; and the Lord also Himself, the teacher of our discipline, and the way of our example, frequently and watchfully prayed, as we read in the Gospel : "He went out into a mountain to pray, and continued all night in prayer to God." [13] And assuredly what He prayed for, He prayed for on our behalf, since He was not a sinner, but bore the sins of others. But He so prayed for us, that in another place we read, "And the Lord said to Peter, Behold, Satan has desired to sift you as wheat : but I have prayed for thee, that thy faith fail not." [14] But if for us and for our sins He both laboured and watched and prayed, how much more ought we to be instant in prayers ; and, first of all, to pray and to entreat the Lord Himself, and then through Him, to make satisfaction to God the Father ! We have an advocate and an intercessor for our sins, Jesus Christ

---

[1] Ps. lxxxix. 30-32.
[2] Satisfacimus.
[3] Ps. lxxxix. 33.
[4] Luke xi. 10.
[5] [A comment on Luke xviii. 3, compared with Matt. xviii. 19. Importunity necessary, even in the latter case.]
[6] Ps. lxviii. 6. [Vulgate and Anglican Psalter version.]
[7] Acts iv. 32.
[8] John xv. 12.
[9] Matt. xviii. 19.

[10] [After the manner of Hermas. Vol. ii. p. 24, note 2.]
[11] Heb. xii. 6.
[12] Col. iv. 2.
[13] Luke vi. 12.
[14] Luke xxii. 31, 32.

the Lord and our God, if only we repent of our sins past, and confess and acknowledge our sins, whereby we now offend the Lord, and for the time to come engage to walk in His ways, and to fear His commandments. The Father corrects and protects us, if we still stand fast in the faith both in afflictions and perplexities, that is to say, cling closely to His Christ ; as it is written, "Who shall separate us from the love of Christ? Shall tribulation, or distress, or persecution, or famine, or nakedness, or peril, or sword?"[1] None of these things can separate believers, nothing can tear away those who are clinging to His body and blood. Persecution of that kind is an examination and searching out of the heart. God wills us to be sifted and proved, as He has always proved His people ; and yet in His trials help has never at any time been wanting to believers.

6. Finally, to the very least of His servants, although placed among very many sins, and unworthy of His condescension, yet He has condescended of His goodness towards us to command :[2] "Tell him," said He, "to be safe, because peace is coming ; but that, in the meantime, there is a little delay, that some who still remain may be proved." But we are admonished by these divine condescensions both concerning a spare diet and a temperate use of drink ; to wit, lest worldly enticement should enervate the breast now elevated with celestial vigour, or lest the mind, weighed down by too abundant feasting, should be less watchful unto prayers and supplication.

7. It was my duty not to conceal these special matters, nor to hide them alone in my own consciousness, — matters by which each one of us may be both instructed and guided. And do not you for your part keep this letter concealed among yourselves, but let the brethren have it to read. For it is the part of one who desires that his brother should not be warned and instructed, to intercept those words with which the Lord condescends to admonish and instruct us. Let them know that we are proved by our Lord, and let them never fail of that faith whereby we have once believed in Him, under the conflict of this present affliction. Let each one, acknowledging his own sins, even now put off the conversation of the old man. "For no man who looks back as he putteth his hand to the plough is fit for the kingdom of God."[3] And, finally, Lot's wife, who, when she was delivered, looked back in defiance of the commandment, lost the benefit of her escape.[4] Let us look not to things which

are behind, whither the devil calls us back, but to things which are before, whither Christ calls us. Let us lift up our eyes to heaven, lest the earth with its delights and enticements deceive us. Let each one of us pray God not for himself only, but for all the brethren, even as the Lord has taught us to pray, when He bids to each one, not private prayer, but enjoined them, when they prayed, to pray for all in common prayer and concordant supplication.[5] If the Lord shall behold us humble and peaceable ; if He shall see us joined one with another ; if He shall see us fearful concerning His anger ; if corrected and amended by the present tribulation, He will maintain us safe from the disturbances of the enemy. Discipline hath preceded ; pardon also shall follow.

8. Let us only, without ceasing to ask, and with full faith that we shall receive, in simplicity and unanimity beseech the Lord, entreating not only with groaning but with tears, as it behoves those to entreat who are situated between the ruins of those who wail, and the remnants of those who fear ; between the manifold slaughter of the yielding, and the little firmness of those who still stand. Let us ask that peace may be soon restored ; that we may be quickly helped in our concealments and our dangers ; that those things may be fulfilled which the Lord deigns to show to his servants, — the restoration of the Church, the security of our salvation ; after the rains, serenity ; after the darkness, light ; after the storms and whirlwinds, a peaceful calm ; the affectionate aids of paternal love, the accustomed grandeurs of the divine majesty whereby both the blasphemy of persecutors may be restrained, the repentance of the lapsed renewed, and the stedfast faith of the persevering may glory. I bid you, beloved brethren, ever heartily farewell ; and have me in remembrance. Salute the brotherhood in my name ; and remind them to remember me. Farewell.

EPISTLE VIII.[6]

TO THE MARTYRS AND CONFESSORS.

ARGUMENT. — CYPRIAN, COMMENDING THE AFRICAN MARTYRS MARVELLOUSLY FOR THEIR CONSTANCY, URGES THEM TO PERSEVERANCE BY THE EXAMPLE OF THEIR COLLEAGUE MAPPALICUS.

Cyprian to the martyrs and confessors in Christ our Lord and in God the Father, everlasting salvation. I gladly rejoice and am thankful, most brave and blessed brethren, at hearing of your faith and virtue, wherein the Church, our Mother, glories. Lately, indeed, she gloried, when, in consequence of an enduring confession,

---

[1] Rom. viii. 35.
[2] [A vision granted to the pastor in behalf of his flock. See Vulgate version of Ps. lxxxix. 19, which Cyprian's, doubtless, anticipated.] This prediction of *settled times* was published in *unsettled* ones; and it was fulfilled by the sudden and unexpected death of Decius, in his expedition against the Goths.
[3] Luke ix. 62.
[4] Gen. xix. 26.

[5] [Saying, " our Father," not " my Father." Vol. i. p. 62.]
[6] Oxford ed.: Ep. x. A.D. 250.

that punishment was undergone which drove the confessors of Christ into exile ; yet the present confession is so much the more illustrious and greater in honour as it is braver in suffering. The combat has increased, and the glory of the combatants has increased also. Nor were you kept back from the struggle by fear of tortures, but by the very tortures themselves you were more and more stimulated to the conflict ; bravely and firmly you have returned with ready devotion, to contend in the extremest contest. Of you I find that some are already crowned, while some are even now within reach of the crown of victory ; but all whom the danger has shut up in a glorious company are animated to carry on the struggle with an equal and common warmth of virtue, as it behoves the soldiers of Christ in the divine camp : that no allurements may deceive the incorruptible stedfastness of your faith, no threats terrify you, no sufferings or tortures overcome you, because " greater is He that is in us, than he that is in the world ; "[1] nor is the earthly punishment able to do more towards casting down, than is the divine protection towards lifting up. This truth is proved by the glorious struggle of the brethren, who, having become leaders to the rest in overcoming their tortures, afforded an example of virtue and faith, contending in the strife, until the strife yielded, being overcome. With what praises can I commend you, most courageous brethren? With what vocal proclamation can I extol the strength of your heart and the perseverance of your faith? You have borne the sharpest examination by torture, even unto the glorious consummation, and have not yielded to sufferings, but rather the sufferings have given way to you. The end of torments, which the tortures themselves did not give, the crown has given. The examination by torture waxing severer, continued for a long time to this result, not to overthrow the stedfast faith, but to send the men of God more quickly to the Lord. The multitude of those who were present saw with admiration the heavenly contest, — the contest of God, the spiritual contest, the battle of Christ, — saw that His servants stood with free voice, with unyielding mind, with divine virtue — bare, indeed, of weapons of this world, but believing and armed with the weapons of faith. The tortured stood more brave than the torturers ; and the limbs, beaten and torn as they were, overcame the hooks that bent and tore them. The scourge, often repeated with all its rage, could not conquer invincible faith, even although the membrane which enclosed the entrails were broken, and it was no longer the limbs but the wounds of the servants of God that were tortured. Blood was

flowing which might quench the blaze of persecution, which might subdue the flames of Gehenna with its glorious gore.[2] Oh, what a spectacle was that to the Lord, — how sublime, how great, how acceptable to the eyes of God in the allegiance and devotion of His soldiers ! As it is written in the Psalms, when the Holy Spirit at once speaks to us and warns us : " Precious in the sight of the Lord is the death of His saints."[3] Precious is the death which has bought immortality at the cost of its blood, which has received the crown from the consummation of its virtues. How did Christ rejoice therein ! How willingly did He both fight and conquer in such servants of His, as the protector of their faith, and giving to believers as much as he who taketh believes that he receives ! He was present at His own contest ; He lifted up, strengthened, animated the champions and assertors of His name. And He who once conquered death on our behalf, always conquers it in us. "When they," says He, " deliver you up, take no thought what ye shall speak : for it shall be given you in that hour what ye shall speak. For it is not ye that speak, but the Spirit of your Father which speaketh in you."[4] The present struggle has afforded a proof of this saying. A voice filled with the Holy Spirit broke forth from the martyr's mouth when the most blessed Mappalicus said to the proconsul in the midst of his torments, "You shall see a contest to-morrow." And that which he said with the testimony of virtue and faith, the Lord fulfilled. A heavenly contest was exhibited, and the servant of God was crowned in the struggle of the promised fight. This is the contest which the prophet Isaiah of old predicted, saying, " It shall be no light contest for you with men, since God appoints the struggle."[5] And in order to show what this struggle would be, he added the words, " Behold, a virgin shall conceive and bear a son, and ye shall call His name Emmanuel."[6] This is the struggle of our faith in which we engage, in which we conquer, in which we are crowned. This is the struggle which the blessed Apostle Paul has shown to us, in which it behoves us to run and to attain the crown of glory. " Do ye not know," says he, " that they which run in a race, run all indeed, but one receiveth the prize? So run that ye may obtain." " Now they do it that they may receive a corruptible crown, but we an incorruptible."[7] Moreover, setting forth his own struggle, and declaring that he himself should

---

[1] John iv. 4.

[2] [There is in the church of S. Stefano Rotondo at Rome a series of delineations of the sufferings of the early martyrs, poorly executed, and too horrible to contemplate; but it all answers to these words of our author. See Ep. xxxiv. *infra*.]
[3] Ps. cxvi. 15.
[4] Matt. x. 19, 20.
[5] Isa. vii. 13; *vide* Lam. iii. 26.
[6] Isa. vii. 14.
[7] 1 Cor. ix. 24, 25.

soon be a sacrifice for the Lord's sake, he says, "I am now ready to be offered, and the time of my assumption is at hand. I have fought a good fight, I have finished my course, I have kept the faith : henceforth there is laid up for me a crown of righteousness, which the Lord, the righteous judge, shall give me at that day ; and not to me only, but unto all them also that love His appearing." [1] This fight, therefore, predicted of old by the prophets, begun by the Lord, waged by the apostles, Mappalicus promised again to the proconsul in his own name and that of his colleagues. Nor did the faithful voice deceive in his promise ; he exhibited the fight to which he had pledged himself, and he received the reward which he deserved. I not only beseech but exhort the rest of you, that you all should follow that martyr now most blessed, and the other partners of that engagement, — soldiers and comrades, stedfast in faith, patient in suffering, victors in tortures, — that those who are united at once by the bond of confession, and the entertainment of a dungeon, may also be united in the consummation of their virtue and a celestial crown ; that you by your joy may dry the tears of our Mother, the Church, who mourns over the wreck and death of very many ; and that you may confirm, by the provocation of your example, the stedfastness of others who stand also. If the battle shall call you out, if the day of your contest shall come, engage bravely, fight with constancy, as knowing that you are fighting under the eyes of a present Lord, that you are attaining by the confession of His name to His own glory ; who is not such a one as that He only looks on His servants, but He Himself also wrestles in us, Himself is engaged, — Himself also in the struggles of our conflict not only crowns, but is crowned. But if before the day of your contest, of the mercy of God, peace shall supervene, let there still remain to you the sound will and the glorious conscience.[2] Nor let any one of you be saddened as if he were inferior to those who before you have suffered tortures, have overcome the world and trodden it under foot, and so have come to the Lord by a glorious road. For the Lord is the "searcher out of the reins and the hearts." [3] He looks through secret things, and beholds that which is concealed. In order to merit the crown from Him, His own testimony alone is sufficient, who will judge us. Therefore, beloved brethren, either case is equally lofty and illustrious, — the former more secure, to wit, to hasten to the Lord with the consummation of our victory, — the latter more joyous ; a leave

of absence, after glory, being received to flourish in the praises of the Church. O blessed Church of ours, which the honour of the divine condescension illuminates, which in our own times the glorious blood of martyrs renders illustrious ! She was white before in the works of the brethren ; now she has become purple in the blood of the martyrs. Among her flowers are wanting neither roses nor lilies. Now let each one strive for the largest dignity of either honour. Let them receive crowns, either white, as of labours, or of purple, as of suffering. In the heavenly camp both peace and strife have their own flowers, with which the soldier of Christ may be crowned for glory. I bid you, most brave and beloved brethren, always heartily farewell in the Lord ; and have me in remembrance. Fare ye well.

EPISTLE IX.[4]

TO THE CLERGY, CONCERNING CERTAIN PRESBYTERS WHO HAD RASHLY GRANTED PEACE TO THE LAPSED BEFORE THE PERSECUTION HAD BEEN APPEASED, AND WITHOUT THE PRIVITY OF THE BISHOPS.

ARGUMENT. — THE ARGUMENT OF THIS EPISTLE IS CONTAINED IN THE FOLLOWING WORDS OF THE XIVTH EPISTLE : — " TO THE PRESBYTERS AND DEACONS," HE SAYS, " WAS NOT WANTING THE VIGOUR OF THE PRIESTHOOD, SO THAT SOME, TOO LITTLE MINDFUL OF DISCIPLINE, AND HASTY WITH A RASH PRECIPITATION, WHO HAD ALREADY BEGUN TO COMMUNICATE WITH THE LAPSED, WERE CHECKED."

1. Cyprian to the presbyters and deacons, his brethren, greeting. I have long been patient, beloved brethren, hoping that my forbearing silence would avail to quietness. But since the unreasonable and reckless presumption of some is seeking by its boldness to disturb both the honour of the martyrs, and the modesty of the confessors, and the tranquillity of the whole people, it behoves me no longer to keep silence, lest too much reticence should issue in danger both to the people and to ourselves. For what danger ought we not to fear from the Lord's displeasure, when some of the presbyters, remembering neither the Gospel nor their own place, and, moreover, considering neither the Lord's future judgment nor the bishop now placed over them, claim to themselves entire authority,[5] — a thing which was never in any wise done under our predecessors, — with discredit and contempt of the bishop?

2. And I wish, if it could be so without the sacrifice of our brethren's safety, that they could make good their claim to all things ; I could dis-

---

[1] 2 Tim. iv. 6-8.
[2] [He contemplates the peace promised in Ep. viii. *supra*. But note the indomitable spirit with which, for successive ages, the Church supplied her martyrs. Heb. xi. 36, 37.]
[3] Rev. ii. 23.

[4] Oxford ed.: Ep. xvi. A.D. 250.
[5] [In letter ii. we have noted a limited exercise of *jurisdiction:* the canons seem not to have allowed them the full powers these presbyters had used.]

semble and bear the discredit of my episcopal authority, as I always have dissembled and borne it. But it is not now the occasion for dissimulating when our brotherhood is deceived by some of you, who, while without the means of restoring salvation they desire to please, become a still greater stumbling-block to the lapsed. For that it is a very great crime which persecution has compelled to be committed, they themselves know who have committed it; since our Lord and Judge has said, "Whosoever shall confess me before men, him will I also confess before my Father which is in heaven; but whosoever shall deny me, him will I also deny."[1] And again He has said, "All sins shall be forgiven unto the sons of men, and blasphemies; but he that shall blaspheme against the Holy Ghost shall not have forgiveness, but is guilty of eternal sin."[2] Also the blessed apostle has said, "Ye cannot drink the cup of the Lord and the cup of devils; ye cannot be partakers of the Lord's table and of the table of devils."[3] He who withholds these words from our brethren deceives them, wretched that they are; so that they who truly repenting might satisfy God, both as the Father and as merciful, with their prayers and works, are seduced more deeply to perish; and they who might raise themselves up fall the more deeply. For although in smaller sins sinners may do penance for a set time, and according to the rules of discipline come to public confession,[4] and by imposition of the hand of the bishop and clergy receive the right of communion: now with their time still unfulfilled, while persecution is still raging, while the peace of the Church itself is not yet restored, they are admitted to communion, and their name is presented; and while the penitence is not yet performed, confession is not yet made, the hands of the bishop and clergy are not yet laid upon them, the eucharist is given to them; although it is written, "Whosoever shall eat the bread and drink the cup of the Lord unworthily, shall be guilty of the body and blood of the Lord."[5]

3. But now they are not guilty who so little observe the law of Scripture; but they will be guilty who are in office and do not suggest these things to brethren, so that, being instructed by those placed above them, they may do all things with the fear of God, and with the observance given and prescribed by Him. Then, moreover, they lay the blessed martyrs open to ill-will, and involve the glorious servants of God with the priest of God; so that although they, mindful of my place, have directed letters to me, and have asked that their wishes should then be ex-

amined, and peace granted them, — when our Mother, the Church herself, should first have received peace for the Lord's mercy, and the divine protection have brought me back to His Church, — yet these, disregarding the honour which the blessed martyrs with the confessors maintain for me, despising the Lord's law and that observance, which the same martyrs and confessors bid to be maintained, before the fear of persecution is quenched, before my return, almost even before the departure of the martyrs, communicate with the lapsed, and offer and give them the eucharist: when even if the martyrs, in the heat of their glory, were to consider less carefully the Scriptures, and to desire anything more, they should be admonished by the presbyters' and deacons' suggestions, as was always done in time past.[6]

4. For this reason the divine rebuke does not cease to chastise us night nor day. For besides the visions of the night, by day also, the innocent age of boys is among us filled with the Holy Spirit, seeing in an ecstasy with their eyes, and hearing and speaking those things whereby the Lord condescends to warn and instruct us.[7] And you shall hear all things when the Lord, who bade me withdraw, shall bring me back again to you. In the meanwhile, let those certain ones among you who are rash and incautious and boastful, and who do not regard man, at least fear God, knowing that, if they shall persevere still in the same course, I shall use that power of admonition which the Lord bids me use; so that they may meanwhile be withheld from offering,[8] and have to plead their cause both before me and before the confessors themselves and before the whole people, when, with God's permission, we begin to be gathered together once more into the bosom of the Church, our Mother. Concerning this matter, I have written to the martyrs and confessors, and to the people, letters; both of which I have bidden to be read to you. I wish you, dearly beloved brethren and earnestly longed-for, ever heartily farewell in the Lord; and have me in remembrance. Fare ye well.

EPISTLE X.[9]

TO THE MARTYRS AND CONFESSORS WHO SOUGHT THAT PEACE SHOULD BE GRANTED TO THE LAPSED.

ARGUMENT. — THE OCCASION OF THIS LETTER IS GIVEN BELOW IN EPISTLE XIV. AS FOLLOWS: — "WHEN I FOUND THAT THOSE WHO HAD POL-

---

[1] Matt. x. 32, 33.
[2] Mark iii. 28, 29.
[3] 1 Cor. x. 21.
[4] "Exomologesis."
[5] 1 Cor. xi. 27.

[6] [Compare Tertullian, *Ad Martyras*, vol. iii. p. 693.]
[7] [Note this persuasion of Cyprian, and compare St. Matt. xxi. 15, 16; Luke xix. 40.]
[8] [Celebrating the Lord's Supper; Rom. xv. 16 (Greek) compared with Mal. i. 11, texts which seem greatly to have influenced the language of the early Church.]
[9] Oxford ed.: Ep. xv. A.D. 250.

LUTED THEIR HANDS AND MOUTHS WITH SACRI-
LEGIOUS CONTACT, OR HAD NO LESS INFECTED
THEIR CONSCIENCE WITH WICKED CERTIFICATES,"
ETC.[1]

1. Cyprian to the martyrs and confessors, his beloved brethren, greeting. The anxiety of my situation and the fear of the Lord constrain me, my brave and beloved brethren, to admonish you in my letters, that those who so devotedly and bravely maintain the faith of the Lord should also maintain the law and discipline of the Lord. For while it behoves all Christ's soldiers to keep the precepts of their commander; to you it is more especially fitting that you should obey His precepts, inasmuch as you have been made an example to others, both of valour and of the fear of God. And I had indeed believed that the presbyters and deacons who are there present with you would admonish and instruct you more fully concerning the law of the Gospel, as was the case always in time past under my predecessors; so that the deacons passing in and out of the prison controlled the wishes of the martyrs by their counsels, and by the Scripture precepts. But now, with great sorrow of mind, I gather that not only the divine precepts are not suggested to you by them, but that they are even rather restrained, so that those things which are done by you yourselves, both in respect of God with caution, and in respect of God's priest[2] with honour, are relaxed by certain presbyters, who consider neither the fear of God nor the honour of the bishop. Although you sent letters to me in which you ask that your wishes should be examined, and that peace should be granted to certain of the lapsed as soon as with the end of the persecution we should have begun to meet with our clergy, and to be gathered together once more; those presbyters, contrary to the Gospel law, contrary also to your respectful petition, before penitence was fulfilled, before confession even of the gravest and most heinous sin was made, before hands were placed upon the repentant by the bishops and clergy, dare to offer on their behalf, and to give them the eucharist, that is, to profane the sacred body of the Lord, although it is written, " Whosoever shall eat the bread and drink the cup of the Lord unworthily, shall be guilty of the body and blood of the Lord."[3]

2. And to the lapsed indeed pardon may be granted in respect of this thing. For what dead person would not hasten to be made alive?

Who would not be eager to attain to his own salvation? But it is the duty of those placed over them to keep the ordinance, and to instruct those that are either hurrying or ignorant, that those who ought to be shepherds of the sheep may not become their butchers. For to concede those things which tend to destruction is to deceive. Nor is the lapsed raised in this manner, but, by offending God, he is more urged on to ruin. Let them learn, therefore, even from you, what they ought to have taught; let them reserve your petitions and wishes for the bishops,[4] and let them wait for ripe and peaceable times to give peace at your requests. The first thing is, that the Mother should first receive peace from the Lord, and then, in accordance with your wishes, that the peace of her children should be considered.

3. And since I hear, most brave and beloved brethren, that you are pressed by the shamelessness of some, and that your modesty suffers violence; I beg you with what entreaties I may, that, as mindful of the Gospel, and considering what and what sort of things in past time your predecessors the martyrs conceded, how careful they were in all respects, you also should anxiously and cautiously weigh the wishes of those who petition you, since, as friends of the Lord, and hereafter to exercise judgment with Him, you must inspect both the conduct and the doings and the deserts of each one. You must consider also the kinds and qualities of their sins, lest, in the event of anything being abruptly and unworthily either promised by you or done by me, our Church[5] should begin to blush, even before the very Gentiles. For we are visited and chastened frequently, and we are admonished, that the commandments of the Lord may be kept without corruption or violation, which I find does not cease to be the case there among you so as to prevent the divine judgment from instructing very many of you also in the discipline of the Church. Now this can all be done, if you will regulate those things that are asked of you with a careful consideration of religion, perceiving and restraining those who, by accepting persons, either make favours in distributing your benefits, or seek to make a profit of an unlawful trade.

4. Concerning this I have written both to the clergy and to the people, both of which letters I have directed to be read to you. But you ought also to bring back and amend that matter according to your diligence, in such a way as to designate those by name to whom you desire that peace should be granted. For I hear that certificates are so given to some as that it is said,

---

[1] That these were everywhere soliciting the martyrs, and were also corrupting the confessors with importunate and excessive entreaty, so that, without any distinction or examination of the individuals, thousands of certificates were given, against the Gospel law, I wrote letters in which I recalled by my advice as much as possible the martyrs and confessors to the Lord's commands.

[2] [Another instance of this word as applied to the bishop, κατ' ἐξοχήν. So in St. Chrysostom, De Sacerdotio = episcopatu.]

[3] 1 Cor. xi. 27.

[4] [He refers to his comprovincials, not arrogating all authority to himself. See Hippolytus, p. 125, note 2, supra.]

[5] [The African Church.]

"Let such a one be received to communion along with his friends," which was never in any case done by the martyrs so that a vague and blind petition should by and by heap reproach upon us. For it opens a wide door to say, "Such a one with his friends;" and twenty or thirty or more, may be presented to us, who may be asserted to be neighbours and connections, and freedmen and servants, of the man who receives the certificate. And for this reason I beg you that you will designate by name in the certificate those whom you yourselves see, whom you have known, whose penitence you see to be very near to full satisfaction, and so direct to us letters in conformity with faith and discipline. I bid you, very brave and beloved brethren, ever heartily in the Lord farewell; and have me in remembrance. Fare ye well.

EPISTLE XI.[1]

TO THE PEOPLE.

ARGUMENT.—THE SUBSTANCE OF THIS LETTER IS ALSO SUGGESTED IN EPISTLE XIV. "AMONG THE PEOPLE ALSO," HE SAYS, "I HAVE DONE WHAT I COULD TO QUIET THEIR MINDS, AND HAVE INSTRUCTED THEM TO BE RETAINED IN ECCLESIASTICAL DISCIPLINE."

1. Cyprian to his brethren among the people who stand fast,[2] greeting. That you bewail and grieve over the downfall of our brethren I know from myself, beloved brethren, who also bewail with you and grieve for each one, and suffer and feel what the blessed apostle said: "Who is weak," said he, " and I am not weak? who is offended, and I burn not?"[3] And again he has laid it down in his epistle, saying, "Whether one member suffer, all the members suffer with it; or one member rejoice, all the members rejoice with it."[4] I sympathize with you in your suffering and grief, therefore, for our brethren, who, having lapsed and fallen prostrate under the severity of the persecution, have inflicted a like pain on us by their wounds, inasmuch as they tear away part of our bowels with them, — to these the divine mercy is able to bring healing. Yet I do not think that there must be any haste, nor that anything must be done incautiously and immaturely, lest, while peace is grasped at, the divine indignation be more seriously incurred. The blessed martyrs have written to me about certain persons, requesting that their wishes may be examined into. When, as soon as peace is given to us all by the Lord, we shall begin to return to the Church, then the wishes of each one shall be looked into in your presence, and with your judgment.[5]

2. Yet I hear that certain of the presbyters, neither mindful of the Gospel nor considering what the martyrs have written to me, nor reserving to the bishop the honour of his priesthood and of his dignity, have already begun to communicate with the lapsed, and to offer on their behalf, and to give them the eucharist, when it was fitting that they should attain to these things in due course. For, as in smaller sins which are not committed against God, penitence may be fulfilled in a set time, and confession may be made with investigation of the life of him who fulfils the penitence, and no one can come to communion unless the hands of the bishop and clergy be first imposed upon him; how much more ought all such matters as these to be observed with caution and moderation, according to the discipline of the Lord, in these gravest and extremest sins! This warning, indeed, our presbyters and deacons ought to have given you, that they might cherish the sheep committed to their care, and by the divine authority might instruct them in the way of obtaining salvation by prayer. I am aware of the peacefulness as well as the fear of our people, who would be watchful in the satisfaction and the deprecation of God's anger, unless some of the presbyters, by way of gratifying them, had deceived them.

3. Even you, therefore, yourselves, guide them each one, and control the minds of the lapsed by counsel and by your own moderation, according to the divine precepts. Let no one pluck the unripe fruit at a time as yet premature. Let no one commit his ship, shattered and broken with the waves, anew to the deep, before he has carefully repaired it. Let none be in haste to accept and to put on a rent tunic, unless he has seen it mended by a skilful workman, and has received it arranged by the fuller. Let them bear with patience my advice, I beg. Let them look for my return, that when by God's mercy I come to you, I, with many of my co-bishops, being called together according to the Lord's discipline,[6] and in the presence of the confessors, and with your opinion also, may be able to examine the letters and the wishes of the blessed martyrs. Concerning this matter I have written both to the clergy and to the martyrs and confessors, both of which letters I have directed to be read to you. I bid you, brethren beloved and most longed-for, ever heartily farewell in the Lord; and have me in remembrance. Fare ye well.

---

[1] Oxford ed.: Ep. xvii. A.D. 250.
[2] [The faithful laity. A technical expression, in the original.]
[3] 2 Cor. xi. 29.
[4] 1 Cor. xii. 26.

[5] [Here is a recognition of the laity as contributing to the decisive action. 1 Cor. v. 4.]
[6] [Elucidation III.; also Ignatius, vol. i. p. 69.]

EPISTLE XII.[1]

TO THE CLERGY, CONCERNING THE LAPSED AND CATECHUMENS, THAT THEY SHOULD NOT BE LEFT WITHOUT SUPERINTENDENCE.

ARGUMENT. — THE BURDEN OF THIS LETTER, AS OF THE SUCCEEDING ONE, IS FOUND BELOW IN THE XIVTH EPISTLE. "BUT AFTERWARDS," HE SAYS, "WHEN SOME OF THE LAPSED, WHETHER OF THEIR OWN ACCORD, OR BY THE SUGGESTION OF ANY OTHER, BROKE FORTH WITH A DARING DEMAND, AS THOUGH THEY WOULD ENDEAVOUR, BY A VIOLENT EFFORT, TO EXTORT THE PEACE THAT HAD BEEN PROMISED TO THEM BY THE MARTYRS AND CONFESSORS," ETC.[2]

1. Cyprian to the presbyters and deacons, his brethren, greeting. I marvel, beloved brethren, that you have answered nothing to me in reply to my many letters which I have frequently written to you, although as well the advantage as the need of our brotherhood would certainly be best provided for if, receiving information from you, I could accurately investigate and advise upon the management of affairs. Since, however, I see that there is not yet any opportunity of coming to you, and that the summer has already begun — a season that is disturbed with continual and heavy sicknesses, — I think that our brethren must be dealt with ; — that they who have received certificates from the martyrs, and may be assisted by their privilege with God, if they should be seized with any misfortune and peril of sickness, should, without waiting for my presence, before any presbyter who might be present, or if a presbyter should not be found and death begins to be imminent, before even a deacon, be able to make confession of their sin, that, with the imposition of hands upon them for repentance, they should come to the Lord with the peace which the martyrs have desired, by their letters to us, to be granted to them.[3]

2. Cherish also by your presence the rest of the people who are lapsed, and cheer them by your consolation, that they may not fail of the faith and of God's mercy. For those shall not be forsaken by the aid and assistance of the Lord, who meekly, humbly, and with true penitence have persevered in good works ; but the divine remedy will be granted to them also. To the hearers[4] also, if there are any overtaken by danger, and placed near to death, let your vigilance not be wanting ; let not the mercy of the Lord be denied to those that are imploring the divine favour.[5] I bid you, beloved brethren, ever heartily farewell ; and remember me. Greet the whole brotherhood in my name, and remind them and ask them to be mindful of me. Fare ye well.

EPISTLE XIII.[6]

TO THE CLERGY, CONCERNING THOSE WHO ARE IN HASTE TO RECEIVE PEACE. A.D. 250.

ARGUMENT. — PEACE MUST BE ATTAINED THROUGH PENITENCE, AND PENITENCE IS REALIZED BY KEEPING THE COMMANDMENTS. THEY WHO ARE OPPRESSED WITH SICKNESS, IF THEY ARE RELIEVED BY THE SUFFRAGES OF THE MARTYRS, MAY BE ADMITTED TO PEACE ; BUT OTHERS ARE TO BE KEPT BACK UNTIL THE PEACE OF THE CHURCH IS SECURED.

1. Cyprian to the presbyters and deacons, his brethren, greeting. I have read your letter, beloved brethren, wherein you wrote that your wholesome counsel was not wanting to our brethren, that, laying aside all rash haste, they should manifest a religious patience to God, so that when by His mercy we come together, we may debate upon all kinds of things, according to the discipline of the Church, especially since it is written, "Remember from whence thou hast fallen, and repent."[7] Now he repents, who, remembering the divine precept, with meekness and patience, and obeying the priests of God, deserves well of the Lord by his obedience and his righteous works.

2. Since, however, you intimate that some are petulant, and eagerly urge their being received to communion, and have desired in this matter that some rule should be given by me to you, I think I have sufficiently written on this subject in the last letter that was sent to you, that they who have received a certificate from the martyrs, and can be assisted by their help with the Lord in respect of their sins, if they begin to be oppressed with any sickness or risk ; when they have made confession, and have received the imposition of hands on them by you in acknowledgment of their penitence, should be remitted to the Lord with the peace promised to them by the martyrs. But others who, without having received any certificate from the martyrs, are envious[8] (since this is the cause not of a few, nor of one church, nor of one province, but of the whole world), must wait, in dependence on the protection of the Lord, for the public peace

---

[1] Oxford ed.: Ep. xviii. A.D. 250.

[2] "Concerning this also I wrote twice to the clergy, and commanded it to be read to them, that for the mitigation of their violence in any manner for the meantime, if any who had received a certificate from the martyrs were departing from this life, having made confession and received the hands imposed upon them for repentance, they should be remitted to the Lord with the peace promised them by the martyrs," etc.

[3] [2 Cor. ii. 10.]

[4] "Audientibus," *scil.* catechumens.

[5] [See *Hermas*, vol. ii. p. 15, note 6.]

[6] Oxford ed.: Ep. xix. [See letter xxvii. *infra*.]

[7] Rev. ii. 5.

[8] Faciunt invidiam: "are producing ill-will to us." Those who were eager to be received into the Church without certificates would produce ill-will to those who refused to receive them, as if they were too strict. Thus Rigaltius explains the passage. "These," Cyprian says, "should wait until the Church in its usual way gives them peace publicly."

of the Church itself. For this is suitable to the modesty and the discipline, and even the life of all of us, that the chief officers meeting together with the clergy in the presence also of the people who stand fast, to whom themselves, moreover, honour is to be shown for their faith and fear, we may be able to order all things with the religiousness of a common consultation.[1] But how irreligious is it, and mischievous, even to those themselves who are eager, that while such as are exiles, and driven from their country, and spoiled of all their property, have not yet returned to the Church, some of the lapsed should be hasty to anticipate even confessors themselves, and to enter into the Church before them! If they are so over-anxious, they have what they require in their own power, the times themselves offering them freely more than they ask. The struggle is still going forward, and the strife is daily celebrated. If they truly and with constancy repent of what they have done, and the fervour of their faith prevails, he who cannot be delayed may be crowned.[2] I bid you, beloved brethren, ever heartily farewell; and have me in remembrance. Greet all the brotherhood in my name, and tell them to be mindful of me. Fare ye well.

EPISTLE XIV.[3]

TO THE PRESBYTERS AND DEACONS ASSEMBLED AT ROME.

ARGUMENT. — HE GIVES AN ACCOUNT OF HIS WITHDRAWAL AND OF THE THINGS WHICH HE DID THEREIN, HAVING SENT TO ROME FOR HIS JUSTIFICATION, COPIES OF THE LETTERS WHICH HE HAD WRITTEN TO HIS PEOPLE; NAY, HE MAKES USE OF THE SAME WORDS WHICH HE HAD EMPLOYED IN THEM.[4]

1. Cyprian to his brethren the presbyters and deacons assembled at Rome, greeting. Having ascertained, beloved brethren, that what I have done and am doing has been told to you in a somewhat garbled and untruthful manner, I have thought it necessary to write this letter to you, wherein I might give an account to you of my doings, my discipline, and my diligence; for, as the Lord's commands teach, immediately the first burst of the disturbance arose, and the people with violent clamour repeatedly demanded me, I, taking into consideration not so much my own safety as the public peace of the brethren, withdrew for a while, lest, by my over-bold presence, the tumult which had begun might be still further provoked. Nevertheless, although absent in body, I was not wanting either in spirit, or in act, or in my advice, so as to fail in any benefit

that I could afford my brethren by my counsel, according to the Lord's precepts, in anything that my poor abilities enabled me.

2. And what I did, these thirteen letters sent forth at various times declare to you, which I have transmitted to you; in which neither counsel to the clergy, nor exhortation to the confessors, nor rebuke, when it was necessary, to the exiles, nor my appeals and persuasions to the whole brotherhood, that they should entreat the mercy of God, were wanting to the full extent that, according to the law of faith and the fear of God, with the Lord's help, my poor abilities could endeavour. But afterwards, when tortures came, my words reached both to our tortured brethren and to those who as yet were only imprisoned with a view to torture, to strengthen and console them. Moreover, when I found that those who had polluted their hands and mouths with sacrilegious contact, or had no less infected their consciences with wicked certificates, were everywhere soliciting the martyrs, and were also corrupting the confessors with importunate and excessive entreaties, so that, without any discrimination or examination of the individuals themselves, thousands of certificates were daily given, contrary to the law of the Gospel, I wrote letters in which I recalled by my advice, as much as possible, the martyrs and confessors to the Lord's commands. To the presbyters and deacons also was not wanting the vigour of the priesthood;[5] so that some, too little mindful of discipline, and hasty, with a rash precipitation, who had already begun to communicate with the lapsed, were restrained by my interposition. Among the people, moreover, I have done what I could to quiet their minds, and have instructed them to maintain ecclesiastical discipline.

3. But afterwards, when some of the lapsed, whether of their own accord, or by the suggestion of any other, broke forth with a daring demand, as though they would endeavour by a violent effort to extort the peace that had been promised to them by the martyrs and confessors; concerning this also I wrote twice to the clergy, and commanded it to be read to them; that for the mitigation of their violence in any manner for the meantime, if any who had received a certificate from the martyrs were departing from this life, having made confession, and received the imposition of hands on them for repentance, they should be remitted to the Lord with the peace promised them by the martyrs. Nor in this did I give them a law, or rashly constitute myself the author of the direction; but as it seemed fit both that honour should be paid to the martyrs, and that the vehemence of those

---

[1] [Elucidation IV.]
[2] [i.e., they can become martyrs, if they will.]
[3] Oxford ed.: Ep. xx.   A.D. 250.
[4] Comp. Ep. xxii. to the Roman clergy.

[5] [Another instance of this usage (κατ' ἐξοχήν), of which see p. 291, *supra*.]

who were anxious to disturb everything should be restrained; and when, besides, I had read your letter which you lately wrote hither to my clergy by Crementius the sub-deacon, to the effect that assistance should be given to those who might, after their lapse, be seized with sickness, and might penitently desire communion; I judged it well to stand by your judgment, lest our proceedings, which ought to be united and to agree in all things, should in any respect be different.[1] The cases of the rest, even although they might have received certificates from the martyrs, I ordered altogether to be put off, and to be reserved till I should be present, that so, when the Lord has given to us peace, and several bishops shall have begun to assemble into one place, we may be able to arrange and reform everything, having the advantage also of your counsel. I bid you, beloved brethren, ever heartily farewell.

EPISTLE XV.[2]

TO MOYSES AND MAXIMUS, AND THE REST OF THE CONFESSORS.

ARGUMENT. — THE BURDEN OF THIS LETTER IS GIVEN IN EPISTLE XXXI. BELOW, WHERE THE ROMAN CLERGY SAY: "ON WHICH SUBJECT WE OWE YOU, AND GIVE YOU OUR DEEPEST AND ABUNDANT THANKS, THAT YOU THREW LIGHT INTO THE GLOOM OF THEIR PRISON BY YOUR LETTERS." [3]

1. Cyprian to Moyses and Maximus, the presbyters and the other confessors, his brethren, greeting. Celerinus, a companion both of your faith and virtue, and God's soldier in glorious engagements, has come to me, beloved brethren, and represented all of you, as well as each individual, forcibly to my affection. I beheld in him, when he came, the whole of you; and when he spoke sweetly and often of your love to me, in his words I heard you. I rejoice very greatly when such things are brought to me from you by such men as he. In a certain manner I am also there with you in prison. I think that I who am thus bound to your hearts, enjoy with you the delights of the divine approval. Your individual love associates me with your honour; the Spirit does not allow our love to be separated. Confession[4] shuts *you* up in prison; affection

shuts *me* up there. And I indeed, remembering you day and night, both when in the sacrifices I offer prayer with many, and when in retirement I pray with private petition, beseech of the Lord a full acknowledgment to your crowns and your praises. But my poor ability is too weak to recompense you; you give more when you remember me in prayer, since, already breathing only celestial things, and meditating only divine things, you ascend to loftier heights, even by the delay of your suffering; and by the long lapse of time, are not wasting, but increasing your glory. A first and single confession makes blessed; you confess as often as, when asked to retire from prison, you prefer the prison with faith and virtue; your praises are as numerous as the days; as the months roll onward, ever your merits increase. He conquers once who suffers at once; but he who continues always battling with punishments, and is not overcome with suffering, is daily crowned.

2. Now, therefore, let magistrates and consuls or proconsuls go by; let them glory in the ensigns of their yearly dignity, and in their twelve fasces. Behold, the heavenly dignity in you is sealed by the brightness of a year's honour, and already, in the continuance of its victorious glory, has passed over the rolling circle of the returning year. The rising sun and the waning moon enlightened the world; but to you, He who made the sun and moon was a greater light in your dungeon, and the brightness of Christ glowing in your hearts and minds, irradiated with that eternal and brilliant light the gloom of the place of punishment, which to others was so horrible and deadly. The winter has passed through the vicissitudes of the months; but you, shut up in prison, were undergoing, instead of the inclemencies of winter, the winter of persecution. To the winter succeeded the mildness of spring, rejoicing with roses and crowned with flowers; but to you were present roses and flowers from the delights of paradise, and celestial garlands wreathed your brows. Behold, the summer is fruitful with the fertility of the harvest, and the threshing-floor is filled with grain; but you who have sown glory, reap the fruit of glory, and, placed in the Lord's threshing-floor, behold the chaff burnt up with unquenchable fire; you yourselves as grains of wheat, winnowed and precious corn, now purged and garnered, regard the dwelling-place of a prison as your granary. Nor is there wanting to the autumn spiritual grace for discharging the duties of the season. The vintage is pressed out of doors, and the grape which shall hereafter flow into the cups is trodden in the presses. You, rich bunches out of the Lord's vineyard, and branches with fruit already ripe, trodden by the tribulation of worldly pressure, fill your wine-press in the tor-

---

[1] [Note the moderation of our author. 1 Pet. v. 5.]

[2] Oxford ed.: Ep. xxxvii. In the autumn of A.D. 250.

[3] "Further, that you came to them in such way as you could enter; that you refreshed their minds, robust in their own faith and confession, by your appeals and your letters; that, accompanying their happiness with deserved praises, you inflamed them to a much more ardent desire for heavenly glory; that you urged them onward in the course; that you animated, as we believe and hope, future victors by the power of your address, so that, although all this may seem to come from the faith of the confessors and the divine indulgence, yet in their martyrdom they may seem in some manner to have become debtors to you."

[4] [i.e., confessorship. As to the time, see Treatise ii. *infra*.]

turing prison, and shed your blood instead of wine ; brave to bear suffering, you willingly drink the cup of martyrdom. Thus the year rolls on with the Lord's servants, — thus is celebrated the vicissitude of the seasons with spiritual deserts, and with celestial rewards.

3. Abundantly blessed are they who, from your number, passing through these footprints of glory, have already departed from the world ; and, having finished their journey of virtue and faith, have attained to the embrace and the kiss of the Lord, to the joy of the Lord Himself. But yet your glory is not less, who are still engaged in contest, and, about to follow the glories of your comrades, are long waging the battle, and with an unmoved and unshaken faith standing fast, are daily exhibiting in your virtues a spectacle in the sight of God. The longer is your strife, the loftier will be your crown. The struggle is one, but it is crowded with a manifold multitude of contests ; you conquer hunger, and despise thirst, and tread under foot the squalor of the dungeon, and the horror of the very abode of punishment, by the vigour of your courage. Punishment is there subdued ; torture is worn out ; death is not feared but desired, being overcome by the reward of immortality, so that he who has conquered is crowned with eternity of life. What now must be the mind in you, how elevated, how large the heart, when such and so great things are resolved, when nothing but the precepts of God and the rewards of Christ are considered ! The will is then only God's will ; and although you are still placed in the flesh, it is the life not of the present world, but of the future, that you now live.

4. It now remains, beloved brethren, that you should be mindful of me ; that, among your great and divine considerations, you should also think of me in your mind and spirit ; and that I should be in your prayers and supplications, when that voice, which is illustrious by the purification of confession, and praiseworthy for the continual tenor of its honour, penetrates to God's ears, and heaven being open to it, passes from these regions of the world subdued, to the realms above, and obtains from the Lord's goodness even what it asks. For what do you ask from the Lord's mercy which you do not deserve to obtain ? — you who have thus observed the Lord's commands, who have maintained the Gospel discipline with the simple vigour of your faith, who, with the glory of your virtue uncorrupted, have stood bravely by the Lord's commands, and by His apostles, and have confirmed the wavering faith of many by the truth of your martyrdom ? Truly, Gospel witnesses, and truly, Christ's martyrs, resting upon His roots, founded with strong foundation upon the Rock, you have

joined discipline with virtue, you have brought others to the fear of God, you have made your martyrdoms, examples. I bid you, brethren, very brave and beloved, ever heartily farewell ; and remember me.

EPISTLE XVI.[1]
THE CONFESSORS TO CYPRIAN.

ARGUMENT. — A CERTIFICATE WRITTEN IN THE NAME OF THE MARTYRS BY LUCIANUS.

All the confessors to father[2] Cyprian, greeting. Know that, to all, concerning whom the account of what they have done since the commission of their sin has been, in your estimation, satisfactory, we have granted peace ; and we have desired that this rescript should be made known by you to the other bishops also. We bid you to have peace with the holy martyrs. Lucianus wrote this, there being present of the clergy, both an exorcist and a reader.

EPISTLE XVII.[3]
TO THE PRESBYTERS AND DEACONS ABOUT THE FOREGOING AND THE FOLLOWING LETTERS.

ARGUMENT. — NO ACCOUNT IS TO BE MADE OF CERTIFICATES FROM THE MARTYRS BEFORE THE PEACE OF THE CHURCH IS RESTORED.

Cyprian to the presbyters and deacons, his brethren, greeting. The Lord speaketh and saith, "Upon whom shall I look, but upon him that is humble and quiet, and that trembleth at my words ?"[4] Although we ought all to be this, yet especially those ought to be so who must labour, that, after their grave lapse, they may, by true penitence and absolute humility, deserve well of the Lord. Now I have read the letter of the whole body of confessors, which they wish to be made known by me to all my colleagues, and in which they requested that the peace given by themselves should be assured to those concerning whom the account of what they have done since their crime has been, in our estimation, satisfactory ; which matter, as it waits for the counsel and judgment of all of us,[5] I do not dare to prejudge, and so to assume a common cause for my own decision. And therefore, in the meantime, let us abide by the letters which I lately wrote to you, of which I have now sent a copy to many of my colleagues,[6] who wrote in

---

[1] Oxford ed.: Ep. xxiii. A.D. 250.
[2] "Cypriano Papæ," to "Pope" Cyprian. [An instance illustrative of what is to be found on p. 54, *supra*. See also Elucidation III. p. 154, *supra*.]
[3] Oxford ed.: Ep. xxvi. A.D. 250.
[4] Isa. lxvi. 2.
[5] [Elucidation V.]
[6] [The affectionate and general usage of primitive bishops to seek the *consensus fratrum*, is noteworthy.]

reply, that they were pleased with what I had decided, and that there must be no departure therefrom, until, peace being granted to us by the Lord, we shall be able to assemble together into one place, and to examine into the cases of individuals. But that you may know both what my colleague Caldonius wrote to me, and what I replied to him, I have enclosed with my letter a copy of each letter, the whole of which I beg you to read to our brethren, that they may be more and more settled down to patience, and not add another fault to what had hitherto been their former fault, not being willing to obey either me or the Gospel, nor allowing their cases to be examined in accordance with the letters of all the confessors. I bid you, beloved brethren, ever heartily farewell; and have me in remembrance. Salute all the brotherhood. Fare ye well!

EPISTLE XVIII.[1]

CALDONIUS TO CYPRIAN.

ARGUMENT. — WHEN, IN THE URGENCY OF A NEW PERSECUTION, CERTAIN OF THE LAPSED HAD CONFESSED CHRIST, AND SO, BEFORE THEY WENT AWAY INTO EXILE, SOUGHT FOR PEACE, CALDONIUS CONSULTS CYPRIAN AS TO WHETHER PEACE SHOULD BE GRANTED THEM.

Caldonius to Cyprian and his fellow-presbyters[2] abiding at Carthage, greeting. The necessity of the times induces us not hastily to grant peace. But it was well to write to you, that they[3] who, after having sacrificed,[4] were again tried, became exiles. And thus they seem to me to have atoned for their former crime, in that they now let go their possessions and homes, and, repenting, follow Christ. Thus Felix, who assisted in the office of presbyter[5] under Decimus, and was very near to me in bonds (I knew that same Felix very thoroughly), Victoria, his wife, and Lucius, being faithful, were banished, and have left their possessions, which the treasury now has in keeping. Moreover, a woman, Bona by name, who was dragged by her husband to sacrifice, and (with no conscience guilty of the crime, but because those who held her hands, sacrificed) began to cry against them, " I did not do it; you it was who did it ! "—was also banished.[6] Since, therefore, all these were asking for peace, saying, " We have recovered the faith which we had lost, we have repented, and have

publicly confessed Christ "—although it seems to me that they ought to receive peace,—yet I have referred them to your judgment, that I might not appear to presume anything rashly. If, therefore, you should wish me to do anything by the common decision, write to me. Greet our brethren; our brethren greet you. I bid you, beloved brethren, ever heartily farewell.

EPISTLE XIX.[7]

CYPRIAN REPLIES TO CALDONIUS.

ARGUMENT.—CYPRIAN TREATS OF NOTHING PECULIAR IN THIS EPISTLE, BEYOND ACQUIESCING IN THE OPINION OF CALDONIUS, TO WIT, THAT PEACE SHOULD NOT BE REFUSED TO SUCH LAPSED AS, BY A TRUE REPENTANCE AND CONFESSION OF THE NAME OF CHRIST, HAVE DESERVED IT, AND HAVE THEREFORE RETURNED TO HIM.

Cyprian to Caldonius, his brother, greeting. We have received your letter, beloved brother, which is abundantly sensible, and full of honesty and faith. Nor do we wonder that, skilled and exercised as you are in the Scriptures of the Lord, you do everything discreetly and wisely. You have judged quite correctly about granting peace to our brethren, which they, by true penitence and by the glory of a confession of the Lord, have restored to themselves, being justified by their words, by which before they had condemned themselves. Since, then, they have washed away all their sin, and their former stain, by the help of the Lord, has been done away by a more powerful virtue, they ought not to lie any longer under the power of the devil, as it were, prostrate; when, being banished and deprived of all their property, they have lifted themselves up and have begun to stand with Christ. And I wish that the others also would repent after their fall, and be transferred into their former condition; and that you may know how we have dealt with these, in their urgent and eager rashness and importunity to extort peace, I have sent a book[8] to you, with letters to the number of five, that I wrote to the clergy and to the people, and to the martyrs also and confessors, which letters have already been sent to many of our colleagues, and have satisfied them; and they replied that they also agree with me in the same opinion according to the Catholic faith; which very thing do you also communicate to as many of our colleagues as you can, that among all these, may be observed one mode of action and one agreement, according to the Lord's precepts.[9] I bid you, beloved brother, ever heartily farewell.

---

1 Oxford ed.: Ep. xxiv. A.D. 250.
2 [The community of this term, *presbyters*, has been noted. See p 156, *supra*.]
3 " Some " would seem to be correct (Goldhorn); but it has no authority.
4 [i.e., to idols, or the imperial image.]
5 " Presbyterium subministrabat; " assisted, probably as vicar or curate.
6 [A very touching incident, dramatically narrated.]

7 Oxford ed.: Ep. xxv. A.D. 250.
8 Probably the treatise, *On the Lapsed.*
9 [A beautiful specimen of obedience to the precept, 1 Pet. v. 5.]

EPISTLE XX.[1]
CELERINUS TO LUCIAN.

ARGUMENT. — CELERINUS, ON BEHALF OF HIS LAPSED SISTERS AT ROME, BESEECHES PEACE FROM THE CARTHAGINIAN CONFESSORS.

1. Celerinus to Lucian, greeting. In writing this letter to you, my lord and brother, I have been rejoicing and sorrowful, — rejoicing in that I had heard that you had been tried on behalf of the name of our Lord Jesus Christ our Saviour, and had confessed His name in the presence of the magistrates of the world ; but sorrowful, in that from the time when I was in your company I have never been able to receive your letters. And now lately a twofold sorrow has fallen upon me ; that although you knew that Montanus, our common brother, was coming to me from you out of the dungeon, you did not intimate anything to me concerning your wellbeing, nor about anything that is done in connection with you. This, however, continually happens to the servants of God, especially to those who are appointed for the confession of Christ. For I know that every one looks not now to the things that are of the world, but that he is hoping for a heavenly crown. Moreover, I said that perhaps you had forgotten to write to me. For if from the lowest place I may be called by you *yours*, or *brother*, if I should be worthy to hear myself named Celerinus ; yet, when I also was in such a purple[2] confession, I remembered my oldest brethren, and I took notice of them in my letters, that their former love was still around me and mine. Yet I beseech, beloved of the Lord, that if, first of all, you are washed in that sacred blood, and have suffered for the name of our Lord Jesus Christ before my letters find you in this world, or should they now reach you, that you would answer them to me. So may He crown you whose name you have confessed. For I believe, that although in this world we do not see each other, yet in the future we shall embrace one another in the presence of Christ. Entreat that I may be worthy, even I, to be crowned along with your company.

2. Know, nevertheless, that I am placed in the midst of a great tribulation ; and, as if you were present with me, I remember your former love day and night, God only knows. And therefore I ask that you will grant my desire, and that you will grieve with me at the (spiritual) death of my sister, who in this time of devastation has fallen from Christ ; for she has sacrificed and provoked our Lord, as seems manifest to us. And for her deeds I in this day

of paschal rejoicing,[3] weeping day and night, have spent the days in tears, in sackcloth, and ashes, and I am still spending them so to this day, until[4] the aid of our Lord Jesus Christ, and affection manifested through you, or through those my lords who have been crowned, from whom you are about to ask it, shall come to the help of so terrible a shipwreck. For I remember your former love, that you will grieve with all the rest for our sisters whom you also knew well — that is, Numeria and Candida, — for whose sin, because they have us as brethren, we ought to keep watch. For I believe that Christ, according to their repentance and the works which they have done towards our banished colleagues who came from you — by whom themselves you will hear of their good works, — that Christ, I say, will have mercy upon them, when you, His martyrs, beseech Him.

3. For I have heard that you have received the ministry of the purpled ones. Oh, happy are you, even sleeping on the ground, to obtain your wishes which you have always desired ! You have desired to be sent into prison for His name's sake, which now has come to pass ; as it is written, "The Lord grant thee according to thine own heart ; "[5] and now made a priest of God over them, and the same their minister has acknowledged it.[6] I ask, therefore my lord, and I entreat by our Lord Jesus Christ, that you will refer the case to the rest of your colleagues, your brethren, my lords, and ask from them, that whichever of you is first crowned, should remit such a great sin to those our sisters, Numeria and Candida. For this latter I have always called Etecusa[7] — God is my witness, — because she gave gifts for herself that she might not sacrifice ; but she appears only to have ascended to the Tria Fata,[8] and thence to have descended. I know, therefore, that she has not sacrificed. Their cause having been lately heard, the chief rulers[9] commanded them in the meantime to remain as they are, until a bishop should be appointed.[10] But, as far as possible, by your holy prayers and petitions, in which we trust, since you are friends as well as witnesses of

---

[3] [Written at Easter, like the first Epistle to the Corinthians, as implied in cap. v. 7. See Conybeare and Howson.]

[4] The Oxford edition has a variation here, as follows: "Until our Lord Jesus Christ afford help, and pity be manifested through you, or through those my lords who may have been crowned, from whom you will entreat that these dreadful shipwrecks may be pardoned."

[5] Ps. xx. 4.

[6] This seems altogether unintelligible: the original is probably corrupt. [It seems to relate to the sort of *priesthood* which was conceded to all martyrs, in view of (Rev. i. 6 and v. 10) the message sent by the angel "to His servants," and by their servant or minister, John.]

[7] Dodwell conjectures this name to be from ἀτυχοῦσα (unhappy) or ἀεκοῦσα (unwilling), and applies it to Candida.

[8] A spot in the Roman Forum which must of necessity be passed by in the ascent to the Capitol. It would appear that Candida therefore repented of her purpose of sacrificing, when she was actually on her way to effect it.

[9] [i.e., the clergy administering jurisdiction.]

[10] i.e., in the room of Fabian.

---

[1] Oxford ed.: Ep. xxi. A.D. 250.

[2] "Florida," *scil.* "purpurea," purpled, that is, with blood. See concluding section of Ep. viii. The Oxford translator has "empurpled."

Christ, (we pray) that you would be indulgent in all these matters.

4. I entreat, therefore, beloved lord Lucian, be mindful of me, and acquiesce in my petition; so may Christ grant you that sacred crown which he has given you not only in confession but also in holiness, in which you have always walked and have always been an example to the saints, as well as a witness, that you will relate to all my lords, your brethren the confessors, all about this matter, that they may receive help from you. For this, my lord and brother, you ought to know, that it is not I alone who ask this on their behalf, but also Statius and Severianus, and all the confessors who have come thence hither from you; to whom these very sisters went down to the harbour [1] and took them up into the city, and they have ministered to sixty-five, and even to this day have tended them in all things. For all are with them. But I ought not to burden that sacred heart of yours any more, since I know that you will labour with a ready will. Macharius, with his sisters Cornelia and Emerita, salute you, rejoicing in your sanguinary confession, as well as in that of all the brethren, and Saturninus, who himself also wrestled with the devil, who also bravely confessed the name of Christ, who moreover, under the torture of the grappling claws, bravely confessed, and who also strongly begs and entreats this. Your brethren Calphurnius and Maria, and all the holy brethren, salute you. For you ought to know this too, that I have written also to my lords your brethren letters, which I request that you will deign to read to them.

EPISTLE XXI.[2]
LUCIAN REPLIES TO CELERINUS.

ARGUMENT. — LUCIAN ASSENTS TO THE PETITION OF CELERINUS.

1. Lucian to Celerinus, his lord, and (if I shall be worthy to be called so) colleague in Christ, greeting. I have received your letter, most dearly beloved lord and brother, in which you have so laden me with expressions of kindness, that by reason of your so burdening me I was almost overcome with such excessive joy; so that I exulted in reading, by the benefit of your so great humility, the letter, which I also earnestly desired after so long a time to read, in which you deigned to call me to remembrance, saying to me in your writing, " if I may be worthy to be called your brother," of a man such as I am who confessed the name of God with trembling before the inferior magistrates. For you, by God's will, when you confessed, not only frightened back the great serpent himself, the pioneer of Antichrist,[3] (but) have conquered him, by that voice and those divine words, whereby I know how you love the faith, and how zealous you are for Christ's discipline, in which I know and rejoice that you are actively occupied.[4] Now beloved, already to be esteemed among the martyrs, you have wished to overload me with your letter, in which you told us concerning our sisters, on whose behalf I wish that we could by possibility mention them without remembering also so great a crime committed. Assuredly we should not then think of them with so many tears as we do now.

2. You ought to know what has been done concerning us. When the blessed martyr Paulus was still in the body, he called me and said to me : " Lucian, in the presence of Christ I say to you, If any one, after my being called away, shall ask for peace from you, grant it in my name." Moreover, all of us whom the Lord has condescended in such tribulation to call away, by our letters, by mutual agreement, have given peace to all. You see, then, brother, how (I have done this) in part of what Paulus bade me, as what we in all cases decreed when we were in this tribulation, wherein by the command of the emperor we were ordered to be put to death by hunger and thirst, and were shut up in two cells, that so they might weaken us by hunger and thirst. Moreover, the fire from the effect of our torture was so intolerable [5] that nobody could bear it. But now we have attained the brightness itself. And therefore, beloved brother, greet Numeria and Candida, who (shall have peace [6]) according to the precept of Paulus, and the rest of the martyrs whose names I subjoin : viz., Bassus in the dungeon of the perjured,[7] Mappalicus at the torture, Fortunio in prison, Paulus after torture, Fortunata, Victorinus, Victor, Herennius, Julia, Martial, and Aristo, who by God's will were put to death in the prison by hunger, of whom in a few days you will hear of me as a companion. For now there are eight days, from the day in which I was shut up again, to the day in which I wrote my letter to you. For before these eight days, for five intervening days, I received a morsel of bread and water by measure. And therefore, brother, as here, since the Lord has begun to give peace to the Church itself, according to the precept of Paulus, and our tractate, the case being set forth before the bishop, and confession being made, I ask that

---

[1] [i e., to Ostia or Portus].
[2] Oxford ed.: Ep. xxii. A.D. 250.

[3] The emperor Decius.
[4] The passage is hopelessly confused.
[5] " And, moreover, by the smoke of fire, and our suffering was so intolerable," etc.; *v. l.*
[6] These parenthical words are necessary to the sense, but are omitted in the original.
[7] " Pejerario." There are many conjectures as to the meaning of this. Perhaps the most plausible is the emendation, " Petrario " — " in the mines."

not only these may have peace, but also (all) those whom you know to be very near to our heart.

3. All my colleagues greet you. Do you greet the confessors of the Lord who are there with you, whose names you have intimated, among whom also are Saturninus, with his companions, but who also is my colleague, and Maris, Collecta, and Emerita, Calphurnius and Maria, Sabina, Spesina, and the sisters, Januaria, Dativa, Donata. We greet Saturus with his family, Bassianus and all the clergy, Uranius, Alexius, Quintianus, Colonica, and all whose names I have not written, because I am already weary. Therefore they must pardon me. I bid you heartily farewell, and Alexius, and Getulicus, and the money-changers, and the sisters. My sisters Januaria and Sophia, whom I commend to you, greet you.[1]

EPISTLE XXII.[2]

TO THE CLERGY ABIDING AT ROME, CONCERNING MANY OF THE CONFESSORS, AND CONCERNING THE FORWARDNESS OF LUCIAN AND THE MODESTY OF CELERINUS THE CONFESSOR.

ARGUMENT. — IN THIS LETTER CYPRIAN INFORMS THE ROMAN CLERGY OF THE SEDITIOUS DEMAND OF THE LAPSED TO BE RESTORED TO PEACE, AND OF THE FORWARDNESS OF LUCIAN. IN ORDER THAT THEY MAY BETTER UNDERSTAND THESE MATTERS, CYPRIAN TAKES CARE THAT NOT ONLY HIS OWN LETTERS, BUT ALSO THOSE OF CELERINUS AND LUCIAN, SHOULD BE SENT TO THEM.

1. Cyprian to the presbyters and deacons abiding at Rome, his brethren, greeting. After the letters that I wrote to you, beloved brethren, in which what I had done was explained, and some slight account was given of my discipline and diligence, there came another matter which, any more than the others, ought not to be concealed from you. For our brother Lucian, who himself also is one of the confessors, earnest indeed in faith, and robust in virtue, but little established in the reading of the Lord's word, has attempted certain things, constituting himself for a time an authority for unskilled people, so that certificates written by his hand were given indiscriminately to many persons in the name of Paulus; whereas Mappalicus the martyr, cautious and modest, mindful of the law and discipline, wrote no letters contrary to the Gospel, but only,

moved with domestic affection for his mother,[3] who had fallen, commanded peace to be given to her. Saturninus, moreover, after his torture, still remaining in prison, sent out no letters of this kind. But Lucian, not only while Paulus was still in prison, gave everywhere in his name certificates written with his own hand, but even after his decease persisted in doing the same things under his name, saying that this had been commanded him by Paulus, ignorant that he must obey the Lord rather than his fellow-servant. In the name also of Aurelius, a young man who had undergone the torture, many certificates were given, written by the hand of the same Lucian, because Aurelius did not know how to write himself.

2. In order, in some measure, to put a stop to this practice, I wrote letters to them, which I have sent to you under the enclosure of the former letter, in which I did not fail to ask and persuade them that consideration might be had for the law of the Lord and the Gospel. But after I sent my letters to them, that, as it were, something might be done more moderately and temperately; the same Lucian wrote a letter in the name of all the confessors, in which well nigh every bond of faith, and fear of God, and the Lord's command, and the sacredness and sincerity of the Gospel were dissolved. For he wrote in the name of all, that they had given peace to all, and that he wished that this decree should be communicated through me to the other bishops, of which letter I transmitted a copy to you. It was added indeed, "of whom the account of what they have done since their crime has been satisfactory;" — a thing which excites a greater odium against me, because I, when I have begun to hear the cases of each one and to examine into them, seem to deny to many what they now are all boasting that they have received from the martyrs and confessors.

3. Finally, this seditious practice has already begun to appear; for in our province, through some of its cities, an attack has been made by the multitude upon their rulers, and they have compelled that peace to be given to them immediately which they all cried out had been once given to them by the martyrs and confessors. Their rulers, being frightened and subdued, were of little avail to resist them, either by vigour of mind or by strength of faith. With us, moreover, some turbulent spirits, who in time past were with difficulty governed by me, and were delayed till my coming, were inflamed by this letter as if by a firebrand, and began to be more violent, and to extort the peace granted to them. I have sent a copy to you of the letters that I wrote to

---

[1] This epistle, as well as the preceding, seems to be very imperfect, having probably been "written," says the Oxford translator, "by persons little versed in writing, — confessors, probably, of the less instructed sort." The meaning in many places is very unsatisfactory.

[2] Oxford ed.: Ep. xxvii. A.D. 250.

[3] Some read, "his mother and sisters, who had fallen."

my clergy about these matters, and, moreover, what Caldonius, my colleague, of his integrity and faithfulness wrote, and what I replied to him. I have sent both to you to read. Copies also of the letter of Celerinus, the good and stout confessor, which he wrote to Lucian the same confessor — also what Lucian replied to him, — I have sent to you; that you may know both my labour in respect of everything, and my diligence, and might learn the truth itself, how moderate and cautious is Celerinus the confessor, and how reverent both in his humility and fear for our faith; while Lucian, as I have said, is less skilful concerning the understanding of the Lord's word, and by his facility, is mischievous on account of the dislike that he causes for my reverential dealing. For while the Lord has said that the nations are to be baptized in the name of the Father, and of the Son, and of the Holy Ghost, and their past sins are to be done away in baptism; this man, ignorant of the precept and of the law, commands peace to be granted and sins to be done away in the name of Paulus; and he says that this was commanded him by Paulus, as you will observe in the letter sent by the same Lucian to Celerinus, in which he very little considered that it is not martyrs that make the Gospel, but that martyrs are made by the Gospel;[1] since Paul also, the apostle whom the Lord called a chosen vessel unto Him, laid down in his epistle: " I marvel that ye are so soon removed from Him that called you into the grace of Christ, unto another gospel: which is not another; but there be some that trouble you, and would pervert the Gospel of Christ. But though we, or an angel from heaven, preach any other gospel unto you than that which we have preached unto you, let him be accursed. As we said before, so say I now again, If any man preach any other gospel unto you than that ye have received, let him be accursed."[2]

4. But your letter, which I received, written to my clergy, came opportunely; as also did those which the blessed confessors, Moyses and Maximus, Nicostratus, and the rest, sent to Saturninus and Aurelius, and the others, in which are contained the full vigour of the Gospel and the robust discipline of the law of the Lord. Your words much assisted me as I laboured here, and withstood with the whole strength of faith the onset of ill-will, so that my work was shortened from above, and that before the letters which I last sent you reached you, you declared to me, that according to the Gospel law, your judgment also strongly and unanimously concurred with mine. I bid you, brethren, beloved and longed-for, ever heartily farewell.

EPISTLE XXIII.[3]

TO THE CLERGY, ON THE LETTERS SENT TO ROME, AND ABOUT THE APPOINTMENT OF SATURUS AS READER, AND OPTATUS AS SUB-DEACON. A.D. 250.

ARGUMENT. — THE CLERGY ARE INFORMED BY THIS LETTER OF THE ORDINATION OF SATURUS AND OPTATUS, AND WHAT CYPRIAN HAD WRITTEN TO ROME.

Cyprian to the presbyters and deacons, his brethren, greeting. That nothing may be unknown to your consciousness, beloved brethren, of what was written to me and what I replied, I have sent you a copy of each letter, and I believe that my rejoinder will not displease you. But I ought to acquaint you in my letter concerning this, that for a very urgent reason I have sent a letter to the clergy who abide in the city. And since it behoved me to write by clergy, while I know that very many of ours are absent, and the few that are there are hardly sufficient for the ministry of the daily duty, it was necessary to appoint some new ones, who might be sent. Know, then, that I have made Saturus a reader, and Optatus, the confessor, a sub-deacon; whom already, by the general advice, we had made next to the clergy, in having entrusted to Saturus on Easter-day, once and again, the reading; and when with the teacher-presbyters[4] we were carefully trying readers — in appointing Optatus from among the readers to be a teacher of the hearers; — examining, first of all, whether all things were found fitting in them, which ought to be found in such as were in preparation for the clerical office. Nothing new, therefore, has been done by me in your absence; but what, on the general advice of all of us had been begun, has, upon urgent necessity, been accomplished. I bid you, beloved brethren, ever heartily farewell; and remember me. Fare ye well.

EPISTLE XXIV.[5]

TO MOYSES AND MAXIMUS AND THE REST OF THE CONFESSORS.

ARGUMENT. — THIS LETTER IS ONE OF CONGRATULATION TO THE ROMAN CONFESSORS.

1. Cyprian to Moyses and Maximus, the presbyters, and to the other confessors, his very

---

[1] [A Cyprianic aphorism applicable to the " The Fathers."]
[2] Gal. i. 6–9. [Applicable to the new Marian dogma.]

[3] Oxford ed.: Ep. xxix. The numbering of the epistles has hitherto been in accordance with Migne's edition of the text; but as he here follows a typographical error in numbering the epistle " xxiv.," and all the subsequent ones accordingly, it has been thought better to continue the correct order in this translation. In each case, therefore, after this, the number of the epistle in the translation will be one earlier than in Migne.
[4] Not " teachers and presbyters," as in the Oxford translation, but " teaching presbyters." For these were a distinct class of presbyters — all not being teachers, — and these were to be judges of the fitness of such as were to be *teachers* of the *hearers*. [According to Cyprian's theory, all presbyters shared in the government and celebrated the Lord's Supper, but only the more learned and gifted were preachers. 1 Tim. iv. 17.]
[5] Oxford ed.: Ep. xxviii. [The See of Rome was now vacant by the death of Fabian. A.D. 250. See letter xxiv. *infra.*]

beloved brethren, greeting. I had already known from rumour, most brave and blessed brethren, the glory of your faith and virtue, rejoicing greatly and abundantly congratulating you, that the highest condescension of our Lord Jesus Christ should have prepared you for the crown by confession of His name. For you, who have become chiefs and leaders in the battle of our day, have set forward the standard of the celestial warfare; you have made a beginning of the spiritual contest which God has purposed to be now waged by your valour; you, with unshaken strength and unyielding firmness, have broken the first onset of the rising war. Thence have arisen happy openings of the fight; thence have begun good auspices of victory. It happened that here martyrdoms were consummated by tortures. But he who, preceding in the struggle, has been made an example of virtue to the brethren, is on common ground with the martyrs in honour. Hence you have delivered to us garlands woven by your hand, and have pledged your brethren from the cup of salvation.

2. To these glorious beginnings of confession and the omens of a victorious warfare, has been added the maintenance of discipline, which I observed from the vigour of your letter that you lately sent to your colleagues joined with you to the Lord in confession, with anxious admonition, that the sacred precepts of the Gospel and the commandments of life once delivered to us should be kept with firm and rigid observance. Behold another lofty degree of your glory; behold, with confession, a double title to deserving well of God, — to stand with a firm step, and to drive away in this struggle, by the strength of your faith, those who endeavour to make a breach in the Gospel, and bring impious hands to the work of undermining the Lord's precepts: — to have before afforded the indications of courage, and now to afford lessons of life. The Lord, when, after His resurrection, He sent forth His apostles, charges them, saying, "All power is given unto me in heaven and in earth. Go ye therefore, and teach all nations, baptizing them in the name of the Father, and of the Son, and of the Holy Ghost: teaching them to observe all things whatsoever I have commanded you." [1] And the Apostle John, remembering this charge, subsequently lays it down in his epistle: "Hereby," says he, "we do know that we know Him, if we keep His commandments. He that saith he knoweth Him, and keepeth not His commandments, is a liar, and the truth is not in him." [2] You prompt the keeping of these precepts; you observe the divine and heavenly commands. This is to be a confessor

of the Lord; this is to be a martyr of Christ, — to keep the firmness of one's profession inviolate among all evils, and secure. [3] For to wish to become a martyr for the Lord, and to try to overthrow the Lord's precepts; to use against Him the condescension that He has granted you; — to become, as it were, a rebel with arms that you have received from Him; — this is to wish to confess Christ, and to deny Christ's Gospel. I rejoice, therefore, on your behalf, most brave and faithful brethren; and as much as I congratulate the martyrs there honoured for the glory of their strength, so much do I also equally congratulate you for the crown of the Lord's discipline. The Lord has shed forth His condescension in manifold kinds of liberality. He has distributed the praises of good soldiers and their spiritual glories in plentiful variety. We also are sharers in your honour; we count your glory our glory, whose times have been brightened by such a felicity, that it should be the fortune of our day to see the proved servants of God and Christ's soldiers crowned. I bid you, most brave and blessed brethren, ever heartily farewell; and remember me.

EPISTLE XXV.[4]

MOYSES, MAXIMUS, NICOSTRATUS, AND THE OTHER CONFESSORS ANSWER THE FOREGOING LETTER. A.D. 250.

ARGUMENT. — THEY GRATEFULLY ACKNOWLEDGE THE CONSOLATION WHICH THE ROMAN CONFESSORS HAD RECEIVED FROM CYPRIAN'S LETTER. MARTYRDOM IS NOT A PUNISHMENT, BUT A HAPPINESS. THE WORDS OF THE GOSPEL ARE BRANDS TO INFLAME FAITH. IN THE CASE OF THE LAPSED, THE JUDGMENT OF CYPRIAN IS ACQUIESCED IN.

1. To Cæcilius Cyprian, bishop of the church of the Carthaginians, Moyses and Maximus, presbyters, and Nicostratus and Rufinus, deacons, and the other confessors persevering in the faith of the truth, in God the Father, and in His Son Jesus Christ our Lord, and in the Holy Spirit, greeting. Placed, brother, as we are among various and manifold sorrows, on account of the present desolations of many brethren throughout almost the whole world,[5] this chief consolation has reached us, that we have been lifted up by the receipt of your letter, and have gathered some alleviation for the griefs of our saddened spirit. From which we can al-

---

[1] Matt. xxviii. 18–20.
[2] 1 John ii. 3, 4.

[3] "And not to become a martyr for the Lord's sake" (or, "by the Lord's help"), "and to endeavour to overthrow the Lord's precepts." Baluz. reads "*præter*," but in notes, "propter," while most MSS. read "*per* Dominum."
[4] Oxford ed.: Ep. xxxi. [This epistle shows that Cyprian's gentle reproof of their former implied regret at his retreat (see p. 280, *supra*) had been effective.]
[5] [Note this testimony to the universality of the persecution. Vol. iv. p. 125, this series.]

ready perceive that the grace of divine providence wished to keep us so long shut up in the prison chains, perhaps for no other reason than that, instructed and more vigorously animated by your letter, we might with a more earnest will attain to the destined crown. For your letter has shone upon us as a calm in the midst of a tempest, and as the longed-for tranquillity in the midst of a troubled sea, and as repose in labours, as health in dangers and pains, as in the densest darkness, the bright and glowing light. Thus we drank it up with a thirsty spirit, and received it with a hungry desire; so that we rejoice to find ourselves by it sufficiently fed and strengthened for encounter with the foe. The Lord will reward you for that love of yours, and will restore you the fruit due to this so good work; for he who exhorts is not less worthy of the reward of the crown than he who suffers; not less worthy of praise is he who has taught, than he who has acted also; he is not less to be honoured who has warned, than he who has fought; except that sometimes the weight of glory more redounds to him who trains, than to him who has shown himself a teachable learner; for the latter, perchance, would not have had what he has practised, unless the former had taught him.

2. Therefore, again, we say, brother Cyprian, we have received great joy, great comfort, great refreshment, especially in that you have described, with glorious and deserved praises, the glorious, I will not say, deaths, but immortalities of martyrs. For such departures should have been proclaimed with such words, that the things which were related might be told in such manner as they were done. Thus, from your letter, we saw those glorious triumphs of the martyrs; and with our eyes in some sort have followed them as they went to heaven, and have contemplated them seated among angels, and the powers and dominions of heaven. Moreover, we have in some manner perceived with our ears the Lord giving them the promised testimony in the presence of the Father. It is this, then, which also raises our spirit day by day, and inflames us to the following of the track of such dignity.

3. For what more glorious, or what more blessed, can happen to any man from the divine condescension, than to confess the Lord God, in death itself, before his very executioners? Than among the raging and varied and exquisite tortures of worldly power, even when the body is racked and torn and cut to pieces, to confess Christ the Son of God with a spirit still free, although departing? Than to have mounted to heaven with the world left behind? Than, having forsaken men, to stand among the angels? Than, all worldly impediments being broken through, already to stand free in the sight of God? Than to enjoy the heavenly kingdom without any delay?

Than to have become an associate of Christ's passion in Christ's name? Than to have become by the divine condescension the judge of one's own judge? Than to have brought off an unstained conscience from the confession of His name? Than to have refused to obey human and sacrilegious laws against the faith? Than to have borne witness to the truth with a public testimony? Than, by dying, to have subdued death itself, which is dreaded by all? Than, by death itself, to have attained immortality? Than when torn to pieces, and tortured by all the instruments of cruelty, to have overcome the torture by the tortures themselves? Than by strength of mind to have wrestled with all the agonies of a mangled body? Than not to have shuddered at the flow of one's own blood? Than to have begun to love one's punishments, after having faith to bear them?[1] Than to think it an injury to one's life not to have left it?

4. For to this battle our Lord, as with the trumpet of His Gospel, stimulates us when He says, "He that loveth father or mother more than me is not worthy of me: and he that loveth his own soul more than me is not worthy of me. And he that taketh not his cross, and followeth after me, is not worthy of me."[2] And again, "Blessed are they which are persecuted for righteousness' sake: for theirs is the kingdom of heaven. Blessed shall ye be, when men shall persecute you, and hate you. Rejoice, and be exceeding glad: for so did their fathers persecute the prophets which were before you."[3] And again, "Because ye shall stand before kings and powers, and the brother shall deliver up the brother to death, and the father the son, and he that endureth to the end shall be saved;"[4] and "To him that overcometh will I give to sit on my throne, even as I also overcame and am set down on the throne of my Father."[5] Moreover the apostle: "Who shall separate us from the love of Christ? shall tribulation, or distress, or persecution, or famine, or nakedness, or peril, or sword? (As it is written, For thy sake are we killed all the day long; we are accounted as sheep for the slaughter.) Nay, in all these things we are more than conquerors for Him who hath loved us."[6]

5. When we read these things,[7] and things of the like kind, brought together in the Gospel, and feel, as it were, torches placed under us, with the Lord's words to inflame our faith, we not only do not dread, but we even provoke[8] the

---

[1] Supplicia sua post fidem amare cœpisse.
[2] Matt. x. 37, 38.
[3] Matt. v. 10–12.
[4] Matt. x. 18, xxi. 22.
[5] Rev. iii. 21.
[6] Rom. viii. 35.
[7] [Note the power of Holy Scripture in creating and supporting the martyr-spirit.]
[8] [See valuable note, Oxford translation, p. 71.]

enemies of the truth ; and we have already conquered the opponents of God, by the very fact of our not yielding to them, and have subdued their nefarious laws against the truth. And although we have not yet shed our blood, we are prepared to shed it. Let no one think that this delay of our departure [1] is any clemency ; for it obstructs us, it makes a hindrance to our glory, it puts off heaven, it withholds the glorious sight of God. For in a contest of this kind, and in the kind of contest when faith is struggling in the encounter, it is not true clemency to put off martyrs by delay. Entreat therefore, beloved Cyprian, that of His mercy the Lord will every day more and more arm and adorn every one of us with greater abundance and readiness, and will confirm and strengthen us by the strength of His power ; and, as a good captain, will at length bring forth His soldiers, whom He has hitherto trained and proved in the camp of our prison, to the field of the battle set before them. May He hold forth to us the divine arms, those weapons that know not how to be conquered, — the breastplate of righteousness, which is never accustomed to be broken, — the shield of faith, which cannot be pierced through, — the helmet of salvation, which cannot be shattered, — and the sword of the Spirit, which has never been wont to be injured. For to whom should we rather commit these things for him to ask for us, than to our so reverend bishop,[2] as destined victims asking help of the priest ?

6. Behold another joy of ours, that, in the duty of your episcopate, although in the meantime you have been, owing to the condition of the times, divided from your brethren, you have frequently confirmed the confessors by your letters ; that you have ever afforded necessary supplies from your own just acquisitions ; that in all things you have always shown yourself in some sense present ; that in no part of your duty have you hung behind as a deserter.[3] But what more strongly stimulated us to a greater joy we cannot be silent upon, but must describe with all the testimony of our voice. For we observe that you have both rebuked with fitting censure, and worthily, those who, unmindful of their sins, had, with hasty and eager desire, extorted peace from the presbyters in your absence, and those who, without respect for the Gospel, had with profane facility granted the *holiness*[4] of the Lord unto dogs, and pearls to swine ; although a great crime, and one which has extended with incredible destructiveness almost over the whole earth, ought only, as you yourself write, to be treated cautiously and with moderation,

with the advice of all the bishops, presbyters, deacons, confessors, and even the laymen who abide fast,[5] as in your letters you yourself also testify ; so that, while wishing unseasonably to bring repairs to the ruins, we may not appear to be bringing about other and greater destruction, for where is the divine word left, if pardon be so easily granted to sinners? Certainly their spirits are to be cheered and to be nourished up to the season of their maturity, and they are to be instructed from the Holy Scriptures how great and surpassing a sin they have committed. Nor let them be animated by the fact that they are many, but rather let them be checked by the fact that they are not few.[6] An unblushing number has never been accustomed to have weight in extenuation of a crime ; but shame, modesty, patience, discipline, humility, and subjection, waiting for the judgment of others upon itself, and bearing the sentence of others upon its own judgment, — this it is which proves penitence ; this it is which skins over a deep wound ; this it is which raises up the ruins of the fallen spirit and restores them, which quells and restrains the burning vapour of their raging sins. For the physician will not give to the sick the food of healthy bodies, lest the unseasonable nourishment, instead of repressing, should stimulate the power of the raging disease, — that is to say, lest what might have been sooner diminished by abstinence, should, through impatience, be prolonged by growing indigestion.

7. Hands, therefore, polluted with impious sacrifices[7] must be purified with good works, and wretched mouths defiled with accursed food[8] must be purged with words of true penitence, and the spirit must be renewed and consecrated in the recesses of the faithful heart. Let the frequent groanings of the penitents be heard ; let faithful tears be shed from the eyes not once only, but again and again, so that those very eyes which wickedly looked upon idols may wash away, with tears that satisfy God, the unlawful things that they had done. Nothing is necessary for diseases but patience : they who are weary and weak wrestle with their pain ; and so at length hope for health, if, by tolerating it, they can overcome their suffering ; for unfaithful is the scar which the physician has too quickly produced ; and the healing is undone by any little casualty, if the remedies be not used faithfully from their very slowness. The flame is quickly recalled again to a conflagration, unless the material of the whole fire be extinguished even to the extremest spark ; so that

---

[1] *Lit.* " of our postponement."
[2] [I have amended the translation here from the Oxford trans]
[3] [An important testimony to Cyprian's judicious retirement, in the spirit of St. Paul, Phil. i. 24.]
[4] " Sanctum." [Note what follows: a rule for our times.]
[5] [An important testimony to the Cyprianic theory from members of the Roman presbytery.]
[6] [The extent of the lapses which Cyprian strove to check by due austerity must be noted.]
[7] [The casting of a grain of incense upon the coals before an image, to escape death.]
[8] [Meats offered to idols.]

men of this kind should justly know that even they themselves are more advantaged by the very delay, and that more trusty remedies are applied by the necessary postponement. Besides, where shall it be said that they who confess Christ are shut up in the keeping of a squalid prison, if they who have denied Him are in no peril of their faith? Where, that they are bound in the cincture of chains in God's name, if they who have not kept the confession of God are not deprived of communion? Where, that the imprisoned martyrs lay down their glorious lives, if those who have forsaken the faith do not feel the magnitude of their dangers and their sins? But if they betray too much impatience, and demand communion with intolerable eagerness, they vainly utter with petulant and unbridled tongues those querulous and invidious reproaches which avail nothing against the truth, since they might have retained by their own right what now by a necessity, which they of their own free will have sought, they are compelled to sue for.[1] For the faith which could confess Christ, could also have been kept by Christ in communion. We bid you, blessed and most glorious father, ever heartily farewell in the Lord; and have us in remembrance.

EPISTLE XXVI.[2]

CYPRIAN TO THE LAPSED.

ARGUMENT. — THE ARGUMENT OF THIS LETTER IS FOUND BELOW IN LETTER XXVII. "THEY WROTE TO ME," SAYS HE, "NOT ASKING THAT PEACE SHOULD BE GRANTED THEM, BUT CLAIMING IT FOR THEMSELVES AS ALREADY GRANTED, BECAUSE THEY SAY THAT PAULUS HAS GIVEN PEACE TO ALL; AS YOU WILL READ IN THEIR LETTER OF WHICH I HAVE SENT YOU A COPY, TOGETHER WITH WHAT I BRIEFLY REPLIED TO THEM." BUT THE LETTER OF THE LAPSED TO WHICH HE REPLIES IS WANTING.

1. Our Lord, whose precepts and admonitions we ought to observe, describing the honour of a bishop[3] and the order of His Church, speaks in the Gospel, and says to Peter: "I say unto thee, That thou art Peter, and upon this rock will I build my Church; and the gates of hell shall not prevail against it. And I will give unto thee the keys of the kingdom of heaven: and whatsoever thou shalt bind on earth shall be bound in heaven: and whatsoever thou shall loose on earth shall be loosed in heaven."[4] Thence, through the changes of times and successions, the ordering of bishops and the plan of the

Church flow onwards; so that the Church is founded upon the bishops, and every act of the Church is controlled by these same rulers.[5] Since this, then, is founded on the divine law, I marvel that some, with daring temerity, have chosen to write to me as if they wrote in the name of the Church; when the Church is established in the bishop and the clergy, and all who stand *fast in the faith.* For far be it from the mercy of God and His uncontrolled might to suffer the number of the lapsed to be called the Church; since it is written, "God is not the God of the dead, but of the living."[6] For we indeed desire that all may be made alive; and we pray that, by our supplications and groans, they may be restored to their original state. But if certain lapsed ones claim to be the Church, and if the Church be among them and in them, what is left but for us to ask of these very persons that they would deign to admit us into the Church? Therefore it behoves them to be submissive and quiet and modest, as those who ought to appease God, in remembrance of their sin, and not to write letters in the name of the Church, when they should rather be aware that they are writing to the Church.

2. But some who are of the lapsed have lately written to me, and are humble and meek and trembling and fearing God, and who have always laboured in the Church gloriously and liberally, and who have never made a boast of their labour to the Lord, knowing that He has said, "When ye shall have done all these things, say, We are unprofitable servants: we have done that which was our duty to do."[7] Thinking of which things, and although they had received certificates from the martyrs, nevertheless, that their satisfaction might be admitted by the Lord, these persons beseeching have written to me that they acknowledge their sin, and are truly repentant, and do not hurry rashly or importunately to secure peace; but that they are waiting for my presence, saying that even peace itself, if they should receive it when I was present, would be sweeter to them. How greatly I congratulate these, the Lord is my witness, who hath condescended to tell what such, and such sort of servants deserve of His kindness. Which letters, as I lately received, and now read that you have written very differently, I beg that you will discriminate between your wishes; and whoever you are who have sent this letter, add your names to the certificate, and transmit the certificate to me with your several names. For I must first know to whom I have to reply; then I will respond to each of the matters that you have written, having regard to the mediocrity of my place and con-

---

[1] [Note the profound convictions in these very lapsers of the truth of the Gospel and of the value of full communion with Christ.]
[2] Oxford ed.: Ep. xxxiii. A.D. 250.
[3] [This is the Cyprianic idea. The idea that this was peculiar to any one bishop had never entered his mind. See vol. iv. p. 99.]
[4] Matt. xvi. 18, 19.

[5] [Elucidated and worked out in the *Treatise on Unity, infra.*]
[6] Matt. xxii. 32.
[7] Luke xvii. 10.

duct. I bid you, beloved brethren, ever heartily farewell, and live quietly and tranquilly according to the Lord's discipline. Fare ye well.

EPISTLE XXVII.[1]
TO THE PRESBYTERS AND DEACONS.

ARGUMENT. — THE ARGUMENT OF THIS LETTER IS SUFFICIENTLY IN AGREEMENT WITH THE PRECEDING, AND IT APPEARS THAT IT IS THE ONE OF WHICH HE SPEAKS IN THE FOLLOWING LETTER ; FOR HE PRAISES HIS CLERGY FOR HAVING REJECTED FROM COMMUNION GAIUS OF DIDDA, A PRESBYTER, AND HIS DEACON, WHO RASHLY COMMUNICATED WITH THE LAPSED ; AND EXHORTS THEM TO DO THE SAME WITH CERTAIN OTHERS.

1. Cyprian to the presbyters and deacons, his brethren, greeting. You have done uprightly and with discipline, beloved brethren, that, by the advice of my colleagues who were present, you have decided not to communicate with Gaius the presbyter of Didda, and his deacon ; who, by communicating with the lapsed, and offering their oblations,[2] have been frequently taken in their wicked errors ; and who once and again, as you wrote to me, when warned by my colleagues not to do this, have persisted obstinately in their presumption and audacity, deceiving certain brethren also from among our people, whose benefit we desire with all humility to consult, and whose salvation we take care for, not with affected adulation, but with sincere faith, that they may supplicate the Lord with true penitence and groaning and sorrow, since it is written, "Remember from whence thou art fallen, and repent."[3] And again, the divine Scripture says, "Thus saith the Lord, When thou shalt be converted and lament, then thou shalt be saved, and shalt know where thou hast been."[4]

2. Yet how can those mourn and repent, whose groanings and tears some of the presbyters obstruct when they rashly think that they may be communicated with, not knowing that it is written, "They who call you happy[5] cause you to err, and destroy the path of your feet?"[6] Naturally, our wholesome and true counsels have no success, whilst the salutary truth is hindered by mischievous blandishments and flatteries, and the wounded and unhealthy mind of the lapsed suffers what those also who are bodily diseased and sick often suffer ; that while they refuse wholesome food and beneficial drink as bitter

and distasteful, and crave those things which seem to please them and to be sweet for the present, they are inviting to themselves mischief and death by their recklessness and intemperance. Nor does the true remedy of the skilful physician avail to their safety, whilst the sweet enticement is deceiving with its charms.

3. Do you, therefore, according to my letters, take counsel about this faithfully and wholesomely, and do not recede from better counsels ; and be careful to read these same letters to my colleagues also, if there are any present, or if any should come to you ; that, with unanimity and concord, we may maintain a healthful plan for soothing and healing the wounds of the lapsed, intending to deal very fully with all when, by the Lord's mercy, we shall begin to assemble together. In the meantime, if any unrestrained and impetuous person, whether of our presbyters or deacons or of strangers, should dare, before our decree, to communicate with the lapsed, let him be expelled from our communion, and plead the cause of his rashness before all of us when, by the Lord's permission, we shall assemble together again.[7] Moreover, you wished me to reply what I thought concerning Philumenus and Fortunatus, sub-deacons, and Favorinus, an acolyte, who retired in the midst of the time of trial, and have now returned. Of which thing I cannot make myself sole judge, since many of the clergy are still absent, and have not considered, even thus late, that they should return to their place ; and this case of each one must be considered separately and fully investigated, not only with my colleagues, but also with the whole of the people themselves.[7] For a matter which hereafter may constitute an example as regards the ministers of the Church must be weighed and adjudged with careful deliberation. In the meanwhile, let them only abstain from the monthly division,[8] not so as to seem to be deprived of the ministry of the Church, but that all matters being in a sound state, they may be reserved till my coming. I bid you, beloved brethren, ever heartily farewell. Greet all the brotherhood, and fare ye well.

EPISTLE XXVIII.[9]
TO THE PRESBYTERS AND DEACONS ABIDING AT ROME.

ARGUMENT.—THE ROMAN CLERGY ARE INFORMED OF THE TEMERITY OF THE LAPSED WHO WERE DEMANDING PEACE.

Cyprian to the presbyters and deacons abiding at Rome, his brethren, greeting. Both our

---

[1] Oxford ed.: Ep. xxxiv. A.D. 250.
[2] [At the Eucharist the alms and oblations were regarded in the light of Matt. v. 23, 24.]
[3] Rev. ii. 5.
[4] Isa. xxx. 15, LXX.
[5] "They which lead thee." — E. V.
[6] Isa. iii. 12, LXX.

[7] [Thus Cyprian keeps in view "the whole Church," and adheres to his principle in letter xiii. p. 294, note 1, *supra*.]
[8] Some read this, "dictione," preaching.
[9] Oxford ed.: Ep. xxxv. A.D. 250.

common love and the reason of the thing demand, beloved brethren, that I should keep back from your knowledge nothing of those matters which are transacted among us, that so we may have a common plan for the advantage of the administration of the Church. For after I wrote to you the letter which I sent by Saturus the reader, and Optatus the sub-deacon, the combined temerity of certain of the lapsed, who refuse to repent and to make satisfaction to God, wrote to me, not asking that peace might be given to them, but claiming it as already given; because they say that Paulus has given peace to all, as you will read in their letter of which I have sent you a copy, as well as what I briefly replied to them in the meantime. But that you may also know what sort of a letter I afterwards wrote to the clergy, I have, moreover, sent you a copy of this. But if, after all, their temerity should not be repressed either by my letters or by yours, and should not yield to wholesome counsels, I shall take such proceedings as the Lord, according to His Gospel, has enjoined to be taken. I bid you, beloved brethren, ever heartily farewell.

EPISTLE XXIX.[1]

THE PRESBYTERS AND DEACONS ABIDING AT ROME, TO CYPRIAN.

ARGUMENT.—THE ROMAN CHURCH DECLARES ITS JUDGMENT CONCERNING THE LAPSED TO BE IN AGREEMENT WITH THE CARTHAGINIAN DECREES. ANY INDULGENCE SHOWN TO THE LAPSED IS REQUIRED TO BE IN ACCORDANCE WITH THE LAW OF THE GOSPEL. THAT THE PEACE GRANTED BY THE CONFESSORS DEPENDS ONLY UPON GRACE AND GOOD-WILL, IS MANIFEST FROM THE FACT THAT THE LAPSED ARE REFERRED TO THE BISHOPS. THE SEDITIOUS DEMAND FOR PEACE MADE BY FELICISSIMUS IS TO BE ATTRIBUTED TO FACTION.

1. The presbyters and deacons abiding at Rome, to Father[2] Cyprian, greeting. When, beloved brother, we carefully read your letter which you had sent by Fortunatus the sub-deacon, we were smitten with a double sorrow, and disordered with a twofold grief, that there was not any rest given to you in such necessities of the persecution, and that the unreasonable petulance of the lapsed brethren was declared to be carried even to a dangerous boldness of expression. But although those things which we have spoken of severely afflicted us and our spirit, yet your vigour and the severity that you have used, according to the proper discipline, moderates the so heavy load of our grief, in that you rightly

restrain the wickedness of some, and, by your exhortation to repentance, show the legitimate way of salvation That they should have wished to hurry to such an extreme as this, we are indeed considerably surprised; as that with such urgency, and at so unseasonable and bitter a time, being in so great and excessive a sin, they should not so much ask for, as claim, peace for themselves; nay, should say that they already have it in heaven. If they have it, why do they ask for what they possess? But if, by the very fact that they are asking for it, it is proved that they have it not, wherefore do they not accept the judgment of those from whom they have thought fit to ask for the peace, which they certainly have not got? But if they think that they have from any other source the prerogative of communion, let them try to compare it with the Gospel, that so at length it may abundantly avail them, if it is not out of harmony with the Gospel law. But on what principle can that give Gospel communion which seems to be established contrary to Gospel truth? For since every prerogative contemplates the privilege of association, precisely on the assumption of its not being out of harmony with the will of Him with whom it seeks to be associated; then, because this is alien from His will with whom it seeks to be associated, it must of necessity lose the indulgence and privilege of the association.

2. Let them, then, see what it is they are trying to do in this matter. For if they say that the Gospel has established one decree, but the martyrs have established another; then they, setting the martyrs at variance with the Gospel, will be in danger on both sides. For, on the one hand, the majesty of the Gospel will already appear shattered and cast down, if it can be overcome by the novelty of another decree; and, on the other, the glorious crown of confession will be taken from the heads of the martyrs, if they be not found to have attained it by the observation of that Gospel whence they become martyrs; so that, reasonably, no one should be more careful to determine nothing contrary to the Gospel, than he who strives to receive the name of martyr from the Gospel. We should like, besides, to be informed of this: if martyrs become martyrs for no other reason than that by not sacrificing they may keep the peace of the Church even to the shedding of their own blood, lest, overcome by the suffering of the torture, by losing peace, they might lose salvation; on what principle do they think that the salvation, which if they had sacrificed they thought that they should not have, was to be given to those who are said to have sacrificed; although they ought to maintain that law in others which they themselves appear to have held before their own eyes? In which thing we observe that they

[1] Oxford ed.: Ep. xxxvi. A.D. 250.
[2] "Papa"=pope. [It may thus be noted what this word meant at Rome: nothing more than the fatherly address of all bishops.]

have put forward against their own cause the very thing which they thought made for them. For if the martyrs thought that peace was to be granted to them, why did not they themselves grant it? Why did they think that, as they themselves say, they were to be referred to the bishops? For he who orders a thing to be done, can assuredly do that which he orders to be done. But, as we understand, nay, as the case itself speaks and proclaims, the most holy martyrs thought that a proper measure of modesty and of truth must be observed on both sides. For as they were urged by many, in remitting them to the bishop they conceived that they would consult their own modesty so as to be no further disquieted; and in themselves not holding communion with them, they judged that the purity of the Gospel law ought to be maintained unimpaired.

3. But of your charity, brother, never desist from soothing the spirits of the lapsed and affording to the erring the medicine of truth, although the temper of the sick is wont to reject the kind offices of those who would heal them. This wound of the lapsed is as yet fresh, and the sore is still rising into a tumour; and therefore we are certain, that when, in the course of more protracted time, that urgency of theirs shall have worn out, they will love that very delay which refers them to a faithful medicine; if only there be not those who arm them for their own danger, and, instructing them perversely, demand on their behalf, instead of the salutary remedies of delay, the fatal poisons of a premature communion. For we do not believe, that without the instigation of certain persons they would all have dared so petulantly to claim peace for themselves. We know the faith of the Carthaginian church,[1] we know her training, we know her humility; whence also we have marvelled that we should observe certain things somewhat rudely suggested against you by letter, although we have often become aware of your mutual love and charity, in many illustrations of reciprocal affection of one another. It is time, therefore, that they should repent of their fault, that they should prove their grief for their lapse, that they should show modesty, that they should manifest humility, that they should exhibit some shame, that, by their submission, they should appeal to God's clemency for themselves, and by due honour for[2] God's priest should draw forth upon themselves the divine mercy. How vastly better would have been the letters of these men themselves, if the prayers of those who stood fast had been aided by their

own humility! since that which is asked for is more easily obtained, when he for whom it is asked is worthy, that what is asked should be obtained.

4. In respect, however, of Privatus of Lambesa, you have acted as you usually do, in desiring to inform us of the matter, as being an object of anxiety; for it becomes us all to watch for the body of the whole Church, whose members are scattered through every various province.[3] But the deceitfulness of that crafty man could not be hid from us even before we had your letters; for previously, when from the company of that very wickedness a certain Futurus came, a standard-bearer of Privatus, and was desirous of fraudulently obtaining letters from us, we were neither ignorant who he was, nor did he get the letters which he wanted. We bid you heartily farewell in the Lord.

EPISTLE XXX.[4]

THE ROMAN CLERGY TO CYPRIAN.

ARGUMENT. — THE ROMAN CLERGY ENTER INTO THE MATTERS WHICH THEY HAD SPOKEN OF IN THE FOREGOING LETTER, MORE FULLY AND SUBSTANTIALLY IN THE PRESENT ONE; REPLYING, MOREOVER, TO ANOTHER LETTER OF CYPRIAN, WHICH IS THOUGHT NOT TO BE EXTANT, AND FROM WHICH THEY QUOTE A FEW WORDS. THEY THANK CYPRIAN FOR HIS LETTERS SENT TO THE ROMAN CONFESSORS AND MARTYRS.[5]

1. To Father[6] Cyprian, the presbyters and deacons abiding at Rome, greeting. Although a mind conscious to itself of uprightness, and relying on the vigour of evangelical discipline, and made a true witness to itself in the heavenly decrees, is accustomed to be satisfied with God for its only judge, and neither to seek the praises nor to dread the charges of any other, yet those are worthy of double praise, who, knowing that they owe their conscience to God alone as the judge, yet desire that their doings should be approved also by their brethren themselves. It is no wonder, brother Cyprian, that you should do this, who, with your usual modesty and inborn industry, have wished that we should be found not so much judges of, as sharers in, your counsels, so that we might find praise with you in your doings while we approve them; and might be able to be fellow-heirs with you in your good counsels, because we entirely accord with them. In the same way we are all thought to have laboured in that in which we are all regarded as

---

[1] [The church at Rome recognises national churches as sisters. The " Roman Catholic " theory was not known, even under the Papacy, till the Trent Council, which destroyed " sister churches."]
[2] Or, we may read *in*.

[3] [On the principles we shall find laid down in Cyprian's *Treatise on Unity*. Also see vol. iv. p. 113.]
[4] Oxford ed.: Ep. xxx. A.D. 250.
[5] This letter was written, as were also the others of the Roman clergy, during the vacancy of the See, after the death of Fabian.
[6] " Pope Cyprian."

allied in the same agreement of censure and discipline.

2. For what is there either in peace so suitable, or in a war of persecution so necessary, as to maintain the due severity of the divine vigour? Which he who resists, will of necessity wander in the unsteady course of affairs, and will be tossed hither and thither by the various and uncertain storms of things; and the helm of counsel being, as it were, wrenched from his hands, he will drive the ship of the Church's safety among the rocks; so that it would appear that the Church's safety can be no otherwise secured, than by repelling any who set themselves against it as adverse waves, and by maintaining the ever-guarded rule of discipline itself as if it were the rudder of safety in the tempest. Nor is it now but lately that this counsel has been considered by us, nor have these sudden appliances against the wicked but recently occurred to us; but this is read of among us as the ancient severity, the ancient faith, the ancient discipline,[1] since the apostle would not have published such praise concerning us, when he said "that your faith is spoken of throughout the whole world,"[2] unless already from thence that vigour had borrowed the roots of faith from those times; from which praise and glory it is a very great crime to have become degenerate.[3] For it is less disgrace never to have attained to the heraldry of praise, than to have fallen from the height of praise; it is a smaller crime not to have been honoured with a good testimony, than to have lost the honour of good testimonies; it is less discredit to have lain without the announcement of virtues, ignoble without praise, than, disinherited of the faith,[4] to have lost our proper praises. For those things which are proclaimed to the glory of any one, unless they are maintained by anxious and careful pains, swell up into the odium of the greatest crime.[5]

3. That we are not saying this dishonestly, our former letters have proved, wherein we have declared our opinion to you with a very plain statement, both against those who had betrayed themselves as unfaithful by the unlawful presentation of wicked certificates, as if they thought that they would escape those ensnaring nets of the devil; whereas, not less than if they had approached to the wicked altars,[6] they were held fast by the very fact that they had testified to him; and against those who had used those certificates when made, although they had not been present when they were made, since they had certainly asserted their presence by ordering that they should be so written. For he is not guiltless of wickedness who has bidden it to be done; nor is he unconcerned in the crime with whose consent it is publicly spoken of, although it was not committed by him. And since the whole mystery[7] of faith is understood to be contained in the confession of the name of Christ, he who seeks for deceitful tricks to excuse himself, has denied Christ; and he who wants to appear to have satisfied either edicts or laws put forth against the Gospel, has obeyed those edicts by the very fact by which he wished to appear to have obeyed them. Moreover, also, we have declared our faith and consent against those, too, who had polluted their hands and their mouths with unlawful sacrifices, whose own minds were before polluted; whence also their very hands and mouths were polluted also.[8] Far be it from the Roman Church to slacken her vigour with so profane a facility, and to loosen the nerves of her severity by overthrowing the majesty of faith; so that, when the wrecks of your ruined brethren are still not only lying, but are falling around, remedies of a too hasty kind, and certainly not likely to avail, should be afforded for communion; and by a false mercy, new wounds should be impressed on the old wounds of their transgression; so that even repentance should be snatched from these wretched beings, to their greater overthrow. For where can the medicine of indulgence profit, if even the physician himself, by intercepting repentance, makes easy way for new dangers, if he only hides the wound, and does not suffer the necessary remedy of time to close the scar? This is not to cure, but, if we wish to speak the truth, to slay.[9]

4. Nevertheless, you have letters agreeing with our letters from the confessors, whom the dignity of their confession has still shut up here in prison, and whom, for the Gospel contest, their faith has once already crowned in a glorious confession; letters wherein they have maintained the severity of the Gospel discipline, and have revoked the unlawful petitions, so that they might not be a disgrace to the Church. Unless they had done this, the ruins of Gospel discipline[10] would not easily be restored, especially since it was to none so fitting to maintain the tenor of evangelical vigour unimpaired, and its dignity, as to those who had given themselves up to be tortured and cut to pieces by raging men on behalf of the Gospel, that they might not deservedly forfeit the honour of martyrdom, if, on the occasion of martyrdom, they had wished to be betrayers of the Gospel. For he who does not guard what he

---

[1] [Note τὰ ἀρχαῖα ἔθη, as in St. Paul, 1 Cor. xi. 16.]
[2] Rom. i. 8.
[3] [God grant this spirit to the modern Christians in Rome.]
[4] [No conception of Roman infallibility here.]
[5] [A concession which illustrates the present awful degeneracy of this See.]
[6] [1 Cor. x. 21, where *tables* and *altars* are used as synonymes.]

[7] Sacramentum.
[8] [See p. 304, note 8, *supra.*]
[9] [The whole system of Roman casuistry, as it now exists in the *authorised* penitential forms of Liguori, is here condemned.]
[10] [See *Alphonsus de' Liguori and the Papal Authorization*, vol. i. p. xxii., ed. Paris, 1852.]

has, in that condition whereon he possesses it, by violating the condition whereon he possesses it, loses what he possessed.

5. In which matter we ought to give you also, and we do give you, abundant thanks, that you have brightened the darkness of their prison by your letters; that you came to them in whatever way you could enter; that you refreshed their minds, robust in their own faith and confession, by your addresses and letters; that, following up their felicities with worthy praises, you have inflamed them to a much more ardent desire of heavenly glory; that you urged them forward; that you animated, by the power of your discourse, those who, as we believe and hope, will be victors by and by; so that although all may seem to come from the faith of those who confess, and from the divine mercy, yet they seem in their martyrdom to have become in some sort debtors to you. But once more, to return to the point whence our discourse appears to have digressed, you shall find subjoined the sort of letters that we also sent to Sicily; although upon us is incumbent a greater necessity of delaying this affair; having, since the departure of Fabian of most noble memory, had no bishop appointed as yet, on account of the difficulties of affairs and times, who can arrange all things of this kind, and who can take account of those who are lapsed, with authority and wisdom. However, what you also have yourself declared in so important a matter, is satisfactory to us, that the peace of the Church must first be maintained; then, that an assembly for counsel being gathered together, with bishops, presbyters, deacons, and confessors, as well as with the laity who stand fast,[1] we should deal with the case of the lapsed. For it seems extremely invidious and burdensome to examine into what seems to have been committed by many, except by the advice of many; or that one should give a sentence when so great a crime is known to have gone forth, and to be diffused among so many; since that cannot be a firm decree which shall not appear to have had the consent of very many.[2] Look upon almost the whole world devastated, and observe that the remains and the ruins of the fallen are lying about on every side, and consider that therefore an extent of counsel is asked for, large in proportion as the crime appears to be widely propagated. Let not the medicine be less than the wound, let not the remedies be fewer than the deaths, that in the same manner as those who fell, fell for this reason that they were too incautious with a blind rashness, so those who strive to set in order this mischief should use every moderation in counsels, lest anything done as it ought not

to be, should, as it were, be judged by all of no effect.

6. Thus, with one and the same counsel, with the same prayers and tears, let us, who up to the present time seem to have escaped the destruction of these times of ours, as well as those who appear to have fallen into those calamities of the time, entreat the divine majesty, and ask peace for the Church's name. With mutual prayers, let us by turns cherish, guard, arm one another; let us pray for the lapsed,[3] that they may be raised up; let us pray for those who stand, that they may not be tempted to such a degree as to be destroyed; let us pray that those who are said to have fallen may acknowledge the greatness of their sin, and may perceive that it needs no momentary nor over-hasty cure; let us pray that penitence may follow also the effects of the pardon of the lapsed; that so, when they have understood their own crime, they may be willing to have patience with us for a while, and no longer disturb the fluctuating condition of the Church, lest they may seem themselves to have inflamed an internal persecution for us, and the fact of their unquietness be added to the heap of their sins. For modesty is very greatly fitting for them in whose sins it is an immodest mind that is condemned. Let them indeed knock at the doors, but assuredly let them not break them down; let them present themselves at the threshold of the church, but certainly let them not leap over it; let them watch at the gates of the heavenly camp, but let them be armed with modesty, by which they perceive that they have been deserters; let them resume the trumpet of their prayers, but let them not therewith sound a point of war; let them arm themselves indeed with the weapons of modesty, and let them resume the shield of faith, which they had put off by their denial through the fear of death, but let those that are even now armed believe that they are armed against their foe, the devil, not against the Church, which grieves over their fall. A modest petition will much avail them; a bashful entreaty, a necessary humility, a patience which is not careless. Let them send tears as their ambassadors for their sufferings; let groanings, brought forth from their deepest heart, discharge the office of advocate, and prove their grief and shame for the crime they have committed.

7. Nay, if they shudder at the magnitude of the guilt incurred; if with a truly medicinal hand they deal with the deadly wound of their heart and conscience and the deep recesses of the subtle mischief, let them blush even to ask; except, again, that it is a matter of greater risk

---

[1] [All-important is this testimony of the Roman clergy to the Cyprianic idea of the Church synods. See this vol. *supra*, p. 283.]
[2] [Note this principle, as a test of synodical decrees.]

[3] [Probably a quotation from a "bidding prayer" in use at Rome in those times. Elucidation VI.]

and shame not to have besought the aid of peace. But let all this be in the sacrament;[1] in the law of their very entreaty let consideration be had for the time ; let it be with downcast entreaty, with subdued petition, since he also who is besought ought to be bent, not provoked ; and as the divine clemency ought to be looked to, so also ought the divine censure ; and as it is written, " I forgave thee all that debt, because thou desiredst me,"[2] so it is written, " Whosoever shall deny me before men, him will I also deny before my Father and before His angels."[3] For God, as He is merciful, so He exacts obedience to His precepts, and indeed carefully exacts it ; and as He invites to the banquet, so the man that hath not a wedding garment He binds hands and feet, and casts him out beyond the assembly of the saints. He has prepared heaven, but He has also prepared hell.[4] He has prepared places of refreshment, but He has also prepared eternal punishment. He has prepared the light that none can approach unto, but He has also prepared the vast and eternal gloom of perpetual night.

8. Desiring to maintain the moderation of this middle course in these matters, we for a long time, and indeed many of us, and, moreover, with some of the bishops who are near to us and within reach, and some whom, placed afar off, the heat of the persecution had driven out from other provinces,[5] have thought that nothing new was to be done before the appointment of a bishop ; but we believe that the care of the lapsed must be moderately dealt with, so that, in the meantime, whilst the grant of a bishop is withheld from us[6] by God, the cause of such as are able to bear the delays of postponement should be kept in suspense ; but of such as impending death does not suffer to bear the delay, having repented and professed a detestation of their deeds with frequency ; if with tears, if with groans, if with weeping they have betrayed the signs of a grieving and truly penitent spirit, when there remains, as far as man can tell, no hope of living ; to them, finally, such cautious and careful help should be ministered, God Himself knowing what He will do with such, and in what way He will examine the balance of His judgment ; while we, however, take anxious care that neither ungodly men should praise our smooth facility, nor truly penitent men accuse our severity as cruel. We bid you, most blessed and

glorious father, ever heartily farewell in the Lord ; and have us in memory.[7]

EPISTLE XXXI.[8]
TO THE CARTHAGINIAN CLERGY, ABOUT THE LETTERS SENT TO ROME, AND RECEIVED THENCE.

ARGUMENT. — THE CARTHAGINIAN CLERGY ARE REQUESTED TO TAKE CARE THAT THE LETTERS OF THE ROMAN CLERGY AND CYPRIAN'S ANSWER ARE COMMUNICATED.

Cyprian to the presbyters and deacons, his brethren, greeting. That you, my beloved brethren, might know what letters I have sent to the clergy acting[9] at Rome, and what they have replied to me, and, moreover, what Moyses and Maximus, the presbyters, and Rufinus and Nicostratus, the deacons, and the rest of the confessors that with them are kept in prison, replied likewise to my letters, I have sent you copies to read. Do you take care, with as much diligence as you can, that what I have written, and what they have replied, be made known to our brethren. And, moreover, if any bishops from foreign places,[10] my colleagues, or presbyters, or deacons, should be present, or should arrive among you, let them hear all these matters from you ; and if they wish to transcribe copies of the letters and to take them to their own people, let them have the opportunity of transcribing them ; although I have, moreover, bidden Saturus the reader, our brother, to give liberty of copying them to any individuals who wish it ; so that, in ordering, for the present, the condition of the Church in any manner, an agreement, one and faithful, may be observed by all. But about the other matters which were to be dealt with, as I have also written to several of my colleagues, we will more fully consider them in a common council, when, by the Lord's permission, we shall begin to assemble into one place. I bid you, brethren, beloved and longed-for, ever heartily farewell. Salute the brotherhood. Fare ye well.

EPISTLE XXXII.[11]
TO THE CLERGY AND PEOPLE, ABOUT THE ORDINATION OF AURELIUS AS A READER.

ARGUMENT. — CYPRIAN TELLS THE CLERGY AND PEOPLE THAT AURELIUS THE CONFESSOR HAS BEEN ORDAINED A READER BY HIM, AND COMMENDS, BY THE WAY, THE CONSTANCY OF HIS VIRTUE AND HIS MIND, WHEREBY HE WAS EVEN DESERVING OF A HIGHER DEGREE IN THE CHURCH.

1. Cyprian to the elders and deacons, and to the whole people, greeting. In ordinations of

---

1 In " sacramento," *scil.* " fidei ; " perhaps in a way in harmony with their religious engagement and with ecclesiastical discipline.
2 Matt. xviii. 32.
3 Matt. x. 33 ; Luke xii. 9.
4 [Note this faithful statement of scriptural doctrine, and no hint of *purgatory.*]
5 [All this illustrates the *Treatise on Unity* (*infra*), and proves the utter absence of anything peculiar in the See of Rome.]
6 [How different the language of the cardinal vicar, now, when he writes, *sede vacante.*]

7 [This eloquent and evangelical letter proves that much dross had been burned away by the fires of persecution since the episcopate of Callistus. It is referred to, p. 309, note 4.]
8 Oxford ed.: Ep. xxxii. A.D. 250.
9 [Administering jurisdiction *sede vacante.*]
10 [Illustrating the *Treatise on Unity.*]
11 Oxford ed.: Ep. xxxviii. A.D. 250.

the clergy, beloved brethren, we usually consult you beforehand, and weigh the character and deserts of individuals, with the general advice.[1] But human testimonies must not be waited for when the divine approval precedes. Aurelius, our brother, an illustrious youth, already approved by the Lord, and dear to God, in years still very young, but, in the praise of virtue and of faith, advanced; inferior in the natural abilities of his age, but superior in the honour *he has merited*, — has contended here in a double conflict, having twice confessed and twice been glorious in the victory of his confession, both when he conquered in the course and was banished, and when at length he fought in a severer conflict, he was triumphant and victorious in the battle of suffering. As often as the adversary wished to call forth the servants of God, so often this prompt and brave soldier both fought and conquered. It had been a slight matter, previously to have engaged under the eyes of a few, when he was banished; he deserved also in the forum to engage with a more illustrious virtue; so that, after overcoming the magistrates, he might also triumph over the proconsul, and, after exile, might vanquish tortures also. Nor can I discover what I ought to speak most of in him, — the glory of his wounds or the modesty of his character; that he is distinguished by the honour of his virtue, or praiseworthy for the admirableness of his modesty. He is both so excellent in dignity and so lowly in humility, that it seems that he is divinely reserved as one who should be an example to the rest for ecclesiastical discipline, of the way in which the servants of God should in confession conquer by their courage, and, after confession, be conspicuous for their character.

2. Such a one, to be estimated not by his years but by his deserts, merited higher degrees of clerical ordination and larger increase. But, in the meantime, I judged it well, that he should begin with the office of reading; because nothing is more suitable for the voice which has confessed the Lord in a glorious utterance, than to sound Him forth in the solemn repetition of the divine lessons; than, after the sublime words which spoke out the witness of Christ, to read the Gospel of Christ whence martyrs are made; to come to the desk after the scaffold; there to have been conspicuous to the multitude of the Gentiles, here to be beheld by the brethren; there to have been heard with the wonder of the surrounding people, here to be heard with the joy of the brotherhood. Know, then, most beloved brethren, that this man has been ordained by me and by my colleagues who were then present. I know that you will both gladly welcome

these tidings, and that you desire that as many such as possible may be ordained in our church. And since joy is always hasty, and gladness can bear no delay, he reads on the Lord's day, in the meantime, for me; that is, he has made a beginning of peace, by solemnly entering on his office of a reader.[2] Do you frequently be urgent in supplications, and assist my prayers by yours, that the Lord's mercy favouring us may soon restore both the priest[3] safe to his people, and the martyr for a reader with the priest. I bid you, beloved brethren in God the Father, and in Jesus Christ, ever heartily farewell.

EPISTLE XXXIII.[4]

TO THE CLERGY AND PEOPLE, ABOUT THE ORDINATION OF CELERINUS AS READER.

ARGUMENT. — THIS LETTER IS ABOUT THE SAME IN PURPORT WITH THE PRECEDING, EXCEPT THAT HE LARGELY COMMENDS THE CONSTANCY OF CELERINUS IN HIS CONFESSION OF THE FAITH. MOREOVER, THAT BOTH OF THESE LETTERS WERE WRITTEN DURING HIS RETREAT, IS SUFFICIENTLY INDICATED BY THE CIRCUMSTANCES OF THE CONTEXT.

1. Cyprian to the presbyters and deacons, and to the whole people, his brethren in the Lord, greeting. The divine benefits, beloved brethren, should be acknowledged and embraced, wherewith the Lord has condescended to embellish and illustrate His Church in our times by granting a respite to His good confessors and His glorious martyrs, that they who had grandly confessed Christ should afterwards adorn Christ's clergy in ecclesiastical ministries. Exult, therefore, and rejoice with me on receiving my letter, wherein I and my colleagues who were then present mention to you Celerinus, our brother, glorious alike for his courage and his character, as added to our clergy, not by human recommendation, but by divine condescension; who, when he hesitated to yield to the Church, was constrained by her own admonition and exhortation, in a vision by night, not to refuse our persuasions; and she had more power, and constrained him, because it was not right, nor was it becoming, that he should be without ecclesiastical honour, whom the Lord honoured with the dignity of heavenly glory.[5]

2. This man was the first in the struggle of our days; he was the leader among Christ's soldiers; he, in the midst of the burning beginnings of the persecution, engaged with the very chief and author of the disturbance, in conquer-

---

[1] [Note again this principle of the Cyprianic freedom and evangelical discipline. Acts xv. 22; Matt. xviii. 17.]

[2] Aurelius not being able to discharge the functions of his office in public, because of the persecution, in the meantime read for Cyprian; which is said to be an augury or beginning of future peace.

[3] [That is himself. Compare Phil. i. 26.]

[4] Oxford ed.: Ep. xxxix. A.D. 250.

[5] [See testimony of Cornelius, in Euseb., *H. E.*, vi. 43.]

ing with invincible firmness the adversary of his own conflict.[1] He made a way for others to conquer; a victor with no small amount of wounds, but triumphant by a miracle, with the long-abiding and permanent penalties of a tedious conflict. For nineteen days, shut up in the close guard of a dungeon, he was racked and in irons; but although his body was laid in chains, his spirit remained free and at liberty. His flesh wasted away by the long endurance of hunger and thirst; but God fed his soul, that lived in faith and virtue, with spiritual nourishments. He lay in punishments, the stronger for his punishments; imprisoned, greater than those that imprisoned him; lying prostrate, but loftier than those who stood; as bound, and firmer than the links which bound him; judged, and more sublime than those who judged him; and although his feet were bound on the rack, yet the serpent was trodden on and ground down and vanquished. In his glorious body shine the bright evidences of his wounds; their manifest traces show forth, and appear on the man's sinews and limbs, worn out with tedious wasting away.[2] Great things are they — marvellous things are they — which the brotherhood may hear of his virtues and of his praises. And should any one appear like Thomas, who has little faith in what he hears, the faith of the eyes is not wanting, so that what one hears he may also see. In the servant of God, the glory of the wounds made the victory; the memory of the scars preserves that glory.

3. Nor is that kind of title to glories in the case of Celerinus, our beloved, an unfamiliar and novel thing. He is advancing in the footsteps of his kindred; he rivals his parents and relations in equal honours of divine condescension. His grandmother, Celerina, was some time since crowned with martyrdom. Moreover, his paternal and maternal uncles, Laurentius and Egnatius, who themselves also were once warring in the camps of the world, but were true and spiritual soldiers of God, casting down the devil by the confession of Christ, merited palms and crowns from the Lord by their illustrious passion. We always offer sacrifices for them,[3] as you remember, as often as we celebrate the passions and days of the martyrs in the annual commemoration. Nor could he, therefore, be degenerate and inferior whom this family dignity and a generous nobility provoked, by domestic examples of virtue and faith. But if in a worldly family it is a matter of heraldry and of praise to be a patrician, of how much greater praise and honour

is it to become of noble rank in the celestial heraldry! I cannot tell whom I should call more blessed, — whether those ancestors, for a posterity so illustrious, or him, for an origin so glorious. So equally between them does the divine condescension flow, and pass to and fro, that, just as the dignity of their offspring brightens their crown, so the sublimity of his ancestry illuminates his glory.

4. When this man, beloved brethren, came to us with such condescension of the Lord, illustrious by the testimony and wonder of the very man who had persecuted him, what else behoved to be done except that he should be placed on the pulpit,[4] that is, on the tribunal of the Church; that, resting on the loftiness of a higher station, and conspicuous to the whole people for the brightness of his honour, he should read the precepts and Gospel of the Lord, which he so bravely and faithfully follows? Let the voice that has confessed the Lord daily be heard in those things which the Lord spoke. Let it be seen whether there is any further degree to which he can be advanced in the Church. There is nothing in which a confessor can do more good to the brethren than that, while the reading of the Gospel is heard from his lips, every one who hears should imitate the faith of the reader. He should have been associated with Aurelius in reading; with whom, moreover, he was associated in the alliance of divine honour; with whom, in all the insignia of virtue and praise, he had been united. Equal both, and each like to the other, in proportion as they were sublime in glory, in that proportion they were humble in modesty. As they were lifted up by divine condescension, so they were lowly in their own peacefulness and tranquillity, and equally affording examples to every one of virtues and character, and fitted both for conflict and for peace; praiseworthy in the former for strength, in the latter for modesty.

5. In such servants the Lord rejoices; in confessors of this kind He glories, — whose way and conversation is so advantageous to the announcement of their glory, that it affords to others a teaching of discipline. For this purpose Christ has willed them to remain long here in the Church; for this purpose He has kept them safe, snatched from the midst of death, — a kind of resurrection, so to speak, being wrought on their behalf; so that, while nothing is seen by the brethren loftier in honour, nothing more lowly in humility, the way of life of the brotherhood[5] may accompany these same persons. Know, then, that these for the present are appointed readers, because it was fitting that the candle

---

[1] [He produced some momentary impression on Decius himself.]
[2] [Gal. vi. 17. St. Paul esteemed such *stigmata* a better ground of glorying in the flesh than his circumcision.]
[3] [Memorial thanksgivings. Ussher argues hereby the absence of all purgatorial ideas, because martyrs were allowed by all to go at once to bliss. Compare Tertull., vol. iv. p. 67.]

[4] [He was called to preach and expound the Scriptures.]
[5] " The brotherhood may follow and imitate these same persons; " *v. l.*

should be placed in a candlestick, whence it may give light to all, and that their glorious countenance should be established in a higher place, where, beheld by all the surrounding brotherhood, they may give an incitement of glory to the beholders. But know that I have already purposed the honour of the presbytery for them, that so they may be honoured with the same presents as the presbyters, and may share the monthly divisions [1] in equalled quantities, to sit with us hereafter in their advanced and strengthened years; although in nothing can he seem to be inferior in the qualities of age who has consummated his age by the dignity of his glory. I bid you, brethren, beloved and earnestly longed-for, ever heartily farewell.

EPISTLE XXXIV.[2]
TO THE SAME, ABOUT THE ORDINATION OF NUMIDICUS AS PRESBYTER.

ARGUMENT. — CYPRIAN TELLS THE CLERGY AND PEOPLE THAT NUMIDICUS HAS BEEN ORDAINED BY HIM PRESBYTER; AND BRIEFLY COMMENDS HIS WORTH.

Cyprian to the presbyters and deacons, and to the whole people, his brethren, very dear and longed-for, greeting. That which belongs, dearest brethren, both to the common joy and to the greatest glory of our Church ought to be told to you; for you must know that I have been admonished and instructed by divine condescension, that Numidicus the presbyter should be appointed in the number of Carthaginian presbyters, and should sit with us among the clergy, — a man illustrious by the brightest light of confession, exalted in the honour both of virtue and of faith; who by his exhortation sent before himself an abundant number of martyrs, slain by stones and by the flames, and who beheld with joy his wife abiding by his side, burned (I should rather say, preserved) together with the rest. He himself, half consumed, overwhelmed with stones, and left for dead, — when afterwards his daughter, with the anxious consideration of affection, sought for the corpse of her father, — was found half dead, was drawn out and revived, and remained unwillingly [3] from among the companions whom he himself had sent before. But the reason of his remaining behind, as we see, was this: that the Lord might add him to our clergy, and might adorn with glorious priests the number of our presbyters that had been desolated by the lapse of some.[4] And when God permits, he shall be advanced to a larger office in his region,

when, by the Lord's protection, we have come into your presence once more. In the meantime, let what is revealed be done, that we receive this gift of God with thanksgiving, hoping from the Lord's mercy more ornaments of the same kind, that so the strength of His Church being renewed, He may make men so meek and lowly to flourish in the honour of our assembly. I bid you, brethren, very dear and longed-for, ever heartily farewell.

EPISTLE XXXV.[5]
TO THE CLERGY, CONCERNING THE CARE OF THE POOR AND STRANGERS.

ARGUMENT. — HE CAUTIONS THEM AGAINST NEGLECTING THE WIDOWS, THE SICK, OR THE POOR, OR STRANGERS.

Cyprian to the presbyters and deacons, his beloved brethren, greeting. In safety, by God's grace, I greet you, beloved brethren, desiring soon to come to you, and to satisfy the wish as well of myself and you, as of all the brethren. It behoves me also, however, to have regard to the common peace, and, in the meantime, although with weariness of spirit, to be absent from you, lest my presence should provoke the jealousy and violence of the heathens, and I should be the cause of breaking the peace, who ought rather to be careful for the quiet of all. When, therefore, you write that matters are arranged, and that I ought to come, or if the Lord should condescend to intimate it to me before, then I will come to you. For where could I be better or more joyful than there where the Lord willed me both to believe and to grow up? I request that you will diligently take care of the widows, and of the sick, and of all the poor. Moreover, you may supply the expenses for strangers, if any should be indigent, from my own portion, which I have left with Rogatianus, our fellow-presbyter;[6] which portion, lest it should be all appropriated, I have supplemented by sending to the same by Naricus the acolyte another share, so that the sufferers may be more largely and promptly dealt with. I bid you, beloved brethren, ever heartily farewell; and have me in remembrance. Greet your brotherhood in my name, and tell them to be mindful of me.

EPISTLE XXXVI.[7]
TO THE CLERGY, BIDDING THEM SHOW EVERY KINDNESS TO THE CONFESSORS IN PRISON.

ARGUMENT. — HE EXHORTS HIS CLERGY THAT EVERY KINDNESS AND CARE SHOULD BE EXERCISED TOWARDS THE CONFESSORS, AS WELL TO-

---

1 [See Bingham, Book v. cap. 6, sec. 3.]
2 Oxford ed.: Ep. xl. A.D. 250.
3 Otherwise, " unconquered."
4 [Let us put ourselves in Cyprian's place, and share his anxiety to fill up the vacant places in his list of presbyters at this terrible period.]

5 Oxford ed.: Ep. vii. A.D. circa 251.
6 [Here, as elsewhere, spoken of in this way, in imitation of 1 Pet. v. 1.]
7 Oxford ed.: Ep. xii. A.D. circa 251.

WARDS THOSE WHO WERE ALIVE, AS THOSE WHO DIED, IN PRISON ; THAT THE DAYS OF THEIR DEATH SHOULD BE CAREFULLY NOTED, FOR THE PURPOSE OF CELEBRATING THEIR MEMORY ANNUALLY ; AND, FINALLY, THAT THEY SHOULD NOT FORGET THE POOR ALSO.

1. Cyprian to the presbyters and deacons, his brethren, greeting. Although I know, dearest brethren, that you have frequently been admonished in my letters to manifest all care for those who with a glorious voice have confessed the Lord, and are confined in prison ; yet, again and again, I urge it upon you, that no consideration be wanting to them to whose glory there is nothing wanting. And I wish that the circumstances of the place and of my station would permit me to present myself at this time with them ; promptly and gladly would I fulfil all the duties of love towards our most courageous brethren in my appointed ministry. But I beseech you, let your diligence be the representative of my duty, and do all those things which behove to be done in respect of those whom the divine condescension has rendered illustrious in such merits of their faith and virtue. Let there be also a more zealous watchfulness and care bestowed upon the bodies of all those who, although they were not tortured in prison, yet depart thence by the glorious exit of death. For neither is their virtue nor their honour too little for them also to be allied with the blessed martyrs. As far as they could, they bore whatever they were prepared and equipped to bear. He who under the eyes of God has offered himself to tortures and to death, has suffered whatever he was willing to suffer ; for it was not he that was wanting to the tortures, but the tortures that were wanting to him. "Whosoever shall confess me before men, him will I also confess before my Father which is in heaven,"[1] saith the Lord. They have confessed Him. "He that endureth to the end, the same shall be saved,"[2] saith the Lord. They have endured and have carried the uncorrupted and unstained merits of their virtues through, even unto the end. And, again, it is written, "Be thou faithful unto death, and I will give thee a crown of life."[3] They have persevered in their faithfulness, and stedfastness, and invincibleness, even unto death. When to the willingness and the confession of the name in prison and in chains is added also the conclusion of dying, the glory of the martyr is consummated.

2. Finally, also, take note of their days on which they depart, that we may celebrate their commemoration among the memorials of the martyrs,[4] although Tertullus, our most faithful and devoted brother, who, in addition to the other solicitude and care which he shows to the brethren in all service of labour, is not wanting besides in that respect in any care of their bodies, has written, and does write and intimate to me the days, in which our blessed brethren in prison pass by the gate of a glorious death to their immortality ; and there are celebrated here by us oblations and sacrifices for their commemorations, which things, with the Lord's protection, we shall soon celebrate with you. Let your care also (as I have already often written) and your diligence not be wanting to the poor, — to such, I mean, as stand fast in the faith and bravely fight with us, and have not left the camp of Christ ; to whom, indeed, we should now show a greater love and care, in that they are neither constrained by poverty nor prostrated by the tempest of persecution, but faithfully serve with the Lord, and have given an example of faith to the other poor. I bid you, brethren beloved, and greatly longed-for, ever heartily farewell ; and remember me. Greet the brotherhood in my name. Fare ye well.

EPISTLE XXXVII.[5]
TO CALDONIUS, HERCULANUS, AND OTHERS, ABOUT THE EXCOMMUNICATION OF FELICISSIMUS.

ARGUMENT. — FELICISSIMUS, TOGETHER WITH HIS COMPANIONS IN SEDITION, IS TO BE RESTRAINED FROM THE COMMUNION OF ALL.

1. Cyprian to Caldonius and Herculanus, his colleagues, also to Rogatianus and Numidicus, his fellow-presbyters, greeting. I have been greatly grieved, dearest brethren, at the receipt of your letter, that although I have always proposed to myself and wished to keep all our brotherhood safe, and to preserve the flock unharmed, as charity requires, you tell me now that Felicissimus has been attempting many things with wickedness and craft ; so that, besides his old frauds and plundering, of which I had formerly known a good deal, he has now, moreover, tried to divide with the bishop a portion of the people ; that is, to separate the sheep from the shepherd, and sons from their parents, and to scatter the members of Christ. And although I sent you as my substitutes to discharge the necessities of our brethren, with funds, and if any, moreover, wished to exercise their crafts, to assist their wishes with such an addition as might be sufficient, and at the same time also to take note of their ages and conditions and deserts, — that I also, upon whom falls the

---

[1] Matt. x. 32.
[2] Matt. x. 22.
[3] Rev. ii. 10.

[4] [The tract of Archbishop Ussher shows what these commemorations were. See vol. iii. p. 701, and Elucidation, p. 706; also vol. i. p. 484.]
[5] Oxford ed.: Ep. xli. A.D. 250.

charge of knowing all of them thoroughly, might promote any that were worthy and humble and meek to the offices of the ecclesiastical administration ; — he has interfered, and directed that no one should be relieved, and that those things which I had desired should not be ascertained by careful examination ; he has also threatened our brethren, who had first approached to be relieved, with a wicked exercise of power, and with a violent dread that those who desired to obey me should not communicate with him in death.[1]

2. And since, after all these things, neither moved by the honour of my station, nor shaken by your authority and presence, but of his own impulse, disturbing the peace of the brethren, he hath rushed forth with many more, and asserted himself as a leader of a faction and chief of a sedition with a hasty madness — in which respect, indeed, I congratulate several of the brethren that they have withdrawn from this boldness, and have rather chosen to consent with you, so that they may remain with the Church, their mother, and receive their stipends from the bishop who dispenses them, which, indeed, I know for certain, that others also will peaceably do, and will quickly withdraw from their rash error, — in the meantime, since Felicissimus has threatened that they should not communicate with him in death[2] who had obeyed us, that is, who communicated with us, let him receive the sentence which he first of all declared, that he may know that he is excommunicated by us ; inasmuch as he adds to his frauds and rapines, which we have known by the clearest truth, the crime also of adultery, which our brethren, grave men, have declared that they have discovered, and have asseverated that they will prove ; all which things we shall then judicially examine, when, with the Lord's permission, we shall assemble in one place with many of our colleagues. But Augendus also, who, considering neither his bishop nor his Church, has equally associated himself with him in this conspiracy and faction, if he should further persevere with him, let him bear the sentence which that factious and impetuous man has provoked on himself. Moreover, whoever shall ally himself with his conspiracy and faction, let him know that he shall not communicate in the Church with us, since of his own accord he has preferred to be separated from the Church. Read this letter of mine to our brethren, and also transmit it to Carthage to the clergy, the names being added of those who have joined themselves with Felicissimus. I bid you, beloved

brethren, ever heartily farewell ; and remember me. Fare ye well.

EPISTLE XXXVIII.[3]
THE LETTER OF CALDONIUS, HERCULANUS, AND OTHERS, ON THE EXCOMMUNICATION OF FELICISSIMUS WITH HIS PEOPLE.

ARGUMENT. — CALDONIUS, HERCULANUS, AND OTHERS CARRY INTO EFFECT WHAT THE PRECEDING LETTER HAD BIDDEN THEM.

Caldonius, with Herculanus and Victor, his colleagues, also with Rogatianus and Numidicus, presbyters.[4] We have rejected Felicissimus and Augendus from communion ; also Repostus from among the exiles, and Irene of the Blood-stained ones ;[5] and Paula the sempstress ; which you ought to 'know from my subscription ; also we have rejected Sophronius and Soliassus (budinarius),[6] — himself also one of the exiles.

EPISTLE XXXIX.[7]
TO THE PEOPLE, CONCERNING FIVE SCHISMATIC PRESBYTERS OF THE FACTION OF FELICISSIMUS.

ARGUMENT. — IN LIKE MANNER, AS IN THE EPISTLE BUT ONE BEFORE THIS, CYPRIAN TOLD THE CLERGY, SO NOW HE TELLS THE PEOPLE, THAT FELICISSIMUS IS TO BE AVOIDED, TOGETHER WITH FIVE PRESBYTERS OF HIS FACTION, WHO NOT ONLY GRANTED PEACE TO THE LAPSED WITHOUT ANY DISCRIMINATION, BUT STIRRED UP SEDITION AND SCHISM AGAINST HIMSELF.

1. Cyprian to the whole people, greeting. Although, dearest brethren, Virtius,[8] a most faithful and upright presbyter, and also Rogatianus and Numidicus, presbyters, confessors, and illustrious by the glory of the divine condescension, and also the deacons, good men and devoted to the ecclesiastical administration in all its duties, with the other ministers, afford you the full attention of their presence, and do not cease to confirm individuals by their assiduous exhortations, and, moreover, to govern and reform the minds of the lapsed by their wholesome counsels, yet, as much as I can, I admonish, and as I can, I visit you with my letters. By my letters I say, dearest brethren ; for the

---

[1] [So the Oxford ed., p. 91.] Or, " in the mount," " in monte ; " *vide* Neander, *K. G.,* i. 252 ; probably in some church or congregation assembled by Felicissimus, on an eminence near or in Carthage.
[2] Or, " on the mount."

[3] Oxford ed.: Ep. xlii. A.D. 251.
[4] *V. l.* " to Cyprian, greeting."
[5] " Rutili," *scil.* confessors who had spilt their blood.
[6] " Budinarius." The exact meaning of this word is unknown. Some read it as another name : " Soliassus and Budinarius." The Oxford editor changes it into Burdonarius, meaning a " carrier on mules." Salmasius, in a long note on a passage in the life of Aurelian (*Hist. Aug.,* p. 408), proposes *butinarius,* which he derives from βυτίνη, a cruet for containing vinegar, etc., and which he identifies with βοῦττις, the original of our *bottle. Butinarius* would then mean a maker of vessels suitable for containing vinegar, etc. See Sophocles' *Glossary of Byzantine Greek, s. v.* βοῦττις. [Probably low Latin for a maker of force-meats. Spanish, *budin.*]
[7] Oxford ed.: Ep. xliii. A.D. 251.
[8] Some read " Britius " or " Briccius."

malignity and treachery of certain of the presbyters has accomplished this, that I should not be allowed to come to you before Easter-day; since mindful of their conspiracy, and retaining that ancient venom against my episcopate, that is, against your suffrage and God's judgment, they renew their old attack upon me, and once more begin their sacrilegious machinations with their accustomed craft. And, indeed, of God's providence, neither by our wish nor desire, nay, although we were forgiving and silent, they have suffered the punishment which they had deserved; so that, not cast out by us, they of their own accord have cast themselves out. They themselves, before their own conscience, have passed sentence on themselves in accordance with your suffrages and the divine. These conspirators and evil men of their own accord have driven themselves from the Church.

2. Now it has appeared whence came the faction of Felicissimus; on what root and by what strength it stood. These men supplied in former times encouragements and exhortations to certain confessors, not to agree with their bishop, not to maintain the ecclesiastical discipline with faith and quietness according to the Lord's precepts, not to keep the glory of their confession with an uncorrupt and unspotted conversation. And lest it should be too little to have corrupted the minds of certain confessors, and to have wished to arm a portion of our broken fraternity against God's priesthood, they have now turned their attention with their envenomed deceitfulness to the ruin of the lapsed, to turn away from the healing of their wound the sick and the wounded, and those who, by the misfortune of their fall, are less fit and less sturdy to take stronger counsel; and invite them, by the falsehood of a fallacious peace, to a fatal rashness, leaving off prayers and supplications, whereby, with long and continual satisfaction, the Lord is to be appeased.

3. But I pray you, brethren, watch against the snares of the devil, and, taking care for your own salvation, be diligently on your guard against this death-bearing fallacy. This is another persecution and another temptation. Those five presbyters are none other than the five leaders who were lately associated with the magistrates in an edict, that they might overthrow our faith, that they might turn away the feeble hearts of the brethren to their deadly nets by the prevarication of the truth. Now the same scheme, the same overturning, is again brought about by the five presbyters, linked with Felicissimus, to the destruction of salvation, that God should not be besought, and that he who has denied Christ should not appeal for mercy to the same Christ whom he had denied; that after the fault of the crime, repentance also should be taken away;

and that the Lord should not be appeased through bishops and priests, but that the Lord's priests being forsaken, a new tradition of a sacrilegious appointment should arise, contrary to the evangelical discipline. And although it was once arranged as well by us as by the confessors and the city[1] clergy, and moreover by all the bishops appointed either in our province or beyond the sea,[2] that no novelty should be introduced in respect of the case of the lapsed unless we all assembled into one place, and our counsels being compared, should decide upon a moderate sentence, tempered alike with discipline and with mercy; — against this our counsel they have rebelled, and all priestly authority and power is destroyed by factious conspiracies.

4. What sufferings do I now endure, dearest brethren, that I myself am not able to come to you at the present juncture, that I myself cannot approach you each one, that I myself cannot exhort you according to the teaching of the Lord and of His Gospel! An exile of, now, two years[3] was not sufficient, and a mournful separation from you, from your countenance, and from your sight, — continual grief and lamentation, which, in my loneliness without you, breaks me to pieces with my constant mourning, nor my tears flowing day and night, that there is not even an opportunity for the priest, whom you made with so much love and eagerness, to greet you, nor to be enfolded in your embraces. This greater grief is added to my worn spirit, that in the midst of so much solicitude and necessity I am not able myself to hasten to you, since, by the threats and by the snares of perfidious men, we are anxious that on our coming a greater tumult may not arise there; and so, although the bishop ought to be careful for peace and tranquillity in all things, he himself should seem to have afforded material for sedition, and to have embittered persecution anew. Hence, however, beloved brethren, I not only admonish but counsel you, not rashly to trust to mischievous words, nor to yield an easy consent to deceitful sayings, nor to take darkness for light, night for day, hunger for food, thirst for drink, poison for medicine, death for safety. Let not the age nor the authority deceive you of those who, answering to the ancient wickedness of the two elders;[4] as they attempted to corrupt and violate the chaste Susannah,[5] are thus also attempting, with their adulterous doctrines, to corrupt the chastity

---

[1] "Clericis urbicis," *scil.* the "Roman city clergy." [A very important example of the concurrent action of the clergy of the metropolis with those of sister churches.]
[2] "Romæ," *scil.* "across the sea, at Rome." [The African canons forbade appeals to any bishop beyond seas.]
[3] [Concerning this exile, see p. 270, *supra.*]
[4] ["The elders," i.e., presbyters. Our author plays upon the word, and compares the corrupt presbyters to their like in the Hebrew Church, from which this name is borrowed. Exod. iii. 16 and *passim.*]
[5] Hist. of Susannah.

of the Church and violate the truth of the Gospel.

5. The Lord cries aloud, saying, "Hearken not unto the words of the false prophets, for the visions of their own hearts deceive them. They speak, but not out of the mouth of the Lord. They say to them that despise the word of the Lord, Ye shall have peace."[1] They are now offering peace who have not peace themselves. They are promising to bring back and recall the lapsed into the Church, who themselves have departed from the Church. There is one God, and Christ is one, and there is one Church, and one chair founded upon the rock by the word of the Lord.[2] Another altar cannot be constituted nor a new priesthood be made, except the one altar and the one priesthood. Whosoever gathereth elsewhere, scattereth. Whatsoever is appointed by human madness, so that the divine disposition is violated, is adulterous, is impious, is sacrilegious. Depart far from the contagion of men of this kind, and flee from their words, avoiding them as a cancer and a plague, as the Lord warns you and says, "They are blind leaders of the blind. But if the blind lead the blind, they shall both fall into the ditch."[3] They intercept your prayers, which you pour forth with us to God day and night, to appease Him with a righteous satisfaction. They intercept your tears with which you wash away the guilt of the sin you have committed; they intercept the peace which you truly and faithfully ask from the mercy of the Lord; and they do not know that it is written, "And that prophet, or that dreamer of dreams, that hath spoken to turn you away from the Lord your God, shall be put to death."[4] Let no one, beloved brethren, make you to err from the ways of the Lord; let no one snatch you, Christians, from the Gospel of Christ; let no one take sons of the Church away from the Church; let them perish alone for themselves who have wished to perish; let them remain outside the Church alone who have departed from the Church; let them alone be without bishops who have rebelled against bishops; let them alone undergo the penalties of their conspiracies who formerly, according to your votes, and now according to God's judgment, have deserved to undergo the sentence of their own conspiracy and malignity.

6. The Lord warns us in His Gospel, saying, "Ye reject the commandment of God, that ye may establish your own tradition."[5] Let them who reject the commandment of God and endeavour to keep their own tradition be bravely and firmly rejected by you; let one downfall be sufficient for the lapsed; let no one by his fraud hurl down those who wish to rise; let no one cast down more deeply and depress those who are down, on whose behalf we pray that they may be raised up by God's hand and arm; let no one turn away from all hope of safety those who are half alive and entreating that they may receive their former health; let no one extinguish every light of the way of salvation to those that are wavering in the darkness of their lapse. The apostle instructs us, saying, "If any man teach otherwise, and consent not to the wholesome words of our Lord Jesus Christ and His doctrine, he is lifted up with foolishness: from such withdraw thyself."[6] And again he says, "Let no man deceive you with vain words; for because of these things cometh the wrath of God upon the children of disobedience. Be not ye therefore partakers with them."[7] There is no reason that you should be deceived with vain words, and begin to be partakers of their depravity. Depart from such, I entreat you, and acquiesce in our counsels, who daily pour out for you continual prayers to the Lord, who desire that you should be recalled to the Church by the clemency of the Lord, who pray for the fullest peace from God, first for the mother, and then for her children. Join also your petitions and prayers with our prayers and petitions; mingle your tears with our wailings. Avoid the wolves who separate the sheep from the shepherd; avoid the envenomed tongue of the devil, who from the beginning of the world, always deceitful and lying, lies that he may deceive, cajoles that he may injure, promises good that he may give evil, promises life that he may put to death. Now also his words are evident, and his poisons are plain. He promises peace, in order that peace may not possibly be attained; he promises salvation, that he who has sinned may not come to salvation; he promises a Church, when he so contrives that he who believes him may utterly perish apart from the Church.

7. It is now the occasion, dearly beloved brethren, both for you who stand fast to persevere bravely, and to maintain your glorious stability, which you kept in persecution with a continual firmness.; and if any of you by the circumvention of the adversary have fallen, that in this second temptation you should faithfully take counsel for your hope and your peace; and in order that the Lord may pardon you, that you should not depart from the priests of the Lord, since it is written, "And the man that will do presumptuously, and will not hearken unto the

---

[1] Jer. xxiii. 16, 17.
[2] [See *Treatise on Unity.* Cyprian considers the universal episcopate as one *cathedra*, like "Moses' seat" in the Church of the Hebrews. This one chair he calls "Peter's chair."]
[3] Matt. xv. 14.
[4] Deut. xiii. 5.
[5] Mark vii. 9.

[6] 1 Tim. vi. 3–5.
[7] Eph. v. 6, 7.

priest or unto the judge that shall be in those days, even that man shall die." [1] Of this persecution this is the latest and final temptation, which itself also, by the Lord's protection, shall quickly pass away; so that I shall be again presented to you after Easter-day with my colleagues, who, being present, we shall be able as well to arrange as to complete the matters which require to be done according to your judgment and to the general advice of all of us as it has been decided before.[2] But if anybody, refusing to repent and to make satisfaction to God, shall yield to the party of Felicissimus and his satellites, and shall join himself to the heretical faction, let him know that he cannot afterwards return to the Church and communicate with the bishops and the people of Christ. I bid you, dearest brethren, ever heartily farewell, and that you plead with me in continual prayer that the mercy of God may be entreated.

EPISTLE XL.[3]

TO CORNELIUS, ON HIS REFUSAL TO RECEIVE NOVATIAN'S ORDINATION.[4]

ARGUMENT. — THE MESSENGERS SENT BY NOVATIAN TO INTIMATE HIS ORDINATION TO THE CHURCH OF CARTHAGE ARE REJECTED BY CYPRIAN.

1. Cyprian to Cornelius, his brother, greeting. There have come to us, beloved brother, sent by Novatian, Maximus the presbyter, and Augendus the deacon, and a certain Machæus and Longinus. But, as we discovered, as well from the letters which they brought with them, as from their discourse and declaration, that Novatian had been made bishop; disturbed by the wickedness of an unlawful ordination made in opposition to the Catholic Church, we considered at once that they must be restrained from communion with us; and having, in the meanwhile, refuted and repelled the things which they pertinaciously and obstinately endeavoured to assert, I and several of my colleagues, who had come together to me, were awaiting the arrival of our colleagues Caldonius and Fortunatus, whom we had lately sent to you as ambassadors, and to our fellow-bishops, who were present at your ordination,[5] in order that, when they came and reported the truth of the matter, the wickedness of the adverse party might be quelled through them, by greater authority and manifest proof. But there came, in addition, Pompeius and Stephanus, our colleagues, who themselves also,

by way of instructing us thereon, put forward manifest proofs and testimonies in conformity with their gravity and faithfulness, so that it was not even necessary that those who had come, as sent by Novatian, should be heard any further. And when in our solemn assembly[6] they burst in with invidious abuse and turbulent clamour, demanding that the accusations, which they said that they brought and would prove, should be publicly investigated by us and by the people, we said that it was not consistent with our gravity to suffer the honour of our colleague, who had already been chosen and ordained and approved by the laudable sentence of many, to be called into question any further by the abusive voice of rivals. And because it would be a long business to collect into a letter the matters in which they have been refuted and repressed, and in which they have been manifested as having caused heresy by their unlawful attempts, you shall hear everything most fully from Primitivus our co-presbyter,[7] when he shall come to you.

2. And lest their raging boldness should ever cease, they are striving here also to distract the members of Christ into schismatical parties, and to cut and tear the one body of the Catholic Church, so that, running about from door to door, through the houses of many, or from city to city, through certain districts, they seek for companions in their obstinacy and error to join to themselves in their schism. To whom we have once given this reply, nor shall we cease to command them to lay aside their pernicious dissensions and disputes, and to be aware that it is an impiety to forsake their Mother; and to acknowledge and understand that when a bishop[8] is once made and approved by the testimony and judgment of his colleagues and the people, another can by no means be appointed.[9] Thus, if they consult their own interest peaceably and faithfully, if they confess themselves to be maintainers of the Gospel of Christ, they must return to the Church. I bid you, dearest brother, ever heartily farewell.

EPISTLE XLI.[10]

TO CORNELIUS, ABOUT CYPRIAN'S APPROVAL OF HIS ORDINATION, AND CONCERNING FELICISSIMUS.

ARGUMENT. — CYPRIAN EXCUSES HIMSELF FOR NOT HAVING WITHOUT HESITATION BELIEVED IN THE ORDINATION OF CORNELIUS, UNTIL HE RECEIVED THE LETTERS OF HIS COLLEAGUES CALDONIUS

---

[1] Deut. xvii. 12.
[2] [The high official tone with which Cyprian upholds his own authority is always balanced by equal zeal for the presbyters and the laity. On which Compare Hooker, *Polity*, book viii. cap. vi. 8.]
[3] Oxford ed.: Ep. xliv. A.D 251.
[4] [Cornelius has succeeded to the *cathedra* in Rome. Here opens a new chapter in the history of Cyprian and of the Roman See.]
[5] [*Ordination* to the episcopate was the term used. *Consecration* is the inferior term now usual in Western Christendom. Elucidation VIII.]

[6] " In statione," " stationary assembly;" these being the Wednesdays and Fridays in each week (Marshall). [See vol. i. p. 33.]
[7] [Note the free use of this phrase by Cyprian This also to the Bishop of Rome.]
[8] [Nothing of a " universal bishop" is intimated or heard of. The election is that of a bishop like any other bishop.]
[9] [Here note, that the episcopate of Rome is in no otherwise regulated or regarded than that of any other See.]
[10] Oxford ed.: Ep. xlv. A.D. 251.

AND FORTUNATUS, WHICH FULLY TESTIFIED TO ITS LEGITIMACY ; AND INCIDENTALLY REPEATS, IN RESPECT OF THE CONTRARY FACTION OF THE NOVATIAN PARTY, THAT HE DID NOT IN THE VERY FIRST INSTANCE GIVE HIS ADHESION TO THAT, BUT RATHER TO CORNELIUS, EVEN TO THE EXTENT OF REFUSING TO RECEIVE ACCU- SATIONS AGAINST HIM.

1. Cyprian to Cornelius his brother, greeting. As was fitting for God's servants, and especially for upright and peaceable priests, dearest brother, we recently sent our colleagues Caldonius and Fortunatus, that they might, not only by the per- suasion of our letters, but by their presence and the advice of all of you, strive and labour with all their power to bring the members of the divided body into the unity of the Catholic Church, and associate them into the bond of Christian charity. But since the obstinate and inflexible pertinacity of the adverse party has not only rejected the bosom and the embrace of its root and Mother, but even, with a discord spreading and reviving itself worse and worse, has appointed a bishop for itself, and, contrary to the sacrament once delivered of the divine appointment and of Cath- olic Unity, has made an adulterous and opposed head outside the Church ; having received your letters as well as those of our colleagues, at the coming also of our colleagues Pompeius and Stephanus, good men and very dear to us, by whom all these things were undoubtedly alleged and proved to us with general gladness,[1] in con- formity with the requirements alike of the sanc- tity and the truth of the divine tradition and ecclesiastical institution, we have directed our letters to you. Moreover, bringing these same things under the notice of our several colleagues throughout the province, we have bidden also that our brethren, with letters from them, be directed to you.

2. *This has been done,* although our mind and intention had been already plainly declared to the brethren, and to the whole of the people in this place, when, having received letters lately from both parties, we read your letters, and intimated your ordination to the episcopate, in the ears of every one. Moreover, remembering the com- mon honour, and having respect for the sacerdo- tal gravity and sanctity, we repudiated those things which from the other party had been heaped together with bitter virulence into a document transmitted to us ; alike considering and weighing, that in so great and so religious an assembly of brethren, in which God's priests were sitting together, and His altar was set, they ought neither to be read nor to be heard. For those things should not easily be put forward, nor

carelessly and rudely published, which may move a scandal by means of a quarrelsome pen in the minds of the hearers, and confuse brethren, who are placed far apart and dwelling across the sea, with uncertain opinions. Let those beware, who, obeying either their own rage or lust, and unmind- ful of the divine law and holiness, rejoice to throw abroad in the meantime things which they can- not prove ; and although they may not be suc- cessful in destroying and ruining innocence, are satisfied with scattering stains upon it with lying reports and false rumours. Assuredly, we should exert ourselves, as it is fitting for prelates and priests to do, that such things, when they are written by any, should be repudiated as far as we are concerned. For otherwise, what will become of that which we learn and which we declare to be laid down in Scripture : "Keep thy tongue from evil, and thy lips from speak- ing guile?"[2] And elsewhere : "Thy mouth abounded in malice, and thy tongue embraced deceit. Thou satest and spakest against thy brother, and slanderedst thine own mother's son."[3] Also what the apostle says : "Let no corrupt communication proceed from thy mouth, but that which is good to the edifying of faith, that it may minister grace unto the hearers."[4] Further, we show what the right course of con- duct to pursue is,[5] if, when such things are writ- ten by the calumnious temerity of some, we do not allow them to be read among us ; and there- fore, dearest brother, when such letters came to me against you, even though they were the let- ters of your co-presbyter sitting with you,[6] as they breathed a tone of religious simplicity, and did not echo with any barkings of curses and re- vilings, I ordered them to be read to the clergy and the people.

3. But in desiring letters from our colleagues,[7] who were present at your ordination at that place, we did not forget the ancient usage, nor did we seek for any novelty. For it was sufficient for you to announce yourself by letters[8] to have been made bishop, unless there had been a dissenting faction on the other side, who by their slander- ous and calumnious fabrications disturbed the minds and perplexed the hearts of our colleagues, as well as of several of the brethren. To set this matter at rest, we judged it necessary to obtain thence the strong and decided authority of our colleagues who wrote to us ; and they, declaring

---

1 The Oxford edition follows some authorities in reading this "sadness" rather than "gladness."

2 Ps. xxxiv. 13.
3 Ps. l. 19, 20.
4 Eph. iv. 29.
5 Lit. : "that these things ought to be done."
6 The co-presbyter here spoken of is Novatian. The Oxford text reads, "When such writings came to me concerning you and your co-presbyters sitting with you, as had the true ring of religious sim- plicity in them." There is a variety of readings. [But think of a modern "Pope" thus addressed about a "co-presbyter."]
7 [Cyprian, however, respectfully demands the canonical evi- dences from his brother Cornelius.]
8 [Every bishop thus announced his ordination.]

the testimony of their letters to be fully deserved by your character, and life, and teaching, have deprived even your rivals, and those who delight either in novelty or evil, of every scruple of doubt or of difference ; and, according to our advice weighed in wholesome reason, the minds of the brethren tossing about in this sea have sincerely and decidedly approved your priesthood. For this, my brother, we especially both labour after, and ought to labour after, to be careful to maintain as much as we can the unity delivered by the Lord, and through His apostles to us their successors, and, as far as in us lies, to gather into the Church the dispersed and wandering sheep which the wilful faction and heretical temptation of some is separating from their Mother ; those only being left outside, who by their obstinacy and madness have persisted, and have been unwilling to return to us ; who themselves will have to give an account to the Lord of the dissension and separation made by them, and of the Church that they have forsaken.

4. But, so far as pertains to the cause of certain presbyters here, and of Felicissimus, that you may know what has been done here, our colleagues have sent you letters subscribed by their own hand, that you may learn, when you have heard the parties, from their letters what they have thought and what they have pronounced. But you will do better,[1] brother, if you will also bid copies of the letters which I had sent lately by our colleagues Caldonius and Fortunatus to you, to be read for the common satisfaction, which I had written concerning the same Felicissimus and his presbytery to the clergy there, and also to the people, to be read to the brethren there ; declaring your ordination, and the course of the whole transaction, that so as well there as here the brotherhood may be informed of all things by us. Moreover, I have here transmitted also copies of the same by Mettius the sub-deacon, sent by me, and by Nicephorus the acolyte. I bid you, dearest brother, ever heartily farewell.

EPISTLE XLII.[2]

TO THE SAME, ON HIS HAVING SENT LETTERS TO THE CONFESSORS WHOM NOVATIAN HAD SEDUCED.

ARGUMENT. — THE ARGUMENT OF THIS LETTER SUFFICIENTLY APPEARS FROM THE TITLE. IT IS MANIFEST THAT THIS LETTER AND THE FOLLOWING WERE SENT BY ONE MESSENGER.

Cyprian to Cornelius his brother, greeting. I have thought it both obligatory on me, and necessary for you, dearest brother, to write a short letter to the confessors who are there with you, and, seduced by the obstinacy and depravity of Novatian and Novatus,[3] have departed from the Church ; in which letter I might induce them, for the sake of our mutual affection, to return to their Mother, that is, to the Catholic Church. This letter I have first of all entrusted to you by Mettius the sub-deacon for your perusal, lest any one should pretend that I had written otherwise than according to the contents of my letter. I have, moreover, charged the same Mettius sent by me to you, that he should be guided by your decision ; and if you should think that this letter should be given to the confessors, then that he should deliver it. I bid you, dearest brother, ever heartily farewell.

EPISTLE XLIII.[4]

TO THE ROMAN CONFESSORS, THAT THEY SHOULD RETURN TO UNITY.

ARGUMENT. — HE EXHORTS THE ROMAN CONFESSORS WHO HAD BEEN SEDUCED BY THE FACTION OF NOVATIAN AND NOVATUS, TO RETURN TO UNITY.

Cyprian to Maximus and Nicostratus, and the other confessors, greeting. As you have frequently gathered from my letters, beloved, what honour I have ever observed in my mode of speaking for your confession, and what love for the associated brotherhood ; believe, I entreat you, and acquiesce in these my letters, wherein I both write and with simplicity and fidelity consult for you, and for your doings, and for your praise. For it weighs me down and saddens me, and the intolerable grief of a smitten, almost prostrate, spirit seizes me, when I find that you there, contrary to ecclesiastical order, contrary to evangelical law, contrary to the unity of the Catholic institution, had consented that another bishop should be made.[5] That is what is neither right nor allowable to be done ; that another church should be set up ; that Christ's members should be torn asunder ; that the one mind and body of the Lord's flock should be lacerated by a divided emulation. I entreat that in you, at all events, that unlawful rending of our brotherhood may not continue ; but remembering both your confession and the divine tradition, you may return to the Mother whence you have gone forth ; whence you came to the glory of confession with the rejoicing of the same Mother. And think not that you are thus maintaining the Gospel of Christ when you separate yourselves from the flock of Christ, and from His peace and

---

[1] [Had such instructions proceeded from the Roman See to Cyprian, what inferences would have been manufactured out of them by the mediæval writers.]

[2] Oxford ed.: Ep. xlvii. A.D. 251.

[3] [On the frequent confusion of these names see Wordsworth, *Hippol.*, p. 109.]

[4] Oxford ed.: Ep. xlvi. A.D. 251.

[5] ["Another bishop should be made." What would have been the outcry of the whole Church, and what the language of Cyprian, had any idea entered their minds that the case was that of the Divine Oracle of Christendom, the Vicar of Christ, the Centre of Unity, the Infallible, etc.]

concord; since it is more fitting for glorious and good soldiers to sit down within their own camp, and so placed within to manage and provide for those things which are to be dealt with in common. For as our unanimity and concord ought by no means to be divided, and because we cannot forsake the Church and go outside her to come to you, we beg and entreat you with what exhortations we can, rather to return to the Church your Mother, and to our brotherhood. I bid you, dearest brethren, ever heartily farewell.

EPISTLE XLIV.[1]

TO CORNELIUS, CONCERNING POLYCARP THE ADRUMETINE.

ARGUMENT. — HE EXCUSES HIMSELF IN THIS LETTER FOR WHAT HAD OCCURRED, IN THAT, DURING THE TIME THAT HE WAS AT ADRUMETUM, LETTERS HAD BEEN SENT THENCE BY THE CLERGY OF POLYCARP, NOT TO CORNELIUS, BUT TO THE ROMAN CLERGY, NOTWITHSTANDING THAT PREVIOUSLY POLYCARP HIMSELF HAD WRITTEN RATHER TO CORNELIUS. IT APPEARS TOLERABLY PLAIN FROM THE CONTEXT ITSELF THAT THIS WAS WRITTEN AFTER THE PRECEDING ONES.

1. Cyprian to Cornelius his brother, greeting. I have read your letters, dearest brother, which you sent by Primitivus our co-presbyter, in which I perceived that you were annoyed that, whereas letters from the Adrumetine colony in the name of Polycarp were directed to you, yet after Liberalis and I came to that place, letters began to be directed thence to the presbyters and to the deacons.

2. In respect of which I wish you to know, and certainly to believe, that it was done from no levity or contempt. But when several of our colleagues who had assembled into one place had determined that, while our co-bishops Caldonius and Fortunatus were sent as ambassadors to you, all things should be in the meantime suspended as they were, until the same colleagues of ours, having reduced matters there to peace, or, having discovered their truth, should return to us; the presbyters and deacons abiding in the Adrumetine colony; in the absence of our co-bishop Polycarp, were ignorant of what had been decided in common by us. But when we came before them, and our purpose was understood, they themselves also began to observe what the others did, so that the agreement of the churches abiding there was in no respect broken.

3. Some persons, however, sometimes disturb men's minds and spirits by their words, in that they relate things otherwise than is the truth. For we, who furnish every person who sails hence with a plan that they may sail without any offence, know that we have exhorted them to

acknowledge and hold the root and *matrix* of the Catholic Church.[2] But since our province is wide-spread, and has Numidia and Mauritania attached to it; lest a schism made in the city should confuse the minds of the absent with uncertain opinions, we decided — having obtained by means of the bishops the truth of the matter, and having got a greater authority for the proof of your ordination, and so at length every scruple being got rid of from the breast of every one — that letters should be sent you by all who were placed anywhere in the province; as in fact is done, that so the whole of our colleagues might decidedly approve of and maintain both you and your communion, that is as well to the unity of the Catholic Church as to its charity. That all which has by God's direction come to pass, and that our design has under Providence been forwarded, we rejoice.

4. For thus as well the truth as the dignity of your episcopate has been established in the most open light, and with the most manifest and substantial approval; so that from the replies of our colleagues, who have thence written to us, and from the account and from the testimonies of our co-bishops Pompeius, and Stephanus, and Caldonius, and Fortunatus, both the needful cause and the right order, and moreover the glorious innocence, of your ordination might be known by all. That we, with the rest of our colleagues, may steadily and firmly administer this office, and keep it in the concordant unanimity of the Catholic Church, the divine condescension will accomplish; so that the Lord who condescends to elect and appoint for Himself priests in His Church, may protect them also when elected and appointed by His good-will and help, inspiring them to govern, and supplying both vigour for restraining the contumacy of the wicked, and gentleness for cherishing the penitence of the lapsed. I bid you, dearest brother, ever heartily farewell.

EPISTLE XLV.[3]

CORNELIUS TO CYPRIAN, ON THE RETURN OF THE CONFESSORS TO UNITY.

ARGUMENT. — CORNELIUS INFORMS CYPRIAN OF THE SOLEMN RETURN OF THE CONFESSORS TO THE CHURCH, AND DESCRIBES IT.

1. Cornelius to Cyprian his brother, greeting. In proportion to the solicitude and anxiety that we sustained in respect of those confessors who had been circumvented and almost deceived and alienated from the Church by the craft and malice of that wily and subtle man,[4] was the joy

---

[1] Oxford ed.: Ep. xlviii. A.D. 251.

[2] [This refers to the episcopate. They had taken letters only to "presbyters and deacons." Or to Christ the root, and the Church the womb or matrix. See *infra*, Letter xlviii. p. 325.

[3] Oxford ed.: Ep. xlix. A.D. 251.

[4] Novatian.

with which we were affected, and the thanks which we gave to Almighty God and to our Lord Christ, when they, acknowledging their error, and perceiving the poisoned cunning of the malignant man, as if of a serpent, came back, as they with one heart profess, with singleness of will to the Church from which they had gone forth. And first, indeed, our brethren of approved faith, loving peace and desiring unity, announced that the swelling pride of these men was already soothed;[1] yet there was no fitting assurance to induce us easily to believe that they were thoroughly changed. But afterwards, Urbanus and Sidonius the confessors came to our presbyters, affirming that Maximus the confessor and presbyter, equally with themselves, desired to return into the Church; but since many things had preceded this which they had contrived, of which you also have been made aware from our co-bishops and from my letters, so that faith could not hastily be reposed in them, we determined to hear from their own mouth and confession those things which they had sent by the messengers. And when they came, and were required by the presbyters to give an account of what they had done, and were charged with having very lately repeatedly sent letters full of calumnies and reproaches, in their name, through all the churches, and had disturbed nearly all the churches; they affirmed that they had been deceived, and that they had not known what was in those letters; that only through being misled they had also committed schismatical acts, and been the authors of heresy, so that they suffered hands to be imposed on him as if upon a bishop.[2] And when these and other matters had been charged upon them, they entreated that they might be done away and altogether discharged from memory.

2. The whole of this transaction therefore being brought before me, I decided that the presbytery[3] should be brought together; (for there were present five bishops, who were also present to-day;) so that by well-grounded counsel it might be determined with the consent of all what ought to be observed in respect of their persons. And that you may know the feeling of all, and the advice of each one, I decided also to bring to your knowledge our various opinions, which you will read subjoined. When these things were done, Maximus, Urbanus, Sidonius, and several brethren who had joined themselves to them, came to the presbytery, desiring with earnest prayers that what had been done before might fall into oblivion, and no mention might be made of it; and *promising* that henceforth, as though nothing had been either done or said, all things on both sides being forgiven, they would now exhibit to God a heart clean and pure, following the evangelical word which says, "Blessed are the pure in heart, for they shall see God."[4] What remained was, that the people should be informed of all this proceeding, that they might see those very men established in the Church whom they had long seen and mourned as wanderers and scattered. Their will being known, a great concourse of the brotherhood was assembled. There was one voice from all, giving thanks to God; all were expressing the joy of their heart by tears, embracing them as if they had this day been set free from the penalty of the dungeon. And to quote their very own words, — "We," they say, "know that Cornelius is bishop of the most holy Catholic Church elected by Almighty God, and by Christ our Lord. We confess our error; we have suffered imposture; we were deceived by captious perfidy and loquacity. For although we seemed, as it were, to have held a kind of communion with a man who was a schismatic and a heretic, yet our mind was always sincere in the Church. For we are not ignorant that there is one God; that there is one Christ the Lord whom we have confessed, and one Holy Spirit; and that in the Catholic Church there ought to be one bishop."[5] Were we not rightly induced by that confession of theirs,[6] to allow that what they had confessed before the power of the world might approve when established in the Church? Wherefore we bade Maximus the presbyter to take his own place; the rest we received with great approbation of the people. But we remitted all things to Almighty God, in whose power all things are reserved.

3. These things therefore, brother, written to you in the same hour, at the same moment, we have transmitted; and I have sent away at once Nicephorus the acolyte, hastening to descend to embarkation, that so, no delay being made, you might, as if you had been present among that clergy and in that assembly of people, give thanks to Almighty God and to Christ our Lord. But we believe — nay, we confide in it for certain — that the others also who have been ranged in this error will shortly return into the Church when they see their leaders acting with us. I think, brother, that you ought to send these letters also to the other churches, that all may know that the craft and prevarication of this schismatic and heretic are from day to day being reduced to nothing. Farewell, dearest brother.

---

1 Baluz.: "Announced the swelling pride of some, the softened temper of others."

2 [i.e., for episcopal ordination and consecration.]

3 [See Ep. xvii. p. 296, *supra*.]

4 Matt. v. 8.

5 [*Episcopatus unus est.* One bishop, i e., one episcopate. See the note, Oxford translation of this letter, p. 108, and Cyprian's theory of the same in his *Treatise on Unity.*]

6 Baluzius reads, without authority: "Who would not be moved by that profession of theirs," etc.

EPISTLE XLVI.[1]

CYPRIAN'S ANSWER TO CORNELIUS, CONGRATULATING HIM ON THE RETURN OF THE CONFESSORS FROM SCHISM.

ARGUMENT. — HE CONGRATULATES HIM ON THE RETURN OF THE CONFESSORS TO THE CHURCH, AND REMINDS HIM HOW MUCH THAT RETURN BENEFITS THE CATHOLIC CHURCH.

1. Cyprian to Cornelius his brother, greeting. I profess that I both have rendered and do render the greatest thanks without ceasing, dearest brother, to God the Father Almighty, and to His Christ the Lord and our God and Saviour, that the Church is thus divinely protected, and its unity and holiness is not constantly nor altogether corrupted by the obstinacy of perfidy and heretical wickedness. For we have read your letter, and have exultingly received the greatest joy from *the fulfilment of* our common desire ; to wit, that Maximus the presbyter, and Urbanus, the confessors, with Sidonius and Macarius, have re-entered into the Catholic Church, that is, that they have laid aside their error, and given up their schismatical, nay, their heretical madness, and have sought again in the soundness of faith the home of unity and truth ; that whence they had gone forth to glory, thither they might gloriously return ; and that they who had confessed Christ should not afterwards desert the camp of Christ, and that they might not tempt the faith of their charity and unity,[2] who had not been overcome in strength and courage. Behold the safe and unspotted integrity of their praise ; behold the uncorrupted and substantial dignity of these confessors, that they have departed from the deserters and fugitives, that they have left the betrayers of the faith, and the impugners of the Catholic Church. With reason did both the people and the brotherhood receive them when they returned, as you write, with the greatest joy ; since in the glory of confessors who had maintained their glory, and returned to unity, there is none who does not reckon himself a partner and a sharer.

2. We can estimate the joy of that day[3] from our own feelings. For if, in this place, the whole number of the brethren rejoiced at your letter which you sent concerning their confession, and received this tidings of common rejoicing with the greatest alacrity, what must have been the joy there when the matter itself, and the general gladness, was carried on under the eyes of all? For since the Lord in His Gospel says that there is the highest "joy in heaven over one sinner

that repenteth,"[4] how much greater is the joy in earth, no less than in heaven, over confessors who return with their glory and with praise to the Church of God, and make a way of returning for others by the faith and approval of their example? For this error had led away certain of our brethren, so that they thought they were following the communion of confessors. When this error was removed, light was infused into the breasts of all, and the Catholic Church has been shown to be one, and to be able neither to be cut nor divided. Nor can any one now be easily deceived by the talkative words of a raging schismatic, since it has been proved that good and glorious soldiers of Christ could not long be detained without the Church by the deceitfulness and perfidy of others. I bid you, dearest brother, ever heartily farewell.

EPISTLE XLVII.[5]

CORNELIUS TO CYPRIAN, CONCERNING THE FACTION OF NOVATIAN WITH HIS PARTY.

ARGUMENT. — CORNELIUS GIVES CYPRIAN AN ACCOUNT OF THE FACTION OF NOVATIAN.[6]

Cornelius to Cyprian his brother, greeting. That nothing might be wanting to the future punishment of this wretched man, when cast down by the powers of God, (on the expulsion by you of Maximus, and Longinus, and Machæus ;) he has risen again ; and, as I intimated in my former letter which I sent to you by Augendus the confessor, I think that Nicostratus, and Novatus, and Evaristus, and Primus, and Dionysius, have already come thither. Therefore let care be taken that it be made known to all our co-bishops and brethren, that Nicostratus is accused of many crimes, and that not only has he committed frauds and plunders on his secular patroness, whose affairs he managed ; but, moreover (which is reserved to him for a perpetual punishment), he has abstracted no small deposits of the Church ; that Evaristus has been the author of a schism ; and that Zetus has been appointed bishop in his room, and his successor to the people over whom he had previously presided. But he contrived greater and worse things by his malice and insatiable wickedness than those which he was then always practising among his own people ; so that you may know what kind of leaders and protectors that schismatic and heretic constantly had joined to his side. I bid you, dearest brother, ever heartily farewell.

---

[1] Oxford ed.: Ep. li. A.D. 251.
[2] Some read, " might not be tried by the faith of their charity and unity."
[3] Some old editions read, " of that thing."

[4] Luke xv. 7.
[5] Oxford ed.: Ep. l. A D. 251.
[6] [Oxford trans., p. 111. Elucidation VIII. and p. 319, *supra.*]

EPISTLE XLVIII.[1]

CYPRIAN'S ANSWER TO CORNELIUS, CONCERNING THE CRIMES OF NOVATUS.

ARGUMENT. — HE PRAISES CORNELIUS, THAT HE HAD GIVEN HIM TIMELY WARNING, SEEING THAT THE DAY AFTER THE GUILTY FACTION HAD COME TO HIM HE HAD RECEIVED CORNELIUS' LETTER. THEN HE DESCRIBES AT LENGTH NOVATUS' CRIMES, AND THE SCHISM THAT HAD BEFORE BEEN STIRRED UP BY HIM IN AFRICA.

1. Cyprian to Cornelius his brother, greeting. You have acted, dearest brother, both with diligence and love, in sending us in haste Nicephorus the acolyte, who both told us the glorious gladness concerning the return of the confessors, and most fully instructed us against the new and mischievous devices of Novatian and Novatus for attacking the Church of Christ. For whereas on the day before, that mischievous faction of heretical wickedness had arrived here, itself already lost and ready to ruin others who should join it, on the day after, Nicephorus arrived with your letter. From which we both learnt ourselves, and have begun to teach and to instruct others, that Evaristus from being a bishop has now not remained even a layman; but, banished from the see and from the people, and an exile from the Church of Christ, he roves about far and wide through other provinces, and, himself having made shipwreck of truth and faith, is preparing for some who are like him, as fearful shipwrecks. Moreover, that Nicostratus, having lost the diaconate of sacred administrations, because he had abstracted the Church's money by a sacrilegious fraud, and disowned the deposits of the widows and orphans, did not wish so much to come into Africa as to escape thither from the city, from the consciousness of his rapines and his frightful crimes. And now a deserter and a fugitive from the Church, as if to have changed the clime were to change the man, he goes on to boast and announce himself a confessor, although *he* can no longer either be or be called a confessor of Christ who has denied Christ's Church. For when the Apostle Paul says, " For this cause shall a man leave his father and mother, and shall cleave unto his wife; and they two shall be one flesh. This is a great mystery; but I speak concerning Christ and the Church; "[2] — when, I say, the blessed apostle says this, and with his sacred voice testifies to the unity of Christ with the Church, cleaving to one another with indivisible links, how can he be with Christ who is not with the spouse of Christ, and in His Church?[3] Or how does he assume to himself the charge of ruling or governing the Church, who has spoiled and wronged the Church of Christ?

2. For about Novatus there need have been nothing told by you to us, since Novatus ought rather to have been shown by us to you, as always greedy of novelty, raging with the rapacity of an insatiable avarice, inflated with the arrogance and stupidity of swelling pride; always known with bad repute to the bishops there; always condemned by the voice of all the priests as a heretic and a perfidious man; always inquisitive, that he may betray: he flatters for the purpose of deceiving, never faithful that he may love; a torch and fire to blow up the flames of sedition; a whirlwind and tempest to make shipwrecks of the faith; the foe of quiet, the adversary of tranquillity, the enemy of peace. Finally, when Novatus withdrew thence from among you, that is, when the storm and the whirlwind departed, calm arose there in part, and the glorious and good confessors who by his instigation had departed from the Church, after he retired from the city, returned to the Church. This is the same Novatus who first sowed among us the flames of discord and schism; who separated some of the brethren here from the bishop; who, in the persecution itself, was to our people, as it were, another persecution, to overthrow the minds of the brethren. He it is who, without my leave or knowledge, of his own factiousness and ambition appointed his attendant Felicissimus a deacon, and with his own tempest sailing also to Rome to overthrow the Church, endeavoured to do similar and equal things there, forcibly separating a part of the people from the clergy, and dividing the concord of the fraternity that was firmly knit together and mutually loving one another. Since Rome from her greatness plainly ought to take precedence of Carthage, he there committed still greater and graver crimes.[4] He who in the one place had made a deacon contrary to the Church, in the other made a bishop. Nor let any one be surprised at this in such men. The wicked are always madly carried away by their own furious passions; and after they have committed crimes, they are agitated by the very consciousness of a depraved mind. Neither can those remain in God's Church, who have not maintained its divine and ecclesiastical discipline, either in the conversation of their life or the peace of their character. Orphans despoiled by him, widows defrauded, moneys moreover of the Church withheld, exact from him those penalties which we behold inflicted in his madness. His father also died of hunger in the street, and afterwards even

---

[1] Oxford ed.: Ep. lii. A.D. 251.
[2] Eph. v. 31, 32.
[3] [See letter xliv. p. 322, *supra*.]

[4] [" From her greatness: " he does not even mention her dignity as the one and only apostolic see of Western Christendom. And this is the case in subsequent action of the Great Councils. Rome, though not *the* root, was yet a " root and *matrix*."]

in death was not buried by him. The womb of his wife was smitten by a blow of his heel; and in the miscarriage that soon followed, the offspring was brought forth, the fruit of a father's murder. And now does he dare to condemn the hands of those who sacrifice, when he himself is more guilty in his feet, by which the son, who was about to be born, was slain?

3. He long ago feared this consciousness of crime. On account of this he regarded it as certain that he would not only be turned out of the presbytery, but restrained from communion; and by the urgency of the brethren, the day of investigation was coming on, on which his cause was to be dealt with before us, if the persecution had not prevented. He, welcoming this, with a sort of desire of escaping and evading condemnation, committed all these crimes, and wrought all this stir; so that he who was to be ejected and excluded from the Church, anticipated the judgment of the priests by a voluntary departure, as if to have anticipated the sentence were to have escaped the punishment.

4. But in respect to the other brethren, over whom we grieve that they were circumvented by him, we labour that they may avoid the mischievous neighbourhood of the crafty impostor, that they may escape the deadly nets of his solicitations, that they may once more seek the Church from which he deserved by divine authority to be expelled. Such indeed, with the Lord's help, we trust may return by His mercy, for one cannot perish unless it is plain that he must perish, since the Lord in His Gospel says, "Every planting which my heavenly Father hath not planted shall be rooted up."[1] He alone who has not been planted in the precepts and warnings of God the Father, can depart from the Church: he alone can forsake the bishops[2] and abide in his madness with schismatics and heretics. But the mercy of God the Father, and the indulgence of Christ our Lord, and our own patience, will unite the rest with us. I bid you, dearest brother, ever heartily farewell.

EPISTLE XLIX.[3]

MAXIMUS AND THE OTHER CONFESSORS TO CYPRIAN, ABOUT THEIR RETURN FROM SCHISM.

ARGUMENT. — THEY INFORM CYPRIAN THAT THEY HAD RETURNED TO THE CHURCH.

Maximus, Urbanus, Sidonius, and Macharius, to Cyprian their brother, greeting. We are certain, dearest brother, that you also rejoice together with us with equal earnestness, that we having taken advice, and especially, considering the interests and the peace of the Church, having passed by all other matters, and reserved them to God's judgment, have made peace with Cornelius our bishop, as well as with the whole clergy.[4] You ought most certainly to know from these our letters that this was done with the joy of the whole Church, and even with the forward affection of the brethren. We pray, dearest brother, that for many years you may fare well.

EPISTLE L.[5]

FROM CYPRIAN TO THE CONFESSORS, CONGRATULATING THEM ON THEIR RETURN FROM SCHISM.

ARGUMENT. — CYPRIAN CONGRATULATES THE ROMAN CONFESSORS ON THEIR RETURN INTO THE CHURCH, AND REPLIES TO THEIR LETTERS.

1. Cyprian to Maximus the presbyter, also to Urbanus, and Sidonius, and Macharius, his brethren, greeting. When I read your letters, dearest brethren, that you wrote to me about your return, and about the peace of the Church, and the brotherly restoration, I confess that I was as greatly overjoyed as I had before been overjoyed when I learnt the glory of your confession, and thankfully received tidings of the heavenly and spiritual renown of your warfare. For this, moreover, is another confession of your faith and praise; to confess that the Church is one, and not to become a sharer in other men's error, or rather wickedness; to seek anew the same camp whence you went forth, whence with the most vigorous strength you leapt forth to wage the battle and to subdue the adversary. For the trophies from the battle-field ought to be brought back thither whence the arms for the field had been received, lest the Church of Christ should not retain those same glorious warriors whom Christ had furnished for glory. Now, however, you have kept in the peace of the Lord the fitting tenor of your faith and the law of undivided charity and concord, and have given by your walk an example of love and peace to others; so that the truth of the Church, and the unity of the Gospel mystery which is held by us, are also linked together by your consent and bond; and confessors of Christ do not become the leaders of error, after having stood forth as praiseworthy originators of virtue and honour.

2. Let others consider how much they may congratulate you, or how much each one may glory for himself: I confess that I congratulate you more, and I more boast of you to others, in respect of this your peaceful return and charity. For you ought in simplicity to hear what was

---

[1] Matt. xv. 13.
[2] [Cyprian's idea of unity as expounded in his treatise, *infra*.]
[3] Oxford ed.: Ep. liii. A.D. 251.

[4] [The language of this letter clearly demonstrates the primitive condition of the Roman clergy and their bishop, and their entire unconsciousness of any exceptional position in their estate or relations to other churches. "Our bishop" — not *Urbis et Orbis papa*.]
[5] Oxford ed.: Ep. liv. A.D. 252.

in my heart. I grieved vehemently, and I was greatly afflicted, that I could not hold communion with those whom once I had begun to love. After the schismatical and heretical error laid hold of you, on your going forth from prison, it seemed as if your glory had been left in the dungeon. For there the dignity of your name seemed to have stayed behind when the soldiers of Christ did not return from the prison to the Church, although they had gone into the prison with the praise and congratulations of the Church.

3. For although there seem to be tares in the Church, yet neither our faith nor our charity ought to be hindered, so that because we see that there are tares in the Church we ourselves should withdraw from the Church: we ought only to labour that we may be wheat, that when the wheat shall begin to be gathered into the Lord's barns, we may receive fruit for our labour and work. The apostle in his epistle says, " In a great house there are not only vessels of gold and silver, but also of wood and of earth, and some to honour and some to dishonour." [1] Let us strive, dearest brethren, and labour as much as we possibly can, that we may be vessels of gold or silver. But to the Lord alone it is granted to break the vessels of earth, to whom also is given the rod of iron. The servant cannot be greater than his lord, nor may any one claim to himself what the Father has given to the Son alone, so as to think that he can take the fan for winnowing and purging the threshing-floor, or can separate by human judgment all the tares from the wheat. That is a proud obstinacy and a sacrilegious presumption which a depraved madness assumes to itself. And while some are always assuming to themselves more dominion than meek justice demands, they perish from the Church ; and while they insolently extol themselves, blinded by their own swelling, they lose the light of truth. For which reason we also, keeping moderation, and considering the Lord's balances, and thinking of the love and mercy of God the Father, have long and carefully pondered with ourselves, and have weighed what was to be done with due moderation.

4. All which matters you can look into thoroughly, if you will read the tracts [2] which I have lately read here, and have, for the sake of our mutual love, transmitted to you also for you to read ; wherein there is neither wanting for the lapsed, censure which may rebuke, nor medicine which may heal. Moreover, my feeble ability has expressed as well as it could the unity of the Catholic Church. [3] Which treatise I now more

and more trust will be pleasing to you, since you now read it in such a way as both to approve and love it ; inasmuch as what we have written in words you fulfil in deeds, when you return to the Church in the unity of charity and peace. I bid you, dearest brethren, and greatly longed-for, ever heartily farewell.

EPISTLE LI.[4]

TO ANTONIANUS ABOUT CORNELIUS AND NOVATIAN.

ARGUMENT. — WHEN ANTONIANUS, HAVING RECEIVED LETTERS FROM NOVATIAN, HAD BEGUN TO BE DISPOSED IN HIS MIND TOWARDS HIS PARTY, CYPRIAN CONFIRMS HIM IN HIS FORMER OPINION, NAMELY, THAT OF CONTINUING TO HOLD COMMUNION WITH HIS BISHOP AND SO WITH THE CATHOLIC CHURCH. HE EXCUSES HIMSELF FOR HIS OWN CHANGE OF OPINION IN RESPECT OF THE LAPSED, AND AT THE END HE EXPLAINS WHEREIN CONSISTS THE NOVATIAN HERESY.[5]

1. Cyprian to Antonianus his brother, greeting. I received your first letters, dearest brother, firmly maintaining the concord of the priestly college, and adhering to the Catholic Church, in which you intimated that you did not hold communion with Novatian, but followed my advice, and held one common agreement with Cornelius our co-bishop.[6] You wrote, moreover, for me to transmit a copy of those same letters to Cornelius our colleague, so that he might lay aside all anxiety, and know at once that you held communion with him, that is, with the Catholic Church.[7]

2. But subsequently there arrived other letters of yours sent by Quintus our co-presbyter, in which I observed that your mind, influenced by the letters of Novatian, had begun to waver. For although previously you had settled your opinion and consent firmly, you desired in these letters that I should write to you once more what heresy Novatian had introduced, or on what grounds Cornelius holds communion with Trophimus and the sacrificers. In which matters, indeed, if you are anxiously careful, from solicitude for the faith, and are diligently seeking out the truth of a doubtful matter, the hesitating anxiety of a mind undecided in the fear of God, is not to be blamed.

3. Yet, as I see that after the first opinion expressed in your letter, you have been disturbed

---

[1] 2 Tim. ii. 20.
[2] [i.e., On Unity and On the Lapsers.]
[3] " Of the Unity of the Church." [And note, Cyprian innocently teaches these Roman clergy the principles of Catholic unity, without an idea that they were in a position to know much more on the subject than they could be taught by a bishop in Africa.]

[4] Oxford ed.: Ep. lv. A.D. 252.
[5] That he may induce him to this, he narrates the history of the whole disturbance between Cornelius and Novatian, and explains that Cornelius was an excellent man, and legitimately elected ; while Novatian was guilty of many crimes, and had obtained an unlawful election.
[6] [" Our co-bishop," — language which reflects our author's idea of Catholic communion. See his Treatise on Unity ; also p 329.]
[7] [His idea is, that to be in communion with the whole Church, one must be in fellowship with his own lawful bishop.]

subsequently by letters of Novatian, I assert this first of all, dearest brother, that grave men, and men who are once established upon the strong rock with solid firmness, are not moved, I say not with a light air, but even with a wind or a tempest, lest their mind, changeable and uncertain, be frequently agitated hither and thither by various opinions, as by gusts of wind rushing on them, and so be turned from its purpose with some reproach of levity. That the letters of Novatian may not do this with you, nor with any one, I will set before you, as you have desired, my brother, an account of the matter in few words. And first of all indeed, as you also seem troubled about what I too have done, I must clear my own person and cause in your eyes, lest any should think that I have lightly withdrawn from my purpose, and while at first and at the commencement I maintained evangelical vigour, yet subsequently I seem to have turned my mind from discipline and from its former severity of judgment, so as to think that those who have stained their conscience with certificates, or have offered abominable sacrifices, are to have peace made easy to them. Both of which things have been done by me, not without long-balanced and pondered reasons.

4. For when the battle was still going on, and the struggle of a glorious contest was raging in the persecution, the courage of the soldiers had to be excited with every exhortation, and with full urgency, and especially the minds of the lapsed had to be roused with the trumpet call, as it were, of my voice, that they might pursue the way of repentance, not only with prayers and lamentations; but, since an opportunity was given of repeating the struggle and of regaining salvation, that they might be reproved by my voice, and stimulated rather to the ardour of confession and the glory of martyrdom. Finally, when the presbyters and deacons had written to me about some persons, that they were without moderation and were eagerly pressing forward to receive communion; replying to them in my letter which is still in existence,[1] then I added also this: " If these are so excessively eager, they have what they require in their own power, the time itself providing for them more than they ask: the battle is still being carried on, and the struggle is daily celebrated: if they truly and substantially repent of what they have done, and the ardour of their faith prevails, he who cannot be delayed may be crowned." But I put off deciding what was to be arranged about the case of the lapsed, so that when quiet and tranquillity should be granted, and the divine indulgence should allow the bishops to assemble into one place, then the advice gathered from the com-

parison of all opinions being communicated and weighed, we might determine what was necessary to be done. But if any one, before our council,[2] and before the opinion decided upon by the advice of all, should rashly wish to communicate with the lapsed, he himself should be withheld from communion.

5. And this also I wrote very fully to Rome, to the clergy who were then still acting without a bishop, and to the confessors, Maximus the presbyter, and the rest who were then shut up in prison, but are now in the Church, joined with Cornelius. You may know that I wrote this from their reply, for in their letter they wrote thus: " However, what you have yourself also declared in so important a matter is satisfactory to us, that the peace of the Church must first be maintained; then, that an assembly for counsel being gathered together, with bishop, presbyters, deacons, and confessors, as well as with the laity who stand fast, we should deal with the case of the lapsed."[3] It was added also — Novatian then writing, and reciting with his own voice what he had written, and the presbyter Moyses, then still a confessor, but now a martyr, subscribing — that peace ought to be granted to the lapsed who were sick and at the point of departure. Which letter was sent throughout the whole world, and was brought to the knowledge of all the churches and all the brethren.[4]

6. According, however, to what had been before decided, when the persecution was quieted, and opportunity of meeting was afforded; a large number of bishops, whom their faith and the divine protection had preserved in soundness and safety, we met together; and the divine Scriptures being brought forward[5] on both sides, we balanced the decision with wholesome moderation, so that neither should hope of communion and peace be wholly denied to the lapsed, lest they should fail still more through desperation, and, because the Church was closed to them, should, like the world, live as heathens; nor yet, on the other hand, should the censure of the Gospel be relaxed, so that they might rashly rush to communion, but that repentance should be long protracted, and the paternal clemency be sorrowfully besought, and the cases, and the wishes, and the necessities of individuals be examined into, according to what is contained in a little book, which I trust has come to you, in which the several heads of our decisions are collected. And lest perchance the number of bishops in Africa should seem unsatisfactory, we also wrote to Rome, to Cornelius our colleague, concerning this thing, who himself

---

[1] Ep. xiii. 2.

[2] [The provincial council, clearly.]
[3] Ep. xxx. p. 310.
[4] [On principles of Catholic unity expounded in his Treatise.]
[5] [Note this appeal to Scripture always, as enthroned *infallibility*, insuring the presence of the *Spirit* of counsel.]

also holding a council with very many bishops, concurred in the same opinion as we had held, with equal gravity and wholesome moderation.[1]

7. Concerning which it has now become necessary to write to you, that you may know that I have done nothing lightly, but, according to what I had before comprised in my letters, had put off everything to the common determination of our council, and indeed communicated with no one of the lapsed as yet, so long as there still was an opening by which the lapsed might receive not only pardon, but also a crown. Yet afterwards, as the agreement of our college, and the advantage of gathering the fraternity together and of healing their wound required, I submitted to the necessity of the times, and thought that the safety of the many must be provided for; and I do not now recede from these things which have once been determined in our council by common agreement, although many things are ventilated by the voices of many, and lies against God's priests uttered from the devil's mouth, and tossed about everywhere, to the rupture of the concord of Catholic unity. But it behoves you, as a good brother and a fellow-priest like-minded, not easily to receive what malignants and apostates may say, but carefully to weigh what your colleagues, modest and grave men, may do, from an investigation of our life and teaching.

8. I come now, dearest brother, to the character of Cornelius our colleague, that with us you may more justly know Cornelius, not from the lies of malignants and detractors, but from the judgment of the Lord God, who made him a bishop, and from the testimony of his fellow-bishops, the whole number of whom has agreed with an absolute unanimity throughout the whole world. For, — a thing which with laudable announcement commends our dearest Cornelius to God and Christ, and to His Church, and also to all his fellow-priests, — he was not one who on a sudden attained to the episcopate; but, promoted through all the ecclesiastical offices, and having often deserved well of the Lord in divine administrations, he ascended by all the grades of religious service to the lofty summit of the Priesthood. Then, moreover, he did not either ask for the episcopate itself, nor did he wish it; nor, as others do when the swelling of their arrogance and pride inflates them, did he seize upon it;[2] but quiet otherwise, and meek, and such as those are accustomed to be who are chosen of God to this office, having regard to the modesty of his virgin continency, and the humility of his inborn and guarded veneration, he did not, as some do, use force to be made a

bishop, but he himself suffered compulsion, so as to be forced to receive the episcopal office. And he was made bishop by very many of our colleagues who were then present in the city of Rome, who sent to us letters concerning his ordination, honourable and laudatory, and remarkable for their testimony in announcement of him. Moreover, Cornelius was made bishop by the judgment of God and of His Christ, by the testimony of almost all the clergy, by the suffrage of the people who were then present, and by the assembly of ancient priests and good men, when no one had been made so before him, when the place of Fabian, that is, when the place of Peter[3] and the degree of the sacerdotal throne was vacant; which being occupied by the will of God, and established by the consent of all of us, whosoever now wishes to become a bishop, must needs be made from without; and he cannot have the ordination of the Church who does not hold the unity of the Church. Whoever he may be, although greatly boasting about himself, and claiming very much for himself, he is profane, he is an alien, he is without. And as after the first there cannot be a second, whosoever is made after one who ought to be alone, is not second to him, but is in fact none at all.

9. Then afterwards, when he had undertaken the episcopate, not obtained by solicitation nor by extortion, but by the will of God who makes priests; what a virtue there was in the very undertaking of his episcopate, what strength of mind, what firmness of faith, — a thing that we ought with simple heart both thoroughly to look into and to praise, — that he intrepidly sate at Rome in the sacerdotal chair at that time when a tyrant, odious to God's priests, was threatening things that can, and cannot be spoken, inasmuch as he would much more patiently and tolerantly hear that a rival prince was raised up against himself, than that a priest of God was established at Rome. Is not this man, dearest brother, to be commended with the highest testimony of virtue and faith? Is not he to be esteemed among the glorious confessors and martyrs, who for so long a time sate awaiting the manglers of his body and the avengers of a ferocious tyrant, who, when Cornelius resisted their deadly edicts, and trampled on their threats and sufferings and tortures by the vigour of his faith, would either rush upon him with the sword, or crucify him, or scorch him with fire, or rend his bowels and his limbs with some unheard-of kind of punishment? Even though the majesty and goodness of the protecting Lord guarded, when made, the priest whom He willed to be made; yet Cornelius, in what pertains to his devotion and fear, suffered[3] whatever he could

---

[1] [A most important reference to the true position of the Roman See. Elucidation IX.]

[2] [Novatian and his like.]

[3] [On the death of Fabian, see Ep. iii. p. 281; sufferings of Cornelius (inference), p. 303; Decius, p. 299.]

suffer, and conquered the tyrant first of all by his priestly office, who was afterwards conquered in arms and in war.

10. But in respect to certain discreditable and malignant things that are bandied about concerning him, I would not have you wonder, when you know that this is always the work of the devil, to wound God's servants with lies, and to defame a glorious name by false opinions, so that they who are bright in the light of their own conscience may be tarnished by the reports of others. Moreover, you are to know that our colleagues have investigated, and have certainly discovered that he has been blemished with no stain of a certificate, as some intimate ; neither has he mingled in sacrilegious communion with the bishops who have sacrificed, but has merely associated with us those whose cause had been heard, and whose innocence was approved.

11. For with respect to Trophimus also, of whom you wished tidings to be written to you, tne case is not as the report and the falsehood of malignant people had conveyed it to you. For, as our predecessors often did, our dearest brother, in bringing together the brethren, yielded to necessity ; and since a very large part of the people had withdrawn with Trophimus, now when Trophimus returned to the Church, and atoned for, and witn the penitence of prayer confessed, his former error, and with perfect humility and satisfaction recalled the brotherhood whom he had lately taken away, his prayers were heard ; and not only Trophimus, but a very great number of brethren who had been with Trophimus, were admitted into the Church of the Lord, who would not all have returned to the Church unless they had come in Trophimus' company. Therefore the matter being considered there with several colleagues,[1] Trophimus was received, for whom the return of the brethren and salvation restored to many made atonement. Yet Trophimus was admitted in such a manner as only to communicate as a layman, not, according to the information given to you by the letters of the malignants, in such a way as to assume the place of a priest.

12. But, moreover, in respect of what has been told you, that Cornelius communicates everywhere with those who have sacrificed, this intelligence has also arisen from the false reports of the apostates. For neither can they praise us who depart from us, nor ought we to expect to please them, who, while they displease us, and revolt against the Church, violently persist in soliciting brethren away from the Church. Wherefore, dearest brethren, do not with facility either hear or believe whatever is currently rumoured against Cornelius and about me.

13. For if any are seized with sicknesses, help is given to them in danger, as it has been decided. Yet after they have been assisted, and peace has been granted to them in their danger, they cannot be suffocated by us, or destroyed,[2] or by our force or hands urged on to the result of death ; as if, because peace is granted to the dying, it were necessary that those who have received peace should die ; although the token of divine love and paternal lenity appears more in this way, that they, who in peace given to them receive the pledge of life, are moreover here bound to life by the peace they have received. And therefore, if with peace received, a reprieve is given by God, no one ought to complain of the priests for this, when once it has been decided that brethren are to be aided in peril. Neither must you think, dearest brother, as some do, that those who receive certificates are to be put on a par with those who have sacrificed ; since even among those who have sacrificed, the condition and the case are frequently different. For we must not place on a level one who has at once leapt forward with good-will to the abominable sacrifice, and one who, after long struggle and resistance, has reached that fatal result under compulsion ; one who has betrayed both himself and all his connections, and one who, himself approaching the trial in behalf of all, has protected his wife and his children, and his whole family, by himself undergoing the danger ; one who has compelled his inmates or friends to the crime, and one who has spared inmates and servants, and has even received many brethren who were departing to banishment and flight, into his house and hospitality ; showing and offering to the Lord many souls living and safe to entreat for a single wounded one.

14. Since, then, there is much difference[3] between those who have sacrificed, what a want of mercy it is, and how bitter is the hardship, to associate those who have received certificates, with those who have sacrificed, when he by whom the certificate has been received may say, " I had previously read, and had been made aware by the discourse of the bishop,[4] that we must not sacrifice to idols, that the servant of God ought not to worship images ; and therefore, in order that I might not do this which was not lawful, when the opportunity of receiving a certificate was offered, which itself also I should not have received, unless the opportunity had been put before me, I either went or charged some other person going to the magistrate, to say that I am a Christian, that I am not allowed

---

[1] [Not by a mere decision, but by consent of " colleagues."]

[2] Opprimi.
[3] [Jude 22.]
[4] [*Episcopo tractante.* See Oxford trans., a valuable note, p. 124; also Vincent, *Common.*, cap. 28.]

to sacrifice, that I cannot come to the devil's altars, and that I pay a price for this purpose, that I may not do what is not lawful for me to do." Now, however, even he who is stained with having received a certificate, — after he has learnt from our admonitions that he ought not even to have done this, and that although his hand is pure, and no contact of deadly food has polluted his lips, yet his conscience is nevertheless polluted, weeps when he hears us, and laments, and is now admonished of the thing wherein he has sinned, and having been deceived, not so much by guilt as by error, bears witness that for another time he is instructed and prepared.

15. If we reject the repentance of those who have some confidence in a conscience that may be tolerated; at once with their wife, with their children, whom they had kept safe, they are hurried by the devil's invitation into heresy or schism; and it will be attributed to us in the day of judgment, that we have not cared for the wounded sheep,[1] and that on account of a single wounded one we have lost many sound ones. And whereas the Lord left the ninety and nine that were whole, and sought after the one wandering and weary, and Himself carried it, when found, upon His shoulders, we not only do not seek the lapsed, but even drive them away when they come to us; and while false prophets are not ceasing to lay waste and tear Christ's flock, we give an opportunity to dogs and wolves, so that those whom a hateful persecution has not destroyed, we ruin by our hardness and inhumanity. And what will become, dearest brother, of what the apostle says: "I please all men in all things, not seeking mine own profit, but the profit of many, that they may be saved. Be ye followers of me, as I also am of Christ."[2] And again: "To the weak I became as weak, that I might gain the weak."[3] And again: "Whether one member suffer, all the members suffer with it; or one member rejoice, all the members rejoice with it."[4]

16. The principle of the philosophers and stoics is different, dearest brother, who say that all sins are equal, and that a grave man ought not easily to be moved. But there is a wide difference between Christians and philosophers. And when the apostle says, "Beware, lest any man spoil you through philosophy and vain deceit,"[5] we are to avoid those things which do not come from God's clemency, but are begotten of the presumption of a too rigid philosophy. Concerning Moses, moreover, we find it said in the Scriptures, "Now the man Moses was very

meek;"[6] and the Lord in His Gospel says, "Be ye merciful, as your Father also had mercy upon you;"[7] and again, "They that be whole need not a physician, but they that are sick."[8] What medical skill can he exercise who says, "I cure the sound only, who have no need of a physician?" We ought to give our assistance, our healing art, to those who are wounded; neither let us think them dead, but rather let us regard them as lying half alive, whom we see to have been wounded in the fatal persecution, and who, if they had been altogether dead, would never from the same men become afterwards both confessors and martyrs.[9]

17. But since in them there is that, which, by subsequent repentance, may be strengthened into faith; and by repentance strength is armed to virtue, which could not be armed if one should fall away through despair; if, hardly and cruelly separated from the Church, he should turn himself to Gentile ways and to worldly works, or, if rejected by the Church, he should pass over to heretics and schismatics; where, although he should afterwards be put to death on account of the name, still, being placed outside the Church, and divided from unity and from charity, he could not in his death be crowned. And therefore it was decided, dearest brother, the case of each individual having been examined into, that the receivers of certificates should in the meantime be admitted, that those who had sacrificed should be assisted at death, because there is no confession in the place of the departed,[10] nor can any one be constrained by us to repentance, if the fruit of repentance be taken away. If the battle should come first, strengthened by us, he will be found ready armed for the battle; but if sickness should press hard upon him before the battle, he departs with the consolation of peace and communion.

18. Moreover, we do not prejudge when the Lord is to be the judge; save that if He shall find the repentance of the sinners full and sound, He will then ratify what shall have been here determined by us. If, however, any one should delude us with the pretence of repentance, God, who is not mocked, and who looks into man's heart, will judge of those things which we have imperfectly looked into, and the Lord will amend the sentence of His servants; while yet, dearest brother, we ought to remember that it is written, "A brother that helpeth a brother shall be exalted;"[11] and that the apostle also has said, "Let all of you severally have regard to yourselves, lest ye also be tempted. Bear ye one another's

---

[1] [Ezek. xxxiv. 4.]
[2] 1 Cor. x. 33, xi. 1.
[3] 1 Cor. ix. 22.
[4] 1 Cor. xii. 26.
[5] Col. ii. 8.

[6] Num. xii. 3.
[7] Luke vi. 36.
[8] Matt. ix. 12.
[9] [Compare Cyprian, in all this, with his less reasonable "master" Tertullian.]
[10] *Apud inferos.* See Ps. vi. 5.
[11] Prov. xviii. 19 (old version).

burdens, and so fulfil the law of Christ;"[1] also that, rebuking the haughty, and breaking down their arrogance, he says in his epistle, "Let him that thinketh he standeth, take heed lest he fall;"[2] and in another place he says, "Who art thou that judgest another man's servant? To his own master he standeth or falleth; yea, he shall stand, for God is able to make him stand."[3] John also proves that Jesus Christ the Lord is our Advocate and Intercessor for our sins, saying, "My little children, these things write I unto you, that ye sin not. And if any man sin, we have an Advocate with the Father, Jesus Christ the Supporter: and He is the propitiation for our sins."[4] And Paul also, the apostle, in his epistle, has written, "If, while we were yet sinners, Christ died for us; much more, being now justified by His blood, we shall be saved from wrath through Him."[5]

19. Considering His love and mercy, we ought not to be so bitter, nor cruel, nor inhuman in cherishing the brethren, but to mourn with those that mourn, and to weep with them that weep, and to raise them up as much as we can by the help and comfort of our love; neither being too ungentle and pertinacious in repelling their repentance; nor, again, being too lax and easy in rashly yielding communion. Lo! a wounded brother lies stricken by the enemy in the field of battle. There the devil is striving to slay him whom he has wounded; here Christ is exhorting that he whom He has redeemed may not wholly perish. Whether of the two do we assist? On whose side do we stand? Whether do we favour the devil, that he may destroy, and pass by our prostrate lifeless brother, as in the Gospel did the priest and Levite; or rather, as priests of God and Christ, do we imitate what Christ both taught and did, and snatch the wounded man from the jaws of the enemy, that we may preserve him cured for God the judge?[6]

20. And do not think, dearest brother, that either the courage of the brethren will be lessened, or that martyrdoms will fail for this cause, that repentance is relaxed to the lapsed, and that the hope of peace is offered to the penitent. The strength of the truly believing remains unshaken; and with those who fear and love God with their whole heart, their integrity continues steady and strong. For to adulterers even a time of repentance is granted by us, and peace is given. Yet virginity is not therefore deficient in the Church, nor does the glorious design of continence languish through the sins of others. The Church, crowned with so many virgins,

flourishes; and chastity and modesty preserve the tenor of their glory. Nor is the vigour of continence broken down because repentance and pardon are facilitated to the adulterer. It is one thing to stand for pardon, another thing to attain to glory: it is one thing, when cast into prison, not to go out thence until one has paid the uttermost farthing; another thing at once to receive the wages of faith and courage. It is one thing, tortured by long suffering for sins, to be cleansed and long purged by fire;[7] another to have purged all sins by suffering. It is one thing, in fine, to be in suspense till the sentence of God at the day of judgment; another to be at once crowned by the Lord.

21. And, indeed, among our predecessors, some of the bishops here in our province thought that peace was not to be granted to adulterers, and wholly closed the gate of repentance against adultery. Still they did not withdraw from the assembly of their co-bishops, nor break the unity of the Catholic Church[8] by the persistency of their severity or censure; so that, because to some peace was granted to adulterers, he who did not grant it should be separated from the Church. While the bond of concord remains, and the undivided sacrament of the Catholic Church endures, every bishop disposes and directs his own acts, and will have to give an account of his purposes to the Lord.[9]

22. But I wonder that some are so obstinate as to think that repentance is not to be granted to the lapsed, or to suppose that pardon is to be denied to the penitent, when it is written, "Remember whence thou art fallen, and repent, and do the first works,"[10] which certainly is said to him who evidently has fallen, and whom the Lord exhorts to rise up again by his works, because it is written, "Alms do deliver from death,"[11] and not, assuredly, from that death which once the blood of Christ extinguished, and from which the saving grace of baptism and of our Redeemer has delivered us, but from that which subsequently creeps in through sins. Moreover, in another place time is granted for repentance; and the Lord threatens him that does not repent: "I have," saith He, "many things against thee, because thou sufferest thy wife Jezebel, which calleth herself a prophetess, to teach and to seduce my servants to commit fornication, and to eat things sacrificed to idols; and I gave her a space to repent, and she will not repent of her forni-

---

[1] Gal. vi. 1, 2.
[2] 1 Cor. x. 12.
[3] Rom. xiv. 4.
[4] 1 John ii. 1, 2.
[5] Rom. v. 8, 9.
[6] [I bespeak admiration for this loving spirit of one often upbraided for his strong expressions and firm convictions.]

[7] These words are variously read, "to be purged divinely," or "to be purged for a long while," *scil.* "purgari divine," or "purgari diutine." [Candid Romish writers concede that this does not refer to their purgatory; but, the idea once accepted, we can *read it into* this place as into 1 Cor. iii. 13. See Oxford trans., p. 128.]
[8] [The unity of the Catholic Church, in his view, consists in this unity of co-bishops in one episcopate, with which every Christian should be in communion through his own bishop.]
[9] [The independence of bishops, and their intercommunion as one episcopate, is his theory of the undivided sacrament of Catholicity.]
[10] Apoc. ii. 5.
[11] Tob. iv. 10.

cation. Behold, I will cast her into a bed, and them that commit adultery with her into great tribulation, except they repent of their deeds;"[1] whom certainly the Lord would not exhort to repentance, if it were not that He promises mercy to them that repent. And in the Gospel He says, " I say unto you, that likewise joy shall be in heaven over one sinner that repenteth, more than over ninety and nine just persons that need no repentance."[2] For since it is written, "God did not make death, neither hath He pleasure in the destruction of the living,"[3] assuredly He who wills that none should perish, desires that sinners should repent, and by repentance should return again to life. Thus also He cries by Joel the prophet, and says, "And now, thus saith the Lord your God, Turn ye even to me with all your heart, and with fasting, and with weeping, and with mourning; and rend your heart, and not your garments, and return unto the Lord your God; for He is gracious and merciful, slow to anger, and of great kindness, and repenteth Him of the evil appointed."[4] In the Psalms, also, we read as well the rebuke as the clemency of God, threatening at the same time as He spares, punishing that He may correct; and when He has corrected, preserving. " I will visit," He says, " their transgressions with the rod, and their iniquity with stripes. Nevertheless, my loving-kindness will I not utterly take from them."[5]

23. The Lord also in His Gospel, setting forth the love of God the Father, says, " What man is there of you, whom, if his son ask bread, will he give him a stone? or if he ask a fish, will he give him a serpent? If ye then, being evil, know how to give good gifts unto your children, how much more shall your heavenly Father give good things to them that ask Him?"[6] The Lord is here comparing the father after the flesh, and the eternal and liberal love of God the Father. But if that evil father upon earth, deeply offended by a sinful and evil son, yet if he should see the same son afterwards reformed, and, the sins of his former life being put away, restored to sobriety and morality and to the discipline of innocence by the sorrow of his repentance, both rejoices and gives thanks, and with the eagerness of a father's exultation, embraces the restored one, whom before he had cast out; how much more does that one and true Father, good, merciful, and loving — yea, Himself Goodness and Mercy and Love — rejoice in the repentance of His own sons ! nor threatens punishment to those who are now repenting, or mourning and lament-

ing, but rather promises pardon and clemency. Whence the Lord in the Gospel calls those that mourn, blessed; because he who mourns calls forth mercy.[7] He who is stubborn and haughty heaps up wrath against himself, and the punishment of the coming judgment. And therefore, dearest brother, we have decided that those who do not repent, nor give evidence of sorrow for their sins with their whole heart, and with manifest profession of their lamentation, are to be absolutely restrained from the hope of communion and peace if they begin to beg for them in the midst of sickness and peril; because it is not repentance for sin, but the warning of urgent death, that drives them to ask; and he is not worthy to receive consolation in death who has not reflected that he was about to die.

24. In reference, however, to the character of Novatian, dearest brother, of whom you desired that intelligence should be written you what heresy he had introduced; know that, in the first place, we ought not even to be inquisitive as to what he teaches, so long as he teaches out of the pale *of unity*. Whoever he may be, and whatever he may be, he who is not in the Church of Christ is not a Christian. Although he may boast himself, and announce his philosophy or eloquence with lofty words, yet he who has not maintained brotherly love or ecclesiastical unity has lost even what he previously had been. Unless he seems to you to be a bishop, who — when a bishop has been made in the Church by sixteen[8] co-bishops — strives by bribery to be made an adulterous and extraneous bishop by the hands of deserters; and although there is one Church, divided by Christ throughout the whole world into many members, and also one episcopate diffused through a harmonious multitude of many bishops;[9] in spite of God's tradition, in spite of the combined and everywhere compacted unity of the Catholic Church, is endeavouring to make a human church, and is sending his new apostles through very many cities, that he may establish some new foundations of his own appointment. And although there have already been ordained in each city, and through all the provinces, bishops old in years, sound in faith, proved in trial, proscribed in persecution, (this one) dares to create over these other *and* false bishops : as if he could either wander over the whole world with the persistence of his new endeavour, or break asunder the structure of the ecclesiastical body, by the propagation of his own discord, not knowing that schismatics are always fervid at the beginning, but that they

[1] Apoc. ii. 20–22.
[2] Luke xv. 7.
[3] Wisd. i. 13.
[4] Joel ii. 12, 13.
[5] Ps lxxxix. 32, 33.
[6] Matt. vii. 9–11.

[7] [Matt. v. 4. A striking exposition. " The quality of mercy is not strained," etc.]
[8] [The primitive canons require the consent of a majority of comprovincials, and *three* at least to ordain.]
[9] [One of the many aphoristic condensations of the Cyprianic theory. Elucidation X.]

cannot increase nor add to what they have unlawfully begun, but that they immediately fail together with their evil emulation. But he could not hold the episcopate, even if he had before been made bishop, since he has cut himself off from the body of his fellow-bishops, and from the unity of the Church; since the apostle admonishes that we should mutually sustain one another, and not withdraw from the unity which God has appointed, and says, "Bearing with one another in love, endeavouring to keep the unity of the Spirit in the bond of peace."[1] He then who neither maintains the unity of the Spirit nor the bond of peace, and separates himself from the band of the Church, and from the assembly of priests, can neither have the power nor the honour of a bishop, since he has refused to maintain either the unity or the peace of the episcopate.[2]

25. Then, moreover, what a swelling of arrogance it is, what oblivion of humility and gentleness, what a boasting of his own arrogance, that any one should either dare, or think that he is able, to do what the Lord did not even grant to the apostles; that he should think that he can discern the tares from the wheat, or, as if it were granted to him to bear the fan and to purge the threshing-floor, should endeavour to separate the chaff from the wheat; and since the apostle says, "But in a great house there are not only vessels of gold and of silver, but also of wood and of earth,"[3] should think to choose the vessels of gold and of silver, to despise, to cast away, and to condemn the vessels of wood and of clay; while the vessels of wood are not burnt up except in the day of the Lord by the flame of the divine burning, and the vessels of clay are only broken by Him to whom is given the rod of iron.

26. Or if he appoints himself a searcher and judge of the heart and reins, let him in all cases judge equally. And as he knows that it is written, "Behold, thou art made whole; sin no more, lest a worse thing happen unto thee,"[4] let him separate the fraudulent and adulterers from his side and from his company, since the case of an adulterer is by far both graver and worse than that of one who has taken a certificate, because the latter has sinned by necessity, the former by free will: the latter, thinking that it is sufficient for him that he has not sacrificed, has been deceived by an error; the former, a violator of the matrimonial tie of another, or entering a brothel, into the sink and filthy gulf of the common people, has befouled by detestable impurity a sanctified body and God's temple,

as says the apostle: "Every sin that a man doeth is without the body, but he that committeth fornication sinneth against his own body."[5] And yet to these persons themselves repentance is granted, and the hope of lamenting and atoning is left, according to the saying of the same apostle: "I fear lest, when I come to you, I shall bewail many of those who have sinned already, and have not repented of the uncleanness, and fornication, and lasciviousness which they have committed."[6]

27. Neither let the new heretics flatter themselves in this, that they say that they do not communicate with idolaters; although among them there are both adulterers and fraudulent persons, who are held guilty of the crime of idolatry, according to the saying of the apostle: "For know this with understanding, that no whoremonger, nor unclean person, nor covetous man, whose guilt is that of idolatry, hath any inheritance in the kingdom of Christ and of God."[7] And again: "Mortify therefore your members which are upon the earth; putting off fornication, uncleanness, and evil concupiscence, and covetousness, which are the service of idols: for which things' sake cometh the wrath of God."[8] For as our bodies are members of Christ, and we are each a temple of God, whosoever violates the temple of God by adultery, violates God; and he who, in committing sins, does the will of the devil, serves demons and idols. For evil deeds do not come from the Holy Spirit, but from the prompting of the adversary, and lusts born of the unclean spirit constrain men to act against God and to obey the devil. Thus it happens that if they say that one is polluted by another's sin, and if they contend, by their own asseveration, that the idolatry of the delinquent passes over to one who is not guilty according to their own word; they cannot be excused from the crime of idolatry, since from the apostolic proof it is evident that the adulterers and defrauders with whom they communicate are idolaters. But with us, according to our faith and the given rule of divine preaching, agrees the principle of truth, that every one is himself held fast in his own sin; nor can one become guilty for another, since the Lord forewarns us, saying, "The righteousness of the righteous shall be upon him, and the wickedness of the wicked shall be upon him."[9] And again: "The fathers shall not die for the children, and the children shall not die for the fathers. Every one shall die in his own sin."[10] Reading and observing this, we certainly think that no one is

---

[1] Eph. iv. 2, 3.
[2] ["The body of his fellow-bishops," as above.]
[3] 2 Tim. ii. 20.
[4] John v. 14.

[5] 1 Cor. vi. 18.
[6] 2 Cor. xii. 21.
[7] Eph. v. 5.
[8] Col. iii. 5, 6.
[9] Ezek. xviii. 20.
[10] Deut. xxiv. 26.

to be restrained from the fruit of satisfaction, and the hope of peace, since we know, according to the faith of the divine Scriptures, God Himself being their author, and exhorting in them, both that sinners are brought back to repentance, and that pardon and mercy are not denied to penitents.[1]

28. And oh, mockery of a deceived fraternity ! Oh, vain deception of miserable and senseless mourners ! Oh, ineffectual and profitless tradition of heretical institution ! to exhort to the repentance of atonement, and to take away the healing from the atonement; to say to our brethren, "Mourn and shed tears, and groan day and night, and labour largely and frequently for the washing away and cleansing of your sin ; but, after all these things, you shall die without the pale of the Church. Whatsoever things are necessary to peace, you shall do, but none of that peace which you seek shall you receive !" Who would not perish at once? Who would not fall away, from very desperation? Who would not turn away his mind from all design of lamentation? Do you think that the husbandman could labour if you should say, "Till the field with all the skill of husbandry, diligently persevere in its cultivation ; but you shall reap no harvest, you shall press no vintage, you shall receive no fruits of your olive-yard, you shall gather no apples from the trees ;" or if, urging upon any one the possession and use of ships, you were to say, "Purchase, my brother, material from excellent woods ; inweave your keel with the strongest and chosen oak ; labour on the rudder, the ropes, the sails, that the ship may be constructed and fitted ; but when you have done this, you shall never behold the result from its doings and its voyages?"

29. This is to shut up and to cut off the way of grief and of repentance ; so that while in all Scripture the Lord God sooths those who return to Him and repent, repentance itself is taken away by our hardness and cruelty, which intercepts the fruits of repentance. But if we find that none ought to be restrained from repenting, and that peace may be granted by His priests to those who entreat and beseech the Lord's mercy, inasmuch as He is merciful and loving, the groaning of those who mourn is to be admitted, and the fruit of repentance is not to be denied to those who grieve. And because in the place of the departed there is no confession, neither can confession be made there,[2] they who have repented from their whole heart, and have

asked for it, ought to be received within the Church, and to be kept in it for the Lord, who will of a surety judge, when He comes to His Church, those whom He shall find within it. But apostates and deserters, or adversaries and enemies, and those who lay waste the Church of Christ, cannot, even if outside the Church they have been slain for His name, according to the apostle, be admitted to the peace of the Church, since they have neither kept the unity of the spirit nor of the Church.

30. These few things for the present, out of many, dearest brother, I have run over as briefly as I could, that I might thereby both satisfy your desire, and might link you more and more closely to the society of our college and body.[3] But if there should arise to you an opportunity and power of coming to us, we shall be able to confer more fully together, and to consider more fruitfully and more at large the things which make for a salutary agreement. I bid you, dearest brother, ever heartily farewell.

EPISTLE LII.[4]

TO FORTUNATUS AND HIS OTHER COLLEAGUES, CONCERNING THOSE WHO HAD BEEN OVERCOME BY TORTUES.

ARGUMENT. — CYPRIAN BEING CONSULTED BY HIS COLLEAGUES, WHETHER CERTAIN LAPSED PERSONS WHO HAD BEEN OVERPOWERED BY TORTURE SHOULD BE ADMITTED TO COMMUNION, REPLIES, THAT INASMUCH AS THEY HAD ALREADY REPENTED FOR THE SPACE OF THREE YEARS, HE THOUGHT THEY SHOULD BE RECEIVED ; BUT AS AFTER THE FESTIVAL OF EASTER THERE WOULD BE A COUNCIL OF BISHOPS WITH HIM, HE WOULD THEN CONSIDER THE MATTER WITH THEM.

1. Cyprian to Fortunatus, Ahymnus, Optatus, Privatianus, Donatulus, and Felix, his brethren, greeting, You have written to me, dearest brethren, that when you were in the city of Capsa for the purpose of ordaining a bishop, Superius, our brother and colleague brought before you, that Ninus, Clementianus, and Florus, our brethren, who had been previously laid hold of in the persecution, and confessing the name of the Lord, had overcome the violence of the magistracy, and the attack of a raging populace, afterwards, when they were tortured before the proconsul with severe sufferings, were vanquished by the acuteness of the torments, and fell, through their lengthened agonies, from the degree of glory to which in the full virtue of

---

[1] [" Fools make a mock at sin." But what serious reflections are inspired by the solemn discipline of primitive Christianity! Mercy is magnified, indeed, but pardon and peace are made worth striving after. Repentance is made a reality, and we hear nothing of mechanical penances and absolutions.]

[2] [He has never heard of indulgences and masses for the dead, nor of a purgatorial remission. See p. 332, note 7.]

[3] [To the unity of our common episcopate. Note this; for, if he had imagined Cornelius to have been a " Pope," he must have said, " to unity with the true pontiff, against whom Novatian has rebelled, and made himself an anti-pope."]

[4] Oxford ed.: Ep. lvi. A.D. 252.

faith they were tending, and after this grave lapse, incurred not willingly but of necessity, had not yet ceased their repentance for the space of three years : of whom you thought it right to consult whether it was well to receive them now to communion.

2. And indeed, in respect of my own opinion, I think that the Lord's mercy will not be wanting to those who are known to have stood in the ranks of battle, to have confessed the name,[1] to have overcome the violence of the magistrates and the rush of the raging populace with the persistency of unshaken faith, to have suffered imprisonment, to have long resisted, amidst the threats of the proconsul and the warring of the surrounding people, torments that wrenched and tore them with protracted repetition ; so that in the last moment to have been vanquished by the infirmity of the flesh, may be extenuated by the plea of preceding deserts. And it may be sufficient for such to have lost their glory, but that we ought not, moreover, to close the place of pardon to them, and deprive them of their Father's love and of our communion ; to whom we think it may be sufficient for entreating the mercy of the Lord, that for three years continually and sorrowfully, as you write, they have lamented with excessive penitential mourning. Assuredly I do not think that peace is incautiously and over-hastily granted to those, who by the bravery of their warfare, have not, we see, been previously wanting to the battle ; and who, if the struggle should come on anew, might be able to regain their glory. For when it was decided in the council that penitents in peril of sickness should be assisted, and have peace granted to them, surely those ought to precede in receiving peace whom we see not to have fallen by weakness of mind, but who, having engaged in the conflict, and being wounded, have not been able to sustain the crown of their confession through weakness of the flesh ; especially since, in their desire to die, they were not permitted to be slain, but the tortures wrenched their wearied frames long enough, not to conquer their faith, which is unconquerable, but to exhaust the flesh, which is weak.

3. Since, however, you have written for me to give full consideration to this matter with many of my colleagues ; and so great a subject claims greater and more careful counsel from the conference of many ; and as now almost all, during the first celebrations of Easter, are dwelling at home with their brethren : when they shall have completed the solemnity to be celebrated among their own people, and have begun to come to me, I will consider it more at large with each one, so that a decided opinion, weighed in the

council of many priests, on the subject on which you have consulted me, may be established among us, and may be written to you. I bid you, dearest brethren, ever heartily farewell.[2]

EPISTLE LIII.[3]
TO CORNELIUS, CONCERNING GRANTING PEACE TO THE LAPSED.

ARGUMENT. — CYPRIAN ANNOUNCES THIS DECREE OF THE BISHOPS IN THE NAME OF THE WHOLE SYNOD TO FATHER CORNELIUS ; AND THEREFORE THIS LETTER IS NOT SO MUCH THE LETTER OF CYPRIAN HIMSELF, AS THAT OF THE ENTIRE AFRICAN SYNOD.[4]

Cyprian, Liberalis, Caldonius, Nicomedes, Cæcilius, Junius, Marrutius, Felix, Successus, Faustinus, Fortunatus, Victor, Saturninus, another Saturninus, Rogatianus, Tertullus, Lucianus, Eutyches, Amplus, Sattius, Secundinus, another Saturninus, Aurelius, Priscus, Herculanus, Victoricus, Quintus, Honoratus, Montanus, Hortensianus, Verianus, Iambus, Donatus, Pompeius, Polycarpus, Demetrius, another Donatus, Privatianus, another Fortunatus, Rogatus and Monulus, to Cornelius their brother,[5] greeting.[6]

1. We had indeed decided some time ago, dearest brother, having mutually taken counsel one with another, that they who, in the fierceness of persecution, had been overthrown by the adversary, and had lapsed, and had polluted themselves with unlawful sacrifices, should undergo a long and full repentance ; and if the risk of sickness should be urgent, should receive peace on the very point of death. For it was not right, neither did the love of the Father nor divine mercy allow, that the Church should be closed to those that knock, or the help of the hope of salvation be denied to those who mourn and entreat, so that when they pass from this world, they should be dismissed to their Lord without communion and peace ; since He Himself who gave the law, that things which were bound on earth should also be bound in heaven, allowed, moreover, that things might be loosed

---

[1] According to some readings, " the name of the Lord."

[2] [The sweetness, moderation, and prudence of this letter are alike commendable. But let us reflect what it meant to confess Christ in those days.]
[3] Oxford ed.: Ep. lvii.
[4] As the African bishops had previously decided in a certain council, that the lapsed, except after long penitence, should not be received to peace, unless perchance peril of sickness was urgent; now on the appearance of a new persecution they decided that peace was to be granted to all those who had repented, so that they might be the more courageous for the contest of suffering.
[5] [" To Cornelius their brother." Now compare this with the abject conduct of Latin bishops at the late council of the Vatican. See Döllinger (On Unity, etc.), Janus, and Quirinus.
[6] The superscription in other texts is as follows: " Cyprian, Liberalis, Caldonius, Nicomedes, Cæcilius, Junius, Marrutius, Felix, Successus, Faustinus, Fortunatus, Victor, Saturninus, another Saturninus, Rogatian, Tertullus, Lucianus, Sattius, Secundinus, another Saturninus, Eutyches, Amplus, another Saturninus, Aurelius, Priscus, Herculaneus, Victoricus, Quintus, Honoratus, Manthaneus, Hortensianus, Verianus, Iambus, Donatus, Pomponius, Polycarp, Demetrius, another Donatus, Privatianus, another Fortunatus, Rogatus and Munnulus, to Cornelius their brother, greeting."

there which were here first loosed in the Church. But now, when we see that the day of another trouble is again beginning to draw near, and are admonished by frequent and repeated intimations that we should be prepared and armed for the struggle which the enemy announces to us, that we should also prepare the people committed to us by divine condescension, by our exhortations, and gather together from all parts all the soldiers of Christ who desire arms, and are anxious for the battle within the Lord's camp : under the compulsion of this necessity, we have decided that peace is to be given to those who have not withdrawn from the Church of the Lord, but have not ceased from the first day of their lapse to repent, and to lament, and to beseech the Lord ; and *we have decided* that they ought to be armed and equipped for the battle which is at hand.

2. For we must comply with fitting intimations and admonitions, that the sheep may not be deserted in danger by the shepherds, but that the whole flock may be gathered together into one place, and the Lord's army may be armed for the contest of the heavenly warfare. For the repentance of the mourners was reasonably prolonged for a more protracted time, help only being afforded to the sick in their departure, so long as peace and tranquillity prevailed, which permitted the long postponement of the tears of the mourners, and late assistance in sickness to the dying. But now indeed peace is necessary, not for the sick, but for the strong ; nor is communion to be granted by us to the dying, but to the living, that we may not leave those whom we stir up and exhort to the battle unarmed and naked, but may fortify them with the protection of Christ's body and blood. And, as the Eucharist is appointed for this very purpose that it may be a safeguard to the receivers, *it is needful* that we may arm those whom we wish to be safe against the adversary with the protection of the Lord's abundance. For how do we teach or provoke them to shed their blood in confession of His name, if we deny to those who are about to enter on the warfare the blood of Christ? Or how do we make them fit for the cup of martyrdom, if we do not first admit them to drink, in the Church, the cup of the Lord [1] by the right of communion?

3. We should make a difference, dearest brother, between those who either have apostatized, and, having returned to the world which they have renounced, are living heathenish lives, or, having become deserters to the heretics, are daily taking up parricidal arms against the Church ; and those who do not depart from the Church's threshold, and, constantly and sorrow-fully imploring divine and paternal consolation, profess that they are now prepared for the battle, and ready to stand and fight bravely for the name of their Lord and for their own salvation. In these times we grant peace, not to those who sleep, but to those who watch. We grant peace, not amid indulgences, but amid arms. We grant peace, not for rest, but for the field of battle. If, according to what we hear, and desire, and believe of them, they shall stand bravely, and shall overthrow the adversary with us in the encounter, we shall not repent of having granted peace to men so brave. Yea, it is the great honour and glory of our episcopate to have granted peace to martyrs, so that we, as priests, who daily celebrate the sacrifices of God, may prepare offerings and victims for God. But if — which may the Lord avert from our brethren — any one of the lapsed should deceive, seeking peace by guile, and at the time of the impending struggle receiving peace without any purpose of doing battle, he betrays and deceives himself, hiding one thing in his heart and pronouncing another with his voice. We, so far as it is allowed to us to see and to judge, look upon the face of each one ; we are not able to scrutinize the heart and to inspect the mind. Concerning these the Discerner and Searcher of hidden things judges, and He will quickly come and judge of the secrets and hidden things of the heart. But the evil ought not to stand in the way of the good, but rather the evil ought to be assisted by the good. Neither is peace, therefore, to be denied to those who are about to endure martyrdom, because there are some who will refuse it, since for this purpose peace should be granted to all who are about to enter upon the warfare, that through our ignorance he may not be the first one to be passed over, who in the struggle is to be crowned.

4. Nor let any one say, " that he who accepts martyrdom is baptized in his own blood, and peace is not necessary to him from the bishop, since he is about to have the peace of his own glory, and about to receive a greater reward from the condescension of the Lord." First of all, he cannot be fitted for martyrdom who is not armed for the contest by the Church ; and his spirit is deficient which the Eucharist received does not raise and stimulate. For the Lord says in His Gospel : " But when they deliver you up, take no thought what ye shall speak ; for it shall be given you in that hour what ye shall speak. For it is not ye that speak, but the Spirit of your Father which speaketh in you." [2] Now, since He says that the Spirit of the Father speaks in those who are delivered up and set

---

[1] [Compare Luke xxii. 15, 42, and Ps. cxvi. 13.]

[2] Matt. x. 19, 20.

in the confession of His name, how can he be found prepared or fit for that confession who has not first, in the reception of peace, received the Spirit of the Father, who, giving strength to His servants, Himself speaks and confesses in us? Then, besides — if, having forsaken everything that he has, a man shall flee, and dwelling in hiding-places and in solitude, shall fall by chance among thieves, or shall die in fever and in weakness, will it not be charged upon us that so good a soldier, who has forsaken all that he hath, and contemning his house, and his parents, and his children, has preferred to follow his Lord, dies without peace and without communion? Will not either inactive negligence or cruel hardness be ascribed to us in the day of judgment, that, pastors though we are, we have neither been willing to take care of the sheep trusted and committed to us in peace, nor to arm them in battle? Would not the charge be brought against us by the Lord, which by His prophet He utters and says? "Behold, ye consume the milk, and ye clothe you with the wool, and ye kill them that are fed; but ye feed not my flock. The weak have ye not strengthened, neither have ye healed that which was sick, neither have ye comforted that which was broken, neither have ye brought again that which strayed, neither have ye sought that which was lost, and that which was strong ye wore out with labour. And my sheep were scattered, because there were no shepherds: and they became meat to all the beasts of the field; and there was none who sought after them, nor brought them back. Therefore thus saith the Lord, Behold, I am against the shepherds; and I will require my sheep of their hand, and cause them to cease from feeding my sheep; neither shall they feed them any more: and I will deliver my sheep from their mouth, and I will feed them with judgment."[1]

5. Lest, then, the sheep committed to us by the Lord be demanded back from our mouth, wherewith we deny peace, wherewith we oppose to them rather the severity of human cruelty than *the benignity* of divine and paternal love; we have determined[2] by the suggestion of the Holy Spirit and the admonition of the Lord, conveyed by many and manifest visions, because the enemy is foretold and shown to be at hand, to gather within the camp the soldiers of Christ, to examine the cases of each one, and to grant peace to the lapsed, yea, rather to furnish arms to those who are about to fight. And this, we trust, will please you in contemplation of the paternal mercy. But if there be any (*one*) of our colleagues who, now that the contest is urgent, thinks that peace should not be granted to our brethren and sisters, he shall give an account to the Lord in the day of judgment, either of his grievous rigour or of his inhuman hardness. We, as befitted our faith and charity and solicitude, have laid before you what was in our own mind, namely, that the day of contest has approached, that a violent enemy will soon rise up against us, that a struggle is coming on, not such as it has been, but much more serious and fierce. This is frequently shown to us from above; concerning this we are often admonished by the providence and mercy of the Lord, of whose help and love we who trust in Him may be secure, because He who in peace foretells to His soldiers that the battle will come, will give to them when they are warring victory in the encounter. We bid you, dearest brother, ever heartily farewell.

EPISTLE LIV.[3]

TO CORNELIUS, CONCERNING FORTUNATUS AND FELICISSIMUS, OR AGAINST THE HERETICS.

ARGUMENT.—CYPRIAN CHIEFLY WARNS CORNELIUS IN THIS LETTER NOT TO HEAR THE CALUMNIES OF FELICISSIMUS AND FORTUNATUS AGAINST HIM, AND NOT TO BE FRIGHTENED BY THEIR THREATS, BUT TO BE OF A BRAVE SPIRIT, AS BECOMES GOD'S PRIESTS IN OPPOSITION TO HERETICS; NAMELY, THOSE WHO, AFTER THE CUSTOM PREVAILING AMONG HERETICS, BEGAN THEIR HERESY AND SCHISMS WITH THE CONTEMPT OF ONE BISHOP IN THE CHURCH.[4]

1. I have read your letter, dearest brother, which you sent by Saturus our brother the acolyte, abundantly full of fraternal love and ecclesiastical discipline and priestly reproof; in which you signified that Felicissimus,[5] no new enemy of Christ, but long ago excommunicated for his very many and grave crimes, and condemned not only by my judgment, but also by that of very many of my fellow-bishops, has been rejected by you there, and that when he came attended by a band and faction of desperadoes, he was driven from the Church with the full vigour with which it behoves a bishop to act. From which Church long ago he was driven, with others like himself, by the majesty of God and the severity of Christ our Lord and Judge; that the author of schism and disagreement, the fraudulent user of money entrusted to him, the violator of virgins, the destroyer and corrupter of many marriages, should not, by the dishonour

---

[1] Ezek. xxxiv. 3–6, 10–16.
[2] ["We have determined." No reference to any revising power in the Bishop of Rome, who is counselled from first to last as a brother, and told what he should do.]

[3] Oxford ed.: Ep. lix. A.D. 252.
[4] Indicating also by the way whence heresy and schisms are wont to take their rise, so that the letter is with good reason inscribed by Morell "Contra Hæreticos."
[5] [He was a purse-proud layman. But see Elucidation XIII. *infra.*]

of his presence and his immodest and incestuous contact, violate further the spouse of Christ, hitherto uncorrupt, holy, modest.

2. But yet, when I read your other letter, brother, which you subjoined to your first one, I was considerably surprised at observing that you were in some degree disturbed by the threats and terrors of those who had come, when, according to what you wrote, they had attacked and threatened you with the greatest desperation, that if you would not receive the letters which they had brought, they would read them publicly, and would utter many base and disgraceful things, and such as were worthy of their mouth. But if the matter is thus, dearest brother, that the audacity of the most wicked men is to be dreaded, and that what evil men cannot do rightly and equitably, they may accomplish by daring and desperation, there is an end of the vigour of the episcopacy, and of the sublime and divine power of governing the Church; nor can we continue any longer, or in fact now be Christians, if it is come to this, that we are to be afraid of the threats or the snares of outcasts. For both Gentiles and Jews threaten, and heretics and all those, of whose hearts and minds the devil has taken possession, daily attest their venomous madness with furious voice. We are not, therefore, to yield because they threaten; nor is the adversary and enemy on that account greater than Christ, because he claims for himself and assumes so much in the world. There ought to abide with us, dearest brother, an immoveable strength of faith; and against all the irruptions and onsets of the waves that roar against us, a steady and unshaken courage should plant itself as with the fortitude and mass of a resisting rock. Nor does it matter whence comes the terror or the danger to a bishop, who lives subject to terrors and dangers, and is nevertheless made glorious by those very terrors and dangers. For we ought not to consider and regard the mere threats of the Gentiles or of the Jews, when we see that the Lord Himself was deserted by His brethren, and was betrayed by him whom He Himself had chosen among His apostles; that also in the beginning of the world it was none other than a brother who slew righteous Abel, and an angry brother pursued the fleeing Jacob, and the youthful Joseph was sold by the act of his brethren. In the Gospel also we read that it was foretold that our foes should rather be of our own household, and that they who have first been associated in the sacrament of unity [1] shall be they who shall betray one another. It makes no difference who delivers up or who rages, since God permits those to be delivered up whom He appoints to be crowned. For it is

no ignominy to us to suffer from our brethren what Christ suffered, nor is it glory to them to do what Judas did. But what insolence it is in them, what swelling and inflated and vain boasting on the part of these threateners, *there* to threaten me in my absence, when here they have me present in their power! I do not fear their reproaches with which they daily wound themselves and their own life; I do not tremble at their clubs and stones and swords, which they brandish with parricidal words: as far as lies in their power such men are homicides before God. Yet they are not able to slay unless the Lord have allowed them to slay; and although I must die but once, yet they daily slay me by their hatred, their words, and their villanies.

3. But, dearest brother, ecclesiastical discipline is not on that account to be forsaken, nor priestly censure to be relaxed, because we are disturbed with reproaches or are shaken with terrors; since Holy Scripture meets and warns us, saying, "But he who presumes and is haughty, the man who boasts of himself, who hath enlarged his soul as hell, shall accomplish nothing." [2] And again: "And fear not the words of a sinful man, for his glory shall be dung and worms. To-day he is lifted up, and to-morrow he shall not be found, because he is turned into his earth, and his thought shall perish." [3] And again: "I have seen the wicked exalted, and raised above the cedars of Libanus: I went by, and, lo, he was not; yea, I sought him, and his place was not found." [4] Exaltation, and puffing up, and arrogant and haughty boastfulness, spring not from the teaching of Christ who teaches humility, but from the spirit of Antichrist, whom the Lord rebukes by His prophet, saying, "For thou hast said in thine heart, I will ascend into heaven, I will place my throne above the stars of God: I will sit on a lofty mountain, above the lofty mountains to the north: I will ascend above the clouds; I will be like the Most High." [5] And he added, saying, "Yet thou shalt descend into hell, to the foundations of the earth; and they that see thee shall wonder at thee." [6] Whence also divine Scripture threatens a like punishment to such in another place, and says, "For the day of the Lord of hosts shall be upon every one that is injurious and proud, and upon every one that is lifted up, and lofty." [7] By his mouth, therefore, and by his words, is every one at once betrayed; and whether he has Christ in his heart, or Antichrist, is discerned in his speaking, according to what the Lord says in His Gospel, "O generation of vipers, how can ye, being evil,

---

1 ["The sacramental host of God's elect."— *The Task*, Cowper.]

2 Hab. ii. 5.
3 1 Mac. ii. 62, 63.
4 Ps. xxxviii. 35, 36.
5 Isa. xiv. 13, 14.
6 Isa. xiv. 15, 16.
7 Isa. ii. 12.

speak good things? for out of the abundance of the heart the mouth speaketh. A good man out of the good treasure bringeth forth good things; and an evil man out of the evil treasure bringeth forth evil things."[1] Whence also that rich sinner who implores help from Lazarus, then laid in Abraham's bosom, and established in a place of comfort, while he, writhing in torments, is consumed by the heats of burning flame, suffers most punishment of all parts of his body in his mouth and his tongue, because doubtless in his mouth and his tongue he had most sinned.[2]

4. For since it is written, "Neither shall revilers inherit the kingdom of God,"[3] and again the Lord says in His Gospel, "Whosoever shall say to his brother, Thou fool; and whosoever shall say, Raca, shall be in danger of the Gehenna of fire,"[4] how can they evade the rebuke of the Lord the avenger, who heap up such expressions, not only on their brethren, but also on the priests, to whom is granted such honour of the condescension of God, that whosoever should not obey his priest, and him that judgeth here for the time, was immediately to be slain? In Deuteronomy the Lord God speaks, saying, "And the man that will do presumptuously, and will not hearken unto the priest or to the judge, whosoever he shall be in those days, that man shall die; and all the people, when they hear, shall fear, and shall do no more wickedly."[5] Moreover, to Samuel, when he was despised by the Jews, God says, "They have not despised thee, but they have despised me."[6] And the Lord also in the Gospel says, "He that heareth you, heareth me, and Him that sent me; and he that rejecteth you, rejecteth me; and he that rejecteth me, rejecteth Him that sent me."[7] And when he had cleansed the leprous man, he said, "Go, show thyself to the priest."[8] And when afterwards, in the time of His passion, He had received a buffet from a servant of the priest, and the servant said to Him, "Answerest thou the high priest so?"[9] the Lord said nothing reproachfully against the high priest, nor detracted anything from the priest's honour; but rather asserting His own innocence, and showing it, He says, "If I have spoken evil, bear witness of the evil; but if well, why smitest thou me?"[10] Also subsequently, in the Acts of the Apostles, the blessed Apostle Paul, when it was said to him, "Revilest thou God's priest?"[11] — although they had begun to be sacrilegious,

and impious, and bloody, the Lord having already been crucified, and had no longer retained anything of the priestly honour and authority — yet Paul, considering the name itself, however empty, and the shadow, as it were, of the priest, said, "I wist not, brethren, that he was the high priest: for it is written, Thou shalt not speak evil of the ruler of thy people."[12]

5. When, then, such and so great examples, and many others, are precedents whereby the priestly authority and power by the divine condescension is established, what kind of people, think you, are they who, being enemies of the priests, and rebels against the Catholic Church, are frightened neither by the threatening of a forewarning Lord, nor by the vengeance of coming judgment? For neither have heresies arisen, nor have schisms originated, from any other source than from this, that God's priest is not obeyed; nor do they consider that there is one person for the time priest in the Church, and for the time judge in the stead of Christ;[13] whom, if, according to divine teaching, the whole fraternity should obey, no one would stir up anything against the college of priests; no one, after the divine judgment, after the suffrage of the people, after the consent of the co-bishops, would make himself a judge, not now of the bishop, but of God. No one would rend the Church by a division of the unity of Christ.[14] No one, pleasing himself, and swelling with arrogance, would found a new heresy, separate and without, unless any one be of such sacrilegious daring and abandoned mind, as to think that a priest is made without God's judgment, when the Lord says in His Gospel, "Are not two sparrows sold for a farthing? and one of them does not fall to the ground without the will of your Father."[15] When He says that not even the least things are done without God's will, does any one think that the highest and greatest things are done in God's Church either without God's knowledge or permission, and that priests — that is, His stewards — are not ordained by His decree? This is not to have faith, whereby we live; this is not to give honour to God, by whose direction and decision we know and believe that all things are ruled and governed. Undoubtedly there are bishops made, not by the will of God, but they are such as are made outside of the Church — such as are made contrary to the ordinance and tradition of the Gospel, as the Lord Himself in the twelve prophets asserts, saying, "They have set up a king for themselves, and not by me."[16] And again:

---

[1] Matt. xii. 34, 35.
[2] [This idea became embedded in the minds of Western Christians. See Southey, *Roderick*, xxv. note 72. The *Fabulous Chronicle* which Southey gives at length is a curious study of this subject.]
[3] 1 Cor. vi. 10.
[4] Matt. v. 22.
[5] Deut. xvii. 12, 13.
[6] 1 Sam. viii. 7.
[7] Luke x. 16.
[8] Matt. viii. 4.
[9] John xviii. 22.
[10] John xviii. 23.
[11] Acts xxiii. 4.

[12] Acts xxiii. 5.
[13] [i.e., in each Church the one episcopate — "the college of priests" — is represented by the one bishop. See note, Oxford trans., p. 155.]
[14] [An illustration again of the Cyprianic theory. See the *Treatise on Unity*. These notes will aid when we reach that Treatise.]
[15] Matt. x. 29.
[16] Hos. viii. 4.

"Their sacrifices are as the bread of mourning; all that eat thereof shall be polluted."[1] And the Holy Spirit also cries by Isaiah, and says, "Woe unto you, children that are deserters. Thus saith the Lord, Ye have taken counsel, but not of me; and ye have made a covenant, but not of my Spirit, that ye may add sin to sin."[2]

6. But — I speak to you as being provoked; I speak as grieving; I speak as constrained — when a bishop is appointed into the place of one deceased, when he is chosen in time of peace by the suffrage of an entire people, when he is protected by the help of God in persecution, faithfully linked with all his colleagues, approved to his people by now four years' experience in his episcopate; observant of discipline in time of peace; in time of disturbance, proscribed with the name of his episcopate applied and attached to him; so often asked for in the circus "for the lions;" in the amphitheatre, honoured with the testimony of the divine condescension; even in these very days on which I have written this letter to you, on account of the sacrifices which, by proclaimed edict, the people were commanded to celebrate, demanded anew in the circus "for the lions" by the clamour of the populace; — when such a one, dearest brother, is seen to be assailed by some desperate and reckless men, and by those who have their place outside the Church, it is manifest who assails him: not assuredly Christ, who either appoints or protects his priests; but he who, as the adversary of Christ and the foe to His Church, for this purpose persecutes with his malice the ruler of the Church, that when the pilot is removed, he may rage more atrociously and more violently with a view to the Church's dispersion.

7. Nor ought it, my dearest brother, to disturb any one who is faithful and mindful of the Gospel, and retains the commands of the apostle who forewarns us; if in the last days certain persons, proud, contumacious, and enemies of God's priests, either depart from the Church or act against the Church, since both the Lord and His apostles have previously foretold that there should be such. Nor let any one wonder that the servant placed over them should be forsaken by some, when His own disciples forsook the Lord Himself, who performed such great and wonderful works, and illustrated the attributes of God the Father by the testimony of His doings. And yet He did not rebuke them when they went away, nor even severely threaten them; but rather, turning to His apostles, He said, "Will ye also go away?"[3] manifestly observing the law whereby a man left to his own liberty, and established in his own choice, himself desires for himself either death or salvation. Nevertheless, Peter,[4] upon whom by the same Lord the Church had been built, speaking one for all, and answering with the voice of the Church, says, "Lord, to whom shall we go? Thou hast the words of eternal life; and we believe, and are sure that Thou art the Christ, the Son of the living God:"[5] signifying, doubtless, and showing that those who departed from Christ perished by their own fault, yet that the Church which believes on Christ, and holds that which it has once learned, never departs from Him at all, and that those are the Church who remain in the house of God; but that, on the other hand, they are not the plantation planted by God the Father, whom we see not to be established with the stability of wheat, but blown about like chaff by the breath of the enemy scattering them, of whom John also in his epistle says, "They went out from us, but they were not of us; for if they had been of us, no doubt they would have continued with us."[6] Paul also warns us, when evil men perish out of the Church, not to be disturbed, nor to let our faith be lessened by the departure of the faithless. "For what," he says, "if some of them have departed from the faith? Hath their unbelief made the faith of God of none effect? God forbid! For God is true, but every man a liar."[7]

8. For our own part, it befits our conscience, dearest brother, to strive that none should perish *going* out of the Church by our fault; but if any one, of his own accord and by his own sin, should perish, and should be unwilling to repent and to return to the Church, that we who are anxious for their well-being should be blameless in the day of judgment, and that they alone should remain in punishment who refused to be healed by the wholesomeness of our advice. Nor ought the reproaches of the lost to move us in any degree to depart from the right path and from the sure rule, since also the apostle instructs us, saying, "If I should please men, I should not be the servant of Christ."[8] There is a great difference whether one desires to deserve well of men or of God. If we seek to please men, the Lord is offended. But if we strive and labour that we may please God, we ought to contemn human reproaches and abuse.

9. But that I did not immediately write to you, dearest brother, about Fortunatus, that pseudo-bishop, constituted by a few, and those,

---

[1] Hos. ix. 4.
[2] Isa. xxx. 1.
[3] John vi. 67.

[4] [Cyprian could not have written this letter to Cornelius had he recognised in him, as a successor of Peter, any other than the gifts which he supposed common to all bishops.]
[5] Matt. xv. 13.
[6] 1 John ii. 19.
[7] Rom. iii. 3, 4.
[8] Gal. i. 10.

inveterate heretics, the matter was not such as ought at once and hastily to be brought under your notice, as if it were great or to be feared; especially since you already know well enough the name of Fortunatus, who is one of the five presbyters who some time back deserted from the Church, and were lately excommunicated by the judgment of our fellow-bishops,[1] men both numerous and entitled to the greatest respect, who on this matter wrote to you last year. Also you would recognise Felicissimus, the standard-bearer of sedition, who himself also is comprised in those same letters long ago written to you by our co-bishops,[1] and who not only was excommunicated by them here, but moreover was lately driven from the Church by you there. Since I was confident that these things were in your knowledge, and knew for certain that they abode in your memory and discipline, I did not think it necessary that the follies of heretics should be told you quickly and urgently. For indeed it ought not to pertain to the majesty or the dignity of the Catholic Church, to concern itself with what the audacity of heretics and schismatics may attempt among themselves. For Novatian's party is also said to have now made Maximus the presbyter — who was lately sent to us as an ambassador for Novatian, and rejected from communion with us — their false bishop in that place; and yet I had not written to you about this, since all these things are slighted by us; and I had sent to you lately the names of the bishops appointed there, who with wholesome and sound discipline govern the brethren in the Catholic Church.[2] And this certainly, therefore, it was decided by the advice of all of us to write to you, that there might be found a short method of destroying error and of finding out truth, that you and our colleagues might know to whom to write, and reciprocally, from whom it behoved you to receive letters; but if any one, except those whom we have comprised in our letter, should dare to write to you, you would know either that he was polluted by sacrifice, or by receiving a certificate, or that he was one of the heretics, and therefore perverted and profane. Nevertheless, having gained an opportunity, by means of a very great friend and a clerk, I have written to you by Felicianus the acolyte, whom you had sent with Perseus our colleague, among other matters which were to be brought under your notice from their party, about that Fortunatus also. But while our brother Felicianus is either retarded there by the wind, or is detained by receiving other letters from us, he has been forestalled by Felicissimus hastening to you.

For thus wickedness always hastens, as if by its speed it could prevail against innocence.

10. But I intimated to you, my brother, by Felicianus, that there had come to Carthage, Privatus, an old heretic in the colony of Lambesa, many years ago condemned for many and grave crimes by the judgment of ninety bishops, and severely remarked upon in the letters of Fabian and Donatus, also our predecessors, as is not hidden from your knowledge;[3] who, when he said that he wished to plead his cause before us in the council which we held on the Ides of May then past, and was not permitted, made for himself that Fortunatus a pretended bishop, worthy of his college. And there had also come with him a certain Felix, whom he himself had formerly appointed a pseudo-bishop outside the Church, in heresy. But Jovinus also, and Maximus, were present as companions with the proved heretic,[4] condemned for wicked sacrifices and crimes proved against them by the judgment of nine bishops, our colleagues, and again excommunicated also by many of us last year in a council. And with these four was also joined Repostus of Suturnica, who not only fell himself in the persecution, but cast down by sacrilegious persuasion the greatest part of his people. These five, with a few who either had sacrificed, or had evil consciences, concurred in desiring Fortunatus as a false bishop for themselves, that so, their crimes agreeing, the ruler should be such as those who are ruled.

11. Hence also, dearest brother, you may now know the other falsehoods which desperate and abandoned men have there spread about, that although, of the sacrificers, or of the heretics, there were not more than five false bishops who came to Carthage, and appointed Fortunatus as the associate of their madness; yet they, as children of the devil, and full of lies, dared, as you write, to boast that there were present twenty-five bishops; which falsehood they boasted here also before among our brethren, saying that twenty-five bishops would come from Numidia to make a bishop for them. After they were detected and confounded in this their lie (only five who had made shipwreck coming together, and these being excommunicated by us), they sailed to Rome with the reward of their lies, as if the truth could not sail after them, and convict their lying tongues by proof of the certainty. And this, my brother, is real madness, not to think nor to know that lies do not long deceive, that the night only lasts so long as until the day brightens; but that when the day is clear and the sun has arisen, the darkness and gloom give place to light, and the robberies which were go-

---

[1] ["Our fellow-bishops." This council was held on the return of Cyprian, A D. 251, soon after Easter.]
[2] [They were not appointed there by any "favour of the Apostolic See," and Cyprian knows much more of their existence as bishops than Cornelius does.]

[3] [Elucidation XI.]
[4] Or, "with Privatus, the proved heretic;" or, according to the Oxford translation, "a proud heretic." [See p. 308.]

ing on through the night cease. In fine, if you were to seek the names from them, they would have none which they could even falsely give. For such among them is the penury even of wicked men, that neither of sacrificers nor of heretics can there be collected twenty-five for them; and yet, for the sake of deceiving the ears of the simple and the absent, the number is exaggerated by a lie, as if, even if this number were true, either the Church would be overcome by heretics, or righteousness by the unrighteous.

12. Nor does it behove me, dearest brother, to do like things to them, and to go through in my discourse those things which they have committed, and still commit, since we have to consider what it becomes God's priests to utter and to write. Nor ought grief to speak among us so much as shame, and I ought not to seem provoked rather to heap together reproaches than crimes and sins. Therefore I am silent upon the deceits practised in the Church. I pass over the conspiracies and adulteries, and the various kinds of crimes. That circumstance alone, however, of their wickedness, in which the cause is not mine, nor man's, but God's, I do not think must be withheld; that from the very first day of the persecution, while the recent crimes of the guilty were still hot, and not only the devil's altars, but the very hands and the mouths of the lapsed, were still smoking with the abominable sacrifices, they did not cease to communicate with the lapsed, and to interfere with their repentance. God cries, "He that sacrificeth unto any gods, save unto the Lord only, shall be rooted out."[1] And in the Gospel the Lord says, "Whosoever shall deny me, him will I deny."[2] And in another place the divine indignation and anger are not silent, saying, "To them hast thou poured out a drink-offering, and to them hast thou offered a meat-offering. Shall I not be angry with these things? saith the Lord."[3] And they interfere that God may not be entreated, who Himself declares that He is angry; they interpose that Christ may not be besought with prayers and satisfactions, who professes that him who denies Him He will deny.

13. In the very time of persecution we wrote letters on this matter, but we were not attended to. A full council being held, we decreed, not only with our consent, but also with our threatening, that the brethren should repent,[4] and that none should rashly grant peace to those who did not repent. And those sacrilegious persons rush with impious madness against God's priests, departing from the Church; and raising their parricidal arms against the Church, in order that the malice of the devil may consummate their work,[5] take pains that the divine clemency may not heal the wounded in His Church. They corrupt the repentance of the wretched men by the deceitfulness of their lies, that it may not satisfy an offended God — that he who has either blushed or feared to be a Christian before, may not afterwards seek Christ his Lord, nor he return to the Church who had departed from Church. Efforts are used that the sins may not be atoned for with just satisfactions and lamentations, that the wounds may not be washed away with tears. True peace is done away by the falsehood of a false peace; the healthful bosom of a mother is closed by the interference of the stepmother, that weeping and groaning may not be heard from the breast and from the lips of the lapsed. And beyond this, the lapsed are compelled with their tongues and lips, in the Capitol[6] wherein before they had sinned, to reproach the priests — to assail with contumelies and with abusive words the confessors and virgins, and those righteous men who are most eminent for the praise of the faith, and most glorious in the Church. By which things, indeed, it is not so much the modesty and the humility and the shame of our people that are smitten, as their own hope and life that are lacerated. For neither is it he who hears, but he who utters the reproach, that is wretched; nor is it he who is smitten by his brother, but he who smites a brother, that is a sinner under the law; and when the guilty do a wrong to the innocent, they suffer the injury who think that they are doing it. Finally, their mind is smitten by these things, and their spirit is dull, and their sense of right is estranged: it is God's wrath that they do not perceive their sins, lest repentance should follow, as it is written, "And God gave them the spirit of torpor,"[7] that is, that they may not return and be healed, and be made whole after their sins by just prayers and satisfactions. Paul the apostle in his epistle lays it down, and says, "They received not the love of the truth, that they might be saved. And for this cause God shall send them strong delusion, that they should believe a lie: that they all might be judged who believed not the truth, but had pleasure in unrighteousness."[8] The highest degree of happiness is, not to sin; the second, to acknowledge our sins. In the former, innocence flows pure and unstained to preserve us; in the latter, there comes a medicine to heal us. Both of these they have lost by offending God, both because the grace is lost which is received from the sanctification of

---

[1] Ex. xxii. 20.
[2] Matt. x. 33.
[3] Isa. lvii. 6.
[4] Strictly, the phrase here as elsewhere is, "should do penance," "pœnitentiam agerent."

[5] "That by the malice of the devil they may consummate their work:" *v. l.*
[6] *Scil.* Capitol of Carthage, for the provinces imitated Rome in this respect. Du Cange gives many instances.
[7] Isa. xxix. 10: orig. "*transpunctionis.*"
[8] 2 Thess. ii. 10-12.

baptism, and repentance comes not to their help, whereby the sin is healed. Think you, brother, that their wickednesses against God are trifling, their sins small and moderate — since by their means the majesty of an angry God is not besought, since the anger and the fire and the day of the Lord is not feared — since, when Antichrist is at hand, the faith of the militant people is disarmed by the taking away of the power of Christ and His fear? Let the laity see to it how they may amend this.[1] A heavier labour is incumbent on the priests in asserting and maintaining the majesty of God, that we seem not to neglect anything in this respect, when God admonishes us, and says, "And now, O ye priests, this commandment is for you. If ye will not hear, and if ye will not lay it to heart, to give glory unto my name, saith the Lord, I will even send a curse upon you, and I will curse your blessing."[2] Is honour, then, given to God when the majesty and decree of God are so contemned, that when He declares that He is indignant and angry with those who sacrifice, and when He threatens eternal penalties and perpetual punishments, it is proposed by the sacrilegious, and said, Let not the wrath of God be considered, let not the judgment of the Lord be feared, let not any knock at the Church of Christ; but repentance being done away with, and no confession of sin being made, the bishops being despised and trodden under foot, let peace be proclaimed by the presbyters in deceitful words; and lest the lapsed should rise up, or those placed without should return to the Church, let communion be offered to those who are not in communion?

14. To these also it was not sufficient that they had withdrawn from the Gospel, that they had taken away from the lapsed the hope of satisfaction and repentance, that they had taken away those involved in frauds or stained with adulteries, or polluted with the deadly contagion of sacrifices, lest they should entreat God, or make confession of their crimes in the Church, from all feeling and fruit of repentance; that they had set up[3] outside for themselves — outside the Church, and opposed to the Church, a conventicle of their abandoned faction, when there had flowed together a band of creatures with evil consciences, and unwilling to entreat and to satisfy God. After such things as these, moreover, they still dare — a false bishop having been appointed for them by heretics — to set sail and to bear letters from schismatic and profane persons to the throne of Peter, and to the chief church whence priestly unity takes its

source;[4] and not to consider that these were the Romans whose faith was praised in the preaching of the apostle, to whom faithlessness could have no access.[5] But what was the reason of their coming and announcing the making of the pseudo-bishop in opposition to the bishops? For either they are pleased with what they have done, and persist in their wickedness; or, if they are displeased and retreat, they know whither they may return. For, as it has been decreed by all of us[6] — and is equally fair and just — that the case of every one should be heard there where the crime has been committed; and a portion of the flock has been assigned to each individual pastor, which he is to rule and govern, having to give account of his doing to the Lord; it certainly behoves those over whom we are placed not to run about nor to break up the harmonious agreement of the bishops with their crafty and deceitful rashness, but there to plead their cause, where they may be able to have both accusers and witnesses of their crime; unless perchance the authority of the bishops constituted in Africa seems to a few desperate and abandoned men to be too little,[7] who have already judged concerning them, and have lately condemned, by the gravity of their judgment, their conscience bound in many bonds of sins. Already their case has been examined, already sentence concerning them has been pronounced; nor is it fitting for the dignity of priests to be blamed for the levity of a changeable and inconstant mind, when the Lord teaches and says, "Let your communication be, Yea, yea; Nay, nay."[8]

15. If the number of those who judged concerning them last year be reckoned with the presbyters and deacons, then there were more present to the judgment and hearing than are those very same persons who now seem to be associated with Fortunatus. For you ought to know, dearest brother, that after he was made a pseudo-bishop by the heretics, he was at once deserted by almost all. For those to whom in past time delusions were offered, and deceitful words were given, to the effect that they were to return to the Church together; after they saw that a false bishop was made there, learned that they had been fooled and deceived, and are daily returning and knocking at the *door of the*

---

[1] [The organization of the laity into their freedom and franchises is part of the Cyprianic system, and gave birth to the whole fabric of free constitutions, in England and elsewhere.]

[2] Mal. ii 1, 2.

[3] "Unless they had set up," *v l.*

[4] [The Apostolic See of the West was necessarily all this in the eyes of an unambitious faithful Western co-bishop; but the letter itself proves that it was not the See of one who had any authority over or apart from his co-bishops. Let us not read into his expressions ideas which are an after-thought, and which conflict with the life and all the testimony of Cyprian.]

[5] [To be interpreted by Epistle xxx. p. 308, *supra.* Elucidation XII.]

[6] [Note this decree, "by all of us," and what follows.]

[7] [Only "desperate and abandoned men" could make light of other bishops, by carrying their case from their own province to Rome This was forbidden by canons. Cyprian's respect for the mother See was like that felt by Anglo-Americans for Canterbury, involving no subjection in the least degree. See Elucidation XIII.]

[8] Matt. v. 37.

Church; while we, meanwhile, by whom account is to be given to the Lord, are anxiously weighing and carefully examining who ought to be received and admitted into the Church. For some are either hindered by their crimes to such a degree, or they are so obstinately and firmly opposed by their brethren, that they cannot be received at all except with offence and risk to a great many. For neither must some putridities be so collected and brought together, that the parts which are sound and whole should be injured; nor is that pastor serviceable or wise who so mingles the diseased and affected sheep with his flock as to contaminate the whole flock with the infection of the clinging evil. (Do not pay attention to their number.[1] For one who fears God is better than a thousand impious sons, as the Lord spoke by the prophet, saying, "O son, do not delight in ungodly sons, though they multiply to thee, except the fear of the Lord be with them."[2]) Oh, if you could, dearest brother, be with us here when those evil and perverse men return from schism, you would see what labour is mine to persuade patience to our brethren, that they should calm their grief of mind, and consent to receive and heal the wicked. For as they rejoice and are glad when those who are endurable and less guilty return, so, on the other hand, they murmur and are dissatisfied as often as the incorrigible and violent, and those who are contaminated either by adulteries or by sacrifices, and who, in addition to this, are proud besides, so return to the Church, as to corrupt the good dispositions within it. Scarcely do I persuade the people; nay, I extort it from them, that they should suffer such to be admitted. And the grief of the fraternity is made the more just, from the fact that one and another who, notwithstanding the opposition and contradiction of the people, have been received by my facility, have proved worse than they had been before, and have not been able to keep the faith of their repentance, because they had not come with true repentance.

16. But what am I to say of those who have now sailed to you with Felicissimus, guilty of every crime, as ambassadors sent by Fortunatus the pseudo-bishop, bringing to you letters as false as he himself is false, whose letters they bring, as his conscience is full of sins, as his life is execrable, as it is disgraceful; so that, even if they were in the Church, such people ought to be expelled from the Church. In addition, since they have known their own conscience, they do not dare to come to us or to approach to the threshold of the Church, but wander about, without her, through the province, for the sake of circumventing and defrauding the brethren; and now, being sufficiently known to all, and everywhere excluded for their crimes, they sail thither also to you. For they cannot have the face to approach to us, or to stand before us, since the crimes which are charged upon them by the brethren are most grievous and grave. If they wish to undergo our judgment, let them come. Finally, if they can find any excuse or defence, let us see what thought they have of making satisfaction, what fruit of repentance they bring forward. The Church is neither closed here to any one, nor is the bishop denied to any. Our patience, and facility, and humanity are ready for those who come. I entreat all to return into the Church. I beg all our fellow-soldiers to be included within the camp of Christ, and the dwelling-place of God the Father. I remit everything. I shut my eyes to many things, with the desire and the wish to gather together the brotherhood. Even those things which are committed against God I do not investigate with the full judgment of religion. I almost sin myself, in remitting sins[3] more than I ought. I embrace with prompt and full love those who return with repentance, confessing their sin with lowly and unaffected atonement.[4]

17. But if there are some who think that they can return to the Church not with prayers but with threats, or suppose that they can make a way for themselves, not with lamentation and atonements, but with terrors, let them take it for certain that against such the Church of the Lord stands closed; nor does the camp of Christ, unconquered and firm with the Lord's protection, yield to threats. The priest of God holding fast the Gospel and keeping Christ's precepts may be slain; he cannot be conquered. Zacharias, God's priest, suggests and furnishes to us examples of courage and faith, who, when he could not be terrified with threats and stoning, was slain in the temple of God, at the same time crying out and saying, what we also cry out and say against the heretics, "Thus saith the Lord, Ye have forsaken the ways of the Lord, and the Lord will forsake you."[5] For because a few rash and wicked men forsake the heavenly and wholesome ways of the Lord, and not doing holy things are deserted by the Holy Spirit, we also ought not therefore to be unmindful of the divine tradition, so as to think that the crimes of madmen are greater than the judgments of priests; or conceive that human endeavours can do

---

[1] [Exod. xxiii. 2. The best comment on Cyprian's system is to be found in the *Commonitory* of Vincent of Lerins (A.D. 450), who lays down the rule, that if the whole Church revolts from the faith save only a few, those few are the Catholics.]

[2] Ecclus. xvi. 1, 2. The words in parenthesis are not found in many editions.

[3] [See vol. ii. pp. 15, 22. And for this ecclesiastical "remission," 2 Cor. ii. 10, which Cyprian imitates.]

[4] [What a contrast to the hierarchical spirit of the Middle Ages, this primitive compassion for penitents! Think of Canossa.]

[5] 2 Chron. xxiv. 20.

more to attack, than divine protection avails to defend.

18. Is the dignity of the Catholic Church, dearest brother, to be laid aside, is the faithful and uncorrupted majesty of the people placed within it,[1] and the priestly authority and power also, all to be laid aside for this, that those who are set without the Church may say that they wish to judge concerning a prelate in the Church? heretics concerning a Christian? wounded men about a whole man? maimed concerning a sound man? lapsed concerning one who stands fast? guilty concerning their judge? sacrilegious men concerning a priest? What is left but that the Church should yield to the Capitol, and that, while the priests depart and remove the Lord's altar, the images and idols should pass over with their altars into the sacred and venerable assembly of our clergy, and a larger and fuller material for declaiming against us and abusing us be afforded to Novatian; if they who have sacrificed and have publicly denied Christ should begin not only to be entreated and admitted without penance done, but, moreover, in addition, to domineer by the power of their terror?

19. If they desire peace, let them lay aside their arms. If they make atonement, why do they threaten? or if they threaten, let them know that they are not feared by God's priests. For even Antichrist, when he shall begin to come, shall not enter into the Church because he threatens; neither shall we yield to his arms and violence, because he declares that he will destroy us if we resist. Heretics arm us when they think that we are terrified by their threatenings; nor do they cast us down on our face, but rather they lift us up and inflame us, when they make peace itself worse to the brethren than persecution. And we desire, indeed, that they may not fill up with crime what they speak in madness, that they who sin with perfidious and cruel words may not also sin in deeds. We pray and beseech God, whom they do not cease to provoke and exasperate, that He will soften their hearts, that they may lay aside their madness, and return to soundness of mind; that their breasts, covered over with the darkness of sins, may acknowledge the light of repentance, and that they may rather seek that the prayers and supplications of the priest may be poured out on their behalf, than themselves pour out the blood of the priest. But if they continue in their madness, and cruelly persevere in these their parricidal deceits and threats, no priest of God is so weak, so prostrate, and so abject, so inefficient by the weakness of human infirmity, as not to be aroused against the enemies and impugners

of God by strength from above; as not to find his humility and weakness animated by the vigour and strength of the Lord who protects him. It matters nothing to us by whom, or when we are slain, since we shall receive from the Lord the reward of our death and of our blood. Their *concision*[2] is to be mourned and lamented, whom the devil so blinds, that, without considering the eternal punishments of Gehenna, they endeavour to imitate the coming of Antichrist, who is now approaching.

20. And although I know, dearest brother, from the mutual love which we owe and manifest one towards another, that you always read my letters to the very distinguished clergy who preside with you there,[3] and to your very holy and large congregation,[4] yet now I both warn and ask you to do by my request what at other times you do of your own accord and courtesy; that so, by the reading of this my letter, if any contagion of envenomed speech and of pestilent propagation has crept in there, it may be all purged out of the ears and of the hearts of the brethren, and the sound and sincere affection of the good may be cleansed anew from all the filth of heretical disparagement.

21. But for the rest, let our most beloved brethren firmly decline, and avoid the words and conversations of those whose word creeps onwards like a cancer; as the apostle says, "Evil communications corrupt good manners."[5] And again: "A man that is an heretic, after one admonition, reject: knowing that he that is such is subverted, and sinneth, being condemned of himself."[6] And the Holy Spirit speaks by Solomon, saying, "A perverse man carrieth perdition in his mouth; and in his lips he hideth a fire."[7] Also again, he warneth us, and says, "Hedge in thy ears with thorns, and hearken not to a wicked tongue."[8] And again: "A wicked doer giveth heed to the tongue of the unjust; but a righteous man does not listen to lying lips."[9] And although I know that our brotherhood there,[10] assuredly fortified by your foresight, and besides sufficiently cautious by their own vigilance, cannot be taken nor deceived by the poisons of heretics, and that the teachings and precepts of God prevail with them only in proportion as the fear of God is in them; yet, even although needlessly, either my solicitude or my

---

[1] [Cyprian's love for the people is always thus conspicuous. Here the majesty and dignity of the Catholic Church is identified with all estates of men therein.]

[2] [Phil. iii. 2. The apostle calls the Judaizers a *concision*, the particle *cut off* and thrown away in the rite of circumcision; a rejected schism. See Joel iii. 14, Eng., margin. Elucidation XII.]
[3] [Note this significant language. Our author has no conception of a pontifical system excluding the presbytery from its part and place in the councils and regimen of the Church.]
[4] [Elucidation XV.; also Elucidation XIII.]
[5] 1 Cor. xv. 33.
[6] Tit. iii. 10, 11.
[7] Prov. xvi. 27.
[8] Ecclus. xxviii. 24 (Vulg. 28).
[9] Prov. xvii. 4.
[10] [It must be seen what all this implies as to the position of Cornelius and (" our brotherhood there ") his comprovincial bishops, i.e., in their relations to Cyprian.]

love persuaded me to write these things to you, that no commerce should be entered into with such; that no banquets nor conferences be entertained with the wicked; but that we should be as much separated from them, as they are deserters from the Church; because it is written, "If he shall neglect to hear the Church, let him be unto thee as a heathen man and a publican."[1] And the blessed apostle not only warns, but also commands us to withdraw from such. "We command you," he says, "in the name of Jesus Christ our Lord, that ye withdraw yourselves from every brother that walketh disorderly, and not after the tradition which he received of us."[2] There can be no fellowship between faith and faithlessness. He who is not with Christ, who is an adversary of Christ, who is hostile to His unity and peace, cannot be associated with us. If they come with prayers and atonements, let them be heard; if they heap together curses and threats, let them be rejected. I bid you, dearest brother, ever heartily farewell.[3]

EPISTLE LV.[4]

TO THE PEOPLE OF THIBARIS, EXHORTING TO MARTYRDOM.

ARGUMENT. — CYPRIAN FIRST OF ALL EXCUSES HIMSELF TO THE THIBARITANS THAT HE HAD NOT BEEN TO VISIT THEM, AND GIVES THEM WARNING OF THE PERSECUTION AT HAND; HE THEN FURNISHES INDUCEMENTS READILY TO UNDERGO MARTYRDOM.[5]

1. Cyprian to the people abiding at Thibaris, greeting. I had indeed thought, beloved brethren, and prayerfully desired — if the state of things and the condition of the times permitted, in conformity with what you frequently desired — myself to come to you; and being present with you, then to strengthen the brotherhood with such moderate powers of exhortation as I possess. But since I am detained by such urgent affairs, that I have not the power to travel far from this place, and to be long absent from the people over whom by divine mercy I am placed, I have written in the meantime this letter, to be to you in my stead. For as, by the condescension of the Lord instructing me, I am very often instigated and warned, I ought to bring unto your conscience also the anxiety of my warning.

For you ought to know and to believe, and hold it for certain, that the day of affliction has begun to hang over our heads, and the end[6] of the world and the time of Antichrist to draw near, so that we must all stand prepared for the battle; nor consider anything but the glory of life eternal, and the crown of the confession of the Lord; and not regard those things which are coming as being such as were those which have passed away. A severer and a fiercer fight is now threatening, for which the soldiers of Christ ought to prepare themselves with uncorrupted faith and robust courage, considering that they drink the cup of Christ's blood daily,[7] for the reason that they themselves also may be able to shed their blood for Christ. For this is to wish to be found with Christ, to imitate that which Christ both taught and did, according to the Apostle John, who said, "He that saith he abideth in Christ, ought himself also so to walk even as He walked."[8] Moreover, the blessed Apostle Paul exhorts and teaches, saying, "We are God's children; but if children, then heirs of God, and joint-heirs with Christ; if so be that we suffer with Him, that we may also be glorified together."[9]

2. Which things must all now be considered by us, that no one may desire anything from the world that is now dying, but may follow Christ, who both lives for ever, and quickens His servants, who are established in the faith of His name. For there comes the time, beloved brethren, which our Lord long ago foretold and taught us was approaching, saying, "The time cometh, that whosoever killeth you will think that he doeth God service. And these things they will do unto you, because they have not known the Father nor me. But these things have I told you, that when the time shall come, ye may remember that I told you of them."[10] Nor let any one wonder that we are harassed with constant persecutions, and continually tried with increasing afflictions, when the Lord before predicted that these things would happen in the last times, and has instructed us for the warfare by the teaching and exhortation of His words. Peter also, His apostle, has taught that persecutions occur for the sake of our being proved, and that we also should, by the example of righteous men who have gone before us, be joined to the love of God by death and sufferings. For he wrote in his epistle, and said, "Beloved, think it not strange concerning the fiery trial which is to try you, nor do ye fall away, as if some new

---

[1] Matt. xviii. 17.
[2] 2 Thess. iii. 6. [Cyprian virtually commands Cornelius, through the Apostle, what course to take. Elucidation XIII.]
[3] [Had such a letter been sent by Cornelius to Cyprian, — so full of warning, advice, and even direction, — what would not have been made of it as a "Decretal"? A.D. 252.]
[4] Oxford ed.: Ep. lviii.
[5] Hence are suggested illustrations of good men from the beginning of the world who have suffered martyrdom, especially that which surpasses all examples, the passion of our Lord. What incitement is afforded to the endurance of martyrdom by the brave and ready enduring of the contests of the stadium and the theatre. Finally, let the reward be considered, which now, moreover, animates and influences us to sustain everything.

[6] Occasum.
[7] [It has been a question whether this *daily* reception of the communion was confined to times of persecution, or was more generally the custom. It seems to me exceptional. Freeman, vol. i. p. 383.]
[8] 1 John ii. 6.
[9] Rom. viii. 16, 17.
[10] John xvi. 2–4.

thing happened unto you; but as often as ye partake in Christ's sufferings, rejoice in all things, that when His glory shall be revealed, ye may be glad also with exceeding joy. If ye be reproached in the name of Christ, happy are ye; for the name of the majesty and power of the Lord resteth on you, which indeed on their part is blasphemed, but on our part is glorified." [1] Now the apostles taught us those things which they themselves also learnt from the Lord's precepts and the heavenly commands, the Lord Himself thus strengthening us, and saying, "There is no man that hath left house, or land, or parents, or brethren, or sisters, or wife, or children, for the kingdom of God's sake, who shall not receive sevenfold more in this present time, and in the world to come life everlasting." [2] And again He says, "Blessed are ye when men shall hate you, and shall separate you from their company, and shall cast you out, and shall reproach your name as evil for the Son of man's sake. Rejoice ye in that day, and leap for joy; for, behold, your reward is great in heaven." [3]

3. The Lord desired that we should rejoice and leap for joy in persecutions, because, when persecutions occur, then are given the crowns of faith, then the soldiers of God are proved, then the heavens are opened to martyrs. For we have not in such a way given our name to warfare that we ought only to think about peace, and draw back from and refuse war, when in this very warfare the Lord walked first — the Teacher of humility, and endurance, and suffering — so that what He taught to be done, He first of all did, and what He exhorts to suffer, He Himself first suffered for us. Let it be before your eyes, beloved brethren, that He who alone received all judgment from the Father, and who will come to judge, has already declared the decree of His judgment and of His future recognition, foretelling and testifying that He will confess those before His Father who confess Him, and will deny those who deny Him. If we could escape death, we might reasonably fear to die. But since, on the other hand, it is necessary that a mortal man should die, we should embrace the occasion that comes by divine promise and condescension, and accomplish the ending provided by death with the reward of immortality; nor fear to be slain, since we are sure when we are slain to be crowned.

4. Nor let any one, beloved brethren, when he beholds our people driven away and scattered by the fear of persecution, be disturbed at not seeing the brotherhood gathered together, nor hearing the bishops discoursing.[4] All are not able to be there together, who may not kill, but who must be killed. Wherever, in those days, each one of the brethren shall be separated from the flock for a time, by the necessity of the season, in body, not in spirit, let him not be moved at the terror of that flight; nor, if he withdraw and be concealed, let him be alarmed at the solitude of the desert place. He is not alone, whose companion in flight Christ is; he is not alone who, keeping God's temple wheresoever he is, is not without God. And if a robber should fall upon you, a fugitive in the solitude or in the mountains; if a wild beast should attack you; if hunger, or thirst, or cold should distress you, or the tempest and the storm should overwhelm you hastening in a rapid voyage over the seas, Christ everywhere looks upon His soldier fighting; and for the sake of persecution, for the honour of His name, gives a reward to him when he dies, as He has promised that He will give in the resurrection. Nor is the glory of martyrdom less that he has not perished publicly and before many, since the cause of perishing is to perish for Christ. That Witness who proves martyrs, and crowns them, suffices for a testimony of his martyrdom.

5. Let us, beloved brethren, imitate righteous Abel, who initiated martyrdoms, he first being slain for righteousness' sake. Let us imitate Abraham, the friend of God, who did not delay to offer his son as a victim with his own hands, obeying God with a faith of devotion. Let us imitate the three children Ananias, Azarias, and Misael, who, neither frightened by their youthful age nor broken down by captivity, Judea being conquered and Jerusalem taken, overcame the king by the power of faith in his own kingdom; who, when bidden to worship the image which Nebuchadnezzar the king had made, stood forth stronger both than the king's threats and the flames, calling out and attesting their faith by these words: "O king Nebuchadnezzar, we are not careful to answer thee in this matter. For the God whom we serve is able to deliver us from the burning fiery furnace; and He will deliver us out of thine hands, O king. But if not, be it known unto thee, that we do not serve thy gods, nor worship the golden image which thou hast set up." [5] They believed that they might escape according to their faith, but they added, "and if not," that the king might know that they could also die for the God they worshipped. For this is the strength of courage and of faith, to believe and to know that God can deliver from present death, and yet not to fear death nor to give way, that faith may be the more mightily proved. The uncorrupted and unconquered might of

---

[1] 1 Pet. iv. 12–14.
[2] Luke xviii. 29, 30.
[3] Luke vi. 22, 23.
[4] [Preaching the eminent duty of true bishops. See letter li p 330, note 4, *supra*.]

[5] Dan. iii. 16–18.

the Holy Spirit broke forth by their mouth, so that the words which the Lord in His Gospel spoke are seen to be true: "But when they shall seize you, take no thought what ye shall speak; for it shall be given you in that hour what ye shall speak. For it is not ye that speak, but the Spirit of your Father which speaketh in you." [1] He said that what we are able to speak and to answer is given to us in that hour from heaven, and supplied; and that it is not then we who speak, but the Spirit of God our Father, who, as He does not depart nor is separated from those who confess Him, Himself both speaks and is crowned in us. So Daniel, too, when he was required to worship the idol Bel, which the people and the king then worshipped, in asserting the honour of his God, broke forth with full faith and freedom, saying, "I worship nothing but the Lord my God, who created the heaven and the earth." [2]

6. What shall we say of the cruel tortures of the blessed martyrs in the Maccabees,[3] and the multiform sufferings of the seven brethren, and the mother comforting her children in their agonies, and herself dying also with her children? Do not they witness the proofs of great courage and faith, and exhort us by their sufferings to the triumphs of martyrdom? What of the prophets whom the Holy Spirit quickened to the foreknowledge of future events? What of the apostles whom the Lord chose? Since these righteous men were slain for righteousness' sake, have they not taught us also to die? The nativity of Christ witnessed at once the martyrdom of infants, so that they who were two years old and under were slain for His name's sake. An age not yet fitted for the battle appeared fit for the crown. That it might be manifest that they who are slain for Christ's sake are innocent, innocent infancy was put to death for His name's sake. It is shown that none is free from the peril of persecution, when even these accomplished martyrdoms. But how grave is the case of a Christian man, if he, a servant, is unwilling to suffer, when his Master first suffered; and that we should be unwilling to suffer for our own sins, when He who had no sin of His own suffered for us! The Son of God suffered that He might make us sons of God, and the son of man will not suffer that he may continue to be a son of God! If we suffer from the world's hatred, Christ first endured the world's hatred. If we suffer reproaches in this world, if exile, if tortures, the Maker and Lord of the world experienced harder things than these, and He also warns us, saying, "If the world hate you, remember that it hated me before you. If ye were of the world, the world would love its own: but because ye are not of the world, but I have chosen you out of the world, therefore the world hateth you. Remember the word that I said unto you, The servant is not greater than his lord. If they have persecuted me, they will also persecute you." [4] Whatever our Lord and God taught, He also did, that the disciple might not be excused if he learns and does not.

7. Nor let any one of you, beloved brethren, be so terrified by the fear of future persecution, or the coming of the threatening Antichrist, as not to be found armed for all things by the evangelical exhortations and precepts, and by the heavenly warnings. Antichrist is coming, but above him comes Christ also.[5] The enemy goeth about and rageth, but immediately the Lord follows to avenge our sufferings and our wounds. The adversary is enraged and threatens, but there is One who can deliver us from his hands. He is to be feared whose anger no one can escape, as He Himself forewarns, and says: "Fear not them which kill the body, but are not able to kill the soul; but rather fear Him which is able to destroy both body and soul in hell." [6] And again: "He that loveth his life, shall lose it; and he that hateth his life in this world, shall keep it unto life eternal." [7] And in the Apocalypse He instructs and forewarns, saying, "If any man worship the beast and his image, and receive his mark in his forehead or in his hand, the same also shall drink of the wine of the wrath of God, mixed in the cup of His indignation, and he shall be tormented with fire and brimstone in the presence of the holy angels, and in the presence of the Lamb; and the smoke of their torments shall ascend up for ever and ever; and they shall have no rest day nor night, who worship the beast and his image." [8]

8. For the secular contest men are trained and prepared, and reckon it a great glory of their honour if it should happen to them to be crowned in the sight of the people, and in the presence of the emperor. Behold a lofty and great contest, glorious also with the reward of a heavenly crown, inasmuch as God looks upon us as we struggle, and, extending His view over those whom He has condescended to make His sons, He enjoys the spectacle of our contest. God looks upon us in the warfare, and fighting in the encounter of faith; His angels look on us, and Christ looks on us. How great is the dignity, and how great the happiness of the

---

[1] Matt. x. 19, 20.
[2] Bel and the Dragon, 5.
[3] [Referred to by St. Paul, Heb. xi. 35. I say St. Paul advisedly. See, to the contrary, Farrar, St. Paul, p. 6.]
[4] John xv. 18–20.
[5] [Valuable note, Oxford trans., Ep. lviii. p. 142, note k.]
[6] Matt. x. 28.
[7] John xii. 25.
[8] Apoc. xiv. 9–11.

glory, to engage in the presence of God, and to be crowned, with Christ for a judge ! Let us be armed, beloved brethren, with our whole strength, and let us be prepared for the struggle with an uncorrupted mind, with a sound faith, with a devoted courage. Let the camp of God go forth to the battle-field which is appointed to us. Let the sound ones be armed, lest he that is sound should lose the advantage of having lately stood ; let the lapsed also be armed, that even the lapsed may regain what he has lost : let honour provoke the whole ; let sorrow provoke the lapsed to the battle. The Apostle Paul teaches us to be armed and prepared, saying, "We wrestle not against flesh and blood, but against powers, and the princes of this world and of this darkness, against spirits of wickedness in high places. Wherefore put on the whole armour, that ye may be able to withstand in the most evil day, that when ye have done all ye may stand ; having your loins girt about with truth, and having put on the breastplate of righteousness ; and your feet shod with the preparation of the Gospel of peace ; taking the shield of faith, wherewith ye shall be able to quench all the fiery darts of the wicked one ; and the helmet of salvation, and the sword of the Spirit, which is the word of God."[1]

9. Let us take these arms, let us fortify ourselves with these spiritual and heavenly safeguards, that in the most evil day we may be able to withstand, and to resist the threats of the devil : let us put on the breastplate of righteousness, that our breast may be fortified and safe against the darts of the enemy : let our feet be shod with evangelical teaching, and armed, so that when the serpent shall begin to be trodden and crushed by us, he may not be able to bite and trip us up : let us bravely bear the shield of faith, by the protection of which, whatever the enemy darts at us may be extinguished : let us take also for protection of our head the helmet of salvation, that our ears may be guarded from hearing the deadly edicts ; that our eyes may be fortified, that they may not see the odious images ; that our brow may be fortified, so as to keep safe the sign of God ;[2] that our mouth may be fortified, that the conquering tongue may confess Christ its Lord : let us also arm the right hand with the sword of the Spirit, that it may bravely reject the deadly sacrifices ; that, mindful of the Eucharist, the hand which has received the Lord's body[3] may embrace the Lord Himself, hereafter to receive from the Lord the reward of heavenly crowns.

10. Oh, what and how great will that day be at its coming, beloved brethren, when the Lord shall begin to count up His people, and to recognise the deservings of each one by the inspection of His divine knowledge, to send the guilty to Gehenna, and to set on fire our persecutors with the perpetual burning of a penal fire, but to pay to us the reward of our faith and devotion ! What will be the glory and how great the joy to be admitted to see God, to be honoured to receive with Christ, thy Lord God, the joy of eternal salvation and light — to greet Abraham, and Isaac, and Jacob, and all the patriarchs, and prophets, and apostles, and martyrs — to rejoice with the righteous and the friends of God in the kingdom of heaven, with the pleasure of immortality given to us — to receive there what neither eye hath seen, nor ear heard, neither hath entered into the heart of man ! For the apostle announces that we shall receive greater things than anything that we here either do or suffer, saying, "The sufferings of this present time are not worthy to be compared with the glory to come hereafter which shall be revealed in us."[4] When that revelation shall come, when that glory of God shall shine upon us, we shall be as happy and joyful, honoured with the condescension of God, as they will remain guilty and wretched, who, either as deserters from God or rebels against Him, have done the will of the devil, so that it is necessary for them to be tormented with the devil himself in unquenchable fire.

11. Let these things, beloved brethren, take hold of our hearts ; let this be the preparation of our arms, this our daily and nightly meditation, to have before our eyes and ever to revolve in our thoughts and feelings the punishments of the wicked and the rewards and the deservings of the righteous : what the Lord threatens by way of punishment against those that deny Him ; what, on the other hand, He promises by way of glory to those that confess Him. If, while we think and meditate on these things, there should come to us a day of persecution, the soldier of Christ instructed in His precepts and warnings is not fearful for the battle, but is prepared for the crown. I bid you, dearest brethren, ever heartily farewell.

EPISTLE LVI.[5]

TO CORNELIUS IN EXILE, CONCERNING HIS CONFESSION.

ARGUMENT. — CYPRIAN PRAISES IN CORNELIUS AND HIS PEOPLE THEIR CONFESSION OF THE NAME OF CHRIST EVEN TO BANISHMENT ; AND EXHORTS THEM TO CONSTANCY AND TO MUTUAL

---

[1] Eph. vi. 12-17.
[2] *Scil. :* the sign of the cross in baptism.
[3] It is observed here that the Eucharist was at this time received by the hand of the communicant, and not placed in his mouth by the minister, as some have pretended was the original mode of administration. [See Cyril of Jerusalem, *Mystagog.*, v. p. 1126, migne.]

[4] Rom. viii. 18.
[5] Oxford ed.: Ep. lx. A.D. 252.

PRAYER FOR ONE ANOTHER, AS WELL IN RE-
SPECT OF THE APPROACHING DAY OF STRUGGLE
IN THIS LIFE, AS AFTER DEATH.[1]

1. Cyprian to Cornelius his brother, greeting.
We have been made acquainted, dearest brother,
with the glorious testimonies of your faith and
courage, and have received with such exultation
the honour of your confession, that we count
ourselves also sharers and companions in your
merits and praises. For as we have one Church,
a mind united, and a concord undivided, what
priest does not congratulate himself on the
praises of his fellow-priest[2] as if on his own ; or
what brotherhood would not rejoice in the joy
of its brethren? It cannot be sufficiently declared how great was the exultation and how
great the joy here, when we had heard of your
success and bravery, that you had stood forth as
a leader of confession to the brethren there ;
and, moreover, that the confession of the leader
had increased by the consent of the brethren ; so
that, while you precede them to glory, you have
made many your companions in glory, and have
persuaded the people to become a confessor by
being first prepared to confess on behalf of all ;
so that we are at a loss what we ought first of
all to commend in you, whether your prompt
and decided faith, or the inseparable love of the
brethren. Among you the courage of the bishop
going before has been publicly proved, and the
unitedness of the brotherhood following has been
shown. As with you there is one mind and one
voice, the whole Roman Church has confessed.[3]

2. The faith, dearest brethren, which the
blessed apostle commended in you has shone
brightly. He even then in the spirit foresaw
this praise of courage and firmness of strength ;
and, attesting your merits by the commendation
of your futur doings, in praising the parents he
provokes the children. While you are thus
unanimous, while you are thus brave, you have
given great examples both of unanimity and of
bravery to the rest of the brethren. You have
taught them deeply to fear God, firmly to cling
to Christ ; that the people should be associated
with the priests in peril ; that the brethren should
not be separated from brethren in persecution ;
that a concord, once established, can by no
means be overcome ; that whatsoever is at the
same time sought for by all, the God of peace
will grant to the peaceful. The adversary had
leapt forth to disturb the camp of Christ with
violent terror ; but, with the same impetuosity
with which he had come, he was beaten back

and conquered ; and as much fear and terror as
he had brought, so much bravery and strength
he also found. He had thought that he could
again overthrow the servants of God, and agitate
them in his accustomed manner, as if they were
novices and inexperienced—as if little prepared
and little cautious. He attacked one first, as a
wolf had tried to separate the sheep from the
flock, as a hawk to separate the dove from the
flying troop ; for he who has not sufficient
strength against all, seeks to gain advantage from
the solitude of individuals. But when beaten
back as well by the faith as by the vigour of the
combined army, he perceived that the soldiers
of Christ are now watching, and stand sober and
armed for the battle ; that they cannot be conquered, but that they can die ; and that by this
very fact they are invincible, that they do not
fear death ; that they do not in turn assail their
assailants, since it is not lawful for the innocent
even to kill the guilty ; but that they readily deliver up both their lives and their blood ; that
since such malice and cruelty rages in the world,
they may the more quickly withdraw from the
evil and cruel. What a glorious spectacle was
that under the eyes of God ! what a joy of His
Church in the sight of Christ, that not single
soldiers, but the whole camp, at once went forth
to the battle which the enemy had tried to begin ! For it is plain that all would have come
if they could have heard, since whoever heard
ran hastily and came. How many lapsed were
there restored by a glorious confession ! They
bravely stood, and by the very suffering of repentance were made braver for the battle, that
it might appear that lately they had been taken
at unawares, and had trembled at the fear of a
new and unaccustomed thing, but that they had
afterwards returned to themselves ; that true
faith and their strength, gathered from the fear
of God, had constantly and firmly strengthened
them to all endurance ; and that now they do
not stand for pardon of their crime, but for the
crown of their suffering.

3. What does Novatian say to these things,
dearest brother? Does he yet lay aside his
error? Or, indeed, as is the custom of foolish
men, is he more driven to fury by our very
benefits and prosperity ; and in proportion as
the glory of love and faith grows here more and
more, does the madness of dissension and envy
break out anew there? Does the wretched man
not cure his own wound, but wound both himself and his friends still more severely, clamour-
ing with his tongue to the ruin of the brethren,
and hurling darts of poisonous eloquence, more
severe in accordance with the wickedness of a
secular philosophy than peaceable with the gentleness of the Lord's wisdom,—a deserter of the
Church, a foe to mercy, a destroyer of repent-

---

[1] Damasus mentions this epistle in the life of Cornelius, as being
that on account of which a calumny arose, whence the tyrant took an
excuse for his death.

[2] [Note the entire equality of these bishops. Carthage and
Rome are of equal sacerdocy.]

[3] [Cornelius the voice of his diocese only because they concur
with him. Compare Leto, *Vat. Council*, p. 223 and *passim*.]

ance, a teacher of arrogance, a corrupter of truth, a murderer of love? Does he now acknowledge who is the priest of God; which is the Church and the house of Christ; who are God's servants, whom the devil molests; who the Christians, whom Antichrist attacks? For neither does he seek those whom he has already subdued, nor does he take the trouble to overthrow those whom he has already made his own. The foe and enemy of the Church despises and passes by those whom he has alienated from the Church, and led without as captives and conquered; he goes on to harass those in whom he sees Christ dwell.

4. Even although any one of such should have been seized, there is no reason for his flattering himself, as if in the confession of the name; since it is manifest that, if people of this sort should be put to death outside the Church, it is no crown of faith, but is rather a punishment of treachery. Nor will those dwell in the house of God among those that are of one mind, whom we see to have withdrawn by the madness of discord from the peaceful and divine household.

5. We earnestly exhort as much as we can, dearest brother, for the sake of the mutual love by which we are joined one to another, that since we are instructed by the providence of the Lord, who warns us, and are admonished by the wholesome counsels of divine mercy, that the day of our contest and struggle is already approaching, we should not cease to be instant with all the people in fastings, in watchings, in prayers. Let us be urgent, with constant groanings and frequent prayers. For these are our heavenly arms, which make us to stand fast and bravely to persevere. These are the spiritual defences and divine weapons which defend us. Let us remember one another in concord and unanimity. Let us on both sides always pray for one another. Let us relieve burdens and afflictions by mutual love, that if any one of us, by the swiftness of divine condescension, shall go hence the first, our love may continue in the presence of the Lord, and our prayers for our brethren and sisters not cease in the presence of the Father's mercy. I bid you, dearest brother, ever heartly farewell.

EPISTLE LVII.[1]

TO LUCIUS[2] THE BISHOP OF ROME, RETURNED FROM BANISHMENT.

ARGUMENT. — CYPRIAN, WITH HIS COLLEAGUES, CONGRATULATES LUCIUS ON HIS RETURN FROM EXILE, REMINDING HIM THAT MARTYRDOM DE-

FERRED DOES NOT MAKE THE GLORY LESS. THEN, POINTING OUT THAT THE MARTYRDOM OF CORNELIUS AND THE BANISHMENT OF LUCIUS HAD HAPPENED BY DIVINE DIRECTION, FOR THE CONFUSION OF THE NOVATIANS, HE FORETELLS TO HIM HIS OWN IMPENDING MARTYRDOM, GOD SO ORDAINING IT THAT IT SHOULD BE CONSUMMATED NOT AWAY FROM HOME, BUT AMONG HIS OWN PEOPLE.

1. Cyprian, with his colleagues, to Lucius his brother, greeting. We had lately also congratulated you indeed, dearest brother, when the divine condescension, by a double honour, appointed you in the administration of God's Church, as well a confessor as a priest. But now also we no less congratulate you and your companions, and the whole fraternity, that the benignant and liberal protection of the Lord has brought you back again to His own with the same glory, and with praises to you; that so the shepherd might be restored to feed his flock, and the pilot to manage the ship, and the ruler to govern the people; and that it might appear that your banishment was so divinely arranged, not that the bishop banished and driven away should be wanting to the Church, but that he should return to the Church greater than he had left it.

2. For the dignity of martyrdom was not the less in the case of the three youths, because, their death being frustrated, they came forth safe from the fiery furnace; nor did Daniel stand forth uncompleted in the praise he deserved, because, when he had been sent to the lions for a prey, he was protected by the Lord, and lived to glory. Among confessors of Christ, martyrdoms deferred do not diminish the merits of confession, but show forth the greatness of divine protection. We see represented in you what the brave and illustrious youths announced before the king, that they indeed were prepared to be burnt in the flames, that they might not serve his gods, nor worship the image which he had made; but that the God whom they worshipped, and whom we also worship, was able even to rescue them from the fiery furnace, and to deliver them from the hands of the king, and from imminent sufferings. This we now find carried out in the faith of your confession, and in the Lord's protection over you; so that while you were prepared and ready to undergo all punishment, yet the Lord withdrew you from punishment, and preserved you for the Church. In your return the dignity of his confession has not been abridged in the bishop, but the priestly authority has rather increased; so that a priest is assisting at the altar of God, who exhorts the people to take up the arms of confession, and to submit to martyrdom, not by his words, but by his deeds; and, now

that Antichrist is near, prepares the soldiers for the battle, not only by the urgency of his speech and his words, but by the example of his faith and courage.

3. We understand, dearest brother, and we perceive with the whole light of our heart, the salutary and holy plans of the divine majesty, whence the sudden persecution lately arose there — whence the secular power suddenly broke forth against the Church of Christ and the bishop Cornelius, the blessed martyr, and all of you ; so that, for the confusion and beating down of heretics, the Lord might show[1] which was the Church — which is its one bishop chosen by divine appointment — which presbyters are associated with the bishop in priestly honour — which is the united and true people of Christ, linked together in the love of the Lord's flock — who they were whom the enemy would harass ; whom, on the other hand, the devil would spare as being his own. For Christ's adversary does not persecute and attack any except Christ's camp and soldiers ; heretics, once prostrated and made his own, he despises and passes by. He seeks to cast down those whom he sees to stand.

4. And I wish, dearest brother, that the power were now given us to be with you there on your return, that we ourselves, who love you with mutual love, might, being present with the rest, also receive the very joyous fruit of your coming. What exultation among all the brethren there ; what running together and embracing of each one as they arrive ! Scarcely can you be satisfied with the kisses of those who cling to you ; scarcely can the very faces and eyes of the people be satiated with seeing. At the joy of your coming the brotherhood there has begun to recognise what and how great a joy will follow when Christ shall come. For because His advent will quickly approach, a kind of representation has now gone before in you ; that just as John, His forerunner and preparer of His way, came and preached that Christ had come, so, now that a bishop returns as a confessor of the Lord, and His priest, it appears that the Lord also is now returning. But I and my colleagues, and all the brotherhood, send this letter to you in the stead of us, dearest brother ; and setting forth to you by our letter our joy, we express the faithful inclination of our love here also in our sacrifices and our prayers, not ceasing to give thanks to God the Father, and to Christ His Son our Lord ; and as well to pray as to entreat, that He who is perfect, and makes perfect, will keep and perfect in you the glorious crown of your confession, who perchance has called you back for this purpose, that your glory should not be hidden, if the martyrdom of your confession should be consummated away

from home. For the victim which affords an example to the brotherhood both of courage and of faith, ought to be offered up when the brethren are present. We bid you, dearest brother, ever heartily farewell.

EPISTLE LVIII.[2]

TO FIDUS, ON THE BAPTISM OF INFANTS.

ARGUMENT. — IN THIS LETTER CYPRIAN IS NOT ESTABLISHING ANY NEW DECREE ; BUT KEEPING MOST FIRMLY THE FAITH OF THE CHURCH, FOR THE CORRECTION OF THOSE WHO THOUGHT THAT AN INFANT MUST NOT BE BAPTIZED BEFORE THE EIGHTH DAY AFTER ITS BIRTH, HE DECREED WITH SOME OF HIS FELLOW-BISHOPS, THAT AS SOON AS IT WAS BORN IT MIGHT PROPERLY BE BAPTIZED. HE TAKES OCCASION, HOWEVER, TO REFUSE TO RECALL THE PEACE THAT HAD BEEN GRANTED TO ONE VICTOR, ALTHOUGH IT HAD BEEN GRANTED AGAINST THE DECREES OF SYNODS CONCERNING THE LAPSED ; BUT FORBIDS THERAPIUS THE BISHOP TO DO IT IN OTHER CASES.[3]

1. Cyprian, and others his colleagues who were present in council, in number sixty-six, to Fidus their brother, greeting. We have read your letter, dearest brother, in which you intimated concerning Victor, formerly a presbyter, that our colleague Therapius, rashly at a too early season, and with over-eager haste, granted peace to him before he had fully repented, and had satisfied the Lord God, against whom he had sinned ; which thing rather disturbed us, that it was a departure from the authority of our decree,[4] that peace should be granted to him before the legitimate and full time of satisfaction, and without the request and consciousness of the people — no sickness rendering it urgent, and no necessity compelling it. But the judgment being long weighed among us, it was considered sufficient to rebuke Therapius our colleague for having done this rashly, and to have instructed him that he should not do the like with any other. Yet we did not think that the peace once granted in any wise by a priest[5] of God was to be taken away, and for this reason have allowed Victor to avail himself of the communion granted to him.

2. But in respect of the case of the infants, which you say ought not to be baptized within the second or third day after their birth, and that the law of ancient circumcision should be regarded, so that you think that one who is just born should not be baptized and sanctified with-

---

[1] [Not Novatian. The organization at Rome is here glanced at, as answering to the Cyprianic theory in all respects.]

[2] Oxford ed.: Ep. lxiv. [It would be unbecoming in me to add comments of my own on this letter. Such are the views of Cyprian; and one may see the opposite views, set forth with extreme candor, by Jeremy Taylor in his *Liberty of Prophesying.*]
[3] This letter was evidently written after both synods concerning the lapsed, of which mention was made above in Epistle liii.; but whether a long time or a short time after is uncertain, although the context indicates that it was written during a time of peace.
[4] [i.e., the decree of the synod, or council.]
[5] [See letter liv. p. 340, *supra.*]

in the eighth day, we all thought very differently in our council. For in this course which you thought was to be taken, no one agreed ; but we all rather judge that the mercy and grace of God is not to be refused to any one born of man. For as the Lord says in His Gospel, "The Son of man is not come to destroy men's lives, but to save them,"[1] as far as we can, we must strive that, if possible, no soul be lost. For what is wanting to him who has once been formed in the womb by the hand of God? To us, indeed, and to our eyes, according to the worldly course of days, they who are born appear to receive an increase. But whatever things are made by God, are completed by the majesty and work of God their Maker.

3. Moreover, belief in divine Scripture declares to us, that among all, whether infants or those who are older, there is the same equality of the divine gift. Elisha, beseeching God, so laid himself upon the infant son of the widow, who was lying dead, that his head was applied to his head, and his face to his face, and the limbs of Elisha were spread over and joined to each of the limbs of the child, and his feet to his feet. If this thing be considered with respect to the inequality of our birth and our body, an infant could not be made equal with a person grown up and mature, nor could its little limbs fit and be equal to the larger limbs *of a man*. But in that is expressed the divine and spiritual equality, that all men are like and equal, since they have once been made by God ; and our age may have a difference in the increase of our bodies, according to the world, but not according to God ; unless that very grace also which is given to the baptized is given either less or more, according to the age of the receivers, whereas the Holy Spirit is not given with measure, but by the love and mercy of the Father alike to all. For God, as He does not accept the person, so does not accept the age ; since He shows Himself a Father to all with well-weighed equality for the attainment of heavenly grace.

4. For, with respect to what you say, that the aspect of an infant in the first days after its birth is not pure, so that any one of us would still shudder at kissing it,[2] we do not think that this ought to be alleged as any impediment to heavenly grace. For it is written, "To the pure all things are pure."[3] Nor ought any of us to shudder at that which God hath condescended to make. For although the infant is still fresh from its birth, yet it is not such that any one should shudder at kissing it in giving grace and in making peace ; since in the kiss of an infant

every one of us ought, for his very religion's sake, to consider the still recent hands of God themselves, which in some sort we are kissing, in the man lately formed and freshly born, when we are embracing that which God has made. For in respect of the observance of the eighth day in the Jewish circumcision of the flesh, a sacrament was given beforehand in shadow and in usage ; but when Christ came, it was fulfilled in truth. For because the eighth day, that is, the first day after the Sabbath, was to be that on which the Lord should rise again, and should quicken us, and give us circumcision of the spirit, the eighth day, that is, the first day after the Sabbath, and the Lord's day, went before in the figure ; which figure ceased when by and by the truth came, and spiritual circumcision was given to us.

5. For which reason we think that no one is to be hindered from obtaining grace by that law which was already ordained, and that spiritual circumcision ought not to be hindered by carnal circumcision, but that absolutely every man is to be admitted to the grace of Christ, since Peter also in the Acts of the Apostles speaks, and says, "The Lord hath said to me that I should call no man common or unclean."[4] But if anything could hinder men from obtaining grace, their more heinous sins might rather hinder those who are mature and grown up and older. But again, if even to the greatest sinners, and to those who had sinned much against God, when they subsequently believed, remission of sins is granted — and nobody is hindered from baptism and from grace — how much rather ought we to shrink from hindering an infant, who, being lately born, has not sinned, except in that, being born after the flesh according to Adam,[5] he has contracted the contagion of the ancient death at its earliest birth, who approaches the more easily on this very account to the reception of the forgiveness of sins — that to him are remitted, not his own sins, but the sins of another.

6. And therefore, dearest brother, this was our opinion in council, that by us no one ought to be hindered from baptism and from the grace of God, who is merciful and kind and loving to all. Which, since it is to be observed and maintained in respect of all, we think is to be even more observed in respect of infants and newly-born persons, who on this very account deserve more from our help and from the divine mercy, that immediately, on the very beginning of their birth, lamenting and weeping, they do nothing else but entreat. We bid you, dearest brother, ever heartily farewell.

---

[1] Luke ix. 56.
[2] [A marvellous relic of pagan ideas. A new-born babe, after its bath, makes no such impression upon civilized minds.]
[3] Tit. i. 15.

[4] Acts x. 28.
[5] [I cannot refrain from quoting a layman's beautiful lines on the death of his son : —

"Pure from all stain save that of human clay,
    Which Christ's atoning blood had washed away."
        GEORGE CANNING, A.D. 1770-1827.]

EPISTLE LIX.[1]

TO THE NUMIDIAN BISHOPS, ON THE REDEMPTION OF THEIR BRETHREN FROM CAPTIVITY AMONG THE BARBARIANS.

ARGUMENT. — CYPRIAN BEGINS BY DEPLORING THE CAPTIVITY OF THE BRETHREN, OF WHICH HE HAD HEARD FROM THE NUMIDIAN BISHOPS, AND SAYS THAT HE IS SENDING THEM A HUNDRED THOUSAND SESTERCES, CONTRIBUTED BY BRETHREN AND SISTERS AND COLLEAGUES.[2]

1. Cyprian to Januarius, Maximus, Proculus, Victor, Modianus, Nemesianus, Nampulus, and Honoratus, his brethren, greeting. With excessive grief of mind, and not without tears, dearest brethren, I have read your letter which you wrote to me from the solicitude of your love, concerning the captivity of our brethren and sisters. For who would not grieve at misfortunes of that kind, or who would not consider his brother's grief his own, since the Apostle Paul speaks, saying, "Whether one member suffer, all the members suffer with it; or one member rejoice, all the members rejoice with it;"[3] and in another place he says, "Who is weak, and I am not weak?"[4] Wherefore now also the captivity of our brethren must be reckoned as our captivity, and the grief of those who are endangered is to be esteemed as our grief, since indeed there is one body of our union; and not love only, but also religion, ought to instigate and strengthen us to redeem the members of the brethren.

2. For inasmuch as the Apostle Paul says again, "Know ye not that ye are the temple of God, and that the Spirit of God dwelleth in you?"[5] — even although love urged us less to bring help to the brethren, yet in this place we must have considered that it was the temples of God which were taken captive, and that we ought not by long inactivity and neglect of their suffering to allow the temples of God to be long captive, but to strive with what powers we can, and to act quickly by our obedience, to deserve well of Christ our Judge and Lord and God. For as the Apostle Paul says, "As many of you as have been baptized into Christ have put on Christ,"[6] Christ is to be contemplated in our captive brethren, and He is to be redeemed from the peril of captivity who redeemed us from the peril of death; so that He who took us out of the jaws of the devil, who abides and dwells in us, may now Himself be rescued and redeemed from the hands of barbarians by a sum of money — who redeemed us by His cross and blood — who suffers these things to happen for this reason, that our faith may be tried, whether each one of us will do for another what he would wish to be done for himself, if he himself were held captive among barbarians. For who that is mindful of humanity, and reminded of mutual love, if he be a father, will not now consider that his sons are there; if he be a husband, will not think that his wife is there kept captive, with as much grief as shame for the marriage tie? But how great is the general grief among all of us, and suffering concerning the peril of virgins who are kept there, on whose behalf we must bewail not only the loss of liberty, but of modesty; and must lament the bonds of barbarians less than the violence of seducers and abominable places, lest the members dedicated to Christ, and devoted for ever in honour of continence by modest virtue, should be sullied by the lust and contagion of the insulter.

3. Our brotherhood, considering all these things according to your letter, and sorrowfully examining, have all promptly and willingly and liberally gathered together supplies of money for the brethren, being always indeed, according to the strength of their faith, prone to the work of God, but now even more stimulated to salutary works by the consideration of so great a suffering. For since the Lord in His Gospel says, "I was sick, and ye visited me,"[7] with how much greater reward for our work will He say now, "I was captive, and ye redeemed me!" And since again He says, "I was in prison, and ye came unto me," how much more will it be when He begins to say, "I was in the dungeon of captivity, and I lay shut up and bound among barbarians, and from that prison of slavery you delivered me," being about to receive a reward from the Lord when the day of judgment shall come! Finally, we give you the warmest thanks that you have wished us to be sharers in your anxiety,[8] and in so great and necessary a work — that you have offered us fruitful fields in which we might cast the seeds of our hope, with the expectation of a harvest of the most abundant fruits which will proceed from this heavenly and saving operation. We have then sent you a sum of one hundred thousand sesterces,[9] which have been collected here in the Church over which by the Lord's mercy we preside, by the contributions of the clergy and people established with us, which you will there dispense with what diligence you may.

4. And we wish, indeed, that nothing of such a kind may happen again, and that our brethren, protected by the majesty of the Lord, may be

---

[1] Oxford ed.: Ep. lxii. A.D. 253.
[2] It is probable that this captivity was the work of those barbarians against whom Decius went to war and was killed.
[3] 1 Cor. xii. 26.
[4] 2 Cor. xi. 29.
[5] 1 Cor. iii. 16.
[6] Gal. iii. 27.

[7] Matt. xxv. 36.
[8] [Primitive Christians were grateful for opportunities to distribute gifts. Rom. xii. 13.]
[9] [An immense contribution, for the times. In our money reckoned (for *temp. Decii*) at $3,757. For the Augustan age it would be $4,294. The text (*sestertia*) dubious. Ed. Paris.

preserved safe from perils of this kind. If, however, for the searching out of the love of our mind, and for the testing of the faith of our heart, any such thing should happen, do not delay to tell us of it in your letters, counting it for certain that our church and the whole fraternity here beseech by their prayers that these things may not happen again ; but if they happen, that they will willingly and liberally render help. But that you may have in mind in your prayers our brethren and sisters who have laboured so promptly and liberally for this needful work, that they may always labour ; and that in return for their good work you may present them in your sacrifices and prayers, I have subjoined the names of each one ; and moreover also I have added the names of my colleagues and fellow-priests, who themselves also, as they were present, contributed some little according to their power, in their own names and the name of their people. And besides our own amount, I have intimated and sent their small sums, all of whom, in conformity with the claims of faith and charity, you ought to remember in your supplications and prayers.[1] We bid you, dearest brethren, ever heartily farewell, and remember us.

EPISTLE LX.[2]

TO EUCHRATIUS, ABOUT AN ACTOR.

ARGUMENT.— HE FORBIDS AN ACTOR, IF HE CONTINUE IN HIS DISGRACEFUL CALLING, FROM COMMUNICATING IN THE CHURCH. NEITHER DOES HE ALLOW IT TO BE AN EXCUSE FOR HIM, THAT HE HIMSELF DOES NOT PRACTICE THE HISTRIONIC ART, SO LONG AS HE TEACHES IT TO OTHERS ; NEITHER DOES HE EXCUSE IT BECAUSE OF THE WANT OF MEANS, SINCE NECESSARIES MAY BE SUPPLIED TO HIM FROM THE RESOURCES OF THE CHURCH ; AND THEREFORE, IF THE MEANS OF THE CHURCH THERE ARE NOT SUFFICIENT, HE RECOMMENDS HIM TO COME TO CARTHAGE.

1. Cyprian to Euchratius his brother, greeting. From our mutual love and your reverence for me you have thought that I should be consulted, dearest brother, as to my opinion concerning a certain actor, who, being settled among you, still persists in the discredit of the same art of his ; and as a master and teacher, not for the instruction, but for the destruction of boys, that which he has unfortunately learnt he also imparts to others : you ask whether such a one ought to communicate with us. This, I think, neither befits the divine majesty nor the discipline of the Gospel, that the modesty and credit of the Church

should be polluted by so disgraceful and infamous a contagion. For since, in the law, men are forbidden to put on a woman's garment, and those that offend in this manner are judged accursed, how much greater is the crime, not only to take women's garments, but also to express base and effeminate and luxurious gestures, by the teaching of an immodest art.

2. Nor let any one excuse himself that he himself has given up the theatre, while he is still teaching the art to others. For he cannot appear to have given it up who substitutes others in his place, and who, instead of himself alone, supplies many in his stead ; against God's appointment, instructing and teaching in what way a man may be broken down into a woman, and his sex changed by art,[3] and how the devil who pollutes the divine image may be gratified by the sins of a corrupted and enervated body. But if such a one alleges poverty and the necessity of small means, his necessity also can be assisted among the rest who are maintained by the support of the Church ; if he be content, that is, with very frugal but innocent food. And let him not think that he is redeemed by an allowance to cease from sinning, since this is an advantage not to us, but to himself. What more he may wish he must seek thence, from such gain as takes men away from the banquet of Abraham, and Isaac, and Jacob, and leads them down, sadly and perniciously fattened in this world, to the eternal torments of hunger and thirst ; and therefore, as far as you can, recall him from this depravity and disgrace to the way of innocence, and to the hope of eternal life, that he may be content with the maintenance of the Church, sparing indeed, but wholesome. But if the Church with you is not sufficient for this, to afford support for those in need, he may transfer himself to us, and here receive what may be necessary to him for food and clothing, and not teach deadly things to others without the Church, but himself learn wholesome things in the Church. I bid you, dearest brother, ever heartily farewell.

EPISTLE LXI.[4]

TO POMPONIUS, CONCERNING SOME VIRGINS.

ARGUMENT. — CYPRIAN, WITH SOME OF HIS COLLEAGUES, REPLIES TO HIS COLLEAGUE POMPONIUS, THAT VIRGINS WHO HAD DETERMINED TO MAINTAIN THEIR STATE WITH CONTINENCY AND FIRMNESS, BUT WHO HAD YET SUBSEQUENTLY BEEN FOUND IN THE SAME BED WITH MEN, IF THEY WERE STILL FOUND TO BE VIRGINS, SHOULD

---

[1] [The *diptychs* are here referred to; that is, lists (read at the Eucharist) in which benefactors, living or dead, were gratefully remembered. *Anglice*, "beadroll."]

[2] Oxford ed.: Ep. ii. *Circa* A.D. 249.

[3] [In the Sistine Chapel of the Vatican, to the disgrace of the pontifical court, the fine music is obtained by recourse to this expedient, inflicted upon children.]

[4] Oxford ed.: Ep. iv. He suggests the kind of discipline by which virgins may be kept in their duty, and some matters concerning the power of excommunication in the Church. *Circa* A.D. 249.

BE RECEIVED INTO COMMUNION AND ADMITTED TO THE CHURCH. BUT IF OTHERWISE, SINCE THEY ARE ADULTEROUS TOWARDS CHRIST, THEY SHOULD BE COMPELLED TO FULL REPENTANCE, AND THOSE WHO SHOULD OBSTINATELY PERSEVERE SHOULD BE EJECTED FROM THE CHURCH.

1. Cyprian, Cæcilius, Victor, Sedatus, Tertullus, with the presbyters who were present with them, to Pomponius their brother, greeting. We have read, dearest brother, your letter which you sent by Paconius our brother, asking and desiring us to write again to you, and say what we thought of those virgins who, after having once determined to continue in their condition, and firmly to maintain their continency, have afterwards been found to have remained in the same bed side by side with men; of whom you say that one is a deacon; and yet that the same virgins who have confessed that they have slept with men declare that they are chaste.[1] Concerning which matters, since you have desired our advice, know that we do not depart from the traditions of the Gospel and of the apostles, but with constancy and firmness take counsel for our brethren and sisters, and maintain the discipline of the Church by all the ways of usefulness and safety, since the Lord speaks, saying, "And I will give you pastors according to mine heart, and they shall feed you with discipline."[2] And again it is written, "Whoso despiseth discipline is miserable;"[3] and in the Psalms also the Holy Spirit admonishes and instructs us, saying, "Keep discipline, lest haply the Lord be angry, and ye perish from the right way, when His anger shall quickly burn against you."[4]

2. In the first place, therefore, dearest brother, both by overseers and people nothing is to be more eagerly sought after, than that we who fear God should keep the divine precepts with every observation of discipline, and should not suffer our brethren to stray, and to live according to their own fancy and lust;[5] but that we should faithfully consult for the life of each one, and not suffer virgins to dwell with men, — I do not say to sleep together, but to live together,[6] — since both their weak sex and their age, still critical, ought to be bridled in all things and ruled by us, lest an occasion should be given to the devil who ensnares us, and desires to rage over us, to hurt them, since the apostle also says, "Do not give place to the devil."[7] The ship is watchfully to be delivered from perilous places, that it may not be broken among the rocks and cliffs; the baggage must swiftly be taken out of the fire, before it is burnt up by the flames reaching it. No one who is near to danger is long safe, nor will the servant of God be able to escape the devil if he has entangled himself in the devil's nets. We must interfere at once with such as these, that they may be separated while yet they can be separated in innocence; because by and by they will not be able to be separated by our interference, after they have become joined together by a very guilty conscience. Moreover, what a number of serious mischiefs we see to have arisen hence; and what a multitude of virgins we behold corrupted by unlawful and dangerous conjunctions of this kind, to our great grief of mind! But if they have faithfully dedicated themselves to Christ, let them persevere in modesty and chastity, without incurring any evil report, and so in courage and steadiness await the reward of virginity. But if they are unwilling or unable to persevere, it is better that they should marry, than that by their crimes they should fall into the fire. Certainly let them not cause a scandal to the brethren or sisters, since it is written, "If meat cause my brother to offend, I will eat no flesh while the world standeth, lest I make my brother to offend."[8]

3. Nor let any one think that she can be defended by this excuse, that she may be examined and proved whether she be a virgin; since both the hands and the eyes of the midwives are often deceived; and if she be found to be a virgin in that particular in which a woman may be so, yet she may have sinned in some other part of her body, which may be corrupted and yet cannot be examined. Assuredly the mere lying together, the mere embracing, the very talking together, and the act of kissing, and the disgraceful and foul slumber of two persons lying together, how much of dishonour and crime does it confess! If a husband come upon his wife, and see her lying with another man, is he not angry and raging, and by the passion of his rage does he not perhaps take his sword into his hand? And what shall Christ and our Lord and Judge think, when He sees His virgin, dedicated to Him, and destined for His holiness, lying with another? How indignant and angry is He, and what penalties does He threaten against such unchaste connections! whose spiritual sword and the coming day of judgment, that every one of the brethren may be able to escape, we ought with all our counsel to provide and to strive. And since it behoves all by all means to keep discipline,[9]

---

[1] [See vol. ii. p. 57, Elucidation II.]
[2] Jer. iii. 15.
[3] Wisd. iii. 11.
[4] Ps. ii. 12 (LXX.).
[5] Some editors read here "fructu" for "ructu;" but Goldhorn observes that a similar collocation of *eructation* with error is found in Horace, *Ep. ad Pis.*, 457.
[6] [How coarse and brutal the pagan manners, which even the Gospel could not immediately refine!"]
[7] Eph. iv. 27.

[8] 1 Cor. viii. 13.
[9] [This abomination may have lingered in Africa much longer than elsewhere among the Punic converts from Canaanite manners. Ezek. viii. 13, 14.]

much more is it right that overseers and deacons should be careful for this, that they may afford an example and instruction to others concerning their conversation and character. For how can they direct the integrity and continence of others, if the corruptions and teachings of sin begin to proceed from themselves?

4. And therefore you have acted advisedly and with vigour, dearest brother, in excommunicating the deacon who has often abode with a virgin ; and, moreover, the others who had been used to sleep with virgins. But if they have repented of this their unlawful lying together, and have mutually withdrawn from one another, let the virgins meantime be carefully inspected by midwives ; and if they should be found virgins, let them be received to communion, and admitted to the Church ; yet with this threatening, that if subsequently they should return to the same men, or if they should dwell together with the same men in one house or under the same roof, they should be ejected with a severer censure, nor should such be afterwards easily received into the Church. But if any one of them be found to be corrupted, let her abundantly repent, because she who has been guilty of this crime is an adulteress, not (indeed) against a husband, but against Christ ; and therefore, a due time being appointed, let her afterwards, when confession has been made, return to the Church. But if they obstinately persevere, and do not mutually separate themselves, let them know that, with this their immodest obstinacy, they can never be admitted by us into the Church, lest they should begin to set an example to others to go to ruin by their crimes. Nor let them think that the way of life or of salvation is still open to them, if they have refused to obey the bishops and priests, since in Deuteronomy the Lord God says, "And the man that will do presumptuously, and will not hearken unto the priest or judge, whosoever he shall be in those days, that man shall die, and all the people shall hear and fear, and do no more presumptuously." [1] God commanded those who did not obey His priests to be slain, and those who did not hearken to His judges who were appointed for the time. And then indeed they were slain with the sword, when the circumcision of the flesh was yet in force ; but now that circumcision has begun to be of the spirit among God's faithful servants, the proud and contumacious are slain with the sword of the Spirit, in that they are cast out of the Church. For they cannot live out of it, since the house of God is one, and there can be no salvation to any except in the Church. But the divine Scripture testifies that the undisciplined

perish, because they do not listen to, nor obey wholesome precepts ; for it says, "An undisciplined man loveth not him that correcteth him. But they who hate reproof shall be consumed with disgrace." [2]

5. Therefore, dearest brother, endeavour that the undisciplined should not be consumed and perish, that as much as you can, by your salutary counsels, you should rule the brotherhood, and take counsel of each one with a view to his salvation. Strait and narrow is the way through which we enter into life, but excellent and great is the reward when we enter into glory. Let those who have once made themselves eunuchs for the kingdom of heaven [3] please God in all things, and not offend God's priests nor the Lord's Church by the scandal of their wickedness. And if, for the present, certain of our brethren seem to be made sorry by us, let us nevertheless remain in our wholesome persuasion, knowing that an apostle also has said, "Am I therefore become your enemy because I tell you the truth?" [4] But if they shall obey us, we have gained our brethren, and have formed them as well to salvation as to dignity by our address. But if some of the perverse persons refuse to obey, let us follow the same apostle, who says, "If I please men, I should not be the servant of Christ." [5] If we cannot please some, so as to make them please Christ, let us assuredly, as far as we can, please Christ our Lord and God, by observing His precepts. I bid you, brother beloved and much longed-for. heartily farewell in the Lord.[6]

EPISTLE LXII.[7]

TO CÆCILIUS, ON THE SACRAMENT OF THE CUP OF THE LORD.

ARGUMENT. — CYPRIAN TEACHES, IN OPPOSITION TO THOSE WHO USED WATER IN THE LORD'S SUPPER, THAT NOT WATER ALONE, BUT WINE MIXED WITH WATER, WAS TO BE OFFERED ; THAT BY WATER WAS DESIGNATED IN SCRIPTURE, BAPTISM, BUT CERTAINLY NOT THE EUCHARIST. BY TYPES DRAWN FROM THE OLD TESTAMENT, THE USE OF WINE IN THE SACRAMENT OF THE LORD'S BODY IS ILLUSTRATED ; AND IT IS DECLARED THAT BY THE SYMBOL OF WATER IS UNDERSTOOD THE CHRISTIAN CONGREGATION.

1. Cyprian to Cæcilius his brother, greeting. Although I know, dearest brother, that very many

---

[1] Deut. xvii. 12, 13.

[2] Prov. xv. 12, 10.
[3] [The frightful condition of heathen society inspired the effort to maintain celibacy, but all this suggests the divine wisdom and clemency in restricting it to the few. Matt. xix. 11.]
[4] Gal. iv. 16.
[5] Gal. i. 10.
[6] [The horrible subject of this letter is treated in a valuable note (k) in the Oxford trans., p 7. It began earlier (see *Hermas*) than that learned annotator supposes; but the silence of Minucius Felix, and the pagan objector of his story, as to this specific reproach, suggests that it was of rare occurrence. Vol. ii. p. 235.]
[7] Oxford ed.: Ep. lxiii. A.D. 253.

of the bishops who are set over the churches of the Lord by divine condescension, throughout the whole world, maintain the plan of evangelical truth, and of the tradition of the Lord, and do not by human and novel institution depart from that which Christ our Master both prescribed and did; yet since some, either by ignorance or simplicity[1] in sanctifying the cup of the Lord, and in ministering to the people, do not do that which Jesus Christ, our Lord and God, the founder and teacher of this sacrifice, did and taught, I have thought it as well a religious as a necessary thing to write to you this letter, that, if any one is still kept in this error, he may behold the light of truth, and return to the root and origin of the tradition of the Lord.[2] Nor must you think, dearest brother, that I am writing my own thoughts or man's; or that I am boldly assuming this to myself of my own voluntary will, since I always hold my mediocrity with lowly and modest moderation. But when anything is prescribed by the inspiration and command of God, it is necessary that a faithful servant should obey the Lord, acquitted by all of assuming anything arrogantly to himself, seeing that he is constrained to fear offending the Lord unless he does what he is commanded.

2. Know then that I have been admonished that, in offering the cup, the tradition of the Lord[2] must be observed, and that nothing must be done by us but what the Lord first did on our behalf, as that the cup which is offered in remembrance of Him should be offered mingled with wine. For when Christ says, "I am the true vine,"[3] the blood of Christ is assuredly not water, but wine; neither can His blood by which we are redeemed and quickened appear to be in the cup, when in the cup there is no wine whereby the blood of Christ is shown forth, which is declared by the sacrament and testimony of all the Scriptures.

3. For we find in Genesis also, in respect of the sacrament in Noe, this same thing was to them a precursor and figure of the Lord's passion; that he drank wine; that he was drunken; that he was made naked in his household; that he was lying down with his thighs naked and exposed; that the nakedness of the father was observed by his second son, and was told abroad, but was covered by two, the eldest and the youngest; and other matters which it is not necessary to follow out, since this is enough for us to embrace alone, that Noe, setting forth a type of the future truth, did not drink water, but wine, and thus expressed the figure of the passion of the Lord.

4. Also in the priest Melchizedek we see prefigured the sacrament of the sacrifice of the Lord, according to what divine Scripture testifies, and says, "And Melchizedek, king of Salem, brought forth bread and wine."[4] Now he was a priest of the most high God, and blessed Abraham. And that Melchizedek bore a type of Christ, the Holy Spirit declares in the Psalms, saying from the person of the Father to the Son: "Before the morning star I begat Thee; Thou art a priest for ever, after the order of Melchizedek;"[5] which order is assuredly this coming from that sacrifice and thence descending; that Melchizedek was a priest of the most high God; that he offered wine and bread; that he blessed Abraham. For who is more a priest of the most high God than our Lord Jesus Christ, who offered a sacrifice to God the Father, and offered that very same thing which Melchizedek had offered, that is, bread and wine, to wit, His body and blood? And with respect to Abraham, that blessing going before belonged to our people. For if Abraham believed in God, and it was accounted unto him for righteousness, assuredly whosoever believes in God and lives in faith is found righteous, and already is blessed in faithful Abraham, and is set forth as justified; as the blessed Apostle Paul proves, when he says, "Abraham believed God, and it was accounted to him for righteousness. Ye know, then, that they which are of faith, these are the children of Abraham. But the Scripture, foreseeing that God would justify the Gentiles through faith, pronounced before to Abraham that all nations should be blessed in him; therefore they who are of faith are blessed with faithful Abraham."[6] Whence in the Gospel we find that "children of Abraham are raised from stones, that is, are gathered from the Gentiles."[7] And when the Lord praised Zacchæus, He answered and said, "This day is salvation come to this house, forasmuch as he also is a son of Abraham."[8] In Genesis, therefore, that the benediction, in respect of Abraham by Melchizedek the priest, might be duly celebrated, the figure of Christ's sacrifice precedes, namely, as ordained in bread and wine; which thing the Lord, completing and fulfilling, offered bread and the cup mixed with wine, and so He who is the fulness of truth fulfilled the truth of the image prefigured.

5. Moreover the Holy Spirit by Solomon shows before the type of the Lord's sacrifice, making mention of the immolated victim, and of the bread and wine, and, moreover, of the altar and of the apostles, and says, "Wisdom hath builded her house, she hath underlaid her seven pillars; she hath killed her victims; she hath mingled

---

[1] [A kindly rebuke of those Encratites who were called *Hydroparastatæ*. Epiphan., iii. p. 9, ed. Oehler.]
[2] [1 Cor. xi. 2. Our author evidently has this in mind. He is *admonished* by such Scriptures to maintain apostolic traditions.]
[3] John xv. 1.

[4] Gen. xiv. 18.
[5] Ps. cx. 4.
[6] Gal. iii. 6-9.
[7] Matt. iii. 9.
[8] Luke xix. 9.

her wine in the chalice ; she hath also furnished her table : and she hath sent forth her servants, calling together with a lofty announcement to her cup, saying, Whoso is simple, let him turn to me ; and to those that want understanding she hath said, Come, eat of my bread, and drink of the wine which I have mingled for you." [1] He declares the wine mingled, that is, he foretells with prophetic voice the cup of the Lord mingled with water and wine, that it may appear that that was done in our Lord's passion which had been before predicted.

6. In the blessing of Judah also this same thing is signified, where there also is expressed a figure of Christ, that He should have praise and worship from his brethren ; that He should press down the back of His enemies yielding and fleeing, with the hands with which He bore the cross and conquered death ; and that He Himself is the Lion of the tribe of Judah, and should couch sleeping in His passion, and should rise up, and should Himself be the hope of the Gentiles. To which things divine Scripture adds, and says, " He shall wash His garment in wine, and His clothing in the blood of the grape." [2] But when the blood of the grape is mentioned, what else is set forth than the wine of the cup of the blood of the Lord?

7. In Isaiah also the Holy Spirit testifies this same thing concerning the Lord's passion, saying, " Wherefore are Thy garments red, and Thy apparel as from the treading of the wine-press full and well trodden?" [3] Can water make garments red? or is it water in the wine-press which is trodden by the feet, or pressed out by the press? Assuredly, therefore, mention is made of wine, that the Lord's blood may be understood, and that which was afterwards manifested in the cup of the Lord might be foretold by the prophets who announced it. The treading also, and pressure of the wine-press, is repeatedly dwelt on ; because just as the drinking of wine cannot be attained to unless the bunch of grapes be first trodden and pressed, so neither could we drink the blood of Christ unless Christ had first been trampled upon and pressed, and had first drunk the cup of which He should also give believers to drink.

8. But as often as water is named alone in the Holy Scriptures, baptism is referred to, as we see intimated in Isaiah : " Remember not," says he, " the former things, and consider not the things of old. Behold, I will do a new thing, which shall now spring forth ; and ye shall know it. I will even make a way in the wilderness, and rivers in the dry place, to give drink to my elected people, my people whom I have pur-

chased, that they might show forth my praise." [4] There God foretold by the prophet, that among the nations, in places which previously had been dry, rivers should afterwards flow plenteously, and should provide water for the elected people of God, that is, for those who were made sons of God by the generation of baptism. [5] Moreover, it is again predicted and foretold before, that the Jews, if they should thirst and seek after Christ, should drink with us, that is, should attain the grace of baptism. " If they shall thirst," he says, " He shall lead them through the deserts, shall bring forth water for them out of the rock ; the rock shall be cloven, and the water shall flow, and my people shall drink ; " [6] which is fulfilled in the Gospel, when Christ, who is the Rock, is cloven by a stroke of the spear in His passion ; who also, admonishing what was before announced by the prophet, cries and says, " If any man thirst, let him come and drink. He that believeth on me, as the Scripture saith, out of his belly shall flow rivers of living water." And that it might be more evident that the Lord is speaking there, not of the cup, but of baptism, the Scripture adds, saying, " But this spake He of the Spirit, which they that believe on Him should receive." [7] For by baptism the Holy Spirit is received ; and thus by those who are baptized, and have attained to the Holy Spirit, is attained the drinking of the Lord's cup. And let it disturb no one, that when the divine Scripture speaks of baptism, it says that we thirst and drink, since the Lord also in the Gospel says, " Blessed are they which do hunger and thirst after righteousness ; " [8] because what is received with a greedy and thirsting desire is drunk more fully and plentifully. As also, in another place, the Lord speaks to the Samaritan woman, saying, " Whosoever drinketh of this water shall thirst again ; but whosoever drinketh of the water that I shall give him, shall not thirst for ever." [9] By which is also signified the very baptism of saving water, which indeed is once received, and is not again repeated. But the cup of the Lord is always both thirsted for and drunk in the Church.

9. Nor is there need of very many arguments, dearest brother, to prove that baptism is always indicated by the appellation of water, and that thus we ought to understand it, since the Lord, when He came, manifested the truth of baptism and the cup in commanding that that faithful water, the water of life eternal, should be given to believers in baptism, but, teaching by the example of His own authority, that the cup should be mingled with a union of wine and

---

[1] Prov. ix. 1–5.
[2] Gen. xlix. 11.
[3] Isa. lxiii. 2.

[4] Isa. xliii. 18–21.
[5] [For a full view of all theories of election, see Faber, *On the Primitive Doctrine of Election*, New York, ed. 1840.]
[6] Isa. xlviii. 21.
[7] John vii. 37–39.
[8] Matt. v. 6.
[9] John iv. 13, 14.

water.[1] For, taking the cup on the eve of His passion, He blessed it, and gave it to His disciples, saying, " Drink ye all of this ; for this is my blood of the New Testament, which shall be shed for many, for the remission of sins. I say unto you, I will not drink henceforth of this fruit of the vine, until that day in which I shall drink new wine with you in the kingdom of my Father."[2] In which portion we find that the cup which the Lord offered was mixed, and that that was wine which He called His blood. Whence it appears that the blood of Christ is not offered if there be no wine in the cup, nor the Lord's sacrifice celebrated with a legitimate consecration unless our oblation and sacrifice respond to His passion. But how shall we drink the new wine of the fruit of the vine with Christ in the kingdom of His Father, if in the sacrifice of God the Father and of Christ we do not offer wine, nor mix the cup of the Lord by the Lord's own tradition?

10. Moreover, the blessed Apostle Paul, chosen and sent by the Lord, and appointed a preacher of the Gospel truth, lays down these very things in his epistle, saying, " The Lord Jesus, the same night in which He was betrayed, took bread ; and when He had given thanks, He brake it, and said, This is my body, which shall be given for you : do this in remembrance of me. After the same manner also He took the cup, when he had supped, saying, This cup is the new testament in my blood : this do, as oft as ye drink it, in remembrance of me. For as often as ye eat this bread and drink this cup, ye shall show forth the Lord's death until He come."[3] But if it is both enjoined by the Lord, and the same thing is confirmed and delivered by His apostle, that as often as we drink, we do in remembrance of the Lord the same thing which the Lord also did, we find that what was commanded is not observed by us, unless we also do what the Lord did ; and that mixing the Lord's cup in like manner we do not depart from the divine teaching ; but that we must not at all depart from the evangelical precepts, and that disciples ought also to observe and to do the same things which the Master both taught and did. The blessed apostle in another place more earnestly and strongly teaches, saying, " I wonder that ye are so soon removed from Him that called you into grace, unto another gospel, which is not another ; but there are some that trouble you, and would pervert the Gospel of Christ. But though we, or an angel from heaven, preach any otherwise than that which we have preached to you, let him be anathema. As we said before, so say I now again, If any

man preach any other gospel unto you than that ye have received, let him be anathema."[4]

11. Since, then, neither the apostle himself nor an angel from heaven can preach or teach any otherwise than Christ has once taught and His apostles have announced, I wonder very much whence has originated this practice, that, contrary to evangelical and apostolical discipline, water is offered in some places in the Lord's cup, which water by itself cannot express the blood of Christ. The Holy Spirit also is not silent in the Psalms on the sacrament of this thing, when He makes mention of the Lord's cup, and says, " Thy inebriating cup, how excellent it is ! "[5] Now the cup which inebriates is assuredly mingled with wine, for water cannot inebriate anybody. And the cup of the Lord in such wise inebriates, as Noe also was intoxicated drinking wine, in Genesis. But because the intoxication of the Lord's cup and blood is not such as is the intoxication of the world's wine, since the Holy Spirit said in the Psalm, " Thy inebriating cup," He added, " how excellent it is," because doubtless the Lord's cup so inebriates them that drink, that it makes them sober ; that it restores their minds to spiritual wisdom ; that each one recovers from that flavour of the world to the understanding of God ; and in the same way, that by that common wine the mind is dissolved, and the soul relaxed, and all sadness is laid aside, so, when the blood of the Lord and the cup of salvation have been drunk, the memory of the old man is laid aside, and there arises an oblivion of the former worldly conversation, and the sorrowful and sad breast which before was oppressed by tormenting sins is eased by the joy of the divine mercy ; because that only is able to rejoice him who drinks in the Church, which, when it is drunk, retains the Lord's truth.[6]

12. But how perverse and how contrary it is, that although the Lord at the marriage made wine of water, we should make water of wine, when even the sacrament of that thing ought to admonish and instruct us rather to offer wine in the sacrifices of the Lord. For because among the Jews there was a want of spiritual grace, wine also was wanting. For the vineyard of the Lord of hosts was the house of Israel ; but Christ, when teaching and showing that the people of the Gentiles should succeed them, and that by the merit of faith we should subsequently attain to the place which the Jews had lost, of water made wine ; that is, He showed that at the marriage of Christ and the Church, as the Jews failed, the people of the nations should rather flow together and assemble : for the divine Scripture in the Apocalypse

---

[1] [See Justin, vol. i. p. 185, this series.]
[2] Matt. xxvi. 28, 29.
[3] 1 Cor. xi. 23–26.

[4] Gal. i. 6–9.
[5] Ps. xxiii. 5. [*Vulgate*, " calix inebrians." Ps. xxii. 5.]
[6] [A happy conception of the *inebriation* of the Spirit, " *where* drinking largely *sobers* us again."]

declares that the waters signify the people, say-ing, "The waters which thou sawest, upon which the whore sitteth, are peoples and multitudes, and nations of the Gentiles, and tongues,"[1] which we evidently see to be contained also in the sac-rament of the cup.

13. For because Christ bore us all, in that He also bore our sins, we see that in the water is understood the people, but in the wine is showed the blood of Christ. But when the water is mingled in the cup with wine, the people is made one with Christ, and the assembly of believers is associated and conjoined with Him on whom it believes; which association and conjunction of water and wine is so mingled in the Lord's cup, that that mixture cannot any more be separated. Whence, moreover, nothing can separate the Church — that is, the people established in the Church, faithfully and firmly persevering in that which they have believed — from Christ, in such a way as to prevent their undivided love from always abiding and adhering. Thus, therefore, in consecrating the cup of the Lord, water alone cannot be offered, even as wine alone cannot be offered. For if any one offer wine only, the blood of Christ is dissociated from us; but if the water be alone, the people are dissociated from Christ; but when both are mingled, and are joined with one another by a close union, there is completed a spiritual and heavenly sacrament. Thus the cup of the Lord is not indeed water alone, nor wine alone, unless each be mingled with the other; just as, on the other hand, the body of the Lord cannot be flour alone or water alone, unless both should be united and joined together and compacted in the mass of one bread; in which very sacrament our people are shown to be made one, so that in like man-ner as many grains, collected, and ground, and mixed together into one mass, make one bread; so in Christ, who is the heavenly bread, we may know that there is one body, with which our number is joined and united.[2]

14. There is then no reason, dearest brother, for any one to think that the custom of certain persons is to be followed, who have thought in time past that water alone should be offered in the cup of the Lord. For we must inquire whom they themselves have followed. For if in the sacrifice which Christ offered none is to be followed but Christ, assuredly it behoves us to obey and do that which Christ did, and what He commanded to be done, since He Himself says in the Gospel, "If ye do whatsoever I command you, henceforth I call you not servants, but friends."[3] And that Christ alone ought to be

heard, the Father also testifies from heaven, say-ing, "This is my well-beloved Son, in whom I am well pleased; hear ye Him."[4] Wherefore, if Christ alone must be heard, we ought not to give heed to what another before us may have thought was to be done, but what Christ, who is before all, first did. Neither is it becoming to follow the practice of man, but the truth of God; since God speaks by Isaiah the prophet, and says, "In vain do they worship me, teach-ing the commandments and doctrines of men."[5] And again the Lord in the Gospel repeats this same saying, and says, "Ye reject the com-mandment of God, that ye may keep your own tradition."[6] Moreover, in another place He establishes it, saying, "Whosoever shall break one of these least commandments, and shall teach men so, he shall be called the least in the kingdom of heaven."[7] But if we may not break even the least of the Lord's commandments, how much rather is it forbidden to infringe such im-portant ones, so great, so pertaining to the very sacrament of our Lord's passion and our own redemption, or to change it by human tradition into anything else than what was divinely ap-pointed! For if Jesus Christ, our Lord and God, is Himself the chief priest of God the Father, and has first offered Himself a sacrifice to the Father, and has commanded this to be done in commemoration of Himself, certainly that priest truly discharges the office of Christ, who imitates that which Christ did; and he then offers a true and full sacrifice in the Church to God the Father, when he proceeds to offer it according to what he sees Christ Himself to have offered.

15. But the discipline of all religion and truth is overturned, unless what is spiritually prescribed be faithfully observed; unless indeed any one should fear in the morning sacrifices,[8] lest by the taste of wine he should be redolent of the blood of Christ. Therefore thus the brotherhood is beginning even to be kept back from the passion of Christ in persecutions, by learning in the offerings to be disturbed concerning His blood and His blood-shedding. Moreover, however, the Lord says in the Gospel, "Whosoever shall be ashamed of me, of him shall the Son of man be ashamed."[9] And the apostle also speaks, saying, "If I pleased men, I should not be the servant of Christ."[10] But how can we shed our

---

[1] Apoc. xvii. 15.
[2] [This figure, copied by St. Augustine (vol. v. p. 1247, ed. Migne), is retained in the liturgy of the Reformed Dutch communion.]
[3] John xv. 14, 15.

[4] Matt. xvii. 5.
[5] Isa. xxix. 13.
[6] Mark vii. 13.
[7] Matt v. 19.
[8] According to some texts is read here, "to offer wine, lest in the morning hours, through the flavour of the wine, its smell should be recognised by its fragrant odour by the perception of unbelievers, and he should be known to be a Christian, since we commemorate the blood of Christ in the oblation of wine." [The heathen detected Christians by this token when searching victims for the persecutor.]
[9] Mark viii. 38. [Bingham, book xv. cap. ii. sec. 7.]
[10] Gal. i. 10.

blood for Christ, who blush to drink the blood of Christ?

16. Does any one perchance flatter himself with this notion, that although in the morning, water alone is seen to be offered, yet when we come to supper we offer the mingled cup? But when we sup, we cannot call the people together to our banquet, so as to celebrate the truth of the sacrament in the presence of all the brotherhood.[1] But still it was not in the morning, but after supper, that the Lord offered the mingled cup. Ought we then to celebrate the Lord's cup after supper, that so by continual repetition of the Lord's supper[2] we may offer the mingled cup? It behoved Christ to offer about the evening of the day, that the very hour of sacrifice might show the setting and the evening of the world; as it is written in Exodus, "And all the people of the synagogue of the children of Israel shall kill it in the evening."[3] And again in the Psalms, "Let the lifting up of my hands be an evening sacrifice."[4] But we celebrate the resurrection of the Lord in the morning.

17. And because we make mention of His passion in all sacrifices (for the Lord's passion is the sacrifice which we offer), we ought to do nothing else than what He did. For Scripture says, "For as often as ye eat this bread and drink this cup, ye do show forth the Lord's death till He come."[5] As often, therefore, as we offer the cup in commemoration of the Lord and of His passion, let us do what it is known the Lord did. And let this conclusion be reached, dearest brother: if from among our predecessors any have either by ignorance or simplicity not observed and kept this which the Lord by His example and teaching has instructed us to do, he may, by the mercy of the Lord, have pardon granted to his simplicity. But we cannot be pardoned who are now admonished and instructed by the Lord to offer the cup of the Lord mingled with wine according to what the Lord offered, and to direct letters to our colleagues also about this, so that the evangelical law and the Lord's tradition may be everywhere kept, and there be no departure from what Christ both taught and did.

18. To neglect these things any further, and to persevere in the former error, what is it else than to fall under the Lord's rebuke, who in the psalm reproveth, and says, "What hast thou to do to declare my statutes, or that thou shouldest take my covenant into thy mouth, seeing thou hatest instruction and castest my words behind thee? When thou sawest a thief, thou consentedst with him, and hast been partaker with adulterers."[6] For to declare the righteousness and the covenant of the Lord, and not to do the same that the Lord did, what else is it than to cast away His words and to despise the Lord's instruction, to commit not earthly, but spiritual thefts and adulteries? While any one is stealing from evangelical truth the words and doings of our Lord, he is corrupting and adulterating the divine precepts, as it is written in Jeremiah. He says, "What is the chaff to the wheat? Therefore, behold, I am against the prophets, saith the Lord, who steal my words every one from his neighbour, and cause my people to err by their lies and by their lightness."[7] Also in the same prophet, in another place, He says, "She committed adultery with stocks and stones, and yet for all this she turned not unto me."[8] That this theft and adultery may not fall unto us also, we ought to be anxiously careful, and fearfully and religiously to watch. For if we are priests of God and of Christ, I do not know any one whom we ought rather to follow than God and Christ, since He Himself emphatically says in the Gospel, "I am the light of the world; he that followeth me shall not walk in darkness, but shall have the light of life."[9] Lest therefore we should walk in darkness, we ought to follow Christ, and to observe his precepts, because He Himself told His apostles in another place, as He sent them forth, "All power is given unto me in heaven and earth. Go, therefore, and teach all nations, baptizing them in the name of the Father, and of the Son, and of the Holy Ghost: teaching them to observe all things whatsoever I have commanded you."[10] Wherefore, if we wish to walk in the light of Christ, let us not depart from His precepts and monitions, giving thanks that, while He instructs for the future what we ought to do, He pardons for the past wherein we in our simplicity have erred. And because already His second coming draws near to us, His benign and liberal condescension is more and more illuminating our hearts with the light of truth.[11]

19. Therefore it befits our religion, and our fear, and the place itself, and the office of our priesthood, dearest brother, in mixing and offering the cup of the Lord, to keep the truth of the Lord's tradition, and, on the warning of the Lord, to correct that which seems with some to have been erroneous; so that when He shall begin to come in His brightness and heavenly majesty, He may find that we keep what He admonished us; that we observe what He taught;

---

1 [Much light is thrown on this by the Hebrew usages. See Freeman, *On the Principles of Divine Service*, vol. ii. p. 293.]
2 "Frequentandis dominicis."
3 Ex. xii. 6.
4 Ps. cxli. 2.
5 1 Cor. xi. 26.
6 Ps. l. 16–18.
7 Jer. xxiii. 28, 30, 32.
8 Jer. iii. 9, 10.
9 John viii. 12.
10 Matt. xxviii. 18–20.
11 [A very important monition that clearer light upon certain Scriptures may break in as time unfolds their purpose. Phil. iii. 15.]

that we do what He did.[1] I bid you, dearest brother, ever heartily farewell.

EPISTLE LXIII.[2]

TO EPICTETUS AND TO THE CONGREGATION OF ASSURÆ, CONCERNING FORTUNATIANUS, FORMERLY THEIR BISHOP.

ARGUMENT. — HE WARNS EPICTETUS AND THE CONGREGATION OF THE ASSURITANS NOT TO ALLOW FORTUNATIANUS, A LAPSER, BUT THEIR FORMER BISHOP, TO RETURN TO HIS EPISCOPATE, AS WELL FOR OTHER REASONS AS BECAUSE IT HAD BEEN DECREED THAT LAPSED BISHOPS SHOULD NOT BE ADMITTED TO THEIR FORMER RANK.

1. Cyprian to Epictetus his brother, and to the people established at Assuræ, greeting. I was gravely and grievously disturbed, dearest brethren, at learning that Fortunatianus, formerly bishop among you, after the sad lapse of his fall, was now wishing to act as if he were sound, and beginning to claim for himself the episcopate. Which thing distressed me; in the first place, on his own account, who, wretched man that he is, being either wholly blinded in the darkness of the devil, or deceived by the sacrilegious persuasion of certain persons; when he ought to be making atonement, and to give himself to the work of entreating the Lord night and day, by tears, and supplications, and prayers, dares still to claim to himself the priesthood which he has betrayed, as if it were right, from the altars of the devil, to approach to the altar of God. Or as if he would not provoke a greater wrath and indignation of the Lord against himself in the day of judgment, who, not being able to be a guide to the brethren in faith and virtue, stands forth as a teacher in perfidy, in boldness, and in temerity; and he who has not taught the brethren to stand bravely in the battle, teaches those who are conquered and prostrate not even to ask *for pardon;* although the Lord says, "To them have ye poured a drink-offering, and to them have ye offered a meat-offering. Shall I not be angry for these things? saith the Lord."[3] And in another place, "He that sacrificeth to any god, save unto the Lord only, shall be destroyed."[4] Moreover, the Lord again speaks, and says, "They have worshipped those whom their own fingers have made : and the mean man boweth down, and the great man humbleth himself: and I will not forgive them."[5] In the Apocalypse also, we read the anger of the Lord

threatening, and saying, "If any man worship the beast and his image, and receive his mark in his forehead or in his hand, the same shall drink of the wine of the wrath of God mixed in the cup of His anger; and he shall be tormented with fire and brimstone in the presence of the holy angels, and in the presence of the Lamb : and the smoke of their torments shall ascend up for ever and ever; neither shall they have rest day nor night, who worship the beast and his image."[6]

2. Since, therefore, the Lord threatens these torments, these punishments in the day of judgment, to those who obey the devil and sacrifice to idols, how does he think that he can act as a priest of God who has obeyed and served the priests of the devil; or how does he think that his hand can be transferred to the sacrifice of God and the prayer of the Lord which has been captive to sacrilege and to crime, when in the sacred Scriptures God forbids the priests to approach to sacrifice even if they have been in lighter guilt; and says in Leviticus : "The man in whom there shall be any blemish or stain shall not approach to offer gifts to God?"[7] Also in Exodus : "And let the priests which come near to the Lord God sanctify themselves, lest perchance the Lord forsake them."[8] And again : "And when they come near to minister at the altar of the Holy One, they shall not bring sin upon them, lest they die."[9] Those, therefore, who have brought grievous sins upon themselves, that is, who, by sacrificing to idols, have offered sacrilegious sacrifices, cannot claim to themselves the priesthood of God, nor make any prayer for their brethren in His sight; since it is written in the Gospel, "God heareth not a sinner; but if any man be a worshipper of God, and doeth His will, him He heareth."[10] Nevertheless the profound gloom of the falling darkness has so blinded the hearts of some, that they receive no light from the wholesome precepts, but, once turned away from the direct path of the true way, they are hurried headlong and suddenly by the night and error of their sins.[11]

3. Nor is it wonderful if now those reject our counsels, or the Lord's precepts, who have denied the Lord. They desire gifts, and offerings, and gain, for which formerly they watched insatiably. They still long also for suppers and banquets, whose debauch they belched forth in the indigestion lately left to the day, most manifestly proving now that they did not before serve religion, but rather their belly and gain, with profane cupidity. Whence also we perceive and

---

[1] [Even these minute maxims show that the spirit of the third century was to adhere to the example of Christ and His Apostles. This gives us confidence that no *intentional* innovations were admitted.]
[2] Oxford ed.: Ep. lxv. A.D. 253.
[3] Isa. lvii. 6.
[4] Ex. xxii. 20.
[5] Isa. ii. 8, 9.

[6] Apoc. xiv. 9-11.
[7] Lev. xxi. 17.
[8] Ex. xix. 22.
[9] Ex. xxviii. 43.
[10] John ix. 31.
[11] [2 Thess. ii. 11. Judicial blindness the result of revolt from known truth.]

believe that this rebuke has come from God's searching out, that they might not continue to stand at the altar; and any further, as unchaste persons, to have to do with modesty; as perfidious, to have to do with faith; as profane, with religion; as earthly, with things divine; as sacrilegious, with things sacred. That such persons may not return again to the profanation of the altar, and to the contagion of the brethren, we must keep watch with all our powers, and strive with all our strength, that, as far as in us lies, we may keep them back from this audacity of their wickedness, that they attempt not any longer to act in the character of priest; who, cast down to the lowest pit of death, have gone headlong with the weight of a greater destruction beyond the lapses of the laity.

4. But if, among these insane persons, their incurable madness shall continue, and, with the withdrawal of the Holy Spirit, the blindness which has begun shall remain in its deep night, our counsel will be to separate individual brethren from their deceitfulness; and, lest any one should run into the toils of their error, to separate them from their contagion. Since neither can the oblation be consecrated where the Holy Spirit is not; nor can the Lord avail to any one by the prayers and supplications of one who himself has done despite to the Lord. But if Fortunatianus, either by the blindness induced by the devil forgetful of his crime, or become a minister and servant of the devil for deceiving the brotherhood, shall persevere in this his madness, do you, as far as in you lies, strive, and in this darkness of the rage of the devil, recall the minds of the brethren from error, that they may not easily consent to the madness of another; that they may not make themselves partakers in the crimes of abandoned men; but being sound, let them maintain the constant tenor of their salvation, and of the integrity preserved and guarded by them.[1]

5. Let the lapsed, however, who acknowledge the greatness of their sin, not depart from entreating the Lord, nor forsake the Catholic Church, which has been appointed one and alone by the Lord; but, continuing in their atonements and entreating the Lord's mercy, let them knock at the *door of the* Church, that they may be received there where once they were, and may return to Christ from whom they have departed, and not listen to those who deceive them with a fallacious and deadly seduction; since it is written, "Let no man deceive you with vain words, for because of these things cometh the wrath of God upon the children of disobedience; be not ye therefore partakers with them."[2] Therefore let no one associate himself with the contumacious, and those who do not fear God, and those who entirely withdraw from the Church. But if any one should be impatient of entreating the Lord who is offended, and should be unwilling to obey us, but should follow desperate and abandoned men, he must take the blame to himself when the day of judgment shall come. For how shall he be able in that day to entreat the Lord, who has both before this denied Christ, and now also the Church of Christ, and not obeying bishops sound and wholesome and living, has made himself an associate and a partaker with the dying? I bid you, dearest brethren and longed-for, ever heartily farewell.

EPISTLE LXIV.[3]

TO ROGATIANUS, CONCERNING THE DEACON WHO CONTENDED AGAINST THE BISHOP.

ARGUMENT.—CYPRIAN WARNS THE BISHOP ROGATIANUS TO RESTRAIN THE PRIDE OF THE DEACON WHO HAD PROVOKED HIM WITH HIS INSULTS, AND TO COMPEL HIM TO REPENT OF HIS BOLDNESS; TAKING OCCASION TO REPEAT ONCE MORE WHATEVER HE HAS SAID IN THE PREVIOUS LETTER, ABOUT THE SACERDOTAL OR EPISCOPAL POWER.[4]

1. Cyprian to his brother Rogatianus, greeting. I and my colleagues who were present with me were deeply and grievously distressed, dearest brother, on reading your letter in which you complained of your deacon, that, forgetful of your priestly station, and unmindful of his own office and ministry, he had provoked you by his insults and injuries. And you indeed have acted worthily, and with your accustomed humility towards us, in rather complaining of him to us; although you have power, according to the vigour of the episcopate and the authority of your See, whereby you might be justified on him at once, assured that all we your colleagues would regard it as a matter of satisfaction, whatever you should do by your priestly power in respect of an insolent deacon, as you have in respect of men of this kind divine commands. Inasmuch as the Lord God says in Deuteronomy, "And the man that will do presumptuously, and will not hearken unto the priest or the judge, whoever he shall be in those days, that man shall die; and all the people, when they hear, shall fear, and shall no more do impiously."[5] And that we may know that this voice of God came forth with His true and highest majesty to honour and avenge His priests; when three of the

---

[1] Otherwise, "the enduring vigour of that soundness which they have preserved and guarded."

[2] Eph. v. 6, 7.
[3] Oxford ed.: Ep. iii.
[4] At what time this letter was written is uncertain, unless we may gather from the similar commencement in both letters, that it was written at the same synod with the following one. Perhaps A.D. 249.
[5] Deut. xvii. 12, 13.

ministers [1] — Korah, Dathan, and Abiram — dared to deal proudly, and to exalt their neck against Aaron the priest, and to equal themselves with the priest set over them; they were swallowed up and devoured by the opening of the earth, and so immediately suffered the penalty of their sacrilegious audacity. Nor they alone, but also two hundred and fifty others, who were their companions in boldness, were consumed by a fire breaking forth from the Lord, that it might be proved that God's priests are avenged by Him who makes priests. In the book of Kings also, when Samuel the priest was despised by the Jewish people on account of his age, as you are now, the Lord in wrath exclaimed, and said, "They have not rejected thee, but they have rejected me." [2] And that He might avenge this, He set over them Saul as a king, who afflicted them with grievous injuries, and trod on the people, and pressed down their pride with all insults and penalties, that the despised priest might be avenged by divine vengeance on a proud people.

2. Moreover also Solomon, established in the Holy Spirit, testifies and teaches what is the priestly authority and power, saying, "Fear the Lord with all thy soul, and reverence His priests;" [3] and again, "Honour God with all thy soul, and honour His priests." [4] Mindful of which precepts, the blessed Apostle Paul, according to what we read in the Acts of the Apostles, when it was said to him, "Revilest thou thus God's high priest?" answered and said, "I wist not, brethren, that he was the high priest; for it is written, Thou shalt not speak evil of the ruler of thy people." [5] Moreover, our Lord Jesus Christ Himself, our King, and Judge, and God, even to the very day of His passion observed the honour to priests and high priests, although they observed neither the fear of God nor the acknowledgment of Christ. For when He had cleansed the leper, He said to him, "Go, show thyself to the priest, and offer the gift." [6] With that humility which taught us also to be humble, He still called him a priest whom He knew to be sacrilegious; also under the very sting of His passion, when He had received a blow, and it was said to Him, "Answerest thou the high priest so?" He said nothing reproachfully against the person of the high priest, but rather maintained His own innocence, saying, "If I have spoken evil, bear witness of the evil; but if well, why smitest thou me?" [7] All which things were therefore done

by Him humbly and patiently, that we might have an example of humility and patience; for He taught that true priests were lawfully and fully to be honoured, in showing Himself such as He was in respect of false priests.

3. But deacons ought to remember that the Lord chose apostles, that is, bishops and overseers; while apostles appointed for themselves deacons [8] after the ascent of the Lord into heaven, as ministers of their episcopacy and of the Church. But if we may dare anything against God who makes bishops, deacons may also dare against us by whom they are made; and therefore it behoves the deacon of whom you write to repent of his audacity, and to acknowledge the honour of the priest, and to satisfy the bishop set over him with full humility. For these things are the beginnings of heretics, and the origins and endeavours of evil-minded schismatics; — to please themselves, and with swelling haughtiness to despise him who is set over them. Thus they depart from the Church — thus a profane altar is set up outside — thus they rebel against the peace of Christ, and the appointment and the unity of God. But if, further, he shall harass and provoke you with his insults, you must exercise against him the power of your dignity, by either deposing him or excommunicating him. For if the Apostle Paul, writing to Timothy, said, "Let no man despise thy youth," [9] how much rather must it be said by your colleagues to you, "Let no man despise thy age? And since you have written, that one has associated himself with that same deacon of yours, and is a partaker of his pride and boldness, you may either restrain or excommunicate him also, and any others that may appear of a like disposition, and act against God's priest. Unless, as we exhort and advise, they should rather perceive that they have sinned and make satisfaction, and suffer us to keep our own purpose; for we rather ask and desire to overcome the reproaches and injuries of individuals by clemency and patience, than to punish them by our priestly power. [10] I bid you, dearest brother, ever heartily farewell.

EPISTLE LXV. [11]

TO THE CLERGY AND PEOPLE ABIDING AT FURNI, ABOUT VICTOR, WHO HAD MADE THE PRESBYTER FAUSTINUS A GUARDIAN.

ARGUMENT. — SINCE, AGAINST THE DECISION OF A COUNCIL OF BISHOPS, GEMINIUS VICTOR HAD NAMED IN HIS WILL GEMINIUS FAUSTINUS THE PRESBYTER AS HIS GUARDIAN OR CURATOR, HE FORBIDS THAT OFFERING SHOULD BE MADE FOR

---

[1] [i.e., Levites = deacons. But Korah and the Levites (Num. xvi. 9, 10) must be regarded apart from the Reubenites (laics) who sinned with them. Jude 11.]
[2] Sam. viii. 7.
[3] Ecclus. vii. 29.
[4] Ecclus. vii. 31.
[5] Acts xxiii. 4, 5.
[6] Matt. viii 4.
[7] John xviii. 23.

[8] [This is the Cyprianic theory.]
[9] 1 Tim. iv. 12.
[10] [See letter liv. sec. 16, p. 345, *supra.*]
[11] Oxford ed.: Ep. i. A.D. 249.

HIM, OR THAT THE SACRIFICE SHOULD BE CELE-BRATED FOR HIS REPOSE, INFERRING BY THE WAY, FROM THE EXAMPLE OF THE LEVITICAL TRIBE, THAT CLERICS OUGHT NOT TO MIX THEM-SELVES UP IN SECULAR CARES.

1. Cyprian to the presbyters, and deacons, and people abiding at Furni, greeting. I and my colleagues who were present with me were greatly disturbed, dearest brethren, as were also our fellow-presbyters who sate with us, when we were made aware that Geminius Victor, our brother, when departing this life, had named Geminius Faustinus the presbyter executor to his will, although long since it was decreed, in a council of the bishops, that no one should appoint any of the clergy and the ministers of God executor or guardian[1] by his will, since every one honoured by the divine priesthood, and ordained in the clerical service, ought to serve only the altar and sacrifices, and to have leisure for prayers and supplications. For it is written: "No man that warreth for God en-tangleth himself with the affairs of this life, that he may please Him to whom he has pledged himself."[2] As this is said of all men, how much rather ought those not to be bound by worldly anxieties and involvements, who, being busied with divine and spiritual things, are not able to withdraw from the Church, and to have leisure for earthly and secular doings! The form of which ordination and engagement the Levites formerly observed under the law, so that when the eleven tribes divided the land and shared the possessions, the Levitical tribe, which was left free for the temple and the altar, and for the divine ministries, received nothing from that portion of the division; but while others culti-vated the soil, that portion only cultivated the favour of God, and received the tithes from the eleven tribes, for their food and mainte-nance, from the fruits which grew. All which was done by divine authority and arrangement, so that they who waited on divine services might in no respect be called away, nor be compelled to consider or to transact secular business. Which plan and rule is now maintained in respect of the clergy, that they who are pro-moted by clerical ordination in the Church of the Lord may be called off in no respect from the divine administration, nor be tied down by worldly anxieties and matters; but in the hon-our of the brethren who contribute, receiving as it were tenths of the fruits, they may not withdraw from the altars and sacrifices, but may serve day and night in heavenly and spiritual things.

2. The bishops our predecessors religiously considering this, and wholesomely providing for it, decided that no brother departing should name a cleric for executor or guardian; and if any one should do this, no offering should be made for him, nor any sacrifice be celebrated for his repose.[3] For he does not deserve to be named at the altar of God in the prayer of the priests, who has wished to call away the priests and ministers from the altar. And therefore, since Victor, contrary to the rule lately made in council by the priests, has dared to appoint Geminius Faustinus, a presbyter, his executor, it is not allowed that any offering be made by you for his repose, nor any prayer be made in the church in his name, that so the decree of the priests, religiously and needfully made, may be kept by us; and, at the same time, an ex-ample be given to the rest of the brethren, that no one should call away to secular anxieties the priests and ministers of God who are occupied with the service of His altar and Church. For care will probably be taken in time to come that this happen not with respect to the person of clerics any more, if what has now been done has been punished. I bid you, dearest brethren, ever heartily farewell.

EPISTLE LXVI.[4]

TO FATHER STEPHANUS, CONCERNING MAR-CIANUS OF ARLES, WHO HAD JOINED HIM-SELF TO NOVATIAN.

ARGUMENT. — AS MARCIANUS, BISHOP OF ARLES, WHEN HE FOLLOWED THE SECT OF NOVATIAN, HAD SEDUCED MANY, AND BY HIS SCHISM HAD SEPARATED HIMSELF FROM THE COMMUNION OF THE REST OF THE BISHOPS, CYPRIAN WARNS STEPHANUS, THAT HE SHOULD BY ANNOUNCING THE EXCOMMUNICATION OF THE OFFENDER, ALIKE BY ROME AND CARTHAGE, ENABLE THE CHURCH AT ARLES, TO ELECT ANOTHER IN HIS PLACE; AND THAT SO PEACE MIGHT BE GRANTED, AS WELL TO THE LAPSED AS TO THOSE SEDUCED BY HIM, UPON THEIR REPENTANCE, AND A RE-TURN TO THE CHURCH CONCEDED TO THEM.

1. Cyprian to his brother Stephen, greeting. Faustinus our colleague, abiding at Lyons, has once and again written to me, dearest brother, informing me of those things which also I cer-tainly know to have been told to you, as well by him as by others our fellow-bishops established

---

[1] The Oxford translator notes here that the Roman law did not permit this office to be declined.
[2] 2 Tim. ii. 4. [Are not these primitive ideas a needed admoni-tion to our times?]

[3] "Pro dormitione ejus." Goldhorn observes here, rather need-lessly, that it was unlucky among the ancient Christians to speak of death. [They counted death as a falling asleep, and the grave as a cœmeterium; and this prayer for the repose of the righteous was strictly such, that they might "rest from their labours," till, in the resurrection, and not before, they should receive their consummation and reward.]
[4] Oxford ed.: Ep. lxviii. This epistle does not appear in many MSS., and its genuineness has been therefore doubted. But the style points to Cyprian as its author, and the documents where it is found are among the oldest, one the most ancient of all. A.D. 254.

in the same province, that Marcianus, who abides at Arles, has associated himself with Novatian, and has departed from the unity of the Catholic Church, and from the agreement of our body and priesthood, holding that most extreme depravity of heretical presumption, that the comforts and aids of divine love and paternal tenderness are closed to the servants of God who repent, and mourn, and knock at the gate of the Church with tears, and groans, and grief; and that those who are wounded are not admitted for the soothing of their wounds, but that, forsaken without hope of peace and communion, they must be thrown to become the prey of wolves and the booty of the devil; which matter, dearest brother, it is our business to advise for and to aid in, since we who consider the divine clemency, and hold the balance in governing the Church, do thus exhibit the rebuke of vigour to sinners in such a way as that, nevertheless, we do not refuse the medicine of divine goodness and mercy in raising the lapsed and healing the wounded.

2. Wherefore it behoves you[1] to write a very copious letter to our fellow-bishops appointed in Gaul, not to suffer any longer that Marcian, froward and haughty, and hostile to the divine mercy and to the salvation of the brotherhood, should insult our assembly, because he does not yet seem to be excommunicated by us;[2] in that he now for a long time boasts and announces that, adhering to Novatian, and following his frowardness, he has separated himself from our communion; although Novatian himself, whom he follows, has formerly been excommunicated, and judged an enemy to the Church; and when he sent ambassadors to us into Africa, asking to be received into our communion, he received back word from a council of several priests who were here present, that he himself had excluded himself, and could not by any of us be received into communion, as he had attempted to erect a profane altar, and to set up an adulterous throne, and to offer sacrilegious sacrifices opposed to the true priest; while the Bishop Cornelius was ordained in the Catholic Church by the judgment of God, and by the suffrages of the clergy and people. Therefore, if he were willing to return to a right mind, and to come to himself, he should repent and return to the Church as a suppliant. How vain it is, dearest brother, when Novatian has lately been repulsed and rejected, and excommunicated by God's priests throughout the whole world, for us still to suffer his flatterers now to jest with us, and to judge of the majesty and dignity of the Church!

3. Let letters be directed by you into the province and to the people abiding at Arles, by which, Marcian being excommunicated, another may be substituted in his place, and Christ's flock, which even to this day is contemned as scattered and wounded by him, may be gathered together. Let it suffice that many of our brethren have departed in these late years in those parts without peace; and certainly let the rest who remain be helped, who groan both day and night, and beseeching the divine and fatherly mercy, entreat the comfort of our succour. For, for that reason, dearest brother, the body of priests is abundantly large, joined together by the bond of mutual concord, and the link of unity; so that if any one of our college should try to originate heresy, and to lacerate and lay waste Christ's flock, others may help, and as it were, as useful and merciful shepherds, gather together the Lord's sheep into the flock. For what if any harbour in the sea shall begin to be mischievous and dangerous to ships, by the breach of its defences; do not the navigators direct their ships to other neighbouring ports where there is a safe[3] and practicable entrance, and a secure station? Or if, on the road, any inn should begin to be beset and occupied by robbers, so that whoever should enter would be caught by the attack of those who lie in wait there; do not the travellers, as soon as this its character is discovered, seek other houses of entertainment on the road, which shall be safer, where the lodging is trustworthy, and the inns safe for the travellers? And this ought now to be the case with us, dearest brother,[4] that we should receive to us with ready and kindly humanity our brethren, who, tossed on the rocks of Marcian,[5] are seeking the secure harbours of the Church; and that we afford such a place of entertainment for the travellers as is that in the Gospel, in which those who are wounded and maimed by robbers may be received and cherished, and protected by the host.

4. For what is a greater or a more worthy care of overseers, than to provide by diligent solicitude and wholesome medicine for cherishing and preserving the sheep? since the Lord speaks, and says, "The diseased have ye not strengthened, neither have ye healed that which was sick, neither have ye bound up that which was broken, neither have ye brought again that which was driven away, neither have ye sought that which was lost. And my sheep were scattered because there is no shepherd; and they became meat to all the beasts of the field, and none did search or seek after them. Therefore

---

1 [With all Cyprian's humility and reverence for the mother See, to which the Church of North Africa owed its origin, he yet, as an older bishop, reminds Stephen of what he ought to do to succour the Church of Irenæus.]
2 [" By us," viz., Rome and Carthage, provinces in communion with Faustinus.]

3 Suppl. "access," according to Baluzius.
4 [Note the language, " with us, dearest brother; " not a thought save that of equal and joint authority.]
5 Some old editions read, "who, having avoided the rocks of Marcian."

thus saith the Lord, Behold, I am against the shepherds, and I will require my flock at their hands, and cause them to cease from feeding the flock ; neither shall they feed them any more : for I will deliver them from their mouth, and I will feed them with judgment." [1]   Since therefore the Lord thus threatens such shepherds by whom the Lord's sheep are neglected and perish, what else ought we to do, dearest brother, than to exhibit full diligence in gathering together and restoring the sheep of Christ, and to apply the medicine of paternal affection to cure the wounds of the lapsed, since the Lord also in the Gospel warns, and says, " They that be whole need not a physician, but they that are sick ? " [2] For although we are many shepherds, yet we feed one flock,[3] and ought to collect and cherish all the sheep which Christ by His blood and passion sought for ; nor ought we to suffer our suppliant and mourning brethren to be cruelly despised and trodden down by the haughty presumption of some, since it is written, " But the man that is proud and boastful shall bring nothing at all to perfection, who has enlarged his soul as hell." [4]   And the Lord, in His Gospel, blames and condemns men of that kind, saying, " Ye are they which justify yourselves before men, but God knoweth your hearts : for that which is highly esteemed among men is abomination in the sight of God." [5]   He says that those are execrable and detestable who please themselves, who, swelling and inflated, arrogantly assume anything to themselves.   Since then Marcian has begun to be of these, and, allying himself with Novatian, has stood forth as the opponent of mercy and love, let him not pronounce sentence, but receive it ; and let him not so act as if he himself were to judge of the college of priests, since he himself is judged by all the priests.

5. For the glorious honour of our predecessors, the blessed martyrs Cornelius and Lucius, must be maintained, whose memory as we hold in honour, much more ought you, dearest brother, to honour and cherish with your weight and authority, since you have become their vicar and successor.[6]   For they, full of the Spirit of God, and established in a glorious martyrdom, judged that peace should be granted to the lapsed, and that when penitence was undergone, the reward of peace and communion was not to be denied ; and this they attested by their letters, and we all everywhere and entirely have judged the

same thing.   For there could not be among us a diverse feeling in whom there was one spirit ; and therefore it is manifest that he does not hold the truth of the Holy Spirit with the rest, whom we observe to think differently.   Intimate plainly to us who has been substituted at Arles in the place of Marcian, that we may know to whom to direct our brethren, and to whom we ought to write.   I bid you, dearest brother, ever heartily farewell.

EPISTLE LXVII.[7]

TO THE CLERGY AND PEOPLE ABIDING IN SPAIN, CONCERNING BASILIDES AND MARTIAL.

ARGUMENT. — BASILIDES AND MARTIAL, BISHOPS, HAVING LAPSED AND BECOME CONTAMINATED BY THE CERTIFICATES OF IDOLATRY, CYPRIAN WITH HIS FELLOW-BISHOPS PRAISES THE CLERGY AND PEOPLE OF SPAIN THAT THEY HAD SUBSTITUTED IN THEIR PLACE BY A LEGITIMATE ELECTION SABINUS AND FELIX ; ESPECIALLY AS, ACCORDING TO THE DECISION OF CORNELIUS AND HIS COLLEAGUES, LAPSED BISHOPS MIGHT INDEED BE RECEIVED TO REPENTANCE, BUT WERE PROHIBITED FROM THE PRIESTLY HONOUR.   MOREOVER, HE ALLUDES BY THE WAY TO CERTAIN MATTERS ABOUT THE ANCIENT RITE OF EPISCOPAL ELECTION.   THE CONTEXT INDICATES THAT THIS WAS WRITTEN DURING THE EPISCOPATE OF STEPHEN.

1. Cyprian, Cæcilius, Primus, Polycarp, Nicomedes, Lucilianus, Successus, Sedatus, Fortunatus, Januarius, Secundinus, Pomponius, Honoratus, Victor, Aurelius, Sattius, Petrus, another Januarius, Saturninus, another Aurelius, Venantius, Quietus, Rogatianus, Tenax, Felix, Faustinus, Quintus, another Saturninus, Lucius, Vincentius, Libosus, Geminius, Marcellus, Iambus, Adelphius, Victoricus, and Paulus, to Felix the presbyter, and to the peoples abiding at Legio [8] and Asturica,[9] also to Lælius the deacon, and the people abiding at Emerita,[10] brethren in the Lord, greeting. When we had come together, dearly beloved brethren, we read your letters, which according to the integrity of your faith and your fear of God you wrote to us by Felix and Sabinus our fellow-bishops, signifying that Basilides and Martial, being stained with the certificates of idolatry, and bound with the consciousness of wicked crimes, ought not to hold the episcopate and administer the priesthood of God ; and you desired an answer to be written to you again concerning these things, and your solicitude, no less just than needful, to be relieved either by the comfort or by the help of our judgment.   Never-

---

[1] Ezek. xxxiv. 4–6, 10, 16.
[2] Matt. ix. 12.
[3] [" We, many shepherds (one episcopate), over one flock." Cyprian's theory is never departed from, practically.]
[4] Heb. ii. 5.
[5] Luke xvi. 15.
[6] [" You ought," etc. Does any modern bishop of the Roman obedience presume to speak thus to the " infallible " oracle of the Vatican?]

[7] Oxford ed.: Ep. lxvii. A.D. 257.
[8] Leon.
[9] Astorga.
[10] Merida.

theless to this your desire not so much our counsels as the divine precepts reply, in which it is long since bidden by the voice of Heaven and prescribed by the law of God, who and what sort of persons ought to serve the altar and to celebrate the divine sacrifices. For in Exodus God speaks to Moses, and warns him, saying, "Let the priests which come near to the Lord God sanctify themselves, lest the Lord forsake them."[1] And again: "And when they come near to the altar of the Holy One to minister, they shall not bring sin upon them, lest they die."[2] Also in Leviticus the Lord commands, and says, "Whosoever hath any spot or blemish upon him, shall not approach to offer gifts to God."[3]

2. Since these things are announced and are made plain to us, it is necessary that our obedience should wait upon the divine precepts; nor in matters of this kind can human indulgence accept any man's person, or yield anything to any one, when the divine prescription has interfered, and establishes a law. For we ought not to be forgetful what the Lord spoke to the Jews by Isaiah the prophet, rebuking, and indignant that they had despised the divine precepts and followed human doctrines. "This people," he says, honoureth me with their lips, but their heart is widely removed from me; but in vain do they worship me, teaching the doctrines and commandments of men."[4] This also the Lord repeats in the Gospel, and says, "Ye reject the commandment of God, that ye may establish your own tradition."[5] Having which things before our eyes, and solicitously and religiously considering them, we ought in the ordinations of priests to choose none but unstained and upright ministers,[6] who, holily and worthily offering sacrifices to God, may be heard in the prayers which they make for the safety of the Lord's people, since it is written, "God heareth not a sinner; but if any man be a worshipper of God, and doeth His will, him He heareth."[7] On which account it is fitting, that with full diligence and sincere investigation those should be chosen for God's priesthood whom it is manifest God will hear.

3. Nor let the people flatter themselves that they can be free from the contagion of sin, while communicating with a priest who is a sinner, and yielding their consent to the unjust and unlawful episcopacy of their overseer, when the divine reproof by Hosea the prophet threatens, and says, "Their sacrifices shall be as the bread of mourning; all that eat thereof shall be pol-

luted;"[8] teaching manifestly and showing that all are absolutely bound to the sin who have been contaminated by the sacrifice of a profane and unrighteous priest. Which, moreover, we find to be manifested also in Numbers, when Korah, and Dathan, and Abiram claimed for themselves the power of sacrificing in opposition to Aaron the priest. There also the Lord commanded by Moses that the people should be separated from them, lest, being associated with the wicked, themselves also should be bound closely in the same wickedness. "Separate yourselves," said He, "from the tents of these wicked and hardened men, and touch not those things which belong to them, lest ye perish together in their sins."[9] On which account a people obedient to the Lord's precepts, and fearing God, ought to separate themselves from a sinful prelate, and not to associate themselves with the sacrifices of a sacrilegious priest, especially since they themselves have the power either of choosing worthy priests, or of rejecting unworthy ones.

4. Which very thing, too, we observe to come from divine authority, that the priest should be chosen in the presence of the people under the eyes of all, and should be approved worthy and suitable by public judgment and testimony; as in the book of Numbers the Lord commanded Moses, saying, "Take Aaron thy brother, and Eleazar his son, and place them in the mount, in the presence of all the assembly, and strip Aaron of his garments, and put them upon Eleazar his son; and let Aaron die there, and be added to his people."[10] God commands a priest to be appointed in the presence of all the assembly; that is, He instructs and shows that the ordination of priests ought not to be solemnized except with the knowledge of the people standing near, that in the presence of the people either the crimes of the wicked may be disclosed, or the merits of the good may be declared, and the ordination, which shall have been examined by the suffrage and judgment of all, may be just and legitimate.[11] And this is subsequently observed, according to divine instruction, in the Acts of the Apostles, when Peter speaks to the people of ordaining an apostle in the place of Judas. "Peter," it says, "stood up in the midst of the disciples, and the multitude were in one place."[12] Neither do we observe that this was regarded by the apostles only in the ordinations of bishops and priests, but also in those of deacons, of which matter itself also it is written in their Acts: "And they

---

1 Ex. xix. 22.
2 Ex. xxviii. 43.
3 Lev. xxi. 17.
4 Isa. xxix. 13.
5 Mark vii. 13.
6 "Antistites."
7 John ix. 31.

8 Hos. ix. 4.
9 Num. xvi. 26.
10 Num. xx. 25, 26.
11 [See sec. 5, *infra*.]
12 Acts i. 15. From some authorities, Baluzius here interpolates, "the number of men was about a hundred and twenty." But this, says a modern editor, smacks of "emendation."

twelve called together," it says, "the whole congregation of the disciples, and said to them;"[1] which was done so diligently and carefully, with the calling together of the whole of the people, surely for this reason, that no unworthy person might creep into the ministry of the altar, or to the office of a priest. For that unworthy persons are sometimes ordained, not according to the will of God, but according to human presumption, and that those things which do not come of a legitimate and righteous ordination are displeasing to God, God Himself manifests by Hosea the prophet, saying, "They have set up for themselves a king, but not by me."[2]

5. For which reason you must diligently observe and keep the practice delivered from divine tradition and apostolic observance, which is also maintained among us, and almost throughout all the provinces;[3] that for the proper celebration of ordinations all the neighbouring bishops of the same province should assemble with that people for which a prelate is ordained. And the bishop should be chosen in the presence of the people, who have most fully known the life of each one, and have looked into the doings of each one as respects his habitual conduct. And this also, we see, was done by you in the ordination of our colleague Sabinus; so that, by the suffrage of the whole brotherhood,[4] and by the sentence of the bishops who had assembled in their presence, and who had written letters to you concerning him, the episcopate was conferred upon him, and hands were imposed on him in the place of Basilides. Neither can it rescind an ordination rightly perfected, that Basilides, after the detection of his crimes, and the baring of his conscience even by his own confession, went to Rome and deceived Stephen our colleague, placed at a distance, and ignorant of what had been done, and of the truth, to canvass that he might be replaced unjustly in the episcopate from which he had been righteously deposed.[5] The result of this is, that the sins of Basilides are not so much abolished as enhanced, inasmuch as to his former sins he has also added the crime of deceit and circumvention. For he is not so much to be blamed who has been through heedlessness surprised by fraud, as he is to be execrated who has fraudulently taken him by surprise. But if Basilides could deceive men, he cannot deceive God, since it is written, "God is not mocked."[6] But neither can deceit advantage Martialis, in such a way as that he

who also is involved in great crimes should hold his bishopric, since the apostle also warns, and says, "A bishop must be blameless, as the steward of God."[7]

6. Wherefore, since as ye have written, dearly beloved brethren, and as Felix and Sabinus our colleagues affirm, and as another Felix of Cæsar Augusta,[8] a maintainer of the faith and a defender of the truth, signifies in his letter, Basilides and Martialis have been contaminated by the abominable certificate of idolatry; and Basilides, moreover, besides the stain of the certificate, when he was prostrate in sickness, blasphemed against God, and confessed that he blasphemed; and because of the wound to his own conscience, voluntarily laying down his episcopate, turned himself to repentance, entreating God, and considering himself sufficiently happy if it might be permitted him to communicate even as a layman : Martialis also, besides the long frequenting of the disgraceful and filthy banquets of the Gentiles in their college, and placing his sons in the same college, after the manner of foreign nations, among profane sepulchres, and burying them together with strangers, has also affirmed, by acts which are publicly taken before a ducenarian procurator,[9] that he had yielded himself to idolatry, and had denied Christ; and as there are many other and grave crimes in which Basilides and Martialis are held to be implicated; such persons attempt to claim for themselves the episcopate in vain; since it is evident that men of that kind may neither rule over the Church of Christ, nor ought to offer sacrifices to God, especially since Cornelius also, our colleague, a peaceable and righteous priest, and moreover honoured by the condescension of the Lord with martyrdom, has long ago decreed with us,[10] and with all the bishops appointed throughout the whole world, that men of this sort might indeed be admitted to repentance, but were prohibited from the ordination of the clergy, and from the priestly honour.

7. Nor let it disturb you, dearest brethren, if with some, in these last times, either an uncertain faith is wavering, or a fear of God without religion is vacillating, or a peaceable concord does not continue. These things have been foretold as about to happen in the end of the world; and it was predicted by the voice of the Lord, and by the testimony of the apostles, that now that the world is failing, and the Antichrist is drawing near, everything good shall fail, but evil and adverse things shall prosper.[11]

8. Yet although, in these last times, evangelic vigour has not so failed in the Church of God, nor

[1] Acts iv. 2.
[2] Hos. viii. 4.
[3] [See Ep. xl. p. 319, *supra*.]
[4] [Elucidation XIV.]
[5] ["Our colleague Stephen," placed at a distance, ignorant of facts and truth, and, in short, incompetent to meddle with the African province in its own business: such was Cyprian's idea of the limits to which even this apostolic See was restricted.]
[6] Gal. vi. 7.

[7] Tit. i. 7.
[8] Saragossa.
[9] A collector of taxes, so called from the amount of his salary.
[10] [Elucidation XV.]
[11] [Surely a significant warning to our own times.]

the strength of Christian virtue or faith so languished, that there is not left a portion of the priests which in no respect gives way under these ruins of things and wrecks of faith ; but, bold and stedfast, they maintain the honour of the divine majesty and the priestly dignity, with full observance of fear. We remember and keep in view that, although others succumbed and yielded, Mattathias boldly vindicated God's law ; that Elias, when the Jews gave way and departed from the divine religion, stood and nobly contended ; that Daniel, deterred neither by the loneliness of a foreign country nor by the harassment of continual persecution, frequently and gloriously suffered martyrdoms ; also that the three youths, subdued neither by their tender years [1] nor by threats, stood up faithfully against the Babylonian fires, and conquered the victor king even in their very captivity itself. Let the number either of prevaricators or of traitors see to it, who have now begun to rise in the Church against the Church, and to corrupt as well the faith as the truth. Among very many there still remains a sincere mind and a substantial religion, and a spirit devoted to nothing but the Lord and its God.[2] Nor does the perfidy of others press down the Christian faith into ruin, but rather stimulates and exalts it to glory, according to what the blessed Apostle Paul exhorts, and says : " For what if some of these have fallen from their faith : hath their unbelief made the faith of God of none effect ? God forbid. For God is true, but every man a liar." [3] But if every man is a liar, and God only true, what else ought we, the servants, and especially the priests, of God, to do, than forsake human errors and lies, and continue in the truth of God, keeping the Lord's precepts ?

9. Wherefore, although there have been found some among our colleagues, dearest brethren, who think that the godly discipline may be neglected, and who rashly hold communion with Basilides and Martialis, such a thing as this ought not to trouble our faith, since the Holy Spirit threatens such in the Psalms, saying, " But thou hatest instruction, and castedst my words behind thee : when thou sawest a thief, thou consentedst unto him, and hast been partaker with adulterers." [4] He shows that they become sharers and partakers of other men's sins who are associated with the delinquents. And besides, Paul the apostle writes, and says the same thing : "Whisperers, backbiters, haters of God, injurious, proud, boasters of themselves, inventors of evil things, who, although they knew the judgment of God, did not understand that they which com-

mit such things are worthy of death, not only they which commit those things, but they also which consent unto those who do these things." [5] Since they, says he, who do such things are worthy of death, he makes manifest and proves that not only they are worthy of death, and come into punishment who do evil things, but also those who consent unto those who do such things —who, while they are mingled in unlawful communion with the evil and sinners, and the unrepenting, are polluted by the contact of the guilty, and, being joined in the fault, are thus not separated in its penalty. For which reason we not only approve, but applaud, dearly beloved brethren, the religious solicitude of your integrity and faith, and exhort you as much as we can by our letters, not to mingle in sacrilegious communion with profane and polluted priests, but maintain the sound and sincere constancy of your faith with religious fear. I bid you, dearest brethren, ever heartily farewell.

EPISTLE LXVIII.[6]

TO FLORENTIUS PUPIANUS, ON CALUMNIATORS.

ARGUMENT.—CYPRIAN CLEARS HIMSELF IN THE EYES OF FLORENTIUS PUPIANUS FROM VARIOUS CRIMES OF WHICH HE IS ACCUSED BY HIM ; AND ARGUES THE LIGHTNESS OF HIS MIND, IN THAT HE HAS SO HASTILY TRUSTED CALUMNIATORS.

1. Cyprian, who is also called Thascius,[7] to Florentius, who is also Pupianus, his brother, greeting. I had believed, brother, that you were now at length turned to repentance for having either rashly heard or believed in time past things so wicked, so disgraceful, so execrable even among Gentiles, concerning me. But even now in your letter I perceive that you are still the same as you were before — that you believe the same things concerning me, and that you persist in what you did believe, and, lest by chance the dignity of your eminence and your martyrdom should be stained by communion with me, that you are inquiring carefully into my character ; and after God the Judge who makes priests, that you wish to judge — I will not say of me, for what am I ? — but of the judgment of God and of Christ. This is not to believe in God — this is to stand forth as a rebel against Christ and His Gospel ; so that although He says, " Are not two sparrows sold for a farthing ? and neither of them falls to the ground

---

[1] Some read, " by the furnaces ; " some " by arms."
[2] [A noteworthy testimony to the Decian period, when to be a Christian, indeed, was to be a confessor or martyr. Soc., *H. E.*, bk. iv. c. 28.]
[3] Rom. iii. 3, 4.
[4] Ps. l. 17, 18.

[5] Rom. i. 30-32.
[6] Oxford ed.: Ep. lxvi. From his saying, that he has now discharged his episcopal office for six years (sec. 5), it is plainly evident that he is writing this letter in the time of Stephen. A.D. 254.
[7] It is suggested with some probability, that this form of superscription was intended to rebuke the rudeness of Florentius, who, in addressing Cyprian, had used his heathen name of Thascius instead of his baptismal name of Cæcilius, which he had adopted from the presbyter who had been the means of his conversion.

without the will of my Father," [1] and His majesty and truth prove that even things of little consequence are not done without the consciousness and permission of God, you think that God's priests are ordained in the Church without His knowledge. For to believe that they who are ordained are unworthy and unchaste, what else is it than to believe that his priests are not appointed in the Church by God, nor through God?

2. Think you that my testimony of myself is better than that of God? when the Lord Himself teaches, and says that testimony is not true, if any one himself appears as a witness concerning himself, for the reason that every one would assuredly favour himself. Nor would any one put forward mischievous and adverse things against himself, but there may be a simple confidence of truth if, in what was announced of us, another is the announcer and witness. "If," He says, "I bear witness of myself, my testimony is not true; but there is another who beareth witness of me." [2] But if the Lord Himself, who will by and by judge all things, was unwilling to be believed on His own testimony, but preferred to be approved by the judgment and testimony of God the Father, how much more does it behove His servants to observe this, who are not only approved by, but even glory in the judgment and testimony of God! But with you the fabrication of hostile and malignant men has prevailed against the divine decree, and against our conscience resting upon the strength of its faith, as if among lapsed and profane persons placed outside the Church, from whose breasts the Holy Spirit has departed, there could be anything else than a depraved mind and a deceitful tongue, and venomous hatred, and sacrilegious lies, which whosoever believes, must of necessity be found with them when the day of judgment shall come.

3. But with respect to what you have said, that priests should be lowly, because both the Lord and His apostles were lowly; both all the brethren and Gentiles also well know and love my humility; and you also knew and loved it while you were still in the Church, and were in communion with me. But which of us is far from humility: I, who daily serve the brethren, and kindly receive with good-will and gladness every one that comes to the Church; or you, who appoint yourself bishop of a bishop, and judge of a judge, [3] given for the time by God? Although the Lord God says in Deuteronomy, " And the man that will do presumptuously, and will not hearken unto the priests or unto the judge

who shall be in those days, even that man shall die; and all the people, when they hear, shall fear, and do no more presumptuously." [4] And again He speaks to Samuel, and says, " They have not despised thee, but they have despised me." [5] And moreover the Lord, in the Gospel, when it was said to Him, " Answerest thou the high priest so?" guarding the priestly dignity, and teaching that it ought to be maintained, would say nothing against the high priest, but only clearing His own innocence, answered, saying, " If I have spoken evil, bear witness of the evil; but if well, why smitest thou me?" [6] The blessed apostle also, when it was said to him, " Revilest thou God's high priest?" spoke nothing reproachfully against the priest, when he might have lifted up himself boldly against those who had crucified the Lord, and who had already sacrificed God and Christ, and the temple and the priesthood; but even although in false and degraded priests, considering still the mere empty shadow of the priestly name, he said, " I wist not, brethren, that he was the high priest; for it is written, Thou shalt not speak evil of the ruler of thy people." [7]

4. Unless perchance I was a priest to you before the persecution, when you held communion with me, and ceased to be a priest after the persecution! For the persecution, when it came, lifted you to the highest sublimity of martyrdom. But it depressed me with the burden of proscription, since it was publicly declared, " If any one holds or possesses any of the property of Cæcilius Cyprian, bishop of the Christians; " so that even they who did not believe in God appointing a bishop, could still believe in the devil proscribing a bishop. Nor do I boast of these things, but with grief I bring them forward, since you constitute yourself a judge [3] of God and of Christ, who says to the apostles, and thereby to all chief rulers, who by vicarious ordination succeed to the apostles: " He that heareth you, heareth me; and he that heareth me, heareth Him that sent me; and he that despiseth you, despiseth me, and Him that sent me." [8]

5. For from this have arisen, and still arise, schisms and heresies, in that the bishop who is one [9] and rules over the Church is contemned by the haughty presumption of some persons; and the man who is honoured by God's condescension, is judged unworthy by men. For what swelling of pride is this, what arrogance of soul, what inflation of mind, to call prelates and priests to one's own recognition, and unless I may be

---

[1] Matt. x. 29.
[2] John v. 31, 32.
[3] [A mild remonstrance against the officious conduct of Stephen, also.]

[4] Deut. xvii. 12, 13.
[5] 1 Sam. viii. 7.
[6] John xviii. 23.
[7] Acts xxiii. 4, 5.
[8] Luke x. 16.
[9] [His aphorism, *Ecclesia in Episcopo*, is here used in another form. " The bishop" here = the episcopate.]

declared clear in your sight and absolved by your judgment, behold now for six years the brotherhood has neither had a bishop, nor the people a prelate,[1] nor the flock a pastor, nor the Church a governor, nor Christ a representative,[2] nor God a priest! Pupianus must come to the rescue, and give judgment, and declare the decision of God and Christ accepted, that so great a number of the faithful who have been summoned away, under my rule, may not appear to have departed without hope of salvation and of peace; that the new crowd of believers may not be considered to have failed of attaining any grace of baptism and the Holy Spirit by my ministry;[3] that the peace conferred upon so many lapsed and penitent persons, and the communion vouchsafed by my examination, may not be abrogated by the authority of your judgment. Condescend for once, and deign to pronounce concerning us, and to establish our episcopate by the authority of your recognition, that God and His Christ may thank you, in that by your means a representative and ruler has been restored as well to their altar as to their people.

6. Bees have a king, and cattle a leader, and *they* keep faith to him. Robbers obey their chief with an obedience full of humility. How much more simple and better than you are the brute cattle and dumb animals, and robbers, although bloody, and raging among swords and weapons! The chief among them is acknowledged and feared, whom no divine judgment has appointed, but on whom an abandoned faction and a guilty band have agreed.

7. You say, indeed, that the scruple into which you have fallen ought to be taken from your mind. You have fallen into it, but it was by your irreligious credulity. You have fallen into it, but it was by your own sacrilegious disposition and will in easily hearkening to unchaste, to impious, to unspeakable things against your brother, against a priest, and in willingly believing them; in defending other men's falsehoods, as if they were your own and your private property; and in not remembering that it is written, "Hedge thine ears with thorns, and hearken not to a wicked tongue;"[4] and again: "A wicked doer giveth heed to the tongue of the unjust; but a righteous man regards not lying lips."[5] Wherefore have not the martyrs fallen into this scruple, full of the Holy Ghost, and already by their passion near to the presence of God and of His Christ; martyrs who, from their dungeon, directed letters to Cyprian the bishop, acknowledging the priest of God, and bearing witness to

him? Wherefore have not so many bishops, my colleagues, fallen into this scruple, who either, when they departed from the midst of us, were proscribed, or being taken were cast into prison and were in chains; or who, sent away into exile, have gone by an illustrious road to the Lord; or who in some places, condemned to death, have received heavenly crowns from the glorification of the Lord? Wherefore have not they fallen into this scruple, from among that people of ours which is with us, and is by God's condescension committed to us — so many confessors who have been put to the question and tortured, and glorious by the memory of illustrious wounds and scars; so many chaste virgins, so many praiseworthy widows; finally, all the churches throughout the whole world who are associated with us in the bond of unity? Unless all these, who are in communion with me, as you have written, are polluted with the pollution of my lips, and have lost the hope of eternal life by the contagion of my communion.[6] Pupianus alone, sound, inviolate, holy, modest, who would not associate himself with us, shall dwell alone in paradise and in the kingdom of heaven.

8. You have written also, that on my account the Church has now a portion of herself in a state of dispersion, although the whole people of the Church are collected, and united, and joined to itself in an undivided concord: they alone have remained without, who even, if they had been within, would have had to be cast out. Nor does the Lord, the protector of His people, and their guardian, suffer the wheat to be snatched from His floor; but the chaff alone can be separated from the Church, since also the apostle says, "For what if some of them have departed from the faith? shall their unbelief make the faith of God of none effect? God forbid; for God is true, but every man a liar."[7] And the Lord also in the Gospel, when disciples forsook Him as He spoke, turning to the twelve, said, "Will ye also go away?" then Peter answered Him, "Lord, to whom shall we go? Thou hast the word of eternal life; and we believe, and are sure, that Thou art the Son of the living God."[8] Peter speaks there, on whom the Church was to be built,[9] teaching and showing in the name of the Church, that although a rebellious and arrogant multitude of those who will not hear and obey may depart, yet the Church does not depart from Christ; and they are the Church who are a people united to the priest, and the flock which adheres to its pastor.[3] Whence you ought to know that the bishop is in the Church, and the

---

[1] [*Præpositum* is the word thus translated.]
[2] Antistitem. [This word occurs in Tertullian, *De Fuga*.]
[3] [In all this his theory comes out; viz., that unity is maintained by communion with one's lawful bishop, not with any foreign See.]
[4] Ecclus. xxviii. 24 (Vulg. 28).
[5] Prov. xvii. 4, LXX.

[6] [See sec. 6, note 3, *supra*.]
[7] Rom. iii. 3, 4.
[8] John vi. 67–69.
[9] [Not any of his successors, but Peter personally, is thus honoured on the strength of Eph. ii. 20. All the apostles were in this foundation also, Rev. xxi. 14; but the figure excludes successors, who are of the superstructure, necessarily.]

Church in the bishop; [1] and if any one be not with the bishop, that he is not in the Church, and that those flatter themselves in vain who creep in, not having peace with God's priests, and think that they communicate secretly with some; while the Church, which is Catholic and one, is not cut nor divided, but is indeed connected and bound together by the cement of priests who cohere with one another.

9. Wherefore, brother, if you consider God's majesty who ordains priests, if you will for once have respect to Christ, who by His decree and word, and by His presence, both rules prelates themselves, and rules the Church by prelates; if you will trust, in respect of the innocence of bishops, not human hatred, but the divine judgment; if you will begin even a late repentance for your temerity, and pride, and insolence; if you will most abundantly make satisfaction to God and His Christ whom I serve, and to whom with pure and unstained lips I ceaselessly offer sacrifices, not only in peace, but in persecution; we may have some ground for communion with you, even although there still remain among us respect and fear for the divine censure; so that first I should consult my Lord whether He would permit peace to be granted to you, and you to be received to the communion of His Church by His own showing and admonition.

10. For I remember what has already been manifested to me, nay, what has been prescribed by the authority of our Lord and God to an obedient and fearing servant; and among other things which He condescended to show and to reveal, He also added this: "Whoso therefore does not believe Christ, who maketh the priest, shall hereafter begin to believe Him who avengeth the priest." Although I know that to some men dreams seem ridiculous and visions foolish, yet assuredly it is to such as would rather believe in opposition to the priest, than believe the priest. But it is no wonder, since his brethren said of Joseph, "Behold, this dreamer cometh; come now therefore, let us slay him." [2] And afterwards the dreamer attained to what he had dreamed; and his slayers and sellers were put to confusion, so that they, who at first did not believe the words, afterwards believed the deeds. But of those things that you have done, either in persecution or in peace, it is foolish for me to pretend to judge you, since you rather appoint yourself a judge over us. These things, of the pure conscience of my mind, and of my confidence in my Lord and my God, I have written at length. You have my letter, and I yours. In

the day of judgment, before the tribunal of Christ, both will be read.

EPISTLE LXIX.[3]

TO JANUARIUS AND OTHER NUMIDIAN BISHOPS, ON BAPTIZING HERETICS.

ARGUMENT. — THE ARGUMENT OF THIS LETTER AND THE NEXT IS FOUND IN A SUBSEQUENT EPISTLE TO STEPHEN: [4] "THAT WHAT HERETICS USE IS NOT BAPTISM; AND THAT NONE AMONG THEM CAN RECEIVE BENEFIT BY THE GRACE OF CHRIST, WHO OPPOSE CHRIST; HAS BEEN LATELY CAREFULLY EXPRESSED IN A LETTER WHICH WAS WRITTEN ON THAT SUBJECT TO QUINTUS, OUR COLLEAGUE, ESTABLISHED IN MAURITANIA; AS ALSO IN A LETTER WHICH OUR COLLEAGUES PREVIOUSLY WROTE TO THE BISHOPS PRESIDING IN NUMIDIA; OF BOTH OF WHICH LETTERS I HAVE SUBJOINED COPIES." [5]

1. Cyprian, Liberalis, Caldonius, Junius, Primus, Cæcilius, Polycarp, Nicomedes, Felix, Marrutius, Successus, Lucianus, Honoratus, Fortunatus, Victor, Donatus, Lucius, Herculanus, Pomponius, Demetrius, Quintus, Saturninus, Januarius, Marcus, another Saturninus, another Donatus, Rogatianus, Sedatus, Tertullus, Hortensianus, still another Saturninus, Sattius, to their brethren Januarius, Saturninus, Maximus, Victor, another Victor, Cassius, Proculus, Modianus, Cittinus, Gargilius, Eutycianus, another Gargilius, another Saturninus, Nemesianus, Nampulus, Antonianus, Rogatianus, Honoratus, greeting. When we were together in council, dearest brethren, we read your letter which you wrote to us concerning those who seem to be baptized by heretics and schismatics, (asking) whether, when they come to the Catholic Church, which is one,[6] they ought to be baptized. On which matter, although you yourselves hold thereupon the truth and certainty of the Catholic rule, yet since you have thought that of our mutual love we ought to be consulted, we put forward our opinion, not as a new one,[7] but we join with you in equal agreement, in an opinion long since decreed by our predecessors, and observed by us, — judging, namely, and holding it for certain that no one can be baptized abroad outside the Church, since there is one baptism appointed in the holy Church. And it is written in the words of the Lord, "They have forsaken me, the fountain of living waters, and hewed them out broken cisterns, which can hold no

---

[1] [See sec. 5, *supra*. This is the famous formula of Cyprian's theory. The whole theory is condensed in what follows.]
[2] Gen. xxxvii. 19, 20. [It seems a beautiful coincidence that another Joseph was a "dreamer" (Matt. ii. 20, 23); and in those days, when prophets and prophesyings were hardly yet extinct, we must not too readily call this credulity. Ps. lxxxix. 19, Vulgate.]

[3] Oxford ed.: Ep. lxx. A.D. 255.
[4] Ep. lxxi.
[5] Mention is made of both letters in the Epistle to Jubaianus, and in the one that follows this.
[6] "And true."
[7] [This is very much to be observed, at this outset of an important historical controversy. Cyprian was not conscious of any innovation. See Oxford Tertull., vol. i. p. 280, note.]

water."[1] And again, sacred Scripture warns, and says, "Keep thee from the strange water, and drink not from a fountain of strange water."[2] It is required, then, that the water should first be cleansed and sanctified by the priest,[3] that it may wash away by its baptism the sins of the man who is baptized; because the Lord says by Ezekiel the prophet: "Then will I sprinkle clean water upon you, and ye shall be cleansed from all your filthiness; and from all your idols will I cleanse you: a new heart also will I give you, and a new spirit will I put within you."[4] But how can he cleanse and sanctify the water who is himself unclean, and in whom the Holy Spirit is not? since the Lord says in the book of Numbers, "And whatsoever the unclean person toucheth shall be unclean."[5] Or how can he who baptizes give to another remission of sins, who himself, being outside the Church, cannot put away his own sins?

2. But, moreover, the very interrogation which is put in baptism is a witness of the truth. For when we say, "Dost thou believe in eternal life and remission of sins through the holy Church?" we mean that remission of sins is not granted except in the Church, and that among heretics, where there is no Church, sins cannot be put away. Therefore they who assert that heretics can baptize, must either change the interrogation or maintain the truth; unless indeed they attribute a church also to those who, they contend, have baptism. It is also necessary that he should be anointed who is baptized; so that, having received the chrism,[6] that is, the anointing, he may be anointed of God, and have in him the grace of Christ. Further, it is the Eucharist whence the baptized are anointed with the oil sanctified on the altar.[7] But he cannot sanctify the creature of oil,[8] who has neither an altar nor a church; whence also there can be no spiritual anointing among heretics, since it is manifest that the oil cannot be sanctified nor the Eucharist celebrated at all among them. But we ought to know and remember that it is written, "Let not the oil of a sinner anoint my head,"[9] which the Holy Spirit before forewarned in the Psalms, lest any one going out of the way and wandering from the path of truth should be anointed by heretics and adversaries of Christ. Besides, what prayer can a priest who is impious

and a sinner offer for a baptized person? since it is written, "God heareth not a sinner; but if any man be a worshipper of God, and doeth His will, him He heareth."[10] Who, moreover, can give what he himself has not? or how can he discharge spiritual functions who himself has lost the Holy Spirit? And therefore he must be baptized and renewed who comes untrained to the Church, that he may be sanctified within by those who are holy, since it is written, "Be ye holy, for I am holy, saith the Lord."[11] So that he who has been seduced into error, and baptized[12] outside *of the Church*, should lay aside even this very thing in the true and ecclesiastical baptism, viz., that he a man coming to God, while he seeks for a priest, fell by the deceit of error upon a profane one.

3. But it is to approve the baptism of heretics and schismatics, to admit that they have *truly* baptized. For therein a part cannot be void, and part be valid. If one could baptize, he could also give the Holy Spirit. But if he cannot give the Holy Spirit, because he that is appointed without is not endowed with the Holy Spirit, he cannot baptize those who come; since both baptism is one and the Holy Spirit is one, and the Church founded by Christ the Lord upon Peter, by a source and principle of unity,[13] is one also. Hence it results, that since with them all things are futile and false, nothing of that which they have done ought to be approved by us. For what can be ratified and established by God which is done by them whom the Lord calls His enemies and adversaries? setting forth in His Gospel, "He that is not with me is against me; and he that gathereth not with me, scattereth."[14] And the blessed Apostle John also, keeping the commandments and precepts of the Lord, has laid it down in his epistle, and said, "Ye have heard that antichrist shall come: even now there are many Antichrists; whereby we know that it is the last time. They went out from us, but they were not of us; for if they had been of us, no doubt they would have continued with us."[15] Whence we also ought to gather and consider whether they who are the Lord's adversaries, and are called antichrists, can give the grace of Christ. Wherefore we who are with the Lord, and maintain the unity of the Lord, and according to His condescension administer His priesthood in the Church, ought to repudiate and reject and regard as profane whatever His adversaries and the antichrists do; and to those who, coming out of error and wickedness, acknowledge the true faith of the one Church, we

---

1 Jer. ii. 13.
2 Prov. ix. 19 (LXX.).
3 [When a deacon baptized, he was regarded as using, not his own "key," but the keys of the priesthood, and as simply supplying a lawful hand to the absent priest. See p. 366, note 8, *supra*.]
4 Ezek. xxxvi. 25, 26.
5 Num. xix. 2.
6 [i.e., confirmation, called chrism, or *unction*, from 1 John ii. 27 and other Scriptures.]
7 An authorized reading here is, "But further, the Eucharist and the oil, whence the baptized are anointed, are sanctified on the altar."
8 [Material oil was not originally used in baptism or confirmation, but was admitted ceremonially, in divers rites, at an early period. Mark vi. 13; Jas. v. 14. Bunsen, *Hippol.*, vol. ii. p. 322, note 1.]
9 Ps. cxli. 5 (LXX.).

10 John ix. 31.
11 Lev. xix. 2.
12 Tinctus.
13 [See Cave, *Prim. Christianity*, p. 365.]
14 Luke xi. 23.
15 1 John ii. 18, 19.

should give the truth both of unity and faith, by means of all the sacraments of divine grace.[1] We bid you, dearest brethren, ever heartily farewell.

EPISTLE LXX.[2]
TO QUINTUS, CONCERNING THE BAPTISM OF HERETICS.

ARGUMENT. — AN ANSWER IS GIVEN TO QUINTUS, A BISHOP IN MAURITANIA, WHO HAS ASKED ADVICE CONCERNING THE BAPTISM OF HERETICS.

1. Cyprian to Quintus his brother, greeting. Lucian, our co-presbyter, has reported to me, dearest brother, that you have wished me to declare to you what I think concerning those who seem to have been baptized by heretics and schismatics ; of which matter, that you may know what several of us fellow-bishops, with the brother presbyters who were present, lately determined in council, I have sent you a copy of the same epistle. For I know not by what presumption some of our colleagues[3] are led to think that they who have been dipped by heretics ought not to be baptized when they come to us, for the reason that they say that there is one baptism ; which indeed is therefore one, because the Church is one, and there cannot be any baptism out of the Church.[4] For since there cannot be two baptisms, if heretics truly baptize, they themselves have this baptism. And he who of his own authority grants this advantage to them, yields and consents to them, that the enemy and adversary of Christ should seem to have the power of washing, and purifying, and sanctifying a man. But we say that those who come thence are not re-baptized among us, but are baptized. For indeed they do not receive anything there, where there is nothing ; but they come to us, that here they may receive where there is both grace and all truth, because both grace and truth are one. But again some of our colleagues[3] would rather give honour to heretics than agree with us ; and while by the assertion of one baptism they are unwilling to baptize those that come, they thus either themselves make two baptisms in saying that there is a baptism among heretics ; or certainly, which is a matter of more importance, they strive to set before and prefer the sordid and profane washing of heretics to the true and only and legitimate baptism of the Catholic Church, not considering that it is written, " He who is baptized by one dead, what

availeth his washing?"[5] Now it is manifest that they who are not in the Church of Christ are reckoned among the dead ; and another cannot be made alive by him who himself is not alive, since there is one Church which, having attained the grace of eternal life, both lives for ever and quickens the people of God.

2. And they say that in this matter they follow ancient custom ;[6] although among the ancients these were as yet the first beginnings of heresy and schisms, so that those were involved in them who departed from the Church, having first been baptized therein ; and these, therefore, when they returned to the Church and repented, it was not necessary to baptize. Which also we observe in the present day, that it is sufficient to lay hands for repentance upon those who are known to have been baptized in the Church, and have gone over from us to the heretics, if, subsequently acknowledging their sin and putting away their error, they return to the truth and to their parent ; so that, because it had been a sheep, the Shepherd may receive into His fold the estranged and vagrant sheep. But if he who comes from the heretics has not previously been baptized in the Church, but comes as a stranger and entirely profane, he must be baptized, that he may become a sheep, because in the holy Church is the one water which makes sheep. And therefore, because there can be nothing common to falsehood and truth, to darkness and light, to death and immortality, to Antichrist and Christ, we ought by all means to maintain the unity of the Catholic Church, and not to give way to the enemies of faith and truth in any respect.

3. Neither must we prescribe this from custom, but overcome *opposite custom* by reason. For neither did Peter, whom first the Lord chose, and upon whom He built His Church, when Paul disputed with him afterwards about circumcision, claim anything to himself insolently, nor arrogantly assume anything ; so as to say that he held the primacy,[7] and that he ought rather to be obeyed by novices and those lately come.[8] Nor did he despise Paul because he had previously been a persecutor of the Church, but admitted the counsel of truth, and easily yielded to the lawful reason which Paul asserted, furnishing thus an illustration to us both of concord and of patience, that we should not obstinately love our own opinions, but should rather adopt as our own those which at any time are usefully and

---

[1] [The vigour of Cyprian's logic must be conceded. The discussion will show, as it proceeds, on what grounds it failed to enlist universal support. It resembled the Easter question, vol. i. p. 569.]

[2] Oxford ed.: Ep. lxxi. A.D. 255.

[3] [Note this, at the outset : it is *presumption* in his colleague Stephen to act otherwise than as a general consent of the provinces seems to rule.]

[4] [Otherwise, " which doubtless is one in the Catholic Church ; and if this Church be one, baptism cannot exist outside the Church." His theory of unity underlies all our author's conduct.]

[5] Ecclus. xxxiv. 25.

[6] [The local custom of the Roman Province seems to have justified Stephen's *local* practice. It is a case similar to that of Polycarp and Anicetus disturbed by Victor, vol. i. 310, and 312.]

[7] [But a primacy involves no supremacy. All the Gallicans, with Bossuet, insist on this point. Cyprian now adopts, as his rule, St. Paul's example, Gal. ii. 5.]

[8] [Here, then, is the whole of Cyprian's idea as to Peter, in a nutshell.]

wholesomely suggested by our brethren and colleagues, if they be true and lawful. Paul, moreover, looking forward to this, and consulting faithfully for concord and peace, has laid down in his epistle this rule : "Moreover, let the prophets speak two or three, and let the rest judge. But if anything be revealed to another that sitteth by, let the first hold his peace." [1] In which place he has taught and shown that many things are revealed to individuals for the better, and that each one ought not obstinately to contend for that which he had once imbibed and held ; but if anything has appeared better and more useful, he should gladly embrace it. For we are not overcome when better things are presented to us, but we are instructed, especially in those matters which pertain to the unity of the Church and the truth of our hope and faith ; so that we, priests of God and prelates of His Church, by His condescension, should know that remission of sins cannot be given save in the Church, nor can the adversaries of Christ claim to themselves anything belonging to His grace.

4. Which thing, indeed, Agrippinus also, a man of worthy memory, with his other fellow-bishops, who at that time governed the Lord's Church in the province of Africa and Numidia, decreed, and by the well-weighed examination of the common council established : whose opinion, as being both religious and lawful and salutary, and in harmony with the Catholic faith and Church, we also have followed.[2] And that you may know what kind of letters we have written on this subject, I have transmitted for our mutual love a copy of them, as well for your own information as for that of our fellow-bishops who are in those parts. I bid you, dearest brother, ever heartily farewell.

EPISTLE LXXI.[3]

TO STEPHEN, CONCERNING A COUNCIL.

ARGUMENT. — CYPRIAN WITH HIS COLLEAGUES IN A CERTAIN COUNCIL TELLS STEPHEN, THE ROMAN BISHOP, THAT IT HAD BEEN DECREED BY THEM, BOTH THAT THOSE WHO RETURNED FROM HERESY INTO THE CHURCH SHOULD BE BAPTIZED, AND THAT BISHOPS OR PRIESTS COMING FROM THE HERETICS SHOULD BE RECEIVED ON NO OTHER CONDITION, THAN THAT THEY SHOULD COMMUNICATE AS LAY PEOPLE. A.D. 255.

1. Cyprian and others, to Stephen their brother, greeting. We have thought it necessary for the arranging of certain matters, dearest brother, and for their investigation by the examination of a common council, to gather together and to hold a council, at which many priests were assembled at once ; at which, moreover, many things were brought forward and transacted. But the subject in regard to which we had chiefly to write to you, and to confer with your gravity and wisdom, is one that more especially pertains both to the priestly authority and to the unity, as well as the dignity, of the Catholic Church, arising as these do from the ordination of the divine appointment ; to wit, that those who have been dipped abroad outside the Church, and have been stained among heretics and schismatics with the taint of profane water, when they come to us and to the Church which is one, ought to be baptized, for the reason that it is a small matter [4] to "lay hands on them that they may receive the Holy Ghost," unless they receive also the baptism of the Church. For then finally can they be fully sanctified, and be the sons of God, if they be born of each sacrament ; [5] since it is written, "Except a man be born again of water, and of the Spirit, he cannot enter into the kingdom of God." [6] For we find also, in the Acts of the Apostles, that this is maintained by the apostles, and kept in the truth of the saving faith, so that when, in the house of Cornelius the centurion, the Holy Ghost had descended upon the Gentiles who were there, fervent in the warmth of their faith, and believing in the Lord with their whole heart ; and when, filled with the Spirit, they blessed God in divers tongues, still none the less the blessed Apostle Peter, mindful of the divine precept and the Gospel, commanded that those same men should be baptized who had already been filled with the Holy Spirit, that nothing might seem to be neglected to the observance by the apostolic instruction in all things of the law of the divine precept and Gospel.[7] But that that is not baptism which the heretics use ; and that none of those who oppose Christ can profit by the grace of Christ ; has lately been set forth with care in the letter which was written on that subject to Quintus, our colleague, established in Mauritania ; as also in a letter which our colleagues previously wrote to our fellow-bishops presiding in Numidia, of both which letters I have subjoined copies.

---

[1] 1 Cor. xiv. 29, 30. [P. 379, note 4, infra.]
[2] [With Cyprian it was an adjudged case. Stephen not only had no authority in the case, but, save by courtesy, even his primacy was confined to his own province.]
[3] Oxford ed.: Ep. lxxii. [Concerning the council (seventh of Carthage), see the Acts, infra. Elucidation XVI.]

[4] [He quotes Acts viii. 17.]
[5] The sense of this passage has been doubted, but seems to be this: "The rite of confirmation, or the giving of the Holy Ghost, is of no avail unless baptism have first been conferred. For only by being born of each sacrament, scil. confirmation and baptism, can they be fully sanctified and be born again: since it is written, ' Except a man be born of water and of the Spirit,' etc ; which quotation is plainly meant to convey, that the birth of water is by baptism, that of the Spirit by confirmation."
[6] John iii. 5. [Bingham, book xii. cap. i. sec. 4.]
[7] [This case (Acts x. 47) was governed by the example of Christ, Matt. iii. 15. The baptism of the Spirit had preceded; yet as an act of obedience to Christ, and in honour of His example, St. Peter "fulfils all righteousness," even to the letter.]

2. We add, however, and connect with what we have said, dearest brother, with common consent and authority, that if, again, any presbyters or deacons, who either have been before ordained in the Catholic Church, and have subsequently stood forth as traitors and rebels against the Church, or who have been promoted among the heretics by a profane ordination by the hands of false bishops and antichrists contrary to the appointment of Christ, and have attempted to offer, in opposition to the one and divine altar, false and sacrilegious sacrifices without, that these also be received when they return, on this condition, that they communicate as laymen, and hold it to be enough that they should be received to peace, after having stood forth as enemies of peace; and that they ought not, on returning, to retain those arms of ordination and honour with which they rebelled against us. For it behoves priests and ministers, who wait upon the altar and sacrifices, to be sound and stainless; since the Lord God speaks in Leviticus, and says, "No man that hath a stain or a blemish shall come nigh to offer gifts to the Lord."[1] Moreover, in Exodus, He prescribes this same thing, and says, "And let the priests which come near to the Lord God sanctify themselves, lest the Lord forsake them."[2] And again: "And when they come near to minister at the altar of the holy place, they shall not bear iniquity upon them, lest they die."[3] But what can be greater iniquity, or what stain can be more odious, than to have stood in opposition to Christ; than to have scattered His Church, which He purchased and founded with His blood; than, unmindful of evangelical peace and love, to have fought with the madness of hostile discord against the unanimous and accordant people of God? Such as these, although they themselves return to the Church, still cannot restore and recall with them those who, seduced by them, and forestalled by death without, have perished outside the Church without communion and peace; whose souls in the day of judgment shall be required at the hands of those who have stood forth as the authors and leaders of their ruin. And therefore to such, when they return, it is sufficient that pardon should be granted; since perfidy ought certainly not to receive promotion in the household of faith. For what do we reserve for the good and innocent, and those who do not depart from the Church, if we honour those who have departed from us, and stood in opposition to the Church?

3. We have brought these things, dearest brother, to your knowledge, for the sake of our mutual honour and sincere affection; believing

that, according to the truth of your religion and faith, those things which are no less religious than true will be approved by you. But we know that some will not lay aside what they have once imbibed, and do not easily change their purpose; but, keeping fast the bond of peace and concord among their colleagues, retain certain things peculiar to themselves, which have once been adopted among them. In which behalf we neither do violence to, nor impose a law upon, any one, since each prelate has in the administration of the Church the exercise of his will free, as he shall give an account of his conduct to the Lord.[4] We bid you, dearest brother, ever heartily farewell.

EPISTLE LXXII.[5]

TO JUBAIANUS, CONCERNING THE BAPTISM OF HERETICS.

ARGUMENT. — CYPRIAN REFUTES A LETTER ENCLOSED TO HIM BY JUBAIANUS, AND WITH THE GREATEST CARE COLLECTS WHATEVER HE THINKS WILL AVAIL FOR THE DEFENCE OF HIS CAUSE. MOREOVER, HE SENDS JUBAIANUS A COPY OF THE LETTER TO THE NUMIDIANS AND TO QUINTUS, AND PROBABLY THE DECREES OF THE LAST SYNOD.[6]

1. Cyprian to Jubaianus his brother, greeting. You have written to me, dearest brother, wishing that the impression of my mind should be signified to you, as to what I think concerning the baptism of heretics; who, placed without, and established outside the Church, arrogate to themselves a matter neither within their right nor their power. This baptism we cannot consider as valid or legitimate, since it is manifestly unlawful among them; and since we have already expressed in our letters what we thought on this matter, I have, as a compendious method, sent you a copy of the same letters, what we decided in council when very many of us were present, and what, moreover, I subsequently wrote back to Quintus, our colleague, when he asked about the same thing. And now also, when we had met together, bishops as well of the province of Africa as of Numidia, to the number of seventy-one, we established this same matter once more[7] by our judgment, deciding that there is one baptism which is appointed in the Catholic Church; and that by this those are not re-baptized, but baptized by us, who at any time come from the adulterous and unhallowed water

---

[1] Lev. xxi. 21.
[2] Ex. xix. 22.
[3] Ex. xxviii. 43.

[4] [Obviously, the law of liberty here laid down might introduce the greatest confusion if not limited by common consent. Yet the tolerant spirit of our author merits praise. P. 378, notes 1, 2.]
[5] Oxford ed.: Ep. lxxiii. A.D. 256.
[6] In the year of Christ 256, a little after the seventh council of Carthage, Cyprian wrote a long letter to the Bishop Jubaianus. He had consulted Cyprian about baptism, and at the same time had sent a letter not written by himself, but by some other person opposed to the opinion of Cyprian.
[7] [Letter lxx. sec. 4, p. 378, *supra.* Jubaian. was of Mauritania.]

to be washed and sanctified by the truth of the saving water.

2. Nor does what you have described in your letters disturb us, dearest brother, that the Novatians re-baptize those whom they entice from us, since it does not in any wise matter to us what the enemies of the Church do, so long as we ourselves hold a regard for our power, and the stedfastness of reason and truth. For Novatian, after the manner of apes — which, although they are not men, yet imitate human doings — wishes to claim to himself the authority and truth of the Catholic Church, while he himself is not in the Church; nay, moreover, has stood forth hitherto as a rebel and enemy against the Church. For, knowing that there is one baptism, he arrogates to himself this one, so that he may say that the Church is with him, and make us heretics. But we who hold the head and root [1] of the one Church know, and trust for certain, that nothing is lawful there outside the Church, and that the baptism which is one [2] is among us, where he himself also was formerly baptized, when he maintained both the wisdom and truth of the divine unity. But if Novatian thinks that those who have been baptized in the Church are to be re-baptized outside — without the Church — he ought to begin by himself, that he might first be re-baptized with an extraneous and heretical baptism, since he thinks that after the Church, yea, and contrary to the Church, people are to be baptized without. But what sort of a thing is this, that, because Novatian dares to do this thing, we are to think that we must not do it! What then? Because Novatian also usurps the honour of the priestly throne, ought we therefore to renounce our throne? Or because Novatian endeavours wrongfully to set up an altar and to offer sacrifices, does it behove us to cease from our altar and sacrifices, lest we should appear to be celebrating the same or like things with him? Utterly vain and foolish is it, that because Novatian arrogates to himself outside the Church the image of the truth, we should forsake the truth of the Church.

3. But among us it is no new or sudden thing for us to judge that those are to be baptized who come to the Church from among the heretics, since it is now many years and a long time ago, that, under Agrippinus — a man of worthy memory — very many bishops assembling together have decided this; [3] and thenceforward until the present day, so many thousands of heretics in our provinces have been converted to the Church, and have neither despised nor delayed, nay, they have both reasonably and gladly embraced, the opportunity to attain the grace of the life-giving laver and of saving baptism. For it is not difficult for a teacher to insinuate true and lawful things into his mind, who, having condemned heretical pravity, and discovered the truth of the Church, comes for this purpose, that he may learn, and learns for the purpose that he may live. We ought not to increase the stolidity of heretics by the patronage of our consent, when they gladly and readily obey the truth.

4. Certainly, since I found in the letter the copy of which you transmitted to me, that it was written, "That it should not be asked who baptized, since he who is baptized might receive remission of sins according to what he believed," I thought that this topic was not to be passed by, especially since I observed in the same epistle that mention was also made of Marcion, saying that "even those that came from him did not need to be baptized, because they seemed to have been already baptized in the name of Jesus Christ." Therefore we ought to consider their faith who believe without, whether in respect of the same faith they can obtain any grace. For if we and heretics have one faith, we may also have one grace. If the Patripassians, Anthropians, Valentinians, Apelletians, Ophites, Marcionites, and other pests, and swords, and poisons of heretics for subverting the truth,[4] confess the same Father, the same Son, the same Holy Ghost, the same Church with us, they may also have one baptism if they have also one faith.

5. And lest it should be wearisome to go through all the heresies, and to enumerate either the follies or the madness of each of them, because it is no pleasure to speak of that which one either dreads or is ashamed to know, let us examine in the meantime about Marcion alone, the mention of whom has been made in the letter transmitted by you to us, whether the ground of his baptism can be made good. For the Lord after His resurrection, sending His disciples, instructed and taught them in what manner they ought to baptize, saying, "All power is given unto me in heaven and in earth. Go ye therefore, and teach all nations, baptizing them in the name of the Father, and of the Son, and of the Holy Ghost." [5] He suggests the Trinity, in whose sacrament the nations were to be baptized. Does Marcion then maintain the Trinity? Does he then assert the same Father, the Creator, as we do? Does he know the same Son, Christ born of the Virgin Mary, who as the Word was made flesh, who bare our sins, who conquered death by dying, who by Himself first of all originated the resurrection of the flesh, and showed to His disciples that He had risen in the

---

[1] [This helps us to understand the expression, p. 322, note 2, *supra*.]
[2] Or, " the source of baptism which is one."
[3] [Note, that Cyprian believes himself to be sustaining a *res adjudicata*, and has no idea that the councils of the African Church need to be revised beyond seas. Letter lxx. p. 378, note 2, *supra*.]

[4] Or otherwise, " and other plagues of heretics subverting the truth with their swords and poisons."
[5] Matt. xxviii. 18, 19. [Elucidation XVII.]

same flesh? Widely different is the faith with Marcion, and, moreover, with the other heretics; nay, with them there is nothing but perfidy, and blasphemy, and contention, which is hostile to holiness and truth. How then can one who is baptized among them seem to have obtained remission of sins, and the grace of the divine mercy, by his faith, when he has not the truth of the faith itself? For if, as some suppose, one could receive anything abroad out of the Church according to his faith, certainly he has received what he believed; but if he believes what is false, he could not receive what is true; but rather he has received things adulterous and profane, according to what he believed.

6. This matter of profane and adulterous baptism Jeremiah the prophet plainly rebukes, saying, "Why do they who afflict me prevail? My wound is hard; whence shall I be healed? while it has indeed become unto me as deceitful water which has no faithfulness."[1] The Holy Spirit makes mention by the prophet of deceitful water which has no faithfulness. What is this deceitful and faithless water? Certainly that which falsely assumes the resemblance of baptism, and frustrates the grace of faith by a shadowy pretence. But if, according to a perverted faith, one could be baptized without, and obtain remission of sins, according to the same faith he could also attain the Holy Spirit; and there is no need that hands should be laid on him when he comes, that he might obtain the Holy Ghost, and be sealed. Either he could obtain both privileges without by his faith, or he who has been without has received neither.

7. But it is manifest where and by whom remission of sins can be given; to wit, that which is given in baptism. For first of all the Lord gave that power to Peter, upon whom He built the Church, and whence He appointed and showed the source of unity — the power, namely, that whatsoever he loosed on earth should be loosed in heaven. And after the resurrection, also, He speaks to the apostles, saying, "As the Father hath sent me, even so I send you. And when He had said this, He breathed on them, and saith unto them, Receive ye the Holy Ghost: whosesoever sins ye remit, they are remitted unto them; and whosesoever sins ye retain, they are retained."[2] Whence we perceive that only they who are set over the Church and established in the Gospel law, and in the ordinance of the Lord, are allowed to baptize and to give remission of sins; but that without, nothing can either be bound or loosed, where there is none who can either bind or loose anything.

8. Nor do we propose this, dearest brother, without the authority of divine Scripture, when we say that all things are arranged by divine direction by a certain law and by special ordinance, and that none can usurp to himself, in opposition to the bishops and priests, anything which is not of his own right and power. For Korah, Dathan, and Abiram endeavoured to usurp, in opposition to Moses and Aaron the priest, the power of sacrificing; and they did not do without punishment what they unlawfully dared. The sons of Aaron also, who placed strange fire upon the altar, were at once consumed in the sight of an angry Lord; which punishment remains to those who introduce strange water by a false baptism, that the divine vengeance may avenge and chastise when heretics do that in opposition to the Church, which the Church alone is allowed to do.

9. But in respect of the assertion of some concerning those who had been baptized in Samaria, that when the Apostles Peter and John came, only hands were imposed on them, that they might receive the Holy Ghost, yet that they were not re-baptized; we see that that place does not, dearest brother, touch the present case. For they who had believed in Samaria had believed with a true faith; and within, in the Church which is one, and to which alone it is granted to bestow the grace of baptism and to remit sins, had been baptized by Philip the deacon, whom the same apostles had sent. And therefore, because they had obtained a legitimate and ecclesiastical baptism, there was no need that they should be baptized any more, but only that which was needed was performed by Peter and John; viz., that prayer being made for them, and hands being imposed, the Holy Spirit should be invoked and poured out upon them, which now too is done among us, so that they who are baptized in the Church are brought to the prelates of the Church, and by our prayers and by the imposition of hands obtain the Holy Spirit, and are perfected with the Lord's seal.

10. There is no ground, therefore, dearest brother, for thinking that we should give way to heretics so far as to contemplate the betrayal to them of that baptism, which is only granted to the one and only Church. It is a good soldier's duty to defend the camp of his general against rebels and enemies. It is the duty of an illustrious leader to keep the standards entrusted to him.[3] It is written, "The Lord thy God is a jealous God."[4] We who have received the Spirit of God ought to have a jealousy for the divine faith; with such a jealousy as that wherewith Phineas both pleased God and justly allayed His wrath when He was angry, and the people were perishing. Why do we receive as

---

[1] Jer. xv. 18 (LXX.).
[2] John xx. 21–23. [See notes of Oxf. edition on this letter.]

[3] [This sounds like Ignatius himself, whose style abounds in aphorisms. See vol. i. p. 45.]
[4] Deut. iv. 24.

allowed an adulterous and alien church, a foe to the divine unity, when we know only one Christ and His one Church? The Church, setting forth the likeness of paradise, includes within her walls fruit-bearing trees, whereof that which does not bring forth good fruit is cut off and is cast into the fire. These trees she waters with four rivers, that is, with the four Gospels, wherewith, by a celestial inundation, she bestows the grace of saving baptism. Can any one water from the Church's fountains who is not within the Church? Can one impart those wholesome and saving draughts of paradise to any one if he is perverted, and of himself condemned, and banished outside the fountains of paradise, and has dried up and failed with the dryness of an eternal thirst?

11. The Lord cries aloud, that "whosoever thirsts should come and drink of the rivers of living water that flowed out of His bosom."[1] Whither is he to come who thirsts? Shall he come to the heretics, where there is no fountain and river of living water at all; or to the Church which is one, and is founded upon one who has received the keys of it by the Lord's voice? It is she who holds and possesses alone all the power of her spouse and Lord. In her we preside; for her honour and unity we fight; her grace, as well as her glory, we defend with faithful devotedness.[2] We by the divine permission water the thirsting people of God; we guard the boundaries of the living fountains. If, therefore, we hold the right of our possession, if we acknowledge the sacrament of unity, wherefore are we esteemed prevaricators against truth? Wherefore are we judged betrayers of unity? The faithful, and saving, and holy water of the Church cannot be corrupted and adulterated, as the Church herself also is uncorrupted, and chaste, and modest. If heretics are devoted to the Church and established in the Church, they may use both her baptism and her other saving benefits. But if they are not in the Church, nay more, if they act against the Church, how can they baptize with the Church's baptism?

12. For it is no small and insignificant matter which is conceded to heretics, when their baptism is recognised by us; since thence springs the whole origin of faith and the saving access to the hope of life eternal, and the divine condescension for purifying and quickening the servants of God. For if any one could be baptized among heretics, certainly he could also obtain remission of sins. If he attained remission of sins, he was also sanctified. If he was sanctified, he also was made the temple of God. I ask, of what God? If of the Creator; he could not be, because he has not believed in Him. If of Christ; he could not become His temple, since he denies that Christ is God. If of the Holy Spirit; since the three are one, how can the Holy Spirit be at peace with him who is the enemy either of the Son or of the Father?

13. Hence it is in vain that some who are overcome by reason oppose to us custom, as if custom were greater than truth;[3] or as if that were not to be sought after in spiritual matters which has been revealed as the better by the Holy Spirit. For one who errs by simplicity may be pardoned, as the blessed Apostle Paul says of himself, "I who at first was a blasphemer, and a persecutor, and injurious; yet obtained mercy, because I did it ignorantly."[4] But after inspiration and revelation made to him, he who intelligently and knowingly perseveres in that course in which he had erred, sins without pardon for his ignorance. For he resists with a certain presumption and obstinacy, when he is overcome by reason. Nor let any one say, "We follow that which we have received from the apostles," when the apostles only delivered one Church, and one baptism, which is not ordained except in the same Church. And we cannot find that any one, when he had been baptized by heretics, was received by the apostles in the same baptism, and communicated in such a way as that the apostles should appear to have approved the baptism of heretics.

14. For as to what some say, as if it tended to favour heretics, that the Apostle Paul declared, " Only every way, whether in pretence or in truth, let Christ be preached,"[5] we find that this also can avail nothing to their benefit who support and applaud heretics. For Paul, in his epistle, was not speaking of heretics, nor of their baptism, so that anything can be shown to have been alleged which pertained to this matter. He was speaking of brethren, whether as walking disorderly and against the discipline of the Church, or as keeping the truth of the Gospel with the fear of God. And he said that certain of them spoke the word of God with constancy and courage, but some acted in envy and dissension; that some maintained towards him a benevolent love, but that some indulged a malevolent spirit of dissension; but yet that he bore all patiently, so long only as, whether in truth or in pretence, the name of Christ which Paul preached might come to the knowledge of many; and the sowing of the word, which as yet had been new and irregular, might increase through the preaching of the

---

[1] John vi. 37, 38. [This quotation is amended by me, in strict accordance with the (ἐκ τῆς κοιλίας) Greek, which refers to the *nobler cavity*, not the inferior, of the human body.]
[2] Or, " with the courage of faith."

[3] [It would seem, then, that " custom " could be pleaded on both sides. This appeal is recognised in Scripture. 1 Cor. xi. 16; and see sec. 23, *infra*. As to preceding sentence, Elucidation XVII.]
[4] 1 Tim. i. 13.
[5] Phil. i. 18.

speakers. Besides, it is one thing for those who are within the Church to speak concerning the name of Christ; it is another for those who are without, and act in opposition to the Church, to baptize in the name of Christ. Wherefore, let not those who favour heretics put forward what Paul spoke concerning brethren, but let them show if he thought anything was to be conceded to the heretic, or if he approved of their faith or baptism, or if he appointed that perfidious and blasphemous men could receive remission of their sins outside the Church.

15. But if we consider what the apostles thought about heretics, we shall find that they, in all their epistles, execrated and detested the sacrilegious wickedness of heretics. For when they say that "their word creeps as a canker," [1] how is such a word as that able to give remission of sins, which creeps like a canker to the ears of the hearers? And when they say that there can be no fellowship between righteousness and unrighteousness, no communion between light and darkness,[2] how can either darkness illuminate, or unrighteousness justify? And when they say that "they are not of God, but are of the spirit of Antichrist,"[3] how can they transact spiritual and divine matters, who are the enemies of God, and whose hearts the spirit of Antichrist has possessed? Wherefore, if, laying aside the errors of human dispute, we return with a sincere and religious faith to the evangelical authority and to the apostolical tradition, we shall perceive that they may do nothing towards conferring the ecclesiastical and saving grace, who, scattering and attacking the Church of Christ, are called adversaries by Christ Himself, but by His apostles, Antichrists.

16. Again, there is no ground for any one, for the circumvention of Christian truth, opposing to us the name of Christ, and saying, "All who are baptized everywhere, and in any manner, in the name of Jesus Christ, have obtained the grace of baptism," — when Christ Himself speaks, and says, "Not every one that saith unto me, Lord, Lord, shall enter into the kingdom of heaven."[4] And again, He forewarns and instructs, that no one should be easily deceived by false prophets and false Christs in His name. "Many," He says, "shall come in my name, saying, I am Christ, and shall deceive many." And afterwards He added: "But take ye heed; behold, I have foretold you all things."[5] Whence it appears that all things are not at once to be received and assumed which are boasted of in the name of Christ, but only those things which are done in the truth of Christ.

17. For whereas in the Gospels, and in the epistles of the apostles, the name of Christ is alleged for the remission of sins; it is not in such a way as that the Son alone, without the Father, or against the Father, can be of advantage to anybody; but that it might be shown to the Jews, who boasted as to their having the Father, that the Father would profit them nothing, unless they believed on the Son whom He had sent. For they who know God the Father the Creator, ought also to know Christ the Son, lest they should flatter and applaud themselves about the Father alone, without the acknowledgment of His Son, who also said, "No man cometh to the Father but by me."[6] But He, the same, sets forth, that it is the knowledge of the two which saves, when He says, "And this is life eternal, that they might know Thee, the only true God, and Jesus Christ, whom thou hast sent."[7] Since, therefore, from the preaching and testimony of Christ Himself, the Father who sent must be first known, then afterwards Christ, who was sent, and there cannot be a hope of salvation except by knowing the two together; how, when God the Father is not known, nay, is even blasphemed, can they who among the heretics are said to be baptized in the name of Christ, be judged to have obtained the remission of sins? For the case of the Jews under the apostles was one, but the condition of the Gentiles is another. The former, because they had already gained the most ancient baptism of the law and Moses, were to be baptized also in the name of Jesus Christ, in conformity with what Peter tells them in the Acts of the Apostles, saying, "Repent, and be baptized every one of you in the name of the Lord Jesus Christ, for the remission of sins, and ye shall receive the gift of the Holy Ghost. For this promise is unto you, and to your children, and to all that are afar off, even as many as the Lord our God shall call."[8] Peter makes mention of Jesus Christ, not as though the Father should be omitted, but that the Son also might be joined to the Father.

18. Finally, when, after the resurrection, the apostles are sent by the Lord to the heathens, they are bidden to baptize the Gentiles "in the name of the Father, and of the Son, and of the Holy Ghost." How, then, do some say, that a Gentile baptized without, outside the Church, yea, and in opposition to the Church, so that it be only in the name of Jesus Christ, everywhere, and in whatever manner, can obtain remission of sin, when Christ Himself commands the heathen to be baptized in the full and united Trinity? Unless while one who denies Christ is denied by Christ, he who denies His Father whom Christ

---

[1] 2 Tim. ii. 17.
[2] 2 Cor. vi. 14.
[3] 1 John iv. 3.
[4] Matt. vii. 21.
[5] Matt. xxiv. 5, 25.

[6] John xiv. 6.
[7] John xvii. 3.
[8] Acts ii. 38, 39.

Himself confessed is not denied; and he who blasphemes against Him whom Christ called His Lord and His God, is rewarded by Christ, and obtains remission of sins, and the sanctification of baptism ! But by what power can he who denies God the Creator, the Father of Christ, obtain, in baptism, the remission of sins, since Christ received that very power by which we are baptized and sanctified, from the same Father, whom He called "greater" than Himself, by whom He desired to be glorified, whose will He fulfilled even unto the obedience of drinking the cup, and of undergoing death? What else is it then, than to become a partaker with blaspheming heretics, to wish to maintain and assert, that one who blasphemes and gravely sins against the Father and the Lord and God of Christ, can receive remission of sins in the name of Christ? What, moreover, is that, and of what kind is it, that he who denies the Son of God has not the Father, and he who denies the Father should be thought to have the Son, although the Son Himself testifies, and says, "No man can come unto me except it were given unto him of my Father?"[1] So that it is evident, that no remission of sins can be received in baptism from the Son, which it is not plain that t' : Father has granted. Especially, since He furtner repeats, and says, "Every plant which my heavenly Father hath not planted shall be rooted up."[2]

19. But if Christ's disciples are unwilling to learn from Christ what veneration and honour is due to the name of the Father, still let them learn from earthly and secular examples, and know that Christ has declared, not without the strongest rebuke, "The children of this world are wiser in their generation than the children of light."[3] In this world of ours, if any one have offered an insult to the father of any; if in injury and frowardness he have wounded his reputation and his honour by a malevolent tongue, the son is indignant, and wrathful, and with what means he can, strives to avenge his injured father's wrong. Think you that Christ grants impunity to the impious and profane, and the blasphemers of His Father, and that He puts away their sins in baptism, who it is evident, when baptized, still heap up evil words on the person of the Father, and sin with the unceasing wickedness of a blaspheming tongue? Can a Christian, can a servant of God, either conceive this in his mind, or believe it in faith, or put it forward in discourse? And what will become of the precepts of the divine law, which say, "Honour thy father and thy mother?"[4] If the name of father, which in man is commanded

to be honoured, is violated with impunity in God, what will become of what Christ Himself lays down in the Gospel, and says, "He that curseth father or mother, let him die the death;"[5] if He who bids that those who curse their parents after the flesh should be punished and slain, Himself quickens those who revile their heavenly and spiritual Father, and are hostile to the Church, their Mother? An execrable and detestable thing is actually asserted by some, that He who threatens the man who blasphemes against the Holy Spirit, that he shall be guilty of eternal sin, Himself condescends to sanctify those who blaspheme against God the Father with saving baptism. And now, those who think that they must communicate with such as come to the Church without baptism, do not consider that they are becoming partakers with other men's, yea, with eternal sins, when they admit without baptism those who cannot, except in baptism, put off the sins of their blasphemies.

20. Besides, how vain and perverse a thing it is, that when the heretics themselves, having repudiated and forsaken either the error or the wickedness in which they had previously been, acknowledge the truth of the Church, we should mutilate the rights and sacrament of that same truth, and say to those who come to us and repent, that they had obtained remission of sins when they confess that they have sinned, and are for that reason come to seek the pardon of the Church! Wherefore, dearest brother, we ought both firmly to maintain the faith and truth of the Catholic Church, and to teach, and by all the evangelical and apostolical precepts to set forth, the plan of the divine dispensation and unity.

21. Can the power of baptism be greater or of more avail than confession, than suffering, when one confesses Christ before men and is baptized in his own blood? And yet even this baptism does not benefit a heretic, although he has confessed Christ, and been put to death outside the Church, unless the patrons and advocates of heretics declare that the heretics who are slain in a false confession of Christ are martyrs, and assign to them the glory and the crown of martyrdom contrary to the testimony of the apostle, who says that it will profit them nothing although they were burnt and slain.[6] But if not even the baptism of a public confession and blood can profit a heretic to salvation, because there is no salvation out of the Church,[7] how much less shall it be of advantage to him, if in a hiding-place and a cave of robbers, stained with the contagion of adulterous water, he has

[1] John vi. 65.
[2] Matt. xv. 13.
[3] Luke xvi. 8.
[4] Ex. xx. 12.

[5] Matt. xv. 4.
[6] 1 Cor. xiii. 3.
[7] [One of the Catholic maxims which has been terribly misunderstood and cruelly abused. See below, p. 385, notes 2 and 3.]

not only not put off his old sins, but rather heaped up still newer and greater ones ! Wherefore baptism cannot be common to us and to heretics, to whom neither God the Father, nor Christ the Son, nor the Holy Ghost, nor the faith, nor the Church itself, is common. And therefore it behoves those to be baptized who come from heresy to the Church, that so they who are prepared, in the lawful, and true, and only baptism of the holy Church, by divine regeneration, for the kingdom of God, may be born of both sacraments, because it is written, "Except a man be born of water and of the Spirit, he cannot enter into the kingdom of God." [1]

22. On which place some, as if by human reasoning they were able to make void the truth of the Gospel declaration, object to us the case of catechumens; asking if any one of these, before he is baptized in the Church, should be apprehended and slain on confession of the name, whether he would lose the hope of salvation and the reward of confession, because he had not previously been born again of water? Let men of this kind, who are aiders and favourers of heretics, know therefore, first, that those catechumens hold the sound faith and truth of the Church, and advance from the divine camp to do battle with the devil, with a full and sincere acknowledgment of God the Father, and of Christ, and of the Holy Ghost; then, that they certainly are not deprived of the sacrament of baptism who are baptized with the most glorious and greatest baptism of blood, concerning which the Lord also said, that He had "another baptism to be baptized with." [2] But the same Lord declares in the Gospel, that those who are baptized in their own blood, and sanctified by suffering, are perfected, and obtain the grace of the divine promise, when He speaks to the thief believing and confessing in His very passion, and promises that he should be with Himself in paradise. Wherefore we who are set over the faith and truth ought not to deceive and mislead those who come to the faith and truth, and repent, and beg that their sins should be remitted to them; but to instruct them when corrected by us, and reformed for the kingdom of heaven by celestial discipline.

23. But some one says, "What, then, shall become of those who in past times, coming from heresy to the Church, were received without baptism?" The Lord is able by His mercy to give indulgence,[3] and not to separate from the gifts of His Church those who by simplicity were admitted into the Church, and in the Church have fallen asleep. Nevertheless it does not follow that, because there was error at one time, there must always be error; since it is more fitting for wise and God-fearing men, gladly and without delay to obey the truth when laid open and perceived, than pertinaciously and obstinately to struggle against brethren and fellow-priests on behalf of heretics.

24. Nor let any one think that, because baptism is proposed to them, heretics will be kept back from coming to the Church, as if offended at the name of a second baptism; nay, but on this very account they are rather driven to the necessity of coming by the testimony of truth shown and proved to them. For if they shall see that it is determined and decreed by our judgment and sentence, that the baptism wherewith they are there baptized is considered just and legitimate, they will think that they are justly and legitimately in possession of the Church also, and the other gifts of the Church; nor will there be any reason for their coming to us, when, as they have baptism, they seem also to have the rest. But further, when they know that there is no baptism without, and that no remission of sins can be given outside the Church, they more eagerly and readily hasten to us, and implore the gifts and benefits of the Church our Mother, assured that they can in no wise attain to the true promise of divine grace unless they first come to the truth of the Church. Nor will heretics refuse to be baptized among us with the lawful and true baptism of the Church, when they shall have learnt from us that they also were baptized by Paul, who already had been baptized with the baptism of John,[4] as we read in the Acts of the Apostles.

25. And now by certain of us the baptism of heretics is asserted to occupy the (like) ground, and, as if by a certain dislike of re-baptizing, it is counted unlawful to baptize after God's enemies. *And this*, although we find that they were baptized whom John had baptized: John, esteemed the greatest among the prophets; John, filled with divine grace even in his mother's womb; who was sustained with the spirit and power of Elias; who was not an adversary of the Lord, but His precursor and announcer; who not only foretold our Lord in words, but even showed Him to the eyes; who baptized Christ Himself by whom others are baptized. But if on that account a heretic could obtain the right of baptism, because he first baptized, then baptism will not belong to the person that has it, but to the person that seizes it. And since baptism and the Church can by no means be separated from one another, and divided, he who has

---

[1] John iii. 5. [His exposition of this passage explains his hyperbole, *nulla salus extra ecclesiam*. Of which sec. 23, *infra*.]
[2] Luke xii. 50. [See p. 386, first line.]
[3] [Here is the qualifying maxim to that other *dictum*. Potens est Dominus misericordia sua, indulgentiam dare. Matt. ix. 13, xii. 7. How emphatic this repeated maxim of Christ! And see Jas. ii. 13.]

[4] [John's baptism was under the Law, and was distinguished from Christ's baptism; which accounts for the plural in Heb. vi. 2.]

first been able to lay hold on baptism has equally also laid hold on the Church; and you begin to appear to him as a heretic, when you being anticipated, have begun to be last, and by yielding and giving way have relinquished the right which you had received. But how dangerous it is in divine matters, that any one should depart from his right and power, Holy Scripture declares when, in Genesis, Esau thence lost his birthright, nor was able afterwards to regain that which he had once given up.

26. These things, dearest brother, I have briefly written to you, according to my abilities, prescribing to none, and prejudging none, so as to prevent any one of the bishops doing what he thinks well, and having the free exercise of his judgment.[1] We, as far as in us lies, do not contend on behalf of heretics with our colleagues and fellow-bishops, with whom we maintain a divine concord and the peace of the Lord;[1] especially since the apostle says, "If any man, however, is thought to be contentious, we have no such custom, neither the Church of God."[2] Charity of spirit, the honour of our college, the bond of faith, and priestly concord, are maintained by us with patience and gentleness. For this reason, moreover, we have with the best of our poor abilities, with the permission and inspiration of the Lord, written a treatise[3] on the "Benefit of Patience," which for the sake of our mutual love we have transmitted to you. I bid you, dearest brother, ever heartily farewell.

EPISTLE LXXIII.[4]

TO POMPEY, AGAINST THE EPISTLE OF STEPHEN ABOUT THE BAPTISM OF HERETICS.

ARGUMENT.— THE PURPORT OF THIS EPISTLE IS GIVEN IN ST. AUGUSTINE'S "CONTRA DONATISTAS," LIB. V. CAP. 23. HE SAYS THERE: "CYPRIAN, MOREOVER, WRITES TO POMPEY ON THE SAME SUBJECT, WHEN HE PLAINLY SIGNIFIES THAT STEPHEN, WHO, AS WE LEARN, WAS THEN A BISHOP OF THE ROMAN CHURCH, NOT ONLY DID NOT AGREE WITH HIM ON THOSE POINTS, BUT EVEN HAD WRITTEN AND CHARGED IN OPPOSITION TO HIM."[5]

1. Cyprian to his brother Pompeius, greeting. Although I have fully comprised what is to be said concerning the baptism of heretics in the letters of which I sent you copies, dearest brother, yet, since you have desired that what Stephen our brother replied to my letters should be brought to your knowledge, I have sent you a copy of his reply; on the reading of which, you will more and more observe his error in endeavouring to maintain the cause of heretics against Christians, and against the Church of God.[6] For among other matters, which were either haughtily assumed, or were not pertaining to the matter, or contradictory to his own view, which he unskilfully and without foresight wrote, he moreover added this saying: "If any one, therefore, come to you from any heresy whatever, let nothing be innovated (or done) which has not been handed down, to wit, that hands be imposed on him for repentance;[7] since the heretics themselves, in their own proper character, do not baptize such as come to them from one another, but only admit them to communion."

2. He forbade one coming from any heresy to be baptized in the Church; that is, he judged the baptism of all heretics to be just and lawful. And although special heresies have special baptisms and different sins, he, holding communion with the baptism of all, gathered up the sins of all, heaped together into his own bosom. And he charged that nothing should be innovated except what had been handed down; as if he were an innovator, who, holding the unity, claims for the one Church one baptism; and not manifestly he who, forgetful of unity, adopts the lies and the contagions of a profane washing. Let nothing be innovated, says he, *nothing maintained*, except what has been handed down. Whence is that tradition? Whether does it descend from the authority of the Lord and of the Gospel, or does it come from the commands and the epistles of the apostles? For that those things which are written must be done, God witnesses and admonishes, saying to Joshua the son of Nun: "The book of this law shall not depart out of thy mouth; but thou shalt meditate in it day and night, that thou mayest observe to do according to all that is written therein."[8] Also the Lord, sending His apostles, commands that the nations should be baptized, and taught to

---

[1] [See Ep. lxxi. sec. 3, p. 379, *supra*. Here is the spirit, not of Tertullian, but of Irenæus (vol. i. p. 310), which seems to have prevailed in the *practical* settlement, between East and West, of one vexed question. As a question of canonical consent and of irresistible logic, *assuming the premiss*, Cyprian appears to me justified.]

[2] 1 Cor. xi 16.

[3] [See this volume, *infra*.] A.D. 256.

[4] Oxford ed.: Ep. lxxiv.

[5] On which subject, again, in chap. 25: "I will not now reconsider what he angrily uttered against Stephen, because there is no necessity for it. The very same things are indeed said which have already been sufficiently discussed, and it is better to pass by what suggested the risk of a mischievous dissension. Stephen, for his part, had thought that they who endeavoured to annul the old custom about receiving heretics were to be excommunicated; but the other, moved

with the difficulty of that very question, and very largely endowed with a sacred charity, thought that unity might be maintained with them who thought differently. Thus, although there was a great deal of keenness, yet it was always in a spirit of brotherhood; and at length the peace of Christ conquered in their hearts, so that in such a dispute none of the mischief of schism arose between them" (Migne). [Ed. Migne adds, assuming the mediæval system to have been known to Cyprian, as follows]: "Thus far Augustine, whom we have quoted at length, because the passage is opposed to those who strive from this to assert his schism from the Roman pontiff."

[6] [It will be seen, more and more, that this entire conviction of Cyprian as to Stephen's absolute equality with himself, results from the Ante-Nicene system, and accords with his theory of the divine organization of the Church. So Augustine, as quoted in the "Argument."]

[7] Meaning, probably, heretics with regard to the doctrine of the Trinity, Stephen not regarding the Novatians as "properly" heretics. [See Oxford translator, note m, p. 261.]

[8] Josh. i. 8.

observe all things which He commanded. If, therefore, it is either prescribed in the Gospel, or contained in the epistles or Acts of the Apostles, that those who come from any heresy should not be baptized, but only hands laid upon them to repentance, let this divine and holy tradition be observed. But if everywhere heretics are called nothing else than adversaries and antichrists, if they are pronounced to be people to be avoided, and to be perverted and condemned of their own selves, wherefore is it that they should not be thought worthy of being condemned by us, since it is evident from the apostolic testimony[1] that they are of their own selves condemned? So that no one ought to defame the apostles as if they had approved of the baptisms of heretics, or had communicated with them without the Church's baptism, when they, the apostles, wrote such things of the heretics. And this, too, while as yet the more terrible plagues of heresy had not broken forth; while Marcion of Pontus had not yet emerged from Pontus, whose master Cerdon came to Rome, — while Hyginus was still bishop, who was the ninth bishop in that city, — whom Marcion followed, and with greater impudence adding other enhancements to his crime, and more daringly set himself to blaspheme against God the Father, the Creator, and armed with sacrilegious arms the heretical madness that rebelled against the Church with greater wickedness and determination.

3. But if it is evident that subsequently heresies became more numerous and worse; and if, in time past, it was never at all prescribed nor written that only hands should be laid upon a heretic for repentance, and that so he might be communicated with; and if there is only one baptism, which is with us, and is within, and is granted of the divine condescension to the Church alone, what obstinacy is that, or what presumption, to prefer human tradition to divine ordinance, and not to observe that God is indignant and angry as often as human tradition relaxes and passes by the divine precepts, as He cries out, and says by Isaiah the prophet, "This people honoureth me with their lips, but their heart is far from me. But in vain do they worship me, teaching the doctrines and commandments of men."[2] Also the Lord in the Gospel, similarly rebuking and reproving, utters and says, "Ye reject the commandment of God, that ye may keep your own tradition."[3] Mindful of which precept, the blessed Apostle Paul himself also warns and instructs, saying, "If any man teach otherwise, and consent not to the wholesome words of our Lord Jesus Christ, and to

His doctrine, he is proud, knowing nothing: from such withdraw thyself."[4]

4. Certainly an excellent and lawful tradition is set before us by the teaching of our brother Stephen, which may afford us a suitable authority! For in the same place of his epistle he has added and continued: "Since those who are specially heretics do not baptize those who come to them from one another, but only receive them to communion." To this point of evil has the Church of God and spouse of Christ been developed, that she follows the examples of heretics; that for the purpose of celebrating the celestial sacraments, light should borrow her discipline from darkness, and Christians should do that which antichrists do. But what is that blindness of soul, what is that degradation of faith, to refuse to recognise the unity[5] which comes from God the Father, and from the tradition of Jesus Christ the Lord and our God! For if the Church is not with heretics, therefore, because it is one, and cannot be divided; and if thus the Holy Spirit is not there, because He is one, and cannot be among profane persons, and those who are without; certainly also baptism, which consists in the same unity, cannot be among heretics, because it can neither be separated from the Church nor from the Holy Spirit.

5. Or if they attribute the effect of baptism to the majesty of the name, so that they who are baptized anywhere and anyhow, in the name of Jesus Christ, are judged to be renewed and sanctified; wherefore, in the name of the same Christ, are not hands laid upon the baptized persons among them, for the reception of the Holy Spirit? Why does not the same majesty of the same name avail in the imposition of hands, which, they contend, availed in the sanctification of baptism? For if any one born out of the Church can become God's temple, why cannot the Holy Spirit also be poured out upon the temple? For he who has been sanctified, his sins being put away in baptism, and has been spiritually re-formed into a new man, has become fitted for receiving the Holy Spirit; since the apostle says, "As many of you as have been baptized into Christ have put on Christ."[6] He who, having been baptized among the heretics, is able to put on Christ, may much more receive the Holy Spirit whom Christ sent. Otherwise He who is sent will be greater than Him who sends; so that one baptized without may begin indeed to put on Christ, but not to be able to receive the Holy Spirit, as if Christ could either be put on without the Spirit, or the Spirit be

---

[1] [Tit. iii. 11.]
[2] Isa. xxix. 13.
[3] Mark vii. 13.

[4] 1 Tim. vi. 3-5.
[5] [This "unity" consisted not at all in agreeing with Stephen, according to our author. See good note (1) Oxford edition, p. 260.]
[6] Gal. iii. 27.

separated from Christ. Moreover, it is silly to say, that although the second birth is spiritual, by which we are born in Christ through the laver of regeneration, one may be born spiritually among the heretics, where they say that the Spirit is not. For water alone is not able to cleanse away sins, and to sanctify a man, unless he have also the Holy Spirit.[1] Wherefore it is necessary that they should grant the Holy Spirit to be there, where they say that baptism is; or else there is no baptism where the Holy Spirit is not, because there cannot be baptism without the Spirit.

6. But what a thing it is, to assert and contend that they who are not born in the Church can be the sons of God! For the blessed apostle sets forth and proves that baptism is that wherein the old man dies and the new man is born, saying, " He saved us by the washing of regeneration."[2] But if regeneration is in the washing, that is, in baptism, how can heresy, which is not the spouse of Christ, generate sons to God by Christ? For it is the Church alone which, conjoined and united with Christ, spiritually bears sons; as the same apostle again says, " Christ loved the Church, and gave Himself for it, that He might sanctify it, cleansing it with the washing of water."[3] If, then, she is the beloved and spouse who alone is sanctified by Christ, and alone is cleansed by His washing, it is manifest that heresy, which is not the spouse of Christ, nor can be cleansed nor sanctified by His washing, cannot bear sons to God.[4]

7. But further, one is not born by the imposition of hands when he receives the Holy Ghost, but in baptism, that so, being already born, he may receive the Holy Spirit, even as it happened in the first man Adam. For first God formed him, and then breathed into his nostrils the breath of life. For the Spirit cannot be received, unless he who receives first have an existence. But as the birth of Christians is in baptism, while the generation and sanctification of baptism are with the spouse of Christ alone, who is able spiritually to conceive and to bear sons to God, where and of whom and to whom is he born, who is not a son of the Church, so as that he should have God as his Father, before he has had the Church for his Mother? But as no heresy at all, and equally no schism, being without, can have the sanctification of saving baptism, why has the bitter obstinacy of our brother Stephen broken forth to such an extent, as to contend that sons

are born to God from the baptism of Marcion; moreover, of Valentinus and Apelles, and of others who blaspheme against God the Father; and to say that remission of sins is granted in the name of Jesus Christ where blasphemy is uttered against the Father and against Christ the Lord God?

8. In which place, dearest brother, we must consider, for the sake of the faith and the religion of the sacerdotal office which we discharge, whether the account can be satisfactory in the day of judgment for a priest of God, who maintains, and approves, and acquiesces in the baptism of blasphemers, when the Lord threatens, and says, " And now, O ye priests, this commandment is for you: if ye will not hear, and if ye will not lay it to heart to give glory unto my name, saith the Lord Almighty, I will even send a curse upon you, and I will curse your blessings."[5] Does he give glory to God, who communicates with the baptism of Marcion? Does he give glory to God, who judges that remission of sins is granted among those who blaspheme against God? Does he give glory to God, who affirms that sons are born to God without, of an adulterer and a harlot? Does he give glory to God, who does not hold the unity and truth that arise from the divine law, but maintains heresies against the Church? Does he give glory to God, who, a friend of heretics and an enemy to Christians, thinks that the priests of God, who support the truth of Christ and the unity of the Church, are to be excommunicated?[6] If glory is thus given to God, if the fear and the discipline of God is thus preserved by His worshippers and His priests, let us cast away our arms; let us give ourselves up to captivity; let us deliver to the devil the ordination of the Gospel, the appointment of Christ, the majesty of God; let the sacraments of the divine warfare be loosed; let the standards of the heavenly camp be betrayed; and let the Church succumb and yield to heretics, light to darkness, faith to perfidy, hope to despair, reason to error, immortality to death, love to hatred, truth to falsehood, Christ to Antichrist! Deservedly thus do heresies and schisms arise day by day, more frequently and more fruitfully grow up, and with serpents' locks shoot forth and cast out against the Church of God with greater force the poison of their venom; whilst, by the advocacy of some, both authority and support are afforded them; whilst their baptism is defended, whilst faith, whilst truth, is betrayed;[7] whilst that which is done without against the Church is defended within in the very Church itself.

---

[1] [Cyprian does not believe in the mere *opus operatum* of the water. And one fears that Stephen's position in this matter bore its fruit long after in that pernicious dogma of the schoolmen.]

[2] Tit. iii. 5.

[3] Eph. v. 25, 26.

[4] [Allowing the premises admitted alike by Stephen and Cyprian (of which it is not my place to speak), the logic of our author appears to me irresistible. *Practically*, how wise the inspired maxim, Rom. xiv. 1.]

[5] Mal. ii. 1, 2. [Compare Tertullian, vol. iv. p. 122.]

[6] [A terrible indictment, indeed, of his brother Stephen: provoked, however, by conduct less warranted. See Ep. lxxiv. *infra*.]

[7] [Stephen's presumption in this step is the dark spot in his record. It was a *brutum fulmen*, however, even in his own province. See Augustine's testimony, Oxf. ed. (note l) p. 258.]

9. But if there be among us, most beloved brother, the fear of God, if the maintenance of the faith prevail, if we keep the precepts of Christ, if we guard the incorrupt and inviolate sanctity of His spouse, if the words of the Lord abide in our thoughts and hearts, when he says, "Thinkest thou, when the Son of man cometh, shall He find faith on the earth?"[1] then, because we are God's faithful soldiers, who war for the faith and sincere religion of God, let us keep the camp entrusted to us by God with faithful valour. Nor ought custom, which had crept in among some, to prevent the truth from prevailing and conquering; for custom without truth is the antiquity of error.[2] On which account, let us forsake the error and follow the truth, knowing that in Esdras also the truth conquers, as it is written: "Truth endureth and grows strong to eternity, and lives and prevails for ever and ever. With her there is no accepting of persons or distinctions; but what is just she does: nor in her judgments is there unrighteousness, but the strength, and the kingdom, and the majesty, and the power of all ages. Blessed be the Lord God of truth!"[3] This truth Christ showed to us in His Gospel, and said, "I am the truth."[4] Wherefore, if we are in Christ, and have Christ in us, if we abide in the truth, and the truth abides in us, let us keep fast those things which are true.

10. But it happens, by a love of presumption and of obstinacy, that one would rather maintain his own evil and false position, than agree in the right and true which belongs to another. Looking forward to which, the blessed Apostle Paul writes to Timothy, and warns him that a bishop must not be "litigious, nor contentious, but gentle and teachable."[5] Now he is teachable who is meek and gentle to the patience of learning. For it behoves a bishop not only to teach, but also to learn; because he also teaches better who daily increases and advances by learning better; which very thing, moreover, the same Apostle Paul teaches, when he admonishes, "that if anything better be revealed to one sitting by, the first should hold his peace."[6] But there is a brief way for religious and simple minds, both to put away error, and to find and to elicit truth. For if we return to the head and source of divine tradition, human error ceases; and having seen the reason of the heavenly sacraments, whatever lay hid in obscurity under the gloom and cloud of darkness, is opened into the light of the truth. If a channel supplying water, which formerly flowed plentifully and freely, suddenly fail, do we not go to the fountain, that there the reason of the failure may be ascertained, whether from the drying up of the springs the water has failed at the fountainhead, or whether, flowing thence free and full, it has failed in the midst of its course; that so, if it has been caused by the fault of an interrupted or leaky channel, that the constant stream does not flow uninterruptedly and continuously, then the channel being repaired and strengthened, the water collected may be supplied for the use and drink of the city, with the same fertility and plenty with which it issues from the spring? And this it behoves the priests of God to do now, if they would keep the divine precepts, that if in any respect the truth have wavered and vacillated, we should return to our original and Lord, and to the evangelical and apostolical tradition; and thence may arise the ground of our action, whence has taken rise both our order and our origin.[7]

11. For it has been delivered to us, that there is one God, and one Christ, and one hope, and one faith, and one Church, and one baptism ordained only in the one Church, from which unity whosoever will depart must needs be found with heretics; and while he upholds them against the Church, he impugns the sacrament of the divine tradition. The sacrament of which unity we see expressed also in the Canticles, in the person of Christ, who says, "A garden enclosed is my sister, my spouse, a fountain sealed, a well of living water, a garden with the fruit of apples."[8] But if His Church is a garden enclosed, and a fountain sealed, how can he who is not in the Church enter into the same garden, or drink from its fountain? Moreover, Peter himself, showing and vindicating the unity, has commanded and warned us that we cannot be saved, except by the one only baptism of one Church. "In the ark," says he, "of Noah, few, that is, eight souls, were saved by water, as also baptism shall in like manner save you."[9] In how short and spiritual a summary has he set forth the sacrament of unity! For as, in that baptism of the world in which its ancient iniquity was purged away, he who was not in the ark of Noah could not be saved by water, so neither can he appear to be saved by baptism who has not been baptized in the Church which is established in the unity[10] of the Lord according to the sacrament of the one ark.

12. Therefore, dearest brother, having explored and seen the truth; it is observed and held by us, that all who are converted from any heresy whatever to the Church must be baptized by the only and lawful baptism of the Church,

---

[1] Luke xviii. 8.
[2] [Another of Cyprian's striking aphorisms: "Consuetudo sine veritate vetustas erroris est."]
[3] Esdras iv. 38-40.
[4] John xiv. 6.
[5] Original, "docibilis." 2 Tim. ii. 24.
[6] 1 Cor. xiv. 30.

[7] [Elucidation XVIII. See pp. 380 (note 1) and 322 (note 2).]
[8] Cant. iv. 12, 13.
[9] 1 Pet. iii. 20, 21.
[10] [It is obvious that the Cyprianic theory of unity has not the least connection with a theory depending on communion with a particular See. But this elucidates the maxim, p. 384, note 7.]

with the exception of those who had previously been baptized in the Church, and so had passed over to the heretics.[1] For it behoves these, when they return, having repented, to be received by the imposition of hands only, and to be restored by the shepherd to the sheep-fold whence they had strayed. I bid you, dearest brother, ever heartily farewell.

EPISTLE LXXIV.[2]

FIRMILIAN, BISHOP OF CÆSAREA IN CAPPADOCIA, TO CYPRIAN, AGAINST THE LETTER OF STEPHEN. A.D. 256.

ARGUMENT. — THE ARGUMENT OF THIS LETTER IS EXACTLY THE SAME AS THAT OF THE PREVIOUS ONE, BUT WRITTEN WITH A LITTLE MORE VEHEMENCE AND ACERBITY THAN BECOMES A BISHOP,[3] CHIEFLY FOR THE REASON, AS MAY BE SUSPECTED, THAT STEPHEN HAD ALSO WRITTEN ANOTHER LETTER TO FIRMILIANUS, HELENUS, AND OTHER BISHOPS OF THOSE PARTS.[4]

1. Firmilianus to Cyprian, his brother in the Lord, greeting. We have received by Rogatian, our beloved deacon, the letter sent by you which you wrote to us, well-beloved brother; and we gave the greatest thanks to the Lord, because it has happened that we who are separated from one another in body are thus united in spirit, as if we were not only occupying one country, but inhabiting together one and the self-same house. Which also it is becoming for us to say, because, indeed, the spiritual house of God is one. "For it shall come to pass in the last days," saith the prophet, "that the mountain of the Lord shall be manifest, and the house of God above the tops of the mountains."[5] Those that come together into this house are united with gladness, according to what is asked from the Lord in the psalm, to dwell in the house of the Lord all the days of one's life. Whence in another place also it is made manifest, that among the saints there is great and desirous love for assembling together. "Behold," he says, "how good and how pleasant a thing it is for brethren to dwell together in unity!"[6]

2. For unity and peace and concord afford the greatest pleasure not only to men who believe and know the truth, but also to heavenly angels themselves, to whom the divine word says it is a joy when one sinner repents and returns to the bond of unity. But assuredly this would not be said of the angels, who have their conversation in heaven, unless they themselves also were united to us, who rejoice at our unity; even as, on the other hand, they are assuredly saddened when they see the diverse minds and the divided wills of some, as if not only they do not together invoke one and the same God, but as if, separated and divided from one another, they can neither have a common conversation nor discourse.[7] Except that we may in this matter give thanks to Stephen, that it has now happened through his unkindness that we receive the proof of your faith and wisdom. But although we have received the favour of this benefit on account of Stephen, certainly Stephen has not done anything deserving of kindness and thanks. For neither can Judas be thought worthy by his perfidy and treachery wherewith he wickedly dealt concerning the Saviour, as though he had been the cause of such great advantages, that through him the world and the people of the Gentiles were delivered by the Lord's passion.

3. But let these things which were done by Stephen be passed by for the present, lest, while we remember his audacity and pride, we bring a more lasting sadness on ourselves from the things that he has wickedly done.[8] And knowing, concerning you, that you have settled this matter, concerning which there is now a question, according to the rule of truth and the wisdom of Christ; we have exulted with great joy, and have given God thanks that we have found in brethren placed at such a distance such a unanimity of faith and truth with us. For the grace of God is mighty to associate and join together in the bond of charity and unity even those things which seem to be divided by a considerable space of earth, according to the way in which of old also the divine power associated in the bond of unanimity Ezekiel and Daniel, though later in their age, and separated from them by a long space of time, to Job and Noah, who were among the first; so that although they were separated by long periods, yet by divine inspiration they felt the same truths. And this also we now observe in you, that you who are separated from us by the most extensive regions, approve yourselves to be, nevertheless, joined with us in mind and spirit. All which arises from the divine unity. For even as the Lord who dwells in us is one and the same, He everywhere joins and couples His own people in the bond of unity, whence their sound has gone out into the whole earth, who are sent by the Lord swiftly running in the spirit of unity; as,

---

[1] [See letter lxxi. p. 378, supra.]

[2] Oxford ed.: Ep lxxv. [This is one of the most important illustrations of ante-Nicene unity and its laws. Elucidation XIX.]

[3] [But observe, in contrast, the language of Stephen, which he rebukes (sec. 26, infra), and his schismatical conduct towards the whole African Church.]

[4] To the effect that he would not hold communion with them so long as they should persist in their opinion concerning the baptism of heretics, as Eusebius tells us from a letter of Dionysius of Alexandria to Xistus, the successor of Stephen, Hist. Eccles., book vii. c. 4.

[5] Isa. ii. 2.

[6] Ps. cxxxiii. 1.

[7] [This is a sentence to be admired, apart from anything in the general subject.]

[8] [Note the ignorance of these Oriental bishops of any superior authority in the Bishop of Rome. Athanas., opp., p. 470, Paris.]

on the other hand, it is of no advantage that some are very near and joined together bodily, if in spirit and mind they differ, since souls cannot at all be united which divide themselves from God's unity. "For, lo," it says, "they that are far from Thee shall perish." [1] But such shall undergo the judgment of God according to their desert, as depart from His words who prays to the Father for unity, and says, " Father, grant that, as Thou and I are one, so they also may be one in us." [2]

4. But we receive those things which you have written as if they were our own; nor do we read them cursorily, but by frequent repetition have committed them to memory. Nor does it hinder saving usefulness, either to repeat the same things for the confirmation of the truth, or, moreover, to add some things for the sake of accumulating proof. But if anything has been added by us, it is not added as if there had been too little said by you; but since the divine discourse surpasses human nature, and the soul cannot conceive or grasp the whole and perfect word, therefore also the number of prophets is so great, that the divine wisdom in its multiplicity may be distributed through many. Whence also he who first speaks in prophecy is bidden to be silent if a revelation be made to a second. For which reason it happens of necessity among us, that year by year we, the elders and prelates, assemble together to arrange those matters which are committed to our care, so that if any things are more serious they may be directed by the common counsel. Moreover, *we do this* that some remedy may be sought for by repentance for lapsed brethren, and for those wounded by the devil after the saving laver, not as though they obtained remission of sins from us, but that by our means they may be converted to the understanding of their sins, and may be compelled to give fuller satisfaction to the Lord.

5. But since that messenger sent by you was in haste to return to you, and the winter season was pressing, we replied what we could to your letter. And indeed, as respects what Stephen has said, as though the apostles forbade those who come from heresy to be baptized, and delivered this also to be observed by their successors, you have replied most abundantly, that no one is so foolish as to believe that the apostles delivered this, when it is even well known that these heresies themselves, execrable and detestable as they are, arose subsequently; when even Marcion the disciple of Cerdo is found to have introduced his sacrilegious tradition against God long after the apostles, and after long lapse of time from them. Apelles, also consenting to

his blasphemy, added many other new and more important matters hostile to faith and truth. But also the time of Valentinus and Basilides is manifest, that they too, after the apostles, and after a long period, rebelled against the Church of God with their wicked lies. It is plain that the other heretics, also, afterwards introduced their evil sects and perverse inventions, even as every one was led by error; all of whom, it is evident, were self-condemned, and have declared against themselves an inevitable sentence before the day of judgment; and he who confirms the baptism of these, what else does he do but adjudge himself with them, and condemn himself, making himself a partaker with such?

6. But that they who are at Rome do not observe those things in all cases which are handed down from the beginning, and vainly pretend the authority of the apostles; [3] any one may know also from the fact, that concerning the celebration of Easter, and concerning many other sacraments of divine matters, he may see that there are some diversities among them, and that all things are not observed among them alike, which are observed at Jerusalem, just as in very many other provinces also many things are varied because of the difference of the places and names. [4] And yet on this account there is no departure at all from the peace and unity of the Catholic Church, such as Stephen has now dared to make; [5] breaking the peace against you, which his predecessors have always kept with you in mutual love and honour, even herein defaming Peter and Paul the blessed apostles, [5] as if the very men delivered this who in their epistles execrated heretics, and warned us to avoid them. Whence it appears that this tradition is of men which maintains heretics, and asserts that they have baptism, which belongs to the Church alone.

7. But, moreover, you have well answered that part where Stephen said in his letter that heretics themselves also are of one mind in respect of baptism; and that they do not baptize such as come to them from one another, but only communicate with them; as if we also ought to do this. In which place, although you have already proved that it is sufficiently ridiculous for any one to follow those that are in error, yet we add this moreover, over and above, that it is not wonderful for heretics to act thus, who, although in some lesser matters they differ, yet in that which is greatest they hold one and the same agreement to blaspheme the Creator, figuring for themselves certain dreams and phantasms of

---

[3] [Apart from the argument, observe the clear inference as to the equal position of Stephen and his " primacy," in the great Western See. For the West, compare Hilar., *Ad Liberium, Frag.*]

[4] Probably " of men," " nominum " in the original having been read for " hominum."

[5] [Peter and Paul could not be quoted, then, as speaking by the mouth of any one bishop; certainly not by any prerogative of his See. See Guettée, *The Papacy*, p. 119. New York, 1866.]

---

[1] Ps. lxxiii. 27.
[2] John xvii. 21.

an unknown God. Assuredly it is but natural that these should agree in having a baptism which is unreal,[1] in the same way as they agree in repudiating the truth of the divinity. Of whom, since it is tedious to reply to their several statements, either wicked or foolish, it is sufficient shortly to say in sum, that they who do not hold the true Lord the Father cannot hold the truth either of the Son or of the Holy Spirit ; according to which also they who are called Cataphrygians, and endeavour to claim to themselves new prophecies, can have neither the Father, nor the Son, *nor the Holy Spirit*,[2] of whom, if we ask what Christ they announce, they will reply that they preach Him who sent the Spirit that speaks by Montanus and Prisca. And in these, when we observe that there has been not the spirit of truth, but of error, we know that they who maintain their false prophesying against the faith of Christ cannot have Christ. Moreover, all other heretics, if they have separated themselves from the Church of God, can have nothing of power or of grace, since all power and grace are established in the Church where the elders[3] preside, who possess the power both of baptizing, and of imposition of hands, and of ordaining. For as a heretic may not lawfully ordain nor lay on hands, so neither may he baptize, nor do any thing holily or spiritually, since he is an alien from spiritual and deifying sanctity. All which we some time back confirmed in Iconium, which is a place in Phrygia, when we were assembled together with those who had gathered from Galatia and Cilicia, and other neighbouring countries, as to be held and firmly vindicated against heretics, when there was some doubt in certain minds concerning that matter.[4]

8. And as Stephen and those who agree with him contend that putting away of sins and second birth may result from the baptism of heretics, among whom they themselves confess that the Holy Spirit is not ; let them consider and understand that spiritual birth cannot be without the Spirit ; in conformity with which also the blessed Apostle Paul baptized anew with a spiritual baptism those who had already been baptized by John before the Holy Spirit had been sent by the Lord, and so laid hands on them that they might receive the Holy Ghost. But what kind of a thing is it, that when we see that Paul, after John's baptism, baptized his disciples again, we are hesitating to baptize those who come to the Church from heresy after their unhallowed and profane dipping. Unless, perchance, Paul was inferior to the bishops of these times, so that these indeed can by imposition of hands alone give the Holy Spirit to those heretics who come (to the Church), while Paul was not fitted to give the Holy Spirit by imposition of hands to those who had been baptized by John, unless he had first baptized them also with the baptism of the Church.

9. That, moreover, is absurd, that they do not think it is to be inquired who was the person that baptized, for the reason that he who has been baptized may have obtained grace by the invocation of the Trinity, of the names of the Father, and of the Son, and of the Holy Ghost. Then this will be the wisdom which Paul writes is in those who are perfected. But who in the Church is perfect and wise who can either defend or believe this, that this bare invocation of names is sufficient to the remission of sins and the sanctification of baptism ; since these things are only then of advantage, when both he who baptizes has the Holy Spirit, and the baptism itself also is not ordained without the Spirit? But, say they, he who in any manner whatever is baptized without, may obtain the grace of baptism by his disposition and faith, which doubtless is ridiculous in itself, as if either a wicked disposition could attract to itself from heaven the sanctification of the righteous, or a false faith the truth of believers. But that not all who call on the name of Christ are heard, and that their invocation cannot obtain any grace, the Lord Himself manifests, saying, "Many shall come in my name, saying, I am Christ, and shall deceive many."[5] Because there is no difference between a false prophet and a heretic. For as the former deceives in the name of God or Christ, so the latter deceives in the sacrament of baptism. Both strive by falsehood to deceive men's wills.

10. But I wish to relate to you *some facts* concerning a circumstance which occurred among us, pertaining to this very matter. About two-and-twenty years ago, in the times after the Emperor Alexander, there happened in these parts many struggles and difficulties, either in general to all men, or privately to Christians. Moreover, there were many and frequent earthquakes, so that many places were overthrown throughout Cappadocia and Pontus ; even certain cities, dragged into the abyss, were swallowed up by the opening of the gaping earth. So that from this also a severe persecution arose against us of the Christian name ; and this after the long peace of the previous age arose suddenly, and with its unusual evils was made more terrible for the disturbance of our people. Serenianus was then governor in our province, a bitter and terrible persecutor. But the faithful being set in this state of disturbance, and fleeing

---

[1] Literally, "in the vanity (or unreality) of a baptism."
[2] These words in italics are conjecturally interpolated, but have no authority.
[3] [Another use of this word as generic for all but deacons.]
[4] [A provincial council of the East; and note, in Asia, not Europe.]

[5] Mark xiii. 6.

hither and thither for fear of the persecution, and leaving their country and passing over into other regions — for there was an opportunity of passing over, for the reason that that persecution was not over the whole world, but was local — there arose among us on a sudden a certain woman, who in a state of ecstasy announced herself as a prophetess, and acted as if filled with the Holy Ghost. And she was so moved by the impetus of the principal demons, that for a long time she made anxious and deceived the brotherhood, accomplishing certain wonderful and portentous things, and promised that she would cause the earth to be shaken. Not that the power of the demon was so great that he could prevail to shake the earth, or to disturb the elements; but that sometimes a wicked spirit, prescient, and perceiving that there will be an earthquake, pretends that he will do what he sees will happen. By these lies and boastings he had so subdued the minds of individuals, that they obeyed him and followed whithersoever he commanded and led. He would also make that woman walk in the keen winter with bare feet over frozen snow, and not to be troubled or hurt in any degree by that walking. Moreover, she would say that she was hurrying to Judea and to Jerusalem, feigning as if she had come thence. Here also she deceived one of the presbyters, a countryman, and another, a deacon, so that they had intercourse with that same woman, which was shortly afterwards detected. For on a sudden there appeared unto her one of the exorcists, a man approved and always of good conversation in respect of religious discipline; who, stimulated by the exhortation also of very many brethren who were themselves strong and praiseworthy in the faith, raised himself up against that wicked spirit to overcome it; which moreover, by its subtile fallacy, had predicted this a little while before, that a certain adverse and unbelieving tempter would come. Yet that exorcist, inspired by God's grace, bravely resisted, and showed that that which was before thought holy, was indeed a most wicked spirit. But that woman, who previously by wiles and deceitfulness of the demon was attempting many things for the deceiving of the faithful, among other things by which she had deceived many, also had frequently dared this; to pretend that with an invocation not to be contemned she sanctified bread and celebrated[1] the Eucharist, and to offer sacrifice to the Lord, not without the sacrament of the accustomed utterance; and also to baptize many, making use of the usual and lawful words of interrogation, that nothing might seem to be different from the ecclesiastical rule.

11. What, then, shall we say about the baptism of this woman, by which a most wicked demon baptized through means of a woman? Do Stephen and they who agree with him approve of this also, especially when neither the symbol of the Trinity nor the legitimate and ecclesiastical interrogatory were wanting to her? Can it be believed that either remission of sins was given, or the regeneration of the saving laver duly completed, when all things, although after the image of truth, yet were done by a demon? Unless, perchance, they who defend the baptism of heretics contend that the demon also conferred the grace of baptism in the name of the Father, and of the Son, and of the Holy Spirit. Among them, no doubt, there is the same error — it is the very deceitfulness of devils, since among them the Holy Spirit is not at all.

12. Moreover, what is the meaning of that which Stephen would assert, that the presence and holiness of Christ is with those who are baptized among heretics? For if the apostle does not speak falsely when he says, "As many of you as are baptized into Christ, have put on Christ,"[2] certainly he who has been baptized among them into Christ, has put on Christ. But if he has put on Christ, he might also receive the Holy Ghost, who was sent by Christ, and hands are vainly laid upon him who comes to us for the reception of the Spirit; unless, perhaps, he has *not* put on the Spirit from Christ, so that Christ indeed may be with heretics, but the Holy Spirit not be with them.

13. But let us briefly run through the other matters also, which were spoken of by you abundantly and most fully, especially as Rogatianus, our well-beloved deacon, is hurrying to you. For it follows that they must be asked by us, when they defend heretics, whether their baptism is carnal or spiritual. For if it is carnal, they differ in no respect from the baptism of the Jews, which they use in such a manner that in it, as if in a common and vulgar laver, only external filth is washed away. But if it is spiritual, how can baptism be spiritual among those among whom there is no Holy Spirit? And thus the water wherewith they are washed is to them only a carnal washing, not a sacrament of baptism.

14. But if the baptism of heretics can have the regeneration of the second birth, those who are baptized among them must be counted not heretics, but children of God. For the second birth, which occurs in baptism, begets sons of God. But if the spouse of Christ is one, which is the Catholic Church, it is she herself who alone bears sons of God. For there are not many spouses of Christ, since the apostle says, "I have espoused you, that I may present you as a chaste

---

[1] Facere. [Demoniacs. See *Apost. lessons*, so called, lxxix.]

[2] Gal. iii. 27.

virgin to Christ;"[1] and, "Hearken, O daughter, and consider, and incline thine ear; forget also thine own people, for the King hath greatly desired thy beauty;"[2] and, "Come with me, my spouse, from Lebanon; thou shalt come, and shalt pass over from the source of thy faith;"[3] and, "I am come into my garden, my sister, my spouse."[4] We see that one person is everywhere set forward, because also the spouse is one. But the synagogue of heretics is not one with us, because the spouse is not an adulteress and a harlot. Whence also she cannot bear children of God; unless, as appears to Stephen, heresy indeed brings them forth and exposes them, while the Church takes them up when exposed, and nourishes those for her own whom she has not born, although she cannot be the mother of strange children. And therefore Christ our Lord, setting forth that His spouse is one, and declaring the sacrament of His unity, says, "He that is not with me is against me, and he that gathereth not with me scattereth."[5] For if Christ is with us, but the heretics are not with us, certainly the heretics are in opposition to Christ; and if we gather with Christ, but the heretics do not gather with us, doubtless they scatter.

15. But neither must we pass over what has been necessarily remarked by you, that the Church, according to the Song of Songs, is a garden enclosed, and a fountain sealed, a paradise with the fruit of apples.[6] They who have never entered into this garden, and have not seen the paradise planted by God the Creator, how shall they be able to afford to another the living water of the saving lava from the fountain which is enclosed within, and sealed with a divine seal? And as the ark of Noah was nothing else than the sacrament of the Church of Christ, which then, when all without were perishing, kept those only safe who were within the ark, we are manifestly instructed to look to the unity of the Church. Even as also the Apostle Peter laid down, saying, "Thus also shall baptism in like manner make you safe;"[7] showing that as they who were not in the ark with Noah not only were not purged and saved by water, but at once perished in that deluge; so now also, whoever are not in the Church with Christ will perish outside, unless they are converted by penitence to the only and saving lava of the Church.

16. But what is the greatness of his error, and what the depth of his blindness, who says that remission of sins can be granted in the synagogues of heretics, and does not abide on the foundation of the one Church which was once based by Christ upon the rock, may be perceived from this, that Christ said to Peter alone, "Whatsoever thou shalt bind on earth shall be bound in heaven, and whatsoever thou shalt loose on earth shall be loosed in heaven."[8] And again, in the Gospel, when Christ breathed on the apostles alone, saying, "Receive ye the Holy Ghost: whose soever sins ye remit they are remitted unto them, and whose soever sins ye retain they are retained."[9] Therefore the power of remitting sins was given to the apostles, and to the churches which they, sent by Christ, established, and to the bishops who succeeded to them by vicarious ordination.[10] But the enemies of the one Catholic Church in which we are, and the adversaries of us who have succeeded the apostles, asserting for themselves, in opposition to us, unlawful priesthoods, and setting up profane altars, what else are they than Korah, Dathan, and Abiram, profane with a like wickedness, and about to suffer the same punishments which they did, as well as those who agree with them, just as their partners and abettors perished with a like death to theirs?

17. And in this respect I am justly indignant at this so open and manifest folly of Stephen, that he who so boasts of the place of his episcopate, and contends that he holds the succession from Peter,[11] on whom the foundations of the Church were laid, should introduce many other rocks and establish new buildings of many churches; maintaining that there is baptism in them by his authority. For they who are baptized, doubtless, fill up the number of the Church. But he who approves their baptism maintains, of those baptized, that the Church is also with them. Nor does he understand that the truth of the Christian Rock is overshadowed, and in some measure abolished, by him when he thus betrays and deserts unity.[12] The apostle acknowledges that the Jews, although blinded by ignorance, and bound by the grossest wickedness, have yet a zeal for God. Stephen, who announces that he holds by succession the throne of Peter, is stirred with no zeal against heretics, when he concedes to them, not a moderate, but the very greatest power of grace: so far as to say and assert that, by the sacrament of baptism, the filth of the old man is washed away by them, that they pardon the former mortal

---

[1] 2 Cor. xi. 2.
[2] Ps. xlv. 11.
[3] Cant. iv. 8.
[4] Cant. v. 1.
[5] Luke xi. 23.
[6] Cant. iv. 12, 13.
[7] 1 Pet. iii. 21.

[8] Matt. xvi. 19.
[9] John xx. 22, 23. [The two texts here quoted lie at the base of Cyprian's own theory: (1) to Peter *alone* this gift to signify its *singleness*, (2) then the same to all the apostles *alone* to signify their common and *undivided partnership* in the use of this gift. Note the two *alones* and one *therefore*. And see Treatise I. *infra*.]
[10] [Cyprian's theory is thus professed by the Orient.]
[11] [This place and succession are conceded in the argument; but Stephen himself does not appear to have claimed to be the Rock or to exercise the authority of Peter. Vol. iii. p. 266.]
[12] [Stephen abolishes the Rock, and "deserts unity;" here, then, is evidence that he was not the one, nor the criterion of the other.]

sins, that they make sons of God by heavenly regeneration, and renew to eternal life by the sanctification of the divine laver. He who concedes and gives up to heretics in this way the great and heavenly gifts of the Church, what else does he do but communicate with them for whom he maintains and claims so much grace? And now he hesitates in vain to consent to them, and to be a partaker with them in other matters also, to meet together with them, and equally with them to mingle their prayers, and appoint a common altar and sacrifice.

18. But, says he, "the name of Christ is of great advantage to faith and the sanctification of baptism; so that whosoever is anywhere soever baptized in the name of Christ, immediately obtains the grace of Christ:" although this position may be briefly met and answered, that if baptism without in the name of Christ availed for the cleansing of man; in the name of the same Christ, the imposition of hands might avail also for the reception of the Holy Spirit; and the other things also which are done among heretics will begin to seem just and lawful when they are done in the name of Christ; as you have maintained in your letter that the name of Christ could be of no avail except in the Church alone, to which alone Christ has conceded the power of heavenly grace.

19. But with respect to the refutation of custom which they seem to oppose to the truth, who is so foolish as to prefer custom to truth, or when he sees the light, not to forsake the darkness?—unless most ancient custom in any respect avail the Jews, upon the advent of Christ, that is, the Truth, in remaining in their old usage, and forsaking the new way of truth. And this indeed you Africans are able to say against Stephen, that when you knew the truth you forsook the error of custom. But we join custom to truth, and to the Romans' custom we oppose custom, but the custom of truth; holding from the beginning that which was delivered by Christ and the apostles.[1] Nor do we remember that this at any time began among us, since it has always been observed here, that we knew none but one Church of God, and accounted no baptism holy except that of the holy Church. Certainly, since some doubted about the baptism of those who, although they receive the new prophets,[2] yet appear to recognise the same Father and Son with us; very many of us meeting together in Iconium very carefully examined the matter, and we decided that every baptism was altogether to be rejected which is arranged for without the Church.[3]

20. But to what they allege and say on behalf of the heretics, that the apostle said, "Whether in pretence or in truth, Christ is preached,"[4] it is idle for us to reply; when it is manifest that the apostle, in his epistle wherein he said this, made mention neither of heretics nor of baptism of heretics, but spoke of brethren only, whether as perfidiously speaking in agreement with himself, or as persevering in sincere faith; nor is it needful to discuss this in a long argument, but it is sufficient to read the epistle itself, and to gather from the apostle himself what the apostle said.

21. What then, say they, will become of those who, coming from the heretics, have been received without the baptism of the Church? If they have departed this life, they are reckoned in the number of those who have been catechumens indeed among us, but have died before they were baptized,—no trifling[5] advantage of truth and faith, to which they had attained by forsaking error, although, being prevented by death, they had not gained the consummation of grace.[6] But they who still abide in life should be baptized with the baptism of the Church, that they may obtain remission of sins, lest by the presumption of others they remain in their old error, and die without the completion of grace. But what a crime is theirs on the one hand who receive, or on the other, theirs who are received, that their foulness not being washed away by the laver of the Church, nor their sins put away, communion being rashly seized, they touch the body and blood of the Lord, although it is written, "Whosoever shall eat the bread or drink the cup of the Lord unworthily, shall be guilty of the body and blood of the Lord!"[7]

22. We have judged, that those also whom they, who had formerly been bishops in the Catholic Church, and afterwards had assumed to themselves the power of clerical ordination, had baptized, are to be regarded as not baptized. And this is observed among us, that whosoever dipped by them come to us are baptized among us as strangers and having obtained nothing, with the only and true baptism of the Catholic Church, and obtain the regeneration of the laver of life. And yet there is a great difference between him who unwillingly and constrained by the necessity of persecution has given way, and him who with a profane will boldly rebels against the Church, or with impious voice blasphemes against the Father and God of Christ and the Creator of the whole world. And Stephen is not ashamed to assert and to say that remission of sins can be

---

[1] [The Roman custom seems to have been a *local* tradition, to which more *general* custom is opposed. See p. 375, *supra*.]
[2] [i.e., Montanists.] Or, "as we do the prophets."
[3] [See sec. 7, *supra*.]

[4] Phil. i. 18.
[5] Or, "they not only speak of, (but have)," is a proposed reading of this obscure passage, "*non modo dicunt*."
[6] [These, as the schoolmen teach, do virtually receive the sacrament, though *in voto tantum*.]
[7] 1 Cor. xi. 27.

granted by those who are themselves set fast in all kinds of sins, as if in the house of death there could be the laver of salvation.

23. What, then, is to be made of what is written, "Abstain from strange water, and drink not from a strange fountain,"[1] if, leaving the sealed fountain of the Church, you take up strange water for your own, and pollute the Church with unhallowed fountains? For when you communicate with the baptism of heretics, what else do you do than drink from their slough and mud; and while you yourself are purged with the Church's sanctification, you become befouled with the contact of the filth of others? And do you not fear the judgment of God when you are giving testimony to heretics in opposition to the Church, although it is written, "A false witness shall not be unpunished?"[2] But indeed you are worse than all heretics. For when many, as soon as their error is known, come over to you from them that they may receive the true light of the Church, you assist the errors of those who come, and, obscuring the light of ecclesiastical truth, you heap up the darkness of the heretical night; and although they confess that they are in sins, and have no grace, and therefore come to the Church, you take away from them remission of sins, which is given in baptism, by saying that they are already baptized and have obtained the grace of the Church outside the Church, and you do not perceive that their souls will be required at your hands when the day of judgment shall come, for having denied to the thirsting the drink of the Church, and having been the occasion of death to those that were desirous of living. And, after all this, you are indignant!

24. Consider with what want of judgment you dare to blame those who strive for the truth against falsehood. For who ought more justly to be indignant against the other? — whether he who supports God's enemies, or he who, in opposition to him who supports God's enemies, unites *with us* on behalf of the truth of the Church? — except that it is plain that the ignorant are also excited and angry, because by the want of counsel and discourse they are easily turned to wrath; so that of none more than of you does divine Scripture say, "A wrathful man stirreth up strifes, and a furious man heapeth up sins."[3] For what strifes and dissensions have you stirred up throughout the churches of the whole world! Moreover, how great sin have you heaped up for yourself, when you cut yourself off from so many flocks! For it is yourself that you have cut off. Do not deceive yourself, since he is really the schismatic who has made himself an apostate from the communion of ec-clesiastical unity.[4] For while you think that all may be excommunicated by you, you have excommunicated yourself alone from all; and not even the precepts of an apostle have been able to mould you to the rule of truth and peace, although he warned, and said, "I therefore, the prisoner of the Lord, beseech you that ye walk worthy of the vocation wherewith ye are called, with all lowliness and meekness, with long-suffering, forbearing one another in love; endeavouring to keep the unity of the Spirit in the bond of peace. There is one body and one Spirit, even as ye are called in one hope of your calling; one Lord, one faith, one baptism; one God and Father of all, who is above all, and through all, and in us all."[5]

25. How carefully has Stephen fulfilled these salutary commands and warnings of the apostle, keeping in the first place lowliness of mind and meekness! For what is more lowly or meek than to have disagreed with so many bishops throughout the whole world, breaking peace with each one of them in various kinds of discord:[6] at one time with the eastern churches, as we are sure you know; at another time with you who are in the south, from whom he received bishops as messengers sufficiently patiently and meekly not to receive them even to the speech of an ordinary conference; and even more, so mindful of love and charity as to command the entire fraternity, that no one should receive them into his house, so that not only peace and communion, but also a shelter and entertainment, were denied to them when they came! This is to have kept the unity of the Spirit in the bond of peace, to cut himself off from the unity of love,[7] and to make himself a stranger in all respects from his brethren, and to rebel against the sacrament and the faith with the madness of contumacious discord! With such a man can there be one Spirit and one body, in whom perchance there is not even one mind, so slippery, and shifting, and uncertain is it?

26. But as far as he is concerned, let us leave him;[7] let us rather deal with that concerning which there is the greatest question. They who contend that persons baptized among the heretics ought to be received as if they had obtained the grace of lawful baptism, say that baptism is one and the same to them and to us, and differs in no respect. But what says the Apostle Paul? "One Lord, one faith, one baptism, one God."[8] If the baptism of heretics be one and the same

---

[1] Prov. ix. 19 (LXX.).
[2] Prov. xix. 5. [Note the charge of schism that follows.]
[3] Prov. xxix. 22.

[4] [This, by the structure of the argument, is supposed to be said to Stephen.]
[5] Eph. iv. 1, 6.
[6] [By Canon XIX. of Nicæa the Paulianists were compelled to observe the Carthaginian discipline, which was a Catholic decision, so far, in Cyprian's favour. His position was not condemned.]
[7] [These passages are noted here, because they all must be borne in mind when we come to the *Treatise on Unity.*]
[8] Eph. iv. 5, 6.

with ours, without doubt their faith also is one; but if our faith is one, assuredly also we have one Lord: if there is one Lord, it follows that we say that He is one.[1] But if this unity which cannot be separated and divided at all, is itself also among heretics, why do we contend any more? Why do we call them heretics and not Christians? Moreover, since we and heretics have not one God, nor one Lord, nor one Church, nor one faith, nor even one Spirit, nor one body, it is manifest that neither can baptism be common to us with heretics, since between us there is nothing at all in common. And yet Stephen is not ashamed to afford patronage to such in opposition to the Church, and for the sake of maintaining heretics to divide the brotherhood; and in addition, to call Cyprian "a false Christ, and a false apostle, and a deceitful worker."[2] And he, conscious that all these characters are in himself, has been in advance of you, by falsely objecting to another those things which he himself ought deservedly to hear. We all bid you, for all our sakes, with all the bishops who are in Africa, and all the clergy, and all the brotherhood, farewell; that, constantly of one mind, and thinking the same thing, we may find you united with us even though afar off.[3]

EPISTLE LXXV.[4]

TO MAGNUS, ON BAPTIZING THE NOVATIANS, AND THOSE WHO OBTAIN GRACE ON A SICK-BED.

ARGUMENT.—THE FORMER PART OF THIS LETTER IS OF THE SAME TENOR WITH THOSE THAT PRECEDE, EXCEPT THAT HE INCULCATES CONCERNING THE NOVATIANS WHAT HE HAD IN SUBSTANCE SAID CONCERNING ALL HERETICS; MOREOVER, INSINUATING BY THE WAY THAT THE LEGITIMATE SUCCESSION OF CORNELIUS AT ROME IS KNOWN, AS THE CHURCH MAY BE KNOWN. IN THE SECOND PART (WHICH HITHERTO, AS THE TITLE SUFFICIENTLY INDICATES, HAS BEEN WRONGLY PUBLISHED AS A SEPARATE LETTER) HE TEACHES THAT THAT IS A TRUE BAPTISM WHEREIN ONE IS BAPTIZED BY SPRINKLING ON A SICK-BED, AS WELL AS BY IMMERSION IN THE CHURCH.

1. Cyprian to Magnus his son, greeting. With your usual religious diligence, you have consulted my poor intelligence, dearest son, as to whether, among other heretics, they also who come from Novatian ought, after his profane washing, to be baptized, and sanctified in the Catholic Church, with the lawful, and true, and only baptism of

the Church. Respecting which matter, as much as the capacity of my faith and the sanctity and truth of the divine Scriptures suggest, I answer, that no heretics and schismatics at all have any power or right. For which reason Novatian neither ought to be nor can be expected, inasmuch as he also is without the Church and acting in opposition to the peace and love of Christ, from being counted among adversaries and antichrists. For our Lord Jesus Christ, when He testified in His Gospel that those who were not with Him were His adversaries, did not point out any species of heresy, but showed that all whatsoever who were not with Him, and who, not gathering with Him, were scattering His flock, were His adversaries; saying, "He that is not with me is against me, and he that gathereth not with me scattereth."[5] Moreover, the blessed Apostle John himself distinguished no heresy or schism, neither did he set down any as specially separated; but he called all who had gone out from the Church, and who acted in opposition to the Church, antichrists, saying, "Ye have heard that Antichrist cometh, and even now are come many antichrists; wherefore we know that this is the last time. They went out from us, but they were not of us; for if they had been of us, they would have continued with us."[6] Whence it appears, that all are adversaries of the Lord and antichrists, who are known to have departed from charity and from the unity of the Catholic Church. In addition, moreover, the Lord establishes it in His Gospel, and says, "But if he neglect to hear the Church, let him be unto thee as a heathen man and a publican."[7] Now if they who despise the Church are counted heathens and publicans, much more certainly is it necessary that rebels and enemies, who forge false altars, and lawless priesthoods, and sacrilegious sacrifices, and corrupted names, should be counted among heathens and publicans; since they who sin less, and are only despisers of the Church, are by the Lord's sentence judged to be heathens and publicans.

2. But that the Church is one, the Holy Spirit declares in the Song of Songs, saying, in the person of Christ, "My dove, my undefiled, is one; she is the only one of her mother, she is the choice one of her that bare her."[8] Concerning which also He says again, "A garden enclosed is my sister, my spouse; a spring sealed up, a well of living water."[9] But if the spouse of Christ, which is the Church, is a garden enclosed; a thing that is closed up cannot lie open to strangers and profane persons. And if it is

---

[1] Otherwise "unity." Some commentators omit this clause.
[2] ["Pseudo-Christum, pseudo-apostolum, et dolosum operarium." Compare Cyprian's meekness (p. 386) with this.]
[3] [This letter may be too much like Stephen's, in a spirit not so meek as is becoming; but it is not less conclusive as a testimony.]
[4] Oxford ed.: Ep. lxix. A.D. 255.

[5] Luke xi. 23. [Bacon wished to see this reconciled with that other text Luke ix. 50.]
[6] 1 John ii. 18, 19.
[7] Matt. xviii. 17.
[8] Cant. vi. 9.
[9] Cant. iv. 12.

a fountain sealed, he who, being placed without, has no access to the spring, can neither drink thence nor be sealed. And the well also of living water, if it is one and the same within, he who is placed without cannot be quickened and sanctified from that water of which it is only granted to those who are within to make any use, or to drink. Peter also, showing this, set forth that the Church is one, and that only they who are in the Church can be baptized; and said, "In the ark of Noah, few, that is, eight souls, were saved by water; the like figure whereunto even baptism shall save you;"[1] proving and attesting that the one ark of Noah was a type of the one Church. If, then, in that baptism of the world thus expiated and purified, he who was not in the ark of Noah could be saved by water, he who is not in the Church to which alone baptism is granted, can also now be quickened by baptism. Moreover, too, the Apostle Paul, more openly and clearly still manifesting this same thing, writes to the Ephesians, and says, "Christ loved the Church, and gave Himself for it, that He might sanctify and cleanse it with the washing of water."[2] But if the Church is one which is loved by Christ, and is alone cleansed by His washing, how can he who is not in the Church be either loved by Christ, or washed and cleansed by His washing?

3. Wherefore, since the Church alone has the living water, and the power of baptizing and cleansing man, he who says that any one can be baptized and sanctified by Novatian must first show and teach that Novatian is in the Church, or presides over the Church. For the Church is one, and as she is one, cannot be both within and without. For if she is with Novatian, she was not with Cornelius.[3] But if she was with Cornelius, who succeeded the bishop Fabian by lawful ordination, and whom, beside the honour of the priesthood, the Lord glorified also with martyrdom, Novatian is not in the Church; nor can he be reckoned as a bishop, who, succeeding to no one, and despising the evangelical and apostolic tradition, sprang from himself. For he who has not been ordained in the Church can neither have nor hold to the Church in any way.

4. For the faith of the sacred Scripture sets forth that the Church is not without, nor can be separated nor divided against itself, but maintains the unity of an inseparable and undivided house; since it is written of the sacrament of the passover, and of the lamb, which Lamb designated Christ: "In one house shall it be eaten: ye shall not carry forth the flesh abroad out of the house."[4] Which also we see expressed concerning Rahab, who herself also bore a type of the Church, who received the command which said, "Thou shalt bring thy father, and thy mother, and thy brethren, and all thy father's household unto thee into thine house; and whosoever shall go out of the doors of thine house into the street, his blood shall be upon him."[5] In which mystery is declared, that they who will live, and escape from the destruction of the world, must be gathered together into one house alone, that is, into the Church; but whosoever of those thus collected together shall go out abroad, that is, if any one, although he may have obtained grace in the Church, shall depart and go out of the Church, that his blood shall be upon him; that is, that he himself must charge it upon himself that he perishes; which the Apostle Paul explains, teaching and enjoining that a heretic must be avoided, as perverse, and a sinner, and as condemned of himself. For that man will be guilty of his own ruin, who, not being cast out by the bishop, but of his own accord deserting from the Church is by heretical presumption condemned of himself.

5. And therefore the Lord, suggesting to us a unity that comes from divine authority, lays it down, saying, "I and my Father are one."[6] To which unity reducing His Church, He says again, "And there shall be one *flock*,[7] and one shepherd."[8] But if the flock is one, how can he be numbered among the flock who is not in the number of the flock? Or how can he be esteemed a pastor, who, — while the true shepherd remains and presides over the Church of God by successive ordination, — succeeding to no one, and beginning from himself, becomes a stranger and a profane person, an enemy of the Lord's peace and of the divine unity, not dwelling in the house of God, that is, in the Church of God, in which none dwell except they are of one heart and one mind, since the Holy Spirit speaks in the Psalms, and says, "It is God who maketh men to dwell of one mind in a house."[9]

6. Besides even the Lord's sacrifices themselves declare that Christian unanimity is linked together with itself by a firm and inseparable charity. For when the Lord calls bread, which is combined by the union of many grains, His body, He indicates our people whom He bore as being united; and when He calls the wine, which is pressed from many grapes and clusters and collected together, His blood, He also signifies our flock linked together by the mingling of a united multitude.[10] If Novatian is united to this bread of the Lord, if he also is mingled

---

[1] 1 Pet. iii. 20, 21.
[2] Eph. v. 25, 26.
[3] [A dilemma which should be borne in mind in studying the subsequent history of the Roman See and its rival popes.]
[4] Ex. xii. 46.

[5] Josh. ii. 18, 19.
[6] John x. 30.
[7] "Grex."
[8] John x. 16.
[9] Ps. lxviii. 6. [Vulgate and Anglican Psalter.]
[10] [See p. 362, *supra*, and Augus., tom. v. p. 1246, ed. Migne.]

with this cup of Christ, he may also seem to be able to have the grace of the one baptism of the Church, if it be manifest that he holds the unity of the Church. In fine, how inseparable is the sacrament of unity, and how hopeless are they, and what excessive ruin they earn for themselves from the indignation of God, who make a schism, and, forsaking their bishop,[1] appoint another false bishop for themselves without, — Holy Scripture declares in the books of Kings; where ten tribes were divided from the tribe of Judah and Benjamin, and, forsaking their king, appointed for themselves another one without. It says, "And the Lord was very angry with all the seed of Israel, and removed them away, and delivered them into the hand of spoilers, until He had cast them out of His sight; for Israel was scattered from the house of David, and they made themselves a king, Jeroboam the son of Nebat."[2] It says that the Lord was very angry, and gave them up to perdition, because they were scattered from unity, and had made another king for themselves. And so great was the indignation of the Lord against those who had made the schism, that even when the man of God was sent to Jeroboam, to charge upon him his sins, and predict the future vengeance, he was forbidden to eat bread or to drink water with them. And when he did not observe this, and took meat against the command of God, he was immediately smitten by the majesty of the divine judgment, so that returning thence he was slain on the way by the jaws of a lion which attacked him. And dares any one to say that the saving water of baptism and heavenly grace can be in common with schismatics, with whom neither earthly food nor worldly drink ought to be in common? Moreover, the Lord satisfies us in His Gospel, and shows forth a still greater light of intelligence, that the same persons who had then divided themselves from the tribe of Judah and Benjamin, and forsaking Jerusalem had seceded to Samaria, should be reckon among profane persons and Gentiles. For when first He sent His disciples on the ministry of salvation, He bade them, saying, "Go not into the way of the Gentiles, and into any city of the Samaritans enter ye not."[3] Sending first to the Jews, He commands the Gentiles as yet to be passed over; but by adding that even the city of the Samaritans was to be omitted, where there were schismatics, He shows that schismatics were to be put on the same level as Gentiles.

7. But if any one objects, by way of saying that Novatian holds the same law which the Catholic Church holds, baptizes with the same symbol with which we baptize, knows the same God and Father, the same Christ the Son, the same Holy Spirit, and that for this reason he may claim the power of baptizing, namely, that he seems not to differ from us in the baptismal interrogatory; let any one that thinks that this may be objected, know first of all, that there is not one law of the Creed, nor the same interrogatory common to us and to schismatics. For when they say, "Dost thou believe the remission of sins and life eternal through the holy Church?" they lie in their interrogatory, since they have not the Church. Then, besides, with their own voice they themselves confess that remission of sins cannot be given except by the holy Church; and not having this, they show that sins cannot be remitted among them.

8. But that they are said to have the same God the Father as we, to know the same Christ the Son, the same Holy Spirit, can be of no avail to such as these. For even Korah, Dathan, and Abiram knew the same God as did the priest Aaron and Moses. Living under the same law and religion, they invoke the one and true God, who was to be invoked and worshipped; yet, because they transgressed the ministry of their office in opposition to Aaron the priest, who had received the legitimate priesthood by the condescension of God and the ordination of the Lord, and claimed to themselves the power of sacrificing, divinely stricken, they immediately suffered punishment for their unlawful endeavours; and sacrifices offered irreligiously and lawlessly, contrary to the right of divine appointment, could not be accepted, nor profit them. Even those very censers in which incense had been lawlessly offered, lest they should any more be used by the priests, but that they might rather exhibit a memorial of the divine vengeance and indignation for the correction of their successors, being by the command of the Lord melted and purged by fire, were beaten out into flexible plates, and fastened to the altars, according to what the Holy Scripture says, "to be," it says, "a memorial to the children of Israel, that no stranger which is not of the seed of Aaron come near to offer incense before the Lord, that he be not as Korah."[4] And yet those men had not made a schism, nor had gone out abroad, and in opposition to God's priests rebelled shamelessly and with hostility; but this these men are now doing who divide the Church, and, as rebels against the peace and unity of Christ, attempt to establish a throne for themselves, and to assume the primacy,[5] and to claim the right of baptizing and

---

[1] [This hinges unity for the individual, according to Cyprian; the individual must be in communion with his lawful bishop, and the bishop with the universal episcopate. It never enters his head that any one See is the test of unity. Vol. i. 415 and 460.]

[2] 2 Kings xvii. 20, 21.

[3] Matt. x. 5.

[4] Num. xvii. 5 [and Jude 11.]

[5] [What would Cyprian have said to Boniface III., A.D. 607, and to Nicholas, A.D. 858? The former attempted to set up a universal throne: the latter founded the papacy on the forged Decretals.]

of offering. How can they complete what they do, or obtain anything by lawless endeavours from God, seeing that they are endeavouring against God what is not lawful to them? Wherefore they who patronize Novatian or other schismatics of that kind, contend in vain that any one can be baptized and sanctified with a saving baptism among them, when it is plain that he who baptizes has not the power of baptizing.

9. And, moreover, that it may be better understood what is the divine judgment against audacity of the like kind, we find that in such wickedness, not only the leaders and originators, but also the partakers, are destined to punishment, unless they have separated themselves from the communion of the wicked; as the Lord by Moses commands, and says, "Separate yourselves from the tents of these most hardened men, and touch nothing of theirs, lest ye be consumed in their sins." [1] And what the Lord had threatened by Moses He fulfilled, that whosoever had not separated himself from Korah, and Dathan, and Abiram, immediately suffered punishment for his impious communion. By which example is shown and proved, that all will be liable to guilt as well as its punishment, who with irreligious boldness mingle themselves with schismatics in opposition to prelates and priests; even as also by the prophet Osea the Holy Spirit witnesses, and says, "Their sacrifices shall be unto them as the bread of mourning; all that eat thereof shall be polluted;" [2] teaching, doubtless, and showing that all are absolutely joined with the leaders in punishment, who have been contaminated by their crime.

10. What, then, can be their deservings in the sight of God, on whom punishments are divinely denounced? or how can such persons justify and sanctify the baptized, who, being enemies of the priests, strive to usurp things foreign and lawless, and by no right conceded to them? And yet we do not wonder that, in accordance with their wickedness, they do contend for them. For it is necessary that each one of them should maintain what they do; nor when vanquished will they easily yield, although they know that what they do is not lawful. That is to be wondered at, yea, rather to be indignant and aggrieved at, that Christians should support antichrists; and that prevaricators of the faith, and betrayers of the Church, should stand within in the Church itself.[3] And these, although otherwise obstinate and unteachable, yet still at least confess this — that all, whether heretics or schismatics, are without the Holy Ghost, and therefore can indeed baptize, but cannot confer the Holy Spirit; and at this very point they are held fast by us, inas-much as we show that those who have not the Holy Ghost are not able to baptize at all.

11. For since in baptism every one has his own sins remitted, the Lord proves and declares in His Gospel that sins can only be put away by those who have the Holy Spirit. For after His resurrection, sending forth His disciples, He speaks to them, and says, "As the Father hath sent me, even so send I you. And when He had said this, He breathed on them, and said to them, Receive ye the Holy Ghost. Whose soever sins ye remit, they shall be remitted unto them; and whose soever sins ye retain, they shall be retained." [4] In which place He shows, that he alone can baptize and give remission of sins who has the Holy Spirit. Moreover, John, who was to baptize Christ our Lord Himself, previously received the Holy Ghost while he was yet in his mother's womb, that it might be certain and manifest that none can baptize save those who have the Holy Spirit. Therefore those who patronize heretics or schismatics must answer us whether they have or have not the Holy Ghost. If they have, why are hands imposed on those who are baptized among them when they come to us, that they may receive the Holy Ghost, since He must surely have been received there, where if He was He could be given? But if heretics and schismatics baptized without have not the Holy Spirit, and therefore hands are imposed on them among us, that *here* may be received what *there* neither is nor can be given; it is plain, also, that remission of sins cannot be given by those who, it is certain, have not the Holy Spirit. And therefore, in order that, according to the divine arrangement and the evangelical truth, they may be able to obtain remission of sins, and to be sanctified, and to become temples of God, they must all absolutely be baptized with the baptism of the Church who come from adversaries and antichrists to the Church of Christ.

12. You have asked also, dearest son, what I thought of those who obtain God's grace in sickness and weakness, whether they are to be accounted legitimate Christians, for that they are not to be washed, but sprinkled, with the saving water. In this point, my diffidence and modesty prejudges none, so as to prevent any from feeling what he thinks right, and from doing what he feels to be right.[5] As far as my poor understanding conceives it, I think that the divine benefits can in no respect be mutilated and weakened; nor can anything less occur in that case, where, with full and entire faith both of the giver and receiver, is accepted what is drawn

---

[1] Num. xvi. 26.
[2] Hos. ix. 4.
[3] " Within the very barriers of the Church; " *v. l.*

[4] John xx. 21-23.
[5] [Here comes into view the question of clinic baptism and of the exceptional mode of sprinkling or affusion. On which let the extreme modesty of our author be a check to me. Elucidation XX.

from the divine gifts. For in the sacrament of salvation the contagion of sins is not in such wise washed away, as the filth of the skin and of the body is washed away in the carnal and ordinary washing, as that there should be need of saltpetre and other appliances also, and a bath and a basin wherewith this vile body must be washed and purified. Otherwise is the breast of the believer washed; otherwise is the mind of man purified by the merit of faith. In the sacraments of salvation, when necessity compels, and God bestows His mercy, the divine methods confer the whole benefit on believers; nor ought it to trouble any one that sick people seem to be sprinkled or affused, when they obtain the Lord's grace, when Holy Scripture speaks by the mouth of the prophet Ezekiel, and says, "Then will I sprinkle clean water upon you, and ye shall be clean: from all your filthiness and from all your idols will I cleanse you. And I will give you a new heart, and a new spirit will I put within you."[1] Also in Numbers: "And the man that shall be unclean until the evening shall be purified on the third day, and on the seventh day shall be clean: but if he shall not be purified on the third day, on the seventh day he shall not be clean. And that soul shall be cut off from Israel: because the water of sprinkling hath not been sprinkled upon him."[2] And again: "And the Lord spake unto Moses, saying, Take the Levites from among the children of Israel, and cleanse them. And thus shalt thou do unto them, to cleanse them: thou shalt sprinkle them with the water of purification."[3] And again: "The water of sprinkling is a purification."[4] Whence it appears that the sprinkling also of water prevails equally with the washing of salvation; and that when this is done in the Church, where the faith both of receiver and giver is sound, all things hold and may be consummated and perfected by the majesty of the Lord and by the truth of faith.

13. But, moreover, in respect of some calling those who have obtained the peace of Christ by the saving water and by legitimate faith, not Christians, but Clinics, I do not find whence they take up this name, unless perhaps, having read more, and of a more recondite kind, they have taken these Clinics from Hippocrates or Soranus.[5] For I, who know of a Clinic in the Gospel, know that to that paralytic and infirm man, who lay on his bed during the long course of his life, his infirmity presented no obstacle to his attainment in the fullest degree of heavenly strength. Nor was he only raised from his bed by the divine indulgence, but he also took up his bed itself with his restored and increased strength. And therefore, as far as it is allowed me by faith to conceive and to think, this is my opinion, that any one should be esteemed a legitimate Christian, who by the law and right of faith shall have obtained the grace of God in the Church. Or if any one think that those have gained nothing by having only been sprinkled with the saving water, but that they are still empty and void, let them not be deceived, so as if they escape the evil of their sickness, and get well, they *should seek* to be baptized.[6] But if they cannot be baptized who have already been sanctified by ecclesiastical baptism, why are they offended in respect of their faith and the mercy of the Lord? Or have they obtained indeed the divine favour, but in a shorter and more limited measure of the divine gift and of the Holy Spirit, so as indeed to be esteemed Christians, but yet not to be counted equal with others?

14. Nay, verily, the Holy Spirit is not given by measure, but is poured out altogether on the believer. For if the day rises alike to all, and if the sun is diffused with like and equal light over all, how much more does Christ, who is the true sun and the true day, bestow in His Church the light of eternal life with the like equality! Of which equality we see the sacrament celebrated in Exodus, when the manna flowed down from heaven, and, prefiguring the things to come, showed forth the nourishment of the heavenly bread and the food of the coming Christ. For there, without distinction either of sex or of age, an omer was collected equally by each one.[7] Whence it appeared that the mercy of Christ, and the heavenly grace that would subsequently follow, was equally divided among all; without difference of sex, without distinction of years, without accepting of persons, upon all the people of God the gift of spiritual grace was shed. Assuredly the same spiritual grace which is equally received in baptism by believers, is subsequently either increased or diminished in our conversation and conduct; as in the Gospel the Lord's seed is equally sown, but, according to the variety of the soil, some is wasted, and some is increased into a large variety of plenty, with an exuberant fruit of either thirty or sixty or a hundred fold. But, once more, when each was called to receive a penny, wherefore should what is distributed equally by God be diminished by human interpretation?

---

[1] Ezek. xxxvi. 25, 26.
[2] Num. xix. 8, 12, 13.
[3] Num. viii. 5-7.
[4] Num. xix. 9.
[5] The Oxford translator has given this name as "Socrates" here, but, as it appears, by an oversight only; for the original text has "Soranus," who is described as "of Ephesus, under Trajan and Adrian, a well-instructed author in methodical medicine," just as the translator describes Socrates. [Elucidation XX.]

[6] The exact meaning of this sentence is very doubtful.
[7] [We may think this fanciful in argument: but this absorption of all Scripture, by primitive believers, into the analogy of faith, is not to be despised. See St. Paul's example, Gal. iv. 21.]

15. But if any one is moved by this, that some of those who are baptized in sickness are still tempted by unclean spirits, let him know that the obstinate wickedness of the devil prevails even up to the saving water, but that in baptism it loses all the poison of his wickedness. An instance of this we see in the king Pharaoh, who, having struggled long, and delayed in his perfidy, could resist and prevail until he came to the water; but when he had come thither, he was both conquered and destroyed. And that that sea was a sacrament of baptism, the blessed Apostle Paul declares, saying, "Brethren, I would not have you ignorant how that all our fathers were under the cloud, and all passed through the sea, and were all baptized unto Moses in the cloud and in the sea;" and he added, saying, "Now all these things were our examples." [1] And this also is done in the present day, in that the devil is scourged, and burned, and tortured by exorcists, by the human voice, and by divine power; [2] and although he often says that he is going out, and will leave the men of God, yet in that which he says he deceives, and puts in practice what was before done by Pharaoh with the same obstinate and fraudulent deceit. When, however, they come to the water of salvation and to the sanctification of baptism, we ought to know and to trust that there the devil is beaten down, and the man, dedicated to God, is set free by the divine mercy. For as scorpions and serpents, which prevail on the dry ground, when cast into water, cannot prevail nor retain their venom; so also the wicked spirits, which are called scorpions and serpents, and yet are trodden under foot by us, by the power given by the Lord, cannot remain any longer in the body of a man in whom, baptized and sanctified, the Holy Spirit is beginning to dwell.

16. This, finally, in very fact also we experience, that those who are baptized by urgent necessity in sickness, and obtain grace, are free from the unclean spirit wherewith they were previously moved, and live in the Church in praise and honour, and day by day make more and more advance in the increase of heavenly grace by the growth of their faith. And, on the other hand, some of those who are baptized in health, if subsequently they begin to sin, are shaken by the return of the unclean spirit, so that it is manifest that the devil is driven out in baptism by the faith of the believer, and returns if the faith afterwards shall fail. Unless, indeed, it seems just to some, that they who, outside the Church among adversaries and antichrists, are polluted with profane water, should be judged to be baptized; while they who are baptized in the Church are thought to have attained less of divine mercy and grace; and so great consideration be had for heretics, that they who come from heresy are not interrogated whether they are washed or sprinkled, whether they be clinics or peripatetics; but among us the sound truth of faith is disparaged, and in ecclesiastical baptism its majesty and sanctity suffer derogation. [3]

17. I have replied, dearest son, to your letter, so far as my poor ability prevailed; and I have shown, as far as I could, what I think; prescribing to no one, so as to prevent any prelate from determining what he thinks right, as he shall give an account of his own doings to the Lord, according to what the blessed Apostle Paul in his Epistle to the Romans writes and says: "Every one of us shall give account for himself: let us not therefore judge one another." [4] I bid you, dearest son, ever heartily farewell.

EPISTLE LXXVI.[5]

CYPRIAN TO NEMESIANUS AND OTHER MARTYRS IN THE MINES.[6]

ARGUMENT. — HE EXTOLS WITH WONDERFUL COMMENDATIONS THE MARTYRS IN THE MINES, OPPOSING, IN A BEAUTIFUL ANTITHESIS, TO THE TORTURES OF EACH, THE CONSOLATIONS OF EACH.

1. Cyprian to Nemesianus, Felix, Lucius, another Felix, Litteus, Polianus, Victor, Jader, and Dativus, his fellow-bishops, also to his fellow-presbyters and deacons, and the rest of the brethren in the mines, martyrs of God the Father Almighty, and of Jesus Christ our Lord, and of God our preserver, everlasting greeting. Your glory, indeed, would demand, most blessed and beloved brethren, that I myself should come to see and to embrace you, if the limits of the place appointed me did not restrain me, banished as I am for the sake of the confession of the Name. But in what way I can, I bring myself into your presence; and even though it is not permitted me to come to you in body and in movement, yet in love and in spirit I come expressing my mind in my letter, in which mind I joyfully exult in those virtues and praises of yours, counting myself a partaker with you, although not in bodily suffering, yet in community of love. Could I be silent and restrain my voice in stillness, when I am made aware of so many and such glorious things concerning my dearest friends, things with which the divine condescension has honoured you, so that part of you have already

---

[1] 1 Cor. x. 1, 2, 6.
[2] [Acts xvi. 16 and xix. 15. We must not overlook such Scriptures in judging the exorcisms of the primitive Church.]

[3] [Clinics, nevertheless, were treated by canonical law as less fit for Holy Orders. See Canon XII., Neo-Cæsarea. Thomassin.]
[4] Rom. xiv. 12, 13.
[5] Oxford ed.: Ep. lxxvi. We gather that this was written in exile from these words, "If the limits of the place appointed me did not restrain me, banished as I am on account of the confession of the Name." A.D. 257.
[6] [Compare vol. iii. p. 693.]

gone before by the consummation of their martyrdom to receive from their Lord the crown of their deserts? Part still abide in the dungeons of the prison, or in the mines and in chains, exhibiting by the very delays of their punishments, greater examples for the strengthening and arming of the brethren, advancing by the tediousness of their tortures to more ample titles of merit, to receive as many payments in heavenly rewards, as days are now counted in their punishments. I do not marvel, most brave and blessed brethren, that these things have happened to you in consideration of the desert of your religion and your faith; that the Lord should thus have lifted you to the lofty height of glory by the honour of His glorification, seeing that you have always flourished in His Church, guarding the tenor of the faith, keeping firmly the Lord's commands; in simplicity, innocence; in charity, concord; modesty in humility, diligence in administration, watchfulness in helping those that suffer, mercy in cherishing the poor, constancy in defending the truth, judgment in severity of discipline. And that nothing should be wanting to the example of good deeds in you, even now, in the confession of your voice and the suffering of your body, you provoke the minds of your brethren to divine martyrdom, by exhibiting yourselves as leaders of virtue, that while the flock follows its pastors, and imitates what it sees to be done by those set over it, it may be crowned with the like merits of obedience by the Lord.

2. But that, being first severely beaten with clubs, and ill-used, you have begun by sufferings of that kind, the glorious firstlings of your confession, is not a matter to be execrated by us. For a Christian body is not very greatly terrified at clubs, seeing all its hope is in the Wood.[1] The servant of Christ acknowledges the sacrament of his salvation: redeemed by wood to life eternal, he is advanced by wood to the crown. But what wonder if, as golden and silver vessels, you have been committed to the mine that is the home of gold and silver, except that now the nature of the mines is changed, and the places which previously had been accustomed to yield gold and silver have begun to receive them? Moreover, they have put fetters on your feet, and have bound your blessed limbs, and the temples of God with disgraceful chains, as if the spirit also could be bound with the body, or your gold could be stained by the contact of iron. To men who are dedicated to God, and attesting their faith with religious courage, such things are ornaments, not chains; nor do they bind the feet of the Christians for infamy, but glorify them for a crown. Oh feet blessedly bound, which

are loosed, not by the smith but by the Lord! Oh feet blessedly bound, which are guided to paradise in the way of salvation! Oh feet bound for the present time in the world, that they may be always free with the Lord! Oh feet, lingering for a while among the fetters and cross-bars,[2] but to run quickly to Christ on a glorious road! Let cruelty, either envious or malignant, hold you here in its bonds and chains as long as it will, from this earth and from these sufferings you shall speedily come to the kingdom of heaven. The body is not cherished in the mines with couch and cushions, but it is cherished with the refreshment and solace of Christ. The frame wearied with labours lies prostrate on the ground, but it is no penalty to lie down with Christ. Your limbs unbathed, are foul and disfigured with filth and dirt; but within they are spiritually cleansed, although without the flesh is defiled. There the bread is scarce; but man liveth not by bread alone, but by the word of God. Shivering, you want clothing; but he who puts on Christ is both abundantly clothed and adorned. The hair of your half-shorn head[3] seems repulsive; but since Christ is the head of the man, anything whatever must needs become that head which is illustrious on account of Christ's name. All that deformity, detestable and foul to Gentiles, with what splendour shall it be recompensed! This temporal and brief suffering, how shall it be exchanged for the reward of a bright and eternal honour, when, according to the word of the blessed apostle, "the Lord shall change the body of our humiliation, that it may be fashioned like to the body of His brightness!"[4]

3. But there cannot be felt any loss of either religion or faith, most beloved brethren, in the fact that now there is given no opportunity there to God's priests for offering and celebrating the divine sacrifices; yea, you celebrate and offer a sacrifice to God equally[5] precious and glorious, and that will greatly profit you for the retribution of heavenly rewards, since the sacred Scripture speaks, saying, "The sacrifice of God is a broken spirit; a contrite and humbled heart God doth not despise."[6] You offer this sacrifice to God; you celebrate this sacrifice without intermission day and night, being made victims to God, and exhibiting yourselves as holy and unspotted offerings, as the apostle exhorts and says, "I beseech you therefore, brethren, by the mercies of God, that ye present your bodies a living sacrifice, holy, acceptable unto God. And be not conformed to this world; but

---

[1] *Scil.*: "of the cross." [Fanciful in *logic*, but our author may be indulged in his *rhetoric*. It was suited to the times.]

[2] [i.e., of the stocks.]
[3] [As of convict criminals. An honourable tonsure.]
[4] Phil. iii. 21.
[5] [This is very strong language, and absolutely disproves transubstantiation and "the eucharistic God" of Dufresne, *Med.*, iii.]
[6] Ps. li. 18.

be ye transformed by the renewing of your mind, that ye may prove what is that good, and acceptable, and perfect will of God." [1]

4. For this it is which especially pleases God; it is this wherein our works with greater deserts are successful in earning God's good-will; this it is which alone the obedience of our faith and devotion can render to the Lord for His great and saving benefits, as the Holy Spirit declares and witnesses in the Psalms: "What shall I render," says He, "to the Lord for all His benefits towards me? I will take the cup of salvation, and I will call upon the name of the Lord. Precious in the sight of the Lord is the death of His saints." [2] Who would not gladly and readily receive the cup of salvation? Who would not with joy and gladness desire that in which he himself also may render somewhat unto His Lord? Who would not bravely and unfalteringly receive a death precious in the sight of the Lord, to please His eyes, who, looking down from above upon us who are placed in the conflict for His name, approves the willing, assists the struggling, crowns the conquering with the recompense of patience, goodness, and affection, rewarding in us whatever He Himself has bestowed, and honouring what He has accomplished?

5. For that it is His doing that we conquer, and that we attain by the subduing of the adversary to the palm of the greatest contest, the Lord declares and teaches in His Gospel, saying, "But when they deliver you up, take no thought how or what ye shall speak; for it shall be given you in that same hour what ye shall speak. For it is not ye that speak, but the Spirit of your Father which speaketh in you." [3] And again: "Settle it therefore in your hearts, not to meditate before what ye shall answer; for I will give you a mouth and wisdom, which your adversaries shall not be able to resist." [4] In which, indeed, is both the great confidence of believers, and the gravest fault of the faithless, that they do not trust Him who promises to give His help to those who confess Him, and do not on the other hand fear Him who threatens eternal punishment to those who deny Him.

6. All which things, most brave and faithful soldiers of Christ, you have suggested to your brethren, fulfilling in deeds what ye have previously taught in words, hereafter to be greatest in the kingdom of heaven, as the Lord promises and says, "Whosoever shall do and teach so, shall be called the greatest in the kingdom of heaven." [5] Moreover, a manifold portion of the people, following your example, have confessed

alike with you, and alike have been crowned, associated with you in the bond of the strongest charity, and separated from their prelates neither by the prison nor by the mines; in the number of whom neither are there wanting virgins in whom the hundred-fold are added to the fruit of sixty-fold, and whom a double glory has advanced to the heavenly crown. In boys also a courage greater than their age has surpassed their years in the praise of their confession, so that every sex and every age should adorn the blessed flock of your martyrdom. [6]

7. What now must be the vigour, beloved brethren, of your victorious consciousness, what the loftiness of your mind, what exultation in feeling, what triumph in your breast, that every one of you stands near to the promised reward of God, are secure from the judgment of God, walk in the mines with a body captive indeed, but with a heart reigning, that you know Christ is present with you, rejoicing in the endurance of His servants, who are ascending by His footsteps and in His paths to the eternal kingdoms! You daily expect with joy the saving day of your departure; and already about to withdraw from the world, you are hastening to the rewards of martyrdom, and to the divine homes, to behold after this darkness of the world the purest light, and to receive a glory greater than all sufferings and conflicts, as the apostle witnesses, and says, "The sufferings of this present time are not worthy to be compared with the glory that shall be revealed in us." [7] And because now your word is more effectual in prayers, and supplication is more quick to obtain what is sought for in afflictions, seek more eagerly, and ask that the divine condescension would consummate the confession of all of us; that from this darkness and these snares of the world God would set us also free with you, sound and glorious; that we who here are united in the bond of charity and peace, and have stood together against the wrongs of heretics and the oppressions of the heathens, may rejoice together in the heavenly kingdom. I bid you, most blessed and most beloved brethren, ever farewell in the Lord, and always and everywhere remember me. [8]

EPISTLE LXXVII. [9]

THE REPLY OF NEMESIANUS, DATIVUS, FELIX, AND VICTOR, TO CYPRIAN.

ARGUMENT.—THIS EPISTLE AND THE TWO FOLLOWING CONTAIN NOTHING ELSE THAN REPLIES TO THE FOREGOING, INASMUCH AS THEY CON-

---

[1] Rom. xii. 1, 2.
[2] Ps. cxvi. 12, 13, 15.
[3] Matt. x. 19, 20.
[4] Luke xxi. 14, 15.
[5] Matt. v. 19.

[6] [No one can read these *obiter dicta* of our author without assurance that the martyrs were a numerous army, beyond what is generally allowed. "A noble army, men and boys" (Heber).]
[7] Rom. viii. 18.
[8] [See next letter. I cannot conceive of any Christian as not profoundly touched and edified by this eloquent and scriptural letter of a martyr to martyrs in a period of fiery trial. They truly believed what is written, "to die is gain." Phil. i. 21.]
[9] Oxford ed.: Ep. lxxvii. A.D. 257.

TAIN THE THANKSGIVING AS WELL FOR THE COMFORT CONVEYED BY THE LETTER AS FOR THE ASSISTANCE SENT THEREWITH. BUT FROM THE FACT THAT THREE DISTINCT LETTERS ARE SENT IN REPLY TO THE SINGLE ONE OF CYPRIAN'S, WE ARE TO GATHER THAT THE BISHOPS WHO WROTE THEM WERE PLACED IN DIFFERENT DEPARTMENTS OF THE MINES.[1]

1. Nemesianus, Dativus, Felix, and Victor, to their brother Cyprian, in the Lord eternal salvation. You speak, dearly beloved Cyprian, in your letters always with deep meaning, as suits the condition of the time, by the assiduous reading of which letters both the wicked are corrected and men of good faith are confirmed. For while you do not cease in your writings to lay bare the hidden mysteries, you thus make us to grow in faith, and men from the world to draw near to belief. For by whatever good things you have introduced in your many books, unconsciously you have described yourself to us. For you are greater than all men in discourse, in speech more eloquent, in counsel wiser, in patience more simple, in works more abundant, in abstinence more holy, in obedience more humble, and in good deeds more innocent. And you yourself know, beloved, that our eager wish was, that we might see you, our teacher and our lover, attain to the crown of a great confession.

2. For, in the proceedings before the proconsul, as a good and true teacher you first have pronounced that which we your disciples, following you, ought to say before the president. And, as a sounding trumpet, you have stirred up God's soldiers, furnished with heavenly arms, to the close encounter; and fighting in the first rank, you have slain the devil with a spiritual sword: you have also ordered the troops of the brethren, on the one hand and on the other, with your words, so that snares were on all sides laid for the enemy, and the severed sinews of the very carcase of the public foe were trodden under foot.[2] Believe us, dearest, that your innocent spirit is not far from the hundred-fold reward, seeing that it has feared neither the first onsets of the world, nor shrunk from going into exile, nor hesitated to leave the city, nor dreaded to dwell in a desert place; and since it furnished many with an example of confession, itself first spoke the martyr-witness. For it provoked others to acts of martyrdom by its own example; and not only began to be a companion of the martyrs already departing from the world, but also linked a heavenly friendship with those who should be so.

3. Therefore they who were condemned with us give you before God the greatest thanks, beloved Cyprian, that in your letter you have refreshed their suffering breasts; have healed their limbs wounded with clubs; have loosened their feet bound with fetters; have smoothed the hair of their half-shorn head; have illuminated the darkness of the dungeon; have brought down the mountains of the mine to a smooth surface; have even placed fragrant flowers to their nostrils, and have shut out the foul odour of the smoke.[3] Moreover, your continued gifts, and those of our beloved Quirinus, which you sent to be distributed by Herennianus the sub-deacon, and Lucian, and Maximus, and Amantius the acolytes, provided a supply of whatever had been wanting for the necessities of their bodies. Let us, then, be in our prayers helpers of one another: and let us ask, as you have bidden us, that we may have God and Christ and the angels as supporters in all our actions. We bid you, lord and brother, ever heartily farewell, and have us in mind. Greet all who are with you. All ours who are with us love you, and greet you, and desire to see you.

EPISTLE LXXVIII.[4]

THE REPLY TO THE SAME OF LUCIUS AND THE REST OF THE MARTYRS.

ARGUMENT. — THE ARGUMENT OF THE PRESENT LETTER IS, IN SUBSTANCE, THE SAME AS THAT OF THE PRECEDING; AND THEREFORE IT IS NOT A LETTER OF LUCIUS THE ROMAN BISHOP, BUT OF LUCIUS THE AFRICAN BISHOP AND MARTYR.

1. To Cyprian our brother and colleague, Lucius, and all the brethren who are with me in the Lord, greeting. Your letter came to us, dearest brother, while we were exulting and rejoicing in God that He had armed us for the struggle, and had made us by His condescension conquerors in the battle; the letter, namely, which you sent to us by Herennianus the sub-deacon, and Lucian, and Maximus, and Amantius the acolytes,[5] which when we read we received a relaxation in our bonds, a solace in our affliction, and a support in our necessity; and we were aroused and more strenuously animated to bear whatever more of punishment might be awaiting us. For before our suffering we were called forth by you to glory, who first afforded us guidance to confession of the name of Christ. We indeed, who follow the footsteps of your confession, hope for an equal grace with you. For he who is first in the race is first also for the reward; and you who first occupied the course thence have com-

---

[1] This is confirmed in Epistle lxxix., where mention is made of one mine in particular.

[2] Otherwise, "the sinews of the common enemy cut in two, his carcase was trodden under foot." [Rom. xvi. 20.]

[3] [A graphic idea of mine-tortures is here afforded.]

[4] Oxford ed.: Ep. lxxviii. A.D. 257.

[5] [These acolytes were of Greek name, but of Western usage only. They were a sort of candidates for Orders; and our Moravian brethren retain this ministry and the name, to this day.]

municated this to us from what you began, showing doubtless the undivided love wherewith you have always loved us, so that we who had one Spirit in the bond of peace might have the grace of your[1] prayers, and one crown of confession.

2. But in your case, dearest brother, to the crown of confession is added the reward of your labours — an abundant measure which you shall receive from the Lord in the day of retribution, who have by your letter presented yourself to us, as you manifested to us that candid and blessed breast of yours which we have ever known, and in accordance with its largeness have uttered praises to God with us, not as much as we deserve to hear, but as much as you are able to utter. For with your words you have both adorned those things which had been less instructed in us, and have strengthened us to the sustaining of those sufferings which we bear,[2] as being certain of the heavenly rewards, and of the crown of martyrdom, and of the kingdom of God, from the prophecy which, being filled with the Holy Spirit, you have pledged to us in your letter. All this will happen, beloved, if you will have us in mind in your prayers, which I trust you do even as we certainly do.

3. And thus, O brother most longed-for, we have received what you sent to us from Quirinus and from yourself, a sacrifice from every clean thing. Even as Noah offered to God, and God was pleased with the sweet savour, and had respect unto his offering, so also may He have respect unto yours, and may He be pleased to return to you the reward of this so good work. But I beg that you will command the letter which we have written to Quirinus to be sent forward. I bid you, dearest brother and earnestly desired, ever heartily farewell, and remember us.[3] Greet all who are with you. Farewell.

EPISTLE LXXIX.[4]

THE ANSWER OF FELIX, JADER, POLIANUS, AND THE REST OF THE MARTYRS, TO CYPRIAN.

ARGUMENT. — THE MARTYRS ABOVE SPOKEN OF ACKNOWLEDGE WITH GRATITUDE THE ASSISTANCE SENT TO THEM BY CYPRIAN.

To our dearest and best beloved Cyprian, Felix, Jader, Polianus, together with the presbyters and all who are abiding with us at the mine of Sigua, eternal health in the Lord. We reply to your salutation, dearest brother, by Herennianus the sub-deacon, Lucian and Maximus our brethren, strong and safe by the aid of your prayers, from whom we have received a sum under the name of an offering, together with

your letter which you wrote, and in which you have condescended to comfort us as if we were sons, out of the heavenly words. And we have given and do give thanks to God the Father Almighty through His Christ, that we have been thus comforted and strengthened by your address, asking from the candour of your mind that you would deign to have us in mind in your constant prayers, that the Lord would supply what is wanting in your confession and ours, which He has condescended to confer on us. Greet all who abide with you. We bid you, dearest brother, ever heartily farewell in God. I Felix wrote this; I Jader subscribed it; I Polianus read it. I greet my lord Eutychianus.

EPISTLE LXXX.[5]

CYPRIAN TO SERGIUS, ROGATIANUS, AND THE OTHER CONFESSORS IN PRISON.

ARGUMENT. — HE CONSOLES ROGATIANUS AND HIS COLLEAGUES, THE CONFESSORS IN PRISON, AND GIVES THEM COURAGE BY THE EXAMPLE OF THE MARTYRS ROGATIANUS THE ELDER AND FELICISSIMUS. THE LETTER ITSELF INDICATES THAT IT WAS WRITTEN IN EXILE.

1. Cyprian to Sergius and Rogatianus, and the rest of the confessors in the Lord, everlasting health. I salute you, dearest and most blessed brethren, myself also desiring to enjoy the sight of you, if the state in which I am placed would permit me to come to you. For what could happen to me more desirable and more joyful than to be now close to you, that you might embrace me with those hands, which, pure and innocent, and maintaining the faith of the Lord, have rejected the profane obedience? What more pleasant and sublime than now to kiss your lips, which with a glorious voice have confessed the Lord, to be looked upon even in presence by your eyes, which, despising the world, have become worthy[6] of looking upon God? But since opportunity is not afforded me to share in this joy, I send this letter in my stead to your ears and to your eyes, by which I congratulate and exhort you that you persevere strongly and steadily in the confession of the heavenly glory; and having entered on the way of the Lord's condescension, that you go on in the strength of the Spirit, to receive the crown, having the Lord as your protector and guide, who said, "Lo, I am with you alway, even unto the end of the world."[7] O blessed prison, which your presence has enlightened! O blessed prison, which sends the men of God to heaven! O darkness, more bright than the sun itself, and

---

[1] Or, "united."
[2] Or, "patiently bear."
[3] [This always means in prayers and at the Lord's Supper, in the common intercessions. Scudamore, *Not. Euch.*, p. 327.]
[4] Oxford ed.: Ep. lxxix. A.D. 257.

[5] Oxford ed.: Ep. vi. A.D. 257; possibly A.D. 250.
[6] [Luke xx. 35, xxi. 36; 1 Thess. ii. 12. Such expressions in our author teach no worthiness apart from the merits of Christ.]
[7] Matt. xxviii. 20.

clearer than the light of this world, where now are placed temples of God, and your members are to be sanctified by divine confessions !

2. Nor let anything now be revolved in your hearts and minds besides the divine precepts and heavenly commands, with which the Holy Spirit has ever animated you to the endurance of suffering. Let no one think of death, but of immortality ; nor of temporary punishment, but of eternal glory ; since it is written, " Precious in the sight of the Lord is the death of His saints ; " [1] and again, " A broken spirit is a sacrifice to God : a contrite and humble heart God doth not despise." [2] And again, where the sacred Scripture speaks of the tortures which consecrate God's martyrs, and sanctify them in the very trial of suffering : " And if they have suffered torments in the sight of men, yet is their hope full of immortality ; and having been a little chastised, they shall be greatly rewarded : for God proved them, and found them worthy of Himself. As gold in the furnace hath He tried them, and received them as a sacrifice of a burnt-offering, and in due time regard shall be had unto them. The righteous shall shine, and shall run to and fro like sparks among the stubble. They shall judge the nations, and have dominion over the people ; and their Lord shall reign for ever." [3] When, therefore, you reflect that you shall judge and reign with Christ the Lord, you must needs exult and tread under foot present sufferings, in the joy of what is to come ; knowing that from the beginning of the world it has been so appointed that righteousness should suffer there in the conflict of the world, since in the beginning, even at the first, the righteous Abel was slain, and thereafter all righteous men, and prophets, and apostles who were sent. To all of whom the Lord also in Himself has appointed an example, teaching that none shall attain to His kingdom but those who have followed Him in His own way, saying, " He that loveth his life in this world shall lose it ; and he that hateth his life in this world shall keep it unto life eternal." [4] And again : " Fear not them which kill the body, but are not able to kill the soul : but rather fear Him who is able to destroy both soul and body in hell." [5] Paul also exhorts us that we who desire to attain to the Lord's promises ought to imitate the Lord in all things. " We are," says he, " the sons of God : but if sons, then heirs ; heirs of God, and joint-heirs with Christ ; if so be that we suffer with Him, that we may also be glorified together." [6] Moreover, he added the comparison of the present time and of the future glory, saying, " The sufferings of this present time are not worthy to be compared with the coming glory which shall be revealed in us." [7] Of which brightness, when we consider the glory, it behoves us to bear all afflictions and persecutions ; because, although many are the afflictions of the righteous, yet those are delivered from them all who trust in God.

3. Blessed women also, who are established with you in the same glory of confession, who, maintaining the Lord's faith, and braver than their sex, not only themselves are near to the crown of glory, but have afforded an example to other women by their constancy ! And lest anything should be wanting to the glory of your number, that each sex and every age also might be with you in honour, the divine condescension has also associated with you boys [8] in a glorious confession ; representing to us something of the same kind as once did Ananias, Azarias, and Misael, the illustrious youths to whom, when shut up in the furnace, the fires gave way, and the flames gave refreshment, the Lord being present with them, and proving that against His confessors and martyrs the heat of hell could have no power, but that they who trusted in God should always continue unhurt and safe in all dangers. And I beg you to consider more carefully, in accordance with your religion, what must have been the faith in these youths which could deserve such full acknowledgment from the Lord. For, prepared for every fate, as we ought all to be, they say to the king, " O king Nebuchadnezzar, we are not careful to answer thee in this matter ; for our God whom we serve is able to deliver us from the burning fiery furnace ; and He will deliver us out of thine hand, O king ! But if not, be it known unto thee, O king, that we will not serve thy gods, nor worship the golden image which thou hast set up." [9] Although they believed, and, in accordance with their faith, knew that they might even be delivered from their present punishment, they still would not boast of this, nor claim it for themselves, saying, " But if not." Lest the virtue of their confession should be less without the testimony of their suffering, they added that God could do all things ; but yet they would not trust in this, so as to wish to be delivered at the moment ; but they thought on that glory of eternal liberty and security.

4. And you also, retaining this faith, and meditating day and night, with your whole heart prepared for God, think of the future only, with contempt for the present, that you may be able to come to the fruit of the eternal kingdom, and

---

[1] Ps. cxvi. 15.
[2] Ps. li. 19.
[3] Wisd. iii. 4–8.
[4] John xii. 25.
[5] Matt. x. 28.
[6] Rom. viii. 16, 17.

---

[7] Rom. viii. 18.
[8] [See p. 404, note 6, *supra*.]
[9] Dan. iii. 16–18.

to the embrace and kiss, and the sight of the Lord, that you may follow in all things Rogatianus the presbyter, the glorious old man who, to the glory of our time, makes a way for you by his religious courage and divine condescension, who, with Felicissimus our brother, ever quiet and temperate, receiving the attack of a ferocious people, first prepared for you a dwelling in the prison, and, marking out the way[1] for you in some measure, now also goes before you. That this may be consummated in you, we beseech the Lord in constant prayers, that from beginnings going on to the highest results, He may cause those whom He has made to confess, also to be crowned. I bid you, dearest and most beloved brethren, ever heartily farewell in the Lord; and may you attain to the crown of heavenly glory. Victor the deacon, and those who are with me, greet you.

EPISTLE LXXXI.[2]

TO SUCCESSUS ON THE TIDINGS BROUGHT FROM ROME, TELLING OF THE PERSECUTION.

ARGUMENT. — CYPRIAN TELLS THE BISHOP SUCCESSUS, THAT IN A SEVERE PERSECUTION THAT HAD BEEN DECREED BY THE EMPEROR VALERIAN[3] XISTUS THE BISHOP HAD SUFFERED AT ROME ON THE EIGHTH OF THE IDES OF AUGUST; AND HE BEGS HIM TO INTIMATE THE SAME TO THE REST OF HIS COLLEAGUES, THAT EACH ONE MIGHT ANIMATE HIS OWN FLOCK TO MARTYRDOM.

1. Cyprian to his brother Successus, greeting. The reason why I could not write to you immediately, dearest brother, was that all the clergy, being placed in the very heat of the contest, were unable in any way to depart hence, all of them being prepared in accordance with the devotion of their mind for divine and heavenly glory. But know that those have come whom I had sent to the City[4] for this purpose, that they might find out and bring back to us the truth, in whatever manner it had been decreed respecting us. For many various and uncertain things are current in men's opinions. But the truth concerning them is as follows, that Valerian had sent a rescript to the Senate, to the effect that bishops and presbyters and deacons should immediately be punished; but that senators, and men of importance, and Roman knights,[5] should lose their dignity, and moreover be deprived of their property; and if, when their means were taken away, they should persist in being Christians, then they should also lose their heads; but that matrons should be deprived of their property, and sent into banishment. Moreover, people of Cæsar's household, whoever of them had either confessed before, or should now confess, should have their property confiscated, and should be sent in chains by assignment to Cæsar's estates. The Emperor Valerian also added to this address a copy of the letters which he sent to the presidents of the provinces concerning us; which letters we are daily hoping will come, waiting according to the strength of our faith for the endurance of suffering, and expecting from the help and mercy of the Lord the crown of eternal life. But know that Xistus was martyred in the cemetery on the eighth day of the Ides of August, and with him four deacons.[6] Moreover, the prefects in the City[7] are daily urging on this persecution; so that, if any are presented to them, they are martyred, and their property claimed by the treasury.

2. I beg that these things may be made known by your means to the rest of our colleagues, that everywhere, by their exhortation, the brotherhood may be strengthened and prepared for the spiritual conflict, that every one of us may think less of death than of immortality; and, dedicated to the Lord, with full faith and entire courage, may rejoice rather than fear in this confession, wherein they know that the soldiers of God and Christ are not slain, but crowned. I bid you, dearest brother, ever heartily farewell in the Lord.[8]

EPISTLE LXXXII.[9]

TO THE CLERGY AND PEOPLE CONCERNING HIS RETIREMENT, A LITTLE BEFORE HIS MARTYRDOM.

ARGUMENT. — WHEN, NEAR THE END OF HIS LIFE, CYPRIAN, ON RETURNING TO HIS GARDENS, WAS TOLD THAT MESSENGERS WERE SENT TO TAKE HIM FOR PUNISHMENT TO UTICA, HE WITHDREW. AND LEST IT SHOULD BE THOUGHT THAT HE HAD DONE SO FROM FEAR OF DEATH, HE GIVES THE REASON IN THIS LETTER, VIZ., THAT HE MIGHT UNDERGO HIS MARTYRDOM NOWHERE ELSE THAN AT CARTHAGE, IN THE SIGHT OF HIS OWN PEOPLE. A.D. 258.

1. Cyprian to the presbyters and deacons, and all the people, greeting. When it had been told to us, dearest brethren, that the gaolers[10] had been sent to bring me to Utica, and I had

---

[1] " Metator."
[2] Oxford ed.: Ep. lxxx. As Cyprian suffered shortly after, in the month of September, there is no doubt but that this letter was written near the close of his life. A.D. 258.
[3] Doubtless with Gallienus.
[4] [Of Rome.] [5] [Elucidation XX.]

[6] Or, " and with him Quartus."
[7] [The modern name, *Istamboul* (εἰς τὴν πόλιν), grows out of like usage in the East. And, as Constantinople was " New Rome," this illustrates Irenæus and his *convenire*, vol i. p. 460.]
[8] [The baptismal question went by default, and was *practically* given up by the African Church, amid greater issues. It has never been dogmatically settled by the Church Catholic: and Roman *usage* is evasive (in spite of its own *anathemas*); for it baptizes again, *sub conditionel.* See useful note, Oxford ed. p. 244.]
[9] Oxford ed.: Ep. lxxxi. [Cyprian's contest with Stephen is practically valueless as to the point at issue between them (see *supra*, p. 396), but it throws a flood of light on the questions raised by papal pretensions. It also illuminates the anti-Nicene doctrine of unity.]
[10] Or, " commissaries."

been persuaded by the counsel of those dearest to me to withdraw for a time from my gardens, as a just reason was afforded I consented. For the reason that it is fit for a bishop, in that city in which he presides over the Church of the Lord, there to confess the Lord, and that the whole people should be glorified by the confession of their prelate in their presence. For whatever, in that moment of confession, the confessor-bishop speaks, he speaks in the mouth of all, by inspiration of God.[1] But the honour of our Church, glorious as it is, will be mutilated if I, a bishop placed over another church, receiving my sentence or my confession at Utica, should go thence as a martyr to the Lord, when indeed, both for my own sake and yours, I pray with continual supplications, and with all my desires entreat, that I may confess among you, and there suffer, and thence depart to the Lord even as I ought. Therefore here in a hidden retreat I await the arrival of the proconsul returning to Carthage, that I may hear from him what the emperors have commanded upon the

subject of Christian laymen and bishops, and may say what the Lord will wish to be said at that hour.

2. But do you, dearest brethren, according to the discipline which you have ever received from me out of the Lord's commands, and according to what you have so very often learnt from my discourse, keep peace and tranquillity ; nor let any of you stir up any tumult for the brethren, or voluntarily offer himself to the Gentiles. For when apprehended and delivered up, he ought to speak, inasmuch as the Lord abiding in us speaks in that hour, who willed that we should rather confess than profess. But for the rest, what it is fitting that we should observe before the proconsul passes sentence on me for the confession of the name of God, we will with the instruction of the Lord arrange in common.[2] May our Lord make you, dearest brethren, to remain safe in His Church, and condescend to keep you. So be it through His mercy.

---

[1] [Matt. x. 19. There is something sublime in the martyr's reliance upon this word of Jesus See sec. 2, *infra*, and Elucidation XXII.]

[2] [Recur to the passion of this holy martyr as related by Pontius, his deacon, p. 390. Stephen had broken communion with him (see p. 390 note) and the African provinces, which had no effect upon his Catholic *status*. (See letter of Firmillian, p. 391 note.) But, *on the Roman theory*, this glorious martyr died in schism. He is, nevertheless, a canonized saint in the Roman Calendar. Elucidation XXII.]

ELUCIDATIONS.

I.

(The presbyterate and the priesthood, p. 268.)

HERE is an instance of a usage just becoming common to the East and West, — to give the name of *priesthood* to the chief ministry as distinguished from the presbyterate. So in Chrysostom *passim*, but notably in his treatise περὶ ἱερωσύνης. The scriptural warrant for this usage is derived, dialectically, from the universal priesthood of Christians (1 Pet. ii. 5), from the Old-Testament prophecies of the Christian ministry (Isa. lxvi. 21), and from the culmination of the *sacerdotium* in the chief ministry of St. Paul. Over and against the Mosaic priesthood he is supposed to assert his own priestly *charisma* in the Epistle to the Romans,[1] where he says, " I have therefore my glorying in Christ Jesus " (i.e., the Great High Priest), " in things pertaining to God ; " that is (according to the Epistle to the Hebrews, v. 1), " as a high priest taken from among men, *in things pertaining to God*, that he may offer both gifts and sacrifices for sins." He asserts himself, therefore, as a better priest than those of the Law, " because of the grace that was given me of God, that I should be a minister of Christ Jesus unto the Gentiles, ministering *in sacrifice*[2] the Gospel of God." He then (according to this theory) adopts the language and the idea of Malachi, and adds, " that the oblation of the Gentiles might be acceptable," etc. ; i.e., the pure *ninchah*, or oblation of bread and wine, commemorative of the one " and only propitiatory sacrifice of Calvary."

These ideas run through all the primitive liturgies,[3] which we are soon to reach in this series. It is no part of my plan to vindicate them, but only to state them. It will be felt by many that these

---

[1] Cap. xv. 15, 16, compared with Mal. i. 11.   [2] Revised Version, margin.   Rather, " ministering hierurgically."

[3] For which, see vol. vii., this series.

were at least exaggerated views of the apostle's ministry, — of the principle underlying his phrase, εἰς τὸ εἶναί με λειτουργὸν . . . ἱερουργοῦντα τὸ εὐαγγέλιον; but let nobody *read into* these primitive expressions concerning a commemoration of the *one only propitiatory* sacrifice "once offered," the monstrous doctrine of the Council of Trent, which, reduced to its mildest form,[1] is as follows : "The sacrifice of the Mass is, and ought to be considered, *one and the same sacrifice with that of the Cross* . . . which being the case, *it must be taught*, without any hesitation, that (as the holy Council of Trent hath moreover explained) the sacred and holy sacrifice of the Mass is not only a sacrifice of praise and eucharist, or a mere commemoration of the sacrifice effected on the Cross, but also truly *a propitiatory sacrifice, by which God is appeased, and rendered propitious to us.*" That such was not the doctrine of the Latin churches, even in the ninth century, sufficiently appears from the treatise of Ratramn ; but it is not less apparent from the ancient liturgies themselves, and even from many primitive features which glitter like gold-dust amid the dross of the Roman missal itself.

II.

(To do nothing on my own private opinion, p. 283.)

Note this golden principle which runs through all the epistles and treatises of our large-minded and free-spirited author, "A primordio episcopatus mei statuerim nihil, sine consilio vestro, *et sine consensu plebis meæ* privata sententia gerere." When, in the midst of persecution, he could not convoke his council, he apologizes, as will appear hereafter,[2] even for taking measures requisite to the emergency without such counsel. Such was *his duty* according to the primitive discipline, no doubt ; but our author knew well that a relaxing of discipline in exceptional circumstances is the fruitful source of corruption. He is jealous against himself : —

> " 'Twill be recorded for a precedent ;
> And many an error, by the same example
> Will rush into the *Church*."

It is instructive to find the views of Baxter harmonizing with those of Cyprian. He speaks for himself and his brethren as not opposed to episcopacy, but only to " the engrossing (by prelates) of *the sole power* of ordination and jurisdiction . . . *excluding wholly the pastors* of particular churches *from all share in it*." This is a sound Cyprianic remonstrance ;[3] but Cyprian always includes the *plebs* as well as the " pastors." In short, if Ignatius, his Gamaliel, teaches primarily, " Do nothing without the bishop," he not less reiterates his own maxim, " Let bishops do nothing without the presbytery and the people."

Here it must be noted, however, that the primitive Fathers never speak of *the episcopate* as a development of *the presbyterate*, as do the Middle-Age writers and the schoolmen. It was the policy of these to write down the bishops to mere presbyters, for the purpose of exalting the papacy, which they made the only episcopate and the universal apostolate. The Universal Bishop might, then, appoint presbyters to be *his local vicars*, and to bear a *titular* episcopate, as such, — the name of an *office*, and not an *order*. The episcopate was no longer, as with Ignatius and Cyprian, the apostolic office from which the presbyterate and diaconate were *precipitated*, but, rather, an ecclesiastical *sublimate* of the presbyterate. By this theory no bishop in the Latin communion can deal with the Bishop of Rome as Cyprian did, — on terms of equality, and as a co-bishop or colleague in a common episcopate. Such is the school doctrine : and the Council of Trent made

---

[1] See the *Trent Catechism*, cap. iv. quæstt. 73, 75.

[2] Epistle xxiii. and Elucidation III.

[3] *Proposals, etc., by the Reverend Ministers of the Presbyterian Persuasion*, London, 1661. An extract may be found in Leighton's *Works*, p. 637, Edinburgh, 1840.

it dogma, abolishing the *order* of bishops as such, and defining that there are only three Holy Orders; viz., presbyters, deacons, and sub-deacons.[1] The order of bishops is thus reduced to a merely ecclesiastical order in "the hierarchy," a vicariate of the papacy.

III.

(According to the Lord's discipline, p. 292.)

Here he lays down, as a divine constitution for the Church, the principle exemplified in the Acts of the Apostles (cap. xv. 4–6, 22, 23). Compare Epistle xiv., where he speaks of some presbyters and deacons as "too little mindful of discipline," and of his instructions to the laity to maintain the same. Observe his language in the exceptional case referred to in the previous elucidation. "In ordinations of the clergy, beloved brethren" (he writes to "presbyters, deacons, *and the whole people*"), "we usually consult you beforehand, and weigh (the matter) with *the general advice*."

It is surprising that the learned and pious Dr. Pusey, always influenced by his essential Gallicanism, and too little devoted to the *primitive* discipline, hastily committed himself, in his work on *The Councils of the Church*, to an erroneous statement of the historic facts[2] as to the participation of the laity in synods. In reply, that American Cyprian, Whittingham of Maryland, called the Doctor's attention to an example he had evidently overlooked, in words worthy of note from so profound a patristic scholar. He says, "It occurred in the middle of the period to which Dr. Pusey's book is limited, and, *as nearly as can be known*, during the episcopate of Cyprian." He adds, "I doubt whether there is another equally particular relation of the circumstances of an episcopal election within the first four centuries." It is given in the life of Gregory Thaumaturgus, by his namesake Gregory of Nyssa.[3] The whole of Bishop Whittingham's searching reviewal[4] of Dr. Pusey's positions is an honour to American scholarship, and ought to be consulted by the student of primitive antiquity.

IV.

(Common consultation, p. 294.)

Again, we have our author's testimony to the free spirit of primitive councils, in which I exult as a Christian believer, and as a loyal supporter of constitutional liberty, i.e., freedom regulated by law. Concerning which, note the saying of Franklin, note 9, vol. i. p. 552, of this series. To primitive discipline and to these free councils of the Cyprianic age the world is indebted for all its free constitutions; and when narrow-minded men presume to assert the contrary, because of mediæval feudalism in the West, let them be reminded that not till the Church's constitutions were superseded by the forged Decretals, was the Western Church so deprived of its freedom as to be made the tool of despotism in violating the liberty of Christians. The last council of the whole West that retained anything of the primitive spirit was that of Frankfort, A.D. 794: but its spirit survived, and not infrequently asserted itself in "the Gallican maxims," so called; while in England it was never smothered, but always survived in the parliaments until the usurpations of the papacy were abolished in the Church and realm. This was done by a *practical re-assertion of Cyprianic principles*. It is well to remind such reckless critics as Draper and Lecky that the Christian Church is responsible only for her own Catholic legislation; not at all for what has been done under the fraudulent pretexts of the Decretals, in defiance of her whole system, which is embodied in the Ante-Nicene Fathers and the Nicene Constitutions.

---

[1] *Catechism of the Council of Trent*, cap. vii. quæst. 12.
[2] See the said work, p. 41.
[3] Bishop Whittingham quotes the edition of Gerard Vossius, pp. 286–291.
[4] *Church Review*, vol. xi. 1859, pp. 88–127.

V.

(Counsel and judgment of all. . . . a common cause, p. 296.)

The language here is indicative of the whole spirit of Catholic canons, to which that of the Latin canonists affords such a contrast after the Isidorian forgeries had been made, by Nicholas, the system of the West. Note the words which our author addresses to his clergy, *omni plebe adstante :* " Quæ res cum omnium nostrum consilium et sententiam spectet, præjudicare ego, et soli mihi rem communem vindicare, non audeo." In other words, " What concerns all, ought by all to be considered and decided." [1]

The fifteenth chapter of Bishop Wordsworth's *History of the Church* (vol. i.) deals with the ante-Nicene councils, and expounds their spirit and organization in a very able and concise manner.

VI.

(Let us pray for the lapsed, p. 310.)

The passage that follows seems to be a quotation from the common prayers then in use. Out of these " bidding prayers " grew the ancient litanies ; the deacon dictating the suffrage, and the people responding with the petition, " Lord, have mercy upon them," or the like.

By arranging the petitions thus, —

$$\left.\begin{array}{l} \text{Pro lapsis,} \\ \text{Pro stantibus,} \end{array}\right\} \text{OREMUS,} \left\{\begin{array}{l} \text{ut erigantur ;} \\ \text{ut non tententur, etc.,} \end{array}\right.$$

we shall see how such prayers were formulated, and how the people, by responding *Amen* to each suffrage, gave their common supplications accordingly. These suffrages might be enlarged indefinitely, as divers subjects for prayer were presented ; and so there was a mingling of what has been called " free prayer " with the liturgical system, without confusion or lack of harmony.

VII.

(The honour of our colleague, p. 319.)

Thus Cyprian speaks of the Bishop of Rome, whose due ordination and rightful jurisdiction Novatian was impugning. The absurdity of calling this heretic Novatian an anti-pope involves a great confusion of ideas, however. For, as Cornelius was no more a pope than Cyprian (to both of whom the title was freely conceded in its primitive sense [2]), how can it be proper to give Novatian a name which implies a mediæval sense, and leads the student to infer that his claim was not merely to the See of Rome,[3] but to a universal bishopric over all Christians? It is needless to say, that, had the churches so understood the case, the whole Christian world would have been convulsed by a matter which, in point of fact, was soon settled by Cyprian's enforcement of the canons. See subsequent letters.

VIII.

(Novatian, pp. 319, 324.)

The similarity of the names of Novatus and Novatian, and their complicity in a common schism, led to great confusions among their contemporaries, which have not been wholly cleared

---

[1] Consult Epistles xxv. (sec. 6, p. 304) and xxx. (sec. 5, p. 310), *supra*. It is interesting to note how the primitive clergy of Rome recognise this free principle, with no suspicion that their own *cathedra* is not only their sufficient resource, but the oracle of God to all mankind.

[2] See Elucidation III. p. 154, *supra*.

[3] Cyprian facetiously remarks (see Ep. xlviii. p. 325) that Novatus reserved his *greater* crimes for the *greater* city; "since Rome, from her magnitude, ought to take precedence of Carthage."

even to this day. See Lardner's elaborate argument against the latter name as a mere blunder. He calls Novatian also *Novatus*, and gives his forcible reasons.

Observe that "ordination" is the term here used for conferring the order of bishops on a presbyter. So always anciently, though now it is customary to speak only of the "consecration" of a bishop. This is the inferior term; for the bishop is supposed to be "consecrated" to his specialty or diocese, while he is raised by "ordination" to the order in which all bishops are equal. Mirabeau says, "Words are things." I quote from a political source the following remarks of a shrewd observer of Mirabeau's principle. Speaking of American phraseology in constitutional affairs, he says, "It is true that *this is a mere matter of words or phrases*, but words and phrases misused have a very potent influence for confusing the minds of men as to real things. In politics, *as in theology*, it is best to stick to the text, and to avoid supposedly equivalent phrases. Such phrases often contain within them the seeds of heresy and schism." Now, it was the policy of the schoolmen to confuse terms, in order to break down the Cyprianic theory; and they denied that bishops were ordained to a "Holy Order." Theirs was only a name of *office;* and their *order* was only an *ecclesiastical* order, as much so as "sacristans." [1] This to, keep them from Cyprian's claim of equality with the Bishop of Rome. But this was debatable *school doctrine* only, till the Council of Trent. Since that, it has been dogma in the Roman communion. Contrast, therefore, the Greek and (modern) Roman dogmas : —

1. *Greek.*[2] "The three orders, by divine institution, are, (1) the episcopate, (2) the priest-hood, (3) the diaconate."

2. *Roman.*[3] "According *to the uniform tradition*[4] of the Catholic Church, the number of these orders is *seven;* and they are called (1) porter, (2) reader, (3) exorcist, (4) acolyte, (5) sub-deacon, (6) deacon, (7) priest." The "bishop," then, is only a *priest*, who acts as vicar for the one "Universal Bishop" at Rome. For the Greek theory, note Cyprian *passim*.

IX.

(Cornelius, our colleague, p. 328.)

Observe the state of the case. "Lest perchance *the number of bishops* in Africa should seem unsatisfactory," etc., he wrote to his *colleague* in Rome, who gathered a council also, "with very many bishops." Imagine such language, and such action in any case, between the French metropolitan and the present Bishop of Rome! The contrast illustrates the absolute nonentity, in the Cyprianic age, of any conception of such relations as now exist between Rome and her vassal episcopate. "Prostrate at the feet of your Holiness," etc.: the noblest bishops and the boldest at the Vatican Council thus signed their feeble and abject remonstrances. Among their names are Schwarzenberg, Furstenberg, and even Strossmayer.[5]

X.

(One episcopate diffused, p. 333.)

Here is the principle expounded in the *Treatise on Unity*. He states it tersely as follows : —

"Episcopatus unus, episcoporum multorum concordi numerositate diffusus."

And he then states in few words his theory of the "compact unity of the Catholic Church," in which the existence of the "provinces" is recognised, and an "ecclesiastical structure;" but not a hint of what must have been laid down as the test and primal law of truth and unity, had

---

[1] Lombard., *Sentences*, p. 394, ed. Migne. Compare Aquinas. [3] *Catechism of the Council of Trent*, cap. vii. quæst. 2.
[2] Macarius, *Théologie Orthodoxe*, vol. iii. p. 244. [4] A monstrous statement. See Ignatius *passim*.
[5] *L'Union Chrétienne*, p. 69, 1870.

any infallible supremacy been imagined to exist. In that case, no need of a *treatise*, no need of words : he would have said nothing of "co-bishops," but simply of communion with the Bishop of Rome.

XI.

(Fabian and Donatus, also our predecessors, p. 342.)

Here the Paris editors of A.D. 1574 take pains to remind us that Cyprian means "Fabian, *your* predecessor, and Donatus, *mine*." Very well. But the implication is that "our predecessors" were persons of the same office and dignity. Let us suppose the present Bishop of *Alger* writing to Leo XIII. in the same manner, as follows : " Bishop Strossmayer was severely remarked upon by Pius and Martial, *our predecessors*, in their letters." Would this be tolerated? The editor of this series answered the invitation of Pius IX. to his council in 1869, after the manner of a contemporary of Cyprian,[1] in order to make the contrast between the third century and the nineteenth palpable to the venerable pontiff and his adviser Antonelli. It was resented with animosity by the Ultramontane journals, on the ground that nobody on earth should address the pontiff as bishop to bishop, or as man to man.

XII.

(To whom perfidy could have no access, p. 344.)

When we put a man in mind of his self-respect, we imply that he is in peril of forgetting the quality we impute to him. " You are a gentleman, and, of course, cannot deceive me : " such language is not complimentary, but involves a gentle reproof. So here our author has to remind the Roman clergy of what is due to themselves if they would keep up the credit assigned to them by St. Paul, but from which, as the apostle himself warned· them, they were in danger of falling. Cyprian goes on to remind them of what they owe to Carthage and its synods, and warns them against " abandoned men " seeking to discredit the African bishops.[2] The Roman clergy had already confessed their sense of what was due to Carthage,[3] and in another epistle,[4] doubtless remembering Zephyrinus and Callistus, they confess their degeneracy, and the ignominy of their actual position as compared with that which the apostle had praised. The passage is often quoted as if it read, "to whom *corrupt faith* can have no access : " but the word is *perfidia*, and has reference, not to faith, but morals ; and, to avoid ambiguity, I have put the word " perfidy " into the translation, where the Edinburgh translator has " faithlessness."

Here note (p. 346, note 2) the reference to St. Paul's term ($\kappa \alpha \tau \alpha \tau o \mu \dot{\eta}$), the *concision*, where the Oxford note (p. 170, Oxford trans.) is to the point. Only let it be more clearly stated, that St. Paul calls the Judaizing schismatics the $\kappa \alpha \tau \alpha \tau o \mu \dot{\eta}$; meaning that, instead of the circumcised body, they are but the *particula præputii* cut off and cast away. Our author uses it here with great effect, therefore. In another place [5] St. Paul carries his scornful anathema farther, with a witty reference to a heathen example ; on which see Canon Farrar in his *St. Paul*, cap. xxii. (Agdistis) p. 235, ed. New York. The " sport with children," in the Canon's note (p. 227), seems to me illustrated by Ex. iv. 24–26. *Trifling* with children, i.e., their salvation.

---

[1] *A Letter to Pius the Ninth, Bishop of Rome*, etc., published by Parker, London, 1870. It also appeared in most of the languages of Europe, and was circulated by the Greeks in their own tongue.

[2] Same epistle and section, farther on. It seems needless to say that these Punic " Africans " were Asiatics, in fact.

[3] Ep. xxix. p. 308, *supra*.

[4] Ep. xxx. p. 309, *supra*.

[5] Gal. v. 12 in the Greek.

XIII.

(I both warn and ask you, p. 346 at note 4.)

The original is, "*admoneo* et peto;" the language of an equal, but yet of an older brother in the episcopate. Here some other points are worthy to be noted in this important letter, and they shall be briefly taken *in serie.*

1. We here encounter the tangled knot of the *triple* schisms, in which the *unhappy* Felicissimus, with Novatus and Novatian, has long presented a scandal to criticism. Thus, our author speaks of Felicissimus as "schismatis et disidii *auctor;*" and difficulties have been raised about the meaning of the text, because Novatus would rather seem entitled to that "bad eminence." I think all difficulty disappears if we drop the idea that a particular schism is here referred to, and understand merely that this bad man was " the *beginner* of schism and dissension," out of which the three specific schisms had cropped. Go back to Epistles xxxvii. (p. 315) and xxxviii. (p. 316) and xxxix. (p. 319) for his antecedents. The "faction of Felicissimus" (sec. 2), and of "five presbyters" with him (sec. 3), is here sufficiently evident to illustrate the point now under consideration. In Epistle xlviii. (p. 325) we find Novatus, it is true, accused as "the first sower of discord and sedition," but in another sense, because Felicissimus was a mere layman. Novatus took him up, and had him unlawfully ordained a deacon; and now Felicissimus becomes a mere appendage, and Novatus becomes formidable. Sailing to Italy, and coming to Rome just in time to inspire the discontent of Novatian with a wicked ambition, he next proceeds to engineer his schismatical ordination to the bishopric of Rome by the hands of three bishops, acting uncanonically and sinfully. So now Novatian becomes the chief character as rival to Cornelius, and pretender to his See; while Novatus returns to Africa to foment new disturbances, but is justly excommunicated, and disappears from history.

2. In this epistle it would seem that Cornelius had vacillated weakly, and was in peril of acting uncanonically. Cyprian gently admonishes him (sec. 2) : "I was considerably surprised," etc.; also (sec. 6), "I speak to you as being *provoked,* as *grieving,* as constrained," etc.

3. Here Fortunatus appears on the scene, to embroil the matter yet more seriously; of whom (sec. 9) enough appears in this letter.

4. Fortunatus, with his wicked allies, sails to Rome (sec. 11) as the nearest apostolic See, hence spoken of (sec. 14) as the chief church (i.e., of the West) and the *matrix* of unity (i.e., to the daughter churches of Africa). Let us read into the pages of Cyprian no Decretalist ideas when he modestly acknowledges the comparative inferiority of his place. Let us find his meaning in this very letter, and others, in which his words contradict all ideas of any official inferiority. Take also the ideas of the epoch for illustration. Recur to Cyprian's master expounding the relations of the primitive churches, one to another, in his *Prescription.* Tertullian points out a root-principle in all apostolic Sees;[1] and then, after elaborate discussion, he thus applies it practically : —

"Run over the apostolic *churches,* in which the very thrones of the apostles," etc. "Achaia, e.g., is proximate to you; then there is Corinth. If you are near Macedonia, there is Philippi. . . . Crossing to Asia, you get Ephesus. . . . Close to Italy you have Rome, *from which comes to us (in Africa) our authority,*" etc. I abridge, but do not alter the sense.[2] Here, then, we find what Cyprian was writing about. The schismatics, on this principle, had rushed to the nearest apostolic See, viz., that of the Imperial City. Cyprian recognises his claims on its bishop; Rome being the source of his own ordination, and the *matrix* of the Carthaginian church. This animates him with a loving humility. But what next? Having expressed all this, he proceeds, as an equal but an elder brother, to assert his rights, and to *admonish* Cornelius that he, too, must obey the ecclesiastical discipline. Nobody, even among the Greeks, would

---

[1] Cap. xx. p. 252, note 7, etc. See vol. iii., this series.   [2] Vol. iii. p. 260, cap. xxxvi. and note 13.

object to such a Roman primacy, even at this day ; but "to give place *by subjection*, even for an hour," is what St. Cyprian would not endure any more than St. Paul.[1] "Supremacy" is another thing.

5. The grounds of his conduct in this and other acts are unfolded in his *Treatise on Unity*. But here is the place to show what Cyprian had in his mind as the ἀρχαῖα ἔθη. A canon[2] of the African church, after providing for local appeals, reads as follows : " Let them not appeal to *tribunals beyond the seas*, but to the primates of their own provinces, or to a general council, as hath been *often ordained* with respect to bishops. But whoso shall persevere in appealing to tribunals beyond seas, let them be received to communion by no one in Africa." And here note that the *plural* is used, illustrating the above quotation from Tertullian. All the apostolic Sees are treated alike, as "tribunals beyond seas." Note, also, that if any one of these tribunals should receive and hear the appellant, its decisions were of no force in Africa.

6. And, still further, let it be noted that the greatness of Rome, *as the capital*, was its only ground, even to a *canonical primacy* afterwards conceded to it for the sake of order. The Council of Chalcedon (Fourth Œcumenical, A.D. 451) states the case, and sets the historical fact beyond dispute, as follows : "The Fathers rightly *granted the seniority* (ἀποδεδώκασι τὰ πρεσβεῖα), *because that city was the capital*, to the throne of the elder Rome, . . . and *equal precedency* (τὰ ἴσα πρεσβεῖα) to the most holy throne of New Rome (Constantinople) ; justly judging that the city which is dignified with the sovereignty and the senate, and enjoys *equal privileges* with the elder imperial Rome, should likewise be magnified with the other in ecclesiastical affairs, and rank second after that See." *Second* as to *order*, that is ; but *equal* as to this *presbeia*.

Cyprian's theory shows why they said nothing of its apostolic dignity ; viz., because in that respect all apostolic Sees were equal, and all older than Rome, and because all other churches in communion with these centres were *practically* apostolic, and each was a See of Peter. For, as Cyprian expounds it, there is but *one episcopate ;* and each bishop, locally, possesses the whole of it. It was given first to Peter to make this principle emphatic ; i.e., it is a gift held whole and entire by each holder. Then he gave *the same* to all the apostles, that each one of them might comprehend that what St. Peter had, he had : it was an undivided and indivisible authority. "Each particular church," says the Oxford translator, "being *the miniature of the whole*, each bishop the representative of Christ, the Chief Bishop ; so that, all bishops being, in *their several stations*, one and the same (as representing the Same), there was, as it were, *but one bishop*." Such was Cyprian's exposition of the ἀρχαῖα ἔθη : I am not so forgetful as to introduce anything of my own. But here it is to be noted that the theory of the Decretals was subversive of all this : there was but one, personally, the representative of Christ, His[3] Vicar ; and his See, *by divine warrant*, was supreme. Hence others, *called* bishops, were not such, as being equals with the Bishop of Rome in the episcopal order, for their "order" was only that of *presbyters ;* and they were *called* "bishops" only as vicars of the one Bishop at Rome, empowered to act *for him* in local stations, but having no real episcopate in themselves. Now, Calvin's memorable sentence was based on this difference between the primitive bishops and those of his day With his strong logic he argued : if, then, bishops are but shadows of a papacy which we have proved fabulous, bishops must be rejected as part of the papacy. But, he said, "Talem nobis hierarchiam si exhibeant, in qua sic emineant episcopi *ut Christo subesse non recusent*, et ab *illo, tanquam unico capite*, pendeant et ad ipsum referantur ; in qua, *sic inter se fraternam societatem colant ut non alio nodo*, quam ejus veritate sint colligati ; tum vero nullo non anathemate dignos fatear, si qui erunt, qui non eam reverenter, summaque obedientia, observent."

It would seem, therefore, that Calvin drew a correct distinction between the Cyprianic theory and that of the Decretists. "A Christo, *unico capite*, pendeant," touches the point of the Western schism, which altered this principle into "A pontifice Romano, unico capite," prorsus pendeant omnes præsules Catholici.

---

[1] Gal. ii. 5.   [2] This canon of the Council of Milevis (A.D. 402), at a much later date, maintains the ancient principle.
[3] Calvin, *De necessitate reformandæ ecclesiæ, Works*, vol. viii. p. 60. Amstelodami, 1667.

XIV.

(The bishop should be chosen in the presence of the people, p. 371.)

Concerning the election of bishops, and the part of the laity therein, enough has been already said to elucidate this important historical point.[1] But here is the place to elucidate Cyprian's relations to Ignatius, by pointing out *his* theory as to " bishops, presbyters, and deacons." The inquiry is, not whether his theory was right or wrong ; but the ante-Nicene Constitutions and Canons cannot be understood without a clear comprehension of it, and it is practically important in the coming collisions with the alien religion now lifting its head aggressively amongst us. To refute its pretensions, Cyprian and Hippolytus are sufficient if cleared from all *ambiguities* thrown back into their expressions from the• mediæval corruption of primitive words, idioms, and modes of thought.

As to presbyters and deacons, then, we must refer to pp. 306, 366, 370 ; sub-deacons are mentioned pp. 301 and 306, with *lectors* under " teaching-presbyters," as preparing for the clerical office. On p. 306 an *acolyte* is mentioned. Now, these readers, sub-deacons, and acolytes (ἀκόλουθος) are all of a class, — persons preparing for Holy Orders, and after a time known as in " ecclesiastical " or *minor* orders.[2] The *lectors* need not be explained. The *sub-deacons* are a class not heard of till this third century, even in the West. Cyprian and Cornelius are the first to mention them. In the East, sub-deacons and acolytes first appear in the fourth century ; they were sub-ministrants and attendants on the clergy, and doubtless had charge of the very trouble-some work of preparing the candidates for immersion, and the waters for that sacrament, besides cleansing the fonts, and superintending the changes of raiment made necessary. Their offices in time of divine service, attending upon the altar, taking the offerings, seating the congregation, watching the children, etc., may be supposed. Apart from the *names*, just such offices, like those of *sextons*, are required in all public worship. The Moravians have *acolyths*, to this day.

XV.

(Cornelius . . . a peaceable and righteous priest, etc., p. 371.)

Now observe his parting tribute in these words, " Cornelius, our colleague, a peaceable and righteous priest, and moreover honoured by the condescension of the Lord with martyrdom, has long ago decreed, *with us and with all the bishops* appointed throughout the whole world," etc. A *colleague*, sharing in the decrees of his *co-bishops* throughout the whole world, is the recognised position of this successor of St. Peter. And Cyprian, who firmly believes that St. Peter, as " a source and principle of unity," had the personal honour of being the first foundation-stone laid on the Corner-Stone Himself, sees nothing in that to make Cornelius the foundation ; nor did Cornelius himself. No, nor St. Peter either, who says (1 Pet. ii. 5) all Christians may become Peters by being laid on the Living Stone, Christ Jesus.

Thus we are prepared to read the *Treatise on Unity*. We may also concede to the bishops of Rome, even now, that as soon as they claim no more than Cornelius and St. Peter himself did, their *primacy* will no longer be a stumbling-block and a schism to the Christian universe.

In parting with Cornelius, it is useful to note that he represents his diocese in his day[3] as numbering " forty-six presbyters, seven deacons and the same number of sub-deacons, with forty-two acolytes and exorcists, readers and sacristans in all fifty-two." More than " fifteen hundred widows and sufferers " dependent on this comparatively small and poor church show the terrible ravages made by persecution.

---

[1] Elucidation III. p. 411, *supra*.   [2] Bingnam, *Antiquities*, book iii. capp. ii., iii.
[3] Eusebius, *H. E.*, book vi. cap. xliii.

XVI.

(Epistle lxxi. . . . To Stephen their brother, p. 378.)

We now reach a very different character from that of his predecessor; and in him we encounter the germinant spirit which, in long after-ages, was able to overcome the discipline of the Church.[1] At this time, and during the great synodical period, these personal caprices were made light of: the canons and constitutions of the Church were strong enough to check them; and such was the predominance of the Eastern mind, for many generations, that the ship of the Church was not thrown out of trim. Let us carefully note this historical point, however, and the spirit in which our great author exposes the elements of error.

XVII.

(In the name of, etc. Since Three are One, pp. 380, 382.)

Having elsewhere touched upon the quotation attributed to Tertullian,[2] I need not repeat what has been said of this once very painfully agitated matter. But, as to the quotations of the African Fathers generally, it ought to be understood that there was a *vetus Itala* before Jerome, — more than one, no doubt, — to which that Father was largely indebted for the text now called the Vulgate. Vercellone assured Dean Burgon that there was indeed one *established* Latin text,[3] an old Itala.

Scrivener[4] says candidly, "It is hard to believe that 1 John v. 7 was not cited by Cyprian;" and again, "The African writers Vigilius of Thapsus (at the end of the fifth century) and Fulgentius (*circa* 520) in two places expressly appeal to *the three heavenly Witnesses.*" So, too, Victor Vitensis, in the notable case of the African king of the Vandals. The admission of Tischendorf is also cited by Scrivener. Tischendorf says, "*Gravissimus est* Cyprianus (in *Tract. de Eccles. Unitate*), Dicit Dominus, Ego et Pater unum sumus (Joann. x. 30); et, iterum, de Patre, Filio, et Spiritu Sancto, scriptum est, *Et tres unum sunt.*" Tischendorf adds the testimony of this epistle to Jubaianus. And Scrivener decides that "it is surely safer and more candid to admit that Cyprian read it in his copies, than to resort to," etc., the usual explainings away. To this note of this same erudite scholar the reader may also turn for satisfaction as to the reasons against authenticity. But primarily, to meet questions as to versions used by Cyprian, let him consult the same invaluable work (p. 269) on the Old Latin before Jerome. I have added an important consideration in a note to the *Anonymous Treatise on Baptism*, which follows (*infra*), with other documents, in our Appendix.[5]

XVIII.

(Return to our Lord and Origin, p. 389.)

Here is an appeal to the ἀρχαῖα ἔθη, that explains other references to "the Root and Origin," which he here identifies with our Lord,[6] and "the *evangelical* and *apostolic* tradition." This was the understanding at Nicæa: "ut si in aliquo nutaverit et vacillaverit veritas, ad originem dominicam et evangelicam et apostolicam traditionem revertamur." Is not this the grand *catholicon* for the disorders of modern Christendom? "Nam consuetudo, *sine veritate*, vetustas

---

[1] Consult Cave, *Dissertation on the Ancient Church Government*, appended to his *Primitive Christianity*, p. 366.

[2] Vol. iii. p. 631.

[3] Burgon, *Letters from Rome*, p. 34. London, 1862.

[4] *Introduction to Criticism*, etc., p. 453, also 564. Compare the *Treatise on Unity*, sec. 6, p. 423, *infra*.

[5] Calling attention to evidence that verse 8 is a sort of *apodosis* implying the *protasis* of verse 7, as read in the Vulgate and English Received.

[6] P. 322, note 2.

erroris est," says Cyprian in this very Epistle.[1]   And, " If we return to the head and source of divine tradition, human error ceases."

XIX.

(Firmilianus to Cyprian, p. 390.)

The contest with Stephen, bishop of Rome, will require no great amount of annotation here, chiefly because the matter has no practical bearings, except as it incidentally proves what was the relation of Stephen to other bishops and to the Catholic Church.   In this letter (sec. 6) Firmilian accuses Stephen of " *daring to make* a departure from the peace and *unity of* the Catholic Church."   And (in sec. 16), further, he sets forth, for the Easterns, the same theory of unity which Cyprian had expounded for the West ; viz., the unity of the episcopate.   He interprets the parallel texts (Matt. xvi. 19 and John xx. 22, 23) of bestowal in the same manner.   His idea is, that, had the latter bestowal been the only one, the apostles might have felt that each had only a *share* in the same respectively ; while, as it stands, there is one episcopate only : in effect, only " one bishop ; " each apostle and every bishop, by " vicarious ordination," holding for his flock in his own See all that Christ gave to Peter himself, save only the personal privilege of a leader in opening the door to the Gentiles,[2] and in teaching the apostles the full meaning of the gift.   The point here is not whether this was the true meaning of our Lord : it is merely that such was the understanding of the Ante-Nicene Fathers.[3]

Further (sec. 17), he complains of Stephen for his *folly* in assuming that he had received some superior privileges as the successor of Peter ; also censures him for " betraying and deserting unity."   So (in sec. 25) he reflects on Stephen for " disagreeing with so many bishops throughout the world . . . with the Eastern churches and with the South."   He adds, " with such a man, can there be one spirit and one body ? "

Firmilian was of Cappadocia, and a disciple of Origen.   The interest of his letter turns upon its entire innocence of any conception that Stephen has a right to dictate ; and, while it shows a dangerous tendency in the latter personally to take airs upon himself as succeeding the primate of the apostolic college, it proves not less that the Church was aware of no ground for it, but held all bishops equally responsible for unity by communion with their brethren.   To make them thus responsible to him and his See had probably not even entered Stephen's head.   He was rash and capricious in his resort to measures by which every bishop felt bound to separate himself from complicity with open heretics, and he seems to have had local usage on his side. But how admirable the contrasted forbearance of Cyprian, whose views were equally strong, but who protested against all coercive measures against others.

XX.

(Clinics, p. 401.)

Cyprian's moderation is conspicuous in his views of clinic baptism ; for, though Novatian knew none other, he forbore to urge this irregularity against him.   Even the good Cornelius was not so forbearing.[4]   St. Cyprian seems to be the earliest apologist for sprinkling.   See Wall, *Reflections on Baptism of Infants* (*Wall's Works*), vol. iii. p. 219, for a refutation of Tertullian's supposed admission of " a little sprinkling."[5]   And see Beveridge on *Trine Immersion, Works,* vol. xii. p. 86 ; also *Canon L., Apostolical Canons.*

---

[1] See secs. 9 and 10.

[2] Acts xv. 7.

[3] See illustrations in Faber's *Difficulties of Romanism*, cap. iii. pp. 46–88, London, 1830.   This work is a succinct reply to Berington and Kirk lately reprinted in New York.   It refutes itself.   Compare vol. i. pp. ix. and x., with the *new dogmas*, vol. iii. pp. 443–460.

[4] See Eusebius, *H. E.*, vi. cap. lxiii.

[5] Tertullian, vol. iii. p. 661.

XXI.

(Senators and men of importance and Roman knights, p. 408.)

1 Cor. i. 26.   We have already seen tokens of the gradual enlightenment of the higher classes in the empire ; " the palace, senate, forum," are mentioned by Tertullian.[1]   The fiercer persecutions seem now to be stimulated by this very fact, and a fear lest Christianity should spread too freely among patricians must have prompted this decree.

XXII.

(The Lord . . . speaks in that hour, p. 409.)

The saying of Christ (Matt. x. 10, Mark xiii. 11), " It is not ye that speak, but the Holy Ghost," was literally accepted, and acted upon.   Is it marvellous that it inspired believing men to be martyrs, or that martyrs were so much venerated?   And ought not the same texts to be more faithfully accepted in explaining the inspiration of the Holy Scriptures?   Language could hardly be stronger : " *It is not ye that speak.*"   So we reach the close of this holy and heroic life of the great, the fervid, the intrepid, but, withal, the gentle and generous Cyprian.   And in these last words we see the spirit of the man cropping out in his proposal to " arrange in common " with the clergy and people what should be observed, as requisite for the diocese after his decease, according to " the instruction of the Lord."   Qui facit voluntatem Dei manet in æternum. 1 St. John ii. 17.

---

[1] Vol. iii. p. 45, this series.

THE TREATISES OF CYPRIAN

TREATISE I.

ON THE UNITY OF THE CHURCH.[1]

ARGUMENT.—ON THE OCCASION OF THE SCHISM OF NOVATIAN, TO KEEP BACK FROM HIM THE CARTHAGINIANS, WHO ALREADY WERE NOT AVERSE TO HIM, ON ACCOUNT OF NOVATUS AND SOME OTHER PRESBYTERS OF HIS CHURCH, WHO HAD ORIGINATED THE WHOLE DISTURBANCE, CYPRIAN WROTE THIS TREATISE. AND FIRST OF ALL, FORTIFYING THEM AGAINST THE DECEITS OF THESE, HE EXHORTS THEM TO CONSTANCY, AND INSTRUCTS THEM THAT HERESIES EXIST BECAUSE CHRIST, THE HEAD OF THE CHURCH, IS NOT LOOKED TO, THAT THE COMMON COMMISSION FIRST ENTRUSTED TO PETER IS CONTEMNED, AND THE ONE CHURCH AND THE ONE EPISCOPATE ARE DESERTED. THEN HE PROVES, AS WELL BY THE SCRIPTURES AS BY THE FIGURES OF THE OLD AND NEW TESTAMENT, THE UNITY OF THE CHURCH.[2]

1. Since the Lord warns us, saying, "Ye are the salt of the earth,"[3] and since He bids us to be simple to harmlessness, and yet with our simplicity to be prudent, what else, beloved brethren, befits us, than to use foresight and watching with an anxious heart, both to perceive and to beware of the wiles of the crafty foe, that we, who have put on Christ the wisdom of God the Father, may not seem to be wanting in wisdom in the matter of providing for our salvation?

For it is not persecution alone that is to be feared ; nor those things which advance by open attack to overwhelm and cast down the servants of God. Caution is more easy where danger is manifest, and the mind is prepared beforehand for the contest when the adversary avows himself. The enemy is more to be feared and to be guarded against, when he creeps on us secretly ; when, deceiving by the appearance of peace, he steals forward by hidden approaches, whence also he has received the name of the Serpent.[4] That is always his subtlety ; that is his dark and stealthy artifice for circumventing man. Thus from the very beginning of the world he deceived ; and flattering with lying words, he misled inexperienced souls by an incautious credulity. Thus he endeavoured to tempt the Lord Himself : he secretly approached Him, as if he would creep on Him again, and deceive ; yet he was understood, and beaten back, and therefore prostrated, because he was recognised and detected.

2. From which an example is given us to avoid the way of the old man, to stand in the footsteps of a conquering[5] Christ, that we may not again be incautiously turned back into the nets of death, but, foreseeing our danger, may possess the immortality that we have received. But how can we possess immortality, unless we keep those commands of Christ whereby death is driven out and overcome, when He Himself warns us, and says, "If thou wilt enter into life, keep the commandments?"[6] And again : "If ye do the things that I command you, henceforth I call you not servants, but friends."[7] Finally, these persons He calls strong and stedfast ; these He declares to be founded in robust security upon the rock, established with immoveable and unshaken firmness, in opposition to all the tempests and hurricanes of the world. "Whosoever," says He, "heareth my words, and doeth them, I will liken him unto a wise man, that built his house upon a rock : the rain descended, the floods came, the winds blew, and beat upon

---

[1] [Written A.D. 251. Although, in order of time, this treatise would be the third, I have placed it here because of its dignity, and because of its importance as a key to the entire writings of Cyprian; for this theory is everywhere the underlying principle of his conduct and of his correspondence. It illustrates the epistles of Ignatius as well as his own, and gives the sense in which the primitive Christians understood these words of the Creed, "the Holy Catholic Church." This treatise has been subjected to falsifying interpolations, long since exposed and detected, to make it less subversive of the counter-theory of Rome as developed by the school doctors. Elucidation I.]
[2] Describing in few words the ambition and dissimulation of Novatian in invading the episcopate of Rome, he argues at length, that neither on the one hand is the passage in Matthew xviii of any avail to compensate for their fewness as against the Church : "Wherever two or three are gathered together in my name," etc. ; nor, on the other, could martyrdom be of any benefit to them outside the Church. Then he tells them that they need not marvel that heresies flourished, since they had been foretold by Christ; nor that certain Roman confessors acquiesced in the schism, because before one's death no one is blessed, and the traitor Judas was found in the very company of the apostles. Yet he charges them to shun the association of schismatics and heretics, and finally exhorts them by the Scriptures to peace and unanimity.
[3] Matt. v. 13.

[4] The creeping, stealing thing.
[5] Or, "living."
[6] Matt. xix. 17.
[7] John xiv. 15.

that house ; and it fell not : for it was founded upon a rock." [1] We ought therefore to stand fast on His words, to learn and do whatever He both taught and did. But how can a man say that he believes in Christ, who does not do what Christ commanded him to do? Or whence shall he attain to the reward of faith, who will not keep the faith of the commandment? He must of necessity waver and wander, and, caught away by a spirit of error, like dust which is shaken by the wind, be blown about ; and he will make no advance in his walk towards salvation, because he does not keep the truth of the way of salvation.

3. But, beloved brethren, not only must we beware of what is open and manifest, but also of what deceives by the craft of subtle fraud. And what can be more crafty, or what more subtle, than for this enemy, detected and cast down by the advent of Christ, after light has come to the nations, and saving rays have shone for the preservation of men, that the deaf might receive the hearing of spiritual grace, the blind might open their eyes to God, the weak might grow strong again with eternal health, the lame might run to the church, the dumb might pray with clear voices and prayers — seeing his idols forsaken, and his fanes and his temples deserted by the numerous concourse of believers — to devise a new fraud, and under the very title of the Christian name to deceive the incautious? He has invented heresies and schisms, whereby he might subvert the faith, might corrupt the truth, might divide the unity.[2] Those whom he cannot keep in the darkness of the old way, he circumvents and deceives by the error of a new way. He snatches men from the Church itself ; and while they seem to themselves to have already approached to the light, and to have escaped the night of the world, he pours over them again, in their unconsciousness, new darkness ; so that, although they do not stand firm with the Gospel of Christ, and with the observation and law of Christ, they still call themselves Christians, and, walking in darkness, they think that they have the light, while the adversary is flattering and deceiving, who, according to the apostle's word, transforms himself into an angel of light, and equips his ministers as if they were the ministers of righteousness, who maintain night instead of day, death for salvation, despair under the offer of hope, perfidy under the pretext of faith, antichrist under the name of Christ ;

so that, while they feign things like the truth, they make void the truth by their subtlety. This happens, beloved brethren, so long as we do not return to the source of truth, as we do not seek the head nor keep the teaching of the heavenly Master.

4. If any one consider and examine these things, there is no need for lengthened discussion and arguments. There is easy proof for faith in a short summary of the truth. The Lord speaks to Peter,[3] saying, " I say unto thee, that thou art Peter ; and upon this rock I will build my Church, and the gates of hell shall not prevail against it. And I will give unto thee the keys of the kingdom of heaven ; and whatsoever thou shalt bind on earth shall be bound also in heaven, and whatsoever thou shalt loose on earth shall be loosed in heaven." [4] And again to the same He says, after His resurrection, " Feed my sheep." [5] And although to all the apostles, after His resurrection, He gives an equal power, and says, " As the Father hath sent me, even so send I you : Receive ye the Holy Ghost : Whose soever sins ye remit, they shall be remitted unto him ; and whose soever sins ye retain, they shall be retained ; " [6] yet, that He might set forth unity, He arranged by His authority the origin of that unity, as beginning from one. Assuredly the rest of the apostles were also the same as was Peter, endowed with a like partnership both of honour and power ; but the beginning proceeds from unity.[7] Which one Church, also, the Holy Spirit in the Song of Songs designated in the person of our Lord, and says, " My dove, my spotless one, is but one. She is the only one of her mother, elect of her that bare her." [8] Does he who does not hold this unity of the Church think that he holds the faith? Does he who strives against and resists the Church [9] trust that he is in the Church, when moreover the blessed Apostle Paul teaches the same thing, and sets forth the sacrament of unity, saying, " There is one body and one spirit, one hope of your calling, one Lord, one faith, one baptism, one God ? " [10]

5. And this unity we ought firmly to hold and assert, especially those of us that are bishops who preside in the Church, that we may

---

[1] Matt. vii 24.
[2] [Here note that our author's *entire ignorance* of any Centre of Unity, of any one See as the test of communion ; in short, of any one bishop as having more of Peter's authority than others, — is a sufficient disproof of the existence of any such things. Otherwise, how could they have been overlooked in a treatise devoted to the subject of unity, its nature and its *criteria ?* The effort to foist into the text something of the kind, by corruption, demonstrates how entirely unsatisfactory to the Middle-Age theorists and dogmatists is the unadulterated work, which they could not let alone.]

[3] [On the falsifying of the text by Romish editors, see Elucidation II.]
[4] Matt. xvi. 18, 19.
[5] John xxi. 15. [Here is interpolated] : " Upon him, being one, He builds His Church, and commits His sheep to be fed."
[6] John xx. 21.
[7] [Here is interpolated] : " And the primacy is given to Peter, that there might be shown one Church of Christ and one See : and they are all shepherds, and the flock is one, which is fed by all the apostles with unanimous consent." This passage, as well as the one a few lines before, is beyond all question spurious.
[8] Cant. vi. 9.
[9] [Here is interpolated] : " Who deserts the chair of Peter, upon whom the Church is founded." This passage also is undoubtedly spurious.
[10] Eph. iv. 4.

also prove the episcopate itself to be one and undivided.[1] Let no one deceive the brotherhood by a falsehood : let no one corrupt the truth of the faith by perfidious prevarication. The episcopate is one, each part of which is held by each one for the whole.[2] The Church also is one, which is spread abroad far and wide into a multitude by an increase of fruitfulness. As there are many rays of the sun, but one light ; and many branches of a tree, but one strength based in its tenacious root ; and since from one spring flow many streams, although the multiplicity seems diffused in the liberality of an overflowing abundance, yet the unity is still preserved in the source. Separate a ray of the sun from its body of light, its unity does not allow a division of light ; break a branch from a tree, — when broken, it will not be able to bud ; cut off the stream from its fountain, and that which is cut off dries up. Thus also the Church, shone over with the light of the Lord, sheds forth her rays over the whole world, yet it is one light which is everywhere diffused, nor is the unity of the body separated. Her fruitful abundance spreads her branches over the whole world. She broadly expands her rivers, liberally flowing, yet her head is one, her source one ; and she is one mother, plentiful in the results of fruitfulness : from her womb we are born, by her milk we are nourished, by her spirit we are animated.

6. The spouse of Christ cannot be adulterous ; she is uncorrupted and pure. She knows one home ; she guards with chaste modesty the sanctity of one couch. She keeps us for God. She appoints the sons whom she has born for the kingdom. Whoever is separated from the Church and is joined to an adulteress, is separated from the promises of the Church ; nor can he who forsakes the Church of Christ attain to the rewards of Christ. He is a stranger ; he is profane ; he is an enemy. He can no longer have God for his Father, who has not the Church for his mother. If any one could escape who was outside the ark of Noah, then he also may escape who shall be outside of the Church. The Lord warns, saying, " He who is not with me is against me, and he who gathereth not with me scattereth." [3] He who breaks the peace and the concord of Christ, does so in opposition to Christ ; he who gathereth elsewhere than in the Church, scatters the Church of Christ. The Lord says, " I and the Father are one ; " [4] and again it is written of the Father, and of the Son, and of the Holy Spirit, " And these three are one." [5] And does any one

believe that this unity which thus comes from the divine strength and coheres in celestial sacraments, can be divided in the Church, and can be separated by the parting asunder of opposing wills? He who does not hold this unity does not hold God's law, does not hold the faith of the Father and the Son, does not hold life and salvation.

7. This sacrament of unity, this bond of a concord inseparably cohering, is set forth where in the Gospel the coat of the Lord Jesus Christ is not at all divided nor cut, but is received as an entire garment, and is possessed as an uninjured and undivided robe by those who cast lots concerning Christ's garment, who should rather put on Christ.[6] Holy Scripture speaks, saying, " But of the coat, because it was not sewed, but woven from the top throughout, they said one to another, Let us not rend it, but cast lots whose it shall be." [7] That coat bore with it an unity that came down from the top, that is, that came from heaven and the Father, which was not to be at all rent by the receiver and the possessor, but without separation we obtain a whole and substantial entireness. He cannot possess the garment of Christ who parts and divides the Church of Christ. On the other hand, again, when at Solomon's death his kingdom and people were divided, Abijah the prophet, meeting Jeroboam the king in the field, divided his garment into twelve sections, saying, " Take thee ten pieces ; for thus saith the Lord, Behold, I will rend the kingdom out of the hand of Solomon, and I will give ten sceptres unto thee ; and two sceptres shall be unto him for my servant David's sake, and for Jerusalem, the city which I have chosen to place my name there." [8] As the twelve tribes of Israel were divided, the prophet Abijah rent his garment. But because Christ's people cannot be rent, His robe, woven and united throughout, is not divided by those who possess it ; undivided, united, connected, it shows the coherent concord of our people who put on Christ. By the sacrament and sign of His garment, He has declared the unity of the Church.

8. Who, then, is so wicked and faithless, who is so insane with the madness of discord, that either he should believe that the unity of God can be divided, or should dare to rend it — the garment of the Lord — the Church of Christ? He Himself in His Gospel warns us, and teaches, saying, " And there shall be one flock and one shepherd." [9] And does any one believe that in

---

[1] [i.e., the universal episcopate is the chair of Peter.]
[2] [This maxim is the essence of the treatise; i.e., " Ecclesia in Episcopo." Compare p. 333, note 9, *supra*.]
[3] Matt. xii. 30.
[4] John x. 30.
[5] I John v. 7.

[6] The above reading of this passage seems hopelessly obscure; and it is not much mended apparently by substituting " ipsam " for Christum, unless " potius " be omitted, as in some editions, in which case we should read, " who should put it on."
[7] John xix. 23, 24.
[8] 1 Kings xi. 31.
[9] John x. 16.

one place there can be either many shepherds or many flocks? The Apostle Paul, moreover, urging upon us this same unity, beseeches and exhorts, saying, " I beseech you, brethren, by the name of our Lord Jesus Christ, that ye all speak the same thing, and that there be no schisms among you; but that ye be joined together in the same mind and in the same judgment." [1] And again, he says, " Forbearing one another in love, endeavouring to keep the unity of the Spirit in the bond of peace." [2] Do you think that you can stand and live if you withdraw from the Church, building for yourself other homes and a different dwelling, when it is said to Rahab, in whom was prefigured the Church, " Thy father, and thy mother, and thy brethren, and all the house of thy father, thou shalt gather unto thee into thine house; and it shall come to pass, whosoever shall go abroad beyond the door of thine house, his blood shall be upon his own head?" [3] Also, the sacrament of the passover contains nothing else in the law of the Exodus than that the lamb which is slain in the figure of Christ should be eaten in one house. God speaks, saying, " In one house shall ye eat it; ye shall not send its flesh abroad from the house." [4] The flesh of Christ, and the holy of the Lord, cannot be sent abroad, nor is there any other home to believers but the one Church. This home, this household [5] of unanimity, the Holy Spirit designates and points out in the Psalms, saying, " God, who maketh men to dwell with one mind in a house." [6] In the house of God, in the Church of Christ, men dwell with one mind, and continue in concord and simplicity.

9. Therefore also the Holy Spirit came as a dove, a simple and joyous creature, not bitter with gall, not cruel in its bite, not violent with the rending of its claws, loving human dwellings, knowing the association of one home; when they have young, bringing forth their young together; when they fly abroad, remaining in their flights by the side of one another, spending their life in mutual intercourse, acknowledging the concord of peace with the kiss of the beak, in all things fulfilling the law of unanimity. This is the simplicity that ought to be known in the Church, this is the charity that ought to be attained, that so the love of the brotherhood may imitate the doves, that their gentleness and meekness may be like the lambs and sheep. What does the fierceness of wolves do in the Christian breast? What the savageness of dogs, and the deadly venom of serpents, and the sanguinary cruelty of wild beasts? We are to

be congratulated when such as these are separated from the Church, lest they should lay waste the doves and sheep of Christ with their cruel and envenomed contagion. Bitterness cannot consist and be associated with sweetness, darkness with light, rain with clearness, battle with peace, barrenness with fertility, drought with springs, storm with tranquillity. Let none think that the good can depart from the Church. The wind does not carry away the wheat, nor does the hurricane uproot the tree that is based on a solid root. The light straws are tossed about by the tempest, the feeble trees are overthrown by the onset of the whirlwind. The Apostle John execrates and severely assails these, when he says, " They went forth from us, but they were not of us; for if they had been of us, surely they would have continued with us." [7]

10. Hence heresies not only have frequently been originated, but continue to be so; while the perverted mind has no peace — while a discordant faithlessness does not maintain unity. But the Lord permits and suffers these things to be, while the choice of one's own liberty remains, so that while the discrimination of truth is testing our hearts and our minds, the sound faith of those that are approved may shine forth with manifest light. The Holy Spirit forewarns and says by the apostle, " It is needful also that there should be heresies, that they which are approved may be made manifest among you." [8] Thus the faithful are approved, thus the perfidious are detected; thus even here, before the day of judgment, the souls of the righteous and of the unrighteous are already divided, and the chaff is separated from the wheat. These are they who of their own accord, without any divine arrangement, set themselves to preside among the daring strangers assembled, who appoint themselves prelates without any law of ordination, who assume to themselves the name of bishop, although no one gives them the episcopate; whom the Holy Spirit points out in the Psalms as sitting in the seat of pestilence, plagues, and spots of the faith, deceiving with serpent's tongue, and artful in corrupting the truth, vomiting forth deadly poisons from pestilential tongues; whose speech doth creep like a cancer, whose discourse forms a deadly poison in the heart and breast of every one.

11. Against people of this kind the Lord cries; from these He restrains and recalls His erring people, saying, " Hearken not unto the words of the false prophets; for the visions of their hearts deceive them. They speak, but not out of the mouth of the Lord. They say to those who cast away the word of God, Ye shall have peace, and every one that walketh after his own will. Every one who walketh in the error of his

---

[1] 1 Cor. i. 10.
[2] Eph. iv. 3.
[3] Josh. ii. 19.
[4] Ex. xii. 46.
[5] " Hospitium."
[6] Ps. lxviii. 6.

[7] 1 John ii. 19.
[8] 1 Cor. xi. 19.

heart, no evil shall come upon him. I have not spoken to them, yet they prophesied. If they had stood on my foundation (*substantia*, ὑποστά- σει), and had heard my words, and taught my people, I would have turned them from their evil thoughts." [1] Again, the Lord points out and designates these same, saying, "They have forsaken me, the fountain of living waters, and have hewed them out broken cisterns which can hold no water." [2] Although there can be no other baptism but one, they think that they can baptize; although they forsake the fountain of life, they promise the grace of living and saving water. Men are not washed among them, but rather are made foul; nor are sins purged away, but are even accumulated. Such a nativity does not generate sons to God, but to the devil. By a falsehood they are born, and they do not receive the promises of truth. Begotten of perfidy, they lose the grace of faith. They cannot attain to the reward of peace, since they have broken the Lord's peace with the madness of discord.

12. Nor let any deceive themselves by a futile interpretation, in respect of the Lord having said, "Wheresoever two or three are gathered together in my name, there am I in the midst of them." [3] Corrupters and false interpreters of the Gospel quote the last words, and lay aside the former ones, remembering part, and craftily suppressing part: as they themselves are separated from the Church, so they cut off the substance of one section. For the Lord, when He would urge unanimity and peace upon His disciples, said, "I say unto you, That if two of you shall agree on earth touching anything that ye shall ask, it shall be given you by my Father which is in heaven. For wheresoever two or three are gathered together in my name, I am with them;" [4] showing that most is given, not to the multitude, but to the unanimity of those that pray. "If," He says, "two of you shall agree on earth:" He placed agreement first; He has made the concord of peace a prerequisite; He taught that we should agree firmly and faithfully. But how can he agree with any one who does not agree with the body of the Church itself, and with the universal brotherhood? How can two or three be assembled together in Christ's name, who, it is evident, are separated from Christ and from His Gospel? For we have not withdrawn from them, but they from us; and since heresies and schisms have risen subsequently, from their establishment for themselves of diverse places of worship, they have forsaken the Head and Source of the truth. But the Lord speaks concerning His Church, and to those also who are in the Church He speaks, that if they are in agreement, if according to what He commanded and admonished, although only two or three gathered together with unanimity should pray — though they be only two or three — they may obtain from the majesty of God what they ask. "Wheresoever two or three are gathered together in my name, I," says He, "am with them;" that is, with the simple and peaceable — with those who fear God and keep God's commandments. With these, although only two or three, He said that He was, in the same manner as He was with the three youths in the fiery furnace; and because they abode towards God in simplicity, and in unanimity among themselves, He animated them, in the midst of the surrounding flames, with the breath of dew: in the way in which, with the two apostles shut up in prison, because they were simple-minded and of one mind, He Himself was present; He Himself, having loosed the bolts of the dungeon, placed them again in the market-place, that they might declare to the multitude the word which they faithfully preached. When, therefore, in His commandments He lays it down, and says, "Where two or three are gathered together in my name, I am with them," He does not divide men from the Church, seeing that He Himself ordained and made the Church; but rebuking the faithless for their discord, and commending peace by His word to the faithful, He shows that He is rather with two or three who pray with one mind, than with a great many who differ, and that more can be obtained by the concordant prayer of a few, than by the discordant supplication of many.

13. Thus, also, when He gave the law of prayer, He added, saying, "And when ye stand praying, forgive, if ye have ought against any; that your Father also which is in heaven may forgive you your trespasses." [5] And He calls back from the altar one who comes to the sacrifice in strife, and bids him first agree with his brother, and then return with peace and offer his gift to God: for God had not respect unto Cain's offerings; for he could not have God at peace with him, who through envious discord had not peace with his brother. What peace, then, do the enemies of the brethren promise to themselves? What sacrifices do those who are rivals of the priests think that they celebrate? Do they deem that they have Christ with them when they are collected together, who are gathered together outside the Church of Christ?

14. Even if such men were slain in confession of the Name, that stain is not even washed away by blood: the inexpiable and grave fault of discord is not even purged by suffering. He cannot be a martyr who is not in the Church; he

---

1 Jer. xxiii. 16-21.
2 Jer. ii. 13.
3 Matt. xviii. 20.
4 Matt. xviii. 19, 20. [Compare John

5 Mark xi. 25. [Freeman, *Principles*, etc. vol. i. 417.]

cannot attain unto the kingdom who forsakes that which shall reign there. Christ gave us peace; He bade us be in agreement, and of one mind. He charged the bonds of love and charity to be kept uncorrupted and inviolate; he cannot show himself a martyr who has not maintained brotherly love. Paul the apostle teaches this, and testifies, saying, "And though I have faith, so that I can remove mountains, and have not charity, I am nothing. And though I give all my goods to feed the poor, and though I give my body to be burned, and have not charity, it profiteth me nothing. Charity is magnanimous; charity is kind; charity envieth not; charity acteth not vainly, is not puffed up, is not easily provoked, thinketh no evil; loveth all things, believeth all things, hopeth all things, endureth all things. Charity never faileth." [1] "Charity," says he, "never faileth." For she will ever be in the kingdom, she will endure for ever in the unity of a brotherhood linked to herself. Discord cannot attain to the kingdom of heaven; to the rewards of Christ, who said, "This is my commandment, that ye love one another, even as I have loved you:" [2] he cannot attain [3] who has violated the love of Christ by faithless dissension. He who has not charity has not God. The word of the blessed Apostle John is: "God," saith he, "is love; and he that dwelleth in love dwelleth in God, and God dwelleth in him." [4] They cannot dwell with God who would not be of one mind in God's Church. Although they burn, given up to flames and fires, or lay down their lives, thrown to the wild beasts, that will not be the crown of faith, but the punishment of perfidy; nor will it be the glorious ending of religious valour, but the destruction of despair. Such a one may be slain; crowned he cannot be. He professes himself to be a Christian in such a way as the devil often feigns himself to be Christ, as the Lord Himself forewarns us, and says, "Many shall come in my name, saying, I am Christ, and shall deceive many." [5] As he is not Christ, although he deceives in respect of the name; so neither can he appear as a Christian who does not abide in the truth of His Gospel and of faith.

15. For both to prophesy and to cast out devils, and to do great acts upon the earth, is certainly a sublime and an admirable thing; but one does not attain the kingdom of heaven although he is found in all these things, unless he walks in the observance of the right and just way. The Lord denounces, and says, "Many shall say to me in that day, Lord, Lord, have

we not prophesied in Thy name, and in Thy name have cast out devils, and in Thy name done many wonderful works? And then will I profess unto them, I never knew you: depart from me, ye that work iniquity." [6] There is need of righteousness, that one may deserve well of God the Judge; we must obey His precepts and warnings, that our merits may receive their reward. The Lord in His Gospel, when He would direct the way of our hope and faith in a brief summary, said, "The Lord thy God is one God: and thou shalt love the Lord thy God with all thy heart, and with all thy soul, and with all thy strength. This is the first commandment; and the second is like unto it: Thou shalt love thy neighbour as thyself. On these two commandments hang all the law and the prophets." [7] He taught, at the same time, love and unity by His instruction. He has included all the prophets and the law in two precepts. But what unity does he keep, what love does he maintain or consider, who, savage with the madness of discord, divides the Church, destroys the faith, disturbs the peace, dissipates charity, profanes the sacrament?

16. This evil, most faithful brethren, had long ago begun, but now the mischievous destruction of the same evil has increased, and the envenomed plague of heretical perversity and schisms has begun to spring forth and shoot anew; because even thus it must be in the decline of the world, since the Holy Spirit foretells and forewarns us by the apostle, saying, "In the last days," says he, "perilous times shall come, and men shall be lovers of their own selves, proud, boasters, covetous, blasphemers, disobedient to parents, unthankful, unholy, without natural affection, truce-breakers, false accusers, incontinent, fierce, hating the good, traitors, heady, high-minded, lovers of pleasures more than lovers of God, having a sort of form [8] of religion, but denying the power thereof. Of this sort are they who creep into houses, and lead captive silly women laden with sins, which are led away with divers lusts; ever learning, and never coming to the knowledge of the truth. And as Jannes and Jambres withstood Moses, so do these also resist the truth; [9] but they shall proceed no further, for their folly shall be manifest unto all men, even as theirs also was." [10] Whatever things were predicted are fulfilled; and as the end of the world is approaching, they have come for the probation as well of the men as of the times. Error deceives as the adversary rages more and more; senselessness lifts up, envy in-

---

[1] 1 Cor. xiii. 2–5, 7, 8.
[2] John xv. 12.
[3] According to some readings, "to Christ," or "to the rewards of Christ."
[4] 1 John iv. 16.
[5] Mark xiii. 6.

[6] Matt. vii. 22.
[7] Mark xii. 29–31.
[8] Deformationem religionis.
[9] Some introduce, "men corrupted in feeling, reprobate concerning the faith."
[10] 2 Tim. iii. 1–9. [Vol. iv. p. 521, this series.]

flames, covetousness makes blind, impiety depraves, pride puffs up, discord exasperates, anger hurries headlong.

17. Yet let not the excessive and headlong faithlessness of many move or disturb us, but rather strengthen our faith in the truthfulness which has foretold the matter. As some have become such, because these things were predicted beforehand, so let other brethren beware of matters of a like kind, because these also were predicted beforehand, even as the Lord instructs us, and says, "But take ye heed : behold, I have told you all things."[1] Avoid, I beseech you, brethren, men of this kind, and drive away from your side and from your ears, as if it were the contagion of death, their mischievous conversation ; as it is written, "Hedge thine ears about with thorns, and refuse to hear a wicked tongue."[2] And again, "Evil communications corrupt good manners."[3] The Lord teaches and warns us to depart from such. He saith, "They are blind leaders of the blind ; and if the blind lead the blind, they shall both fall into the ditch."[4] Such a one is to be turned away from and avoided, whosoever he may be, that is separated from the Church. Such a one is perverted and sins, and is condemned of his own self. Does he think that he has Christ, who acts in opposition to Christ's priests, who separates himself from the company of His clergy and people? He bears arms against the Church, he contends against God's appointment. An enemy of the altar, a rebel against Christ's sacrifice, for the faith faithless, for religion profane, a disobedient servant, an impious son, a hostile brother, despising the bishops, and forsaking God's priests, he dares to set up another altar, to make another prayer with unauthorized words, to profane the truth of the Lord's offering by false sacrifices, and not[5] to know that he who strives against the appointment of God, is punished on account of the daring of his temerity by divine visitation.

18. Thus Korah, Dathan, and Abiram, who endeavoured to claim to themselves the power of sacrificing in opposition to Moses and Aaron the priest, underwent immediate punishment for their attempts. The earth, breaking its fastenings, gaped open into a deep gulf, and the cleft of the receding ground swallowed up the men standing and living. Nor did the anger of the indignant God strike only those who had been the movers (of the sedition) ; but two hundred and fifty sharers and associates of that madness besides, who had been mingled with them in that boldness, the fire that went out from the

Lord consumed with a hasty revenge ; doubtless to admonish and show that whatever those wicked men had endeavoured, in order by human will to overthrow God's appointment, had been done in opposition to God. Thus also Uzziah the king, —when he bare the censer and violently claimed to himself to sacrifice against God's law, and when Azariah the priest withstood him, would not be obedient and yield, — was confounded by the divine indignation, and was polluted upon his forehead by the spot of leprosy : he was marked by an offended Lord in that part of his body where they are signed who deserve well of the Lord. And the sons of Aaron, who placed strange fire upon the altar, which the Lord had not commanded, were at once extinguished in the presence of an avenging Lord.

19. These, doubtless, they imitate and follow, who, despising God's tradition, seek after strange doctrines, and bring in teachings of human appointment, whom the Lord rebukes and reproves in His Gospel, saying, "Ye reject the commandment of God, that ye may keep your own tradition."[6] This is a worse crime than that which the lapsed seem to have fallen into, who nevertheless, standing as penitents for their crime, beseech God with full satisfactions. In this case, the Church is sought after and entreated ; in that case, the Church is resisted : here it is possible that there has been necessity ; there the will is engaged in the wickedness : on the one hand, he who has lapsed has only injured himself ; on the other, he who has endeavoured to cause a heresy or a schism has deceived many by drawing them with him. In the former, it is the loss of one soul ; in the latter, the risk of many. Certainly the one both understands that he has sinned, and laments and bewails it ; the other, puffed up in his heart, and pleasing himself in his very crimes, separates sons from their Mother, entices sheep from their shepherd, disturbs the sacraments of God ; and while the lapsed has sinned but once, he sins daily. Finally, the lapsed, who has subsequently attained to martyrdom, may receive the promises of the kingdom ; while the other, if he have been slain without the Church, cannot attain to the rewards of the Church.

20. Nor let any one marvel, beloved brethren, that even some of the confessors advance to these lengths, and thence also that some *others* sin thus wickedly, thus grievously. For neither does confession make a man free from the snares of the devil, nor does it defend a man who is still placed in the world, with a perpetual security from temptations, and dangers, and onsets, and attacks of the world ; otherwise we should never see in confessors those subsequent frauds, and

---

[1] Mark xiii. 23.
[2] Ecclus. xxviii. 24, Vulg.
[3] 1 Cor. xv. 33.
[4] Matt. xv. 14.
[5] According to some, "does not deign," or "disdains to know."

[6] Mark vii. 9.

fornications, and adulteries, which now with groans and sorrow we witness in some. Whosoever that confessor is, he is not greater, or better, or dearer to God than Solomon, who, although so long as he walked in God's ways, retained that grace which he had received from the Lord, yet after he forsook the Lord's way he lost also the Lord's grace.[1] And therefore it is written, "Hold fast that which thou hast, lest another take thy crown."[2] But assuredly the Lord would not threaten that the crown of righteousness might be taken away, were it not that, when righteousness departs, the crown must also depart.

21. Confession is the beginning of glory, not the full desert of the crown; nor does it perfect our praise, but it initiates our dignity; and since it is written, "He that endureth to the end, the same shall be saved,"[3] whatever has been before the end is a step by which we ascend to the summit of salvation, not a terminus wherein the full result of the ascent is already gained. He is a confessor; but after confession his peril is greater, because the adversary is more provoked. He is a confessor; for this cause he ought the more to stand on the side of the Lord's Gospel, since he has by the Gospel attained glory from the Lord. For the Lord says, "To whom much is given, of him much shall be required; and to whom more dignity is ascribed, of him more service is exacted."[4] Let no one perish by the example of a confessor; let no one learn injustice, let no one learn arrogance, let no one learn treachery, from the manners of a confessor. He is a confessor, let him be lowly and quiet; let him be in his doings modest with discipline, so that he who is called a confessor of Christ may imitate Christ whom he confesses. For since He says, "Whosoever exalteth himself shall be abased, and he who humbleth himself shall be exalted;"[5] and since He Himself has been exalted by the Father, because as the Word, and the strength, and the wisdom of God the Father, He humbled Himself upon earth, how can He love arrogance, who even by His own law enjoined upon us humility, and Himself received the highest name from the Father as the reward of His humility? He is a confessor of Christ, but only so if the majesty and dignity of Christ be not afterwards blasphemed by him. Let not the tongue which has confessed Christ be evil-speaking; let it not be turbulent, let it not be heard jarring with reproaches and quarrels, let it not after words of praise, dart forth serpents' venom against the brethren and God's priests. But if one shall

have subsequently been blameworthy and obnoxious; if he shall have wasted his confession by evil conversation; if he shall have stained his life by disgraceful foulness; if, finally, forsaking the Church in which he has become a confessor, and severing the concord of unity, he shall have exchanged his first faith for a subsequent unbelief, he may not flatter himself on account of his confession that he is elected to the reward of glory, when from this very fact his deserving of punishment has become the greater.

22. For the Lord chose Judas also among the apostles, and yet afterwards Judas betrayed the Lord. Yet not on that account did the faith and firmness of the apostles fail, because the traitor Judas failed from their fellowship: so also in the case in question the holiness and dignity of confessors is not forthwith diminished, because the faith of some of them is broken. The blessed Apostle Paul in his epistle speaks in this manner: "For what if some of them fall away from the faith, shall their unbelief make the faith of God without effect? God forbid: for God is true, though every man be a liar."[6] The greater and better part of the confessors stand firm in the strength of their faith, and in the truth of the law and discipline of the Lord; neither do they depart from the peace of the Church, who remember that they have obtained grace in the Church by the condescension of God; and by this very thing they obtain a higher praise of their faith, that they have separated from the faithlessness of those who have been associated with them in the fellowship of confession, and withdrawn from the contagion of crime. Illuminated by the true light of the Gospel, shone upon with the Lord's pure and white brightness, they are as praiseworthy in maintaining the peace of Christ, as they have been victorious in their combat with the devil.

23. I indeed desire, beloved brethren, and I equally endeavour and exhort, that if it be possible, none of the brethren should perish, and that our rejoicing Mother may enclose in her bosom the one body of a people at agreement. Yet if wholesome counsel cannot recall to the way of salvation certain leaders of schisms and originators of dissensions, who abide in blind and obstinate madness, yet do you others, if either taken in simplicity, or induced by error, or deceived by some craftiness of misleading cunning, loose yourselves from the nets of deceit, free your wandering steps from errors, acknowledge the straight way of the heavenly road. The word of the witnessing apostle is: "We command you," says he, "in the name of our Lord Jesus Christ, that ye withdraw yourselves from all brethren that walk disorderly, and not after

---

[1] Some read, "As it is written, And the Lord stirred up the adversary (Satan) against Solomon; and therefore in the Apocalypse the Lord solemnly warns John."
[2] Apoc. iii. 11.
[3] Matt. x. 22.
[4] Luke xii. 48.
[5] Luke xviii. 14.

[6] Rom. iii. 3.

the tradition that they have received from us."[1] And again he says, " Let no man deceive you with vain words ; for because of these things cometh the wrath of God upon the children of disobedience. Be not ye therefore partakers with them."[2] We must withdraw, nay rather must flee, from those who fall away, lest, while any one is associated with those who walk wickedly, and goes on in ways of error and of sin, he himself also, wandering away from the path of the true road, should be found in like guilt. God is one, and Christ is one, and His Church is one, and the faith is one, and the people[3] is joined into a substantial unity of body by the cement of concord. Unity cannot be severed ; nor can one body be separated by a division of its structure, nor torn into pieces, with its entrails wrenched asunder by laceration. Whatever has proceeded from the womb cannot live and breathe in its detached condition, but loses the substance of health.

24. The Holy Spirit warns us, and says, "What man is he that desireth to live, and would fain see good days? Refrain thy tongue from evil, and thy lips that they speak no guile. Eschew evil, and do good ; seek peace, and ensue it."[4] The son of peace ought to seek peace and ensue it. He who knows and loves the bond of charity, ought to refrain his tongue from the evil of dissension. Among His divine commands and salutary teachings, the Lord, when He was now very near to His passion, added this one, saying, " Peace I leave with you, my peace I give unto you."[5] He gave this to us as an heritage ; He promised all the gifts and rewards of which He spoke through the preservation of peace. If we are fellow-heirs with Christ, let us abide in the peace of Christ ; if we are sons of God, we ought to be peacemakers. " Blessed," says He, " are the peacemakers ; for they shall be called the sons of God."[6] It behoves the sons of God to be peacemakers, gentle in heart, simple in speech, agreeing in affection, faithfully linked to one another in the bonds of unanimity.

25. This unanimity formerly prevailed among the apostles ; and thus the new assembly of believers, keeping the Lord's commandments, maintained its charity. Divine Scripture proves this, when it says, " But the multitude of them which believed were of one heart and of one soul."[7] And again : " These all continued with one mind in prayer with the women, and Mary the mother of Jesus, and with His brethren."[8]

And thus[9] they prayed with effectual prayers ; thus they were able with confidence to obtain whatever they asked from the Lord's mercy.

26. But in us unanimity is diminished in proportion as liberality of working is decayed. Then they used to give for sale houses and estates ; and that they might lay up for themselves treasures in heaven, presented to the apostles the price of them, to be distributed for the use of the poor. But now we do not even give the tenths from our patrimony ; and while our Lord bids us sell, we rather buy and increase our store. Thus has the vigour of faith dwindled away among us ; thus has the strength of believers grown weak. And therefore the Lord, looking to our days, says in His Gospel, " When the Son of man cometh, think you that He shall find faith on the earth?"[10] We see that what He foretold has come to pass. There is no faith in the fear of God, in the law of righteousness, in love, in labour ; none considers the fear of futurity, and none takes to heart the day of the Lord, and the wrath of God, and the punishments to come upon unbelievers, and the eternal torments decreed for the faithless. That which our conscience would fear if it believed, it fears not because it does not at all believe. But if it believed, it would also take heed ; and if it took heed, it would escape.

27. Let us, beloved brethren, arouse ourselves as much as we can ; and breaking the slumber of our ancient listlessness, let us be watchful to observe and to do the Lord's precepts. Let us be such as He Himself has bidden us to be, saying, " Let your loins be girt, and your lamps burning ;[11] and ye yourselves like unto men that wait for their Lord, when He shall come from the wedding, that when He cometh and knocketh, they may open to Him. Blessed are those servants whom their Lord, when He cometh, shall find watching."[12] We ought to be girt about, lest, when the day of setting forth comes, it should find us burdened and entangled. Let our light shine in good works, and glow in such wise as to lead us from the night of this world to the daylight of eternal brightness. Let us always with solicitude and caution wait for the sudden coming of the Lord, that when He shall knock, our faith may be on the watch, and receive from the Lord the reward of our vigilance. If these commands be observed, if these warnings and precepts be kept, we cannot be overtaken in slumber by the deceit of the devil ; but we shall reign with Christ in His kingdom as servants that watch.

---

[1] 2 Thess. iii. 6.
[2] Eph. v. 6.
[3] " is one."
[4] Ps. xxxiv. 12, 13.
[5] John xiv. 27.
[6] Matt. v. 9.
[7] Acts iv. 32. [Bernard., Epist. ccxxxviii., *Opp.* i. 502.]
[8] Acts i. 14.

[9] Some interpolate " because."
[10] Luke xviii. 8.
[11] Some read, " in your hands."
[12] Luke xii. 35.

TREATISE II.[1]

ON THE DRESS OF VIRGINS.

ARGUMENT. — CYPRIAN CELEBRATES THE PRAISES OF DISCIPLINE, AND PROVES ITS USEFULNESS FROM SCRIPTURE. THEN, DESCRIBING THE GLORY, HONOUR, AND MERITS OF VIRGINITY, AND OF THOSE WHO HAD VOWED AND DEDICATED THEIR VIRGINITY TO CHRIST, HE TEACHES THAT CONTINENCE NOT ONLY CONSISTS IN FLESHLY PURITY, BUT ALSO IN SEEMLINESS OF DRESS AND ORNAMENT, AND THAT EVEN WEALTH DID NOT EXCUSE SUPERFLUOUS CARE FOR DRESS ON THE PART OF THOSE WHO HAD ALREADY RENOUNCED THE WORLD. RATHER, SINCE THE APOSTLE PRESCRIBES EVEN TO MARRIED WOMEN A DRESS TO BE REGULATED BY FITTING LIMITS, MODERATION OUGHT EVEN MORE TO BE OBSERVED BY A VIRGIN. THEREFORE, EVEN IF SHE BE WEALTHY, SHE SHOULD CONSIDER CERTAINLY HOW TO USE WEALTH, BUT FOR GOOD PURPOSES, FOR THOSE THINGS WHICH GOD HAS COMMANDED, TO WIT, FOR BEING SPENT ON THE POOR.[2] MOREOVER, ALSO, HE FORBIDS TO VIRGINS THOSE THINGS WHICH HAD NEGLIGENTLY COME INTO USE, AS BEING PRESENT AT WEDDINGS, AS WELL AS GOING TO PROMISCUOUS BATHING-PLACES. FINALLY, IN A BRIEF EPILOGUE,[3] DECLARING WHAT BENEFIT THE VIRTUE OF CONTINENCY AFFORDS, AND WHAT EVIL IT IS WITHOUT, HE CONCLUDES THE BOOK.

1. Discipline, the safeguard of hope, the bond of faith, the guide of the way of salvation, the stimulus and nourishment of good dispositions, the teacher of virtue, causes us to abide always in Christ, and to live continually for God, and to attain to the heavenly promises and to the divine rewards. To follow her is wholesome, and to turn away from her and neglect her is deadly. The Holy Spirit says in the Psalms, " Keep discipline, lest perchance the Lord be angry, and ye perish from the right way, when His wrath is quickly kindled against you." [4] And again : " But unto the ungodly saith God, " Why dost thou preach my laws, and takest my covenant into thy mouth? Whereas thou hatest discipline, and hast cast my words behind thee." [5] And again we read : " He that casteth away discipline

is miserable." [6] And from Solomon we have received the mandates of wisdom, warning us : " My son, despise not thou the discipline of the Lord, nor faint when thou art rebuked of Him : for whom the Lord loveth He correcteth." [7] But if God rebukes whom He loves, and rebukes him for the very purpose of amending him, brethren also, and especially priests, do not hate, but love those whom they rebuke, that they may amend them ; since God also before predicted by Jeremiah, and pointed to our times, when he said, "And I will give you shepherds according to my heart : and they shall feed you with the food of discipline." [8]

2. But if in Holy Scripture discipline is frequently and everywhere prescribed, and the whole foundation of religion and of faith proceeds from obedience and fear ; what is more fitting for us urgently to desire, what more to wish for and to hold fast, than to stand with roots strongly fixed, and with our houses based with solid mass upon the rock unshaken by the storms and whirlwinds of the world, so that we may come by the divine precepts to the rewards of God? considering as well as knowing that our members, when purged from all the filth of the old contagion by the sanctification of the laver of life, are God's temples, and must not be violated nor polluted, since he who does violence to them is himself injured. We are the worshippers and priests of those temples ; let us obey Him whose we have already begun to be. Paul tells us in his epistles, in which he has formed us to a course of living by divine teaching, "Ye are not your own, for ye are bought with a great price ; glorify and bear God in your body." [9] Let us glorify and bear God in a pure and chaste body, and with a more complete obedience ; and since we have been redeemed by the blood of Christ, let us obey and give furtherance to the empire of our Redeemer by all the obedience of service, that nothing impure or profane may be brought into the temple of God, lest He should be offended, and forsake the temple which He inhabits. The words of the Lord giving health and teaching, as well curing as warning, are : " Behold, thou art made whole : sin no more, lest a worse thing come unto thee." [10] He gives the course of life, He gives the law of innocency after He has conferred health, nor suffers the man afterwards to wander with free and unchecked reins, but more severely threatens him who is again enslaved by those same things of which he had been healed, because it is doubtless a smaller fault to have sinned before, while as yet you had not known God's discipline ; but there is no further pardon for

---

[1] The deacon Pontius, in his life of Cyprian, in few words comprises the argument of the following treatise. " Who," says he, " would restrain virgins into a fitting discipline of modesty, and a dress meet for holiness, as if with a bridle of the Lord's lessons ? "

[2] After this he teaches from the Apostle, and from the third chapter of Isaiah also, that distinctions of dress and ornaments are more suited to prostitutes than to virgins; and he infers that, while so many things are offensive to God, more especially are the sumptuous ornaments of women; and therefore making a transition from superfluous ornament to the different kinds of dyes and paints, he forbids such things, not only to virgins, but absolutely also to married women, who assuredly cannot with impunity strive to improve, to transfigure, and to adulterate God's work.

[3] [Written, A D. 248. Compare Tertullian, vol. iv. p. 14.]

[4] Ps. ii. 12.

[5] Ps. l. 17.

[6] Wisd. iii. 11.

[7] Prov. iii. 11.

[8] Jer. iii. 15.

[9] 1 Cor. vi. 19.

[10] John v. 14.

sinning after you have begun to know God. And, indeed, let as well men as women, as well boys as girls ; let each sex and every age observe this, and take care in this respect, according to the religion and faith which they owe to God, that what is received holy and pure from the condescension of the Lord be preserved with a no less anxious fear.[1]

3. My address is now to virgins, whose glory, as it is more eminent, excites the greater interest. This is the flower of the ecclesiastical seed,[2] the grace and ornament of spiritual endowment, a joyous disposition, the wholesome and uncorrupted work of praise and honour, God's image answering to the holiness of the Lord, the more illustrious portion of Christ's flock. The glorious fruitfulness of Mother Church rejoices by their means, and in them abundantly flourishes ; and in proportion as a copious virginity is added to her number, so much the more it increases the joy of the Mother. To these I speak, these I exhort with affection rather than with power ; not that I would claim — last and least, and very conscious of my lowliness as I am — any right to censure, but because, being unceasingly careful even to solicitude, I fear more from the onset of Satan.

4. For that is not an empty carefulness nor a vain fear, which takes counsel for the way of salvation, which guards the commandments of the Lord and of life ; so that they who have dedicated themselves to Christ, and who depart from carnal concupiscence, and have vowed themselves to God as well in the flesh as in the spirit, may consummate their work, destined as it is to a great reward, and may not study any longer to be adorned or to please anybody but their Lord, from whom also they expect the reward of virginity ; as He Himself says : "All men cannot receive this word, but they to whom it is given. For there are some eunuchs, which were so born from their mother's womb ; and there are some eunuchs, which were made eunuchs of men ; and there are eunuchs which have made themselves eunuchs for the kingdom of heaven's sake."[3] Again, also by this word of the angel the gift of continency is set forth, and virginity is preached : "These are they which have not defiled themselves with women, for they have remained virgins ; these are they which follow the Lamb whithersoever He goeth."[4] For not only thus does the Lord promise the grace of continency to men, and pass over women ; but since the woman is a portion of the man, and is taken and formed from him, God in Scripture almost always speaks to the Protoplast, the first formed, because

they are two in one flesh, and in the male is at the same time signified the woman also.

5. But if continency follows Christ, and virginity is destined for the kingdom of God, what have they to do with earthly dress, and with ornaments, wherewith while they are striving to please men they offend God ? Not considering that it is declared, "They who please men are put to confusion, because God hath despised them ; "[5] and that Paul also has gloriously and sublimely uttered, "If I yet pleased men, I should not be the servant of Christ."[6] But continence and modesty consist not alone in purity of the flesh, but also in seemliness, as well as in modesty of dress and adornment ; so that, according to the apostle, she who is unmarried may be holy both in body and in spirit. Paul instructs and teaches us, saying, "He that is unmarried careth for the things of the Lord, how he may please God : but he who has contracted marriage careth for the things which are of this world, how he may please his wife. So both the virgin and the unmarried woman consider those things which are the Lord's, that they may be holy both in body and spirit."[7] A virgin ought not only to be so, but also to be perceived and believed to be so : no one on seeing a virgin should be in any doubt as to whether she is one. Perfectness should show itself equal in all things ; nor should the dress of the body discredit the good of the mind. Why should she walk out adorned? Why with dressed hair, as if she either had or sought for a husband? Rather let her dread to please if she is a virgin ; and let her not invite her own risk, if she is keeping herself for better and divine things. They who have not a husband whom they profess that they please, should persevere, sound and pure not only in body, but also in spirit. For it is not right that a virgin should have her hair braided for the appearance of her beauty, or boast of her flesh and of its beauty, when she has no struggle greater than that against her flesh, and no contest more obstinate than that of conquering and subduing the body.

6. Paul proclaims in a loud and lofty voice, "But God forbid that I should glory, save in the cross of our Lord Jesus Christ, by whom the world is crucified unto me, and I unto the world."[8] And yet a virgin in the Church glories concerning her fleshly appearance and the beauty of her body ! Paul adds, and says, "For they that are Christ's have crucified their flesh, with its faults and lusts."[9] And she who professes to have renounced the lusts and vices of the flesh, is found in the midst of those very things which she has renounced ! Virgin, thou art taken, thou

---

[1] One codex adds here: "since it is written, 'He who perseveres unto the end, the same shall be saved.'"
[2] Otherwise, "These are the flowers of the ecclesiastical seed."
[3] Matt. xix. 11.
[4] Apoc. xiv. 4.

[5] Ps. liii. 5.
[6] Gal. i. 10.
[7] 1 Cor. vii. 32.
[8] Gal. vi. 14.
[9] Gal. v. 24.

art exposed, thou boastest one thing and affect-est another. You sprinkle yourself with the stains of carnal concupiscence, although you are a candidate of purity and modesty. "Cry," says the Lord to Isaiah, "All flesh is grass, and all the glory of it as the flower of the grass : the grass withereth, and the flower fadeth ; but the word of the Lord endureth for ever." [1] It is becoming for no Christian, and especially it is not becoming for a virgin, to regard any glory and honour of the flesh, but only to desire the word of God, to embrace benefits which shall endure for ever. Or, if she must glory in the flesh, then assuredly let her glory when she is tortured in confession of the name ; when a woman is found to be stronger than the tortures ; when she suffers fire, or the cross, or the sword, or the wild beasts, that she may be crowned. These are the precious jewels of the flesh, these are the better ornaments of the body.

7. But there are some rich women, and wealthy in the fertility of means, who prefer their own wealth, and contend that they ought to use these blessings. Let them know first of all that she is rich who is rich in God ; that she is wealthy who is wealthy in Christ ; that those are blessings which are spiritual, divine, heavenly, which lead us to God, which abide with us in perpetual possession with God. But whatever things are earthly, and have been received in this world, and will remain here with the world, ought so to be contemned even as the world itself is contemned, whose pomps and delights we have already renounced when by a blessed passage we came to God. John stimulates and exhorts us, witnessing with a spiritual and heavenly voice. "Love not the world," says he, "neither the things that are in the world. If any man love the world, the love of the Father is not in him. For all that is in the world, is lust of the flesh, and the lust of the eyes, and the pride of life, which is not from the Father, but is of the lust of the world. And the world passeth away, and the lust thereof : but he that doeth the will of God abideth for ever, even as God also abideth for ever." [2] Therefore eternal and divine things are to be followed, and all things must be done after the will of God, that we may follow the divine footsteps and teachings of our Lord, who warned us, and said, "I came down from heaven, not to do my own will, but the will of Him that sent me." [3] But if the servant is not greater than his lord, and he that is freed owes obedience to his deliverer, we who desire to be Christians ought to imitate what Christ said and did. It is written, and it is read and heard, and is celebrated for our example by the Church's

mouth, "He that saith he abideth in Christ, ought himself also so to walk even as He walked." [4] Therefore we must walk with equal steps ; we must strive with emulous walk. Then the following of truth answers to the faith of our name, and a reward is given to the believer, if what is believed is also done.

8. You call yourself wealthy and rich ; but Paul meets your riches, and with his own voice prescribes for the moderating of your dress and ornament within a just limit. "Let women," said he, "adorn themselves with shamefacedness and sobriety, not with broidered hair, nor gold, nor pearls, nor costly array, but as becometh women professing chastity, with a good conversation." [5] Also Peter consents to these same precepts, and says, "Let there be in the woman not the outward adorning of array, or gold, or apparel, but the adorning of the heart." [6] But if these also warn us that the women who are accustomed to make an excuse for their dress by reference to their husband, should be restrained and limited by religious observance to the Church's discipline, how much more is it right that the virgin should keep that observance, who has no excuse for adorning herself, nor can the deceitfulness of her fault be laid upon another, but she herself remains in its guilt !

9. You say that you are wealthy and rich. But not everything that can be done ought also to be done ; nor ought the broad desires that arise out of the pride of the world to be extended beyond the honour and modesty of virginity ; since it is written, "All things are lawful, but all things are not expedient : all things are lawful, but all things edify not." [7] For the rest, if you dress your hair sumptuously, and walk so as to draw attention in public, and attract the eyes of youth upon you, and draw the sighs of young men after you, nourish the lust of concupiscence, and inflame the fuel of sighs, so that, although you yourself perish not, yet you cause others to perish, and offer yourself, as it were, a sword or poison to the spectators ; you cannot be excused on the pretence that you are chaste and modest in mind. Your shameful dress and immodest ornament accuse you ; nor can you be counted now among Christ's maidens and virgins, since you live in such a manner as to make yourselves objects of desire.

10. You say that you are wealthy and rich ; but it becomes not a virgin to boast of her riches, since Holy Scripture says, "What hath pride profited us? or what benefit hath the vaunting of riches conferred upon us? And all these

1 Isa. xl. 6.
2 1 John ii. 15-17.
3 John vi. 38.

4 1 John ii. 6.
5 1 Tim. ii. 9, 10.
6 1 Pet. iii. 3, 4.
7 1 Cor. x. 23.

things have passed away like a shadow." [1] And the apostle again warns us, and says, "And they that buy, as though they bought not; and they that possess, as though they possessed not; and they that use this world, as though they used it not. For the fashion of this world passeth away." [2] Peter also, to whom the Lord commends His sheep to be fed and guarded, on whom He placed and founded the Church, says indeed that he has no silver and gold, but says that he is rich in the grace of Christ — that he is wealthy in his faith and virtue — wherewith he performed many great works with miracle, wherewith he abounded in spiritual blessings to the grace of glory. These riches, this wealth, she cannot possess, who had rather be rich to this world than to Christ.

11. You say that you are wealthy and rich, and you think that you should use those things which God has willed you to possess. Use them, certainly, but for the things of salvation; use them, but for good purposes; use them, but for those things which God has commanded, and which the Lord has set forth. Let the poor feel that you are wealthy; let the needy feel that you are rich. Lend your estate to God; give food to Christ. Move *Him* by the prayers of many [3] to grant you to carry out the glory of virginity, and to succeed in coming to the Lord's rewards. There entrust your treasures, where no thief digs through, where no insidious plunderer breaks in. Prepare for yourself possessions; but let them rather be heavenly ones, where neither rust wears out, nor hail bruises, nor sun burns, nor rain spoils your fruits constant and perennial, and free from all contact of worldly injury. For in this very matter you are sinning against God, if you think that riches were given you by Him for this purpose, to enjoy them thoroughly, without a view to salvation. For God gave man also a voice; and yet love-songs and indecent things are not on that account to be sung. And God willed iron to be for the culture of the earth, but not on that account must murders be committed. Or because God ordained incense, and wine, and fire, are we thence to sacrifice to idols? Or because the flocks of cattle abound in your fields, ought you to immolate victims and offerings to the gods? Otherwise a large estate is a temptation, unless the wealth minister to good uses; so that every man, in proportion to his wealth, ought by his patrimony rather to redeem his transgressions than to increase them.

12. The characteristics of ornaments, and of garments, and the allurements of beauty, are not fitting for any but prostitutes and immodest women; and the dress of none is more precious than of those whose modesty is lowly. [4] Thus in the Holy Scriptures, by which the Lord wished us to be both instructed and admonished, the harlot city is described more beautifully arrayed and adorned, and with her ornaments; and the rather on account of those very ornaments about to perish. "And there came," it is said, "one of the seven angels, which had the seven phials, and talked with me, saying, Come hither, I will show thee the judgment of the great whore, that sitteth upon many waters, with whom the kings of the earth have committed fornication. And he carried me away in spirit; and I saw a woman sit upon a beast, and that woman was arrayed in a purple and scarlet mantle, and was adorned with gold, and precious stones, and pearls, having a golden cup in her hand, full of curses, and filthiness, and fornication of the whole earth." [5] Let chaste and modest virgins avoid the dress of the unchaste, the manners of the immodest, the ensigns of brothels, the ornaments of harlots.

13. Moreover Isaiah, full of the Holy Spirit, cries out and chides the daughters of Sion, corrupted with gold, and silver, and raiment, and rebukes them, affluent as they were in pernicious wealth, and departing from God for the sake of the world's delights. "The daughters of Sion," says he, "are haughty, and walk with stretched-out neck and beckoning of the eyes, trailing their gowns as they go, and mincing with their feet. And God will humble the princely daughters of Sion, and the Lord will unveil their dress; and the Lord will take away the glory of their apparel, and their ornaments, and their hair, and their curls, and their round tires like the moon, and their crisping-pins, and their bracelets, and their clusters of pearls, and their armlets and rings, and ear-rings, and silks woven with gold and hyacinth. And instead of a sweet smell there shall be dust; and thou shall be girt with a rope instead of with a girdle; and for a golden ornament of thy head thou shalt have baldness." [6] This God blames, this He marks out: hence He declares that virgins are corrupted; hence, that they have departed from the true and divine worship. Lifted up, they have fallen; with their heads adorned, they merited dishonour and disgrace. Having put on silk and purple, they cannot put on Christ; adorned with gold, and pearls, and necklaces, they have lost the ornaments of the heart and spirit. Who would not execrate and avoid that which has been the destruction of another? Who would desire and

---

[1] Wisd. v. 8.
[2] 1 Cor. vii. 30, 31.
[3] The meaning is, — gifts to the poor will induce them to pray for the virgin, and in answer to their prayers, God will grant her the glory of virginity. [Luke xvi. 9.]

[4] Perhaps this sentence would be more literally translated, "and the dress of no women is, generally speaking, more expensive than the dress of those whose modesty is cheap;" i.e., who have no modesty at all, or very little.
[5] Apoc. xvii. 1.
[6] Isa. iii. 16.

take up that which has served as the sword and weapon for the death of another? If he who had drunk should die by draining the cup, you would know that what he had drunk was poison; if, on taking food, he who had taken it were to perish, you would know that what, when taken, could kill, was deadly; nor would you eat or drink of that whence you had before seen that others had perished. Now what ignorance of truth is it, what madness of mind, to wish for that which both has hurt and always will hurt; and to think that you yourself will not perish by those means whereby you know that others have perished!

14. For God neither made the sheep scarlet or purple, nor taught the juices of herbs and shell-fish to dye and colour wool, nor arranged necklaces with stones set in gold, and with pearls distributed in a woven series or numerous cluster, wherewith you would hide the neck which He made; that what God formed in man may be covered, and that may be seen upon it which the devil has invented in addition. Has God willed that wounds should be made in the ears, wherewith infancy, as yet innocent, and unconscious of worldly evil, may be put to pain, that subsequently from the scars and holes of the ears precious beads may hang, heavy, if not by their weight, still by the amount of their cost? All which things sinning and apostate angels put forth by their arts, when, lowered to the contagions of earth, they forsook their heavenly vigour. They taught them also to paint the eyes with blackness drawn round them in a circle, and to stain the cheeks with a deceitful red, and to change the hair with false colours, and to drive out all truth, both of face and head, by the assault of their own corruption.

15. And indeed in that very matter, for the sake of the fear which faith suggests to me, for the sake of the love which brotherhood requires, I think that not virgins only and widows, but married women also, and all of the sex alike, should be admonished, that the work of God and His fashioning and formation ought in no manner to be adulterated, either with the application of yellow colour, or with black dust or rouge, or with any kind of medicament which can corrupt the native lineaments. God says, "Let us make man in our image and likeness;"[1] and does any one dare to alter and to change what God has made? They are laying hands on God when they try to re-form that which He formed, and to transfigure it, not knowing that everything which comes into being is God's work, everything that is changed is the devil's. If any artist, in painting, were to delineate in envious colouring the countenance and likeness and

bodily appearance of any one; and the likeness being now painted and completed, another person were to lay hands on it, as if, when it was already formed and already painted, he, being more skilled, could amend it, a serious wrong and a just cause of indignation would seem natural to the former artist. And do you think yourself likely with impunity to commit a boldness of such wicked temerity, an offence to God the artificer? For although you may not be immodest among men, and are not unchaste with your seducing dyes, yet when those things which belong to God are corrupted and violated, you are engaged in a worse adultery. That you think yourself to be adorned, that you think your hair to be dressed, is an assault upon the divine work, is a prevarication of the truth.

16. The voice of the warning apostle is, "Purge out the old leaven, that ye may be a new lump, as ye are unleavened; for even Christ our passover is sacrificed. Therefore let us keep the feast, not with old leaven, neither with the leaven of malice and wickedness, but with the unleavened bread of sincerity and truth."[2] But are sincerity and truth preserved, when what is sincere is polluted by adulterous colours, and what is true is changed into a lie by the deceitful dyes of medicaments? Your Lord says, "Thou canst not make one hair white or black;"[3] and you, in order to overcome the word of your Lord, will be more mighty than He, and stain your hair with a daring endeavour and with profane contempt. With evil presage of the future, you make a beginning to yourself already of flame-coloured hair; and sin (oh, wickedness!) with your head—that is, with the nobler part of your body! And although it is written of the Lord, "His head and His hair were white like wool or snow,"[4] you curse that whiteness and hate that hoariness which is like to the Lord's head.

17. Are you not afraid, I entreat you, being such as you are, that when the day of resurrection comes, your Maker may not recognise you again, and may turn you away when you come to His rewards and promises, and may exclude you, rebuking you with the vigour of a Censor and Judge, and say: "This is not my work, nor is this our image. You have polluted your skin with a false medicament, you have changed your hair with an adulterous colour, your face is violently taken possession of by a lie, your figure is corrupted, your countenance is another's. You cannot see God, since your eyes are not those which God made, but those which the devil has spoiled. You have followed him, you have imitated the red and painted eyes of the serpent. As you are adorned in the fashion of your enemy,

---

[1] Gen. i. 26.

[2] 1 Cor. v. 7.
[3] Matt. v. 36.
[4] Apoc. i. 14.

with him also you shall burn by and by." Are not these, I beg, matters to be reflected on by God's servants? Are they not always to be dreaded day and night? Let married women see to it, in what respect they are flattering themselves concerning the solace of their husbands with the desire of pleasing them, and while they put them forward indeed as their excuse, they make them partners in the association of guilty consent. Virgins, assuredly, to whom this address is intended to appeal, who have adorned themselves with arts of this kind, I should think ought not to be counted among virgins, but, like infected sheep and diseased cattle, to be driven from the holy and pure flock of virginity, lest by living together they should pollute the rest with their contagion ; lest they ruin others even as they have perished themselves.

18. And since we are seeking the advantage of continency, let us also avoid everything that is pernicious and hostile to it. And I will not pass over those things, which while by negligence they come into use, have made for themselves a usurped licence, contrary to modest and sober manners. Some are not ashamed to be present at marriage parties, and in that freedom of lascivious discourse to mingle in unchaste conversation, to hear what is not becoming, to say what is not lawful, to expose themselves, to be present in the midst of disgraceful words and drunken banquets, by which the ardour of lust is kindled, and the bride is animated to bear, and the bridegroom to dare lewdness.[1] What place is there at weddings for her whose mind is not towards marriage? Or what can there be pleasant or joyous in those engagements for her, where both desires and wishes are different from her own? What is learnt there — what is seen? How greatly a virgin falls short of her resolution, when she who had come there modest goes away immodest ! Although she may remain a virgin in body and mind, yet in eyes, in ears, in tongue, she has diminished the virtues that she possessed.

19. But what of those who frequent promiscuous baths ; who prostitute to eyes that are curious to lust, bodies that are dedicated to chastity and modesty? They who disgracefully behold naked men, and are seen naked by men, do they not themselves afford enticement to vice, do they not solicit and invite the desires of those present to their own corruption and wrong? "Let every one," say you, "look to the disposition with which he comes thither : my care is only that of refreshing and washing my poor body." That kind of defence does not clear you, nor does it excuse the crime of lasciviousness and wantonness. Such a washing defiles ; it does not purify nor cleanse the limbs, but stains them. You behold no one immodestly, but you yourself are gazed upon immodestly. You do not pollute your eyes with disgraceful delight, but in delighting others you yourself are polluted. You make a show of the bathing-place ; the places where you assemble are fouler than a theatre. There all modesty is put ; off together with the clothing of garments, the honour and modesty of the body is laid aside ; virginity is exposed, to be pointed at and to be handled. And now, then, consider whether when you are clothed you are modest among men, when the boldness of nakedness has conduced to immodesty.

20. For this reason, therefore, the Church frequently mourns over her virgins ; hence she groans at their scandalous and detestable stories ; hence the flower of her virgins is extinguished, the honour and modesty of continency are injured, and all its glory and dignity are profaned. Thus the hostile besieger insinuates himself by his arts ; thus by snares that deceive, by secret ways, the devil creeps in. Thus, while virgins wish to be more carefully adorned, and to wander with more liberty, they cease to be virgins, corrupted by a furtive dishonour ; widows before they are married, adulterous, not to their husband, but to Christ. In proportion as they had been as virgins destined to great rewards, so will they experience great punishments for the loss of their virginity.

21. Therefore hear me, O virgins, as a parent ; hear, I beseech you, one who fears while he warns ; hear one who is faithfully consulting for your advantage and your profit. Be such as God the Creator made you ; be such as the hand of your Father ordained you. Let your countenance remain in you incorrupt, your neck unadorned, your figure simple ; let not wounds be made in your ears, nor let the precious chain of bracelets and necklaces circle your arms or your neck ; let your feet be free from golden bands, your hair stained with no dye, your eyes worthy of beholding God. Let your baths be performed with women, among whom your bathing is modest.[2] Let the shameless feasts and lascivious banquets of marriages be avoided, the contagion of which is perilous. Overcome dress, since you are a virgin ; overcome gold, since you overcome the flesh and the world. It is not consistent to be unable to be conquered by the greater, and to be found no match for the less. Strait and narrow is the way which leadeth to life ; hard and difficult is the track which tends to glory. By this pathway the martyrs pro-

---

[1] [The utterly intolerable paganism here exposed, and fully sustained by Martial and other Latin poets, accounts for much of the discipline of the early Church, and its excessive laudations of virginity.]

[2] Otherwise read, "among you; " or possibly, "whose bathing is modest towards you."

gress, the virgins pass, the just of all kinds advance. Avoid the broad and roomy ways. There are deadly snares and death-bringing pleasures; there the devil flatters, that he may deceive; smiles, that he may do mischief; entices, that he may slay. The first fruit for the martyrs is a hundred-fold; the second is yours, sixty-fold. As with the martyrs there is no thought of the flesh and of the world, no small, and trifling, and delicate encounter; so also in you, whose reward is second in grace, let there be the strength in endurance next to theirs. The ascent to great things is not easy. What toil we suffer, what labour, when we endeavour to ascend the hills and the tops of mountains! What, then, that we may ascend to heaven? If you look to the reward of the promise, your labour is less. Immortality is given to the persevering, eternal life is set before them; the Lord promises a kingdom.

22. Hold fast, O virgins! hold fast what you have begun to be; hold fast what you shall be. A great reward awaits you, a great recompense of virtue, the immense advantage of chastity. Do you wish to know what ill the virtue of continence avoids, what good it possesses? " I will multiply," says God to the woman, " thy sorrows and thy groanings; and in sorrow shalt thou bring forth children; and thy desire shall be to thy husband, and he shall rule over thee." [1] You are free from this sentence. You do not fear the sorrows and the groans of women. You have no fear of child-bearing; nor is your husband lord over you; but your Lord and Head is Christ, after the likeness and in the place of the man; *with that of men* your lot and your condition is equal. It is the word of the Lord which says, " The children of this world beget and are begotten; but they who are counted worthy of that world, and of the resurrection from the dead, neither marry nor are given in marriage: neither shall they die any more: for they are equal to the angels of God, being the children of the resurrection." [2] That which we shall be, you have already begun to be. You possess already in this world the glory of the resurrection. You pass through the world without the contagion of the world; in that you continue chaste and virgins, you are equal to the angels of God. Only let your virginity remain and endure substantial and uninjured; and as it began bravely, let it persevere continuously, and not seek the ornaments of necklaces nor garments, but of conduct. Let it look towards God and heaven, and not lower to the lust of the flesh and of the world, the eyes uplifted *to things* above, or set them upon earthly things.

23. The first decree commanded to increase and to multiply; the second enjoined continency. While the world is still rough and void, we are propagated by the fruitful begetting of numbers, and we increase to the enlargement of the human race. Now, when the world is filled and the earth supplied, they who can receive continency, living after the manner of eunuchs, are made eunuchs unto the kingdom. Nor does the Lord command this, but He exhorts it; nor does He impose the yoke of necessity, since the free choice of the will is left. But when He says that in His Father's house are many mansions, He points out the dwellings of the better habitation. Those better habitations you are seeking; cutting away the desires of the flesh, you obtain the reward of a greater grace in the heavenly home. All indeed who attain to the divine gift and inheritance by the sanctification of baptism, therein put off the old man by the grace of the saving laver, and, renewed by the Holy Spirit from the filth of the old contagion, are purged by a second nativity. But the greater holiness and truth of that repeated birth belongs to you, who have no longer any desires of the flesh and of the body. Only the things which belong to virtue and the Spirit have remained in you to glory. It is the apostle's word whom the Lord called His chosen vessel, whom God sent to proclaim the heavenly command: " The first man," says he, " is from the earth, of earth; the second man is from heaven. Such as is the earthy, such are they also who are earthy; and such as is the heavenly, such also are the heavenly. As we have borne the image of him who is earthy, let us also bear the image of Him who is heavenly." [3] Virginity bears this image, integrity bears it, holiness bears it, and truth. Disciplines which are mindful of God bear it, retaining righteousness with religion, stedfast in faith, humble in fear, brave to all suffering, meek to sustain wrong, easy to show mercy, of one mind and one heart in fraternal peace.

24. Every one of which things, O good virgins, you ought to observe, to love, to fulfil, who, giving yourselves to God and Christ, are advancing in both the higher and better part to the Lord, to whom you have dedicated yourselves. You that are advanced in years, suggest a teaching to the younger. You that are younger, give a stimulus to your coevals. Stir one another up with mutual exhortations; provoke to glory by rival proofs of virtue. Endure bravely, go on spiritually, attain happily. Only remember us at that time, when virginity shall begin to be rewarded in you.

---

[1] Gen. iii. 16.
[2] Luke xx. 35, 36.

[3] 1 Cor. xv. 47.

TREATISE III.[1]

ON THE LAPSED.[2]

ARGUMENT. — HAVING ENLARGED UPON THE UNLOOKED-FOR PEACE OF THE CHURCH, AND THE CONSTANCY OF THE CONFESSORS AND THOSE WHO HAD STOOD FAST IN THE FAITH; AND THEN WITH EXTREME GRIEF HAVING POINTED TO THE DOWNFALL OF THE LAPSED, AND UNFOLDED THE CAUSES OF THE BYGONE PERSECUTION, NAMELY, THE NEGLECT OF DISCIPLINE, AND THE SINS OF THE FAITHFUL; OUR AUTHOR SEVERELY REPROACHES THE LAPSED, THAT, AT THE VERY FIRST WORDS OF THE ENEMY THREATENING THEM, THEY HAD SACRIFICED TO IDOLS, AND HAD NOT RATHER WITHDRAWN, ACCORDING TO CHRIST'S COUNSEL.[3] LASTLY, HE WARNS HIS READERS TO AVOID THE NOVATIANS, CONFUTING THEIR HERESY WITH MANY SCRIPTURES.

1. Behold, beloved brethren, peace is restored to the Church; and although it lately seemed to incredulous people difficult, and to traitors impossible, our security is by divine aid and retribution re-established. Our minds return to gladness; and the season of affliction and the cloud being dispersed, tranquillity and serenity have shone forth once more. Praises must be given to God, and His benefits and gifts must be celebrated with giving of thanks, although even in the time of persecution our voice has not ceased to give thanks. For not even an enemy has so much power as to prevent us, who love the Lord with our whole heart, and life, and strength, from declaring His blessings and praises always and everywhere with glory. The day earnestly desired, by the prayers of all has come; and after the dreadful and loathsome darkness of a long night, the world has shone forth irradiated by the light of the Lord.

2. We look with glad countenances upon confessors illustrious with the heraldry of a good name, and glorious with the praises of virtue and of faith; clinging to them with holy kisses, we embrace them long desired with insatiable eagerness. The white-robed cohort of Christ's soldiers is here, who in the fierce conflict have broken the ferocious turbulence of an urgent persecu-

tion, having been prepared for the suffering of the dungeon, armed for the endurance of death. Bravely you have resisted the world: you have afforded a glorious spectacle in the sight of God; you have been an example to your brethren that shall follow you. That religious voice has named the name of Christ, in whom it has once confessed that it believed; those illustrious hands, which had only been accustomed to divine works, have resisted the sacrilegious sacrifices; those lips, sanctified by heavenly food after the body and blood of the Lord, have rejected the profane contacts and the leavings of the idols. Your head has remained free from the impious and wicked veil[4] with which the captive heads of those who sacrificed were there veiled; your brow, pure with the sign of God, could not bear the crown of the devil, but reserved itself for the Lord's crown. How joyously does your Mother Church receive you in her bosom, as you return from the battle! How blissfully, how gladly, does she open her gates, that in united bands you may enter, bearing the trophies from a prostrate enemy! With the triumphing men come women also, who, while contending with the world, have also overcome their sex; and virgins also come with the double glory of their warfare, and boys transcending their years with their virtues.[5] Moreover, also, the rest of the multitude of those who stand fast follow your glory, and accompany your footsteps with the insignia of praise, very near to, and almost joined with, your own. In them also is the same sincerity of heart, the same soundness of a tenacious faith. Resting on the unshaken roots of the heavenly precepts, and strengthened by the evangelical traditions, the prescribed banishment, the destined tortures, the loss of property, the bodily punishments, have not terrified them. The days for proving their faith were limited beforehand; but he who remembers that he has renounced the world knows no day of worldly appointment, neither does he who hopes for eternity from God calculate the seasons of earth any more.

3. Let none, my beloved brethren, let none depreciate this glory; let none by malignant dispraise detract from the uncorrupted stedfastness of those who have stood. When the day appointed for denying was gone by, every one who had not professed within that time not to be a Christian, confessed that he was a Christian. It is the first title to victory to confess the Lord under the violence of the hands of the Gentiles. It is the second step to glory to be withdrawn by a cautious retirement, and to be

---

[1] [Written A.D. 251.]

[2] Cyprian had frequently promised, that as soon as peace should be restored to the Church, he would write something definite on the subject of the lapsed; and in the following treatise he fulfils his promise.

[3] Now that they had been polluted with sacrifices, contrary to the law of the Gospel, before their sins were atoned for, before confession of their crime had been made, they were doing violence to the body and blood of the Lord, and were extorting communion and peace from certain presbyters, without the bishop's judgment. He exhorts them accordingly, in many words, that, — deterred by the divine vengeance on certain of the lapsed who had communicated unworthily, and animated by the example of those, who, although under the bondage of no crime, either of sacrifice or of certificate, yet, because they had even thought of these things, confessed with grief and sincerity the actual sin to God's priests and made avowal, — they should confess their sin, to public repentance and full satisfaction.

[4] The veiled head was the sign of Roman worship. — *Oxford trans.* [This helps to interpret 1 Cor. xi. 4, which was equally against the Jewish practice.]

[5] Some read, with very uncertain authority, "with the virtues of continency."

reserved for the Lord. The former is a public, the latter is a private confession. The former overcomes the judge of this world; the latter, content with God as its judge, keeps a pure conscience in integrity of heart. In the former case there is a readier fortitude; in the latter, solicitude is more secure. The former, as his hour approached, was already found mature; the latter perhaps was delayed, who, leaving his estate, withdrew for a while, because he would not deny, but would certainly confess if he too had been apprehended.

4. One cause of grief saddens these heavenly crowns of martyrs, these glorious spiritual confessions, these very great and illustrious virtues of the brethren who stand; which is, that the hostile violence has torn away a part of our own bowels, and thrown it away in the destructiveness of its own cruelty. What shall I do in this matter, beloved brethren? Wavering in the various tide of feeling, what or how shall I speak? I need tears rather than words to express the sorrow with which the wound of our body should be bewailed, with which the manifold loss of a people once numerous should be lamented. For whose heart is so hard or cruel, who is so unmindful of brotherly love, as, among the varied ruins of his friends, and the mournful relics disfigured with all degradation, to be able to stand and to keep dry eyes, and not in the breaking out of his grief to express his groanings rather with tears than with words? I grieve, brethren, I grieve with you; nor does my own integrity and my personal soundness beguile me to the soothing of my griefs, since it is the shepherd that is chiefly wounded in the wound of his flock. I join my breast with each one, and I share in the grievous burden of sorrow and mourning. I wail with the wailing, I weep with the weeping, I regard myself as prostrated with those that are prostrate. My limbs are at the same time stricken with those darts of the raging enemy; their cruel swords have pierced through my bowels; my mind could not remain untouched and free from the inroad of persecution among my downfallen brethren; sympathy has cast me down also.

5. Yet, beloved brethren, the cause of truth is to be had in view; nor ought the gloomy darkness of the terrible persecution so to have blinded the mind and feeling, that there should remain no light and illumination whence the divine precepts may be beheld. If the cause of disaster is recognised, there is at once found a remedy for the wound. The Lord has desired His family to be proved; and because a long peace had corrupted the discipline[1] that had been divinely delivered to us, the heavenly re-

buke has aroused our faith, which was giving way, and I had almost said slumbering; and although we deserved[2] more for our sins, yet the most merciful Lord has so moderated all things, that all which has happened has rather seemed a trial than a persecution.

6. Each one was desirous of increasing his estate; and forgetful of what believers had either done before in the times of the apostles, or always ought to do, they, with the insatiable ardour of covetousness, devoted themselves to the increase of their property. Among the priests there was no devotedness of religion; among the ministers[3] there was no sound faith: in their works there was no mercy; in their manners there was no discipline. In men, their beards were defaced;[4] in women, their complexion was dyed: the eyes were falsified from what God's hand had made them; their hair was stained with a falsehood. Crafty frauds were used to deceive the hearts of the simple, subtle meanings for circumventing the brethren. They united in the bond of marriage with unbelievers; they prostituted the members of Christ to the Gentiles. They would swear not only rashly, but even more, would swear falsely; would despise those set over them with haughty swelling, would speak evil of one another with envenomed tongue, would quarrel with one another with obstinate hatred. Not a few bishops[5] who ought to furnish both exhortation and example to others, despising their divine charge, became agents in secular business, forsook their throne, deserted their people, wandered about over foreign provinces, hunted the markets for gainful merchandise, while brethren were starving in the Church.[6] They sought to possess money in hoards, they seized estates by crafty deceits, they increased their gains by multiplying usuries. What do not such as we deserve to suffer for sins of this kind, when even already the divine rebuke has forewarned us, and said, "If they shall forsake my law, and walk not in my judgments; if they shall profane my statutes, and shall not observe my precepts, I will visit their offences with a rod, and their sins with scourges?"[7]

7. These things were before declared to us, and predicted. But we, forgetful of the law and obedience required of us, have so acted by our sins, that while we despise the Lord's commandments, we have come by severer remedies to the correction of our sin and probation of our faith. Nor indeed have we at last been converted to the fear of the Lord, so as to undergo patiently

---

[1] [This and the whole passage which follows are cited by Wordsworth, to illustrate the times that produced a Callistus. See his *Hippol.*, p. 140.]

[2] Some read, "to suffer."
[3] A late version gives, "in the ministries."
[4] [Vol. iv. p. 22. Here Cyprian's "master" seems to speak again.]
[5] [The state of things at Rome under Callistus and his predecessor is here very delicately reflected.]
[6] Or, "brought no aid to starving brethren in the Church."
[7] Ps. lxxxix. 30.

and courageously this our correction and divine proof. Immediately at the first words of the threatening foe, the greatest number of the brethren betrayed their faith, and were cast down, not by the onset of persecution, but cast themselves down by voluntary lapse. What unheard-of thing, I beg of you, what new thing had happened, that, as if on the occurrence of things unknown and unexpected, the obligation to [1] Christ should be dissolved with headlong rashness? Have not prophets aforetime, and subsequently apostles, told of these things? Have not they, full of the Holy Spirit, predicted the afflictions of the righteous, and always the injuries of the heathens? Does not the sacred Scripture, which ever arms our faith and strengthens with a voice from heaven the servants of God, say, "Thou shalt worship the Lord thy God, and Him only shalt thou serve?" [2] Does it not again show the anger of the divine indignation, and warn of the fear of punishment beforehand, when it says, "They worshipped them whom their fingers have made; and the mean man boweth down, and the great man humbleth himself, and I will forgive them not?" [3] And again, God speaks, and says, "He that sacrifices unto any gods, save unto the Lord only, shall be destroyed." [4] In the Gospel also subsequently, the Lord, who instructs by His words and fulfils by His deeds, teaching what should be done, and doing whatever He had taught, did He not before admonish us of whatever is now done and shall be done? Did He not before ordain both for those who deny Him eternal punishments, and for those that confess Him saving rewards?

8. From some — ah, misery! — all these things have fallen away, and have passed from memory. They indeed did not wait to be apprehended ere they ascended, or to be interrogated ere they denied. Many were conquered before the battle, prostrated before the attack. Nor did they even leave it to be said for them, that they seemed to sacrifice to idols unwillingly. They ran to the market-place of their own accord; freely they hastened to death, as if they had formerly wished it, as if they would embrace an opportunity now given which they had always desired. How many were put off by the magistrates at that time, when evening was coming on; how many even asked that their destruction might not be delayed! What violence can such a one plead as an excuse? How can he purge his crime, when it was he himself who rather used force to bring about his own ruin? When they came voluntarily to the Capitol, — when they freely approached to the obedience of the terrible wick-

edness, — did not their tread falter? Did not their sight darken, their heart tremble, their arms fall helplessly down? Did not their senses fail, their tongue cleave to their mouth, their speech grow weak? Could the servant of God stand there, and speak and renounce Christ, when he had already renounced the devil and the world? Was not that altar, whither he drew near to perish, to him a funeral pile? Ought he not to shudder at and flee from the devil's altar, which he had seen to smoke, and to be redolent of a foul fœtor, as if it were the funeral and sepulchre of his life? Why bring with you, O wretched man, a sacrifice? why immolate a victim? You yourself have come to the altar an offering; you yourself have come a victim: there you have immolated your salvation, your hope; there you have burnt up your faith in those deadly fires. [5]

9. But to many their own destruction was not sufficient. With mutual exhortations, people were urged to their ruin; death was pledged by turns in the deadly cup. And that nothing might be wanting to aggravate the crime, infants also, in the arms of their parents, either carried or conducted, lost, while yet little ones, what in the very first beginning of their nativity they had gained. [6] Will not they, when the day of judgment comes, say, "We have done nothing; [7] nor have we forsaken the Lord's bread and cup to hasten freely to a profane contact; the faithlessness of others has ruined us. We have found our parents our murderers; they have denied to us the Church as a Mother; they have denied God as a Father: so that, while we were little, and unforeseeing, and unconscious of such a crime, we were associated by others to the partnership of wickedness, and we were snared by the deceit of others?"

10. Nor is there, alas, any just and weighty reason which excuses such a crime. One's country was to be left, and loss of one's estate was to be suffered. Yet to whom that is born and dies is there not a necessity at some time to leave his country, and to suffer the loss of his estate? But let not Christ be forsaken, so that the loss of salvation and of an eternal home should be feared. Behold, the Holy Spirit cries by the prophet, "Depart ye, depart ye, go ye out from thence, touch not the unclean thing; go ye out from the midst of her, and be ye separate, that bear the vessels of the Lord." [8] Yet those who are the vessels of the Lord and the temple of God do not go out from the midst, nor depart, that they may not be compelled to touch the unclean thing, and to be polluted and corrupted with deadly food. Elsewhere also a voice is

---

[1] "Christi sacramentum." [Like a panic in an undisciplined army.]
[2] Deut. vi. 13.
[3] Isa. ii. 8, 9.
[4] Ex. xxii. 20.

[5] [Mark viii. 36.]
[6] [The baptism of infants seems now to be general, and also the communion of infants. See sec. 25, *infra*.]
[7] Some read, "evil."
[8] Isa. lii. 11.

heard from heaven, forewarning what is becoming for the servants of God to do, saying, "Come out of her, my people, that ye be not partakers of her sins, and that ye receive not of her plagues."[1] He who goes out and departs does not become a partaker of the guilt; but he will be wounded with the plagues who is found a companion in the crime. And therefore the Lord commanded us in the persecution to depart and to flee; and both taught that this should be done, and Himself did it. For as the crown is given of the condescension of God, and cannot be received unless the hour comes for accepting it, whosoever abiding in Christ departs for a while does not deny his faith, but waits for the time; but he who has fallen, after refusing to depart, remained to deny it.

11. The truth, brethren, must not be disguised; nor must the matter and cause of our wound be concealed. A blind love of one's own property has deceived many; nor could they be prepared for, or at ease in, departing when their wealth fettered them like a chain. Those were the chains to them that remained — those were the bonds by which both virtue was retarded, and faith burdened, and the spirit bound, and the soul hindered; so that they who were involved in earthly things[2] might become a booty and food for the serpent, which, according to God's sentence, feeds upon earth. And therefore the Lord the teacher of good things, forewarning for the future time, says, " If thou wilt be perfect, go, sell all that thou hast, and give to the poor, and thou shalt have treasure in heaven: and come and follow me."[3] If rich men did this, they would not perish by their riches; if they laid up treasure in heaven, they would not now have a domestic enemy and assailant. Heart and mind and feeling would be in heaven, if the treasure were in heaven; nor could he be overcome by the world who had nothing in the world whereby he could be overcome.[4] He would follow the Lord loosed and free, as did the apostles, and many in the times of the apostles, and many who forsook both their means and their relatives, and clave to Christ with undivided ties.

12. But how can they follow Christ, who are held back by the chain of their wealth? Or how can they seek heaven, and climb to sublime and lofty heights, who are weighed down by earthly desires? They think that they possess, when they are rather possessed; as slaves of their profit, and not lords with respect to their own money, but rather the bond-slaves of their money. These times and these men are indicated by the apostle, when he says, "But they that will be rich, fall into temptation, and a snare, and into many foolish and hurtful lusts, which drown men in destruction and in perdition. For the root of all evil is the love of money, which, while some have coveted, they have erred[5] from the faith, and pierced themselves through with many sorrows."[6] But with what rewards does the Lord invite us to contempt of worldly wealth? With what compensations does He atone for the small and trifling losses of this present time? " There is no man," saith He, " that leaves house, or land, or parents, or brethren, or wife, or children, for the kingdom of God's sake, but he shall receive seven fold[7] even in this time, but in the world to come life everlasting."[8] If we know these things, and have found them out from the truth of the Lord who promises, not only is not loss of this kind to be feared, but even to be desired; as the Lord Himself again announces and warns us, " Blessed are ye when men shall persecute you, and when they shall separate you from their company, and shall cast you out, and shall speak of your name as evil, for the Son of man's sake! Rejoice ye in that day, and leap for joy; for, behold, your reward is great in heaven."[9]

13. But (say they) subsequently tortures had come,[10] and severe sufferings were threatening those who resisted. He may complain of tortures who has been overcome by tortures; he may offer the excuse of suffering who has been vanquished in suffering. Such a one may ask, and say, " I wished indeed to strive bravely, and, remembering my oath, I took up the arms of devotion and faith; but as I was struggling in the encounter, varied tortures and long-continued sufferings overcame me. My mind stood firm, and my faith was strong, and my soul struggled long, unshaken with the torturing pains; but when, with the renewed barbarity of the most cruel judge, wearied out as I was, the scourges were now tearing me,[11] the clubs bruised me, the rack strained me, the claw dug into me, the fire roasted me; my flesh deserted me in the struggle, the weakness of my bodily frame gave way, — not my mind, but my body, yielded in the suffering." Such a plea may readily avail to forgiveness; an apology of that kind may excite compassion. Thus at one time the Lord forgave Castus and Æmilius; thus, overcome in the first encounter, they were made victors in the second battle. So that they who had formerly given way to the fires became stronger than the fires,

---

[1] Apoc. xviii. 4.
[2] According to some, for " things " read " desires."
[3] Matt. xix. 21.
[4] Otherwise, " could be bound."

[5] Some substitute, " have made shipwreck of."
[6] 1 Tim. vi. 9.
[7] Or, " a hundred-fold."
[8] Mark x. 29.
[9] Luke vi. 22.
[10] " Were at hand."
[11] Or, " the scourges were lacerating my already wearied body."

and in that in which they had been vanquished they were conquerors. They entreated not for pity of their tears, but of their wounds; nor with a lamentable voice alone, but with laceration and suffering of body. Blood flowed instead of weeping; and instead of tears, gore poured forth from their half-scorched entrails.

14. But now, what wounds can those who are overcome show? what gashes of gaping entrails, what tortures of the limbs, in cases where it was not faith that fell in the encounter, but faithlessness that anticipated the struggle? Nor does the necessity of the crime excuse the person compelled, where the crime is committed of free will. Nor do I say this in such a way as that I would burden the cases of the brethren, but that I may rather instigate the brethren to a prayer of atonement. For, as it is written, "They who call you happy cause you to err, and destroy the paths of your feet," [1] he who soothes the sinner with flattering blandishments furnishes the stimulus to sin; nor does he repress, but nourishes wrong-doing. But he who, with braver counsels, rebukes at the same time that he instructs a brother, urges him onward to salvation. "As many as I love," saith the Lord, "I rebuke and chasten." [2] And thus also it behoves the Lord's priest not to mislead by deceiving concessions, but to provide with salutary remedies. He is an unskilful physician who handles the swelling edges of wounds with a tender hand, and, by retaining the poison shut up in the deep recesses of the body, increases it. The wound must be opened, and cut, and healed by the stronger remedy of cutting out the corrupting parts. The sick man may cry out, may vociferate, and may complain, in impatience of the pain; but he will afterwards give thanks when he has felt that he is cured.

15. Moreover, beloved brethren, a new kind of devastation has appeared; and, as if the storm of persecution had raged too little, there has been added to the heap, under the title of mercy, a deceiving mischief and a fair-seeming calamity. Contrary to the vigour of the Gospel, contrary to the law of the Lord and God, by the temerity of some, communion is relaxed to heedless persons, — a vain and false peace, dangerous to those who grant it, and likely to avail nothing to those who receive it. They do not seek for the patience necessary to health, nor the true medicine derived from atonement. Penitence is driven forth from their breasts, and the memory of their very grave and extreme sin is taken away. The wounds of the dying are covered over, and the deadly blow that is planted in the deep and secret entrails is concealed by a dissimulated suffering. Returning from the altars of the devil, they draw near to the holy place of the Lord, with hands filthy and reeking with smell, still almost breathing of the plague-bearing idol-meats; and even with jaws still exhaling their crime, and reeking with the fatal contact, they intrude on the body of the Lord, although the sacred Scripture stands in their way, and cries, saying, "Every one that is clean shall eat of the flesh; and whatever soul eateth of the flesh of the saving sacrifice, which is the Lord's, having his uncleanness upon him, that soul shall be cut off from his people." [3] Also, the apostle testifies, and says, "Ye cannot drink the cup of the Lord and the cup of devils; ye cannot be partakers of the Lord's table and of the table of devils." [4] He threatens, moreover, the stubborn and froward, and denounces them, saying, "Whosoever eateth the bread or drinketh the cup of the Lord unworthily, is guilty of the body and blood of the Lord." [5]

16. All these warnings being scorned and contemned, — before their sin is expiated, before confession has been made of their crime, before their conscience has been purged by sacrifice and by the hand of the priest,[6] before the offence of an angry and threatening Lord has been appeased, violence is done to His body and blood; and they sin now against their Lord more with their hand and mouth than when they denied their Lord. They think that that is peace which some with deceiving words are blazoning forth: [7] that is not peace, but war; and he is not joined to the Church who is separated from the Gospel. Why do they call an injury a kindness? Why do they call impiety by the name of piety? Why do they hinder those who ought to weep continually and to entreat their Lord, from the sorrowing of repentance, and pretend to receive them to communion? This is the same kind of thing to the lapsed as hail to the harvests; as the stormy star to the trees; as the destruction of pestilence to the herds; as the raging tempest to shipping. They take away the consolation of eternal hope; they overturn the tree from the roots; they creep on to a deadly contagion with their pestilent words; they dash the ship on the rocks, so that it may not reach to the harbour. Such a facility does not grant peace, but takes it away; nor does it give communion, but it hinders from salvation. This is another persecution, and another temptation, by which the crafty enemy still further assaults the lapsed; attacking them by a secret corruption, that their

---

[1] Isa. iii. 12.
[2] Apoc. iii. 19.

[3] Lev. vii. 20.
[4] 1 Cor. x. 21.
[5] 1 Cor. xi. 27.
[6] By some, the rest of the sentence after this word ("priest") is placed at the beginning of the paragraph, after the word "contemned."
[7] Venditant.

lamentation may be hushed, that their grief may be silent, that the memory of their sin may pass away, that the groaning of their heart may be repressed, that the weeping of their eyes may be quenched ; nor long and full penitence deprecate the Lord so grievously offended, although it is written, " Remember from whence thou art fallen, and repent." [1]

17. Let no one cheat himself, let no one deceive himself. The Lord alone can have mercy. He alone can bestow pardon for sins which have been committed against Himself, who bare our sins, who sorrowed for us, whom God delivered up for our sins. Man cannot be greater than God, nor can a servant remit or forego by his indulgence what has been committed by a greater crime against the Lord, lest to the person lapsed this be moreover added to his sin, if he be ignorant that it is declared, "Cursed is the man that putteth his hope in man." [2] The Lord must be besought. The Lord must be appeased by our atonement, who has said, that him that denieth Him He will deny, who alone has received all judgment from His Father. We believe, indeed, that the merits of martyrs and the works of the righteous are of great avail with the Judge ; but that will be when the day of judgment shall come ; [3] when, after the conclusion of this life and the world, His people shall stand before the tribunal of Christ.

18. But if any one, by an overhurried haste, rashly thinks that he can give remission of sins to all,[4] or dares to rescind the Lord's precepts, not only does it in no respect advantage the lapsed, but it does them harm. Not to have observed His judgment is to have provoked His wrath, and to think that the mercy of God must not first of all be entreated, and, despising the Lord, to presume on His power.[5] Under the altar of God the souls of the slain martyrs cry with a loud voice, saying, " How long, O Lord, holy and true, dost Thou not judge and avenge our blood upon those who dwell on the earth ?"[6] And they are bidden to rest, and still to keep patience. And does any one think that, in opposition to the Judge, a man can become of avail [7] for the general remission and pardon of sins, or that he can shield others before he himself is vindicated? The martyrs order something to be done ; [8] but only if this thing be just and lawful, if it can be done without opposing the Lord Himself by God's priest, if the consent of the obeying party be easy and yielding, if the moderation of the asking party be religious. The martyrs order something to be done ; but if what they order be not written in the law of the Lord, we must first know that they have obtained what they ask from God, and then do what they command. For that may not always appear to be immediately conceded by the divine majesty, which has been promised by man's undertaking.

19. For Moses also besought for the sins of the people ; and yet, when he had sought pardon for these sinners, he did not receive it. " I pray Thee," said he, " O Lord, this people have sinned a great sin, and have made them gods of gold. Yet now, if Thou wilt forgive their sin, forgive it ; but if not, blot me out of the book which Thou hast written. And the Lord said unto Moses, Whosoever hath sinned against me, him will I blot out of my book." [9] He, the friend of God ; he who had often spoken face to face with the Lord, could not obtain what he asked, nor could appease the wrath of an indignant God by his entreaty. God praises Jeremiah, and announces, saying, " Before I formed thee in the belly, I knew thee ; and before thou camest out of the womb I sanctified thee, and I ordained thee a prophet unto the nations." [10] And to the same man He saith, when he often entreated and prayed for the sins of the people, " Pray not thou for this people, neither lift up cry nor prayer for them ; for I will not hear them in the time wherein they call on me, in the time of their affliction." [11] But who was more righteous than Noah, who, when the earth was filled with sins, was alone found righteous on the earth? Who more glorious than Daniel? Who more strong for suffering martyrdom in firmness of faith, more happy in God's condescension, who so many times, both when he was in conflict conquered, and, when he had conquered, lived on? Was any more ready in good works than Job, braver in temptations, more patient in sufferings, more submissive in his fear, more true in his faith? And yet God said that He would not grant to them if they were to seek. When the prophet Ezekiel entreated for the sin of the people, " Whatsoever land," said He, " shall sin against me by trespassing grievously, I will stretch out mine hand upon it, and will break the staff of bread thereof, and will send famine upon it, and will cut off man and beast from it. Though these three men, Noah, Daniel, and Job, were in it, they should deliver neither sons nor daughters ; but

---

[1] Apoc. ii. 5.
[2] Jer. xvii. 5. [Here is an emphatic repudiation of what produced mediæval indulgences, saint-worship, and Mariolatry. Of the latter, so pre-eminently the system of modern Rome, not a syllable in all these Fathers. " Quam ritus eccles. nescit." Bernard, Ep. clxxiv., *Opp.*, i. 389.]
[3] [All the whole base on which " indulgences" and the like rest, is here shown to be worthless]
[4] " To any."
[5] " On his facility; " *v. l.*
[6] Apoc. vi. 10.
[7] " Worthy of."
[8] [i.e., the confessors awaiting martyrdom. See vol. iv. p. 693, note 2.]

[9] Ex. xxxii. 31.
[10] Jer. i. 5.
[11] Jer. vii. 16.

they only should be delivered themselves." [1] Thus, not everything that is asked is in the pre-judgment of the asker, but in the free will of the giver; neither can human judgment claim to itself or usurp anything, unless the divine pleasure approve.

20. In the Gospel the Lord speaks, and says, "Whosoever shall confess me before men, him will I also confess before my Father which is in heaven : but he that denieth me, him will I also deny." [2] If He does not deny him that denies, neither does He confess him that confesses; the Gospel cannot be sound in one part and waver in another. Either both must stand firm, or both must lose the force of truth. If they who deny shall not be guilty of a crime, neither shall they who confess receive the reward of a virtue. Again, if faith which has conquered be crowned, it is of necessity that faithlessness which is con-quered should be punished. Thus the martyrs can either do nothing if the Gospel may be broken; or if the Gospel cannot be broken, they can do nothing against the Gospel, since they become martyrs on account of the Gospel. Let no one, beloved brethren, let no one decry the dignity of martyrs, let no one degrade their glories and their crowns. The strength of their uncorrupted faith abides sound; nor can he either say or do anything against Christ, whose hope, and faith, and virtue, and glory, are all in Christ : those cannot be the authority for the bishops doing anything against God's command, who themselves have done God's command. Is any one greater than God, or more merciful than God's goodness, that he should either wish that undone which God has suffered to be done, or, as if God had too little power to protect His Church, should think that we could be preserved by his help?

21. Unless, perchance, these things have been done without God's knowledge, or all these things have happened without His permission; although Holy Scripture teaches the indocile, and admon-ishes the unmindful, where it speaks, saying, "Who gave Jacob for a spoil, and Israel to those who made a booty of him? Did not the Lord against whom they sinned, and would not walk in His ways, neither were obedient unto His law? And He has poured upon them the fury of His anger." [3] And elsewhere it testifies and says, "Is the Lord's hand shortened, that it cannot save; or His ear heavy, that it cannot hear? But your iniquities separate between you and your God; and because of your sins He hath hid His face from you, that He may not have mercy." [4] Let us rather consider our of-fences, revolving our doings and the secrets of our mind; let us weigh the deserts of our con-science; let it come back upon our heart that we have not walked in the Lord's ways, and have cast away God's law, and have never been will-ing to keep His precepts and saving counsels.

22. What good can you think of him, what fear can you suppose to have been with him, or what faith, whom neither fear could correct nor persecution itself could reform? His high and rigid neck, even when it has fallen, is unbent; his swelling and haughty soul is not broken, even when it is conquered. Prostrate, he threat-ens those who stand; and wounded, the sound. And because he may not at once receive the body of the Lord in his polluted hands, the sac-rilegious one is angry with the priests. And — oh your excessive madness, O frantic one — you are angry with him who endeavours to avert the anger of God from you; you threaten him who beseeches the divine mercy on your behalf, who feels your wound which you yourself do not feel, who sheds tears for you, which perhaps you never shed yourself. You are still aggravating and enhancing your crime; and while you yourself are implacable [5] against the ministers and priests [6] of God, do you think that the Lord can be appeased concerning you?

23. Receive rather, and admit what we say. Why do your deaf ears not hear the salutary pre-cepts with which we warn you? Why do your blind eyes not see the way of repentance which we point out? Why does your stricken and alienated mind not perceive the lively remedies which we both learn and teach from the heavenly Scriptures? [7] Or if some unbelievers have little faith in future events, let them be terrified with present ones. Lo, what punishments do we be-hold of those who have denied ! what sad deaths of theirs do we bewail ! Not even here can they be without punishment, although the day of punishment has not yet arrived. Some are punished in the meantime, that others may be corrected. The torments of a few are the ex-amples of all.

24. One of those who of his own will ascended the Capitol to make denial, after he had denied Christ, became dumb. The punishment began from that point whence the crime also began; [8] so that now he could not ask, since he had no words for entreating mercy. [9] Another, who was in the baths, (for this was wanting to her crime and to her misfortunes, that she even went at once to the baths, when she had lost the grace of the laver of life) ; there, unclean as she was,

---

[1] Ezek. xiv. 13.
[2] Luke xii. 8.
[3] Isa. xlii. 24.
[4] Isa. lix. 1.

[5] ' And are angry."
[6] Some omit " and priests."
[7] [There can be no doubt where Cyprian would have been found in the times of Savonarola. See Perrens, *Vie*, etc., tom. ii. p. 350.]
[8] [See p. 340, note 2, *supra*.]
[9] Otherwise, " for the mercifulness of prayers."

was seized by an unclean spirit,[1] and tore with her teeth the tongue with which she had either impiously eaten or spoken. After the wicked food had been taken, the madness of the mouth was armed to its own destruction. She herself was her own executioner, nor did she long continue to live afterwards : tortured with pangs of the belly and bowels, she expired.

25. Learn what occurred when I myself was present and a witness.[2] Some parents who by chance were escaping, being little careful[3] on account of their terror, left a little daughter under the care of a wet-nurse. The nurse gave up the forsaken child to the magistrates. They gave it, in the presence of an idol whither the people flocked (because it was not yet able to eat flesh on account of its years), bread mingled with wine, which however itself was the remainder of what had been used in the immolation of those that had perished. Subsequently the mother recovered her child. But the girl was no more able to speak, or to indicate the crime that had been committed, than she had before been able to understand or to prevent it. Therefore it happened unawares in their ignorance, that when we were sacrificing, the mother brought it in with her. Moreover, the girl mingled with the saints, became impatient of our prayer and supplications, and was at one moment shaken with weeping, and at another tossed about like a wave of the sea by the violent excitement of her mind ; as if by the compulsion of a torturer the soul of that still tender child confessed a consciousness of the fact with such signs as it could. When, however, the solemnities were finished, and the deacon began to offer the cup to those present, and when, as the rest received it, its turn approached, the little child, by the instinct of the divine majesty, turned away its face, compressed its mouth with resisting lips, and refused the cup.[4] Still the deacon persisted, and, although against her efforts, forced on her some of the sacrament of the cup. Then there followed a sobbing and vomiting. In a profane body and mouth the Eucharist could not remain ; the draught sanctified in the blood of the Lord burst forth from the polluted stomach. So great is the Lord's power, so great is His majesty. The secrets of darkness were disclosed under His light, and not even hidden crimes deceived God's priest.

26. This much about an infant, which was not yet of an age to speak of the crime committed by others in respect of herself. But the woman

who in advanced life and of more mature age secretly crept in among us when we were sacrificing, received not food, but a sword for herself ; and as if taking some deadly poison[5] into her jaws and body, began presently to be tortured, and to become stiffened with frenzy ; and suffering the misery no longer of persecution, but of her crime, shivering and trembling, she fell down. The crime of her dissimulated conscience was not long unpunished or concealed. She who had deceived man, felt that God was taking vengeance. And another woman, when she tried with unworthy hands to open her box,[6] in which was the holy (body) of the Lord, was deterred by fire rising from it from daring to touch it. And when one,[7] who himself was defiled, dared with the rest to receive secretly a part of the sacrifice celebrated by the priest ; he could not eat nor handle the holy of the Lord, but found in his hands[8] when opened that he had a cinder. Thus by the experience of one it was shown that the Lord withdraws when He is denied ; nor does that which is received benefit the undeserving for salvation, since saving grace is changed by the departure of the sanctity into a cinder. How many there are daily who do not repent nor make confession of the consciousness of their crime, who are filled with unclean spirits ![9] How many are shaken even to unsoundness of mind and idiotcy by the raging of madness ! Nor is there any need to go through the deaths of individuals, since through the manifold lapses occurring in the world the punishment of their sins is as varied as the multitude of sinners is abundant. Let each one consider not what another has suffered, but what he himself deserves to suffer ; nor think that he has escaped if his punishment delay for a time, since he ought to fear it the more that the wrath of God the judge has reserved it for Himself.

27. Nor let those persons flatter themselves that they need repent the less, who, although they have not polluted their hands with abominable sacrifices, yet have defiled their conscience with certificates.[10] That profession of one who denies, is the testimony of a Christian disowning what he had been. He says that he has done what another has actually committed ; and although it is written, "Ye cannot serve two masters,"[11] he has served an earthly master in that

---

[1] Some read, " and fell down."

[2] [What Cyprian testifies as of his own knowledge, we must accept as fact, however it be accounted for. For the rest, we may believe that the terrible excitements of the times led him to accept as real the exaggerated stories which became current. In our own days " the faith-cure " excites a like credulity.]

[3] Some read, " of themselves ; " others, " of their belongings."

[4] [Infant communion.]

[5] " And receiving the blood as if some deadly poison," etc.; v. l.

[6] [They carried the sacred bread in this manner to invalids at home. The idea of " worshipping the host," therefore, could not have been possible.]

[7] Or, " a certain one."

[8] [The holy bread was delivered into the hands of the recipient. See Cyril of Jerusalem, Mystagog., xxiii. 21.]

[9] [Luke xi. 20. The whole of scriptural teachings concerning these, requires renewed study. Consult Tillotson, Works, ii. 508, ed. 1722.]

[10] [The kindly but unwise interposition of the confessors in their behalf. See vol. iii. p. 693, note 2.]

[11] Matt. vi. 24.

he has obeyed his edict; he has been more obedient to human authority than to God. It matters not whether he has published what he has done with less either of disgrace or of guilt among men. Be that as it may, he will not be able to escape and avoid God his judge, seeing that the Holy Spirit says in the Psalms, "Thine eyes did see my substance, that it was imperfect, and in Thy book shall all men be written."[1] And again: "Man seeth the outward appearance, but God seeth the heart."[2] The Lord Himself also forewarns and prepares us, saying, "And all the churches shall know that I am He which searcheth the reins and the heart."[3] He looks into the hidden and secret things, and considers those things which are concealed; nor can any one evade the eyes of the Lord, who says, "I am a God at hand, and not a God afar off. If a man be hidden in secret places, shall not I therefore see him? Do not I fill heaven and earth?"[4] He sees the heart and mind of every person; and He will judge not alone of our deeds, but even of our words and thoughts. He looks into the minds, and the wills, and conceptions of all men, in the very lurking-places of the heart that is still closed up.

28. Moreover, how much are they both greater in faith and better in their fear, who, although bound by no crime of sacrifice *to idols* or of certificate, yet, since they have even thought of such things, with grief and simplicity confess this very thing to God's priests, and make the conscientious avowal, put off from them the load of their minds, and seek out the salutary medicine even for slight and moderate wounds, knowing that it is written, "God is not mocked."[5] God cannot be mocked, nor deceived, nor deluded by any deceptive cunning. Yea, he sins the more, who, thinking that God is like man, believes that he evades the penalty of his crime if he has not openly admitted his crime. Christ says in His precepts, "Whosoever shall be ashamed of me, of him shall the Son of man be ashamed."[6] And does he think that he is a Christian, who is either ashamed or afraid to be a Christian? How can he be one with Christ, who either blushes or fears to belong to Christ? He will certainly have sinned less, by not seeing the idols, and not profaning the sanctity of the faith under the eyes of a people standing round and insulting, and not polluting his hands by the deadly sacrifices, nor defiling his lips with the wicked food. This is advantageous to this extent, that the fault is less, not that the conscience is guiltless. He can more easily attain to pardon of his crime, yet he is not free from crime; and let him not cease to carry out his repentance, and to entreat the Lord's mercy, lest what seems to be less in the quality of his fault, should be increased by his neglect of atonement.

29. I entreat you, beloved brethren, that each one should confess his own sin, while he who has sinned is still in this world, while his confession may be received, while the satisfaction and remission made by the priests are pleasing to the Lord.[7] Let us turn to the Lord with our whole heart, and, expressing our repentance for our sin with true grief, let us entreat God's mercy. Let our soul lie low before Him. Let our mourning atone to Him. Let all our hope lean upon Him. He Himself tells us in what manner we ought to ask. "Turn ye," He says, "to me with all your heart, and at the same time with fasting, and with weeping, and with mourning; and rend your hearts, and not your garments."[8] Let us return to the Lord with our whole heart. Let us appease His wrath and indignation with fastings, with weeping, with mourning, as He Himself admonishes us.

30. Do we believe that a man is lamenting with his whole heart, that he is entreating the Lord with fasting, and with weeping, and with mourning, who from the first day of his sin daily frequents the bathing-places with women; who, feeding at rich banquets, and puffed out with fuller dainties, belches forth on the next day his indigestions, and does not dispense of his meat and drink so as to aid the necessity of the poor? How does he who walks with joyous and glad step mourn for his death? And although it is written, "Ye shall not mar the figure of your beard,"[9] he plucks out his beard, and dresses his hair; and does he now study to please any one who displeases God? Or does she groan and lament who has time to put on the clothing of precious apparel, and not to consider the robe of Christ which she has lost; to receive valuable ornaments and richly wrought necklaces, and not to bewail the loss of divine and heavenly ornament? Although thou clothest thyself in foreign garments and silken robes, thou art naked; although thou adornest thyself to excess both in pearls, and gems, and gold, yet without the adornment of Christ thou art unsightly. And you who stain your hair, now at least cease in the midst of sorrows; and you who paint the edges of your eyes with a line drawn around them of black powder, now at least wash your eyes with tears. If you had lost any dear one of your friends by the death incident to mortality, you would groan grievously, and weep with disordered countenance, with changed dress,

---

[1] Ps. cxxxix. 16.
[2] 1 Sam. xvi. 7.
[3] Apoc. ii. 23.
[4] Jer. xxiii. 23.
[5] Gal. vi. 7.
[6] Mark viii. 83.

[7] [See sec. 32, p. 446, *infra*. Note, not after this life.]
[8] Joel ii. 12.
[9] Lev. xix. 27.

with neglected hair, with clouded face, with dejected appearance, you would show the signs of grief. Miserable creature, you have lost your soul; spiritually dead here, you are continuing to live to yourself, and although yourself walking about, you have begun to carry your own death with you. And do you not bitterly moan; do you not continually groan; do you not hide yourself, either for shame of your sin or for continuance of your lamentation? Behold, these are still worse wounds of sinning; behold, these are greater crimes—to have sinned, and not to make atonement—to have committed crimes, and not to bewail your crimes.

31. Ananias, Azarias, and Misael, the illustrious and noble youths, even amid the flames and the ardours of a raging furnace, did not desist from making public confession to God. Although possessed of a good conscience, and having often deserved well of the Lord by obedience of faith and fear, yet they did not cease from maintaining their humility, and from making atonement to the Lord, even amid the glorious martyrdoms of their virtues. The sacred Scripture speaks, saying, "Azarias stood up and prayed, and, opening his mouth, made confession before God together with his companions in the midst of the fire." [1] Daniel also, after the manifold grace of his faith and innocency, after the condescension of the Lord often repeated in respect of his virtues and praises, strives by fastings still further to deserve well of God, wraps himself in sackcloth and ashes, sorrowfully making confession, and saying, " O Lord God, great, and strong, and dreadful, keeping Thy covenant and mercy for them that love Thee and keep Thy commandments, we have sinned, we have committed iniquity, and have done wickedly: we have transgressed, and departed from Thy precepts, and from Thy judgments; neither have we hearkened to the words of Thy servants the prophets, which they spake in Thy name to our kings, and to all the nations, and to all the earth. O Lord, righteousness [2] belongs unto Thee, but unto us confusion." [3]

32. These things were done by men, meek, simple, innocent, in deserving well of the majesty of God; and now those who have denied the Lord refuse to make atonement to the Lord, and to entreat Him. I beg you, brethren, acquiesce in wholesome remedies, obey better counsels, associate your tears with our tears, join your groans with ours; we beseech you in order that we may beseech God for you: we turn our very prayers to you first; our prayers with which we pray [4] God for you that He would pity you.

Repent abundantly, prove the sorrow of a grieving and lamenting mind.

33. Neither let that imprudent error or vain stupor of some move you, who, although they are involved in so grave a crime, are struck with blindness of mind, so that they neither understand nor lament their sins. This is the greater visitation of an angry God; as it is written, "And God gave them the spirit of deadness." [5] And again: "They received not the love of the truth, that they might be saved. And for this cause God shall send them the working of error, that they should believe a lie; that they all might be damned who believed not the truth, but had pleasure in unrighteousness." [6] Unrighteously pleasing themselves, and mad with the alienation of a hardened mind, they despise the Lord's precepts, neglect the medicine for their wound, and will not repent. Thoughtless before their sin was acknowledged, after their sin they are obstinate; neither stedfast before, nor suppliant afterwards: when they ought to have stood fast, they fell; when they ought to fall and prostrate themselves to God, they think they stand fast. They have taken peace for themselves of their own accord when nobody granted it; seduced by false promises, and linked with apostates and unbelievers, they take hold of error instead of truth: they regard a communion as valid with those who are not communicants; they believe men against God, although they have not believed God against men.

34. Flee from such men as much as you can; avoid with a wholesome caution those who adhere to their mischievous contact. Their word doth eat as doth a cancer; [7] their conversation advances like a contagion; their noxious and envenomed persuasion kills worse than persecution itself. In such a case there remains only penitence which can make atonement. But they who take away repentance for a crime, close the way of atonement. Thus it happens that, while by the rashness of some a false safety is either promised or trusted, the hope of true safety is taken away.

35. But you, beloved brethren, whose fear is ready towards God, and whose mind, although it is placed in the midst of lapse, is mindful of its misery, do you in repentance and grief look into your sins; acknowledge the very grave sin of your conscience; open the eyes of your heart to the understanding of your sin, neither despairing of the Lord's mercy nor yet at once claiming His pardon. God, in proportion as with the affection of a Father He is always indulgent and good, in the same proportion is to be dreaded with the majesty of a judge. Even as we have

---

1 Song of the Three Children.
2 Some add, "to Thee, glory."
3 Dan. ix. 4.
4 [Sec. 29, *supra*. "While still *in this world*."]

5 Isa. xxix. 10; Vulg. "transpunctionis."
6 2 Thess. ii. 10.
7 [2 Tim. ii. 17.]

sinned greatly, so let us greatly lament. To a deep wound let there not be wanting a long and careful treatment; let not the repentance be less than the sin. Think you that the Lord can be quickly appeased, whom with faithless words you have denied, to whom you have rather preferred your worldly estate, whose temple you have violated with a sacrilegious contact? Think you that He will easily have mercy upon you whom you have declared not to be your God? You must pray more eagerly and entreat; you must spend the day in grief; wear out nights in watchings and weepings; occupy all your time in wailful lamentations; lying stretched on the ground, you must cling close to the ashes, be surrounded with sackcloth and filth; after losing the raiment of Christ, you must be willing now to have no clothing; after the devil's meat, you must prefer fasting; be earnest in righteous works, whereby sins may be purged; frequently apply yourself to almsgiving, whereby souls are freed from death.[1] What the adversary took from you, let Christ receive; nor ought your estate now either to be held or loved, by which you have been both deceived and conquered. Wealth must be avoided as an enemy; must be fled from as a robber; must be dreaded by its possessors as a sword and as poison.[2] To this end only so much as remains should be of service, that by it the crime and the fault may be redeemed. Let good works be done without delay, and largely; let all your estate be laid out for the healing of your wound; let us lend of our wealth and our means to the Lord, who shall judge concerning us. Thus faith flourished in the time of the apostles; thus the first people of believers kept Christ's commands: they were prompt, they were liberal, they gave their all to be distributed by the apostles; and yet they were not redeeming sins of such a character as these.

36. If a man make prayer with his whole heart, if he groan with the true lamentations and tears of repentance, if he incline the Lord to pardon of his sin by righteous and continual works, he who expressed His mercy in these words may pity such men: "When you turn and lament, then shall you be saved, and shall know where you have been."[3] And again: "I have no pleasure in the death of him that dieth, saith the Lord, but that he should return and live."[4] And Joel the prophet declares the mercy of the Lord in the Lord's own admonition, when he says: "Turn ye to the Lord your God, for He is merciful and gracious, and patient, and of great mercy, and repenteth Him with respect to the evil that He hath inflicted."[5] He can show mercy; He can turn back His judgment. He can mercifully pardon the repenting, the labouring, the beseeching sinner. He can regard as effectual whatever, in behalf of such as these, either martyrs have besought or priests have done. Or if any one move Him still more by his own atonement, if he appease His anger, if he appease the wrath of an indignant God by righteous entreaty, He gives arms again whereby the vanquished may be armed; He restores and confirms the strength whereby the refreshed faith may be invigorated. The soldier will seek his contest anew; he will repeat the fight, he will provoke the enemy, and indeed by his very suffering he is made braver for the battle. He who has thus made atonement to God; he who by repentance for his deed, who by shame for his sin, has conceived more both of virtue and of faith from the very grief of his fall, heard and aided by the Lord, shall make the Church which he had lately saddened glad, and shall now deserve of the Lord not only pardon, but a crown.

TREATISE IV.[6]

ON THE LORD'S PRAYER.

ARGUMENT. — THE TREATISE OF CYPRIAN ON THE LORD'S PRAYER COMPRISES THREE PORTIONS, IN WHICH DIVISION HE IMITATES TERTULLIAN IN HIS BOOK ON PRAYER. IN THE FIRST PORTION, HE POINTS OUT THAT THE LORD'S PRAYER IS THE MOST EXCELLENT OF ALL PRAYERS, PROFOUNDLY SPIRITUAL, AND MOST EFFECTUAL FOR OBTAINING OUR PETITIONS. IN THE SECOND PART, HE UNDERTAKES AN EXPLANATION OF THE LORD'S PRAYER; AND, STILL TREADING IN THE FOOTSTEPS OF TERTULLIAN, HE GOES THROUGH ITS SEVEN CHIEF CLAUSES. FINALLY, IN THE THIRD PART, HE CONSIDERS THE CONDITIONS OF PRAYER, AND TELLS US WHAT PRAYER OUGHT TO BE.[7] —

1. The evangelical precepts, beloved brethren, are nothing else than divine teachings, — foundations on which hope is to be built, supports to strengthen faith, nourishments for cheering the heart, rudders for guiding our way, guards for obtaining salvation, — which, while they instruct the docile minds of believers on the earth, lead them to heavenly kingdoms. God, moreover, willed many things to be said and to be heard by means of the prophets His

---

[1] [In view of Matt. xxv. 36.]
[2] Instead of "and a poison," some read, "and sold."
[3] Isa. xxx. 51.
[4] Ezek. xxxiii. 11.

[5] Joel ii 13.
[6] [Written A.D. 252. Compare Tertullian, vol. iii. p. 681.]
[7] 1st, persevering and continuous, after the example of Christ our Lord; 2dly, watchful, and poured forth from the heart, after the example of the priest who, in the preface which precedes the prayer, prepares the minds of the brethren by saying *Sursum Corda*, to which the people answer *Habemus ad Dominum;* 3dly, associated with good works and alms, like that of Tobias and Cornelius; 4thly, at every hour of the day, and especially at the three hours appointed by the Church for prayer, to wit, the third, the sixth, and the ninth hour; and, moreover, we must pray morning and evening.

servants; but how much greater are those which the Son speaks, which the Word of God who was in the prophets testifies with His own voice; not now bidding to prepare the way for His coming, but Himself coming and opening and showing to us the way, so that we who have before been wandering in the darkness of death, without forethought and blind, being enlightened by the light of grace, might keep the way of life, with the Lord for our ruler and guide !

2. He, among the rest of His salutary admonitions and divine precepts wherewith He counsels His people for their salvation, Himself also gave a form of praying—Himself advised and instructed us what we should pray for. He who made us to live, taught us also to pray, with that same benignity, to wit, wherewith He has condescended to give and confer all things else; in order that while we speak to the Father in that prayer and supplication which the Son has taught us, we may be the more easily heard. Already He had foretold that the hour was coming "when the true worshippers should worship the Father in spirit and in truth;"[1] and He thus fulfilled what He before promised, so that we who by His sanctification[2] have received the Spirit and truth, may also by His teaching worship truly and spiritually. For what can be a more spiritual prayer than that which was given to us by Christ, by whom also the Holy Spirit was given to us? What praying to the Father can be more truthful than that which was delivered to us by the Son who is the Truth, out of His own mouth? So that to pray otherwise than He taught is not ignorance alone, but also sin; since He Himself has established, and said, "Ye reject the commandments of God, that ye may keep your own traditions."[3]

3. Let us therefore, brethren beloved, pray as God our Teacher has taught us. It is a loving and friendly prayer to beseech God with His own word, to come up to His ears in the prayer of Christ. Let the Father acknowledge the words of His Son when we make our prayer, and let Him also who dwells within in our breast Himself dwell in our voice. And since we have Him as an Advocate with the Father for our sins, let us, when as sinners we petition on behalf of our sins, put forward the words of our Advocate. For since He says, that "whatsoever we shall ask of the Father in His name, He will give us,"[4] how much more effectually do we obtain what we ask in Christ's name, if we ask for it in His own prayer![5]

4. But let our speech and petition when we pray be under discipline, observing quietness and modesty. Let us consider that we are standing in God's sight. We must please the divine eyes both with the habit of body and with the measure of voice. For as it is characteristic of a shameless man to be noisy with his cries, so, on the other hand, it is fitting to the modest man to pray with moderated petitions. Moreover, in His teaching the Lord has bidden us to pray in secret—in hidden and remote places, in our very bed-chambers—which is best suited to faith, that we may know that God is everywhere present, and hears and sees all, and in the plenitude of His majesty penetrates even into hidden and secret places, as it is written, "I am a God at hand, and not a God afar off. If a man shall hide himself in secret places, shall I not then see him? Do not I fill heaven and earth?"[6] And again: "The eyes of the Lord are in every place, beholding the evil and the good."[7] And when we meet together with the brethren in one place, and celebrate divine sacrifices with God's priest, we ought to be mindful of modesty and discipline—not to throw abroad our prayers indiscriminately, with unsubdued voices, nor to cast to God with tumultuous wordiness a petition that ought to be commended to God by modesty; for God is the hearer, not of the voice, but of the heart. Nor need He be clamorously reminded, since He sees men's thoughts, as the Lord proves to us when He says, "Why think ye evil in your hearts?"[8] And in another place: "And all the churches shall know that I am He that searcheth the hearts and reins."[9]

5. And this Hannah in the first book of Kings, who was a type of the Church, maintains and observes, in that she prayed to God not with clamorous petition, but silently and modestly, within the very recesses of her heart. She spoke with hidden prayer, but with manifest faith. She spoke not with her voice, but with her heart, because she knew that thus God hears; and she effectually obtained what she sought, because she asked it with belief. Divine Scripture asserts this, when it says, "She spake in her heart, and her lips moved, and her voice was not heard; and God did hear her."[10] We read also in the Psalms, "Speak in your hearts, and in your beds, and be ye pierced."[11] The Holy Spirit, moreover, suggests these same things by Jeremiah, and teaches, saying, "But in the heart ought God to be adored by thee."[12]

---

[1] John iv. 23.
[2] "Satisfaction."
[3] Mark vii 9. [On the *Shemoneh Eshreh*, Prideaux, I. vi. 2]
[4] John xvi. 23.
[5] [Compare John xiv. 6. How can we come to the Father by the Son more effectually than by using the words which the Son has taught? Dr. Johnson thought extemporaneous prayers very good if the Lord's Prayer were not omitted.]

[6] Jer. xxiii. 23, 24.
[7] Prov. xv. 3.
[8] Matt. ix. 4.
[9] Apoc. ii. 23.
[10] 1 Sam. i. 13.
[11] Ps. iv. 4, "transpungimini."
[12] Or, "In the heart, O God, ought we to worship Thee." (Baruch vi. 6.)

6. And let not the worshipper, beloved brethren, be ignorant in what manner the publican prayed with the Pharisee in the temple. Not with eyes lifted up boldly to heaven, nor with hands proudly raised ; but beating his breast, and testifying to the sins shut up within, he implored the help of the divine mercy. And while the Pharisee was pleased with himself, this man who thus asked, the rather deserved to be sanctified, since he placed the hope of salvation not in the confidence of his innocence, because there is none who is innocent ; but confessing his sinfulness, he humbly prayed, and He who pardons the humble heard the petitioner. And these things the Lord records in His Gospel, saying, "Two men went up into the temple to pray ; the one a Pharisee, and the other a publican. The Pharisee stood, and prayed thus with himself: God, I thank Thee that I am not as other men are, unjust, extortioners, adulterers, even as this publican. I fast twice in the week, I give tithes of all that I possess. But the publican stood afar off, and would not so much as lift up his eyes unto heaven, but smote upon his breast, saying, God, be merciful to me a sinner. I say unto you, this man went down to his house justified rather than the Pharisee : for every one that exalteth himself shall be abased ; and whosoever humbleth himself shall be exalted." [1]

7. These things, beloved brethren, when we have learnt from the sacred reading, and have gathered in what way we ought to approach to prayer, let us know also from the Lord's teaching what we should pray. "Thus," says He, " pray ye : —

"Our Father, which art in heaven, Hallowed be Thy name. Thy kingdom come. Thy will be done, as in heaven so in earth. Give us this day our daily bread. And forgive us our debts, as we forgive our debtors. And suffer us not to be led into temptation ; but deliver us from evil. Amen." [2]

8. Before all things, the Teacher of peace and the Master of unity would not have prayer to be made singly and individually, as for one who prays to pray for himself alone. For we say not " My Father, which art in heaven," nor " Give me this day my daily bread ;" nor does each one ask that only his own debt should be forgiven him ; nor does he request for himself alone that he may not be led into temptation, and delivered from evil. Our prayer is public and common ; and when we pray, we pray not for one, but for the whole people, because we the whole people are one. The God of peace and the Teacher of concord, who taught unity, willed that one should thus pray for all, even as He Himself bore us all in one.[3] This law of prayer the three children

observed when they were shut up in the fiery furnace, speaking together in prayer, and being of one heart in the agreement of the spirit ; and this the faith of the sacred Scripture assures us, and in telling us how such as these prayed, gives an example which we ought to follow in our prayers, in order that we may be such as they were : "Then these three," it says, " as if from one mouth sang an hymn, and blessed the Lord." [4] They spoke as if from one mouth, although Christ had not yet taught them how to pray. And therefore, as they prayed, their speech was availing and effectual, because a peaceful, and sincere, and spiritual prayer deserved well of the Lord. Thus also we find that the apostles, with the disciples, prayed after the Lord's ascension : "They all," says the Scripture, " continued with one accord in prayer, with the women, and Mary who was the mother of Jesus, and with His brethren." [5] They continued with one accord in prayer, declaring both by the urgency and by the agreement [6] of their praying, that God, " who maketh men to dwell of one mind in a house," [7] only admits into the divine and eternal home those among whom prayer is unanimous.

9. But what matters of deep moment [8] are contained in the Lord's prayer ! How many and how great, briefly collected in the words, but spiritually abundant in virture ! so that there is absolutely nothing passed over that is not comprehended in these our prayers and petitions, as in a compendium of heavenly doctrine. "After this manner," says He, " pray ye : Our Father, which art in heaven." The new man, born again and restored to his God by His grace, says " Father," in the first place because he has now begun to be a son. " He came," He says, " to His own, and His own received Him not. But as many as received Him, to them gave He power to become the sons of God, even to them that believe in His name." [9] The man, therefore, who has believed in His name, and has become God's son, ought from this point to begin both to give thanks and to profess himself God's son, by declaring that God is his Father in heaven ; and also to bear witness, among the very first words of his new birth, that he has renounced an earthly and carnal father, and that he has begun to know as well as to have as a father Him only who is in heaven, as it is written : "They who say unto their father and their mother, I have not known thee, and who have not acknowledged their own children ; these have observed Thy precepts, and have kept Thy covenant." [10] Also the Lord in

---

[1] Luke xviii. 10-14.
[2] Matt. vi. 9.
[3] [Unity is never out of our author's mind or heart.]

[4] Song of the Three Children, v. 28.
[5] Acts i. 14.
[6] " Both the urgency and the agreement."
[7] Ps. lxviii. 6.
[8] *Sacramenta.*
[9] John i. 11.
[10] Deut. xxxiii. 9.

His Gospel has bidden us to call "no man our father upon earth, because there is to us one Father, who is in heaven." [1] And to the disciple who had made mention of his dead father, He replied, "Let the dead bury their dead;" [2] for he had said that his father was dead, while the Father of believers is living.

10. Nor ought we, beloved brethren, only to observe and understand that we should call Him *Father* who is in heaven; but we add to it, and say *our* Father, that is, the Father of those who believe — of those who, being sanctified by Him, and restored by the nativity of spiritual grace, have begun to be sons of God. A word this, moreover, which rebukes and condemns the Jews, who not only unbelievingly despised Christ, who had been announced to them by the prophets, and sent first to them, but also cruelly put Him to death; and these cannot now call God their Father, since the Lord confounds and confutes them, saying, "Ye are born of your father the devil, and the lusts of your father ye will do. For he was a murderer from the beginning, and abode not in the truth, because there is no truth in him." [3] And by Isaiah the prophet God cries in wrath, "I have begotten and brought up children; but they have despised me. The ox knoweth his owner, and the ass his master's crib; but Israel hath not known me, and my people hath not understood me. Ah sinful nation, a people laden with sins, a wicked seed, corrupt children! [4] Ye have forsaken the Lord; ye have provoked the Holy One of Israel to anger." [5] In repudiation of these, we Christians, when we pray, say Our Father; because He has begun to be ours, and has ceased to be the Father of the Jews, who have forsaken Him. Nor can a sinful people be a son; but the name of sons is attributed to those to whom remission of sins is granted, and to them immortality is promised anew, in the words of our Lord Himself: "Whosoever committeth sin is the servant of sin. And the servant abideth not in the house for ever, but the son abideth ever." [6]

11. But how great is the Lord's indulgence! how great His condescension and plenteousness of goodness towards us, seeing that He has wished us to pray in the sight of God in such a way as to call God Father, and to call ourselves sons of God, even as Christ is the Son of God,— a name which none of us would dare to venture on in prayer, unless He Himself had allowed us thus to pray! We ought then, beloved brethren, to remember and to know, that when we call God Father, we ought to act as God's children;

so that in the measure in which we find pleasure in considering God as a Father, He might also be able to find pleasure in us. Let us converse as temples of God, that it may be plain that God dwells in us. Let not our doings be degenerate from the Spirit; so that we who have begun to be heavenly and spiritual, may consider and do nothing but spiritual and heavenly things; since the Lord God Himself has said, "Them that honour me I will honour; and he that despiseth me shall be despised." [7] The blessed apostle also has laid down in his epistle: "Ye are not your own; for ye are bought with a great price. Glorify and bear about God in your body." [8]

12. After this we say, "Hallowed be Thy name;" not that we wish for God that He may be hallowed by our prayers, but that we beseech of Him that His name may be hallowed in us. But by whom is God sanctified, since He Himself sanctifies? Well, because He says, "Be ye holy, even as I am holy," [9] we ask and entreat, that we who were sanctified in baptism may continue in that which we have begun to be. And this we daily pray for; for we have need of daily sanctification, that we who daily fall away may wash out our sins by continual sanctification. And what the sanctification is which is conferred upon us by the condescension of God, the apostle declares, when he says, "neither fornicators, nor idolaters, nor adulterers, nor effeminate, nor abusers of themselves with mankind, nor thieves, nor deceivers, nor drunkards, nor revilers, nor extortioners, shall inherit the kingdom of God. And such indeed were you; but ye are washed; but ye are justified; but ye are sanctified in the name of our Lord Jesus Christ, and by the Spirit of our God." [10] He says that we are sanctified in the name of our Lord Jesus Christ, and by the Spirit of our God. We pray that this sanctification may abide in us; and because our Lord and Judge warns the man that was healed and quickened by Him, to sin no more lest a worse thing happen unto him, we make this supplication in our constant prayers, we ask this day and night, that the sanctification and quickening which is received from the grace of God may be preserved by His protection.

13. There follows in the prayer, Thy kingdom come. We ask that the kingdom of God may be set forth to us, even as we also ask that His name may be sanctified in us. For when does God not reign, or when does that begin with Him which both always has been, and never ceases to be? We pray that our kingdom, which has been promised us by God, may come, which was acquired by the blood and passion of Christ; that

---

[1] Matt. xxiii. 9.
[2] Matt. viii. 22.
[3] John viii. 44.
[4] "A very evil seed, lawless children."
[5] Isa. i. 3.
[6] John viii. 34.

[7] 1 Sam. ii. 30.
[8] 1 Cor. vi. 20.
[9] Lev. xx. 7.
[10] 1 Cor. vi. 9.

we who first are His subjects in the world, may hereafter reign with Christ when He reigns, as He Himself promises and says, "Come, ye blessed of my Father, receive the kingdom which has been prepared for you from the beginning of the world." [1] Christ Himself, dearest brethren, however, may be the kingdom of God, whom we day by day desire to come, whose advent we crave to be quickly manifested to us. For since He is Himself the Resurrection,[2] since in Him we rise again, so also the kingdom of God may be understood to be Himself, since in Him we shall reign. But we do well in seeking the kingdom of God, that is, the heavenly kingdom, because there is also an earthly kingdom. But he who has already renounced the world, is moreover greater than its honours and its kingdom. And therefore he who dedicates himself to God and Christ, desires not earthly, but heavenly kingdoms. But there is need of continual prayer and supplication, that we fall not away from the heavenly kingdom, as the Jews, to whom this promise had first been given, fell away; even as the Lord sets forth and proves: "Many," says He, "shall come from the east and from the west, and shall recline with Abraham, and Isaac, and Jacob in the kingdom of heaven. But the children of the kingdom shall be cast out into outer darkness: there shall be weeping and gnashing of teeth." [3] He shows that the Jews were previously children of the kingdom, so long as they continued also to be children of God; but after the name of Father ceased to be recognised among them, the kingdom also ceased; and therefore we Christians, who in our prayer begin to call God our Father, pray also that God's kingdom may come to us.

14. We add, also, and say, "Thy will be done, as in heaven so in earth;" not that God should do what He wills, but that we may be able to do what God wills. For who resists God, that He may not do what He wills? But since we are hindered by the devil from obeying with our thought and deed God's will in all things, we pray and ask that God's will may be done in us; and that it may be done in us we have need of God's good will, that is, of His help and protection, since no one is strong in his own strength, but he is safe by the grace and mercy of God. And further, the Lord, setting forth the infirmity of the humanity which He bore, says, "Father, if it be possible, let this cup pass from me;" and affording an example to His disciples that they should do not their own will, but God's, He went on to say, "Nevertheless not as I will, but as Thou wilt." [4] And in another place He says, "I came down from heaven not to do my own will, but the will of Him that sent me." [5] Now if the Son was obedient to do His Father's will, how much more should the servant be obedient to do his Master's will! as in his epistle John also exhorts and instructs us to do the will of God, saying, "Love not the world, neither the things that are in the world. If any man love the world, the love of the Father is not in him. For all that is in the world is the lust of the flesh, and the lust of the eyes, and the ambition of life, which is not of the Father, but of the lust of the world. And the world shall pass away, and the lust thereof: but he that doeth the will of God abideth for ever, even as God also abideth for ever." [6] We who desire to abide for ever should do the will of God, who is everlasting.

15. Now that is the will of God which Christ both did and taught. Humility in conversation; stedfastness in faith; modesty in words; justice in deeds; mercifulness in works; discipline in morals; to be unable to do a wrong, and to be able to bear a wrong when done; to keep peace with the brethren; to love God with all one's heart; to love Him in that He is a Father; to fear Him in that He is God; to prefer nothing whatever to Christ, because He did not prefer anything to us; to adhere inseparably to His love; to stand by His cross bravely and faithfully; when there is any contest on behalf of His name and honour, to exhibit in discourse that constancy wherewith we make confession; in torture, that confidence wherewith we do battle; in death, that patience whereby we are crowned; — this is to desire to be fellow-heirs with Christ; this is to do the commandment of God; this is to fulfil the will of the Father.

16. Moreover, we ask that the will of God may be done both in heaven and in earth, each of which things pertains to the fulfilment of our safety and salvation. For since we possess the body from the earth and the spirit from heaven, we ourselves are earth and heaven; and in both — that is, both in body and spirit — we pray that God's will may be done. For between the flesh and spirit there is a struggle; and there is a daily strife as they disagree one with the other, so that we cannot do those very things that we would, in that the spirit seeks heavenly and divine things, while the flesh lusts after earthly and temporal things; and therefore we ask [7] that, by the help and assistance of God, agreement may be made between these two natures, so that while the will of God is done both in the spirit and in the flesh, the soul which is new-born by Him may be preserved. This is what the Apostle

---

[1] Matt. xxv. 34.
[2] Or, "our resurrection."
[3] Matt. viii. 11.
[4] Matt. xxvi. 39.

[5] John vi. 38.
[6] 1 John ii. 15-17.
[7] Some add "earnestly."

Paul openly and manifestly declares by his words : "The flesh," says he, "lusteth against the spirit, and the spirit against the flesh : for these are contrary the one to the other ; so that ye cannot do the things that ye would. Now the works of the flesh are manifest, which are these ; adulteries, fornications, uncleanness, lasciviousness, idolatry, witchcraft, murders, hatred, variance, emulations, wraths, strife, seditions, dissensions, heresies, envyings, drunkenness, revellings, and such like : of the which I tell you before, as I have also told you in times past, that they which do such things shall not inherit the kingdom of God. But the fruit of the spirit is love, joy, peace, magnanimity, goodness, faith, gentleness, continence, chastity." [1] And therefore we make it our prayer in daily, yea, in continual supplications, that the will of God concerning us should be done both in heaven and in earth ; because this is the will of God, that earthly things should give place to heavenly, and that spiritual and divine things should prevail.

17. And it may be thus understood, beloved brethren, that since the Lord commands and admonishes us even to love our enemies, and to pray even for those who persecute us, we should ask, moreover, for those who are still earth, and have not yet begun to be heavenly, that even in respect of these God's will should be done, which Christ accomplished in preserving and renewing humanity. For since the disciples are not now called by Him earth, but the salt of the earth, and the apostle designates the first man as being from the dust of the earth, but the second from heaven, we reasonably, who ought to be like God our Father, who maketh His sun to rise upon the good and bad, and sends rain upon the just and the unjust, so pray and ask by the admonition of Christ as to make our prayer for the salvation of all men ; that as in heaven — that is, in us by our faith — the will of God has been done, so that we might be of heaven ; so also in earth [2] — that is, in those who believe not [3] — God's will may be done, that they who as yet are by their first birth of earth, may, being born of water and of the Spirit, begin to be of heaven.

18. As the prayer goes forward, we ask and say, "Give us this day our daily bread." And this may be understood both spiritually and literally, because either way of understanding it is rich in divine usefulness to our salvation. For Christ is the bread of life ; and this bread does not belong to all men, but it is ours. And according as we say, " Our Father," because He is the Father of those who understand and believe ; so also we call it " our bread," because Christ is

the bread of those who are in union with His body.[4] And we ask that this bread should be given to us daily, that we who are in Christ, and daily [5] receive the Eucharist for the food of salvation, may not, by the interposition of some heinous sin, by being prevented, as withheld and not communicating, from partaking of the heavenly bread, be separated from Christ's body, as He Himself predicts, and warns, " I am the bread of life which came down from heaven. If any man eat of my bread, he shall live for ever : and the bread which I will give is my flesh, for the life of the world." [6] When, therefore, He says, that whoever shall eat of His bread shall live for ever ; as it is manifest that those who partake of His body and receive the Eucharist by the right of communion are living, so, on the other hand, we must fear and pray lest any one who, being withheld from communion, is separate from Christ's body should remain at a distance from salvation ; as He Himself threatens, and says, " Unless ye eat the flesh of the Son of man, and drink His blood, ye shall have no life in you." [7] And therefore we ask that our bread — that is, Christ — may be given to us daily, that we who abide and live in Christ may not depart from His sanctification and body.[8]

19. But it may also be thus understood, that we who have renounced the world, and have cast away its riches and pomps in the faith of spiritual grace, should only ask for ourselves food and support, since the Lord instructs us, and says, "Whosoever forsaketh not all that he hath, cannot be my disciple." [9] But he who has begun to be Christ's disciple, renouncing all things according to the word of his Master, ought to ask for his daily food, and not to extend the desires of his petition to a long period, as the Lord again prescribes, and says, " Take no thought for the morrow, for the morrow itself shall take thought for itself. Sufficient for the day is the evil thereof." [10] With reason, then, does Christ's disciple ask food for himself for the day, since he is prohibited from thinking of the morrow ; because it becomes a contradiction and a repugnant thing for us to seek to live long in this world, since we ask that the kingdom of God should come quickly. Thus also the blessed apostle admonishes us, giving substance and strength to the stedfastness of our hope and faith : " We brought nothing," says he, " into this world, nor indeed

---

[1] Gal. v. 17-22.
[2] [See Hooker (a beautiful passage) in Walton's *Life*, " on the angels in heaven; " also, *E. P.*, book v. cap. xxxv. at close.]
[3] Some editions omit this " not."

[4] This passage is differently read as follows: " And according as we say Our Father, so also we call Christ our bread, because He is ours as we come in contact with His body."
[5] [Probably in times of persecution. See Freeman, *Principles of Divine Service.*]
[6] John vi. 58.
[7] John vi. 53.
[8] [Not tied to actual daily reception, however. See the figure, 1 Kings xix. 7, 8. But see valuable note on (ἐπιούσιος) the supersubstantial bread. Cyril of Jerusalem, p. 277, Oxford trans. of the *Mystagogic Lectures.*]
[9] Luke xiv. 33.
[10] Matt. vi. 34.

can we carry anything out. Having therefore food and raiment, let us be herewith content. But they that will be rich fall into temptation and a snare, and into many and hurtful lusts, which drown men in perdition and destruction. For the love of money is the root of all evil; which while some coveted after, they have made shipwreck from the faith, and have pierced themselves through with many sorrows." [1]

20. He teaches us that riches are not only to be contemned, but that they are also full of peril; that in them is the root of seducing evils, that deceive the blindness of the human mind by a hidden deception. Whence also God rebukes the rich fool, who thinks of his earthly wealth, and boasts himself in the abundance of his overflowing harvests, saying, "Thou fool, this night thy soul shall be required of thee; then whose shall those things be which thou hast provided?" [2] The fool who was to die that very night was rejoicing in his stores, and he to whom life already was failing, was thinking of the abundance of his food. But, on the other hand, the Lord tells us that he becomes perfect and complete who sells all his goods, and distributes them for the use of the poor, and so lays up for himself treasure in heaven. He says that that man is able to follow Him, and to imitate the glory of the Lord's passion, who, free from hindrance, and with his loins girded, is involved in no entanglements of worldly estate, but, at large and free himself, accompanies his possessions, which before have been sent to God. For which result, that every one of us may be able to prepare himself, let him thus learn to pray, and know, from the character of the prayer, what he ought to be.

21. For daily bread cannot be wanting to the righteous man, since it is written, "The Lord will not slay the soul of the righteous by hunger;" [3] and again, "I have been young, and now am old, yet have I not seen the righteous forsaken, nor his seed begging their bread." [4] And the Lord moreover promises and says, "Take no thought, saying, "What shall we eat, or what shall we drink, or wherewithal shall we be clothed? For after all these things do the nations seek. And your Father knoweth that ye have need of all these things. Seek ye first the kingdom of God and His righteousness, and all these things shall be added unto you." [5] To those who seek God's kingdom and righteousness, He promises that all things shall be added. [6] For since all things are God's, nothing will be wanting to him who possesses God, if God Himself be not wanting to him. Thus a meal was divinely provided for Daniel: when he was shut up by the king's command in the den of lions, and in the midst of wild beasts who were hungry, and yet spared him, the man of God was fed. Thus Elijah in his flight was nourished both by ravens ministering to him in his solitude, and by birds bringing him food in his persecution. And — oh detestable cruelty of the malice of man! — the wild beasts spare, the birds feed, while men lay snares, and rage!

22. After this we also entreat for our sins, saying, "And forgive us our debts, as we also forgive our debtors." After the supply of food, pardon of sin is also asked for, that he who is fed by God may live in God, and that not only the present and temporal life may be provided for, but the eternal also, to which we may come if our sins are forgiven; and these the Lord calls debts, as He says in His Gospel, "I forgave thee all that debt, because thou desiredst me." [7] And how necessarily, how providently and salutarily, are we admonished that we are sinners, since we are compelled to entreat for our sins, and while pardon is asked for from God, the soul recalls its own consciousness of sin! Lest any one should flatter himself that he is innocent, [8] and by exalting himself should more deeply perish, he is instructed and taught that he sins daily, in that he is bidden to entreat daily for his sins. Thus, moreover, John also in his epistle warns us, and says, "If we say that we have no sin, we deceive ourselves, and the truth is not in us; but if we confess our sins, the Lord is faithful and just to forgive us our sins." [9] In his epistle he has combined both, that we should entreat for our sins, and that we should obtain pardon when we ask. Therefore he said that the Lord was faithful to forgive sins, keeping the faith of His promise; because He who taught us to pray for our debts and sins, has promised that His fatherly mercy and pardon shall follow.

23. He has clearly joined herewith and added the law, and has bound us by a certain condition and engagement, that we should ask that our debts be forgiven us in such a manner as we ourselves forgive our debtors, knowing that that which we seek for our sins cannot be obtained unless we ourselves have acted in a similar way in respect of our debtors. Therefore also He says in another place, "With what measure ye mete, it shall be measured to you again." [10] And the servant who, after having had all his debt forgiven him by his master, would not forgive his fellow-servant, is cast back into prison; be-

---

[1] 1 Tim. vi. 7.
[2] Luke xii. 20.
[3] Prov. x. 3.
[4] Ps. xxxvii. 25.
[5] Matt. vi. 31.
[6] [Thus the petition covers (1) our spiritual food, John vi. 27; and (2) our bodily sustenance, Matt. vi. 8.]

[7] Matt. xviii. 32.
[8] "Although none is innocent" is here added by some.
[9] 1 John i. 8. [Connect with this, Matt. vi. 15, and compare Freeman on the *Principles of Divine Service*, vol. i. p. 417.]
[10] Matt. vii. 2.

cause he would not forgive his fellow-servant, he lost the indulgence that had been shown to himself by his lord. And these things Christ still more urgently sets forth in His precepts with yet greater power of His rebuke. "When ye stand praying," says He, "forgive if ye have aught against any, that your Father which is in heaven may forgive you your trespasses. But if ye do not forgive, neither will your Father which is in heaven forgive you your trespasses." [1] There remains no ground of excuse in the day of judgment, when you will be judged according to your own sentence; and whatever you have done, that you also will suffer. For God commands us to be peacemakers, and in agreement, and of one mind in His house; [2] and such as He makes us by a second birth, such He wishes us when new-born to continue, that we who have begun to be sons of God may abide in God's peace, and that, having one spirit, we should also have one heart and one mind. Thus God does not receive the sacrifice of a person who is in disagreement, but commands him to go back from the altar and first be reconciled to his brother, that so God also may be appeased by the prayers of a peacemaker. Our peace and brotherly agreement [3] is the greater sacrifice to God, — and a people united in one in the unity of the Father, and of the Son, and of the Holy Spirit.

24. For even in the sacrifices which Abel and Cain first offered, God looked not at their gifts, but at their hearts, so that he was acceptable in his gift who was acceptable in his heart. Abel, peaceable and righteous in sacrificing in innocence to God, taught others also, when they bring their gift to the altar, thus to come with the fear of God, with a simple heart, with the law of righteousness, with the peace of concord. With reason did he, who was such in respect of God's sacrifice, become subsequently himself a sacrifice to God; so that he who first set forth martyrdom, and initiated the Lord's passion by the glory of his blood, had both the Lord's righteousness and His peace. Finally, such are crowned by the Lord, such will be avenged [4] with the Lord in the day of judgment; but the quarrelsome and disunited, and he who has not peace with his brethren, in accordance with what the blessed apostle and the Holy Scripture testifies, even if he have been slain for the name of Christ, shall not be able to escape the crime of fraternal dissension, because, as it is written, "He who hateth his brother is a murderer," [5] and no murderer attains to the kingdom of heaven, nor does he live with God. He cannot be with Christ, who had rather be an imitator of Judas than of Christ. How great is the sin which cannot even be washed away by a baptism of blood — how heinous the crime which cannot be expiated by martyrdom!

25. Moreover, the Lord of necessity admonishes us to say in prayer, "And suffer us not to be led into temptation." In which words it is shown that the adversary can do nothing against us except God shall have previously permitted it; so that all our fear, and devotion, and obedience may be turned towards God, since in our temptations nothing is permitted to evil unless power is given from Him. This is proved by divine Scripture, which says, "Nebuchadnezzar king of Babylon came to Jerusalem, and besieged it; and the Lord delivered it into his hand." [6] But power is given to evil against us according to our sins, as it is written, "Who gave Jacob for a spoil, and Israel to those who make a prey of Him? Did not the Lord, against whom they sinned, and would not walk in His ways, nor hear His law? and He has brought upon them the anger of His wrath." [7] And again, when Solomon sinned, and departed from the Lord's commandments and ways, it is recorded, "And the Lord stirred up Satan against Solomon himself." [8]

26. Now power is given against us in two modes: either for punishment when we sin, or for glory when we are proved, as we see was done with respect to Job; as God Himself sets forth, saying, "Behold, all that he hath I give unto thy hands; but be careful not to touch himself." [9] And the Lord in His Gospel says, in the time of His passion, "Thou couldest have no power against me unless it were given thee from above." [10] But when we ask that we may not come into temptation, we are reminded of our infirmity and weakness in that we thus ask, lest any should insolently vaunt himself, lest any should proudly and arrogantly assume anything to himself, lest any should take to himself the glory either of confession or of suffering as his own, when the Lord Himself, teaching humility, said, "Watch and pray, that ye enter not into temptation; the spirit indeed is willing, but the flesh is weak;" [11] so that while a humble and submissive confession comes first, and all is attributed to God, whatever is sought for suppliantly with fear and honour of God, may be granted by His own loving-kindness.

27. After all these things, in the conclusion of the prayer comes a brief clause, which shortly

---

[1] Mark xi. 25. [Elucidation III.]
[2] [Ps. lxviii. 6. Vulgate and Angl. Psalter.]
[3] [Cyprian was very mild in his position against the accusations of Stephen. Sec. 26, p. 386, *supra;* also Treatise ix., *infra.*]
[4] Or, "will judge."
[5] 1 John iii. 15.

[6] 2 Kings xxiv. 11.
[7] Isa. xlii. 24.
[8] 1 Kings xi. 14.
[9] Job i. 12.
[10] John xix. 11.
[11] Mark xiv. 38.

and comprehensively sums up all our petitions and our prayers. For we conclude by saying, "But deliver us from evil," comprehending all adverse things which the enemy attempts against us in this world, from which there may be a faithful and sure protection if God deliver us, if He afford His help to us who pray for and implore it. And when we say, Deliver us from evil, there remains nothing further which ought to be asked. When we have once asked for God's protection against evil, and have obtained it, then against everything which the devil and the world work against us we stand secure and safe. For what fear is there in this life, to the man whose guardian in this life is God?

28. What wonder is it, beloved brethren, if such is the prayer which God taught, seeing that He condensed in His teaching all our prayer in one saving sentence? This had already been before foretold by Isaiah the prophet, when, being filled with the Holy Spirit, he spoke of the majesty and loving-kindness of God, "consummating and shortening His word,"[1] He says, "in righteousness, because a shortened word[2] will the Lord make in the whole earth."[3] For when the Word of God, our Lord Jesus Christ, came unto all, and gathering alike the learned and unlearned, published to every sex and every age the precepts of salvation He made a large compendium of His precepts, that the memory of the scholars might not be burdened in the celestial learning, but might quickly learn what was necessary to a simple faith. Thus, when He taught what is life eternal, He embraced the sacrament of life in a large and divine brevity, saying, "And this is life eternal, that they might know Thee, the only and true God, and Jesus Christ, whom Thou hast sent."[4] Also, when He would gather from the law and the prophets the first and greatest commandments, He said, "Hear, O Israel; the Lord thy God is one God: and thou shalt love the Lord thy God with all thy heart, and with all thy mind, and with all thy strength. This is the first commandment. And the second is like unto it, Thou shalt love thy neighbour as thyself."[5] "On these two commandments hang all the law and the prophets."[6] And again: "Whatsoever good things ye would that men should do unto you, do ye even so to them. For this is the law and the prophets."[7]

29. Nor was it only in words, but in deeds also, that the Lord taught us to pray, Himself praying frequently and beseeching, and thus showing us, by the testimony of His example,

what it behoved us to do, as it is written, "But Himself departed into a solitary place, and there prayed."[8] And again: "He went out into a mountain to pray, and continued all night in prayer to God."[9] But if He prayed who was without sin, how much more ought sinners to pray; and if He prayed continually, watching through the whole night in uninterrupted petitions, how much more ought we to watch[10] nightly in constantly repeated prayer!

30. But the Lord prayed and besought not for Himself—for why should He who was guiltless pray on His own behalf?—but for our sins, as He Himself declared, when He said to Peter, "Behold, Satan hath desired that he might sift you as wheat. But I have prayed for thee, that thy faith fail not."[11] And subsequently He beseeches the Father for all, saying, "Neither pray I for these alone, but for them also which shall believe on me through their word; that they all may be one; as Thou, Father, art in me, and I in Thee, that they also may be one in us."[12] The Lord's loving-kindness, no less than His mercy, is great in respect of our salvation, in that, not content to redeem us with His blood, He in addition also prayed for us. Behold now what was the desire of His petition, that like as the Father and Son are one, so also we should abide in absolute unity; so that from this it may be understood how greatly he sins who divides unity and peace, since for this same thing even the Lord besought, desirous doubtless that His people should thus be saved and live in peace, since He knew that discord cannot come into the kingdom of God.[13]

31. Moreover, when we stand praying, beloved brethren, we ought to be watchful and earnest with our whole heart, intent on our prayers. Let all carnal and worldly thoughts pass away, nor let the soul at that time think on anything but the object only of its prayer. For this reason also the priest, by way of preface before his prayer, prepares the minds of the brethren by saying, "Lift up your hearts," that so upon the people's response, "We lift them up unto the Lord," he may be reminded that he himself ought to think of nothing but the Lord.[14] Let the breast be closed against the adversary, and be open to God alone; nor let it suffer God's enemy to approach to it at the time of prayer. For frequently he steals upon us, and penetrates within, and by crafty deceit calls away our prayers from God, that we may have one thing in our heart and another in our voice,

---

1 Verbum.
2 Sermonem.
3 Isa. x. 22.
4 John xvii. 3.
5 Matt. xii. 29–31.
6 Matt. xxii. 40.
7 Matt. vii. 12.

8 Luke v. 16.
9 Luke vi. 12.
10 [Such was the example of Cotton Mather. *Magnalia*, i. 35.]
11 Luke xxii. 31.
12 John xvii. 20.
13 [Unity again enforced.]
14 [The antiquity of the *Sursum Corda* is here shown. Elucidation IV.]

when not the sound of the voice, but the soul and mind, ought to be praying to the Lord with a simple intention. But what carelessness it is, to be distracted and carried away by foolish and profane thoughts when you are praying to the Lord, as if there were anything which you should rather be thinking of than that you are speaking with God! How can you ask to be heard of God, when you yourself do not hear yourself? Do you wish that God should remember you when you ask, if you yourself do not remember yourself? This is absolutely to take no precaution against the enemy; this is, when you pray to God, to offend the majesty of God by the carelessness of your prayer; this is to be watchful with your eyes, and to be asleep with your heart, while the Christian, even though he is asleep with his eyes, ought to be awake with his heart, as it is written in the person of the Church speaking in the Song of Songs, " I sleep, yet my heart waketh." [1] Wherefore the apostle anxiously and carefully warns us, saying, " Continue in prayer, and watch in the same; " [2] teaching, that is, and showing that those are able to obtain from God what they ask, whom God sees to be watchful in their prayer.

32. Moreover, those who pray should not come to God with fruitless or naked prayers. Petition is ineffectual when it is a barren entreaty that beseeches God.[3] For as every tree that bringeth not forth fruit is cut down and cast into the fire; assuredly also, words that do not bear fruit cannot deserve anything of God, because they are fruitful in no result. And thus Holy Scripture instructs us, saying, " Prayer is good with fasting and almsgiving." [4] For He who will give us in the day of judgment a reward for our labours and alms, is even in this life a merciful hearer of one who comes to Him in prayer associated with good works. Thus, for instance, Cornelius the centurion, when he prayed, had a claim to be heard. For he was in the habit of doing many alms-deeds towards the people, and of ever praying to God. To this man, when he prayed about the ninth hour, appeared an angel bearing testimony to his labours, and saying, " Cornelius, thy prayers and thine alms are gone up in remembrance before God." [5]

33. Those prayers quickly ascend to God which the merits of our labours urge upon God. Thus also Raphael the angel was a witness to the constant prayer and the constant good works of Tobias, saying, " It is honourable to reveal and confess the works of God. For when thou didst pray, and Sarah, I did bring the remembrance

of your prayers before the holiness of God. And when thou didst bury the dead in simplicity, and because thou didst not delay to rise up and to leave thy dinner, but didst go out and cover the dead, I was sent to prove thee; and again God has sent me to heal thee, and Sarah thy daughter-in-law. For I am Raphael, one of the seven holy angels which stand and go in and out before the glory of God." [6] By Isaiah also the Lord reminds us, and teaches similar things, saying, " Loosen every knot of iniquity, release the oppressions of contracts which have no power, let the troubled go into peace, and break every unjust engagement. Break thy bread to the hungry, and bring the poor that are without shelter into thy house. When thou seest the naked, clothe him; and despise not those of the same family and race as thyself. Then shall thy light break forth in season, and thy raiment shall spring forth speedily; and righteousness shall go before thee, and the glory of God shall surround thee. Then shalt thou call, and God shall hear thee; and while thou shalt yet speak, He shall say, Here I am." [7] He promises that He will be at hand, and says that He will hear and protect those who, loosening the knots of unrighteousness from their heart, and giving alms among the members of God's household according to His commands, even in hearing what God commands to be done, do themselves also deserve to be heard by God. The blessed Apostle Paul, when aided in the necessity of affliction by his brethren, said that good works which are performed are sacrifices to God. " I am full," saith he, " having received of Epaphroditus the things which were sent from you, an odour of a sweet smell, a sacrifice acceptable, well pleasing to God." [8] For when one has pity on the poor, he lends to God; and he who gives to the least gives to God — sacrifices spiritually to God an odour of a sweet smell.

34. And in discharging the duties of prayer, we find that the three children with Daniel, being strong in faith and victorious in captivity, observed the third, sixth, and ninth hour, as it were, for a sacrament of the Trinity, which in the last times had to be manifested. For both the first hour in its progress to the third shows forth the consummated number of the Trinity, and also the fourth proceeding to the sixth declares another Trinity; and when from the seventh the ninth is completed, the perfect Trinity is numbered every three hours, which spaces of hours the worshippers of God in time past having spiritually decided on, made use of for determined and lawful times for prayer. And subsequently the thing was manifested, that

---

[1] Cant. v. 2.
[2] Col. i. 2.
[3] [Should not this principle be more effectually taught?]
[4] Tob. xx. 8.
[5] Acts x. 2, 4.

[6] Tob. xii. 12–15.
[7] Isa. lviii. 6–9.
[8] Phil. iv. 18.

these things were of old Sacraments, in that anciently righteous men prayed in this manner. For upon the disciples at the third hour the Holy Spirit descended, who fulfilled the grace of the Lord's promise. Moreover, at the sixth hour, Peter, going up unto the house-top, was instructed as well by the sign as by the word of God admonishing him to receive all to the grace of salvation, whereas he was previously doubtful of the receiving of the Gentiles to baptism. And from the sixth hour to the ninth, the Lord, being crucified, washed away our sins by His blood; and that He might redeem and quicken us, He then accomplished His victory by His passion.

35. But for us, beloved brethren, besides the hours of prayer observed of old,[1] both the times and the sacraments have now increased in number. For we must also pray in the morning, that the Lord's resurrection may be celebrated by morning prayer. And this formerly the Holy Spirit pointed out in the Psalms, saying, "My King, and my God, because unto Thee will I cry; O Lord, in the morning shalt Thou hear my voice; in the morning will I stand before Thee, and will look up to Thee."[2] And again, the Lord speaks by the mouth of the prophet: "Early in the morning shall they watch for me, saying, Let us go, and return unto the Lord our God."[3] Also at the sunsetting and at the decline of day, of necessity we must pray again. For since Christ is the true sun and the true day, as the worldly sun and worldly day depart, when we pray and ask that light may return to us again, we pray for the advent of Christ, which shall give us the grace of everlasting light. Moreover, the Holy Spirit in the Psalms manifests that Christ is called the day. "The stone," says He, "which the builders rejected, is become the head of the corner. This is the Lord's doing; and it is marvellous in our eyes. This is the day which the Lord hath made; let us walk and rejoice in it."[4] Also the prophet Malachi testifies that He is called the Sun, when he says, "But to you that fear the name of the Lord shall the Sun of righteousness arise, and there is healing in His wings."[5] But if in the Holy Scriptures the true sun and the true day is Christ, there is no hour excepted for Christians wherein God ought not frequently and always to be worshipped; so that we who are in Christ — that is, in the true Sun and the true Day — should be instant throughout the entire day in petitions, and should pray; and when, by the law of the world, the revolving night, recurring in its alternate changes, succeeds, there can be no harm arising

from the darkness of night to those who pray, because the children of light have the day even in the night. For when is he without light who has light in his heart? or when has not he the sun and the day, whose Sun and Day is Christ?

36. Let not us, then, who are in Christ — that is, always in the light — cease from praying even during night. Thus the widow Anna, without intermission praying and watching, persevered in deserving well of God, as it is written in the Gospel: "She departed not," it says, "from the temple, serving with fastings and prayers night and day."[6] Let the Gentiles look to this, who are not yet enlightened, or the Jews who have remained in darkness by having forsaken the light. Let us, beloved brethren, who are always in the light of the Lord, who remember and hold fast what by grace received we have begun to be, reckon night for day; let us believe that we always walk in the light, and let us not be hindered by the darkness which we have escaped. Let there be no failure of prayers in the hours of night — no idle and reckless waste of the occasions of prayer. New-created and new-born of the Spirit by the mercy of God, let us imitate what we shall one day be. Since in the kingdom we shall possess day alone, without intervention of night, let us so watch in the night as if in the daylight. Since we are to pray and give thanks to God for ever, let us not cease in this life also to pray and give thanks.[7]

TREATISE V.[8]

AN ADDRESS TO DEMETRIANUS.

ARGUMENT. — CYPRIAN, IN REPLY TO DEMETRIANUS THE PROCONSUL OF AFRICA, WHO CONTENDED THAT THE WARS, AND FAMINE, AND PESTILENCE WITH WHICH THE WORLD WAS THEN PLAGUED MUST BE IMPUTED TO THE CHRISTIANS BECAUSE THEY DID NOT WORSHIP THE GODS; FAIRLY URGES (HAVING ARGUED THAT ALL THINGS ARE GRADUALLY DETERIORATING WITH THE OLD AGE OF THE WORLD) THAT IT WAS RATHER THE HEATHENS THEMSELVES WHO WERE THE CAUSE OF SUCH MISCHIEFS, BECAUSE THEY DID NOT WORSHIP GOD, AND, MOREOVER, WERE DISTRESSING THE CHRISTIANS WITH UNJUST PERSECUTIONS.[9]

1. I had frequently, Demetrianus, treated with contempt your railing and noisy clamour with

---

[1] [By the apostles, as here mentioned. Acts iii. 1 and *passim.*]
[2] Ps. v. 2.
[3] Hos. vi. 1.
[4] Ps. cxviii. 22.
[5] Mal. iv. 2.

[6] Luke ii. 37.
[7] [On the *Amen* see Elucidation V. See vol. i. p. 186.]
[8] [Written A.D. 252.]
[9] Next, having reproached him with the unaccustomed kinds of tortures with which he tormented the Christians more severely than any other criminals, not for the purpose of making them confess, but of making them deny their faith, he shows the impotence of the gods, — as well because they themselves cannot defend themselves, and so Demetrianus, who pretended to avenge them, should rather be worshipped by them, than himself worship them; — as because, when expelled by Christians from possessed bodies, they themselves confess what they are. Nor indeed must the fall of kings, the destruction of

sacrilegious mouth and impious words against the one and true God, thinking it more modest and better, silently to scorn the ignorance of a mistaken man, than by speaking to provoke the fury of a senseless one. Neither did I do this without the authority of the divine teaching,[1] since it is written, "Speak not in the ears of a fool, lest when he hear thee he should despise the wisdom of thy words;"[2] and again, "Answer not a fool according to his folly, lest thou also be like unto him."[3] And we are, moreover, bidden to keep what is holy within our own knowledge, and not expose it to be trodden down by swine and dogs, since the Lord speaks, saying, "Give not that which is holy unto the dogs, neither cast ye your pearls before swine, lest they trample them under their feet, and turn again and rend you."[4] For when you used often to come to me with the desire of contradicting rather than with the wish to learn, and preferred impudently to insist on your own views, which you shouted with noisy words, to patiently listening to mine, it seemed to me foolish to contend with you; since it would be an easier and slighter thing to restrain the angry waves of a turbulent sea with shouts, than to check your madness by arguments. Assuredly it would be both a vain and ineffectual labour to offer light to a blind man, discourse to a deaf one, or wisdom to a brute; since neither can a brute apprehend, nor can a blind man admit the light, nor can a deaf man hear.

2. In consideration of this, I have frequently held my tongue, and overcome an impatient man with patience; since I could neither teach an unteachable man, nor check an impious one with religion, nor restrain a frantic man with gentleness. But yet, when you say that very many are complaining that to us it is ascribed that wars arise more frequently, that plague, that famines rage, and that long droughts are suspending the showers and rains, it is not fitting that I should be silent any longer, lest my silence should begin to be attributed to mistrust rather than to modesty; and while I am treating the false charges with contempt, I may seem to be acknowledging the crime. I reply, therefore, as well to you, Demetrianus, as to others whom perhaps you have stirred up, and many of whom, by sowing hatred against us with malicious words, you have made your own partisans, from the

budding forth of your own root and origin, who, however, I believe, will admit the reasonableness of my discourse; for he who is moved to evil by the deception of a lie, will much more easily be moved to good by the cogency of truth.

3. You have said that all these things are caused by us, and that to us ought to be attributed the misfortunes wherewith the world is now shaken and distressed, because your gods are not worshipped by us. And in this behalf, since you are ignorant of divine knowledge, and a stranger to the truth, you must in the first place know this, that the world has now grown old, and does not abide in that strength in which it formerly stood; nor has it that vigour and force which it formerly possessed. This, even were we silent, and if we alleged no proofs from the sacred Scriptures and from the divine declarations, the world itself is now announcing, and, bearing witness to its decline by the testimony of its failing estate.[5] In the winter there is not such an abundance of showers for nourishing the seeds; in the summer the sun has not so much heat for cherishing the harvest; nor in the spring season are the corn-fields so joyous; nor are the autumnal seasons so fruitful in their leafy products. The layers of marble are dug out in less quantity from the disembowelled and wearied mountains; the diminished quantities of gold and silver suggest the early exhaustion of the metals, and the impoverished veins are straitened and decreased day by day; the husbandman is failing in the fields, the sailor at sea, the soldier in the camp, innocence in the market, justice in the tribunal, concord in friendships, skilfulness in the arts, discipline in morals. Think you that the substantial character of a thing that is growing old remains so robust as that wherewith it might previously flourish in its youth while still new and vigorous? Whatever is tending downwards to decay, with its end nearly approaching, must of necessity be weakened. Thus, the sun at his setting darts his rays with a less bright and fiery splendour; thus, in her declining course, the moon wanes with exhausted horns; and the tree, which before had been green and fertile, as its branches dry up, becomes by and by misshapen in a barren old age; and the fountain which once gushed forth liberally from its overflowing veins, as old age causes it to fail, scarcely trickles with a sparing moisture. This is the sentence passed on the world, this is God's law, that everything that has had a beginning should perish, and things that have grown should become old, and that strong things should become weak, and great things become small, and that, when they have become weakened and diminished, they should come to an end.

---

property, and such like evils which accompanied the persecutions of Christians as a punishment from Heaven, be judged not to be punishments, because they were shared by the Christians themselves; inasmuch as all these things are a joy to them rather than a punishment. Accordingly, while there is time, he urges him to return to a better mind, or at least to dread the judgment and an ever burning fiery Gehenna. In this tract Cyprian partly imitates Tertullian's *Apology* and his treatise to Scapula, partly the *Octavius* of Minucius Felix.

[1] Some add, "and name."
[2] Prov. xxiii. 9.
[3] Prov. xxvi. 4.
[4] Matt. vii. 6.

---

[5] [Elucidation VI. See Commodian, vol. iv. 219.]

4. You impute it to the Christians that everything is decaying as the world grows old. What if old men should charge it on the Christians that they grow less strong in their old age ; that they no longer, as formerly, have the same faculties, in the hearing of their ears, in the swiftness of their feet, in the keenness of their eyes, in the vigour of their strength, in the freshness of their organic powers, in the fulness of their limbs, and that although once the life of men endured beyond the age of eight and nine hundred years, it can now scarcely attain to its hundredth year? We see grey hairs in boys — the hair fails before it begins to grow ; and life does not cease in old age, but it begins with old age. Thus, even at its very commencement, birth hastens to its close ;[1] thus, whatever is now born degenerates with the old age of the world itself; so that no one ought to wonder that everything begins to fail in the world, when the whole world itself is already in process of failing, and in its end.

5. Moreover, that wars continue frequently to prevail, that death and famine accumulate anxiety, that health is shattered by raging diseases, that the human race is wasted by the desolation of pestilence, know that this was foretold ; that evils should be multiplied in the last times, and that misfortunes should be varied ; and that as the day of judgment is now drawing nigh, the censure of an indignant God should be more and more aroused for the scourging of the human race. For these things happen not, as your false complaining and ignorant inexperience of the truth asserts and repeats, because your gods are not worshipped by us, but because God is not worshipped by you. For since He is Lord and Ruler of the world, and all things are carried on by His will and direction, nor can anything be done save what He Himself has done or allowed to be done, certainly when those things occur which show the anger of an offended God, they happen not on account of us by whom God is worshipped, but they are called down by your sins and deservings, by whom God is neither in any way sought nor feared, because your vain superstitions are not forsaken, nor the true religion known in such wise that He who is the one God over all might alone be worshipped and petitioned.

6. In fine, listen to Himself speaking ; Himself with a divine voice at once instructing and warning us : " Thou shalt worship the Lord thy God," says He, " and Him only shalt thou serve."[2] And again, " Thou shalt have none other gods but me."[3] And again, " Go not after other gods, to serve them ; and worship them not, and provoke not me to anger with the works of your

hands to destroy you."[4] Moreover, the prophet, filled with the Holy Spirit, attests and denounces the anger of God, saying, " Thus saith the Lord Almighty : Because of mine house that is waste, and ye run every man to his own house, therefore the heavens shall be stayed from dew, and the earth shall withhold her fruits : and I will bring a sword upon the earth, and upon the corn, and upon the wine, and upon the oil, and upon men, and upon cattle, and upon all the labours of their hands."[5] Moreover, another prophet repeats, and says, " And I will cause it to rain upon one city, and upon another city I will cause it not to rain. One piece shall be rained upon, and the piece whereon I send no rain shall be withered. And two and three cities shall be gathered into one city to drink water, and shall not be satisfied ; and ye are not converted unto me, saith the Lord."[6]

7. Behold, the Lord is angry and wrathful, and threatens, because you turn not unto Him. And you wonder or complain in this your obstinacy and contempt, if the rain comes down with unusual scarcity ; and the earth falls into neglect with dusty corruption ; if the barren glebe hardly brings forth a few jejune and pallid blades of grass ; if the destroying hail weakens the vines ; if the overwhelming whirlwind roots out the olive ; if drought stanches the fountain ; a pestilent breeze corrupts the air ; the weakness of disease wastes away man ; although all these things come as the consequence of the sins that provoke them, and God is more deeply indignant when such and so great evils avail nothing ! For that these things occur either for the discipline of the obstinate or for the punishment of the evil, the same God declares in the Holy Scriptures, saying, " In vain have I smitten your children ; they have not received correction."[7] And the prophet devoted and dedicated to God answers to these words in the same strain, and says, " Thou hast stricken them, but they have not grieved ; Thou hast scourged them, but they have refused to receive correction."[8] Lo, stripes are inflicted from God, and there is no fear of God. Lo, blows and scourgings from above are not wanting, and there is no trembling, no fear. What if even no such rebuke as that interfered in human affairs ? How much greater still would be the audacity in men, if it were secure in the impunity of their crimes !

8. You complain that the fountains are now less plentiful to you, and the breezes less salubrious, and the frequent showers and the fertile earth afford you less ready assistance ; that the elements no longer subserve your uses and your pleasures as of old. But do you serve God, by

---

[1] [Wisd. v. 13.]
[2] Deut. vi. 13.
[3] Ex. xxix. 3.

[4] Jer. xxv. 6.
[5] Hag. i. 9.
[6] Amos iv. 7.
[7] Jer. ii. 30. [Compare Aug., *City of God, passim.*]
[8] Jer. v. 3.

whom all things are ordained to your service; do you wait upon Him by whose good pleasure all things wait upon you?[1] From your slave you yourself require service; and though a man, you compel your fellow-man to submit, and to be obedient to you; and although you share the same lot in respect of being born, the same condition in respect of dying; although you have like bodily substance and a common order of souls, and although you come into this world of ours and depart from it after a time with equal rights,[2] and by the same law; yet, unless you are served by him according to your pleasure, unless you are obeyed by him in conformity to your will, you, as an imperious and excessive exactor of his service, flog and scourge him: you afflict and torture him with hunger, with thirst and nakedness, and even frequently with the sword and with imprisonment. And, wretch that you are, do you not acknowledge the Lord your God while you yourself are thus exercising lordship?[3]

9. And therefore with reason in these plagues that occur, there are not wanting God's stripes and scourges; and since they are of no avail in this matter, and do not convert individuals to God by such terror of destructions, there remains after all the eternal dungeon, and the continual fire, and the everlasting punishment; nor shall the groaning of the suppliants be heard there, because here the terror of the angry God was not heard, crying by His prophet, and saying, "Hear the word of the Lord, ye children of Israel: for the judgment of the Lord is against the inhabitants of the earth; because there is neither mercy, nor truth, nor knowledge of God upon the earth. But cursing, and lying, and killing, and stealing, and committing adultery, is broken out over the land, they mingle blood with blood. Therefore shall the land mourn, with every one that dwelleth therein, with the beasts of the field, with things that creep on the earth, and with the fowls of heaven; and the fishes of the sea shall languish, so that no man shall judge, no man shall rebuke."[4] God says He is wrathful and angry, because there is no acknowledgment of God in the earth, and God is neither known nor feared. The sins of lying, of lust, of fraud, of cruelty, of impiety, of anger, God rebukes and finds fault with, and no one is converted to innocency. Lo, those things are happening which were before foretold by the words of God; nor is any one admonished by the belief of things present to take thought for what is to come. Amongst those very misfortunes wherein the soul, closely bound and shut up, can scarcely breathe, there is still found opportunity for men to be evil, and in such great dangers to judge not so much of themselves as of others. You are indignant that God is angry, as if by an evil life you were deserving any good, as if all things of that kind which happen were not infinitely less and of smaller account than your sins.

10. You who judge others, be for once also a judge of yourself; look into the hiding-places of your own conscience; nay, since now there is not even any shame in your sin,[5] and you are wicked, as if it were rather the very wickedness itself that pleased you, do you, who are seen clearly and nakedly by all other men, yourself also look upon yourself. For either you are swollen with pride, or greedy with avarice, or cruel with anger, or prodigal with gambling, or flushed with intemperance, or envious with jealousy, or unchaste with lust, or violent with cruelty; and do you wonder that God's anger increases in punishing the human race, when the sin that is punished is daily increasing? You complain that the enemy rises up, as if, though an enemy were wanting, there could be peace for you even among the very togas of peace. You complain that the enemy rises up, as if, even although external arms and dangers from barbarians were repressed, the weapons of domestic assault from the calumnies and wrongs of powerful citizens, would not be more ferocious and more harshly wielded within. You complain of barrenness and famine, as if drought made a greater famine than rapacity, as if the fierceness of want did not increase more terribly from grasping at the increase of the year's produce, and the accumulation of their price. You complain that the heaven is shut up from showers, although in the same way the barns are shut up on earth. You complain that now less is produced, as if what had already been produced were given to the indigent. You reproach plague and disease, while by plague itself and disease the crimes of individuals are either detected or increased, while mercy is not manifested to the weak, and avarice and rapine are waiting open-mouthed for the dead. The same men are timid in the duties of affection, but rash in quest of impious gains; shunning the deaths of the dying, and craving the spoils of the dead, so that it may appear as if the wretched are probably forsaken in their sickness for this cause, that they may not, by being cured, escape: for he who enters so eagerly upon the estate of the dying, *probably* desired the sick man to perish.

---

[1] Some read, "But you do not serve God, by whom all things are ordained to your service; you do not wait upon Him," etc.
[2] ["Æquali jure et pari lege." This would have furnished ground for Jefferson's famous sentence in the American Declaration of Independence. See also Franklin's sentiment, vol. i. p. 552, note 9. There is a very remarkable passage in Massillon which might have engendered the French Revolution had it been known to the people. See Petit Carême, *On Palm Sunday*, p 189, etc., ed. 1745.]
[3] Some add, "over man."
[4] Hos. iv. 1-4.

[5] Some texts read, "fear or shame in sinning."

11. So great a terror of destruction cannot give the teaching of innocency ; and in the midst of a people dying with constant havoc, nobody considers that he himself is mortal. Everywhere there is scattering, there is seizure, there is taking possession ; no dissimulation about spoiling, and no delay.[1] As if it were all lawful, as if it were all becoming, as if he who does not rob were suffering loss and wasting his own property, thus every one hastens to the rapine. Among thieves there is at any rate some modesty in their crimes. They love pathless ravines and deserted solitudes ; and they do wrong in such a way, that still the crime of the wrong-doers is veiled by darkness and night. Avarice, *however*, rages openly, and, safe by its very boldness, exposes the weapons of its headlong craving in the light of the market-place. Thence cheats, thence poisoners, thence assassins in the midst of the city, are as eager for wickedness as they are wicked with impunity. The crime is committed by the guilty, and the guiltless who can avenge it is not found. There is no fear from accuser or judge : the wicked obtain impunity, while modest men are silent ; accomplices are afraid, and those who are to judge are for sale. And therefore by the mouth of the prophet the truth of the matter is put forth with the divine spirit and instinct : it is shown in a certain and obvious way that God can prevent adverse things, but that the evil deserts of sinners prevent His bringing aid. " Is the Lord's hand," says he, " not strong to save you ; or has He made heavy His ear, that He cannot hear you? But your sins separate between you and God ; and because of your sins He hath hid His face from you, that He may not have mercy."[2] Therefore let your sins and offences be reckoned up ; let the wounds of your conscience be considered ; and let each one cease complaining about God, or about us, if he should perceive that himself deserves what he suffers.

12. Look what that very matter is of which is chiefly our discourse — that you molest us, although innocent ; that, in contempt of God, you attack and oppress God's servants. It is little, *in your account*, that your life is stained with a variety of gross vices, with the iniquity of deadly crimes, with the summary of all bloody rapines ; that true religion is overturned by false superstitions ; that God is neither sought at all, nor feared at all ; but over and above this, you weary[3] God's servants, and those who are dedicated to His majesty and His name, with unjust persecutions. It is not enough that you yourself do not worship God, but, over and above, you persecute those who do worship, with a sacrile-gious hostility. You neither worship God, nor do you at all permit Him to be worshipped ; and while others who venerate not only those foolish idols and images made by man's hands, but even portents and monsters besides, are pleasing to you, it is only the worshipper of God who is displeasing to you. The ashes of victims and the piles of cattle everywhere smoke in your temples, and God's altars are either nowhere or are hidden. Crocodiles, and apes, and stones, and serpents are worshipped by you ; and God alone in the earth is not worshipped, or if worshipped, not with impunity. You deprive the innocent, the just, the dear to God, of their home ; you spoil them of their estate, you load them with chains, you shut them up in prison, you punish them with the sword, with the wild beasts, with the flames. Nor, indeed, are you content with a brief endurance of our sufferings, and with a simple and swift exhaustion of pains. You set on foot tedious tortures, by tearing our bodies ; you multiply numerous punishments, by lacerating our vitals ; nor can your brutality and fierceness be content with ordinary tortures ; your ingenious cruelty devises new sufferings.

13. What is this insatiable madness for blood-shedding, what this interminable lust of cruelty? Rather make your election of one of two alternatives. To be a Christian is either a crime, or it is not. If it be a crime, why do you not put the man that confesses it to death? If it be not a crime, why do you persecute an innocent man? For I ought to be put to the torture if I denied it. If in fear of your punishment I should conceal, by a deceitful falsehood, what I had previously been, and the fact that I had not worshipped your gods, then I might deserve to be tormented, then I ought to be compelled to confession of my crime by the power of suffering, as in other examinations the guilty, who deny that they are guilty of the crime of which they are accused, are tortured in order that the confession of the reality of the crime, which the tell-tale voice refuses to make, may be wrung out by the bodily suffering. But now, when of my own free will I confess, and cry out, and with words frequent and repeated to the same effect bear witness that I am a Christian, why do you apply tortures to one who avows it, and who destroys your gods, not in hidden and secret places, but openly, and publicly, and in the very market-place, in the hearing of your magistrates and governors ; so that, although it was a slight thing which you blamed in me before, that which you ought rather to hate and punish has increased, that by declaring myself a Christian in a frequented place, and with the people standing around, I am confounding both you and your gods by an open and public announcement?

---

[1] Or, " no pretence." Some add, " no fear."
[2] Isa. lix. 1.
[3] Or, " distress ; " *v. l.*

14. Why do you turn your attention to the weakness of our body? why do you strive with the feebleness of this earthly flesh? Contend rather with the strength of the mind, break down the power of the soul, destroy our faith, conquer if you can by discussion, overcome by reason; or, if your gods have any deity and power, let them themselves rise to their own vindication, let them defend themselves by their own majesty. But what can they advantage their worshippers, if they cannot avenge themselves on those who worship them not? For if he who avenges is of more account than he who is avenged, then you are greater than your gods. And if you are greater than those whom you worship, you ought not to worship them, but rather to be worshipped and feared by them as their lord. Your championship defends them when injured, just as your protection guards them when shut up from perishing. You should be ashamed to worship those whom you yourself defend; you should be ashamed to hope for protection from those whom you yourself protect.

15. Oh, would you but hear and see them when they are adjured by us, and tortured with spiritual scourges, and are ejected from the possessed bodies with tortures of words,[1] when howling and groaning at the voice of man and the power of God, feeling the stripes and blows, they confess the judgment to come! Come and acknowledge that what we say is true; and since you say that you thus worship gods, believe even those whom you worship. Or if you will even believe yourself, he—i.e., the demon—who has now possessed your breast, who has now darkened your mind with the night of ignorance, shall speak concerning yourself in your hearing. You will see that we are entreated by those whom you entreat, that we are feared by those whom you fear, whom you adore. You will see that under our hands they stand bound, and tremble as captives, whom you look up to and venerate as lords: assuredly even thus you might be confounded in those errors of yours, when you see and hear your gods, at once upon our interrogation betraying what they are, and even in your presence unable to conceal those deceits and trickeries of theirs.

16. What, then, is that sluggishness of mind; yea, what blind and stupid madness of fools, to be unwilling to come out of darkness into light, and to be unwilling, when bound in the toils of eternal death, to receive the hope of immortality, and not to fear God when He threatens and says, "He that sacrifices unto any gods, but unto the Lord only, shall be rooted out?"[2] And again: "They worshipped them whom

their fingers made; and the mean man hath bowed down, and the great man hath humbled himself, and I will not forgive them."[3] Why do you humble and bend yourself to false gods? Why do you bow your body captive before foolish images and creations of earth? God made you upright; and while other animals are downlooking, and are depressed in posture bending towards the earth, yours is a lofty attitude; and your countenance is raised upwards to heaven, and to God. Look thither, lift your eyes thitherward, seek God in the highest, that you may be free from things below; lift your heart to a dependence on high and heavenly things. Why do you prostrate yourself into the ruin of death with the serpent whom you worship? Why do you fall into the destruction of the devil, by his means and in his company? Keep the lofty estate in which you were born. Continue such as you were made by God. To the posture of your countenance and of your body, conform your soul. That you may be able to know God, first know yourself. Forsake the idols which human error has invented. Be turned to God, whom if you implore He will aid you. Believe in Christ, whom[4] the Father has sent to quicken and restore us. Cease to hurt the servants of God and of Christ with your persecutions, since when they are injured the divine vengeance defends them.

17. For this reason it is that none of us, when he is apprehended, makes resistance, nor avenges himself against your unrighteous violence, although our people are numerous and plentiful. Our certainty of a vengeance to follow makes us patient. The innocent give place to the guilty; the harmless acquiesce in punishments and tortures, sure and confident that whatsoever we suffer will not remain unavenged, and that in proportion to the greatness of the injustice of our persecution so will be the justice and the severity of the vengeance exacted for those persecutions. Nor does the wickedness of the impious ever rise up against the name we bear, without immediate vengeance from above attending it. To say nothing of the memories of ancient times, and not to recur with wordy commemoration to frequently repeated vengeance on behalf of God's worshippers, the instance of a recent matter is sufficient to prove that our defence, so speedily, and in its speed so powerfully, followed of late in the ruins of things,[5] in the destruction of wealth, in the waste of soldiers, and the diminution of forts. Nor let any one think that this occurred by chance, or think that it was fortuitous, since long ago Scripture has laid down, and said. "Vengeance

---

[1] [Vol. iii. pp. 176, 180.]
[2] Ex. xxii. 20.

[3] Isa. ii. 8.
[4] Some read, "the Son whom."
[5] Or, according to some, "of kings."

is mine; I will repay, saith the Lord."[1] And again the Holy Spirit forewarns, and says, "Say not thou, I will avenge myself of mine enemy, but wait on the Lord, that He may be thy help."[2] Whence it is plain and manifest, that not by our means, but for our sakes, all those things are happening which come down from the anger of God.

18. Nor let anybody think that Christians are not avenged by those things that are happening, for the reason that they also themselves seem to be affected by their visitation. A man feels the punishment of worldly adversity, when all his joy and glory are in the world. He grieves and groans if it is ill with him in this life, with whom it cannot be well after this life, all the fruit of whose life is received here, all whose consolation is ended here, whose fading and brief life here reckons some sweetness and pleasure, but when it has departed hence, there remains for him only punishment added to sorrow. But they have no suffering from the assault of present evils who have confidence in future good things. In fact, we are never prostrated by adversity, nor are we broken down, nor do we grieve or murmur in any external misfortune or weakness of body: living by the Spirit rather than by the flesh, we overcome bodily weakness by mental strength. By those very things which torment and weary us, we know and trust that we are proved and strengthened.[3]

19. Do you think that we suffer adversity equally with yourselves, when you see that the same adverse things are not borne equally by us and by you? Among you there is always a clamorous and complaining impatience; with us there is a strong and religious patience, always quiet and always grateful to God. Nor does it claim for itself anything joyous or prosperous in this world, but, meek and gentle and stable against all the gusts of this tossing world, it waits for the time of the divine promise; for as long as this body endures, it must needs have a common lot with others, and its bodily condition must be common. Nor is it given to any of the human race to be separated one from another, except by withdrawal from this present life. In the meantime, we are all, good and evil, contained in one household. Whatever happens within the house, we suffer with equal fate, until, when the end of the temporal life shall be attained, we shall be distributed among the homes either of eternal death or immortality. Thus, therefore, we are not on the same level, and equal with you, because, placed in this present world and in this flesh, we incur equally with you the annoyances of the world and of the flesh; for since in the sense of pain is all punishment,

it is manifest that he is not a sharer of your punishment who, you see, does not suffer pain equally with yourselves.[4]

20. There flourishes with us the strength of hope and the firmness of faith. Among these very ruins of a decaying world our soul is lifted up, and our courage unshaken: our patience is never anything but joyous; and the mind is always secure of its God, even as the Holy Spirit speaks through the prophet, and exhorts us, strengthening with a heavenly word the firmness of our hope and faith. "The fig-tree," says He, "shall not bear fruit, and there shall be no blossom in the vines. The labour of the olive shall fail, and the fields shall yield no meat. The flock shall be cut off from the fold, and there shall be no herd in the stalls. But I will rejoice in the Lord, and I will joy in the God of my salvation."[5] He says that the man of God and the worshipper of God, depending on the truth of his hope, and founded on the stedfastness of his faith, is not moved by the attacks of this world and this life. Although the vine should fail, and the olive deceive, and the field parched with grass dying with drought should wither, what is this to Christians? what to God's servants whom paradise is inviting, whom all the grace and all the abundance of the kingdom of heaven is waiting for? They always exult in the Lord, and rejoice and are glad in their God; and the evils and adversities of the world they bravely suffer, because they are looking forward to gifts and prosperities to come: for we who have put off our earthly birth, and are now created and regenerated by the Spirit, and no longer live to the world but to God, shall not receive God's gifts and promises until we arrive at the presence of God. And yet we always ask for the repulse of enemies, and for obtaining showers, and either for the removal or the moderating of adversity; and we pour forth our prayers, and, propitiating and appeasing God, we entreat constantly and urgently, day and night, for your peace and salvation.

21. Let no one, however, flatter himself, because there is for the present to us and to the profane, to God's worshippers and to God's opponents,[6] by reason of the equality of the flesh and body, a common condition of worldly troubles, in such a way as to think from this, that all those things which happen are not drawn down by you; since by the announcement of God Himself, and by prophetic testimony, it has previously been foretold that upon the unjust should come the wrath of God, and that persecutions which humanly would hurt us should not

---

[1] Rom. xii. 19.
[2] Prov. xx. 22.
[3] [Beautiful triumph of faith, "peace in believing!"]

[4] Or, "whom you do not see not to suffer with yourself."
[5] Hab. iii. 17.
[6] Otherwise read, "to us the worshippers of God, and to His profane opponents."

be wanting; but, moreover, that vengeance, which should defend with heavenly defence those who were hurt, should attend them.

22. And how great, too, are those things which in the meantime are happening in that respect on our behalf! Something is given for an example, that the anger of an avenging God may be known. But the day of judgment is still future which the Holy Scripture denounces, saying, "Howl ye, for the day of the Lord is at hand, and destruction from God shall come; for, lo, the day of the Lord cometh, cruel with wrath and anger, to lay the earth desolate, and to destroy the sinners out of it." [1] And again: "Behold, the day of the Lord cometh, burning as an oven; and all the aliens and all that do wickedly shall be as stubble, and the day that cometh shall burn them up, saith the Lord." [2] The Lord prophesies that the aliens shall be burnt up and consumed; that is, aliens from the divine race, and the profane, those who are not spiritually new-born, nor made children of God. For that those only can escape who have been new-born and signed with the sign of Christ, God says in another place, when, sending forth His angels to the destruction of the world and the death of the human race, He threatens more terribly in the last time, saying, "Go ye, and smite, and let not your eye spare. Have no pity upon old or young, and slay the virgins and the little ones and the women, that they may be utterly destroyed. But touch not any man upon whom is written the mark." [3] Moreover, what this mark is, and in what part of the body it is placed, God sets forth in another place, saying, "Go through the midst of Jerusalem, and set a mark upon the foreheads of the men that sigh and that cry for all the abominations that be done in the midst thereof." [4] And that the sign pertains to the passion and blood of Christ, and that whoever is found in this sign is kept safe and unharmed, is also proved by God's testimony, saying, "And the blood shall be to you for a token upon the houses in which ye shall be; and I will see the blood, and will protect you, and the plague of diminution shall not be upon you when I smite the land of Egypt." [5] What previously preceded by a figure in the slain lamb is fulfilled in Christ, the truth which followed afterwards. As, then, when Egypt was smitten, the Jewish people could not escape except by the blood and the sign of the lamb; so also, when the world shall begin to be desolated and smitten, whoever is found in the blood and the sign of Christ alone shall escape. [6]

23. Look, therefore, [7] while there is time, to the true and eternal salvation; and since now the end of the world is at hand, turn your minds to God, in the fear of God; nor let that powerless and vain dominion in the world over the just and meek delight you, since in the field, even among the cultivated and fruitful corn, the tares and the darnel have dominion. Nor say ye that ill fortunes happen because your gods are not worshipped by us; but know that this is the judgment of God's anger, that He who is not acknowledged on account of His benefits may at least be acknowledged through His judgments. Seek the Lord even late; for long ago, God, forewarning by His prophet, exhorts and says, "Seek ye the Lord, and your soul shall live." [8] Know God even late; for Christ at His coming admonishes and teaches this, saying, "This is life eternal, that they might know Thee, the only true God, and Jesus Christ, whom Thou hast sent." [9] Believe Him who deceives not at all. Believe Him who foretold that all these things should come to pass. Believe Him who will give to all that believe the reward of eternal life. Believe Him who will call down on them that believe not, eternal punishments in the fires of Gehenna.

24. What will then be the glory of faith? what the punishment of faithlessness? When the day of judgment shall come, what joy of believers, what sorrow of unbelievers; that they should have been unwilling to believe here, and now that they should be unable to return that they might believe! An ever-burning Gehenna will burn up the condemned, and a punishment devouring with living flames; nor will there be any source whence at any time they may have either respite or end to their torments. Souls with their bodies will be reserved in infinite tortures for suffering. Thus the man will be for ever seen by us who here gazed upon us for a season; and the short joy of those cruel eyes in the persecutions that they made for us will be compensated by a perpetual spectacle, according to the truth of Holy Scripture, which says, "Their worm shall not die, and their fire shall not be quenched; and they shall be for a vision to all flesh." [10] And again: "Then shall the righteous men stand in great constancy before the face of those who have afflicted them, and have taken away their labours. When they see it, they shall be troubled with horrible fear, and shall be amazed at the suddenness of their unexpected salvation; and they, repenting and groaning for anguish of spirit, shall say within themselves, These are they whom we had some

---

[1] Isa. xiii. 6–9.
[2] Mal. iv. 1.
[3] Ezek. ix. 5.
[4] Ezek. ix. 4.
[5] Ex. xii. 13.
[6] [Ezek. ix. 4; Rev. vii. 3, ix. 4.]

[7] Or, according to some readings, "Be wise, therefore."
[8] Amos v. 6.
[9] John xvii. 3.
[10] Isa. lxvi. 24.

time in derision, and a proverb of reproach ; we fools counted their life madness, and their end to be without honour. How are they numbered among the children of God, and their lot is among the saints! Therefore have we erred from the way of truth, and the light of righteousness hath not shined upon us, and the sun rose not on us. We wearied ourselves in the way of wickedness and destruction ; we have gone through deserts where there lay no way ; but we have not known the way of the Lord. What hath pride profited us, or what good hath the boasting of riches done us? All those things are passed away like a shadow." [1] The pain of punishment will then be without the fruit of penitence ; weeping will be useless, and prayer ineffectual. Too late they will believe in eternal punishment who would not believe in eternal life.

25. Provide, therefore, while you may, for your safety and your life. We offer you the wholesome help of our mind and advice. And because we may not hate, and we please God more by rendering no return for wrong, we exhort you while you have the power, while there yet remains to you something of life, to make satisfaction to God, and to emerge from the abyss of darkling superstition [2] into the bright light of true religion. We do not envy your comforts, nor do we conceal the divine benefits. We repay kindness for your hatred ; and for the torments and penalties which are inflicted on us, we point out to you the ways of salvation. Believe and live, and do ye who persecute us in time rejoice with us for eternity. When you have once departed thither, there is no longer any place for repentance, and no possibility of making satisfaction. Here life is either lost or saved ; here eternal safety is provided for by the worship of God and the fruits of faith. Nor let any one be restrained either by his sins or by his years from coming to obtain salvation. To him who still remains in this world no repentance is too late. The approach to God's mercy is open, and the access is easy to those who seek and apprehend the truth. Do you entreat for your sins, although it be in the very end of life, and at the setting of the sun of time ; and implore God, who is the one and true God, in confession and faith of acknowledgment of Him, and pardon is granted to the man who confesses, and saving mercy is given from the divine goodness to the believer, and a passage is opened to immortality even in death itself. This grace Christ bestows ; this gift of His mercy He confers upon us, by overcoming death in the trophy of the cross, by redeeming the believer with the price of His blood, by reconciling man to God the Father, by quickening our mortal nature with a heavenly regeneration. If it be possible, let us all follow Him ; let us be registered in His sacrament and sign. He opens to us the way of life ; He brings us back to paradise ; He leads us on to the kingdom of heaven. Made by Him the children of God, with Him we shall ever live ; with Him we shall always rejoice, restored by His own blood. We Christians shall be glorious together with Christ, blessed of God the Father, always rejoicing with perpetual pleasures in the sight of God, and ever giving thanks to God. For none can be other than always glad and grateful, who, having been once subject to death, has been made secure in the possession of immortality. [3]

TREATISE VI. [4]

ON THE VANITY OF IDOLS: SHOWING THAT THE IDOLS ARE NOT GODS, AND THAT GOD IS ONE, AND THAT THROUGH CHRIST SALVATION IS GIVEN TO BELIEVERS.

ARGUMENT. — THIS HEADING EMBRACES THE THREE LEADING DIVISIONS OF THIS TREATISE. THE WRITER FIRST OF ALL SHOWS THAT THEY IN WHOSE HONOUR TEMPLES WERE FOUNDED, STATUES MODELLED, VICTIMS SACRIFICED, AND FESTAL DAYS CELEBRATED, WERE KINGS AND MEN AND NOT GODS ; AND THEREFORE THAT THEIR WORSHIP COULD BE OF NO AVAIL EITHER TO STRANGERS OR TO ROMANS, AND THAT THE POWER OF THE ROMAN EMPIRE WAS TO BE ATTRIBUTED TO FATE RATHER THAN TO THEM, INASMUCH AS IT HAD ARISEN BY A CERTAIN GOOD FORTUNE, AND WAS ASHAMED OF ITS OWN ORIGIN. [5]

1. That those are no gods whom the common people worship, is known from this. They were formerly kings, who on account of their royal memory subsequently began to be adored by their people even in death. Thence temples were founded to them ; thence images were sculptured to retain the countenances of the deceased by the likeness ; and men sacrificed victims, and celebrated festal days, by way of giving them honour. Thence to posterity those rites became sacred which at first had been adopted as a consolation. And now let us see

---

[1] Wisd. v. 1-9.
[2] "From the deep and darkling night of superstition" is another reading.

[3] [Compare the *Octavius* of Minucius Felix with this treatise, and also the other apologists, e.g., vol. ii. 93.]
[4] [Written A.D. 247. Compare vol. ii. pp. 79, 136, 184, etc.]
[5] Moreover, that it was manifest from their deceitful results, that nothing could be referred to auspices or auguries; nay, even those who acknowledged both one God and the demons, allowed that these illusions were the work of the demons, according to the testimony of the poets themselves, and Socrates, Plato, Trismegistus, and Hostanes. The second point, that God is one, he makes evident in a few words, as well from the greater dignity of a monarchy than of other forms of government, as from the very expressions of the heathen and of the common people — "O God!" and the like. Finally, he treats of Christ more at large, from the Jewish prophets and from the evangelical history.

whether this truth is confirmed in individual instances.

2. Melicertes and Leucothea are precipitated into the sea, and subsequently become sea-divinities. The Castors [1] die by turns, that they may live. Æsculapius is struck by lightning, that he may rise into a god. Hercules, that he may put off the man, is burnt up in the fires of Oeta. Apollo fed the flocks of Admetus; Neptune founded walls for Laomedon, and received — unfortunate builder — no wages for his work. The cave of Jupiter is to be seen in Crete, and his sepulchre is shown; and it is manifest that Saturn was driven away by him, and that from him Latium received its name, as being his lurking-place. [2] He was the first that taught to print letters; he was the first that taught to stamp money in Italy, [3] and thence the treasury is called the treasury of Saturn. And he also was the cultivator of the rustic life, whence he is painted as an old man [4] carrying a sickle. Janus had received him to hospitality when he was driven away, from whose name the Janiculum is so called, and the month of January is appointed. He himself is portrayed with two faces, because, placed in the middle, he seems to look equally towards the commencing and the closing year. The Mauri, indeed, manifestly worship kings, and do not conceal their name by any disguise.

3. From this the religion of the gods is variously changed among individual nations and provinces, inasmuch as no one god is worshipped by all, but by each one the worship of its own ancestors is kept peculiar. Proving that this is so, Alexander the Great writes in the remarkable volume addressed to his mother, that through fear of his power the doctrine of the gods being men, which was kept secret, [5] had been disclosed to him by a priest, that it was the memory of ancestors and kings that was (really) kept up, and that from this the rites of worship and sacrifice have grown up. But if gods were born at any time, why are they not born in these days also? — unless, indeed, Jupiter possibly has grown too old, or the faculty of bearing has failed Juno.

4. But why do you think that the gods can avail on behalf of the Romans, when you see that they can do nothing for their own worshippers in opposition to the Roman arms? For we know that the gods of the Romans are indigenous. Romulus was made a god by the perjury of Proculus, and Picus, and Tiberinus, and Pilum-

nus, and Consus, whom as a god of treachery Romulus would have to be worshipped, just as if he had been a god of counsels, when his perfidy resulted in the rape of the Sabines. Tatius also both invented and worshipped the goddess Cloacina; Hostilius, Fear and Paleness. By and by, I know not by whom, Fever was dedicated, and Acca and Flora the harlots. [6] These are the Roman gods. But Mars is a Thracian, and Jupiter a Cretan, and Juno either Argive or Samian or Carthaginian, and Diana of Taurus, and the mother of the gods of Ida; and there are Egyptian monsters, not deities, who assuredly, if they had had any power, would have preserved their own and their people's kingdoms. Certainly there are also among the Romans the conquered Penates whom the fugitive Æneas introduced thither. There is also Venus the bald, — far more dishonoured by the fact of her baldness in Rome than by her having been wounded in Homer.

5. Kingdoms do not rise to supremacy through merit, but are varied by chance. Empire was formerly held by both Assyrians and Medes and Persians; and we know, too, that both Greeks and Egyptians have had dominion. Thus, in the varying vicissitudes of power, the period of empire has also come to the Romans as to the others. But if you recur to its origin, you must needs blush. A people is collected together from profligates and criminals, and by founding an asylum, impunity for crimes makes the number great; and that their king himself may have a superiority in crime, Romulus becomes a fratricide; [7] and in order to promote marriage, he makes a beginning of that affair of concord by discords. They steal, they do violence, they deceive in order to increase the population of the state; their marriage consists of the broken covenants of hospitality and cruel wars with their fathers-in-law. The consulship, moreover, is the highest degree in Roman honours, yet we see that the consulship began even as did the kingdom. Brutus puts his sons to death, that the commendation of his dignity may increase by the approval of his wickedness. The Roman kingdom, therefore, did not grow from the sanctities of religion, nor from auspices and auguries, but it keeps its appointed time within a definite limit. Moreover, Regulus observed the auspices, yet was taken prisoner; and Mancinus observed their religious obligation, yet was sent under the yoke. Paulus had chickens that fed, and yet he was slain at Cannæ. Caius Cæsar despised

---

[1] Most editors read, "Castor and Pollux."

[2] *Latebra.*

[3] ["Litteras imprimere . . . signare nummos." How could the art of printing have failed to follow such inventions and such words? Every coin was a hint of the printer's art. God only could have restrained the invention till the set time. Dan. xii. 4.]

[4] According to some readings, the words "an old man" are omitted.

[5] The readings here vary much. The first part of the sentence is found in Minucius Felix, c. 21. [Vol. iv. p. 185.]

[6] The following passage, accepted in some editions, is of doubtful authenticity: "To such an extent, indeed, were feigned the names of gods among the Romans, that there is even among them a god, Viduus, who widows the body from the soul — who, as being sad and funereal, is not kept within the walls, but placed outside; but who nevertheless, in that he is excluded, is rather condemned by the Roman religion than worshipped. There is also Scansus, so called from ascents, and Forculus from doors, and Limentinus from thresholds, and Cardea from hinges, and Orbona from bereavement."

[7] "Parricida."

the auguries and auspices that were opposed to his sending ships before the winter to Africa; yet so much the more easily he both sailed and conquered.

6. Of all these, however, the principle is the same, which misleads and deceives, and with tricks which darken the truth, leads away a credulous and foolish rabble. They are impure and wandering spirits, who, after having been steeped in earthly vices, have departed from their celestial vigour by the contagion of earth, and do not cease, when ruined themselves, to seek the ruin of others; and when degraded themselves, to infuse into others the error of their own degradation. These demons the poets also acknowledge, and Socrates declared that he was instructed and ruled at the will of a demon; and thence the Magi have a power either for mischief or for mockery, of whom, however, the chief Hostanes both says that the form of the true God cannot be seen, and declares that true angels stand round about His throne. Wherein Plato also on the same principle concurs, and, maintaining one God, calls the rest angels or demons. Moreover, Hermes Trismegistus speaks of one God, and confesses that He is incomprehensible, and beyond our estimation.

7. These spirits, therefore, are lurking under the statues and consecrated images: these inspire the breasts of their prophets with their afflatus, animate the fibres of the entrails, direct the flights of birds, rule the lots, give efficiency to oracles, are always mixing up falsehood with truth, for they are both deceived and they deceive;[1] they disturb their life, they disquiet their slumbers; their spirits creeping also into their bodies, secretly terrify their minds, distort their limbs, break their health, excite diseases to force them to worship of themselves, so that when glutted with the steam of the altars and the piles of cattle, they may unloose what they had bound, and so appear to have effected a cure. The only remedy from them is when their own mischief ceases; nor have they any other desire than to call men away from God, and to turn them from the understanding of the true religion, to superstition with respect to themselves; and since they themselves are under punishment, (they wish) to seek for themselves companions in punishment whom they may by their misguidance make sharers in their crime. These, however, when adjured by us through the true God, at once yield and confess, and are constrained to go out from the bodies possessed. You may see them at our voice, and by the operation of the hidden majesty, smitten with stripes, burnt with fire, stretched out with the increase of a growing punishment, howling, groaning, entreat-

ing, confessing whence they came and when they depart, even in the hearing of those very persons who worship them, and either springing forth at once or vanishing gradually, even as the faith of the sufferer comes in aid, or the grace of the healer effects. Hence they urge the common people to detest our name, so that men begin to hate us before they know us, lest they should either imitate us if known, or not be able to condemn us.[2]

8. Therefore the one Lord of all is God. For that sublimity cannot possibly have any compeer, since it alone possesses all power. Moreover, let us borrow an illustration for the divine government from the earth. When ever did an alliance in royalty either begin with good faith or end without bloodshed? Thus the brotherhood of the Thebans was broken, and discord endured even in death in their disunited ashes. And one kingdom could not contain the Roman twins, although the shelter of one womb had held them. Pompey and Cæsar were kinsmen, and yet they did not maintain the bond of their relationship in their envious power. Neither should you marvel at this in respect of man, since herein all nature consents. The bees have one king, and in the flocks there is one leader, and in the herds one ruler. Much rather is the Ruler of the world one; who commands all things, whatsoever they are, with His word, disposes them by His wisdom, and accomplishes them by His power.

9. He cannot be seen — He is too bright for vision; nor comprehended — He is too pure for our discernment; nor estimated — He is too great for our perception; and therefore we are only worthily estimating Him when we say that He is inconceivable. But what temple can God have, whose temple is the whole world? And while man dwells far and wide, shall I shut up the power of such great majesty within one small building? He must be dedicated in our mind; in our breast He must be consecrated. Neither must you ask the name of God. God is His name. Among those there is need of names where a multitude is to be distinguished by the appropriate characteristics of appellations. To God who alone is, belongs the whole name of God; therefore He is one, and He in His entirety is everywhere diffused. For even the common people in many things naturally confess God, when their mind and soul are admonished of their author and origin. We frequently hear it said, "O God," and "God sees," and "I commend to God," and "God give you," and "as God will," and "if God should grant;" and this is the very height of sinfulness, to refuse to acknowledge Him whom you cannot but know.[3]

---

[1] [2 Tim. iii. 13. See vol. iii. 68.]

[2] [Vol. iii. p. 111; also other apologists.]
[3] [See vol. iii. p. 179, elucidation.]

10. But that Christ is, and in what way salvation came to us through Him, after this manner is the plan, after this manner is the means. First of all, favour with God was given to the Jews. Thus they of old were righteous; thus their ancestors were obedient to their religious engagements. Thence with them both the loftiness of their rule flourished, and the greatness of their race advanced. But subsequently becoming neglectful of discipline, proud, and puffed up with confidence in their fathers, they despised the divine precepts, and lost the favour conferred upon them. But how profane became their life, what offence to their violated religion was contracted, even they themselves bear witness, since, although they are silent with their voice, they confess it by their end. Scattered and straggling, they wander about; outcasts from their own soil and climate, they are thrown upon the hospitality of strangers.[1]

11. Moreover, God had previously foretold that it would happen, that as the ages passed on, and the end of the world was near at hand, God would gather to Himself from every nation, and people, and place, worshippers much better in obedience and stronger in faith,[2] who would draw from the divine gift that mercy which the Jews had received and lost by despising their religious ordinances. Therefore of this mercy and grace[3] the Word and Son of God is sent as the dispenser and master, who by all the prophets of old was announced as the enlightener and teacher of the human race. He is the power of God, He is the reason, He is His wisdom and glory; He enters into a virgin; being the holy Spirit,[4] He is endued with flesh; God is mingled with man. This is our God, this is Christ, who, as the mediator of the two, puts on man that He may lead them to the Father. What man is, Christ was willing to be, that man also may be what Christ is.

12. And the Jews knew that Christ was to come, for He was always being announced to them by the warnings of prophets. But His advent being signified to them as twofold — the one which should discharge the office and example of a man, the other which should avow Him as God — they did not understand the first advent which preceded, as being hidden in His passion, but believe in the one only which will be manifest in power.[5] But that the people of the Jews could not understand this, was the desert of their sins. They were so punished by their blindness of wisdom and intelligence, that they

who were unworthy of life, had life before their eyes, and saw it not.

13. Therefore when Christ Jesus, in accordance with what had been previously foretold by the prophets, drove out from men the demons by His word, and by the command of His voice nerved up the paralytics, cleansed the leprous, enlightened the blind, gave power of movement to the lame, raised the dead again, compelled the elements to obey Him as servants, the winds to serve Him, the seas to obey Him, the lower regions to yield to Him; the Jews, who had believed Him man only from the humility of His flesh and body, regarded Him as a sorcerer for the authority of His power. Their masters and leaders — that is, those whom He subdued both by learning and wisdom — inflamed with wrath and stimulated with indignation,[6] finally seized Him and delivered Him to Pontius Pilate, who was then the procurator of Syria on behalf of the Romans, demanding with violent and obstinate urgency His crucifixion and death.

14. That they would do this He Himself also had foretold; and the testimony of all the prophets had in like manner preceded Him, that it behoved Him to suffer, not that He might feel death, but that He might conquer death, and that, when He should have suffered, He should return again into heaven, to show the power of the divine majesty. Therefore the course of events fulfilled the promise. For when crucified, the office of the executioner being forestalled,[7] He Himself of His own will yielded up His spirit, and on the third day freely rose again from the dead. He appeared to His disciples like as He had been. He gave Himself to the recognition of those that saw Him, associated together with Him; and being evident by the substance of His bodily existence, He delayed for forty days, that they might be instructed by Him in the precepts of life, and might learn what they were to teach. Then in a cloud spread around Him He was lifted up into heaven, that as a conqueror He might bring to the Father, Man whom He loved, whom He put on, whom He shielded from death; soon to come from heaven for the punishment of the devil and to the judgment of the human race, with the force of an avenger and with the power of a judge; whilst the disciples, scattered over the world, at the bidding of their Master and God gave forth His precepts for salvation, guided men from their wandering in darkness to the way of light, and gave eyes to the blind and ignorant for the acknowledgment of the truth.

15. And that the proof might not be the less substantial, and the confession of Christ might not be a matter of pleasure, they are tried by

---

[1] [Ps. lix. 11; and see p. 202, *supra.*]
[2] "Of greater obedience and of stronger faith" is a varied reading here.
[3] Some add, "and discipline."
[4] "With the co-operation of the Holy Spirit," is perhaps a more probable reading. [See vol. iii. p. 609.]
[5] [See Treatise xii. book ii. secs. 13 and 28, *infra.*]

[6] "Set upon Him and" is here interpolated by some.
[7] [John x. 18 See Pearson, *Creed*, art. v. p. 424]

tortures, by crucifixions, by many kinds of punishments. Pain, which is the test of truth, is brought to bear, that Christ the Son of God, who is trusted in as given to men for their life, might not only be announced by the heralding of the voice, but by the testimony of suffering. Therefore we accompany Him, we follow Him, we have Him as the Guide of our way, the Source of light, the Author of salvation, promising as well the Father as heaven to those who seek and believe. What Christ is, we Christians shall be, if we imitate Christ.

TREATISE VII.

ON THE MORTALITY.[1]

ARGUMENT. — THE DEACON PONTIUS IN A FEW WORDS UNFOLDS THE BURTHEN OF THIS TREATISE IN HIS LIFE OF CYPRIAN.[2] FIRST OF ALL, HAVING POINTED OUT THAT AFFLICTIONS OF THIS KIND HAD BEEN FORETOLD BY CHRIST, HE TELLS THEM THAT THE MORTALITY OR PLAGUE WAS NOT TO BE FEARED, IN THAT IT LEADS TO IMMORTALITY, AND THAT THEREFORE, THAT MAN IS WANTING IN FAITH WHO IS NOT EAGER FOR A BETTER WORLD. NOR IS IT WONDERFUL THAT THE EVILS OF THIS LIFE ARE COMMON TO THE CHRISTIANS WITH THE HEATHENS, SINCE THEY HAVE TO SUFFER MORE THAN OTHERS IN THE WORLD, AND THENCE, AFTER THE EXAMPLE OF JOB AND TOBIAS, THERE IS NEED OF PATIENCE WITHOUT MURMURING. FOR UNLESS THE STRUGGLE PRECEDED, THE VICTORY COULD NOT ENSUE; AND HOW MUCH SOEVER DISEASES ARE COMMON TO THE VIRTUOUS AND VICIOUS, YET THAT DEATH IS NOT COMMON TO THEM, FOR THAT THE RIGHTEOUS ARE TAKEN TO CONSOLATION, WHILE THE UNRIGHTEOUS ARE TAKEN TO PUNISHMENT.[3]

1. Although in very many of you, dearly beloved brethren, there is a stedfast mind and a firm faith, and a devoted spirit that is not disturbed at the frequency of this present mortality, but, like a strong and stable rock, rather shatters the turbulent onsets of the world and the raging waves of time, while it is not itself shattered, and is not overcome but tried by these temptations; yet because I observe that among the people some, either through weakness of mind, or through decay of faith, or through the sweetness of this worldly life, or through the softness of their sex, or what is of still greater account, through error from the truth, are standing less steadily, and are not exerting the divine and unvanquished vigour of their heart, the matter may not be disguised nor kept in silence, but as far as my feeble powers suffice with my full strength, and with a discourse gathered from the Lord's lessons, the slothfulness of a luxurious disposition must be restrained, and he who has begun to be already a man of God and of Christ, must be found worthy of God and of Christ.

2. For he who wars for God, dearest brethren, ought to acknowledge himself as one who, placed in the heavenly camp, already hopes for [4] divine things, so that we may have no trembling at the storms and whirlwinds of the world, and no disturbance, since the Lord had foretold that these would come. With the exhortation of His foreseeing word, instructing, and teaching, and preparing, and strengthening the people of His Church for all endurance of things to come, He predicted and said that wars, and famines, and earthquakes, and pestilences would arise in each place; and lest an unexpected and new dread of mischiefs should shake us, He previously warned us that adversity would increase more and more in the last times. Behold, the very things occur which were spoken; and since those occur which were foretold before, whatever things were promised will also follow; as the Lord Himself promises, saying, "But when ye see all these things come to pass, know ye that the kingdom of God is at hand." [5] The kingdom of God, beloved brethren, is beginning to be at hand; the reward of life, and the rejoicing of eternal salvation, and the perpetual gladness [6] and possession lately lost of paradise, are now coming, with the passing away of the world; already heavenly things are taking the place of earthly, and great things of small, and eternal things of things that fade away. What room is there here for anxiety and solicitude? Who, in the midst of these things, is trembling and sad, except he who is without hope and faith? For it is for him to fear death who is not willing to go to Christ. It is for him to be unwilling to go to Christ who does not believe that he is about to reign [7] with Christ.

---

[1] Eusebius in his *Chronicon* makes mention of the occasion on which Cyprian wrote this treatise, saying, "A pestilent disease took possession of many provinces of the whole world, and especially Alexandria and Egypt; as Dionysius writes, and the treatise of Cyprian 'concerning the Mortality' bears witness." A.D. 252.

[2] He says: "By whom were Christians, — grieved with excessive fondness at the loss of their friends, or what is of more consequence, with their decrease of faith, — comforted with the hope of things to come?" [See p. 269, *supra*.]

[3] Then to the tacit objection that by this mortality they would be deprived of martyrdom, he replies that martyrdom is not in our power, and that even the spirit that is ready for martyrdom is crowned by God the judge. Finally, he tells them that the dead must not be bewailed in such a matter as that we should become a stumbling-block to the Gentiles, as if we were without the hope of a resurrection. But if also the day of our summons should come, we must depart hence with a glad mind to the Lord, especially since we are departing to our country, where the large number of those dear to us are waiting for us: a dense and abundant multitude are longing for us, who, being already secure of their own immortality, are still solicitous about our salvation.

[4] Some read "breathes."
[5] Luke xxi. 31.
[6] Or, "security."
[7] Some add, "for ever."

3. For it is written that the just lives by faith.[1] If you are just, and live by faith, if you truly believe in Christ, why, since you are about to be with Christ, and are secure of the Lord's promise, do you not embrace the assurance that you are called to Christ, and rejoice that you are freed from the devil? Certainly Simeon, that just man, who was truly just, who kept God's commands with a full faith, when it had been pledged him from heaven that he should not die before he had seen the Christ, and Christ had come an infant into the temple with His mother, acknowledged in spirit that Christ was now born, concerning whom it had before been foretold to him; and when he had seen Him, he knew that he should soon die. Therefore, rejoicing concerning his now approaching death, and secure of his immediate summons, he received the child into his arms, and blessing the Lord, he exclaimed, and said, "Now lettest Thou Thy servant depart in peace, according to Thy word; for mine eyes have seen Thy salvation;"[2] assuredly proving and bearing witness that the servants of God then had peace, then free, then tranquil repose, when, withdrawn from these whirlwinds of the world, we attain the harbour of our home and eternal security, when having accomplished this death we come to immortality. For that is our[3] peace, that our faithful tranquillity, that our stedfast, and abiding, and perpetual security.

4. But for the rest, what else in the world than a battle against the devil is daily carried on, than a struggle against his darts and weapons in constant conflicts? Our warfare is with avarice, with immodesty, with anger, with ambition; our diligent and toilsome wrestle with carnal vices, with enticements of the world. The mind of man besieged, and in every quarter invested with the onsets of the devil, scarcely in each point meets the attack, scarcely resists it. If avarice is prostrated, lust springs up. If lust is overcome, ambition takes its place. If ambition is despised, anger exasperates, pride puffs up, wine-bibbing entices, envy breaks concord, jealousy cuts friendship; you are constrained to curse, which the divine law forbids; you are compelled to swear, which is not lawful.

5. So many persecutions the soul suffers daily, with so many risks is the heart wearied, and yet it delights to abide here long among the devil's weapons, although it should rather be our craving and wish to hasten to Christ by the aid of a quicker death; as He Himself instructs us, and says, "Verily, verily, I say unto you, That ye shall weep and lament, but the world shall rejoice; and ye shall be sorrowful, but your sorrow shall be turned into joy."[4] Who would not desire to be without sadness? who would not hasten to attain to joy? But when our sadness shall be turned into joy, the Lord Himself again declares, when He says, "I will see you again, and your heart shall rejoice; and your joy no man shall take from you."[5] Since, therefore, to see Christ is to rejoice, and we cannot have joy unless when we shall see Christ, what blindness of mind or what folly is it to love the world's afflictions, and punishments, and tears, and not rather to hasten to the joy which can never be taken away!

6. But, beloved brethren, this is so, because faith is lacking, because no one believes that the things which God promises are true, although He is true, whose word to believers is eternal and unchangeable. If a grave and praiseworthy man should promise you anything, you would assuredly have faith in the promiser, and would not think that you should be cheated and deceived by him whom you knew to be stedfast in his words and his deeds. Now God is speaking with you; and do you faithlessly waver in your unbelieving mind? God promises to you, on your departure from this world, immortality and eternity; and do you doubt? This is not to know God at all; this is to offend Christ, the Teacher[6] of believers, with the sin of incredulity; this is for one established in the Church not to have faith in the house of faith.

7. How great is the advantage of going out of the world, Christ Himself, the Teacher of our salvation and of our good works, shows to us, who, when His disciples were saddened that He said that He was soon to depart, spoke to them, and said, "If ye loved me, ye would surely rejoice because I go to the Father;"[7] teaching thereby, and manifesting that when the dear ones whom we love depart from the world, we should rather rejoice than grieve. Remembering which truth, the blessed Apostle Paul in his epistle lays it down, saying, "To me to live is Christ, and to die is gain;"[8] counting it the greatest gain no longer to be held by the snares of this world, no longer to be liable to the sins and vices of the flesh, but taken away from smarting troubles, and freed from the envenomed fangs of the devil, to go at the call of Christ to the joy of eternal salvation.

8. But nevertheless it disturbs some that the power of this Disease attacks our people equally with the heathens, as if the Christian believed for this purpose, that he might have the enjoyment of the world and this life free from the

---

[1] [To live by faith = to be just, through Christ the object of faith. The Fathers always accept "justification by faith." See Faber's *Primitive Doctrine of Justification;* and compare Bull, *Harmonia Apostolica.*]
[2] Luke. ii. 29.
[3] Baluzius interpolates here, without authority, "true."

[4] John xvi. 20.
[5] John xvi. 22.
[6] Or, "Master and Teacher."
[7] John xvi. 28.
[8] Phil. i. 21.

contact of ills; and not as one who undergoes all adverse things here and is reserved for future joy. It disturbs some that this mortality is common to us with others; and yet what is there in this world which is not common to us with others, so long as this flesh of ours still remains, according to the law of our first birth, common to us with them? So long as we are here in the world, we are associated with the human race in fleshly equality,[1] but are separated in spirit. Therefore until this corruptible shall put on incorruption, and this mortal receive immortality, and the Spirit[2] lead us to God the Father, whatsoever are the disadvantages of the flesh are common to us with the human race. Thus, when the earth is barren with an unproductive harvest, famine makes no distinction; thus, when with the invasion of an enemy any city is taken, captivity at once desolates all; and when the serene clouds withhold the rain, the drought is alike to all; and when the jagged rocks rend the ship, the shipwreck is common without exception to all that sail in her; and the disease of the eyes, and the attack of fevers, and the feebleness of all the limbs is common to us with others, so long as this common flesh of ours is borne by us in the world.

9. Moreover, if the Christian know and keep fast under what condition and what law he has believed, he will be aware that he must suffer more than others in the world, since he must struggle more with the attacks of the devil. Holy Scripture teaches and forewarns, saying, "My son, when thou comest to the service of God, stand in righteousness and fear, and prepare thy soul for temptation."[3] And again: "In pain endure, and in thy humility have patience; for gold and silver is tried in the fire, but acceptable men in the furnace of humiliation."[4]

10. Thus Job, after the loss of his wealth, after the death of his children, grievously afflicted, moreover, with sores and worms, was not overcome, but proved; since in his very struggles and anguish, showing forth the patience of a religious mind, he says, "Naked came I out of my mother's womb, naked also I shall go under the earth: the Lord gave, the Lord hath taken away; as it seemed fit to the Lord, so it hath been done. Blessed be the name of the Lord."[5] And when his wife also urged him, in his impatience at the acuteness of his pain, to speak something against God with a complaining and envious voice, he answered and said, "Thou speakest as one of the foolish women. If we have received good from the hand of the Lord, why shall we not suffer evil? In all these things which befell him, Job sinned not with his lips in the sight of the Lord."[6] Therefore the Lord God gives him a testimony, saying, "Hast thou considered my servant Job? for there is none like him in all the earth, a man without complaint, a true worshipper of God."[7] And Tobias, after his excellent works, after the many and glorious illustrations of his merciful spirit, having suffered the loss of his sight, fearing and blessing God in his adversity, by his very bodily affliction increased in praise; and even him also his wife tried to pervert, saying, "Where are thy righteousnesses? Behold what thou sufferest!"[8] But he, stedfast and firm in respect of the fear of God, and armed by the faith of his religion to all endurance of suffering, yielded not to the temptation of his weak wife in his trouble, but rather deserved better from God by his greater patience; and afterwards Raphael the angel praises him, saying, "It is honourable to show forth and to confess the works of God. For when thou didst pray, and Sara thy daughter-in-law, I did offer the remembrance of your prayer in the presence of the glory of God. And when thou didst bury the dead in singleness of heart, and because thou didst not delay to rise up and leave thy dinner, and wentest and didst bury the dead, I was sent to make proof of thee. And God again hath sent me to heal thee and Sara thy daughter-in-law. For I am Raphael, one of the seven holy angels, who are present, and go in and out before the glory of God."[9]

11. Righteous men have ever possessed this endurance. The apostles maintained this discipline from the law of the Lord, not to murmur in adversity, but to accept bravely and patiently whatever things happen in the world; since the people of the Jews in this matter always offended, that they constantly murmured against God, as the Lord God bears witness in the book of Numbers, saying, "Let their murmuring cease from me, and they shall not die."[10] We must not murmur in adversity, beloved brethren, but we must bear with patience and courage whatever happens, since it is written, "The sacrifice to God is a broken spirit; a contrite and humbled heart God does not despise;"[11] since also in Deuteronomy the Holy Spirit warns by Moses, and says, "The Lord thy God will vex thee, and will bring hunger upon thee; and it shall be known in thine heart if thou hast well kept His commandments or no."[12] And again: "The

---

[1] [The Christian is not exempted from the common lot of humanity; but all men, if they would live godly, would escape many evils (1 Tim. vi. 6), even in the light of 2 Tim. iii. 12.]
[2] A few codices read, for "the Spirit," "Christ."
[3] Ecclus. ii. 1, 4.
[4] Ecclus. ii. 5.
[5] Job i. 21. ["The Christian's sorrow," says Bishop Horne, "is better than the world's joy." John xvi. 33.]
[6] Job ii. 10.
[7] Job i. 8.
[8] Tob. ii. 14.
[9] Tob. xii. 11-15.
[10] Num. xvii. 10.
[11] Ps. li. 17.
[12] Deut. viii. 2.

Lord your God proveth you, that He may know whether ye love the Lord your God with all your heart, and with all your soul." [1]

12. Thus Abraham pleased God, who, that he might please God, did not shrink even from losing his son, or from doing an act of parricide. You, who cannot endure to lose your son by the law and lot of mortality, what would you do if you were bidden to slay your son? The fear and faith of God ought to make you prepared for everything, although it should be the loss of private estate, although the constant and cruel harassment of your limbs by agonizing disorders, although the deadly and mournful wrench from wife, from children, from departing dear ones; let not these things be offences to you, but battles: nor let them weaken nor break the Christian's faith, but rather show forth his strength in the struggle, since all the injury inflicted by present troubles is to be despised in the assurance of future blessings. Unless the battle has preceded, there cannot be a victory: when there shall have been, in the onset of battle, the victory, then also the crown is given to the victors. For the helmsman [2] is recognised in the tempest; in the warfare the soldier is proved. It is a wanton display when there is no danger. Struggle in adversity is the trial of the truth. [3] The tree which is deeply founded in its root is not moved by the onset of winds, and the ship which is compacted of solid timbers is beaten by the waves and is not shattered; and when the threshing-floor brings out the corn, the strong and robust grains despise the winds, while the empty chaff is carried away by the blast that falls upon it.

13. Thus, moreover, the Apostle Paul, after shipwrecks, after scourgings, after many and grievous tortures of the flesh and body, says that he is not grieved, but benefited by his adversity, in order that while he is sorely afflicted he might more truly be proved. "There was given to me," he says, "a thorn in the flesh, the messenger of Satan to buffet me, that I should not be lifted up: for which thing I besought the Lord thrice, that it might depart from me; and He said unto me, My grace is sufficient for thee, for strength is made perfect in weakness." [4] When, therefore, weakness and inefficiency and any destruction seize us, then our strength is made perfect; then our faith, if when tried it shall stand fast, is crowned; as it is written, "The furnace trieth the vessels of the potter, and the trial of tribulation just men." [5] This, in short, is the difference between us and others who

know not God, that in misfortune they complain and murmur, while adversity does not call us away from the truth of virtue and faith, but strengthens us by its suffering.

14. This trial, that now the bowels, relaxed into a constant flux, discharge the bodily strength; that a fire originated in the marrow ferments into wounds of the fauces; that the intestines are shaken with a continual vomiting; that the eyes are on fire with the injected blood; that in some cases the feet or some parts of the limbs are taken off by the contagion of diseased putrefaction; that from the weakness arising by the maiming and loss of the body, either the gait is enfeebled, or the hearing is obstructed, or the sight darkened; — is profitable as a proof of faith. What a grandeur of spirit it is to struggle with all the powers of an unshaken mind against so many onsets of devastation and death! what sublimity, to stand erect amid the desolation of the human race, and not to lie prostrate with those who have no hope in God; but rather to rejoice, [6] and to embrace the benefit of the occasion; that in thus bravely showing forth our faith, and by suffering endured, going forward to Christ by the narrow way that Christ trod, we may receive the reward of His life [7] and faith according to His own judgment! Assuredly he may fear to die, who, not being regenerated of water and the Spirit, is delivered over to the fires of Gehenna; he may fear to die who is not enrolled in the cross and passion of Christ; he may fear to die, who from this death shall pass over to a second death; he may fear to die, whom on his departure from this world eternal flame shall torment with never-ending punishments; he may fear to die who has this advantage in a lengthened delay, that in the meanwhile his groanings and his anguish are being postponed.

15. Many of our people die in this mortality, that is, many of our people are liberated from this world. This mortality, as it is a plague to Jews and Gentiles, and enemies of Christ, so it is a departure to salvation to God's servants. The fact that, without any difference made between one and another, the righteous die as well as the unrighteous, is no reason for you to suppose that it is a common death for the good and evil alike. The righteous are called to their place of refreshing, the unrighteous are snatched away to punishment; safety is the more speedily given to the faithful, penalty to the unbelieving. We are thoughtless and ungrateful, beloved brethren, for the divine benefits, and do not acknowledge what is conferred upon us. Lo, virgins depart in peace, safe with their glory, not fearing the threats of the coming Antichrist,

---

[1] Deut. xiii. 3.
[2] According to some, "the ship's helmsman." [Vol. i. 94.]
[3] Some read, "of virtue." [In the Ignatian manner. Compare vol. i. p. 45.]
[4] 2 Cor. xii. 7–9.
[5] Ecclus. xxvii. 5.

[6] Some read, "rather it behoves us to rejoice."
[7] Or, "of the way."

and his corruptions and his brothels. Boys escape the peril of their unstable age, and in happiness attain the reward of continence and innocence. Now the delicate matron does not fear the tortures ; for she has escaped by a rapid death the fear of persecution, and the hands and the torments of the executioner. By the dread of the mortality and of the time the lukewarm are inflamed, the slack are nerved up, the slothful are stimulated, the deserters are compelled to return, the heathens are constrained to believe, the ancient congregation of the faithful is called to rest, the new and abundant army is gathered to the battle with a braver vigour, to fight without fear of death when the battle shall come, because it comes to the warfare in the time of the mortality.

16. And further, beloved brethren, what is it, what a great thing is it, how pertinent, how necessary, that that pestilence and plague which seems horrible and deadly, searches out the righteousness of each one, and examines the minds of the human race, to see whether they who are in health tend the sick ; whether relations affectionately love their kindred ; whether masters pity their languishing servants ; whether physicians do not forsake the beseeching patients ; whether the fierce suppress their violence ; whether the rapacious can quench the ever insatiable ardour of their raging avarice even by the fear of death ; whether the haughty bend their neck ; whether the wicked soften their boldness ; whether, when their dear ones perish, the rich, even then bestow anything,[1] and give, when they are to die without heirs. Even although this mortality conferred nothing else, it has done this benefit to Christians and to God's servants, that we begin gladly to desire martyrdom as we learn not to fear death. These are trainings for us, not deaths : they give the mind the glory of fortitude ; by contempt of death they prepare for the crown.

17. But perchance some one may object, and say, " It is this, then, that saddens me in the present mortality, that I, who had been prepared for confession, and had devoted myself to the endurance of suffering with my whole heart and with abundant courage, am deprived of martyrdom, in that I am anticipated by death." In the first place, martyrdom is not in your power, but in the condescension of God ; neither can you say that you have lost what you do not know whether you would deserve to receive. Then, besides, God the searcher of the reins and heart, and the investigator and knower of secret things, sees you, and praises and approves you ; and He who sees that your virtue was ready in you, will give you a reward for your

virtue. Had Cain, when he offered his gift to God, already slain his brother? And yet God, foreseeing the fratricide conceived in his mind, anticipated its condemnation. As in that case the evil thought and mischievous intention were foreseen[2] by a foreseeing God, so also in God's servants, among whom confession is purposed and martyrdom conceived in the mind, the intention dedicated to good is crowned by God the judge. It is one thing for the spirit to be wanting for martyrdom, and another for martyrdom to have been wanting for the spirit. Such as the Lord finds you when He calls you, such also He judges you ; since He Himself bears witness, and says, " And all the churches shall know that I am the searcher of the reins and heart."[3] For God does not ask for our blood, but for our faith.[4] For neither Abraham, nor Isaac, nor Jacob were slain ; and yet, being honoured by the deserts of faith and righteousness, they deserved to be first among the patriarchs, to whose feast is collected every one that is found faithful, and righteous, and praiseworthy.

18. We ought to remember that we should do not our own will, but God's, in accordance with what our Lord has bidden us daily to pray. How preposterous and absurd it is, that while we ask that the will of God should be done, yet when God calls and summons us from this world, we should not at once obey the command of His will ! We struggle and resist, and after the manner of froward servants we are dragged to the presence of the Lord with sadness and grief, departing hence under the bondage of necessity, not with the obedience of free will ; and we wish to be honoured with heavenly rewards by Him to whom we come unwillingly. Why, then, do we pray and ask that the kingdom of heaven may come, if the captivity of earth delights us ? Why with frequently repeated prayers do we entreat and beg that the day of His kingdom may hasten, if our greater desires and stronger wishes are to obey the devil here, rather than to reign with Christ?

19. Besides, that the indications of the divine providence may be more evidently manifest, proving that the Lord, prescient of the future, takes counsel for the true salvation of His people, when one of our colleagues and fellow-priests, wearied out with infirmity, and anxious about the present approach of death, prayed for a respite to himself ; there stood by him as he prayed, and when he was now at the point of death, a youth, venerable in honour and majesty, lofty in stature and shining in aspect, and on whom, as he stood by him, the human glance

---

[1] Some add, " on the poor."

[2] Or " perceived."
[3] Apoc. ii. 23.
[4] Some originals read, " does not desire our blood, but asks for our faith."

could scarcely look with fleshly eyes, except that he who was about to depart from the world could already behold such a one. And he, not without a certain indignation of mind and voice, rebuked him, and said, You fear to suffer, you do not wish to depart; what shall I do to you? It was the word of one rebuking and warning, one who, when men are anxious about persecution, and indifferent concerning their summons, consents not to their present desire, but consults for the future. Our dying brother and colleague heard what he was to say to others. For he who heard when he was dying, heard for the very purpose that he might tell it; he heard not for himself, but for us. For what could he, who was already on the eve of departure, learn for himself? Yea, doubtless, he learnt it for us who remain, in order that, when we find the priest who sought for delay rebuked, we might acknowledge what is beneficial for all.

20. To myself also, the very least and last, how often has it been revealed, how frequently and manifestly has it been commanded by the condescension of God, that I should diligently bear witness and publicly declare that our brethren who are freed from this world by the Lord's summons are not to be lamented, since we know that they are not lost, but sent before;[1] that, departing from us, they precede us as travellers, as navigators are accustomed to do; that they should be desired, but not bewailed; that the black garments should not be taken upon us here,[2] when they have already taken upon them white raiment there; that occasion should not be given to the Gentiles for them deservedly and rightly to reprehend us, that we mourn for those, who, we say, are alive with God, as if they were extinct and lost; and that we do not approve with the testimony of the heart and breast the faith which we express with speech and word. We are prevaricators of our hope and faith: what we say appears to be simulated, feigned, counterfeit. There is no advantage in setting forth virtue by our words, and destroying the truth by our deeds.

21. Finally, the Apostle Paul reproaches, and rebukes, and blames any who are in sorrow at the departure of their friends. "I would not," says he, have you ignorant, brethren, concerning them which are asleep, that ye sorrow not, even as others which have no hope. For if we believe that Jesus died and rose again, even so them which are asleep in Jesus will God bring with Him."[3] He says that those have sorrow in the departure of their friends who have no hope. But we who live in hope, and believe in God,

and trust that Christ suffered for us and rose again, abiding in Christ, and through Him and in Him rising again, why either are we ourselves unwilling to depart hence from this life, or do we bewail and grieve for our friends when they depart as if they were lost, when Christ Himself, our Lord and God, encourages us and says, " I am the resurrection and the life: he that believeth in me, though he die, yet shall live; and whosoever liveth and believeth in me shall not die eternally?"[4] If we believe in Christ, let us have faith in His words and promises; and since we shall not die eternally, let us come with a glad security unto Christ, with whom we are both to conquer and to reign for ever.

22. That in the meantime we die, we are passing over to immortality by death; nor can eternal life follow, unless it should befall us to depart from this life. That is not an ending, but a transit, and, this journey of time being traversed, a passage to eternity. Who would not hasten to better things? Who would not crave to be changed and renewed[5] into the likeness of Christ, and to arrive more quickly to the dignity of heavenly glory, since Paul the apostle announces and says, "For our conversation is in heaven, from whence also we look for the Lord Jesus Christ; who shall change the body of our humiliation, and conform it to the body of His glory?"[6] Christ the Lord also promises that we shall be such, when, that we may be with Him, and that we may live with Him in eternal mansions, and may rejoice in heavenly kingdoms, He prays the Father for us, saying, "Father, I will that they also whom Thou hast given me be with me where I am, and may see the glory which Thou hast given me before the world was made."[7] He who is to attain to the throne of Christ, to the glory of the heavenly kingdoms, ought not to mourn nor lament, but rather, in accordance with the Lord's promise, in accordance with his faith in the truth, to rejoice in this his departure and translation.

23. Thus, moreover, we find that Enoch also was translated, who pleased God, as in Genesis the Holy Scripture bears witness, and says, "And Enoch pleased God; and afterwards he was not found, because God translated him."[8] To have been pleasing in the sight of God was thus to have merited to be translated from this contagion of the world. And moreover, also, the Holy Spirit teaches by Solomon, that they who please God are more early taken hence, and are more quickly set free, lest while they are delaying longer in this world they should be polluted

---

[1] [Sciamus non eos amitti sed præmitti. Current even in our day.]
[2] [The clouds of black which are still customary in affliction are not according to the faith, in Cyprian's idea. Leighton, *St. Peter*, ii. 24.]
[3] 1 Thess. iv. 13.

[4] John xi. 25.
[5] " Transformed."
[6] Phil. iii. 21.
[7] John xvii. 24.
[8] Gen. v. 24.

with the contagions of the world. "He was taken away," says he, "lest wickedness should change his understanding. For his soul was pleasing to God; wherefore hasted He to take him away from the midst of wickedness."[1] So also in the Psalms, the soul that is devoted to its God in spiritual faith hastens to the Lord, saying, "How amiable are thy dwellings, O God of hosts! My soul longeth, and hasteth unto the courts of God."[2]

24. It is for him to wish to remain long in the world whom the world delights, whom this life, flattering and deceiving, invites by the enticements of earthly pleasure. Again, since the world hates the Christian, why do you love that which hates you? and why do you not rather follow Christ, who both redeemed you and loves you? John in his epistle cries and says, exhorting that we should not follow carnal desires and love the world. "Love not the world," says he, "neither the things which are in the world. If any man love the world, the love of the Father is not in him. For all that is in the world is the lust of the flesh, and the lust of the eyes, and the pride of life, which is not of the Father, but of the lust of the world. And the world shall pass away, and the lust thereof; but he who doeth the will of God abideth for ever, even as God abideth for ever."[3] Rather, beloved brethren, with a sound mind, with a firm faith, with a robust virtue, let us be prepared for the whole will of God: laying aside the fear of death, let us think on the immortality which follows. By this let us show ourselves to be what we believe, that we do not grieve over the departure of those dear to us, and that when the day of our summons shall arrive, we come witnout delay and without resistance to the Lord when He Himself calls us.

25. And this, as it ought always to be done by God's servants, much more ought to be done now — now that the world is collapsing and is oppressed with the tempests of mischievous ills; in order that we who see that terrible things have begun, and know that still more terrible things are imminent, may regard it as the greatest advantage to depart from it as quickly as possible. If in your dwelling the walls were shaking with age, the roofs above you were trembling, and the house, now worn out and wearied, were threatening an immediate destruction to its structure crumbling with age, would you not with all speed depart? If, when you were on a voyage, an angry and raging tempest, by the waves violently aroused, foretold the coming

shipwreck, would you not quickly seek the harbour? Lo, the world is changing and passing away, and witnesses to its ruin not now by its age, but by the end of things. And do you not give God thanks, do you not congratulate yourself, that by an earlier departure you are taken away, and delivered from the shipwrecks and disasters that are imminent?

26. We should consider, dearly beloved brethren — we should ever and anon reflect that we have renounced the world, and are in the meantime living here as guests and strangers. Let us greet the day which assigns each of us to his own home, which snatches us hence, and sets us free from the snares of the world, and restores us to paradise and the[4] kingdom. Who that has been placed in foreign lands would not hasten to return to his own country? Who that is hastening to return to his friends would not eagerly desire a prosperous gale, that he might the sooner embrace those dear to him? We regard paradise as our country — we already begin to consider the patriarchs as our parents: why do we not hasten and run, that we may behold our country, that we may greet our parents? There a great number of our dear ones is awaiting us, and a dense crowd of parents, brothers, children, is longing for us, already assured of their own safety, and still solicitous for our salvation. To attain to their presence and their embrace, what a gladness both for them and for us in common! What a pleasure is there in the heavenly kingdom, without fear of death; and how lofty and perpetual a happiness with eternity of living! There the glorious company of the apostles[5] — there the host of the rejoicing prophets — there the innumerable multitude of martyrs, crowned for the victory of their struggle and passion — there the triumphant virgins, who subdued the lust of the flesh and of the body by the strength of their continency — there are merciful men rewarded, who by feeding and helping the poor have done the works of righteousness — who, keeping the Lord's precepts, have transferred their earthly patrimonies to the heavenly treasuries. To these, beloved brethren, let us hasten with an eager desire; let us crave quickly to be with them, and quickly to come to Christ. May God behold this our eager desire; may the Lord Christ look upon this purpose of our mind and faith, He who will give the larger rewards of His glory to those whose desires in respect of Himself were greater!

---

[1] Wisd. iv. 11.
[2] Ps. lxxxiv. 1.
[3] 1 John ii. 15.

[4] Some have "heavenly."
[5] [A prelude to the *Te Deum*, and very possibly from a Western hymn: —

Apostolorum gloriosus chorus;
Prophetarum exultantium numerus;
Martyrum innumerabilis populus.]

TREATISE VIII.[1]

ON WORKS AND ALMS.

ARGUMENT. — HE POWERFULLY EXHORTS TO THE MANIFESTATION OF FAITH BY WORKS, AND ENFORCES THE WISDOM OF OFFERINGS TO THE CHURCH AND OF BOUNTY TO THE POOR AS THE BEST INVESTMENT OF A CHRISTIAN'S ESTATE. THIS HE PROVES OUT OF MANY SCRIPTURES.

1. Many and great, beloved brethren, are the divine benefits wherewith the large and abundant mercy of God the Father and Christ both has laboured and is always labouring for our salvation : that the Father sent the Son to preserve us and give us life, in order that He might restore us ; and that the Son was willing[2] to be sent and to become the Son of man, that He might make us sons of God ; humbled Himself, that He might raise up the people who before were prostrate ; was wounded that He might heal our wounds ; served, that He might draw out to liberty those who were in bondage ; underwent death, that He might set forth immortality to mortals. These are many and great boons of divine compassion. But, moreover, what is that providence, and how great the clemency, that by a plan of salvation it is provided for us, that more abundant care should be taken for preserving man after he is already redeemed ! For when the Lord at His advent had cured those wounds which Adam had borne,[3] and had healed the old poisons of the serpent,[4] He gave a law to the sound man, and bade him sin no more, lest a worse thing should befall the sinner. We had been limited and shut up into a narrow space by the commandment of innocence. Nor would the infirmity and weakness of human frailty have any resource, unless the divine mercy, coming once more in aid, should open some way of securing salvation by pointing out works of justice and mercy, so that by almsgiving we may wash away whatever foulness we subsequently contract.[5]

2. The Holy Spirit speaks in the sacred Scriptures, and says, " By almsgiving and faith sins are purged."[6] Not assuredly those sins which had been previously contracted, for those are purged by the blood and sanctification of Christ. Moreover, He says again, "As water extinguisheth fire, so almsgiving quencheth sin."[7] Here also it is shown and proved, that as in the laver of saving water the fire of Gehenna is extinguished, so by almsgiving and works of righteousness the flame of sins is subdued. And because in baptism remission of sins is granted once for all, constant and ceaseless labour, following the likeness of baptism, once again bestows the mercy of God. The Lord teaches this also in the Gospel. For when the disciples were pointed out, as eating and not first washing their hands, He replied and said, " He that made that which is within, made also that which is without. But give alms, and behold all things are clean unto you ; "[8] teaching hereby and showing, that not the hands are to be washed, but the heart, and that the foulness from inside is to be done away rather than that from outside ; but that he who shall have cleansed what is within has cleansed also that which is without ; and that if the mind is cleansed, a man has begun to be clean also in skin and body. Further, admonishing, and showing whence we may be clean and purged, He added that alms must be given. He who is pitiful teaches and warns us that pity must be shown ; and because He seeks to save those whom at a great cost He has redeemed, He teaches that those who, after the grace of baptism, have become foul, may once more be cleansed.

3. Let us then acknowledge, beloved brethren, the wholesome gift of the divine mercy ; and let us, who cannot be without some wound of conscience, heal our wounds by the spiritual remedies for the cleansing and purging of our sins. Nor let any one so flatter himself with the notion of a pure and immaculate heart, as, in dependence on his own innocence, to think that the medicine needs not to be applied to his wounds ; since it is written, " Who shall boast that he hath a clean heart, or who shall boast that he is pure from sins ? "[9] And again, in his epistle, John lays it down, and says, " If we say that we have no sin, we deceive ourselves, and the truth is not in us."[10] But if no one can be without sin, and whoever should say that he is without fault is either proud or foolish, how needful, how kind is the divine mercy, which, knowing that there are still found some wounds in those that have been healed, even after their healing, has given wholesome remedies for the curing and healing of their wounds anew !

4. Finally, beloved brethren, the divine admonition in the Scriptures, as well old as new, has never failed, has never been silent in urging God's people always and everywhere to works of mercy ; and in the strain and exhortation of the Holy Spirit, every one who is instructed into the hope of the heavenly kingdom is com-

---

1 [Numbered x. in Oxford ed., and assigned to A.D. 254.]
2 A slight and scarcely noticeable difference occurs here in the Oxford text, which reads the passage, " that the Son was sent, and willed to be called the Son of man."
3 Portaverat; " had brought " (Oxf. transl.).
4 " Poisons of the old serpent."
5 [The beauty of Cyprian's exordiums and perorations proves that he was a true orator. " Great and manifold," etc., *Translators of King James.*]
6 Prov. xvi. 6. [" By mercy and truth," etc., Eng. Version]
7 Ecclus. iii. 30.

8 Luke xi. 41.
9 Prov. xx. 9.
10 1 John i. 8, 9. Oxford editors add: " If we confess our sins, the Lord is faithful and just to forgive us our sins." [They remind us that this passage is expounded in the Anglican *Book of Homilies*, Hom. xi. part ii. p. 347, ed. Philadelphia, 1844.]

manded to give alms. God commands and prescribes to Isaiah: "Cry," says He, "with strength, and spare not. Lift up thy voice as a trumpet, and declare to my people their transgressions, and to the house of Jacob their sins." [1] And when He had commanded their sins to be charged upon them, and with the full force of His indignation had set forth their iniquities, and had said, that not even though they should use supplications, and prayers, and fastings, should they be able to make atonement for their sins; nor, if they were clothed in sackcloth and ashes, be able to soften God's anger, yet in the last part showing that God can be appeased by almsgiving alone, he added, saying, "Break thy bread to the hungry, and bring the poor that are without a home into thy house. If thou seest the naked, clothe him; and despise not the household of thine own seed. Then shall thy light break forth in season, and thy garments shall arise speedily; and righteousness shall go before thee, and the glory of God shall surround thee. Then shalt thou cry, and God shall hear thee; whilst yct thou art speaking, He shall say, Here I am." [2]

5. The remedies for propitiating God are given in the words of God Himself; the divine instructions have taught what sinners ought to do, that by works of righteousness God is satisfied, that with the deserts of mercy sins are cleansed. And in Solomon we read, "Shut up alms in the heart of the poor, and these shall intercede for thee from all evil." [3] And again: "Whoso stoppeth his ears that he may not hear the weak, he also shall call upon God, and there will be none to hear him." [4] For he shall not be able to deserve the mercy of the Lord, who himself shall not have been merciful; nor shall he obtain aught from the divine pity in his prayers, who shall not have been humane towards the poor man's prayer. And this also the Holy Spirit declares in the Psalms, and proves, saying, "Blessed is he that considereth of the poor and needy; the Lord will deliver him in the evil day." [5] Remembering which precepts, Daniel, when king Nebuchodonosor was in anxiety, being frightened by an adverse dream, gave him, for the turning away of evils, a remedy to obtain the divine help, saying, "Wherefore, O king, let my counsel be acceptable to thee; and redeem thy sins by almsgivings, and thine unrighteousness by mercies to the poor, and God will be patient [6] to thy sins." [7] And as the king did not obey him, he underwent the misfortunes and mischiefs which he had seen, and which he might have escaped and avoided had he redeemed his sins by almsgiving. Raphael the angel also witnesses the like, and exhorts that alms should be freely and liberally bestowed, saying, "Prayer is good, with fasting and alms; because alms doth deliver from death, and it purgeth away sins." [8] He shows that our prayers and fastings are of less avail, unless they are aided by almsgiving; that entreaties alone are of little force to obtain what they seek, unless they be made sufficient [9] by the addition of deeds and good works. The angel reveals, and manifests, and certifies that our petitions become efficacious by almsgiving, that life is redeemed from dangers by almsgiving, that souls are delivered from death by almsgiving.

6. Neither, beloved brethren, are we so bringing forward these things, as that we should not prove what Raphael the angel said, by the testimony of the truth. In the Acts of the Apostles the faith of the fact is established; and that souls are delivered by almsgiving not only from the second, but from the first death, is discovered by the evidence of a matter accomplished and completed. When Tabitha, being greatly given to good works and to bestowing alms, fell sick and died, Peter was summoned to her lifeless body; and when he, with apostolic humanity, had come in haste, there stood around him widows weeping and entreating, showing the cloaks, and coats, and all the garments which they had previously received, and praying for the deceased not by their words, but by her own deeds. Peter felt that what was asked in such a way might be obtained, and that Christ's aid would not be wanting to the petitioners, since He Himself was clothed in the clothing of the widows. When, therefore, falling on his knees, he had prayed, and — fit advocate for the widows and poor — had brought to the Lord the prayers entrusted to him, turning to the body, which was now lying washed on the bier, [10] he said, "Tabitha, in the name of Jesus Christ, arise!" [11] Nor did He fail to bring aid to Peter, who had said in the Gospel, that whatever should be asked in His name should be given. Therefore death is suspended, and the spirit is restored, and, to the marvel and astonishment of all, the revived body is quickened into this worldly light once more; so effectual were the merits of mercy, so much did righteous works avail! She who had conferred upon suffering widows the help needful to live, deserved to be recalled to life by the widows' petition.

7. Therefore in the Gospel, the Lord, the

---

[1] Isa. lviii. 1.
[2] Isa. lviii. 1–9.
[3] Ecclus. xxix. 12.
[4] Prov. xxi. 13.
[5] Ps. xli. 1.
[6] Some editors read "parcens" instead of "patiens," making the meaning "sparing to thy sins."
[7] Dan. iv. 27.

[8] Tob. xii. 8, 9.
[9] Some have read for "satientur," "farciantur," and others "socientur," "be filled up," or "be associated."
[10] Other translators read, "in the upper chamber."
[11] Acts ix. 40.

Teacher of our life and Master of eternal salvation, quickening the assembly of believers, and providing for them for ever when quickened, among His divine commands and precepts of heaven, commands and prescribes nothing more frequently than that we should devote ourselves to almsgiving, and not depend on earthly possessions, but rather lay up heavenly treasures. "Sell," says He, "your goods, and give alms."[1] And again : "Lay not up for yourselves treasures upon the earth, where moth and rust do corrupt, and where thieves break through and steal. But lay up for yourselves treasures in heaven, where neither moth nor rust doth corrupt, and where thieves do not break through nor steal. For where thy treasure is, there will thy heart be also."[2] And when He wished to set forth a man perfect and complete by the observation of the law,[3] He said, "If thou wilt be perfect, go and sell that thou hast, and give to the poor, and thou shalt have treasure in heaven ; and come and follow me."[4] Moreover, in another place He says that a merchant of the heavenly grace, and a gainer of eternal salvation, ought to purchase the precious pearl — that is, eternal life — at the price of the blood of Christ, from the amount of his patrimony, parting with all his wealth for it. He says : "The kingdom of heaven is like unto a merchantman seeking goodly pearls. And when he found a precious pearl, he went away and sold all that he had, and bought it."[5]

8. In fine, He calls those the children of Abraham whom He sees to be laborious in aiding and nourishing the poor. For when Zacchæus said, "Behold, the half of my goods I give to the poor ; and if I have done any wrong to any man, I restore fourfold," Jesus answered and said, "That salvation has this day come to this house, for that he also is a son of Abraham."[6] For if Abraham believed in God, and it was counted unto him for righteousness, certainly he who gives alms according to God's precept believes in God, and he who has the truth of faith maintains the fear of God ; moreover, he who maintains the fear of God considers God in showing mercy to the poor. For he labours thus because he believes — because he knows that what is foretold by God's word is true, and that the Holy Scripture cannot lie — that unfruitful trees, that is, unproductive men, are cut off and cast into the fire, but that the merciful are called into the kingdom. He also, in another place, calls laborious and fruitful men faithful ; but He denies faith to unfruitful and barren ones, saying, "If ye have not been faithful in the unrighteous mammon, who will commit to you that which is true? And if ye have not been faithful in that which is another man's, who shall give you that which is your own?"[7]

9. If you dread and fear, lest, if you begin to act thus abundantly, your patrimony being exhausted with your liberal dealing, you may perchance be reduced to poverty ; be of good courage in this respect, be free from care : that cannot be exhausted whence the service of Christ is supplied, whence the heavenly work is celebrated. Neither do I vouch for this on my own authority ; but I promise it on the faith of the Holy Scriptures, and on the authority of the divine promise. The Holy Spirit speaks by Solomon, and says, "He that giveth unto the poor shall never lack, but he that turneth away his eye shall be in great poverty ;"[8] showing that the merciful and those who do good works cannot want, but rather that the sparing and barren hereafter come to want. Moreover, the blessed Apostle Paul, full of the grace of the Lord's inspiration, says : "He that ministereth seed to the sower, shall both minister bread for your food, and shall multiply your seed sown, and shall increase the growth of the fruits of your righteousness, that in all things ye may be enriched."[9] And again : "The administration of this service shall not only supply the wants of the saints, but shall be abundant also by many thanksgivings unto God ;"[10] because, while thanks are directed to God for our almsgivings and labours, by the prayer of the poor, the wealth of the doer is increased by the retribution of God. And the Lord in the Gospel, already considering the hearts of men of this kind, and with prescient voice denouncing faithless and unbelieving men, bears witness, and says : "Take no thought, saying, What shall we eat? or, What shall we drink? or, Wherewithal shall we be clothed? For for these things the Gentiles seek. And your Father knoweth that ye have need of all these things. Seek first the kingdom of God, and His righteousness ; and all these things shall be added unto you."[11] He says that all these things shall be added and given to them who seek the kingdom and righteousness of God. For the Lord says, that when the day of judgment shall come, those who have laboured in His Church are admitted to receive the kingdom.

10. You are afraid lest perchance your estate should fail, if you begin to act liberally from it ; and you do not know, miserable man that you are, that while you are fearing lest your family property should fail you, life itself, and salvation,

---

[1] Luke xii. 33.
[2] Matt. vi. 19-21.
[3] "When He would show to one who had observed the law how to become perfect and finished" (Oxf. transl.).
[4] Matt. xix. 21.
[5] Matt. xiii. 45, 46.
[6] Luke xix. 8, 9.
[7] Luke xvi. 11, 12.
[8] Prov. xxviii 27.
[9] 2 Cor. ix. 10.
[10] 2 Cor. ix. 12.
[11] Matt. vi. 31-33.

are failing; and whilst you are anxious lest any of your wealth should be diminished, you do not see that you yourself are being diminished, in that you are a lover of mammon more than of your own soul; and while you fear, lest for the sake of yourself, you should lose your patrimony, you yourself are perishing for the sake of your patrimony. And therefore the apostle well exclaims, and says: "We brought nothing into this world, neither indeed can we carry anything out. Therefore, having food and clothing, let us therewith be content. For they who will be rich fall into temptation and a snare, and into many and hurtful desires, which drown a man in perdition and in destruction. For covetousness is a root of all evils, which some desiring, have made shipwreck from the faith, and pierced themselves through with many sorrows."[1]

11. Are you afraid that your patrimony perchance may fall short, if you should begin to do liberally from it? Yet when has it ever happened that resources[2] could fail the righteous man, since it is written, "The Lord will not slay with famine the righteous soul?"[3] Elias in the desert is fed by the ministry of ravens; and a meal from heaven is made ready for Daniel in the den, when shut up by the king's command for a prey to the lions; and you are afraid that food should be wanting to you, labouring and deserving well of the Lord, although He Himself in the Gospel bears witness, for the rebuke of those whose mind is doubtful and faith small, and says: "Behold the fowls of heaven, that they sow not, nor reap, nor gather into barns; and your heavenly Father feedeth them: are you not of more value than they?"[4] God feeds the fowls, and daily food is afforded to the sparrows; and to creatures which have no sense of things divine there is no want of drink or food. Thinkest thou that to a Christian — thinkest thou that to a servant of the Lord — thinkest thou that to one given up to good works — thinkest thou that to one that is dear to his Lord, anything will be wanting?

12. Unless you imagine that he who feeds Christ is not himself fed by Christ, or that earthly things will be wanting to those to whom heavenly and divine things are given, whence this unbelieving thought, whence this impious and sacrilegious consideration? What does a faithless heart do in the home of faith? Why is he who does not altogether trust in Christ named and called a Christian? The name of Pharisee is more fitting for you. For when in the Gospel the Lord was discoursing concerning almsgiving, and faithfully and wholesomely

warned us to make to ourselves friends of our earthly lucre by provident good works, who might afterwards receive us into eternal dwellings, the Scripture added after this, and said, "But the Pharisees heard all these things, who were very covetous, and they derided Him."[5] Some suchlike we see now in the Church, whose closed ears and darkened hearts admit no light from spiritual and saving warnings, of whom we need not wonder that they contemn the servant in his discourses, when we see the Lord Himself despised by such.

13. Wherefore do you applaud yourself in those vain and silly conceits, as if you were withheld from good works by fear and solicitude for the future? Why do you lay out before you certain shadows and omens of a vain excuse? Yea, confess what is the truth; and since you cannot deceive those who know,[6] utter forth the secret and hidden things of your mind. The gloom of barrenness has besieged your mind; and while the light of truth has departed thence, the deep and profound darkness of avarice has blinded your carnal heart. You are the captive and slave of your money; you are bound with the chains and bonds of covetousness; and you whom Christ had once loosed, are once more in chains. You keep your money, which, when kept, does not keep you.[7] You heap up a patrimony which burdens you[8] with its weight; and you do not remember what God answered to the rich man, who boasted with a foolish exultation of the abundance of his exuberant harvest: "Thou fool," said He, "this night thy soul is required of thee; then whose shall those things be which thou hast provided?"[9] Why do you watch in loneliness over your riches? why for your punishment do you heap up the burden of your patrimony, that, in proportion as you are rich in this world, you may become poor to God? Divide your returns with the Lord your God; share your gains with Christ; make Christ a partner with you in your earthly possessions, that He also may make you a fellow-heir with Him in His heavenly kingdom.

14. You are mistaken, and are deceived, whosoever you are, that think yourself rich in this world. Listen to the voice of your Lord in the Apocalypse, rebuking men of your stamp with righteous reproaches: "Thou sayest," says He, "I am rich, and increased with goods, and have need of nothing; and knowest not that thou art wretched, and miserable, and poor, and blind, and naked. I counsel thee to buy of me gold

---

[1] 1 Tim. vi. 7-10.
[2] Some editors read, "the resources of life."
[3] Prov. x. 3.
[4] Matt. v. 26.

[5] Luke xvi. 14.
[6] "Him who knows it," Oxford translation.
[7] [Prov. i. 19 "The eagle stole a lamb from the altar," say the Rabbins, "to feed his young; but a coal from the altar came with it, and burnt up nest and all."]
[8] According to Manutius, Pamelius, and others, "too heavily" is here added.
[9] Luke xii. 20.

tried in the fire, that thou mayest be rich ; and white raiment, that thou mayest be clothed, and that the shame of thy nakedness may not appear in thee ; and anoint thine eyes with eye-salve, that thou mayest see." [1] You therefore, who are rich and wealthy, buy for yourself of Christ gold tried by fire ; that you may be pure gold, with your filth burnt out as if by fire, if you are purged by almsgiving and righteous works. Buy for yourself white raiment, that you who had been naked according to Adam, and were before frightful and unseemly, may be clothed with the white garment of Christ. And you who are a wealthy and rich matron in Christ's Church,[2] anoint your eyes, not with the collyrium of the devil,[3] but with Christ's eye-salve, that you may be able to attain to see God, by deserving well of God, both by good works and character.

15. But you who are such as this, cannot labour in the Church. For your eyes, overcast with the gloom of blackness, and shadowed in night, do not see the needy and poor. You are wealthy and rich, and do you think that you celebrate the Lord's Supper, not at all considering the offering,[4] who come to the Lord's Supper without a sacrifice, and yet take part of the sacrifice which the poor man has offered? Consider in the Gospel the widow that remembered the heavenly precepts, doing good even amidst the difficulties and straits of poverty, casting two mites, which were all that she had, into the treasury ; whom when the Lord observed and saw, regarding her work not for its abundance, but for its intention, and considering not how much, but *from* how much, she had given, He answered and said, " Verily I say unto you, that widow hath cast in more than they all into the offerings of God. For all these have, of that which they had in abundance, cast in unto the offerings of God ; but she of her penury hath cast in all the living that she had." [5] Greatly blessed and glorious woman, who even before the day of judgment hast merited to be praised by the voice of the Judge ! Let the rich be ashamed of their barrenness and unbelief. The widow, the widow needy in means,[6] is found rich in works. And although everything that is given is conferred upon widows and orphans, she gives, whom it behoved to receive, that we may know thence what punishment awaits the barren rich man, when by this very instance even the poor ought to labour in good works. And in order that we may understand

that their labours are given to God, and that whoever performs them deserves well of the Lord, Christ calls this " the offerings of God," and intimates that the widow has cast in two farthings into the offerings of God, that it may be more abundantly evident that he who hath pity on the poor lendeth to God.

16. But neither let the consideration, dearest brethren, restrain and recall the Christian from good and righteous works, that any one should fancy that he could be excused for the benefit of his children ; since in spiritual expenditure we ought to think of Christ, who has declared that He receives them ; and not prefer our fellow-servants, but the Lord, to our children, since He Himself instructs and warns us, saying, " He that loveth father or mother more than me is not worthy of me, and he that loveth son or daughter more than me is not worthy of me." [7] Also in Deuteronomy, for the strengthening of faith and the love of God, similar things are written : " Who say," he saith, " unto their father or mother, I have not known thee ; neither did they acknowledge their children, these have observed Thy words, and kept Thy covenant." [8] For if we love God with our whole heart, we ought not to prefer either our parents or children to God. And this also John lays down in his epistle, that the love of God is not in them whom we see unwilling to labour for the poor. " Whoso," says he, " hath this world's goods, and seeth his brother have need, and shutteth up his bowels from him, how dwelleth the love of God in him ? " [9] For if by almsgiving to the poor we are lending to God — and when it is given to the least it is given to Christ — there is no ground for any one preferring earthly things to heavenly, nor for considering human things before divine.

17. Thus that widow in the third book of Kings, when in the drought and famine, having consumed everything, she had made of the little meal and oil which was left, a cake upon the ashes, and, having used this, was about to die with her children, Elias came and asked that something should first be given him to eat, and then of what remained that she and her children should eat. Nor did she hesitate to obey ; nor did the mother prefer her children to Elias in her hunger and poverty. Yea, there is done in God's sight a thing that pleases God : promptly and liberally is presented what is asked for. Neither is it a portion out of abundance, but the whole out of a little, that is given, and another is fed before her hungry children ; nor in penury and want is food thought of before mercy ; so that while in a saving work the life according to

---

[1] Rev. iii. 17, 18.
[2] These words, " in Christ's Church," are omitted in a few texts.
[3] [See Tertullian, vol. iv. p. 19; and for men, p. 22. Also, " eye-lid-powder," p. 23.]
[4] " Corban." [The note of the Oxford translation is useful in this place, quoting from Palmer, *Antiq.*, iv. 8. But see Pellicia, *Polity*, etc., p. 237, trans. London, Masters, 1883.]
[5] Luke xxi. 3, 4.
[6] This is differently read " a widow, a poor widow is found," etc.; or, " a woman widowed and poor."

[7] Matt. x. 37.
[8] Deut. xxxiii. 9.
[9] 1 John iii. 17.

the flesh is contemned, the soul according to the spirit is preserved. Therefore Elias, being the type of Christ, and showing that according to His mercy He returns to each their reward, answered and said : "Thus saith the Lord, The vessel of meal shall not fail, and the cruse of oil shall not be diminished, until the day that the Lord giveth rain upon the earth."[1] According to her faith in the divine promise, those things which she gave were multiplied and heaped up to the widow; and her righteous works and deserts of mercy taking augmentations and increase, the vessels of meal and oil were filled. Nor did the mother take away from her children what she gave to Elias, but rather she conferred upon her children what she did kindly and piously.[2] And she did not as yet know Christ; she had not yet heard His precepts; she did not, as redeemed by His cross and passion, repay meat and drink for His blood. So that from this it may appear how much he sins in the Church, who, preferring himself and his children to Christ, preserves his wealth, and does not share an abundant estate with the poverty of the needy.

18. Moreover, also, (you say) there are many children at home; and the multitude of your children checks you from giving yourself freely to good works. And yet on this very account you ought to labour the more, for the reason that you are the father of many pledges. There are the more for whom you must beseech the Lord. The sins of many have to be redeemed, the consciences of many to be cleansed, the souls of many to be liberated. As in this worldly life, in the nourishment and bringing up of children, the larger the number the greater also is the expense; so also in the spiritual and heavenly life, the larger the number of children you have, the greater ought to be the outlay of your labours. Thus also Job offered numerous sacrifices on behalf of his children; and as large as was the number of the pledges in his home, so large also was the number of victims given to God. And since there cannot daily fail to be sins committed in the sight of God, there wanted not daily sacrifices wherewith the sins might be cleansed away. The Holy Scripture proves this, saying : "Job, a true and righteous man, had seven sons and three daughters, and cleansed them, offering for them victims to God according to the number of them, and for their sins one calf."[3] If, then, you truly love your children, if you show to them the full and paternal sweetness of love, you ought to be the more charitable, that by your righteous works you may commend your children to God.

19. Neither should you think that he is father to your children who is both changeable and infirm, but you should obtain Him who is the eternal and unchanging Father of spiritual children. Assign to Him your wealth which you are saving up for your heirs. Let Him be the guardian for your children; let Him be their trustee; let Him be their protector, by His divine majesty, against all worldly injuries. The state neither takes away the property entrusted to God, nor does the exchequer intrude on it, nor does any forensic calumny overthrow it. That inheritance is placed in security which is kept under the guardianship of God.[4] This is to provide for one's dear pledges for the coming time; this is with paternal affection to take care for one's future heirs, according to the faith of the Holy Scripture, which says : "I have been young, and now am old; yet have I not seen the righteous forsaken, nor his seed wanting bread. All the day long he is merciful, and lendeth;[5] and his seed is blessed."[6] And again : "He who walketh without reproach in his integrity shall leave blessed children after him."[7] Therefore you are an unfair and traitorous father, unless you faithfully consult for your children, unless you look forward to preserve them in religion and true piety. You who are careful rather for their earthly than for their heavenly estate, rather to commend your children to the devil than to Christ, are sinning twice, and allowing a double and twofold crime, both in not providing for your children the aid of God their Father, and in teaching your children to love their property more than Christ.

20. Be rather such a father to your children as was Tobias. Give useful and saving precepts to your pledges, such as he gave to his son; command your children what he also commanded his son, saying : "And now, my son, I command thee, serve God in truth, and do before Him that which pleaseth Him; and command thy sons, that they exercise righteousness and alms, and be mindful of God, and bless His name always."[8] And again : "All the days of thy life, most dear son, have God in your mind, and be not willing to transgress His commandments. Do righteousness all the days of thy life, and be not willing to walk in the way of iniquity; because if thou deal truly, there will be respect of thy works. Give alms of thy substance, and turn not away thy face from any poor man. So

---

4 [" The howse shall be preserved and
never will decaye
Wheare the Almightie God is honored
and served, daye by daye."
This motto I copied from an old oaken beam in the hall of Rockingham Castle, with date A.D. 1579. In 1875 I saw the householder kneeling under this motto, with all his family and servants, daily.]
5 The original is variously read " fœnerat " and " commodat."
6 Ps. xxxvii. 25, 26.
7 Prov. xx. 7.
8 Tob. xiv 10, 11.

---

1 1 Kings xvii. 14.
2 [See p. 479, *supra*, note 7. [Prov. xi. 24.]
3 Job i. 5, LXX.

shall it be, that neither shall the face of God be turned away from thee. As thou hast, my son, so do. If thy substance is abundant, give alms of it the more. If thou hast little, communicate of that little. And fear not when thou doest alms ; for thou layest up a good reward for thyself against the day of necessity, because that alms do deliver from death, and suffereth not to come into Gehenna. Alms is a good gift to all that give it, in the sight of the most high God." [1]

21. What sort of gift is it, beloved brethren, whose setting forth is celebrated in the sight of God? If, in a gift of the Gentiles, it seems a great and glorious thing to have proconsuls or emperors present, and the preparation and display is the greater among the givers, in order that they may please the higher classes ; how much more illustrious and greater is the glory to have God and Christ as the spectators of the gift ! How much more sumptuous the preparation and more liberal the expense to be set forth in that case, when the powers of heaven assemble to the spectacle, when all the angels come together : where it is not a four-horsed chariot or a consulship that is sought for the giver, but life eternal is bestowed ; nor is the empty and fleeting favour of the rabble grasped at, but the perpetual reward of the kingdom of heaven is received !

22. And that the indolent and the barren, and those, who by their covetousness for money do nothing in respect of the fruit of their salvation, may be the more ashamed, and that the blush of dishonour and disgrace may the more strike upon their sordid conscience, let each one place before his eyes the devil with his servants, that is, with the people of perdition and death, springing forth into the midst, and provoking the people of Christ with the trial of comparison — Christ Himself being present, and judging — in these words : " I, for those whom thou seest with me, neither received buffets, nor bore scourgings, nor endured the cross, nor shed my blood, nor redeemed my family at the price of my suffering and blood ; but neither do I promise them a celestial kingdom, nor do I recall them to paradise, having again restored to them immortality. But they prepare for me gifts how precious ! how large ! with how excessive and tedious a labour procured ! and that, with the most sumptuous devices, either pledging or selling their means in the procuring of the gift ! and, unless a competent manifestation followed, they are cast out with scoffings and hissings, and by the popular fury sometimes they are almost stoned ! Show, O Christ, such givers as these of Thine [2] — those rich men, those men affluent

with abounding wealth — whether in the Church wherein Thou presidest and beholdest, they set forth a gift of that kind, — having pledged or scattered their riches, yea, having transferred them, by the change of their possessions for the better, into heavenly treasures ! In those spectacles of mine, perishing and earthly as they are, no one is fed, no one is clothed, no one is sustained by the comfort either of any meat or drink. All things, between the madness of the exhibitor and the mistake of the spectator, are perishing in a prodigal and foolish vanity of deceiving pleasures. There, in Thy poor, Thou art clothed and fed ; Thou promisest eternal life to those who labour for Thee ; and scarcely are Thy people made equal to mine that perish, although they are honoured by Thee with divine wages and heavenly rewards.

23. What do we reply to these things, dearest brethren? With what reason do we defend the minds of rich men, overwhelmed with a profane barrenness and a kind of night of gloom? With what excuse do we acquit them, seeing that we are less than the devil's servants, so as not even moderately to repay Christ for the price of His passion and blood? He has given us precepts ; what His servants ought to do He has instructed us ; promising a reward to those that are charitable, and threatening punishment to the unfruitful. He has set forth His sentence. He has before announced what He shall judge. What can be the excuse for the laggard? what the defence for the unfruitful? But when the servant does not do what is commanded, the Lord will do what He threatens, seeing that He says : " When the Son of man shall come in His glory, and all the angels with Him, then shall He sit in the throne of His glory : and before Him shall be gathered all nations ; and He shall separate them one from another, as a shepherd divideth his sheep from the goats : and He shall set the sheep on His right hand, but the goats on the left. Then shall the King say unto them that shall be on His right hand, Come, ye blessed of my Father, receive the kingdom that is prepared for you from the foundation of the world. For I was an hungered, and ye gave me to eat : I was thirsty, and ye gave me to drink : I was a stranger, and ye took me in : naked, and ye clothed me : I was sick, and ye visited me : I was in prison, and ye came to me. Then shall the righteous answer Him, saying, Lord, when saw we Thee an hungered, and fed Thee? thirsty, and gave Thee drink? When saw we Thee a stranger, and took Thee in? naked, and clothed Thee? Or when saw we Thee sick, and in prison, and came unto Thee? Then shall the King answer and say unto them, Verily I say unto you, Insomuch as you did it to one of the least of these my brethren, ye did it unto me. Then

---

[1] Tob. iv. 5-11.
[2] Some editors add here, " warned by Thy precepts, and who shall receive heavenly things instead of earthly."

shall He say also unto those that shall be at His left hand, Depart from me, ye cursed, into everlasting fire, which my Father hath prepared for the devil and his angels. For I was an hungered, and ye gave me not to eat: I was thirsty, and ye gave me not to drink: I was a stranger, and ye took me not in: naked, and ye clothed me not: sick, and in prison, and ye visited me not. Then shall they also answer Him, saying, Lord, when saw we Thee an hungered, or athirst, or a stranger, or naked, or sick, or in prison, and ministered not unto Thee? And He shall answer them, Verily I say unto you, In so far as ye did it not to one of the least of these, ye did it not unto me. And these shall go away into everlasting burning: but the righteous into life eternal." [1] What more could Christ declare unto us? How more could He stimulate the works of our righteousness and mercy, than by saying that whatever is given to the needy and poor is given to Himself, and by saying that He is aggrieved unless the needy and poor be supplied? So that he who in the Church is not moved by consideration for his brother, may yet be moved by contemplation of Christ; and he who does not think of his fellow-servant in suffering and in poverty, may yet think of his Lord, who abideth in that very man whom he is despising.

24. And therefore, dearest brethren, whose fear is inclined towards God, and who having already despised and trampled under foot the world, have lifted up your mind to things heavenly and divine, let us with full faith, with devoted mind, with continual labour, give our obedience, to deserve well of the Lord. Let us give to Christ earthly garments, that we may receive heavenly raiment; let us give food and drink of this world, that we may come with Abraham, and Isaac, and Jacob to the heavenly banquet. That we may not reap little, let us sow abundantly. Let us, while there is time, take thought for our security and eternal salvation, according to the admonition of the Apostle Paul, who says: "Therefore, while we have time, let us labour in what is good unto all men, but especially to them that are of the household of faith. But let us not be weary in welldoing, for in its season we shall reap." [2]

25. Let us consider, beloved brethren, what the congregation of believers did in the time of the apostles, when at the first beginnings the mind flourished with greater virtues, when the faith of believers burned with a warmth of faith as yet new. Then they sold houses and farms, and gladly and liberally presented to the apostles the proceeds to be dispensed to the poor; selling and alienating their earthly estate, they transferred their lands thither where they might re-

ceive the fruits of an eternal possession, and there prepared homes where they might begin an eternal habitation. Such, then, was the abundance in labours, as was the agreement in love, as we read in the Acts of the Apostles: "And the multitude of them that believed acted with one heart and one soul; neither was there any distinction among them, nor did they esteem anything their own of the goods which belonged to them, but they had all things common." [3] This is truly to become sons of God by spiritual birth; this is to imitate by the heavenly law the equity of God the Father. For whatever is of God is common in our use; nor is any one excluded from His benefits and His gifts, so as to prevent the whole human race from enjoying equally the divine goodness and liberality. Thus the day equally enlightens, the sun gives radiance, the rain moistens, the wind blows, and the sleep is one to those that sleep, and the splendour of the stars and of the moon is common. In which example of equality,[4] he who, as a possessor in the earth, shares his returns and his fruits with the fraternity, while he is common and just in his gratuitous bounties, is an imitator of God the Father.

26. What, dearest brethren, will be that glory of those who labour charitably — how great and high the joy when the Lord begins to number His people, and, distributing to our merits and good works the promised rewards, to give heavenly things for earthly, eternal things for temporal, great things for small; to present us to the Father, to whom He has restored us by His sanctification; to bestow upon us immortality and eternity, to which He has renewed us by the quickening of His blood; to bring us anew to paradise, to open the kingdom of heaven, in the faith and truth of His promise! Let these things abide firmly in our perceptions, let them be understood with full faith, let them be loved with our whole heart, let them be purchased by the magnanimity of our increasing labours. An illustrious and divine thing, dearest brethren, is the saving labour of charity; a great comfort of believers, a wholesome guard of our security, a protection of hope, a safeguard of faith, a remedy for sin, a thing placed in the power of the doer, a thing both great and easy, a crown of peace without the risk of persecution; the true and greatest gift of God, needful for the weak, glorious for the strong, assisted by which the Christian accomplishes spiritual grace, deserves well of Christ the Judge, accounts God his debtor. For this palm of works of salvation let us gladly and readily strive; let us all, in the struggle of righteousness, run

---

[1] Matt. xxv. 31–46.
[2] Gal. vi. 10, 9.

[3] Acts iv. 32.
[4] This appears to be the less usual reading, the ordinary one being "equity."

with God and Christ looking on; and let us who have already begun to be greater than this life and the world, slacken our course by no desire of this life and of this world. If the day shall find us, whether it be the day of reward [1] or of persecution, furnished, if swift, if running in this contest of charity, the Lord will never fail of giving a reward for our merits : in peace He will give to us who conquer, a white crown for our labours ; in persecution, He will accompany it with a purple one for our passion.

TREATISE IX.

ON THE ADVANTAGE OF PATIENCE.[2]

ARGUMENT. — CYPRIAN HIMSELF BRIEFLY SETS FORTH THE OCCASION OF THIS TREATISE AT THE CONCLUSION OF HIS EPISTLE TO JUBAIANUS AS FOLLOWS : " CHARITY OF SPIRIT, THE HONOUR OF OUR COLLEGE, THE BOND OF FAITH, AND PRIESTLY CONCORD, ARE MAINTAINED BY US WITH PATIENCE AND GENTLENESS. FOR THIS REASON, MOREOVER, WE HAVE, WITH THE BEST OF OUR POOR ABILITIES, BY THE PERMISSION AND INSPIRATION OF THE LORD, WRITTEN A PAMPHLET ' ON THE BENEFIT OF PATIENCE,' WHICH, FOR THE SAKE OF OUR MUTUAL LOVE, WE HAVE TRANSMITTED TO YOU." A.D. 256.

1. As I am about to speak, beloved brethren, of patience, and to declare its advantages and benefits, from what point should I rather begin than this, that I see that even at this time, for your audience of me, patience is needful, as you cannot even discharge this duty of hearing and learning without patience ? For wholesome discourse and reasoning are then effectually learnt, if what is said be patiently heard. Nor do I find, beloved brethren, among the rest of the ways of heavenly discipline wherein the path of our hope and faith is directed to the attainment of the divine rewards, anything of more advantage, either as more useful for life or more helpful to glory, than that we who are labouring in the precepts of the Lord with the obedience of fear and devotion, should especially, with our whole watchfulness, be careful of patience.[3]

2. Philosophers also profess that they pursue this virtue ; but in their case the patience is as false as their wisdom also is. For whence can he be either wise or patient, who has neither known the wisdom nor the patience of God? since He Himself warns us, and says of those who seem to themselves to be wise in this world, " I will destroy the wisdom of the wise, and I will reprove the understanding also of the prudent." [4] Moreover, the blessed Apostle Paul, filled with the Holy Spirit, and sent forth for the calling and training of the heathen, bears witness and instructs us, saying, " See that no man despoil you through philosophy and vain deceit, after the tradition of men, after the elements of the world, and not after Christ, because in Him dwelleth all the fulness of divinity." [5] And in another place he says : " Let no man deceive himself ; if any man among you thinketh himself to be wise, let him become a fool to this world, that he may become wise. For the wisdom of this world is foolishness with God. For it is written, I will rebuke the wise in their own craftiness." And again : " The Lord knoweth the thoughts of the wise, that they are foolish." [6] Wherefore if the wisdom among them be not true, the patience also cannot be true. For if he is wise [7] who is lowly and meek — but we do not see that philosophers are either lowly or meek, but greatly pleasing themselves, and, for the very reason that they please themselves, displeasing God — it is evident that the patience is not real among them where there is the insolent audacity of an affected liberty, and the immodest boastfulness of an exposed and half-naked bosom.

3. But for us, beloved brethren, who are philosophers, not in words, but in deeds, and do not put forward our wisdom in our garb, but in truth — who are better acquainted with the consciousness, than with the boast, of virtues — who do not speak great things, but live them, — let us, as servants and worshippers of God, show, in our spiritual obedience, the patience which we learn from heavenly teachings. For we have this virtue in common with God. From Him patience begins ; from Him its glory and its dignity take their rise. The origin and greatness of patience proceed from God as its author. Man ought to love the thing which is dear to God ; the good which the Divine Majesty loves, it commends. If God is our Lord and Father, let us imitate the patience of our Lord as well as our Father ; because it behoves servants to be obedient, no less than it becomes sons not to be degenerate.

4. But what and how great is the patience in God, that, most patiently enduring the profane temples and the images of earth, and the sacri-

---

[1] A more ancient reading seems to be, " of return " (scil. " reditionis ").

[2] Having at the outset distinguished true patience from the false patience of philosophers, he commends Christian patience by the patience of God, of Christ, and of all righteous men. He further proves, as well by Scripture as by reason, and, moreover, by the instances of Job and Tobias, that not only is patience useful, but that it is needful also; and in order that the excellence of patience may shine forth the more by contrast with the vice opposed to it, he sets forth what is the evil of impatience. Finally, he reproves the desire of vengeance, and teaches that revenge ought, according to Scripture, to be left to God rather than to be arrogated to ourselves. If in any writing Cyprian is an imitator of Tertullian, assuredly in this he imitates that writer's treatise On Patience. [See vol. iii. p. 707.]

[3] [Hermas, vol. ii. 23, 49; also Tertullian, iii. 714, and elucidation, p. 717.]

[4] Isa. xxix. 14.
[5] Col. ii. 8, 10.
[6] 1 Cor. iii. 18-20.
[7] The Oxford edition (Treatise ix.), and many others read " patient."

legious rites instituted by men, in contempt of His majesty and honour, He makes the day to begin and the light of the sun to arise alike upon the good and the evil; and while He waters the earth with showers, no one is excluded from His benefits, but upon the righteous equally with the unrighteous He bestows His undiscriminating rains. We see that with undistinguishing [1] equality of patience, at God's behest, the seasons minister to the guilty and the guiltless, the religious and the impious — those who give thanks and the unthankful; that the elements wait on them; the winds blow, the fountains flow, the abundance of the harvests increases, the fruits of the vineyards ripen,[2] the trees are loaded with apples, the groves put on their leaves, the meadows their verdure; and while God is provoked with frequent, yea, with continual offences, He softens His indignation, and in patience waits for the day of retribution, once for all determined; and although He has revenge in His power, He prefers to keep patience for a long while, bearing, that is to say, mercifully, and putting off, so that, if it might be possible, the long protracted mischief may at some time be changed, and man, involved in the contagion of errors and crimes, may even though late be converted to God, as He Himself warns and says, "I do not will the death of him that dieth, so much as that he may return and live." [3] And again, "Return unto me, saith the Lord." [4] And again: "Return to the Lord your God; for He is merciful, and gracious, and patient, and of great pity, and who inclines His judgment towards the evils inflicted." [5] Which, moreover, the blessed apostle referring to, and recalling the sinner to repentance, sets forward, and says: "Or despisest thou the riches of His goodness, and forbearance, and long-suffering, not knowing that the patience and goodness of God leadeth thee to repentance? But after thy hardness and impenitent heart thou treasurest up unto thyself wrath in the day of wrath and of revelation of the righteous judgment of God, who shall render to every one according to his works." [6] He says that God's judgment is just, because it is tardy, because it is long and greatly deferred, so that by the long patience of God man may be benefited for life eternal.[7] Punishment is then executed on the impious and the sinner, when repentance for the sin can no longer avail.

5. And that we may more fully understand, beloved brethren, that patience is a thing of God, and that whoever is gentle, and patient, and meek, is an imitator of God the Father; when the Lord in His Gospel was giving precepts for salvation, and, bringing forth divine warnings, was instructing His disciples to perfection, He laid it down, and said, "Ye have heard that it is said, Thou shalt love thy neighbour, and have thine enemy in hatred. But I say unto you, Love your enemies, and pray for them which persecute you; that ye may be the children of your Father which is in heaven, who maketh His sun to rise on the good and on the evil, and raineth upon the just and on the unjust. For if ye love them which love you, what reward shall ye have? do not even the publicans the same? And if ye shall salute your brethren only, what do ye more (than others)? do not even the heathens the same thing? Be ye therefore perfect, even as your Father in heaven is perfect." [8] He said that the children of God would thus become perfect. He showed that they were thus completed, and taught that they were restored by a heavenly birth, if the patience of God our Father dwell in us — if the divine likeness, which Adam had lost by sin, be manifested and shine in our actions. What a glory is it to become like to God! what and how great a felicity, to possess among our virtues, that which may be placed on the level of divine praises!

6. Nor, beloved brethren, did Jesus Christ, our God and Lord, teach this in words only; but He fulfilled it also in deeds. And because He had said that He had come down for this purpose, that He might do the will of His Father; among the other marvels of His virtues, whereby He showed forth the marks of a divine majesty, He also maintained the patience of His Father in the constancy of His endurance. Finally, all His actions, even from His very advent, are characterized by patience as their associate; in that, first of all, coming down from that heavenly sublimity to earthly things, the Son of God did not scorn to put on the flesh of man, and although He Himself was not a sinner, to bear the sins of others. His immortality being in the meantime laid aside, He suffers Himself to become mortal, so that the guiltless may be put to death for the salvation of the guilty. The Lord is baptized by the servant; and He who is about to bestow remission of sins, does not Himself disdain to wash His body in the laver of regeneration. For forty days He fasts, by whom others are feasted. He is hungry, and suffers famine, that they who had been in hunger of the word and of grace may be satisfied with heavenly bread. He wrestles with the devil tempting Him; and, content only to have overcome the enemy, He strives no

---

[1] "Inseparabili."
[2] The original here is read variously "maturescere" and "mitescere."
[3] Ezek. xviii. 32.
[4] Mal. iii. 7. The Oxford edition omits this quotation, and introduces the next with the words, "And again the prophet."
[5] Joel ii. 13.
[6] Rom. ii. 4-6.
[7] ["Deus patiens quia æternus" (Augustine).]

[8] Matt. v. 43-48.

further than by words. He ruled over His disciples not as servants in the power of a master; but, kind and gentle, He loved them with a brotherly love. He deigned even to wash the apostles' feet, that since the Lord is such among His servants, He might teach, by His example, what a fellow-servant ought to be among his peers and equals. Nor is it to be wondered at, that among the obedient [1] He showed Himself such, since He could bear Judas even to the last with a long patience — could take meat with His enemy — could know the household foe, and not openly point him out, nor refuse the kiss of the traitor. Moreover, in bearing with the Jews, how great equanimity and how great patience, in turning the unbelieving to the faith by persuasion, in soothing the unthankful by concession, in answering gently to the contradictors, in bearing the proud with clemency, in yielding with humility to the persecutors, in wishing to gather together the slayers of the prophets, and those who were always rebellious against God, even to the very hour of His cross and passion!

7. And moreover, in His very passion and cross, before they had reached the cruelty of death and the effusion of blood, what infamies of reproach were patiently heard, what mockings of contumely were suffered, so that *He* received [2] the spittings of insulters, who with His spittle had a little before made eyes for a blind man; and He in whose name the devil and his angels is now scourged by His servants, Himself suffered scourgings! He was crowned with thorns, who crowns martyrs with eternal flowers. He was smitten on the face with palms, who gives the true palms to those who overcome. He was despoiled of His earthly garment, who clothes others in the vesture of immortality. He was fed with gall, who gave heavenly food. He was given to drink of vinegar, who appointed the cup of salvation. That guiltless, that just One, — nay, He who is innocency itself and justice itself, — is counted among transgressors, and truth is oppressed with false witnesses. He who shall judge is judged; and the Word of God is led silently to the slaughter. And when at the cross of the Lord the stars are confounded, the elements are disturbed, the earth quakes, night shuts out the day, the sun, that he may not be compelled to look on the crime of the Jews, withdraws both his rays and his eyes, He speaks not, nor is moved, nor declares His majesty even in His very passion itself. Even to the end, all things are borne perseveringly and constantly, in order that in Christ a full and perfect patience may be consummated.[3]

8. And after all these things, He still receives His murderers, if they will be converted and come to Him; and with a saving patience, He who is benignant [4] to preserve, closes His Church to none. Those adversaries, those blasphemers, those who were always enemies to His name, if they repent of their sin, if they acknowledge the crime committed, He receives, not only to the pardon of their sin, but to the reward of the heavenly kingdom. What can be said more patient, what more merciful? Even he is made alive by Christ's blood who has shed Christ's blood. Such and so great is the patience of Christ; and had it not been such and so great, the Church would never have possessed Paul as an apostle.[5]

9. But if we also, beloved brethren, are in Christ; if we put Him on, if He is the way of our salvation, who follow Christ in the footsteps of salvation, let us walk by the example of Christ, as the Apostle John instructs us, saying, "He who saith he abideth in Christ, ought himself also to walk even as He walked."[6] Peter also, upon whom by the Lord's condescension the Church was founded,[7] lays it down in his epistle, and says, "Christ suffered for us, leaving you an example, that ye should follow His steps, who did no sin, neither was deceit found in His mouth; who, when He was reviled, reviled not again; when He suffered, threatened not, but gave Himself up to him that judged Him unjustly."[8]

10. Finally, we find that both patriarchs and prophets, and all the righteous men who in their preceding likeness wore the figure of Christ, in the praise of their virtues were watchful over nothing more than that they should preserve patience with a strong and stedfast equanimity. Thus Abel, who first initiated and consecrated the origin of martyrdom, and the passion of the righteous man, makes no resistance nor struggles against his fratricidal [9] brother, but with lowliness and meekness he is patiently slain. Thus Abraham, believing God, and first of all instituting the root and foundation of faith, when tried in respect of his son, does not hesitate nor delay, but obeys the commands of God with all the patience of devotion. And Isaac, prefigured as the likeness of the Lord's victim, when he is presented by his father for immolation, is found patient. And Jacob, driven forth by his brother from his country, departs with patience; and afterwards with greater patience, he suppliantly brings him back to concord with peaceful gifts,

---

[1] Baluzius reads, "compares obaudientes" — His obedient peers. The mss. have "obaudientes" only.

[2] Erasmus adds, "with patience."

[3] [This sublime passage recalls Bacon's *Paradoxes*. See p. 237, note 3, *supra*.]

[4] Some editors insert "and patient."

[5] [1 Tim. i. 3. A striking suggestion, put in our author's terse way.]

[6] 1 John ii. 6.

[7] [See Elucidation VII. The Trent Council itself (on Matt. xvi. 18) affirms this of the Creed, not Peter. Vol. iv. pp. 99 and 101.]

[8] 1 Pet. ii. 21-23, with a singular departure from the received text.

[9] According to some, "parricidal."

when he is even more impious and persecuting. Joseph, sold by his brethren and sent away, not only with patience pardons them, but even bountifully and mercifully bestows gratuitous supplies of corn on them when they come to him. Moses is frequently contemned by an ungrateful and faithless people, and almost stoned ; and yet with gentleness and patience he entreats the Lord for those people. But in David, from whom, according to the flesh, the nativity of Christ springs, how great and marvellous and Christian is the patience, that he often had it in his power to be able to kill king Saul, who was persecuting him and desiring to slay him ; and yet, chose rather to save him when placed in his hand, and delivered up to him, not repaying his enemy in turn, but rather, on the contrary, even avenging him when slain ! In fine, so many prophets were slain, so many martyrs were honoured with glorious deaths, who all have attained to the heavenly crowns by the praise of patience. For the crown of sorrows and sufferings cannot be received unless patience in sorrow and suffering precede it.

11. But that it may be more manifestly and fully known how useful and necessary patience is, beloved brethren ; let the judgment of God be pondered, which even in the beginning of the world and of the human race, Adam, forgetful of the commandment, and a transgressor of the given law, received. Then we shall know how patient in this life we ought to be who are born in such a state, that we labour here with afflictions and contests. "Because," says He, "thou hast hearkened to the voice of thy wife, and hast eaten of the tree of which alone I had charged thee that thou shouldest not eat, cursed shall be the ground in all thy works : in sorrow and in groaning shalt thou eat of it all the days of thy life. Thorns and thistles shall it give forth to thee, and thou shalt eat the food of the field. In the sweat of thy face shalt thou eat thy bread, till thou return into the ground from which thou wast taken : for dust thou art, and to dust shalt thou go."[1] We are all tied and bound with the chain of this sentence, until, death being expunged, we depart from this life. In sorrow and groaning we must of necessity be all the days of our life : it is necessary that we eat our bread with sweat and labour.

12. Whence every one of us, when he is born and received in the inn of this world, takes his beginning from tears ; and, although still unconscious and ignorant of all things, he knows nothing else in that very earliest birth except to weep. By a natural foresight, the untrained soul laments the anxieties and labours of the mortal life, and even in the beginning bears witness by its wails and groans to the storms of the world which it

is entering. For the sweat of the brow and labour is the condition of life so long as it lasts. Nor can there be supplied any consolations to those that sweat and toil other than patience ; which consolations, while in this world they are fit and necessary for all men, are especially so for us who are more shaken by the siege of the devil, who, daily standing in the battle-field, are wearied with the wrestlings of an inveterate and skilful enemy ; for us who, besides the various and continual battles of temptations, must also in the contest of persecutions[2] forsake our patrimonies, undergo imprisonment, bear chains, spend our lives, endure the sword, the wild beasts, fires, crucifixions — in fine, all kinds of torments and penalties, to be endured in the faith and courage of patience ; as the Lord Himself instructs us, and says, "These things have I spoken unto you, that in me ye might have peace. But in the world ye shall have tribulation ; yet be confident, for I have overcome the world."[3] And if we who have renounced the devil and the world, suffer the tribulations and mischiefs of the devil and the world with more frequency and violence, how much more ought we to keep patience, wherewith as our helper and ally, we may bear all mischievous things !

13. It is the wholesome precept of our Lord and Master : "He that endureth," saith He, "unto the end, the same shall be saved ; "[4] and again, "If ye continue," saith He, "in my word, ye shall be truly my disciples ; and ye shall know the truth, and the truth shall make you free."[5] We must endure and persevere, beloved brethren, in order that, being admitted to the hope of truth and liberty, we may attain to the truth and liberty itself; for that very fact that we are Christians is the substance of faith and hope. But that hope and faith may attain to their result, there is need of patience. For we are not following after present glory, but future, according to what Paul the apostle also warns us, and says, "We are saved by hope ; but hope that is seen is not hope : for what a man seeth, why doth he hope for? But if we hope for that which we see not, then do we by patience wait for it."[6] Therefore, waiting and patience are needful, that we may fulfil that which we have begun to be, and may receive that which we believe and hope for, according to God's own showing.[7] Moreover, in another place, the same apostle instructs the righteous and the doers of good works, and them who lay up for themselves

---

[1] Gen. iii. 17-19.

[2] [How practical this treatise in an age when to be a Christian meant to be prepared for all these things! "Fiery trials" the chronic state.]
[3] John xvi. 33.
[4] Matt. x. 22.
[5] John viii. 31, 32.
[6] Rom. viii. 24, 25.
[7] A common reading here is "giving" instead of "showing," *scil.* "præstante" for "representante."

treasures in heaven with the increase of the divine usury, that they also should be patient; and teaches them, saying, " Therefore, while we have time, let us labour in that which is good unto all men, but especially to them who are of the household of faith. But let us not faint in well-doing, for in its season we shall reap." [1] He admonishes that no man should impatiently faint in his labour, that none should be either called off or overcome by temptations and desist in the midst of the praise and in the way of glory; and the things that are past perish, while those which have begun cease to be perfect; as it is written, " The righteousness of the righteous shall not deliver him in whatever day he shall transgress;" [2] and again, " Hold that which thou hast, that another take not thy crown." [3] Which word exhorts us to persevere with patience and courage, so that he who strives towards the crown with the praise now near at hand, may be crowned by the continuance of patience.

14. But patience, beloved brethren, not only keeps watch over what is good, but it also repels what is evil. In harmony with the Holy Spirit, and associated with what is heavenly and divine, it struggles with the defence of its strength against the deeds of the flesh and the body, wherewith the soul is assaulted and taken. Let us look briefly into a few things out of many, that from a few the rest also may be understood. Adultery, fraud, manslaughter, are mortal crimes. Let patience be strong and stedfast in the heart; and neither is the sanctified body and temple of God polluted by adultery, nor is the innocence dedicated to righteousness stained with the contagion of fraud; nor, after the Eucharist carried in it, [4] is the hand spotted with the sword and blood.

15. Charity is the bond of brotherhood, the foundation of peace, the holdfast and security of unity, which is greater than both hope and faith, which excels both good works and martyrdoms, which will abide with us always, eternal with God in the kingdom of heaven. Take from it patience; and deprived of it, it does not endure. Take from it the substance of bearing and of enduring, and it continues with no roots nor strength. The apostle, finally, when he would speak of charity, joined to it endurance and patience. " Charity," he says, " is large-souled; charity is kind; charity envieth not, is not puffed up, is not provoked, thinketh not evil; loveth all things, believeth all things, hopeth all things, beareth all things." [5] Thence

he shows that it can tenaciously persevere, because it knows how to endure all things. And in another place : " Forbearing one another," he says, " in love, using every effort to keep the unity of the spirit in the bond of peace." [6] He proved that neither unity nor peace could be kept unless brethren should cherish one another with mutual toleration, and should keep the bond of concord by the intervention of patience.

16. What beyond ; — that you should not swear nor curse ; that you should not seek again your goods when taken from you; that, when you receive a buffet, you should give your other cheek to the smiter; that you should forgive a brother who sins against you, not only seven times, but seventy times seven times, [7] but, moreover, all his sins altogether ; that you should love your enemies ; that you should offer prayer for your adversaries and persecutors? Can you accomplish these things unless you maintain [8] the stedfastness of patience and endurance? And this we see done in the case of Stephen, who, when he was slain by the Jews with violence and stoning, did not ask for vengeance for himself, but for pardon for his murderers, saying, " Lord, lay not this sin to their charge." [9] It behoved the first martyr of Christ thus to be, who, fore-running the martyrs that should follow him in a glorious death, was not only the preacher of the Lord's passion, but also the imitator of His most patient gentleness. What shall I say of anger, of discord, of strife, which things ought not to be found in a Christian? Let there be patience in the breast, and these things cannot have place there ; or should they try to enter, they are quickly excluded and depart, that a peaceful abode may continue in the heart, where it delights the God of peace to dwell. Finally, the apostle warns us, and teaches, saying : " Grieve not the Holy Spirit of God, in whom ye are sealed unto the day of redemption. Let all bitterness, and anger, and wrath, and clamour, and blasphemy, be put away from you." [10] For if the Christian have departed from rage and carnal contention as if from the hurricanes of the sea, and have already begun to be tranquil and meek in the harbour of Christ, he ought to admit neither anger nor discord within his breast, since he must neither return evil for evil, nor bear hatred.

17. And moreover, also, for the varied ills of the flesh, and the frequent and severe torments of the body, wherewith the human race is daily wearied and harassed, patience is necessary. For since in that first transgression of the com-

---

1 Gal. vi. 10, 9.
2 Ezek. xxxiii. 12.
3 Rev. iii 11.
4 The older editions have " gustatam," " tasted," instead of " gestatam," " carried," as above. [See page p. 350, supra. Also St. Cyril. Elucidation VIII.]
5 1 Cor. xiii. 4–7.

6 Eph. iv. 2, 3.
7 Manutius, Pamelius, and others add, " not only seventy times seven times."
8 Or, " them with the stedfastness of patience," etc.
9 Acts vii. 60.
10 Eph. iv. 30, 31.

mandment strength of body departed with immortality, and weakness came on with death — and strength cannot be received unless when immortality also has been received — it behoves us, in this bodily frailty and weakness, always to struggle and to fight. And this struggle and encounter cannot be sustained but by the strength of patience. But as we are to be examined and searched out, diverse sufferings are introduced; and a manifold kind of temptations is inflicted by the losses of property, by the heats of fevers, by the torments of wounds, by the loss of those dear to us. Nor does anything distinguish between the unrighteous and the righteous more, than that in affliction the unrighteous man impatiently complains and blasphemes, while the righteous is proved by his patience, as it is written: "In pain endure, and in thy low estate have patience; for gold and silver are tried in the fire."[1]

18. Thus Job was searched out and proved, and was raised up to the very highest pinnacle of praise by the virtue of patience. What darts of the devil were sent forth against him! what tortures were put in use! The loss of his estate is inflicted, the privation of a numerous offspring is ordained for him. The master, rich in estate, and the father, richer in children, is on a sudden neither master nor father! The wasting of wounds is added; and, moreover, an eating pest of worms consumes his festering and wasting limbs. And that nothing at all should remain that Job did not experience in his trials, the devil arms his wife also, making use of that old device of his wickedness, as if he could deceive and mislead all by women, even as he did in the beginning of the world. And yet Job is not broken down by his severe and repeated conflicts, nor the blessing of God withheld from being declared in the midst of those difficulties and trials of his, by the victory of patience. Tobias also, who, after the sublime works of his justice and mercy, was tried with the loss of his eyes, in proportion as he patiently endured his blindness, in that proportion deserved greatly of God by the praise of patience.

19. And, beloved brethren, that the benefit of patience may still more shine forth, let us consider, on the contrary, what mischief impatience may cause. For as patience is the benefit of Christ, so, on the other hand, impatience is the mischief of the devil; and as one in whom Christ dwells and abides is found patient, so he appears always impatient whose mind the wickedness of the devil possesses. Briefly let us look at the very beginnings. The devil suffered with impatience that man was made in the image of God.[2]

Hence he was the first to perish and to ruin others. Adam, contrary to the heavenly command with respect to the deadly food, by impatience fell into death; nor did he keep the grace received from God under the guardianship of patience. And in order that Cain should put his brother to death, he was impatient of his sacrifice and gift; and in that Esau descended from the rights of the first-born to those of the younger, he lost his priority by impatience for the pottage. Why was the Jewish people faithless and ungrateful in respect of the divine benefits? Was it not the crime of impatience, that they first departed from God? Not being able to bear the delays of Moses conferring with God, they dared to ask for profane gods, that they might call the head of an ox and an earthen image leaders of their march; nor did they ever desist from their impatience, until, impatient always of docility and of divine admonition, they put to death their prophets and all the righteous men, and plunged even into the crime of the crucifixion and bloodshedding of the Lord. Moreover, impatience makes heretics in the Church, and, after the likeness of the Jews, drives them in opposition to the peace and charity of Christ as rebels, to hostile and raging hatred.[3] And, not at length to enumerate single cases, absolutely everything which patience, by its works, builds up to glory, impatience casts down into ruin.

20. Wherefore, beloved brethren, having diligently pondered both the benefits of patience and the evils of impatience, let us hold fast with full watchfulness the patience whereby we abide in Christ, that with Christ we may attain to God; which patience, copious and manifold, is not restrained by narrow limits, nor confined by strait boundaries. The virtue of patience is widely manifest, and its fertility and liberality proceed indeed from a source of one name, but are diffused by overflowing streams through many ways of glory; nor can anything in our actions avail for the perfection of praise, unless from this it receives the substance of its perfection. It is patience which both commends and keeps us to God. It is patience, too, which assuages anger, which bridles the tongue, governs the mind, guards peace, rules discipline, breaks the force of lust, represses the violence of pride, extinguishes the fire of enmity, checks the power of the rich, soothes the want of the poor, protects a blessed integrity in virgins, a careful purity in widows, in those who are united and married a single affection. It makes men humble in prosperity, brave in adversity, gentle towards

---

[1] Ecclus. ii. 4, 5.
[2] [Admirably worked out in *Messias and Anti-Messias*, by the Rev. C. I. Black, ed. London, Masters, 1854.]

[3] [The downfall of Novatian and of Arius and others seems largely attributable to this sin. They could not await God's time to give them influence and power for good. See quotation from Massillon, vol. iii. p. 718, this series. Also Tertull., iii. p. 677.]

wrongs and contempts. It teaches us quickly to pardon those who wrong us ; and if you yourself do wrong, to entreat long and earnestly. It resists temptations, suffers persecutions, perfects passions and martyrdoms. It is patience which firmly fortifies the foundations of our faith. It is this which lifts up on high the increase of our hope. It is this which directs our doing, that we may hold fast the way of Christ while we walk by His patience. It is this that makes us to persevere as sons of God, while we imitate our Father's patience.

21. But since I know, beloved brethren, that very many are eager, either on account of the burden or the pain of smarting wrongs, to be quickly avenged of those who act harshly and rage against them,[1] we must not withhold the fact in the furthest particular, that placed as we are in the midst of these storms of a jarring world, and, moreover, the persecutions both of Jews or Gentiles, and heretics, we may patiently wait for the day of (God's) vengeance, and not hurry to revenge our suffering with a querulous[2] haste, since it is written, "Wait ye upon me, saith the Lord, in the day of my rising up for a testimony ; for my judgment is to the congregations of the nations, that I may take hold on the kings, and pour out upon them my fury."[3] The Lord commands us to wait,[4] and to bear with brave patience the day of future vengeance ; and He also speaks in the Apocalypse, saying, "Seal not the sayings of the prophecy of this book : for now the time is at hand for them that persevere in injuring to injure, and for him that is filthy to be filthy still ; but for him that is righteous to do things still more righteous, and likewise for him that is holy to do things still more holy. Behold, I come quickly ; and my reward is with me, to render to every man according to his deeds."[5] Whence also the martyrs, crying out and hastening with grief breaking forth to their revenge, are bidden still to wait, and to give patience for the times to be fulfilled and the martyrs to be completed. "And when He had opened," says he, "the fifth seal, I saw under the altar of God the souls of them that were slain for the word of God, and for their testimony ; and they cried with a loud voice, saying, How long, O Lord, holy and true, dost Thou not judge and avenge our blood on them that dwell on the earth ? And there were given to them each white robes ; and it was said unto them that they should rest yet for a little season,

until the number of their fellow-servants and brethren is fulfilled, who afterwards shall be slain after their example."[6]

22. But when shall come the divine vengeance for the righteous blood, the Holy Spirit declares by Malachi the prophet, saying, "Behold, the day of the Lord cometh, burning as an oven ; and all the aliens and all the wicked shall be stubble ; and the day that cometh shall burn them up, saith the Lord."[7] And this we read also in the Psalms, where the approach of God the Judge is announced as worthy to be reverenced for the majesty of His judgment : "God shall come manifest, our God, and shall not keep silence ; a fire shall burn before Him, and round about Him a great tempest. He shall call the heaven above, and the earth beneath, that He may separate His people. Gather His saints together unto Him, who establish His covenant in sacrifices ; and the heavens shall declare His righteousness, for God is the Judge."[8] And Isaiah foretells the same things, saying : "For, behold, the Lord shall come like a fire, and His chariot as a storm, to render vengeance in anger ; for in the fire of the Lord they shall be judged, and with His sword shall they be wounded."[9] And again : "The Lord God of hosts shall go forth, and shall crumble the war to pieces ; He shall stir up the battle, and shall cry out against His enemies with strength, I have held my peace ; shall I always hold my peace?"[10]

23. But who is this that says that he has held his peace before, and will not hold his peace for ever? Surely it is He who was led as a sheep to the slaughter ; and as a lamb before its shearer is without voice, so He opened not His mouth. Surely it is He who did not cry, nor was His voice heard in the streets. Surely He who was not rebellious, neither contradicted, when He offered His back to stripes, and His cheeks to the palms of the hands ; neither turned away His face from the foulness of spitting. Surely it is He who, when He was accused by the priests and elders, answered nothing, and, to the wonder of Pilate, kept a most patient silence. This is He who, although He was silent in His passion, yet by and by will not be silent in His vengeance. This is our God, that is, not the God of all, but of the faithful and believing ; and He, when He shall come manifest in His second advent, will not be silent.[11] For although He came first shrouded in humility, yet He shall come manifest in power.

24. Let us wait for Him, beloved brethren, our Judge and Avenger, who shall equally avenge

---

[1] The Oxford edition adds here, according to some authorities, "and will not put off the recompense of evils until that day of last judgment, we exhort you, for the meanwhile, embrace with us this benefit of patience, that," etc.; and it omits the following ten words.
[2] On the authority of one codex, Pamelius here adds, "and envious."
[3] Zeph. iii. 8.
[4] "Dearest brethren," Oxford edit.
[5] Rev. xxii. 10-12.

[6] Rev. vi. 9-11.
[7] Mal. iv. 1.
[8] Ps. l. 3 6.
[9] Isa. lxvi. 15, 16.
[10] Isa. xlii. 13, 14.
[11] [Ps. l. 3.]

with Himself the congregation of His Church, and the number of all the righteous from the beginning of the world. Let him who hurries, and is too impatient for his revenge, consider that even He Himself is not yet avenged who is the Avenger. God the Father ordained His Son to be adored; and the Apostle Paul, mindful of the divine command, lays it down, and says: "God hath exalted Him, and given Him a name which is above every name, that in the name of Jesus every knee should bow, of things heavenly, and things earthly, and things beneath." [1] And in the Apocalypse the angel withstands John, who wishes to worship him,[2] and says: "See thou do it not; for I am thy fellow-servant, and of thy brethren. Worship Jesus the Lord." [3] How great is the Lord Jesus, and how great is His patience, that He who is adored in heaven is not yet avenged on earth! Let us, beloved brethren, consider His patience in our persecutions and sufferings; let us give an obedience full of expectation to His advent; and let us not hasten, servants as we are, to be defended before our Lord with irreligious and immodest eagerness. Let us rather press onward and labour, and, watching with our whole heart, and stedfast to all endurance, let us keep the Lord's precepts; so that when that day of anger and vengeance shall come, we may not be punished with the impious and sinners, but may be honoured with the righteous and those that fear God.

TREATISE X.[4]

ON JEALOUSY AND ENVY.

ARGUMENT.[5] — AFTER POINTING OUT THAT JEAL-OUSY OR ENVY IS A SIN ALL THE MORE HEINOUS IN PROPORTION AS ITS WICKEDNESS IS HIDDEN, AND THAT ITS ORIGIN IS TO BE TRACED TO THE DEVIL, HE GIVES ILLUSTRATIONS OF ENVY FROM THE OLD TESTAMENT, AND GATHERS, BY REFER-ENCE TO SPECIAL VICES, THAT ENVY IS THE ROOT OF ALL WICKEDNESS. THEREFORE WITH REASON WAS FRATERNAL HATRED FORBIDDEN NOT IN ONE PLACE ONLY, BUT BY CHRIST AND HIS APOSTLES. FINALLY, EXHORTING TO THE LOVE OF ONE'S ENEMIES BY GOD'S EXAMPLE, HE DISSUADES FROM THE SIN OF ENVY, BY URGING THE REWARDS SET BEFORE THE INDULGENCE OF LOVE.

1. To be jealous of what you see to be good, and to be envious of those who are better than yourself, seems, beloved brethren, in the eyes of some people to be a slight and petty wrong; and, being thought trifling and of small account, it is not feared; not being feared, it is contemned; being contemned, it is not easily shunned: and it thus becomes a dark and hidden mischief, which, as it is not perceived so as to be guarded against by the prudent, secretly distresses incautious minds. But, moreover, the Lord bade us be prudent, and charged us to watch with careful solicitude, lest the adversary, who is always on the watch and always lying in wait, should creep stealthily into our breast, and blow up a flame from the sparks, magnifying small things into the greatest; and so, while soothing the unguarded and careless with a milder air and a softer breeze, should stir up storms and whirlwinds, and bring about the destruction of faith and the shipwreck of salvation and of life. Therefore, beloved brethren, we must be on our guard, and strive with all our powers to repel, with solicitous and full watchfulness, the enemy, raging and aiming his darts against every part of our body in which we can be stricken and wounded, in accordance with what the Apostle Peter, in his epistle, forewarns and teaches, saying, "Be sober, and watch; because your adversary the devil, as a roaring lion, goeth about seeking any one to devour." [6]

2. He goeth about every one of us; and even as an enemy besieging those who are shut up (in a city), he examines the walls, and tries whether there is any part of the walls [7] less firm and less trustworthy, by entrance through which he may penetrate to the inside. He presents to the eyes seductive forms and easy pleasures, that he may destroy chastity by the sight. He tempts the ears with harmonious music, that by the hearing of sweet sounds he may relax and enervate Christian vigour.[8] He provokes the tongue by reproaches; he instigates the hand by exasperating wrongs to the wrecklessness of murder; to make the cheat, he presents dishonest gains; to take captive the soul by money, he heaps together mischievous hoards; he promises earthly honours, that he may deprive of heavenly ones; he makes a show of false things, that he may steal away the true; and when he cannot hiddenly deceive, he threatens plainly and openly, holding forth the fear of turbulent persecution to vanquish God's servants — always restless, and always hostile, crafty in peace, and fierce in persecution.

3. Wherefore, beloved brethren, against all the devil's deceiving snares or open threatenings, the mind ought to stand arrayed and armed,

---

[1] Phil. ii. 9, 10.
[2] [Origen, vol. iv. p. 544, this series.]
[3] Rev. xxii. 9; [also xix. 10. And compare Acts x. 26, and xiv. 14, 15; also Col. ii. 18.]
[4] [This is numbered xii. in Oxford trans., and is assigned to A.D. 256.]
[5] The deacon Pontius thus briefly suggests the purpose of this treatise in his Life of Cyprian: "Who was there to restrain the ill blood arising from the envenomed malignity of envy with the sweetness of a wholesome remedy?"

[6] 1 Pet. v. 8.
[7] According to some, "of our members."
[8] [The nude in art, the music of the opera, and sensual luxury of all sorts, are here condemned. And compare Clem. Alex., vol. ii. p. 249, note 11, this series.]

ever as ready to repel as the foe is ever ready to attack. And since those darts of his which creep on us in concealment are more frequent, and his more hidden and secret hurling of them is the more severely and frequently effectual to our wounding, in proportion as it is the less perceived, let us also be watchful to understand and repel these, among which is the evil of jealousy and envy. And if any one closely look into this, he will find that nothing should be more guarded against by the Christian, nothing more carefully watched, than being taken captive by envy and malice, that none, entangled in the blind snares of a deceitful enemy, in that the brother is turned by envy to hatred of his brother, should himself be unwittingly destroyed by his own sword. That we may be able more fully to collect and more plainly to perceive this, let us recur to its fount and origin. Let us consider whence arises jealousy, and when and how it begins. For so mischievous an evil will be more easily shunned by us, if both the source and the magnitude of that same evil be known.[1]

4. From this source, even at the very beginnings of the world, the devil was the first who both perished (himself) and destroyed (others). He who[2] was sustained in angelic majesty, he who was accepted and beloved of God, when he beheld man made in the image of God, broke forth into jealousy with malevolent envy — not hurling down another by the instinct of his jealousy before he himself was first hurled down by jealousy, captive before he takes captive, ruined before he ruins others. While, at the instigation of jealousy, he robs man of the grace of immortality conferred, he himself has lost that which he had previously been. How great an evil is that, beloved brethren, whereby an angel fell, whereby that lofty and illustrious grandeur could be defrauded and overthrown, whereby he who deceived was himself deceived! Thenceforth envy rages on the earth, in that he who is about to perish by jealousy obeys the author of his ruin, imitating the devil in his jealousy; as it is written, "But through envy of the devil death entered into the world."[3] Therefore they who are on his side imitate him.[1]

5. Hence, in fine, began the primal hatreds of the new brotherhood, hence the abominable fratricides, in that the unrighteous Cain is jealous of the righteous Abel, in that the wicked persecutes the good with envy and jealousy. So far prevailed the rage of envy to the consummation of that deed of wickedness, that neither the love of his brother, nor the immensity of the crime, nor the fear of God, nor the penalty

of the sin, was considered.[4] He was unrighteously stricken who had been the first to show righteousness; he endured hatred who had not known how to hate; he was impiously slain, who, dying, did not resist. And that Esau was hostile to his brother Jacob, arose from jealousy also. For because the latter had received his father's blessing, the former was inflamed to a persecuting hatred by the brands of jealousy. And that Joseph was sold by his brethren, the reason of their selling him proceeded from envy. When in simplicity, and as a brother to brethren, he set forth to them the prosperity which had been shown to him in visions, their malevolent disposition broke forth into envy. Moreover, that Saul the king hated David, so as to seek by often repeated persecutions to kill him — innocent, merciful, gentle, patient in meekness — what else was the provocation save the spur of jealousy? Because, when Goliath was slain, and by the aid and condescension of God so great an enemy was routed, the wondering people burst forth with the suffrage of acclamation into praises of David, Saul through jealousy conceived the rage of enmity and persecution. And, not to go to the length of numbering each one, let us observe the destruction of a people that perished once for all.[5] Did not the Jews perish for this reason, that they chose rather to envy Christ[6] than to believe Him? Disparaging those great works which He did, they were deceived by blinding jealousy, and could not open the eyes of their heart to the knowledge of divine things.

6. Considering which things, beloved brethren, let us with vigilance and courage fortify our hearts dedicated to God against such a destructiveness of evil. Let the death of others avail for our safety; let the punishment of the unwise confer health upon the prudent. Moreover, there is no ground for any one to suppose that evil of that kind is confined in one form, or restrained within brief limits in a narrow boundary. The mischief of jealousy, manifold and fruitful, extends widely. It is the root of all evils, the fountain of disasters, the nursery of crimes, the material of transgressions. Thence arises hatred, thence proceeds animosity. Jealousy inflames avarice, in that one cannot be content with what is his own, while he sees another more wealthy. Jealousy stirs up ambition, when one sees another more exalted in honours.[7] When jealousy darkens our perceptions, and reduces the secret agencies of the

---

[1] [Chrysostom, vol. iv. p. 473, ed. Migne. This close practical preaching is a lesson to the younger clergy of our days.]
[2] Some add "long ago."
[3] Wisd. ii. 24. [So Lactantius, *Institutes*, book ii. cap. ix. in vol. vii., this series.]

[4] [Chrysostom, *ut. supra.*]
[5] Variously "semel" or "simul."
[6] [Matt. xxvi. 18.]
[7] Or, with some editors, "more increased in honours." [To be purged from a Christian's heart like a leprosy from the body. See Jeremy Taylor, sermon xix., *Apples of Sodom.* Quotation from Ælian, vol. i. p. 717.]

mind under its command, the fear of God is despised, the teaching of Christ is neglected, the day of judgment is not anticipated. Pride inflates, cruelty embitters, faithlessness prevaricates, impatience agitates, discord rages, anger grows hot; nor can he who has become the subject of a foreign authority any longer restrain or govern himself. By this the bond of the Lord's peace is broken; by this is violated brotherly charity; by this truth is adulterated, unity is divided; men plunge into heresies and schisms when priests are disparaged, when bishops are envied, when a man complains that he himself was not rather ordained, or disdains to suffer that another should be put over him.[1] Hence the man who is haughty through jealousy, and perverse through envy, kicks, hence he revolts, in anger and malice the opponent, not of the man, but of the honour.

7. But what a gnawing worm of the soul is it, what a plague-spot of our thoughts, what a rust of the heart, to be jealous of another, either in respect of his virtue or of his happiness; that is, to hate in him either his own deservings or the divine benefits — to turn the advantages of others into one's own mischief — to be tormented by the prosperity of illustrious men — to make other people's glory one's own penalty, and, as it were, to apply a sort of executioner to one's own breast, to bring the tormentors to one's own thoughts and feelings, that they may tear us with intestine pangs, and may smite the secret recesses of the heart with the hoof of malevolence! To such, no food is joyous, no drink can be cheerful. They are ever sighing, and groaning, and grieving; and since envy is never put off by the envious, the possessed heart is rent without intermission day and night. Other ills have their limit; and whatever wrong is done, is bounded by the completion of the crime. In the adulterer the offence ceases when the violation is perpetrated; in the case of the robber, the crime is at rest when the homicide is committed; and the possession of the booty puts an end to the rapacity of the thief; and the completed deception places a limit to the wrong of the cheat. Jealousy has no limit; it is an evil continually enduring, and a sin without end. In proportion as he who is envied has the advantage of a greater success, in that proportion the envious man burns with the fires of jealousy to an increased heat.[2]

8. Hence the threatening countenance, the lowering aspect, pallor in the face, trembling on the lips, gnashing of the teeth, mad words, unbridled revilings, a hand prompt for the violence of slaughter; even if for the time deprived of a sword, yet armed with the hatred of an infuriate mind. And accordingly the Holy Spirit says in the Psalms: "Be not jealous against him who walketh prosperously in his way."[3] And again: "The wicked shall observe the righteous, and shall gnash upon him with his teeth. But God shall laugh at him; for He seeth that his day is coming."[4] The blessed Apostle Paul designates and points out these when he says, "The poison of asps is under their lips, and their mouth is full of cursing and bitterness. Their feet are swift to shed blood, destruction and misery are in their ways, who have not known the way of peace; neither is the fear of God before their eyes."[5]

9. The mischief is much more trifling, and the danger less, when the limbs are wounded with a sword. The cure is easy where the wound is manifest; and when the medicament is applied, the sore that[6] is seen is quickly brought to health. The wounds of jealousy are hidden and secret; nor do they admit the remedy of a healing cure, since they have shut themselves in blind suffering within the lurking-places of the conscience. Whoever you are that are envious and malignant, observe how crafty, mischievous, and hateful you are to those whom you hate. Yet you are the enemy of no one's well-being more than your own. Whoever he is whom you persecute with jealousy, can evade and escape you. You cannot escape yourself.[7] Wherever you may be, your adversary is with you; your enemy is always in your own breast; your mischief is shut up within; you are tied and bound with the links of chains from which you cannot extricate yourself; you are captive under the tyranny of jealousy; nor will any consolations help you. It is a persistent evil to persecute a man who belongs to the grace of God. It is a calamity without remedy to hate the happy.

10. And therefore, beloved brethren, the Lord, taking thought for this risk, that none should fall into the snare of death through jealousy of his brother, when His disciples asked Him which among them should be the greatest, said, "Whosoever shall be least among you all, the same shall be great."[8] He cut off all envy by His reply.[9] He plucked out and tore away every cause and matter of gnawing envy. A disciple of Christ must not be jealous, must not be envious. With us there can be no contest for exaltation; from

---

[1] [The sin of Novatian and Arius. See p. 489, note 3, *supra*.]
[2] [Another specimen of our author's pithy condensations of thought and extraordinary eloquence.]

[3] Ps. xxxvii. 7.
[4] Ps. xxxvii. 12, 13.
[5] Rom. iii. 13-18.
[6] Erasmus and others give this reading. Baluzius, Routh, and many codices, omit "vulnus," and thus read, "what is seen."
[7] ["It punishes the delinquent in the very act." Jer. Taylor, *ut supra*, p. 492, also Anselm, *Opp.*, i. 682, ed. Migne.]
[8] Luke ix. 48. [Elucidation IX.]
[9] [And all ground for a *supremacy* among brethren was here absolutely ejected from the Christian system. The last of the canonical primates of Rome named himself *Servus Servorum Dei*, to rebuke those who would make him "Universal Bishop."]

humility we grow to the highest attainments; we have learnt in what way we may be pleasing. And finally, the Apostle Paul, instructing and warning, that we who, illuminated by the light of Christ, have escaped from the darkness of the conversation of night, should walk in the deeds and works of light, writes and says, "The night has passed over, and the day is approaching: let us therefore cast away the works of darkness, and let us put upon us the armour of light. Let us walk honestly, as in the day; not in rioting and drunkenness, not in lusts and wantonness, not in strifes and jealousy." [1] If the darkness has departed from your breast, if the night is scattered therefrom, if the gloom is chased away, if the brightness of day has illuminated your senses, if you have begun to be a man of light, do those things which are Christ's, because Christ is the Light and the Day.

11. Why do you rush into the darkness of jealousy? why do you enfold yourself in the cloud of malice? why do you quench all the light of peace and charity in the blindness of envy? why do you return to the devil, whom you had renounced? why do you stand like Cain? For that he who is jealous of his brother, and has him in hatred, is bound by the guilt of homicide, the Apostle John declares in his epistle, saying, "Whosoever hateth his brother is a murderer; and ye know that no murderer hath life abiding in him." [2] And again: "He that saith he is in the light, and hateth his brother, is in darkness even until now, and walketh in darkness, and knoweth not whither he goeth, because that darkness hath blinded his eyes." [3] Whosoever hates, says he, his brother, walketh in darkness, and knoweth not whither he goeth. For he goeth unconsciously to Gehenna, in ignorance and blindness; he is hurrying into punishment, departing, that is, from the light of Christ, who warns and says, "I am the light of the world. He that followeth me shall not walk in darkness, but shall have the light of life." [4] But he follows Christ who stands in His precepts, who walks in the way of His teaching, who follows His footsteps and His ways, who imitates that which Christ both did and taught; in accordance with what Peter also exhorts and warns, saying, "Christ suffered for us, leaving you an example that ye should follow His steps." [5]

12. We ought to remember by what name Christ calls His people, by what title He names His flock. He calls them sheep, that their Christian innocence may be like that of sheep; He calls them lambs, that their simplicity of mind may imitate the simple nature of lambs.

Why does the wolf lurk under the garb of sheep? why does he who falsely asserts himself to be a Christian, dishonour the flock of Christ? To put on the name of Christ, and not to go in the way of Christ, what else is it but a mockery of the divine name, but a desertion of the way of salvation; since He Himself teaches and says that he shall come unto life who keeps His commandments, and that he is wise who hears and does His words; that he, moreover, is called the greatest doctor in the kingdom of heaven who thus does and teaches; [6] that, then, will be of advantage to the preacher what has been well and usefully preached, if what is uttered by his mouth is fulfilled by deeds following? But what did the Lord more frequently instil into His disciples, what did He more charge to be guarded and observed among His saving counsels and heavenly precepts, than that with the same love wherewith He Himself loved the disciples, we also should love one another? And in what manner does he keep either the peace or the love of the Lord, who, when jealousy intrudes, can neither be peaceable nor loving?

13. Thus also the Apostle Paul, when he was urging the merits of peace and charity, and when he was strongly asserting and teaching that neither faith nor alms, nor even the passion itself of the confessor and the martyr, [7] would avail him, unless he kept the requirements of charity entire and inviolate, added, and said: "Charity is magnanimous, charity is kind, charity envieth not;" [8] teaching, doubtless, and showing that whoever is magnanimous, and kind, and averse from jealousy and rancour, such a one can maintain charity. Moreover, in another place, when he was advising that the man who has already become filled with the Holy Spirit, and a son of God by heavenly birth, should observe nothing but spiritual and divine things, he lays it down, and says: "And I indeed, brethren, could not speak unto you as unto spiritual, but as unto carnal, even as unto babes in Christ. I have fed you with milk, not with meat: [9] for ye were not able hitherto; moreover, neither now are ye able. For ye are yet carnal: for whereas there are still among you jealousy, and contention, and strifes, are ye not carnal, and walk as men?" [10]

14. Vices and carnal sins must be trampled down, beloved brethren, and the corrupting plague of the earthly body must be trodden under foot with spiritual vigour, lest, while we are turned back again to the conversation of the old man,

---

1 Rom. xiii. 12, 13.
2 1 John iii. 15.
3 1 John ii. 9–11.
4 John viii. 12.
5 1 Pet. ii. 21.

6 [Matt. v. 19.]
7 Or, according to ancient authority, "of confession and martyrdom." [Note this clear conception of the root-principle of the true martyr, and compare Treatise xi. *infra.*]
8 1 Cor. xiii. 4.
9 Or, "I have given you milk to drink, not meat," is read by some.
10 1 Cor. iii. 1–3.

we be entangled in deadly snares, even as the apostle, with foresight and wholesomeness, forewarned us of this very thing, and said : "Therefore, brethren, let us not live after the flesh ; for if ye live after the flesh, ye shall begin to die ; but if ye, through the Spirit, mortify the deeds of the flesh, ye shall live. For as many as are led by the Spirit of God they are the sons of God." [1] If we are the sons of God, if we are already beginning to be His temples, if, having received the Holy Spirit, we are living holily and spiritually, if we have raised our eyes from earth to heaven, if we have lifted our hearts, filled with God and Christ, to things above and divine, let us do nothing but what is worthy of God and Christ, even as the apostle arouses and exhorts us, saying : "If ye be risen with Christ, seek those things which are above, where Christ is sitting at the right hand of God ; occupy your minds with things that are above, not with things which are upon the earth. For ye are dead, and your life is hid with Christ in God. But when Christ, who is your life, shall appear, then shall ye also appear with Him in glory." [2] Let us, then, who in baptism have both died and been buried in respect of the carnal sins of the old man, who have risen again with Christ in the heavenly regeneration, both think upon and do the things which are Christ's, even as the same apostle again teaches and counsels, saying : "The first man is of the dust of the earth ; the second man is from heaven. Such as he is from the earth, such also are they who are from the earth ; and such as He the heavenly is, such also are they who are heavenly. As we have borne the image of him who is of the earth, let us also bear the image of Him who is from heaven." [3] But we cannot bear the heavenly image, unless in that condition wherein we have already begun to be, we show forth the likeness of Christ.

15. For this is to change what you had been, and to begin to be what you were not, that the divine birth might shine forth in you, that the godly discipline might respond to God, the Father, that in the honour and praise of living, God may be glorified in man ; as He Himself exhorts, and warns, and promises to those who glorify Him a reward in their turn, saying, "Them that glorify me I will glorify, and he who despiseth me shall be despised." [4] For which glorification the Lord, forming and preparing us, and the Son of God instilling [5] the likeness of God the Father, says in His Gospel : "Ye have heard that it hath been said, Thou shalt love thy neighbour, and hate thine enemy. But I say unto you, Love your enemies, and pray for them which persecute you ; that ye may be the children of your Father which is in heaven, who maketh His sun to rise on the good and on the evil, and sendeth rain upon the just and on the unjust." [6] If it is a source of joy and glory to men to have children like to themselves — and it is more agreeable to have begotten an offspring then when the remaining [7] progeny responds to the parent with like lineaments — how much greater is the gladness in God the Father, when any one is so spiritually born that in his acts and praises the divine eminence of race [8] is announced ! What a palm of righteousness is it, what a crown, to be such a one [9] as that the Lord should not say of you, "I have begotten and brought up children, but they have despised me !" [10] Let Christ rather applaud you, and invite you to the reward, saying, "Come, ye blessed of my Father, receive the kingdom which is prepared for you from the beginning of the world." [11]

16. The mind must be strengthened, beloved brethren, by these meditations. By exercises of this kind it must be confirmed against all the darts of the devil. Let there be the divine reading in the hands, [12] the Lord's thoughts in the mind ; let constant prayer never cease at all ; let saving labour persevere. Let us be always busied in spiritual actions, that so often as the enemy approaches, however often he may try to come near, he may find the breast closed and armed against him. For a Christian man's crown is not only that which is received in the time of persecution : peace [13] also has its crowns, wherewith the victors, from a varied and manifold engagement, are crowned, when their adversary is prostrated and subdued. To have overcome lust is the palm of continency. To have resisted against anger, against injury, is the crown of patience. It is a triumph over avarice to despise money. It is the praise of faith, by trust in the future, to suffer the adversity of the world. And he who is not haughty in prosperity, obtains glory for his humility ; and he who is disposed to the mercifulness of cherishing the poor, obtains the retribution of a heavenly treasure ; and he who knows not to be jealous, and who with one heart and in meekness loves his brethren, is honoured with the recompense of love and peace. In this course of virtues we daily run ; to these palms and crowns of justice we attain without intermission of time.

17. To these rewards that you also may come who had been possessed with jealousy and ran-

---

[1] Rom. viii. 12-14.
[2] Col. iii. 1-4.
[3] 1 Cor. xv. 47-49.
[4] 1 Sam. ii. 30.
[5] " And engendering in the sons of God." — Oxford ed.

[6] Matt. v. 43-45.
[7] Or, " successive."
[8] " Generositas."
[9] Or, " that one should be such; " or, " that thou shouidst be such."
[10] Isa. i. 2.
[11] Matt. xxv. 34.
[12] Pamelius, from four codices, reads, " Let there be the divine reading before the eyes, good works in the hands."
[13] [" Habet et pax coronas suas." Comp. Milton, *Sonnet* xi.]

cour, cast away all that malice wherewith you were before held fast, and be reformed to the way of eternal life in the footsteps of salvation. Tear out from your breast thorns and thistles, that the Lord's seed may enrich you with a fertile produce, that the divine and spiritual cornfield may abound to the plentifulness of a fruitful harvest. Cast out the poison of gall, cast out the virus of discords. Let the mind which the malice [1] of the serpent had infected be purged; let all bitterness which had settled within be softened by the sweetness of Christ. If you take both meat and drink from the sacrament of the cross, let the wood which at Mara [2] availed in a figure for sweetening the taste, avail to you in in reality for soothing your softened breast; and you shall not strive for a medicine for your increasing health. Be cured by that whereby you had been wounded.[3] Love those whom you previously had hated; favour those whom you envied with unjust disparagements. Imitate good men, if you are able to follow them; but if you are not able to follow them, at least rejoice with them, and congratulate those who are better than you. Make yourself a sharer [4] with them in united love; make yourself their associate in the alliance of charity and the bond of brotherhood. Your debts shall be remitted to you when you yourself shall have forgiven. Your sacrifices shall be received when you shall come in peace to God. Your thoughts and deeds shall be directed from above, when you consider those things which are divine and righteous, as it is written: "Let the heart of a man consider righteous things, that his steps may be directed by the Lord." [5]

18. And you have many things to consider. Think of paradise, whither Cain does not enter,[6] who by jealousy slew his brother. Think of the heavenly kingdom, to which the Lord does not admit any but those who are of one heart and mind. Consider that those alone can be called sons of God who are peacemakers, who in heavenly [7] birth and by the divine law are made one, and respond to the likeness of God the Father and of Christ. Consider that we are standing under the eyes of God, that we are pursuing the course of our conversation and our life, with God Himself looking on and judging, that we may then at length be able to attain to the result of beholding Him, if we now delight Him who sees us, by our actions, if we show ourselves worthy of His favour and indulgence;

if we, who are always to please Him in His kingdom, previously please Him in the world.

TREATISE XI.[8]

EXHORTATION TO MARTYRDOM, ADDRESSED TO FORTUNATUS.

PREFACE.

1. You have desired, beloved Fortunatus,[9] that, since the burden of persecutions and afflictions is lying heavy upon us, and in the ending and completion of the world the hateful time of Antichrist is already beginning to draw near,[10] I would collect from the sacred Scriptures some exhortations for preparing and strengthening the minds of the brethren, whereby I might animate the soldiers of Christ for the heavenly and spiritual contest. I have been constrained to obey your so needful wish, so that as much as my limited powers, instructed by the aid of divine inspiration, are sufficient, some arms, as it were, and defences might be brought forth from the Lord's precepts for the brethren who are about to fight. For it is little to arouse God's people by the trumpet call of our voice, unless we confirm the faith of believers, and their valour dedicated and devoted to God, by the divine readings.[11]

2. But what more fitly or more fully agrees with my own care and solicitude, than to prepare the people divinely entrusted to me, and an army established in the heavenly camp, by assiduous exhortations against the darts and weapons of the devil? For he cannot be a soldier fitted for the war who has not first been exercised in the field; nor will he who seeks to gain the crown of contest be rewarded on the racecourse, unless he first considers the use and skilfulness of his powers. It is an ancient adversary and an old enemy with whom we wage our battle: six thousand years are now nearly completed since the devil first attacked man.[12] All kinds of temptation, and arts, and snares for his overthrow, he has learned by the very practice of long years. If he finds Christ's soldier unprepared, if unskilled, if not careful and watching with his whole heart; he circumvents him if ignorant, he deceives him incautious, he cheats him inexperienced. But if a man, keeping the Lord's precepts, and bravely adhering to Christ,[13] stands against him, he must needs be conquered, because Christ, whom that man confesses, is unconquered.

---

[1] The Oxford translator gives "blackness;" the original is "livor."
[2] Or "myrrh," variously given in originals as "myrrham" or "merrham."
[3] ["Unde vulneratus fueras, inde curare." *Lear*, act ii. sc. 4.]
[4] "A fellow-heir," according to Baluzius and Routh.
[5] Prov. xv. 1, LXX.
[6] "Return" is a more common reading.
[7] Routh omits the word "heavenly," on the authority of fourteen codices.

[8] [Oxford number, xiii. Assigned to A.D. 252 or 257.]
[9] [In the Council of Carthage, A.D. 256, a bishop of Tucca is so named.]
[10] [Hippol., p. 242, *supra*.]
[11] [Compare, *On the Glory of Martyrdom*, this volume, *infra*. This treatise seems a prescient admonition against the evils which soon after began to infect the Latin theology.]
[12] [Note this chronological statement, and compare vol. ii. p. 334, note 5, and Elucidation XV. p. 346, same volume.]
[13] Some read, "bravely abiding in the footsteps of Christ."

3. And that I might not extend my discourse, beloved brother, to too great a length, and fatigue my hearer or reader by the abundance of a too diffuse style, I have made a compendium; so that the titles being placed first, which every one ought both to know and to have in mind, I might subjoin sections of the Lord's word, and establish what I had proposed by the authority of the divine teaching, in such wise as that I might not appear to have sent you my own treatise so much, as to have suggested material for others to discourse on; a proceeding which will be of advantage to individuals with increased benefit. For if I were to give a man a garment finished and ready, it would be my garment that another was making use of, and probably the thing made for another would be found little fitting for his figure of stature and body. But now I have sent you the very wool and the purple [1] from the Lamb, by whom we were redeemed and quickened; which, when you have received, you will make into a coat for yourself according to your own will, and the rather that you will rejoice in it as your own private and special garment. And you will exhibit to others also what we have sent, that they themselves may be able to finish it according to their will; so that that old nakedness being covered, they may all bear the garments of Christ robed in the sanctification of heavenly grace.

4. Moreover also, beloved brethren, I have considered it a useful and wholesome plan in an exhortation so needful as that which may make martyrs, to cut off all delays and tardiness in our words, and to put away the windings of human discourse, and set down only those things which God speaks, wherewith Christ exhorts His servants to martyrdom. Those divine precepts themselves must be supplied, as it were, for arms for the combatants. Let them be the incitements of the warlike trumpet; let them be the clarion-blast for the warriors. Let the ears be roused by them; let the minds be prepared by them; let the powers both of soul and body be strengthened to all endurance of suffering. Let us only who, by the Lord's permission, have given the first baptism to believers, also prepare each one for the second; urging and teaching that this is a baptism greater in grace, more lofty in power, more precious in honour — a baptism wherein angels baptize — a baptism in which God and His Christ exult — a baptism after which no one sins any more [2] — a baptism which completes the increase of our faith — a baptism which, as we withdraw from the world, immediately associates us with God. In the baptism of water is received the remission of sins, in the baptism of blood the crown of virtues. This thing is to be embraced and desired, and to be asked for in all the entreaties of our petitions, that we who are God's servants should be also His friends.

HEADS OF THE FOLLOWING BOOK.

1. Therefore, in exhorting and preparing our brethren, and in arming them with firmness of virtue and faith for the heralding forth of the confession of the Lord, and for the battle of persecution and suffering, we must declare, in the first place, that the idols which man makes for himself are not gods. For things which are made are not greater than their maker and fashioner; nor can these things protect and preserve anybody, which themselves perish out of their temples, unless they are preserved by man. But neither are those elements to be worshipped [3] which serve man according to the disposition and ordinance of God.

2. The idols being destroyed, and the truth concerning the elements being manifested, we must show that God only is to be worshipped.

3. Then we must add, what is God's threatening against those who sacrifice to idols.

4. Besides, we must teach that God does not easily pardon idolaters.

5. And that God is so angry with idolatry, that He has even commanded those to be slain who persuade others to sacrifice and serve idols.

6. After this we must subjoin, that being redeemed and quickened by the blood of Christ, we ought to prefer nothing to Christ, because He preferred nothing to us, and on our account preferred evil things to good, poverty to riches, servitude to rule, death to immortality; that we, on the contrary, in our sufferings are preferring the riches and delights of paradise to the poverty of the world, eternal dominion and kingdom to the slavery of time, immortality to death, God and Christ to the devil and Antichrist.

7. We must urge also, that when snatched from the jaws of the devil, and freed from the snares of this world, if they begin to be in difficulty and trouble, they must not desire to return again to the world, and so lose the advantage of their withdrawal therefrom.

8. That we must rather urge on and persevere in faith and virtue, and in completion of heavenly and spiritual grace, that we may attain to the palm and to the crown.

9. For that afflictions and persecutions are brought about for this purpose, that we may be proved.

10. Neither must we fear the injuries and penalties of persecutions, because greater is the Lord to protect than the devil to assault.

---

[1] [Compare the paradox of Rev. vii. 14.]
[2] ["Baptisma post quod nemo jam peccat." This gave "the baptism of blood" its grand advantage in the martyrs' eyes.]

[3] The Oxford edition here adds, "in the place of gods."

11. And lest any one should be frightened and troubled at the afflictions and persecutions which we suffer in this world, we must prove that it was before foretold that the world would hold us in hatred, and that it would arouse persecutions against us ; that from this very thing, that these things come to pass, is manifest the truth of the divine promise, in recompenses and rewards which shall afterwards follow ; that it is no new thing which happens to Christians, since from the beginning of the world the good have suffered, and have been oppressed and slain by the unrighteous.

12. In the last place, it must be laid down what hope and what reward await the righteous and martyrs after the struggles and the sufferings of this time, and that we shall receive more in the reward of our suffering than what we suffer here in the passion itself.

ON THE EXHORTATION TO MARTYRDOM.

1. That idols are not gods, and that the elements are not to be worshipped in the place of gods.[1]

In the cxiiith Psalm it is shown that "the idols of the heathen are silver and gold, the work of men's hands. They have a mouth, and speak not ; eyes have they, and see not. They have ears, and hear not ; neither is there any breath in their mouth. Let those that make them be made like unto them."[2] Also in the Wisdom of Solomon : "They counted all the idols of the nations to be gods, which neither have the use of eyes to see, nor noses to draw breath, nor ears to hear, nor fingers on their hands to handle ; and as for their feet, they are slow to go. For man made them, and he that borrowed his own spirit fashioned them ; but no man can make a god like unto himself. For, since he is mortal, he worketh a dead thing with wicked hands ; for he himself is better than the things which he worshippeth, since he indeed lived once, but they never."[3] In Exodus also : "Thou shalt not make to thee an idol, nor the likeness of anything."[4] Moreover, in Solomon, concerning the elements : "Neither by considering the works did they acknowledge who was the workmaster ; but deemed either fire, or wind, or the swift air, or the circle of the stars, or the violent water, or the sun, or the moon, to be gods.[5] On account of whose beauty, if they

thought this, let them know how much more beautiful is the Lord than they. Or if they admired their powers and operations, let them understand by them, that He that made these mighty things is mightier than they."[6]

2. That God alone must be worshipped.

"As it is written, Thou shalt worship the Lord thy God, and Him only shalt thou serve."[7] Also in Exodus : "Thou shalt have none other gods beside me."[8] Also in Deuteronomy : "See ye, see ye that I am He, and that there is no God beside me. I will kill, and will make alive ; I will smite, and I will heal ; and there is none who can deliver out of mine hands."[9] In the Apocalypse, moreover : "And I saw another angel fly in the midst of heaven, having the everlasting Gospel to preach over the earth, and over all nations, and tribes, and tongues, and peoples, saying with a loud voice, Fear God rather, and give glory to Him : for the hour of His judgment is come ; and worship Him that made heaven and earth, and the sea, and all that therein is."[10] So also the Lord, in His Gospel, makes mention of the first and second commandment, saying, "Hear, O Israel, The Lord thy God is one God ;"[11] and, "Thou shalt love thy Lord with all thy heart, and with all thy soul, and with all thy strength. This is the first ; and the second is like unto it, Thou shalt love thy neighbour as thyself. On these two commandments hang all the law and the prophets."[12] And once more : "And this is life eternal, that they may know Thee, the only and true God, and Jesus Christ, whom Thou hast sent."[13]

3. What is God's threatening against those who sacrifice to idols?

In Exodus : "He that sacrificeth unto any gods but the Lord only, shall be rooted out."[14] Also in Deuteronomy : "They sacrificed unto demons, and not to God."[15] In Isaiah also : "They worshipped those which their fingers have made ; and the mean man was bowed down, and the great man was humbled : and I will not forgive them."[16] And again : "To them hast thou poured out drink-offerings, and to them thou hast offered sacrifices. For these, therefore, shall I not be angry, saith the Lord?"[17] In Jeremiah also : "Walk ye not after other gods, to serve them ; and worship them not, and provoke me

---

[1] [The astronomical idols seem to have been the earliest adopted (Job xxxi. 27), and so the soul degraded itself to lower forms and to mere *fetichism* by a process over and over again repeated among men. Rom. i. 21, 23.]
[2] Ps. cxxxv. 15–18, cxv. 4–8.
[3] Wisd. xv. 15–17.
[4] Ex. xx. 4.
[5] Pamelius and others read here, "the gods who rule over the world," apparently. taking the words from the thirteenth chapter of the book of Wisdom, and from the *Testimonies*, iii. 59, below, where they are quoted.

[6] Wisd. xiii. 1–4.
[7] Deut. vi. 13, x. 20.
[8] Ex. xx. 3.
[9] Deut. xxxii. 39.
[10] Rev. xiv. 6, 7.
[11] Mark xii. 29–31.
[12] Matt. xxii. 37–40.
[13] John xvii. 3.
[14] Ex. xxii. 20.
[15] Deut. xxxii. 17.
[16] Isa. ii. 8, 9.
[17] Isa. lvii. 6.

not in the works of your hands, to destroy you." [1] In the Apocalypse too : " If any man worship the beast and his image, and receive his mark in his forehead or in his hand, he shall also drink of the wine of the wrath of God, which is mixed in the cup of His wrath, and shall be punished with fire and brimstone before the eyes of the holy angels, and before the eyes of the Lamb : and the smoke of their torments shall ascend for ever and ever : and they shall have no rest day or night, whosoever worship the beast and his image." [2]

4. That God does not easily pardon idolaters.

Moses in Exodus prays for the people, and does not obtain his prayer, saying : " I pray, O Lord, this people hath sinned a great sin. They have made them gods of gold. And now, if Thou forgivest them their sin, forgive it ; but if not, blot me out of the book which Thou hast written. And the Lord said unto Moses, If any one hath sinned against me, him will I blot out of my book." [3] Moreover, when Jeremiah besought for the people, the Lord speaks to him, saying : " And pray not thou for this people, and entreat not for them in prayer and supplication ; because I will not hear in the time wherein they shall call upon me in the time of their affliction." [4] Ezekiel also denounces this same anger of God upon those who sin against God, and says : " And the word of the Lord came unto me, saying, Son of man, whatsoever land sinneth against me, by committing an offence, I will stretch forth mine hand upon it, and will crush the support of the bread thereof ; and I will send into it famine, and I will take away from it man and beast. And though these three men were in the midst of it, Noah, Daniel, and Job, they shall not deliver sons nor daughters ; they themselves only shall be delivered." [5] Likewise in the first book of Kings : " If a man sin by offending against another, they shall beseech the Lord for him ; but if a man sin against God, who shall entreat for him ? " [6]

5. That God is so angry against idolatry, that He has even enjoined those to be slain who persuade others to sacrifice and serve idols.

In Deuteronomy : " But if thy brother, or thy son, or thy daughter, or thy wife which is in thy bosom, or thy friend which is the fellow of thine own soul, should ask thee secretly, saying, Let us go and serve other gods, the gods of the nations, thou shalt not consent unto him, and thou shalt not hearken unto him, neither shall thine eye spare him, neither shalt thou conceal him, declaring thou shalt declare concerning him. Thine hand shall be upon him first of all to put him to death, and afterwards the hand of all the people ; and they shall stone him, and he shall die, because he hath sought to turn thee away from the Lord thy God." [7] And again the Lord speaks, and says, that neither must a city be spared, even though the whole city should consent to idolatry : " Or if thou shalt hear in one of the cities which the Lord thy God shall give thee, to dwell there, saying, Let us go and serve other gods, which thou hast not known,[8] slaying thou shalt kill all who are in the city with the slaughter of the sword, and burn the city with fire, and it shall be without habitation for ever. Moreover, it shall no more be rebuilt, that the Lord may be turned from the indignation of His anger. And He will show thee mercy, and He will pity thee, and will multiply thee, if thou wilt hear the voice of the Lord thy God, and wilt observe His precepts." [9] Remembering which precept and its force, Mattathias slew him who had approached the altar to sacrifice. But if before the coming of Christ these precepts concerning the worship of God and the despising of idols were observed, how much more should they be regarded since Christ's advent ; since He, when He came, not only exhorted us with words, but with deeds also, but after all wrongs and contumelies, suffered also, and was crucified, that He might teach us to suffer and to die by His example, that there might be no excuse for a man not to suffer for Him,[10] since He suffered for us ; and that since He suffered for the sins of others, much rather ought each to suffer for his own sins. And therefore in the Gospel He threatens, and says : " Whosoever shall confess me before men, him will I also confess before my Father which is in heaven ; but whosoever shall deny me before men, him will I also deny before my Father which is in heaven." [11] The Apostle Paul also says : " For if we die with Him, we shall also live with Him ; if we suffer, we shall also reign with Him ; if we deny Him, He also will deny us." [12] John too : " Whosoever denieth the Son, the same hath not the Father ; he that acknowledgeth the Son, hath both the Son and the Father." [13] Whence the Lord exhorts and strengthens us to contempt of death, saying : " Fear not them which kill the body, but are not able to kill the soul ; but rather fear Him

---

[1] Jer. vii. 6.
[2] Rev. xiv. 9-11.
[3] Ex. xxxii. 31-33.
[4] Jer. vii. 16.
[5] Ezek. xiv. 12-14.
[6] 1 Sam. ii. 25.

[7] Deut. xiii. 6-10.
[8] The Oxford edition inserts here, " Thou shalt inquire diligently ; and if thou shalt find that that is certain which is said."
[9] Deut. xiii. 12-18.
[10] Or, " for a man who does not suffer."
[11] Matt. x. 32, 33.
[12] 2 Tim. ii. 11, 12.
[13] 1 John ii. 23.

which is able to kill soul and body in Gehenna."[1] And again: "He that loveth his life shall lose it; and he who hateth his life in this world, shall keep it unto life eternal."[2]

6. That, being redeemed and quickened by the blood of Christ, we ought to prefer nothing to Christ.[3]

In the Gospel the Lord speaks, and says: "He that loveth father or mother more than me, is not worthy of me; and he that loveth son or daughter more than me, is not worthy of me; and he that taketh not his cross and followeth me, is not worthy of me."[4] So also it is written in Deuteronomy: "They who say to their father and their mother, I have not known thee, and have not acknowledged their own children, these have kept Thy precepts, and have observed Thy covenant."[5] Moreover, the Apostle Paul says: "Who shall separate us from the love of Christ? shall tribulation, or distress, or persecution, or hunger, or nakedness, or peril, or sword? As it is written, Because for Thy sake we are killed all the day long, we are counted as sheep for the slaughter. Nay, in all these things we overcome on account of Him who hath loved us."[6] And again: "Ye are not your own, for ye are bought with a great price. Glorify and bear God in your body."[7] And again: "Christ died for all, that both they which live may not henceforth live unto themselves, but unto Him which died for them, and rose again."[8]

7. That those who are snatched from the jaws of the devil, and delivered from the snares of this world,[9] ought not again to return to the world, lest they should lose the advantage of their withdrawal therefrom.

In Exodus the Jewish people, prefigured as a shadow and image of us, when, with God for their guardian and avenger, they had escaped the most severe slavery of Pharaoh and of Egypt — that is, of the devil and the world — faithless and ungrateful in respect of God, murmur against Moses, looking back to the discomforts of the desert and of their labour; and, not understanding the divine benefits of liberty and salvation, they seek to return to the slavery of Egypt — that is, of the world whence they had been drawn forth — when they ought rather to have

trusted and believed on God, since He who delivers His people from the devil and the world, protects them also when delivered. "Wherefore hast thou thus done with us," say they, "in casting us forth out of Egypt? It is better for us to serve the Egyptians than to die in this wilderness. And Moses said unto the people, Trust, and stand fast, and see the salvation which is from the Lord, which He shall do to you to-day. The Lord Himself shall fight for you, and ye shall hold your peace."[10] The Lord, admonishing us of this in His Gospel, and teaching that we should not return again to the devil and to the world, which we have renounced, and whence we have escaped, says: "No man looking back, and putting his hand to the plough, is fit for the kingdom of God."[11] And again: "And let him that is in the field not return back. Remember Lot's wife."[12] And lest any one should be retarded by any covetousness of wealth or attraction of his own people from following Christ, He adds, and says: "He that forsaketh not all that he hath, cannot be my disciple."[13]

8. That we must press on and persevere in faith and virtue, and in completion of heavenly and spiritual grace, that we may attain to the palm and the crown.

In the book of Chronicles: "The Lord is with you so long as ye also are with Him; but if ye forsake Him, He will forsake you."[14] In Ezekiel also: "The righteousness of the righteous shall not deliver him in what day soever he may transgress."[15] Moreover, in the Gospel the Lord speaks, and says: "He that shall endure to the end, the same shall be saved."[16] And again: "If ye shall abide in my word, ye shall be my disciples indeed; and ye shall know the truth, and the truth shall make you free."[17] Moreover, forewarning us that we ought always to be ready, and to stand firmly equipped and armed, He adds, and says: "Let your loins be girded about, and your lamps burning, and ye yourselves like unto men that wait for their lord when he shall return from the wedding, that when he cometh and knocketh they may open unto him. Blessed are those servants whom their lord, when he cometh, shall find watching."[18] Also the blessed Apostle Paul, that our faith may advance and grow, and attain to the highest point, exhorts us, saying: "Know ye not, that they which run in a race run all indeed, yet one receiveth the prize?

---

[1] Matt. x. 28.
[2] John xii. 25.
[3] The Oxford edition adds, "because neither did He account of anything before us."
[4] Matt. x. 37, 38.
[5] Deut. xxxiii. 9.
[6] Rom. viii. 35-37.
[7] 1 Cor. vi. 20.
[8] 2 Cor. v. 15.
[9] The Oxford edition here interpolates, "if they find themselves in straits and tribulations."

[10] Ex. xiv. 11-14.
[11] Luke ix. 62.
[12] Luke xvii. 31, 32.
[13] Luke xiv. 33.
[14] 2 Chron. xv. 2.
[15] Ezek. xxxiii. 12.
[16] Matt. x. 22.
[17] John viii. 31, 32.
[18] Luke xii. 35-37.

So run, that ye may obtain.[1] And they, indeed, that they may receive a corruptible crown; but ye an incorruptible."[2] And again: "No man that warreth for God binds himself to anxieties of this world, that he may be able to please Him to whom he hath approved himself. Moreover, also, if a man should contend, he will not be crowned unless he have fought lawfully."[3] And again: "Now I beseech you, brethren, by the mercy of God, that ye constitute your bodies a living sacrifice, holy, acceptable unto God; and be not conformed to this world, but be ye transformed in the renewing of your spirit, that ye may prove what is the will of God, good, and acceptable, and perfect."[4] And again: "We are children of God: but if children, then heirs; heirs indeed of God, but joint-heirs with Christ, if we suffer together, that we may also be glorified together."[5] And in the Apocalypse the same exhortation of divine preaching speaks, saying, "Hold fast that which thou hast, lest another take thy crown;"[6] which example of perseverance and persistence is pointed out in Exodus, when Moses, for the overthrow of Amalek, who bore the type of the devil, raised up his open hands in the sign and sacrament of the cross,[7] and could not conquer his adversary unless when he had stedfastly persevered in the sign with hands continually lifted up. "And it came to pass," says he, "when Moses raised up his hands, Israel prevailed; but when he let down his hands, Amalek grew mighty. And they took a stone and placed it under him, and he sate thereon. And Aaron and Hur held up his hands on the one side and on the other side, and Moses' hands were made steady even to the going down of the sun. And Jesus routed Amalek and all his people. And the Lord said unto Moses, Write this, and let it be a memorial in a book, and tell it in the ears of Jesus; because in destroying I will destroy the remembrance of Amalek from under heaven."[8]

9. That afflictions and persecutions arise for the sake of our being proved.

In Deuteronomy, "The Lord your God proveth you, that He may know if ye love the Lord your God with all your heart, and with all your soul, and with all your strength."[9] And again, in Solomon: "The furnace proveth the potter's vessel, and righteous men the trial of tribulation."[10] Paul also testifies similar things, and

speaks, saying: "We glory in the hope of the glory of God. And not only so, but we glory in tribulations also; knowing that tribulation worketh patience, and patience experience, and experience hope; and hope maketh not ashamed, because the love of God is shed abroad in our hearts by the Holy Spirit who is given unto us."[11] And Peter, in his epistle, lays it down, and says: "Beloved, be not surprised at the fiery heat which falleth upon you, which happens for your trial; and fail not, as if some new thing were happening unto you. But as often as ye communicate with the sufferings of Christ, rejoice in all things, that also in the revelation made of His glory you may rejoice with gladness. If ye be reproached in the name of Christ, happy are ye; because the name of the majesty and power of the Lord resteth upon you; which indeed according to them is blasphemed, but according to us is honoured."[12]

10. That injuries and penalties of persecutions are not to be feared by us, because greater is the Lord to protect than the devil to assault.

John, in his epistle, proves this, saying: "Greater is He who is in you than he that is in the world."[13] Also in the cxviith Psalm: "I will not fear what man can do unto me; the Lord is my helper."[14] And again: "These in chariots, and those in horses; but we will glory in the name of the Lord our God. They themselves are bound,[15] and they have fallen; but we have risen up, and stand upright."[16] And even more strongly the Holy Spirit, teaching and showing that the army of the devil is not to be feared, and that, if the foe should declare war against us, our hope consists rather in that war itself; and that by that conflict the righteous attain to the reward of the divine abode and eternal salvation, — lays down in the twenty-sixth Psalm, and says: "Though an host should be arrayed against me, my heart shall not fear; though war should rise up against me, in that will I put my hope. One hope have I sought of the Lord, this will I require; that I may dwell in the house of the Lord all the days of my life."[17] Also in Exodus, the Holy Scripture declares that we are rather multiplied and increased by afflictions, saying: "And the more they afflicted them, so much the more they became greater, and waxed stronger."[18] And in the Apocalypse, divine protection is promised to our sufferings. "Fear nothing of these things," it says, "which

[1] Oxford edition: "For every one that striveth for the mastery is temperate in all things."
[2] 1 Cor. ix. 24, 25.
[3] 2 Tim. ii. 4, 5.
[4] Rom. xii. 1. 2.
[5] Rom. viii. 16, 17.
[6] Rev. iii. 11.
[7] [Vol. i., Justin, pp. 242, 244; Barnabas, *ibid.*, pp. 144, 145.]
[8] Ex. xvii. 11–14.
[9] Deut. xiii. 3.
[10] Ecclus. xxvii. 5.

[11] Rom. v. 2–5.
[12] 1 Pet. iv. 12–14.
[13] 1 John iv. 4.
[14] Ps. cxviii. 6. [The text adopts the old Latin numbering.]
[15] The Oxford editor reads, "Their feet are bound."
[16] Ps. xx. 7, 8.
[17] Ps. xxvii. 3, 4. [The text is numbered by the old Latin.]
[18] Ex. i. 12.

thou shalt suffer." [1] Nor does any one else promise to us security and protection, than He who also speaks by Isaiah the prophet, saying: "Fear not; for I have redeemed thee, and called thee by thy name: thou art mine. And if thou passest through the water, I am with thee, and the rivers shall not overflow thee. And if thou passest through the fire, thou shalt not be burned, and [2] the flame shall not burn thee; for I, the Lord thy God, the Holy One of Israel, am He who maketh thee safe." [3] Who also promises in the Gospel that divine help shall not be wanting to God's servants in persecutions, saying: "But when they shall deliver you up, take no thought how or what ye shall speak. For it shall be given you in that hour what ye shall speak. For it is not ye who speak, but the Spirit of your Father who speaketh in you." [4] And again: "Settle it in your hearts not to meditate before how to answer. For I will give you a mouth and wisdom, which your adversaries shall not be able to resist." [5] As in Exodus God speaks to Moses when he delayed and trembled to go to the people, saying: "Who hath given a mouth to man? and who hath made the stammerer? and who the deaf man? and who the seeing, and the blind man? Have not I, the Lord God? And now go, and I will open thy mouth, and will instruct thee what thou shalt say." [6] Nor is it difficult for God to open the mouth of a man devoted to Himself, and to inspire constancy and confidence in speech to His confessor; since in the book of Numbers He made even a she-ass to speak against the prophet Balaam. [7] Wherefore in persecutions let no one think what danger the devil is bringing in, but let him indeed consider what help God affords; nor let human mischief overpower the mind, but let divine protection strengthen the faith; since every one, according to the Lord's promises and the deservings of his faith, receives so much from God's help as he thinks that he receives. Nor is there anything which the Almighty is not able to grant, unless the failing faith of the receiver be deficient and give way.

11. That it was before predicted that the world would hold us in abhorrence, and that it would stir up persecutions against us, and that no new thing is happening to the Christians, since from the beginning of the world the good

have suffered, and the righteous have been oppressed and slain by the unrighteous.

The Lord in the Gospel forewarns and foretells, saying: "If the world hates you, know that it first hated me. If ye were of the world, the world would love what is its own: but because ye are not of the world, and I have chosen you out of the world, therefore the world hateth you. Remember the word that I spoke unto you, The servant is not greater than his master. If they have persecuted me, they will persecute you also." [8] And again: "The hour will come, that every one that killeth you will think that he doeth God service; but they will do this because they have not known the Father nor me. But these things have I told you, that when the hour shall come ye may remember them, because I told you." [9] And again: "Verily, verily, I say unto you, That ye shall weep and lament, but the world shall rejoice; ye shall be sorrowful, but your sorrow shall be turned into joy." [10] And again: "These things have I spoken unto you, that in me ye may have peace; but in the world ye shall have tribulation: but be of good confidence, for I have overcome the world." [11] And when He was interrogated by His disciples concerning the sign of His coming, and of the consummation of the world, He answered and said: "Take care lest any deceive you: for many shall come in my name, saying, I am Christ; and shall deceive many. And ye shall begin to hear of wars, and rumours of wars; see that ye be not troubled: for these things must needs come to pass, but the end is not yet. For nation shall rise against nation, and kingdom against kingdom: and there shall be famines, and earthquakes, and pestilences, in every place. But all these things are the beginnings of travailings. Then they shall deliver you up into affliction, and shall kill you: and ye shall be hateful to all nations for my name's sake. And then shall many be offended, and shall betray one another, and shall hate one another. And many false prophets shall arise, and shall seduce many; and because wickedness shall abound, the love of many shall wax cold. But he who shall endure to the end, the same shall be saved. And this Gospel of the kingdom shall be preached through all the world, for a testimony to all nations; and then shall come the end. When, therefore, ye shall see the abomination of desolation which is spoken of by Daniel the prophet, standing in the holy place (let him who readeth understand), then let them which are in Judea flee to the mountains; and let him which is on

---

[1] Rev. ii. 10.
[2] The common reading is, "through the fire, the flame," etc.
[3] Isa. xliii. 1–3.
[4] Matt. x. 19, 20.
[5] Luke xxi. 14, 15.
[6] Ex. vi. 11, 12.
[7] [Confirmed in the New Testament, as if on purpose to silence unbelief (2 Pet. ii. 16). Cyprian is one of the few divines who note the light thrown on Balaam's inspiration by the fact that even a dumb beast might be made to speak words, not of his own will.]

[8] John xv. 18–20.
[9] John xvi. 2–4.
[10] John xvi. 20.
[11] John xvi. 33.

the house-roof not go down to take anything from the house ; and let him who is in the field not return back to carry away his clothes. But woe to them that are pregnant, and to those that are giving suck in those days ! But pray ye that your flight be not in the winter, nor on the Sabbath-day : for there shall be great tribulation, such as has not arisen from the beginning of the world until now, neither shall arise. And unless those days should be shortened, no flesh should be saved ; but for the elect's sake those days shall be shortened. Then if any one shall say unto you, Lo, here is Christ, or, Lo, there ; believe him not. For there shall arise false Christs, and false prophets, and shall show great signs and wonders, to cause error, if it be possible, even to the elect. But take ye heed : behold, I have foretold you all things. If, therefore, they shall say to you, Lo, he is in the desert ; go not forth : lo, he is in the sleeping chambers ; believe it not. For as the flashing of lightning goeth forth from the east, and appeareth even to the west, so also shall the coming of the Son of man be. Wheresoever the carcase shall be, there shall the eagles be gathered together. But immediately after the affliction of those days the sun shall be darkened, and the moon shall not give her light, and the stars shall fall from heaven, and the powers of heaven shall be moved : and then shall appear the sign of the Son of man in heaven : and all the tribes of the earth shall lament, and shall see the Son of man coming in the clouds of heaven with great power and glory. And He shall send His angels with a great trumpet, and they shall gather together His elect from the four winds, from the heights of heaven, even into the farthest bounds thereof." [1] And these are not new or sudden things which are now happening to Christians ; since the good and righteous, and those who are devoted to God in the law of innocence and the fear of true religion, advance always through afflictions, and wrongs, and the severe and manifold penalties of troubles, in the hardship of a narrow path. Thus, at the very beginning of the world, the righteous Abel was the first to be slain by his brother ; and Jacob was driven into exile, and Joseph was sold, and king Saul persecuted the merciful David ; and king Ahab endeavoured to oppress Elias, who firmly and bravely asserted the majesty of God. Zacharias the priest was slain between the temple and the altar, that himself might there become a sacrifice where he was accustomed to offer sacrifices to God. So many martyrdoms of the righteous have, in fact, often been celebrated ; so many examples of faith and virtue have been set forth to future generations. The three youths, Ananias,

Azarias, and Misäel, equal in age, agreeing in love, stedfast in faith, constant in virtue, stronger than the flames and penalties that urged them, proclaim that they only obey God, that they know Him alone, that they worship Him alone, saying : " O king Nebuchodonosor, there is no need for us to answer thee in this matter. For the God whom we serve is able to deliver us out of the furnace of burning fire ; and He will deliver us from thy hands, O king. And if not, be it known unto thee, that we do not serve thy gods, and we do not adore the golden image which thou hast set up." [2] And Daniel, devoted to God, and filled with the Holy Spirit, exclaims and says : " I worship nothing but the Lord my God, who founded the heaven and the earth." [3] Tobias also, although under a royal and tyrannical slavery, yet in feeling and spirit free, maintains his confession to God, and sublimely announces both the divine power and majesty, saying : " In the land of my captivity I confess to Him, and I show forth His power in a sinful nation." [4] What, indeed, do we find in the Maccabees of seven brethren, equals alike in their lot of birth and virtues, filling up the number seven in the sacrament of a perfected completion? Seven brethren were thus associating in martyrdom. As the first seven days in the divine arrangement containing seven thousand of years, [5] as the seven spirits and seven angels which stand and go in and out before the face of God, and the seven-branched lamp in the tabernacle of witness, and the seven golden candlesticks in the Apocalypse, and the seven columns in Solomon upon which Wisdom built her house ; so here also the number seven of the brethren, embracing, in the quantity of their number, the seven churches, as likewise in the first book of Kings we read that the barren hath borne seven. And in Isaiah seven women lay hold on one man, whose name they ask to be called upon them. And the Apostle Paul, who refers to this lawful and certain number, writes to the seven churches. And in the Apocalypse the Lord directs His divine and heavenly precepts to the seven churches and their angels, which number is now found in this case, in the seven brethren, that a lawful consummation may be completed. With the seven children is manifestly associated also the mother, their origin and root, who subsequently begat seven churches, she herself having been first, and alone founded upon a rock [6] by the voice of the Lord. [7] Nor is it of no account that in their sufferings the

---

[1] Matt. xxiv. 4–31.

[2] Dan. iii. 16–18.
[3] Bel and Dragon, ver. 5.
[4] Tob. xiii. 6.
[5] [Irenæus, vol. i. p. 557: also p. 551, and Barnabas, ib., p. 146.]
[6] " Petrum " is the reading of Migne; but by far the more authoritative reading is " Petram," " a rock."
[7] [The seven churches were none of them founded by St. Peter. The mother here referred to is therefore the *Ecclesia Catholica*.]

mother alone is with her children. For martyrs who witness themselves as the sons of God in suffering are now no more counted as of any father but God, as in the Gospel the Lord teaches, saying, "Call no man your father upon earth; for one is your Father, which is in heaven."[1] But what utterances of confessions did they herald forth! how illustrious, how great proofs of faith did they afford! The king Antiochus, their enemy — yea, in Antiochus Antichrist was set forth — sought to pollute the mouths of martyrs, glorious and unconquered in the spirit of confession, with the contagion of swine's flesh; and when he had severely beaten them with whips, and could prevail nothing, commanded iron plates to be heated, which being heated and made to glow, he commanded him who had first spoken, and had more provoked the king with the constancy of his virtue and faith, to be brought up and roasted, his tongue having first been pulled out and cut off, which had confessed God; and this happened the more gloriously to the martyr. For the tongue which had confessed the name of God, ought itself first to go to God. Then in the second, sharper pains having been devised, before he tortured the other limbs, he tore off the skin of his head with the hair, doubtless with a purpose in his hatred. For since Christ is the head of the man, and God is the head of Christ, he who tore the head in the martyr was persecuting God and Christ in that head. But he, trusting in his martyrdom, and promising to himself from the retribution of God the reward of resurrection, exclaimed and said, "Thou indeed impotently destroyest us out of this present life; but the King of the world will raise us up, who die for His laws, unto the eternal resurrection of life."[2] The third being challenged, quickly put forth his tongue; for he had learned from his brother to despise the punishment of cutting off the tongue. Moreover, he firmly held forth his hands to be cut off, greatly happy in such a mode of punishment, since it was his lot to imitate, by stretching forth his hands, the form of his Lord's passion. And also the fourth, with like virtue, despising the tortures, and answering, to restrain the king, with a heavenly voice exclaimed, and said, "It is better that those who are given to death by men should wait for hope from God, to be raised up by Him again to eternal life.[3] For to thee there shall be no resurrection to life."[4] The fifth, besides treading under foot the torments of the king, and his severe and various tortures, by the strength of faith, animated to prescience also and knowledge of future events by the Spirit of divinity, foretold to the king the wrath of God, and the vengeance that should swiftly follow. "Having power," said he, "among men, though thou art corruptible, thou doest what thou wilt. But think not that our race is forsaken of God. Abide, and see His great power, how He will torment thee and thy seed."[5] What alleviation was that to the martyr![6] how substantial a comfort in his sufferings, not to consider his own torments, but to predict the penalties of his tormentor! But in the sixth, not his bravery only, but also his humility, is to be set forth; that the martyr claimed nothing to himself, nor even made an account of the honour of his own confession with proud words, but rather ascribed it to his sins that he was suffering persecution from the king, while he attributed to God that afterwards he should be avenged. He taught that martyrs are modest, that they were confident of vengeance, and boasted nothing in their suffering. "Do not," said he, "needlessly err; for we on our own account suffer these things, as sinning against our God. But think not thou that thou shalt be unpunished, who darest to fight against God."[7] Also the admirable mother, who, neither broken down by the weakness of her sex, nor moved by her manifold bereavement, looked upon her dying children with cheerfulness, and did not reckon those things punishments of her darlings, but glories, giving as great a witness to God by the virtue of her eyes, as her children had given by the tortures and suffering of their limbs; when, after the punishment and slaying of six, there remained one of the brethren, to whom the king promised riches, and power, and many things, that his cruelty and ferocity might be soothed by the satisfaction of even one being subdued, and asked that the mother would entreat that her son might be cast down with herself; she entreated, but it was as became a mother of martyrs — as became one who was mindful of the law and of God — as became one who loved her sons not delicately, but bravely. For she entreated, but it was that he would confess God. She entreated that the brother would not be separated from his brothers in the alliance of praise and glory; then only considering herself the mother of seven sons, if it should happen to her to have brought forth seven sons, not to the world, but to God. Therefore arming him, and strengthening him, and so bearing her son by a more blessed birth, she said, "O son, pity me that bare thee ten[8] months in the womb, and gave thee milk for three years, and nourished

---

[1] Matt. xxiii. 9.
[2] 2 Macc. vii. 9. [Heb. xi. 35.]
[3] " To eternal life" is omitted in the Oxford edition.
[4] 2 Macc. vii. 14.

[5] 2 Macc. vii. 16.
[6] "How great" is added in some editions.
[7] 2 Macc. vii. 18.
[8] Otherwise "nine."

thee and brought thee up to this age; I pray thee, O son, look upon the heaven and the earth; and having considered all the things which are in them, understand that out of nothing God made these things and the human race. Therefore, O son,[1] do not fear that executioner; but being made worthy of thy brethren, receive death, that in the same mercy I may receive thee with thy brethren."[2] The mother's praise was great in her exhortation to virtue, but greater in the fear of God and in the truth of faith, that she promised nothing to herself or her son from the honour of the six martyrs, nor believed that the prayer of the brothers would avail[3] for the salvation of one who should deny, but rather persuaded him to become a sharer in their suffering, that in the day of judgment he might be found with his brethren. After this the mother also dies with her children; for neither was anything else becoming, than that she who had borne and made martyrs, should be joined in the fellowship of glory with them, and that she herself should follow those whom she had sent before to God. And lest any, when the opportunity either of a certificate or of any such matter is offered to him whereby he may deceive, should embrace the wicked part of deceivers, let us not be silent, moreover, about Eleazar, who, when an opportunity was offered him by the ministers of the king, that having received the flesh which it was allowable for him to partake of, he might pretend, for the misguiding of the king, that he ate those things which were forced upon him from the sacrifices and unlawful meats, would not consent to this deception, saying that it was fitting neither for his age nor nobility to feign that, whereby others would be scandalized and led into error; if they should think that Eleazar, being ninety years old, had left and betrayed the law of God, and had gone over to the manner of aliens; and that it was not of so much consequence to gain the short moments of life, and so incur eternal punishment from an offended God. And he having been long tortured, and now at length reduced to extremity, while he was dying in the midst of stripes and tortures, groaned and said, "O Lord, that hast the holy knowledge, it is manifest that although I might be delivered from death, I suffer the severest pains of body, being beaten with scourges; but with my mind, on acconnt of Thy fear, I willingly suffer these things."[4] Assuredly his faith was sincere and his virtue sound, and abundantly pure, not to have regarded king Antiochus, but God the Judge, and to have known that it could not avail him for salvation if he should mock

and deceive man, when God, who is the judge of our conscience, and who only is to be feared, cannot at all be mocked nor deceived. If, therefore, we also live as dedicated and devoted to God — if we make our way over the ancient and sacred footsteps of the righteous, let us go through the same proofs of sufferings, the same testimonies of passions, considering the glory of our time the greater on this account, that while ancient examples may be numbered, yet that subsequently, when the abundance of virtue and faith was in excess, the Christian martyrs cannot be numbered, as the Apocalypse testifies and says: "After these things I beheld a great multitude, which no man could number, of every nation, and of every tribe, and people, and language, standing in the sight of the throne and of the Lamb; and they were clothed in white robes, and palms were in their hands; and they said with a loud voice, Salvation to our God, who sitteth upon the throne, and unto the Lamb! And one of the elders answered and said unto me, Who are those which are arrayed in white robes, and whence come they? And I said unto him, My lord, thou knowest. And he said unto me, These are they who have come out of great tribulation, and have washed their robes, and made them white in the blood of the Lamb. Therefore are they before the throne of God, and serve Him day and night in His temple."[5] But if the assembly of the Christian martyrs is shown and proved to be so great, let no one think it a hard or a difficult thing to become a martyr, when he sees that the crowd of martyrs cannot be numbered.

12. What hope and reward remains for the righteous and for martyrs after the conflicts and sufferings of this present time,

The Holy Spirit shows and predicts by Solomon, saying: "And although in the sight of men they suffered torments, yet their hope is full of immortality. And having been troubled in a few things, they shall be in many happily ordered, because God has tried them, and has found them worthy of Himself. As gold in the furnace, He hath tried them; and as whole burnt-offerings of sacrifice, He hath received them, and in its season there will be respect of them. They will shine and run about as sparks in a place set with reeds.[6] They shall judge the nations, and have dominion over the peoples; and their Lord shall reign for ever."[7] In the same also our vengeance is described, and the repentance of those who persecute and molest us is announced. "Then," saith he, "shall the righteous stand in great constancy before such as have

---

[1] " Thus it shall turn out that you," etc., is the Oxford reading.
[2] 2 Macc. vii. 27.
[3] [This is noteworthy, for obvious reasons.]
[4] 2 Macc. vi. 30.

[5] Rev. vii. 9–15.
[6] In many editions this clause is wanting.
[7] Wisd. iii. 4–8.

afflicted them, and who have taken away their labours; when they see it, they shall be troubled with a horrible fear: and they shall marvel at the suddenness of their unexpected salvation, saying among themselves, repenting and groaning for anguish of spirit, These are they whom we had sometime in derision and as a proverb of reproach. We fools counted their life madness, and their end to be without honour. How are they numbered among the children of God, and their lot is among the saints! Therefore have we erred from the way of truth, and the light of righteousness hath not shined unto us, and the sun hath not risen upon us. We have been wearied in the way of unrighteousness and perdition, and have walked through hard deserts, but have not known the way of the Lord. What hath pride profited us, or what hath the boasting of riches brought to us? All these things have passed away like a shadow." Likewise in the cxvth Psalm is shown the price and the reward of suffering: "Precious," it says, "in the sight of the Lord is the death of His saints." [1] In the cxxvth Psalm also is expressed the sadness of the struggle, and the joy of the retribution: "They who sow," it says, "in tears, shall reap in joy. As they walked, they walked and wept, casting their seeds; but as they come again, they shall come in exultation, bearing their sheaves." [2] And again, in the cxviiith Psalm: "Blessed are those that are undefiled in the way, who walk in the law of the Lord. Blessed are they who search His testimonies, and seek Him out with their whole heart." [3] Moreover, the Lord in the Gospel, Himself the avenger of our persecution and the rewarder of our suffering, says: "Blessed are they who suffer persecution for righteousness' sake, for theirs is the kingdom of heaven." [4] And again: "Blessed shall ye be when men shall hate you, and shall separate you, and shall expel you, and shall revile your name as evil, for the Son of man's sake. Rejoice ye in that day, and leap for joy; for, behold, your reward is great in heaven." [5] And once more: "Whosoever shall lose his life for my sake, the same shall save it." [6] Nor do the rewards of the divine promise attend those alone who are reproached and slain; but if the passion itself be wanting to the faithful, while their faith has remained sound and unconquered, and having forsaken and contemned all his possessions, the Christian has shown that he is following Christ, even he also is honoured by Christ among the martyrs, as He Himself promises and says: "There is no man that leaveth house, or land,

or parents, or brethren, or wife, or children, for the kingdom of God's sake, but shall receive seven times as much in this present time, and in the world to come eternal life." [7] In the Apocalypse also He says the same thing: "And I saw," saith he, "the souls of them that were slain for the name of Jesus and the word of God." And when he had placed those who were slain in the first place, he added, saying: "And whosoever had not worshipped the image of the beast, neither had received his mark upon their forehead or in their hand;" all these he joins together, as seen by him at one time in the same place, and says, "And they lived and reigned with Christ." [8] He says that all live and reign with Christ, not only who have been slain; but even whosoever, standing in firmness of the faith and in the fear of God, have not worshipped the image of the beast, and have not consented to his deadly and sacrilegious edicts.

13. That we receive more as the reward of our suffering than what we endure here in the suffering itself,

The blessed Apostle Paul proves; who by the divine condescension, being caught up into the third heaven and into paradise, testifies that he heard unspeakable words, who boasts that he saw Jesus Christ by the faith of sight, who professes that which he both learnt and saw with the greater truth of consciousness, and says: "The sufferings of this present time are not worthy to be compared with the coming glory which shall be revealed in us." [9] Who, then, does not with all his powers labour to attain to such a glory that he may become the friend of God, that he may at once rejoice with Christ, that after earthly tortures and punishments he may receive divine rewards? If to soldiers of this world it is glorious to return in triumph to their country when the foe is vanquished, how much more excellent and greater is the glory, when the devil is overcome, to return in triumph to paradise, and to bring back victorious trophies to that place whence Adam was ejected as a sinner, after casting down him who formerly had cast him down; to offer to God the most acceptable gift — an uncorrupted faith, and an unyielding virtue of mind, an illustrious praise of devotion; to accompany Him when He shall come to receive vengeance from His enemies, to stand at His side when He shall sit to judge, to become co-heir of Christ, to be made equal to the angels; with the patriarchs, with the apostles, with the prophets, to rejoice in the possession of the heavenly kingdom! Such thoughts as these, what persecution can conquer,

---

[1] Ps. cxvi. 15.
[2] Ps. cxxvi. 5, 6.
[3] Ps. cxix. 1, 2.
[4] Matt. v. 10.
[5] Luke vi. 22, 23.
[6] Luke ix. 24.

[7] Luke xviii. 29, 30.
[8] Rev. xx. 4, 5
[9] Rom. viii. 18.

what tortures can overcome? The brave and stedfast mind, founded in religious meditations, endures; and the spirit abides unmoved against all the terrors of the devil and the threats of the world, when it is strengthened by the sure and solid faith of things to come. In persecutions, earth is shut up,[1] but heaven is opened; Antichrist is threatening, but Christ is protecting; death is brought in, but immortality follows; the world is taken away from him that is slain, but paradise is set forth to him restored; the life of time is extinguished, but the life of eternity is realized. What a dignity it is, and what a security, to go gladly from hence, to depart gloriously in the midst of afflictions and tribulations; in a moment to close the eyes with which men and the world are looked upon, and at once to open them to look upon God and Christ! Of such a blessed departure how great is the swiftness! You shall be suddenly taken away from earth, to be placed in the heavenly kingdoms. It behoves us to embrace these things in our mind and consideration, to meditate on these things day and night. If persecution should fall upon such a soldier of God, his virtue, prompt for battle, will not be able to be overcome. Or if his call should come to him before, his faith shall not be without reward, seeing it was prepared for martyrdom; without loss of time, the reward is rendered by the judgment of God. In persecution, the warfare, — in peace, the purity of conscience, is crowned.[2]

TREATISE XII.[3]

THREE BOOKS OF TESTIMONIES AGAINST THE JEWS.

Cyprian to his son Quirinus, greeting. It was necessary, my beloved son, that I should obey your spiritual desire, which asked with most urgent petition for those divine teachings wherewith the Lord has condescended to teach and instruct us by the Holy Scriptures, that, being led away from the darkness of error, and enlightened by His pure and shining light, we may keep the way of life through the saving sacraments. And indeed, as you have asked, so has this discourse been arranged by me; and this treatise has been ordered in an abridged compendium, so that I should not scatter what was written in too diffuse an abundance, but, as far as my poor memory suggested, might collect all that was necessary in selected and connected heads, under which I may seem, not so much to have treated the subject, as to have afforded material for others

to treat it. Moreover, to readers also, brevity of the same kind is of very great advantage, in that a treatise of too great length dissipates the understanding and perception of the reader, while a tenacious memory keeps that which is read in a more exact compendium. But I have comprised in my undertaking two books of equally moderate length: one wherein I have endeavoured to show that the Jews, according to what had before been foretold, had departed from God, and had lost God's favour, which had been given them in past time, and had been promised them for the future; while the Christians had succeeded to their place, deserving well of the Lord by faith, and coming out of all nations and from the whole world. The second book likewise contains the sacrament of Christ, that He has come who was announced according to the Scriptures, and has done and perfected all those things whereby He was foretold as being able to be perceived and known.[4] And these things may be of advantage to you meanwhile, as you read, for forming the first lineaments of your faith. More strength will be given you, and the intelligence of the heart will be effected more and more, as you examine more fully the Scriptures, old and new, and read through the complete volumes of the spiritual books.[5] For now we have filled a small measure from the divine fountains, which in the meantime we would send to you. You will be able to drink more plentifully, and to be more abundantly satisfied, if you also will approach to drink together with us at the same springs of the divine fulness.[6] I bid you, beloved son, always heartily farewell.

FIRST BOOK.

HEADS.

1. That the Jews have fallen under the heavy wrath of God, because they have departed from the Lord, and have followed idols.

2. Also because they did not believe the prophets, and put them to death.

3. That it was previously foretold that they would neither know the Lord, nor understand nor receive Him.

4. That the Jews would not understand the Holy Scriptures, but that they would be intelligible in the last times, after Christ had come.

5. That the Jews could understand nothing of the Scriptures unless they first believed on Christ.

6. That they would lose Jerusalem, and leave the land which they had received.

---

[1] "The eyes of the earth are closed" is the reading of other editions.

[2] [It is hard for us to retain the fact that for three hundred years to be a Christian was to be a martyr, at least in spirit and in daily liability. 1 Cor. xv. 31; 1 Pet. iv. 12.]

[3] [Addressed to Quirinus, and dated A.D. 248.]

[4] This sentence is otherwise read, "whereby it may be perceived and known that it is He Himself who was foretold."

[5] [P. 227, note 3, *supra*. I cannot but note repeatedly how absolutely the primitive Fathers relied on the Holy Scriptures, and commended a Berean use of them. Acts xvii. 11.]

[6] [The canon assumed to be universally known.]

7. That they would also lose the Light of the Lord.

8. That the first circumcision of the flesh was made void, and a second circumcision of the spirit was promised instead.

9. That the former law, which was given by Moses, was about to cease.

10. That a new law was to be given.

11. That another dispensation and a new covenant was to be given.

12. That the old baptism was to cease, and a new one was to begin.

13. That the old yoke was to be made void, and a new yoke was to be given.

14. That the old pastors were to cease, and new ones to begin.

15. That Christ should be God's house and temple, and that the old temple should pass away, and a new one should begin.

16. That the old sacrifice should be made void, and a new one should be celebrated.

17. That the old priesthood should cease, and a new priest should come who should be for ever.

18. That another prophet, such as Moses, was promised, to wit, who should give a new testament, and who was rather to be listened to.

19. That two peoples were foretold, the elder and the younger; that is, the ancient people of the Jews, and the new one which should be of us.

20. That the Church, which had previously been barren, should have more sons from among the Gentiles than the synagogue had had before.

21. That the Gentiles should rather believe in Christ.

22. That the Jews should lose the bread and the cup of Christ, and all His grace; while we should receive them, and that the new name of Christians should be blessed in the earth.

23. That rather the Gentiles than the Jews should attain to the kingdom of heaven.

24. That by this alone the Jews could obtain pardon of their sins, if they wash away the blood of Christ slain in His baptism, and, passing over into the Church, should obey His precepts.[1]

TESTIMONIES.

1. That the Jews have fallen under the heavy wrath of God because they have forsaken the Lord, and have followed idols.

In Exodus the people said to Aaron: "Arise, and make us gods which shall go before us: because as for this man Moses, who brought us out of Egypt, we know not what has become of him."[2] In the same place also Moses says to the Lord: "O Lord, I pray thee, this people have sinned a great sin. They have made to themselves gods of gold and silver. And now, if thou wilt forgive them their sin, forgive; but if not, blot me out of the book which Thou hast written. And the Lord said unto Moses, If any one hath sinned against me, him will I blot out of my book."[3] Likewise in Deuteronomy: "They sacrificed unto demons, and not unto God."[4] In the book of Judges too: "And the children of Israel did evil in the sight of the Lord God of their fathers, who brought them out of the land of Egypt, and followed the gods of the peoples that were round about them, and offended the Lord, and forsook God, and served Baal."[5] Also in the same place: "And the children of Israel added again to do evil[6] in the sight of the Lord, and served Baal and the gods of the strangers, and forsook the Lord, and served Him not."[7] In Malachi: "Judah is forsaken, and has become an abomination in Israel and in Jerusalem, because Judah has profaned the holiness of the Lord in those things wherein He hath loved, and courted strange gods. The Lord will cut off the man who doeth this, and he shall be made base in the tabernacles of Jacob."[8]

2. Also because they did not believe the prophets, and put them to death.

In Jeremiah the Lord says: "I have sent unto you my servants the prophets. Before the daylight I sent them (and ye heard me not, and did not listen with your ears), saying, Let every one of you be converted from his evil way, and from your most wicked desires; and ye shall dwell in that land which I have given you and your fathers for ever and ever."[9] And again:[10] "Go not after other gods, to serve them, and do not worship them; and provoke me not to anger in the works of your hands to scatter you abroad; and ye have not hearkened unto me."[11] Also in the third book of the Kings, Elias saith unto the Lord: "In being jealous I have been jealous for the Lord God Almighty; because the children of Israel have forsaken Thee, have demolished Thine altars, and have slain Thy prophets with the sword; and I have remained solitary, and they seek my life, to take it away from me."[12] In Ezra also: "They have fallen away from Thee, and have cast Thy law behind their backs, and have killed Thy prophets which testified against them that they should return to Thee."[13]

---

1 [These twenty-four propositions are specially worthy of the consideration of the young theologian who would clearly comprehend the Old Law and the New as St. Paul has expounded them in his Epistle to the Romans, and elsewhere.]
2 Ex. xxxii. 1.
3 Ex. xxxii. 31–33.
4 Deut. xxxii. 17.
5 Judg. ii 11–13.
6 " And again they did evil."
7 Judg. iv. 1.
8 Mal. ii. 11.
9 Jer. vii. 25, xxv. 4.
10 The words " and again " are sometimes omitted; and sometimes read " Moreover, in the same place."
11 Jer xxv. 6, 7.
12 1 Kings xix. 10.
13 Neh. ix. 26.

3. That it was previously foretold that they would neither know the Lord, nor understand, nor receive Him.

In Isaiah : " Hear, O heaven, and give ear, O earth : for the Lord hath spoken ; I have begotten and brought up children, but they have rejected me. The ox knoweth his owner, and the ass his master's crib : but Israel hath not known me, and my people hath not perceived me. Ah sinful nation, a people filled with sins, a wicked seed, corrupting children : ye have forsaken the Lord, and have sent that Holy One of Israel into anger." [1] In the same also the Lord says : " Go and tell this people, Ye shall hear with the ear, and shall not understand ; and seeing, ye shall see, and shall not perceive. For the heart of this people hath waxed gross, and they hardly hear with their ears, and they have shut up their eyes, lest haply they should see with their eyes, and hear with their ears, and understand with their heart, and should return, and I should heal them." [2] Also in Jeremiah the Lord says : " They have forsaken me, the fountain of living water, and have dug for themselves worn-out cisterns, which could not hold water." [3] Moreover, in the same : " Behold, the word of the Lord has become unto them a reproach, and they do not wish for it." [4] Again in the same the Lord says : " The kite knoweth his time, the turtle, and the swallow ; [5] the sparrows of the field keep the time of their coming in ; but my people doth not know the judgment of the Lord. How say ye, We are wise, and the law of the Lord is with us? The false measurement [6] has been made vain ; the scribes are confounded ; the wise men have trembled, and been taken, because they have rejected the word of the Lord." [7] In Solomon also : " Evil men seek me, and shall not find me ; for they held wisdom in hatred, and did not receive the word of the Lord." [8] Also in the twenty-seventh Psalm : " Render to them their deserving, because they have not perceived in the works of the Lord." [9] Also in the eighty-first Psalm : " They have not known, neither have they understood ; they shall walk on in darkness." [10] In the Gospel, too, according to John : " He came unto His own, and His own received Him not. As many as received Him, to them gave He power to become the sons of God who believe on His name." [11]

4. That the Jews would not understand the Holy Scriptures, but that they would be intelligible in the last times, after that Christ had come.

In Isaiah : " And all these words shall be unto you as the words of a book that is sealed, which, if you shall give to a man that knoweth letters to read, he shall say, I cannot read, for it is sealed. But in that day the deaf shall hear the words of the book, and they who are in darkness and in a cloud ; the eyes of the blind shall see." [12] Also in Jeremiah : " In the last of the days ye shall know those things." [13] In Daniel, moreover : " Secure the words, and seal the book until the time of consummation, until many learn, and knowledge is fulfilled, because when there shall be a dispersion they shall know all these things." [14] Likewise in the first Epistle of Paul to the Corinthians : " Brethren, I would not that ye should be ignorant, that all our fathers were under the cloud." [15] Also in the second Epistle to the Corinthians : " Their minds are blinded even unto this day, by this same veil which is taken away in Christ, while this same veil remains in the reading of the Old Testament, which is not unveiled, because it is made void in Christ ; and even to this day, if at any time Moses is read, the veil is upon their heart. But by and by, when they shall be turned unto the Lord, the veil shall be taken away." [16] In the Gospel, the Lord after His resurrection says : " These are the words which I spake unto you while I was yet with you, that all things must be fulfilled which are written in the law of Moses, and in the prophets, and in the Psalms, concerning me. Then opened He their understanding, that they might understand the Scriptures ; and said unto them, That thus it is written, and thus it behoved Christ to suffer, and to rise again from the dead the third day ; and that repentance and remission of sins should be preached in His name even among all nations." [17]

5. That the Jews could understand nothing of the Scriptures unless they first believed in Christ.

In Isaiah : " And if ye will not believe, neither will ye understand." [18] Also the Lord in the Gospel : " For if ye believe not that I am He, ye shall die in your sins." [19] Moreover, that righteousness should subsist by faith, and that in it was life, was predicted in Habakkuk : " Now

[1] Isa. i. 2–4.
[2] Isa. vi. 9, 10.
[3] Jer. ii. 13.
[4] Jer. vi. 10.
[5] According to the Oxford edition: " The turtle and the swallow knoweth its time," etc.
[6] Six ancient authorities have " your measurement."
[7] Jer. viii. 7–9.
[8] Prov. i. 28, 29.
[9] Ps. xxviii. 4, 5.
[10] Ps. lxxxii. 5.
[11] John i. 11, 12.

[12] Isa. xxix. 11–18.
[13] Jer. xxiii. 20.
[14] Dan. xii. 4–7.
[15] 1 Cor. x. 1.
[16] 2 Cor. iii. 14–16. There is a singular confusion in the reading of this quotation. The translator has followed Migne's text.
[17] Luke xxiv. 44–47.
[18] Isa. vii. 9.
[19] John viii. 24.

the just shall live by faith of me." [1] Hence Abraham, the father of the nations, believed ; in Genesis : "Abraham believed in God, and it was counted unto him for righteousness." [2] In like manner, Paul to the Galatians : "Abraham believed in God, and it was counted unto him for righteousness. Ye know, therefore, that they which are of faith, the same are children of Abraham. But the Scripture, foreseeing that God justifieth the heathens by faith, foretold to Abraham that all nations should be blessed in him. Therefore they who are of faith are blessed [3] with faithful Abraham." [4]

6. That the Jews should lose Jerusalem, and should leave the land which they had received.

In Isaiah : "Your country is desolate, your cities are burned with fire : your land, strangers shall devour it in your sight ; and the daughter of Zion shall be left deserted, and overthrown by foreign peoples, as a cottage in a vineyard, and as a keeper's lodge in a garden of cucumbers, as a city which is besieged. And unless the Lord of Sabaoth had left us a seed, we should have been as Sodoma, and we should have been like unto Gomorrah." [5] Also in the Gospel the Lord says : "Jerusalem, Jerusalem, that killest the prophets, and stonest them that are sent unto thee, how often would I have gathered thy children as a hen gathereth her chickens under her wings, and thou wouldst not! Behold, your house shall be left unto you desolate." [6]

7. Also that they should lose the Light of the Lord.

In Isaiah : "Come ye, and let us walk in the light of the Lord. For He hath sent away His people, the house of Israel." [7] In His Gospel also, according to John : "That was the true light which lighteth every man that cometh into this world. He was in this world, and the world was made by Him, and the world knew Him not." [8] Moreover, in the same place : "He that believeth not is judged already, because he hath not believed in the name of the only begotten Son of God. And this is the judgment, that light is come into the world, and men loved darkness rather than light." [9]

8. That the first circumcision of the flesh is made void, and the second circumcision of the spirit is promised instead.

In Jeremiah : "Thus saith the Lord to the men of Judah, and to them who inhabit Jerusalem, Renew newness among you, and do not sow among thorns : circumcise yourselves to your God, and circumcise the foreskin of your heart ; lest my anger go forth like fire, and burn you up, and there be none to extinguish it." [10] Also Moses says : "In the last days God will circumcise thy heart, and the heart of thy seed, to love the Lord thy God." [11] Also in Jesus the son of Nave : "And the Lord said unto Jesus, Make thee small knives of stone, very sharp, and set about to circumcise the children of Israel for the second time." [12] Paul also, to the Colossians : "Ye are circumcised with the circumcision not made with hands in the putting off of the flesh, but with the circumcision of Christ." [13] Also, because Adam was first made by God uncircumcised, and righteous Abel, and Enoch, who pleased God and was translated ; and Noah, who, when the world and men were perishing on account of transgressions, was chosen alone, that in him the human race might be preserved ; and Melchizedek, the priest according to whose order Christ was promised. Then, because that sign did not avail women, [14] but all are sealed by the sign of the Lord.

9. That the former law which was given by Moses was to cease.

In Isaiah : "Then shall they be manifest who seal the law, that they may not learn ; and he shall say, I wait upon the Lord, who turneth away His face from the house of Jacob, and I shall trust in Him." [15] In the Gospel also : "All the prophets and the law prophesied until John." [16]

10. That a new law was to be given.

In Micah : "For the law shall go forth out of Sion, and the word of the Lord from Jerusalem. And He shall judge among many peoples, and He shall subdue and uncover strong nations." [17] Also in Isaiah : "For from Sion shall go forth the law, and the word of the Lord from Jerusalem ; and He shall judge among the nations." [18] Likewise in the Gospel according to Matthew : "And behold a voice out of the cloud, saying, This is my beloved Son, in whom I am well pleased ; hear ye Him." [19]

---

[1] Hab. ii. 4.
[2] Gen. xv. 6.
[3] The Burgundian codex reads, "are justified."
[4] Gal. iii. 6–9.
[5] Isa. i. 7–9.
[6] Matt. xxiii. 37, 38.
[7] Isa. ii. 5, 6.
[8] John i. 9, 10.
[9] John iii. 18, 19.

[10] Jer. iv. 3, 4.
[11] Deut. xxx. 6.
[12] Josh. v. 2.
[13] Col ii. 11.
[14] This appears to be the natural reading, but it rests on slight authority; the better accredited reading being "seminis" for "feminis."
[15] Isa. viii. 16, 17.
[16] Matt. xi. 13.
[17] Mic. iv. 2, 3.
[18] Isa. ii. 3, 4.
[19] Matt. xvii. 5.

11. That another dispensation and a new covenant was to be given.

In Jeremiah: "Behold, the days come, saith the Lord, and I will complete for the house of Israel, and for the house of Judah, a new testament, not according to the testament which I ordered with their fathers in that day in which I took hold of their hands to bring them out of the land of Egypt, because they remained not in my testament, and I disregarded them, saith the Lord: Because this is the testament which I will establish with the house of Israel after those days, saith the Lord: I will give them my laws, and into their minds I will write them; and I will be to them for a God, and they shall be to me for a people; and they shall not teach every man his brother, saying, Know the Lord: for all shall know me, from the least even to the greatest of them: for I will be merciful to their iniquities, and will no more be mindful of their sins." [1]

12. That the old baptism should cease, and a new one should begin.

In Isaiah: "Therefore remember ye not the former things, neither reconsider the ancient things. Behold, I make new the things which shall now arise, and ye shall know it; and I will make in the desert a way, and rivers in a dry place, to give drink to my chosen race, my people whom I acquired, that they should show forth my praises." [2] In the same also: "If they thirst, He will lead them through the deserts; He will bring forth water from the rock; the rock shall be cloven, and the water shall flow: and my people shall drink." [3] Moreover, in the Gospel according to Matthew, John says: "I indeed baptize you with water unto repentance: but He that cometh after me is mightier than I, whose shoes I am not worthy to bear; He shall baptize you with the Holy Ghost, and with fire." [4] Also according to John: "Except a man be born of water, and of the Spirit, he cannot enter into the kingdom of God. For that which is born of the flesh is flesh, and that which is born of the Spirit is spirit." [5]

13. That the old yoke should be made void, and a new yoke should be given.

In the second Psalm: "For what purpose have the heathen raged, and the people imagined vain things? The kings of the earth stood up, and the rulers have gathered together against the Lord, and against His Christ. Let us break their bonds asunder, and cast away their yoke from us." [6] Likewise in the Gospel according to Matthew, the Lord says: "Come unto me, all ye that labour and are burdened, and I will cause you to rest. Take my yoke upon you, and learn of me; for I am meek and lowly in heart: and ye shall find rest unto your souls. For my yoke is excellent, and my burden is light." [7] In Jeremiah: "In that day I will shatter the yoke from their neck, and will burst their fetters; and they shall not labour for others, but they shall labour for the Lord God; and I will raise up David a king unto them." [8]

14. That the old pastors should cease and new ones begin.

In Ezekiel: "Wherefore thus saith the Lord, Behold, I am above the shepherds; and I will require my sheep from their hands, and I will turn them away from feeding my sheep; and they shall feed them no more, and I will deliver my sheep from their mouth, and I will feed them with judgment." [9] In Jeremiah the Lord says: "And I will give you shepherds according to my own heart, and they shall feed you with the food of discipline." [10] In Jeremiah, moreover: "Hear the word of the Lord, ye nations, and tell it to the islands which are afar off. Say, He that scattereth Israel will gather him, and will keep him as a shepherd his flock: for the Lord hath redeemed Jacob, and taken him out from the hand of him that was stronger than he." [11]

15. That Christ should be the house and temple of God, and that the old temple should cease, and the new one should begin.

In the second book of Kings: "And the word of the Lord came to Nathan, saying, Go and tell my servant David, Thus saith the Lord, Thou shalt not build me an house to dwell in; but it shall be, when thy days shall be fulfilled, and thou shalt sleep with thy fathers, I will raise up thy seed after thee, which shall come from thy bowels, and I will make ready his kingdom. He shall build me an house in my name, and I will raise up his throne for ever; and I will be to him for a father, and he shall be to me for a son: and his house shall obtain confidence, and his kingdom for evermore in my sight." [12] Also in the Gospel the Lord says: "There shall not be left in the temple one stone upon another that shall not be thrown down." [13] And "After three days another shall be raised up without hands." [14]

---

[1] Jer. xxxi. 31–34.
[2] Isa. xliii. 18–21.
[3] Isa. xlviii. 21.
[4] Matt. iii. 11.
[5] John iii. 5, 6.
[6] Ps. ii. 1–3.
[7] Matt. xi. 28–30.
[8] Jer. xxx. 8, 9.
[9] Ezek. xxxiv. 10–16.
[10] Jer. iii. 15.
[11] Jer. xxxi. 10, 11.
[12] 2 Sam. vii. 4, 5, 12–16.
[13] Matt. xxiv. 2.
[14] John ii. 19; Mark xiv. 58.

16. That the ancient sacrifice should be made void, and a new one should be celebrated.

In Isaiah: "For what purpose to me is the multitude of your sacrifices? saith the Lord: I am full; I will not have the burnt sacrifices of rams, and fat of lambs, and blood of bulls and goats. For who hath required these things from your hands?"[1]   Also in the forty-ninth Psalm: "I will not eat the flesh of bulls, nor drink the blood of goats. Offer to God the sacrifice of praise, and pay your vows to the Most High. Call upon me in the day of trouble, and I will deliver thee: and thou shalt glorify me."[2]   In the same Psalm, moreover: "The sacrifice of praise shall glorify me: therein is the way in which I will show him the salvation of God."[3]   In the fourth Psalm too: "Sacrifice the sacrifice of righteousness, and hope in the Lord."[4]   Likewise in Malachi: "I have no pleasure concerning you, saith the Lord, and I will not have an accepted offering from your hands. Because from the rising of the sun, even unto the going down of the same, my name is glorified among the Gentiles; and in every place odours of incense are offered to my name, and a pure sacrifice, because great is my name among the nations, saith the Lord."[5]

17. That the old priesthood should cease, and a new priest should come, who should be for ever.

In the cixth Psalm: "Before the morning star I begat thee. The Lord hath sworn, and He will not repent, Thou art a priest for ever, after the order of Melchizedek."[6]   Also in the first book of Kings, God says to the priest Eli: "And I will raise up to me a faithful priest, who shall do all things which are in my heart: and I will build him a sure house; and he shall pass in the presence of my anointed ones for all days. And it shall be, whosoever shall remain in thine house, shall come to worship for an obolus of money, and for one loaf of bread."[7]

18. That another Prophet such as Moses was promised, to wit, one who should give a new testament, and who rather ought to be heard.

In Deuteronomy God said to Moses: "And the Lord said to me, A Prophet will I raise up to them from among their brethren, such as thee, and I will give my word in His mouth; and He shall speak unto them that which I shall command Him. And whosoever shall not hear whatsoever things that Prophet shall speak in my name, I will avenge it."[8]   Concerning whom also Christ says in the Gospel according to John: "Search the Scriptures, in which ye think ye have eternal life. These are they which set forth testimony concerning me; and ye will not come to me, that ye might have life. Do not think that I accuse you to the Father: there is one that accuseth you, even Moses, on whom ye hope. For if ye had believed Moses, ye would also believe me: for he wrote of me. But if ye believe not his writings, how shall ye believe my words?"[9]

19. That two peoples were foretold, the elder and the younger; that is, the old people of the Jews, and the new one which should consist of us.

In Genesis: "And the Lord said unto Rebekah, Two nations are in thy womb, and two peoples shall be separated from thy belly; and the one people shall overcome the other people; and the elder shall serve the younger."[10]   Also in Hosea: "I will call them my people that are not my people, and her beloved that was not beloved. For it shall be, in that place in which it shall be called not my people, they shall be called the sons of the living God."[11]

20. That the Church which before had been barren should have more children from among the Gentiles than what the synagogue had had before.

In Isaiah: "Rejoice, thou barren, that barest not; and break forth and cry, thou that travailest not: because many more are the children of the desolate one than of her who hath an husband. For the Lord hath said, Enlarge the place of thy tabernacle, and of thy curtains, and fasten them: spare not, make long thy measures, and strengthen thy stakes: stretch forth yet to thy right hand and to thy left hand; and thy seed shall possess the nations, and shall inhabit the deserted cities. Fear not; because thou shalt overcome: nor be afraid because thou art cursed; for thou shalt forget thy eternal confusion."[12]   Thus also to Abraham, when his former son was born of a bond-woman, Sarah remained long barren; and late in old age bare her son Isaac, of promise, who was the type of Christ. Thus also Jacob received two wives: the elder Leah, with weak eyes, a type of the

---

[1] Isa. i. 11, 12.
[2] Ps. l. 13-15.
[3] Ps. l. 23.
[4] Ps. iv. 5.
[5] Mal. i. 10, 11. [P. 251, note 1, *supra*. The oblation of Melchizedek. Gen. xiv. 18. The Oxford translator adds, "with the incense of pious prayers." See Justin, vol. i. p. 215, cap. xli., and Irenæus, vol. i. p. 484.]
[6] Ps. cx. 3.
[7] 1 Sam. ii. 35, 36.

[8] Deut. xviii. 18, 19.
[9] John v. 39, 40, 45-47.
[10] Gen. xxv. 23.
[11] Hos. ii. 23, i. 10.
[12] Isa. liv. 1-4.

synagogue; the younger the beautiful Rachel, a type of the Church, who also remained long barren, and afterwards brought forth Joseph, who also was himself a type of Christ. And in the first of Kings it is said that Elkanah had two wives: Peninnah, with her sons; and Hannah, barren, from whom is born Samuel, not according to the order of generation, but according to the mercy and promise of God, when she had prayed in the temple; and Samuel being born, was a type of Christ. Also in the first book of Kings: "The barren hath borne seven; and she that had many children has grown weak." [1] But the seven children are the seven churches. Whence also Paul wrote to seven churches; and the Apocalypse sets forth seven churches, that the number seven may be preserved; as the seven days in which God made the world; as the seven angels who stand and go in and out before the face of God, as Raphael the angel says in Tobit; and the sevenfold lamp in the tabernacle of witness; and the seven eyes of God, which keep watch over the world; and the stone with seven eyes, as Zechariah says; and the seven spirits; and the seven candlesticks in the Apocalypse; and the seven pillars upon which Wisdom hath builded her house in Solomon.

21. That the Gentiles should rather believe in Christ.

In Genesis: "And the Lord God said unto Abraham, Go out from thy country, and from thy kindred, and from thy father's house, and go into that land which I shall show thee: and I will make of thee a great nation, and I will bless thee, and I will magnify thy name; and thou shalt be blessed: and I will bless him that blesseth thee, and I will curse him that curseth thee: and in thee shall all the tribes of the earth be blessed." [2] On this same point in Genesis: "And Isaac blessed Jacob.[3] Behold, the smell of my son is as the smell of a plentiful field which the Lord hath blessed: and God give thee of the dew of heaven, and of the fertility of the earth, abundance of corn, and wine, and oil: and peoples shall obey thee, and princes shall worship thee: and thou shalt be lord over thy brother, and the sons of thy father shall worship thee: and he that curseth thee shall be cursed, and he that blesseth thee shall be blessed." [4] On this matter too in Genesis: "But when Joseph saw that his father placed his right hand on the head of Ephraim, it seemed displeasing to him: and Joseph laid hold of his father's hand, to lift it from the head of Ephraim

on to the head of Manasseh. Moreover, Joseph said unto his father, Not so, my father: this is my first-born; place thy right hand upon his head. But he would not, and said, I know it, my son, I know it: and he also shall be a people, and he shall be exalted; but his younger brother shall be greater than he, and his seed shall become a multitude of nations." [5] Moreover in Genesis: "Judah, thy brethren shall praise thee: thine hand shall be upon the back of thine enemies; the sons of thy father shall worship thee. Judah is a lion's whelp: from the slender twig,[6] my son, thou hast ascended: thou layedst down and sleepedst as a lion, and as a lion's whelp. Who shall stir him up? There shalt not fail a prince from Judah, and a leader from his loins, until those things entrusted to him shall come; and he is the hope of the nations: binding his foal unto the vine, and his ass's colt unto the branch of the vine;[7] he shall wash his garments in wine, and his clothing in the blood of the grape: terrible are his eyes with wine, and his teeth are whiter than milk." [8] Hence in Numbers it is written concerning our people: "Behold, the people shall rise up as a lion-like people." [9] In Deuteronomy: "Ye Gentiles shall be for the head; but this unbelieving people shall be for the tail." [10] Also in Jeremiah: "Hear the sound of the trumpet. And they said, We will not hear: for this cause the nations shall hear, and they who shall feed their cattle among them." [11] In the seventeenth Psalm: "Thou shalt establish me the head of the nations: a people whom I have not known have served me: at the hearing of the ear they have obeyed me." [12] Concerning this very thing the Lord says in Jeremiah: "Before I formed thee in the belly, I knew thee; and before thou wentest forth from the womb, I sanctified thee, and established thee as a prophet among the nations." [13] Also in Isaiah: "Behold, I have manifested him for a witness to the nations, a prince and a commander to the peoples." [14] Also in the same: "Nations which have not known Thee shall call upon Thee; and peoples which were ignorant of Thee shall flee to Thee." [15] In the same, moreover: "And in that

---

[1] 1 Sam. ii. 5. [Compare Treatise xi. p. 503, *supra*.]
[2] Gen. xi. 1–3.
[3] The quotation in the Oxford edition begins from this point.
[4] Gen. xxvii. 27–29.

[5] Gen. xlviii. 17–19. The whole of this quotation is wanting in more than one codex.
[6] "Frutice." The Oxford translator has here, without any authority as it appears, from the text, adopted the reading of the Vulgate, "ad prædam." Cyprian has used the LXX., reading apparently, ἐκ βλαστοῦ. The Hebrew מִטֶּרֶף gives a colour to either reading. See Gesenius, *Lex. in voce* טֶרֶף. [Elucidation X.]
[7] Original, "ad cilicium;" LXX. τῇ ἕλικι, "the tendril of the vine;" Oxford trans. "the choice vine."
[8] Gen. xlix. 8–12.
[9] Num. xxiii. 14.
[10] Deut. xxviii. 44.
[11] Jer. vi. 18.
[12] Ps. xviii. 43, 44.
[13] Jer. i. 5.
[14] Isa. lv. 4.
[15] Isa. lv. 5.

day there shall be a root of Jesse, which shall rise to rule in all the nations; in Him shall the Gentiles hope: and His rest shall be honour."[1] In the same again: "The land of Zebulon, and the land of Nephtalim, by the way of the sea, and ye others who inhabit the maritime places, and beyond Jordan[2] of the nations. People that walk in darkness, behold ye a great light; ye who dwell in the region of the shadow of death, the light shall shine upon you."[3] Also in the same: "Thus saith the Lord God to Christ my Lord, whose right hand I hold, that the nations may hear Him; and I will break asunder the strength of kings, I will open before Him gates; and cities shall not be shut."[4] Also in the same: "I come to gather together all nations and tongues; and they shall come, and see my glory. And I will send out over them a standard, and I will send those that are preserved among them to the nations which are afar off, which have not heard my name nor seen my glory; and they shall declare my glory to the nations."[5] Also in the same: "And in all these things they are not converted; therefore He shall lift up a standard to the nations which are afar, and He will draw them from the end of the earth."[6] Also in the same: "Those who had not been told of Him shall see, and they who have not heard shall understand."[7] Also in the same: "I have been made manifest to those who seek me not: I have been found of those who asked not after me. I said, Lo, here am I, to a nation that has not called upon my name."[8] Of this same thing, in the Acts of the Apostles, Paul says: "It was necessary that the word of God should first be shown to you; but since ye put it from you, and judged yourselves unworthy of eternal life, lo, we turn to the Gentiles: for thus said the Lord by the Scriptures, Behold, I have set Thee a light among the nations, that Thou shouldest be for salvation even to the ends of the earth."[9]

22. That the Jews would lose while we should receive the bread and the cup of Christ and all His grace, and that the new name of Christians should be blessed in the earth.

In Isaiah: "Thus saith the Lord, Behold, they who serve me shall eat, but ye shall be hungry: behold, tney who serve me shall drink, but ye shall be thirsty:[10] behold, they who serve me shall rejoice, but ye shall be confounded; the Lord shall slay you. But to those who serve me a new name shall be named, which shall be blessed in the earth."[11] Also in the same place: "Therefore shall He lift up an ensign to the nations which are afar off, and He will draw them from the end of the earth; and, behold, they shall come swiftly with lightness; they shall not hunger nor thirst."[12] Also in the same place: "Behold, therefore, the Ruler, the Lord of Sabaoth, shall take away from Judah and from Jerusalem the healthy man and the strong man, the strength of bread and the strength of water."[13] Likewise in the thirty-third Psalm: "O taste and see how sweet is the Lord. Blessed is the man that hopeth in Him. Fear the Lord God, all ye His saints: for there is no want to them that fear Him. Rich men have wanted and have hungered; but they who seek the Lord shall never want any good thing."[14] Moreover, in the Gospel according to John, the Lord says: "I am the bread of life: he that cometh to me shall not hunger, and he that trusteth in me shall never thirst."[15] Likewise He saith in that place: "If any one thirst, let him come and drink. He that believeth on me, as the Scripture saith, out of his belly shall flow rivers of living water."[16] Moreover, He says in the same place: "Except ye eat the flesh of the Son of man, and drink His blood, ye shall have no life in you."[17]

23. That the Gentiles rather than the Jews attain to the kingdom of heaven.

In the Gospel the Lord says: "Many shall come from the east and from the west, and shall lie down with Abraham, and Isaac, and Jacob, in the kingdom of heaven; but the children of the kingdom shall go out into outer darkness: there shall be weeping and gnashing of teeth."[18]

24. That by this alone the Jews can receive pardon of their sins, if they wash away the blood of Christ slain, in His baptism, and, passing over into His Church, obey His precepts.

In Isaiah the Lord says: "Now I will not release your sins. When ye stretch forth your hands, I will turn away my face from you; and if ye multiply prayers, I will not hear you: for your hands are full of blood. Wash you, make you clean; take away the wickedness from your souls from the sight of mine eyes; cease from your wickedness; learn to do good; seek judg-

---

[1] Isa. xi. 10.
[2] Oxford edition adds "Galilee."
[3] Isa. ix. 1, 2.
[4] Isa. xlv. 1.
[5] Isa. lxvi. 18, 19.
[6] Isa v. 25, 26.
[7] Isa. lii. 15.
[8] Isa. lxv. 1.
[9] Acts xiii. 46, 47.
[10] This second clause, "Behold, they who serve me shall drink," etc., is wanting in some editions.

[11] Isa. lxv. 13–15.
[12] Isa. v. 26, 27.
[13] Isa. iii. 1, 2.
[14] Ps. xxxiv. 8–10.
[15] John vi. 35.
[16] John vii. 37, 38.
[17] John vi. 53.
[18] Matt. viii. 11, 12.

ment; keep him who suffers wrong; judge for the orphan, and justify the widow. And come, let us reason together, saith the Lord: and although your sins be as scarlet, I will whiten [1] them as snow; and although they were as crimson, I will whiten [2] them as wool. And if ye be willing and listen to me, ye shall eat of the good of the land; but if ye be unwilling, and will not hear me, the sword shall consume you; for the mouth of the Lord hath spoken these things." [3]

SECOND BOOK.

HEADS.

1. That Christ is the First-born, and that He is the Wisdom of God, by whom all things were made.

2. That Christ is the Wisdom of God; and about the sacrament of His incarnation, and passion, and cup, and altar, and the apostles who were sent and preached.

3. That Christ also is Himself the Word of God.

4. That the same Christ is God's hand and arm.

5. That the same is Angel and God.

6. That Christ is God.

7. That Christ our God should come as the Illuminator and Saviour of the human race.

8. That although from the beginning He had been Son of God, He had yet to be begotten again according to the flesh.

9. That this should be the sign of His nativity, that He should be born of a virgin — man and God — Son of man and of God.

10. That Christ is man and God, compounded of either nature, that He might be a mediator between us and the Father.

11. That He was to be born of the seed of David after the flesh.

12. That He should be born in Bethlehem.

13. That He should come in lowly condition on His first advent.

14. That He was the righteous One whom the Jews should put to death.

15. That He was called a Sheep and a Lamb who would have to be slain, and concerning the sacrament of the passion.

16. That He is also called a Stone.

17. That subsequently that stone should become a mountain, and should fill the whole earth.

18. That in the last times the same mountain should be manifested, upon which the Gentiles should come, and on which the righteous should go up.

19. That He is the Bridegroom, having the

Church as His bride, from whom children should be spiritually born.

20. That the Jews should fasten Him to the cross.

21. That in the passion and the sign of the cross is all virtue and power.

22. That in this sign of the cross is salvation for all who are marked on their foreheads.

23. That at mid-day, during His passion, there should be darkness.

24. That He should not be overcome of death, nor should remain in hell.

25. That He should rise again from hell on the third day.

26. That when He had risen, He should receive from His Father all power, and His power should be eternal.

27. That it is impossible to attain to God the Father, except through the Son Jesus Christ.

28. That He is to come as a Judge.

29. That He is to reign as a King for ever.

30. That He is both Judge and King.

TESTIMONIES.

1. That Christ is the First-born, and that He is the Wisdom of God, by whom all things were made.

In Solomon in the Proverbs: "The Lord established [4] me in the beginning of His ways, into His works: before the world He founded me. In the beginning, before He made the earth, and before He appointed the abysses, before the fountains of waters gushed forth, before the mountains were settled, before all the hills, the Lord begot me. He made the countries, and the uninhabitable places, and the uninhabitable bounds under heaven. When He prepared the heaven, I was present with Him; and when He set apart His seat. When He made the strong clouds above the winds, and when He placed the strengthened fountains under heaven, when He made the mighty foundations of the earth, I was by His side, ordering them: I was He in whom He delighted: moreover, I daily rejoiced before His face in all time, when He rejoiced in the perfected earth." [5] Also in the same in Ecclesiasticus: "I went forth out of the mouth of the Most High, first-born before every creature: I made the unwearying light to rise in the heavens, and I covered the whole earth with a cloud: I dwelt in the high places, and my throne in the pillar of the cloud: I compassed the circle of heaven, and I penetrated into the depth of the abyss, and I walked on the waves of the sea, and I stood in all the earth; and in

---

[1] " Exalbabo."
[2] " Inalbabo."
[3] Isa. i. 15-20.

[4] [Condidit. Bull, *Opp.*, v. p. 515. ἐκτήσατο, Jerome; ἔκτισε, *alii*. See Justin, vol. i. p. 264; Athenagoras, vol. ii. p. 133; Clement, *ib.*, p. 194; and see note, Oxford translation. See Irenæus, vol. i. p. 488.]
[5] Prov. viii. 22-31.

every people and in every nation I had the pre-eminence, and by my own strength I have trodden the hearts of all the excellent and the humble: in me is all hope of life and virtue: pass over to me, all ye who desire me."[1] Also in the eighty-eighth Psalm: "And I will establish Him as my first-born, the highest among the kings of the earth. I will keep my mercy for Him for ever, and my faithful covenant for Him; and I will establish his seed for ever and ever. If his children forsake my law, and walk not in my judgments; if they profane my judgments, and do not observe my precepts, I will visit their wickednesses with a rod, and their sins with scourges; but my mercy will I not scatter away from them."[2] Also in the Gospel according to John, the Lord says: "And this is life eternal, that they should know Thee, the only and true God, and Jesus Christ, whom Thou hast sent. I have glorified Thee on the earth: I have finished the work which Thou gavest me to do. And now, do Thou glorify me with Thyself, with the glory which I had with Thee before the world was made."[3] Also Paul to the Colossians: "Who is the image of the invisible God, and the first-born of every creature."[4] Also in the same place: "The first-born from the dead, that He might in all things become the holder of the pre-eminence."[5] In the Apocalypse too: "I am Alpha and Omega, the beginning and the end. I will give unto Him that is thirsting from the fountain of the water of life freely."[6] That He also is both the wisdom and the power of God, Paul proves in his first Epistle to the Corinthians. "Because the Jews require a sign, and the Greeks seek after wisdom: but we preach Christ crucified, to the Jews indeed a stumbling-block, and to the Gentiles foolishness; but to them that are called, both Jews and Greeks, Christ the power of God and the wisdom of God."[7]

2. That Christ is the Wisdom of God; and concerning the sacrament of His incarnation and of His passion, and cup and altar; and of the apostles who were sent, and preached.

In Solomon in the Proverbs: "Wisdom hath builded herself an house, and she has placed under it seven pillars; she has slain her victims; she hath mingled her wine in the goblet, and hath made ready her table,[8] and hath sent her servants, calling with a loud announcement to the cup, saying, Let him who is foolish turn to me: and to them that want understanding she has said, Come, eat of my loaves, and drink the wine which I have mingled for you. Forsake foolishness, and seek wisdom, and correct knowledge by understanding."[9]

3. That the same Christ is the Word of God.

In the forty-fourth Psalm: "My heart hath breathed out a good Word. I tell my works to the King."[10] Also in the thirty-second Psalm: "By the Word of God were the heavens made fast; and all their strength by the breath of His mouth."[11] Also in Isaiah: "A Word completing and shortening in righteousness, because a shortened word will God make in the whole earth."[12] Also in the cviith Psalm: "He sent His Word, and healed them."[13] Moreover, in the Gospel according to John: "In the beginning was the Word, and the Word was with God, and God was the Word. The same was in the beginning with God. All things were made by Him, and without Him was nothing made that was made. In Him was life; and the life was the light of men. And the light shineth in darkness; and the darkness comprehended it not."[14] Also in the Apocalypse: "And I saw the heaven opened, and lo, a white horse; and he who sate upon him was called Faithful and True, judging rightly and justly; and He made war. And He was covered with a garment sprinkled with blood; and His name is called the Word of God."[15]

4. That Christ is the Hand and Arm of God.[16]

In Isaiah: "Is God's Hand not strong to save? or has He made His ear heavy, that He cannot hear? But your sins separate between you and God; and on account of your sins He turns His face away from you, that He may not pity. For your hands are defiled with blood, and your fingers with sins. Moreover, your lips have spoken wickedness, and your tongue meditates unrighteousness. No one speaketh truth, nor is there true judgment: they trust in vanity, and speak emptiness, who conceive sorrow, and bring forth wickedness."[17] Also in the same place: "Lord, who hath believed our report? and to whom is the Arm of God revealed?"[18] Also in the same: "Thus saith the Lord, Heaven is my throne, and the earth is the support of my

---

[1] Ecclus. xxiv. 3–7.
[2] Ps. lxxxix. 27–33.
[3] John xvii. 3–5.
[4] Col. i. 15.
[5] Col. i. 18.
[6] Rev. xxi. 6.
[7] 1 Cor. i. 22–24.
[8] [The house = the Church; the seven pillars = Isa. xi. 2, 3; her table = the Lord's table; her cup = the sacrament of the Blood; her loaves = of the Body. Then her servants = preachers. So old authors.]

[9] Prov. ix. 1–6.
[10] Ps. xlv. 1. [דָּבָר טוֹב, *Hebrew.* λογόν, *Sept.* Verbum, *Vulg.* Matter, *Eng.* and *Angl. Psalter.*]
[11] Ps. xxxiii. 6.
[12] Isa. x. 23.
[13] Ps. cvii. 20.
[14] John i. 1–5.
[15] Rev. xix. 11–13.
[16] [Hence the Spirit, "the finger of God." Luke xi. 20.]
[17] Isa. lix. 1–4.
[18] Isa. liii. 1.

feet. What house will ye build unto me? or what is the place for my rest? For all these things hath mine hand made." [1] Also in the same: "O Lord God, Thine Arm is high, and they knew it not; but when they know it, they shall be confounded." [2] Also in the same: "The Lord hath revealed His Arm, that holy Arm, in the sight of all nations; all nations, even the ends of the earth, shall see salvation from God." [3] Also in the same place: "Behold, I have made thee as the wheels of a thrashing chariot, new and turned back upon themselves;" [4] and thou shalt thrash the mountains, and shalt beat the hills small, and shalt make them as chaff, and shalt winnow them; and the wind shall seize them, and the whirlwind shall scatter them: but thou shalt rejoice in the saints of Israel; and the poor and needy shall exult. For they shall seek water, and there shall be none. For their tongue shall be dry for thirst. I the Lord God, I the God of Israel, will hear them, and will not forsake them; but I will open rivers in the mountains, and fountains in the midst of the fields. I will make the wildernesses watery groves, and a thirsty land into water-courses. I will establish in the land of drought the cedar-tree and the box-tree, and the myrtle and the cypress, and the elm [5] and the poplar, that they may see and acknowledge, and know and believe together, that the Hand of the Lord hath done these things, and the Holy One of Israel hath shown them." [6]

5. That Christ is at once Angel and God. [7]

In Genesis, to Abraham: "And the Angel of the Lord called him from heaven, and said unto him, Abraham, Abraham! And he said, Here am I. And He said, Lay not thine hand upon the lad, neither do thou anything unto him. For now I know that thou fearest thy God, and hast not spared thy son, thy beloved son, for my sake." [8] Also in the same place, to Jacob: "And the Angel of the Lord spake unto me in dreams, I am God, whom thou sawest in the place of God [9] where thou anointedst me a pillar of stone, and vowedst to me a vow." [10] Also in Exodus: "But God went before them by day indeed in a pillar of cloud, to show them the way; and by night in a pillar of fire." [11] And

afterwards, in the same place: "And the Angel of God moved forward, which went before the army of the children of Israel." [12] Also in the same place: "Lo, I send my Angel before thy face, to keep thee in the way, that He may lead thee into the land which I have prepared for thee. Observe Him, and obey Him, and be not disobedient to Him, and He will not be wanting to thee. For my Name is in Him." [13] Whence He Himself says in the Gospel: "I came in the name of my Father, and ye received me not. When another shall come in his own name, him ye will receive." [14] And again in the cxviith Psalm: "Blessed is He who cometh in the name of the Lord." [15] Also in Malachi: "My covenant of life and peace was with Levi; [16] and I gave him fear, that he should fear me, that he should go from the face of my name. The law of truth was in his mouth, and unrighteousness was not found in his lips. In the peace of the tongue correcting, he walked with us, and turned many away from unrighteousness. Because the lips of the priests shall keep knowledge, and they shall seek the law at His mouth; for He is the Angel of the Almighty." [17]

6. That Christ is God.

In Genesis: "And God said unto Jacob, Arise, and go up to the place of Bethel, and dwell there; and make there an altar to that God who appeared unto thee when thou fleddest from the face of thy brother Esau." [18] Also in Isaiah: "Thus saith the Lord, the God of Sabaoth, Egypt is wearied; and the merchandise of the Ethiopians, and the tall men of the Sabeans, shall pass over unto Thee, and shall be Thy servants; and shall walk after Thee bound with chains; and shall worship Thee, and shall pray to Thee, because God is in Thee, and there is no other God beside Thee. For Thou art God, and we knew it not, O God of Israel, our Saviour. They shall all be confounded and fear who oppose Thee, and shall fall into confusion." [19] Likewise in the same: "The voice of one crying in the wilderness, Prepare ye the way of the Lord, make straight the paths of our God. Every channel shall be filled up, and every mountain and hill shall be made low, and all crooked places shall be made straight, and rough places plain; and the glory of the Lord shall be seen, and all flesh shall see the salvation of God, because the Lord hath spoken it." [20] Moreover, in Jeremiah:

---

[1] Isa. lxvi. 1, 2.
[2] Isa. xxvi. 11.
[3] Isa. lii. 10.
[4] Original: "Rotas vehiculi triturantis novas in se retornatas." The Oxford edition reads the three last words, "in serras formatas:" and the translator gives, "the wheels of a thrashing instrument made with new teeth."
[5] Some editions omit "and the elm."
[6] Isa. xli. 15-20. [Irenæus, vol. i. p. 487. "Word and Wisdom = hands."]
[7] [i.e., the Jehovah-Angel. See Tertullian, vol. iii. p. 335.]
[8] Gen. xxii. 11, 12.
[9] Scil. "Beth-el," "the house of God."
[10] Gen. xxxi. 13.
[11] Ex. xiii. 21.

[12] Ex. xiv. 19.
[13] Ex. xxiii. 20, 21. [See Tertullian, vol. iii. p. 335, a valuable passage. De Maistre has something to say on this, quite to the purpose. See Bull *passim*: e.g., vol. v. pp. 21-26, 33, 40; 745-760.]
[14] John v. 43.
[15] Ps. cxviii. 26.
[16] Otherwise, "My covenant was with life and peace."
[17] Mal. ii. 5-7.
[18] Gen. xxxv. 1.
[19] Isa. xlv. 14-16.
[20] Isa. xl. 3-5.

This is our God, and no other shall be esteemed beside Him, who hath found all the way of knowledge, and hath given it to Jacob His son, and to Israel His beloved. After this He was seen upon earth, and He conversed with men." [1] Also in Zechariah God says: "And they shall cross over through the narrow sea, and they shall smite the waves in the sea, and they shall dry up all the depths of the rivers; and all the haughtiness of the Assyrians shall be confounded, and the sceptre of Egypt shall be taken away. And I will strengthen them in the Lord their God, and in His name shall they glory, saith the Lord." [2] Moreover, in Hosea the Lord saith: "I will not do according to the anger of mine indignation, I will not allow Ephraim to be destroyed: for I am God, and there is not a holy man in thee: and I will not enter into the city; I will go after God." [3] Also in the forty-fourth Psalm: "Thy throne, O God, is for ever and ever: the sceptre of righteousness is the sceptre of Thy kingdom. Thou hast loved righteousness, and hated iniquity: wherefore God, Thy God, hath anointed Thee with the oil of gladness above Thy fellows." [4] So, too, in the forty-fifth Psalm: "Be still, and know that I am God. I will be exalted among the nations, and I will be exalted in the earth." [5] Also in the eighty-first Psalm: "They have not known, neither have they understood: they will walk on in darkness." [6] Also in the sixty-seventh Psalm: "Sing unto God, sing praises unto His name: make a way for Him who goeth up into the west: God is His name." [7] Also in the Gospel according to John: "In the beginning was the Word, and the Word was with God, and God was the Word." [8] Also in the same: "The Lord said to Thomas, Reach hither thy finger, and behold my hands: and be not faithless, but believing. Thomas answered and said unto Him, My Lord and my God. Jesus saith unto him, Because thou hast seen me, thou hast believed: blessed are they who have not seen, and yet have believed." [9] Also Paul to the Romans: "I could wish that I myself were accursed from Christ for my brethren and my kindred according to the flesh: who are Israelites: whose are the adoption, and the glory, and the covenant, and the appointment of the law, and the service (of God), and the promises; whose are the fathers, of whom, according to the flesh, Christ came, who is God over all, blessed for evermore." [10] Also in the Apocalypse: "I am Alpha and Omega, the beginning and the end:

I will give to him that is athirst, of the fountain of living water freely. He that overcometh shall possess these things, and their inheritance; and I will be his God, and he shall be my son." [11] Also in the eighty-first Psalm: "God stood in the congregation of gods, and judging gods in the midst." [12] And again in the same place: "I have said, Ye are gods; and ye are all the children of the Highest: but ye shall die like men." [13] But if they who have been righteous, and have obeyed the divine precepts, may be called gods, how much more is Christ, the Son of God, God! Thus He Himself says in the Gospel according to John: "Is it not written in the law, that I said, Ye are gods? If He called them gods to whom the word of God was given, and the Scripture cannot be relaxed, do ye say to Him whom the Father hath sanctified and sent into the world, that thou blasphemest, because I said, I am the Son of God? But if I do not the works of my Father, believe me not; but if I do, and ye will not believe me, believe the works, and know that the Father is in me, and I in Him." [14] Also in the Gospel according to Matthew: "And ye shall call His name Emmanuel, which is, being interpreted, God with us." [15]

7. That Christ our God should come, the Enlightener and Saviour of the human race.

In Isaiah: "Be comforted, ye weakened hands; and ye weak knees, be strengthened. Ye who are of a timorous heart, fear not. Our God will recompense judgment, He Himself will come, and will save us. Then shall be opened the eyes of the blind, and the ears of the deaf shall hear. Then the lame man shall leap as a stag, and the tongue of the dumb shall be intelligible; because in the wilderness the water is broken forth, and the stream in the thirsty land." [16] Also in that place: "Not an elder nor an angel, but the Lord Himself shall deliver them; because He shall love them, and shall spare them, and He Himself shall redeem them." [17] Also in the same place: "I the Lord God have called Thee in righteousness, that I may hold Thine hand, and I will comfort Thee; and I have given Thee for a covenant of my people, for a light of the nations; to open the eyes of the blind, to bring forth them that are bound from chains, and those who sit in darkness from the prison-house. I am the Lord God, that is my name. I will not give my glory to another, nor my powers to graven images." [18] Also in the twenty-fourth Psalm: "Show me Thy ways, O Lord, and teach

[1] Baruch iii. 35-37.
[2] Zech. x. 11, 12.
[3] Hos. xi. 9, 10.
[4] Ps. xlv. 6, 7.
[5] Ps. xlv. 10.
[6] Ps. lxxxii. 5.
[7] Ps. lxviii. 4.
[8] John i. 1.
[9] John xx. 27-29.
[10] Rom. ix. 3-5.

[11] Rev. xxi. 6, 7.
[12] Ps. lxxxii. 1.
[13] Ps. lxxxii. 6, 7.
[14] John x. 34-38.
[15] Matt. i. 23.
[16] Isa. xxxv. 3-6.
[17] Isa. lxiii. 9.
[18] Isa. xlii. 6-8.

me Thy paths, and lead me unto Thy truth, and teach me ; for Thou art the God of my salvation." [1] Whence, in the Gospel according to John, the Lord says : "I am the light of the world. He that will follow me shall not walk in darkness, but shall have the light of life." [2] Moreover, in that according to Matthew, the angel Gabriel says to Joseph : "Joseph, thou son of David, fear not to take unto thee Mary thy wife. For that which shall be born to her is of the Holy Ghost. And she shall bring forth a son, and thou shalt call His name Jesus ; for He shall save His people from their sins." [3] Also in that according to Luke : "And Zacharias was filled with the Holy Ghost, and prophesied, saying, Blessed be the Lord God of Israel, who hath foreseen redemption for His people, and hath raised up an horn of salvation for us in the house of His servant David." [4] Also in the same place, the angel said to the shepherds : "Fear not ; for, behold, I bring you tidings that unto you is born this day in the city of David a Saviour, which is Christ Jesus." [5]

8. That although from the beginning He had been the Son of God, yet He had to be begotten again according to the flesh.

In the second Psalm : "The Lord said unto me, Thou art my Son ; this day have I begotten Thee. Ask of me, and I will give Thee the nations for Thine inheritance, and the bounds of the earth for Thy possession." [6] Also in the Gospel according to Luke : "And it came to pass, when Elisabeth heard the salutation of Mary, the babe leaped in her womb ; and she was filled with the Holy Ghost, and she cried out with a loud voice, and said, Blessed art thou among women, and blessed is the fruit of thy womb. And whence does this happen to me, that the mother of my Lord should come to me?" [7] Also Paul to the Galatians : "But when the fulness of the time was come, God sent His Son, born of a woman." [8] Also in the Epistle of John : "Every spirit which confesses that Jesus Christ is come in the flesh is of God. But whosoever denies that He is come in the flesh is not of God, but is of the spirit of Antichrist." [9]

9. That this should be the sign of His nativity, that He should be born of a virgin — man and God — a son of man and a Son of God.

In Isaiah : "And the Lord went on to speak to Ahaz, saying, Ask thee a sign from the Lord thy God, in the height above and in the depth below. And Ahaz said, I will not ask, and I will not tempt the Lord my God. And He said, Hear ye, therefore, O house of David : it is no trifling contest unto you with men, since God supplies the struggle. On this account God Himself will give you a sign. Behold, a virgin shall conceive, and shall bear a son, and ye shall call His name Emmanuel. Butter and honey shall He eat ; before that He knows to prefer the evil, He shall exchange the good." [10] This seed God had foretold would proceed from the woman that should trample on the head of the devil. In Genesis : "Then God said unto the serpent, Because thou hast done this, cursed art thou from every kind of the beasts of the earth. Upon thy breast and thy belly shalt thou crawl, and earth shall be thy food all the days of thy life. And I will place enmity between thee and the woman and her·seed. He shall regard thy head, and thou shalt watch his heel." [11]

10. That Christ is both man and God, compounded of both natures, that He might be a Mediator between us and the Father.

In Jeremiah : "And He is man, and who shall know Him?" [12] Also in Numbers : "A Star shall arise out of Jacob, and a man shall rise up from Israel." [13] Also in the same place : "A Man shall go forth out of his seed, [14] and shall rule over many nations ; and His kingdom shall be exalted as Gog, [15] and His kingdom shall be increased ; and God brought Him forth out of Egypt. His glory is as of the unicorn, and He shall eat the nations of His enemies, and shall take out the marrow of their fatnesses, and will pierce His enemy with His arrows. He couched and lay down as a lion, and as a lion's whelp. Who shall raise Him up? Blessed are they who bless Thee, and cursed are they who curse Thee." [16] Also in Isaiah : "The Spirit of the Lord is upon me ; on account whereof He hath anointed me : He hath sent me to tell good tidings to the poor ; to heal the bruised in heart, to preach deliverance to the captives, and sight to the blind, to proclaim the acceptable year of the Lord, and the day of retribution." [17] Whence, in the Gospel according to Luke, Gabriel says to Mary : "And the angel, answering, said to her, The Holy Ghost

---

[10] Isa. vii. 10-15. The ordinary reading here is, "before He knows, to refuse the evil and to choose the good." The reading in the text, however, is more authentic.
[11] Gen. iii. 14, 15.
[12] Jer. xvii. 9.
[13] Num. xxiv. 17.
[14] [Here the English (q. v.) gives the more literal reading, which the Septuagint treats as a proverb, unfolding its sense. "Water from the bucket" seems to have signified the same as our low proverb "a chip from the block," hence = a Son from the Father. Num. xxiv. 7.]
[15] The Oxford translator follows the English version, and reads, "over Agag."
[16] Num. xxiv. 7-9.
[17] Isa. lxi. 1, 2.

---

[1] Ps. xxv. 4, 5.
[2] John viii. 12.
[3] Matt. i. 20, 21.
[4] Luke i. 67-69.
[5] Luke ii. 10, 11.
[6] Ps. ii. 7, 8.
[7] Luke i. 41-43.
[8] Gal. iv. 4.
[9] 1 John iv. 2, 3.

shall come upon thee, and the power of the Highest shall overshadow thee. Wherefore that holy thing which is born of thee shall be called the Son of God." [1]   Also in the first Epistle of Paul to the Corinthians : " The first man is of the mud [2] of the earth ; the second man is from heaven. As was he from the soil, such are they also that are of the earth ; and as is the heavenly, such also are the heavenly. As we have borne the image of him who is of the earth, let us also bear the image of Him who is from heaven." [3]

11. That Christ was to be born of the seed of David, according to the flesh.

In the second of Kings : " And the word of the Lord came to Nathan, saying, Go and tell my servant David, Thus saith the Lord, Thou shalt not build me an house to dwell in ; but it shall come to pass, when thy days shall be fulfilled, and thou shalt sleep with thy fathers, I will raise up thy seed after thee who shall come from thy loins, and I will establish His kingdom. He shall build me a house in my name, and I will set up His throne for ever ; and I will be to Him a Father, and He shall be to me a Son ; and His house shall obtain confidence, and His kingdom for ever in my sight." [4]   Also in Isaiah : " And a rod shall go forth of the root of Jesse, and a flower shall go up from his root ; and the Spirit of the Lord shall rest upon Him, the spirit of wisdom and of understanding, the spirit of counsel and might, the spirit of knowledge and piety ; and the spirit of the fear of the Lord shall fill Him." [5]   Also in the cxxxist Psalm : " God hath sworn the truth unto David himself, and He has not repudiated it ; of the fruit of thy belly will I set upon my throne." [6]   Also in the Gospel according to Luke : " And the angel said unto her, Fear not, Mary. For thou hast found favour before God. Behold, thou shalt conceive, and shalt bring forth a son, and shalt call His name Jesus. The same shall be great, and He shall be called the Son of the Highest ; and the Lord God shall give Him the throne of His father David, and He shall reign over the house of Jacob for ever, and of His kingdom there shall be no end." [7]   Also in the Apocalypse : " And I saw in the right hand of God, who sate on the throne, a book written within, and on the back sealed with seven seals ; and I saw a strong angel proclaiming with a loud voice, Who is worthy to receive the book, and to open its seals ?   Nor was there any one either in heaven or upon the earth, or under the earth, who was able to open the book, nor even to look into it. And I wept much because nobody was found worthy to open the book, nor to look into it. And one of the elders said unto me, Weep not ; behold, the Lion of the tribe of Judah, the Root of David, hath prevailed to open the book, and to loose its seven seals." [8]

12. That Christ should be born in Bethlehem.

In Micah : " And thou, Bethlehem, house of Ephrata, art not little, that thou shouldst be appointed among the thousands of Judah. Out of thee shall He come forth to me, that He may be a prince in Israel, and His goings forth from the beginning from the days of old." [9]   Also in the Gospel : " And when Jesus was born in Bethlehem of Judah, in the days of Herod the king, behold, Magi came from the east to Jerusalem, saying, Where is He that is born King of the Jews? For we have seen His star in the east, and we have come with gifts to worship Him." [10]

13. That Christ was to come in low estate in His first advent.

In Isaiah : " Lord, who hath believed our report, and to whom is the Arm of the Lord revealed ? We have declared in His presence as children, as a root in a thirsty ground. There is no form nor glory in Him ; and we saw Him, and He had no form nor beauty ; but His form was without honour, and lacking beyond other men. He was a man set in a plague, and knowing how to bear weakness ; because His face was turned away, He was dishonoured, and was not accounted of. He bears our sins, and grieves for us ; and we thought that He was in grief, and in wounding, and in affliction ; but He was wounded for our transgressions, and He was weakened [11] for our sins. The discipline of our peace was upon Him, and with His bruise we are healed. We all like sheep have gone astray ; man has gone out of his way. And God has delivered Him for our sins ; and He, because He was afflicted, opened not His mouth." [12]   Also in the same : " I am not rebellious, nor do I contradict. I gave my back to the stripes, and my cheeks to the palms of the hands. Moreover, I did not turn away my face from the foulness of spitting, and God was my helper." [13]   Also in the same : " He shall not cry, nor will any one hear His voice in the streets. He shall not break a bruised reed, and a smoking flax He shall not extinguish ; but He shall bring forth

---

[1] Luke i. 35.
[2] " Limo."
[3] 1 Cor. xv. 47-49.
[4] 2 Sam. vii. 5, 12-16.
[5] Isa. xi. 1-3.
[6] Ps. cxxxii. 11.
[7] Luke i. 30-33.

[8] Rev. v. 1-5.
[9] Mic. v. 2
[10] Matt. ii. 1, 2.
[11] " Infirmatus; " Oxford transl. " bruised."
[12] Isa. liii. 1-7. [See p. 516, *supra*.]
[13] Isa. l. 5-7.

judgment in truth. He shall shine forth, and shall not be shaken, until He set judgment in the earth, and in His name shall the nations trust." [1] Also in the twenty-first Psalm : " But I am a worm, and no man ; the accursed of man, and the casting away of the people. All they who saw me despised me, and spoke within their lips, and moved their head. He hoped in the Lord, let Him deliver him ; let Him save him, since he will have Him." [2] Also in that place : " My strength is dried up like a potsherd, and my tongue is glued to my jaws." [3] Also in Zechariah : " And the Lord showed me Jesus, that great priest, standing before the face of the Angel of the Lord, and the devil was standing at his right hand to oppose him. And Jesus was clothed in filthy garments, and he stood before the face of the Angel Himself ; and He answered and said to them who were standing before His face, saying, Take away his filthy garments from him. And he said to him, Behold, I have taken away thine iniquities. And put upon him a priestly garment,[4] and set a fair mitre[5] upon his head." [6] Also Paul to the Philippians : " Who, being established in the form of God, thought it not robbery that He was equal with God, but emptied Himself, taking the form of a servant, and was made in the likeness of men ; and being found in fashion as a man, He humbled Himself, becoming obedient even unto death, even the death of the cross. Wherefore also God exalted Him, and gave Him a name which is above every name, that in the name[7] of Jesus every knee should bow, of things in heaven, of things in earth, and of infernal things, and every tongue should confess that Jesus Christ is Lord in the glory of God the Father." [8]

14. That He is the righteous One whom the Jews should put to death.

In the Wisdom of Solomon : " Let us lay hold of the righteous, because He is disagreeable to us, and is contrary to our works, and reproacheth us with our transgressions of the law.[9] He professeth that He has the knowledge of God, and calls Himself the Son of God ; He has become to us an exposure of our thoughts ; He is grievous unto us even to look upon, because His life is unlike to others, and His ways are changed.

We are esteemed by Him as frivolous, and He restraineth Himself from our ways, as if from uncleanness ; and He extols the last end of the righteous, and boasts that He has God for His Father. Let us see, then, if His words are true, and let us try what will come to Him. Let us interrogate Him with reproach and torture, that we may know His reverence and prove His patience. Let us condemn Him with a most shameful death. These things they considered, and erred. For their maliciousness hath blinded them, and they knew not the sacraments of God." [10] Also in Isaiah : " See ye how the righteous perisheth, and no man understandeth ; and righteous men are taken away, and no man regardeth. For the righteous man is taken away from the face of unrighteousness, and his burial shall be in peace." [11] Concerning this very thing it was before foretold in Exodus : " Thou shalt not slay the innocent and the righteous." [12] Also in the Gospel : " Judas, led by penitence, said to the priests and elders, I have sinned, in that I have betrayed the innocent blood." [13]

15. That Christ is called a sheep and a lamb who was to be slain, and concerning the sacrament (mystery) of the passion.

In Isaiah : " He was led as a sheep to the slaughter, and as a lamb before his shearer is dumb, so He opened not His mouth. In His humiliation His judgment was taken away : who shall relate His nativity ? Because His life shall be taken away from the earth. By the transgressions of my people He was led to death ; and I will give the wicked for His burial, and the rich themselves for His death ; because He did no wickedness, nor deceits with His mouth. Wherefore He shall gain many, and shall divide the spoils of the strong ; because His soul was delivered up to death, and He was counted among transgressors. And He bare the sins of many, and was delivered for their offences." [14] Also in Jeremiah : " Lord, give me knowledge, and I shall know it : then I saw their meditations. I was led like a lamb without malice to the slaughter ; against me they devised a device, saying, Come, let us cast the tree into His bread,[15] and let us erase His life from the earth, and His name shall no more be a remembrance." [16] Also in Exodus God said to Moses : " Let them take to themselves each man a sheep, through the houses of the tribes, a sheep without blemish, perfect, male, of a year old it shall be to you. Ye shall take it from the lambs and

---

[1] Isa. xlii. 2–4.
[2] Ps. xxii. 6–8.
[3] Ps. xxii. 15.
[4] " Poderem," " a long priestly robe reaching to the heels " (Migne's *Lexicon*). The Oxford translation gives the meaning " an alb," which also is given in Migne.
[5] Cidarim, the head-dress for the Jewish high priest.
[6] Zech. iii. 1, 3, 5.
[7] " *In* nomine : " Oxford translator, " at the name," following the Eng. ver. But see the Greek, ἐν τῷ ὀνόματι.
[8] Phil. ii 6–11.
[9] The Oxford translation here inserts from the Apocrypha, without authority even for its text, " and objecteth to us the transgressions of the law."

[10] Wisd. ii. 12–22.
[11] Isa. lvii. 1, 2. [Justin, vol. i. 203.]
[12] Ex. xxiii. 7.
[13] Matt. xxvii. 3, 4.
[14] Isa. liii. 7–9, 12.
[15] [Tertull., iii. p. 166. Note also " the *mystery* of the passion."]
[16] Jer. xi. 18, 19.

from the goats, and all the congregation of the synagogue of the children of Israel shall kill it in the evening; and they shall take of its blood, and shall place it upon the two posts,[1] and upon the threshold in the houses, in the very houses in which they shall eat it. And they shall eat the flesh on the same night, roasted with fire; and they shall eat unleavened bread with bitter herbs.[2] Ye shall not eat of them raw nor dressed in water, but roasted with fire; the head with the feet and the inward parts. Ye shall leave nothing of them to the morning; and ye shall not break a bone of it. But what of it shall be left to the morning shall be burnt with fire. But thus ye shall eat it; your loins girt, and your sandals on your feet, and your staff in your hands; and ye shall eat it in haste: for it is the Lord's passover."[3] Also in the Apocalypse: "And I saw in the midst of the throne, and of the four living creatures, and in the midst of the elders, a Lamb standing as if slain, having seven horns and seven eyes, which are the seven spirits of God sent forth throughout all the earth. And He came and took the book from the right hand of God, who sate on the throne. And when He had taken the book, the four living creatures and the four and twenty elders cast themselves before the Lamb, having every one of them harps and golden cups[4] full of odours of supplications, which are the prayers of the saints; and they sang a new song, saying, Worthy art Thou, O Lord, to take the book, and to open its seals: for Thou wast slain, and hast redeemed us with Thy blood from every tribe, and tongue, and people, and nation; and Thou hast made us a kingdom unto our God, and hast made us priests, and they shall reign upon the earth."[5] Also in the Gospel: "On the next day John saw Jesus coming to him, and saith, Behold the Lamb of God, and behold Him that taketh away the sins of the world!"[6]

16. That Christ also is called a Stone.

In Isaiah: "Thus saith the Lord, Behold, I place on the foundations of Sion a precious stone, elect, chief, a corner stone, honourable; and he who trusteth in Him shall not be confounded."[7] Also in the cxviith Psalm: "The stone which the builders rejected, the same is become the head of the corner. This is done by the Lord, and it is wonderful in our eyes. This is the day which the Lord hath made; let us rejoice and be glad in it. O Lord, save therefore, O Lord, direct therefore. Blessed is He who cometh in the name of the Lord."[8] Also in Zechariah: "Behold, I bring forth my servant. The Orient is his name, because the stone which I have placed before the face of Jesus; upon that one stone are seven eyes."[9] Also in Deuteronomy: "And thou shalt write upon the stone all this law, very plainly."[10] Also in Jesus the son of Nave: "And he took a great stone, and placed it there before the Lord; and Jesus said unto the people, Behold, this stone shall be to you for a testimony, because it hath heard all the things which were spoken by the Lord, which He hath spoken to you to-day; and it shall be for a testimony to you in the last of the days, when ye shall have departed from your God."[11] Also in the Acts of the Apostles, Peter: "Ye princes of the people, and elders of Israel, hearken: Behold, we are this day interrogated by you about the good deed done to the impotent man, by means of which he is made whole. Be it known unto you all, and to all the people of Israel, that in the name of Jesus Christ of Nazareth, whom ye have crucified, whom God hath raised up from the dead, by Him he stands whole in your presence, but by none other. This is the stone which was despised by you builders, which has become the head of the corner. For there is no other name given to men under heaven in which we must be saved."[12] This is the stone in Genesis, which Jacob places at his head, because the head of the man is Christ; and as he slept he saw a ladder reaching to heaven, on which the Lord was placed, and angels were ascending and descending.[13] And this stone he designating Christ consecrated and anointed with the sacrament of unction. This is the stone in Exodus upon which Moses sate on the top of a hill when Jesus the son of Nave fought against Amalek; and by the sacrament of the stone, and the stedfastness of his sitting, Amalek was overcome by Jesus, that is, the devil was overcome by Christ. This is the great stone in the first book of Kings, upon which was placed the ark of the covenant when the oxen brought it back in the cart, sent back and returned by the strangers. Also, this is the stone in the first book of Kings, with which David smote the forehead of Goliath and slew him; signifying that the devil and his servants are thereby thrown down — that part of the head, namely,

---

[1] Migne's reading differs considerably from this, and is as follows: "They shall take from the lambs and the goats of its blood, and shall place it upon the two posts," etc.
[2] Erasmus reads for "picridibus," "lactucis agrestibus," wild lettuces.
[3] Ex. xii. 3-12.
[4] "Pateras."
[5] Rev. v. 6-10.
[6] John i. 29.
[7] Isa. xxviii. 16. [See Tertull., "stumbling-stone," vol. iii. p. 165.]

[8] Ps. cxviii. 21-26.
[9] Zech. iii. 8, 9.
[10] Deut. xxvii. 8.
[11] Josh. xxiv. 26, 27.
[12] Acts iv. 8-12.
[13] [The *anointing* of this stone gave it the name of *Messiah* in our author's account; and this interpretation gives great dignity to Jacob's dying reference to Him, Gen. xlix. 24.] The Oxford edition omits "and descending."

being conquered [1] which they have not had sealed. And by this seal we also are always safe and live. This is the stone which, when Israel had conquered the aliens, Samuel set up and called its name Ebenezer; that is, the stone that helpeth.

17. That afterwards this Stone should become a mountain, and should fill the whole earth.

In Daniel: "And behold a very great image; and the aspect of this image was fearful, and it stood erect before thee; whose head was of fine gold, its breast and arms were silver, its belly and thighs were of brass, and its feet were partly indeed of iron, and partly of clay, until that a stone was cut [2] out of the mountain, without the hands of those that should cut it, and struck the image upon the feet of iron and clay, and brake them into small fragments. And the iron, and the clay, and the brass, and the silver, and the gold, was made altogether; and they became small as chaff, or dust in the threshing-floor in summer; and the wind blew them away, so that nothing remained of them. And the stone which struck the image became a great mountain, and filled the whole earth." [3]

18. That in the last times the same mountain should be manifested, and upon it the Gentiles should come, and on it all the righteous should go up.

In Isaiah: "In the last times the mountain of the Lord shall be revealed, and the house of God upon the tops of the mountains; and it shall be exalted above the hills, and all nations shall come upon it, and many shall walk and say, Come, and let us go up into the mountain of the Lord, and into the house of the God of Jacob; and He will tell us His way, and we will walk in it. For from Sion shall proceed the law, and the word of the Lord from Jerusalem; and He shall judge among the nations, and shall rebuke much people; and they shall beat their swords into ploughshares, and their spears into pruning-hooks, and they shall no more learn to fight." [4] Also in the twenty-third Psalm: "Who shall ascend into the hill of the Lord, or who shall stand in His holy place? He that is innocent in his hands, and of a clean heart; who hath not received his life in vanity, and hath not sworn craftily to his neighbour. He shall receive the blessing from the Lord, and mercy [5] from the God that saveth him. This is the generation of those who seek Him, that seek the face of the God of Jacob." [6]

19. That Christ is the Bridegroom, having the Church as His bride, from which spiritual children were to be born.

In Joel: "Blow with the trumpet in Sion; sanctify a fast, and call a healing; assemble the people, sanctify the Church, gather the elders, collect the little ones that suck the breast; let the Bridegroom go forth of His chamber, and the bride out of her closet." [7] Also in Jeremiah: "And I will take away from the cities of Judah, and from the streets of Jerusalem, the voice of the joyous, and the voice of the glad; the voice of the bridegroom, and the voice of the bride." [8] Also in the eighteenth Psalm: "And he is as a bridegroom going forth from his chamber; he exulted as a giant to run his course. From the height of heaven is his going forth, and his circuit even to the end of it; and there is nothing which is hid from his heat." [9] Also in the Apocalypse: "Come, I will show thee the new bride, the Lamb's wife. And he took me in the Spirit to a great mountain, and he showed me the holy city Jerusalem descending out of heaven from God, having the glory of God." [10] Also in the Gospel according to John: "Ye are my witnesses, that I said to them who were sent from Jerusalem to me, that I am not the Christ, but that I am sent before Him. For he who has the bride is the bridegroom; but the friend of the bridegroom is he who standeth and heareth him with joy, and rejoiceth because of the voice of the bridegroom." [11] The mystery of this matter was shown in Jesus the son of Nave, when he was bidden to put his shoes from off him, doubtless because he himself was not the bridegroom. For it was in the law, that whoever should refuse marriage should put off his shoe, but that he should be shod who was to be the bridegroom: "And it happened, when Jesus was in Jericho, he looked around with his eyes, and saw a man standing before his face, and holding a javelin [12] in his hand, and said, Art thou for us or for our enemies? And he said, I am the leader of the host of the Lord; now draw near. And Jesus fell on his face to the earth, and said to him, Lord, what dost Thou command unto Thy servant. And the leader of the Lord's host said, Loose thy shoe from thy feet, for the place whereon thou standest is holy ground." [13] Also, in Exodus, Moses is bidden to put off his shoe,

---

[1] The Oxford edition reads, "conquered, that is, in that part of the head."
[2] [Hippolytus, p. 209, *supra*.]
[3] Dan. ii. 31–35.
[4] Isa. ii. 2–4.
[5] "Misericordiam."

[6] Ps. xxiv. 3–6.
[7] Joel ii. 15, 16.
[8] Jer. xvi. 9.
[9] Ps. xix. 5, 6.
[10] Rev. xxi. 9–11.
[11] John iii. 28, 29.
[12] Frameam.
[13] Josh. v. 13–15.

because he, too, was not the bridegroom: "And there appeared unto him the angel of the Lord in a flame of fire out of a bush; and he saw that the bush burned with fire, but the bush was not consumed. And Moses said, I will pass over and see this great sight, why the bush is not consumed. But when He saw that he drew near to see, the Lord God called him from the bush, saying, Moses, Moses. And he said, What is it? And He said, Draw not nigh hither, unless thou hast loosed thy shoe from off thy feet; for the place on which thou standest is holy ground. And He said unto him, I am the God of thy father, the God of Abraham, and the God of Isaac, and the God of Jacob." [1] This was also made plain in the Gospel according to John: "And John answered them, I indeed baptize with water, but there standeth One in the midst of you whom ye know not: He it is of whom I said, The man that cometh after me is made before me, the latchet of whose shoe I am not worthy to unloose." [2] Also according to Luke: "Let your loins be girt, and your lamps burning, and ye like to men that wait for their master when he shall come from the wedding, that when he cometh and knocketh, they may open unto him. Blessed are those servants whom their Lord, when He cometh, shall find watching." [3] Also in the Apocalypse: "The Lord God omnipotent reigneth: let us be glad and rejoice, and let us give to Him the honour of glory; for the marriage of the Lamb is come, and His wife hath made herself ready." [4]

20. That the Jews would fasten Christ to the cross.

In Isaiah: "I have spread out my hands all day to a people disobedient and contradicting me, who walk in ways that are not good, but after their own sins." [5] Also in Jeremiah: "Come, let us cast the tree into His bread, and let us blot out His life from the earth." [6] Also in Deuteronomy: "And Thy life shall be hanging (in doubt) before Thine eyes; and Thou shalt fear day and night, and shalt not trust to Thy life." [7] Also in the twenty-first Psalm: "They tore my hands and my feet; [8] they numbered all my bones. And they gazed upon me, and saw me, and divided my garments among them, and upon my vesture they cast a lot. But Thou, O Lord, remove not Thy help far from me; attend unto my help. Deliver my soul from the

sword, and my only one from the paw [9] of the dog. Save me from the mouth of the lion, and my lowliness from the horns of the unicorns. I will declare Thy name unto my brethren; in the midst of the Church I will praise Thee." [10] Also in the cxviiith Psalm: "Pierce my flesh with nails through fear of Thee." [11] Also in the cxlth Psalm: "The lifting up of my hands is an evening sacrifice." [12] Of which sacrifice Sophonias said: "Fear from the presence of the Lord God, since His day is near, because the Lord hath prepared His sacrifice, He hath sanctified His elect." [13] Also in Zechariah: "And they shall look upon me, whom they have pierced." [14] Also in the eighty-seventh Psalm: "I have called unto Thee, O Lord, the whole day; I have stretched out my hands unto Thee." [15] Also in Numbers: "Not as a man is God suspended, nor as the son of man does He suffer threats." [16] Whence in the Gospel the Lord says: "As Moses lifted up the serpent in the wilderness, even so must the Son of man be lifted up, that whosoever believeth in the Son may have life eternal." [17]

21. That in the passion and the sign of the cross is all virtue and power.

In Habakkuk: "His virtue covered the heavens, and the earth is full of His praise, and His splendour shall be as the light; there shall be horns in His hands. And there the virtue of His glory was established, and He founded His strong love. Before His face shall go the Word, and shall go forth unto the plains according to His steps." [18] In Isaiah also: "Behold, unto us a child is born, and to us a Son is given, upon whose shoulders shall be government; and His name shall be called the Messenger of a mighty thought." [19] By this sign of the cross also Amalek was conquered by Jesus through Moses. In Exodus Moses said to Jesus: "Choose thee out men, and go forth, and order yourselves with Amalek until the morrow. Behold, I will stand on the top of the hill, and the rod of God in mine hand. And it came to pass, when Moses lifted up his hands, Israel prevailed; but when Moses had let down his hands, Amalek waxed strong. But the hands of Moses were heavy; and they took a stone, and placed it under him, and he sate upon it; and Aaron and Hur held up his hands, on the one side and on the other side; and the hands of Moses were made steady even to the setting of the sun. And Jesus routed

1 Ex. iii. 2-6.
2 John i. 26, 27.
3 Luke xii. 35-37.
4 Rev. xix. 6, 7.
5 Isa. lxv. 2. [So Justin, vol. i. pp. 179 and 206. But compare Isa. xxv. 11, a remarkable simile.]
6 Jer. xi. 19.
7 Deut. xxviii. 66.
8 [This is one of the passages corrupted by the Jews since the crucifixion. See Pearson, *On the Creed*, p. 534. All his notes on "crucified" are most precious.]

9 "Manu."
10 Ps. xxii. 16-22.
11 Ps. cxix. 120.
12 Ps. cxli. 2.
13 Zeph. i. 7.
14 Zech. xii. 10.
15 Ps. lxxxviii. 9.
16 Num xxiii. 19.
17 John iii. 14, 15.
18 Hab. iii. 3-5.
19 Isa. ix. 6.

Amalek and all his people. And the Lord said unto Moses, Write this, that it may be a memorial in a book, and tell it unto the ears of Jesus, that I may utterly destroy the memory of Amalek from under heaven." [1]

22. That in this sign of the Cross is salvation for all people who are marked on their foreheads. [2]

In Ezekiel the Lord says : " Pass through the midst of Jerusalem, and thou shalt mark the sign upon the men's foreheads, who groan and grieve for the iniquities which are done in the midst of them." [3] Also in the same place : " Go and smite, and do not spare your eyes. Have no pity on the old man, and the youth, and the virgin, and slay little children and women, that they may be utterly destroyed. But ye shall not touch any one upon whom the sign is written, and begin with my holy places themselves." [4] Also in Exodus God says to Moses : " And there shall be blood for a sign to you upon the houses wherein ye shall be ; and I will look on the blood, and will protect you. And there shall not be in you the plague of wasting when I shall smite the land of Egypt." [5] Also in the Apocalypse : " And I saw [6] a Lamb standing on Mount Sion, and with Him a hundred and forty and four thousand ; and they had His name and the name of His Father written on their foreheads." [7] Also in the same place : " I am Alpha and Omega, the first and the last, the beginning and the end. Blessed are they that do His commandments, that they may have power over the tree of life." [8]

23. That at mid-day in His passion there should be darkness.

In Amos : " And it shall come to pass in that day, saith the Lord, the sun shall set at noonday, and the day of light shall be darkened ; and I will turn your feast-days into grief, and all your songs into lamentation." [9] Also in Jeremiah : " She is frightened that hath borne children, and her soul hath grown weary. Her sun hath gone down while as yet it was mid-day ; she hath been confounded and accursed : I will give the rest of them to the sword in the sight of their enemies." [10] Also in the Gospel : " Now from the sixth hour there was darkness over all the earth even to the ninth hour." [11]

24. That He was not to be overcome of death, nor should remain in Hades.

In the twenty-ninth Psalm : " O Lord, Thou hast brought back my soul from hell." [12] Also in the fifteenth Psalm : " Thou wilt not leave my soul in hell, neither wilt Thou suffer Thine Holy One to see corruption." [13] Also in the third Psalm : " I laid me down and slept, and rose up again, because the Lord helped me." [14] Also according to John : " No man taketh away my life from me ; but I lay it down of myself. I have the power of laying it down, and I have the power of taking it again. For this commandment I have received from my Father." [15]

25. That He should rise again from the dead on the third day.

In Hosea : " After two days He will revive us ; we shall rise again on the third day." [16] Also in Exodus : " And the Lord said unto Moses, Go down and testify to the people, and sanctify them to-day and to-morrow ; and let them wash their garments, and let them be prepared against the day after to-morrow. For on the third day the Lord will come down on Mount Sinai." [17] Also in the Gospel : " A wicked and adulterous generation seeketh after a sign ; and there shall no sign be given unto it but the sign of the prophet Jonas : for as Jonas was in the whale's belly three days and three nights, so shall the Son of man be three days and three nights in the heart of the earth." [18]

26. That after He had risen again He should receive from His Father all power, and His power should be everlasting.

In Daniel : " I saw in a vision by night, and behold as it were the Son of man, coming in the clouds of heaven, came even to the Ancient of days, and stood in His sight. And they who stood beside Him brought Him before Him : and to Him was given a royal power, and all the kings of the earth by their generation, and all glory obeying Him : and His power is eternal, which shall not be taken away, and His kingdom shall not be destroyed." [19] Also in Isaiah : " Now will I arise, saith the Lord ; now will I be glorified, now will I be exalted, now ye shall see, now ye shall understand, now ye shall be confounded. Vain will be the strength of your spirit : the fire shall consume you." [20] Also in the cixth Psalm : " The Lord said unto my Lord, Sit Thou on my

---

[1] Ex. xvii. 9-14.
[2] [i.e., baptized; but probably after immersion this symbolic ceremony was already in use.]
[3] Ezek. ix. 4.
[4] Ezek. ix. 4-6.
[5] Ex. xii. 13.
[6] " And behold," Oxford text.
[7] Rev. xiv. 1.
[8] Rev. xxii. 13, 14.
[9] Amos viii. 9, 10. [Lardner, Credib., vol. vii. pp. 107-124.]
[10] Jer. xv. 9. [I admire Lardner's caution: possibly he carries it too far.]
[11] Matt. xxvii. 45. [See vol. iii. p. 58.]

[12] Ps. xxx. 3.
[13] Ps. xvi. 10.
[14] Ps. iii. 5.
[15] John x. 18.
[16] Hos. vi. 2.
[17] Ex. xix. 10, 11.
[18] Matt. xii. 39, 40.
[19] Dan. vii. 13, 14.
[20] Isa. xxxiii. 10, 11.

right hand, until I make Thine enemies the footstool of Thy feet. God will send the rod of Thy power out of Sion, and Thou shalt rule in the midst of Thine enemies." [1] Also in the Apocalypse: "And I turned and looked to see the voice which spake with me. And I saw seven golden candlesticks, and in the midst of the candlesticks one like unto the Son of man, clothed with a long garment,[2] and He was girt about the paps with a golden girdle. And His head and His hairs were white as wool or snow, and His eyes as a flame of fire, and His feet like to fine brass from a furnace of fire, and His voice like the sound of many waters. And He had in His right hand seven stars; and out of His mouth went a sharp two-edged sword; and His face shone as the sun in his might. And when I saw Him, I fell at His feet as dead. And He laid His right hand upon me, and said, Fear not; I am the first and the last, and He that liveth and was dead; and, lo, I am living for evermore,[3] and I have the keys of death and of hell." [4] Likewise in the Gospel, the Lord after His resurrection says to His disciples: "All power is given unto me in heaven and in earth. Go therefore and teach all nations, baptizing them in the name of the Father, and of the Son, and of the Holy Ghost, teaching them to observe all things whatsoever I have commanded you." [5]

27. That it is impossible to attain to God the Father, except by His Son Jesus Christ.

In the Gospel: "I am the way, and the truth, and the life: no one cometh to the Father but by me." [6] Also in the same place: "I am the door: by me if any man shall enter in, he shall be saved." [7] Also in the same place: "Many prophets and righteous men have desired to see the things which ye see, and have not seen them; and to hear those things which ye hear, and have not heard them." [8] Also in the same place: "He that believeth on the Son hath eternal life: he that is not obedient in word to the Son hath not life; but the wrath of God shall abide upon him." [9] Also Paul to the Ephesians: "And when He had come, He preached peace to you, to those which are afar off, and peace to those which are near, because through Him we both have access in one Spirit unto the Father." [10] Also to the Romans: "For all have sinned, and fail of the glory of God; but they are justified by His gift and grace, through the redemption which is in Christ Jesus." [11] Also in the Epistle of Peter the apostle: "Christ hath died once for our sins, the just for the unjust, that He might present us to God." [12] Also in the same place: "For in this also was it preached to them that are dead, that they might be raised again." [13] Also in the Epistle of John: "Whosoever denieth the Son, the same also hath not the Father. He that confesseth the Son, hath both the Son and the Father." [14]

28. That Jesus Christ shall come as a Judge.

In Malachi: "Behold, the day of the Lord cometh, burning as an oven; and all the aliens and all the wicked shall be as stubble; and the day that cometh shall burn them up, saith the Lord." [15] Also in the forty-ninth (or fiftieth) Psalm: "God the Lord of gods hath spoken, and called the earth. From the rising of the sun even to the going down thereof, out of Sion is the beauty of His glory. God shall come manifestly, our God, and shall not keep silence. A fire shall burn before Him, and round about Him shall be a great storm. He hath called the heaven above, and the earth, that He may separate His people. Gather together His saints unto Him, those who arrange His covenant with sacrifices. And the heavens shall announce His righteousness, for God is the judge." [16] Also in Isaiah: "The Lord God of strength shall go forth, and shall break war in pieces: He shall stir up contest, and shall cry over His enemies with strength. I have been silent; shall I always be silent?" [17] Also in the sixty-seventh Psalm: "Let God arise, and let His enemies be scattered: and let those who hate Him flee from His face. As smoke vanisheth, let them vanish: as wax melteth from the face of fire, thus let the sinners perish from the face of God. And let the righteous be glad and rejoice in the sight of God: and let them be glad with joyfulness. Sing unto God, sing praises unto His name: make a way to Him who goeth up into the west. God is His name. They shall be put to confusion from the face of Him who is the Father of the orphans, and the Judge of the widows. God is in His holy place: God, who maketh men to dwell with one mind in an house, bringing forth them that are bound with might, and equally those who provoke unto anger, who dwell in the sepulchres: God, when Thou wentest forth in the sight of Thy people, in passing into the desert." [18] Also in the eighty-first

---

1 Ps. cx. 1, 2.
2 "Podere."
3 One codex reads here, "living in the assembly of the saints."
4 Rev. i. 12–18.
5 Matt. xxviii. 18–20.
6 John xiv. 6.
7 John x. 9.
8 Matt. xiii. 17.
9 John iii. 36.
10 Eph. ii. 17, 18.

11 Rom. iii. 23, 24.
12 1 Pet. iii. 18.
13 1 Pet. iv. 6.
14 1 John ii. 23.
15 Mal. iv. 1.
16 Ps. l. 1–6.
17 Isa. xlii. 13, 14.
18 Ps. lxviii. 1–7.

Psalm : "Arise, O God ; judge the earth : for Thou wilt exterminate among all nations."[1] Also in the Gospel according to Matthew : "What have we to do with Thee, Thou Son of David? why art Thou come hither to punish us before the time?"[2] Likewise according to John : "The Father judgeth nothing, but hath given all judgment to the Son, that all may honour the Son as they honour the Father. He that honoureth not the Son, honoureth not the Father who hath sent Him."[3] So too in the second Epistle of Paul to the Corinthians : "We must all appear before the judgment-seat of Christ, that every one may bear the things proper to his body, according to those things which he hath done, whether they be good or evil."[4]

29. That He will reign as a King for ever.

In Zechariah : "Tell ye the daughter of Zion, Behold, thy King cometh unto thee : just, and having salvation ; meek, sitting upon an ass that hath not been tamed."[5] Also in Isaiah : "Who will declare to you that eternal place? He that walketh in righteousness, and holdeth back his hands from gifts ; stopping his ears, that he may not hear the judgment of blood ; and closing his eyes, that he may not see unrighteousness : this man shall dwell in the lofty cavern of the strong rock ; bread shall be given him, and his water shall be sure. Ye shall see the King with glory."[6] Likewise in Malachi : "I am a great King, saith the Lord, and my name is illustrious among the nations."[7] Also in the second Psalm : "But I am established as a King by Him upon His holy hill of Zion, announcing His empire."[8] Also in the twenty-first Psalm : "All the ends of the world shall be reminded, and shall turn to the Lord : and all the countries of the nations shall worship in Thy sight. For the kingdom is the Lord's : and He shall rule over all nations."[9] Also in the twenty-third Psalm : "Lift up your gates, ye princes ; and be ye lifted up, ye everlasting doors ; and the King of glory shall come in. Who is this King of glory? The Lord strong and mighty, the Lord strong in battle. Lift up your gates, O ye princes ; and be ye lifted up, ye everlasting doors ; and the King of glory shall come in. Who is this King of glory? The Lord of hosts, He is the King of glory."[10] Also in the forty-fourth Psalm : "My heart hath breathed forth a good discourse :[11] I tell my works to the king :

my tongue is the pen of a writer intelligently writing. Thou art lovely in beauty above the children of men : grace is shed forth on Thy lips, because God hath blessed Thee for ever. Be girt with Thy sword on Thy thigh, O most mighty. To Thy honour and to Thy beauty both attend, and direct Thyself, and reign, because of truth, and meekness, and righteousness."[12] Also in the fifth Psalm : "My King, and my God, because unto Thee will I pray. O Lord, in the morning Thou shalt hear my voice ; in the morning I will stand before Thee, and will contemplate Thee."[13] Also in the ninety-sixth Psalm : "The Lord hath reigned ; let the earth rejoice ; let the many isles be glad."[14] Moreover, in the forty-fourth Psalm : "The queen stood at thy right hand in a golden garment ; she is clothed in many colours. Hear, O daughter, and see, and incline thine ear, and forget thy people and thy father's house ; for the King hath desired thy beauty, for He is thy Lord God."[15] Also in the seventy-third Psalm : "But God is our King before the world ; He hath wrought salvation in the midst of the earth."[16] Also in the Gospel according to Matthew : "And when Jesus was born in Bethlehem of Judah in the days of Herod the king, behold, Magi from the east came to Jerusalem, saying, Where is He who is born King of the Jews? for we have seen His star in the east, and have come to worship Him."[17] Also, according to John, Jesus said : "My kingdom is not of this world. If my kingdom were of this world, my servants would be in trouble, that I should not be delivered to the Jews ; but now is my kingdom not from hence. Pilate said, Art thou a king, then? Jesus answered, Thou sayest that I am a king. For this cause I was born, and for this cause I am come into the world, that I might bear testimony to the truth. Every one that is of the truth heareth my voice."[18]

30. That He Himself is both Judge and King.

In the seventy-first Psalm : "O God, give Thy judgment to the king, and Thy righteousness to the king's son, to judge Thy people in righteousness."[19] Also in the Apocalypse : "And I saw the heaven opened, and behold a white horse ; and He who sate upon him was called Faithful and True ; and He judgeth justice and righteousness, and maketh war. And His eyes were. as it were, a flame of fire, and upon His head were many crowns ; and He bare a name written that was known to none other than Himself :

---

[1] Ps. lxxxii. 8.
[2] Matt. viii. 29.
[3] John v. 22, 23.
[4] 2 Cor. v. 10.
[5] Zech. ix. 9.
[6] Isa. xxxiii. 14-17.
[7] Mal. i. 14.
[8] Ps. ii. 6.
[9] Ps. xxii. 27, 28.
[10] Ps. xxiv. 7-10.
[11] [i.e., rather "a good Word." See p. 516, *supra*.]

[12] Ps. xlv. 1-4.
[13] Ps. v. 2, 3.
[14] Ps. xcvii. 1.
[15] Ps. xlv. 9-11.
[16] Ps. lxxiv. 12.
[17] Matt. ii. 1, 2.
[18] John i. 36, 37.
[19] Ps. lxxii. 1, 2.

and He was clothed with a garment sprinkled with blood, and His name is called the Word of God. And the armies which are in heaven followed Him on white horses, clothed in linen, white and clean. And out of His mouth went forth a sword with two edges, that with it He should smite the nations, which He shall shepherd [1] with a rod of iron; and He shall tread the winepress of the wrath of God Almighty. Also He has on His garment and on His thigh the name written, King of kings, and Lord of lords." [2] Likewise in the Gospel: "When the Son of man shall come in His glory, and all the angels with Him, then He shall sit in the throne of His glory; and all nations shall be gathered together before Him, and He shall separate them one from another, even as a shepherd separates the sheep from the goats; and He shall place the sheep at His right hand, but the goats at His left hand. Then shall the King say unto them who shall be at His right hand, Come, ye blessed of my Father, receive the kingdom which is prepared for you from the beginning of the world: for I was hungry, and ye gave me to eat: I was thirsty, and ye gave me to drink: I was a stranger, and ye received me: naked, and ye clothed me: sick, and ye visited me: I was in prison, and ye came unto me. Then shall the righteous answer, and say unto Him, Lord, when saw we Thee hungry, and fed Thee? thirsty, and gave Thee to drink? And when saw we Thee a stranger, and received Thee? naked, and clothed Thee? And when saw we Thee sick, and in prison, and came unto Thee? And the King, answering, shall say unto them, Verily I say unto you, In as far as ye have done it to the least of these my brethren, ye have done it unto me. Then shall He say unto them who shall be on His left hand, Depart from me, ye cursed, into everlasting fire, which my Father hath prepared [3] for the devil and his angels: for I have been hungry, and ye gave me not to eat: I have been thirsty, and ye gave me not to drink: I was a stranger, and ye received me not: naked, and ye clothed me not: sick, and in prison, and ye visited me not. Then shall they also answer and say, Lord, when saw we Thee hungry, or thirsty, or a stranger, or naked, or sick, or in prison, and have not ministered unto Thee? And He shall answer unto them, Verily I say unto you, Inasmuch as ye have not done it to one of the least of these, ye have not done it unto me. And these shall go away into everlasting burning, but the righteous into life eternal." [4]

THIRD BOOK.

Cyprian to his son Quirinus,[5] greeting. Of your faith and devotion which you manifest to the Lord God, beloved son, you asked me to gather out for your instruction from the Holy Scriptures some heads bearing upon the religious teaching of our school;[5] seeking for a succinct course of sacred reading, so that your mind, surrendered to God, might not be wearied with long or numerous volumes of books, but, instructed with a summary of heavenly precepts, might have a wholesome and large compendium for nourishing its memory. And because I owe you a plentiful and loving obedience, I have done what you wished. I have laboured for once, that you might not always labour.[6] Therefore, as much as my small ability could embrace, I have collected certain precepts of the Lord, and divine teachings, which may be easy and useful to the readers, in that a few things digested into a short space are both quickly read through, and are frequently repeated. I bid you, beloved son, ever heartily farewell.

HEADS.[7]

1. On the benefit of good works and mercy.

2. In works and alms, even if by smallness of power less be done, that the will itself is enough.

3. That charity and brotherly love must be religiously and stedfastly practised.

4. That we must boast in nothing, since nothing is our own.

5. That humility and quietness is to be maintained in all things.

6. That all good and righteous men suffer more, but ought to endure because they are proved.

7. That we must not grieve the Holy Spirit whom we have received.

8. That anger must be overcome, lest it constrain us to sin.

9. That brethren ought to sustain one another.

10. That we must trust in God only, and in Him we must glory.

11. That he who has attained to faith, having put off the former man, ought to regard only celestial and spiritual things, and to give no heed to the world which he has already renounced.

12. That we must not swear.

13. That we are not to curse.

14. That we must never murmur, but bless God concerning all things that happen.

15. That men are tried by God for this purpose, that they may be proved.

---

[1] The words "which He shall feed," or "shepherd," are wanting in the Apocalypse; and they are not found in many authorities.
[2] Rev. xix. 11-16.
[3] [Said to be in the old *Itala*, as in some Greek mss. So Irenæus, vol. i. p. 524.]
[4] Matt. xxv. 31-46.

[5] [Whom he had probably baptized. Elucidation XI.]
[6] [May the American editor of these volumes venture to trust that he has in some degree lightened the labours of those who come after him: "laboravi semel ne tu semper laborares."]
[7] [Six-score precepts to be compared with the heathen maxims and morals with which they so generally conflict. See Elucidation XII.]

16. Of the benefit of martyrdom.

17. That what we suffer in this world is of less account than is the reward which is promised.

18. That nothing must be preferred to the love of God and of Christ.

19. That we must not obey our own will, but that of God.

20. That the foundation and strength of hope and faith is fear.

21. That we must not rashly judge of another.

22. That when we have received a wrong, we must remit and forgive it.

23. That evil is not to be returned for evil.

24. That it is impossible to attain to the Father but by Christ.

25. That unless a man have been baptized and born again, he cannot attain to the kingdom of God.

26. That it is of small account to be baptized and to receive the Eucharist, unless one profits by it both in deeds and works.

27. That even a baptized person loses the grace which he has attained, unless he keep innocency.

28. That remission cannot in the Church be granted unto him who has sinned against God.

29. That it was before predicted concerning the hatred of the Name.

30. That what any one has vowed to God, he must quickly pay.

31. That he who does not believe is judged already.

32. Of the benefit of virginity and of continency.

33. That the Father judgeth nothing, but the Son ; and the Father is not honoured by him by whom the Son is not honoured.

34. That the believer ought not to live like the Gentiles.

35. That God is patient for this end, that we may repent of our sin and be reformed.

36. That a woman ought not to be adorned in a worldly manner.

37. That the believer ought not to be punished for other offences but for the name he bears only.

38. That the servant of God ought to be innocent, lest he fall into secular punishment.

39. That the example of living is given to us in Christ.

40. That we must not labour boastfully or noisily.

41. That we must not speak foolishly and offensively.

42. That faith is of advantage altogether, and that we can do as much as we believe.

43. That he who truly believes can immediately obtain.

44. That the believers who differ among themselves ought not to refer to a Gentile judge.

45. That hope is of future things, and therefore that faith concerning those things which are promised ought to be patient.

46. That a woman ought to be silent in the church.

47. That it arises from our fault and our desert that we suffer, and do not perceive God's help in everything.

48. That we must not take usury.

49. That even our enemies are to be loved.

50. That the sacrament of the faith must not be profaned.

51. That no one should be uplifted in his doing.

52. That the liberty of believing or of not believing is placed in free choice.

53. That the secrets of God cannot be seen through, and therefore that our faith ought to be simple.

54. That none is without filth and without sin.

55. That we must not please men, but God.

56. That nothing that is done is hidden from God.

57. That the believer is amended and reserved.

58. That no one should be made sad by death, since in living is labour and peril, in dying peace and the certainty of resurrection.

59. Of the idols which the Gentiles think gods.

60. That too great lust of food is not to be desired.

61. That the lust of possessing, and money, are not to be desired.

62. That marriage is not to be contracted with Gentiles.

63. That the sin of fornication is grievous.

64. What are those carnal things which beget death, and what are the spiritual things which lead to life.

65. That all sins are put away in baptism.

66. That the discipline of God is to be observed in Church precepts.

67. That it was foretold that men would despise sound discipline.

68. That we must depart from him who lives irregularly and contrary to discipline.

69. That the kingdom of God is not in the wisdom of the world, nor in eloquence, but in the faith of the cross and in virtue of conversation.

70. That we must obey parents.

71. And that fathers ought not to be bitter against their children.

72. That servants, when they believe, ought the more to be obedient to their fleshly masters.

73. Likewise that masters ought to be more gentle.

74. That every widow that is approved ought to be honoured.

75. That every person ought to have care rather of his own people, and especially of believers.

76. That one who is older must not rashly be accused.

77. That the sinner is to be publicly reproved.

78. That we must not speak with heretics.

79. That innocency asks with confidence, and obtains.

80. That the devil has no power against man unless God have allowed it.

81. That wages be quickly paid to the hireling.

82. That divination must not be used.

83. That a tuft of hair [1] is not to be worn on the head.

84. That the beard must not be plucked.

85. That we must rise when a bishop or a presbyter comes.

86. That a schism must not be made, even although he who withdraws should remain in one faith and in the same tradition.

87. That believers ought to be simple with prudence.

88. That a brother must not be deceived.

89. That the end of the world comes suddenly.

90. That a wife must not depart from her husband; or if she departs, she must remain unmarried.

91. That every one is tempted so much as he is able to bear.

92. That not everything is to be done which is lawful.

93. That it was foretold that heresies would arise.

94. That the Eucharist is to be received with fear and honour.

95. That we are to live with the good, but to avoid the evil.

96. That we must labour with deeds, not with words.

97. That we must hasten to faith and to attainment. [2]

98. That the catechumen ought to sin no more.

99. That judgment will be in accordance with the terms, before the law, of equity; after Moses, of the law.

100. That the grace of God ought to be gratuitous.

101. That the Holy Spirit has often appeared in fire.

102. That all good men ought willingly to hear rebuke.

103. That we must abstain from much speaking.

104. That we must not lie.

105. That they are frequently to be corrected who do wrong in domestic service.

106. That when a wrong is received, patience is to be maintained, and that vengeance is to be left to God.

107. That we must not use detraction.

108. That we must not lay snares against our neighbour.

109. That the sick are to be visited.

110. That tale-bearers are accursed.

111. That the sacrifices of evil men are not acceptable.

112. That those are more severely judged who in this world have more power.

113. That widows and orphans ought to be protected.

114. That while one is in the flesh, he ought to make confession.

115. That flattery is pernicious.

116. That God is more loved by him who has had many sins forgiven in baptism.

117. That there is a strong conflict to be waged against the devil, and that therefore we ought to stand bravely, that we may be able to conquer.

118. Of Antichrist, that he will come as a man.

119. That the yoke of the law was heavy, which is cast off by us; and that the Lord's yoke is light, which is taken up by us.

120. That we are to be urgent in prayers.

TESTIMONIES.

1. Of the benefit of good works and mercy.

In Isaiah: "Cry aloud," saith He, "and spare not; lift up thy voice like a trumpet; tell my people their sins, and the house of Jacob their wickednesses. They seek me from day to day, and desire to know my ways, as a people which did righteousness, and did not forsake the judgment of God. They ask of me now a righteous judgment, and desire to approach to God, saying, What! because we have fasted, and Thou hast not seen: we have humiliated our souls, and Thou hast not known. For in the days of fasting are found your own wills; for either ye torment those who are subjected to you, or ye fast for strifes and judgments, or ye strike your neighbours with fists. For what do you fast unto me, that to-day your voice should be heard in clamour? This fast I have not chosen, save that a man should humble his soul. And if thou shalt bend thy neck like a ring, and spread under thee sackcloth and ashes, neither thus shall it be called an acceptable fast. Not such a fast have I chosen, saith the Lord; but loose every knot of unrighteousness, let go the

---

[1] "Cirrum in capite non habendum." "Cirrus" means "a tuft of hair," or a curl or lovelock. [But compare Clement, vol. ii. p. 286 (and note 9, on the chrism), for the more probable meaning.]

[2] *Scil.* "of baptism," Oxford transl.

chokings of impotent engagements.[1] Send away the harassed into rest, and scatter every unrighteous contract. Break thy bread to the hungry, and bring the houseless poor into thy dwelling. If thou seest the naked, clothe him; and despise not them of thy own seed in thy house. Then shall thy seasonable light break forth, and thy garments shall quickly arise; and righteousness shall go before thee: and the glory of God shall surround thee. Then thou shalt cry out, and God shall hear thee; while thou art yet speaking, He shall say, Here I am."[2] Concerning this same thing in Job: "I have preserved the needy from the hand of the mighty; and I have helped the orphan, to whom there was no helper. The mouth of the widow blessed me, since I was the eye of the blind; I was also the foot of the lame, and the father of the weak."[3] Of this same matter in Tobit: "And I said to Tobias, My son, go and bring whatever poor man thou shalt find out of our brethren, who still has God in mind with his whole heart. Bring him hither, and he shall eat my dinner together with me. Behold, I attend thee, my son, until thou come."[4] Also in the same place: "All the days of thy life, my son, keep God in mind, and transgress not His precepts. Do justice all the days of thy life, and do not walk in the way of unrighteousness; because if thou act truly, there will be respect of thy works. Give alms of thy substance, and turn not thy face from any poor man. So shall it come to pass that the face of God shall not be turned away from thee. Even as thou hast, my son, so do: if thou hast abundant substance, give the more alms therefrom; if thou hast little, communicate even of that little. And do not fear when thou givest alms: thou layest up for thyself a good reward against the day of need; because alms delivereth from death, and does not suffer to go into darkness. Alms is a good office for all who do it in the sight of the most high God."[5] On this same subject in Solomon in Proverbs: "He that hath pity on the poor lendeth unto the Lord."[6] Also in the same place: "He that giveth to the poor shall never want; but he who turns away his eye shall be in much penury."[7] Also in the same place: "Sins are purged away by alms-giving and faith."[8] Again, in the same place: "If thine enemy hunger, feed him; and if he thirst, give him to drink: for by doing this thou shalt scatter live coals upon his head."[9] Again,

in the same place: "As water extinguishes fire, so alms-giving extinguishes sin."[10] In the same in Proverbs: "Say not, Go away, and return, to-morrow I will give; when you can do good immediately. For thou knowest not what may happen on the coming day."[11] Also in the same place: "He who stoppeth his ears that he may not hear the weak, shall himself call upon God, and there shall be none to hear him."[12] Also in the same place: "He who has his conversation without reproach in righteousness, leaves blessed children."[13] In the same in Ecclesiasticus: "My son, if thou hast, do good by thyself, and present worthy offerings to God; remember that death delayeth not."[14] Also in the same place: "Shut up alms in the heart of the poor, and this will entreat for thee from all evil."[15] Concerning this thing in the thirty-sixth Psalm, that mercy is beneficial also to one's posterity: "I have been young, and I have also grown old; and I have not seen the righteous forsaken, nor his seed begging their bread. The whole day he is merciful, and lendeth; and his seed is in blessing."[16] Of this same thing in the fortieth Psalm: "Blessed is he who considereth over the poor and needy: in the evil day God will deliver him."[17] Also in the cxith Psalm: "He hath distributed, he hath given to the poor; his righteousness shall remain from generation to generation."[18] Of this same thing in Hosea: "I desire mercy rather than sacrifice, and the knowledge of God more than whole burnt-offerings."[19] Of this same thing also in the Gospel according to Matthew: "Blessed are they who hunger and thirst after righteousness: for they shall be satisfied."[20] Also in the same place: "Blessed are the merciful: for they shall obtain mercy."[21] Also in the same place: "Lay up for yourselves treasures in heaven, where neither moth nor rust doth corrupt, and where thieves do not dig through and steal: for where your treasure is, there will your heart be also."[22] Also in the same place: "The kingdom of heaven is like unto a merchant-man seeking goodly pearls: and when he hath found a precious pearl, he went away and sold all that he had, and bought it."[23] That even a small work is of advantage, also in the same place: "And whoever shall give to drink to one of the least of these a cup of cold water in the name

---

1 "Impotentium commerciorum."
2 Isa. lviii. 1–9.
3 Job xxix. 12, 13, 15, 16.
4 Tob. ii. 2.
5 Tob. iv. 5–11.
6 Prov. xix. 17.
7 Prov. xxviii. 27.
8 Prov. xvi. 6.
9 Prov. xxv. 21.

10 Ecclus. iii. 30.
11 Prov. iii. 28.
12 Prov. xxi. 13.
13 Prov. xx. 7.
14 Ecclus. xiv. 11.
15 Ecclus. xxix. 12.
16 Ps. xxxvii. 25, 26.
17 Ps. xli. 1.
18 Ps. cxii. 9.
19 Hos. vi. 6.
20 Matt. v. 6.
21 Matt. v. 7.
22 Matt. vi. 20, 21.
23 Matt. xiii. 45, 46

of a disciple, verily I say unto you, His reward shall not perish." [1] That alms are to be denied to none, also in the same place : "Give to every one that asketh thee ; and from him who would wish to borrow, be not turned away." [2] Also in the same place : "If thou wilt enter into life, keep the commandments. He saith, Which? Jesus saith unto him, Thou shalt not kill, Thou shalt not commit adultery, Thou shalt not bear false witness, Honour thy father and mother : and, Thou shalt love thy neighbour as thyself. The young man saith unto Him, All these things have I observed : what lack I yet? Jesus saith unto him, If thou wilt be perfect, go and sell all that thou hast, and give to the poor, and thou shalt have treasure in heaven ; and come, follow me." [3] Also in the same place : "When the Son of man shall come in His majesty, and all the angels with Him, then He shall sit on the throne of His glory : and all nations shall be gathered together before Him ; and He shall separate them one from another, even as a shepherd separates the sheep from the goats : and He shall place the sheep on the right hand, but the goats on the left hand. Then shall the King say unto them that are on His right hand, Come, ye blessed of my Father, receive the kingdom prepared for you from the beginning of the world. For I was hungry, and ye gave me to eat : I was thirsty, and ye gave me to drink : I was a stranger, and ye took me in : naked, and ye clothed me : I was sick, and ye visited me : I was in prison, and ye came unto me. Then shall the righteous answer Him, and say, Lord, when saw we Thee [4] a stranger, and took Thee in : naked, and clothed Thee? And when saw we Thee sick, and in prison, and came to Thee? And the King, answering, shall say unto them, Verily I say unto you, Inasmuch as ye did it to one of the least of these my brethren, ye did it unto me. Then shall He say unto them who are on His left hand, Depart from me, ye cursed, into everlasting fire, which my Father hath prepared for the devil and his angels : for I was hungry, and ye gave me not to eat : I was thirsty, and ye gave me not to drink : I was a stranger, and ye took me not in : I was naked, and ye clothed me not : sick, and in prison, and ye visited me not. Then shall they also answer, and say, Lord, when saw we Thee hungry, or thirsty, or a stranger, or naked, or sick, or in prison, and did not minister unto Thee? And He shall answer them, Verily I say unto you, Inasmuch as ye did it not to one of the least of these, ye did it not unto me. And these shall go away into everlasting burning : but the righteous into life eternal." [5] Concerning this same matter in the Gospel according to Luke : "Sell your possessions, and give alms." [6] Also in the same place : "He who made that which is within, made that which is without also. But give alms, and, behold, all things are pure unto you." [7] Also in the same place : "Behold, the half of my substance I give to the poor ; and if I have defrauded any one of anything, I restore him fourfold. And Jesus said unto him, that salvation has this day been wrought for this house, since he also is a son of Abraham." [8] Of this same thing also in the second Epistle to the Corinthians : "Let your abundance supply their want, that their abundance also may be the supplement of your want, that there may be equality : as it is written, He who had much had not excess ; and he who had little had no lack." [9] Also in the same place : "He who soweth sparingly shall reap also sparingly ; and he who soweth in blessing shall reap also of blessing. But let every one do as he has proposed in his heart : not as if sorrowfully, or of necessity : for God loveth a cheerful giver." [10] Also in the same place : "As it is written, He hath dispersed abroad ; he hath given to the poor : his righteousness remaineth for ever." [11] Likewise in the same place : "Now he who ministereth seed to the sower, shall both supply bread to be eaten, and shall multiply your seed, and shall increase the growth of the fruits of your righteousness : that in all things ye may be made rich." [12] Also in the same place : "The administration of this service has not only supplied that which is lacking to the saints, but has abounded by much giving of thanks unto God." [13] Of this same matter in the Epistle of John : "Whoso hath this world's substance, and seeth his brother desiring, and shutteth up his bowels from him, how dwelleth the love of God in him?" [14] Of this same thing in the Gospel according to Luke : "When thou makest a dinner or a supper, call not thy friends, nor brethren, nor neighbours, nor the rich ; lest haply they also invite thee again, and a recompense be made thee. But when thou makest a banquet, call the poor, the weak, the blind, and lame : and thou shalt be blessed ; because they have not the means of rewarding thee : but thou shalt be recompensed in the resurrection of the just." [15]

---

[1] Matt. x. 42.
[2] Matt. v. 42.
[3] Matt. xix. 17–21.
[4] The Oxford edition inserts here, "an hungered, and fed Thee : thirsty, and gave Thee drink? when saw we Thee —"

[5] Matt. xxv. 31–46.
[6] Luke xii. 33.
[7] Luke xi. 40, 41.
[8] Luke xix. 8, 9.
[9] 2 Cor. viii. 14, 15.
[10] 2 Cor. ix. 6, 7.
[11] 2 Cor. ix. 9.
[12] 2 Cor. ix. 10, 11.
[13] 2 Cor. ix. 12.
[14] 1 John iii. 17.
[15] Luke xiv. 12–14.

2. In works and alms, even if by smallness of power less be done, that the will itself is sufficient.

In the second Epistle of Paul to the Corinthians : " If there be a ready will, it is acceptable according to what a man hath, not according to that which he hath not ; nor let there be to others a mitigation, but to you a burdening.[1]

3. That charity and brotherly affection are to be religiously and stedfastly practised.

In Malachi : " Hath not one God created us? Is there not one Father of us all ? Why have ye certainly deserted every one his brother ? "[2] Of this same thing according to John : " Peace I leave with you, my peace I give unto you."[3] Also in the same place : "This is my commandment, That ye love one another, even as I have loved you. Greater love than this has no man, than that one should lay down his life for his friends."[4] Also in the same place : " Blessed are the peacemakers, for they shall be called the sons of God."[5] Also in the same place : "Verily I say unto you, That if two of you shall agree on earth concerning everything, whatever you shall ask it shall be given you from my Father which is in heaven. For wherever two or three are gathered together in my name, I am with them."[6] Of this same thing in the first Epistle to the Corinthians : " And I indeed, brethren, could not speak unto you as to spiritual, but as to carnal, as to babes in Christ. I have given you milk for drink, not meat : for while ye were yet little ye were not able to bear it, neither now are ye able. For ye are still carnal : for where there are in you emulation, and strife, and dissensions, are ye not carnal, and walk after man ? "[7] Likewise in the same place : " And if I should have all faith, so that I can remove mountains, but have not charity, I am nothing. And if I should distribute all my goods for food, and if I should deliver up my body to be burned, but have not charity, I avail nothing. Charity is great-souled ; charity is kind ; charity envieth not ; charity dealeth not falsely ; is not puffed up ; is not irritated ; thinketh not evil ; rejoiceth not in injustice, but rejoiceth in the truth. It loveth all things, believeth all things, hopeth all things, beareth all things. Charity shall never fail."[8] Of this same thing to the Galatians : " Thou shalt love thy neighbour as thyself. But if ye bite and accuse one another, see that ye be not consumed one of another."[9] Of this same thing

in the Epistle of John : " In this appear the children of God and the children of the devil. Whosoever is not righteous is not of God, and he who loveth not his brother. For he who hateth his brother is a murderer ; and ye know that no murderer hath eternal life abiding in him."[10] Also in the same place : " If any one shall say that he loves God, and hates his brother, he is a liar : for he who loveth not his brother whom he seeth, how can he love God whom he seeth not ? "[11] Of this same thing in the Acts of the Apostles : " But the multitude of them that had believed acted with one soul and mind : nor was there among them any distinction, neither did they esteem as their own anything of the possessions that they had ; but all things were common to them."[12] Of this same thing in the Gospel according to Matthew : If thou wouldest offer thy gift at the altar, and there rememberest that thy brother hath ought against thee ; leave thou thy gift before the altar, and go ; first be reconciled to thy brother, and then come and offer thy gift at the altar."[13] Also in the Epistle of John : "God is love ; and he that dwelleth in love dwelleth in God, and God in him."[14] Also in the same place : " He who saith he is in the light, and hateth his brother, is a liar, and walketh in darkness even until now."[15]

4. That we must boast in nothing, since nothing is our own.

In the Gospel according to John : " No one can receive anything, except it were given him from heaven."[16] Also in the first Epistle of Paul to the Corinthians : "For what hast thou that thou hast not received? But if thou hast received it, why boastest thou, as if thou hadst not received it ? "[17] Also in the first of Kings : " Boast not, neither speak lofty things, and let not great speeches proceed out of your mouth, for the Lord is a God of knowledge."[18] Also in the same place : "The bow of the mighty men has been made weak, and the weak are girt about with strength."[18] Of this same thing in the Maccabees : " It is just to be subjected to God, and that a mortal should not think things equal to God."[19] Also in the same place : " And fear not the words of a man that is a sinner, because his glory shall be filth and worms. To-day he shall be lifted up, and to-morrow he shall not be found ; because he is turned into his earth, and his thought has perished."[20]

---

1 2 Cor. viii. 12, 13.
2 Mal. ii. 10.
3 John xiv. 27.
4 John xv. 12, 13.
5 Matt. v. 9.
6 Matt. xviii. 19, 20.
7 1 Cor. iii. 1–3.
8 1 Cor. xiii. 2–8.
9 Gal. v. 14, 15.

10 1 John iii. 10, 15.
11 1 John iv. 20.
12 Acts. iv. 32.
13 Matt. v. 23, 24. [I think this harmonizes with Heb. xiii. 10.]
14 1 John iv. 16.
15 1 John ii. 9.
16 John iii. 27.
17 1 Cor. iv. 7.
18 1 Sam. ii. 3, 4.
19 2 Macc. ix. 12.
20 1 Macc. ii. 62, 63.

5. That humility and quietness are to be maintained in all things.

In Isaiah: "Thus saith the Lord God, The heaven is my throne, and the earth is the stool of my feet. What seat will ye build for me, or what is the place for my rest? For all those things hath my hand made, and all those things are mine. And upon whom else will I look, except upon the lowly and quiet man, and him that trembleth at my words?"[1] On this same thing in the Gospel according to Matthew: "Blessed are the meek, for they shall inherit the earth."[2] Of this same thing, too, according to Luke: "He that shall be least among you all, the same shall be great."[3] Also in the same place: "Whosoever exalteth himself shall be made low, and whosoever abaseth himself shall be exalted."[4] Of this same thing to the Romans: "Be not high-minded, but fear; for if God spared not the natural branches, (take heed) lest He also spare not thee."[5] Of this same thing in the thirty-third Psalm: "And He shall save the lowly in spirit."[6] Also to the Romans: "Render to all what is due: tribute to whom tribute is due, custom to whom custom, fear to whom fear, honour to whom honour; owe no man anything, except to love another."[7] Also in the Gospel according to Matthew: "They love the first place of reclining at feasts, and the chief seat in the synagogues, and salutations in the market, and to be called of men Rabbi. But call not ye Rabbi, for One is your Master."[8] Also in the Gospel according to John: "The servant is not greater than his lord, nor the apostle greater than He that sent himself. ·If ye know these things, blessed shall ye be if ye shall do them."[9] Also in the eighty-first Psalm: "Do justice to the poor and lowly."[10]

6. That all good and righteous men suffer more, but ought to endure because they are proved.

In Solomon: "The furnace proveth the vessels of the potter, and the trial of tribulation righteous men."[11] Also in the fiftieth Psalm: "The sacrifice to God is a contrite spirit; a contrite and humbled heart God will not despise."[12] Also in the thirty-third Psalm: "God is nearest to them that are contrite in heart, and

He will save the lowly in spirit."[13] Also in the same place: "Many are the afflictions of the righteous, but out of them all the Lord will deliver them."[14] Of this same matter in Job: "Naked came I out of my mother's womb, naked also shall I go under the earth: the Lord gave, and the Lord hath taken away: as it hath pleased the Lord, so it is done; blessed be the name of the Lord. In all these things which happened to him Job sinned in nothing with his lips in the sight of the Lord."[15] Concerning this same thing in the Gospel according to Matthew: "Blessed are they that mourn, for they shall be comforted."[16] Also according to John: "These things have I spoken unto you, that in me ye may have peace. But in the world ye shall have affliction; but have confidence, for I have overcome the world."[17] Concerning this same thing in the second Epistle to the Corinthians: "There was given to me a thorn in the flesh, a messenger of Satan to buffet me, that I should not be exalted. For which thing I thrice besought the Lord, that it should depart from me. And He said unto me, My grace is sufficient for thee; for strength is perfected in weakness."[18] Concerning this same thing to the Romans: "We glory in hope of the glory of God. And not only so, but we also glory in afflictions: knowing that affliction worketh patience; and patience, experience; and experience, hope: and hope does not confound; because the love of God is infused in our hearts by the Holy Spirit, which is given unto us."[19] On this same subject, according to Matthew: "How broad and spacious is the way which leadeth unto death, and many there are who go in thereby: how straight and narrow is the way that leadeth to life, and few there are that find it!"[20] Of this same thing in Tobias: "Where are thy righteousnesses? behold what thou sufferest."[21] Also in the Wisdom of Solomon: "In the places of the wicked the righteous groan; but at their ruin the righteous will abound."[22]

7. That we must not grieve the Holy Spirit, whom we have received.

Paul the apostle to the Ephesians: "Grieve not the Holy Spirit of God, in which ye were sealed in the day of redemption. Let all bitterness, and wrath, and indignation, and clamour, and blasphemy, be taken away from you."[23]

---

[1] Isa. lxvi. 1, 2.
[2] Matt. v. 5.
[3] Luke ix. 48.
[4] Luke xiv. 11.
[5] Rom. xi. 20, 21.
[6] Ps. xxxiv. 18.
[7] Rom. xiii. 7, 8.
[8] Matt. xxiii. 6–8.
[9] John xiii. 16, 17.
[10] Ps. lxxxii. 3.
[11] Ecclus. xxvii. 5.
[12] Ps. li. 17.

[13] Ps. xxxiv. 18.
[14] Ps. xxxiv. 19.
[15] Job i. 21, 22.
[16] Matt. v. 4.
[17] John xvi. 33.
[18] 2 Cor. xii. 7–9.
[19] Rom. v. 2–5.
[20] Matt. vii. 13, 14.
[21] Tob. ii. 14.
[22] Prov. xxviii. 28.
[23] Eph. iv. 30, 31. [For the *sealing*, see Acts xix. 6, Heb. vi. 2.]

8. That anger must be overcome, lest it constrain us to sin.

In Solomon in the Proverbs: "Better is a patient man than a strong man; for he who restrains his anger is better than he who taketh a city."[1] Also in the same place: "The imprudent man declareth his anger on the same day, but the crafty man hideth away his dishonour."[2] Of this same thing to the Ephesians: "Be ye angry, and sin not. Let not the sun set upon your wrath."[3] Also in the Gospel according to Matthew: "Ye have heard that it was said by the ancients, Thou shalt not kill; and whoever shall kill shall be guilty of the judgment. But I say unto you, That every one who is angry with his brother without cause shall be guilty of the judgment."[4]

9. That brethren ought to support one another.

To the Galatians: "Each one having others in consideration, lest ye also should be tempted. Bear ye one another's burdens, and so ye shall fulfil the law of Christ."[5]

10. That we must trust in God only, and in Him we must glory.

In Jeremiah: "Let not the wise man glory in his wisdom, neither let the strong man glory in his strength, nor let the rich man glory in his riches; but let him that glorieth glory in this, that he understands and knows that I am the Lord, who do mercy, and judgment, and righteousness upon the earth, because in them is my pleasure, saith the Lord."[6] Of the same thing in the fifty-fourth Psalm: "In the Lord have I hoped; I will not fear what man can do unto me."[7] Also in the same place: "To none but God alone is my soul subjected."[8] Also in the cxviith Psalm: "I will not fear what man can do unto me; the Lord is my helper."[9] Also in the same place: "It is good to trust in the Lord rather than to trust in man; it is good to hope in the Lord rather than to hope in princes."[10] Of this same thing in Daniel: "But Shadrach, Meshach, and Abednego answered and said to king Nebuchadnezzar, O king, there is no need to answer thee concerning this word. For God, whom we serve, is able to deliver us from the furnace of burning fire; and He will deliver us from thine hand, O

king. And if not, be it known unto thee that we serve not thy gods, and we adore not the golden image which thou hast set up."[11] Likewise in Jeremiah: "Cursed is the man who hath hope in man; and blessed is the man who trusts in the Lord, and his hope shall be in God."[12] Concerning this same thing in Deuteronomy: "Thou shalt worship the Lord thy God, and Him only shalt thou serve."[13] Of this same thing to the Romans: "And they worshipped and served the creature, forsaking the Creator. Wherefore also God gave them up to ignominious passions."[14] Of this thing also in John: "Greater is He who is in you than he who is in this world."[15]

11. That he who has attained to trust, having put off the former man, ought to regard only celestial and spiritual things, and to give no heed to the world which he has already renounced.

In Isaiah: "Seek ye the Lord; and when ye have found Him, call upon Him. But when He hath come near unto you, let the wicked forsake his ways, and the unrighteous man his thoughts: and let him be turned unto the Lord, and he shall obtain mercy, because He will plentifully pardon your sins."[16] Of this same thing in Solomon: "I have seen all the works which are done under the sun; and, lo, all are vanity."[17] Of this same thing in Exodus: "But thus shall ye eat it; your loins girt, and your shoes on your feet, and your staves in your hands: and ye shall eat it in haste, for it is the Lord's passover."[18] Of this same thing in the Gospel according to Matthew: "Take no thought, saying, What shall we eat? or, What shall we drink? or, Wherewith shall we be clothed? for these things the nations seek after. But your Father knoweth that ye have need of all these things. Seek first the kingdom of God, and His righteousness; and all these things shall be added unto you."[19] Likewise in the same place: "Think not for the morrow, for the morrow shall take thought for itself. Sufficient unto the day is its own evil."[20] Likewise in the same place: "No one looking back, and putting his hands to the plough, is fit for the kingdom of God."[21] Also in the same place: "Behold the fowls of the heaven: for they sow not, nor reap, nor gather into barns; and your heavenly Father feedeth

---

[1] Prov. xvi. 32.
[2] Prov. xii. 16.
[3] Eph. iv. 26.
[4] Matt. v. 21, 22.
[5] Gal. vi. 1, 2.
[6] Jer. ix. 23, 24.
[7] Ps. lvi. 11.
[8] Ps. lxii. 1.
[9] Ps. cxviii. 6.
[10] Ps. cxviii. 8.

[11] Dan. iii. 16-18.
[12] Jer. xvii. 5-7.
[13] Deut. vi. 13.
[14] Rom. i. 25, 26.
[15] 1 John iv. 4.
[16] Isa. lv. 6, 7.
[17] Eccles. i. 14.
[18] Ex. xii. 11.
[19] Matt. vi. 31-33.
[20] Matt. vi. 34.
[21] Luke ix. 62.

them. Are not ye of more value than they?"[1] Concerning this same thing, according to Luke: "Let your loins be girded, and your lamps burning; and ye like unto men that wait for their lord, when he cometh from the wedding; that, when he cometh and knocketh, they may open to him. Blessed are those servants, whom their lord, when he cometh, shall find watching."[2] Of this same thing in Matthew: "The foxes have holes, and the birds of the heaven have nests; but the Son of man hath not where He may lay His head."[3] Also in the same place: "Whoso forsaketh not all that he hath, cannot be my disciple."[4] Of this same thing in the first to the Corinthians: "Ye are not your own, for ye are bought with a great price. Glorify and bear God in your body."[5] Also in the same place: "The time is limited. It remaineth, therefore, that both they who have wives be as though they have them not, and they who lament as they that lament not, and they that rejoice as they that rejoice not, and they who buy as they that buy not, and they who possess as they who possess not, and they who use this world as they that use it not; for the fashion of this world passeth away."[6] Also in the same place: "The first man is of the clay of the earth, the second man from heaven. As he is of the clay, such also are they who are of the clay; and as is the heavenly, such also are the heavenly. Even as we have borne the image of him who is of the clay, let us bear His image also who is from heaven."[7] Of this same matter to the Philippians: "All seek their own, and not those things which are Christ's; whose end is destruction, whose god is their belly, and their glory is to their confusion, who mind earthly things. For our conversation is in heaven, whence also we expect the Saviour, our Lord Jesus Christ, who shall transform the body of our humiliation conformed to the body of His glory."[8] Of this very matter to Galatians: "But be it far from me to boast, except in the cross of our Lord Jesus Christ, by whom the world is crucified unto me, and I unto the world."[9] Concerning this same thing to Timothy: "No man that warreth for God bindeth himself with worldly annoyances, that he may please Him to whom he hath approved himself. But and if a man should contend, he will not be crowned unless he fight lawfully."[10] Of this same thing to the Colossians: "If ye be dead with Christ from the elements of the world, why still, as if living in the world, do ye follow vain things?"[11] Also concerning this same thing: "If ye have risen together with Christ, seek those things which are above, where Christ is sitting on the right hand of God. Give heed to the things that are above, not to those things which are on the earth; for ye are dead, and your life is hidden with Christ in God. But when Christ your life shall appear, then shall ye also appear with Him in glory."[12] Of this same thing to the Ephesians: "Put off the old man of the former conversation, who is corrupted, according to the lusts of deceit. But be ye renewed in the spirit of your mind, and put on the new man, him who according to God is ordained in righteousness, and holiness, and truth."[13] Of this same thing in the Epistle of Peter: "As strangers and pilgrims, abstain from fleshly lusts, which war against the soul; but having a good conversation among the Gentiles, that while they detract from you as if from evildoers, yet, beholding your good works, they may magnify God."[14] Of this same thing in the Epistle of John: "He who saith he abideth in Christ, ought himself also to walk even as He walked."[15] Also in the same place: "Love not the world, neither the things that are in the world. If any man loveth the world, the love of the Father is not in him. Because everything which is in the world is lust of the flesh, and lust of the eyes, and the ambition of this world, which is not of the Father, but of the lust of this world. And the world shall pass away with its lust. But he that doeth the will of God abideth for ever, even as God abideth for ever."[16] Also in the first Epistle of Paul to the Corinthians: "Purge out the old leaven, that ye may be a new dough, as ye are unleavened. For also Christ our passover is sacrificed. Therefore let us celebrate the feast, not in the old leaven, nor in the leaven of malice and wickedness, but in the unleavened bread of sincerity and truth."[17]

12. That we must not swear.

In Solomon: "A man that sweareth much shall be filled with iniquity, and the plague shall not depart from his house; and if he swear vainly, he shall not be justified."[18] Of this same matter, according to Matthew: "(Again, ye have heard that it was said to them of old, Thou shalt not swear falsely, but shalt perform unto the Lord thine oaths.) I say unto you, Swear not at all: (neither by heaven, because it is God's throne; nor by the earth, because it is His footstool; nor

---

[1] Matt. vi. 26.
[2] Luke xii. 35-37.
[3] Matt. viii. 20.
[4] Luke xiv. 33.
[5] 1 Cor. vi. 19, 20.
[6] 1 Cor. vii. 29-31.
[7] 1 Cor. xv. 47-49.
[8] Phil. ii. 21, iii. 19-21.
[9] Gal. vi. 14.
[10] 2 Tim. ii. 4, 5.

[11] Col. ii. 20.
[12] Col. iii. 1-4.
[13] Eph. iv. 22-24.
[14] 2 Pet. ii. 11, 12.
[15] 1 John ii. 6.
[16] 1 John ii. 15-17.
[17] 1 Cor v. 7, 8.
[18] Ecclus. xxiii. 11. From some ancient text the Oxford edition adds here, "Et si frustra juraverit dupliciter punietur" — "and if he swear with no purpose, he shall be punished doubly."

by Jerusalem, because it is the city of the great King; neither shalt thou swear by thy head, because thou canst not make one hair white or black.) But let your discourse be, Yea, yea; Nay, nay: (for whatever is fuller than these is of evil.")[1] Of this same thing in Exodus: "Thou shalt not take the name of the Lord thy God in vain."[2]

13. That we must not curse.

In Exodus: "Thou shalt not curse nor speak ill of the ruler of thy people."[3] Also in the thirty-third Psalm: "Who is the man who desires life, and loveth to see good days? Restrain thy tongue from evil, and thy lips that they speak no guile."[4] Of this same thing in Leviticus: "And the Lord spoke to Moses, saying, Bring forth him who hath cursed abroad outside the camp; and all who heard him shall place their hands upon his head, and all the assembly of the children of Israel shall stone him."[5] Of this same thing in Paul's Epistle to the Ephesians: "Let no evil discourse proceed out of your mouth, but that which is good for the edification of faith, that it may give grace to the hearers."[6] Of this same thing to the Romans: "Blessing, and not cursing."[7] Of this same thing in the Gospel according to Matthew: "He who shall say to his brother, Thou fool! shall be liable to the Gehenna of fire."[8] Of this same matter, according to the same Matthew: "But I say unto you, That every idle word which men shall speak, they shall give account for it in the day of judgment. For by thy words thou shalt be justified, and by thy words thou shalt be condemned."[9]

14. That we must never murmur, but bless God concerning all things that happen.

In Job: "Say some word against the Lord, and die. But he, looking upon her, said, Thou speakest as one of the foolish women. If we have received good things from the Lord's hand, why shall we not endure evil things? In all these things which happened unto him, Job sinned not with his lips in the sight of the Lord."[10] Also in the same place: "Hast thou regarded my servant Job? for there is none like unto him in the earth: a man without complaint: a true worshipper of God, restraining himself from all evil."[11] Of the same thing in the thirty-third

Psalm: "I will bless the Lord at all times: His praise shall ever be in my mouth."[12] Of this same thing in Numbers: "Let their murmuring cease from me, and they shall not die."[13] Of this same thing in the Acts of the Apostles: "But about the middle of the night Paul and Silas prayed and gave thanks to God, and the prisoners heard them."[14] Also in the Epistle of Paul to the Philippians: "But doing all things for love, without murmurings and revilings,[15] that ye may be without complaint, and spotless sons of God."[16]

15. That men are tried by God for this purpose, that they may be proved.

In Genesis: "And God tempted Abraham, and said to him, Take thy only son whom thou lovest, Isaac, and go into the high land, and offer him there as a burnt-offering on one of the mountains of which I will tell thee."[17] Of this same thing in Deuteronomy: "The Lord your God proveth you, that He may know if ye love the Lord your God with all your heart, and with all your soul."[18] Of this same thing in the Wisdom of Solomon: "Although in the sight of men they suffered torments, their hope is full of immortality; and having been in few things distressed, yet in many things they shall be happily ordered, because God tried them, and found them worthy of Himself. As gold in the furnace He proved them, and as a burnt-offering He received them. And in their time there shall be respect of them; they shall judge the nations, and shall rule over the people; and their Lord shall reign for ever."[19] Of this same thing in the Maccabees: "Was not Abraham found faithful in temptation, and it was accounted unto him for righteousness?"[20]

16. Of the benefits of martyrdom.

In the Proverbs of Solomon: "The faithful martyr delivers his soul from evils."[21] Also in the same place: "Then shall the righteous stand in great boldness against them who have afflicted them, and who took away their labours. When they see them, they shall be disturbed with a horrible fear; and they shall wonder at the suddenness of their unhoped-for salvation, saying among themselves, repenting and groaning with distress of spirit, These are they whom some time we had in derision, and in the likeness of a proverb; we fools counted their life madness,

[1] Matt. v. 34-37. All these passages are wanting in the Oxford text; [also in ed. Paris, 1574].
[2] Ex. xx. 7. [Compare old Paris ed. on this section.]
[3] Ex. xxii. 28.
[4] Ps. xxxiv. 12, 13.
[5] Lev. xxiv. 13, 14.
[6] Eph. iv. 29.
[7] Rom. xii. 14.
[8] Matt. v. 22.
[9] Matt. xii. 36, 37.
[10] Job ii. 9, 10.
[11] Job i. 8.

[12] Ps. xxxiv. 1.
[13] Num. xvii. 10.
[14] Acts xvi. 25.
[15] Reputationibus; possibly "complainings."
[16] Phil. ii. 14, 15.
[17] Gen. xxii. 1, 2.
[18] Deut. xiii. 3.
[19] Wisd. iii. 4-8.
[20] 1 Macc. ii. 52.
[21] Prov. xiv. 25.

and their end without honour. How are they reckoned among the children of God, and their lot among the saints! Therefore we have wandered from the way of truth, and the light of righteousness has not shined upon us, and the sun has not risen upon us. We have been wearied in the way of iniquity and of perdition, and we have walked through difficult solitudes; but we have not known the way of the Lord. What hath pride profited us? or what hath the boasting of riches brought to us? All these things have passed away as a shadow." [1] Of this same thing in the cxvth Psalm: "Precious in the sight of the Lord is the death of His saints." [2] Also in the cxxvth Psalm: "They who sow in tears shall reap in joy. Walking they walked, and wept as they cast their seeds; but coming they shall come in joy, raising up their laps." [3] Of this same thing in the Gospel according to John: "He who loveth his life shall lose it; and he that hateth his life in this world shall find it to life eternal." [4] Also in the same place: "But when they shall deliver you up, take no thought what ye shall speak; for it is not ye who speak, but the Spirit of your Father which speaketh in you." [5] Also in the same place: "The hour shall come, that every one that killeth you shall think he doeth service to God; but they shall do this also because they have not known the Father nor me." [6] Of this same matter, according to Matthew: "Blessed are they which shall suffer persecution for righteousness' sake; for theirs is the kingdom of heaven." [7] Also in the same place: "Fear not them which kill the body, but are not able to kill the soul; but rather fear Him which is able to kill the soul and body in Gehenna." [8] Also in the same place: "Whosoever shall confess me before men, him also will I confess before my Father which is in heaven; but he who shall deny me before men, him also will I deny before my Father which is in heaven. And he that shall endure to the end, the same shall be saved." [9] Of this same thing, according to Luke: "Blessed shall ye be when men shall hate you, and shall separate you (from their company), and shall drive you out, and shall speak evil of your name, as wicked, for the Son of man's sake. Rejoice in that day, and exult; for, lo, your reward is great in heaven." [10] Also in the same place: "Verily I say unto you, There is no man that leaveth house, or parents, or brethren, or wife, or children, for the sake of the kingdom of God, and does not receive seven times as much in this present time, but in the world to come life everlasting." [11] Of this same thing in the Apocalypse: "And when he had opened the fifth seal, I saw under the altar of God the souls of them that were slain on account of the word of God and His testimony. And they cried with a loud voice, saying, How long, O Lord, holy and true, dost Thou not judge and avenge our blood on them that dwell on the earth? And unto every one of them were given white robes; and it was said to them, that they should rest still for a short time, until the number of their fellow-servants, and of their brethren, should be fulfilled, and they who shall afterwards be slain, after their example." [12] Also in the same place: "After these things I saw a great crowd, which no one among them could number, from every nation, and from every tribe, and from every people and tongue, standing before the throne and before the Lamb; and they were clothed with white robes, and palms were in their hands. And they said with a loud voice, Salvation to our God, that sitteth upon the throne, and to the Lamb. And one of the elders answered and said to me, What are these which are clothed with white robes? who are they, and whence have they come? And I said unto him, My lord, thou knowest. And he said unto me, These are they who have come out of great tribulation, and have washed their robes, and made them white in the blood of the Lamb. Therefore they are before the throne of God, and serve Him day and night in His temple; and He who sitteth upon the throne shall dwell among them. They shall neither hunger nor thirst ever; and neither shall the sun fall upon them, nor shall they suffer any heat: for the Lamb who is in the midst of the throne shall protect them, and shall lead them to the fountains of the waters of life; and God shall wipe away every tear from their eyes." [13] Also in the same place: "He who shall overcome I will give him to eat of the tree of life, which is in the paradise of my God." [14] Also in the same place: "Be thou faithful even unto death, and I will give thee a crown of life." [15] Also in the same place: "Blessed shall they be who shall watch, and shall keep their garments, lest they walk naked, and they see their shame." [16] Of this same thing, Paul in the second Epistle to Timothy: "I am now offered up, and the time of my assumption is at hand. I have fought a good fight, I have finished my course, I have kept the faith. There now remains for me a crown of righteousness, which the Lord, the righteous Judge, will give

---

[1] Wisd. v. 1-9.
[2] Ps. cxvi. 5.
[3] Ps. cxxvi. 5, 6.
[4] John xii. 25.
[5] Matt. x. 19, 20.
[6] John xvi. 2, 3.
[7] Matt. v. 10.
[8] Matt. x. 28.
[9] Matt. x. 32, 33.
[10] Luke vi. 22, 23.

[11] Luke xviii. 29, 30.
[12] Rev. vi. 9-11.
[13] Rev. vii. 9-17.
[14] Rev. ii. 7.
[15] Rev. ii. 10.
[16] Rev. xvi. 15.

me in that day; and not only to me, but to all also who love His appearing." [1] Of this same thing to the Romans: "We are the sons of God: but if sons and heirs of God, we are also joint-heirs with Christ; if we suffer together, that we may also be magnified together." [2] Of this same thing in the cxviiith Psalm: "Blessed are they who are undefiled in the way, and walk in the law of the Lord. Blessed are they who search into His testimonies." [3]

17. That what we suffer in this world is of less account than is the reward which is promised.

In the Epistle of Paul to the Romans: "The sufferings of this present time are not worthy of comparison with the glory that is to come after, which shall be revealed in us." [4] Of this same thing in the Maccabees: "O Lord, who hast the holy knowledge, it is manifest that while I might be delivered from death, I am suffering most cruel pains of body, being beaten with whips; yet in spirit I suffer these things willingly, because of the fear of thine own self." [5] Also in the same place: "Thou indeed, being power-less, destroyest us out of this present life; but the King of the world shall raise us up who have died for His laws into the eternal resurrection of life." [6] Also in the same place: "It is better that, given up to death by men, we should expect hope from God to be raised again by Him. For there shall be no resurrection to life for thee." [7] Also in the same place: "Having power among men, although thou art corruptible, thou doest what thou wilt. But think not that our race is forsaken of God. Sustain, and see how His great power will torment thee and thy seed." [8] Also in the same place: "Do not err without cause; for we suffer these things on our own accounts, as sinners against our God. But think not thou that thou shalt be unpunished, having undertaken to fight against God." [9]

18. That nothing is to be preferred to the love of God and Christ.

In Deuteronomy: "Thou shalt love the Lord thy God with all thy heart, and with all thy soul, and with all thy might." [10] Also in the Gospel according to Matthew: "He that loveth father or mother above me, is not worthy of me; and he that loveth son or daughter above me, is not worthy of me; and he that taketh not up his cross and followeth me, is not my disciple." [11] Also in the Epistle of Paul to the Romans: "Who shall separate us from the love of Christ? shall tribulation, or distress, or persecution, or famine, or nakedness, or peril, or sword? As it is written, Because for thy sake we are killed all the day long, we are counted as sheep for the slaughter. But in all these things we are more than conquerors for His sake who loved us." [12]

19. That we are not to obey our own will, but the will of God.

In the Gospel according to John: "I came not down from heaven to do mine own will, but the will of Him that sent me." [13] Of this same matter, according to Matthew: "Father, if it be possible, let this cup pass from me; neverthe-less, not what I will, but what Thou wilt." [14] Also in the daily prayer: "Thy will be done, as in heaven, so in earth." [15] Also according to Mat-thew: "Not every one who saith unto me, Lord, Lord, shall enter into the kingdom of heaven; but he who doeth the will of my Father which is in heaven, he shall enter into the kingdom of heaven." [16] Also according to Luke: "But that servant which knoweth his Lord's will, and obeyed not His will, shall be beaten with many stripes." [17] In the Epistle of John: "But he that doeth the will of God abideth for ever, even as He Him-self also abideth for ever." [18]

20. That the foundation and strength of hope and faith is fear.

In the cxth Psalm: "The fear of the Lord is the beginning of wisdom." [19] Of the same thing in the Wisdom of Solomon: "The beginning of wisdom is to fear God." [20] Also in the Proverbs of the same: "Blessed is the man who rever-ences all things with fear." [21] Of the same thing in Isaiah: "And upon whom else will I look, except upon him that is lowly and peaceful, and that trembleth at my words?" [22] Of this same thing in Genesis: "And the angel of the Lord called him from heaven, and said unto him, Abraham, Abraham: and he said, Here am I. And he said, Lay not thine hand upon the lad, neither do anything unto him: for now I know that thou fearest thy God, and hast not spared thy beloved son for my sake." [23] Also in the second Psalm: "Serve the Lord in fear, and

---

[1] 2 Tim. iv. 6-8.
[2] Rom. viii. 16, 17.
[3] Ps. cxix. 1, 2.
[4] Rom. viii. 18.
[5] 2 Macc. vi. 30.
[6] 2 Macc. vii. 9.
[7] 2 Macc. vii. 14.
[8] 2 Macc. vii. 16, 17.
[9] 2 Macc. vii. 18, 19.
[10] Deut. vi. 5.

[11] Matt. x. 37, 38.
[12] Rom. viii. 35-37.
[13] John vi. 38.
[14] Matt. xxvi. 39.
[15] Matt. vi. 10.
[16] Matt. vii. 21.
[17] Luke xii. 47.
[18] 1 John ii. 17.
[19] Ps. cxi. 10. [Tertull., vol. iii. 264.]
[20] Ecclus. i. 14.
[21] Prov. xxviii. 14.
[22] Isa. lxvi. 2.
[23] Gen. xxii. 11, 12.

rejoice unto Him in trembling." [1] Also in Deuteronomy, the word of God to Moses: "Call the people together to me, and let them hear my words, that they may learn to fear me all the days that they themselves shall live upon the earth." [2] Also in Jeremiah: "Behold, the days come, saith the Lord, that I will perfect upon the house of Israel, and in the house of Judah, a new covenant: not according to the covenant that I had ordered with their fathers in the day when I laid hold of their hand to bring them out of the land of Egypt; because they have not abode in my covenant, and I have been unmindful of them, saith the Lord; because this is the covenant which I will ordain for the house of Israel; After those days, saith the Lord, I will give my law, and will write it in their mind; and I will be to them for a God, and they shall be to me for a people. And they shall not teach every man his brother, saying, Know the Lord: because all shall know me, from the least even to the greatest of them: because I will be favourable to their iniquities, and their sins I will not remember any more. If the heaven should be lifted up on high, saith the Lord, and if the earth should be made low from beneath, yet I will not cast away the people of Israel, saith the Lord, for all the things which they have done. Behold, I will gather them together from every land in which I have scattered them in anger, and in my fury, and in great indignation; and I will grind them down into that place, and I will leave them in fear; and they shall be to me for a people, and I will be to them for a God: and I will give them another way, and another heart, that they may fear me all their days in prosperity with their children: and I will perfect for them an everlasting covenant, which I will not turn away after them; and I will put my fear into their heart, that they may not depart from me: and I will visit upon them to do them good, and to plant them in their land in faith, and with all the heart, and with all the mind." [3] Also in the Apocalypse: "And the four and twenty elders which sit on their thrones in the sight (of God), fell upon their faces, and worshipped God, saying, We give Thee thanks, O Lord God omnipotent, which art and which wast; because Thou hast taken Thy great power, and hast reigned. And the nations were angry, and Thy wrath is come, and the time in which it should be judged concerning the dead, and the reward should be given to Thy servants the prophets, and the saints that fear Thy name, small and great; and to disperse those who have corrupted the earth." [4]

Also in the same place: "And I saw another angel flying through the midst of the heaven, having the everlasting Gospel to preach to those who dwell upon the earth, and to all the nations, and tribes, and tongues, and peoples, saying with a loud voice, Fear God, and give Him honour, because the hour of His judgment is come; and adore Him who made the heaven, and the earth, and the sea, and the fountains of waters." [5] Also in the same place: "And I saw as it were a sea of glass mingled with fire; and the beasts were feeding with His lambs; [6] and the number of His name a hundred and forty and four, standing upon the sea of glass, having the harps of God; and they sing the song of Moses, the servant of God, and the song of the Lamb, saying, Great and marvellous are Thy works, O Lord God Almighty; just and true are Thy ways, Thou King of the nations. Who would not fear Thee, and give honour to Thy name? for Thou only art holy: and because all nations shall come and worship in Thy sight, because Thy righteousnesses have been made manifest." [7] Also in Daniel: "There was a man dwelling in Babylon whose name was Joachim; and he took a wife by name Susanna, the daughter of Helchias, a very beautiful woman, and one that feared the Lord. And her parents were righteous, and taught their daughter according to the law of Moses." [8] Moreover, in Daniel: "And we are lowly this day in all the earth because of our sins, and there is not at this time any prince, or prophet, or leader, or burnt-offering, or oblation, or sacrifice, or incense, or place to sacrifice before Thee, and to find mercy from Thee. And yet in the soul and spirit of lowliness let us be accepted as the burnt-offerings of rams and bulls, and as it were many thousands of lambs which are fattest. If our offering may be made in Thy presence this day, their power shall be consumed, for they shall not be ashamed who put their trust in Thee. And now we follow with our whole heart, and we fear and seek Thy face. Give us not over unto reproach, but do with us according to Thy tranquillity, and according to the multitude of Thy mercy deliver us." [9] Also in the same place: "And the king exceedingly rejoiced, and commanded Daniel to be taken up out of the den of lions; and the lions had done him no hurt, because he trusted and had believed in his God. And the king commanded, and they brought those men who had accused Daniel; and they cast them in the den of lions, and their wives and their children. And before they had

---

[1] Ps. ii. 11. The whole of the remainder of this section, except the two concluding quotations from the Psalms, is wanting in many editions.
[2] Deut. iv. 10.
[3] Jer. xxxi. 31-41.
[4] Rev. xi. 16, 17.

[5] Rev. xiv. 16, 17.
[6] There is considerable departure here from the Apocalyptic text, for which it is not easy to account. [But this is an interesting fact as bearing upon the question of an original African version made from a family of MSS. now extinct.]
[7] Rev. xv. 2-4.
[8] Hist. of Susannah, 1-3.
[9] Song of the Three Children, 14-19.

reached the pavement of the den they were seized by the lions, and they brake all their bones in pieces. Then Darius the king wrote, To all peoples, tribes, and languages which are in my kingdom, peace be unto you from my face. I decree and ordain that all those who are in my kingdom shall fear and tremble before the most high God whom Daniel serves, because He is the God who liveth and abideth for ever, and His kingdom shall not pass away, and His dominion goeth on for ever; and He alone doeth signs, and prodigies, and marvellous things in the heaven and the earth, who snatched Daniel from the den of lions." [1] Also in Micah : "Wherewith shall I approach the Lord, and lay hold upon Him? in sacrifices, in burnt-offerings, in calves of a year old? Does the Lord favour and receive me with thousands of fat goats? or shall I give my first-fruits of unrighteousness, the fruit of my belly, the sin of my soul? It is told thee, O man, what is good ; or what else the Lord doth require, save that thou shouldst do judgment and justice, and love mercy, and be ready to go with the Lord thy God. The voice of the Lord shall be invoked in the city, and He will save those who fear His name." [2] Also in Micah : "Feed Thy people with Thy rod, the sheep of Thine inheritance ; and pluck up those who dwell separately in the midst of Carmel. They shall prepare Bashan and Gilead according to the days of the age ; and according to the days of their going forth from the land of Egypt I will show them wonderful things. The nations shall see, and be confounded at all their might ; and they shall place their hand upon their mouth. Their ears shall be deafened, and they shall lick the dust as do serpents. Dragging the earth, they shall be disturbed, and they shall lick the dust : in their end they shall be afraid towards the Lord their God, and they shall fear because of Thee. Who is a God as Thou art, raising up unrighteousness, and passing over impiety?" [3] And in Nahum : "The mountains were moved at Him, and the hills trembled ; and the earth was laid bare before His face, and all who dwell therein. From the face of His anger who shall bear it, and who withstandeth in the fury of His soul? His rage causes the beginnings to flow, and the rocks were melted by Him. The Lord is good to those who sustain Him in the day of affliction, and knoweth those who fear Him." [4] Also in Haggai : "And Zerubbabel the son of Salathiel, of the tribe of Judah, and Jesus the son of Josedech, the high priest, and all who remained of the people, obeyed the voice of the Lord their God, because the Lord sent him to

them, and the people feared from the face of God." [5] Also in Malachi : "The covenant was with life and peace ; and I gave to them the fear to fear me from the face of my name." [6] Also in the thirty-third Psalm : "Fear the Lord, all ye His saints : for there is no want to them that fear Him." [7] Also in the eighteenth Psalm : "The fear of the Lord is chaste, abiding for ever." [8]

21. That we must not rashly judge of another.

In the Gospel according to Luke : "Judge not, that ye be not judged : condemn not, that ye be not condemned." [9] Of this same subject to the Romans : "Who art thou that judgest another man's servant? to his own master he standeth or falleth. But he shall stand ; for God is able to make him stand." [10] And again : "Wherefore thou art without excuse, O every man that judgest : for in that in which thou judgest another, thou condemnest thyself ; for thou doest the same things which thou judgest. But dost thou hope, who judgest those who do evil, and doest the same, that thou thyself shalt escape the judgment of God?" [11] Also in the first Epistle of Paul to the Corinthians : "And let him that thinketh he standeth take heed lest he fall." [12] And again : "If any man thinketh that he knoweth anything, he knoweth not yet in what manner he ought to know." [13]

22. That when we have received a wrong, we must remit and forgive it.

In the Gospel, in the daily prayer : "Forgive us our debts, even as we forgive our debtors." [14] Also according to Mark : "And when ye stand for prayer, forgive, if ye have ought against any one ; that also your Father who is in heaven may forgive you your sins. But if ye do not forgive, neither will your Father which is in heaven forgive you your sins." [15] Also in the same place : "In what measure ye mete, in that shall it be measured to you again." [16]

23. That evil is not to be returned for evil.

In the Epistle of Paul to the Romans : "Rendering to no man evil for evil." [17] Also in the same place : "Not to be overcome of evil, but overcome evil with good." [18] Of this same thing in the Apocalypse : "And He said unto me,

---

[1] Dan. vi. 24–28.
[2] Mic. vi. 6–9.
[3] Mic. vii. 14–18.
[4] Nah. i. 5–7.

[5] Hag. i. 12.
[6] Mal. ii. 5.
[7] Ps. xxxiv. 9.
[8] Ps. xix. 9.
[9] Luke vi. 37.
[10] Rom. xiv. 4.
[11] Rom. ii. 1–3.
[12] 1 Cor. x. 12.
[13] 1 Cor. viii. 2.
[14] Matt. vi. 12.
[15] Matt. xi. 25, 26.
[16] Mark iv. 24.
[17] Rom. xii. 17.
[18] Rom. xii. 21.

Seal not the words of the prophecy of this book; because now the time is at hand. And let those who persist in hurting, hurt: and let him who is filthy, be filthy still: but let the righteous do still more righteousness: and in like manner, let him that is holy do still more holiness. Behold, I come quickly; and my reward is with me, to render to every man according to his deeds."[1]

24. That it is impossible to attain to the Father but by His Son Jesus Christ.

In the Gospel according to John: "I am the way, the truth, and the life: no man cometh unto the Father, but by me."[2] Also in the same place: "I am the door: by me if any man enter in, he shall be saved."[3]

25. That unless a man have been baptized and born again, he cannot attain unto the kingdom of God.

In the Gospel according to John: "Except a man be born again of water and the Spirit, he cannot enter into the kingdom of God. For that which is born of the flesh is flesh; and that which is born of the Spirit is spirit."[4] Also in the same place: "Unless ye eat the flesh of the Son of man, and drink His blood, ye shall not have life in you."[5]

26. That it is of small account to be baptized and to receive the Eucharist, unless one profit by it both in deeds and works.

In the first Epistle of Paul to the Corinthians: "Know ye not, that they which run in a race run indeed all, although one receiveth the prize? So run, that ye may obtain. And those indeed that they may receive a corruptible crown, but we an incorruptible."[6] In the Gospel according to Matthew: "Every tree that bringeth not forth good fruit shall be cut down, and cast into the fire."[7] Also in the same place: "Many shall say unto me in that day, Lord, Lord, have we not prophesied in Thy name, and in Thy name have cast out devils, and in Thy name have done great works? And then shall I say to them, I never knew you; depart from me, ye who work iniquity."[8] Also in the same place: "Let your light shine before men, that they may see your good works, and glorify your Father which is in heaven."[9] Also Paul to the Philippians: "Shine as lights in the world."[10]

27. That even a baptized person loses the grace that he has attained, unless he keep innocency.

In the Gospel according to John: "Lo, thou art made whole: sin no more, lest a worse thing happen unto thee."[11] Also in the first Epistle of Paul to the Corinthians: "Know ye not that ye are the temple of God, and the Spirit of God abideth in you? If any one violate the temple of God, him will God destroy."[12] Of this same thing in the Chronicles: "God is with you, while ye are with Him: if ye forsake Him, He will forsake you."[13]

28. That remission cannot in the Church be granted unto him who has sinned against God (i.e., the Holy Ghost).

In the Gospel according to Matthew: "Whosoever shall say a word against the Son of man, it shall be forgiven him; but whosoever shall speak against the Holy Ghost, it shall not be forgiven him, neither in this world nor in the world to come."[14] Also according to Mark: "All sins shall be forgiven, and blasphemies, to the sons of men; but whoever shall blaspheme against the Holy Ghost, it shall not be forgiven him, but he shall be guilty of eternal sin."[15] Of this same thing in the first book of Kings: "If a man sin by offending against a man, they shall pray the Lord for him; but if a man sin against God, who shall pray for him?"[16]

29. That it was before predicted, concerning the hatred of the Name,

In the Gospel according to Luke: "And ye shall be hated of all men for my name's sake."[17] Also according to John: "If the world hate you, know ye that it first hated me. If ye were of the world, the world would love what would be its own: but because ye are not of the world, and I have chosen you out of the world, therefore the world hateth you. Remember the word which I said unto you, The servant is not greater than his lord. If they have persecuted me, they will also persecute you."[18] Also in Baruch:[19] "For the time shall come, and ye shall seek me, both ye and those who shall be after you, to hear the word of wisdom and of understanding; and ye shall not find me. But the nations shall desire to

---

1 Rev. xxii. 10–12.
2 John xiv. 6.
3 John x. 9.
4 John iii. 5, 6.
5 John vi. 53.
6 1 Cor. ix. 24, 25.
7 Matt. iii. 10.
8 Matt. vii. 22, 23.
9 Matt. v. 16.
10 Phil. ii. 15.

11 John v. 14.
12 1 Cor. iii. 16, 17.
13 2 Chron. xv. 2.
14 Matt. xii. 32.
15 Mark iii. 28, 29.
16 1 Sam. ii. 25. [i.e , he regards this text as expounded by the preceding words of Christ. Compare 1 John v. 16.]
17 Luke xxi. 17.
18 John xv. 18–20.
19 The whole of this quotation, as it is called, from Baruch, is wanting in all codices but two. It is remarkable, as finding no place in any text of Scripture, nor in any translation, whether Greek or Latin.

see the wise man, and it shall not happen to them; not because the wisdom of this world shall be wanting, or shall fail to the earth; but neither shall the word of the law be wanting to the world. For wisdom shall be in a few who watch, and are silent and quiet, and who hold converse with one another; because some shall dread them, and shall fear them as evil. But some do not believe the word of the law of the Highest. But some who are amazed in their countenance will not believe; and they also who contradict will believe, and will be contrary to and hindering the spirit of truth. Moreover, others will be wise to the spirit of error, and declaring the edicts, as if of the Highest and the Strong One. More-over, others are *possessors of faith*.[1] Others are mighty and strong in the faith of the Highest, and hateful to the stranger."

30. That what any one has vowed to God, he must quickly repay.

In Solomon: "According as thou hast vowed a vow to God, delay not to pay it."[2] Concern-ing this same thing in Deuteronomy: "But if thou hast vowed a vow to the Lord thy God, thou shalt not delay to pay it: because the Lord thy God inquiring shall seek it of thee; and it shall be for a sin. Thou shalt observe those things that shall go forth out of thy lips, and shalt perform the gift which thou hast spoken with thy mouth."[3] Of this same matter in the forty-ninth Psalm: "Sacrifice to God the sacri-fice of praise, and pay thy vows to the Most High. Call upon me in the day of trouble, and I will deliver thee, and thou shalt glorify me."[4] Of this same thing in the Acts of the Apostles: "Why hath Satan filled thine heart, that thou shouldst lie to the Holy Ghost, when thy estate was in thine own power? Thou hast not lied unto men, but unto God."[5] Also in Jeremiah: "Cursed is he who doeth the work of God negligently."[6]

31. That he who does not believe is judged already.

In the Gospel according to John: "He that believeth not is already judged, because he hath not believed in the name of the only[7] Son of God. And this is the judgment, that light has come into the world, and men have loved dark-ness rather than light."[8] Of this also in the first Psalm: "Therefore the ungodly shall not

rise up in judgment, nor sinners in the council of the righteous."[9]

32. Of the benefit of virginity and of con-tinency.[10]

In Genesis: "Multiplying I will multiply thy sorrows and thy groanings, and in sorrow shalt thou bring forth children; and thy turning shall be to thy husband, and he shall rule over thee."[11] Of this same thing in the Gospel according to Matthew: "All men do not receive the word, but they to whom it is given: for there are some eunuchs who were born so from their mother's womb, and there are eunuchs who have been constrained by men, and there are eunuchs who have made themselves eunuchs for the kingdom of heaven's sake. He who can re-ceive it, let him receive it."[12] Also according to Luke: "The children of this world beget, and are begotten. But they who have been consid-ered worthy of that world, and the resurrection from the dead, do not marry, nor are married: for neither shall they begin to die: for they are equal to the angels of God, since they are the children of the resurrection. But, that the dead rise again, Moses intimates when he says in the bush, The Lord, the God of Abraham, and the God of Isaac, and the God of Jacob. He is not the God of the dead, but of the living: for all live unto Him."[13] Also in the first Epistle of Paul to the Corinthians: "It is good for a man not to touch a woman. But, on account of fornication, let every man have his own wife, and every woman have her own husband. Let the husband render what is due to the wife, and similarly the wife to the husband. The wife hath not power over her own body, but the hus-band. And in like manner, the husband hath not power over his own body, but the wife. Defraud not one the other, except by agreement for a time, that ye may have leisure for prayer; and again return to the same point, lest Satan tempt you on account of your incontinency. This I say by way of allowance, not by way of command. But I wish that all men should be even as I am. But every one has his proper gift from God; one in one way, but another in another way."[14] Also in the same place: "An unmarried man thinks of those things which are the Lord's, in what way he may please God; but he who has contracted marriage thinks of those things that are of this world, in what way he may please his wife. Thus also, both the woman and the unmarried virgin thinketh of

---

[1] Personales fidei. This, like many other expressions in this strange passage, gives no clue to a meaning.
[2] Eccles. v. 4.
[3] Deut. xxiii. 21-23.
[4] Ps. l. 14, 15.
[5] Acts v. 3, 4.
[6] Jer. xlviii. 10.
[7] *Unice;* but some read *unigeniti*, "only-begotten."
[8] John iii. 18, 19.

[9] Ps. i 5.
[10] [This section is confined to Scripture, and goes not beyond the word of the Divine Wisdom, as do some of the Fathers.]
[11] Gen. iii. 16.
[12] Matt. xix. 11, 12.
[13] Luke xx. 34-38.
[14] 1 Cor. vii. 1-7.

those things which are the Lord's, that she may be holy both in body and in spirit; but she that hath married thinks of those things which are of this world, in what way she may please her husband."[1] Also in Exodus, when the Lord had commanded Moses that he should sanctify the people for the third day, he sanctified them, and added: "Be ye ready, for three days ye shall not approach to women."[2] Also in the first book of Kings: "And the priest answered to David, and said, There are no profane loaves in my hand, except one sacred loaf. If the young men have been kept back from women, they shall eat."[3] Also in the Apocalypse: "These are they who have not defiled themselves with women, for they have continued virgins; these are they who follow the Lamb whithersoever He shall go."[4]

33. That the Father judgeth nothing, but the Son; and that the Father is not glorified by him by whom the Son is not glorified.

In the Gospel according to John: "The Father judgeth nothing, but hath given all judgment unto the Son, that all may honour the Son as they honour the Father. He who honoureth not the Son, honoureth not the Father who hath sent Him."[5] Also in the seventy-first Psalm: "O God, give the king Thy judgment, and Thy righteousness to the king's son, to judge Thy people in righteousness."[6] Also in Genesis: "And the Lord rained upon Sodom and Gomorrah sulphur, and fire from heaven from the Lord."[7]

34. That the believer ought not to live like the Gentile.

In Jeremiah: "Thus saith the Lord, Walk ye not according to the way of the Gentiles."[8] Of this same thing, that one ought to separate himself from the Gentiles, lest he should be a companion of their sin, and become a partaker of their penalty, in the Apocalypse: "And I heard another voice from heaven, saying, Go forth from her, my people, lest thou be partaker of her crimes, and lest thou be stricken with her plagues; because her crimes have reached even to heaven, and the Lord God hath remembered her iniquities. Therefore He hath returned unto her double, and in the cup which she hath mixed double is mingled for her; and in how much she hath glorified herself and possessed of de-

lights, in so much is given unto her both torment and grief. For in her heart she says, I am a queen, and cannot be a widow, nor shall I see sorrow. Therefore in one hour her plagues shall come on her, death, grief, and famine; and she shall be burned with fire, because the Lord God is strong who shall judge her. And the kings of the earth shall weep and lament themselves for her, who have committed fornication with her, and have been conversant in her sins."[9] Also in Isaiah: "Go forth from the midst of them, ye who bear the vessels of the Lord."[10]

35. That God is patient for this end, that we may repent of our sin, and be reformed.

In Solomon, in Ecclesiasticus: "Say not, I have sinned, and what sorrow hath happened to me? For the Highest is a patient repayer."[11] Also Paul to the Romans: "Or despisest thou the riches of His goodness, and forbearance, and patience, not knowing that the goodness of God leadeth thee to repentance? But, according to thy hardness and impenitent heart, thou treasurest up to thyself wrath in the day of wrath and of revelation of the just judgment of God, who will render to every man according to his deeds."[12]

36. That a woman ought not to be adorned in a worldly fashion.

In the Apocalypse: "And there came one of the seven angels having vials, and approached me, saying, Come, I will show thee the condemnation of the great whore, who sitteth upon many waters, with whom the kings of the earth have committed fornication. And I saw a woman who sate upon a beast. And that woman was clothed with a purple and scarlet robe; and she was adorned with gold, and precious stones, and pearls, holding a golden cup in her hand full of curses, and impurity, and fornication of the whole earth."[13] Also to Timothy: "Let your women be such as adorn themselves with shamefacedness and modesty, not with twisted hair, nor with gold, nor with pearls, or precious garments, but as becometh women professing chastity, with a good conversation."[14] Of this same thing in the Epistle of Peter to the people at Pontus: "Let there be in a woman not the outward adorning of ornament, or of gold, or of apparel, but the adorning of the heart."[15] Also in Genesis: "Thamar covered herself with a cloak, and adorned herself;

[1] 1 Cor. vii. 32–34.
[2] Ex. xix. 15.
[3] 1 Sam. xxi. 4.
[4] Rev. xiv. 4.
[5] John v. 22, 23.
[6] Ps. lxxii. 1, 2.
[7] Gen. xix. 24.
[8] Jer. x. 2.

[9] Rev. xviii. 4–9. The Oxford text reads "deliciis" instead of "delictis," — making the last clause, "and have walked in delicacies."
[10] Isa. lii. 11.
[11] Ecclus. v. 4.
[12] Rom. ii. 4–6.
[13] Rev. xvii. 1–4.
[14] 1 Tim. ii. 9, 10.
[15] 1 Pet. iii. 4. [This limitation to "Pontus" is curious.]

and when Judah beheld her, she appeared to him to be a harlot."[1]

37. That the believer ought not to be punished for other offences, except for the name he bears.

In the Epistle of Peter to them of Pontus: "Nor let any of you suffer as a thief, or a murderer, or as an evil-doer, or as a minder of other people's business,[2] but as a Christian.[3]

38. That the servant of God ought to be innocent, lest he fall into secular punishment.

In the Epistle of Paul to the Romans: "Wilt thou not be afraid of the power? Do that which is good, and thou shalt have praise of it."[4]

39. That there is given to us an example of living in Christ.

In the Epistle of Peter to them of Pontus: "For Christ suffered for us, leaving you an example, that ye may follow His steps; who did no sin, neither was guile found in His mouth; who, when He was reviled, reviled not again; when He suffered, threatened not, but gave Himself up to him that judgeth unrighteously."[5] Also Paul to the Philippians: "Who, being appointed in the figure of God, thought it not robbery that He was equal with God; but emptied Himself, taking the form of a servant, He was made in the likeness of man, and was found in fashion as a man. He humbled Himself, becoming obedient even unto death, and the death of the cross. For which cause also God hath exalted Him, and hath given Him a name, that it may be above every name, that in the name of Jesus every knee should be bowed, of things heavenly, and earthly, and infernal; and that every tongue should confess that the Lord Jesus Christ is in glory of God the Father."[6] Of this same thing in the Gospel according to John: "If I have washed your feet, being your Master and Lord, ye also ought to wash the feet of others. For I have given you an example, that as I have done, ye also should do to others."[7]

40. That we must not labour noisily nor boastfully.

In the Gospel according to Matthew: "Let not thy left hand know what thy right hand doeth, that thine alms may be in secret; and thy Father, which seeth in secret, shall render to thee."[8] Also in the same place: "When thou doest an alms, do not sound a trumpet before thee, as the hypocrites do in the streets and in the synagogues, that they may be glorified of men. Verily I say unto you, They have fulfilled their reward."[9]

41. That we must not speak foolishly and offensively.

In Paul's Epistle to the Ephesians: "Foolish speaking and scurrility, which are not fitting for the occasion, let them not be even named among you."[10]

42. That faith is of advantage altogether, and that we can do as much as we believe.

In Genesis: "And Abraham believed God, and it was counted unto him for righteousness."[11] Also in Isaiah: "And if ye do not believe, neither shall ye understand."[12] Also in the Gospel according to Matthew: "O thou of little faith, wherefore didst thou doubt?"[13] Also in the same place: "If you have faith as a grain of mustard seed, ye shall say to this mountain, Pass over from here to that place, and it shall pass over; and nothing shall be impossible unto you."[14] Also according to Mark: "All things whatsoever ye pray and ask for, believe that ye shall receive them, and they shall be yours."[15] Also in the same place: "All things are possible to him that believeth."[16] In Habakkuk: "But the righteous liveth by my faith."[17] Also in Daniel: "Ananias, Azarias, and Misael, trusting in God, were delivered from the fiery flame."

43. That he who believes can immediately obtain (i.e., pardon and peace).

In the Acts of the Apostles: "Lo, here is water; what is there which hinders me from being baptized? Then said Philip, If thou believest with all thine heart, thou mayest."[18]

44. That believers who differ among themselves ought not to refer to a Gentile judge.[19]

In the first Epistle of Paul to the Corinthians: "Dares any of you, having a matter against an-

---

[1] Gen. xxxviii. 14, 15.
[2] [Gr. ὡς ἀλλοτριοεπίσκοπος; a strange expression. This is St. Paul's canon (Greek) of jurisdiction, which he expounds, 2 Cor. x. 13, 14. Comp. Gal. ii. 9. Showing, by the way, the limits of Peter's jurisdiction, "measure," or μετρόν τοῦ κανόνος. Note 15, p. 544, *supra*.]
[3] 1 Pet. iv. 15, 16.
[4] Rom. xiii. 3.
[5] 1 Pet. ii. 21–23.
[6] Phil. ii. 6–11.
[7] John xiii. 14, 15.

[8] Matt. vi. 3, 4.
[9] Matt. vi. 2.
[10] Eph. v. 4.
[11] Gen. xv. 6.
[12] Isa. vii. 9.
[13] Matt. xiv. 31.
[14] Matt. xvii. 20.
[15] Mark xi. 24.
[16] Mark ix. 22.
[17] Hab. ii. 4.
[18] Acts viii. 36, 37.
[19] [The oath on the Bible in our courts, and other Christian forms, are important in Christian morals, as bearing upon our right to seek redress at the law, while it is *Christian* law.]

other, to discuss it among the unrighteous, and not among the saints? Know ye not that the saints shall judge this world?"[1]   And again: "Now indeed there is altogether a fault among you, because ye have judgments one against another. Wherefore do ye not rather suffer injury? or wherefore are ye not rather defrauded? But ye do wrong, and defraud, and this your brethren. Know ye not that the unrighteous shall not obtain the kingdom of God?"[2]

45. That hope is of future things, and therefore that our faith concerning those things which are promised ought to be patient.

In the Epistle of Paul to the Romans: "We are saved by hope. But hope that is seen is not hope; for what a man seeth, why doth he hope for? But if we hope for what we see not, we hope[3] for it in patience."[4]

46. That a woman ought to be silent in the church.

In the first Epistle of Paul to the Corinthians: "Let women be silent in the church. But if any wish to learn anything, let them ask their husbands at home."[5]   Also to Timothy: "Let a woman learn with silence, in all subjection. But I permit not a woman to teach, nor to be set over the man, but to be in silence. For Adam was first formed, then Eve; and Adam was not seduced, but the woman was seduced."[6]

47. That it arises from our fault and our desert that we suffer, and do not perceive God's help in everything.

In Hosea: "Hear ye the word of the Lord, ye children of Israel: because judgment is from the Lord against the inhabitants of the earth, because there is neither mercy nor truth, nor acknowledgment of God upon the earth; but cursing, and lying, and slaughter, and theft, and adultery is scattered abroad upon the earth: they mingle blood to blood. Therefore the land shall mourn, with all its inhabitants, with the beasts of the field, with the creeping things of the earth, with the birds of heaven; and the fishes of the sea shall fail: so that no man may judge, no man may refute."[7]   Of this same thing in Isaiah: "Is not the Lord's hand strong to save, or has He weighed down His ear that He may not hear?

But your sins separate between you and God; and on account of your iniquities He turns away His face from you, lest He should pity. For your hands are polluted with blood, and your fingers with sins; and your lips have spoken wickedness, and your tongue devises unrighteousness. No one speaks true things, neither is judgment true. They trust in vanity, and speak emptiness, who conceive sorrow, and bring forth wickedness."[8]   Also in Zephaniah: "In failing, let it fail from the face of the earth, saith the Lord. Let man fail, and cattle; let the birds of heaven fail, and the fishes of the sea; and I will take away the unrighteous from the face of the earth."[9]

48. That we must not take usury.

In the thirteenth Psalm:[10] "He that hath not given his money upon usury, and has not received gifts concerning the innocent. He who doeth these things shall not be moved for ever."[11]   Also in Ezekiel: "But the man who will be righteous, shall not oppress a man, and shall return the pledge of the debtor, and shall not commit rapine, and shall give his bread to the hungry, and shall cover the naked, and shall not give his money for usury."[12]   Also in Deuteronomy: "Thou shalt not lend to thy brother with usury of money, and with usury of victuals."[13]

49. That even our enemies must be loved.

In the Gospel according to Luke: "If ye love those who love you, what thank have ye? For even sinners love those who love them."[14]   Also according to Matthew: "Love your enemies, and pray for those who persecute you, that ye may be the children of your Father who is in heaven, who maketh His sun to rise upon the good and the evil, and giveth rain upon the righteous and the unrighteous."[15]

50. That the sacrament of faith must not be profaned.

In Solomon, in the Proverbs: "Say not anything in the ears of a foolish man; lest, when he hears it, he may mock at thy wise words."[16]   Also in the Gospel according to Matthew: "Give not that which is holy to dogs; neither cast ye your pearls before the swine, lest perchance they trample them down with their feet, and turn again and crush you."[17]

---

[1] 1 Cor. vi. 1, 2.
[2] 1 Cor. vi. 7–9.
[3] Some read " exspectamus," " we wait for it."
[4] Rom. viii. 24, 25.
[5] 1 Cor. xiv. 34, 35. [Women might have spiritual gifts, like the daughters of Philip, Acts xxi. 9; but even such are here forbidden to use them in the public worship of the Church.]
[6] 1 Tim. ii. 11–14.
[7] Hos. iv. 1–4.

[8] Isa. lix. 1–4.
[9] Zeph. i. 2, 3.
[10] The Oxford edition has "the fourteenth."   [Elucidation XIII.]
[11] Ps. xv. 6.
[12] Ezek. xviii. 7, 8.
[13] Deut. xxiii. 19.
[14] Luke vi. 32.
[15] Matt. v. 44, 45.
[16] Prov. xxiii. 9.
[17] Matt. vii. 6.

51. That no one should be uplifted in his labour.[1]

In Solomon, in Ecclesiasticus: "Extol not thyself in doing thy work."[2] Also in the Gospel according to Luke: "Which of you, having a servant ploughing, or a shepherd, says to him when he cometh from the field, Pass forward and recline? But he says to him, Make ready somewhat that I may sup, and gird thyself, and minister to me, until I eat and drink; and afterwards thou shalt eat and drink? Does he thank that servant because he has done what was commanded him? So also ye, when ye shall have done that which is commanded you, say, We are unprofitable servants; we have done what we had to do."[3]

52. That the liberty of believing or of not believing is placed in free choice.

In Deuteronomy: "Lo, I have set before thy face life and death, good and evil. Choose for thyself life, that thou mayest live."[4] Also in Isaiah: "And if ye be willing, and hear me, ye shall eat the good of the land. But if ye be unwilling, and will not hear me, the sword shall consume you. For the mouth of the Lord hath spoken these things."[5] Also in the Gospel according to Luke: "The kingdom of God is within you."[6]

53. That he secrets of God cannot be seen through, and therefore that our faith ought to be simple.[7]

In the first Epistle of Paul to the Corinthians: "We see now through the glass in an enigma, but then with face to face. Now I know partly; but then I shall know even as also I am known."[8] Also in Solomon, in Wisdom: "And in simplicity of heart seek Him."[9] Also in the same: "He who walketh with simplicity, walketh trustfully."[10] Also in the same: "Seek not things higher than thyself, and look not into things stronger than thyself."[11] Also in Solomon: "Be not excessively righteous, and do not reason more than is required."[12] Also in Isaiah: "Woe unto them who are convicted in themselves."[13] Also in the Maccabees: "Daniel in his simplicity was delivered from the mouth of the lions."[14]

Also in the Epistle of Paul to the Romans: "Oh the depth of the riches of the wisdom and knowledge of God! How incomprehensible are His judgments, and how unsearchable are His ways! For who has known the mind of the Lord? or who has been His counsellor? or who has first given to Him, and it shall be recompensed to him again? Because from Him, and through Him, and in Him, are all things: to Him be glory for ever and ever."[15] Also to Timothy: "But foolish and unlearned questions avoid, knowing that they generate strifes. But the servant of God ought not to strive, but to be gentle towards all men."[16]

54. That no one is without filth and without sin.

In Job: "For who is pure from filth? Not one; even if his life be of one day on the earth."[17] Also in the fiftieth Psalm: "Behold, I was conceived in iniquities, and in sins hath my mother conceived me."[18] Also in the Epistle of John: "If we say that we have no sin, we deceive ourselves, and the truth is not in us."[19]

55. That we must not please men, but God.

In the fifty-second Psalm: "They that please men are confounded, because God hath made them nothing."[20] Also in the Epistle of Paul to the Galatians: "If I wished to please men, I should not be the servant of Christ."[21]

56. That nothing that is done is hidden from God.

In the Wisdom of Solomon: "In every place the eyes of God look upon the good and evil."[22] Also in Jeremiah: "I am a God at hand, and not a God afar off. If a man should be hidden in the secret place, shall I not therefore see him? Do not I fill heaven and earth? saith the Lord."[23] Also in the first of Kings: "Man looketh on the face, but God on the heart."[24] Also in the Apocalypse: "And all the churches shall know that I am the searcher of the reins and heart; and I will give to every one of you according to his works."[25] Also in the eighteenth Psalm: "Who understands his faults? Cleanse Thou me from my secret sins, O Lord."[26] Also in the second Epistle of Paul to the Corinthians: "We must all be manifested before the tribunal of Christ,

---

1 [Hab. i. 16; Ps. cxxxi. 1.]
2 Ecclus. x. 26.
3 Luke xvii. 7–10.
4 Deut. xiii. 19.
5 Isa. i. 19.
6 Luke xvii. 21.
7 [The aphoristic force of these "heads" is often striking in the original; e.g., "Dei arcana perspici non posse, et ideo fidem nostram simplicem esse debere."]
8 1 Cor. xiii. 12.
9 Wisd. i. 1.
10 Prov. x. 9.
11 Eccles. iii. 21.
12 Ecclus. vii. 17.
13 Isa. xxix. 15.
14 1 Macc. ii. 60.

15 Rom. xi. 33–36.
16 2 Tim. ii. 23, 24.
17 Job xiv. 4, 5.
18 Ps. li. 5.
19 1 John i. 8.
20 Ps. liii. 5.
21 Gal. i. 10.
22 Prov. xv. 3.
23 Jer. xxiii. 23, 24.
24 1 Sam. xvi. 7.
25 Rev. ii. 23.
26 Ps. xix. 12.

that every one may bear again the things which belong to his own body, according to what he hath done, whether good or evil." [1]

57. That the believer is amended and reserved.

In the cxviith Psalm: "The Lord amending hath amended me, and hath not delivered me to death." [2] Also in the eighty-eighth Psalm: " I will visit their transgressions with a rod, and their sins with scourges. But my mercy will I not scatter away from them." [3] Also in Malachi: "And He shall sit melting and purifying, as it were, gold and silver; and He shall purify the sons of Levi." [4] Also in the Gospel: "Thou shalt not go out thence until thou pay the uttermost farthing." [5]

58. That no one should be made sad by death; since in living is labour and peril, in dying peace and the certainty of resurrection.

In Genesis: "Then said the Lord to Adam, Because thou hast hearkened to the voice of thy wife, and hast eaten of that tree of which alone I commanded thee that thou shouldest not eat, cursed shall be the ground in all thy works; in sadness and groaning shalt thou eat of it all the days of thy life: thorns and thistles shall it cast forth to thee; and thou shalt eat the herb of the field in the sweat of thy brow. Thou shalt eat thy bread until thou return unto the earth from which also thou wast taken; because earth thou art, and to earth thou shalt go." [6] Also in the same place: "And Enoch pleased God, and was not found afterwards; because God translated him." [7] And in Isaiah: "All flesh is grass, and all the glory of it as the flower of grass. The grass withered, and the flower hath fallen away; but the word of the Lord abideth for ever." [8] In Ezekiel: "They say, Our bones are become dry, our hope hath perished: we have expired. Therefore prophesy, and say, Thus saith the Lord, Behold, I open your monuments, and I will bring you forth from your monuments, and I will bring you into the land of Israel; and I will put my Spirit upon you, and ye shall live; and I will place you into your land: and ye shall know that I the Lord have spoken, and will do it, saith the Lord." [9] Also in the Wisdom of Solomon: "He was taken away, lest wickedness should change his understand-

ing; for his soul was pleasing to God." [10] Also in the eighty-third Psalm: "How beloved [11] are thy dwellings, Thou Lord of hosts? My soul desires and hastes to the courts of God." [12] And in the Epistle of Paul to the Thessalonians: "But we would not that you should be ignorant, brethren, concerning those who sleep, that ye sorrow not as others which have no hope. For if we believe that Jesus died and rose again, so also them which have fallen asleep in Jesus God bring with Him." [13] Also in the first Epistle to the Corinthians: "Thou fool, that which thou sowest is not quickened except it have first died." [14] And again: "Star differeth from star in glory: so also the resurrection. The body is sown in corruption, it rises without corruption; it is sown in ignominy, it rises again in glory; it is sown in weakness, it rises again in power; it is sown an animal body, it rises again a spiritual body." [15] And again: "For this corruptible must put on incorruption, and this mortal put on immortality. But when this corruptible shall have put on incorruption, and this mortal shall have put on immortality, then shall come to pass the word that is written, Death is absorbed into striving. Where, O death, is thy sting? Where, O death, is thy striving?" [16] Also in the Gospel according to John: "Father, I will that those whom Thou hast given me be with me where I shall be, and may see my glory which Thou hast given me before the foundation of the world." [17] Also according to Luke: "Now lettest Thou Thy servant depart in peace, O Lord, according to the word; for mine eyes have seen Thy salvation." [18] Also according to John: "If ye loved me, ye would rejoice because I go to the Father; for the Father is greater than I." [19]

59. Of the idols which the Gentiles think to be gods.

In the Wisdom of Solomon: "All the idols of the nations they counted gods, which neither have the use of their eyes for seeing, nor their nostrils to receive breath, nor their ears for hearing, nor the fingers on their hands for handling; but their feet also are slow to walk. For man made them; and he who has borrowed his breath, he fashioned them. But no man will be able to fashion a god like to himself. For since he is mortal, he fashioneth a dead thing with wicked hands. But he himself is better than they whom he worships, since he indeed lived, but

---

[1] 2 Cor. v. 10.
[2] Ps. cxviii. 18.
[3] Ps. lxxxix. 32, 33.
[4] Mal. iii. 3.
[5] Matt. v. 26.
[6] Gen. iii. 17–19.
[7] Gen. v. 24.
[8] Isa. xl. 6, 7.
[9] Ezek. xxxvii. 11–14.

[10] Wisd. iv. 11, 14.
[11] Some read "amabiles," "amiable."
[12] Ps. lxxxiv. 1, 2.
[13] 1 Thess. iv. 13, 14.
[14] 1 Cor. xv. 36.
[15] 1 Cor. xv. 41–44.
[16] 1 Cor. xv. 53–55.
[17] John xvii. 24.
[18] Luke ii. 29, 30.
[19] John xiv. 28.

they never." [1] On this same matter : " Neither have they who have regarded the works known who was the artificer, but have thought that either fire, or wind, or the rapid air, or the circle of the stars, or the abundant water, or the sun and moon, were the gods that rule over the world ; and if, on account of the beauty of these, they have thought thus, let them know how much more beautiful than these is the Lord ; or if they have admired their powers and operations, let them perceive from these very things that He who has established these mighty things is stronger than they." [2] Also in the cxxxivth Psalm : " The idols of the nations are silver and gold, the work of men's hands. They have a mouth, and speak not ; they have eyes, and see not ; they have ears, and hear not ; and neither is there any breath in their mouth. Let them who make them become like unto them, and all those who trust in them." [3] Also in the ninety-fifth Psalm : " All the gods of the nations are demons, but the Lord made the heavens." [4] Also in Exodus : " Ye shall not make unto yourselves gods of silver nor of gold." [5] And again : " Thou shalt not make to thyself an idol, nor the likeness of any thing." [6] Also in Jeremiah : " Thus saith the Lord, Walk not according to the ways of the heathen ; for they fear those things in their own persons, because the lawful things of the heathen are vain. Wood cut out from the forest is made the work of the carpenter, and melted silver and gold are beautifully arranged : they strengthen them with hammers and nails, and they shall not be moved, for they are fixed. The silver is brought from Tharsis, the gold comes from Moab. All things are the works of the artificers ; they will clothe it with blue and purple ; lifting them, they will carry them, because they will not go forward. Be not afraid of them, because they do no evil, neither is there good in them. Say thus, The gods that have not made the heaven and the earth perish from the earth, and from under this heaven. The heaven hath trembled at this, and hath shuddered much more vehemently, saith the Lord. These evil things hath my people done. They have forsaken the fountain of living water, and have dug out for themselves worn-out wells, which could not hold water. Thy love hath smitten thee, and thy wickedness shall accuse thee. And know and see that it shall be a bitter thing for thee that thou hast forsaken me, saith the Lord thy God, and thou hast not hoped in me, saith thy Lord. Because of old time thou hast resented my yoke, and hast broken thy bonds,

and hast said, I will not serve, but I will go upon every lofty mountain, and upon every high hill, and upon every shady tree : there I will be confounded with fornication. To the wood and to the stone they have said, Thou art my father ; and to the stone, Thou hast begotten me : and they turned to me their back, and not their face." [7] In Isaiah : " The dragon hath fallen or is dissolved ; their carved works have become as beasts and cattle. Labouring and hungry, and without strength, ye shall bear them bound upon your neck as a heavy burden." [8] And again : " Gathered together, they shall not be able to be saved from war ; but they themselves have been led captive with thee." [9] And again : " To whom have ye likened me ? See and understand that ye err in your heart, who lavish gold out of the bag, and weigh silver in the balance, bringing it up to the weight. The workmen have made with their hand the things made ; and, bowing themselves, they have adored it, and have raised it on their shoulders : and thus they walked. But if they should place them down, they will abide in their place, and will not be moved ; and they will not hear those who cry unto them : they will not save them from evils." [10] Also in Jeremiah : " The Lord, who made heaven and earth, in strength hath ordered the world, in His wisdom hath stretched forth the heaven, and the multitude of the waters in the heaven. He hath brought out the clouds from the end of the earth, the lightnings in the clouds ; and He hath brought forth the winds from His treasures. Every man is made foolish by his knowledge, every artificer is confounded by his graven images ; because he hath molten a falsehood : there is no breath in them. The works shut up in them are made vain ; in the time of consideration they shall perish." [11] And in the Apocalypse : " And the sixth angel sounded with his trumpet. And I heard one of the four corners of the golden ark, which is in the presence of God, saying to the sixth angel who had the trumpet, Loose the four angels which are bound upon the great river Euphrates. And the four angels were loosed, which were prepared for an hour, and a day, and a month, and a year, to slay the third part of men ; and the number of the army of the horsemen was two hundred thousand of thousand : I heard the number of them. And then I saw the horses in the vision, and those that sate upon them, having breast-plates of fire, and of hyacinth, and of sulphur : and the heads of the horses (as the heads of lions) ; and out of their mouth went fire, and

---

[1] Wisd. xv. 15–17.
[2] Wisd. xiii. 1–4.
[3] Ps. cxxxv. 16–18.
[4] Ps. xcvi. 5.
[5] Ex. xx. 23.
[6] Ex. xx. 4. This section closes here, according to the Oxford text. The Leipzic edition continues as in the above reading.

[7] Jer. x. 2–5, 9, 11, ii. 12, 13, 19, 20, 27.
[8] Isa. xlvi. 1, 2, 5.
[9] Migne refers this to Jer. li. 15–18, but there is nothing corresponding to it in the passage.
[10] Isa. xlvi. 6, 7.
[11] Jer. li. 16–19.

smoke, and sulphur. By these three plagues the third part of men was slain, by the fire, and the smoke, and the sulphur which went forth from their mouth, and is in their tails : for their tails were like unto eels ; for they had heads, and with them they do mischief. And the rest of the men who were not slain by these plagues, nor repented of the works of the deeds of their hands, that they should not worship demons and idols, that is, images of gold, and of silver, and of brass, and of stone, and of wood, which can neither see nor walk, repented not also of their murders." [1] Also in the same place : " And the third angel followed them, saying with a loud voice, If any man worship the beast and his image, and hath received his mark in his forehead or upon his hand, the same shall drink of the wine of His wrath, and shall be punished with fire and sulphur, under the eyes of the holy angels, and under the eyes of the Lamb ; and the smoke of their torments shall ascend up for ever and ever." [2]

60. That too great lust of food is not to be desired.

In Isaiah : " Let us eat and drink, for to-morrow we shall die. This sin shall not be remitted to you even until ye die." [3] Also in Exodus : " And the people sate down to eat and drink, and rose up to play." [4] Paul, in the first to the Corinthians : " Meat commendeth us not to God ; neither if we eat shall we abound, nor if we eat not shall we want." [5]. And again : " When ye come together to eat, wait one for another. If any is hungry, let him eat at home, that ye may not come together for judgment." [6] Also to the Romans : " The kingdom of God is not meat and drink, but righteousness, and peace, and joy in the Holy Ghost." [7] In the Gospel according to John : " I have meat which ye know not of. My meat is, that I should do His will who sent me, and should finish His work." [8]

61. That the lust of possessing, and money, are not to be sought for.

In Solomon, in Ecclesiasticus : " He that loveth silver shall not be satisfied with silver." [9] Also in Proverbs : " He who holdeth back the corn is cursed among the people ; but blessing is on the head of him that communicateth it." [10] Also in Isaiah : " Woe unto them who join house to house, and lay field to field, that they may

take away something from their neighbour. Will ye dwell alone upon the earth?" [11] Also in Zephaniah : " They shall build houses, and shall not dwell in them ; and they shall appoint vineyards, and shall not drink the wine of them, because the day of the Lord is near." [12] Also in the Gospel according to Luke : " For what does it profit a man to make a gain of the whole world, but that he should lose himself?" [13] And again : " But the Lord said unto him, Thou fool, this night thy soul is required of thee. Whose, then, shall those things be which thou hast provided?" [14] And again : " Remember that thou hast received thy good things in this life, and likewise Lazarus evil things. But now he is besought, and thou grievest." [15] And in the Acts of the Apostles : " But Peter said unto him, Silver and gold indeed I have not ; but what I have I give unto you : In the name of Jesus Christ of Nazareth, rise up and walk. And, taking hold of his right hand, he lifted him up." [16] Also in the first to Timothy : " We brought nothing into this world, but neither can we take anything away. Therefore, having maintenance and clothing, let us with these be content. But they who will become rich fall into temptation and a snare, and many and hurtful lusts, which drown man in perdition and destruction. For the root of all evils is covetousness, which some coveting, have made shipwreck from the faith, and have plunged themselves in many sorrows." [17]

62. That marriage is not to be contracted with Gentiles.

In Tobias : " Take a wife from the seed of thy parents, and take not a strange woman who is not of the tribe of thy parents." [18] Also in Genesis, Abraham sends his servant to take from his seed Rebecca, for his son Isaac. Also in Esdras, it was not sufficient for God when the Jews were laid waste, unless they forsook their foreign wives, with the children also whom they had begotten of them. Also in the first Epistle of Paul to the Corinthians : " The woman is bound so long as her husband liveth ; but if he die, she is freed to marry whom she will, only in the Lord. But she will be happier if she abide thus." [19] And again : " Know ye not that your bodies are the members of Christ? Shall I take the members of Christ, and make them the members of an harlot? Far be it from me. Or know ye not that he who is joined together with an harlot is one body? for two shall be in

---

[1] Rev. ix. 1, 13–21.
[2] Rev. xiv. 9–11.
[3] Isa. xxii. 13, 14.
[4] Ex. xxxii. 6.
[5] 1 Cor viii. 8.
[6] 1 Cor. xi. 33.
[7] Rom. xiv. 17.
[8] John iv. 32, 34.
[9] Eccles. v. 10.
[10] Prov. xi. 26.

[11] Isa. v. 8.
[12] Zeph. i. 13, 14.
[13] Luke ix. 25.
[14] Luke xii. 20.
[15] Luke xvi. 25.
[16] Acts iii. 6.
[17] 1 Tim. vi. 7–10.
[18] Tob. iv. 12.
[19] 1 Cor. vii. 39, 40.

one flesh. But he who is joined to the Lord is one spirit." [1] Also in the second to the Corinthians : " Be not joined together with unbelievers. For what participation is there between righteousness and unrighteousness? or what communication hath light with darkness?" [2] Also concerning Solomon in the third book of Kings : " And foreign wives turned away his heart after their gods." [3]

63. That the sin of fornication is grievous.

In the first Epistle of Paul to the Corinthians : " Every sin whatsoever a man doeth is outside the body ; but he who committeth fornication sinneth against his own body. Ye are not your own, for ye are bought with a great price. Glorify and bear the Lord in your body." [4]

64. What are those carnal things which beget death, and what are the spiritual things which lead to life.

Paul to the Galatians : " The flesh lusteth against the Spirit, and the Spirit against the flesh : for these are contrary the one to the other, that ye cannot do even those things which ye wish. But the deeds of the flesh are manifest, which are : adulteries, fornications, impurities, filthiness, idolatries, sorceries, murders, hatreds, strifes, emulations, animosities, provocations, hatreds, dissensions, heresies, envyings, drunkenness, revellings, and such like : with respect to which I declare, that they who do such things shall not possess the kingdom of God. But the fruit of the Spirit is charity, joy, peace, magnanimity, goodness, faith, gentleness, continency, chastity. For they who are Christ's have crucified their flesh, with its vices and lusts." [5]

65. That all sins are put away in baptism.

In the first Epistle of Paul to the Corinthians : " Neither fornicators, nor those who serve idols, nor adulterers, nor effeminate, nor the lusters after mankind, nor thieves, nor cheaters, nor drunkards, nor revilers, nor robbers, shall obtain the kingdom of God. And these things indeed ye were : but ye are washed, but ye are sanctified in the name of our Lord Jesus Christ, and in the Spirit of our God." [6]

66. That the discipline of God is to be observed in Church precepts.

In Jeremiah : " And I will give to you shepherds according to my own heart ; and they shall feed the sheep, feeding them with discipline." [7] Also in Solomon, in the Proverbs : " My son, neglect not the discipline of God, nor fail when rebuked by Him. For whom God loveth, He rebuketh." [8] Also in the second Psalm : " Keep discipline, lest perchance the Lord should be angry, and ye perish from the right way, when His anger shall burn up quickly against you. Blessed are all they who trust in Him." [9] Also in the forty-ninth Psalm : " But to the sinner saith God, For what dost thou set forth my judgments, and takest my covenant into thy mouth? But thou hatest discipline, and hast cast my words behind thee." [10] Also in the Wisdom of Solomon : " He who casteth away discipline is miserable." [11]

67. That it was foretold that men should despise sound discipline.

Paul, in the second to Timothy : " There will be a time when they will not endure sound doctrine ; but according to their own lusts will heap to themselves teachers itching in hearing, tickling their ears ; and shall turn away their hearing indeed from the truth, but they shall be converted unto fables." [12]

68. That we must depart from him who lives irregularly and contrary to discipline.

Paul to the Thessalonians : " But we have commanded you, in the name of Jesus Christ, that ye depart from all brethren who walk disorderly, and not according to the tradition which they have received from us." [13] Also in the forty-ninth Psalm : " If thou sawest a thief, at once thou rannest with him, and placedst thy portion with the adulterers." [14]

69. That the kingdom of God is not in the wisdom of the world, nor in eloquence, but in the faith of the cross, and in virtue of conversation.

In the first Epistle of Paul to the Corinthians : " Christ sent me to preach, not in wisdom of discourse, lest the cross of Christ should become of no effect. For the word of the cross is foolishness to those who perish ; but to those who are saved it is the power of God. For it is written, I will destroy the wisdom of the wise, and I will reprove the prudence of the prudent. Where is the wise? where is the scribe? where is the disputer of this world? Hath not God

---

[1] 1 Cor. vi. 15-17.
[2] 2 Cor. vi. 14.
[3] 1 Kings xi. 4. [Surely this principle is important in teaching fathers and mothers how to guard the social relations of children.]
[4] 1 Cor. vi. 18-20.
[5] Gal. v. 17-24.
[6] 1 Cor. vi. 9-11.

[7] Jer. iii. 15.
[8] Prov. iii. 11, 12.
[9] Ps. ii. 12.
[10] Ps. l. 16.
[11] Wisd. iii. 11.
[12] 2 Tim. iv. 3, 4.
[13] 2 Thess. iii. 6. [A very noteworthy safeguard of apostolic ordinances; but mark the charity with which it is softened, 2 Thess. iii. 14, 15. Compare also cap. ii. 15.]
[14] Ps. l. 18.

made foolish the wisdom of this world? Since indeed, in the wisdom of God, the world by wisdom knew not God, it pleased God by the foolishness of preaching to save them that believe. Because the Jews desire signs, and the Greeks seek for wisdom : but we preach Christ crucified, to the Jews indeed a stumbling-block, and to the Gentiles foolishness ; but to them that are called, Jews and Greeks, Christ the power of God, and the wisdom of God." [1] And again : "Let no man deceive himself. If any man think that he is wise among you, let him become a fool to this world, that he may be wise. For the wisdom of this world is foolishness with God. For it is written, Thou shalt rebuke the wise in their own craftiness." [2] And again : "The Lord knoweth the thoughts of the wise, that they are foolish." [3]

70. That we must obey parents.

In the Epistle of Paul to the Ephesians : "Children, be obedient to your parents : for this is right. Honour thy father and thy mother (which is the first command with promise), that it may be well with thee, and thou mayest be long-lived on the earth." [4]

71. And that fathers also should not be harsh in respect of their children.

Also in the same place : "And, ye fathers, drive not your children to wrath : but nourish them in the discipline and rebuke of the Lord." [5]

72. That servants, when they have believed, ought to serve their carnal masters the better.

In the Epistle of Paul to the Ephesians : "Servants, obey your fleshly masters with fear and trembling, and in simplicity of your heart, as to Christ ; not serving for the eye, as if you were pleasing men ; but as servants of God." [6]

73. Moreover, that masters should be the more gentle.

Also in the same place : "And, ye masters, do the same things to them, forbearing anger : knowing that both your Master and theirs is in heaven ; and there is no choice of persons with Him." [7]

74. That all widows that are approved are to be held in honour.

In the first Epistle of Paul to Timothy : "Honour widows which are truly widows. But the widow that is wanton, is dead while she liveth." [8] And again : "But the younger widows pass by : for when they shall be wanton in Christ, they wish to marry ; having judgment, because they have cast off their first faith." [9]

75. That every person ought to have care rather of his own people, and especially of believers.

The apostle in his first Epistle to Timothy : "But if any take not care of his own, and especially of those of his own household, he denies the faith, and is worse than an infidel." [10] Of this same thing in Isaiah : "If thou shalt see the naked, clothe him ; and despise not those who are of the household of thine own seed." [11] Of which members of the household it is said in the Gospel : "If they have called the master of the house Beelzebub, how much rather them of his household !" [12]

76. That an elder must not be rashly accused.

In the first to Timothy : "Against an elder receive not an accusation." [13]

77. That the sinner must be publicly reproved.

In the first Epistle of Paul to Timothy : "Rebuke them that sin in the presence of all, that others also may be afraid." [14]

78. That we must not speak with heretics.

To Titus : "A man that is an heretic, after one rebuke avoid ; knowing that one of such sort is perverted, and sinneth, and is by his own self condemned." [15] Of this same thing in the Epistle of John : "They went out from among us, but they were not of us ; for if they had been of us, they would doubtless have remained with us." [16] Also in the second to Timothy : "Their word doth creep as a canker." [17]

79. That innocency asks with confidence, and obtains.

In the Epistle of John : "If our heart blame us not, we have confidence towards God ; and whatever we ask, we shall receive from Him." [18] Also in the Gospel according to Matthew : "Blessed are they of a pure heart, for they shall see God." [19] Also in the twenty-third Psalm : "Who shall ascend into the hill of the Lord?

---

[1] 1 Cor. i. 17-24.
[2] 1 Cor. iii. 18-20.
[3] Ps. xciii. 11.
[4] Eph. vi. 1-3.
[5] Eph. vi. 4.
[6] Eph. vi. 5, 6.
[7] Eph. vi. 9.

[8] 1 Tim. v. 3, 6.
[9] 1 Tim. v. 11, 12.
[10] 1 Tim. v. 8.
[11] Isa. lviii. 7.
[12] Matt. x. 25.
[13] 1 Tim. v. 19.
[14] 1 Tim. v. 20.
[15] Tit. iii. 10, 11.
[16] 1 John ii. 19.
[17] 2 Tim. ii. 17.
[18] 1 John ii. 21, 22.
[19] Matt. v. 8.

or who shall stand in His holy place? The innocent in hands and of a pure heart."[1]

80. That the devil has no power against man unless God have allowed it.

In the Gospel according to John: "Jesus said, Thou couldest have no power against me, unless it were given thee from above."[2] Also in the third of Kings: "And God stirred up Satan against Solomon himself."[3] Also in Job, first of all God permitted, and then it was allowed to the devil; and in the Gospel, the Lord first permitted, by saying to Judas, "What thou doest, do quickly."[4] Also in Solomon, in the Proverbs: "The heart of the king is in God's hand."[5]

81. That wages be quickly paid to the hireling.

In Leviticus: "The wages of thy hireling shall not sleep with thee until the morning."[6]

82. That divination must not be used.

In Deuteronomy: "Do not use omens nor auguries."[7]

83. That a tuft of hair is not to be worn on the head.

In Leviticus: "Ye shall not make a tuft from the hair of your head."[8]

84. That the beard must not be plucked.

"Ye shall not deface the figure of your beard."[9]

85. That we must rise when a bishop or a presbyter comes.

In Leviticus: "Thou shalt rise up before the face of the elder, and shalt honour the person of the presbyter."[10]

86. That a schism must not be made, even although he who withdraws should remain in one faith, and in the same tradition.

In Ecclesiasticus, in Solomon: "He that cleaveth firewood shall be endangered by it if the iron shall fall off."[11] Also in Exodus: "In one house shall it be eaten: ye shall not cast forth the flesh abroad out of the house."[12] Also in the cxxxiid Psalm: "Behold how good and how pleasant a thing it is that brethren should

dwell in unity!"[13] Also in the Gospel according to Matthew: "He that is not with me is against me; and he that gathereth not with me scattereth."[14] Also in the first Epistle of Paul to the Corinthians: "But I beseech you, brethren, by the name of our Lord Jesus Christ, that ye all say the same thing, and that there be no schisms among you; but that ye be all joined together in the same mind and in the same opinion."[15] Also in the sixty-seventh Psalm: "God, who maketh men to dwell with one mind in a house."[16]

87. That believers ought to be simple, with prudence.

In the Gospel according to Matthew: "Be ye prudent as serpents, and simple as doves."[17] And again: "Ye are the salt of the earth. But if the salt have lost his savour, in what shall it be salted? It is good for nothing, but to be cast out abroad, and to be trodden under foot of men."[18]

88. That a brother must not be deceived.

In the first Epistle of Paul to the Thessalonians: "That a man do not deceive his brother in a matter, because God is the avenger for all these."[19]

89. That the end of the world comes suddenly.

The apostle says: "The day of the Lord shall so come as a thief in the night. When they shall say, Peace and security, then on them shall come sudden destruction."[20] Also in the Acts of the Apostles: "No one can know the times or the seasons which the Father has placed in His own power."[21]

90. That a wife must not depart from her husband; or if she should depart, she must remain unmarried.

In the first Epistle of Paul to the Corinthians: "But to them that are married I command, yet not I, but the Lord, that the wife should not be separated from her husband; but if she should depart, that she remain unmarried or be reconciled to her husband: and that the husband should not put away his wife."[22]

91. That every one is tempted so much as he is able to bear.

In the first Epistle of Paul to the Corinthians: "No temptation shall take you, except

---

[1] Ps. xxiv. 3, 4.
[2] John xix. 11.
[3] 1 Kings xi. 23.
[4] John xiii. 27.
[5] Prov. xxi. 1.
[6] Lev. xix. 13.
[7] Deut. xviii. 10.
[8] Lev. xix. 27. [See p. 530, *supra*, the note and reference.]
[9] Lev. xix. 27. [Compare Clement, vol. ii. p. 280, this series.]
[10] Lev. xix. 32.
[11] Eccles. x. 9.
[12] Ex. xii. 4.

[13] Ps. cxxxiii. 1.
[14] Matt. xii. 30.
[15] 1 Cor. i. 10.
[16] Ps. lxviii. 6. [So Vulgate and Anglican Psalter.]
[17] Matt. x. 16.
[18] Matt. v. 13.
[19] 1 Thess. iv. 6.
[20] 1 Thess. v. 2, 3.
[21] Acts i. 7.
[22] 1 Cor. vii. 10, 11.

such is human. But God is faithful, who will not suffer you to be tempted above that ye are able ; but will with the temptation also make a way to escape, that ye may be able to bear it." [1]

92. That not everything is to be done which is lawful.

Paul, in the first Epistle to the Corinthians : " All things are lawful, but all things are not expedient : all things are lawful, but all things edify not." [2]

93. That it was foretold that heresies would arise.

In the first epistle of Paul to the Corinthians : " Heresies must needs be, in order that they which are approved may be made manifest among you." [3]

94. That the Eucharist is to be received with fear and honour.[4]

In Leviticus : " But whatever soul shall eat of the flesh of the sacrifice of salvation, which is the Lord's, and his uncleanness is still upon him, that soul shall perish from his people." [5] Also in the first to the Corinthians : " Whosoever shall eat the bread or drink the cup of the Lord unworthily, shall be guilty of the body and blood of the Lord." [6]

95. That we are to live with the good, but to avoid the evil.

In Solomon, in the Proverbs : " Bring not the impious man into the habitation of the righteous." [7] Also in the same, in Ecclesiasticus : " Let righteous men be thy guests." [8] And again : " The faithful friend is a medicine of life and of immortality." [9] Also in the same place : " Be thou far from the man who has the power to slay, and thou shalt not suspect fear." [10] Also in the same place, : " Blessed is he who findeth a true friend, and who speaketh righteousness to the listening ear." [11] Also in the same place : " Hedge thine ears with thorns, and hear not a wicked tongue." [12] Also in the seventeenth Psalm : " With the righteous Thou shalt be justified ; and with the innocent man Thou shalt be innocent ; and with the froward man Thou shalt be froward." [13] Also in the first Epistle of Paul to the Corinthians : " Evil communications corrupt good dispositions." [14]

96. That we must labour not with words, but with deeds.

In Solomon, in Ecclesiasticus : " Be not hasty in thy tongue, and in thy deeds useless and remiss." [15] And Paul, in the first to the Corinthians : " The kingdom of God is not in word, but in power." [16] Also to the Romans : " Not the hearers of the law are righteous before God, but the doers of the law shall be justified." [17] Also in the Gospel according to Matthew : " He who shall do and teach so, shall be called greatest in the kingdom of heaven." [18] Also in the same place : " Every one who heareth my words, and doeth them, I will liken him to a wise man who built his house upon a rock. The rain descended, the floods came, the winds blew, and beat upon that house, and it fell not : for it was founded upon a rock. And every one who heareth my words, and doeth them not, I will liken him to the foolish man, who built his house upon the sand. The rain descended, the floods came, the winds blew, and beat upon that house ; and it fell : and its ruin became great." [19]

97. That we must hasten to faith and to attainment.

In Solomon, in Ecclesiasticus : " Delay not to be converted to God, and do not put off from day to day ; for His anger cometh suddenly." [20]

98. That the catechumen ought now no longer to sin.[21]

In the Epistle of Paul to the Romans : " Let us do evil until the good things come ; whose condemnation is just." [22]

99. That judgment will be according to the times, either of equity before the law, or of law after Moses.

Paul to the Romans : " As many as have sinned without law, shall perish without law ; and as many as have sinned in the law, shall be judged also by the law." [23]

100. That the grace of God ought to be without price.

In the Acts of the Apostles : " Thy money be in perdition with thyself, because thou hast

---

1 1 Cor. x. 13.
2 1 Cor. x. 23.
3 1 Cor. xi. 19.
4 [Note, not to be worshipped, but received.]
5 Lev. vii. 20.
6 1 Cor. xi. 27.
7 Prov. xxiv. 15.
8 Ecclus. ix. 16.
9 Ecclus. vi. 16.
10 Ecclus. ix. 13.
11 Ecclus. xxv. 9.
12 Ecclus. xxviii. 24.
13 Ps. xviii. 25, 26.

14 1 Cor. xv. 33.
15 Ecclus. iv. 29.
16 1 Cor. iv. 20.
17 Rom. ii. 13.
18 Matt. v. 19.
19 Matt. vii. 24–27.
20 Ecclus. v. 7.
21 [Converts preparing for baptism. Apostolical Constitutions, and Bunsen's *Hippolytus*, vol. iii. pp. 3–24.]
22 Rom. iii. 8.
23 Rom. ii. 12.

thought that the grace of God is possessed by money."[1] Also in the Gospel: "Freely ye have received, freely give."[2] Also in the same place: "Ye have made my Father's house a house of merchandise; and ye have made the house of prayer a den of thieves."[3] Also in Isaiah: "Ye who thirst, go to the water, and as many as have not money: go, and buy, and drink without money."[4] Also in the Apocalypse: "I am Alpha and Omega, the beginning and the end. I will give to him that thirsteth from the fountain of the water of life freely. He who shall overcome shall possess these things, and their inheritance; and I will be his God, and he shall be my son."[5]

101. That the Holy Spirit has frequently appeared in fire.

In Exodus: "And the whole of Mount Sinai smoked, because God had come down upon it in fire."[6] Also in the Acts of the Apostles: "And suddenly there was made a sound from heaven, as if a vehement blast were borne along, and it filled the whole of that place in which they were sitting. And there appeared to them cloven tongues as if of fire, which also settled upon each of them; and they were all filled with the Holy Ghost."[7] Also in the sacrifices, whatsoever God accounted accepted, fire descended from heaven, which consumed what was sacrificed. In Exodus: "The angel of the Lord appeared in a flame of fire from the bush."[8]

102. That all good men ought willingly to hear rebuke.

In Solomon, in the Proverbs: "He who reproveth a wicked man shall be hated by him. Rebuke a wise man, and he will love you."[9]

103. That we must abstain from much speaking.

In Solomon: "Out of much speaking thou shalt not escape sin; but sparing thy lips, thou shalt be wise."[10]

104. That we must not lie.

"Lying lips are an abomination to the Lord."[11]

105. That they are frequently to be corrected who do wrong in domestic duty.

In Solomon: "He who spareth the rod, hateth his son."[12] And again: "Do not cease from correcting the child."[13]

106. That when a wrong is received, patience is to be maintained, and vengeance to be left to God.

Say not, I will avenge me of mine enemy; but wait for the Lord, that He may be thy help."[14] Also elsewhere: "To me belongeth vengeance; I will repay, saith the Lord."[15] Also in Zephaniah: "Wait on me, saith the Lord, in the day of my rising again to witness; because my judgment is to the congregations of the Gentiles, that I may take kings, and pour out upon them my anger."[16]

107. That we must not use detraction.

In Solomon, in the Proverbs: "Love not to detract, lest thou be taken away."[17] Also in the forty-ninth Psalm: "Thou sattest, and spakest against thy brother; and against the son of thy mother thou placedst a stumbling-block."[18] Also in the Epistle of Paul to the Colossians:[19] "To speak ill of no man, nor to be litigious."[20]

108. That we must not lay snares against our neighbour.

In Solomon, in the Proverbs: "He who diggeth a pit for his neighbour, himself shall fall into it."[21]

109. That the sick are to be visited.[22]

In Solomon, in Ecclesiasticus: "Be not slack to visit the sick man; for from these things thou shalt be strengthened in love."[23] Also in the Gospel: "I was sick, and ye visited me; I was in prison, and ye came unto me."[24]

110. That tale-bearers are accursed.

In Ecclesiasticus, in Solomon: "The tale-bearer and the double-tongued is accursed; for he will disturb many who have peace."[25]

[1] Acts viii. 20.
[2] Matt. x. 8.
[3] Matt. xxi. 13. The latter clause of this quotation is omitted by the Oxford editor.
[4] Isa. lv. 1.
[5] Rev. xxi. 6, 7.
[6] Ex. xix. 18.
[7] Acts ii. 2-4.
[8] Ex. iii. 2.
[9] Prov. ix. 8.
[10] Prov. x. 19.
[11] Prov. xii. 22.
[12] Prov. xiii. 24.
[13] Prov. xix. 18.
[14] Lev. xix. 18.
[15] Deut. xxxii. 35.
[16] Zeph. iii 8.
[17] Prov. xx. 13 (LXX.).
[18] Ps. l. 20.
[19] Oxford edition, " to Titus."
[20] Tit. iii. 2.
[21] Prov. xxvi. 27.
[22] [Elucidation XII. See p. 528, *supra*.]
[23] Ecclus. vii. 39.
[24] Matt. xxv. 36.
[25] Ecclus. xxviii. 15.

111. That the sacrifices of the wicked are not acceptable.

In the same: " The Highest approveth not the gifts of the unrighteous."[1]

112. That those are more severely judged, who in this world have had more power.

In Solomon: " The hardest judgment shall be made on those who govern. For to a mean man mercy is granted; but the powerful shall suffer torments mightily."[2] Also in the second Psalm: " And now, ye kings, understand; be amended, ye who judge the earth."[3]

113. That the widow and orphans ought to be protected.

In Solomon: " Be merciful to the orphans as a father, and as a husband to their mother; and thou shalt be the son of the Highest if thou shalt obey."[4] Also in Exodus: " Ye shall not afflict any widow and orphan. But if ye afflict them, and they cry out and call unto me, I will hear their cryings, and will be angry in mind against you; and I will destroy you with the sword, and your wives shall be widows, and your children orphans."[5] Also in Isaiah: " Judge for the fatherless, and justify the widow; and come, let us reason, saith the Lord."[6] Also in Job: " I have preserved the poor man from the hand of the mighty, and I have helped the fatherless, who had no helper: the mouth of the widow hath blessed me."[7] Also in the sixty-seventh Psalm: " The Father of the orphans, and the Judge of the widows."[8]

114. That one ought to make confession while he is in the flesh.

In the fifth Psalm: " But in the grave who will confess unto Thee?"[9] Also in the twenty-ninth Psalm: " Shall the dust make confession to Thee?"[10] Also elsewhere that confession is to be made: " I would rather have the repentance of the sinner than his death."[11] Also in Jeremiah: " Thus saith the Lord, Shall not he that falleth arise? or shall not he that is turned away be converted?"[12]

115. That flattery is pernicious.

In Isaiah: " They who call you blessed, lead you into error, and trouble the paths of your feet."[13]

116. That God is more loved by him who has had many sins forgiven in baptism.

In the Gospel according to Luke: " To whom much is forgiven, he loveth much; and to whom little is forgiven, the same loveth little."[14]

117. That there is a strong conflict to be waged against the devil, and that therefore we ought to stand bravely, that we may be able to conquer.

In the Epistle of Paul to the Ephesians: " Our wrestle is not against flesh and blood, but against the powers and princes of this world, and of this darkness; against the spiritual things of wickedness in the heavenly places. Because of this, put on the whole armour of God, that ye may be able to resist in the most evil day; that when ye have accomplished all, ye may stand, having your loins girt in the truth of the Gospel, putting on the breastplate of righteousness, and having your feet shod with the preparation of the Gospel of peace; in all things taking the shield of faith, in which ye may extinguish all the fiery darts of the most wicked one; and take the helmet of salvation, and the sword of the Spirit, which is the word of God."[15]

118. Also of Antichrist, that he will come as a man.

In Isaiah: " This is the man who arouseth the earth, who disturbeth kings, who maketh the whole earth a desert."[16]

119. That the yoke of the law was heavy, which is cast off by us, and that the Lord's yoke is easy, which is taken up by us.

In the second Psalm: " Wherefore have the heathen been in tumult, and the peoples meditated vain things? The kings of the earth have stood up, and their princes have been gathered together against the Lord, and against His Christ. Let us break their bonds asunder, and cast away from us their yoke."[17] Also in the Gospel according to Matthew: " Come unto me, ye who labour and are burdened, and I will make you to rest. Take my yoke upon you, and learn of

---

[1] Ecclus. xxxiv. 19.
[2] Wisd. vi. 6.
[3] Ps. ii. 10.
[4] Ecclus. iv. 10.
[5] Ex. xxii. 22–24.
[6] Isa. i. 17, 18.
[7] Job xxix. 12, 13.
[8] Ps. lxviii. 5.
[9] Ps. vi. 5. [Here, as often, the grave is represented as enjoying a temporary victory, for the flesh is no longer capable of worship. Not till the whole man is restored comes 1 Cor. xv. 54, 55.]
[10] Ps. xxx. 9.
[11] Ezek. xxxiii. 11.
[12] Jer. viii. 4.

[13] Isa. iii. 12.
[14] Luke vii. 47.
[15] Eph. vi. 12–17.
[16] Isa. xiv. 16.
[17] Ps. ii. 1–3.

me : for I am meek and lowly of heart,[1] and ye shall find rest for your souls. For my yoke is good, and my burden is light."[2] Also in the Acts of the Apostles : " It seemed good to the Holy Ghost, and to us, to impose upon you no other burden than those things which are of necessity, that you should abstain from idolatries, from shedding of blood, and from fornication. And whatsoever you would not to be done unto you, do not to others."[3]

[1] In one codex, from this point all the rest is wanting.
[2] Matt. xi. 28-30.
[3] Acts xv. 28, 29.

120. That we are to be urgent in prayers.

In the Epistle of Paul to the Colossians : " Be instant in prayer, and watch therein."[4] Also in the first Psalm : " But in the law of the Lord is his will, and in His law will he meditate day and night."[5]

[4] Col. iv. 2.
[5] Ps. i. 2. The Oxford editon continues: " Likewise in Solomon; ' Be not hindered from praying ever, and delay not unto death to be justified; for the repayment of the Lord abideth for ever.'" [In a day when there were few Bibles, and no printed books, no concordances, and no published collections of this sort, reflect on the value of this treatise to a young believer, and on the labour of his pastor in making it.]

ELUCIDATIONS.

I.

(On the unity of the Church, p. 421.)

THE epistles have already been elucidated as the best exposition of this treatise. Little need be added. But, to illustrate the bearings of this treatise upon the history of Christian unity, we need only refer to the manner in which the subject was treated as soon as the papacy was created by Nicholas I. Thus, he astounded the Greeks by his consummate audacity (A.D. 860) in the matter of the disputed succession in Constantinople.[1] " *It is our will*," he says, " that Ignatius should appear before our envoys," etc. He declares it the rule of the Fathers, that, " without the consent of the Roman See and the Roman pontiff, nothing should be decided." Also, he affirms, " The Creator of all things has established the Princedom of the Divine Power, which He granted to His chosen apostles. He has firmly established it on the firm faith of the Prince of the Apostles, — that is to say, Peter, — to whom he pre-eminently granted the first See," etc. He was now speaking on the strength of the forged Decretals, to which he appeals, and which he succeeded in making law for the West. He thus created the lasting schism with the Easterns, who had never heard the like before his time.

Obviously, therefore, had Cyprian entertained such ideas, his treatise could never have been written ; for it is a masterly exposition of a curious point, viz., the fact that (1) the Apostle Peter received the first grant alone, and yet (2) all the apostles received precisely the same ; while (1) Peter had thus a primacy of honour, but (2) in no respect any power or authority over his brethren. On these admitted facts he constructs his theory of unity, expounding by it the actual state of the Church's constitution. Peter's memory he honours, but without any less reverence for all the apostolic Sees, which over and over again he maintains to be of equal authority and sanctity. That the Church was founded on Stephen any more than on the Bishop of Carthage, he never imagines ; for it is one thing to allow that a bishop has succeeded an apostle at the place of his last labours, and quite another to assume that therefore such a bishop is virtually the apostle himself. Yet this assumption is the ground of all Roman doctrine on this point.[2]

Had such been Cyprian's idea, his *Treatise on Unity* must have proceeded thus: (1) " Our Lord said to Peter only, I will give unto thee the keys ; (2) to the rest of the apostles He gave only an inferior and subject authority ; (3) to the successor of Peter, therefore, at Rome, all other

[1] For the Ultramontane side, consult the *Histoire de Photius*, etc., par M. l'Abbé Jager, p. 41, ed. Paris, 1854. For the Greeks, *La Papauté Schismatique*, etc., par M. l'Abbé Guettée (pp. 286, 288, etc.), Paris, 1863.

[2] " Whatever is said in commendation of St. Peter is at once transferred to the occupant of the papacy, as if *pasce oves meas* had been said to Pius IX." Burgon, *Letters from Rome*, p. 411, ed. 1862.

bishops and churches must be subject; for (4) in this subjection the law of unity consists; and (5) if even all the other apostles were alive to this day, they would be subject to Stephen, as Prince of the Apostles, or would be rebels against Christ."

Compare this treatise of Cyprian, then, with any authorized treatise on the subject proceeding from modern Rome, and it will be seen that the two systems are irreconcilable. Thus, in few words, says the Confession[1] of Pius IV.: "I acknowledge the Holy Catholic Apostolic *Roman* Church for the mother and mistress of all churches; and I promise true obedience to the Bishop of Rome, successor to St. Peter, Prince of the Apostles, and Vicar of Jesus Christ." This is the voice of Italy in the ninth century; but Cyprian speaks for Œcumenical Christendom in the third, and the two systems are as contrary as darkness and light.

II.

(Falsifying of the text, p. 422.)

Cyprian is often innocently quoted by Romanist controvertists against the very principles of Cyprian himself, of his life and his writings. This is due to the fact that they have in their hands vitiated and interpolated copies. Thus, take a famous passage as follows: —

CYPRIAN.	INTERPOLATED.
Loquitur Dominus ad Petrum, Ego tibi dico Tu es Petrus, etc.[a]	[a] Et iterum eidem, post resurrectionem suam dicit, Pasce oves meas.
Super unum [b] ædificat ecclesiam.	[b] Super *illum* unum . . . et illi pascendas mandat oves suas.
Hoc erant utique et cæteri apostoli quod fuit Petrus, qui consortio prædati et honoris et potestatis, sed exordium ab unitate proficisitur,[c] ut [d] Christi ecclesia [e] una monstretur.[f]	[c] Et primatus Petro datur.
	[d] Una.
	[e] Et cathedra.
	[f] Et pastores sunt omnes et grex unus ostenditur, qui ab apostolis omnibus, unanimi consensione pascatur, etc.
Qui Ecclesiæ resistitur et resistit,[g] in ecclesia se esse confidit?	[g] Qui cathedram Petri, super quem fundata est ecclesia deserit, etc.

This is but a specimen of the way in which Cyprian has been "doctored," in order to bring him into a shape capable of being misinterpreted. But you will say where is the proof of such interpolations? The greatly celebrated Benedictine edition reads as the interpolated column does, and who would not credit Baluzius? Now note, Baluzius rejected these interpolations and others; but, dying (A.D. 1718) with his work unfinished, the completion of the task was assigned to a nameless monk, who confesses that he corrupted the work of Baluzius, or rather glories in the exploit.[2] "Nay, further," he says, "it was necessary to alter not a few things in the notes of Baluzius; and more would have been altered if *it could have been done conveniently.*" Yet the edition came forth, and passes as the genuine work of the erudite Baluzius himself.

An edition of this treatise, with valuable annotations, appeared (A.D. 1852) from the press of Burlington, N.J., under the very creditable editorship of Professor Hyde, who was soon after called to depart this life. It exhibits the interpolations, and gives a useful catalogue of codices and of editions. Though its typographical execution is imperfect, I know not where so much condensed information on the subject is to be had at so little cost.[3] I am grateful for the real advantage I derived from it on its first appearance.

---

[1] *Compendium Ritualis Romani,* etc., Baltimori, 1842, p. 195.

[2] Burgon, *Letters from Rome,* p. 417.

[3] Th. C. Cypriani *de Unitate Ecclesiæ* ad optimorum librorum fidem expressa, cum variis lectionibus, ad notationibus Fellii, Baluzii, etc., instructa. Curante M. F. Hyde, M.A., etc, Burlingtoniæ, MDCCCLII.

III.

(If ye do not forgive, etc., p. 454.)

The Jewish liturgies contained the petitions of the Lord's Prayer essentially; but our divine Lord framed this comprehensive and sublime compend, and gave it to His children for ever, with His own seal upon it in the exceptional petition which imparts to it the impress of His own cross and passion. In the Gospel of St. Matthew [1] we find our Master commenting on the fifth petition in a very striking manner, as if it were the essence of the whole prayer; and, indeed, it is so, regarded as its evangelical feature, i.e., something added to the law in the spirit of the Atonement. As such, it surprised the apostles; and He who knew their thoughts instantly anticipated their inquiries: " For if ye forgive men," etc.

From the criticism of a very able editorial hand,[2] I feel it a privilege to insert the following valuable comments: —

"The petitions of the Lord's Prayer, as is well known, are to be found for the most part in the Talmud and Jewish liturgies. In the latter we have frequently the phrases, 'our Father, our King,' 'our Father, Father of mercies,' and 'our Father that art in heaven.' The third petition in the *Shemone esre* is, 'Let us hallow the Name in the world as it is hallowed in the high heaven. We will hallow Thee, and Thy praise, O God, shall not leave our mouth for ever and ever; since Thou, O God, art a great and holy King. Praised be Thou, O Lord, thou holy God. Thou art holy, and Thy name is holy, and holy men praise Thee everlastingly every day.' The ineffable name of God represented all His attributes, and is consequently frequently substituted for Him. The end of the first petition in the Kaddish prayer runs thus: 'May He extend His kingdom in your days, and in those of the whole house of Israel very soon.' In Berakhoth (29 *b*) we have, 'What is a short prayer? Rabbi Eliezer said, "Thy will be done in heaven, and peace of heart be unto those who fear Thee on earth."' The same tract gives another prayer: 'The needs of Thy people Israel are many, but its discernment is small. Do Thou, O everlasting One, our God, give to each man what he needs for his support, and what his body wants; but do what seemeth Thee good.' In the Mekhilta we read that Rabbi Eliezer of Modin, near Jerusalem, said: 'Whosoever has enough for the day to eat, and says, What shall I eat to-morrow? is of little faith.' This passage seems to illustrate the meaning of the Greek ἐπιούσιον. The third petition in the *Shemone esre* runs · "Forgive us, O our Father, for we have sinned; forgive us, O our King, for we have transgressed: since Thou art He that forgiveth and pardoneth.' In reference to this the Midrash Shemoth (par. 31) states, 'There is no creature who does not owe thanks to the Lord; but He is pitiful and long-suffering, and remitteth old debts.' The daily morning prayer of the Jews contains this petition: 'Lead us not into the power of sin, of transgression and crime, of temptation and shame. Let not passion have dominion over us, and keep us far from wicked men and evil company.' In one of the prayers composed in Aramaic for the rabbis and leading men of the Jewish community, the passage occurs, 'Defend and deliver them from all evil, and from all evil hap,' which may be compared with the petition, 'Deliver us from evil.' The Doxology at the end of the Lord's Prayer has equally Jewish parallels. Thus, one of the daily evening prayers concludes with the words, 'For Thine is the kingdom;' i.e., God alone is ruler of the world. The words 'the power and the glory' seem to come from 1 Chron. xxix. 11, which is quoted in the Talmud; and the Mishna Berakhoth (ix. 5) states, 'In the temple all blessings did not end with "Amen," but with the words "for ever and ever."' When the heretics multiplied, however, there was only one world; so the concluding formula became 'from everlasting to everlasting.'"

IV.

(Lift up your hearts, p. 455.)

It is demonstrated by Sir William Palmer that the *Sursum Corda* is of a date to which no history runneth contrary, and is to be found in all the primitive liturgies of whatever family. For a very early example of its use, I must refer to the Alexandrian liturgy cited by Bunsen;[3] and, in short, I beg to refer the reader to all the resources of the fourth volume of his *Hippolytus*. Little as I can approve of the magisterial air with which Dr. Bunsen undertakes to decide all

---

[1] Cap. vi. 14.   [2] *New-York Independent*, April 25, 1878.   [3] *Hippolytus*, vol. iv. p. 161.

questions, and little as I sympathize with his abnormal religion, which seems to coincide with that of no existing church or sect in the world, I feel grateful for his industry in collecting materials, and am always interested in the ingenuity with which he works them into his theories. Although he possesses some touchstone unknown to the rest of mankind, by which he reaches and utters pontifical decisions as to what is genuine and what is corrupt, I must record my doubts as to many of his facts, and my dissent from most of his inferences. But, unwilling to refer to Anglican authorities on points so much disputed, I cordially turn to the learned Chevalier, and to the treasures he has collected. See the Greek forms on p. 335 of his fourth volume, followed by the preface on p. 336, and the *Tersanctus* on p. 337 : Ἅγιος, ἅγιος, ἅγιος, κύριε Σαβαώθ, κ.τ.λ.

V.

(To pray and give thanks, p. 457.)

Here comes into view that reference of the apostle [1] to the usages of the primitive assemblies : " How shall he that occupieth the room of the unlearned say *Amen* at thy giving of thanks." Though Cyprian omits the final *Amen* from his express commentary, it is to be noted that our Lord makes it virtually part of this prayer, by His precept (St. John xvi. 23, 24), to ask in His name. Now, He makes this word *Amen* one of His own names [2] in the Apocalypse ; throwing back a new character upon His frequent use of it, especially in St. John's Gospel, and giving it as a sort of appropriation of 2 Cor. i. 20, when He calls Himself " The Amen, the faithful and true Witness." He thus makes it infinitely dear to Christians.[3] As in the Jewish usages,[4] with which the disciples were familiar, it was a matter of course, we may suppose they added *Amen* in reciting this prayer, but not with their subsequent knowledge that it implies the merits, and claims the mediation, of the Great Intercessor. Rev. v. 8, viii. 3, 4 ; St. John xvii. 8.

Tertullian [5] refers to the responsive " Hallelujah " as " enriched prayer," and the *Amen* usually accompanied this ejaculation.

VI.

(Its failing estate, p. 458.)

Hippolytus [6] foresaw the democratic age into which the feudal era of iron should pass, corroding in the toes by contact with the miry clay of the despised *plebs*, " the seed of men." No lasting strength was to be imparted to imperialism by the *plébiscite* (Dan. ii. 43) ; and the prophet might almost be supposed to have the epoch of *dynamite* in his sight, as he speaks of the unwillingness of the people to cleave to the effete system of empire. Now, then, if " the failing estate " of the world was apparent in the days of Philip and Decius, how much more in our own ! Sixteen human lives span the gulf of time between us and them, for we have many centenarians among us ; and with the Lord " a thousand years are as one day." Compare 2 Pet. iii. 9. And, putting such Scriptures together, is it not clear that " the last time " (i.e., the last of the seven *times* of the Gentiles) is drawing to its close ? The *three and a half* times of Daniel extend to the convulsive epoch of Mohammed ; the second moiety (of the seven) to our own age. See Faber, *Sacred Calendar*,[7] vol. i. cap. iii. pp. 308, 309, etc.

---

[1] 1 Cor. xiv. 16.
[2] Rev. iii. 14.
[3] Note a striking use of it, as a name of Christ, by Commodian, vol. iv. 43, p. 211.
[4] Num. v. 22; Deut. xxvii. 15; 1 Kings i. 36; 1 Chron. xvi. 36; Jer. xxviii. 6; in the Psalms *passim*.
[5] Vol. iii. cap. xxvii. p. 690, this series.
[6] P. 178.
[7] A most instructive work, though I by no means accept his theories in full.

VII.

(Peter, upon whom, etc., p. 486.)

Launoi, the eminent Gallican, found but *seventeen* of the Fathers and Doctors of the Church (among whom he reckons " Fathers " down to the twelfth century) who understand St. Peter to be " the rock," and he cites *forty* of the contrary opinion.[1]   Yet of the " seventeen," most of them speak only rhetorically, and with justifiable freedom.   I have often done the same myself, on the principle which the same apostle applies to *all* Christians : " Ye also as lively *stones*," [2] etc. But it is quite noteworthy that the Council of Trent itself momentarily adopts the prevailing patristic and therefore the Catholic interpretation, speaking of the Nicene Creed : [3] " In quo omnes qui fidem Christi profitentur necessario conveniunt, ac *fundamentum* firmum et *unicum*, contra quod portæ inferi nunquam prævalebunt (Matt. xvi. 18)."   Thus, *the faith* of Peter is confessed the only foundation, in a direct exposition of the text so often quoted with another intent. In spite of all this, the Creed of Pius IV. was enjoined as soon as that council closed ; and every member of the late Vatican Council was made to profess the same verbally before any other business was undertaken.   Now, even this spurious creed forced them to swear concerning the Holy Scriptures, " I will never take and interpret them otherwise than according to the *unanimous consent* of the Fathers."   Obviously, according to this rule, there is no Catholic doctrine on the subject ; much less any Catholic teaching to the effect that the modern bishops of Rome are " the rock," as really as St. Peter himself.

VIII.

(The Eucharist carried in it, p. 488.)

The modern usage of the Latin churches is for the priest to put the wafer into the communicant's mouth, an ordinance dating no farther back than A.D. 880.   A new doctrine having been forged, and faith in the *corporal* presence of Christ being forced upon the conscience, a change of ceremonial followed, which indicates the novelty of the idea.   Contrast the teaching of St. Cyril of Jerusalem,[4] informing his catechumens how they should receive, as follows : —

" Approaching, therefore, come not with thy wrists extended, or thy fingers open ; but make thy left hand a sort of cushion for thy right, which is about to receive the King.   And having hollowed thy palm, receive the Body of Christ, saying after it, *Amen*."   " *Not discerning* the Lord's body," etc., is the language of Scripture ; but, had the apostles taught transubstantiation, this could not be said, for everybody can discern the host when it is uplifted.   The Lord's Body is therefore discerned *by faith*, and so taken and received.

IX.

(Which should be greatest, p. 493.)

How differently our Lord must have settled this inquiry had He given the supremacy to one of the Apostles, or had He designed the supremacy of any single pastor to be perpetual in His Church !   " Who should be greatest?" ask this question of any Romanist theologian, and he answers, in the words of the Creed of Pius IV., " the Bishop of Rome, successor to St. Peter, Prince of the Apostles, and Vicar of Christ."   But why was no such answer given by our Lord? And why does St. Peter know nothing of it when he says, " The elders who are among you I

---

[1] Guettée, p. 143, ed. New York.
[2] Compare *Peshito Syriac*, where *Cephas* is the very word applied to all believers.   Ed. Trostii, 1621.
[3] Richter, *Canones et Decreta*, etc., p. 10, ed. Lipsiæ, 1853.
[4] A.D. 348.

exhort, who am also an elder . . . feed the flock of God, taking the oversight . . . not as being lords over God's heritage," etc. So also in the Council of Jerusalem, how humbly he sits under the presidency of James,[1] and again how cheerfully he permits the apostles to send him forth, and "give him mission" to Samaria![2] St. Paul, moreover, who was "not a whit behind the chiefest of the Apostles,"[3] overrules him, and reforms his judgment.[4]

If I have forborne in these notes to refer frequently to the Treatise of Bishop Sage, who often elucidates our author in a very learned manner, it is because he is almost wholly a controvertist, and therefore not to my purpose in this work. For his *Cyprian*,[5] however, I entertain a sincere respect; and, as it might seem otherwise should I omit all reference to that work, I place its title in the footnote. Profoundly do I feel what another Scottish Doctor[6] has beautifully said, "It is a loss, even to those that oppose errors and divisions, that they are forced to be busied that way."

X.

(From the slender twig, my son, thou hast ascended, p. 513.)

The text of Cyprian[7] is: "Catulus leonis Juda, de *frutice* fili mi ascendisti, recubans obdormisti velut leo, et velut catulus leonis." Now, with this compare the comment of Calmet, citing the Septuagint (ἐκ βλαστοῦ = *e germine*), and rendering by metaphrase, "*e medio plantarum*, sive herbarum germinantium, ascendisti."

Here, then, we have the idea precisely equivalent to Jer. xlix. 19: "Ecce *quasi leo ascendet* de superbia Jordanis." The lion is recumbent among the sprouting twigs (*frutice*, or foliage) of the Jordan's banks in the springtime. The swelling of the river, which the melting of snows from Lebanon causes to overflow, rouses the reposing creature; and he goes up into the mountains. But Cyprian had in hand the old African,[8] which seems to follow the LXX., and St. Jerome's Vulgate did not; and this word *frutice* animates Cyprian's poetic genius. Its springtide imagery corresponding with Easter,[9] he *reads into it* all the New Testament fulfilment: "Thou layedst down and sleepedst as a lion, and as a lion's whelp — *but, from the shooting of the first verdure in spring, thou hast gone up on high* — thou hast ascended." "Quis excitabit illum" is separated from this in the Paris text, and in the Septuagint, which the Old Latin followed, and so I have pointed it, though the Edinburgh reads: "and as a lion's whelp; who shall stir him up?"

XI.

(Third Book . . . religious teaching of our school, p. 528.)

Quirinus, Cyprian's "son" in the Gospel, seems to me to have been a catechumen of the *competent* class, i.e., preparing for baptism at Easter; or possibly of the higher sort, preparing for the first communion. Many tokens lead me to surmise that he may have been of Jewish birth; and, if so, he was probably baptized *Quirinus* after St. Luke ii. 2, as St. Paul borrowed his Roman name from Sergius Paulus.[10] The use of the word *secta*, here rendered "school," suggests to me that the Vulgate got it (and so our English version) out of the old African Latin in Acts xxviii. 22.

---

[1] Acts xv. 13.
[2] Acts viii. 14.
[3] See Barrow, *Works*, vol. iii. p. 95, ed. New York, 1845.
[4] Gal. ii. 11-14.
[5] *The Principles of the Cyprianic Age*, etc., A.D. 1695. Reprinted, Edinburgh, 1846.
[6] Leighton, *On St. Peter*, i. 2, *Works*, i. p. 30, London, 1870.
[7] Ed. Paris, 1574.
[8] Scrivener, *Introduction*, etc., p. 302, ed. 1874.
[9] Jordan overflows its banks at the time of the passover, Josh. iii. 15, v. 10, 11.
[10] Acts xiii. 7-9.

If Quirinus was a Hebrew, there is a playful irony in Cyprian's use of the word in expounding the pure morality of "the *sect*" everywhere spoken against.

Origen's treatise *Against Celsus* shows how cunningly the adversaries of the Gospel could assume a Jewish position against it;[1] and the first two books of that work are designed to establish a perfect harmony between the Old Testament and the New, proving Christ to be the substance and sum of both. Cyprian may have foreseen the perils menacing the Church from the school of Plotinus, already rising, and which soon sent forth the venomous Porphyry. He was but a presbyter when he wrote this excellent defence of the faith; and his earnest pastoral care for his pupil is shown by his addition of a third book, entirely practical. The catechetical system of St. Luke's day[2] had become a developed feature of the Church (St. Cyril's lectures in the succeeding century show how it was further expanded), and it also illustrates the purity of her moral teaching. Our author harmonizes faith and works, and presents her simple scriptural precepts in marked contrast with the putrid casuistry[3] which Pascal exposes, and which grew up in the West with the enforcement of auricular confession by Innocent III., A.D. 1215. The theory of transubstantiation was also made a dogma at the same time, and operated, with the other, to the total extinguishment of the primitive discipline and worship. The withholding of the chalice in the Holy Communion followed, A.D. 1415.

XII.

(Good works and mercy, p. 528.)

Clement was able to remind the heathen, half a century before,[4] that Christ had "*already* made the universe an ocean of blessings." Here we have the moral canons of Christianity reflecting the Light of the World, and they show us how practically it operated. As I have noted, the first Christian hospital was founded (A.D. 350) by Ephraem Syrus. His example was followed by St. Basil, who also founded another for lepers. The founding of hostels as refuges for travellers was an institution of the Nicene period. "In the time of Chrysostom," says one not too well disposed towards the Gospel,[5] "the church of Antioch supported three thousand widows and virgins, besides strangers and sick. Legacies for the poor became common; and it was not infrequent for men and women who desired to live a life of especial sanctity, and especially for priests who attained the episcopacy, as a first act, to bestow their properties in charity. A Christian, it was maintained, should devote at least one-tenth of his profits to the poor. A priest named Thalasius collected blind beggars in an asylum on the banks of the Euphrates. A merchant named Apollinus founded on Mount Nitria a gratuitous dispensary."

So here our author's canons enforce (1) works of mercy; (2) almsdeeds; (3) brotherly love; (4) mutual support; (5) forgiveness of injuries; (6) the example of Christ's holy living; (7) forbearance; (8) suppression of idle talk; (9) love of enemies; (10) abhorrence of usury, (11) and avarice, (12) and carnal impurity: also, (13) obedience to parents; (14) parental love; (15) consideration of servants; (16) respect for the aged; (17) moderation, even in use of things lawful; (18) control of the tongue; (19) abstinence from detraction; (20) to visit the sick; (21) care of widows and orphans; (22) not to flatter; (23) to practise the Golden Rule; and (24) to abstain from bloodshed. In short, we have here the outgrowth of the Sermon on the Mount, and of St. Paul's epitome, "Whatsoever things are true," etc.[6]

---

[1] Vol. iv. p. 462.
[2] Luke i. 4. Greek.
[3] See that very useful little publication of the S. P. C. K., Dr. Littledale's *Plain Reasons against Joining the Church of Rome*, pp. 18 and 205.
[4] See vol. ii. p. 202, note 5.
[5] Lecky, *History of European Morals*, vol. ii. p. 86, ed. New York, 1872. See vol. ii. p. 202, note 5.
[6] Phil. iv. 8.

XIII.

(In the thirteenth Psalm, p. 546.)

The note says that the Oxford edition gives it as the *fourteenth*, while in our English Bibles it is the *fifteenth*. As I find that some of the readers of these works are puzzled by such confusions, I note *retrospectively*, as well as for future reference, the origin of such apparent blunders.

1. Our English version follows the Hebrew numbering, which is reputed the most accurate. By that a psalm is cited in the New Testament as if the numbering itself were important, and the product of inspired wisdom.[1]

2. But the Greek Psalter differs from the Hebrew; Psalms ix. and x. being made into one, as confessedly their material suggests. The Seventy joined also Psalms cxiv. and cxv. But they divided Psalm cxvi., and also Psalm cxlvii.

3. The Vulgate Latin follows the LXX.; and our Ante-Nicene Fathers usually quote the Septuagint, or else the Old Latin, by which the Vulgate was probably governed. In the Vulgate, also, the Hebrew prefaces are often numbered as if they were verses, which is another source of confusion.

4. By the fusion of Psalms ix. and x., our Psalm xv. becomes the xiv., and so the Vulgate gives it; and the Oxford translators follow that.

5. But our text says " Psalm xiii.," and for this it is not easy to account. The Oxford editors regard it as a mere corruption of the text, and change it accordingly.

---

[1] Acts xiii. 33.

THE SEVENTH COUNCIL OF CARTHAGE UNDER CYPRIAN.[1]

CONCERNING THE BAPTISM OF HERETICS.

THE JUDGMENT OF EIGHTY-SEVEN BISHOPS ON THE BAPTISM OF HERETICS.

PROŒMIUM.—WHEN STEPHEN, BISHOP OF ROME, HAD BY HIS LETTERS CONDEMNED THE DECREES OF THE AFRICAN COUNCIL ON THE BAPTISM OF HERETICS, CYPRIAN LOST NO TIME IN HOLDING ANOTHER COUNCIL AT CARTHAGE WITH A GREATER NUMBER OF BISHOPS. HAVING THEREFORE SUMMONED EIGHTY-SEVEN BISHOPS FROM AFRICA, NUMIDIA, AND MAURITANIA, WHO ASSEMBLED AT CARTHAGE IN THE KALENDS OF SEPTEMBER, A.D. 258, THIS THIRD COUNCIL ON THE SAME MATTER OF BAPTISM WAS THEN CELEBRATED; AT THE BEGINNING OF WHICH, AFTER THE LETTERS ON EITHER SIDE HAD BEEN READ, CYPRIAN, BY IMPLICATION, CONDEMNS THE ASSUMPTION OF STEPHEN.[2]

WHEN, in the kalends of September, a great many bishops from the provinces of Africa, Numidia, and Mauritania, had met together at Carthage, together with the presbyters and deacons, and a considerable part of the congregation who were also present; and when the letter of Jubaianus written to Cyprian had been read, as also the reply of Cyprian to Jubaianus, about baptizing heretics, and what the same Jubaianus had subsequently rejoined to Cyprian,—Cyprian said: You have heard, my dearly beloved colleagues, what Jubaianus our co-bishop has written to me, taking counsel of my poor intelligence concerning the unlawful and profane baptism of heretics, as well as what I wrote in answer to him, decreeing, to wit, what we have once and again and frequently determined, that heretics who come to the Church must be baptized and sanctified by the baptism of the Church. More-over, another letter of Jubaianus has also been read to you, wherein, replying, in accordance with his sincere and religious devotion, to my letter, he not only acquiesced in what I had said, but, confessing that he had been instructed thereby, he returned thanks for it. It remains, that upon this same matter each of us should bring forward what we think, judging no man, nor rejecting any one from the right of communion, if he should think differently from us. For neither does any of us set himself up as a bishop of bishops,[3] nor by tyrannical terror does any compel his colleague to the necessity of obedience; since every bishop, according to the allowance of his liberty and power, has his own proper right of judgment, and can no more be judged by another than he himself can judge another.[4] But let us all wait for the judgment of our Lord Jesus Christ, who is the only one that has the power both of preferring us in the government of His Church, and of judging us in our conduct there.

Cæcilius of Bilta[5] said: I know only one baptism in the Church, and none out of the Church. This one will be here, where there is the true hope and the certain faith. For thus it is written: "One faith, one hope, one baptism;"[6] not among heretics, where there is no hope, and the faith is false, where all things are carried on by lying; where a demoniac exorcises; where one[7] whose mouth and words send forth a cancer puts the sacramental interrogation;[8] the faithless gives faith; the wicked bestows pardon of sins; and Antichrist baptizes in the name of

---

[1] [On councils, see Oxford trans., pp. 232, 240.]
[2] Of this council there exists no further memorials than such as have been here collected from Cyprian, and from St. Augustine, *De Baptismo contra Donatistas*, book iii. ch. iv., v., and vi., and book vii. ch. i.; and in these nothing else is contained than the judgments of the eighty-seven bishops on the nullity of baptism administered by heretics. If any one desires to see these judgments impugned, let him consult Augustine as above. The results of this council are given in Ep. lxxi. p. 378, *supra*.

[3] Of course this implies a rebuke to the assumption of Stephen, ["their brother," and forcibly contrasts the spirit of Cyprian with that of his intolerant compeer].
[4] [This, then, is the primitive idea of the relations existing, mutually, among bishops as brethren.]
[5] *Scil.* of Mauritania; possibly, says the Oxford translator, Bidil, Bita, or "urbs Abitensis."
[6] Eph. iv. 5.
[7] According to some editions, "the sacrilegious man," etc
[8] "Sacramentum interrogat."

565

Christ; he who is cursed of God blesses; he who is dead promises life; he who is unpeaceful gives peace; the blasphemer calls upon God; the profane person administers the office of the priesthood; the sacrilegious person establishes an altar. In addition to all these things, there is also this evil, that the priests of the devil dare to celebrate the Eucharist; or else let those who stand by them say that all these things concerning heretics are false. Behold to what kind of things the Church is compelled[1] to consent, and is constrained without baptism, without pardon of sins, to hold communion. And this thing, brethren, we ought to flee from and avoid, and to separate ourselves from so great a wickedness, and to hold one baptism, which is granted by the Lord to the Church alone.

Primus of Misgirpa[2] said: I decide, that every man who comes to us from heresy must be baptized. For in vain does he think that he has been baptized there, seeing that there is no baptism save the one and true baptism in the Church; because not only is God one, but the faith is one, and the Church is one, wherein stands the one baptism, and holiness, and the rest. For whatever is done without, has no effect of salvation.

Polycarp from Adrumetum[3] said: They who approve the baptism of heretics make void our baptism.

Novatus of Thamugada[4] said: Although we know that all the Scriptures give witness concerning the saving baptism, still we ought to declare our faith, that heretics and schismatics who come to the Church, and appear to have been falsely baptized, ought to be baptized in the everlasting fountain; and therefore, according to the testimony of the Scriptures, and according to the decree of our colleagues, men of most holy memory, that all schismatics and heretics who are converted to the Church must be baptized; and moreover, that those who appeared to have been ordained must be received among lay people.

Nemesianus of Thubunæ[5] said: That the baptism which heretics and schismatics bestow is not the true one, is everywhere declared in the Holy Scriptures, since their very leading men are false Christs and false prophets, as the Lord says by Solomon: "He who trusteth in that which is false, he feedeth the winds; and the very same, moreover, followeth the flight of birds. For he forsaketh the ways of his own vineyard, he has wandered from the paths of his own little field. But he walketh through pathless places,

and dry, and a land destined for thirst; moreover, he gathereth together fruitless things in his hands."[6] And again: "Abstain from strange water, and from the fountain of another do not drink, that you may live a long time; also that the years of life may be added to thee."[7] And in the Gospel our Lord Jesus Christ spoke with His divine voice, saying, "Except a man be born again of water and the Spirit, he cannot enter the kingdom of God."[8] This is the Spirit which from the beginning was borne over the waters; for neither can the Spirit operate without the water, nor the water without the Spirit. Certain people therefore interpret for themselves ill, when they say that by imposition of the hand they receive the Holy Ghost, and are thus received, when it is manifest that they ought to be born again in the Catholic Church by both sacraments. Then indeed they will be able to be sons of God, as says the apostle: "Taking care to keep the unity of the Spirit in the bond of peace. There is one body, and one Spirit, as ye have been called in one hope of your calling; one Lord, one faith, one baptism, one God."[9] All these things speaks the Catholic Church.[10] And again, in the Gospel the Lord says: "That which is born of the flesh is flesh, and that which is born of the Spirit is spirit; because God is a Spirit, and he is born of God."[11] Therefore, whatsoever things all heretics and schismatics do are carnal, as the apostle says: "For the works of the flesh are manifest, which are, fornications, uncleannesses, incest, idolatries, witchcrafts, hatreds, contentions, jealousy, anger, divisions, heresies, and the like to these; concerning which I have told you before, as I also foretell you now, that whoever do such things shall not inherit the kingdom of God."[12] And thus the apostle condemns, with all the wicked, those also who cause division, that is, schismatics and heretics. Unless therefore they receive saving baptism in the Catholic Church, which is one, they cannot be saved, but will be condemned with the carnal in the judgment of the Lord Christ.

Januarius of Lambesis[13] said: According to the authority[14] of the Holy Scriptures, I decree that all heretics must be baptized, and so admitted into the holy Church.

Lucius of Castra Galbæ[15] said: Since the Lord in His Gospel said, "Ye are the salt of the earth: but if the salt should have lost its savour, wherewith shall it be salted? It is thenceforth good

---

[1] By the despotism of Stephen.
[2] A city of Zeugitana. Augustine calls this bishop Felix, and speaks of him as the *first* of that name who spoke. — *Fell*.
[3] This is the Polycarp referred to in Ep. xliv. p. 322, *supra*. Adrumetum was a colony on the coast, about eighty-five miles from Carthage.
[4] In Numidia.
[5] In Mauritania Cæsariensis.

[6] Prov. ix. 12, LXX.
[7] Prov. ix. 19.
[8] John iii. 5.
[9] Eph. iv. 3-6.
[10] [He has no idea that this voice proceeds from any one bishop.]
[11] John iii. 6.
[12] Gal. v. 19-21.
[13] In Numidia.
[14] [This appeal to Scripture against Stephen must be noted, whatever we may think of his conclusions.]
[15] Or Gilba.

for nothing, but to be cast out of doors, and to be trodden under foot of men."[1] And again, after His resurrection, sending His apostles, He gave them charge, saying, "All power is given unto me, in heaven and in earth. Go and teach all nations, baptizing them in the name of the Father, and of the Son, and of the Holy Ghost."[2] Since, therefore, it is manifest that heretics — that is, the enemies of Christ — have not the sound confession of the sacrament; moreover, that schismatics cannot season others with spiritual wisdom, since they themselves, by departing from the Church, which is one, having lost the savour, have become contrary to it, — let it be done as it is written, "The house of those that are contrary to the law owes a cleansing."[3] And it is a consequence that those who, having been baptized by people who are contrary to the Church, are polluted, must first be cleansed, and then at length be baptized.

Crescens of Cirta[4] said: In such an assembly of most holy fellow-priests, as the letters of our most beloved Cyprian to Jubaianus and also to Stephen have been read, containing in them so much of the holy testimonies which descend from the divinely made Scriptures, that with reason we ought, all being made one by the grace of God, to consent to them; I judge that all heretics and schismatics who wish to come to the Catholic Church, shall not be allowed to enter without they have first been exorcised and baptized; with the exception of those indeed who may previously have been baptized in the Catholic Church, and these in such a way that they may be reconciled to the penitence of the Church by the imposition of hands.

Nicomedes of Segermæ[5] said: My opinion is this, that heretics coming to the Church should be baptized, for the reason that among sinners without they can obtain no remission of sins.

Munnulus[6] of Girba[7] said: The truth of our Mother[8] the Catholic Church, brethren, hath always remained and still remains with us, and even especially in the Trinity of baptism, as our Lord says, "Go ye and baptize the nations, in the name of the Father, of the Son, and of the Holy Spirit."[9] Since, then, we manifestly know that heretics have not either Father, or Son, or Holy Spirit, they ought, when they come to the Church our Mother, truly to be born again and to be baptized; that the cancer which they had,

and the anger of damnation, and the witchery of error, may be sanctified by the holy and heavenly laver.

Secundinus of Cedias[10] said: Since our Lord Christ says, "He who is not with me is against me;"[11] and John the apostle calls those who depart from the Church Antichrists — undoubtedly enemies of Christ — any such as are called Antichrists cannot minister the grace of saving baptism. And therefore I think that those who flee from the snares of the heretics to the Church must be baptized by us, who are called friends of God, of His condescension.

Felix of Bagai[12] said: As, when the blind leads the blind, they fall together into the ditch; so, when the heretic baptizes a heretic, they fall together into death. And therefore a heretic must be baptized and made alive, lest we who are alive should hold communion with the dead.

Polianus of Mileum[13] said: It is right that a heretic be baptized in the holy Church.

Theogenes of Hippo Regius[14] said: According to the sacrament of God's heavenly grace which we have received, we believe one baptism which is in the holy Church.

Dativus of Badis[15] said: We, as far as in us lies, do not hold communion with heretics, unless they have been baptized in the Church, and have received remission of their sins.

Successus of Abbir Germaniciana[16] said: Heretics can either do nothing, or they can do all. If they can baptize, they can also bestow the Holy Spirit. But if they cannot give the Holy Spirit, because they have not the Holy Spirit, neither can they spiritually baptize. Therefore we judge that heretics must be baptized.

Fortunatus of Tuccaboris[17] said: Jesus Christ our Lord and God, Son of God the Father and Creator, built His Church upon a rock,[18] not upon heresy; and gave the power of baptizing to bishops, not to heretics. Wherefore they who are without the Church, and, standing in opposition to Christ, disperse His sheep and flock, cannot baptize, being without.

Sedatus of Tuburbo[19] said: In the degree in which water sanctified in the Church by the prayer of the priest, washes away sins; in that degree, if infected with heretical discourse as with a cancer, it heaps up sins. Wherefore we must endeavour with all peaceful powers, that no one infected and stained with heretical error

---

[1] Matt. v. 13.
[2] Matt. xxviii. 18, 19.
[3] Prov. xiv. 9, LXX.
[4] Cirta Julia in Numidia.
[5] In Numidia.
[6] Ep. liii. p. 336, *supra*. Munnulus is mentioned as one of the bishops who write with Cyprian to Cornelius. He is there called "Monulus."
[7] Gerra.
[8] [Testimony to the meaning of the Holy Catholic Church in the Nicene Creed.]
[9] Matt. xxviii. 19.

[10] Perhaps Quidias in Mauritania Cæsariensis.
[11] Matt. xii. 30.
[12] In Numidia. Here was held the Donatist "Concilium Bagaiense" of 310 bishops (Oxford ed.).
[13] In Numidia.
[14] The See of St. Augustine in Numidia, 218 miles from Carthage, and 160 miles from Hippo Diarrhytus. See p. 571, *infra*.
[15] Badea, or Badel, in Numidia.
[16] In Zeugitana.
[17] Tucca-terebinthina in Zeugitana.
[18] [Evidently he never suspects that Stephen is the rock.]
[19] Thuburbo, or Thuburbis, in Zeugitana.

refuse to receive the single and true baptism of the Church, by which whosoever is not baptized, shall become an alien from the kingdom of heaven.

Privatianus of Sufetula[1] said: Let him who says that heretics have the power of baptizing, say first who founded heresy. For if heresy is of God, it also may have the divine indulgence. But if it is not from God, how can it either have the grace of God, or confer it upon any one?

Privatus of Sufes[2] said: He who approves the baptism of heretics, what else does he do than communicate with heretics?

Hortensianus of Lares[3] said: Let either these presumptuous ones,[4] or those who favour heretics, consider how many baptisms there are. We claim for the Church one baptism, which we know not except in the Church. Or how can they baptize any one in the name of Christ, whom Christ Himself declares to be His adversaries?

Cassius of Macomadæ[5] said: Since there cannot be two baptisms, he who yields baptism to the heretics takes it away from himself. I judge therefore that heretics, lamentable and corrupt, must be baptized when they begin to come to the Church; and that when washed by the sacred and divine washing, and illuminated by the light of life, they may be received into the Church, not as enemies, but as made peaceful; not as foreigners, but as of the household of the faith of the Lord; not as children of adultery, but as sons of God; not of error, but of salvation; except those who once faithful have been supplanted, and have passed over from the Church to the darkness of heresy, but that these must be restored by the imposition of hands.

Another Januarius of Vicus Cæsaris[6] said: If error does not obey truth, much more truth does not consent to error; and therefore we stand by the Church in which we preside, that, claiming her baptism for herself alone, we should baptize those whom the Church has not baptized.

Another Secundinus of Carpi[7] said: Are heretics Christians or not? If they are Christians, why are they not in the Church of God? If they are not Christians, how come they to make Christians? Or whither will tend the Lord's discourse, when He says, "He that is not with me is against me, and he who gathereth not with me scattereth?"[8] Whence it appears plain that upon strange children, and on the offspring of Antichrist, the Holy Ghost cannot descend only by imposition of hands, since it is manifest that heretics have not baptism.

Victoricus of Thabraca[9] said: If heretics are allowed to baptize and to give remission of sins, wherefore do we brand them with infamy and call them heretics?

Another Felix of Uthina[10] said: Nobody doubts, most holy fellow-priests, that human presumption is not able to do so much as the adorable and venerable majesty of our Lord Jesus Christ. Therefore, remembering the danger, we ought not only to observe this also, but moreover to confirm it by the voice of all of us, that all heretics who come to the bosom of Mother Church should be baptized, that thus the heretical mind that has been polluted by a long decay, purged by the sanctification of the laver, may be reformed for the better.

Quietus of Baruch[11] said: We who live by faith ought to obey with careful observance those things which before have been foretold for our instruction. For it is written in Solomon: "He that is baptized from the dead, (and again toucheth the dead,[12]) what availeth his washing?"[13] which certainly speaks of those who are washed by heretics, and of those that wash them. For if those who are baptized among them obtain by remission of their sins life eternal, why do they come to the Church? But if from a dead person no salvation is received, and therefore, acknowledging their previous error, they return to the truth with penitence, they ought to be sanctified with the one vital baptism which is in the Catholic Church.

Castus of Sicca[14] said: He who with contempt of the truth presumes to follow custom, is either envious and malignant in respect of his brethren to whom the truth is revealed, or is ungrateful in respect of God, by whose inspiration His Church is instructed.

Euchratius of Thenæ[15] said: God and our Lord Jesus Christ, teaching the apostles with His own mouth, has entirely completed our faith, and the grace of baptism, and the rule of the ecclesiastical law, saying: "Go ye and teach all nations, baptizing them in the name of the Father, and of the Son, and of the Holy Ghost."[16] Thus the false and wicked baptism of heretics must be rejected by us, and refuted with all detestation, from whose mouth is expressed poison, not life, not celestial grace, but blasphemy of the Trinity.[17] And therefore it is

[1] A city of Numidia Byzacenæ.
[2] In Byzacena.
[3] A city of Numidia Ptolemais.
[4] [Stephen and those who accept his ideas.]
[5] Or Macodama in Numidia.
[6] Perhaps Nova Cæsaris in Numidia.
[7] In Zeugitana, on the borders of Tunis.
[8] Matt. xii. 30.

[9] A colony variously called Tabraca or Tabathra.
[10] Οὔθινα in Zeugitana.
[11] Or Buruch, probably Bourka in Numidia.
[12] This clause is omitted in the larger number of editions.
[13] Ecclus. xxxiv. 25.
[14] Sicca Veneria, a city of Zeugitana.
[15] A city of Byzacena.
[16] Matt. xxviii. 18.
[17] "Let the reader observe here, as elsewhere, that the word 'Trinity' is simply used for the persons of the Godhead" (Oxford edit.).

manifest that heretics who come to the Church ought to be baptized with the sound and Catholic baptism, in order that, being purified from the blasphemy of their presumption, they may be reformed by the grace of the Holy Spirit.

Libosus of Vaga[1] said: In the Gospel the Lord says, "I am the truth."[2] He said not, "I am the custom." Therefore the truth being manifest, let custom yield to truth; so that, although for the past any one was not in the habit of baptizing heretics in the Church, let him now begin to baptize them.[3]

Lucius of Thebeste[1] said: I determine that blasphemous and unrighteous heretics, who with various words tear asunder the holy and adorable words of the Scriptures, are to be accursed, and therefore that they must be exorcised and baptized.

Eugenius of Ammedera[1] said: And I determine the same — that heretics must be baptized.

Also another Felix of Amaccora[4] said: And I myself, following the authority of the divine Scriptures,[5] judge that heretics must be baptized; and, moreover, those also who contend that they have been baptized among the schismatics. For if, according to Christ's warning, our font is private to us, let all the adversaries of our Church understand that it cannot be for another. Nor can He who is the Shepherd of the one flock give the saving water to two peoples. And therefore it is plain that neither heretics nor schismatics can receive anything heavenly, seeing that they dare to receive from men who are sinners, and from those who are external to the Church. When there is no place for the giver, assuredly there is no profit for the receiver.

Also another Januarius of Muzzuli[6] said: I am surprised, since all confess that there is one baptism, that all do not perceive the unity of the same baptism. For the Church and heresy are two things, and different things. If heretics have baptism, we have it not; but if we have it, heretics cannot have it. But there is no doubt that the Church alone possesses the baptism of Christ, since she alone possesses both the grace and the truth of Christ.

Adelphius of Thasvalte[7] said: Certain persons without reason impugn the truth by false and envious words, in saying that we rebaptize, when the Church does not rebaptize heretics, but baptizes them.

Demetrius of Leptiminus[8] said: We maintain one baptism, because we demand for the Church Catholic alone her own property. But they who say that heretics truly and legitimately baptize, are themselves the people who make not one, but many baptisms. For since heresies are many, according to their number will be reckoned baptisms.

Vincentius of Thibaris[9] said: We know that heretics are worse than Gentiles. If, therefore, being converted, they should wish to come to the Lord, we have assuredly the rule of truth which the Lord by His divine precept commanded to His apostles, saying, "Go ye, lay on hands in my name, expel demons."[10] And in another place: "Go ye and teach the nations, baptizing them in the name of the Father, of the Son, and of the Holy Ghost."[11] Therefore first of all by imposition of hands in exorcism, secondly by the regeneration of baptism, they may then come to the promise of Christ. Otherwise I think it ought not to be done.

Marcus of Mactaris[12] said: It is not to be wondered at if heretics, enemies, and impugners of the truth claim to themselves a matter in the power and condescension of others. But it is to be wondered at, that some of us, prevaricators of the truth, support heretics and oppose themselves to Christians. Therefore we decree that heretics must be baptized.

Sattius of Sicilibba[13] said: If to heretics in baptism their sins are remitted, they come to the Church without reason. For since, in the day of judgment, they are sins which are punished, there is nothing which the heretics can fear from Christ's judgment, if they have already obtained remission of their sins.

Victor of Gor[14] said: Since sins are not remitted[15] save in the baptism of the Church, he who admits a heretic to communion without baptism does two things against reason: he does not cleanse the heretics, and he befouls the Christians.

Aurelius of Utica[16] said: Since the apostle says that we are not to communicate with other people's sins, what else does he do but communicate with other people's sins, who holds communion with heretics without the Church's baptism? And therefore I judge that heretics must be baptized, that they may receive forgiveness of their sins; and thus communion may be had with them.

---

[1] A city of Numidia.
[2] John xiv. 6.
[3] [Here is a concession that at least the *local* custom could be pleaded by Stephen.]
[4] "Damatcore," or "Vamaccore," in Numidia.
[5] [Here we may think as we choose as to this conclusion, but the appeal to Holy Scripture proves that this is the only infallible authority.]
[6] Mazula in Numidia.
[7] A city of Byzacena.
[8] Λέπτις μικρά — a city of Byzacena.
[9] Tabora, a city of Mauritania Cæsariensis.
[10] Apparently in reference to Mark xvi. 17, 18.
[11] Matt. xxviii. 19.
[12] A city of Byzacena.
[13] A city of Zeugitana — "Sicilibra," thirty-four miles from Carthage.
[14] Probably "Garra," a city of Mauritania Cæsariensis, or "Garriana," a city of Byzacena.
[15] [Referring to Acts xxii. 16 and John xx. 23.]
[16] A city of Zeugitana, famous as being the place of Cato's death, now called Byzerta.

Iambus of Germaniciana [1] said : They who approve of the baptism of heretics, disapprove of ours, in denying that they who are, I will not say washed, but befouled, outside the Church, ought to be baptized in the Church.

Lucianus of Rucuma [2] said : It is written, "And God saw the light, that it was good, and divided between the light and the darkness." [3] If there can be agreement between light and darkness, there may be something in common between us and heretics. Therefore I determine that heretics must be baptized.

Pelagianus of Luperciana [4] said : It is written, "Either the Lord is God, or Baal is God." [5] Therefore in the present case also, either the Church is the Church, or heresy is the Church. On the other hand, if heresy is not the Church, how can the Church's baptism be among heretics?

Jader of Midila [6] said : We know that there is but one baptism in the Catholic Church, and therefore we ought not to receive a heretic unless he has been baptized among us ; lest he should think that he has been baptized out of the Catholic Church.

Also another Felix of Marazana [7] said : There is one faith, one baptism, but of the Catholic Church, which alone has the right to baptize.

Paulus of Obba [8] said : It does not disturb me if any man does not assert the faith and truth of the Church, since the apostle says, " For what if some of them have fallen away from the faith? Has their unbelief made the faith of God of no effect? By no means. For God is true, but every man a liar." [9] But if God is true, how can the truth of baptism be among the heretics, among whom God is not?

Pomponius of Dionysiana [7] said : It is evident that heretics cannot baptize and give remission of sins, seeing that they have not power to be able to loose or to bind anything on earth.

Venantius of Timisa [2] said : If a husband, going into foreign parts, had commended his wife to the guardianship of his friend, that friend would take care of her who was commended to him with all possible diligence, that her chastity and holiness should not be corrupted by any one. Christ the Lord and our God, going to His Father, has commended to us His bride. Shall we guard her incorrupt and inviolate, or shall we betray her integrity and chastity to adulterers and corrupters? For he who makes the Church's baptism common to heretics, betrays the spouse of Christ to adulterers.

Ahymnus of Ausvaga [10] said : We have received one baptism, and that same we maintain and practise. But he who says that heretics also may lawfully baptize, makes two baptisms.

Saturninus of Victoriana [7] said : If heretics may baptize, they who do unlawful things are excused and defended ; nor do I see why either Christ should have called them adversaries, or the apostle should have called them Antichrists.

Saturninus [11] of Thucca [6] said : The Gentiles, although they worship idols, do yet know and confess a supreme God [12] as Father and Creator. Against Him Marcion blasphemes, and some persons do not blush to approve the baptism of Marcion. How do such priests either observe or vindicate God's priesthood, who do not baptize God's enemies, and hold communion with them as they are !

Marcellus of Zama [13] said : Since sins are not remitted [14] save in the baptism of the Church, he who does not baptize a heretic holds communion with a sinner.

Irenæus of Ululi [15] said : If the Church does not baptize a heretic, for the reason that he is said to be already baptized, it is the greater heresy.

Donatus of Cibaliana [16] said : I know one Church and her one baptism. If there is any who says that the grace of baptism is with heretics, he must first show and prove that the Church is among them.

Zosimus of Tharassa [6] said : When a revelation of the truth is made, let error give place to truth ; because Peter also, who previously circumcised, yielded to Paul when he preached the truth. [17]

Julianus of Telepte [18] said : It is written, " No man can receive anything unless it have been given him from heaven." [19] If heresy is from heaven, it can also give baptism.

Faustus of Timida Regia [20] said : Let not them who are in favour of heretics flatter themselves. He who interferes with the baptism of the Church on behalf of heretics, makes them Christians, and us heretics.

---

[1] *Scil.* " urbs," a city of Byzacena. The epithet refers to its being a place frequented by the veterans of German cohorts, and distinguishes it from " Abbiritana."
[2] A city of Zeugitana.
[3] Gen. i. 4.
[4] Possibly " Lubertina."
[5] 1 Kings xviii. 21.
[6] A city of Numidia.
[7] A city of Byzacena.
[8] Otherwise " Bobba," a city of Mauritania.
[9] Rom. iii. 3, 4.

[10] This seems to be " Ausana " or " Ausagga."
[11] The Oxford reads " Another Saturninus."
[12] Manifestly, says the Oxford editor, this expression refers to " Jupiter the father of gods and men."
[13] A city of Numidia; the scene of Hannibal's overthrow by Scipio.
[14] [The Nicene Creed is emphatic in the article based on this idea; and it proves that the primitive discipline of penitence was not in those days a " sacrament of absolution," to which all were compelled to submit. Private confessions seem to have been unknown.]
[15] " Usilla," a city of Byzacena.
[16] Possibly " Cerbaliana " in Byzacena.
[17] [The bearings of this simple statement upon the later claims of Stephen's See must not be overlooked.]
[18] A city of Numidia Byzacenæ.
[19] John iii 27.
[20] A city of Zeugitana; some read " Tumida."

Geminius of Furni [1] said: Some of our colleagues may prefer heretics to themselves, they cannot to us: and therefore what we have once determined we maintain — that we baptize those who come to us from the heretics.

Rogatianus of Nova [2] said: Christ instituted the Church; the devil, heresy. How can the synagogue of Satan have the baptism of Christ?

Therapius of Bulla [3] said: He who concedes and betrays the Church's baptism to heretics, what else has he been to the spouse of Christ than a Judas?

Also another Lucius of Membresa [4] said: It is written, "God heareth not a sinner." [5] How can a heretic who is a sinner be heard in baptism?

Also another Felix of Bussacene [6] said: In the matter of receiving heretics without the baptism of the Church, let no one prefer custom to reason and truth, because reason and truth always exclude custom. [7]

Another Saturninus of Avitini [8] said: If Antichrist can give to any one the grace of Christ, heretics also are able to baptize, for they are called antichrists.

Quintus of Aggya: [9] He can give something who has something. But what can heretics give, who, it is plain, have nothing?

Another Julianus of Marcelliana [10] said: If a man can serve two masters, God and mammon, baptism also can serve two masters, the Christian and the heretic.

Tenax of Horrea Cæliæ [11] said: Baptism is one, but it is the Church's. Where the Church is not there, there can be no baptism.

Another Victor of Assuri [1] said: It is written, that "God is one, and Christ is one, and the Church is one, and baptism is one." [12] How, therefore, can any one be baptized there, where God, and Christ, and the one Church is not?

Donatulus of Capse [13] said: And I also have always thought this, that heretics, who can obtain nothing without the Church, when they are converted to the Church, must be baptized.

Verulus [14] of Rusiccada [15] said: A man who is a heretic cannot give what he has not; much more a schismatic, who has lost what he once had.

Pudentianus of Cuiculis [15] said: The novelty of my episcopal office, [16] beloved brethren, has caused me to await what my elders should judge. For it is manifest that heresies have nothing, nor can have any thing. And thus, if any one comes from them, it is most justly decreed that they must be baptized.

Peter of Hippo Diarrhytus [17] said: Since there is one baptism in the Catholic Church, it is manifest that one cannot be baptized outside the Church. And therefore I judge that those who have been dipped in heresy or in schism, when they come to the Church, should be baptized.

Also another Lucius of Ausafa [18] said: According to the direction of my mind, and of the Holy Spirit, as there is one God and Father of our Lord Jesus Christ, and one Christ, and one hope, and one Spirit, and one Church, there ought also to be one baptism. And therefore I say, that if any thing had been set on foot or accomplished by heretics, it ought to be rescinded, and that those who come thence must be baptized in the Church.

Also another Felix of Gurgites [13] said: I judge that, according to the precepts of the holy Scriptures, he who is unlawfully baptized by heretics outside the Church, when he wishes to take refuge in the Church, should obtain the grace of baptism where it is lawfully given.

Pusillus of Lamasba [19] said: I believe that there is no saving baptism except in the Catholic Church. Whatsoever is apart from the Catholic Church is a pretence.

Salvianus of Gazaufala [20] said: It is certain that heretics have nothing, and therefore they come to us that they may receive what they have not.

Honoratus of Thucca [21] said: Since Christ is the Truth, we ought rather to follow truth than custom; so that we should sanctify heretics with the Church's baptism, seeing that they come to us for the reason that they could receive nothing without.

Victor of Octavum [22] said: As yourselves also know, I have not long been appointed a bishop, and I therefore waited for the decision [16]

---

[1] A city of Zeugitana.
[2] A city of Mauritania Cæsariensis. Fell observes that in Numidia are many cities of the name of "Nova" or "Noba."
[3] A city of Zeugitana. There were two cities of the name — Βουλλαρία, or Bulla Regia, and Βουλλαμίνσα, or Bulla Minor. The latter is probably referred to.
[4] Otherwise "Memosita," a city of Zeugitana. It is also written "Membrosa."
[5] John ix. 31.
[6] Probably "Byzacene."
[7] [Custom, then, was elsewhere established: and it ultimately prevailed; whether against truth or not, need not here be discussed.]
[8] This is supposed to be "Autenti," a city of Byzacene.
[9] Supposed to be Aggiva.
[10] Mention of the Bishop of Marcelliana is found in *Notitia Episcopatus Africæ*.
[11] A village belonging to Byzacene, seventy-five miles from Carthage.
[12] Eph. iv. 5.
[13] A city of Byzacene.
[14] Called in some editions "a martyr from the schismatics."
[15] A city of Numidia.

[16] [Noteworthy examples of episcopal modesty. In the colleges of bishops, however, it is now usual to call upon juniors first, that, if they should think differently from older brethren, their free opinion need not be restrained by deference.]
[17] A city of Zeugitana, called Diarrhytus because of the number of the streams that water it. The name is otherwise read "Hippo Diarrhytorum."
[18] A city of Zeugitana, sometimes written "Assapha."
[19] "Lambesa," a city of Numidia.
[20] A city of Numidia, otherwise Γανσάφνα (Ptol.) and Γαζόφυλα (Procop.)
[21] There are four cities in Africa of this name.
[22] A city of Numidia, otherwise called "Octabum."

of my predecessors. I therefore think this, that as many as come from heresy should undoubtedly be baptized.

Clarus of Mascula [1] said : The sentence of our Lord Jesus Christ is plain, when He sent His apostles, and accorded to them alone the power given to Him by His Father ; and to them we have succeeded, governing the Lord's Church with the same power,[2] and baptizing the faith of believers. And therefore heretics, who neither have power without, nor have the Church of Christ, are able to baptize no one with His baptism.

Secundianus of Thambei [3] said : We ought not to deceive heretics by our presumption ; so that they who have not been baptized in the Church of our Lord Jesus Christ, and have not obtained by this means remissions of their sins, when the day of judgment shall come, should impute to us that through us they were not baptized, and did not obtain the indulgence of divine grace. On which account, since there is one Church and one baptism, when they are converted to us they should obtain, together with the Church, the Church's baptism also.

Also another Aurelius of Chullabi [4] said : John the apostle laid it down in his epistle, saying : "If any one come unto you, and have not the doctrine of Christ, receive him not into your house, and say not to him, Hail. For he that saith to him, Hail, partakes with his evil deeds."[5] How can such be rashly admitted into God's house, who are prohibited from being admitted into our private dwelling? Or how can we hold communion with them without the Church's baptism, to whom, if we should only say Hail, we are partakers of their evil deeds?

Litteus [6] of Gemelli [7] said : If the blind lead the blind, both fall into the ditch. Since, then, it is manifest that heretics cannot give light to any, as being themselves blind, their baptism does not avail.

Natalis of Oëa [8] said : As well I who am present, as Pompey [9] of Sabrata,[8] as also Dioga of Leptis Magna [10] — who, absent indeed in body, but present in spirit, have given me charge — judge the same as our colleagues, that heretics cannot hold communion with us, unless they shall be baptized with ecclesiastical baptism.

Junius of Neapolis [8] said : From the judgment which we once determined on I do not recede, that we should baptize heretics who come to the Church.

Cyprian of Carthage said : The letter which was written to our colleague Jubaianus very fully expresses my opinion, that, according to evangelical and apostolic testimony, heretics, who are called adversaries of Christ and Antichrists, when they come to the Church, must be baptized with the one baptism of the Church, that they may be made of adversaries, friends, and of Antichrists, Christians.[11]

---

[6] This Litteus is mentioned in Ep. lxxvi. p. 402, *supra*.
[7] A city of Numidia. A Roman colony was planted there under the Emperor Hadrian.
[8] A city of Tripolis.
[9] Probably the same to whom Ep. lxxiii. (p. 386, *supra*) was written.
[10] A city of Tripolis, thus distinguished from Leptis parva.
[11] [Here Cyprian sums up, and gives the sentence of the council, after the example of St. James, who presided in the Council of Jerusalem, Acts xv. 13, 19.]

---

[1] A city of Numidia.
[2] [This is Cyprian's theory of the origin of the episcopate. Elucidation *infra*.]
[3] A city of Byzacena.
[4] This is otherwise called " Cululi," a city of Byzacena.
[5] 2 John 10, 11.

ELUCIDATION.

(To them we have succeeded, p. 572.)

THE theory of Cyprian is thus recognised in full council, by his colleagues, with respect to the unity of the Church Catholic. They have never heard of any counter theory, and they state it as a matter of course. Fortunatus of "Tuccaboris" had shortly before referred to the Church as " built upon a *rock*," with evident reference to *the faith*, for he adds, " not upon *heresy*." Of a perpetuated *construction*, of which any one bishop was the perpetuated *foundation*, nobody as yet seems to have dreamed. " Other *foundation* can no man lay than that is laid," says St. Paul ; viz., "Christ." On Him, "the Stone, Elect, precious," St. Peter and all the apostles (the prophets as well) are built as foundation-stones ; and we also, as " lively stones," are built upon that foundation,[1] into a holy temple.

This Council of Carthage sustains Cyprian also in his judgment concerning the question of baptism, and it is a mistake to say that it was ever overruled. Compare St. Basil, *Ad Amphilochium* (*Epist. Canonica prima*, p. 19, vol. iii., ed. Paris, 1638), where he refers to Cyprian and Firmilian ("*our* Firmilian ") as " ancient men," and treats the question as still an open one.

---

[1] See p. 522, sec. 16, *supra*. All this interprets the *Petra*, not " Petrus."

TRANSLATOR'S INTRODUCTION

TO

TREATISES ATTRIBUTED TO CYPRIAN ON QUESTIONABLE AUTHORITY.

THE treatises which follow are usually classed under the doubtful works of Cyprian. Baluzius, however, gives the two first, *On the Public Shows*, and *On the Glory of Martyrdom*, among the genuine *Opuscula*, and says: "I have not thought it fit to prejudice any one amid the diversity of opinions on the subject, but have refrained from separating the following from the genuine works of the blessed martyr, especially since many have observed that there is no such difference of style in these writings as to justify the denial of their authorship to Cyprian."

Of course the question is one almost entirely of criticism, and the translator leaves the discussion of it to abler hands. He ventures, however, to record his impression, that the style of the following writings throughout is more pretentious and laboured, and far more wordy and involved, than that of Cyprian's undoubted works. With a more copious vocabulary, there is manifested less skill in the use of words; and if the text be not in some places most elaborately and unintelligibly corrupt, the accumulation of epithets, as well as their collocation, seems the very wantonness of rhetoric. The text, however, is undoubtedly far less to be depended upon than in the case of the genuine works.

The treatises *On the Discipline and Benefit of Chastity* and the *Exhortation to Repentance* are generally placed under the *Opuscula dubia*. The former was first edited by Baluzius, with the title "Epistle of an Unknown Author." Its Cyprianic authorship was maintained by Bellarmin, Pamelius, and others; while Erasmus, Tillemont, and others have rejected it as spurious. The second treatise was first published by Joannes Chrysostomus Trombellius (in 1751), who regarded it as a genuine work of Cyprian's. And indeed, as far as internal evidence goes, the treatise, consisting merely of a collection of quotations from Scripture, in the manner of the *Testimonies against the Jews*, may probably be attributed to him with as much reason as the *Testimonies*.

It is, however, right to add, that Professor Blunt quotes from the *Treatise on the Glory of Martyrdom* as being Cyprian's, without referring to any doubts on the subject.[1]

---

[1] [A strong testimony in its favour. It is quite possible that the less worthy portions are corrupt interpolations.]

TREATISES ATTRIBUTED TO CYPRIAN ON QUESTIONABLE AUTHORITY.

ON THE PUBLIC SHOWS.[1]

ARGUMENT.[2] — THE WRITER FIRST OF ALL TREATS AGAINST THOSE WHO ENDEAVOURED TO DEFEND THE PUBLIC EXHIBITIONS OF THE HEATHENS BY SCRIPTURAL AUTHORITY ; AND HE PROVES THAT, ALTHOUGH THEY ARE NEVER PROHIBITED BY THE EXPRESS WORDS OF SCRIPTURE, YET THAT THEY ARE CONDEMNED IN THE SCRIPTURAL PROHIBITION OF IDOLATRY, FROM THE FACT THAT THERE IS NO KIND OF PUBLIC SHOW WHICH IS NOT CONSECRATED TO IDOLS.[3]

1. Cyprian to the congregation who stand fast in the Gospel, sends greeting. As it greatly saddens me, and deeply afflicts my soul, when no opportunity of writing to you is presented to me, for it is my loss not to hold converse with you ; so nothing restores to me such joyfulness and hilarity, as when that opportunity is once more afforded me. I think that I am with you when I am speaking to you by letter. Although, therefore, I know that you are satisfied that what I tell you is even as I say, and that you have no doubt of the truth of my words, nevertheless an actual proof will also attest the reality of the matter. For my affection (for you) is proved, when absolutely no opportunity (of writing) is passed over. However certain I may be, then, that you are no less respectable in the conduct of your life than faithful in respect of your sacramental vow ;[4] still, since there are not wanting smooth-tongued advocates of vice, and indulgent patrons who afford authority to vices, and, what is worse, convert the rebuke of the heavenly Scriptures into an advocacy of crimes ; as if the pleasure derived from the public exhibitions might be sought after as being innocent, by way of a mental relaxation ; — for thereby the vigour of ecclesiastical discipline is so relaxed, and is so deteriorated by all the languor of vice that it is no longer apology, but authority, that is given for wickedness, — it seemed good in a few words not now to instruct you, but to admonish you who are instructed, lest, because the wounds are badly bound up, they should break through the cicatrix of their closed soundness. For no mischief is put an end to with so much difficulty but that its recurrence is easy, so long as it is both maintained by the consent, and caressed by the excuses[5] of the multitude.

2. Believers, and men who claim for themselves the authority of the Christian name, are not ashamed — are not, I repeat, ashamed to find a defence in the heavenly Scriptures for the vain superstitions associated with the public exhibitions of the heathens, and thus to attribute divine authority to idolatry. For how is it, that what is done by the heathens in honour of any idol is resorted to in a public show by faithful Christians, and the heathen idolatry is maintained, and the true and divine religion is trampled upon in contempt of God? Shame binds me to relate their pretexts and defences in this behalf. "Where," say they, "are there such Scriptures? where are these things prohibited? On the contrary, both Elias is the charioteer of Israel, and David himself danced before the ark. We read of psalteries, horns,[6] trumpets, drums, pipes, harps, and choral dances. Moreover, the apostle, in his struggle, puts before us the contest of the Cæstus, and of our wrestle against the spiritual things of wickedness. Again, when he borrows his illustrations from the racecourse, he also proposes the prize of the crown. Why, then, may not a faithful Christian man gaze upon that which the divine pen might write about?" At this point I might not unreasonably say that

---

[1] [See Ben Jonson, *Volpone*, Ep. Dedicatory.]
[2] Obviously imitating Tertullian's treatise *De Spectaculis.* [See vol. iii. p. 79.]
[3] He then prosecutes the subject, by going through the several kinds of public exhibitions, and sets forth, a little more diffusely than in the Epistle to Donatus, what risks are incurred by the spectators, and especially in respect of those exhibitions wherein, as he says, " representations of lust convey instruction in obscenity." Finally, he briefly enumerates such exhibitions as are worthy of the interest of a Christian man, and in which he ought rightfully to find pleasure. [For *Epistle to Donatus*, see p. 275, *supra.*]
[4] " In sacramento."

[5] Elucidation I.
[6] " Nabla."

it would have been far better for them not to know any writings at all, than thus to read the Scriptures.[1] For words and illustrations which are recorded by way of exhortation to evangelical virtue, are translated by them into pleas for vice ; because those things are written of, not that they should be gazed upon, but that a greater eagerness might be aroused in our minds in respect of things that will benefit us, seeing that among the heathens there is manifest so much eagerness in respect of things which will be of no advantage.

3. These are therefore an argument to stimulate virtue, not a permission or a liberty to look upon heathen error, that by this consideration the mind may be more inflamed to Gospel virtue for the sake of the divine rewards, since through the suffering of all these labours and pains it is granted to attain to eternal benefits. For that Elias is the charioteer of Israel is no defence for gazing upon the public games ; for he ran his race in no circus. And that David in the presence of God led the dances, is no sanction for faithful Christians to occupy seats in the public theatre ; for David did not twist his limbs about in obscene movements, to represent in his dancing the story of Grecian lust. Psalteries, horns, pipes, drums, harps, were used in the service of the Lord, and not of idols. Let it not on this account be objected that unlawful things may be gazed upon ; for by the artifice of the devil these are changed from things holy to things unlawful. Then let shame demur to these things, even if the Holy Scriptures cannot. For there are certain things wherein the Scripture is more careful in giving instruction. Acquiescing in the claim of modesty, it has forbidden more where it has been silent. The truth, if it descended low enough to deal with such things, would think very badly of its faithful votaries. For very often, in matters of precept, some things are advantageously said nothing about ; they often remind when they are expressly forbidden. So also there is an implied silence even in the writings of the Scripture ; and severity speaks in the place of precepts ; and reason teaches where Scripture has held its peace. Let every man only take counsel with himself, and let him speak consistently with the character of his profession,[2] and then he will never do any of these things.[3] For that conscience will have more weight which shall be indebted to none other than itself.

4. What has Scripture interdicted? Certainly it has forbidden gazing upon what it forbids to be done. It condemned, I say, all those kinds of exhibitions when it abrogated idolatry — the mother of all public amusements,[4] whence these prodigies of vanity and lightness came. For what public exhibition is without an idol? what amusement without a sacrifice? what contest is not consecrated to some dead person? And what does a faithful Christian do in the midst of such things as these? If he avoids idolatry, why does he [5] who is now sacred take pleasure in things which are worthy of reproach? Why does he approve of superstitions which are opposed to God, and which he loves while he gazes upon them? Besides, let him be aware that all these things are the inventions of demons, not of God. He is shameless who in the church exorcises demons while he praises their delights in public shows ; and although, once for all renouncing him, he has put away everything in baptism, when he goes to the devil's exhibition after (receiving) Christ, he renounces Christ as much as (he had done) the devil. Idolatry, as I have already said, is the mother of all the public amusements ; and this, in order that faithful Christians may come under its influence, entices them by the delight of the eyes and the ears. Romulus was the first who consecrated the games of the circus to Consus as the god of counsel, in reference to the rape of the Sabine women. But the rest of the scenic amusements were provided to distract the attention of the people while famine invaded the city, and were subsequently dedicated to Ceres and Bacchus, and to the rest of the idols and dead men. Those Grecian contests, whether in poems, or in instrumental music, or in words, or in personal prowess, have as their guardians various demons ; and whatever else there is which either attracts the eyes or allures the ears of the spectators, if it be investigated in reference to its origin and institution, presents as its reason either an idol, or a demon, or a dead man. Thus the devil, who is their original contriver, because he knew that naked idolatry would by itself excite repugnance, associated it with public exhibitions, that for the sake of their attraction it might be loved.

5. What is the need of prosecuting the subject further, or of describing the unnatural kinds of sacrifices in the public shows, among which sometimes even a man becomes the victim by the fraud of the priest, when the gore, yet hot from the throat, is received in the foaming cup while it still steams, and, as if it were thrown into the face of the thirsting idol, is brutally drunk in pledge to it ; and in the midst of the pleasures of the spectators the death of some is eagerly besought, so that by means of a bloody exhibition men may learn fierceness, as if a

---

[1] [In Edin. trans. needlessly " the writings *of the Scriptures*."]
[2] " Cum persona professionis suæ loquatur."
[3] Baluzius reads with less probability " indecorum," " anything unbecoming." The reading adopted in the text is, according to Fell, " inde eorum."

[4] *Vid.* Ovid's *Fasti*, lib. v.
[5] The Oxford text here has the reading, " Why does he speak of it? why does he," etc.

man's own private frenzy were of little account to him unless he should learn it also in public? For the punishment of a man, a rabid wild beast is nourished with delicacies, that he may become the more cruelly ferocious under the eyes of the spectators. The skilful trainer instructs the brute, which perhaps might have been more merciful had not its more brutal master taught it cruelty. Then, to say nothing of whatever idolatry more generally recommends, how idle are the contests themselves; strifes in colours, contentions in races, acclamations in mere questions of honour; rejoicing because a horse has been more fleet, grieving because it was more sluggish, reckoning up the years of cattle, knowing the consuls *under whom they ran*, learning their age, tracing their breed, recording their very grandsires and great-grandsires! How unprofitable a matter is all this; nay, how disgraceful and ignominious! This very man, I say, who can compute by memory the whole family of his equine race, and can relate it with great quickness without interfering with the exhibition — were you to inquire of this man who were the parents of Christ, he cannot tell, or he is the more unfortunate if he can. But if, again, I should ask him by what road he has come to that exhibition, he will confess (that he has come) by the naked bodies of prostitutes and of profligate women, by (scenes of) public lust, by public disgrace, by vulgar lasciviousness, by the common contempt of all men. And, not to object to him what perchance he has done, still he has seen what was not fit to be done, and he has trained his eyes to the exhibition of idolatry by lust: he would have dared, had he been able, to take that which is holy into the brothel with him; since, as he hastens to the spectacle when dismissed from the Lord's *table*, and still bearing within him, as often occurs, the Eucharist, that unfaithful man has carried about the holy body of Christ among the filthy bodies of harlots, and has deserved a deeper condemnation for the way *by which he has gone 'hither*, than for the pleasure he has received from the exhibition.

6. But now to pass from this to the shameless corruption of the stage. I am ashamed to tell what things are said; I am even ashamed to denounce the things that are done — the tricks of arguments, the cheatings of adulterers, the immodesties of women, the scurrile jokes, the sordid parasites, even the toga'd fathers of families themselves, sometimes stupid, sometimes obscene, but in all cases dull, in all cases immodest. And though no individual, or family, or profession, is spared by the discourse [1] of

these reprobates, yet every one flocks to the play. The general infamy is delightful to see or to recognise; it is a pleasure, nay, even to learn it. People flock thither to the public disgrace of the brothel for the teaching of obscenity, that nothing less may be done in secret than what is learnt in public; and in the midst of the laws themselves is taught everything that the laws forbid. What does a faithful Christian do among these things, since he may not even think upon wickedness? Why does he find pleasure in the representations of lust, so as among them to lay aside his modesty and become more daring in crimes? He is learning to do, while he is becoming accustomed to see. Nevertheless, those women whom their misfortune has introduced and degraded to this slavery, conceal their public wantonness, and find consolation for their disgrace in their concealment. Even they who have sold their modesty blush to appear to have done so. But that public prodigy is transacted in the sight of all, and the obscenity of prostitutes is surpassed. A method is sought to commit adultery with the eyes. To this infamy an infamy fully worthy of it is superadded: a human being broken down in every limb, a man melted to something beneath the effeminacy of a woman, has found the art to supply language with his hands; and on behalf of one — I know not what, but neither man nor woman — the whole city is in a state of commotion, that the fabulous debaucheries of antiquity may be represented in a ballet. Whatever is not lawful is so beloved, that what had even been lost sight of by the lapse of time is brought back again into the recollection of the eyes.

7. It is not sufficient for lust to make use of its present means of mischief, unless by the exhibition it makes its own that in which a former age had also gone wrong. It is not lawful, I say, for faithful Christians to be present; it is not lawful, I say, at all, even for those whom for the delight of their ears Greece sends everywhere to all who are instructed in her vain arts.[2] One imitates the hoarse warlike clangours of the trumpet; another with his breath blowing into a pipe regulates its mournful sounds; another with dances, and with the musical voice of a man, strives with his breath, which by an effort he had drawn from his bowels into the upper parts of his body, to play upon the stops of pipes; now letting forth the sound, and now closing it up inside, and forcing it into the air by certain openings of the stops; now breaking the sound in measure, he endeavours to speak with his fingers, ungrateful to the Artificer who gave him a tongue. Why should I speak of comic and useless efforts? Why of those great tragic vocal

---

[1] [It is painful to recognise, in the general licence of the press in our country, this very feature of a corrupt civilization, — a delight in scandal, and in the invasion of homes and private affairs, for the gratification of the popular appetite.]

[2] [Compare Clement, vol. ii. p. 248, note 5, and p. 249, notes 2, 11.]

ravings? Why of strings set vibrating with noise? These things, even if they were not dedicated to idols,[1] ought not to be approached and gazed upon by faithful Christians; because, even if they were not criminal, they are characterized by a worthlessness which is extreme, and which is little suited to believers.

8. Now that other folly of others is an obvious source of advantage to idle men; and the first victory is for the belly to be able to crave food beyond the human limit, — a flagitious traffic for the claim to the crown of gluttony: the wretched face is hired out to bear wounding blows, that the more wretched belly may be gorged. How disgusting, besides, are those struggles! Man lying below man is enfolded in abominable embraces and twinings. In such a contest, whether a man looks on or conquers, still his modesty is conquered. Behold, one naked man bounds forth towards you; another with straining powers tosses a brazen ball into the air. This is not glory, but folly. In fine, take away the spectator, and you will have shown its emptiness. Such things as these should be avoided by faithful Christians, as I have frequently said already; spectacles so vain, so mischievous, so sacrilegious, from which both our eyes and our ears should be guarded. We quickly get accustomed to what we hear and what we see. For since man's mind is itself drawn towards vice, what will it do if it should have inducements of a bodily nature as well as a downward tendency in its slippery will? What will it do if it should be impelled *from without?*[2] Therefore the mind must be called away from such things as these.

9. The Christian has nobler exhibitions, if he wishes for them. He has true and profitable pleasures, if he will recollect himself. And to say nothing of those which he cannot yet contemplate, he has that beauty of the world to look upon and admire.[3] He may gaze upon the sun's rising, and again on its setting, as it brings round in their mutual changes days and nights; the moon's orb, designating in its waxings and wanings the courses of the seasons; the troops of shining stars, and those which glitter from on high with extreme mobility, — their members divided through the changes of the entire year, and the days themselves with the nights distributed into hourly periods; the heavy mass of the earth balanced by the mountains, and the flowing rivers with their sources; the expanse of seas, with their waves and shores; and meanwhile, the air, subsisting equally everywhere in

perfect harmony, expanded in the midst of all, and in concordant bonds animating all things with its delicate life, now scattering showers from the contracted clouds, now recalling the serenity of the sky with its refreshed purity; and in all these spheres their appropriate tenants — in the air the birds, in the waters the fishes, on the earth man. Let these, I say, and other divine works, be the exhibitions for faithful Christians. What theatre built by human hands could ever be compared to such works as these? Although it may be reared with immense piles of stones, the mountain crests are loftier; and although the fretted roofs glitter with gold, they will be surpassed by the brightness of the starry firmament.[4] Never will any one admire the works of man, if he has recognised himself as the son of God. He degrades himself from the height of his nobility, who can admire anything but the Lord.

10. Let the faithful Christian, I say, devote himself to the sacred Scriptures,[5] and there he shall find worthy exhibitions for his faith. He will see God establishing His world, and making not only the other animals, but that marvellous and better fabric of man. He will gaze upon the world in its delightfulness, righteous shipwrecks, the rewards of the good, and the punishments of the impious, seas drained dry by a people, and again from the rock seas spread out by a people. He will behold harvests descending from heaven, not pressed in by the plough; rivers with their hosts of waters bridled in, exhibiting dry crossings. He will behold in some cases faith struggling with the flame, wild beasts overcome by devotion and soothed into gentleness. He will look also upon souls brought back even from death. Moreover, he will consider the marvellous souls brought back to the life of bodies which themselves were already consumed. And in all these things he will see a still greater exhibition — that devil who had triumphed over the whole world lying prostrate under the feet of Christ. How honourable is this exhibition, brethren! how delightful, how needful ever to gaze upon one's hope, and to open our eyes to one's salvation! This is a spectacle which is beheld even when sight is lost. This is an exhibition which is given by neither prætor nor consul, but by Him who is alone and above all things, and before all things, yea, and of whom are all things, the Father of our Lord Jesus Christ, to whom be glory and honour for ever and ever. I bid you, brethren, ever heartily farewell. Amen.[6]

---

[1] [This touches a point important to the modern question. It is said, "Oh! but these Fathers denounced only those heathen spectacles of which idolatry was part," etc. The reply is sufficiently made by our author.]

[2] There is much confusion in the reading of this passage, which in the original runs, according to Baluzius: "Nam cum mens hominis ad vitia ipsa ducatur, quid faciet, si habuerit exempla naturæ corporis lubrica quæ sponte corruit? Quid faciet si fuerit impulsa?"

[3] [Compare Clement, vol. ii. p. 256, and note 1.]

[4] [De Maistre, who is a Christian, with all his hereditary prejudice and enslavement, has a fine passage in the opening of his *Soirées de St. Pétersbourg*, which the reader will enjoy. It concludes with this saying: "Les cœurs pervers n'ont jamais de belles nuits ni de beaux jours." P. 7. vol. i. See vol. iv. p. 173, this series.]

[5] [Always the sacred Scriptures are held up as capable of yielding delight as well as profit to the believer. The works of God and His word go together. Col. iii. 16.]

[6] [There is much in the above treatise which is not unworthy of Cyprian. As to questions of authenticity, however, experts alone should venture upon an opinion. *Non nobis tantas componere lites.*]

ON THE GLORY OF MARTYRDOM.[1]

ARGUMENT. — THE GLORY OF MARTYRDOM, — NAMELY, WHAT MARTYRDOM IS, HOW GREAT IT IS, AND OF WHAT ADVANTAGE IT IS. BY SIMILITUDES, AND BY ARGUMENT DEDUCED FROM THE DAILY DEATHS, THE AUTHOR EXHORTS TO A JOYOUS SUBMISSION TO DEATH FOR CHRIST'S SAKE.[2] AMONG THE BENEFITS OF MARTYRDOM HE MAINTAINS THAT WITHOUT EXPERIENCE OF THE UNIVERSAL SUFFERING THAT PREVAILS, THE PROPITIATION OF CHRIST CROWNS MARTYRS IN SUCH A WAY THAT HIS SAYING ABOUT THE VERY LAST FARTHING IS NOT APPLICABLE TO THEM.

1. Although, beloved brethren, it is unfitting, while my speaking to you receives this indulgence, to profess any trepidation, and it very little becomes me to diminish the glory of so great a devotion by the confession of an incipient doubt ; yet at the same time I say that my mind is divided by that very deliberation, being influenced by the desire of describing the glory, and restrained from speaking by the magnitude of the virtue (to be described) ; since it is either not becoming to be silent, or it is perilous to say too little, save that to one who is tossing in doubt this consideration alone is helpful, that it would appear easy for him to be pardoned who has not feared to dare. Wherefore, beloved brethren, although my mental capacity is burdened by the importance of the subject in such a way, that in proportion as it puts itself forth in declaring the dignity of martyrdom, in that degree it is overwhelmed by the very weight of the glory, and by its estimation of all those things concerning which, when it speaks most, it fails, by its address being weakened, and broken, and self-entangled, and does not with free and loosened reins display the might of such glory in the liberal eloquence of discourse ; yet, if I am not mistaken, some power there will be in my utterance, which, when fortified by the appeal of the work itself, may here and there pour forth what the unequal consciousness of my ability withheld from my words. Since, therefore, beloved brethren, involved as we are in affairs so many and important, we are endeavouring with all eagerness and labour to confirm the excellent and most beautiful issues of salvation, I do not fear being so deterred by any slothful dread as to be withheld or rendered powerless ; since, if any one should desire to look into that of which we are considering, the hope of devotion being taken into account, and the very magnitude of the thing being weighed, he would rather wonder that I could have dared at all, in a matter wherein both the vastness of the subject oppressed me, and the earnestness of its own desire drove my mind, confused with its joy, into mental difficulties. For who is there whom such a subject would not alarm? who is there whom it would not overthrow with the fear of its own wonder !

2. For there is indeed, unless I am mistaken, even in the very power of conscience, a marvellous fear which at once disturbs and inflames us ; whose power, the more closely you look into, the more the dreadful sense of its obligation is gathered from its very aspect of venerable majesty. For assuredly you ought to consider what glory there is in expiating any kind of defilement of life, and the foulness of a polluted body, and the contagions gathered from the long putrefaction of vices, and the worldly guilt incurred by so great a lapse of time, by the remedial agency of one stroke, whereby both reward may be increased, and guilt may be excluded. Whence every perfection and condition of life is included in martyrdom. This is the foundation of life and faith, this is the safeguard of salvation, this is the bond of liberty and honour ; and although there are also other means whereby the light may be attained, yet we more easily arrive at nearness to the promised reward, by help of these punishments, which sustain us.

3. For consider what glory it is to set aside the lusts of this life, and to oppose a mind withdrawn from all commerce with nature and the world, to all the opposition of the adversary, and to have no dread of the cruelty of the torturer ; that a man should be animated by the suffering whereby he might be believed to be destroyed, and should take to himself, as an enhancement of his strength, that which the punisher thinks will aggravate his torments. For although the hook, springing forth from the stiffening ribs, is put back again into the wound, and with the repeated strokes of the whip the returning lash[3] is drawn away with the rent portions of the flesh ; still he stands immoveable, the stronger for his sufferings, revolving only this in his mind, that

---

[1] [Erasmus doubts as to the authorship, judging from the style. Pamelius is sure it is Cyprian's.]

[2] In place of reward, he sets before them not only security from the fear of Gehenna, but also the attainment of everlasting life, describing both alternatives briefly in a poetical manner. He points out, that to some, martyrdom serves as a crown, while to others who are baptized in their own blood, it serves as redemption. Finally, when from the Scriptures he has stirred up his readers to confession of the name of Christ, he asks them to remember him when the Lord begins to honour martyrdom in them, since the Lord is known not to deny such as they when they ask Him for anything.

[3] "Habena;" but according to Baluzius "avena," "an oat-straw."

in that brutality of the executioners Christ Himself is suffering[1] more in proportion to what he suffers. For since, if he should deny the Lord, he would incur guilt on His behalf for whom he ought to have overcome, it is essential that He should be seen to bear all things to whom the victory is due, even in the suffering.

4. Therefore, since martyrdom is the chief thing, there are three points arising out of it on which we have proposed to ourselves to speak : What it is, how great it is, and of what advantage it is. What, then, is martyrdom? It is the end of sins, the limit of dangers, the guide of salvation, the teacher of patience, the home of life, on the journey to which those things moreover befall which in the coming crisis might be considered torments. By this also testimony is borne to the Name, and the majesty of the Name is greatly enhanced : not that in itself that majesty can be diminished, or its magnitude detracted from, by the guilt of one who denies it ; but that it redounds to the increase of its glory, when the terror of the populace that howls around is giving to suffering, fearless minds, and by the threats of snarling hatred is adding to the title whereby Christ has desired to crown the man, that in proportion as he has thought that he conquered, in that proportion his courage has grown in the struggle. It is then, therefore, that all the vigour of faith is brought to bear, then facility of belief is approved, when you encounter the speeches and the reproaches of the rabble,[2] and when you strengthen yourself by a religious mind against those madnesses of the people, — overcoming, that is, and repelling whatever their blasphemous speech may have uttered to wrong Christ in your person ; as when the resisting breakwater repels the adverse sea, although the waves dash and the rolling water again and again beats upon it, yet its immoveable strength abides firm, and does not yield even when covered over by the waves that foam around, until its force is scattered over the rocks and loses itself, and the conquered billow lying upon the rocks retires forth into the open spaces of the shore.

5. For what is there in these *speeches* other than empty discourse, and senseless talk, and a depraved pleasure in meaningless words? As it is written : "They have eyes, and they see not ; ears have they, and they hear not."[3] "Their foolish heart is made sluggish, lest at any time they should be converted, and I should heal

them."[4] For there is no doubt but that He said this of all whose hardened mind and obstinate brutality of heart is always driven away and repugnates from a vital devotion, folly leading them, madness dragging them, in fine, every kind of ferocity enraging them, whereby they are instigated as well as carried away, so that in their case their own deeds would be sufficient for their punishment, their guilt would burden the very penalty of the persecution inflicted.

6. The whole of this tends to the praise of martyrdom, the whole illuminates the glory of suffering wherein the hope of time future is beheld, wherein Christ Himself is engaged, of whom are given the examples that we seek, and whose is the strength by which we resist. And that in this behalf something is supplied to us to present, is surely a lofty and marvellous condescension, and such as we are able neither mentally to conceive nor fully to express in words. For what could He with His liberal affection bestow upon us more, than that He should be the first to show forth in Himself what He would reward with a crown in others? He became mortal that we might be immortal, and He underwent the issue of human destiny, by whom things human are governed ; and that He might appear to have given to us the benefit of His having suffered, He gave us confession. He suggested martyrdoms ; finally, He, by the merits of His nativity, imputed all those things whereby the light (of life) may be quenched, to a saving remedy, by His excellent humility, by His divine strength. Whoever have deserved to be worthy of this have been without death, have overcome all the foulest stains of the world, having subdued the condition of death.

7. For there is no doubt how much they obtain from the Lord, who have preferred God's name to their own safety, so that in that judgment-day their blood-shedding would make them better, and the blood spilt would show them to be spotless. Because death makes life more complete, death rather leads to glory. Thus, whenever on the rejoicing wheat-stalks the ears of corn distended by rains grow full, the abundant harvests are forced[5] by the summer ; thus, as often as the vine is pruned by the knife from the tendrils that break forth upon it, the bunch of grapes is more liberally clothed. For whatever is of advantage by its injury turns out for the increase of the time to come ; just as it has often been of avail to the fields to let loose the flames, that by the heat of the wandering conflagration the blind breathing-holes of the earth might be relaxed. It has been useful to parch the light stalks with the crackling fire, that the pregnant corn-field might raise itself

---

[1] [Acts ix. 5. The principle is recognised in the words, "Ye did it unto me," where Christ identifies Himself with members of His body. Oh, the condescension! Heb. ii. 11.]
[2] [Ps. lxiv. 3. The revilings of the multitude are reckoned by the Psalmist among the most cruel tortures of Christ; and we cannot doubt that the early Christians found the like cruelty of the heathen a daily martyrdom, before they came to their crowning passion. Compare Tertullian, vol. iii. p. 712.]
[3] Ps. cxiii. 13.

[4] Isa. vi. 10.
[5] "Coguntur," or "coquuntur," — "are matured."

higher, and a more abundant grain might flourish on the breeding stems. Therefore such also is first of all the calamity, and by and by the fruit of martyrdom, that it so contemns death, that it may preserve life in death.

8. For what is so illustrious and sublime, as by a robust devotion to preserve all the vigour of faith in the midst of so many weapons of executioners? What so great and honourable, as in the midst of so many swords of the surrounding guards, again and again to profess in repeated words the Lord of one's liberty and the author of one's salvation?—and especially if you set before your eyes that there is nothing more detestable than dishonour, nothing baser than slavery, that now you ought to seek nothing else, to ask for nothing else, than that you should be snatched from the slaughters of the world, be delivered from the ills of the world, and be engaged only as an alien from the contagion of earth, among the ruins of a globe that is speedily to perish? For what have you to do with this light, if you have the promise of an eternal light? What interest have you in this commerce of life and nature, if the amplitude of heaven is awaiting you? Doubtless let that lust of life keep hold, but let it be of those whom for unatoned sin the raging fire will torture with eternal vengeance for their crimes. Let that lust of life keep hold, but let it be of those to whom it is both a punishment to die, and a torment to endure (after death). But to you both the world itself is subjected, and the earth yields, if, when all are dying, you are reserved for this fate of being a martyr. Do we not behold daily dyings? We behold new kinds of death of the body long worn out with raging diseases, the miserable results of some plague hitherto unexperienced; and we behold the destruction of wasted cities, and hence we may acknowledge how great is to be considered the dignity of martyrdom, to the attainment of the glory of which even the pestilence is beginning to compel us.[1]

9. Moreover, beloved brethren, regard, I beseech you, this consideration more fully; for in it both salvation is involved, and sublimity accounted of, although I am not unaware that you abundantly know that we are supported by the judgments of all who stand fast, and that you are not ignorant that this is the teaching handed down to us, that we should maintain the power of so great a Name without any dread of the warfare; because we whom once the desire of an everlasting remembrance has withheld from the longing for this light, and whom the anticipations of the future have wrenched away, and whom the society of Christ so longed for has

kept aloof from all wickedness, shrink from offering our soul to death except it be in the way of yielding to a mischief, and that those benefits of God must no longer be retained and clung to by us, since beyond the burning up of these things the reward is so great as that human infirmity can hardly attain sufficiently to speak of it. Heaven lies open to our blood; the dwelling-place of Gehenna gives way to our blood; and among all the attainments of glory, the title of blood is sealed as the fairest, and its crown is designated as most complete.

10. Thus, whenever the soldier returns from the enemy laden with triumphant spoils, he rejoices in his wounds. Thus, whenever the sailor, long harassed with tempests, arrives at safe shores, he reckons his happiness by the dangers that he has suffered. For, unless I am mistaken, that is assuredly a joyous labour whereby safety is found. Therefore all things must be suffered, all things must be endured; nor should we desire the means of rejoicing for a brief period, and being punished with a perpetual burning. For you ought to remember that you are bound, as it were, by a certain federal paction, out of which arises the just condition either of obtaining salvation, or the merited fearfulness of punishment. You stand equally among adverse things and prosperous, in the midst of arms and darts; and on the one hand, worldly ambition, on the other heavenly greatness, incites you.

11. If you fear to lose salvation, know that you can die; and, moreover, death should be contemned by you, for whom Christ was slain. Let the examples of the Lord's passion, I beseech you, pass before your eyes; let the offerings, and the rewards, and the distinctions prepared come together before you, and look carefully at both events, how great a difficulty they have between them. For you will not be able to confess unless you know what a great mischief you do if you deny. Martyrs rejoice in heaven; the fire will consume those who are enemies of the truth. The paradise of God blooms for the witnesses; Gehenna will enfold the deniers, and eternal fire will burn them up. And, to say nothing of other matters, this assuredly ought rather to urge us, that the confession of one word is maintained by the everlasting confession of Christ; as it is written, "Whosoever shall confess me on earth before men, him also will I confess before my Father, and before His angels."[2] To this are added, by way of an enhancement of glory, the adornments of virtue; for He says, "The righteous shall shine as sparks that run to and fro among the stubble; they shall judge the nations, and shall have dominion over the peoples."[3]

---

[1] [The heathen attributed this pestilence to the "atheism" of Christians, and hence persecuted them the more fiercely; and, as it was better to die by martyrdom than by the pestilence, he thus speaks. Death an advantage. Shaks., *Hen. V.*, act. iv. sc. 1.]

[2] Luke xxii. 8.
[3] Wisd. iii. 7.

12. For it is a great glory, beloved brethren, to adorn the life of eternal salvation with the dignity of suffering : it is a great sublimity before the face of the Lord, and under the gaze of Christ, to contemn without a shudder the torments inflicted by human power. Thus Daniel, by the constancy of his faith, overcame the threats of the king and the fury of raging lions, in that he believed that none else than God was to be adored. Thus, when the young men were thrown into the furnace, the fire raged against itself, because, being righteous, they endured the flames, and guarded against those of Gehenna, by believing in God, whence also they received things worthy of them : they were not delayed to a future time : they were not reserved for the reward of eternal salvation. God saw their faith ; that what they had promised to themselves to see after their death, they merited to see in their body. For how great a reward was given them in the present tribulation could not be estimated. If there was cruelty, it gave way ; if there was flame, it stood still. For there was one mind to all of them, which neither violence could break down nor wrath could subvert ; nor could the fear of death restrain them from the obedience of devotion. Whence by the Lord's grace it happened, that in this manner the king himself appeared rather to be punished in those men (who were slain), whilst they escape whom he had thought to slay.

13. And now, beloved brethren, I shall come to that point whence I shall very easily be able to show you how highly the virtue of martyrdom is esteemed, which, although it is well known to all, and is to be desired on account of the insignia of its inborn glory, yet in the desire of its enjoyment has received more enhancement from the necessity of the times. Because if any one be crowned at that season in which he supposes himself to be crowned, if perchance he should die, he is greatly rewarded. Therefore, sublime and illustrious as martyrdom is, it is the more needful now, when the world itself is turned upside down, and, while the globe is partially shattered, failing nature is giving evidence of the tokens of its final destruction. For the rain-cloud hangs over us in the sky, and the very air stretches forth the mournful rain-(curtain) ; and as often as the black tempest threatens the raging sea, the glittering lightning-flashes glow terribly in the midst of the opening darkness of the clouds. Moreover, when the deep is lashed into immense billows, by degrees the wave is lifted up, and by degrees the foam whitens, until at length you behold it rush in such a manner, that on those rocks on which it is hurled, it throws its foam higher than the wave that was vomited forth by the swelling sea. You read that it is written, that we must pay even the uttermost farthing. But the martyrs alone are relieved of this obligation ; because they who trust to their desires for eternal salvation, and have overcome their longings for this life, have been made by the Lord's precepts free from the universal suffering.[1] Therefore from this especially, beloved brethren, we shall be able to set forth what great things the virtue of martyrdom is able to fulfil.

14. And, to pass over everything else, we ought to remember what a glory it is to come immaculate to Christ — to be a sharer in His suffering, and to reign in a perpetual eternity with the Lord — to be free from the threatening destruction of the world, and not to be mixed up with the bloody carnage of wasting diseases in a common lot with others ; and, not to speak of the crown itself, if, being situated in the midst of these critical evils of nature, you had the promise of an escape from this life, would you not rejoice with all your heart? If, I say, while tossing amid the tempests of this world, a near repose should invite you, would you not consider death in the light of a remedy? Thus, surrounded as you are with the knives of the executioners, and the instruments of testing tortures, stand sublime and strong, considering how great is the penalty of denying, in a time when you are unable to enjoy, the world for the sake of which you would deny, because indeed the Lord knew that cruel torments and mischievous acts of punishment would be armed against us for our destruction, in order that He might make us strong to endure them all. " My son," says He, " if thou come to serve God, stand fast in righteousness, and fear, and prepare thy soul for temptation."[2] Moreover, also, the blessed Apostle Paul exclaimed, and said, " To me to live is Christ, and to die is gain."[3]

15. Wherefore, beloved brethren, with a firm faith, with a robust devotion, with a virtue opposed to the fierce threatenings of the world, and the savage murmurs of the attending crowds, we must resist and not fear, seeing that ours is the hope of eternity and heavenly life, and that our ardour is inflamed with the longing for the light, and our salvation rejoices in the promise of immortality. But the fact that our hands are bound with tightened bonds, and that heavy links fastened round our necks oppress us with their solid weight, or that our body strained on the rack hisses on the red-hot plates, is not for the sake of seeking our blood, but for the sake of trying us.[4] For in what manner should we

---

[1] [The sufferings of this life are here supposed to be retributive in the case of those who must be weaned from the world. Martyrs have weaned themselves, and go gladly to their rest.]
[2] Ecclus. ii. 1.
[3] Phil. i. 21.
[4] [The terrible pictures in S. Stefano Rotondo (see p. 288, *supra*) might seem to have been taken from this graphic treatise. Can our faith and love be compared with that of these sufferers?]

be able to recognise even the dignity of martyrdom, if we were not constrained to desire it, even at the price of the sacrifice of our body? I indeed have known it, and I am not deceived in the truth of what I say, when the cruel hands of the persecutors were wrenching asunder the martyr's limbs, and the furious torturer was ploughing up his lacerated muscles, and still could not overcome him. I have known it by the words of those who stood around.[1] "This is a great matter. Assuredly I know not what it is — that he is not subdued by suffering, that he is not broken down by wearing torments." Moreover, there were other words of those who spoke: "And yet I believe he has children: for he has a wife associated with him in his house; and yet he does not give way to the bond of his offspring, nor is he withdrawn by the claim of his family affection from his stedfast purpose. This matter must be known, and this strength must be investigated, even to the very heart; for that is no trifling confession, whatever it may be, for which a man suffers, even so as to be able to die."

16. Moreover, beloved brethren, so great is the virtue of martyrdom, that by its means even he who has wished to slay you is constrained to believe. It is written, and we read: "Endure in suffering, and in thy humiliation have patience, because gold and silver are tried by the fire."[2] Since, therefore, the Lord proves us by earthly temptations, and Christ the Judge weighs us by these worldly ills, we must congratulate ourselves, and rejoice that He does not reserve us for those eternal destructions, but rejoices over us as purged from all contagion. But from those whom He adopts as partners of His inheritance, and is willing to receive into the kingdom of heaven, what else indeed does He ask than a walk in integrity? He Himself has said that all things are His, both those things which are displayed upon the level plains, and which lift themselves up into sloping hills; and moreover, whatever the greatness of heaven surrounds, and what the gliding water embraces in the circumfluent ocean. But if all things are within His ken, and He does not require of us anything but sincere actions, we ought, as He Himself has said, to be like to gold. Because, when you behold in the glistening ore[3] the gold glittering under the tremulous light, and melting into a liquid form by the roaring flames (for this also is generally the care of the workmen), whenever from the panting furnaces is vomited forth the glowing fire, the rich flame is drawn away from the access of the earth in a narrow channel, and is kept back by sand from the refluent masses of earth. Whence it is necessary to suffer all things, that we may be free from all wickedness, as He has said by His prophet: "And though in the sight of men they have suffered torments, yet is their hope full of immortality; and being vexed in a few things, they shall be well rewarded in many things, because God has tried them, and has found them worthy of Himself, and has received them as a sacrifice of burnt-offering."[4]

17. But if ambitious dignity deter you, and the amount of your money heaped up in your stores influence you — a cause which ever distracts the intentions of a virtuous heart, and assails the soul devoted to its Lord with a fearful trembling — I beg that you would again refer to the heavenly words. For it is the very voice of Christ who speaks, and says, "Whosoever shall lose his life for my name's sake, shall receive in this world a hundred fold, and in the world to come shall possess eternal life."[5] And we ought assuredly to reckon nothing greater, nothing more advantageous, than this. For although in the nature of your costly garments the purple dye flows into figures, and in the slackening threads the gold strays into a pattern, and the weighty metals to which you devote yourselves are not wanting in your excavated treasures; still, unless I am mistaken, those things will be esteemed vain and purposeless, if, while all things else are added to you, salvation alone is found to be wanting; even as the Holy Spirit declares that we can give nothing in exchange for our soul. For He says, "If you should gain the whole world, and lose your own soul, what shall it profit you, or what exchange shall a man give for his soul?"[6] For all those things which we behold are worthless, and such as resting on weak foundations, are unable to sustain the weight of their own mass. For whatever is received from the world is made of no account by the antiquity of time. Whence, that nothing should be sweet or dear that might be preferred to the desires of eternal life, things which are of personal right and individual law are cut off by the Lord's precepts; so that in the undergoing of tortures, for instance, the son should not soften the suffering father, and private affection should not change the heart that was previously pledged to enduring strength, into another disposition. Christ of His own right ordained that truth and salvation alone must be embraced in the midst of great sufferings, under which wife, and children, and grandchildren, under which all the offspring of one's bowels, must be forsaken, and the victory be claimed.

---

[1] [To me, these dramatic narrations of what was going on among the crowds that gazed upon the tortures of Christ's witnesses, are very suggestive of the whole scene. Compare pp. 295-296, *supra*.]
[2] Ecclus. ii. 4.
[3] Or, " earth."

[4] Wisd. iii. 4.
[5] Matt. x. 39.
[6] Matt. xv. 26.

18. For Abraham also thus pleased God, in that he, when tried by God, spared not even his own son, in behalf of whom perhaps he might have been pardoned had he hesitated to slay him. A religious devotion armed his hands; and his paternal love, at the command of the Lord who bade it, set aside all the feelings of affection. Neither did it shock him that he was to shed the blood of his son, nor did he tremble at the word; nevertheless for him Christ had not yet been slain. For what is dearer than He who, that you might not sustain anything unwillingly in the present day, first of all Himself suffered that which He taught *others to suffer?* What is sweeter than He who, although He is our God and Lord, nevertheless makes the man who suffers for His sake His fellow-heir in the kingdom of heaven? Oh grand — I know not what ! — whether that reason scarcely bears to receive that consciousness, although it always marvels at the greatness of the rewards; or that the majesty of God is so abundant, that to all who trust in it, it even offers those things which, while we were considering what we have done, it had been sin to desire. Moreover, if only eternal salvation should be given, for that very perpetuity of living we should be thankful. But now, when heaven and the power of judging concerning others is bestowed in the eternal world, what is there wherein man's mediocrity may not find itself equal to all these trials? If you are assailed with injuries, He was first so assailed. If you are oppressed with reproaches, you are imitating the experience of God. Whence also it is but a little matter whatever you undergo for Him, seeing that you can do nothing more, unless that in this consists the whole of salvation, that He has promised the whole to martyrdom. Finally, the apostle, to whom all things were always dear, while he deeply marvelled at the greatness of the promised benefits, said, " I reckon that the sufferings of this present time are not worthy to be compared to the glory that is to follow, which shall be revealed in us." [1] Because he was musing in his own mind how great would be the reward, that to him to whom it would be enough to be free from death, should be given not only the prerogative of salvation, but also to ascend to heaven : to heaven which is not constrained into darkness, even when light is expelled from it, and the day does not unfold into light by alternate changes; but the serene temperature of the liquid air unfolds a pure brightness through a clearness that reddens with a fiery glow.

19. It now remains, beloved brethren, that we are bound to show what is the advantage of martyrdom, and that we should teach that especially,

so that the fear of the future may stimulate us to this glorious title. Because those to whom great things are promised, seem to have greater things which they are bound to fear. For the soldier does not arouse himself to arms before the enemy have brandished their hostile weapons ; nor does a man withdraw his ship in an anchorage, unless the fear of the deep have checked his courage. Moreover also, while eager for his wealth, the considerate husbandman does not stir up the earth with a fortunate ploughshare, before the crumbling glebe is loosened into dust by the rain that it has received. Thus this is the natural practice of every man, to be ignorant of what is of advantage, unless you recognise what has been mischievous. Whence also a reward is given to all the saints, in that the punishment of their deeds is inflicted on the unrighteous. Therefore what the Lord has promised to His people is doubtful to none, however ignorant he is ; but neither is there any doubt what punitive fires He threatens. And since my discourse has led me thus to argue about both these classes of things in a few words, as I have already spoken of both, I will briefly explain them.

20. A horrible place, of which the name is Gehenna, with an awful murmuring and groaning of souls bewailing, and with flames belching forth through the horrid darkness of thick night, is always breathing out the raging fires of a smoking furnace, *while* the confined mass of flames is restrained or relaxed for the various purposes of punishment. Then there are very many degrees of its violence, as it gathers into itself whatever tortures the consuming fire of the heat emitted can supply. Those by whom the voice of the Lord has been rejected, and His control contemned, it punishes with different dooms ; and in proportion to the different degree of deserving of the forfeited salvation it applies its power, while a portion assigns its due distinction to crime. And some, for example, are bowed down by an intolerable load, some are hurried by a merciless force over the abrupt descent of a precipitous path, and the heavy weight of clanking chains bends over them its bondage. Some there are, also, whom a wheel is closely turning, and an unwearied dizziness *tormenting;* and *others* whom, bound to one another with tenacious closeness, body clinging to body compresses : so that both fire is devouring, and the load of iron is weighing down, and the uproar of many is torturing.

21. But those by whom God has always been sought or known, have never lost the position which Christ has given them, where grace is found, where in the verdant fields the luxuriant earth clothes itself with tender grass, and is pastured with the scent of flowers ; where the groves

---

[1] Rom. viii. 18.

are carried up to the lofty hill-top, and where the tree clothes with a thicker foliage whatever spot the canopy, expanded by its curving branches, may have shaded. There is no excess of cold or of heat, nor is it needed that in autumn the fields should rest, or, again in the young spring, that the fruitful earth should bring forth. All things are of one season: fruits are borne of a continued summer, since there neither does the moon serve the purpose of her months, nor does the sun run his course along the moments of the hours, nor does the banishment of the light make way for night. A joyous repose possesses the people, a calm home shelters them, where a gushing fountain in the midst issues from the bosom of a broken hollow, and flows in sinuous mazes by a course deep-sounding, at intervals to be divided among the sources of rivers springing from it. Here there is the great praise of martyrs, here is the noble crown of the victors, who have the promise of greater things than those whose rewards are more abundant. And that either their body is thrown to wild beasts, or the threatening sword is not feared, is shown as the reason of their dignity, is manifested as *the ground of* their election. Because it would have been inconsistent, that he who had been judged equal to such a duty, should be kept among earthly vices and corruptions.

22. For you deserve, O excellent martyrs, that nothing should be denied to you who are nourished with the hope of eternity and of light; whose absolute devotion, and whose mind dedicated to the service of heaven, is evidently seen. Deservedly, I say deservedly, nothing to you is forbidden to wish for, since by your soul this world is looked down upon, and the alienated appearance of the time has made you to shudder, as if it were a confused blindness of darkness; to whom this world is always regarded in the light of a dungeon, its dwellings for restraints, in a life which has always been esteemed by you as a period of delay on a journey. Thus, indeed, in the triumph of victory he is snatched from these evils, whom no vain ambition with pompous step has subdued, nor popular greatness has elated, but whom, burning with heavenly desire, Christ has added to His kingdom.

23. There is nothing, then, so great and venerable as the deliverance from death, and the causing to live, and the giving to reign for ever. This is fitting for the saints, needful for the wretched, pleasing to all, in which the good rejoice, the abject are lifted up, the elect are crowned. Assuredly God, who cares for all, gave to life a certain medicine as it were in martyrdom, when to some He assigned it on account of their deserving, to others He gave it on account of His mercy. We have assuredly seen very many distinguished by their faith, come to claim this illustrious name, that death might ennoble the obedience of their devotion. Moreover, also, we have frequently beheld others stand undismayed, that they might redeem their sins committed, and be regarded as washed in their gore by *His* blood; and so being slain they might live again, who when alive were counted slain. Death assuredly makes life more complete, death finds the glory that was lost. For in this the hope once lost is regained, in this all salvation is restored. Thus, when the seed-times shall fail on the withering plains, and the earth shall be parched with its dying grass, the river has delighted to spring forth from the sloping hills, and to soothe the thirsty fields with its gushing streams, so that the vanquished poverty of the land might be dissolved into fruitful wheat-stems, and the corn-field might bristle up the thicker for the counterfeited showers of rain.

24. What then, beloved brethren, shall I chiefly relate, or what shall I say? When all dignified titles thus combine in one, the mind is confused, the perception is misled; and in the very attempt to speak with brilliancy, my unworthy discourse vanishes away. For what is there to be said which can be sufficient, when, if you should express the power of eternal salvation, its attending glories come in your way; if you would speak of its surroundings, its greatness prevents you? The things at the same time are both in agreement and in opposition, and there is nothing which appears worthy to be uttered. Thus the instances of martyrdom have held in check the impulses of daring speech, as if entangled and ensnared by an opponent. What voice, what lungs, what strength, can undertake to sustain the form of such a dignity? At the confession of one voice, adverse things give way, joyous things appear, kingdoms are opened, empires are prepared, suffering is overcome, death is subdued, life is preferred, and the resisting weapons of a mischievous enemy are broken up. If there is sin, it perishes; if there is crime, it is left behind. Wherefore I beseech you, weigh this in your minds, and from my address receive so much as you know that you can feel.

25. Let it present itself to your eyes, what a day that is, when, with the people looking on, and all men watching, an undismayed devotion is struggling against earthly crosses and the threats of the world; how the minds in suspense, and hearts anxious about the tremblings of doubt, are agitated by the dread of the timid fearfulness of those who are congratulating them! What an anxiety is there, what a prayerful entreaty, what desires are recorded, when, with the victory still wavering, and the crown of conquest hanging in doubt over the head while the results are still uncertain, and when that pestilent and raving confession is inflamed by passion, is kindled

by madness, and finally, is heated by the fury of the heart, and by gnashing threats! For who is ignorant how great a matter this is, that our, as it were, despised frailty, and the unexpected boldness of human strength, should not yield to the pangs of wounds, nor to the blows of tortures,—that a man should stand fast and not be moved, should be tortured and still not be overcome, but should rather be armed by the very suffering whereby he is tormented?

26. Consider what it is, beloved brethren: set before your perceptions and your minds all the endurance of martyrdom. Behold, indeed, in the passion of any one you will, they who are called martyrs rejoice as being already summoned out of the world; they rejoice as being messengers of all good men; they rejoice in like manner as elected. Thus the Lord rejoices in His soldier,[1] Christ rejoices in the witness to His name. It is a small matter that I am speaking of, beloved brethren; it is a small matter, so great a subject in this kind of address, and so marvellous a difficulty has been undertaken by me; but let the gravity of the issue, I beseech you, not be wanting for my own purpose, knowing that as much can be said of martyrdom as could be appreciated. Whence also this alone has been the reason of my describing its glory, not that I judged myself equal and fitted for its praise, but that I saw that there was such a virtue in it, that however little I might say about it, I should profess that I had said as much as possible. For although the custody of faith may be preferred to the benefit of righteousness, and an immaculate virginity may recognise itself as better than the praises of all; yet it is necessary that even it should give place to the claim of blood, and be made second to a gory death. The former have chosen what is good, the latter have imitated Christ.

27. But now, beloved brethren, lest any one should think that I have placed all salvation in no other condition than in martyrdom, let him first of all look especially at this, that it is not I who seem to speak, that am of so great importance, nor is the order of things so arranged that the promised hope of immortality should depend on the strength of a partial advocacy. But since the Lord has testified with His own mouth, that in the Father's possession are many dwellings, I have believed that there is nothing greater than that glory whereby those men are proved who are unworthy of this worldly life. Therefore, beloved brethren, striving with a religious rivalry, as if stirred up with some incentive of reward, let us submit to all the abundance and the endurance of strength. For things passing

away ought not to move us, seeing that they are always being pressed forward to their own overthrow, not only by the law proposed to them, but even by the very end of time. John exclaims, and says, "Now is the axe laid to the root of the tree;"[2] showing, to wit, and pointing out that it is the last old age of all things. Moreover, also, the Lord Himself says, "Walk while ye have the light, lest the darkness lay hold upon you."[3] But if He has foretold that we must walk in that time, certainly He shows that we must at any rate walk.

28. And to return to the praise of martyrdom, there is a word of the blessed Paul, who says: "Know ye not that they who run in a race strive many, but one receiveth the prize? But do ye so run, that all of you may obtain."[4] Moreover also elsewhere, that he may exhort us to martyrdom, he has called us fellow-heirs with Christ; nay, that he might omit nothing, he says, "If ye are dead with Christ, why, as if living in the world, do ye make distinctions?"[5] Because, dearest brethren, we who bear the rewards of resurrection, who seek for the day of judgment, who, in fine, are trusting that we shall reign with Christ, ought to be dead to the world. For you can neither desire martyrdom till you have first hated the world, nor attain to God's reward unless you have loved Christ. And he who loves Christ does not love the world. For Christ was given up by the world, even as the world also was given up by Christ; as it is written, "The world is crucified unto me, and I unto the world."[6] The world has been an object of affection to none whom the Lord has not previously condemned; nor could he enjoy eternal salvation who has gloried in the life of the world. That is the very voice of Christ, who says: "He that loveth his life in this world, shall lose it in the world to come; but he that hateth his life in this world, shall find it in the world to come."[7] Moreover, also, the Apostle Paul says: "Be ye imitators of me, as I also am of Christ."[8] And the same elsewhere says: "I wish that all of you, if it were possible, should be imitators of me."[9]

29. He said this who suffered, and who suffered for this cause, that he might imitate the Lord; and assuredly he wished us also to suffer for this cause, that through him we might imitate Christ. If thou art righteous, and believest in God, why fearest thou to shed thy blood for Him whom thou knowest to have so often suffered for thee? In Isaiah He was sawn asunder, in Abel

---

[1] [The adoption of "the sign of the cross," after the immersion of baptism, is referable to this martyr-age. It was meant to impress the idea of soldiership.]

[2] Matt. iii. 10. [Elucidation II.]
[3] John xii. 35.
[4] 1 Cor. ix. 24.
[5] Col. ii. 20; "decernitis."
[6] Gal. vi. 14. [Compare Ep. xxv. p. 303, supra.]
[7] Matt. x. 39.
[8] 1 Cor. vi. 4.
[9] 1 Cor. vii. 7

He was slain, in Isaac He was offered up, in Joseph He was sold into slavery, in man He was crucified. And I say nothing of other matters, such as neither my discourse is able to tell nor my mind to bear. My consciousness is overcome by the example of His humility; and when it considers what things befell when He suffered, it marvels that He should suffer on whose behalf all things quaked. The day fled into the night; the light gave up all things into darkness; and, its mass being inclined backwards and forwards, the whole earth was jarred, and burst open; the dead[1] were disturbed, the graves were laid bare, and as the tombs gaped open into the rent of the earth, bodies returning to the light were restored; the world trembled at the flowing of His blood; and the veil which hung from the opening of the temple was rent, and all the temple uttered a groan. For which cause it is a great matter to imitate Him who, in dying, convicted the world. Therefore when, after the example of the Lord's passion, and after all the testimony of Christ, you lay down your life, and fear not to shed your blood, everything must absolutely give way to martyrdom. Inestimable is the glory of martyrdom, infinite its measure, immaculate its victory, invaluable its title, immense its triumph; because he who is presented to Him with the special glory of a confessor, is adorned with the kindred blood of Christ.

30. Therefore, beloved brethren, although this is altogether of the Lord's promise and gift, and although it is given from on high, and is not received except by His will, and moreover, can neither be expressed in words nor described by speech, nor can be satisfied by any

kind of powers of eloquence, still such will be your benevolence, such will be your charity and love, as to be mindful of me when the Lord shall begin to glorify martyrdom in your experience. That holy altar[2] encloses you within itself, that great dwelling-place of the venerable Name encloses you within itself, as if in the folds of a heart's embrace: the powers of the everlasting age sustain you, and that by which you shall ever reign and shall ever conquer. O blessed ones! and such as truly have your sins remitted, if, however, you who are Christ's peers ever have sinned![3] O blessed ones! whom the blood of the Lord has dyed from the beginning of the world, and whom such a brightness of snowy clothing has deservedly invested, and the whiteness of the enfolding robe has adorned! Finally, I myself seem to myself to behold already, and, as far as is possible to the mind of man, that divine and illustrious thing occurs to my eyes and view. I seem, I say to myself, already to behold, that that truly noble army accompanies the glory and the path of their Christ. The blessed band of victors will go before His face; and as the crowds become denser, the whole army, illuminated as it were by the rising of the sun, will ascribe to Him the power. And would that it might be the lot of such a poor creature as myself to see that sight! But the Lord can do what He is believed not to deny to your petitions.[4]

---

[2] [Rev. vi. 9; also vol. i. p. 486, note 10, this series.]
[3] ["Si tamen qui Christi compares estis aliquando peccastis;" not very happily translated, but extravagant at best.]
[4] [Think, I say again, of three hundred years of such "fiery trial," so marvellously sustained, and we shall gain new views of Christ's power to perfect His own strength in human weakness. The life of these Christians was a conscious daily warfare against "the world, the flesh, and the devil;" and we must recognise this in all judgments of their discipline and their modes of thought.]

---

[1] Or, "Manes."

OF THE DISCIPLINE AND ADVANTAGE OF CHASTITY.[1]

1. I do not conceive that I have exceeded any portions of my duty, in always striving as much as possible, by daily discussions of the Gospels, to afford to you from time to time the means of growth, by the Lord's help, in faith and knowledge. For what else can be effected in the Lord's Church with greater advantage, what can be found more suitable to the office of a bishop, than that, by the teaching of the divine words, recommended and commented on by Him, believers should be enabled to attain to the promised kingdom of heaven? This assuredly, as the desired result day by day of my work as

well as of my office, I endeavour, notwithstanding my absence, to accomplish; and by my letters I try to make myself present to you, addressing you in faith, in my usual manner, by the exhortations that I send you. I call upon you, therefore, to be established in the power of the Root[2] of the Gospel, and to stand always armed against all the assaults of the devil. I shall not believe myself to be absent from you, if I shall be sure of you. Nevertheless, everything which is advantageously set forth, and which either defines or promises the condition of eternal life to those who are investigating it, is then only profitable, if it be aided in attaining

---

[1] [Not reckoned by Erasmus as worthy of Cyprian. Pamelius thinks otherwise.]

[2] [This illustrates pp. 322 and 389, note 7.]

the reward of the effort by the power of the divine mercy. We not only set forth words which come from the sacred fountains of the Scriptures, but with these very words we associate prayers to the Lord, and wishes, that, as well to us as to you, He would not only unfold the treasures of His sacraments, but would bestow strength for the carrying into act of what we know. For the danger is all the greater if we know the Lord's will, and loiter in the work of the will of God.

2. Although, therefore, I exhort you always, as you are aware, to many things, and to the precepts of the Lord's admonition — for what else can be desirable or more important to me, than that in all things you should stand perfect in the Lord? — yet I admonish you, that you should before all things maintain the barriers of chastity, as also you do: knowing that you are the temple of the Lord, the members of Christ, the habitation of the Holy Spirit, elected to hope, consecrated to faith, destined to salvation, sons of God, brethren of Christ, associates of the Holy Spirit, owing nothing any longer to the flesh, as born again of water, that the chastity, over and above the will, which we should always desire to be ours, may be afforded to us also, on account of the redemption, that that which has been consecrated by Christ might not be corrupted. For if the apostle declares the Church to be the spouse of Christ, I beseech you *consider* what chastity is required, where the Church is given in marriage as a betrothed virgin. And I indeed, except that I have proposed to admonish you with brevity, think the most diffuse praises due, and could set forth abundant laudations of chastity; but I have thought it superfluous to praise it at greater length among those who practise it. For you adorn it while you exhibit it; and in its exercise you set forth its more abundant praises, being made its ornament, while it also is yours, each lending and borrowing honour from the other. It adds to you the discipline of good morals; you confer upon it the ministry of saintly works. For how much and what it can effect has on the one hand been manifest by your means, and on the other it has shown and taught what you are wishing for, — the two advantages of precepts and practice being combined into one, that nothing should appear maimed, as would be the case if either principles were wanting to service, or service to principles.

3. Chastity is the dignity of the body, the ornament of morality, the sacredness of the sexes, the bond of modesty, the source of purity, the peacefulness of home, the crown of concord.[1]

Chastity is not careful whom it pleases but itself. Chastity is always modest, being the mother of innocency; chastity is ever adorned with modesty alone, then rightly conscious of its own beauty if it is displeasing to the wicked. Chastity seeks nothing in the way of adornments: it is its own glory. It is this which commends us to the Lord, unites us with Christ; it is this which drives out from our members all the illicit conflicts of desire, instils peace into our bodies: blessed itself, and making those blessed, whoever they are, in whom it condescends to dwell. It is that which even they who possess it not can never accuse; it is even venerable to its enemies, since they admire it much more because they are unable to capture it. Moreover, as mature, it is both always excellent in men, and to be earnestly desired by women; so its enemy, unchastity, is always detestable, making an obscene sport for its servants, sparing neither bodies nor souls. For, their own proper character being overcome, it sends the entire man under its yoke of lust, alluring at first, that it may do the more mischief by its attraction, — the foe of continency, exhausting both means and modesty; the perilous madness of lust frequently attaining to the blood, the destruction of a good conscience, the mother of impenitence, the ruin of a more virtuous age, the disgrace of one's race, driving away all confidence in blood and family, intruding one's own children upon the affections of strangers, interpolating the offspring of an unknown and corrupted stock into the testaments of others. And this also, very frequently burning without reference to sex, and not restraining itself within the permitted limits, thinks it little satisfaction to itself, unless even in the bodies of men it seeks, not a new pleasure, but goes in quest of extraordinary and revolting extravagances, contrary to nature itself, of men with men.

4. But chastity maintains the first rank in virgins, the second in those who are continent, the third in the case of wedlock. Yet in all it is glorious, with all its degrees. For even to maintain the marriage-faith is a matter of praise in the midst of so many bodily strifes; and to have determined on a limit in marriage defined by continency is more virtuous still, because herein even lawful things are refused.[2] Assuredly to have guarded one's purity from the womb, and to have kept oneself an infant even to old age throughout the whole of life, is certainly the part of an admirable virtue; only that *if* never to have known the body's seductive capacities is the greater blessedness, to have overcome them when once known is the greater virtue; yet still in such a sort that that virtue comes of God's gift, al-

---

[1] [" So dear to Heaven is saintly Chastity, etc." — MILTON, *Comus*, 455.]

[2] [Holy men have generally recognised this rule as ennobling the estate of matrimony. See Jeremy Taylor, *Holy Living*, cap. ii. sec. 3.]

though it manifests itself to men in their members.

5. The precepts of chastity, brethren, are ancient. Wherefore do I say ancient? Because they were ordained at the same time as men themselves. For both her own husband belongs to the woman, for the reason that besides him she may know no other ; and the woman is given to the man for the purpose that, when that which had been his own had been yielded to him, he should seek for nothing belonging to another.[1] And in such wise it is said, "Two shall be in one flesh,"[2] that what had been made one should return together, that a separation without return should not afford any occasion to a stranger. Thence also the apostle declares that the man is the head of the woman, that he might commend chastity in the conjunction of the two. For as the head cannot be suited to the limbs of another, so also one's limbs cannot be suited to the head of another : for one's head matches one's limbs, and one's limbs one's head ; and both of them are associated by a natural link in mutual concord, lest, by any discord arising from the separation of the members, the compact of the divine covenant should be broken. Yet he adds, and says : " Because he who loves his wife, loves himself. For no one hates his own flesh ; but nourishes and cherishes it, even as Christ the Church."[3] From this passage there is great authority for charity with chastity, if wives are to be loved by their husbands even as Christ loved the Church, and wives ought so to love their husbands also as the Church loves Christ.

6. Christ gave this judgment when, being inquired of, He said that a wife must not be put away, save for the cause of adultery ; such honour did He put upon chastity. Hence arose the decree : " Ye shall not suffer adulteresses to live."[4] Hence the apostle says : "This is the will of God, that ye abstain from fornication."[5] Hence also he says the same thing : "That the members of Christ must not be joined with the members of an harlot."[6] Hence the man is delivered over unto Satan for the destruction of the flesh, who, treading under foot the law of chastity, practises the vices of the flesh. Hence with reason adulterers do not attain the kingdom of heaven. Hence it is that every sin is without the body, but that the adulterer alone sins against his own body. Hence other authoritative utterances of the instructor, all of which it is not necessary at this time to collect, especially among you, who for the most part know and do them ;

and you cannot find cause for complaint concerning these things, even though they are not described. For the adulterer has not an excuse, nor could he have, because he might take a wife.

7. But as laws are prescribed to matrons, who are so bound that they cannot thence be separated, while virginity and continency are beyond all law, there is nothing in the laws of matrimony which pertains to virginity ; for by its loftiness it transcends them all. If any evil undertakings of men endeavour to transcend laws, virginity places itself on an equality with angels ; moreover, if we investigate, it even excels them, because struggling in the flesh it gains the victory even against a nature which angels have not. What else is virginity than the glorious preparation for the future life? Virginity is of neither sex. Virginity is the continuance of infancy. Virginity is the triumph over pleasures. Virginity has no children ; but what is more, it has contempt for offspring : it has not fruitfulness, but neither has it bereavement ; blessed that it is free from the pain of bringing forth, more blessed still that it is free from the calamity of the death of children. What else is virginity than the freedom of liberty? It has no husband for a master. Virginity is freed from all affections : it is not given up to marriage, nor to the world, nor to children. It cannot dread persecution, since it cannot provoke it from its security.

8. But since the precepts of chastity have thus briefly been set forth to us, let us now give an instance of chastity. For it is more profitable when we come in the very presence of the thing ; nor will there be any doubt about the virtue, when that which is prescribed is also designated by illustrations. The example of chastity begins with Joseph. A Hebrew youth, noble by his parentage, nobler by his innocence, on account of the envy excited by his revelations exposed for sale by his brethren to the Israelites, had attained to the household of a man of Egypt. By his obedience and his innocence, and by the entire faithfulness of his service, he had aroused in his favour the easy and kindly disposition of his master ; and his appearance had commended itself to all men, alike by his gracious speech as by his youthfulness. But that same nobility of manner was received by his master's wife in another manner than was becoming ; in a secret part of the house, and without witnesses, — a place high up, and fitted for deeds of wickedness, the unrestrained unchastity of the woman thought that it could overcome the youth's chastity, now by promises, now by threats. And when he was restrained from attempting flight by her holding his garments, shocked at the audacity of such a crime, tearing his very gar-

---

[1] [This natural law, renewed in Christ, is part of the honour which He has restored to womanhood ; honouring His mother therein as the second Eve. Matt. xix. 8 ; Gen. ii. 24.]

[2] Matt. xix. 5.

[3] Eph. v. 28, 29

[4] Lev. xx. 10.

[5] 1 Thess. iv. 3.

[6] 1 Cor. vi. 15.

ments, and able to appeal to the sincerity of his naked body as a witness of his innocence, the rash woman did not shrink from adding calumny to the crime of her unchastity. Dishevelled, and raging that her desire should be despised, she complained both to others and to her husband that the Hebrew youth had attempted to use that force to her which she herself had striven to exercise.[1] The husband's passion, unconscious of the truth, and terribly inflamed by his wife's accusation, is aroused; and the modest youth, because he did not defile his conscience with the crime, is thrust into the lowest dungeon of the prison. But chastity is not alone in the dungeon; for God is with Joseph, and the guilty are given into his charge, because he had been guiltless. Moreover, he dissolves the obscurities of dreams, because his spirit was watchful in temptations, and he is freed from chains by the master *of the prison*. He who had been an inferior in the house with peril, was made lord of the palace without risk; restored to his noble station, he received the reward of chastity and innocence by the judgment of God, from whom he had deserved it.

9. But not less from a different direction arises to us another similar instance of chastity from the continence of women. Susanna, as we read, the daughter of Chelcias, the wife of Joachim, was exceedingly beautiful — more beautiful still in character. Her outward appearance added no charm to her, for she was simple: chastity had cultivated her; and in addition to chastity, nature alone. With her, two of the elders had begun to be madly in love, mindful of nothing, neither of the fear of God, nor even of their age, already withering with years. Thus the flame of resuscitated lust recalled them into the glowing heats of their bygone youth. Robbers of chastity, they profess love, while they really hate. They threaten her with calumnies when she resists; the adulterers in wish declare themselves the accusers of adultery. And between these rocks of lust she sought help of the Lord, because she was not equal to prevailing against them by bodily strength. And the Lord heard from heaven chastity crying to Him; and when she, overwhelmed with injustice, was being led to punishment, she was delivered, and saw her revenge upon her enemies. Twice victorious, and in her peril so often and so fatally hedged in, she escaped both the lust and death. It will be endless if I continue to produce more examples; I am content with these two, especially as in these cases chastity has been defended with all their might.

10. The memory of noble descent could not enervate them, although to some this is a suggestive licence to lasciviousness; nor the comeliness of their bodies, and the beauty of their well-ordered limbs, although for the most part this affords a hint, that being, as it were, the short-lived flower of an age that rapidly passes away, it should be fed with the offered opportunity of pleasure; nor the first years of a green but mature age, although the blood, still inexperienced, grows hot, and stimulates the natural fires, and the blind flames that stir in the marrow, to seek a remedy, even if they should break forth at the risk of modesty; nor any opportunity afforded by secrecy, or by freedom from witnesses, which to some seems to ensure safety, although this is the greatest temptation to the commission of crime, that there is no punishment for meditating it. Neither was a necessity laid upon them by the authority of those who bade them yield, and in the boldness of association and companionship, by which kind of temptations also righteous determinations are often overcome. Neither did the very rewards nor the kindliness, nor did the accusations, nor threats, nor punishments, nor death, move them; nothing was counted so cruel, so hard, so distressing, as to have fallen from the lofty stand of chastity. They were worthy of such a reward of the Divine Judge, that one of them should be glorified on a throne almost regal; that the other, endowed with her husband's sympathy, should be rescued by the death of her enemies. These, and such as these, are the examples ever to be placed before our eyes, the like of them to be meditated on day and night.

11. Nothing so delights the faithful soul as the healthy consciousness of an unstained modesty.[2] To have vanquished pleasure is the greatest pleasure; nor is there any greater victory than that which is gained over one's desires. He who has conquered an enemy has been stronger, but it was stronger than another; he who has subdued lust has been stronger than himself. He who has overthrown an enemy has beaten a foreign foe; he who has cast down desire has vanquished a domestic adversary. Every evil is more easily conquered than pleasure; because, whatever it is, the former is repulsive, the latter is attractive. Nothing is crushed with such difficulty as that which is armed by it. He who gets rid of desires has got rid of fears also; for from desires come fears. He who overcomes desires, triumphs over sin; he who overcomes desires, shows that the mischief of the human family lies prostrate under his feet; he who has overcome desires, has given to himself perpetual peace; he who has overcome desires, restores to himself liberty, — a most difficult matter even for noble natures. Therefore

---

[1] " Irrogare."

[2] [Tertullian, vol. iv pp. 74, 97, etc.]

we should always meditate, brethren, as these matters teach us, on chastity. That it may be the more easy, it is based upon no acquired skill. For the right will that is therein carried to perfection — which, were it not checked, is remote (*scil.* from our consciousness) — is still our will; so that it is not a will to be acquired, but that which is our own is to be cherished.[1]

12. For what is chastity but a virtuous mind added to watchfulness over the body; so that modesty observed in respect of the sexual relations, attested by strictness (of demeanour), should maintain honourable faith by an uncorrupted offspring? Moreover, to chastity, brethren, are suited and are known first of all divine modesty, and the sacred meditation of the divine precepts, and a soul inclined to faith, and a mind attuned to the sacredness of religion : then carefulness that nothing in itself should be elaborated beyond measure, or extended beyond propriety ; that nothing should be made a show of, nothing artfully coloured ; that there should be nothing to pander to the excitement or the renewal of wiles. She is not a modest woman who strives to stir up the fancy of another, even although her bodily chastity be preserved. Away with such as do not adorn, but prostitute their beauty. For anxiety about beauty is not only the wisdom of an evil mind, but belongs to deformity. Let the bodily nature be free, nor let any sort of force be intruded upon God's works. She is always wretched who is not satisfied to be such as she is. Wherefore is the colour of hair changed? Why are the edges of the eyes darkened? Why is the face moulded by art into a different form? Finally, why is the looking-glass consulted, unless from fear lest a woman should be herself? Moreover, the dress of a modest woman should be modest ; a believer should not be conscious of adultery even in the mixture of colours. To wear gold in one's garments is as if it were desirable to corrupt one's garments. What do rigid metals do among the delicate threads of the woven textures, except to press upon the enervated shoulders, and unhappily to show the extravagance of a boastful soul? Why are the necks oppressed and hidden by outlandish stones, the prices of which, without workmanship, exceed the entire fortune[2] of many a one?

It is not the woman that is adorned, but the woman's vices that are manifested. What, when the fingers laden with so much gold can neither close nor open, is there any advantage sought for, or is it merely to show the empty parade of one's estate? It is a marvellous thing that women, tender in all things else, in bearing the burden of their vices are stronger than men.

13. But to return to what I began with : chastity is ever to be cultivated by men and women ; it is to be kept with all watchfulness within its bounds. The bodily nature is quickly endangered in the body, when the flesh, which is always falling, carries it away with itself. Because under the pretext of a nature which is always urging men to desires whereby the ruins of a decayed race are restored, deceiving with the enticement of pleasure, it does not lead its offspring to the continence of legitimate intercourse, but hurls them into crime. Therefore, in opposition to these fleshly snares, by which the devil both obtrudes himself as a companion and makes himself a leader, we must struggle with every kind of strength. Let the aid of Christ be appropriated, according to the apostle, and let the mind be withdrawn as much as possible from the association of the body ; let consent be withheld from the body ; let vices be always chastised, that they may be hated ; let that misshapen and degraded shame which belongs to sin be kept before our eyes. Repentance itself, with all its struggles, is a discreditable testimony to sins committed. Let not curiosity be indulged in scanning other people's countenances. Let one's speech be brief, and one's laughter moderate, for laughter is the sign of an easy and a negligent disposition ; and let all contact, even that which is becoming, be avoided.[3] Let no indulgence be permitted to the body, when bodily vice is to be avoided. Let it be considered how honourable it is to have conquered dishonour, how disgraceful to have been conquered by dishonour.

14. It must be said, moreover, that adultery is not pleasure, but mutual contempt ; nor can it delight, because it kills both the soul and modesty. Let the soul restrain the provocations of the flesh ; let it bridle the impulses of the body. For it has received this power, that the limbs should be subservient to its command ; and as a lawful and accomplished charioteer, it should turn about the fleshly impulses when they lift themselves above the allowed limits of the body, by the reins of the heavenly precepts, lest that chariot of the body, carried away beyond its limits, should hurry into its own peril the charioteer himself as well as it. But in the midst of these things, nay, before these things,

---

[1] This passage is allowed by all to be corrupt. If we were to punctuate differently, to insert " nisi " before " consummata," and change " longe est " into " non deesset," we get the following sense: " Therefore we should always meditate, brethren, on chastity, as circumstances teach us, that it may be more easy for us. It depends on no arts; for what is it but perfected will, which, if it were not checked, would certainly not fail to arise? And it is our own will, too: therefore it has not to be acquired, but we have to cherish what is already our own."

[2] [" Kalendarium cujusvis excedunt." The *kalendaria* were tablets of monthly accounts, in which the monthly interest due, etc., were set down. " Exceed the entire monthly income " would be better. Tertullian uses the same word, " exhaust the *kalendarium*," rendered by our Edinburgh translator (vol. iv. p. 18), a " fortune." In this treatise Tertullian is constantly copied and quoted.]

[3] [Laughter, vol. ii. p. 249, and contact p. 291.]

in opposition to disturbances and all vices, help must be sought for from the divine camp; for God alone, who has condescended to make men, is powerful also to afford sufficient help to men. I have composed a few words, because I did not propose to write a volume, but to send you an address. Look ye to the Scriptures; seek out for yourselves from those precepts greater illustrations of this matter.[1] Beloved brethren, farewell.

---

[1] [Everything in antiquity breathes this spirit of "searching the Scriptures." Compare Hippol., p. 219, note 4, *supra*.]

EXHORTATION TO REPENTANCE.[1]

That all sins may be forgiven him who has turned to God with his whole heart.

In the eighty-eighth Psalm: "If his children forsake my law, and walk not in my judgments, and keep not my commandments, I will visit their iniquities with a rod, and their sins with stripes; nevertheless my loving-kindness will I not scatter away from them."[2]

Also in Isaiah: "Thus saith the Lord, the Holy One of Israel, When thou shalt turn and mourn, then thou shalt be saved, and shalt know where thou wast."[3]

Also in the same place: "Woe unto you, children of desertion, saith the Lord! ye have made counsel not by me, and my covenant not by my Spirit, to add sin to sin."[4]

Also in Jeremiah: "Withdraw thy foot from a rough way, and thy face from thirst. But she said, I will be comforted, I am willing; for she loved strangers, and went after them."[5]

Also in Isaiah: "Be ye converted, because ye devise a deep and wicked counsel."[6]

Also in the same place: "I am He, I am He that blotteth out thy iniquities, and will not remember them; but do thou remember them, and let us be judged together; do thou first tell thine unrighteousnesses."[7]

Also in the same: "Seek the Lord; and when ye shall have found Him, call upon Him. But when He has drawn near to you, let the wicked forsake his ways, and the unrighteous man his thoughts; and let him be converted to the Lord, and mercy shall be prepared for him, because He does not much[8] forgive your sins."[9]

Also in the same: "Remember these things, O Jacob and Israel, because thou art my servant. I have called thee my servant; and thou, Israel, forget me not. Lo, I have washed away thy unrighteousness as . . . , and thy sins as a rain-cloud. Be converted to me, and I will redeem thee."[10]

Also in the same: "Have these things in mind, and groan. Repent, ye that have been seduced; be converted in heart unto me, and have in mind the former ages, because I am God."[11]

Also in the same: "For a very little season I have forsaken thee, and with great mercy I will pity thee. In a very little wrath I turned away my face from thee; in everlasting mercy I will pity thee."[12]

Also in the same: "Thus said the Most High, who dwelleth on high, for ever Holy in the holies, His name is the Lord, the Most High, resting in the holy places, and giving calmness of mind to the faint-hearted, and giving life to those that are broken-hearted: I am not angry with you for ever, neither will I be avenged in all things on you: for my Spirit shall go forth from me, and I have made all inspiration; and on account of a very little sin I have grieved him, and have turned away my face from him; and he has suffered the vile man, and has gone away sadly in his ways. I have seen his ways, and have healed him, and I have comforted him, and I have given to him the true consolation, and peace upon peace to those who are afar off, and to those that are near. And the Lord said, I have healed them; but the unrighteous, as a troubled sea, are thus tossed about and cannot rest. There is no joy to the wicked, saith the Lord."[13]

Also in Jeremiah: "Shall a bride forget her adornment, or[14] a virgin the girdle of her breast? But my people has forgotten my days,[15] whereof there is no number."[16]

Also in the same: "For a decree, I will speak upon the nation or upon the kingdom, or I will take them away and destroy them. And if the nation should be converted from its evils, I will

---

[1] [Almost wholly made up of Scripture, and useful in any age to all Christians. Whatever its origin, it breathes a truly primitive spirit. Compare Tertullian, vol. iii. p. 657.]
[2] Ps. lxxxix. 30.
[3] Isa. xxx. 15, LXX.
[4] Isa. xxx. 1, LXX.
[5] Jer. ii. 25, LXX.
[6] Isa. xxxi. 6, LXX.
[7] Isa. xliii. 25, LXX.
[8] Non multum remittit — probably a misprint for "permultum."
[9] Isa. lv. 6, 7, LXX.

[10] Isa. xliv. 21, 22, LXX.
[11] Isa. xlvi. 8, LXX.
[12] Isa. liv. 7, 8, LXX.
[13] Isa. lvii. 15 et seq., LXX.
[14] It is taken for granted that the "ut" of the original is a misprint for "aut."
[15] Otherwise, "has forgotten me days without number."
[16] Jer. ii. 32, LXX.

repent of the ills which [1] I have thought to do unto them. And I will speak the decree upon the nation or the people, that I should rebuild it and plant it; and they will do evil before me, that they should not hearken to my voice, and I will repent of the good things which I spoke of doing to them." [2]

Also in the same: "Return to me, O dwelling of Israel, saith the Lord, and I will not harden my face upon you; because I am merciful, saith the Lord, and I will not be angry against you for ever." [3]

Also in the same: "Be converted, ye children that have departed, saith the Lord; because I will rule over you, and will take you one of a city, and two of a family, and I will bring you into Sion: and I will give you shepherds after my heart, and they shall feed you, feeding you with discipline." [4]

Also in the same: "Be converted, ye children who are turning, and I will heal your affliction." [5]

Also in the same: "Wash thine heart from wickedness, O Jerusalem, that thou mayest be healed: how long shall there be in thee thoughts of thy sorrows?" [6]

Also in the same: "Thus saith the Lord, Does not he that falleth arise? or he that turns away, shall he not be turned back? Because this people hath turned itself away by a shameless vision, and they have persisted in their presumption, and would not be converted." [7]

Also in the same: "There is no man that repenteth of his iniquity, saying, What have I done? The runner has failed from his course, as the sweating horse in his neighing." [8]

Also in the same: "Therefore let every one of you turn from his evil way, and make your desires better. And they said, We will be comforted, because we will go after your [9] inventions, and every one of us will do the sins which please his own heart." [10]

Also in the same: "Pour down as a torrent tears, day and night give thyself no rest, let not the pupil of thine eye be silent." [11]

Also in the same: "Let us search out our ways, and be turned to the Lord. Let us purge our hearts with our hands, and let us look unto the Lord who dwelleth in the heavens. We have sinned, and we have provoked Thee, and Thou hast not been propitiated." [12]

Also in the same: "And the Lord said to me

in the days of Josias the king, Thou hast seen what the dwelling of the house, [13] the house of Israel, has done to me. It has gone away upon every lofty mountain, and has gone under every shady [14] tree, and has committed fornication there; and I said, after she had committed all these fornications, Return unto me, and she has not returned." [15]

Also in the same: "The Lord will not reject for ever; and when He has made low, He will have pity according to the multitude of His mercy. Because He will not bring low from His whole heart, neither will He reject the children of men." [16]

Also in Ezekiel: "And the righteous shall not be able to be saved in the day of transgression. When I shall say to the righteous, Thou shalt surely live; but [17] he will trust to his own righteousness, and will do iniquity: all his righteousnesses shall not be remembered; in his iniquity which he has done, in that he shall die. And when I shall say to the wicked, Thou shalt surely die, and he turns himself from his sin, and doeth righteousness and judgment, and restoreth to the debtor his pledge, and giveth back his robbery, and walketh in the precepts of life, that he may do no iniquity, he shall surely live, and shall not die; none of his sins which he hath sinned shall be stirred up against him: because he hath done justice and judgment, he shall live in them." [18]

Also in the same: "I am the Lord, because I bring low the high tree, and exalt the low tree, and dry up the green tree, and cause the dry tree to flourish." [19]

Also in the same: "And thou, son of man, say unto the house of Israel, Even as ye have spoken, saying, Our errors and our iniquities are in us, and we waste away in them, and how shall we live? Say unto them, I live, saith the Lord: if I will the death of a sinner, only let him turn from his way, and he shall live." [20]

Also in the same: "I the Lord have built up the ruined places, and have planted the wasted places." [21]

Also in the same: "And the wicked man, if he turn himself from all his iniquities that he has done, and keep all my commandments, and do judgment, and justice, and mercy, shall surely live, and shall not die. None of his sins which he has committed shall be in remembrance; in his righteousness which he hath done he shall

---

[1] Here also the emendation of "quæ" for "quod" is obviously necessary.
[2] Jer. xviii. 7.
[3] Jer. iii. 12, LXX.
[4] Jer. iii. 14, LXX.
[5] Jer. iii. 22, LXX.
[6] Jer. iv. 14, LXX.
[7] Jer. viii. 4, LXX.
[8] Jer. viii. 6, LXX.
[9] Otherwise "our."
[10] Jer. xviii. 12, LXX.
[11] Lam. ii. 18, LXX.
[12] Lam. iii. 40.

[13] There is evident confusion here, and no place can be found for the word "vocem."
[14] It has been taken for granted that "numerosum" is a misprint for "nemorosum."
[15] Jer. iii. 6, LXX.
[16] Lam. iii. 31, LXX.
[17] Trombellius suggests "if" instead of "but."
[3] Ezek. xxxii. 12, etc., LXX.
[19] Ezek. xvii. 24, LXX.
[20] Ezek. xxxiii. 10, LXX.
[21] Ezek. xxxvi. 36, LXX.

live.   Do I willingly desire the death of the un-righteous man, saith Adonai the Lord, rather than that he should turn him from his evil way, that he should live?"[1]

Also in the same: "Be ye converted, and turn you from all your wickednesses, and they shall not be to you for a punishment.   Cast away from you all your iniquities which ye have wickedly committed against me, and make to yourselves a new heart and a new spirit; and why will ye die, O house of Israel? For I de-sire not the death of him that dieth, saith Adonai the Lord."[2]

Also in Daniel: "And after the end of the days, I Nabuchodonosor lifted up my eyes to heaven, and my sense returned to me, and I praised the Most High, and blessed the King of heaven, and praised Him that liveth for ever; because His power is eternal, His kingdom is for generations,[3] and all who inhabit the earth are as nothing."[4]

Also in Micah: "Alas for me, O my soul, be-cause truth has perished from the earth, and among all there is none that correcteth; all judge in blood.   Every one treadeth down his neighbour with tribulation; they prepare their hands for evil."[5]

Also in the same: "Rejoice not against me, O mine enemy, because I have fallen, but I shall arise; because although I shall sit in darkness, the Lord will give me light: I will bear the Lord's anger, because I have sinned against Him, until He justify my cause."[6]

Also in Zephaniah: "Come ye together and pray, O undisciplined people; before ye be made as a flower that passeth away, before the anger of the Lord come upon you, before the day of the Lord's fury come upon you, seek ye the Lord, all ye humble ones of the earth; do judgment and seek justice, and seek for gentleness; and answer ye to Him that ye may be protected in the day of the Lord's anger."[7]

Also in Zechariah: "Be ye converted unto me, and I will be turned unto you."[8]

Also in Hosea: "Be thou converted, O Israel, to the Lord thy God, because thou art weakened by thine iniquities.   Take many with you, and be converted to the Lord your God; worship Him, and say, Thou art mighty to put away our sins; that ye may not receive iniquity, but that ye may receive good things."[9]

Also in Ecclesiasticus: "Be thou turned to the Lord, and forsake thy sins, and exceedingly

hate cursing, and know righteousness and God's judgments, and stand in the lot of the propitia-tion of the Most High: and go into the portion of life with the living, and those that make con-fession.   Delay not in the error of the wicked. Confession perisheth from the dead man, as if it were nothing.   Living and sound, thou shalt confess to the Lord, and thou shalt glory in His mercies; for great is the mercy of the Lord, and His propitiation unto such as turn unto Him."[10]

Also in the same: "How good is it for a true heart to show forth repentance! For thus shalt thou escape voluntary sin."[11]

Also in the Acts of the Apostles: "But Peter saith unto him, thy money perish with thee, be-cause thou thinkest to be able to obtain the grace of God by money.   Thou hast no part nor lot in this faith, for thy heart is not right with God. Therefore repent of this thy wickedness, and pray the Lord, if haply the thought of thy heart may be forgiven thee.   For I see that thou art in the bond of iniquity, and in the bitterness of gall."[12]

Also in the second Epistle of the blessed[13] Paul to the Corinthians: "For the sorrow which is according to God worketh a stedfast repent-ance unto salvation, but the sorrow of the world worketh death."[14]

Also in the same place of this very matter: "But if ye have forgiven anything to any one, I also forgive him; for I also forgave what I have forgiven for your sakes in the person of Christ, that we may not be circumvented by Satan, for we are not ignorant of his wiles."[15]

Also in the same: "But I fear lest perchance, when I come to you, God may again humble me among you, and I shall bewail many of those who have sinned before, and have not repented, for that they have committed fornication and lasciviousness."[16]

Also in the same: "I told you before, and foretell you as I sit present; and absent now from those who before have sinned, and to all others; as, if I shall come again, I will not spare."[17]

Also in the second to Timothy: "But shun profane novelties of words, for they are of much advantage to impiety.   And their word creeps as a cancer: of whom is Hymenæus and Phile-tus, who have departed from the truth, saying that the resurrection has already happened, and have subverted the faith of certain ones.   But the foundation of God standeth firm, having this seal, God knoweth them that are His.   And,

---

[1] Ezek. xviii. 21, LXX.
[2] Ezek. xviii 30, LXX.
[3] "In generatione."
[4] Dan. iv. 34.
[5] Mic. vii. 1, 2, 3. LXX.
[6] Mic. vii. 8, LXX.
[7] Zeph. ii. 1, LXX.
[8] Zech. i. 3.
[9] Hos. xiv. 2.

[10] Ecclus. xvii. 26.
[11] Ecclus xx. 3.
[12] Acts viii. 20, etc.
[13] The original has only "ben," which Trombellius reasonably assumes to be meant for "benedicti."
[14] 2 Cor. vii. 10.
[15] 2 Cor. ii. 10.
[16] 2 Cor. xii. 21.
[17] 2 Cor. xiii. 2.

Every one who nameth the name of the Lord shall depart from all iniquity. But in a great house there are not only vessels of gold and silver, but also of wood and of clay; and some indeed for honour, and some for contempt. Therefore if any one shall amend [1] himself from these things, he shall be a vessel sanctified for honour, and useful for the Lord, prepared for every good work. Moreover, flee youthful lusts: but follow after righteousness, faith, charity, peace, with them that call upon the Lord from a pure heart. But avoid questions that are foolish and without learning, knowing that they be-

get strifes. And the servant of the Lord ought not to strive; but to be gentle, docile to all men, patient with modesty, correcting those who resist, lest at any time God may give them repentance to the acknowledgment of the truth, and recover themselves from the snares of the devil, by whom they are held captive at his will." [2]

Also in the Apocalypse: " Remember whence thou hast fallen, and repent; but if not, I will come to thee quickly, and remove thy candlestick out of its place." [3]

---

[1] " Emendaverit," probably a mistake for " emundaverit," " shall purge," as in the Vulg.; *scil.* ἐκκαθάρῃ.

---

[2] 2 Tim. ii. 16. [On true penitence see Epistle xxv. p. 304. *supra.*]

[3] Rev. ii. 5. [This selection of texts seems made on the same principle which dictated the compilation of texts against the Jews; a *breviarium*, the author calls it, — *quædam utilia collecta et digesta*, — to be read with readiness, and frequently referred to.]

ELUCIDATIONS.

I.

(Maintained by consent, and caressed by excuses, p. 557.)

THE severer discipline of early Christianity must not be discarded by those who claim it for the canon of Scripture; for modes of baptism, confirmation, and other rites; for Church polity, in short; and for the Christian year. Let us note that the whole spirit of antiquity is opposed to *worldliness*. It reflects the precept, " Be not conformed to this world," and in nothing more emphatically than in hostility to theatrical amusements, which in our days are re-asserting the deadly influence over Christians which Cyprian and Tertullian and other Fathers so solemnly denounced. If they were " maintained by consent, and caressed by excuses," even in the martyr-age, no wonder that in our Laodicean period they baffle all exertions of faithful watchmen, who enforce the baptismal vow against " *pomps* and vanities," always understood of theatrical shows, and hence part of that " world, the flesh, and the devil " which Christians have renounced.

II.

(Now is the axe laid to the root, p. 586.)

Matt. iii. 10. " Securis ad radicem arboris *posita est,*" says Cyprian, quoting the Old Latin, with which the Vulgate substantially agrees.[1] A very diligent biblical scholar directs attention to the vulgar abuse of this saying,[2] which turns upon a confusion of the active verb *to lay*, with the neuter verb *to lie.*[3] It is quoted as if it read, *Lay the axe to the root*, and is " interpreted, popularly, as of felling a tree, an incumbrance or a nuisance. . . . Hence it often makes radical reformers in Church and State, and becomes the motto of many a reckless leader whose way has been to teach, not upward by elevating the ignoble, but downward by sinking the elevated. . . . There is something similar in Latin: *jacio* to hurl; and *jaceo*, to lie, recline, or remain at rest. Beza follows the Vulgate (*posita est*) ; but the original is clear, — κεῖται,[4] *is laid, or lieth.* . . . It

---

[1] It has arbor*um*, however, instead of the singular.

[2] *Theopneuston*, by Samuel Hanson Cox, D.D., New York, 1842.

[3] Note, an extraordinary instance, *Childe Harold*, Canto iv. st. 180.

[4] Lexicographers give κεῖμαι = jaceo.

means, The axe is ready; it lieth near the root, in mercy and in menace. . . . The *long-suffering of God waiteth as in the days of Noah* . . . waiteth, i.e., for good fruit."

Compare Luke xiii. 9: "If it bear fruit, well: and if not, then after that thou shalt cut it down." Such is the argument of Cyprian, in view of the approaching "end of time."

III.

(General Note.)

Let me here call attention to the mischievous use of words common among modern Latins, even the best of them. Thus, Pellicia [1] mentions Cyprian as referring his synodical judgment to "*the supreme chair* of the Church of Rome." No need to say that his reference proves nothing of the kind. "Supremacy," indeed! Consult Bossuet and the Gallicans on that point, even after Trent. The case cited is evidence of the very reverse. Cyprian and his Carthaginian colleagues wished, also, the conspicuous co-operation of their Italian brethren; and so he writes to "Cornelius, *our colleague*," who, "with very many comprovincial bishops, having held a council, *concurred* in the same opinion." It is an instance of *fraternal concurrence* on grounds of entire equality; and Cyprian's courteous invitation to his "colleague" Cornelius and his comprovincials to co-operate, is a striking illustration of the maxim, "*Totus* apellandus sit *orbis*, ubi totum orbem causa spectat." Compare St. Basil's letters to the Western bishops, in which he reminds them that the Gospel came to them from the East. This is a sort of *primacy* recognised by St. Paul himself,[2] as it was afterwards, when Jerusalem was recognised as "the mother of all the churches"[3] by a general council, writing to Damasus, bishop of Rome, himself.

---

[1] *Polity*, etc., p. 416 (translation). This valuable work, translated and edited by the Rev. J. C. Bellett, M.A. (London, 1883), is useful as to mediæval usages, and as supplementing Bingham. But the learned editor has not been sufficiently prudent in noting his author's perpetual misconceptions of antiquity.

[2] 1 Cor. xiv. 36.

[3] Theodoret, book v. cap. ix. A.D. 382. The bishops say "last year" (A.D. 381), speaking of the council in session.

CAIUS

[TRANSLATED BY THE REV. S. D. F. SALMOND, M.A.]

INTRODUCTORY NOTICE

TO

CAIUS, PRESBYTER OF ROME

[A.D. 180–217.] During the episcopate of Zephyrinus, Caius, one of his presbyters, acquired much credit by his refutation of Proclus, a Montanist. He became known as an eloquent and erudite doctor, and to him has often been ascribed the *Philosophumena* of Hippolytus, and also *The Labyrinth*. He wrote in Greek, and finally seems to have been promoted to an episcopal See, possibly among the Easterns.[1] To him also has been ascribed the celebrated "Muratorian Canon," which is therefore given in this volume, with other fragments less dubiously associated with his name. He has been supposed by some to have been a pupil of Irenæus, but of this there is no conclusive evidence. If his reputation suffers somewhat from his supposed rejection of the Apocalypse, it is apologized for by Wordsworth, in a paragraph that deserves to be quoted entire : " Let it be remembered that the church of Rome was not eminent for learning at that time. It was induced, by fear of erroneous consequences, to surrender another canonical book, — the Epistle to the Hebrews. The learning of the Church was then mainly in the East. It was by the influence of the East, in the West, that the church of Rome was enabled to recover that epistle. It was also the influence of the Apocalyptic churches of Asia that preserved the Apocalypse as an inspired work of St. John to the church of Rome." By the deference with which the author of the *Refutation* speaks of the Apocalypse, we are able, among other evidences, to decide that it is not the work of Caius.

In an interesting chapter of his *Hippolytus*, Bishop Wordsworth considers the possibility of the authorship of that work as his, and discusses it with ability and learning. Nearly all that is known or conjectured concerning Caius is there condensed and elucidated. But Lardner devotes a yet more learned chapter to him ; and to that the inquirer is referred, as a sufficient elucidation of all that was known or conjectured about him before the present century. He is quoted by Eusebius ;[2] and the traveller is reminded, when he visits the gorgeous Church of St. Paul on the Ostian Road, that so early an author as Caius may be cited as evidence that it probably stands very near the spot where St. Paul fulfilled his prophecy, " I am now ready to be offered, and the time of my departure is at hand." We can only conjecture the time of his birth by the age he must have attained in the time of Zephyrinus ; but of his death, the secret is with the Master in whom he believed, as we may trust, until he fell asleep.

Here follows, from the Edinburgh series, the learned editor's INTRODUCTORY NOTICE : —

EUSEBIUS states that Caius lived in the time of Zephyrinus.[3] He speaks of him as a member of the Catholic Church,[4] and as being most learned. And he mentions that a dialogue of his

---

[1] The ingenious conjecture of Wordsworth, who surmises that καὶ ἐθνῶν ἐπίσκοπον, in Photius, should be read καὶ ἑωθινῶν. *Hippolytus*, p. 30. Another conjecture is 'Αθηνῶν. For the originals of these Fragments and learned notes, see Routh, *Reliqu.*, ii. p. 127.

[2] Eusebius quotes him in several places (book ii. cap. xxv., book iii. capp. xxviii. and xxxi.), and cites him in proof that St. Peter suffered on the Vatican, and St. Paul on the *Via Ostiensis*. See Lardner, *Credib.*, vol. ii. pp. 394, 410.

[3] *Hist. Eccl.*, ii. 25, vi. 20.

[4] ἐκκλησιαστικὸς ἀνήρ.

was extant in his time, in which he argued with Proclus, the leader of the Cataphrygian heresy; and that Caius in this dialogue spoke of only thirteen epistles of the Apostle Paul, "not counting the Epistle to the Hebrews with the rest." [1]

Eusebius mentions no other work of Caius. He makes extracts from a work against the heresy of Artemon in the fifth book of his *Ecclesiastical History*, but he states distinctly that the work was anonymous. He evidently did not know who was the author. Theodoret and Nicephorus affirm that the work from which Eusebius made these extracts bore the title of *The Little Labyrinth*. Photius has the following notice of Caius: "Read the work of Josephus on the universe, bearing in some manuscripts the inscription *On the Cause of the Universe*, and in others, *On the Substance of the Universe*. . . . But I found that this treatise is not the work of Josephus, but of one Gaius a presbyter, who lived in Rome, who they say composed *The Labyrinth* also, and whose dialogue with Proclus, the champion of the Montanistic heresy, is in circulation. . . . They say also that he composed another treatise specially directed against the heresy of Artemon." [2] Photius here ascribes four works to Caius: 1. *On the Universe;* 2. *The Labyrinth;* 3. *The Dialogue between himself and Proclus;* 4. *The Treatise against the Heresy of Artemon.* He does not say that he read any of them but the first. This treatise is now assigned to Hippolytus. The information of Photius in regard to the other three, derived as it is from the statements of others, cannot be trusted.

NOTE BY THE AMERICAN EDITOR.

IT is to be observed that the Fragment of *Muratori* proves that the *Apocalypse* was received in the church at Rome in the times of Pius, A.D. 160. It is quoted in *Hermas* freely. Also, see the Epistle of Roman clergy to Cyprian (p. 303, note 5, *supra*), about A.D. 250. But the *Fragment* aforesaid is the earliest direct evidence on the subject. Note, that its author says, "*We* receive the Apocalypse," etc. "*Some amongst us* will not have," etc. (see p. 602, *infra*). Thus, the comprovincials have a voice, as in the cases cited by Hippolytus. See (pp. 157, 159, *supra*) Elucidations VI. and XI. The Bishop of Rome seems, by this *Fragment*, to have received the *Apocalypse of Peter* (Eusebius, *H. E.*, book iii. cap. 25), but it was thrown out as spurious by the Church nevertheless.

---

[1] *Hist. Eccl.*, vi. 20.　　　　　[2] Cod. 48.

FRAGMENTS OF CAIUS

I. — FROM A DIALOGUE OR DISPUTATION AGAINST PROCLUS.[1]

I.

(Preserved in Eusebius' *Eccles. Hist.*, ii. 25.)

AND I can show the trophies of the apostles.[2] For if you choose to go to the Vatican or to the Ostian Road,[3] you will find the trophies of those who founded this church.

II.

(In the same, iii. 28.)

But Cerinthus, too, through revelations written, as he would have us believe, by a great apostle, brings before us marvellous things, which he pretends were shown him by angels ; alleging that after the resurrection the kingdom of Christ is to be on earth, and that the flesh[4] dwelling in Jerusalem is again to be subject to desires and pleasures. And being an enemy to the Scriptures of God, wishing to deceive men, he says that there is to be a space of a thousand years for marriage festivals.

III.

(In the same, iii. 31.)

And after this there were four prophetesses, daughters of Philip, at Hierapolis in Asia. Their tomb is there, and that, too, of their father.[5]

II. — AGAINST THE HERESY OF ARTEMON.[6]

I.

(In Eusebius' *Eccl. Hist.*, v. 28.)

For they say that all those of the first age, and the apostles themselves, both received and taught those things which these *men* now maintain ;

and that the truth of Gospel preaching was preserved until the times of Victor, who was the thirteenth bishop in Rome from Peter, and that from his successor Zephyrinus the truth was falsified. And perhaps what they allege might be credible, did not the Holy Scriptures, in the first place, contradict them. And then, besides, there are writings of certain brethren older than the times of Victor, which they wrote against the heathen in defence of the truth, and against the heresies of their time : I mean Justin and Miltiades, and Tatian and Clement, and many others, in all which divinity is ascribed to Christ. For who is ignorant of the books of Irenæus and Melito, and the rest, which declare Christ to be God and man? All the psalms, too, and hymns[7] of brethren, which have been written from the beginning by the faithful, celebrate Christ the Word of God, ascribing divinity to Him. Since the doctrine of the Church, then, has been proclaimed so many years ago, how is it possible that men have preached, up to the time of Victor, in the manner asserted by these? And how are they not ashamed to utter these calumnies against Victor, knowing well that Victor excommunicated Theodotus the tanner,[8] the leader and father of this God-denying apostasy, who first affirmed that Christ was a mere man? For if, as they allege, Victor entertained the very opinions which their blasphemy teaches, how should he have cast off Theodotus, the author of this heresy?

II.

(In Eusebius, as above.)

I shall, at any rate, remind many of the brethren of an affair that took place in our own time, — an affair which, had it taken place in Sodom, might, I think, have been a warning even to them. There was a certain confessor, Natalius,[9]

---

[1] A defender of the sect of the Cataphrygians.
[2] So Jerome, in the Epistle to Marcellus, says: " There, too, is a holy church; there are the trophies of the apostles and martyrs."
[3] The MSS. and the *Chronicon* of Georgius Syncellus read *Vasican*, Βασικανόν. The reference is to the Vatican as the traditional burial place of Peter, and to the Ostian Road as that of Paul.
[4] [Vol. i. pp. 351-352, 416.]
[5] This extract is taken from the Disputation of Caius, but the words are those of Proclus, as is shown by the citation in Eusebius.
[6] Two fragments of an anonymous work ascribed by some to Caius. Artemon and his followers maintained that Christ was mere (ψιλόν) man.

[7] [Elucidation, I.]
[8] [See cap. xxiii. p. 114, *supra*, and Euseb., iii. cap. 28.]
[9] This *may*, perhaps, be the Cæcilius Natalis who appears in the *Octavius* of Minucius Felix, as maintaining the cause of paganism against Octavius Januarius, and becoming a convert to the truth through the discussion. Name, time, and profession at least suit. [A painful conjecture, and quite gratuitous. See the *Octavius*, cap. xvi. note 6, p. 181, vol. iv., this series.]

who lived not in distant times, but in our own day. He was deluded once by Asclepiodotus, and another Theodotus, a banker. And these were both disciples of Theodotus the tanner, the first who was cut off from communion on account of this sentiment, or rather senselessness, by Victor, as I said, the bishop of the time.[1] Now Natalius was persuaded by them to let himself be chosen[2] bishop of this heresy, on the understanding that he should receive from them a salary of a hundred and fifty *denarii* a month. Connecting himself, therefore, with them, he was on many occasions admonished by the Lord in visions. For our merciful God and Lord Jesus Christ was not willing that a witness of His own sufferings should perish, being without the Church. But as he gave little heed to the visions, being ensnared by the dignity of presiding among them, and by that sordid lust of gain which ruins very many, he was at last scourged by holy angels, and severely beaten through a whole night, so that he rose early in the morning, and threw himself, clothed with sackcloth and covered with ashes, before Zephyrinus the bishop, with great haste and many tears, rolling beneath the feet not only of the clergy, but even of the laity, and moving the pity of the compassionate Church of the merciful Christ by his weeping. And after trying many a prayer, and showing the weals left by the blows which he had received, he was at length with difficulty admitted to communion.

III.

(In Eusebius, as above)

The sacred Scriptures they have boldly falsified, and the canons of the ancient faith[3] they have rejected, and Christ they have ignored, not inquiring what the sacred Scriptures say, but laboriously seeking to discover what form of syllogism might be contrived to establish their impiety.[4] And should any one lay before them a word of divine Scripture, they examine whether it will make a connected or disjoined form of syllogism;[5] and leaving the Holy Scriptures of God, they study geometry, as men who are of the earth, and speak of the earth, and are ignorant of Him who cometh from above. Euclid,

indeed, is laboriously measured[6] by some of them, and Aristotle and Theophrastus are admired; and Galen,[7] forsooth, is perhaps even worshipped by some of them. But as to those men who abuse the arts of the unbelievers to establish their own heretical doctrine, and by the craft of the impious adulterate the simple faith of the divine Scriptures, what need is there to say that these are not near the faith? For this reason is it they have boldly laid their hands upon the divine Scriptures, alleging that they have corrected them. And that I do not state this against them falsely, any one who pleases may ascertain. For if any one should choose to collect and compare all their copies together, he would find many discrepancies among them. The copies of Asclepiades,[8] at any rate, will be found at variance with those of Theodotus. And many such copies are to be had, because their disciples were very zealous in inserting the corrections, as they call them, i.e., the corruptions made by each of them. And again, the copies of Hermophilus do not agree with these; and as for those of Apollonius,[9] they are not consistent even with themselves. For one may compare those which were formerly prepared by them[10] with those which have been afterwards corrupted with a special object, and many discrepancies will be found. And as to the great audacity implied in this offence, it is not likely that even they themselves can be ignorant of that. For either they do not believe that the divine Scriptures were dictated by the Holy Spirit, and are thus infidels; or they think themselves wiser than the Holy Spirit, and what are they then but demoniacs? Nor can they deny that the crime is theirs, when the copies have been written with their own hand; nor[11] did they receive such copies of the Scriptures from those by whom they were first instructed in the faith, and they cannot produce copies from which these were transcribed. And some of them did not even think it worth while to corrupt them; but simply denying the law and the prophets for the sake of their lawless and impious doctrine, under pretexts of grace, they sunk down to the lowest abyss of perdition.[12]

---

1 [-οὖ τότε ἐπισκόπου, " the then bishop." *Text of Routh.*]
2 There is another reading — *named* (κληθῆναι) instead of *chosen* or *elected* (:Δηρωθῆναι).
3 [Thus early, primitive canons are recognised as in force.]
4 [Here we have an early foreshadowing of the schoolmen, whose rise was predicted by St. Bernard in his protest against Abelard. See Bernard, *Opp.*, tom. i. p. 410, *et alibi.*]
5 The *connected* form here is the *hypothetical*, as e.g., "If it is day, it is light." The *disjoined* is the *disjunctive*, as e.g., "It is either day or night." The words admit another rendering, viz., "Whether it, when connected or disjoined, will make the form of a syllogism."

6 There is a play in the original on the word *geometry.*
7 Galen composed treatises on the figures of syllogisms, and on philosophy in general. This is also a notable testimony, as proceeding from a very ancient author, almost contemporary with Galen himself. And from a great number of other writers, as well as this one. it is evident that Galen was ranked as the equal of Aristotle, Theophrastus, and even Plato. [Galen died *circa* A.D. 200.]
8 In Nicephorus it is *Asclepiodotus*, which is also the reading of Rufinus.
9 It appears from Theodoret (*Hæret. Fab.*, book ii. ch. v.), as well as from Nicephorus and Rufinus, that we should read *Apolloui-des* for Apollonius.
10 There is another reading — *by him.*
11 This paragraph, down to the word "transcribed," is wanting in the Codex Regius.
12 [Note the care and jealousy with which the integrity of the *codices* was guarded. Comp. *Uncan. and Apoc. Scriptures*, by Churton, London, 1884.]

III.—CANON MURATORIANUS.[1]

(In Muratori, *V. C. Antiq. Ital. Med. æv.*, vol. iii. col. 854.)

1. . . . . those things at which he was present he placed thus.[2] The third book of the Gospel, that according to Luke, the well-known physician Luke wrote in his own name[3] in order after the ascension of Christ, and when Paul had associated him with himself[4] as one studious of right.[5] Nor did he himself see the Lord in the flesh; and he, according as he was able to accomplish it, began[6] his narrative with the nativity of John. The fourth Gospel is that of John, one of the disciples. When his fellow-disciples and bishops entreated him, he said, "Fast ye now with me for the space of three days, and let us recount to each other whatever may be revealed to each of us." On the same night it was revealed to Andrew, one of the apostles, that John should narrate all things in his own name as they called them to mind.[7] And hence, although different points[8] are taught us in the several books of the Gospels, there is no difference as regards the faith of believers, inasmuch as in all of them all things are related under one imperial Spirit,[9] which concern the *Lord's* nativity, His passion, His resurrection, His conversation with His disciples, and His twofold advent, — the first in the humiliation of rejection, which is now past, and the second in the glory of royal power, which is yet in the future. What marvel is it, then, that John brings forward these several things[10] so constantly in his epistles also, saying in his own person, "What we have seen with our eyes, and heard with our ears, and our hands have handled, that have we written."[11] For thus he professes himself to be not only the eye-witness, but also the hearer; and besides that, the historian of all the wondrous facts concerning the Lord in their order.

2. Moreover, the Acts of all the Apostles are comprised by Luke in one book, and addressed to the most excellent Theophilus, because these different events took place when he was present himself; and he shows this clearly — i.e., that the principle on which he wrote was, to give only what fell under his own notice — by the omission[12] of the passion of Peter, and also of the journey of Paul, when he went from the city — Rome — to Spain.

3. As to the epistles[13] of Paul, again, to those who will understand the matter, they indicate of themselves what they are, and from what place or with what object they were directed. He wrote first of all, and at considerable length, to the Corinthians, to check the schism of heresy; and then to the Galatians, to forbid circumcision; and then to the Romans on the rule of the *Old Testament* Scriptures, and also to show them that Christ is the first object[14] in these; — which it is needful for us to discuss severally,[15] as the blessed Apostle Paul, following the rule of his predecessor John, writes to no more than seven churches by name, in this order: the first to the Corinthians, the second to the Ephesians, the third to the Philippians, the fourth to the Colossians, the fifth to the Galatians, the sixth to the Thessalonians, the seventh to the Romans. Moreover, though he writes twice to the Corinthians and Thessalonians for their correction, it is yet shown — i.e., by this sevenfold writing — that there is one Church spread abroad through the whole world. And John too, indeed, in the Apocalypse, although he writes only to seven churches, yet addresses all. He wrote, besides these, one to Philemon, and one to Titus, and two to Timothy, in simple personal affection and love indeed; but yet these are hallowed in the esteem of the Catholic Church, *and* in the regulation of ecclesiastical discipline. There are also in circulation one to the Laodiceans, and another to the Alexandrians, forged under the name of Paul, *and* addressed against the heresy of Marcion; and there are also several others which cannot be received into the Catholic Church, for it is not suitable for gall to be mingled with honey.

4. The Epistle of Jude, indeed,[16] and two belonging to the above-named John — or bearing the name of John — are reckoned among the Catholic *epistles*.[17] And the *book of* Wisdom,

---

[1] An acephalous fragment on the canon of the sacred Scriptures, ascribed by some to Caius. This very important fragment [vol. ii. pp. 4 and 56, this series] was discovered by Muratori in the Ambrosian Library at Milan, and published by him in his *Antiquitates Italicæ* in 1740. This manuscript belongs to the seventh or eighth century. Muratori ascribed it to Caius, Bunsen to Hegesippus; but there is no clue whatever to the authorship. From internal evidence the writer of the fragment is believed to belong to the latter half of the second century. The fragment has been much discussed. For a full account of it, see Westcott's *General Survey of the History of the Canon of the New Testament*, 2d ed. p. 184 ff., and Tregelles' *Canon Muratorianus;* [also Routh, *Rel.*, i. pp. 394-434].

[2] The text is, "quibus tamen interfuit et ita posuit." Westcott omits the "et." Bunsen proposes "*ipse non* interfuit." The reference probably is to the statement of Papias (Euseb., *Histor. Eccles.*, iii. 39) as to Mark's Gospel being a narrative not of what he himself witnessed, but of what he heard from Peter.

[3] The text gives "numine suo ex opinione concriset," for which we read "nomine suo ex ordine conscripsit" with Westcott.

[4] Reading "secum" for "secundum."

[5] The text gives "quasi ut juris studiosum," for which "quasi et virtutis studiosum," = "as one devoted to virtue," has been proposed. Bunsen reads "itineris socium" = "as his companion in the way."

[6] "Incepit" for "incipet."

[7] Or as they revised them, *recognoscentibus*.

[8] *Principia*.

[9] *Principali*, leading. [Note this theory of inspiration.]

[10] *Singula*.

[11] 1 John i. 1.

[12] The text is, "semote passionem Petri," etc., for which Westcott reads "semotâ." [A noteworthy statement.]

[13] Reading "epistolæ" and "directæ" instead of "epistola" and "directe," and "volentibus" for "voluntatibus."

[14] *Principium*.

[15] The text is, "de quibus singulis necesse est a nobis disputari cum," etc. Bunsen reads, "de quibus non necesse est a nobis disputari cur" = "on which we need not discuss the reason why."

[16] *Sane*.

[17] The text is "in catholica," which may be "in the Catholic Church." Bunsen, Westcott, etc., read "in catholicis."

written by the friends of Solomon in his honour. We receive also the Apocalypse of John and *that of* Peter, though some amongst us will not have this latter read in the Church. The *Pastor*, moreover, did Hermas write very recently in our times in the city of Rome, while his brother bishop Pius sat in the chair of the Church of Rome. And therefore it also ought to be read; but it cannot be made public [1] in the Church to the people, nor *placed* among the prophets, as their number is complete, nor among the apostles to the end of time. Of *the writings of* Arsinous, called also Valentinus, or of Miltiades, we receive nothing at all. Those *are rejected* too who wrote the new *Book of Psalms* for Marcion, together with Basilides and the founder of the Asian Cataphrygians.[2]

[1] Reading " sed publicari " for " se publicare." [Vol. ii. p. 3.]

[2] [For remarks of my own on the *Muratorian Canon*, see vol. ii. p. 56, this series.]

ELUCIDATIONS.

I.

(Psalms and hymns, p. 601.)

I SUBJOIN as an elucidation, to which I have suffixed references of my own, a valuable note of the Edinburgh editor,[1] which is found on p. 156 of vol. ix. in that series : " From this it appears that it was a very ancient custom in the Church to compose hymns and psalms in honour of Christ. Pliny, in his letter to Trajan, also states that the Christians were accustomed to meet together and sing hymns to Christ.[2] Hippolytus also may be understood to refer to these hymns and psalms towards the close of his oration on the end of the world,[3] where he says : ' Your mouth I made to give glory and praise, and to utter psalms and spiritual songs.' A hymn of this kind in honour of Jesus Christ, composed by Clement of Alexandria, is extant at the end of his books entitled *Pædagogi*." [4]

II.

(The Dialogue between himself and Proclus, p. 600.)

I have been unable to get a copy of the work of John de Soynes on *Montanism*, which possibly throws some light upon the *Dialogue with Proclus*, attributed to him by Photius. It is praised by Adolf Harnack, and highly spoken of by English critics. It was a Hulsean prize essay, published Cambridge, 1878.

[1] The Rev. S. D. F. Salmond, M.A.

[2] " Soliti essent *Christiani*, stato die, ante lucem convenire, *carmenque* Christo, quasi Deo, *dicere secum invicem.* Compare (Greek) Eph. v. 19 and Col. iii. 16. Lardner gives Pliny's letter entire, vol. vii. p. 22.

[3] Sec. xlvi. p. 254, *supra*.

[4] Vol. ii. p, 295, this series.

NOVATIAN

[TRANSLATED BY THE REV. ROBERT ERNEST WALLIS.]

INTRODUCTORY NOTICE

TO

NOVATIAN, A ROMAN PRESBYTER

[A.D. 210–280.] When we reflect upon the history of Solomon, and his marvellous contributions to the sacred canon of Scripture, we must not be surprised to find a Tatian, a Tertullian, and a Novatian among the Fathers. We deplore the lapse of such characters, but after death they are not subject to human judgment. Let us cherish the gratitude we owe to them for their good works, and use their testimony so far as it was faithful; covering their shame with the mantle of charity, and praying for grace never to imitate their faults. "If any teacher have wandered from the faith, it is permitted," says St. Vincent of Lerins,[1] "by Divine Providence *for our trial*, whether we love God or not, with all our heart and with all our soul."

We find Novatian apparently exercising jurisdiction, *sede vacante*, in Rome, with his co-presbyters, and as *vicar-general* (to use a later term) corresponding with Cyprian. This was about A.D. 250, after the death of Fabian. His marked abilities and real services had fitted him to preside thus over the Roman presbytery, and to be their "secretary for foreign affairs." But he laboured under the impediment of clinic baptism, and had not an unblemished record, if we credit Eusebius,[2] in his conduct during persecution.

He was not called, therefore, to the episcopate. Cornelius was made bishop June 4, A.D. 251; and, apparently, disappointed ambition soon bore its thorny fruits. "Emulation of the episcopal office is the mother of schisms," said Tertullian;[3] even in that period when to be a bishop was so often to be a martyr. And we find Novatian grasping a shadowy titular bishopric, which, wholly irregular and universally disowned, could have been to such a man the source of nothing but misery. I say, "to such a man," for, *without hearing the other side*, I cannot accept what was unquestionably supposed to be fact amid the excitements of the times. And Novatian was not a common or a vulgar character. The arguments of Lardner[4] teach us at least to be Christians,— to accept the facts, but "forbear to judge," seeing, as that writer observes, "we have not one remaining line of his in self-defence or against his adversaries."

Now as to his orthodoxy, so far as his extant writings are concerned, I think any scholar, not anxious to make out a case, will abide by the candid judgment of Bull, who defends his reputation against Petavius.[5] "By no means," he says, "should we tolerate that injustice of the Jesuit Petau towards the ancient writers, against their manifest mind and purpose; twisting, as he everywhere does, their sound and Catholic sayings into a sense alien and heretical."

The work upon the Trinity, which is a most valuable contribution to ante-Nicene theology, is said by Cave to have been written about A.D. 257; and that upon the Jewish meats seems to

---

[1] In his *Commonitory*, cap. xix. p. 57, ed. Baltimore, 1847. This useful edition contains the text, and a translation, with valuable notes, by the late Bishop Whittingham of Maryland.

[2] *H E.*, vi.

[3] Vol. iii. cap. 17, p. 677, this series.

[4] His elaborate chapter (xlvii. and the note) must be read by all students who wish to understand the matter, or even to read Cyprian advantageously.

[5] *Defensio Fid. Nicæn., Works*, vol. v. p. 374.

have been composed during the Decian persecution. His heresy, such as it was, turned upon unrelenting discipline, and was a sin against charity, which is greater than faith itself. It violated the "seventy times seven" maxim of our Lord, and the comprehensive precept, "Forgive, and ye shall be forgiven." It wounded Christian unity at a perilous period, and when every breach in the wall of the fold was sure to let in the wolves.

"He may have aspired to *the papal chair,*" says a contemporary writer[1] of no mean repute, adding, "to which he had the best claim." Then he says, "Novatian was elected *anti-pope* by a minority, and consecrated by three Italian bishops." Is this history? What impression must it give to the young student? The learned writer whom I quote shows clearly enough that there was no "papacy" in primitive times, as that word is universally understood. Why, then, put a face upon Antiquity so utterly misleading? Neither Novatian, nor his consecrators, nor Cornelius, against whom he rebelled, ever dreamed of anything more than of an episcopal chair ; venerable, indeed, for its succession of pastors from the times of SS. Peter and Paul, but as yet hardly felt in the Christian brotherhood ; which for two centuries had produced many pious but few eminent men, and in which Novatian himself was the earliest contributor to the "Latin Christianity," already founded and flourishing, not in Italy, but in Northern Africa.

The following is the INTRODUCTORY NOTICE of the Edinburgh translator, the Rev. Dr. Wallis, who, I am glad to observe, is tender towards our author's memory : —

THE biography of Novatian belongs to the ecclesiastical history of the third century. He was, or is reputed to have been, the founder of a sect which claimed for itself the name of "Puritan"[2] (καθαροί). For a long time he was in determined opposition to Cornelius, bishop of Rome, in regard to the admission of the lapsed and penitent into the Church ; but the facts of the controversy and much of our information in regard to Novatian are to be got only from his enemies, the Roman bishop and his adherents. Accordingly, some have believed all the accusations that have been brought against him, while others have been inclined to doubt them all.[3]

It is not known where Novatian was born. Some have appealed to Philostorgius[4] in behalf of the opinion that he was a Phrygian ; but others maintain that, supposing this to be a statement of the historian, it is a mere conjecture of his, based on the character of Novatian's teaching. It is also stated by Cyprian, that he was a Stoic before he passed over to the Christian Church ; but this also has been doubted. While amongst the catechumens, he was seized by a violent disease, attributed to demoniac agency ; and, being near death, he received baptism. He was ordained presbyter by Fabian, bishop of Rome, against the wishes of the rest of the clergy, who objected thereto because he had received clinic baptism.[5] The subsequent circumstances of his schism and his contest with Cornelius, are stated at length with no friendly spirit in a letter to Antonianus by Cyprian.[6] Socrates[7] states that he suffered martyrdom ; but his authority, amid the silence of all others, is not sufficient to guarantee the fact.

Novatian composed many works. The following are extant : —

I. *De Trinitate,* formerly attributed by some to Tertullian, by others to Cyprian ; but now on all hands allowed to be the work of Novatian, to whom Jerome expressly assigns it.[8] It was written after the heresy of Sabellius, which appeared 256 A.D.

---

[1] Dr. Schaff, *History of Christian Church,* vol. ii. p. 851.

[2] [This is again putting a false face upon Antiquity. *Purists,* rather; i.e., in morals.]

[3] See the last portion of Section Second of Neander's *Church History.*

[4] *Hist. Eccl.,* lib. viii. c. 15. The text of Valesius has Οὐατον, not Novatus or Novatian.

[5] [See p. 400, note 5, *supra.*]

[6] Ep. li. p. 327, *supra.* [How could it be stated truly and yet seem friendly? The unfortunate man had violated discipline, and broken his most sacred obligations to the Christian flock, at a time when the heathen persecutions made all such scandals little less than mutiny against Christ Himself. Consult Matt. xviii. 7 and Luke xvii. 1. We owe to such discipline the sure canon of Scripture.]

[7] *Hist. Eccl.,* lib. iv. c. 28.

[8] *De viris Illustribus,* c. 70.

II. *De Cibis Judaicis:* at first also attributed by some to Tertullian or Cyprian; but now assigned to Novatian on the testimony of Jerome. It was written during the time of the Decian persecution, about 250 A.D.

III. Novatian was the author of the letter[1] addressed by the Roman clergy to Cyprian. So Cyprian himself states.[2] Some have also attributed to him Ep. xxix. without any authority.

IV. Jerome attributes to him writings on Circumcision, on the Sabbath, on the Passover, on the Priesthood, on Prayer, on Attalus, on the Present Crisis, and Letters.

The best editions of Novatian are by Welchman, Oxford, 1724; and by Jackson, London, 1728.

---

[1] Ep. xxx. p. 308, *supra.*   [2] Ep. li. 5, p. 328, *supra.*   [Also, see Ep. xli. 2, p. 320, *supra.*]

A TREATISE OF NOVATIAN CONCERNING THE TRINITY.

PREFACE.

NOVATIAN's treatise concerning the Trinity is divided into thirty-one chapters. He first of all, from chapter first to the eighth, considers those words of the Rule of Truth or Faith,[1] which bid us believe on God the Father and Lord Almighty, the absolutely perfect Creator of all things. Wherein among the other divine attributes he moreover ascribes to Him, partly from reason and partly from the Holy Scriptures, immensity, eternity, unity, goodness, immutability, immortality, spirituality; and adds that neither passions nor members can be attributed to God, and that these things are only asserted of God in Scripture anthropopathically.[2]

CHAP. I. *ARGUMENT.* — NOVATIAN, WITH THE VIEW OF TREATING OF THE TRINITY, SETS FORTH FROM THE RULE OF FAITH THAT WE SHOULD FIRST OF ALL BELIEVE IN GOD THE FATHER AND LORD OMNIPOTENT, THE ABSOLUTE FOUNDER OF ALL THINGS. THE WORKS OF CREATION ARE BEAUTIFULLY DESCRIBED. MAN'S FREE-WILL IS ASSERTED; GOD'S MERCY IN INFLICTING PENALTY ON MAN IS SHOWN; THE CONDITION AFTER DEATH OF THE SOULS OF THE RIGHTEOUS AND UNRIGHTEOUS IS DETERMINED.

The Rule of truth requires that we should first of all things believe on God the Father and Lord Omnipotent; that is, the absolutely perfect Founder of all things, who has suspended the heavens in lofty sublimity, has established the earth with its lower mass, has diffused the seas with their fluent moisture, and has distributed all these things, both adorned and supplied with their appropriate and fitting instruments. For in the solid vault of heaven He has both awakened the light-bringing Sunrisings; He has filled up the white globe of the moon in its monthly[3] waxings as a solace for the night; He, moreover, kindles the starry rays with the varied splendours of glistening light; and He has willed all these things in their legitimate tracks to circle the entire compass of the world, so as to cause days, months, years, signs, and seasons, and benefits of other kinds for the human race. On the earth, moreover, He has lifted up the loftiest mountains to a peak, He has thrown down valleys into the depths, He has smoothly levelled the plains, He has ordained the animal herds usefully for the various services of men. He has also established the oak trees of the woods for the future benefit of human uses. He has developed the harvests into food. He has unlocked the mouths of the springs, and has poured them into the flowing rivers. And after these things, lest He should not also provide for the very delights of the eyes, He has clothed all things with the various colours of the flowers for the pleasure of the beholders. Even in the sea itself, moreover, although it was in itself marvellous both for its extent and its utility, He has made manifold creatures, sometimes of moderate, sometimes of vast bodily size, testifying by the variety of His appointment to the intelligence of the Artificer. And, not content with these things, lest perchance the roaring and rushing waters should seize upon a foreign element at the expense of its human possessor, He has enclosed its limits with shores;[4] so that when the raving billow and the foaming water should come from its deep bosom, it should return again unto itself, and not transgress its concealed bounds, but keep its prescribed laws, so that man might the rather be careful to observe the divine laws, even

---

[1] Which we call the Creed.

[2] From the ninth chapter to the twenty-eighth he enters upon the diffuse explanation also of those words of our creed which commend to us faith in the Son of God, Jesus Christ, the Lord our God, the Christ promised in the Old Testament, and proves by the authority of the old and new covenant that He is very man and very God. In chapter eighteen he refutes the error of the Sabellians, and by the authority of the sacred writings he establishes the distinction of the Father and of the Son, and replies to the objections of the above-named heresiarchs and others. In the twenty-ninth chapter he treats of faith in the Holy Spirit, saying that finally the authority of the faith admonishes us, after the Father and the Son, to believe also on the Holy Spirit, whose operations he recounts and proves from the Scriptures. He then labours to associate the unity of God with the matters previously contended for, and at length sets forth the sum of the doctrines above explained. [Anthropopathy, see cap. v. p. 615.]

[3] " Mensurnis," or otherwise " menstruis."

[4] [Jer..v. 22. Compare this sublime page with paganism.]

as the elements themselves observed them. And after these things He also placed man at the head of the world, and man, too, made in the image of God, to whom He imparted mind, and reason, and foresight, that he might imitate God ; and although the first elements of his body were earthly, yet the substance was inspired by a heavenly and divine breathing. And when He had given him all things for his service, He willed that he alone should be free. And lest, again, an unbounded freedom should fall into peril, He laid down a command, in which man was taught that there was no evil in the fruit of the tree ; but he was forewarned that evil would arise if perchance he should exercise his free will, in the contempt of the law that was given. For, on the one hand, it had behoved him to be free, lest the image of God should unfittingly be in bondage ; and on the other, the law was to be added, so that an unbridled liberty might not break forth even to a contempt of the Giver. So that he might receive as a consequence both worthy rewards and a deserved punishment, having in his own power that which he might choose to do, by the tendency of his mind in either direction : whence, therefore, by envy, mortality comes back upon him ; seeing that, although he might escape it by obedience, he rushes into it by hurrying to be God under the influence of perverse counsel. Still, nevertheless, God indulgently tempered his punishment by cursing, not so much himself, as his labours upon earth. And, moreover, what is required does not come without man's knowledge ; but He shows forth man's hope of future discovery [1] and salvation in Christ. And that he is prevented from touching of the wood of the tree of life, is not caused by the malignant poison of envy, but lest, living for ever without Christ's previous pardon of his sins, he should always bear about with him for his punishment an immortality of guilt. Nevertheless also, in higher regions ; that is, above even the firmament itself, regions which are not now discernible by our eyes, He previously ordained angels, he arranged spiritual powers, He put in command thrones and powers, and founded many other infinite spaces of heavens, and unbounded works of His mysteries ; so that this world, immense as it is, might almost appear rather as the latest, than the only work of corporeal things. And truly,[2] what lies beneath the earth is not itself void of distributed and arranged powers. For there is a place whither the souls of the just and the unjust are taken, conscious of the anticipated dooms of future judgment ; so that we might behold the overflowing greatness of God's works in all directions, not shut up within the bosom of this world, however capacious as we have said, but might also be able to conceive of them beneath both the abysses and the depths of the world itself. And thus considering the greatness of the works, we should worthily admire the Artificer of such a structure.

CHAP. II. *ARGUMENT.* — GOD IS ABOVE ALL THINGS, HIMSELF CONTAINING ALL THINGS, IMMENSE, ETERNAL, TRANSCENDING THE MIND OF MAN ; INEXPLICABLE IN DISCOURSE, LOFTIER THAN ALL SUBLIMITY.

And over all these things He Himself, containing all things, having nothing vacant beyond Himself, has left room for no superior God, such as some people conceive. Since, indeed, He Himself has included all things in the bosom of perfect greatness and power, He is always intent upon His own work, and pervading all things, and moving all things, and quickening all things, and beholding all things, and so linking together discordant materials into the concord of all elements, that out of these unlike principles one world is so established by a conspiring union, that it can by no force be dissolved, save when He alone who made it commands it to be dissolved, for the purpose of bestowing other and greater things upon us. For we read that He contains all things, and therefore that there could have been nothing beyond Himself. Because, since He has not any beginning, so consequently He is not conscious of an ending ; unless perchance — and far from us be the thought — He at some time began to be, and is not above all things, but as He began to be after something else, He would be beneath that which was before Himself, and would so be found to be of less power, in that He is designated as subsequent even in time itself. For this reason, therefore, He is always unbounded, because nothing is greater than He ; always eternal, because nothing is more ancient than He. For that which is without beginning can be preceded by none, in that He has no time. He is on that account immortal, that He does not come to an end by any ending of His completeness. And since everything that is without beginning is without law, He excludes the mode of time by feeling Himself debtor to none. Concerning Him, therefore, and concerning those things which are of Himself, and are in Him, neither can the mind of man worthily conceive what they are, how great they are, and what they are like ; nor does the eloquence of human discourse set forth a power that approaches the level of His majesty. For to conceive and to speak of His majesty, as well all eloquence is with reason mute, as all mind poor. For He is greater than mind itself ; nor can it be conceived how great He is, seeing that, if He could be conceived, He would be smaller than the human

---

[1] " Inventionis." " Redemptionis " is a reasonable emendation.
[2] Or probably, " Neither indeed is," etc. [Vol. iii. p. 428.]

mind wherein He could be conceived. He is greater, moreover, than all discourse, nor can He be declared; for if He could be declared, He would be less than human discourse, whereby being declared, He can both be encompassed and contained. For whatever could be thought concerning Him must be less than Himself; and whatever could be declared must be less than He, when compared in respect of Himself. Moreover, we can in some degree be conscious of Him in silence, but we cannot in discourse unfold Him as He is. For should you call Him *Light*, you would be speaking of His creature rather than of Himself — you would not declare Him; or should you call Him *Strength*, you would rather be speaking of and bringing out His power than speaking of Himself; or should you call Him *Majesty*, you would rather be describing His honour than Himself. And why should I make a long business of going through His attributes one by one? I will at once unfold the whole. Whatever in any respect you might declare of Him, you would rather be unfolding some condition and power of His than Himself. For what can you fittingly either say or think concerning Him who is greater than all discourses and thoughts? Except that in one manner — and how can we do this? how can we by possibility conceive how we may grasp these very things? — we shall mentally grasp what God is, if we shall consider that He is that which cannot be understood either in quality or quantity, nor, indeed, can come even into the thought itself. For if the keenness of our eyes grows dull on looking at the sun, so that the gaze, overcome by the brightness of the rays that meet it, cannot look upon the orb itself, the keenness of our mental perception suffers the same thing in all our thinking about God, and in proportion as we give our endeavours more directly to consider God, so much the more the mind itself is blinded by the light of its own thought. For — to repeat once more — what can you worthily say of Him, who is loftier than all sublimity, and higher than all height, and deeper than all depth, and clearer than all light, and brighter than all brightness, more brilliant than all splendour, stronger than all strength, more powerful [1] than all power, and more mighty than all might, and greater than all majesty, and more potent than all potency, and richer than all riches, more wise than all wisdom, and more benignant than all kindness, better than all goodness, juster than all justice, more merciful than all clemency? For all kinds of virtues must needs be less than Himself, who is both God and Parent of all virtues, so that it may truly be said that God is that, which is such that

nothing can be compared to Him. For He is above all that can be said. For He is a certain Mind generating and filling all things, which, without any beginning or end of time, controls, by the highest and most perfect reason, the naturally linked causes of things, so as to result in benefit to all.

CHAP. III. *ARGUMENT.* — THAT GOD IS THE FOUNDER OF ALL THINGS, THEIR LORD AND PARENT, IS PROVED FROM THE HOLY SCRIPTURES.

Him, then, we acknowledge and know to be God, the Creator of all things — Lord on account of His power, Parent on account of His discipline — Him, I say, who "spake, and all things were made;" [2] He commanded, and all things went forth: of whom it is written, "Thou hast made all things in wisdom;" [3] of whom Moses said, "God in heaven above, and in the earth beneath;" [4] who, according to Isaiah, "hath meted out the heaven with a span, the earth with the hollow of His hand;" [5] "who looketh on the earth, and maketh it tremble; who boundeth the circle of the earth, and those that dwell in it like locusts; who hath weighed the mountains in a balance, and the groves in scales," [6] that is, by the sure test of divine arrangement; and lest its greatness, lying unequally, should easily fall into ruins if it were not balanced with equal weights, He has poised this burden of the earthly mass with equity. Who says by the prophet, "I am God, and there is none beside me." [7] Who says by the same prophet, "Because I will not give my majesty to another," [8] that He may exclude all heathens and heretics with their figments; proving that that is not God who is made by the hand of the workman, nor that which is feigned by the intellect of a heretic. For he is not God for whose existence the workman must be asked. And He has added hereto by the prophet, "The heaven is my throne, and the earth is my footstool: what house will ye build me, and where is the place of my rest?" [9] that He may show that He whom the world does not contain is much less contained in a temple; and He says these things not for boastfulness of Himself, but for our knowledge. For He does not desire from us the glory of His magnitude; but He wishes to confer upon us, even as a father, a religious wisdom. And He, wishing moreover to attract to gentleness our minds, brutish, and swelling, and stubborn with cloddish ferocity, says, "And upon whom shall my Spirit rest, save upon him that is lowly, and quiet, and

---

[1] Viritior. [See Robert Hall on *French Atheism*.]

[2] Ps. cxlviii. 5.
[3] Ps. ciii. 24.
[4] Deut. iv. 39.
[5] Ps. ciii. 32.
[6] Isa. xl. 22, 12.
[7] Isa. xlv. 22.
[8] Isa. xlii. 8.
[9] Isa. lxvi. 1. [No portable or pocket god.]

that trembleth at my words?"[1] — so that in some degree one may recognise how great God is, in learning to fear Him by the Spirit given to him : Who, similarly wishing still more to come into our knowledge, and, by way of stirring up our minds to His worship, said, " I am the Lord, who made the light and created the darkness ;"[2] that we might deem not that some Nature, — what I know not, — was the artificer of those vicissitudes whereby nights and days are controlled, but might rather, as is more true, recognise God as their Creator. And since by the gaze of our eyes we cannot see Him, we rightly learn of Him from the greatness, and the power, and the majesty of His works. " For the invisible things of Him," says the Apostle Paul, " from the creation of the world, are clearly seen, being understood by those things which are made, even His eternal power and godhead ;"[3] so that the human mind, learning hidden things from those that are manifest, from the greatness of the works which it should behold, might with the eyes of the mind consider the greatness of the Architect. Of whom the same apostle, " Now unto the King eternal, immortal, invisible, the only God, be honour and glory."[4] For He has gone beyond the contemplation of the eyes who has surpassed the greatness of thought. " For," it is said, " of Him, and through Him, and in Him are all things."[5] For all things are by His command, because they are *of Him;* and are ordered by His word as being *through Him;* and all things return to His judgment; as *in Him* expecting liberty when corruption shall be done away, they appear to be recalled *to Him.*

CHAP. IV. *ARGUMENT.* — MOREOVER, HE IS GOOD, ALWAYS THE SAME, IMMUTABLE, ONE AND ONLY, INFINITE ; AND HIS OWN NAME CAN NEVER BE DECLARED, AND HE IS INCORRUPTIBLE AND IMMORTAL.

Him alone the Lord rightly declares good, of whose goodness the whole world is witness ; which world He would not have ordained if He had not been good. For if " everything was very good,"[6] consequently, and reasonably, both those things which were ordained have proved that He that ordained them is good, and those things which are the work of a good Ordainer cannot be other than good ; wherefore every evil is a departure from God. For it cannot happen that He should be the originator or architect of any evil work, who claims to Himself the name of " the Perfect," both Parent and Judge, especially when He is the avenger and judge of every evil work ; because, moreover, evil does not occur to man from any other cause than by his departure from the good God. Moreover, this very thing is specified in man, not because it was necessary, but because he himself so willed it. Whence it manifestly appeared also what was evil ; and lest there should seem to be envy in God, it was evident whence evil had arisen. He, then, is always like to Himself ; nor does He ever turn or change Himself into any forms, lest by change He should appear to be mortal. For the change implied in turning from one thing to another is comprehended as a portion of a certain death. Thus there is never in Him any accession or increase of any part or honour, lest anything should appear to have ever been wanting to His perfection, nor is any loss sustained in Him, lest a degree of mortality should appear to have been suffered by Him. But what He is, He always is ; and who He is, He is always Himself ; and what character He has, He always has.[7] For increasing argues beginning, as well as losses prove death and perishing. And therefore He says, " I am God, I change not ;"[8] in that, what is not born cannot suffer change, holding His condition always. For whatever it be in Him which constitutes Divinity, must necessarily exist always, maintaining itself by its own powers, so that He should always be God. And thus He says, " I am that I am."[9] For what He is has this name, because it always maintains the same quality of Himself. For change takes away the force of that name " That I Am ; " for whatever, at any time, is changed, is shown to be mortal in that very particular which is changed. For it ceases to be that which it had been, and consequently begins to be what it was not ; and therefore, reasonably, there remains always in God His position, in that without any loss arising from change, He is always like and equal to Himself. And what is not born cannot be changed : for only those things undergo change which are made, or which are begotten ; in that those things which had not been at one time, learn to be by coming into being, and therefore to suffer change by being born. Moreover, those things which neither have nativity nor maker, have excluded from themselves the capacity of change, not having a beginning wherein is cause of change. And thus He is declared to be one, having no equal. For whatever can be God, must as God be of necessity the Highest. But whatever is the Highest, must certainly be the Highest in such sense as to be without any equal. And thus that must needs be alone and one on

[1] Isa. lxvi. 2.
[2] Isa. xlv. 7. [A lesson to our age.]
[3] Rom. i. 20. [" So that they are without excuse."]
[4] 1 Tim. i. 17.
[5] Rom. xi. 33.
[6] Gen. i. 31.

[7] In other words, God is always the same in essence, in personality, and in attributes.
[8] Mal. iii. 6.
[9] Ex. iii. 14. [The ineffable name of the Self-Existent.]

which nothing can be conferred, having no peer; because there cannot be two infinites, as the very nature of things dictates. And that is infinite which neither has any sort of beginning nor end. For whatever has occupied the whole excludes the beginning of another. Because if He does not contain all which is, whatever it is — seeing that what is found in that whereby it is contained is found to be less than that whereby it is contained — He will cease to be God; being reduced into the power of another, in whose greatness He, being smaller, shall have been included. And therefore what contained Him would then rather claim to be God. Whence it results that God's own name also cannot be declared, because He cannot be conceived. For that is contained in a name which is, in any way, comprehended from the condition of His nature. For the name is the signification of that thing which could be comprehended from a name. But when that which is treated of is such that it cannot be worthily gathered into one form by the very understanding itself, how shall it be set forth fittingly in the one word of an appellation, seeing that as it is beyond the intellect, it must also of necessity be above the significancy of the appellation? As with reason when He applies and prefers from certain reasons and occasions His name of God, we know that it is not so much the legitimate propriety of the appellation that is set forth, as a certain significancy determined for it, to which, while men betake themselves, they seem to be able thereby to obtain God's mercy. He is therefore also both immortal and incorruptible, neither conscious of any kind of loss nor ending. For because He is incorruptible, He is therefore immortal; and because He is immortal, He is certainly also incorruptible, — each being involved by turns in the other, with itself and in itself, by a mutual connection, and prolonged by a vicarious concatenation to the condition of eternity; immortality arising from incorruption, as well as incorruption coming from immortality.

CHAP. V. *ARGUMENT.* — IF WE REGARD THE ANGER, AND INDIGNATION, AND HATRED OF GOD DESCRIBED IN THE SACRED PAGES, WE MUST REMEMBER THAT THEY ARE NOT TO BE UNDERSTOOD AS BEARING THE CHARACTER OF HUMAN VICES.

Moreover, if we read of His wrath, and consider certain descriptions of His indignation, and learn that hatred is asserted of Him, yet we are not to understand these to be asserted of Him in the sense in which they are human vices. For all these things, although they may corrupt man, cannot at all corrupt the divine power. For such passions as these will rightly be said to be in men, and will not rightly be judged to be

in God. For man may be corrupted by these things, because he can be corrupted; God may not be corrupted by them, because He cannot be corrupted. These things, forsooth, have their force which they may exercise, but only where a material capable of impression precedes them, not where a substance that cannot be impressed precedes them. For that God is angry, arises from no vice in Him. But He is so for our advantage; for He is merciful even then when He threatens, because by these threats men are recalled to rectitude. For fear is necessary for those who want the motive to a virtuous life, that they who have forsaken reason may at least be moved by terror. And thus all those, either angers of God or hatreds, or whatever they are of this kind, being displayed for our medicine, — as the case teaches, — have arisen of wisdom, not from vice, nor do they originate from frailty; wherefore also they cannot avail for the corruption of God. For the diversity in us of the materials of which we consist, is accustomed to arouse the discord of anger which corrupts us; but this, whether of nature or of defect, cannot subsist in God, seeing that He is known to be constructed assuredly of no associations of bodily parts. For He is simple and without any corporeal commixture, being wholly of that essence, which, whatever it be, — He alone knows, — constitutes His being, since He is called Spirit. And thus those things which in men are faulty and corrupting, since they arise from the corruptibility of the body, and matter itself, in God cannot exert the force of corruptibility, since, as we have said, they have come, not of vice, but of reason.

CHAP. VI. *ARGUMENT.* — AND THAT, ALTHOUGH SCRIPTURE OFTEN CHANGES THE DIVINE APPEARANCE INTO A HUMAN FORM, YET THE MEASURE OF THE DIVINE MAJESTY IS NOT INCLUDED WITHIN THESE LINEAMENTS OF OUR BODILY NATURE.

And although the heavenly Scripture often turns the divine appearance into a human form, — as when it says, "The eyes of the Lord are over the righteous;"[1] or when it says, "The Lord God smelled the smell of a good savour;"[2] or when there are given to Moses the tables "written with the finger of God;"[3] or when the people of the children of Israel are set free from the land of Egypt "with a mighty hand and with a stretched out arm;"[4] or when it says, "The mouth of the Lord hath spoken these things;"[5] or when the earth is set forth as "God's footstool;"[6] or when it says, "Incline thine ear,

---

[1] Ps. xxxiv. 15. [Anthropopathy, p. 611.]
[2] Gen. viii. 21.
[3] Ex. xxxi. 18.
[4] Ps. cxxxvi. 12.
[5] Isa. i. 20.
[6] Isa. lxvi. 1. [Capp. v. and vi. are specimens of vigorous thought.]

and hear," [1]—we who say that the law is spiritual do not include within these lineaments of our bodily nature any mode or figure of the divine majesty, but diffuse that character of unbounded magnitude (so to speak) over its plains without any limit. For it is written, "If I shall ascend into heaven, Thou art there; if I shall descend into hell, Thou art there also; and if I shall take my wings, and go away across the sea, there Thy hand shall lay hold of me, and Thy right hand shall hold me." [2] For we recognise the plan of the divine Scripture according to the proportion of its arrangement. For the prophet then was still speaking about God in parables according to the period of the faith, not as God was, but as the people were able to receive Him. And thus, that such things as these should be said about God, must be imputed not to God, but rather to the people. Thus the people are permitted to erect a tabernacle, and yet God is not contained within the enclosure of a tabernacle. Thus a temple is reared, and yet God is not at all bounded within the restraints of a temple. It is not therefore God who is limited, but the perception of the people is limited; nor is God straitened, but the understanding of the reason of the people is held to be straitened. Finally, in the Gospel the Lord said, "The hour shall come when neither in this mountain nor in Jerusalem shall ye worship the Father;" [3] and gave the reasons, saying, "God is a Spirit; and those therefore who worship, must worship in spirit and in truth." [4] Thus the divine agencies are there [5] exhibited by means of members; it is not the appearance of God nor the bodily lineaments that are described. For when the eyes are spoken of, it is implied that He sees all things; and when the ear, it is set forth that He hears all things; and when the finger, a certain energy of His will is opened up; and when the nostrils, His recognition of prayers is shown forth as of odours; and when the hand, it is proved that He is the author of every creature; and when the arm, it is announced that no nature can withstand the power of His arm; and when the feet, it is unfolded that He fills all things, and that there is not any place where God is not. For neither members nor the offices of members are needful to Him to whose sole judgment, even unexpressed, all things serve and are present. For why should He require eyes who is Himself the light? or why should He ask for feet who is everywhere? or why should He wish to go when there is nowhere where He can go beyond Himself? or why should He seek for hands whose will is, even when silent, the architect for the foundation of all things? He needs no ears who knows the wills that are even unexpressed; or for what reason should He need a tongue whose thought is a command? These members assuredly were necessary to men, but not to God, because man's design would be ineffectual if the body did not fulfil the thought. Moreover, they are not needful to God, whose will the works attend not so much without any effort, as that the works themselves proceed simultaneously with the will. Moreover, He Himself is all eye, because He all sees; and all ear, because He all hears; and all hand, because He all works; and all foot, because He all is everywhere. For He is the same, whatever it is. He is all equal, and all everywhere. For He has not in Him any diversity in Himself, being simple. For those are the things which are reduced to diversity of members, which arise from birth and go to dissolution. But things which are not concrete cannot be conscious of these things. [6] And what is immortal, whatever it is, that very thing is one and simple, and for ever. And thus because it is one it cannot be dissolved; since whatever is that very thing which is placed beyond the claim of dissolution, it is freed from the laws of death.

CHAP. VII. *ARGUMENT.*—MOREOVER, THAT WHEN GOD IS CALLED A SPIRIT, BRIGHTNESS, AND LIGHT, GOD IS NOT SUFFICIENTLY EXPRESSED BY THOSE APPELLATIONS.

But when the Lord says that God is a Spirit, I think that Christ spoke thus of the Father, as wishing that something still more should be understood than merely that God is a Spirit. For although, in His Gospel, He is reasoning for the purpose of giving to men an increase of intelligence, nevertheless He Himself speaks to men concerning God, in such a way as they can as yet hear and receive; although, as we have said, He is now endeavouring to give to His hearers religious additions to their knowledge of God. For we find it to be written that God is called *Love*, and yet from this the substance of God is not declared to be *Love;* and that He is called *Light*, while in this is not the substance of God. But the whole that is thus said of God is as much as can be said, so that reasonably also, when He is called a Spirit, it is not all that He is which is so called; but so that, while men's mind by understanding makes progress even to the Spirit itself, being already changed in spirit, it may conjecture God to be something even greater through the Spirit. For that which *is*, according to what it is, can neither be declared by human discourse, nor received by human ears, nor gathered by human perceptions. For if "the things which God hath prepared for them

[1] 2 Chron. xix. 16.
[2] Ps. cxxxix. 8, 9, 10.
[3] John iv. 21.
[4] John iv. 24.
[5] *sc.* in the Old Testament.

[6] That is to say, "of birth and dissolution." [He is the Now.]

that love Him, neither eye hath seen, nor ear hath heard, nor the heart of man, nor even his mind has perceived;"[1] what and how great is He Himself who promises these things, in understanding which both the mind and nature of man have failed! Finally, if you receive the Spirit as the substance of God, you will make God a creature. For every spirit is a creature. And therefore, then, God will be made. In which manner also, if, according to Moses, you should receive God to be *fire*, in saying that He is a creature, you will have declared what is ordained, you will not have taught who is its ordainer. But these things are rather used as figures than as being so in fact. For as, in the Old Testament,[2] God is for this reason called *Fire*, that fear may be struck into the hearts of a sinful people, by suggesting to them a Judge; so in the New Testament He is announced as Spirit, that, as the Renewer and Creator of those who are dead in their sins, He may be attested by this goodness of mercy granted to those that believe.

CHAP. VIII. *ARGUMENT.* — IT IS THIS GOD, THEREFORE, THAT THE CHURCH HAS KNOWN AND ADORES; AND TO HIM THE TESTIMONY OF THINGS AS WELL VISIBLE AS INVISIBLE IS GIVEN, BOTH AT ALL TIMES AND IN ALL FORMS, BY THE NATURE WHICH HIS PROVIDENCE RULES AND GOVERNS.

This God, then, setting aside the fables and figments of heretics, the Church knows and worships, to whom the universal and entire nature of things as well visible as invisible gives witness; whom angels adore, stars wonder at, seas bless, lands revere, and all things under the earth look up to; whom the whole mind of man is conscious of, even if it does not express *itself;* at whose command all things are set in motion, springs gush forth, rivers flow, waves arise, all creatures bring forth their young, winds are compelled to blow, showers descend, seas are stirred up, all things everywhere diffuse their fruitfulness. Who ordained, peculiar to the protoplasts of eternal life, a certain beautiful paradise in the east; He planted the tree of life, and similarly placed near it another tree of the knowledge of good and evil, gave a command, and decreed a judgment against sin; He preserved the most righteous Nöe from the perils of the deluge, for the merit of His innocence and faith; He translated Enoch: He elected Abraham into the society of his friendship; He protected Isaac: He increased Jacob; He gave Moses for a leader unto the people; He delivered the groaning children of Israel from the yoke of slavery; He wrote the law;

He brought the offspring of our fathers into the land of promise; He instructed the prophets by His Spirit, and by all of them He promised His Son Christ; and at the time at which He had covenanted that He would give Him, He sent Him, and through Him He desired to come into our knowledge, and shed forth upon us the liberal stores of His mercy, by conferring His abundant Spirit on the poor and abject. And, because He of His own free-will is both liberal and kind, lest the whole of this globe, being turned away from the streams of His grace, should wither, He willed the apostles, as founders of our family, to be sent by His Son into the whole world, that the condition of the human race might be conscious of its Founder; and, if it should choose to follow Him, might have One whom even in its supplications it might now call Father instead of God.[3] And His providence has had or has its course among men, not only individually, but also among cities themselves, and states whose destructions have been announced by the words of prophets; yea, even through the whole world itself; whose end, whose miseries, and wastings, and sufferings on account of unbelief He has allotted. And lest moreover any one should think that such an indefatigable providence of God does not reach to even the very least things, "One of two sparrows," says the Lord, "shall not fall without the will of the Father; but even the very hairs of your head are all numbered."[4] And His care and providence did not permit even the clothes of the Israelites to be worn out, nor even the vilest shoes on their feet to be wasted; nor, moreover, finally, the very garments of the captive young men to be burnt. And this is not without reason; for if He embraces all things, and contains all things, — and all things, and the whole, consist of individuals, — His care will consequently extend even to every individual thing, since His providence reaches to the whole, whatever it is. Hence it is that He also sitteth above the Cherubim; that is, He presides over the variety of His works, the living creatures which hold the control over the rest being subjected to His throne:[5] a crystal covering being thrown over all things; that is, the heaven covering all things, which at the command of God had been consolidated into a firmament[6] from the fluent material of the waters, that the strong hardness that divides the midst of the waters that covered the earth before,

---

[1] 1 Cor. ii. 9.
[2] [Ex. iii. 2. Not consuming. Heb. xii. 29, "consuming."]

[3] [Madame de Staël has beautifully remarked on the benefit conferred upon humanity by Him who authorized us to say, "Our Father." "Scientific" atheism gives nothing instead.]
[4] Matt. x. 29, 30.
[5] [Ezek. i. 10 and Rev. iv. 7.]
[6] [The science of the third century had overruled the Pythagorean system, and philosophers bound the Church and the human mind in the chains of false science for ages. The revival of true science was due to Copernicus, a Christian priest, and to Galileo, and other Christians. Let this be noted.]

might sustain as if on its back the weight of the superincumbent water, its strength being established by the frost. And, moreover, wheels lie below — that is to say, the seasons — whereby all the members of the world are always being rolled onwards; such feet being added by which those things do not stand still for ever, but pass onward. And, moreover, throughout all their limbs they are studded with eyes; for the works of God must be contemplated with an ever watchful inspection : in the heart of which things, a fire of embers is in the midst, either because this world of ours is hastening to the fiery day of judgment; or because all the works of God are fiery, and are not darksome, but flourish.[1] Or, moreover, lest, because those things had arisen from earthly beginnings, they should naturally be inactive, from the rigidity of their origin, the hot nature of an interior spirit was added to all things; and that this nature concreted with the cold bodies might minister[2] for the purpose of life equal measures for all.[3] This, therefore, according to David, is God's chariot. "For the chariot of God," says he, "is multiplied ten thousand times;"[4] that is, it is innumerable, infinite, immense. For, under the yoke of the natural law given to all things, some things are restrained, as if withheld by reins; others, as if stimulated, are urged on with relaxed reins. For the world,[5] which is that chariot of God with all things, both the angels themselves and the stars guide; and their movements, although various, yet bound by certain laws, we watch them guiding by the bounds of a time prescribed to themselves; so that rightly we also are now disposed to exclaim with the apostle, as he admires both the Architect and His works : "Oh the depth of the riches of the wisdom and knowledge of God ! how inscrutable are His judgments, and His ways past finding out ! " And the rest.[6]

CHAP. IX. *ARGUMENT.* — FURTHER, THAT THE SAME RULE OF TRUTH TEACHES US TO BELIEVE, AFTER THE FATHER, ALSO IN THE SON OF GOD, JESUS CHRIST OUR LORD GOD, BEING THE SAME THAT WAS PROMISED IN THE OLD TESTAMENT, AND MANIFESTED IN THE NEW.

The same rule of truth teaches us to believe, after the Father, also on the Son of God, Christ Jesus, the Lord our God, but the Son of God — of that God who is both one and alone, to wit the Founder of all things, as already has been expressed above. For this Jesus Christ, I will once more say, the Son of this God, we read of as having been promised in the Old Testament, and we observe to be manifested in the New, fulfilling the shadows and figures of all the sacraments, with the presence of the truth embodied. For as well the ancient prophecies as the Gospels testify Him to be the son of Abraham and the son of David. Genesis itself anticipates Him, when it says : "To thee will I give it, and to thy seed."[7] He is spoken of when it shows how a man wrestled with Jacob; He too, when it says : "There shall not fail a prince from Judah, nor a leader from between his thighs, until He shall come to whom it has been promised; and He shall be the expectation of the nations."[8] He is spoken of by Moses when he says : "Provide another whom thou mayest send."[9] He is again spoken of by the same, when he testifies, saying : "A Prophet will God raise up to you from your brethren; listen to Him as if to me."[10] It is He, too, that he speaks of when he says : "Ye shall see your life hanging in doubt night and day, and ye shall not believe Him."[11] Him, too, Isaiah alludes to : "There shall go forth a rod from the root of Jesse, and a flower shall grow up from his root."[12] The same also when he says : "Behold, a virgin shall conceive, and bear a son."[13] Him he refers to when he enumerates the healings that were to proceed from Him, saying : "Then shall the eyes of the blind be opened, and the ears of the deaf shall hear : then shall the lame man leap as an hart, and the tongue of the dumb shall be eloquent."[14] Him also, when he sets forth the virtue of patience, saying : "His voice shall not be heard in the streets; a bruised reed shall He not destroy, and the smoking flax shall He not quench."[15] Him, too, when he described His Gospel : "And I will ordain for you an everlasting covenant, even the sure mercies of David."[16] Him, too, when he foretells that the nations should believe on Him : "Behold, I have given Him for a Chief and a Commander to the nations. Nations that knew not Thee shall call upon Thee, and peoples that knew Thee not shall flee unto Thee."[17] It is the same that he refers to when, concerning His passion, he exclaims, saying : "As a sheep He is led to the slaughter; and as a lamb before his shearer is dumb, so He opened not His mouth in His

---

[1] "Vigent," or otherwise "lucent."
[2] "Ministraret" seems to be preferable to "monstraret."
[3] [Our author's genius actually suggests a theory, in this chapter, concerning the *zoa*, or "living creatures," which anticipates all that is truly demonstrated by the "evolutionists," and which harmonizes the variety of animated natures. Rev. v. 13, 14.]
[4] Ps. lxviii. 18.
[5] [The universe is here intended, as in Milton, "this pendent world." *Parad. Lost*, book ii. 1052.]
[6] Rom. xi. 33. "*Note* also the rest *of the text*" is our author's additional comment.

[7] Gen. xvii. 8.
[8] Gen. xlix. 10.
[9] Ex. iv. 13.
[10] Deut. xviii. 15.
[11] Deut. xxviii. 66.
[12] Isa. xi. 1.
[13] Isa. vii. 13.
[14] Isa. xxxv. 3–6.
[15] Isa. xlii. 2, 3.
[16] Isa. lv. 3.
[17] Isa. lv. 4, 5.

humility." [1] Him, moreover, when he described the blows and stripes of His scourgings: "By His bruises we were healed." [2] Or His humiliation: "And we saw Him, and He had neither form nor comeliness, a man in suffering, and who knoweth how to bear infirmity." [3] Or that the people would not believe on Him: "All day long I have spread out my hands unto a people that believeth not." [4] Or that He would rise again from the dead: "And in that day there shall be a root of Jesse, and one who shall rise to reign over the nations; on Him shall the nations hope, and His rest shall be honour." [5] Or when he speaks of the time of the resurrection: "We shall find Him, as it were, prepared in the morning." [6] Or that He should sit at the right hand of the Father: "The Lord said unto my Lord, Sit Thou at my right hand, until I shall place Thine enemies as the stool of Thy feet." [7] Or when He is set forth as possessor of all things: "Ask of me, and I will give Thee the heathen for Thine inheritance, and the boundaries of the earth for Thy possession." [8] Or when He is shown as Judge of all: "O God, give the King Thy judgment, and Thy righteousness to the King's Son." [9] And I shall not in this place pursue the subject further: the things which are announced of Christ are known to all heretics, but are even better known to those who hold the truth.

CHAP. X. *ARGUMENT.* — THAT JESUS CHRIST IS THE SON OF GOD AND TRULY MAN, AS OPPOSED TO THE FANCIES OF HERETICS, WHO DENY THAT HE TOOK UPON HIM TRUE FLESH.

But of this I remind *you*, that Christ was not to be expected in the Gospel in any other wise than as He was promised before by the Creator, in the Scriptures of the Old Testament; especially as the things that were predicted of Him were fulfilled, and those things that were fulfilled had been predicted. As with reason I might truly and constantly say to that fanciful — I know not what — of those heretics who reject the authority of the Old Testament, as to a Christ feigned and coloured up from old wives' fables: "Who art thou? Whence art thou? By whom art thou sent? Wherefore hast thou now chosen to come? Why such as thou art? Or how hast thou been able to come? Or wherefore hast thou not gone to thine own, except that thou hast proved that thou hast none of thine own, by coming to those of another? What hast thou to do with the Creator's world? What hast thou to do with the Creator's man? What hast thou to do with the image of a body from which thou takest away the hope of resurrection? Why comest thou to another man's servant, and desirest thou to solicit another man's son? Why dost thou strive to take me away from the Lord? Why dost thou compel me to blaspheme, and to be impious to my Father? Or what shall I gain from thee in the resurrection, if I do not receive myself when I lose my body? If thou wishest to save, thou shouldest have made a man to whom to give salvation. If thou desirest to snatch from sin, thou shouldest have granted to me previously that I should not fall into sin. But what approbation of law dost thou carry about with thee? What testimony of the prophetic word hast thou? Or what substantial good can I promise myself from thee, when I see that thou hast come in a phantasm and not in a bodily substance? What, then, hast thou to do with the form of a body, if thou hatest a body? Nay, thou wilt be refuted as to the hatred of bearing about the substance of a body, since thou hast been willing even to take up its form. For thou oughtest to have hated the imitation of a body, if thou hatedst the reality; because, if thou art something else, thou oughtest to have come as something else, lest thou shouldest be called the Son of the Creator if thou hadst even the likeness of flesh and body. Assuredly, if thou hatedst being born because thou hatedst 'the Creator's marriage-union,' thou oughtest to refuse even the likeness of a man who is born by the 'marriage of the Creator.'"

Neither, therefore, do we acknowledge that that is a Christ of the heretics who was — as it is said — in appearance and not in reality; for of those things which he did, he could have done nothing real, if he himself was a phantasm, and not reality. Nor him who wore nothing of our body in himself, seeing "he received nothing from Mary;" neither did he come to us, since he appeared "as a vision, not in our substance." Nor *do we acknowledge* that *to be Christ* who chose an ethereal or starry flesh, as some heretics have pretended. Nor can we perceive any salvation of ours in him, if *in him* we do not even recognise the substance of our body; nor, in short, any other who may have worn any other kind of fabulous body of heretical device. For all such fables as these are confuted as well by the nativity as by the death itself of our Lord. For John says: "The Word was made flesh, and dwelt among us;" [10] so that, reasonably, our body should be in Him, because indeed the Word took on Him our flesh. And for this reason blood flowed forth from His hands and feet,

1 Isa. liii. 7.
2 Isa. liii. 5.
3 Isa. liii. 2.
4 Isa. lxv. 2.
5 Isa. xi. 10.
6 Hos. vi. 3.
7 Ps. cx. 1, 2.
8 Ps. ii. 8.
9 Ps. lxxii. 1.

10 John i. 14. [Of fables and figments, see cap. viii. p. 617.]

and from His very side, so that He might be proved to be a sharer in our body by dying according to the laws of our dissolution. And that He was raised again in the same bodily substance in which He died, is proved by the wounds of that very body, and thus He showed the laws of our resurrection in His flesh, in that He restored the same body in His resurrection which He had from us. For a law of resurrection is established, in that Christ is raised up in the substance of the body as an example for the rest; because, when it is written that "flesh and blood do not inherit the kingdom of God,"[1] it is not the substance of the flesh that is condemned, which was built up by the divine hands that it should not perish, but only the guilt of the flesh is rightly rebuked, which by the voluntary daring of man rebelled against the claims of divine law. Because in baptism and in the dissolution of death the flesh is raised up and returns to salvation, by being recalled to the condition of innocency when the mortality of guilt is put away.

CHAP. XI. — AND INDEED THAT CHRIST WAS NOT ONLY MAN, BUT GOD ALSO; THAT EVEN AS HE WAS THE SON OF MAN, SO ALSO HE WAS THE SON OF GOD.

But lest, from the fact of asserting that our Lord Jesus Christ, the Son of God, the Creator, was manifested in the substance of the true body, we should seem either to have given assent to other heretics, who in this place maintain that He is man only and alone, and therefore desire to prove that He was a man bare and solitary; and lest we should seem to have afforded them any ground for objecting, we do not so express *doctrine* concerning the substance of His body, as to say that He is only and alone man, but so as to maintain, by the association of the divinity of the Word in that very materiality, that He was also God according to the Scriptures. For there is a great risk of saying that the Saviour of the human race *was only man;* that the Lord of all, and the Chief of the world, to whom all things were delivered, and all things were granted by His Father, by whom all things were ordained, all things were created, all things were arranged, the King of all ages and times, the Prince of all the angels, before whom there is none but the Father, was only man, and denying to Him divine authority in these things. For this contempt of the heretics will recoil also upon God the Father, if God the Father could not beget God the Son. But, moreover, no blindness of the heretics shall prescribe to the truth. Nor, because they maintain one thing in Christ and do not maintain another, they see one side of

Christ and do not see another, shall there be taken away from us that which they do not see for the sake of that which they do. For they regard the weaknesses in Him as if they were a man's weaknesses, but they do not count the powers as if they were a God's powers. They keep in mind the infirmities of the flesh, they exclude the powers of the divinity; when if this argument from the infirmities of Christ is of avail to the result of proving Him to be man from His infirmities, the argument of divinity in Him gathered from His powers avails to the result also of asserting Him to be God from His works. For if His sufferings show in Him human frailty, why may not His works assert in Him divine power? For if this should not avail to assert Him to be God from His powers, neither can His sufferings avail to show Him to be man also from them. For whatever principle be adopted on one or the other side, will be found to be maintained.[2] For there will be a risk that He should not be shown to be man from His sufferings, if He could not also be approved as God by His powers. We must not then lean to one side and evade the other side, because any one who should exclude one portion of the truth will never hold the perfect truth. For Scripture as much announces Christ as also God, as it announces God Himself as man. It has as much described Jesus Christ to be man, as moreover it has also described Christ the Lord to be God. Because it does not set forth Him to be the Son of God only, but also the Son of man; nor does it only say, the Son of man, but it has also been accustomed to speak of Him as the Son of God. So that being of both, He is both, lest if He should be one only, He could not be the other. For as nature itself has prescribed that he must be believed to be a man who is of man, so the same nature prescribes also that He must be believed to be God who is of God; but if he should not also be God when he is of God, no more should he be man although he should be of man. And thus both doctrines would be endangered in one and the other way, by one being convicted to have lost belief in the other. Let them, therefore, who read that Jesus Christ the Son of man is man, read also that this same Jesus is called also God and the Son of God. For in the manner that as man He is of Abraham, so also as God He is before Abraham himself. And in the same manner as He is as man the "Son of David,"[3] so as God He is proclaimed David's Lord. And in the same manner as He was made as man "under the law,"[4] so as God He is declared to be "Lord of the Sabbath."[5]

---

[1] 1 Cor. xvi 50. [Vol. iii. p. 521, this series.]

[2] *Scil.* in its alternative.
[3] Matt xxiii. 42 et seq.
[4] Gal. iv. 4.
[5] Luke vi. 5.

And in the same manner as He suffers, as man, the condemnation, so as God He is found to have all judgment of the quick and dead. And in the same manner as He is born as man subsequent to the world, so as God He is manifested to have been before the world. And in the same way as He was begotten as man of the seed of David, so also the world is said to have been ordained by Him as God. And in the same way as He was as man after many, so as God He was before all. And in the same manner as He was as man inferior to others, so as God He was greater than all. And in the same manner as He ascended as man into heaven, so as God He had first descended thence. And in the same manner as He goes as man to the Father, so as the Son in obedience to the Father He shall descend thence. So if imperfections in Him prove human frailty, majesties in Him affirm divine power. For the risk is, in reading of both, to believe not both, but one of the two. Wherefore as both are read of in Christ, let both be believed; that so finally the faith may be true, being also complete. For if of two principles one gives way in the faith, and the other, and that indeed which is of least importance, be taken up for belief, the rule of truth is thrown into confusion; and that boldness will not confer salvation, but instead of salvation will effect a great risk of death from the overthrow of the faith.

CHAP. XII. *ARGUMENT.*—THAT CHRIST IS GOD, IS PROVED BY THE AUTHORITY OF THE OLD TESTAMENT SCRIPTURES.

Why, then, should we hesitate to say what Scripture does not shrink from declaring? Why shall the truth of faith hesitate in that wherein the authority of Scripture has never hesitated? For, behold, Hosea the prophet says in the person of the Father: " I will not now save them by bow, nor by horses, nor by horsemen; but I will save them by the Lord their God." [1] If God says that He saves by God, still God does not save except by Christ. Why, then, should man hesitate to call Christ God, when he observes that He is declared to be God by the Father according to the Scriptures? Yea, if God the Father does not save except by God, no one can be saved by God the Father unless he shall have confessed Christ to be God, in whom and by whom the Father promises that He will give him salvation: so that, reasonably, whoever acknowledges Him to be God, may find salvation in Christ God; whoever does not acknowledge Him to be God, would lose salvation which he could not find elsewhere than in Christ God. For in the same way as Isaiah says, " Behold, a virgin shall conceive and bear a son, and ye shall call His name Emmanuel, which is, interpreted, God with us; " [2] so Christ Himself says, " Lo, I am with you, even to the consummation of the world." [3] Therefore He is " God with us; " yea, and much rather, He is in us. Christ is with us, therefore it is He whose name is God with us, because He also is with us; or is He not with us? How then does He say that He is with us? He, then, *is* with us. But because He is with us He was called Emmanuel, that is, God with us. God, therefore, because He is with us, was called God with us. The same prophet says: " Be ye strengthened, ye relaxed hands, and ye feeble knees; be consoled, ye that are cowardly in heart; be strong; fear not. Lo, our God shall return judgment; He Himself shall come, and shall save you: then shall the eyes of the blind be opened, and the ears of the deaf shall hear; then shall the lame man leap as an hart, and the tongue of the dumb shall be eloquent." [4] Since the prophet says that at God's advent these should be the signs which come to pass; let men acknowledge either that Christ is the Son of God, at whose advent and by whom these wonders of healings were performed; or, overcome by the truth of Christ's divinity, let them rush into the other heresy, and refusing to confess Christ to be the Son of God, and God, let them declare Him to be the Father. For, being bound by the words of the prophets, they can no longer deny Christ to be God. What, then, do they reply when those signs are said to be about to take place on the advent of God, which were manifested on the advent of Christ? In what way do they receive Christ as God? For now they cannot deny Him to be God. As God the Father, or as God the Son? If as the Son, why do they deny that the Son of God is God? If as the Father, why do they not follow those who appear to maintain blasphemies of that kind? unless because in this contest against them concerning the truth, this is in the meantime sufficient for us, that, being convinced in any kind of way, they should confess Christ to be God, seeing they have even wished to deny that He is God. He says by Habakkuk the prophet: " God shall come from the south, and the Holy One from the dark and dense mountain." [5] Whom do they wish to represent as coming from the south? If they say that it is the Almighty God the Father, then God the Father comes from a place, from which place, moreover, He is thus excluded, and He is bounded within the straitnesses of some abode; and thus by such as these, as we have said, the sacrilegious heresy of Sabellius is

---

[1] Hos. i. 7.

[2] Isa. vii. 14.
[3] Matt. xxviii. 20.
[4] Isa. xxxv. 3, etc.
[5] Hab. iii. 3. [See English *margin*, and Robinson, i. p. 552.]

embodied. Since Christ is believed to be not the Son, but the Father; since by them He is asserted to be in strictness a bare man, in a new manner, by those, again, Christ is proved to be God the Father Almighty. But if in Bethlehem, the region of which local division looks towards the southern portion of heaven, Christ is born, who by the Scriptures is also said to be God, this God is rightly described as coming from the south, because He was foreseen as about to come from Bethlehem. Let them, then, choose of the two alternatives, the one that they prefer, that He who came from the south is the Son, or the Father; for God is said to be about to come from the south. If the Son, why do they shrink from calling Him Christ and God? For the Scripture says that God shall come. If the Father, why do they shrink from being associated with the boldness of Sabellius, who says that Christ is the Father? unless because, whether they call Him Father or Son, from his heresy, however unwillingly, they must needs withdraw if they are accustomed to say that Christ is merely man; when compelled by the facts themselves, they are on the eve of exalting Him as God, whether in wishing to call Him Father or in wishing to call Him Son.

CHAP. XIII. *ARGUMENT.*— THAT THE SAME TRUTH IS PROVED FROM THE SACRED WRITINGS OF THE NEW COVENANT.

And thus also John, describing the nativity of Christ, says: "The Word was made flesh, and dwelt among us, and we saw His glory, the glory as of the only begotten of the Father, full of grace and truth." [1] For, moreover, "His name is called the Word of God," [2] and not without reason. "My heart has emitted a good word;" [3] which word He subsequently calls by the name of the King inferentially, "I will tell my works to the King." [3] For "by Him were made all the works, and without Him was nothing made." [4] "Whether," says the apostle, "they be thrones, or dominations, or powers, or mights, visible things and invisible, all things subsist by Him." [5] Moreover, this is that Word which "came unto His own, and His own received Him not. For the world was made by Him, and the world knew Him not." [6] Moreover, this Word "was in the beginning with God, and God was the Word." [7] Who then can doubt, when in the last clause it is said, "The Word was made flesh, and dwelt among us," that Christ, whose is the

nativity, and because He was made flesh, is man; and because He is the Word of God, who can shrink from declaring without hesitation that He is God, especially when he considers the evangelical Scripture, that it has associated both of these substantial natures into one concord of the nativity of Christ? For He it is who "as a bridegroom goeth forth from his bride-chamber; He exulted as a giant to run his way. His going forth is from the end of the heaven, and His return unto the ends of it." [8] Because, even to the highest, "not any one hath ascended into heaven save He who came down from heaven, the Son of man who is in heaven." [9] Repeating this same thing, He says: "Father, glorify me with that glory wherewith I was with Thee before the world was." [10] And if this Word came down from heaven as a bridegroom to the flesh, that by the assumption of flesh He might ascend thither as the Son of man, whence the Son of God had descended as the Word, reasonably, while by the mutual connection both flesh wears the Word of God, and the Son of God assumes the frailty of the flesh; when the flesh being espoused ascending thither, whence without the flesh it had descended, it at length receives that glory which in being shown to have had before the foundation of the world, it is most manifestly proved to be God. And, nevertheless, while the world itself is said to have been founded after Him, it is found to have been created by Him; by that very divinity in Him whereby the world was made, both His glory and His authority are proved. Moreover, if, whereas it is the property of none but God to know the secrets of the heart, Christ beholds the secrets of the heart; and if, whereas it belongs to none but God to remit sins, the same Christ remits sins; and if, whereas it is the portion of no man to come from heaven, He descended by coming from heaven; and if, whereas this word can be true of no man, "I and the Father are one," [11] Christ alone declared this word out of the consciousness of His divinity; and if, finally, the Apostle Thomas, instructed in all the proofs and conditions of Christ's divinity, says in reply to Christ, "My Lord and my God;" [12] and if, besides, the Apostle Paul says, "Whose are the fathers, and of whom Christ came according to the flesh, who is over all, God blessed for evermore," [13] writing in his epistles; and if the same apostle declares that he was ordained "an apostle not by men, nor of man, but by Jesus Christ;" [14] and if the same contends that he learned the Gospel not from men

---

[1] John i. 14. [For Sabellius, see p. 128, *supra.*]
[2] Rev. xix. 13.
[3] Ps. xlv. 1.
[4] John i. 3.
[5] Col. i. 16.
[6] John i. 10, 11.
[7] John i. 1.

[8] Ps. xix. 6, 7.
[9] John iii. 13.
[10] John xvii. 5. [Note this exposition.]
[11] John x. 30.
[12] John xx. 28.
[13] Rom. ix. 5.
[14] Gal. i. 1 and 12.

or by man, but received it from Jesus Christ, reasonably Christ is God. Therefore, in this respect, one of two things must needs be established. For since it is evident that all things were made by Christ, He is either before all things, since all things were by Him, and so He is justly God; or because He is man He is subsequent to all things, and justly nothing was made by Him. But we cannot say that nothing was made by Him, when we observe it written that all things were made by Him. He is not therefore subsequent to all things; that is, He is not man only, who is subsequent to all things, but God also, since God is prior to all things. For He is before all things, because all things are by Him, while if He were only man, nothing would be by Him; or if all things were by Him, He would not be man only, because if He were only man, all things would not be by Him; nay, nothing would be by Him. What, then, do they reply? That nothing is by Him, so that He is man only? How then are all things by Him? Therefore He is not man only, but God also, since all things are by Him; so that we reasonably ought to understand that Christ is not man only, who is subsequent to all things, but God also, since by Him all things were made. For how can you say that He is man only, when you see Him also in the flesh, unless because when both aspects are considered, both truths are rightly believed?

CHAP. XIV. *ARGUMENT.* — THE AUTHOR PROSE-
CUTES THE SAME ARGUMENT.

And yet the heretic still shrinks from urging that Christ is God, whom he perceives to be proved God by so many words as well as facts. If Christ is only man, how, when He came into this world, did He come unto His own, since a man could have made no world? If Christ was only man, how is the world said to have been made by Him, when the world was not by man, but man was ordained after the world? If Christ was only man, how was it that Christ was not only of the seed of David; but He was the Word made flesh and dwelt among us? For although the Protoplast was not born of seed, yet neither was the Protoplast formed of the conjunction of the Word and the flesh. For He is not the Word made flesh, nor dwelt in us. If Christ was only man, how does He "who cometh from heaven testify what He hath seen and heard,"[1] when it is plain that man cannot come from heaven, because he cannot be born there? If Christ be only man, how are "visible things and invisible, thrones, powers, and dominions," said to be created by Him and in Him; when the heavenly powers could not have been

made by man, since they must needs have been prior to man? If Christ is only man, how is He present wherever He is called upon; when it is not the nature of man, but of God, that it can be present in every place? If Christ is only man, why is a man invoked in prayers as a Mediator, when the invocation of a man to afford salvation is condemned as ineffectual? If Christ is only man, why is hope rested upon Him, when hope in man is declared to be accursed? If Christ is only man, why may not Christ be denied without destruction of the soul, when it is said that a sin committed against man may be forgiven? If Christ is only man, how comes John the Baptist to testify and say, "He who cometh after me has become before me, because He was prior to me;"[2] when, if Christ were only man, being born after John, He could not be before John, unless because He preceded him, in that He is God? If Christ is only man, how is it that "what things the Father doeth, these also doeth the Son likewise,"[3] when man cannot do works like to the heavenly operations of God? If Christ is only man, how is it that "even as the Father hath life in Himself, so hath He given to the Son to have life in Himself,"[4] when man cannot have life in him after the example of God the Father, because he is not glorious in eternity, but made with the materials of mortality? If Christ is only man, how does He say, "I am the bread of eternal life which came down from heaven,"[5] when man can neither be the bread of life, he himself being mortal, nor could he have come down from heaven, since no perishable material is established in heaven? If Christ is only man, how does He say that "no man hath seen God at any time, save He which is of God; He hath seen God?"[6] Because if Christ is only man, He could not see God, because no man has seen God; but if, being of God, He has seen God, He wishes it to be understood that He is more than man, in that He has seen God. If Christ is only man, why does He say, "What if ye shall see the Son of man ascending thither where He was before?"[7] But He ascended into heaven, therefore He was there, in that He returned thither where He was before. But if He was sent from heaven by the Father, He certainly is not man only; for man, as we have said, could not come from heaven. Therefore as man He was not there before, but ascended thither where He was not. But the Word of God descended which was there, — the Word of God, I say, and God by whom all things were

---

[1] John iii. 31.

[2] John i. 15.
[3] John v. 19.
[4] John v. 26.
[5] John vi. 51.
[6] John vi. 46.
[7] John vi. 62.

made, and without whom nothing was made. It was not therefore man that thus came thence from heaven, but the Word of God; that is, God descended thence.

CHAP. XV.[1] ARGUMENT. — AGAIN HE PROVES FROM THE GOSPEL THAT CHRIST IS GOD.

If Christ is only man, how is it that He says, "Though I bear record of myself, yet my record is true: because I know whence I came, and whither I go; ye know not whence I came, and whither I go. Ye judge after the flesh?"[2] Behold, also He says, that He shall return thither whence He bears witness that He came before, as being sent, — to wit, from heaven. He came down therefore from whence He came, in the same manner as He goes thither from whence He descended. Whence if Christ were only man, He would not have come thence, and therefore would not depart thither, because He would not have come thence. Moreover, by coming thence, whence as man He could not have come, He shows Himself to have come as God. For the Jews, ignorant and untaught in the matter of this very descent of His, made these heretics their successors, seeing that to them it is said, "Ye know not whence I come, and whither I go: ye judge after the flesh." As much they as the Jews, holding that the carnal birth of Christ was the only one, believed that Christ was nothing else than man; not considering this point, that as man could not come from heaven, so as that he might return thither, He who descended thence must be God, seeing that man could not come thence. If Christ is only man, how does He say, "Ye are from below, I am from above; ye are of this world, I am not of this world?"[3] But therefore if every man is of this world, and Christ is for that reason in this world, is He only man? God forbid! But consider what He says: "I am not of this world." Does He then speak falsely when He says "of this world," if He is only man? Or if He does not speak falsely, He is not of this world; He is therefore not man only, because He is not of this world. But that it should not be a secret who He was, He declared whence He was: "I," said He, "am from above," that is, from heaven, whence man cannot come, for he was not made in heaven. He is God, therefore, who is from above, and therefore He is not of this world; although, moreover, in a certain manner He is of this world: wherefore Christ is not God only, but man also. As reasonably in the way in which He is not of this world according to the divinity of the Word, so He is of this world according to the frailty of the body that

He has taken upon Him. For man is joined with God, and God is linked with man. But on that account this Christ here laid more stress on the one aspect of His sole divinity, because the Jewish blindness contemplated in Christ the aspect alone of the flesh; and thence in the present passage He passed over in silence the frailty of the body, which is of the world, and spoke of His divinity alone, which is not of the world: so that in proportion as they had inclined to believe Him to be only man, in that proportion Christ might draw them to consider His divinity, so as to believe Him to be God, desirous to overcome their incredulity concerning His divinity by omitting in the meantime any mention of His human condition, and by setting before them His divinity alone. If Christ is man only, how does He say, "I proceeded forth and came from God,"[4] when it is evident that man was made by God, and did not proceed forth from Him? But in the way in which as man He proceeded not from God, thus the Word of God proceeded, of whom it is said, "My heart hath uttered forth a good Word;"[5] which, because it is from God, is with reason also with God. And this, too, since it was not uttered without effect, reasonably makes all things: "For all things were made by Him, and without Him was nothing made."[6] But this Word whereby all things were made (is God). "And God," says he, "was the Word."[7] Therefore God proceeded from God, in that the Word which proceeded is God, who proceeded forth from God. If Christ is only man, how does He say, "If any man shall keep my word, he shall not see death for ever?"[8] Not to see death for ever! what is this but immortality? But immortality is the associate of divinity, because both the divinity is immortal, and immortality is the fruit of divinity. For every man is mortal; and immortality cannot be from that which is mortal. Therefore from Christ, as a mortal man, immortality cannot arise. "But," says He, "whosoever keepeth my word, shall not see death for ever;" therefore the word of Christ affords immortality, and by immortality affords divinity. But although it is not possible to maintain that one who is himself mortal can make another immortal, yet this word of Christ not only sets forth, but affords immortality: certainly He is not man only who gives immortality, which if He were only man He could not give; but by giving divinity by immortality, He proves Himself to be God by offering divinity, which if He were not God He could not give. If Christ was only man, how did He say, "Before Abraham was,

---

[1] According to Pamelius, ch. xxiii.
[2] John viii. 14, 15.
[3] John viii. 23.

[4] John viii. 42.
[5] Ps. xlv. 1.
[6] John i. 3.
[7] John i. 1.
[8] John viii. 51.

I Am?"[1] For no man can be before Him from whom he himself is; nor can it be that any one should have been prior to him of whom he himself has taken his origin. And yet Christ, although He is born of Abraham, says that He is before Abraham. Either, therefore, He says what is not true, and deceives, if He was not before Abraham, seeing that He was of Abraham; or He does not deceive, if He is also God, and was before Abraham. And if this were not so, it follows that, being of Abraham, He could not be before Abraham. If Christ was only man, how does He say, "And I know them, and my sheep follow me; and I give unto them eternal life, and they shall never perish?"[2] And yet, since every man is bound by the laws of mortality, and therefore is unable to keep himself for ever, much more will he be unable to keep another for ever. But Christ promises to give salvation for ever, which if He does not give, He is a deceiver; if He gives, He is God. But He does not deceive, for He gives what He promises. Therefore He is God who proffers eternal salvation, which man, being unable to keep himself *for ever*, cannot be able to give to another. If Christ is only man, what is that which He says, "I and the Father are one?"[3] For how can it be that "I and the Father are one," if He is not both God and the Son?—who may therefore be called one, seeing that He is of Himself, being both His Son, and being born of Him, being declared to have proceeded from Him, by which He is also God; which when the Jews thought to be hateful, and believed to be blasphemous, for that He had shown Himself in these discourses to be God, and therefore rushed at once to stoning, and set to work passionately to hurl stones, He strongly refuted His adversaries by the example and witness of the Scriptures. "If," said He, "He called them gods to whom the words of God were given, and the Scriptures cannot be broken, ye say of Him whom the Father sanctified, and sent into this world, Thou blasphemest, because I said, I am the Son of God."[4] By which words He did not deny Himself to be God, but rather He confirmed the assertion that He was God. For because, undoubtedly, they are said to be gods unto whom the words of God were given, much more is He God who is found to be superior to all these. And nevertheless He refuted the calumny of blasphemy in a fitting manner with lawful tact.[5] For He wishes that He should be thus understood to be God, as the Son of God, and He would not wish to be understood to be the Father Himself. Thus He said that

He was *sent*, and showed them that He had manifested many good works from the Father; whence He desired that He should not be understood to be the Father, but the Son. And in the latter portion of His defence He made mention of the Son, not the Father, when He said, "Ye say, Thou blasphemest, because I said, I am the Son of God." Thus, as far as pertains to the guilt of blasphemy, He calls Himself the Son, not the Father; but as pertaining to His divinity, by saying, "I and the Father are one," He proved that He was the Son of God. He is God, therefore, but God in such a manner as to be the Son, not the Father.

CHAP. XVI.[6] *ARGUMENT.*— AGAIN FROM THE GOSPEL HE PROVES CHRIST TO BE GOD.

If Christ was only man, how is it that He Himself says, "And every one that believeth in me shall not die for evermore?"[7] And yet he who believes in man by himself alone is called accursed; but he who believes on Christ is not accursed, but is said not to die for evermore. Whence, if on the one hand He is man only, as the heretics will have it, how shall not anybody who believes in Him die eternally, since he who trusts in man is held to be accursed? Or on the other, if he is not accursed, but rather, as it is read, destined for the attainment of everlasting life, Christ is not man only, but God also, in whom he who believes both lays aside all risk of curse, and attains to the fruit of righteousness. If Christ was only man, how does He say that the Paraclete "shall take of His, those things which He shall declare?"[8] For neither does the Paraclete receive anything from man, but the Paraclete offers knowledge to man; nor does the Paraclete learn things future from man, but instructs man concerning futurity. Therefore either the Paraclete has not received from Christ, as man, what He should declare, since man could give nothing to the Paraclete, seeing that from Him man himself ought to receive, and Christ in the present instance is both mistaken and deceives, in saying that the Paraclete shall receive from Him, being a man, the things which He may declare; or He does not deceive us,—as in fact He does not,—and the Paraclete has received from Christ what He may declare. But if He has received from Christ what He may declare to us, Christ is greater than the Paraclete, because the Paraclete would not receive from Christ unless He were less than Christ. But the Paraclete being less than Christ, moreover, by this very fact proves Christ to be God, from whom He has received what He declares: so that the testimony of Christ's divinity is immense,

---

[1] John viii. 58.
[2] John x. 27, 28.
[3] John x. 30.
[4] John x. 35, 36.
[5] "Dispositione," *scil.* οἰκονομία. — JACKSON.

[6] According to Pamelius, ch. xxiv.
[7] John xi. 26.
[8] John xvi. 14.

in the Paraclete being found to be *in this economy* less than Christ, and taking from Him what He gives to others; seeing that if Christ were only man, Christ would receive from the Paraclete what He should say, not the Paraclete receive from Christ what He should declare. If Christ was only man, wherefore did He lay down for us such a rule of believing as that in which He said, "And this is life eternal, that they should know Thee, the only and true God, and Jesus Christ, whom Thou hast sent?"[1] Had He not wished that He also should be understood to be God, why did He add, "And Jesus Christ, whom Thou hast sent," except because He wished to be received as God also? Because if He had not wished to be understood to be God, He would have added, "And the man Jesus Christ, whom Thou hast sent;" but, in fact, He neither added this, nor did Christ deliver Himself to us as man only, but associated Himself with God, as He wished to be understood by this conjunction to be God also, as He is. We must therefore believe, according to the rule prescribed,[2] on the Lord, the one true God, and consequently on Him whom He has sent, Jesus Christ, who by no means, as we have said, would have linked Himself to the Father had He not wished to be understood to be God also: for He would have separated Himself from Him had He not wished to be understood to be God. He would have placed Himself among men only, had He known Himself to be only man; nor would He have linked Himself with God had He not known Himself to be God also. But in this case He is silent about His being man, because no one doubts His being man, and with reason links Himself to God, that He might establish the formula of His divinity[2] for those who should believe. If Christ was only man, how does He say, "And now glorify me with the glory which I had with Thee before the world was?"[3] If, before the world was, He had glory with God, and maintained His glory with the Father, He existed before the world, for He would not have had the glory unless He Himself had existed before, so as to be able to keep the glory. For no one could possess anything, unless he himself should first be in existence to keep anything. But now Christ has the glory before the foundation of the world; therefore He Himself *was* before the foundation of the world. For unless He were before the foundation of the world, He could not have glory before the foundation of the world, since He Himself was not in existence. But indeed man could not have glory before the foundation of the world, seeing that he was after

the world; but Christ had — therefore He was before the world. Therefore He was not man only, seeing that He was before the world. He is therefore God, because He was before the world, and held His glory before the world. Neither let this be explained by predestination, since this is not so expressed, or let them add this who think so, but woe is denounced to them who add to, even as to those who take away from, that which is written. Therefore that may not be said, which may not be added. And thus, predestination being set aside, seeing it is not so laid down, Christ was in substance before the foundation of the world. For He is "the Word by which all things were made, and without which nothing was made." Because even if He is said to be glorious in predestination, and that this predestination was before the foundation of the world, let order be maintained, and before Him a considerable number of men was destined to glory. For in respect of that destination, Christ will be perceived to be less than others if He is designated subsequent to them. For if this glory was in predestination, Christ received that predestination to glory last of all; for prior to Him Adam will be seen to have been predestinated, and Abel, and Enoch, and Noah, and Abraham, and many others. For since with God the order of all, both persons and things, is arranged, many will be said to have been predestinated before this predestination of Christ to glory. And on these terms Christ is discovered to be inferior to other men, although He is really found to be better and greater, and more ancient than the angels themselves. Either, then, let all these things be set on one side, that Christ's divinity may be destroyed; or if these things cannot be set aside, let His proper divinity be attributed to Christ by the heretics.

CHAP. XVII.[4] *ARGUMENT.* — IT IS, MOREOVER, PROVED BY MOSES IN THE BEGINNING OF THE HOLY SCRIPTURES.

What if Moses pursues this same rule of truth, and delivers to us in the beginning of his sacred writings, this principle by which we may learn that all things were created and founded by the Son of God, that is, by the Word of God? For He says the same that John and the rest say; nay, both John and the others are perceived to have received from Him what they say. For if John says, "All things were made by Him, and without Him was nothing made,"[5] the prophet *David* too says, "I tell my works to the King."[6] Moses, moreover, introduces God commanding that there should be light at the first, that the heaven should be established, that the waters

---

[1] John xvii. 3.
[2] [That is, "the prescribed rule" of our Catholic orthodoxy reflects the formula of our Lord's testimony concerning Himself. Here is a reference to testimony of the early creeds and canons.]
[3] John xvii. 5.

[4] According to Pamelius, ch. xxv.
[5] John i. 3.
[6] Ps. xlv. 1.

should be gathered into one place, that the dry land should appear, that the fruit should be brought forth according to its seed, that the animals should be produced, that lights should be established in heaven, and stars. He shows that none other was then present to God — by whom these works were commanded that they should be made — than He by whom all things were made, and without whom nothing was made. And if He is the Word of God — "for my heart has uttered forth a good Word".[1] — He shows that in the beginning the Word was, and that this Word was with the Father, and besides that the Word was God, and that all things were made by Him. Moreover, this "Word was made flesh and dwelt among us,"[2] — to wit, Christ the Son of God; whom both on receiving subsequently as man according to the flesh, and seeing before the foundation of the world to be the Word of God, and God, we reasonably, according to the instruction of the Old and New Testament, believe and hold to be as well God as man, Christ Jesus. What if the same Moses introduces God saying, "Let us make man after our image and likeness;"[3] and below, "And God made man; in the image of God made He him, male and female made He them?"[4] If, as we have already shown, it is the Son of God by whom all things were made, certainly it was the Son of God by whom also man was ordained, on whose account all things were made. Moreover, when God commands that man should be made, He is said to be God who makes man; but the Son of God makes man, that is to say, the Word of God, "by whom all things were made, and without whom nothing was made." And this Word was made flesh, and dwelt among us: therefore Christ is God; therefore man was made by Christ as by the Son of God. But God made man in the image of God; He is therefore God who made man in the image of God; therefore Christ is God: so that with reason neither does the testimony of the Old Testament waver concerning the person of Christ, being supported by the manifestation of the New Testament; nor is the power of the New Testament detracted from, while its truth is resting on the roots of the same Old Testament. Whence they who presume Christ the Son of God and man to be only man, and not God also, do so in opposition to both Old and New Testaments, in that they corrupt the authority and the truth both of the Old and New Testaments. What if the same Moses everywhere introduces God the Father infinite and without end, not as being enclosed in any place, but as one who includes every place; nor as one who is in a place, but rather one in whom every place is, containing all things and embracing all things, so that with reason He can neither descend nor ascend, because He Himself both contains and fills all things, and yet nevertheless introduces God descending to consider the tower which the sons of men were building, asking and saying, "Come;" and then, "Let us go down and there confound their tongues, that each one may not understand the words of his neighbour."[5] Whom do they pretend here to have been the God who descended to that tower, and asking to visit those men at that time? God the Father? Then thus He is enclosed in a place; and how does He embrace all things? Or does He say that it is an angel descending with angels, and saying, "Come;" and subsequently, "Let us go down and there confound their tongues?" And yet in Deuteronomy we observe that God told these things, and that God said, where it is written, "When He scattered abroad the children of Adam, He determined the bounds of the nations according to the number of the angels of God."[6] Neither, therefore, did the Father descend, as the subject itself indicates; nor did an angel command these things, as the fact shows. Then it remains that He must have descended, of whom the Apostle Paul says, "He who descended is the same who ascended above all the heavens, that He might fill all things,"[7] that is, the Son of God, the Word of God. But the Word of God was made flesh, and dwelt among us. This must be Christ. Therefore Christ must be declared to be God.

CHAP. XVIII.[8] *ARGUMENT.* — MOREOVER ALSO, FROM THE FACT THAT HE WHO WAS SEEN OF ABRAHAM IS CALLED GOD; WHICH CANNOT BE UNDERSTOOD OF THE FATHER, WHOM NO MAN HATH SEEN AT ANY TIME; BUT OF THE SON IN THE LIKENESS OF AN ANGEL.

Behold, the same Moses tells us in another place that "God was seen of Abraham."[9] And yet the same Moses hears from God, that "no man can see God and live."[10] If God cannot be seen, how was God seen? Or if He was seen, how is it that He cannot be seen? For John also says, "No man hath seen God at any time;"[11] and the Apostle Paul, "Whom no man hath seen, nor can see."[12] But certainly the Scripture does not lie; therefore, truly, God was

---

[1] Ps. xlv. 1. [As understood by the Father *passim*. See Justin, vol. i. p. 213; Theophilus, ii. 98; Tertullian, iii. 365; Origen, iv. 352, 421; and Cyprian, v. p. 516, *supra*.]
[2] John i. 14.
[3] Gen. i. 26.
[4] Gen. i. 27.

[5] Gen. xi. 7.
[6] Deut. xxxii. 8. [ἐστησεν ὅρια ἐθνῶν κατὰ ἀριθμὸν ἀγγέλων Θεοῦ, Sept.]
[7] Eph. iv. 10.
[8] According to Pamelius, ch. xxvi.
[9] Gen. xii. 7.
[10] Ex. xxxiii. 20.
[11] 1 John iv. 12.
[12] 1 Tim. vi. 16.

seen. Whence it may be understood that it was not the Father who was seen, seeing that He never was seen; but the Son, who has both been accustomed to descend, and to be seen because He has descended. For He is the image of the invisible God, as the imperfection and frailty of the human condition was accustomed sometimes even then to see God the Father in the image of God, that is, in the Son of God. For gradually and by progression human frailty was to be strengthened by the image to that glory of being able one day to see God the Father. For the things that are great are dangerous if they are sudden. For even the sudden light of the sun after darkness, with its too great splendour, will not make manifest the light of day to unaccustomed eyes, but will rather strike them with blindness.

And lest this should occur to the injury of human eyes, the darkness is broken up and scattered by degrees; and the rising of that luminary, mounting by small and unperceived increments, gently accustoms men's eyes to bear its full orb by the *gentle* increase of its rays. Thus, therefore, Christ also — that is, the image of God, and the Son of God — is looked upon by men, inasmuch as He could be seen. And thus the weakness and imperfection of the human destiny is nourished, led up, and educated by Him; so that, being accustomed to look upon the Son, it may one day be able to see God the Father Himself also as He is, that it may not be stricken by His sudden and intolerable brightness, and be hindered from being able to see God the Father, whom it has always desired.[1] Wherefore it is the Son who is seen; but the Son of God is the Word of God: and the Word of God was made flesh, and dwelt among us; and this is Christ. What in the world is the reason that we should hesitate to call Him God, who in so many ways is acknowledged to be proved God? And if, moreover, the angel meets with Hagar, Sarah's maid, driven from her home as well as turned away, near the fountain of water in the way to Shur; asks and learns the reason of her flight, and after that offers her advice that she should humble herself; and, moreover, gives her the hope of the name of mother, and pledges and promises that from her womb there should be a numerous seed, and that she should have Ishmael to be born from her; and with other things unfolds the place of his habitation, and describes his mode of life; yet Scripture sets forth this angel as both Lord and God — for He would not have promised the blessing of seed unless the angel had also been God. Let them ask what the heretics can make of this present passage. Was that the Father

that was seen by Hagar or not? For He is declared to be God. But far be it from us to call God the Father an angel, lest He should be subordinate to another whose angel He would be. But they will say that it was an angel. How then shall He be God if He was an angel? Since this name is nowhere conceded to angels, except that on either side the truth compels us into this opinion, that we ought to understand it to have been God the Son, who, because He is of God, is rightly called God, because He is the Son of God. But, because He is subjected[3] to the Father, and the Announcer of the Father's will, He is declared to be the Angel of Great Counsel.[2] Therefore, although this passage neither is suited to the person of the Father, lest He should be called an angel, nor to the person of an angel, lest he should be called God; yet it is suited to the person of Christ that He should be both God because He is the Son of God, and should be an angel because He is the Announcer of the Father's mind. And the heretics ought to understand that they are setting themselves against the Scriptures, in that, while they say that they believe Christ to have been also an angel, they are unwilling to declare Him to have been also God, when they read in the Old Testament that He often came to visit the human race. To this, moreover, Moses added the instance of God seen of Abraham at the oak of Mamre, when he was sitting at the opening of his tent at noon-day. And nevertheless, although he had beheld three men, *note* that he called one of them Lord; and when he had washed their feet, he offers them bread baked on the ashes, with butter and abundance of milk itself, and urges them that, being detained as guests, they should eat. And after this he hears also that he should be a father, and learns that Sarah his wife should bring forth a son by him; and acknowledges concerning the destruction of the people of Sodom, what they deserve to suffer; and learns that God had come down on account of the cry of Sodom. In which place, if they will have it that the Father was seen at that time to have been received with hospitality in company with two angels, the heretics have believed the Father to be visible. But if an angel, although of the three angels one is called Lord, why, although it is not usual, is an angel called God? Unless because, in order that His proper invisibility may be restored to the Father, and the proper inferiority[3] be remitted to the angel, it was only God the Son, who also is God, who was seen by Abraham, and was believed to have been re-

---

[1] [This leading up and educating of humanity to "see God" is here admirably put. Heb. i. 3.]

[2] [Isa. ix. 6, according to the Seventy. Ex. xxiii. 20. See Bull, *Defensio*, etc., vol. v. p. 30. Comp. Hippol., p. 225, *supra;* Novatian, p. 632, *infra.*]

[3] [*De subordinatione*, etc.: Bull, *Defensio*, etc., vol. v. pp. 767, 685. The Nicene doctrine includes the *subordination* of the Son.]

ceived with hospitality. For He anticipated sacramentally what He was hereafter to become. He was made a guest of Abraham, being about to be among the sons of Abraham. And his children's feet, by way of proving what He was, He washed; returning in the children the claim of hospitality which formerly the Father had put out to interest to Him. Whence also, that there might be no doubt but that it was He who was the guest of Abraham on the destruction of the people of Sodom, it is declared: "Then the Lord rained upon Sodom and upon Gomorrha fire and brimstone from the Lord out of heaven." [1] For thus also said the prophet in the person of God: "I have overthrown you, as the Lord overturned Sodom and Gomorrha." [2] Therefore the Lord overturned Sodom, that is, God overturned Sodom; but in the overturning of Sodom, the Lord rained fire from the Lord. And this Lord was the God seen by Abraham; and this God was the guest of Abraham, certainly seen because He was also touched. But although the Father, being invisible, was assuredly not at that time seen, He who was accustomed to be touched and seen was seen and received to hospitality. But-this the Son of God, "The Lord rained from the Lord upon Sodom and Gomorrha brimstone and fire." And this is the Word of God. And the Word of God was made flesh, and dwelt among us; and this is Christ. It was not the Father, then, who was a guest with Abraham, but Christ. Nor was it the Father who was seen then, but the Son; and Christ was seen. Rightly, therefore, Christ is both Lord and God, who was not otherwise seen by Abraham, except that as God the Word He was begotten of God the Father before Abraham himself. Moreover, says the Scripture, the same Angel and God visits and consoles the same Hagar when driven with her son from the dwelling of Abraham. For when in the desert she had exposed the infant, because the water had fallen short from the pitcher; and when the lad had cried out, and she had lifted up her weeping and lamentation, "God heard," says the Scripture, "the voice of the lad from the place where he was." [3] Having told that it was God who heard the voice of the infant, it adds: "And the angel of the Lord called Hagar herself out of heaven," saying that that was an angel [4] whom it had called God, and pronouncing Him to be Lord whom it had set forth as an angel; which Angel and God moreover promises to Hagar herself greater consolations, in saying, "Fear not; for I have heard the voice of the lad from the place where he was. Arise, take up the lad, and hold him; for I will make of

him a great nation." [5] Why does this angel, if angel only, claim to himself this right of saying, I will make of him a great nation, since assuredly this kind of power belongs to God, and cannot belong to an angel? Whence also He is confirmed to be God, since He is able to do this; because, by way of proving this very point, it is immediately added by the Scripture: "And God opened her eyes, and she saw a well of running water; and she went and filled the bottle from the well, and gave to the lad: and God was with the lad." [6] If, then, this God was with the Lord, who opened the eyes of Hagar that she might see the well of running water, and might draw the water on account of the urgent need of *the lad's* thirst, and this God who calls her from heaven is called an angel when, in previously hearing the voice of the lad crying, He was rather God; is not understood to be other than angel, in like manner as He was God also. And since this cannot be applicable or fitting to the Father, who is God only, but may be applicable to Christ, who is declared to be not only God, but angel also, [7] it manifestly appears that it was not the Father who thus spoke to Hagar, but rather Christ, since He is God; and to Him also is applied the name of angel, since He became the "angel of great counsel." [8] And He is the angel, in that He declares the bosom of the Father, as John sets forth. For if John himself says, that He Himself who sets forth the bosom of the Father, as the Word, became flesh in order to declare the bosom of the Father, assuredly Christ is not only man, but angel also; and not only angel, but He is shown by the Scriptures to be God also. And this is believed to be the case by us; so that, if we will not consent to apprehend that it was Christ who then spoke to Hagar, we must either make an angel God, or we must reckon God the Father Almighty among the angels. [9]

CHAP. XIX. [10] ARGUMENT. — THAT GOD ALSO APPEARED TO JACOB AS AN ANGEL; NAMELY, THE SON OF GOD.

What if in another place also we read in like manner that God was described as an angel? For when, to his wives Leah and Rachel, Jacob complained of the injustice of their father, and when he told them that he desired now to go and return into his own land, he moreover interposed the authority of his dream; and at this time he says that the angel of God had said to him in a dream, "Jacob, Jacob. And I said,"

---

[1] Gen. xix. 24.
[2] Amos iv. 11.
[3] Gen. xxi. 17, etc.
[4] [See note 2, p. 628, *supra*.]

[5] Gen. xxi. 18.
[6] Gen. xxi. 20.
[7] [See vol. i. p. 184.]
[8] Isa. ix. 6, LXX.
[9] [Among the *apparitions* are noted Gen. xxxii. 24, Ex. iii., Num. xxii. 21, Josh. v. 13, 1 Kings xxviii. 11.]
[10] According to Pamelius, ch. xxvii.

says he, "What is it? Lift up thine eyes, said He, and see, the he-goats and the rams leaping upon the sheep, and the she-goats are black and white, and many-coloured, and grizzled, and speckled: for I have seen all that Laban hath done to thee. I am God, who appeared to thee in the place of God, where thou anointedst for me there the standing stone, and there vowedst a vow unto me: now therefore arise, and go forth from this land, and go unto the land of thy nativity, and I will be with thee."[1] If the Angel of God speaks thus to Jacob, and the Angel himself mentions and says, "I am God, who appeared unto thee in the house of God," we see without any hesitation that this is declared to be not only an angel, but God also; because He speaks of the vow directed to Himself by Jacob in the place of God, and He does not say, in *my place*. It is then the place of God, and He also is God. Moreover, it is written simply in the place of God, for it is not said in the place of the angel and God, but only of God; and He who promises those things is manifested to be both God and Angel, so that reasonably there must be a distinction between Him who is called God only, and Him who is declared to be not God simply, but Angel also. Whence if so great an authority cannot here be regarded as belonging to any other angel, that He should also avow Himself to be God, and should bear witness that a vow was made to Him, except to Christ alone, to whom not as angel only, but as to God, a vow can be vowed; it is manifest that it is not to be received as the Father, but as the Son, God and Angel.[2] Moreover, if this is Christ, as it is, he is in terrible risk who says that Christ is either man or angel alone, withholding from Him the power of the divine name, — an authority which He has constantly received on the faith of the heavenly Scriptures, which continually say that He is both Angel and God. To all these things, moreover, is added this, that in like manner as the divine Scripture has frequently declared Him both Angel and God, so the same divine Scripture declares Him also both man and God, expressing thereby what He should be, and depicting even then in figure what He was to be in the truth of His substance. "For," it says, "Jacob remained alone; and there wrestled with him a man even till daybreak. And He saw that He did not prevail against him; and He touched the broad part of Jacob's thigh while He was wrestling with him and he with Him, and said to him, Let me go, for the morning has dawned. And he said, I will not let Thee go, except Thou bless me. And He said, What is thy name?

And he said, Jacob. And He said to him, Thy name shall no longer be called Jacob, but Israel shall be thy name; because thou hast prevailed with God, and thou art powerful with men."[3] And it adds, moreover: "And Jacob called the name of that place the Vision of God: for I have seen the Lord face to face, and my soul has been made safe. And the sun arose upon him. Afterwards he crossed over the Vision of God, but he halted upon his thigh."[4] A man, it says, wrestled with Jacob. If this was a mere man, who is he? Whence is he? Wherefore does he contend and wrestle with Jacob? What had intervened? What had happened? What was the cause of so great a dispute as that, and so great a struggle? Why, moreover, is Jacob, who is found to be strong enough to hold the man with whom he is wrestling, and asks for a blessing from Him whom he is holding, asserted to have asked therefore, except because this struggle was prefigured as that which should be between Christ and the sons of Jacob, which is said to be completed in the Gospel? For against this man Jacob's people struggled, in which struggle Jacob's people was found to be the more powerful, because against Christ it gained the victory of its iniquity: at which time, on account of the crime that it committed, hesitating and giving way, it began most sorely to halt in the walk of its own faith and salvation; and although it was found the stronger, in respect of the condemnation of Christ, it still needs His mercy, still needs His blessing. But, moreover, the man who wrestled with Jacob says, "Moreover, thy name shall no longer be called Jacob, but Israel shall be thy name;" and if Israel is the man who sees God, the Lord was beautifully showing that it was not only a man who was then wrestling with Jacob, but God also. Certainly Jacob saw God, with whom he wrestled, although he was holding the man in his own struggle. And in order that there might still be no hesitation, He Himself laid down the interpretation by saying, "Because thou hast prevailed with God, and art powerful with men." For which reason the same Jacob, perceiving already the force of the Mystery, and apprehending the authority of Him with whom he had wrestled, called the name of that place in which he had wrestled, the Vision of God. He, moreover, superadded the reason for his interpretation being offered of the Vision of God: "For I have seen," said he, "God face to face, and my soul has been saved." Moreover, he saw God, with whom he wrestled as with a man; but still indeed he held the man as a conqueror, though as an inferior he asked a blessing as from God. Thus he wrestled with God and with man; and

---

[1] Gen. xxxi. 11-13.
[2] [Eccles. v. 6. A striking text when compared with the "Angel of the Covenant" (*Angelus Testamenti*, Vulgate), Mal. iii. 1.]

[3] Gen. xxxii. 24-27. [Vol. iv. 390, this series.]
[4] Gen. xxxii. 30, 31.

thus truly was that struggle prefigured, and in the Gospel was fulfilled, between Christ and the people of Jacob, wherein, although the people had the mastery, yet it proved to be inferior by being shown to be guilty. Who will hesitate to acknowledge that Christ, in whom this type of a wrestling was fulfilled, was not man only, but God also, since even that very type of a wrestling seems to have proved Him man and God? And yet, even after this, the same divine Scripture justly does not cease to call the Angel God, and to pronounce God the Angel. For when this very Jacob was about to bless Manasseh and Ephraim, the sons of Joseph, with his hands placed across on the heads of the lads, he said, "The God which fed me from my youth even unto this day, the Angel who delivered me from all evils, bless these lads." [1] Even to such a point does he affirm the same Being to be an Angel, whom he had called God, as in the end of his discourse, to express the person of whom he was speaking as one, when he said [2] "bless these lads." For if he had meant the one to be understood as God, and the other as an angel, he would have comprised the two persons in the plural number; but now he defined the singular number of one person in the blessing, whence he meant it to be understood that the same person is God and Angel. But yet He cannot be received as God the Father; but as God and Angel, as Christ He can be received. And Him, as the author of this blessing, Jacob also signified by placing his hands crossed upon the lads, as if their father was Christ, and showing, from thus placing his hands, the figure and future form of the passion. [3] Let no one, therefore, who does not shrink from speaking of Christ as an Angel, thus shrink from pronouncing Him God also, when he perceives that He Himself was invoked in the blessing of these lads, by the sacrament of the passion, intimated in the type of the *crossed* hands, as both God and Angel.

CHAP. XX. [4] *ARGUMENT.* — IT IS PROVED FROM THE SCRIPTURES THAT CHRIST WAS CALLED AN ANGEL. BUT YET IT IS SHOWN FROM OTHER PARTS OF HOLY SCRIPTURE THAT HE IS GOD ALSO.

But if some heretic, obstinately struggling against the truth, should persist in all these instances either in understanding that Christ was properly an angel, or should contend that He must be so understood, he must in this respect also be subdued by the force of truth. For if, since all heavenly things, earthly things, and things under the earth, are subjected to Christ,

even the angels themselves, with all other creatures, as many as are subjected to Christ, are called gods, [5] rightly also Christ is God. And if any angel at all subjected to Christ can be called God, and this, if it be said, is also professed without blasphemy, certainly much more can this be fitting for Christ, Himself the Son of God, for Him to be pronounced God. For if an angel who is subjected to Christ is exalted as God, much more, and more consistently, shall Christ, to whom all angels are subjected, be said to be God. For it is not suitable to nature, that what is conceded to the lesser should be denied to the greater. Thus, if an angel be inferior to Christ, and yet an angel is called god, rather by consequence is Christ said to be God, who is discovered to be both greater and better, not than one, but than all angels. And if "God standeth in the assembly of the gods, and in the midst God distinguisheth between the gods," [6] and Christ stood at various times in the synagogue, then Christ stood in the synagogue as God, — judging, to wit, between the gods, to whom He says, "How long do ye accept the persons of men?" That is to say, consequently, charging the men of the synagogue with not practising just judgments. Further, if they who are reproved and blamed seem even for any reason to attain this name without blasphemy, that they should be called gods, assuredly much more shall He be esteemed God, who not only is said to have stood as God in the synagogue of the gods, but moreover is revealed by the same authority of the reading as distinguishing and judging between gods. But *even* if they who "fall like one of the princes" are still called gods, much rather shall He be said to be God, who not only does not fall like one of the princes, but even overcomes both the author and prince of wickedness himself. And what in the world is the reason, that although they say that this name was given even to Moses, since it is said, "I have made thee as a god to Pharaoh," [7] it should be denied to Christ, who is declared to be ordained [8] not to Pharaoh *only*, but to every creature, as both Lord and God? And in the former case indeed this name is given with reserve, in the latter lavishly; in the former by measure, in the latter above all kind of measure: "For," it is said, "the Father giveth not to the Son by measure, for the Father loveth the Son." [9] In the former for the time, in the latter without reference to time; [10] for He received the power of the divine name, both above all things and for all time. But if he who has received the power

---

[1] Gen. xlviii. 14, 15.
[2] Benedicat.
[3] [A very beautiful patristic idea of the dim vision of the cross to which the Fathers were admitted, but which they understood not, even when they predicted it. 1 Pet. x. 11.]
[4] According to Pamelius, ch. xv.

[5] [Ps. xcvii. 7; John x. 36; Hippol., p. 153, *supra*.]
[6] Ps. lxxxii. 1, 2, etc.
[7] Ex. vii. 1.
[8] [The full meaning of which only comes out in the Gospel and in 2 Pet. i. 4. The lie of Gen. iii. 5, is made true in Christ.]
[9] John iii. 34, 35.
[10] [Rev. xi. 15.

of one man, in respect to this limited power given him, still without hesitation attains that name of God, how much more shall He who has power over Moses himself as well be believed to have attained the authority of that name?

CHAP. XXI.[1]   ARGUMENT. — THAT THE SAME DIVINE MAJESTY IS AGAIN CONFIRMED IN CHRIST BY OTHER SCRIPTURES.

And indeed I could set forth the treatment of this subject by all heavenly Scriptures, and set in motion, so to speak, a perfect forest of *texts* concerning that manifestation of the divinity of Christ, except that I have not so much undertaken to speak against this special form of heresy, as to expound the rule of truth concerning the person of Christ. Although, however, I must hasten to other matters, I do not think that I must pass over this point, that in the Gospel the Lord declared, by way of signifying His majesty, saying, " Destroy this temple, and in three days I will build it up again." [2]   Or when, in another passage, and on another subject, He declares, "I have power to lay down my life, and again to take it up ; for this commandment I have received of my Father."[3]   Now who is it who says that He can lay down His life, or can Himself recover His life again, because He has received it of His Father?   Or who says that He can again resuscitate and rebuild the destroyed temple of His body, except because He is the Word who is from the Father, who is with the Father, "by whom all things were made, and without whom nothing was made ;"[4] the imitator[5] of His Father's works and powers, "the image of the invisible God ;"[6] "who came down from heaven ;"[7] who testified what things he had seen and heard ; who "came not to do His own will, but rather to do the will of the Father,"[8] by whom He had been sent for this very purpose, that being made the "Messenger of Great Counsel,"[9] He might unfold to us the laws of the heavenly mysteries ; and who as the Word made flesh dwelt among us, of us this Christ is proved to be not man only, because He was the son of man, but also God, because He is the Son of God?   And if by the apostle Christ is called "the first-born of every creature,"[10] how could He be the first-born

of every creature, unless because according to His divinity the Word proceeded from the Father before every creature?   And unless the heretics receive it thus, they will be constrained to show that Christ the man was the first-born of every creature ; which they will not be able to do. Either, therefore, He is before every creature, that He may be the first-born of every creature, and He is not man only, because man is after every creature ; or He is man only, and He is after every creature.   And how is He the first-born of every creature, except because being that Word which is before every creature ; and therefore, the first-born of every creature, He becomes flesh and dwells in us, that is, assumes that man's nature which is after every creature, and so dwells with him and in him, in us, that neither is humanity taken away from Christ, nor His divinity denied?   For if He is only before every creature, humanity is taken away from Him ; but if He is only man, the divinity which is before every creature is interfered with.   Both of these, therefore, are leagued together in Christ, and both are conjoined, and both are linked with one another.   And rightly, as there is in Him something which excels the creature, the agreement of the divinity and the humanity seems to be pledged in Him : for which reason He who is declared as made the " Mediator between God and man " [11] is revealed to have associated in Himself God and man.   And if the same apostle says of Christ, that " having put off the flesh, He spoiled powers, they being openly triumphed over in Himself," [12] he certainly did not without a meaning propound that the flesh was put off, unless because he wished it to be understood that it was again put on also at the resurrection.   Who, therefore, is He that thus put off and put on *the flesh ?*   Let the heretics seek out.   For we know that the Word of God was invested with the substance of flesh, and that He again was divested of the same bodily material, which again He took up in the resurrection and resumed as a garment.   And yet Christ could neither have been divested of nor invested with manhood, had He been only man : for man is never either deprived of nor invested with himself.   For that must be something else, whatever it may be, which by any other is either taken away or put on.   Whence, reasonably, it was the Word of God who put off the flesh, and again in the resurrection put it on, since He put it off because at His birth He had been invested with it.   Therefore in Christ it is God who is invested, and moreover must be divested, because He who is invested must also likewise be He who is divested ; whereas, as man, He is invested with and divested of, as it were, a certain tunic of the

---

[1] According to Pamelius, ch. xvi.
[2] John ii. 19.
[3] John x. 18.
[4] John i. 3.
[5] [John v. 19   The infirmities of language are such that cunning men like Petavius can construct *anti*-Nicene doctrine out of Scripture itself: and the marvel is, that the Christian Fathers before the Council of Nicæa generally use such precision of language, although they lacked the synodical definitions.]
[6] Col. i. 15.
[7] John iii. 31, 32.
[8] John iv. 38.
[9] Isa. ix. 6.
[10] Col. i. 15.   [But not a *creature*, for the apostle immediately subjoins that He is the *Creator* and final Cause of the universe. Moreover, the *first-born* here seems to mean the *heir* of all creation, for such is the logical force of the verse following. So, πρωτοτοκεία (in the Seventy) = heirship. Gen. xxv. 31.]

[11] 1 Tim. ii. 5.
[12] Col. ii. 15.

compacted body.[1] And therefore by consequence He was, as we have said, the Word of God, who is revealed to be at one time invested, at another time divested *of the flesh*. For this, moreover, He before predicted in blessings: " He shall wash His garment in wine, and His clothing in the blood of the grape."[2] If the garment in Christ be the flesh, and the clothing itself be the body, let it be asked who is He whose body is clothing, and garment flesh? For to us it is evident that the flesh is the garment, and the body the clothing of the Word ; and He washed His bodily substance, and purified the material of the flesh in blood, that is, in wine, by His passion, in the human character that He had undertaken. Whence, if indeed He is washed, He is man, because the garment which is washed is the flesh ; but He who washes is the Word of God, who, in order that He might wash the garment, was made the taker-up of the garment. Rightly, from that substance which is taken that it might be washed, He is revealed as a man, even as from the authority of the Word who washed it He is manifested to be God.

CHAP. XXII.[3] *ARGUMENT.*—THAT THE SAME DIVINE MAJESTY IS IN CHRIST, HE ONCE MORE ASSERTS BY OTHER SCRIPTURES.

But why, although we appear to hasten to another branch of the argument, should we pass over that passage in the apostle : " Who, although He was in the form of God, did not think it robbery that He should be equal with God ; but emptied Himself, taking up the form of a servant, being made in the likeness of men ; and found in fashion as a man, He humbled Himself, becoming obedient even unto death, even the death of the cross. Wherefore also God hath highly exalted Him, and hath given Him a name which is above every name ; that in the name of Jesus every knee should be bent, of things in heaven, and things in earth, and things under the earth ; and every tongue should confess that Jesus is Lord, in the glory of God the Father?"[4] " Who, although He was in the form of God," he says. If Christ had been only man, He would have been spoken of as in " the image " of God, not " in the form " of God. For we know that man was made after the image or likeness, not after the form, of God. Who then is that angel who, as we have said, was made in the form of God? But neither do we read of the form of God in angels, except because this one is chief and royal above all — the Son of God, the Word of God, the

imitator of all His Father's works, in that He Himself worketh even as His Father. He is — as we have declared — in the form of God the Father. And He is reasonably affirmed to be in the form of God, in that He Himself, being above all things, and having the divine power over every creature, is also God after the example of the Father. Yet He obtained this from His own Father, that He should be both God of all and should be Lord, and be begotten and made known from Himself as God in the form of God the Father. He then, although He was in the form of God, thought it not robbery that He should be equal with God. For although He remembered that He was God from God the Father, He never either compared or associated Himself with God the Father, mindful that He was from His Father, and that He possessed that very thing that He is, because the Father had given it Him.[5] Thence, finally, both before the assumption of the flesh, and moreover after the assumption of the body, besides, after the resurrection itself, He yielded all obedience to the Father, and still yields it as ever. Whence it is proved that He thought that *the claim of a* certain divinity would be robbery, to wit, that of equalling Himself with God the Father ; but, on the other hand, obedient and subject to all His rule and will, He even was contented to take on Him the form of a servant — that is, to become man ; and the substance of flesh and body which, as it came to Him from the bondage of His forefathers' sins according to His manhood, He undertook by being born, at which time moreover He emptied Himself, in that He did not refuse to take upon Him the frailty incident to humanity. Because if He had been born man only, He would not have been emptied in respect of this ; for man, being born, is increased, not emptied. For in beginning to be that which He could not possess, so long as He did not exist, as we have said, He is not emptied, but is rather increased and enriched. But if Christ is emptied in being born, in taking the form of a servant, how is He man only? Of whom it could more truly have been said that He was enriched, not emptied, at the time that He was born, except because the authority of the divine Word, reposing for awhile in taking upon itself humanity, and not exercising itself with its real strength, casts itself down, and puts itself off for the time, in bearing the humanity which it has undertaken? It empties itself in descending to injuries and reproaches, in bearing abominatiohs, in experiencing things unworthy ; and yet of this humility there is present at once an eminent reward. For He has " received a name which is above every name," which assuredly we

---

[1] Perhaps the emendation *homine* instead of *homo* is right. " He puts on and puts off humanity, as if it were a kind of tunic for a compacted body."
[2] Gen. xlix. 11.
[3] According to Pamelius, ch. xvii.
[4] Phil. ii. 6-11.

[5] [Not " *a seipso* Deus." See Bull, *Defens.*, vol. v. p. 685.]

understand to be none other than the name of God. For since it belongs to God alone to be above all things, it follows that the name which is that God's who is above all things, is above every name ; which name by consequence is certainly His who, although He was "in the form of God, thought it not robbery for Him to be equal with God." For neither, if Christ were not God, would every knee bend itself in His name, "of things in heaven, and things in earth, and things under the earth ; " nor would things visible and invisible, even every creature of all things, be subjected or be placed under man, when they might remember that they were before man. Whence, since Christ is said to be in the form of God, and since it is shown that for His nativity according to the flesh He emptied Himself; and since it is declared that He received from the Father that name which is above every name ; and since it is shown that in His name "every knee of things in heaven, and things in earth, and things under the earth, bend and bow" themselves ; and this very thing is asserted to be a furtherance of the glory of God the Father ; consequently He is not man only, from the fact that He became obedient to the Father, even to death, yea, the death of the cross ; but, moreover, from the proclamation by these higher matters of the divinity of Christ, Christ Jesus is shown to be Lord and God, which the heretics will not have.

CHAP. XXIII.[1] ARGUMENT. — AND THIS IS SO MANIFEST, THAT SOME HERETICS HAVE THOUGHT HIM TO BE GOD THE FATHER, OTHERS THAT HE WAS ONLY GOD WITHOUT THE FLESH.

In this place I may be permitted also to collect arguments from the side of other heretics. It is a substantial kind of proof which is gathered even from an adversary, so as to prove the truth even from the very enemies of truth. For it is so far manifest that He is declared in the Scriptures to be God, that many heretics, moved by the magnitude and truth of this divinity, exaggerating His honours above measure, have dared to announce or to think Him not the Son, but God the Father Himself.[2] And this, although it is contrary to the truth of the Scriptures, is still a great and excellent argument for the divinity of Christ, who is so far God, except as Son of God, born of God, that very many heretics — as we have said — have so accepted Him as God, as to think that He must be pronounced not the Son, but the Father. Therefore let it be considered whether He is God or not, since His authority has so affected some, that, as we have already said above, they have thought Him God the Father Himself, and have confessed the

divinity in Christ with such impetuosity and effusion — compelled to it by the manifest divinity in Christ — that they thought that He whom they read of as the Son, because they perceived Him to be God, must be the Father. Moreover, other heretics •have so far embraced the manifest divinity of Christ, as to say that He was without flesh, and to withdraw from Him the whole humanity which He took upon Him, lest, by associating with Him a human nativity, as they conceived it, they should diminish in Him the power of the divine name.[3] This, however, we do not approve ; but we quote it as an argument to prove that Christ is God, to this extent, that some, taking away the manhood, have thought Him God only, and some have thought Him God the Father Himself ; when reason and the proportion of the heavenly Scriptures show Christ to be God, but as the Son of God ; and the Son of man, having been taken up, moreover, by God, that He must be believed to be man also. Because if He came to man, that He might be Mediator of God and men, it behoved Him to be. with man, and the Word to be made flesh, that in His own self He might link together the agreement of earthly things with heavenly things, by associating in Himself pledges of both natures, and uniting God to man and man to God ; so that reasonably the Son of God might be made by the assumption of flesh the Son of man, and the Son of man by the reception of the Word of God the Son of God. This most profound and recondite mystery, destined before the worlds for the salvation of the human race, is found to be fulfilled in the Lord Jesus Christ, both God and man, that the human race might be placed within the reach of the enjoyment of eternal salvation.

CHAP. XXIV.[4] ARGUMENT. — THAT THESE HAVE THEREFORE ERRED, BY THINKING THAT THERE WAS NO DIFFERENCE BETWEEN THE SON OF GOD AND THE SON OF MAN ; BECAUSE THEY HAVE ILL UNDERSTOOD THE SCRIPTURE.

But the material of that heretical error has arisen, as I judge, from this, that they think that there is no distinction between the Son of God and the Son of man ; because if a distinction were made, Jesus Christ would easily be proved to be both man and God. For they will have it that the self-same that is man, the Son of man, appears also as the Son of God ; that man and flesh and that same frail substance may be said to be also the Son of God Himself. Whence, since no distinction is discerned between the Son of man and the Son of God, but the Son of man Himself is asserted to be the Son of God, the same Christ and the Son of God is

---

[1] According to Pamelius, ch. xviii.
[2] [The Noetians, Hippol., p. 148, *supra*.]
[3] [Irenæus, vol. i. p. 527.]
[4] According to Pamelius, ch. xix.

asserted to be man only; by which they strive to exclude, "The Word was made flesh, and dwelt among us."[1] And ye shall call His name Emmanuel; which is, interpreted, God with us."[2] For they propose and put forward what is told in the Gospel of Luke, whence they strive to maintain not what is the truth, but only what they want it to be: "The Holy Spirit shall come upon thee, and the power of the Highest shall overshadow thee; therefore also the Holy Thing which is born of thee shall be called the Son of God."[3] If, then, say they, the angel of God says to Mary, "that Holy Thing which is born of thee," the substance of flesh and body is of Mary; but he has set forth that this substance, that is, that Holy Thing which is born of her, is the Son of God. Man, say they, himself, and that bodily flesh; that which is called holy, itself is the Son of God. That also when the Scripture says that "Holy Thing," we should understand thereby Christ the man, the Son of man; and when it places before us the Son of God, we ought to perceive, not man, but God. And yet the divine Scripture easily convicts and discloses the frauds and artifices of the heretics. For if it were thus only, "The Spirit shall come upon thee, and the power of the Highest shall overshadow thee; therefore that Holy Thing which is born of thee shall be called the Son of God," perchance we should have had to strive against them in another sort, and to have sought for other arguments, and to have taken up other weapons, with which to overcome both their snares and their wiles; but since the Scripture itself, abounding in heavenly fulness, divests itself of the calumnies of these heretics, we easily depend upon that that is written, and overcome those errors without any hesitation. For it said, not as we have already stated, "Therefore the Holy Thing which shall be born of thee;" but added the conjunction, for it says, "Therefore also that Holy Thing which shall be born of thee," so as to make it plain that that Holy Thing which is born of her — that is, that substance of flesh and body — is not the Son of God primarily, but consequently, and in the secondary place;[4] but primarily, that the Son of God is the Word of God, incarnate by that Spirit of whom the angel says, "The Spirit shall come upon thee, and the power of the Highest shall overshadow thee." For He is the legitimate Son of God who is of God Himself; and He, while He assumes that Holy Thing, and links to Himself the Son of man, and draws Him and transfers Him to Him-

self, by His connection and mingling of association becomes responsible for and makes Him the Son of God, which by nature He was not, so that the original cause[5] of that name Son of God is in the Spirit of the Lord, who descended and came, and that there is only the continuance of the name in the case of the Son of man;[6] and by consequence He reasonably became the Son of God, although originally He is not the Son of God. And therefore the angel, seeing that arrangement, and providing for that order of the mystery, did not confuse every thing in such a way as to leave no trace of a distinction, but established the distinction by saying, "Therefore *also* that Holy Thing which shall be born of thee shall be called the Son of God;" lest, had he not arranged that distribution with his balances, but had left the matter all mixed up in confusion, it had really afforded occasion to heretics to declare that the Son of man, in that He is man, is the same as the Son of God and man. But now, explaining severally the ordinance and the reason of so great a mystery, he evidently set forth in saying, "And that Holy Thing which shall be born of thee shall be called the Son of God;" the proof that the Son of God descended, and that He, in taking up into Himself the Son of man, consequently made Him the Son of God, because the Son of God associated and joined Him to Himself. So that, while the Son of man cleaves in His nativity to the Son of God, by that very mingling He holds that as pledged and derived which of His own nature He could not possess. And thus by the word of the angel the distinction is made, against the desire of the heretics, between the Son of God and man; yet with their association, by pressing them to understand that Christ the Son of man is man, and also to receive the Son of God and man the Son of God; that is, the Word of God as it is written as God; and thus to acknowledge that Christ Jesus the Lord, connected on both sides, so to speak, is on both sides woven in and grown together, and associated in the same agreement of both substances, by the binding to one another of a mutual alliance — man and God by the truth of the Scripture which declares this very thing.

CHAP. XXV.[7]   *ARGUMENT.* — AND THAT IT DOES NOT FOLLOW THENCE, THAT BECAUSE CHRIST DIED IT MUST ALSO BE RECEIVED THAT GOD DIED; FOR SCRIPTURE SETS FORTH THAT NOT ONLY WAS CHRIST GOD, BUT MAN ALSO.

Therefore, say they, if Christ is not man only, but God also — and Scripture tells us that He

---

[1] John i. 14.
[2] Matt. i. 23.
[3] Luke i. 35.
[4] "The miraculous generation is here represented as the natural, but by no means as the only cause for which He who had no human father was to receive the name of God's Son." — OOSTERZEE, *in loco*, on Luke. — TR.

[5] Principalitas.
[6] The edition of Pamelius reads: ut sequela nominis in Filio Dei et hominis sit. The words *Dei et* were expelled by Welchman, whom we have followed.
[7] According to Pamelius, ch. xx.

died for us, and was raised again — then Scripture teaches us to believe that God died; or if God does not die, and Christ is said to have died, then Christ will not be God, because God cannot be admitted to have died. If they ever could understand or had understood what they read, they would never speak after such a perilous fashion. But the folly of error is always hasty in its descent, and it is no new thing if those who have forsaken the lawful faith descend even to perilous results. For if Scripture were to set forth that Christ is God only, and that there was no association of human weakness mingled in His nature, this intricate argument of theirs might reasonably avail something. If Christ is God, and Christ died, then God died. But when Scripture determines, as we have frequently shown, that He is not only God, but man also, it follows that what is immortal may be held to have remained uncorrupted. For who cannot understand that the divinity is impassible, although the human weakness is liable to suffering? When, therefore, Christ is understood to be mingled and associated as well of that which God is, as of that which man is — for "the Word was made flesh, and dwelt in us" — who cannot easily apprehend of himself, without any teacher and interpreter, that it was not that in Christ that died which is God, but that in Him died which is man? For what if the divinity in Christ does not die, but the substance of the flesh only is destroyed, when in other men also, who are not flesh only, but flesh and soul, the flesh indeed alone suffers the inroads of wasting and death, while the soul is seen to be uncorrupted, and beyond the laws of destruction and death? For this also our Lord Himself said, exhorting us to martyrdom and to contempt of all human power: "Fear not those who slay the body, but cannot kill the soul." [1] But if the immortal soul cannot be killed or slain in any other, although the body and flesh by itself can be slain, how much rather assuredly could not the Word of God and God in Christ be put to death at all, although the flesh alone and the body was slain! For if in any man whatever, the soul has this excellence of immortality that it cannot be slain, much more has the nobility of the Word of God this power of not being slain. For if the power of men fails to slay the sacred power of God, and if the cruelty of man fails to destroy the soul, much more ought it to fail to slay the Word of God. For as the soul itself, which was made by the Word of God, is not killed by men, certainly much rather will it be believed that the Word of God cannot be destroyed. And if the sanguinary cruelty of men cannot do more against men than only to

slay the body, how much more certainly it will not have power against Christ beyond in the same way slaying the body! So that, while from these considerations it is gathered that nothing but the human nature in Christ was put to death, it appears that the Word in Him was not drawn down into mortality. For if Abraham, and Isaac, and Jacob, who, it is admitted, were only men, are manifested to be alive — for all they,[2] says He, "live unto God;" and death in them does not destroy the soul, although it dissolves the bodies themselves: for it could exercise its power on the bodies, it did not avail to exercise it on the souls: for the one in them was mortal, and therefore died; the other in them was immortal, and therefore is understood not to have been extinguished: for which reason they are affirmed and said to live unto God, — much rather death in Christ could have power against the material of His body alone, while against the divinity of the Word it could not bring itself to bear. For the power of death is broken when the authority of immortality intervenes.

CHAP. XXVI.[3] *ARGUMENT.* — MOREOVER, AGAINST THE SABELLIANS HE PROVES THAT THE FATHER IS ONE, THE SON ANOTHER.

But from this occasion of Christ being proved from the sacred authority of the divine writings not man only, but God also, other heretics, breaking forth, contrive to impair the religious position in Christ; by this very fact wishing to show that Christ is God the Father, in that He is asserted to be not man only, but also is declared to be God. For thus say they, If it is asserted that God is one, and Christ is God, then say they, If the Father and Christ be one God, Christ will be called the Father. Wherein they are proved to be in error, not knowing Christ, but following the sound of a name; for they are not willing that He should be the second person after the Father, but the Father Himself. And since these things are easily answered, few words shall be said. For who does not acknowledge that the person of the Son is second after the Father, when he reads that it was said by the Father, consequently to the Son, "Let us make man in our image and our likeness;" [4] and that after this it was related, "And God made man, in the image of God made He him?" Or when he holds in his hands: "The Lord rained upon Sodom and Gomorrha fire and brimstone from the Lord from heaven?" [5] Or when he reads

---

[1] Matt. x. 28.

[2] [Luke xx. 38. A solemn admonition is found in the parallel Scripture, Matt. xxii. 29, which teaches us how much we ought to find beneath the surface of Holy Writ.]
[3] According to Pamelius, ch. xxi.
[4] Gen. i. 26.
[5] Gen. xix. 24.

(as having been said) to Christ : "Thou art my Son, this day have I begotten Thee. Ask of me, and I will give Thee the heathens for Thine inheritance, and the ends of the earth for Thy possession ? "[1] Or when also that beloved writer says : "The Lord said unto my Lord, Sit Thou on my right hand, until I shall make Thine enemies the stool of Thy feet?"[2] Or when, unfolding the prophecies of Isaiah, he finds it written thus : "Thus saith the Lord to Christ my Lord?"[3] Or when he reads : "I came not down from heaven to do mine own will, but the will of Him that sent me?"[4] Or when he finds it written : "Because He who sent me is greater than I?"[5] Or when he considers the passage : "I go to my Father, and your Father; to my God, and your God?"[6] Or when he finds it placed side by side with others : "Moreover, in your law it is written that the witness of two is true. I bear witness of myself, and the Father who sent me beareth witness of me?"[7] Or when the voice from heaven is : "I have both glorified Him, and I will glorify Him again?"[8] Or when by Peter it is answered and said : "Thou art the Son of the living God?"[9] Or when by the Lord Himself the sacrament of this revelation is approved, and He says : "Blessed art thou, Simon Barjona, because flesh and blood hath not revealed this to thee, but my Father which is in heaven?"[10] Or when by Christ Himself it is expressed : "Father, glorify me with that glory with which I was with Thee before the world was made?"[11] Or when it was said by the same : "Father, I knew that Thou hearest me always ; but on account of those who stand around I said it, that they may believe that Thou hast sent me?"[12] Or when the definition of the rule is established by Christ Himself, and it is said : "And this is life eternal, that they should know Thee, the only and true God, and Jesus Christ, whom Thou hast sent. I have glorified Thee upon the earth, I have finished the work which Thou gavest me?"[13] Or when, moreover, by the same it is asserted and said : "All things are delivered to me by my Father?"[14] Or when the session at the right hand of the Father is proved both by apostles and prophets? And I should have enough to do were I to endeavour to gather together all

the passages[15] whatever on this side ; since the divine Scripture, not so much of the Old as also of the New Testament, everywhere shows Him to be born of the Father, by whom all things were made, and without whom nothing was made, who always has obeyed and obeys the Father ; that He always has power over all things, but as delivered, as granted, as by the Father Himself permitted to Him. And what can be so evident *proof* that this is not the Father, but the Son ; as that He is set forth as being obedient to God the Father, unless, if He be believed to be the Father, Christ may be said to be subjected to another God the Father?

CHAP. XXVII.[16] *ARGUMENT.* — HE SKILFULLY REPLIES TO A PASSAGE WHICH THE HERETICS EMPLOYED IN DEFENCE OF THEIR OWN OPINION.

But since they frequently urge upon us the passage where it is said, "I and the Father are one,"[17] in this also we shall overcome them with equal facility. For if, as the heretics think, Christ were the Father, He ought to have said, "I and the Father are one."[18] But when He says I, and afterwards introduces the Father by saying, "I and the Father," He severs and distinguishes the peculiarity of His, that is, the Son's person, from the paternal authority, not only in respect of the sound of the name, but moreover in respect of the order of the distribution of power, since He might have said, "I the Father," if He had had it in mind that He Himself was the Father. And since He said "*one*" *thing*, let the heretics understand that He did not say "*one*" *person*. For *one* placed in the neuter, intimates the social concord, not the personal unity. He is said to be one *neuter*, not one *masculine*, because the expression is not referred to the number, but it is declared with reference to the association of another. Finally, He adds, and says, "We are," not "I am," so as to show, by the fact of His saying "I and the Father are," that they are two persons. Moreover, that He says *one*,[19] has reference to the agreement, and to the identity of judgment, and to the loving association itself, as reasonably the Father and Son are one in agreement, in love, and in affection ; and because He is of the Father, whatsoever He is, He is the Son ; the distinction however remaining, that He is not the Father who is the Son, because He is not the Son who is the Father. For He would not have added "*We are*," if He had had it in mind that He, the only and sole Father, had become the Son. In fine, the Apostle Paul

---

1 Ps. ii. 7, 8.
2 Ps. cx. 1.
3 Isa. xlv. 1. Some transcriber has written Κυρίῳ for Κύρῳ, "the Lord" for "Cyrus," and the mistake has been followed by the author.
4 John vi. 38.
5 John xiv. 28.
6 John xx. 17.
7 John viii. 17, 18.
8 John xii. 20.
9 Matt. xvi. 16.
10 Matt. xvi. 17.
11 John xvii. 5.
12 John xi. 12.
13 John xvii. 3, 4.
14 Luke x. 22.

15 [Cap. xxi. p. 632, *supra.*]
16 According to Pamelius, ch. xxii.
17 John x. 30; *scil.* "unum," Gr. ἕν.
18 Original, "unas." *Scil.* person.
19 Neuter.

also apprehended this agreement of unity, with the distinction of persons notwithstanding: for in writing to the Corinthians he said, "I have planted, Apollos watered, but God gave the increase. Therefore neither is he that planteth anything, nor he that watereth, but God who gives the increase. Now he that planteth and he that watereth are one." [1] And who does not perceive that Apollos is one person and Paul another, and that Apollos and Paul are not one and the same person? Moreover, also, the offices mentioned of each one of them are different; for one is he who plants, and another he who waters. The Apostle Paul, however, put forward these two not as being one *person*, but as being " one ; " so that although Apollos indeed is one, and Paul another, so far as respects the distinction of persons, yet as far as respects their agreement both are "one." For when two persons have one judgment, one truth, one faith, one and the same religion, one fear of God also, they are one even although they are two persons : they are the same, in that they have the same mind. Since those whom the consideration of person divides from one another, these same again are brought together as one by the consideration of religion. And although they are not actually the self-same people, yet in feeling the same, they are the same ; and although they are two, are still one, as having an association in faith, even although they bear diversity in persons. Besides, when at these words of the Lord the Jewish ignorance had been aroused, so that hastily they ran to take up stones, and said, " For a good work we stone thee not, but for blasphemy ; and because thou, being a man, makest thyself God," [2] the Lord established the distinction, in giving them the principle on which He had either said that He was God, or wished it to be understood, and says, " Say ye of Him, whom the Father sanctified, and sent into this world, Thou blasphemest; because I said, I am the Son of God?" [3] Even here also He said that He had the Father. He is therefore the Son, not the Father : for He would have confessed that He was the Father had He considered Himself to be the Father ; and He declares that He was sanctified by His Father. In receiving, then, sanctification from the Father, He is inferior to the Father. Now, consequently, He who is inferior to the Father, is *not the Father*, but the Son ; for had He been the Father, He would have given, and not received, sanctification. Now, however, by declaring that He has received sanctification from the Father, by the very fact of proving Himself to be less than the Father, by receiving from Him sanctification,

He has shown that He is the Son, and not the Father. Besides, He says that He is sent : so that by that obedience wherewith the Lord Christ came, being sent, He might be proved to be not the Father, but the Son, who assuredly would have sent had He been the Father ; but being sent, He was not the Father, lest the Father should be proved, in being sent, to be subjected to another God. And still after this He added what might dissolve all ambiguity, and quench all the controversy of error : for He says, in the last portion of His discourse, " Ye say, Thou blasphemest, because I said I am the Son of God." Therefore if He plainly testifies that He is the Son of God, and not the Father, it is an instance of great temerity and excessive madness to stir up a controversy of divinity and religion, contrary to the testimony of the Lord Christ Himself, and to say that Christ Jesus is the Father, when it is observed that He has proved Himself to be, not the Father, but the Son.

CHAP. XXVIII.   *ARGUMENT.*— HE PROVES ALSO THAT THE WORDS SPOKEN TO PHILIP MAKE NOTHING FOR THE SABELLIANS.

Hereto also I will add that view wherein the heretic, while he rejoices as if at the loss of some power of seeing special truth and light, acknowledges the total blindness of his error. For again and again, and frequently, he objects that it was said, " Have I been so long time with you, and do ye not know me, Philip? He who hath seen me, hath seen the Father also." [4] But let him learn what he does not understand. Philip is reproved, and rightly, and deservedly indeed, because he has said, "Lord, show us the Father, and it sufficeth us." [5] For when had he either heard from Christ, or learnt that Christ was the Father? although, on the other hand, he had frequently heard, and had often learned, rather that He was the Son, not that He was the Father. For what the Lord said, " If ye have known me, ye have known my Father also : and henceforth ye have known Him, and have seen Him," [6] He said not as wishing to be understood Himself to be the Father, but *implying* that he who thoroughly, and fully, and with all faith and all religiousness, drew near to the Son of God, by all means shall attain, through the Son Himself, in whom he thus believes, to the Father, and shall see Him. "For no one," says He, " can come to the Father, but by me." [7] And therefore he shall not only come to God the Father, and shall know the Father Himself ; but, moreover, he ought thus to hold, and so to pre-

---

[1] 1 Cor. iii. 6, 7, 8 (*scil. ἐν*).
[2] John x. 33.
[3] John x. 36.

[4] John xiv. 9.
[5] John xiv. 8.
[6] John xiv. 7.
[7] John xiv. 6.

sume in mind and heart, that he has henceforth not only known, but seen the Father. For often the divine Scripture announces things that are not yet done as being done, because thus they shall be; and things which by all means have to happen, it does not predict as if they were future, but narrates as if they were done. And thus, although Christ had not been born as yet in the times of Isaiah the prophet, he said, "For unto us a child is born;"[1] and although Mary had not yet been approached, he said, "And I approached unto the prophetess; and she conceived, and bare a son."[2] And when Christ had not yet made known the mind of the Father, it is said, "And His name shall be called the Angel of Great Counsel."[3] And when He had not yet suffered, he declared, "He is as a sheep led to the slaughter."[4] And although the cross had never yet existed, He said, "All day long have I stretched out my hands to an unbelieving people."[5] And although not yet had He been scornfully given to drink, the Scripture says, "In my thirst they gave me vinegar to drink."[6] And although He had not yet been stripped, He said, "Upon my vesture they did cast lots, and they numbered my bones: they pierced my hands and my feet."[7] For the divine Scripture, foreseeing, speaks of things which it knows shall be as being already done, and speaks of things as perfected which it regards as future, but which shall come to pass without any doubt. And thus the Lord in the present passage said, "Henceforth ye have known and have seen Him." Now He said that the Father should be seen by whomsoever had followed the Son, not as if the Son Himself should be the Father seen, but that whosoever was willing to follow Him, and be His disciple, should obtain the reward of being able to see the Father. For He also is the image of God the Father; so that it is added, moreover, to these things, that "as the Father worketh, so also the Son worketh."[8] And the Son is an imitator[9] of all the Father's works, so that every one may regard it just as if he saw the Father, when he sees Him who always imitates the invisible Father in all His works. But if Christ is the Father Himself, in what manner does He immediately add, and say, "Whosoever believeth in me, the works that I do he shall do also; and greater works than these shall he do; because I go to my Father?"[10] And He further subjoins, "If ye love me, keep my commandments; and I will ask the Father, and He will

give you another Comforter."[11] After which also He adds this: "If any one loveth me, he shall keep my word: and my Father will love him; and we will come unto him, and will make our abode with him."[12] Moreover, also, He added this too: "But the Advocate, that Holy Spirit whom the Father will send, He will teach you, and bring all things to your remembrance, whatsoever I have said unto you."[13] He utters, further, that passage when He shows Himself to be the Son, and reasonably subjoins, and says, "If ye loved me, ye would rejoice because I go unto the Father: for the Father is greater than I."[14] But what *shall we say* when He also continues in these words: "I am the true vine, and my Father is the husbandman. Every branch in me that beareth not fruit He taketh away; and every branch that beareth fruit He purgeth, that it may bring forth more fruit?"[15] Still He persists, and adds: "As the Father hath loved me, so also have I loved you: remain in my love. If ye have kept my commandments, ye shall remain in my love; even as I have kept the Father's commandments, and remain in His love."[16] Further, He says in addition: "But I have called you friends; for all things which I have heard of my Father I have made known unto you."[17] Moreover, He adds to all this: "But all these things will they do unto you for my name's sake, because they know not Him that sent me."[18] These things then, after the former, evidently attesting Him to be not the Father but the Son, the Lord would never have added, if He had had it in mind, either that He was the Father, or wished Himself to be understood as the Father, except that He might declare this, that every man ought henceforth to consider, in seeing the image of God the Father through the Son, that it was as if he saw the Father; since every one believing on the Son may be exercised in the contemplation of the likeness, so that, being accustomed to seeing the divinity in likeness, he may go forward, and grow even to the perfect contemplation of God the Father Almighty. And since he who has imbibed this truth into his mind and soul, and has believed of all things that thus it shall be, he shall even now see, as it were, in some measure the Father whom he will see *hereafter;* and he may so regard it, as if he actually held, what he knows for certain that he shall one day hold. But if Christ Himself had been the Father, why did He promise as future, a reward which He had already granted and given? For that He says, "Blessed are they of

---

1 Isa. ix. 6.
2 Isa. viii. 3.
3 Isa. ix. 6, LXX. [See pp. 628, 632, *supra.*]
4 Isa. liii. 7.
5 Isa. lxv. 2.
6 Ps. lxix. 21.
7 Ps. xxii. 18, 17.
8 John v. 17.
9 [Cap. xxi. note 5, 632, *supra.*]
10 John xiv. 12.

11 John xiv. 15, 16.
12 John xiv. 23.
13 John xiv. 26.
14 John xiv. 28.
15 John xv. 1.
16 John xv. 9, 10.
17 John xv. 15.
18 John xv. 21.

a pure heart, for they shall see God," [1] it is understood to promise the contemplation and vision of the Father; therefore He had not given this; for why should He promise if He had already given? For He had given if He was the Father: for He was seen, and He was touched. But since, when Christ Himself is seen and touched, He still promises, and says that he who is of a pure heart shall see God, He proves by this very saying that He who was then present was not the Father, seeing that He was seen, and yet promised that whoever should be of a pure heart should see the Father. It was therefore not the Father, but the Son, who promised this, because He who was the Son promised that which had yet to be seen; and His promise would have been superfluous unless He had been the Son. For why did He promise to the pure in heart that they should see the Father, if already they who were then present saw Christ as the Father? But because He was the Son, not the Father, rightly also He was then seen as the Son, because He was the image of God; and the Father, because He is invisible, is promised and pointed out as to be seen by the pure in heart. Let it then be enough to have suggested even these points against that heretic; a few words about many things. For a field which is indeed both wide and expansive would be laid open if we should desire to discuss that heretic more fully; seeing that bereaved, in these two particulars, as it were of his eyes plucked out, he is altogether overcome in the blindness of his doctrine.

CHAP. XXIX. *ARGUMENT.* — HE NEXT TEACHES US THAT THE AUTHORITY OF THE FAITH ENJOINS, AFTER THE FATHER AND THE SON, TO BELIEVE ALSO ON THE HOLY SPIRIT, WHOSE OPERATIONS HE ENUMERATES FROM SCRIPTURE.

Moreover, the order of reason, and the authority of the faith in the disposition of the words and in the Scriptures of the Lord, admonish us after these things to believe also on the Holy Spirit, once promised to the Church, and in the appointed occasions of times given. For He was promised by Joel the prophet, but given by Christ. "In the last days," says the prophet, "I will pour out of my Spirit upon my servants and my handmaids." [2] And the Lord said, "Receive ye the Holy Ghost: whose sins ye remit, they shall be remitted; and whose ye retain, they shall be retained." [3] But this Holy Spirit the Lord Christ calls at one time "the Paraclete," at another pronounces to be the "Spirit of truth." [4] And He is not new in

the Gospel, nor yet even newly given; for it was He Himself who accused the people in the prophets, and in the apostles gave them the appeal to the Gentiles. For the former deserved to be accused, because they had contemned the law; and they of the Gentiles who believe deserve to be aided by the defence of the Spirit, because they earnestly desire to attain to the Gospel law. Assuredly in the Spirit there are different kinds of offices, because in the times there is a different order of occasions; and yet, on this account, He who discharges these offices is not different, nor is He another in so acting, but He is one and the same, distributing His offices according to the times, and the occasions and impulses of things. Moreover, the Apostle Paul says, "Having the same Spirit; as it is written, I believed, and therefore have I spoken; we also believe, and therefore speak." [5] He is therefore one and the same Spirit who was in the prophets and apostles, except that in the former He was occasional, in the latter always. But in the former not as being always in them, in the latter as abiding always in them; and in the former distributed with reserve, in the latter all poured out; in the former given sparingly, in the latter liberally bestowed; not yet manifested before the Lord's resurrection, but conferred after the resurrection. For, said He, "I will pray the Father, and He will give you another Advocate, that He may be with you for ever, even the Spirit of truth." [6] And, "When He, the Advocate, shall come, whom I shall send unto you from my Father, the Spirit of truth who proceedeth from my Father." [7] And, "If I go not away, that Advocate shall not come to you; but if I go away, I will send Him to you." [8] And, "When the Spirit of truth shall come, He will direct you into all the truth." [9] And because the Lord was about to depart to the heavens, He gave the Paraclete out of necessity to the disciples; so as not to leave them in any degree orphans, [10] which was little desirable, and forsake them without an advocate and some kind of protector. For this is He who strengthened their hearts and minds, who marked out the Gospel sacraments, who was in them the enlightener of divine things; and they being strengthened, feared, for the sake of the Lord's name, neither dungeons nor chains, nay, even trod under foot the very powers of the world and its tortures, since they were henceforth armed and strengthened by the same Spirit, having in themselves the gifts which this same Spirit distributes, and appropriates to the Church, the

---

[1] Matt. v. 8.
[2] Joel ii. 28; Acts ii. 17.
[3] John xx. 22, 23.
[4] John xiv. 16, 17.

[5] 2 Cor. iv. 13.
[6] John xiv. 16, 17.
[7] John xv. 20.
[8] John xvi. 7.
[9] John xvi. 13.
[10] [John xiv. 18, *Greek*.]

spouse of Christ, as her ornaments. This is He who places prophets in the Church, instructs teachers, directs tongues, gives powers and healings, does wonderful works, offers discrimination of spirits, affords powers of government, suggests counsels, and orders and arranges whatever other gifts there are of *charismata;* and thus make the Lord's Church everywhere, and in all, perfected and completed. This is He who, after the manner of a dove, when our Lord was baptized, came and abode upon Him, dwelling in Christ full and entire, and not maimed in any measure or portion; but with His whole overflow copiously distributed and sent forth, so that from Him others might receive some enjoyment of His graces: the source of the entire Holy Spirit remaining in Christ, so that from Him might be drawn streams of gifts and works, while the Holy Spirit dwelt affluently in Christ. For truly Isaiah, prophesying this, said: "And the Spirit of wisdom and understanding shall rest upon Him, the Spirit of counsel and might, the Spirit of knowledge and piety; and the Spirit of the fear of the Lord shall fill Him." [1] This self-same thing also he said in the person of the Lord Himself, in another place: "The Spirit of the Lord is upon me; because He has anointed me, He has sent me to preach the Gospel to the poor." [2] Similarly David: "Wherefore God, even Thy God, hath anointed Thee with the oil of gladness above thy fellows." [3] Of Him the Apostle Paul says: "For he who hath not the Spirit of Christ is none of His." [4] "And where the Spirit of the Lord is, there is liberty." [5] He it is who effects with water the second birth, as a certain seed of divine generation, and a consecration of a heavenly nativity, the pledge of a promised inheritance, and as it were a kind of handwriting of eternal salvation; who can make us God's temple, and fit us for His house; who solicits the divine hearing for us with groanings that cannot be uttered; filling the offices of advocacy, and manifesting the duties of our defence, — an inhabitant given for our bodies and an effector of their holiness. Who, working in us for eternity, can also produce our bodies at the resurrection of immortality, accustoming them to be associated in Himself with heavenly power, and to be allied with the divine eternity of the Holy Spirit. For our bodies are both trained in Him and by Him to advance to immortality, by learning to govern themselves with moderation according to His decrees. For this is He who "desireth against the flesh," because "the flesh resisteth against the Spirit." [6]

This is He who restrains insatiable desires, controls immoderate lusts, quenches unlawful fires, conquers reckless impulses, repels drunkenness, checks avarice, drives away luxurious revellings, links love, binds together affections, keeps down sects, orders the rule of truth, overcomes heretics, turns out the wicked, guards the Gospel. Of this says the same apostle: "We have not received the spirit of the world, but the Spirit which is of God." [7] Concerning Him he exultingly says: "And I think also that I have the Spirit of God." [8] Of Him he says: "The Spirit of the prophets is subject to the prophets." [9] Of Him also he tells: "Now the Spirit speaketh plainly, that in the last times some shall depart from the faith, giving heed to seducing spirits, doctrines of demons, who speak lies in hypocrisy, having their conscience cauterized." [10] Established in this Spirit, "none ever calleth Jesus anathema;" [11] no one has ever denied Christ to be the Son of God, or has rejected God the Creator; no one utters any words of his own contrary to the Scriptures; no one ordains other and sacrilegious decrees; no one draws up different laws. [12] Whosoever shall blaspheme against Him, "hath not forgiveness, not only in this world, but also not in the world to come." [13] This is He who in the apostles gives testimony to Christ; in the martyrs shows forth the constant faithfulness of their religion; in virgins restrains the admirable continency of their sealed chastity; in others, guards the laws of the Lord's doctrine incorrupt and uncontaminated; destroys heretics, corrects the perverse, condemns infidels, makes known pretenders; moreover, rebukes the wicked, keeps the Church uncorrupt and inviolate, in the sanctity of a perpetual virginity and truth.

CHAP. XXX. *ARGUMENT.* — IN FINE, NOTWITHSTANDING THE SAID HERETICS HAVE GATHERED THE ORIGIN OF THEIR ERROR FROM CONSIDERATION OF WHAT IS WRITTEN: [14] ALTHOUGH WE CALL CHRIST GOD, AND THE FATHER GOD, STILL SCRIPTURE DOES NOT SET FORTH TWO GODS, ANY MORE THAN TWO LORDS OR TWO TEACHERS.

And now, indeed, concerning the Father, and the Son, and the Holy Spirit, let it be sufficient to have briefly said thus much, and to have laid down these points concisely, without carrying them out in a lengthened argument. For they could be presented more diffusely and continued in a more expanded disputation, since the whole

---

[1] Isa. xi. 2, 3.
[2] Isa. lxi. 1.
[3] Ps. xlv. 7.
[4] Rom. viii. 9.
[5] 2 Cor. iii. 17.
[6] Gal. v. 17.

[7] 1 Cor. ii. 12.
[8] 1 Cor. vii. 40.
[9] 1 Cor. xiv. 32.
[10] 1 Tim. iv. 1.
[11] 1 Cor. xii. 3.
[12] [To commit any one of these errors, he thinks, is to prove one's self "sensual, having not the Spirit." Jude 19; Rom. viii. 7.]
[13] Matt. xii. 32.
[14] "There is one God."

of the Old and New Testaments might be adduced in testimony that thus the true faith stands. But because heretics, ever struggling against the truth, are accustomed to prolong the controversy of pure tradition and Catholic faith, being offended against Christ; because He is, moreover, asserted to be God by the Scriptures also, and this is believed to be so by us; we must rightly — that every heretical calumny may be removed from our faith — contend, concerning the fact that Christ is God also, in such a way as that it may not militate against the truth of Scripture; nor yet against our faith, how there is declared to be one God by the Scriptures, and *how* it is held and believed by us. For as well they who say that Jesus Christ Himself is God the Father, as moreover they who would have Him to be only man, have gathered thence[1] the sources and reasons of their error and perversity; because when they perceived that it was written[2] that "God is one," they thought that they could not otherwise hold such an opinion than by supposing that it must be believed either that Christ was man only, or really God the Father. And they were accustomed in such a way to connect their sophistries as to endeavour to justify their own error. And thus they who say that Jesus Christ is the Father argue as follows: — If God is one, and Christ is God, Christ is the Father, since God is one. If Christ be not the Father, because Christ is God the Son, there appear to be two Gods introduced, contrary to the Scriptures. And they who contend that Christ is man only, conclude on the other hand thus: — If the Father is one, and the Son another, but the Father is God and Christ is God, then there is not one God, but two Gods are at once introduced, the Father and the Son; and if God is one, by consequence Christ must be a man, so that rightly the Father may be one God. Thus indeed the Lord is, as it were, crucified between two thieves,[3] even as He was formerly placed; and thus from either side He receives the sacrilegious reproaches of such heretics as these. But neither the Holy Scriptures nor we suggest to them the reasons of their perdition and blindness, if they either will not, or cannot, see what is evidently written in the midst of the divine documents. For we both know, and read, and believe, and maintain that God is one, who made the heaven as well as the earth, since we neither know any other, nor shall we at any time know such, seeing that there is none. "I," says He, "am God, and there is none beside me, righteous and a Saviour."[4] And in another place: "I am the first and the last, and beside me there

is no God who is as I."[5] And, "Who hath meted out heaven with a span, and the earth with a handful? Who has suspended the mountains in a balance, and the woods on scales?"[6] And Hezekiah: "That all may know that Thou art God alone."[7] Moreover, the Lord Himself: "Why askest thou me concerning that which is good? God alone is good."[8] Moreover, the Apostle Paul says: "Who only hath immortality, and dwelleth in the light that no man can approach unto, whom no man hath seen, nor can see."[9] And in another place: "But a mediator is not a mediator of one, but God is one."[10] But even as we hold, and read, and believe this, thus we ought to pass over no portion of the heavenly Scriptures, since indeed also we ought by no means to reject those marks of Christ's divinity which are laid down in the Scriptures, that we may not, by corrupting the authority of the Scriptures, be held to have corrupted the integrity of our holy faith. And let us therefore believe this, since it is most faithful that Jesus Christ the Son of God is our Lord and God; because "in the beginning was the Word, and the Word was with God, and God was the Word. The same was in the beginning with God."[11] And, "The Word was made flesh, and dwelt in us."[12] And, "My Lord and my God."[13] And, "Whose are the fathers, and of whom according to the flesh Christ came, who is over all, God blessed for evermore."[14] What, then, shall we say? Does Scripture set before us two Gods? How, then, does it say that "God is one?" Or is not Christ God also? How, then, is it said to Christ, "My Lord and my God?" Unless, therefore, we hold all this with fitting veneration and lawful argument, we shall reasonably be thought to have furnished a scandal to the heretics, not assuredly by the fault of the heavenly Scriptures, which never deceive; but by the presumption of human error, whereby they have chosen to be heretics. And in the first place, we must turn the attack against them who undertake to make against us the charge of saying that there are two Gods. It is written, and they cannot deny it, that "there is one Lord."[15] What, then, do they think of Christ? — that He is Lord, or that He is not Lord at all? But they do not doubt absolutely that He is Lord; therefore, if their reasoning be true, here are already two Lords. How, then, is it true according to the Scriptures, there is one Lord? And Christ

---

[1] *Scil.* from Scripture.
[2] [Gal. iii. 20; Deut. vi. 4.]
[3] ["Non semper pendebit inter latrones Christus: aliquando resurget Crucifixa Veritas." — SEBASTIAN CASTALIO.]
[4] Isa. xliii. 11.

[5] Isa. xliv. 6, 7.
[6] Isa. xl. 12.
[7] Isa. xxxvii. 20.
[8] Matt. xix. 17.
[9] 1 Tim. vi. 16.
[10] Gal. iii. 20.
[11] John i. 1, 2.
[12] John i. 14.
[13] John xx. 28.
[14] Rom. ix. 5.
[15] Deut. vi. 4.

is called the "one Master." [1] Nevertheless we read that the Apostle Paul also is a master.[2] Then, according to this, our Master is not one, for from these things we conclude that there are two masters. How, then, according to the Scriptures, is "one our Master, even Christ?" In the Scriptures there is one "called good, even God;" but in the same Scriptures Christ is also asserted to be good. There is not, then, if they rightly conclude, one good, but even two good. How, then, according to the scriptural faith, is there said to be only one good? But if they do not think that it can by any means interfere with the truth that there is one Lord, that Christ also is Lord, nor with the truth that one is our Master, that Paul also is our master, or with the truth that one is good, that Christ also is called good; on the same reasoning, let them understand that, from the fact that God is one, no obstruction arises to the truth that Christ also is declared to be God.

CHAP. XXXI. *ARGUMENT.* — BUT THAT GOD, THE SON OF GOD, BORN OF GOD THE FATHER FROM EVERLASTING, WHO WAS ALWAYS IN THE FATHER, IS THE SECOND PERSON TO THE FATHER, WHO DOES NOTHING WITHOUT HIS FATHER'S DECREE; AND THAT HE IS LORD, AND THE ANGEL OF GOD'S GREAT COUNSEL, TO WHOM THE FATHER'S GODHEAD IS GIVEN BY COMMUNITY OF SUBSTANCE.

Thus God the Father, the Founder and Creator of all things, who only knows no beginning, invisible, infinite, immortal, eternal, is one God; to whose greatness, or majesty, or power, I would not say nothing can be preferred, but nothing can be compared; of whom, when He willed it, the Son, the Word, was born, who is not received[3] in the sound of the stricken air, or in the tone of voice forced from the lungs, but is acknowledged in the substance of the power put forth by God, the mysteries of whose sacred and divine nativity neither an apostle has learnt, nor prophet has discovered, nor angel has known, nor creature has apprehended. To the Son alone they are known, who has known the secrets of the Father. He then, since He was begotten of the Father, is always in the Father. And I thus say always, that I may show Him not to be unborn, but born. But He who is before all time must be said to have been always in the Father; for no time can be assigned to Him who is before all time. And He is always in the Father, unless the Father be not always Father, only that the Father also precedes Him, — in a certain sense, — since it is necessary — in some degree — that He should *be* before He is Father.

Because it is essential that He who knows no beginning must go before Him who has a beginning;[4] even as He is the less as knowing that He is in Him, having an origin because He is born, and of like nature with the Father in some measure by His nativity, although He has a beginning in that He is born, inasmuch as He is born of that Father who alone has no beginning. He, then, when the Father willed it, proceeded from the Father, and He who was in the Father came forth from the Father; and He who was in the Father because He was of the Father, was subsequently with the Father, because He came forth from the Father, — that is to say, that divine substance whose name is the Word, whereby all things were made, and without whom nothing was made. For all things are after Him, because they are by Him. And reasonably, He is before all things, but after the Father, since all things were made by Him, and He proceeded from Him of whose will all things were made. Assuredly God proceeding from God, causing a person second to the Father as being the Son, but not taking from the Father that characteristic that He is one God. For if He had not been born — compared with Him who was unborn, an equality being manifested in both — He would make two unborn beings, and thus would make two Gods. If He had not been begotten — compared with Him who was not begotten, and as being found equal — they not being begotten, would have reasonably given two Gods, and thus Christ would have been the cause of two Gods. Had He been formed without beginning as the Father, and He Himself the beginning of all things as is the Father, this would have made two beginnings, and consequently would have shown to us two Gods also. Or if He also were not the Son, but the Father begetting from Himself another Son, reasonably, as compared with the Father, and designated as great as He, He would have caused two Fathers, and thus also He would have proved the existence of two Gods. Had He been invisible, as compared with the Invisible, and declared equal, He would have shown forth two Invisibles, and thus also He would have proved them to be two Gods. If incomprehensible,[5] if also whatever other attributes belong to the Father, reasonably we say, He would have given rise to the allegation of two Gods, as these people feign. But now, whatever He is, He is not of Himself, because He is not unborn; but He is of the Father, because He is begotten, whether as being the Word, whether as being the Power, or as being the Wisdom, or as being the Light, or as being the Son; and whatever of these He is, in that He is not from any other source, as we have

---

[1] Matt. xxiii. 8-10.
[2] διδάσκαλος.
[3] As the Word formed. [He expounds Ps. xliv. (xlv.), Sept.]

[4] ["In a sense;" i.e, in logic, not time.]
[5] [Compare the Athanasian Confession.]

already said before, than from the Father, owing His origin to His Father, He could not make a disagreement in the divinity by the number of two Gods, since He gathered His beginning by being born of Him who is one God. In which kind, being both as well only-begotten as first-begotten of Him who has no beginning, He is the only one, of all things both Source and Head. And therefore He declared that God is one, in that He proved Him to be from no source nor beginning, but rather the beginning and source of all things. Moreover, the Son does nothing of His own will, nor does anything of His own determination; nor does He come from Himself, but obeys all His Father's commands and precepts; so that, although birth proves Him to be a Son, yet obedience even to death declares Him the minister of the will of His Father, of whom He is. Thus making Himself obedient to His Father in all things, although He also is God, yet He shows the one God the Father by His obedience, from whom also He drew His beginning. And thus He could not make two Gods, because He did not make two beginnings, seeing that from Him who has no beginning He received the source of His nativity before all time.[1] For since that is the beginning to other creatures which is unborn, — which God the Father only is, being beyond a beginning of whom He is who was born, — while He who is born of Him reasonably comes from Him who has no beginning, proving that to be the beginning from which He Himself is, even although He is God who is born, yet He shows Him to be one God whom He who was born proved to be without a beginning. He therefore is God, but begotten for this special result, that He should be God. He is also the Lord, but born for this very purpose of the Father, that He might be Lord. He is also an Angel, but He

was destined of the Father as an Angel to announce the Great Counsel of God. And His divinity is thus declared, that it may not appear by any dissonance or inequality of divinity to have caused two Gods. For all things being subjected to Him as the Son by the Father, while He Himself, with those things which are subjected to Him, is subjected to His Father, He is indeed proved to be Son of His Father; but He is found to be both Lord and God of all else. Whence, while all things put under Him are delivered to Him who is God, and all things are subjected to Him, the Son refers all that He has received to the Father, remits again to the Father the whole authority of His divinity. The true and eternal Father is manifested as the one God, from whom alone this power of divinity is sent forth, and also given and directed upon the Son, and is again returned by the communion of substance to the Father. God indeed is shown as the Son, to whom the divinity is beheld to be given and extended. And still, nevertheless, the Father is proved to be one God; while by degrees in reciprocal transfer that majesty and divinity are again returned and reflected as sent by the Son Himself to the Father, who had given them; so that reasonably God the Father is God of all, and the source also of His Son Himself whom He begot as Lord. Moreover, the Son is God of all else, because God the Father put before all Him whom He begot. Thus the Mediator of God and men, Christ Jesus, having the power of every creature subjected to Him by His own Father, inasmuch as He is God; with every creature subdued to Him, found at one with His Father God, has, by abiding in that condition that He moreover "was heard,"[2] briefly proved God His Father to be one and only and true God.

---

[1] [As in the Athanasian Confession.]

[2] There is apparently some indistinct reference here to the passage in Heb. v. 7, "and was heard in that He feared" — ἀπὸ τῆς εὐλαβείας. [For the Angel of Great Counsel, see p. 629, *supra*.]

TWO NOTES BY THE AMERICAN EDITOR.

P. 609.   The author's elucidation of the figure, *anthropopathy*, is an enlargement of Clement's casual remarks in the *Stromata* (cap. xvi. vol. ii. p. 363, this series).   Consult *On the Figurative Language of Holy Scripture*, Jones of Nayland, *Works*, vol. iv. ed. 1801.

P. 630, note 5.   Compare Waterland, vol. ii. p. 210, ed. 1823; also *Life of Bishop Bull*, by Robert Nelson, p. 260.   For the extraordinary history of Bull's work in France, see the said *Life*, pp. 327–333.   For Petavius, Waterland, vol. ii. p. 277, and Bull's *Life*, p. 243.   *Petavius* seems to have had a crafty design to sustain the Council of Trent by arguing that the Council of Nicæa also made *new* dogmas.   Bull proves that it only *bore witness to the old*.   To the honour of the assembled bishops of the Gallican Church, they sustained Bull against the Jesuit.

ON THE JEWISH MEATS.

CHAP. I. *ARGUMENT.* — NOVATIAN, A ROMAN PRES-
BYTER, DURING HIS RETIREMENT AT THE TIME
OF THE DECIAN PERSECUTION, BEING URGED
BY VARIOUS LETTERS FROM HIS BRETHREN, HAD
WRITTEN TWO EARLIER EPISTLES AGAINST THE
JEWS ON THE SUBJECTS OF CIRCUMCISION AND
THE SABBATH, AND NOW WRITES THE PRESENT
ONE ON THE JEWISH MEATS.

Although, most holy brethren, the day in which
I receive your letters and writings is most ardent-
ly longed for by me, and to be reckoned among
the chief and happiest — for what else is there
now to make me more joyous?[2] — still I think
that the day is to be deemed not less notable,
and among special days, wherein I return to you
similar communications, with the affection of
love that I owe you, and write you letters with
a corresponding interest. For nothing, most
holy brethren, holds me bound with such bonds,
nothing stirs and arouses me with such a stimulus of care and anxiety, as the fear lest you should
think that any disadvantage is suffered by you
by reason of my absence; and this I strive to
remedy, in labouring to show myself present
with you by frequent letters. Although, therefore, the duty which I owe, and the charge I
have undertaken, and the very ministerial office
imposed upon me, require of me this necessity
of writing letters, yet you still further enhance
it, by stirring me up to write through means of
your continual communications. And inclined
although I am to those periodical expressions of
love, you urge me the more by showing that you
stand fast continually in the Gospel: whence it
results, that by my letters I am not so much instructing you who are already informed, as incit-
ing you who are already prepared. For you, who
not only hold the Gospel pure and purged from
all stain of perverse doctrine, but also energeti-
cally teach the same, seek not man for a master,
since you show yourselves by these very things
to be teachers. Therefore as you run, I exhort
you; and as you watch, I stir you up; and as
you contend against "the spiritual things of

wickedness,"[3] I address you; and as you press
"in your course to the prize of your calling in
Christ,"[4] I urge you on, — that, treading under
foot and rejecting as well the sacrilegious calumnies of heretics as also the idle fables of Jews,
you may hold the sole word[5] and teaching of
Christ, so as worthily to claim for yourselves the
authority of His name. But how perverse are
the Jews, and remote from the understanding
of their law, I have fully shown, as I believe, in
two former letters,[6] wherein it was absolutely
proved that they are ignorant of what is the true
circumcision, and what the true Sabbath; and
their ever increasing blindness is confuted in
this present epistle, wherein I have briefly discoursed concerning their meats, because that in
them they consider that they only are holy, and
that all others are defiled.[7]

CHAP. II. *ARGUMENT.* — HE FIRST OF ALL ASSERTS
THAT THE LAW IS SPIRITUAL; AND THENCE, AS
MAN'S FIRST FOOD WAS ONLY THE FRUIT OF
TREES, AND THE USE OF FLESH WAS ADDED,
THAT THE LAW THAT FOLLOWED SUBSEQUENTLY[8]
WAS TO BE UNDERSTOOD SPIRITUALLY.[9]

Therefore, first of all, we must avail ourselves
of that passage, "that the law is spiritual;"[10]
and if they deny it to be spiritual, they assuredly
blaspheme; if, avoiding blasphemy, they confess
it to be spiritual, let them read it spiritually.
For divine things must be divinely received, and
must assuredly be maintained as holy. But a
grave fault is branded on those who attach earthly and human doctrine to sacred and spiritual
words; and this we must beware of doing.

---

[1] Entitled "A Letter of Novatian, the Roman Presbyter."
[2] "Liberiorem," translated, according to a plausible emendation,
as "hilariorem."

[3] Eph. vi. 12.
[4] Phil. iii. 14.
[5] Traditionem.
[6] These letters are not extant, but they are mentioned by Jerome,
De vir. Illustr., ch. lxx.
[7] [1 Cor. vi. 13. A passage probably connected with the Jewish
superstition. But see the Peshito-Syriac version on Mark vii. 19.
Compare Murdock's version *ad loc.*, ed. 1855.]
[8] Which, distinguishing between meats, granted certain animals as
clean, and interdicted certain others as not clean, especially as all
animals were declared "very good," and even unclean animals were
reserved for offspring in Noah's ark, although they otherwise might
have been got rid of, if they ought to have been destroyed on account
of their uncleanness.
[9] [The divers animals are also *parables* illustrating human passions and appetites. See Jones of Nayland, vol. xi. p. 1.]
[10] Rom. vii. 14.

Moreover, we may beware, if any things enjoined by God be so treated as if they were assumed to diminish His authority, lest, in calling some things impure and unclean, their institution should dishonour their ordainer. For in reprobating what He has made, He will appear to have condemned His own works, which He had approved as good; and He will be designated as seeming capricious in both cases, as the heretics indeed would have it; either in having blessed things which were not clean, or in subsequently reprobating as not good, creatures which He had blessed as both clean and good. And of this the enormity and contradiction will remain for ever if that Jewish doctrine is persisted in, which must be got rid of with all our ability; so that whatever is irregularly delivered by them, may be taken away by us, and a suitable arrangement of His works, and an appropriate and spiritual application of the divine law, may be restored. But to begin from the beginning of things, whence it behoves me to begin; the only food for the first men was fruit and the produce of the trees. For afterwards, man's sin transferred his need from the fruit-trees to the produce of the earth, when the very attitude of his body attested the condition of his conscience. For although innocency raised men up towards the heavens to pluck their food from the trees so long as they had a good conscience, yet sin, when committed, bent men down to the earth and to the ground to gather its grain. Moreover, afterwards the use of flesh was added, the divine favour supplying for human necessities the kinds of meats generally fitting for suitable occasions. For while a more tender meat was needed to nourish men who were both tender and unskilled, it was still a food not prepared without toil, doubtless for their advantage, lest they should again find a pleasure in sinning, if the labour imposed upon sin did not exhort innocence. And since now it was no more a paradise to be tended, but a whole world to be cultivated, the more robust food of flesh is offered to men, that for the advantage of culture something more might be added to the vigour of the human body. All these things, as I have said, were by grace and by divine arrangement: so that either the most vigorous food should not be given in too small quantity for men's support, and they should be enfeebled for labour; or that the more tender meat should not be too abundant, so that, oppressed beyond the measure of their strength, they should not be able to bear it.[1] But the law which followed subsequently ordained[2] the flesh foods with distinction: for some animals it gave

and granted for use,[3] as being clean; some it interdicted as not clean, and conveying pollution to those that eat them. Moreover, it gave this character to those that were clean, that those which chew the cud and divide the hoofs are clean; those are unclean which do neither one nor other of these things. So, in fishes also, the law said that those indeed were clean which were covered with scales and supplied with fins, but that those which were otherwise were not clean. Moreover, it established a distinction among the fowls, and laid down what was to be judged either an abomination, or clean. Thus the law ordained *the exercise of* very great subtlety in making a separation among those animals which the ancient appointment had gathered together into one form of blessing. What, then, are we to say? Are the animals therefore unclean? But what else is it *to say* that they are not clean, than that the law has separated them from the uses of food? And what, moreover, is that that we have just now said? Then God is the ordainer of things which are not clean; and the blame attached to things which are made will recoil upon their Maker, who did not produce them clean; to say which is certainly characteristic of extreme and excessive folly: it is to accuse God as having created unclean things, and to charge upon the divine majesty the guilt of having made things which are abomination, especially when they were both pronounced "very good,"[4] and as being good have obtained the blessing from God Himself "that they should increase and multiply." Moreover also they were reserved by the command of the Creator in Noah's ark for the sake of their offspring, that so being kept they might be proved to be needful; and being needful, they might be proved to be good, although even in that case also there is a distinction appended. But still, even then, the creation of those very creatures that were not clean might have been utterly abolished, if it had needed to be abolished on account of its own pollution.

CHAP. III. *ARGUMENT.* — AND THUS UNCLEAN ANIMALS ARE NOT TO BE REPROACHED, LEST THE REPROACH BE THROWN UPON THEIR AUTHOR; BUT WHEN AN IRRATIONAL ANIMAL IS REJECTED ON ANY ACCOUNT, IT IS RATHER THAT THAT VERY THING SHOULD BE CONDEMNED IN MAN WHO IS RATIONAL; AND THEREFORE THAT IN ANIMALS THE CHARACTER, THE DOINGS, AND THE WILLS OF MEN ARE DEPICTED.

How far, then, must that law, which — as I have shown by the authority of the apostle — is spiritual, be spiritually received in order that the

---

[1] This sentence is very unintelligible, but it is the nearest approach to a meaning that can be gathered from the original.
[2] [Gen. ix. 3. The Noachic covenant was Catholic, and foreshadowed Acts x. 15, although clean and unclean beasts were recognised as by natural classification. Gen. vii. 2. Argue as in Gal. iii. 17.]

[3] Or, as some read, "for eating," substituting "esum" for "usum."
[4] Gen. i. 31.

divine and sure idea of the law may be carried out? Firstly, we must believe that whatever was ordained by God is clean and purified by the very authority of His creation; neither must it be reproached, lest the reproach should be thrown back upon its Author. Then *too* that the law was given to the children of Israel for this purpose, that they might profit by it, and return to those virtuous manners which, although they had received them from their fathers, they had corrupted in Egypt by reason of their intercourse with a barbarous people. Finally, also, those ten commandments on the tables teach nothing new, but remind them of what had been obliterated — that righteousness in them, which had been put to sleep, might revive again as it were by the afflatus of the law, after the manner of a *smothered* fire. But they could profit by the perception that those vices were especially to be avoided in men which the law had condemned even in beasts.[1] For when an irrational animal is rejected on any account, it is rather that very thing which is condemned in the man, who is rational. And if in it anything which it has by nature is characterized as a defilement, that same thing is most to be blamed when it is found in man opposed to his nature. Therefore, in order that men might be purified, the cattle were censured — to wit, that men also who had the same vices might be esteemed on a level with the brutes. Whence it results, that not only were the animals not condemned by their Creator because of His agency;[2] but that men might be instructed in the brutes to return to the unspotted nature of their own creation. For we must consider how the Lord distinguishes clean and not clean. The creatures that are clean, it says, both chew the cud and divide the hoof; the unclean do neither, or only one of the two. All these things were made by one Workman, and He who made them Himself blessed them. Therefore I regard the creation of both as clean, because both He who created them is holy, and those things which were created are not in fault in being that which they were made. For it has never been customary for nature, but for a perverted will, to bear the blame of guilt. What, then, is the case? In the animals it is the characters, and doings, and wills of men that are depicted.[3] They are clean if they chew the cud; that is, if they ever have in their mouth as food the divine precepts. They divide the hoof, if with the firm step of innocency they tread the ways of righteousness, and of every virtue of life. For of those creatures which divide the foot into two hoofs the walk is always vigorous; the ten-

dency to slip of one part of the hoof being sustained by the firmness of the other, and so retained in the substantial footstep. Thus they who do neither are unclean, whose walk is neither firm in virtues; nor do they digest the food of the divine precepts after the manner of that chewing of the cud. And they, too, who do one of these things are not themselves clean either, inasmuch as they are maimed of the other, and not perfect in both. And these are they who do both, as believers, and are clean; or one of the two, as Jews and heretics, and are blemished; or neither, as the Gentiles, and are consequently unclean. Thus in the animals, by the law, as it were, a certain mirror of human life is established, wherein men may consider the images of penalties; so that everything which is vicious in men, as committed against nature, may be the more condemned, when even those things, although naturally ordained in brutes, are in them blamed.[4] For that in fishes the roughness of scales is regarded as constituting their cleanness; rough, and rugged, and unpolished, and substantial, and grave manners are approved in men; while those that are without scales are unclean; because trifling, and fickle, and faithless, and effeminate manners are disapproved. Moreover, what does the law mean when it says, "Thou shalt not eat the camel?"[5] — except that by the example of that animal it condemns a life nerveless[6] and crooked with crimes. Or when it forbids the swine to be taken for food? It assuredly reproves a life filthy and dirty, and delighting in the garbage of vice, placing its supreme good not in generosity of mind, but in the flesh alone. Or when it forbids the hare? It rebukes men deformed into women. And who would use the body of the weasel for food? But in this case it reproves theft. Who would eat the lizard? But it hates an aimless waywardness of life. Who the eft? But it execrates mental stains. Who would eat the hawk, who the kite, who the eagle? But it hates plunderers and violent people who live by crime. Who the vulture? But it holds accursed those who seek for booty by the death of others. Or who the raven? But it holds accused crafty wills. Moreover, when it forbids the sparrow, it condemns intemperance; when the owl, it hates those who fly from the light of truth; when the swan, the proud with high neck; when the sea-mew, too talkative an intemperance of tongue; when the bat, those who seek the darkness of night as well as of error. These things, then, and the like to these, the law holds accursed in animals, which in them indeed are not blameworthy, because they are born in this condition;

---

[1] [See chap. ii. p. 645, *supra*, note 9.]
[2] Sui culpa.
[3] [The moral uses of the animal creation are recognised in all languages: as when we say of men, a serpent, a fox, a hog, an ass, etc: so otherwise, a lion, a lamb, an eagle, a dove, etc.]

[4] [Novatian was a keen analyst, and his allegorial renderings are logical generally, though sometimes fanciful.]
[5] Lev. xi. 4. [Jones of Nayland, vol. iii., *Disquisition*, ed. 1801.]
[6] " Enervem," but more probably " informem."

in man they are blamed, because they are sought for contrary to his nature, not by his creation, but by his error.

CHAP. IV. *ARGUMENT.* — TO THESE THINGS ALSO WAS ADDED ANOTHER REASON FOR PROHIBITING MANY KINDS OF MEATS TO THE JEWS ; TO WIT, FOR THE RESTRAINT OF THE INTEMPERANCE OF THE PEOPLE, AND THAT THEY MIGHT SERVE THE ONE GOD.

To these considerations, then, thus enumerated, were added also other reasons for which many kinds of meats were withheld from the Jews ; and that this might be so, many things were called unclean, not as being condemned in themselves, but that the Jews might be restrained to the service of one God ; because frugality and moderation in appetite were becoming to those who were chosen for this purpose. And such moderation is always found to be approximate to religion, nay, so to speak, rather related and akin to it ; for luxury is inimical to holiness. For how shall religion be spared by it, when modesty is not spared ? Luxury does not entertain the fear of God ; since while pleasures hurry it on, it is carried forward to the sole daring of its desires : for the reins being loosened, it increases in the application of expense without measure, as if it were its food, exceeding its patrimony with its modesty ; or as a torrent rushing from the mountain-peaks not only overleaps what is opposed to it, but carries with it those very hindrances for the destruction of other things. Therefore these remedies were sought for to restrain the intemperance of the people, that in proportion as luxury was diminished, virtuous manners might be increased. For what else did they deserve, than that they should be restrained from using all the pleasures of divers meats, who dared to prefer the vilest meats of the Egyptians to the divine banquets of manna, preferring the juicy meats of their enemies and masters to their liberty ? They were truly worthy that the slavery which they had coveted should pamper them, if the food that was more desirable and free was so ill pleasing to them.

CHAP. V. *ARGUMENT.* — BUT THERE WAS A LIMIT TO THE USE OF THESE SHADOWS OR FIGURES ; FOR AFTERWARDS, WHEN THE END OF THE LAW, CHRIST, CAME, ALL THINGS WERE SAID BY THE APOSTLE TO BE PURE TO THE PURE, AND THE TRUE AND HOLY MEAT WAS A RIGHT FAITH AND AN UNSPOTTED CONSCIENCE.

And thus there was a certain ancient time, wherein those shadows or figures were to be used, that meats should be abstained from which had indeed been commended by their creation, but had been prohibited by the law. But now

Christ, the end of the law, has come, disclosing all the obscurities of the law — all those things which antiquity had covered with the clouds of sacraments. For the illustrious Master, and the heavenly Teacher, and the ordainer of the perfected truth, has come, under whom at length it is rightly said : "To the pure all things are pure ; but unto them that are defiled and unbelieving is nothing pure, but even their mind and conscience is defiled."[1] Moreover, in another place : "For every creature of God is good, and nothing to be refused which is received with thanksgiving ; for it is sanctified by the Word of God and prayer."[2] Again, in another place : "The Spirit expressly says that in the last days some shall depart from the faith, giving heed to seducing spirits, doctrines of demons, speaking lies in hypocrisy, having their conscience seared with a hot iron, forbidding to marry, and *commanding to* abstain from meats which God hath created to be received with thanksgiving by them which believe and those who know God."[3] Moreover, in another passage : "Everything that is sold in the market-place eat, asking nothing."[4] From these things it is plain that all those things are returned to their *original* blessedness now that the law is finished, and that we must not revert to the special observances of meats, which observances were ordained for a certain reason, but which evangelical liberty has now taken away, their discharge being given. The apostle cries out : "The kingdom of God is not meat and drink, but righteousness, and peace, and joy."[5] Also elsewhere : "Meats for the belly, and the belly for meats : but God shall destroy both it and them. Now the body is not for fornication, but for the Lord ; and the Lord for the body."[6] God is not worshipped by the belly nor by meats, which the Lord says will perish, and are "purged" by natural law in the draught.[7] For he who worships the Lord by meats, is merely as one who has his belly for his Lord. The meat, I say, true, and holy, and pure, is a true faith, an unspotted conscience, and an innocent soul. Whosoever is thus fed, feeds also with Christ. Such a banqueter is God's guest : these are the feasts that feed the angels, these are the tables which the martyrs make. Hence is that word of the law : "Man doth not live by bread alone, but by every word which proceedeth out of the mouth of God."[8] Hence, too, that saying of Christ : "My meat is to do the will of Him that sent me, and to finish His work."[9] Hence,

---

1 Tit. i. 15.
2 1 Tim. iv. 4, 5.
3 1 Tim. iv. 1, 2, 3.
4 1 Cor. x. 25.
5 Rom. xiv. 17.
6 1 Cor. vi. 13.
7 [Or lower bowel, Mark vii. 19 ; Matt. xv. 17. See cap. i. note 7, p. 645, *supra.* It throws off refuse, leaving food only to the system.]
8 Deut. viii. 3.
9 John iv. 34.

"Ye seek me not because ye saw the miracles, but because ye did eat of my loaves and were filled. But labour not for the meat which perisheth, but for the meat which endureth to life eternal, which the Son of man will give you; for Him hath the Father sealed." [1] By righteousness, I say, and by continency, and by the rest of the virtues, God is worshipped. For Zecharias also tells us, saying: "If ye eat or drink, is it not *ye* that eat or drink?" [2] — declaring thereby that meat or drink attain not unto God, but unto man: for neither is God fleshly, so as to be pleased with flesh; nor is He careful [3] for these pleasures, so as to rejoice in our food. [4] God rejoices in our faith alone, in our innocency alone, in our truth alone, in our virtues alone. And these dwell not in our belly, but in our soul; and these are acquired for us by divine awe and heavenly fear, and not by earthly food. And such the apostle fitly rebuked, as "obeying the superstitions of angels, puffed up by their fleshly mind; not holding Christ the head, from whom all the body, joined together by links, and inwoven and grown together by mutual members in the bond of charity, increaseth to God;" [5] but observing those things: "Touch not, taste not, handle not; which indeed seem to have a form of religion, in that the body is not spared." [6] Yet there is no advantage at all of righteousness, while we are recalled by a voluntary slavery to those elements to which by baptism we have died.

CHAP. VI. *ARGUMENT.* — BUT, ON THE GROUND THAT LIBERTY IN MEATS IS GRANTED TO US, THERE IS NO PERMISSION OF LUXURY, THERE IS NO TAKING AWAY OF CONTINENCE AND FASTING: FOR THESE THINGS GREATLY BECOME THE FAITHFUL, — TO WIT, THAT THEY SHOULD PRAY TO GOD, AND GIVE HIM THANKS, NOT ONLY BY DAY, BUT BY NIGHT.

But from the fact that liberty of meats is granted to us, it does not of necessity follow that luxury is allowed us; nor because the Gospel has dealt with us very liberally, has it taken away continency. By this, I say, the belly is not provided for, but the form of meats was shown: it was made manifest what was right, not that we might go into the gulf of desire, but to give a reason for the law. But nothing has so restrained intemperance as the Gospel; nor has any one given such strict laws against gluttony as Christ, who is said to have pronounced even the poor blessed, and the hungering and thirsting happy, the rich miserable; to whom, obeying the government of their belly and their palate, the material of their lusts could never be wanting, so that their servitude could not cease; who think it an argument of their happiness to desire as much as they can, except that they are thus able to attain less than they desire. For, moreover, preferring Lazarus in his very hunger and in his sores themselves, and with the rich man's dogs, He restrained the destroyers of salvation, the belly and the palate, by examples. The apostle also, when he said, "Having food and raiment, we are therewith content," [7] laid down the law of frugality and continency; and thinking that it would be of little advantage that he had written, he also gave himself as an example of what he had written, adding not without reason, that "avarice is the root of all evils;" [8] for it follows in the footsteps of luxury. Whatever the latter has wasted by vice, the former restores by crime; the circle of crimes being re-trodden, that luxury may again take away whatever avarice had heaped together. Nor yet are there wanting, among such things, those who, although they have claimed to themselves the sound of the Christian name, afford instances and teachings of intemperance; whose vices have come even to that pitch, that while fasting they drink in the early morning, not thinking it Christian to drink after meat, unless the wine poured into their empty and unoccupied veins should have gone down directly after sleep: for they seem to have less relish of what they drink if food be mingled with the wine. Thus you may see such in a new kind, still fasting and already drunk, not running to the tavern, but carrying the tavern about with them; and if any one of them offers a salute, he gives not a kiss, but drinks a health. What can they do after meat, whom meat finds intoxicated? Or in what kind of state does the sun at his setting leave them, whom at his rising he looks upon as already stupid with wine? But things which are detestable are not to be taken as our examples. For those things only are to be taken by which our soul may be made better; and although in the Gospel the use of meats is universally given to us, yet it is understood to be given to us only with the law of frugality and continence. For these things are even greatly becoming to the faithful, — to wit, those who are about to pray to God and to give Him thanks, not only by day, but by night also; which cannot be if the mind, stupefied by meat and wine, should not prevail to shake off heavy sleep and the load heaped upon the breast.

---

[1] John vi. 26, 27.
[2] Zech. vii. 6, LXX.
[3] "Attonitus" is assumed to be rightly read "attentus."
[4] [1 Tim. iv. 4, vi. 17. Against the Encratites (vol. i. p. 353), but not against moderation (vol. ii. p. 237, this series).]
[5] Col. ii. 18, 19.
[6] Col. ii. 21, 23.

[7] 1 Tim. vi. 8.
[8] 1 Tim. vi. 10.

CHAP. VII. *ARGUMENT.* — MOREOVER, WE MUST BE CAREFUL THAT NO ONE SHOULD THINK THAT THIS LICENCE MAY BE CARRIED TO SUCH AN EXTENT AS THAT HE MAY APPROACH TO THINGS OFFERED TO IDOLS.

But it must be very greatly guarded against in the use of food, and we must be warned lest any should think that liberty is permitted to that degree that even he may approach to what has been offered to idols. For, as far as pertains to God's creation, every creature is clean. But when it has been offered to demons, it is polluted so long as it is offered to the idols; and as soon as this is done, it belongs no longer to God, but to the idol. And when this creature is taken for food, it nourishes the person who so takes it for the demon, not for God, by making him a fellow-guest with the idol, not with Christ, as rightly do the Jews also.[1] And the meaning of these meats being perceived, and the counsel of the law being considered, and the kindness of the Gospel grace being known, and the rigour of temperance being observed, and the pollution of things offered to idols being rejected, we who keep the rule of truth throughout all things, ought to give thanks to God through Jesus Christ, His Son, our Lord, to whom be praise, and honour, and glory, for ever and ever. Amen.

---

[1] *Scil.* abstain. [But see 1 Cor. viii. 4, etc.]

A letter written to Cyprian by Novatian the Roman presbyter, in the name of the Roman clergy, will be found translated (Ep. xxx.) at p. 308, this volume.

APPENDIX

ACTS AND RECORDS OF THE FAMOUS CONTROVERSY ABOUT THE BAPTISM OF HERETICS.

A ROMAN COUNCIL CELEBRATED UNDER STEPHEN.

FROM THE SYNODAL ROLL.

A DIVINE and sacred provincial synod, gathered together at Rome by Stephen, the blessed martyr and *father* [1] which excommunicated those who in an African synod had, without reason, conceded that they who came to the Catholic Church from any heresy should be re-baptized. [2]

CARTHAGINIAN COUNCILS.

THE THIRD CARTHAGINIAN COUNCIL UNDER CYPRIAN, ON THE BAPTISM OF INFANTS ; HELD ANNO DOMINI 253.

This document is translated at p. 353, Ep. lviii.

THE FOURTH CARTHAGINIAN COUNCIL UNDER CYPRIAN ; HELD ANNO DOMINI 254. ABOUT BASILIDES AND MARTIAL, BISHOPS OF SPAIN, WHO HAD RECEIVED CERTIFICATES.

This document is translated at p. 369, Ep. lxvii.

---

[1] " Papa" [as applied to all bishops. See p. 154, *supra*.]
[2] Reference is made to this council in *Epistles of Cyprian*, No. lxxiii., and at large in Epistles lxix. to lxxiv., pp. 375–396, *supra*.

THE FIFTH CARTHAGINIAN COUNCIL UNDER CYPRIAN, THE FIRST ABOUT BAPTISM ; HELD ANNO DOMINI 255, THE THIRD YEAR OF ST. STEPHEN'S EPISCOPATE.

This will be found translated at p. 375, Ep. lxix.

THE SIXTH CARTHAGINIAN COUNCIL UNDER CYPRIAN, THE SECOND ABOUT BAPTISM, FROM A PROVINCE OF AFRICA AND NUMIDIA ; HELD ANNO DOMINI 256, IN THE THIRD YEAR OF STEPHEN'S EPISCOPATE.

This will be found translated at p. 378, Ep. lxxi.

THE SEVENTH CARTHAGINIAN COUNCIL UNDER CYPRIAN, THE THIRD ABOUT BAPTISM, FROM THREE PROVINCES OF AFRICA ; HELD ANNO DOMINI 256, IN THE THIRD YEAR OF STEPHEN'S EPISCOPATE.

This will be found translated and given in full on p. 565 of the present volume.

INTRODUCTORY NOTICE[1]

TO AN

ANONYMOUS TREATISE AGAINST THE HERETIC NOVATIAN.

THE writer of the following treatise was undoubtedly a contemporary of Cyprian, and wrote in the early part of the reign of Valerian (254–256), during an interval of peace to the Church. This much may be collected from the fact that he names one, and only one, persecution after that of Decius — namely, that of Gallus and Volusianus — and speaks of those who had lapsed under the former, as having been stedfast and victorious in the latter.[2] He is generally believed to have been an African, and Tillemont is only withheld from attributing the work to Cyprian himself by what he judges to be a difference of style. But although from the exordium it may be concluded that the writer was a bishop, yet, from his manifest uncertainty as to the fitting way to treat those who had lapsed, it is evident that Cyprian cannot have been the author; for that prelate, when the persecution of Gallus and Volusianus was just threatening, had already decided upon receiving to communion the penitents who had yielded to temptation under Decius.[3]

Ceillier[4] says that this treatise was written about the year 255, while Novatian was still alive,[5] and when the schism of Felicissimus was all but extinct.

Erasmus first published it among the known works of Cyprian in the year 1520.

---

[1] [By Dr. Wallis, editor of vol. xiii., Edinb. series.]
[2] Ch. (or sec.) 6, p. 659, *infra*.
[3] *Epistles*, liii. p. 336, *supra*.
[4] *Hist. Gén. des Auteurs*, tom. iii. ch. i. art. 4, sec. 2, note 4.
[5] Ch. (or sec.) 1, p. 657, *infra*.

NOTE.

THE American editor subjoins as follows : Cyprian, and Cornelius afterward, had decided, with their councils, that the lapsed should be classed, and dealt with accordingly, as (1) *Libellatici*, those who had compounded with the heathen, and *bought off* from offering sacrifice ; and (2) *Sacrificati*, those who had actually offered sacrifice to idols. Different degrees of discipline were awarded, but all were admitted to pardon finally.

A TREATISE AGAINST THE HERETIC NOVATIAN BY AN ANONYMOUS BISHOP.

THAT THE HOPE OF PARDON SHOULD NOT BE DENIED TO THE LAPSED.

1. WHILE I was meditating and impatiently tossing in my mind what I ought to do concerning those pitiable brethren who, wounded, not of their own will, but by the onset of a raging devil, have lived until now, that is, through a long course of time, in the endurance of their punishment; lo, there appeared opposed to me another enemy, and the adversary of his own paternal affection—the heretic Novatian—who not only, as it is signified in the Gospel, passed by the prostrate wounded man, as did the priest or the Levite, but by an ingenious and novel cruelty rather would slay the wounded man, by taking away the hope of salvation, by denying the mercy of his Father, by rejecting the repentance of his brother. Marvellous, how bitter, how harsh, how perverse are many things! But one more easily perceives the straw in another's eye than the beam in one's own. Let not the abrupt madness of that perfidious heretic move or disturb us however, beloved brethren, who, although he is placed in such great guilt of dissension and schism, and is separated from the Church, with sacrilegious temerity does not shrink from hurling back his charges upon us: for although he is now by himself made unclean, defiled with the filth of sacrilege, he contends that we are so. And although it is written that the dogs should remain without, and the apostle has taught that these same dogs must be shunned, as we read, for he says, "Beware of dogs, beware of evil workers,"[1] he does not cease stirring up his frenzy with barkings, after the manner of wolves seeking the gloomy darkness, where with his brutal cruelty he may easily rend in his dark caves the sheep snatched away from the Shepherd. Certainly he declares that he and his friends whom he collects are gold. Nor do we doubt but that deserters of the Church who have become apostates could now easily be converted into gold, but it must be that gold in which the first sins of the people of Israel were designated. But the gold and silver vessels which were wrested from the Egyptians continue in the Lord's power, that is, in Christ's Church; in which house if thou hadst continued, Novatian, thou hadst perchance been also a precious vessel; but now thou neither perceivest nor complainest that thou art changed into chaff and straw.

2. Why, therefore, shouldst thou be lifted up with vain things? Thou wilt gain loss rather than profit. Why, from the very fact that thou art become poorer, believest thou thyself rich? Hear in the Apocalypse the Lord's voice rebuking thee with righteous reproaches: "Thou sayest," says He, "I am rich, and increased with goods, and have need of nothing; and knowest not that thou art wretched, and miserable, and blind, and poor, and naked."[2] Let him think for certain that he possesses these riches of poverty, whoever he may be, that, forsaking the Church of Christ, with his darkened reason does not shrink from being turned to those rash leaders of schisms and authors of dissension, whom John calls antichrists, whom the Evangelist likens to chaff, whom the Lord Christ characterizes as thieves and robbers, as He Himself declares in the Gospel, saying that "he who entereth not by the door into the sheep-fold, but goeth down by some other way, the same is a thief and a robber."[3] Moreover, in the same He also says, "All who have come are thieves and robbers."[4] Who are such but the deserters of the faith, and the transgressors of God's Church, who strive against God's ordinance;—whom the Holy Spirit rightly rebukes by the prophet, saying, "Ye have taken counsel, but not by me; and *have made* a confederacy, but not by my Spirit, to add sin to sin."[5] What now can those most perverse friends of Novatian, even now the most unhappy[6] few, reply to

---

[1] Phil. iii. 2.

[2] Rev. iii. 17.
[3] John x. 1.
[4] John x. 8.
[5] Isa. xxx. 1.
[6] Infelicissimi. This is supposed to be a play upon the name of Felicissimus, referred to in Cyprian's letter, [xlviii. p. 325, *supra*].

these things, who have broken forth to such a folly of madness as to have no reverence either for God or man? Among them, shamelessly, and without any law of ordination, the episcopate is sought after; but among us in its own Sees, and in those of the throne delivered to it by God, it is renounced.[1] There the Truth says, "They reject me, that they may sacrifice to me; nor do they offer the holy oblations of the children of Israel, nor do they approach to offer the holy of holies, but they shall receive their ignominy in the error wherein they have erred."[2] Let it be enough in a few words to have proved what they are. Hear, therefore, O Novatians, among whom the heavenly Scriptures are read rather than understood; well, if they are not interpolated.[3] For your ears are closed, and your hearts darkened, seeing that ye admit no light from spiritual and saving warnings; as Isaiah says, "The servants of God are blinded."[4] And deservedly blinded, because the desire of schismatics is not in the law; which law points out to us the one and only Church in that ark, to wit, which was fashioned, by the providence of God, under Noah before the deluge, in which — to answer you quickly, O Novatian — we find that there were shut up not only clean animals, but also unclean; which ark was saved alone, with those who were in it, whereas the other things which were not found therein perished in the deluge. From that ark there were loosed two birds, a raven and a dove; and this raven truly bore the figure or type of impure men, and men who would be in perpetual darkness through the world's broad road, and of apostates who should arise, feeding on unclean things, and not turning themselves eventually to the Church; and as we read, we find that it was sent forth, and returned no more. Whoever should be found to resemble this bird, then, that is, the impure spirit, will no more be able to return to the Church, seeing that the Lord will forbid them, even if they should wish it, as He commanded Moses, saying, "Everything leprous[5] and impure, cast abroad outside the camp."[6] But the dove sent forth that returned, is signified by the man who does not delay, because he would have no rest for his feet. And Noah received it into the ark; and when it was sent forth again on the seventh day, received it, bearing in its mouth an olive leaf.

3. And I, beloved brethren, — as I not heedlessly meditate these things, and not in harmony with human wisdom, but as it is permitted to our minds by the condescension of the heavenly Lord, needfully and pertinently to conceive, — say that that dove signifies to us of itself a double type. Formerly, that is, from the beginning of the divine administration, it suggests its own figure, the first indeed and chief — that is, the figure of the Spirit. And by its mouth the sacrament of baptism which is provided for the salvation of the human race, and that by the heavenly plan it is celebrated in the Church only.[7] Moreover, three times sent forth from the ark, flying about through the air over the water, it already signified the sacraments of our Church. Whence also the Lord Christ charges upon Peter, and moreover also upon the rest of His disciples, "Go ye and preach the Gospel to the nations, baptizing them in the name of the Father, and of the Son, and of the Holy Ghost."[8] That is, that that same Trinity which operated figuratively in Noah's days through the dove, now operates in the Church spiritually through the disciples.

4. Let us now take the second character also of the dove sent forth from the ark, that is to say, in the time of the deluge, when all the abysses broke forth; when the cataracts of heaven were opened upon the earth, on account of the wickedness of men which they daily practised before the Lord; as said Moses, "And the Lord God saw that the wickednesses of men were overflowing upon the earth, and that all of them were remembering for evil from the beginning of their days; and He said, I will destroy man whom I have made from off the face of the earth, from man even unto cattle, and from the creeping thing even unto the fowls of the air."[9] Therefore in the time of the flood the dove is sent forth from the ark, when the waters were violently rushing with all their force upon the earth.

5. That ark bore the figure of the Church, as we have said above, which was stricken hither and thither to such a degree by the tumultuous waters. Therefore that deluge which happened under Noah showed forth the figure of the persecution which now lately was poured forth over the whole world. Moreover, by the waters, the cataracts broken forth meeting together on all sides, and growing, were signified the peoples which grew up for the desolation of the Church; as the Apocalypse teaches, saying, "The waters which thou sawest are peoples, and nations, and kingdoms."[10] Moreover, the dove which could not find rest for its feet, bore the likeness of the lapsed, who fell forgetful of the divine announcements, either ignorant in simplicity, or feigning in audacity. Of whom the Lord had intimated the future destruction in the Gospel in these

---

1 [Ep. xl. p. 319, *supra: et alibi.*]
2 Ezek. xliv. 10-13.
3 [See p. 602, note 12, *supra.*]
4 Isa. xlii. 19.
5 Varium.
6 Num. v. 2.

7 This passage is altogether corrupt and unintelligible; some force is necessary even to give it an appearance of meaning.
8 Matt. xxviii. 19. [For the next sentence see Acts ii. 33.]
9 Gen. vi. 5-7.
10 Rev. xvii. 15.

words, saying, "He who heareth my words and doeth them not, I will liken him to a foolish man, who built his house upon the sand: the tempests came and beat upon that house, and it fell; and great was its destruction."[1] And lest we should seem to have made the comparison inconsiderately of that dove bearing the image of the lapsed, the prophet rebukes the city as a dove, that is, the character of the lapsed, saying, "The dove hearkens not to the voice; that is, the illustrious and redeemed city receives not teaching, and trusted not in the Lord."[2]

6. Moreover, that that dove could not find rest for her feet, as we have said above, this signified the footsteps of those who deny; that is, those, wounded by the poison of the shining serpent, who sacrifice, turned towards their fall; which could not any further step upon the asp and the basilisk, and tread upon the dragon and the lion. For this power the Lord gave to His disciples, as He says in the Gospel: "Lo, I give unto you power to tread on all the power of the enemy, and upon serpents and scorpions; and they shall not harm you."[3] When, therefore, these so many and such malignant spirits are attacking and bestirring themselves for the destruction of the lapsed, a way of salvation is provided for the wounded, that with whatever strength they have they may drag themselves with their whole body, and betake themselves to their camp, wherein being received, they may heal their wounds with spiritual medicaments. Thus the dove received, after the intervention of a few days, is again sent forth from the ark; and returning, not only shows its firm footsteps, but moreover the signs of its peace and victory, in those olive leaves which it bore in its mouth. Therefore that twofold sending forth shows to us a twofold trial of persecution: the first, in which they who have lapsed have fallen conquered; the second, in which they who have fallen have come out conquerors. For to none of us is it doubtful or uncertain, beloved brethren, that they who in the first struggle — that is, in the Decian persecution — were wounded; afterwards, that is in the second encounter, persevered so bravely, that, despising the edicts of the princes of the world,[4] they maintained that unconquered; in that they did not fear, after the example of the good Shepherd, to give up their life, and to shed their blood, and not to shrink from any barbarity of the raging tyrant.

7. Behold how glorious, how dear to the Lord, are the people whom these schismatics do not shrink from calling "wood, hay, stubble;"[5] the equals of whom, that is, those who are even still

placed in the same guilt of their lapse, they presume must not be admitted to repentance. *This they judge* from that utterance of the Lord, where He says, "Whosoever shall deny me before men, him will I deny before my Father which is in heaven."[6] Oh grief! why do they strive against the Lord's precepts, that this offspring of Novatian, following the example of his father the devil, should now endeavour to put in force those things which Christ will do in the time of His judgment? *that is*, when Scripture says, "Vengeance is mine; and I will repay, saith the Lord."[7]

8. We will answer them *as to* that utterance of the Lord, which they ill understand, and ill explain to themselves. For that He says, "Whosoever shall deny me before men, him will I also deny before my Father which is in heaven," its meaning is assuredly with respect to future time — to the time at which the Lord shall begin to judge the secrets of men — to the time at which we must all stand before the judgment-seat of Christ — to the time at which many shall begin to say, "Lord, Lord, have we not prophesied in Thy name, and in Thy name cast out devils, and in Thy name done many wonderful works?"[8] And yet *they* shall hear the voice of the Lord saying, "Depart from me, all ye that have worked iniquity: I know you not."[8] Then shall it be fulfilled that He says, "I also will deny them." But whom will the Lord Christ chiefly deny, if not all of you heretics, and schismatics, and strangers to His name? For ye who were some time Christians, but now are Novatians, no longer Christians, have changed your first faith by a subsequent perfidy in the calling of your name. I should wish you to reply to your own proposition. Read and teach: whom of those who had failed or denied Him, while He was still with them, did our Lord deny? Yet also to the others of the disciples who had remained with Him He saith, "Will ye also go away?"[9] Even Peter, whom He had previously foretold as about to deny Him, when he had denied Him, He did not deny, but sustained; and He Himself soothed him when subsequently bitterly bewailing his denial.

9. What sort of folly is thine, Novatian, only to read what tends to the destruction of salvation, and to pass by what tends to mercy, when Scripture cries, and says, "Repent, ye who err: be converted in heart;"[10] and when the same prophet also exhorts, and says, "Be converted unto me with all your heart, in fasting, and weeping, and mourning; and rend your hearts, and not your garments; be ye converted to the

---

[1] Matt. vii. 26, 27.
[2] Zeph. iii. 1, 2, 3, LXX.
[3] Luke x. 19.
[4] *Scil.* Gallus and Volusianus (Pamel.).
[5] 1 Cor. iii. 12.

[6] Matt. x. 33.
[7] Heb. x. 30.
[8] Matt. vii. 22, 23.
[9] John vi. 67.
[10] Ezek. xviii. 30.

Lord your God: for He is merciful, and one who pities with great compassion?"[1]

10. Thus we have heard that the Lord is of great compassion. Let us hear what the Holy Spirit testifies by David: "If his children forsake my law, and walk not in my commandments; if they should profane my righteousness, and should not keep my precepts; I will visit their crimes with a rod, and their sins with stripes. But my mercy will I not utterly disperse from them."[2] Words like to these we read that the Lord said also by Ezekiel: "Son of man, the house of Israel has dwelt on its own land, and they have defiled it by their crimes: their uncleanness has become like that of a menstruous woman before my face. I have poured out my anger upon them, and I have scattered them among the nations; and I have judged them according to their sins, because they have defiled my holy name; and because it was said of them, This is the people of the Lord, I have spared them, because of my holy name, which the house of Israel despised among the nations."[3] And in conjunction with this he says, "Therefore say to the people of Israel, Thus saith the Lord, I spare you not, O house of Israel; but I will spare you on account of my holy name, which ye have defiled among the nations: and ye shall know that I am the Lord, when I shall be sanctified in you." Also the Lord to the same: "Son of man, say unto the people of Israel, Wherefore have ye spoken, saying, We are pining away in our sins, and how shall we be able to be saved? Say unto them, I live, saith the Lord: for I do not desire the death of the sinner; but I desire that the sinner should turn from his evil way, and live: therefore return ye from your evil way: why do ye give yourselves over to death, O house of Israel?"[4] So, too, by Isaiah the prophet: "I will not be angry with you for ever, nor will I abstain from defending you always."[5] And because Jeremiah the prophet, in the person of the sinful people, prays to the Lord, saying, "Amend us, O Lord, but in judgment, and not in anger, lest Thou make us few;"[6] Isaiah also added, and said, "For his sin I have slightly afflicted him; and I have stricken him, and have turned away my face from him: and he was afflicted, and went away sadly in his ways."[7] And because he labours, he added and said, "I have seen his ways, and I have healed him; and I have given him a true exhortation, peace upon peace;"[8] that to those who repent, and pray, and labour,

restoration is possible, because they would miserably perish, and because they would decline from Christ.

11. Moreover, this is proved in the Gospel, where is described that woman who was a sinner, who came to the house of a certain Pharisee whither the Lord had been bidden with His disciples, and she brought a vessel of ointment, and stood at the Lord's feet, and washed His feet with her tears, and wiped them with her hair, and pressed kisses upon them; so that that Pharisee was provoked, and said, "If this man were a prophet, he would know who and what sort of a woman this is who touches him; for she is a sinner."[9] Whence immediately the Lord, the remitter of sins and the receiver of the penitent, says, "Simon, I have somewhat to say unto thee. And he answered, saying, Master, say on. And the Lord, There was a certain creditor which had two debtors; one who had[10] five hundred pence, and the other fifty. When they had nothing to pay, he forgave both. And He asked, Which of these loved most? And Simon answered, Assuredly he to whom he forgave most. And He added, saying, Seest thou that woman? I entered into thy house, thou gavest me no kiss; but she hath not ceased to kiss my feet; thou washedst not my feet, but she has washed them with her tears, and wiped them with her hair; thou didst not anoint my feet with oil, but she hath anointed them. Wherefore I say unto thee, Simon, that her sins are forgiven her." Behold, the Lord grants the debt with His liberal kindness to both debtors; behold Him who pardons sins; behold the woman who was a sinner, penitent, weeping, praying, and receiving remission of her sins!

12. And now blush if thou canst, Novatian; cease to deceive the unwary with thy impious arguments; cease to frighten them with the subtlety of one particular. We read, and adore, and do not pass over the heavenly judgment of the Lord, where he says that He will deny him who denies Him. But does this mean the penitent? And why should I be taking pains so long to prove individual cases of mercies? since the mercy of God is not indeed denied to the Ninevites, although strangers, and placed apart from the law of the Lord, when they beseech it on account of the overthrow announced to their city. Nor to Pharaoh himself, resisting with sacrilegious boldness, when formerly he was stricken with plagues from heaven, and, turning to Moses and to his brother, said, "Pray to the Lord for me, for I have sinned."[11] At once the anger of God was suspended from him. And yet thou, O Novatian, judgest and declarest that the lapsed

---

[1] Joel ii. 12, 13.
[2] Ps. lxxxix. 30 et seq.
[3] Ezek. xxxvi. 17-23.
[4] Ezek. xxxiii. 10, 11.
[5] Isa. lvii. 16.
[6] Jer. x. 24.
[7] Isa. lvii. 17.
[8] Isa. lvii. 19.

[9] Luke vii. 39 et seq.
[10] "Habebat," but probably "debebat" — owed.
[11] Ex. ix. 28.

have no hope of peace and mercy, nor inclinest thine ear to the rebuke of the apostle, when he says, "Who art thou, who judgest another man's servant? To his own master he standeth or falleth. Yea, he shall stand. God is mighty to establish him." [1] Whence pertinently and needfully the Holy Spirit, in the person of those same lapsed people, rebukes you when He says, "Rejoice not over me, O mine enemy: because if I have fallen, I shall also rise again; and if I shall walk in darkness, the Lord is my light. I will bear the indignation of the Lord, because I have sinned against Him, until He justify my cause, and execute judgment and justice, and bring me forth to the light. I shall behold His righteousness; and she that is mine enemy shall see me, and shall cover herself with confusion." [2]

13. I beseech thee, hast thou not read, "Boast not, and speak not loftily, and let not arrogancy proceed out of your mouth: for the Lord lifteth the poor from the earth; He raiseth up the beggar from the dunghill, and maketh him to sit with the mighty ones of the people?" [3] Hast thou not read, that "the Lord resisteth the proud, and giveth grace to the humble?" [4] Hast thou not read, "Whoso exalteth himself shall be humbled?" [5] Hast thou not read, that "God destroys the remembrance of the proud, and does not forsake the memory of the lowly?" Hast thou not read, that "with what judgment a man shall judge he must be judged?" [6] Hast thou not read, that "he who hateth his brother is in darkness, and walketh in darkness, and knoweth not whither he goeth, because the darkness hath blinded his eyes?" [7] Whence, then, this Novatian has become both so wicked and so lost, so mad with rage of discord, I cannot discover, since he always in one household — that is, the Church of Christ — would have bewailed the sins of his neighbours as his own; [8] would have borne the burthens of his brethren, as the apostle exhorts; would have strengthened the faltering in the faith with heavenly counsel. But now, from the time when he began to practise that heresy of Cain which only delights in slaying, he does not even of late spare himself. But if he had read, that "the righteousness of the righteous shall not deliver him in the day on which he shall have erred, and the wickedness of the wicked shall not harm him from the day in which he shall have been converted," [9] he would long ago have repented in ashes, who is always opposed to penitents; who labours more readily in the destruction of those

things which are built and standing, than in the building up of those which are prostrate; who has once more made heathens of many most wretched brethren of ours, terrified by his false oppositions, by saying that the repentance of the lapsed is vain, and cannot avail them for salvation, although the Scripture cries aloud and says, "Remember whence thou hast fallen, and repent, or else I will come to thee except thou repent." [10] And indeed, writing to the seven churches, rebuking each one of them with its own crimes and sins, it said, Repent. To whom but to them, doubtless, whom He had redeemed at the great price of His blood?

14. O impious and wicked as thou art, thou heretic Novatian! who after so many and great crimes which in past times thou hadst known to be voluntarily committed in the Church, and before thou thyself wast an apostate in the family of God, hadst certainly taught that these might be abolished from memory if well-doing followed; according to the faith of the Scripture which says, "But if the wicked will turn from all his sins which he hath committed, and will do righteousness, he shall live in eternal life, and shall not die in his wickedness." [11] For the sins which he has committed shall be abolished from memory by the good deeds which succeed. Thou reconsiderest now, whether the wounds of the lapsed who have fallen, stripped bare by the devil, ought to be cured; *dashed down, as they are*, by the "violence of the flood which the serpent sent forth from his mouth after the woman." [12] But "What shall I say?" says the apostle. "Do I praise you? In this I praise you not; that ye come together not for the better, but for the worse." [13] For where there are "rivalries and dissensions among you, are ye not carnal, and walk according to man?" [14] Nor indeed ought we to wonder why this Novatian should dare now to practise such wicked, such severe things against the person of the lapsed, since we have previous examples of this kind of prevarication. Saul, that *once good* [15] man, besides other things, is subsequently overthrown by envy, and strives to do everything that is harsh and hostile against David. That Judas, who was chosen among the apostles, who was always of one mind and faithful in the house of God, himself subsequently betrayed God. [16]

And indeed the Lord had foretold that many should come as ravening wolves in the skins of sheep. Who are those ravening wolves but such as conspire with treacherous intent to waste the

---

[1] Rom. xiv. 4.
[2] Mic. vii. 8-10.
[3] 1 Sam. ii. 3-8.
[4] Jas. iv. 6.
[5] Matt. xxiii. 12.
[6] Matt. vii. 2.
[7] 1 John ii. 11.
[8] This refers to Novatian's letter in the name of the Roman people. [See p. 308. Compare p. 320, note 6.]
[9] Ezek. xxxiii. 12.

[10] Rev. ii. 5.
[11] Ezek. xviii. 21.
[12] Rev. xii. 15.
[13] 1 Cor. xi. 17.
[14] 1 Cor. iii. 3.
[15] 1 Sam. ix. 2.
[16] [A misconception of Judas, who seems to have been hypocritical from the first. John vi. 64.]

flock of Christ? As we read it written in Zechariah : " Lo, I raise up a shepherd in the land, who shall not visit that which is turned away, and will eat the flesh of the chosen, and tear their claws in pieces." [1] Similarly also in Ezekiel he rebukes shepherds of this kind, to wit, robbers and butchers (I will speak as he had thought [2]), saying, " O shepherds, wherefore do ye drink the milk, and eat up the curdled milk, and have brought that which is strong to nothing, and have not visited the weak, have not healed the halting, and have not recalled the wandering, and have permitted my people to wander among thorns and briers? For these things, says the Lord, lo, I will come against the shepherds, and I will require my sheep of their hands ; and I will drive them away, that they may not feed my sheep ; and my sheep shall no more be for them to devour, and I will seek them out as a shepherd his flock in the day in which there shall be darkness and cloud. Thus I will seek out my sheep, and I will seek them out in every place wherever they are scattered ; and I will seek out what had perished, and I will recall what had wandered, and what had halted I will heal, and what is weak I will watch over ; and I will feed my sheep with judgment." [3]

15. Who is it that says these things? Certainly He who, having left the ninety and nine sheep, went to seek that one which had wandered from His flock ; as David says, " I have gone astray like a sheep which was lost," [4] which being found Christ brings back, bearing on His shoulder the tender sinful one ; and He, rejoicing and exulting, having called His friends and domestics, says, " Rejoice with me ; for my sheep which was lost is found. I say," says He, " unto you, that there will be such joy in heaven over one sinner that repenteth." [5] And in continuation, He says : " Or what woman, having ten *denarii*, if she should lose one of the *denarii*, does not light a lamp, and all the day long clean out her house, seeking till she finds it? And when she has found it, she calls together her friends and neighbours, saying, Rejoice with me ; for I have found the denarius that I had lost. I say unto you, that such joy shall be in the sight of the angels of God over one sinner that repenteth." [5] But, on the other hand, they who do not repent of their wickedness, let them know from the answer of the Lord Himself what remaineth for them ; for we read in the Gospel, that " certain men came from the Galileans to the Lord, telling Him of those whose blood Pilate mingled with their sacrifices ; to whom

the Lord answered, saying, Think ye that those Galileans had been sinners above other Galileans, because they suffered such things? No ; for I say unto you, unless ye repent, ye shall all likewise perish. Or those eighteen upon whom the tower in Siloam fell, think ye that they were debtors to death above all men who dwell in Jerusalem? No ; I say unto you," said He, " that unless ye repent, ye shall all likewise perish." [6]

16. Let us then arouse ourselves as much as we can, beloved brethren ; and breaking away from the slumber of indolence and security, let us be watchful for the observance of the Lord's precepts. Let us with all our hearts seek for what we have lost, that we may be able to find ; because " to him that seeketh," says the Scripture, " it shall be given, and to him that knocketh it shall be opened." [7] Let us cleanse our house with spiritual cleanliness, that every secret and hidden place of our breast, truly enlightened by the light of the Gospel, may say, " Against Thee only have I sinned, and done this great evil in Thy sight." [8] Because the death of sinners is evil, and in hell there is no repentance. Let us have in contemplation especially the day of judgment and retribution, and what must be believed by all of us, and firmly maintained, that " there is no acceptance of persons with God ;" [9] since He commanded in Deuteronomy, that the person must not be accepted in judgment : " Thou shalt not accept," says He, " the person, neither shalt thou judge according to the least nor according to the greatest." [10] Like words to these He also said by Ezekiel : " All souls," said He, " are mine ; as the soul of the father, so is the soul of the son : the soul that hath sinned, it shall die." [11] It is then He who must be revered by us ; He must be held fast ; He must be propitiated by our full and worthy confession, " who has the power of sending soul and body to the Gehenna of fire," [12] — as it is written, " Behold, He cometh with many thousands of His messengers, to execute judgment upon all, and to destroy all the wicked, and to condemn all flesh, for all the deeds of the wicked which they have wickedly done, and for all the impious words which sinners have spoken about God." [13]

17. Like things to these also says Daniel : " I beheld a throne placed, and the Ancient of days sat upon it, and His clothing was as it were snow, and the hairs of His head as it were white wool : His throne was a flame of fire, its wheels were burning fire. A river of fire came forth before Him : thousand thousands ministered to

---

[1] Zech. xi. 16.
[2] This parenthesis is unintelligible. [i.e., not *shepherds*, but " butchers," in the prophet's thought, who speaks as follows, etc.]
[3] Ezek. xxxiv.
[4] Ps. cxix. 176.
[5] Luke xv. 6–10.

[6] Luke xiii. 1–5.
[7] Luke xi. 10.
[8] Ps. li. 4.
[9] Rom. ii. 11.
[10] Deut. i. 17.
[11] Ezek. xviii. 4.
[12] Matt. x. 28.
[13] Jude 14, 15.

Him, and thousand thousands stood before Him : He sat to judgment, and the books were opened." [1] And John still more plainly declares, both about the day of judgment and the consummation of the world, saying, " And when," said he, " He had opened the sixth seal, lo, there was a great earthquake ; and the sun became black as sackcloth of hair, and the whole moon became as of blood ; and the stars fell to the earth, even as a fig-tree, shaken by a mighty wind, casteth her unripe figs. And the heaven departed as a book when it is rolled up, and every mountain and island were moved from their places. And the kings of the earth, and all the great men, and the tribunes, and the rich men, and the strong men, and every slave, and every free man, hid themselves in the caves and in the caverns of the mountains ; saying to the mountains and to the rocks, Fall upon us, and hide us from the sight of the Father that sitteth upon the throne, and from the wrath of the Lamb : because the day of destruction cometh ; and who shall be able to stand ? " [2] Also in the same Apocalypse John says that this too was revealed to him. " I saw," says he, " a great throne, and one in white who sat upon it, from whose face the heaven and the earth fled away ; and their place was not found. And I saw the dead, great and small, standing before the sight of the Lord's throne : and the books were opened ; and another book was opened, which is (the book) of life : and every one was judged according to those things that were written in the book, according to their own works." [3] Moreover, too, the apostle, giving good advice, thus exhorts us, saying, " Let no one deceive you with vain words : for because of these things the wrath of God cometh upon the children of disobedience. Be not partakers with them." [4]

18. Let us, then, with the whole strength of our faith, give praise to God ; let us give our full confession, since the powers of heaven rejoice over our repentance, all the angels rejoice, and Christ also rejoices, who once again with full and merciful moderation exhorts us, laden with sins, overwhelmed with crimes, to cease from wickedness, saying, " Turn ye, and return from your impieties, and your iniquities shall not be to you for a punishment. Cast away from you all your impieties which ye have committed against me ; and make to yourselves a new heart and a new spirit. And why do ye deliver yourselves over to death, O house of Israel? For I do not desire the death of the sinner." [5] " I am He, I am He who blot out thy crimes, and I will not remember them. But do thou have in mind, and let us judge ; tell thou thy wickednesses first, that thou mayest be justified." [6] While the way of mercy, brethren, is open,[7] let us entreat God with full atonements ; let us humble ourselves, that we may be exalted ; let us acquiesce in the divine exhortation, whereby we may escape the day of the Lord and His anger. For thus He says : " Look, my son, upon the nations of men, and know who hath hoped in the Lord, and has been confounded ; or has remained in His commandments, and has been forsaken ; or has called upon Him, and He has despised him. For the Lord is loving and merciful, and forgiving in time of tribulation their sins to all those that seek after Him in truth." [8] Therefore He says, " First tell thou thy sins, that thou mayest be justified." Let there be first in your hand that prayer full of confession.[9]

---

[1] Dan. vii. 9, 10.
[2] Rev. vi. 12-17.
[3] Rev. xx. 11-13.
[4] Eph. v. 6, 7.

[5] Ezek. xviii. 30-32.
[6] Isa. xliii. 25, 26.
[7] [A virtual refutation of the dogma of purgatory, and all the trading in Masses which it involves. The pious Hirscher, in his *Kirchlichen Zustände der Gegenwart* (Tübingen, 1849; a translation of which, by the American editor of this series, was published, Oxford, 1852), bewails the corrupting influences of this system, though he died in the Papal communion.]
[8] Ecclus. ii. 10, 11.
[9] [The Lord's prayer; p. 454, note 1, *supra*.]

INTRODUCTORY NOTICE[1]

TO

ANONYMOUS TREATISE ON RE-BAPTISM.

THE following treatise on Re-baptism has been attributed by some authorities to the pen of one Ursinus,[1] a monk, who is said to have written in the fourth century. But internal evidence seems to point to a bishop as having been the writer;[2] and it seems very probable that it was written while the baptismal controversy was still agitating the Church, from the manner in which he refers to it. Moreover, the bitter attack contained in the first chapter was probably levelled against Cyprian, as the leader of the party in favour of the re-baptism of heretics. And this would hardly have been the case, at least the attack would not have been characterized by the same rancour, if Cyprian had already suffered martyrdom, and the controversy had lost its acrimony and intensity.

Rigaltius, who first edited the treatise, among his notes to the works of Cyprian, judged that it was written about the time of that Father. And Fell, Cave, Tillemont, and Galland, are of the same opinion. The two latter, indeed, conjecture that it was actually intended against Cyprian.

The difficulty arising to the translator from a loose and rambling style, and very involved argument, has been enhanced by a text singularly uncertain; but he ventures to think that there are points in the treatment of the subject which will not be without interest to the theological student of the present day, although its immediate purpose has passed away.

---

[1] [By Dr. Wallis, as before, p. 655.]   [2] Gennadius, *de Script. Eccles.*, cap. xxvii.   [3] Sec. x.

A TREATISE ON RE-BAPTISM BY AN ANONYMOUS WRITER.

***

ARGUMENT. — THAT THEY WHO HAVE ONCE BEEN WASHED IN THE NAME OF THE LORD JESUS CHRIST, OUGHT NOT TO BE RE-BAPTIZED.

1. I OBSERVE that it has been asked among the brethren what course ought specially to be adopted towards the persons of those who, although baptized in heresy, have yet been baptized in the name of our Lord Jesus Christ,[1] and subsequently departing from their heresy, and fleeing as supplicants to the Church of God, should repent with their whole hearts, and only now perceiving the condemnation of their error, implore from the Church the help of salvation. *The point is* whether, according to the most ancient custom and ecclesiastical tradition, it would suffice, after that baptism which they have received outside *the Church* indeed, but still in the name of Jesus Christ our Lord, that only hands should be laid upon them by the bishop for their reception of the Holy Spirit, and this imposition of hands would afford them the renewed and perfected seal of faith; or whether, indeed, a repetition of baptism would be necessary for them, as if they should receive nothing if they had not obtained baptism afresh, just as if they were never baptized in the name of Jesus Christ. And therefore some things were talked about as having been written and replied on this new question, wherein both sides endeavoured with the greatest eagerness to demolish what had been written by their antagonists. In which kind of debate, as it appears to me, no controversy or discussion could have arisen at all if each one of us had been content with the venerable authority of all the churches,[2] and with becoming humility had desired to innovate nothing, as observing no kind of room for contradiction. For everything which is both doubtful and ambiguous, and is established in opinions differing *among those* of prudent and faithful men, if it is judged to be against the ancient and memorable and most solemn observance of all those holy and faithful men who have deserved well, ought assuredly to be condemned; since in a matter once arranged and ordained, whatever that is which is brought forward against the quiet and peace of the Church, will result in nothing but discords, and strifes, and schisms. And in this no other fruit can be found but this alone; that one man, whoever he is, should be vaingloriously declared among certain fickle men to be of great prudence and constancy: and, being gifted with the arrogance of heretics, whose only consolation in destruction is the not appearing to sin alone, should be renowned among those that are most similar and agreeable to himself, as having corrected the errors and vices of all the churches. For this is the desire and purpose of all heretics, to frame as many calumnies of this kind as possible against our most holy mother the Church, and to deem it a great glory to have discovered anything that can be imputed to her as a crime, or even as a folly. And since it becomes no faithful man of sound mind to dare to hold such a view, especially no one who is ordained in any clerical office at all, and much more in the episcopal order, it is like a prodigy for bishops themselves to devise such scandals, and not to fear to unfold too irreverently against the precept of the law and of all the Scriptures, with their own disgrace and risk, the disgrace of their mother the Church — if they think that there is any disgrace in this matter; although the Church has no disgrace in this instance, save in the error of such men as these themselves. Therefore it is the more grievous sin in men of this kind, if that which is blamed by them in the most ancient observance, as if it were not rightly done, is manifestly and forcibly shown as well to have been rightly observed by those who were before us, as to be rightly observed also by us; so that even if we should engage in the controversy with equal arguments on both sides, yet, since that which was innovated could not be

---

[1] [" In the name," etc., implies as Jesus Christ commanded, St. Matt. xxviii. 19.]
[2] [This was assumed by the Westerns to be the *general* rule, whereas it was only *local.* See p. 408, note 7, *supra.*]

established without dissension among the brethren and mischief to the Church, assuredly it ought not, — right or wrong, as they say, that is, contrary to what is good and proper — rashly to be flung like a stain upon our mother the Church; and the ignominy of this audacity and impiety ought with reason to be attached to those who should attempt this. But since it is not in our power, according to the apostle's precept, "to speak the same thing, that there be not schisms among us;"[1] yet, as far as we can, we strive to demonstrate the true condition of this argument, and to persuade turbulent men, even now, to mind their own business, as we shall even attain a great deal if they will at length acquiesce in this sound advice.[2] And therefore we shall, as is needful, collect into one mass whatever passages of the Holy Scriptures are pertinent to this subject. And we shall manifestly harmonize, as far as possible, those which seem to be differing or of various meaning; and we shall to the extent of our poor ability examine both the utility and advantage of each method, that we may recommend to all the brethren, that the most wholesome form and peaceful custom be adopted in the Church.

2. To such, then, as approach to a discussion of saving and modern, that is, of spiritual and evangelical baptism, there occurs first of all the announcement universally well known, made and begun by John the Baptist, who, somewhat departing from the law, that is, from the most ancient baptism of Moses, and preparing the way of the new and true grace, both preoccupied the ears of the Jews gradually by the baptism of water and of repentance which for the time he practised, and took possession of them with the announcement of a spiritual baptism that was to come, exhorting them, and saying, "He that cometh after me is mightier than I, whose shoe's latchet I am not worthy to unloose: He shall baptize you with the Holy Ghost, and with fire;"[3] and for this reason we also ought to make a beginning of this discourse from this point. For in the Acts of the Apostles, the Lord after His resurrection, confirming this same word of John, "commanded them that they should not depart from Jerusalem, but wait for that promise of the Father which, *saith He*, ye have heard from me; for John truly baptized with water, but ye shall be baptized with the Holy Ghost not many days hence."[4] And Peter also related these same words of the Lord, when he gave an account of himself to the apostles, saying: "And as I began to speak, the Holy

Ghost fell upon them as on us at the beginning; and I remembered the word of the Lord, how that He said, John indeed baptized with water, but ye shall be baptized with the Holy Ghost. If, therefore, He gave them a like gift as to us, who believe on the Lord Jesus Christ, who was I, that I could withstand the Lord?"[5] And again: "Men and brethren, ye know how from ancient days God made choice among us, that the Gentiles by my mouth should hear the word of the Gospel, and believe. And God, who knoweth the hearts, bare them witness, giving them the Holy Spirit, even as He did unto us."[6] And on this account we ought to consider what is the force and power of this saying. For the Lord says to them who would have to be subsequently baptized because they should believe, that they must be baptized not in like manner as by Him in water, unto repentance, but in the Holy Ghost. And of this announcement, as assuredly none of us can doubt it, it is plain on what principle men were baptized in the Holy Spirit. For it was peculiarly in the Holy Spirit Himself alone that they who believed were baptized. For John distinguished, and said that he indeed baptized in water, but that one should come who would baptize in the Holy Ghost, by the grace and power of God; and they are so by the *Spirit's* bestowal and operation of hidden results. Moreover, they are so no less in the baptism of the Spirit and of water. They are so, besides, also in the baptism of every one in his own proper blood.[7] Even as the Holy Scriptures declare to us, from which we shall adduce evident proofs throughout each individual instance of those things which we shall narrate.

3. And to these things thou perchance, who art bringing in some novelty, mayest immediately and impatiently reply, as thou art wont, that the Lord said in the Gospel: "Except a man be born again of water and of the Spirit, he cannot enter into the kingdom of heaven."[8] Whence it manifestly appears that that baptism alone is profitable wherein also the Holy Spirit can dwell; for that upon the Lord Himself, when He was baptized, the Holy Spirit descended, and that His deed and word are quite in harmony, and that such a mystery can consist with no other principle. To which reply none of us is found either so senseless or so stubborn as to dare, contrary to right or contrary to truth, to object, for instance, so to the doing of things in their integrity, and by all means in the Church, and the observation of them according to the order of discipline perpetually by us. But if, in the same New Testament, those things which in that mat-

---

[1] 1 Cor. i. 10.
[2] [The bitterness with which Vincent follows up the assumption that there was a general custom of all the churches, shows how sadly this controversy became envenomed in the West. Cap. vi. is a blemish on his *Commonitory*.]
[3] Matt. iii. 11.
[4] Acts i. 4, 5.

[5] Acts xi. 15–17.
[6] Acts xv. 7, 8.
[7] There is something needed to make the connection of this passage complete.
[8] John iii. 3, 5.

ter we come upon as associated, be sometimes found in some sort divided, and separated, and arranged, and ordered just as if they were by themselves; let us see whether these solitary instances by themselves may not sometimes be such as are not imperfect, but, as it were, entire and complete. For when by imposition of the bishop's hands the Holy Spirit is given to every one that believes, as in the case of the Samaritans, after Philip's baptism, the apostles did to them by laying on of hands; in this manner also they conferred on them the Holy Spirit. And that this might be the case, they themselves prayed for them, for as yet the Holy Spirit had not descended upon any of them, but they had only been baptized in the name of the Lord Jesus. Moreover, our Lord after His resurrection, when He had breathed upon His apostles, and had said to them, "Receive ye the Holy Ghost,"[1] thus and thus only bestowed upon them the Spirit.

4. And this being found to be so, what thinkest thou, my brother? If a man be not baptized by a bishop, so as even at once to have the imposition of hands, and should yet die before having received the Holy Spirit, should you judge him to have received salvation or not? Because, indeed, both the apostles themselves and the disciples, who also baptized others, and were themselves baptized by the Lord, did not at once receive the Holy Spirit, for He had not as yet been given, because that Jesus had not as yet been glorified. And after His resurrection no small interval of time elapsed before that took place, — even as also the Samaritans, when they were baptized by Philip, *did not receive the gift* until the apostles invited from Jerusalem to Samaria went down to them to lay hands upon them, and conferred on them the Holy Spirit by the imposition of hands. Because in that interval of time any one of them who had not attained the Holy Spirit, might have been cut off by death, and die defrauded of the grace of the Holy Spirit. And it cannot be doubted also, that in the present day this sort of thing is usual, and happens frequently, that many after baptism depart from this life without imposition of the bishop's hands, and yet are esteemed perfected believers. Just as the Ethiopian eunuch, when he was returning from Jerusalem and reading the prophet Isaiah, and was in doubt, having at the Spirit's suggestion heard the truth from Philip the deacon, believed and was baptized; and when he had gone up out of the water, the Spirit of the Lord took away Philip, and the eunuch saw him no more. For he went on his way rejoicing, although, as thou observest, hands were not laid on him by the bishop, that he might receive the Holy Spirit. But if thou ad-

mittest this, and believest it to be saving, and dost not gainsay the opinion of all the faithful, thou must needs confess this, that even as this principle proceeds to be more largely discussed, that other also can be more broadly established; that is, that by the imposition of hands alone of the bishop — because baptism in the name of our Lord Jesus Christ has gone before it — may the Holy Spirit also be given to another man who repents and believes. Because the Holy Scripture has affirmed that they who should believe in Christ, must needs be baptized in the Spirit; so that these also may not seem to have anything less than those who are perfectly Christians; lest it should be needful to ask what sort of a thing was that baptism which they have attained in the name of Jesus Christ. Unless, perchance, in that former discussion also, about those who should only have been baptized in the name of Jesus Christ, thou shouldst decide that they can be saved even without the Holy Spirit, or that the Holy Spirit is not accustomed to be bestowed in this manner only, but by the imposition of the bishop's hands; or even shouldst say that it is not the bishop alone who can bestow the Holy Spirit.

5. And if this be so, and the occurrence of any of these things cannot deprive a man who believes, of salvation, thou thyself also affirmest that the fact of the mystery of the faith being divided in a manner, and its not being, as thou contendest, consummated, where necessity intervenes, cannot take away salvation from a believing and penitent man. Or if thou sayest that a man of this kind cannot be saved, we deprive all bishops of salvation, whom thou thus engagest, under risks as assured as possible, to be bound themselves to afford help to all those who live under their care, and are in weak health, in their districts, scattered up and down, because other men of less degree among the clerics who venture cannot confer the same benefit; so that the blood of those who shall appear to have departed from this life without the benefit would have, of necessity, to be required at the hands of the bishops. And further, as you are not ignorant, the Holy Spirit is found to have been given to men who believe, by the Lord without baptism of water, as is contained in the Acts of the Apostles after this manner: "While Peter was still speaking these words, the Holy Ghost fell upon all them who heard the word. And they who were of the circumcision which believed were astonished, as many as came with Peter, because that on the Gentiles also was poured out the gift of the Holy Spirit. For they heard them speak with their tongues, and they magnified God. Then answered Peter, Can any man forbid water, that these should not be baptized, who have received the Holy Ghost as well as we?

---

[1] John xx. 22.

And he commanded them to be baptized in the name of Jesus Christ."[1] Even as Peter also subsequently most abundantly taught us about the same Gentiles, saying: "And He put no difference between us and them, their hearts being purified by faith."[2] And there will be no doubt that men may be baptized with the Holy Ghost without water, — as thou observest that these were baptized before they were baptized with water; that the announcements of both John and of our Lord Himself were satisfied, — forasmuch as they received the grace of the promise both without the imposition of the apostle's hands and without the laver, which they attained afterwards. And their hearts being purified, God bestowed upon them at the same time, in virtue of their faith, remission of sins; so that the subsequent baptism conferred upon them this benefit alone, that they received also the invocation of the name of Jesus Christ, that nothing might appear to be wanting to the integrity of their service and faith.[3]

6. And this also, — looking at it from the opposite side of this discussion, — those disciples of our Lord themselves attained, upon whom, being previously baptized, the Holy Spirit at length came down on the day of Pentecost, descending from heaven indeed by the will of God, not of His own accord, but effused for this very office, and moreover upon each one of them. Although these were already righteous, and, as we have said, had been baptized by the Lord's baptism even as the apostles themselves, who nevertheless are found on the night on which He was apprehended to have all deserted Him. And even Peter himself, who boasted that he would persevere in his faith, and most obstinately resisted the prediction of the Lord Himself, yet at last denied Him, that by this means it might be shown to us, that whatever sins they had contracted in the meantime and in any manner, these same sins, by the faith in them subsequently attested as sincere, were without doubt put away by the baptism of the Holy Spirit. Nor, as I think, was it for any other reason that the apostles had charged those whom they addressed in the Holy Spirit, that they should be baptized in the name of Christ Jesus, except that the power of the name of Jesus invoked upon any man by baptism might afford to him who should be baptized no slight advantage for the attainment of salvation, as Peter relates in the Acts of the Apostles, saying: "For there is none other name under heaven given among men whereby we must be saved."[4] As also the Apostle Paul unfolds, showing that God hath exalted our Lord Jesus, and "given Him a name, that it may be above every name, that in the name of Jesus all should bow the knee, of things heavenly and earthly, and under the earth, and every tongue should confess that Jesus is Lord in the glory of God the Father." And he on whom, when he should be baptized, invocation should be made in the name of Jesus, although he might obtain baptism under some error, still would not be hindered from knowing the truth at some time or another, and correcting his error, and coming to the Church and to the bishop, and sincerely confessing our Jesus before men; so that then, when hands were laid upon him by the bishop, he might also receive the Holy Spirit, and he would not lose that former invocation of the name of Jesus. Which none of us may disallow, although this invocation, if it be standing bare and by itself, could not suffice for affording salvation, lest on this principle we should believe that even Gentiles and heretics, who abuse the name of Jesus, could attain unto salvation without the true and entire thing. Yet it is extremely useful to believe that this invocation of the name of Jesus, together with the correction of error and the acknowledgment of the belief of the truth, and with the putting away of all stain of past conversation, if rightly performed with the mystery of God among men of this kind, obtains a place which it would not have had, and finally, in the true faith and for the maintenance of the integrity of the sign, is no hindrance, when its supplement which had been wanting is added; and that it is consistent with good reason, with the authority of so many years, and so many churches and apostles and bishops; even as it is the very greatest disadvantage and damage to our most holy mother Church, now for the first time suddenly and without reason to rebel against former decisions after so long a series of so many ages. For not for any other reason Peter — who had already been baptized and had been asked what he thought of the Lord by the Lord Himself, and the truth of the revelation of the Father in heaven being bestowed on him had confessed that Christ was not only our Lord, but was the Son of the living God — was shown subsequently to have withstood the same Christ when He made announcement of His passion, and therefore was set forth as being called Satan. *For no other reason* except because it would come to pass that some, although varying in their own judgment, and somewhat halting in faith and doctrine, although they were baptized in the name of Jesus, yet, if they had been able to rescind their error in some interval of time, were not on that account cut off from salvation; but at any time that they had come to the right mind, obtained by repentance a sound hope of salvation, espe-

---

[1] Acts x. 44–48.
[2] Acts xv. 9.
[3] [It was a notable compliance with the example of Christ, Matt. iii. 15. "They had received," etc., yet that was no reason why the ordinance of Christ should be slighted.]
[4] Acts iv. 12.

cially when they received the Holy Spirit, to be baptized by Whom is the duty of every man, they would have intended some such thing. Even as we do not apprehend that Peter in the Gospel suffered this alone, but all the disciples, to whom, though already baptized, the Lord afterwards says, that "all ye shall be offended in me," [1] all of whom, as we observe, having amended their faith, were baptized after the Lord's resurrection with the Holy Spirit. So that not without reason we also in the present day may believe that men, amended from their former error, may be baptized in the Holy Spirit, who, although they were baptized with water in the name of the Lord, might have had a faith somewhat imperfect. Because it is of great importance whether a man is not baptized at all in the name of our Lord Jesus Christ, or indeed whether in some respect he halts when he is baptized with the baptism of water, which is of less account provided that afterwards a sincere faith in the truth is evident in the baptism of the Spirit, which undoubtedly is of greater account.

7. Neither must you esteem what our Lord said as being contrary to this treatment: "Go ye, teach the nations; baptize them in the name of the Father, and of the Son, and of the Holy Ghost." [2] Because, although this is true and right, and to be observed by all means in the Church, and moreover has been used to be observed, yet it behoves us to consider that invocation of the name of Jesus ought not to be thought futile by us on account of the veneration and power of that very name, in which name all kinds of power are accustomed to be exercised, and occasionally some even by men outside the Church. But to what effect are those words of Christ, who said that He would deny, and not know, those who should say to Him in the day of judgment, "Lord, Lord, have we not prophesied in Thy name, and in Thy name cast out demons, and in Thy name done many wonderful works," when He answered them, even with emphasis,[3] "I never knew you; depart from me, ye who work iniquity," [4] unless that it should be shown to us, that even by those who work iniquity might these good works also be done, by the superfluous [5] energy of the name of Christ? Therefore ought this invocation of the name of Jesus to be received as a certain beginning of the mystery of the Lord common to us and to all others, which may afterwards be filled up with the remaining things. Otherwise such an invocation would not avail if it should remain alone, because after the death of a man in this position there cannot be added to him anything

at all, nor supplemented, nor can, in anything, avail him in the day of judgment, when they shall begin to be reproached by our Lord with those things which we have above mentioned, none of whom notwithstanding in this present time may by any man be so hardly and cruelly prohibited from aiding themselves in those ways which we have above shown.

8. But these things thou wilt, as thou art wont, contradict, by objecting to us, that when they were baptized, the disciples were baptized perfectly, and rightly, and not as these heretics; and this thou must needs assume from their condition, and His who baptized them. And therefore we reply to this proposition of thine, not as accusers of the Lord's disciples, but as we are constrained, because it is necessary that we should investigate by reasons where and when, and in what measure, salvation has been bestowed on each of us. For that our Lord was born, and that He was the Christ, appeared by many reasons to be believed, not unjustly, by His disciples, because He had been born of the tribe of Judah, of the family of David, and in the city of Bethlehem; and because He had been announced to the shepherds by the angels at the same moment that there was born to them a Saviour; because His star being seen in the east, He had been most anxiously sought for and adored by the Magi, and honoured with illustrious presents and distinguished offerings; because while still a youth, sitting in the temple with the doctors of the law, He wisely, and with the admiration of all, had disputed; because when He was baptized He had been glorified, as had happened to none others, by the descent of the Holy Spirit from the opened heavens, and by its abode upon Him; and moreover by the testimony of His Father, and also of John the Baptist; because, beyond the inferior capacity of man, He understood the hearts and thoughts of all men; because He cured and healed weaknesses, and vices, and diseases, with very great power; because He bestowed remissions of sins, with manifest attestation; because He expelled demons at His bidding; because He purified lepers with a word; because, by converting water into wine, He enlarged the nuptial festivity with marvellous joyfulness; because He restored or granted sight to the blind; because He maintained the doctrine of the Father with all confidence; because in a desert place He satisfied five thousand men with five loaves; because the remains and the fragments filled more than twelve baskets; because He everywhere raised up the dead, according to His mercy; because He commanded the winds and the sea to be still; because He walked with His feet upon the sea; because He absolutely performed all miracles.

[1] Mark xiv. 27.
[2] Matt. xxviii. 19.
[3] " Jurejurando."
[4] Mark xiv. 27.
[5] [Query, superabounding?]

9. By which things, and by many deeds of this kind tending to His glory, it appeared to follow as a consequence, that in whatever manner the Jews think about Christ, and although they do not believe concerning Jesus Christ our Lord, that even they themselves thought that such and so great a one would without any death endure to eternity, and would possess the kingdom of Israel, and of the whole world for ever; and that it should not be destroyed. Whence, moreover, the Jews dared to seize Him by force, and anoint Him for the kingdom, which indeed He was compelled to evade; and therefore His disciples thought that in no other way would He bestow upon them eternal life, except He Himself had first continued this temporal life into that eternal one in His own experience. In fine, when they were passing through Galilee, Jesus said to them, "The Son of man is to be delivered into the hands of men, and they will kill Him; and after three days He shall rise again." [1] and they were greatly grieved, because, as we have said, they had formed a very different notion previously in their minds and hearts. And again, this also was the speech of the Jews, in contradiction against Him, when He taught them of Himself, and announced future things to them, and they said, "We have heard out of the law that Christ abideth for ever: and how sayest thou that the Son of man must be lifted up?" [2] And so there was this same presumption concerning Christ in the mind of the disciples, even as Peter himself, the leader and chief of the apostles, broke forth into that expression of his own incredulity. For when he, together with the others, had been asked by the Lord what he thought about Him, that is, whom he thought Him to be, and had first of all confessed the truth, saying that He was the Christ the Son of the living God, and therefore was judged blessed by Him because he had arrived at this truth, not after the flesh, but by the revelation of the heavenly Father; yet this same *Peter*, when Jesus began to show His disciples that He must go to Jerusalem, and suffer many things from the elders, and priests, and scribes, and be killed, and after the third day rise again from the dead; nevertheless that true confessor of Christ, after a few days, taking Him aside, began to rebuke Him, saying, "Be propitious to Thyself: this shall not be;" [3] so that on that account he deserved to hear from the Lord, "Get thee behind me, Satan; [4] thou art an offence unto me, because he savoured not the

things which are of God, but those things which are of men." Which rebuke against Peter became more and more apparent when the Lord was apprehended, and, frightened by the damsel, he said, "I know not what thou sayest, neither know I thee;" [5] and again when, using an oath, he said this same thing; and for the third time, cursing and swearing, he affirmed that he knew not the man, and not once, but frequently, denied Him. [6] And this disposition, because it was to continue to him even to the Lord's passion, was long before made manifest by the Lord, that we also might not be ignorant of it. Again, after the Lord's resurrection, one of His disciples, Cleopas, when he was, according to the error of all his fellow-disciples, sorrowfully telling what had happened to the Lord Himself, as if to some unknown person, spoke thus, saying of Jesus the Nazarene, "who was a prophet mighty in deed and in word before God and all the people; how the chief priests and our rulers delivered Him to be condemned to death, and fastened Him to the cross. But we trusted that it had been He which should have redeemed Israel." [7] And in addition to these things, all the disciples also judged the declaration of the women who had seen the Lord after the resurrection to be idle tales; and some of themselves, when they had seen Him, believed not, but doubted; and they who were not then present believed not at all until they had been subsequently by the Lord Himself in all ways rebuked and reproached; because His death had so offended them that they thought that He had not risen again, who they had believed ought not to have died, because contrary to their belief He had died once. And thus, as far as concerns the disciples themselves, they are found to have had a faith neither sound nor perfect in such matters as we have referred to; and what is much more serious, they moreover baptized others, as it is written in the Gospel according to John.

10. Besides, what wilt thou say of those who are in many cases baptized by bishops of very bad character, who yet at length, when God so wills it, convicted of their crimes, are even deprived of their office itself, or absolutely of communion? Or what wilt thou decide of those who may have been baptized by bishops, whose opinions are unsound, or who are very ignorant — when they may not have spoken clearly and honestly, or even have spoken otherwise than is fit in the tradition of the sacrament, or at least may have asked anything, or asking, have heard from those who answered what ought by no means

---

[1] Mark ix. 30.
[2] John xii. 34.
[3] Matt. xvi. 22.
[4] [Isa. xiv. 12. The sin of Lucifer had, very possibly, been this of rebelling against the Incarnation and the introduction thereby of an order of beings higher than himself. Hence our Lord recognised in Peter's words the voice of the old adversary, and called him "Satan." A premonition of his lapse.]

[5] Matt. xxvi. 70.
[6] [It has been profoundly felt, that, as the Church of Rome in her early rectitude (Rom. i. 8) reflected Peter's *confession*, so in her lapse (Rom. xi. 20, 21) she reflects this terrible rebuke. If she was once identified with Peter's *Rock*, so now, alas! with Peter's *Satan*.]
[7] Luke xxiv. 20, 21.

to be so asked or answered? And still this does not greatly injure that true faith of ours, although, moreover, these more simple men may deliver the mystery of the faith without the elegance and order that thou wouldst use. And thou wilt assuredly say, with that marvellous carefulness of thine, that these too should be baptized again, since this is especially the thing which is wanting to them, or hinders their being able to receive, uncorrupted, that divine and inviolable mystery of the faith. And yet, O excellent man, let us attribute and allow to the heavenly agencies their power, and let us concede to the condescension of the divine majesty its appropriate operations; and understanding how great is the advantage therein, let us gladly acquiesce in it. And thus, as our salvation is founded in the baptism of the Spirit, which for the most part is associated with the baptism of water, if indeed baptism shall be given by us, let it be conferred in its integrity and with solemnity, and with all those means which are written; and let it be administered without any disconnection of anything. Or if, by the necessity of the case, it should be administered by an inferior cleric, let us wait for the result, that it may either be supplied by us,[1] or reserved to be supplied by the Lord. If, however, it should have been administered by strangers, let this matter be amended as it can and as it allows. Because outside the Church there is no Holy Spirit, sound faith moreover cannot exist, not alone among heretics, but even among those who are established in schism. And for that reason, they who repent and are amended by the doctrine of the truth, and by their own faith, which subsequently has been improved by the purification of their heart, ought to be aided only by spiritual baptism, that is, by the imposition of the bishop's hands, and by the ministration of the Holy Spirit. Moreover, the perfect seal of faith has been rightly accustomed to be given in this manner and on this principle in the Church. So that the invocation of the name of Jesus, which cannot be done away, may not seem to be held in disesteem by us; which assuredly is not fitting; although such an invocation, if none of those things of which we have spoken should follow it, may fail and be deprived of the effect of salvation. For when the apostle said that there was " one baptism,"[2] it must needs have been by the continued effect of the invocation of the name of Jesus, because, once invoked, it cannot be taken away by any man, even although we might venture, against the decision of the apostles, to repeat it by giving too much, yea, by the desire of superadding baptism. If he who returns to the Church be unwilling again to be baptized, the re-

sult will be that we may defraud him of the baptism of the Spirit, whom we think we must not defraud of the baptism of water.

11. And what wilt thou determine against the person of him who hears the word,[3] and haply taken up in the name of Christ, has at once confessed, and has been punished before it has been granted him to be baptized with water? Wilt thou declare him to have perished because he has not been baptized with water? Or, indeed, wilt thou think that there may be something from without that helps him to salvation, although he is not baptized with water? Thy thinking him to have perished will be opposed by the sentence of the Lord, who says, "Whosoever shall confess me before men, him will I also confess before my Father which is in heaven;"[4] because it is no matter whether he who confesses for the Lord is a hearer of the word or a believer, so long as he confesses that same Christ whom he ought to confess; because the Lord, by confessing him, in turn Himself graces His confessor before his Father with the glory of his martyrdom, as He promised. But this assuredly ought not to be taken too liberally, as if it could be stretched to such a point as that any heretic can confess the name of Christ who notwithstanding denies Christ Himself; that he believes on another Christ, when Christ avows that it cannot avail him at all; forasmuch as the Lord said that He[5] must needs be brought to confession by us before men, which cannot be done without Him, and without veneration of His name. And therefore both[6] ought to stand by the confessor, sound, and sincere, and uncontaminated, and inviolated, without any choice being made of the confessor himself, whether he is righteous or a sinner, and a perfect Christian or an imperfect one, who has not feared to confess the Lord at his own greatest peril. And this is not contrary to the former discussion, because there is left therein time for the correction of many things which are bad, and because certain things are conceded to the very name only of our Lord; while martyrdom cannot be consummated except in the Lord and by the Lord Himself, and therefore nobody can confess Christ without His name, nor can the name of Christ avail any one for confession without Christ Himself.

12. Wherefore the whole of this discussion must be considered, that it may be made clearer. For the invocation of the name of Jesus can only be an advantage if it shall be subsequently properly supplemented, because both prophets

---

[1] *Scil.* the bishop. [The plural of "solidarity." See p. 128, note 5, *supra*, and Elucidation XI. p. 159.]
[2] Eph. iv. 5.

[3] By him who hears the word is meant a catechumen (Rigaltius). [Bunsen, vol. ii. p. 317. He quotes the *Apostolical Constitutions* (Alexandria), "Let the catechumens be three years hearing the word," etc.]
[4] Matt. x. 32.
[5] The original interpolates " non."
[6] [*Scil.* baptisms (?) i.e., of water and of blood.]

and apostles have so declared. For James says in the Acts of the Apostles: "Men and brethren, hearken: Simon hath declared how God at the first visited the Gentiles, to take out of them a people for His name. And to this agree the words of the prophets; as it is written, After this I will return, and will build again the tabernacle of David, which has fallen down; and I will build again the ruins thereof, and I will raise it up anew; that the residue of men may seek the Lord, and all the Gentiles, upon whom my name is called upon them, saith the Lord, who doeth these things." [1] Therefore also the residue of men, that is, some of the Jews and all the Gentiles upon whom the name of the Lord is called, may and of necessity must seek the Lord, because that very invocation of the name affords them the opportunity, or even imposes on them the necessity, of seeking the Lord. And with these they prescribe the Holy Scriptures — whether all or only some of them — to discuss still more boldly concerning the truth than with the Gentiles upon whom the name of the Lord Jesus, the Son of the living God, has not been invoked, as it likewise has not upon the Jews who only receive the Old Testament Scriptures. And thus men of both of these kinds, that is, Jews and Gentiles, fully believing as they ought, are in like manner baptized. But heretics who are already baptized in water in the name of Jesus Christ must only be baptized with the Holy Spirit; and in Jesus, which is " the only name given under heaven whereby we must be saved," death is reasonably despised, although, if they continue as they are, they cannot be saved, because they have not sought the Lord after the invocation of His name upon them, — even as those who, on account of false Christs, perchance have refused to believe, of whom the Lord says, "Take heed that no man lead you into error. For many shall come in my name, saying, I am Christ, and shall lead many into error." [2] And again He says: "Then if any man shall say unto you, Lo here is Christ, or lo there; believe it not. For there shall arise false Christs, and false prophets, and shall show great signs and wonders; so that, if it were possible, even the very elect shall be deceived." [3] And these miracles, without doubt, they shall then do under the name of Christ; in which name some even now appear to do certain miracles, and to prophesy falsely. But it is certain that those, because they are themselves not of Christ, therefore do not belong to Christ, in like manner as if one should depart from Christ, abiding only in His name, he would not be much advantaged; nay, rather, he is even burdened by that name, al-

though he may have been previously very faithful, or very righteous, or honoured with some clerical office, or endowed with the dignity of confession. For all those, by denying the true Christ, and by introducing or following another — although there is no other at all — leave themselves no hope or salvation; not otherwise than they who have denied Christ before men, who must needs be denied by Christ; no consideration for them being made from their previous conversation, or feeling, or dignity, equally as they themselves have dared to do away with Christ, that is, their own salvation, they are condemned by the short sentence of this kind, because it was manifestly said by the Lord, "Whosoever shall deny me before men, I also will deny him before my Father which is in heaven." As this word "whosoever," also in the sentence of confession, most fully shows us that no condition of the confessor himself can stand in the way, although he may have been before a denier, or a heretic, or a hearer, or one who is beginning to hear, who has not yet been baptized or converted from heresy to the truth of the faith, or one who has departed from the Church and has afterwards returned, and then when he returned, before the bishop's hands could be laid upon him, being apprehended, should be compelled to confess Christ before men; even as to one who again denies Christ, no special ancient dignity can be effectual to him for salvation.

13. For any one of us will hold it necessary, that whatever is the last thing to be found in a man in this respect, is that whereby he must be judged, all those things which he has previously done being wiped away and obliterated.[4] And therefore, although in martyrdom there is so great a change of things in a moment of time, that in a very rapid case all things may be changed; let nobody flatter himself who has lost the occasion of a glorious salvation, if by chance he has excluded himself therefrom by his own fault; even as that wife of Lot,[5] who in a similar manner in time of trouble only, contrary to the angel's command, looked behind her, and she became a pillar of salt. On which principle also, that heretic who, by confessing Christ's name, is put to death, can subsequently correct nothing, if he should have thought anything erroneously of God or of Christ, although by believing on another God or on another Christ he has deceived himself: he is not a confessor of Christ, but in the name only of Christ; since also the apostle goes on to say, "And if I shall give up my body so that I may

[1] Acts xv. 13–17.
[2] Matt. xxiv. 4, etc.
[3] Matt. xxiv. 23, 24.

[4] [Ezek. xxxiii. 12. On the principle that what is deepest in man's heart proves, finally, the character; Phil. ii. 12. A very solemn consideration in human accountability (1 Pet. i. 17), but not to be disjoined from 2 Cor. vi. 10.]
[5] [Vol. i. p. 505, note 12, this series.]

be burnt up with fire, but have not love, I profit nothing."[1] Because by this deed he profits nothing who has not the love of that God and Christ who is announced by the law and the prophets and in the Gospel in this manner: "Thou shalt love the Lord thy God, with all thy heart, and with all thy mind, and with all thy thought; and thou shalt love thy neighbour as thyself. For on these two commandments hang all the law and the prophets;"[2] — even as John the evangelist said, "And every one that loveth is born of God, and knoweth God; for God is love;"[3] even as God also says, "For God so loved the world, that He gave His only-begotten Son, that every one that believeth on Him should not perish, but have everlasting life,"[4] — as it manifestly appears that he who has not in him this love, of loving us and of being loved by us, profits nothing by an empty confession and passion, except that thereby it appears and is plain that he is a heretic who believes on another God, or receives another Christ than Him whom the Scriptures of the Old and New Testament manifestly declare, which announce without any obscurity the Father omnipotent, Creator of all things, and His Son. For it shall happen to them as to one who expects salvation from another God. Then, finally, contrary to their notion, they are condemned to eternal punishment by Christ, the Son of God the Father omnipotent, the Creator whom they have blasphemed, when God shall begin to judge the hidden things of men according to the Gospel by Christ Jesus, because they did not believe in Him, although they were washed in His name.

14. And even to this point the whole of that heretical baptism may be amended, after the intervention of some space of time, if a man should survive and amend his faith, as our God, in the Gospel according to Luke, spoke to His disciples, saying, "But I have another baptism to be baptized with."[5] Also according to Mark He said, with the same purpose, to the sons of Zebedee: "Are ye able to drink of the cup which I drink of, or to be baptized with the baptism wherewith I am baptized?"[6] Because He knew that those men had to be baptized not only with water, but also in their own blood; so that, as well baptized in this baptism only, they might attain the sound faith and the simple love of the laver, and, baptized in both ways, they might in like manner to the same extent attain the baptism of salvation and glory. For what was said by the Lord, "I have another baptism to be

baptized with," signifies in this place not a second baptism, as if there were two baptisms, but demonstrates that there is moreover a baptism of another kind given to us, concurring to the same salvation. And it was fitting that both these kinds should first of all be initiated and sanctified by our Lord Himself, so that either one of the two or both kinds might afford to us this one twofold saving and glorifying baptism; and certain ways of the one baptism might so be laid open to us, that at times some one of them might be wanting without mischief, even as in the case of martyrs that hear the word, the baptism of water is wanting without evil; and yet we are certain that these, if they had any indulgence, would also be used to be baptized with water. And also to those who are made lawful believers, the baptism of their own blood is wanting without mischief, because, being baptized in the name of Christ, they have been redeemed with the most precious blood of the Lord; since both of these rivers of the baptism of the Lord proceed out of one and the same fountain, that every one who thirsts may come and drink, as says the Scripture, "From his belly flowed rivers of living water;"[7] which rivers were manifested first of all in the Lord's passion, when from His side, pierced by the soldier's spear, flowed blood and water, so that the one side of the same person emitted two rivers of a different kind, that whosoever should believe and drink of both rivers might be filled with the Holy Spirit. For, speaking of these rivers, the Lord set this forth, signifying the Holy Spirit whom they should receive who should believe on Him: "But the Spirit was not yet *given*, because Jesus was not yet glorified."[8] And when He thus said how baptism might be produced, which the apostle declares to be one, it is assuredly manifest on that principle that there are different kinds of one and the same baptism that flow from one wound into water and blood; since there are there two baptisms of water of which we have spoken, that is, of one and the same kind,[9] although the baptism of each kind ought to be one, as we have more fully spoken.

15. And since we seem to have divided all spiritual baptism in a threefold manner, let us come also to the proof of the statement proposed, that we may not appear to have done this of our own judgment, and with rashness. For John says of our Lord in his epistle, teaching us: "This is He who came by water and blood, Jesus Christ; not by water only, but by water and blood: and it is the Spirit that beareth witness, because the Spirit is truth. For three bear witness, the Spirit, and the water, and the

[1] 1 Cor. xiii. 3.
[2] Matt. xxii. 37.
[3] 1 John iv. 7, 8.
[4] John iii. 16.
[5] Luke xii. 50.
[6] Mark x. 38.
[7] John vii. 38.
[8] John vii. 39.
[9] Unius atque ejusdem *species*.

blood : and these three are one ; " [1] — that we may gather from these words both that water is wont to confer *the Spirit*, and that men's own blood is wont to confer the Spirit, and that the Spirit Himself also is wont to confer the Spirit. For since water is poured forth even as blood, the Spirit also was poured out by the Lord upon all who believed. Assuredly both in water, and none the less in their own blood, and then especially in the Holy Spirit, men may be baptized. For Peter says : " But this is that which was spoken by the prophet ; It shall come to pass in the last days, saith the Lord, I will pour out my Spirit upon all flesh : and their sons and their daughters shall prophesy, and their young men shall see visions, and their old men shall dream dreams : and upon my servants, and upon my handmaidens, will I pour out of my Spirit ; " [2] — which Spirit we discover to have been communicated in the Old Testament, not indeed everywhere nor at large, but with other gifts ; or, moreover, to have sprung of His own will into certain men, or to have invested them, or to have been upon them, even as we observe that it was said by the Lord to Moses, about the seventy elders, " And I will take of the Spirit which is upon thee, and will put it upon them." [3] For which reason also, according to His promise, God put upon them from another of the Spirit which had been upon Moses, and they prophesied in the camp. And Moses, as a spiritual man, rejoiced that this had so happened, although he was unwillingly persuaded by Jesus the son of Nave to oppose this thing, and was not thereby induced. Further, also in the book of Judges, and in the books of Kings too, we observe that upon several, there either was the Spirit of the Lord, or that He came unto them, as upon Gothoniel, Gideon, Jephthah, Samson, Saul, David, and many others. Which comes to this result, that the Lord has taught us most plainly by them the liberty and power of the Holy Spirit, approaching of His own will, saying, " The Spirit breathes where He will ; and thou hearest His voice, and knowest not whence He cometh or whither He goeth." [4] So that the same Spirit is, moreover, sometimes found to be upon those who are unworthy of Him ; not certainly in vain or without reason, but for the sake of some needful operation ; as He was upon Saul, upon whom came the Spirit of God, and he prophesied. However, in later days, after the Spirit of the Lord departed from him, and after a malign spirit from the Lord vexed him, because then he had come, after the messengers whom he had previously sent

before with care, with intent to kill David ; and they therefore fell into the chorus of the prophets, and they prophesied, so that they neither were able nor willing to do what they had been bidden. And we believe that the Spirit which was upon them all effected this with an admirable wisdom, by the will of God. Which Spirit also filled John the Baptist even from his mother's womb ; and it fell upon those who were with Cornelius the centurion before they were baptized with water. Thus, cleaving to the baptism of men, the Holy Spirit either goes before or follows it ; or failing the baptism of water, it falls upon those who believe. We are counselled that either we ought duly to maintain the integrity of baptism, or if by chance baptism is given by any one in the name of Jesus Christ, we ought to supplement it, guarding the most holy invocation of the name of Jesus Christ, as we have most abundantly set forth ; guarding, moreover, the custom and authority which so much claim our veneration for so long a time and for such great men.

16. But since the first part of this argument seems to be unfolded, we ought to touch on its subsequent part, on account of the heretics ; because it is very necessary not to pass over that discussion which once falls into our hands, lest perchance some heretic should dare, of his subtlety, to assail those of our brethren who are more simple. For because John said that we must be baptized in the Holy Ghost and in fire, from the fact that he went on to say *and fire*, some desperate men have dared to such an extent to carry their depravity, and therefore very crafty men seek how they can thus corrupt and violate, and even neutralize the baptism of holiness. Who derive the origin of their notion from Simon Magus, practising it with manifold perversity through various errors ; to whom Simon Peter, in the Acts of the Apostles, said, " Thy money perish with thee, because thou hast thought that the grace of God could be possessed by money ; thou hast neither part nor lot in this work ; for thy heart is not right with God." [5] And such men as these do all these things in the desire to deceive those who are more simple or more inquisitive. And some of them try to argue that they only administer a sound and perfect, not as we, a mutilated and curtailed baptism, which they are in such wise said to designate, that immediately they have descended into the water, fire at once appears upon the water. Which if it can be effected by any trick, as several tricks of this kind are affirmed to be — of Anaxilaus — whether it is anything natural, by means of which this may happen, or whether they think that they behold this, or whether the work and

---

[1] 1 John v. 6.
[2] Acts ii. 17, 18.
[3] Num. xi. 17.
[4] John iii. 5. [*Greek*, πνευμα. *Syriac* as here rendered.]

[5] Acts viii. 20, 21.

magical poison of some malignant being can force fire from the water ; still they declare such a deceit and artifice to be a perfect baptism, which if faithful men have been forced to receive, there will assuredly be no doubt but that they have lost that which they had. Just as, if a soldier after taking an oath should desert his camp, and in the very different camp of the enemy should wish to take an oath of a far other kind, it is plain that in this way he is discharged from his old oath.

17. Moreover, if a man of this sort should again return to thee, thou wilt assuredly hesitate whether he may have baptism or no ; and yet it will behove thee, in whatever way thou canst, to aid even this man if he repent. For of this adulterous, yea, murderous baptism, if there is any other author, it is then certainly a book devised by these same heretics on behalf of this same error, which is inscribed *The Preaching of Paul;*[1] in which book, contrary to all Scriptures, thou wilt find both Christ confessing His own sin — although He alone did no sin at all — and almost compelled by His mother Mary unwillingly to receive John's baptism. Also, that when He was baptized, fire was seen to be upon the water, which is written in neither of the Gospels. And that after such long time, Peter and Paul, after the collation of the Gospel in Jerusalem, and the mutual consideration and altercation and arrangement of things to be done finally, were known to one another, as if then for the first time ; and certain other things devised of this kind disgracefully and absurdly ; — all which things thou wilt find gathered together into that book. But they who are not ignorant of the nature of the Holy Spirit, understand that what is said of fire is said of the Spirit Himself. For in the Acts of the Apostles, according to that same promise of our Lord, on the very day of Pentecost, when the Holy Spirit had descended upon the disciples, that they might be baptized in Him, there were seen sitting upon each one tongues as if of fire, that it might be manifest that they were baptized with the Holy Ghost and with fire — that is, with that Spirit which was, whether fire, or as fire, such as was the fire which burned in the bush, and did not consume the bush ; and such as is that fire which is the Spirit of the Angel, as saith the Scripture, " Who maketh His angels spirits, and His ministers a burning fire ; "[2] whom if thou shouldst resemble, or be a companion or sharer with, thou shalt be able to dread no fire, not even that which, going before the Lord in the day of judgment, shall burn up the whole world, save those who are baptized in the Holy Spirit and in fire.

18. And the Spirit, indeed, continues to this day invisible to men, as the Lord says, " The Spirit breathes where He will ; and thou knowest not whence He cometh, or whither He goeth."[3] But in the beginning of the mystery of the faith and of spiritual baptism, the same Spirit was manifestly seen to have sat upon the disciples as it had been fire. Moreover, the heavens being opened, to have descended upon the Lord like a dove ; because many things, yea, almost all things which were to be, are manifest — which, however, were only invisible nevertheless, — now also are shown to the eyes and to the incredulity of men, either partially, or at times, or in figure, for the strengthening and confirming of our faith. But neither should I omit that which the Gospel well announces. For our Lord says to the paralytic man, " Be of good cheer, my son, thy sins are forgiven thee,"[4] that He might show that hearts were purified by faith for the forgiveness of sins that should follow. And this remission of sins that woman also which was a sinner in the city obtained, to whom the Lord said, " Thy sins are forgiven thee."[5] And when they who were reclining around began to say among themselves, " Who is this that forgiveth sins ? "[6] — because concerning the paralytic the scribes and Pharisees had murmured crossly — the Lord says to the woman, " Thy faith hath made thee whole ; go in peace."[6] From all which things it is shown that hearts are purified by faith, but that souls are washed by the Spirit ; further, also, that bodies are washed by water, and moreover that by blood we may more readily attain at once to the rewards of salvation.

19. I think that we have fully followed out the announcement of John the Baptist, whence we began our discourse, when he said to the Jews, " I indeed baptize you with water unto repentance ; but He who cometh after me is greater than I, whose shoe's latchet I am not worthy to unloose : He shall baptize you with the Holy Ghost, and with fire."[7] Moreover, I think also that we have not unsuitably set in order the teaching of the Apostle John, who says that " three bear witness, the Spirit, and the water, and the blood ; and these three are one."[8] And, unless I am mistaken, we have also explained what our Lord says : " John indeed bap-

---

[1] Rigaltius says that Jerome mentions this document, and regards it as apocryphal. And Eusebius refers to the Περίοδοι Πέτρου, which, according to the common reading of Peter for Paul in the text, may point to the same document. [Vol. ii. 341, note 10; and vol. iv. p. 246.]
[2] Ps. civ. 4.

[3] John iii. 8.
[4] Matt. ix. 2.
[5] Luke vii. 48.
[6] Luke vii. 50.
[7] Luke iii. 16.
[8] 1 John v. 8. [It is noteworthy that he quotes the Latin formula, and not that (εἰς τὸ ἕν εἰσιν) of the Greek. Now, the Latin, repeating (in verse 8) the formula (*hi tres unum sunt*) which belongs to the dubious *protasis*, is so far evidence that such a verse existed in the old Greek. It is important that the Latin is not conformed to the received formula of the *apodosis*, " the three *agree* in one."]

tized with water, but ye shall be baptized with the Holy Ghost."[1] Moreover, I think that we have given no weak reason as the cause of the custom. Let us have a care, although we do that in a subsequent place, that none may think that we are stirring up the present debate on a single article; although this custom even alone ought, among men who have the fear of God, and are lowly, to maintian a chief place.

[1] Acts i. 5.

NOTE BY THE EDINBURGH TRANSLATOR.

Letters of Cyprian to *Quintus*, to *Jubaianus*, to *Pompey*, on "the baptism of heretics;" and to *Magnus* on "baptizing the Novatians, and those who obtain grace on a sick-bed," may be found translated in Ep. lxx. (p. 377, *supra*), Ep. lxxii. (p. 379, *supra*), Ep. lxxiii. (p. 386, *supra*), and Ep. lxxv. (p. 397, *supra*), respectively; and the Letter of *Firmilian* to Cyprian against the *Letter of Stephen*, at p. 390, *supra*, Ep. lxxiv. All these letters are repeated, *in extenso*, in the *Monumenta Veterum*.

Eusebius says, by way of introduction to the fragment of a letter written to Stephen by Dionysius of Alexandria, as follows: "Dionysius indited to Stephen the first of those letters which were written on the subject of baptism, when no small controversy had arisen whether they who are converted from any kind of heresy ought to be purged by baptism (because an ancient custom had prevailed, that in receiving such there should only be hands laid upon them, with prayers). Cyprian, who then ruled the Church of Carthage, was the first who judged that they must not be admitted to communion unless they were first purified from error by baptism. But Stephen, thinking that nothing should be innovated contrary to the tradition which had already obtained in that matter from the beginning, was indignant at this. And as Dionysius had already written many letters to him on this argument, he intimates to him finally, that all the churches everywhere, now that the fury of persecution was abated, detesting the turbulent novelty of Novatian,[1] had established peace with one another."[2]

[1] Eusebius calls him Novatus. [2] See *H. E.*, book viii. chaps. ii., iii., and iv.; and vol. vi., this series.

INDEXES

HIPPOLYTUS

INDEX OF TEXTS.

CYPRIAN

INDEX OF SUBJECTS.

CYPRIAN

INDEX OF TEXTS.

CAIUS, NOVATIAN, APPENDIX

INDEX OF SUBJECTS.

Angel of the Covenant, the Son of God, 627–631.

Apocalypse, early received at Rome, 600.

Apostles Peter and Paul, remains of. at Rome, 601.

Ark, type of the Church, 658.

Baptism of the Spirit, 669, 671; of water, 670; of blood, 676; of fire, 676.

Caius, presbyter, historical notice of, and his works, 599.

Cerinthus, heresies of, 601.

Christ, divinity of, a primitive doctrine, 601; psalms and hymns in honour of, 601, 604 (note); prophecies of, 618, 621; truly man, 619, and God, 620, proved by Holy Scripture, 621; testimony of Moses, 626; Christ seen by Abraham, 627, by Hagar, and Jacob, 629; equal with God, 633; His divinity acknowledged by heretics making Him the Father, 634; Son of God distinguished from Son of man, 634; suffered as man only, 635; Scripture testimonies of the Son of God, 636; one with the Father in substance, not in person, 637–

640, 642; of the Father, 643–644; why acknowledged by the first disciples, 671, but with imperfect faith, 672.

Creation, works of God in, 611, 617.

Cross, sign of, in Jacob's blessing, 631.

Deluge, the, symbol of persecution, 658.

Dove of Noah, type of baptism, 658.

God, over all things, attributes of, 612; Creator of all, 613; perfect, 614; without human passions or form, 615; ineffable, 616; His providence, 617.

Heretical baptism, acts and records of, noted, 653; not to be repeated, 667, but completed by imposition of hands, 668, 673, but valid without such complement, 669, 673; note from Eusebius on, 678.

Holy Spirit, person and office of, 640.

Intemperance among Christians, 649.

Lapsed, not to be denied mercy, 659; instances from Scripture, 660–661.

Law of Jewish meats, to be understood spiritually, 645.

Laying on of hands, complement of baptism, 668; given by bishops only, 669.

Martyrdom, not possible to deniers of Christ, 673–674.

Meats, law of, spiritual, 645; animal, given after the Fall, 646; distinction of clean and unclean for man's sake only, and spiritually interpreted, 647, done away by Christ, 648, but not to permit luxury or intemperance, 649, nor partaking of idol-meats, 650.

Natalius, heretic, account of, 601.

Novatian, historical notice of, 607: orthodoxy of his writings, 608; extant works, 608; anonymous treatise against his heresy, 657–663.

Paraclete, the, receives from Christ what He reveals to man, 625: His person and office, 640.

Scriptures, perverted by heretics, 602; canon of, in the second century, 603.

697

CAIUS, NOVATIAN, APPENDIX

INDEX OF TEXTS.